CW00361961

Well Rob

Now you have this,

Perhaps we can have one

to stuff & put on the wall.

David & Renee

Christmas 1998.

Where to Fish 1998-1999

86th EDITION

EDITED BY
D. A. ORTON

THOMAS HARMSWORTH PUBLISHING
COMPANY

86th Edition published 1998 by
Thomas Harmsworth Publishing Company
Old Rectory Offices
Stoke Abbott
Beaminster
Dorset DT8 3JT
United Kingdom

ISBN 0-948807-42-3
ISSN 1362-3842
Internet address: www.where-to-fish.com

Advertisements in this book have been inserted in the form in which they have been received from the advertisers. Care has been exercised in the acceptance of them, but the publisher accepts no responsibility for any loss through advertisers' malpractice. Advertisements have been accepted on the understanding that they do not contravene the Trades Descriptions Act 1968, the Sex Discrimination Act 1975, the Wildfowl and Countryside Act 1981 or any other Act of Parliament.

British Library
Cataloguing-in-Publication Data
A catalogue record of this book is
available from the British Library
ISBN 0 948807-42-3

Printed in Great Britain by
Bookcraft (Bath) Ltd.

CONTENTS

FISHING IN THE BRITISH ISLES

FISHING ABROAD

Abbreviations: The following abbreviations are used throughout the book: S, salmon; T, trout; MT, migratory trout, NT, non-migratory trout; C, char; FF or FW, freshwater (ie coarse fish); RD, River Division (or its equivalent); s, season; m, month (National Rivers Authority list only); f, fortnight; w, week; d, day; t, ticket; ns, nearest railway station; m means mile or miles, except when it is used in conjunction with t, ie, mt, when it means monthly ticket. Likewise, st means season ticket, wt weekly ticket, dt daily ticket, and so on.

The late Peter Tombleson OBE., Executive Director, National Anglers' Council: the last official to date empowered to speak for the whole sport of angling in Britain. As shown here, not merely a theoretician. *Photo: Derek Rowe.*

Action now!!!

In 1923 legislation was enacted under which all folk fishing in English and Welsh freshwater might be required to take out a licence. There were certain exceptions, but licenses became general; for coarse fishers, an innovation. As years and governments rolled by, the exceptions became fewer. Ministry of Agriculture and Fisheries, then Agriculture, Fisheries and Food, exercised a general supervision.

Under that watchful eye, Fisheries Boards, Regional Water Authorities, organised catchment by catchment and exercising some discretion board by board in the detail of the by-laws, reigned. Then came the National Rivers Authority which sought to rationalise so far that salmon and roach could be fished for nationwide on a single licence: a dream destined to fade like others with the coming of daylight.

Now, the National Rivers Authority, too, has passed into history; its functions absorbed into the far wider remit of The Environment Agency. Like all changes preceding it, this one was introduced as offering promising prospects of environmental improvement. So it may have been intended, as were its forerunners. Some, however, now regard its remit - Pollution Registers notwithstanding - as a polluters' charter. Let us hope they are wrong.

This lineage of public bodies controlled and provided for angling, but it was not part of the original duty to protect or develop the sport. That was taken on board progressively, to a limited extent, after 1948.

Private action, though, inspired by public spirit, was already there. The Salmon & Trout Association, the National Federation of Anglers (catering for coarse fishing) and the National Federation of Sea Anglers are bodies of long standing: the principal protectors of the sport. About 30 years ago, serious talk began about their joining forces in a composite body, with official standing and government support. Government was taking a keener interest in the electorate's leisure but did not wish to negotiate with three bodies representing what it saw as a single sport.

So came into being the National Anglers' Council, on which these three bodies sat with the Fishmongers' Company as the founder members. Later, the Council was joined by other bodies with an interest. Sports Council, Water Space Amenity Commission, MAFF, the tackle trade, The Anglers' Co-operative Association. Thus reinforced, the National Anglers' Council made progress, although some matters it tackled might have been dealt with as expeditiously by the founder members acting independently; some matters of importance failed to appear on the agenda. But all in all, angling received a worthwhile service.

For most anglers, all of us perhaps to some extent, our sport is an escapism. Thus one explains why so small a percentage of anglers join and contribute funds towards their protective bodies and raised no vigorous objection when National Anglers' Council, too, passed into history as the present decade began.

Now, there is no body in existence to represent anglers as a whole: just as there is now no official body in existence with its principal focus the protection of the element in which our fish swim, and without it in reasonably good condition they cannot survive. All in an era in which industrial pollution, although somewhat abated, has been reinforced by agricultural pollution into which changes in Statute Law, however well-meant, have not succeeded in sinking teeth as deeply as we anglers wish to see.

It will not happen until anglers get up off their bottoms and escape from the escapist dream. No-one but anglers will protect angling effectively. Action now! ... but don't bleat for government funds to finance it. Those to whom it gives money often find themselves working for it, one way or another.

FISHERY AGENTS

ENGLAND

Harris & Stokes, 125 Eign Street, Hereford HR4 0AJ (Tel: 01432-354455). Some 500 rods to let each season on the Wye, Usk and other rivers.

Hatton Fishing Tackle, 64 St Owen Street, Hereford (Tel: 01432 272317). Up-to-the-minute information on fishing on Wye and Lugg.

Sale & Partners, 18-20 Glendale Road, Wooler, Northumberland (Tel: 01668 281611, Fax: 01668 281113). Tweed salmon fishing *(see advt).*

Knight Frank, 20 Hanover Square, London W1R 0AH (Tel: 0171-629 8171, Fax 491 0854, Internet http://www.knightfrank.co.uk).

Savills, 20 Grosvenor Hill, Berkeley Square, London, W1X 0HQ (Tel: 0171-499 8644).

Strutt & Parker, 37 Davies Street, London, WIY 2SP (Tel: 0171-629 7282, Fax: 0171 499 1657) *(see advt).*

WALES

Knight Frank, 14 Broad Street, Hereford, HR4 9AL (Tel: 01432-273087, Fax 275935, Internet http://www.knightfrank.co.uk2).

Strutt and Parker, Dolgarreg, North Road, Builth Wells, Powys, LD2 3DD. Salmon fishing on Wye, Usk and tributaries. By the day or week (Tel: 01982-553248, fax: 553154) *(see advt).*

SCOTLAND

Bell-Ingram, Durn, Isla Rd, Perth PH2 7HF (Tel: 01738-621121, fax: 630904). Deveron, Cassley, Dee, etc.

Knight, Frank, 2 North Charlotte Street, Edinburgh EH2 4HR (Tel: 0131 225 8171, Fax: 4151, Internet http://www.knightfrank.co.uk).

J H Leeming, Stichill House, Kelso, Roxburghshire TD5 7TB. (Tel: 01573 470280, fax: 01573 470259, Internet www.scotborders.co.uk.). 24 hour information service, Freephone 0800 387 675. River Tweed.

Strutt & Parker, 37 Davies Street, London, WIY 2SP (Tel: 0171-629 7282, Fax: 0171 499 1657, telex: 8955508 STRUTT G) *(see advt).*

Thurso Fisheries Ltd, Thurso East, Thurso, Caithness KW14 8HP (Tel: 01847 8963134). River Thurso.

FISHING HOLIDAY AGENTS

Arthur Oglesby, 9 Oatlands Drive, Harrogate, N Yorks HG2 8JT. Tel/Fax: 01423 883565. Host to parties on such rivers as the Spey in Scotland, the Varzuga and Kitza in Russia, Orkla in Norway, Alagnak in Alaska and the Ranga in Iceland *(see advt).*

Top End Sportfishing Safaris, P O Box 194, Howard Springs, NT 0835, Australia. Tel: 00 61 8 8983 1495. Fax: 00 61 8 8983 1456.

Roxton Bailey Robinson, Field Sports and Safaris, 25 High Street, Hungerford, Berkshire RG17 0NF. Tel: 01488 683222. Fax: 682977. Internet http:\\www.roxtons.com. Salmon fishing in Russia, Norway, Iceland, Alaska, Scotland. Saltwater and deep sea fishing in Bahamas, Cuba, Kenya, and elsewhere. Trout fishing in UK, USA, Argentina, New Zealand and elsewhere.

Viv's Barramundi & Sportfishing Safaris, P O Box 95, Howard Springs, NT 0835, Australia. Tel: 00 61 8 8983 2044. Fax 00 61 8 8983 2786. E-mail: helent@taunet.net.au *(see advt).*

BRITISH FISH FARMS

Anna Valley Trout Farm Ltd, Andover, Hants (Tel: 01264 710382).

Berkshire Trout Farm, Hungerford, Berkshire, RG17 0UN. (Tel: 01488-682520, Fax: 01488 685002). Brown and rainbow trout.

Bibury Trout Farm, Bibury, near Cirencester, Gloucestershire GL7 5NL. Rainbow and brown trout bred on Coln. (Tel: 0128574 0212/215, Fax: 01285 740392). Catch Your Own fishery on R Coln.

Clearwater Fish Farm, East Hendred, Wantage, Oxon OX12 8LN. (Tel: 01235 833732, Fax: 01235 835586).

Exe Valley Fishery Ltd, Exbridge, Dulverton, Somerset, TA22 9AY. Rainbow trout available. (Tel: 01398 323328, Fax: 01398 24079).

Kilnsey Park Trout Farm, Kilnsey, Skipton, North Yorkshire ID23 5PS, (Tel: 01756 752150, fax: 752224).

Loch Leven Fishery, Kinross Estates Office, Kinross KY13 7UF. Trout. (Tel: 01577 863407, fax: 863180.)

Ludworth Trout Farm, Marple Bridge, Cheshire SK6 5NS. (Tel: 0161 449 9520).

Ruskin Mill Aquaculture Project, Harsley Mill, Harsley, Stroud, Gloucestershire GL6 0Pl. Trout and carp. (Tel: 01453 833379.)

Trent Fish Culture Co Ltd, Mercaston, Ashbourne, Derbyshire DE6 3BL. Brown, rainbow and American brook trout. Ova, fry, yearlings and two-year-olds 1.5lb to 2lb; larger fish on application. (Tel: 01335 360318).

Upper Mills Trout Farm, Glyn Ceiriog, Nr Llangollen LL20 7HB. (Tel: 01691 718225, fax: 01691 718188.)

Watermill Trout Farms Ltd, Welton Springs, Louth, Lincs LN11 0QT. Brown and rainbow trout. (Tel: 01507 602524, Fax: 01507 600592, Telex: 56528.)

Westacre Trout Farm, King's Lynn, Norfolk. Brown and rainbow trout for immediate delivery. (Tel/Fax: 01760 755240.)

Further information about **British Fish Farms** can be had from **British Trout Farmers' Restocking Association**, Secretary, T Whyatt, Allenbrook Trout Farm, Brockington, Wimbourne, St Giles, Dorset BH21 5LT. (Tel: 01725 517369, fax: 517769.)

FISHING SCHOOLS AND COURSES

A.P.G.A.I. (Association of Professional Game Angling Instructors), Little Saxby's Farm, Cowden, Kent TN8 7DN. Tel: 01342 850765, Fax: 01342 850926. The Association has approximately 80 members both in the UK and abroad offering a range of tuition from simple casting lessons to full residential courses. Members can be contacted through the Association.

Arthur Oglesby, 9 Oatlands Drive, Harrogate, N Yorks HG2 8JT. (Tel/Fax: 01423 883565).

The Arundell Arms, Lifton, Devon PL16 0AA. (Tel: 01566 784666, Fax: 01566 784494). A full range of residential courses from beginners' to advanced. Private tuition also offered.

School of Casting, Salmon & Trout Fishing, Michael Waller and Margaret Cockburn, Station House, Clovenfords, Galashiels, Selkirkshire TD1 3LU. (Tel/fax: 01896 850293). Brown trout, sea trout and salmon on River Tweed and other waters in area.

Seafield Lodge Hotel, Alasdair Buchanan, Grantown on Spey, Moray PH26 3JN. (Tel: 01479 872152. Fax: 01479 872340). Access to seven miles of Association water.

These below are members of the **Register of Experienced Fly Fishing Instructors and Schools** (Reffis), sponsored by Farlow's of Pall Mall, 5 Pall Mall, London SW1Y 5NP. (Tel: 0171 839 2423, fax: 01285 6437, Internet http://www.farlows.co.uk/farlows/). For full list of members, contact Reffis Chairman, Charles Bingham (*below*).

Charles Bingham, West Down, Whitchurch, Tavistock, Devon PL19 9LD. (Tel/fax: 01822

613899). Wild brown trout, sea trout and salmon on Dartmoor rivers. Also stillwater trout.

Clonanav Fly Fishing Centre, Andrew Ryan, Ballymacarbry, Clonmel, Co Waterford, Eire. (Tel/fax: 052 36141).

Colebrook Park Fly Fishing School, Patrick Trotter, Colebrook estate, Brookeborough, Co. Fermanagh, Northern Ireland BT94 4DW. (Tel 01365 531402).

Fishing Breaks Ltd, Simon Cooper, 23 Compton Terrace, London N1 2UN. Tel: (0171 359 8818, fax: 4540). Stillwater and chalkstream trout (R Test and others).

Half Stone Sporting Agency, Roddy Rae, 6 Hescane Park, Cheriton Bishop, Exeter EX6 6SP. (Tel: 01647 24643). Brown trout, sea trout and salmon on Teign and Exe.

Highland Angling Services, Robert Brighton, 12 Fyrish Crescent, Evanton, Ross-shire, Scotland IV16 9YS. (Tel: 01349 830159). Highland loch fishing.

Ian Moutter, South Wing, Borthwick Hall, Heriot, Midlothian, scotland EH38 5YE. (Tel 0131 557 8333, fax: 0131 556 3707). Instruction on river and stillwater fisheries in the Scottish borders.

Tom Pass, 4 Putty Row, Macclesfield Road, Eaton, Congleton, Cheshire, CW12 2NP. (Tel: 01260 223472). Teaches fly fishing techniques on Marton Heath Trout Pools.

Simon Ward, 20 Primrose Way, Locks Heath, Southampton, Hampshire SO31 6WX. (Tel: 01489 579295). Chalk streams in southern England.

Wessex Fly Fishing School, Southover, Tolpuddle, Dorchester, Dorset DT2 7HF. (Tel: 01305 848460, fax: 01305 849060). Lakes, pools, chalk-stream fishing for trout on Rivers Piddle and Frome.

West Wales School of Fly Fishing, Pat O'Reilly A.P.G.A.I., Ffoshelyg, Lancych, Boncath, Pembrokeshire SA37 0LJ. (Tel/Fax: 01239 698678). Trout, sea trout and salmon on Rivers Teifi, Cych and Gwili, and private lakes. Beginners' and advanced courses. Personal tuition also offered.

A sport for the young.

Environment Agency Regions

North West
North East
Midlands
Welsh
Anglian
Thames
South West
Southern

FISHING IN ENGLAND and WALES

Environment Agency structure, close seasons, licence duties etc.

The Environment Agency was created in 1996 from the National Rivers Authority, which had come into existence with the privatisation of the Regional Water Authorities. The Agency works to improve fish stocks, by checking, rescue and stocking; to improve water quality, habitat and river flows; to protect fisheries from poaching, and enforce fishing and water byelaws generally; and to help anglers through supply of information, restoration and promotion of fisheries, and protection of wildlife.

The Agency is also responsible for the issue of compulsory rod licences. In England and Wales anyone aged 12 years or older who fishes for salmon, trout, freshwater fish or eels must hold an Environment Agency rod licence, and in addition, permission to fish, if necessary, must be gained from the owners or tenants of the fishing rights. Failure to produce a valid Agency rod licence when fishing is a criminal offence. Rod licence income helps the Agency to perform its necessary duties.

Rod licences are available from post offices in England and Wales. Licences are also obtainable from some larger fisheries, Regional Environment Agency offices, or by post from Environment Agency National Rod licence Administration Centre, PO Box 432, Richard Fairclough House, Knutsford Road, Warrington WA4 1HH. Concessionary rates are available for persons aged 12 to 16, aged 65 years and over, or in receipt of invalidity benefit or severe disability allowance. War pensioners in receipt of an unemployability supplement are also entitled to the concession. Licence charges are as follows:

Salmon and Migratory Trout - Full season £55.00 (concessionary rate £27.50), 8 consecutive days £15.00, Single day £5.00.

Non-migratory Trout and Coarse - Full season £16.00 (concessionary rate £8.00), 8 consecutive days £6.00, Single day £2.00.

Where local rules and regulations permit, up to 4 rods may be used when fishing for coarse fish and eels; 1 rod may be used when fishing for salmon and migratory trout on rivers, streams, drains and canals; 2 rods on reservoirs, lakes and ponds; 1 rod may be used when fishing for non-migratory trout and coarse fish on rivers, streams, drains and canals; 2 rods on reservoirs, lakes and ponds.

Anglers are reminded that the expression 'immature' in relation to salmon means that the fish is less than 12in long; taking immature salmon is prohibited throughout England and Wales. In relation to other fish the expression 'immature' means that the fish is of a length less than that prescribed by bye-law. Unless otherwise stated, it may be assumed that the length is measured from the tip of the snout to the fork of the tail.

The word 'salmon' means all fish of the salmon species. The word 'trout' means all fish of the salmon species commonly known as trout. The expression 'migratory trout' means trout that migrate to and from the sea. The expression 'freshwater (ie coarse) fish' means any fish living in fresh water except salmon, trout, all kinds of fish which migrate to and from tidal water, eels and their fry.

NOTE: In the following lists the telephone numbers are those at which to contact officers during office hours. For the reporting of pollution an emergency hotline exists on a 24 hour free service: 0800 807060. Environment Agency general enquiries may be made through tel: 0645 333111.

Abbreviations: The following abbreviations are used throughout the book: S, salmon; T, trout; MT, migratory trout, NT, non-migratory trout; C, char; FF or FW, freshwater (ie coarse fish); s, season; m, month (Following list only); f, fortnight; w, week; d, day; t, ticket, ns, nearest railway station. In the lists of fishing stations the abbreviation m means mile or miles, except when it is used in conjunction with t, ie, mt, when it means monthly ticket. Likewise, st means season ticket, wt weekly ticket, dt daily ticket, and so on.

Environment Agency

For general enquiries, you should call your *local* Enviroment Agency office. The national general enquiry line (0645 333 111) should only be used if you are unsure who to contact at the local office.

There is a 24-hour **emergency hot-line** for reporting all **enviromental incidents** relating to air, land and water: 0800 80 70 60.

Regions of the Environment Agency.

SOUTHERN REGION, Guildbourne House, Chatsworth Road, Worthing, Sussex BN11 1LD. (Tel: 01903 832000, Fax: 01903 821832).

Regional Fisheries, Recreation, Conservation and Navigation Manager: Ian Johnson.

Rivers controlled: Darent, Cray, Medway, Stour, Eastern Rother, RM Canal, Adur, Arun, Ouse, Cuckmere, all rivers in Pevensey Levels, Test, Itchen, Hamble, Meon, Beaulieu, Lymington, Fletch, Keyhaven, Eastern Yar, Medina, and the tributaries of all these rivers.

Divisional offices.

Kent: Kent Fisheries Officer, Millbrook House, Mill Street, East Malling, Kent ME19 6BU. Tel: 01732 875587. Fax: 01732 875057.

Sussex: Sussex Fisheries Officer, Rivers House, 3 Liverpool Gardens, Worthing BN11 1TG. Tel: 01903 215835.

Pollution reporting: emergency hotline: 0800 807060.

Hampshire/Isle of Wight. Hampshire Fisheries Officer, Sarum Court, Sarum Road, Winchester, Hampshire SO22 5DP. Tel: 01962 713267.

Pollution reporting, outside office hours: Winchester and Isle of Wight, Tel: 01962 713267; Chichester, Tel: 01243 786431; Pevensey, Tel: 01323 762691; Rye, Tel: 01797 223256; Leigh 01732 838858; Canterbury, Tel: 01634 830655. 24 hour emergencies - Freephone: 0800 807060.

SOUTH WEST REGION, Headquarters: Manley House, Kestrel Way, Exeter, Devon, EX2 7LQ. (Tel: 01392 444000, fax: 01392 444238).

Regional Headquarters: Fisheries, Recreation Conservation and Navigation Manager: E S Bray.

Regional General Manager: Katharine Bryan.

Cornwall Area: Sir John Moore House, Victoria Square, Bodmin, Cornwall PL31 1EB. (Tel: 01208 78301, fax: 78321.)

Fisheries, Recreation and Conservation Manager: M P Willans.

Rivers controlled: Camel, Fowey, Looe, Lynher, Plym, Tamar, Tavy, Yealm and tributaries, including Bude Canal.

Devon Area: Manley House, Kestrel Way, Exeter EX2 7LQ. (Tel: 01392 444000. Fax: 444238.)

Fisheries, Recreation and Conservation Manager: N A Reader.

Rivers controlled: Avon, Axe, Dart, Erme, Exe, Lyn, Otter, Taw, Teign, Torridge and tributaries, including Exeter and Tiverton Canal.

North Wessex Area: Rivers House, East Quay, Bridgwater, Somerset TA6 4YS. (Tel: 01278 457333. Fax: 01278 452985.)

Fisheries, Recreation and Conservation Manager: E R Merry.

Rivers controlled: Axe, Bristol Avon, Brue, Parrett and their tributaries, including Tone, Huntspill, King's Sedgemoor Drain and Bridgwater and Taunton Canal.

South Wessex Area: Rivers House, Sunrise Business Park, Higher Shaftesbury Road, Blandford Forum, Dorset DT11 8ST (Tel: 01258 456080. Fax: 455998).

Fisheries, Recreation and Conservation Manager: G Lightfoot.

Rivers controlled: Hampshire Avon and Stour, Frome, Piddle, Brit and Char. (All riyers entering the sea between Lyme Regis and Christchurch).

Rod Seasons:

Devon and Cornwall Areas
Salmon: Avon - 15 April to 30 November (E). Erme - 15 March to 31 October. Axe, Otter, Sid - 15 March to 31 October. Camel - 1 April to 15 December. Dart - 1 February to 30 September. Exe - 14 February to 30 September. Fowey, Looe - 1 April to 15 December. Tamar, Tavy, Lynher - 1 March to 14 October. Plym - 1 April to 15 December. Yealm - 1 April to 15 December. Taw, Torridge - 1 March to 30 September. Lyn - 1 February to 31 October. Teign - 1 February to 30 September. Lim - 1 March to 30 September. **Migratory trout:** Avon - 15 April to 30 September. Erme - 15 March to 30 September. Axe, Otter, Sid - 15 April to 31 October. Camel, Gannel, Menalhyl, Valency - 1 April to 30 September. Dart - 15 March to 30 September. Exe - 15 March to 30 September. Fowey, Looe, Seaton, Tresillian - 1 April to 30 September. Tamar, Lynher, Plym, Tavy, Yealm - 3 March to 30 September. Taw, Torridge, Lyn - 15 March to 30 September. Teign, - 15 March to 30 September. Lim - 16 April to 31 October. **Brown trout:** Camel, Fowey - 1 April to 30 September. Other rivers and streams - 15 March to 30 September. All rivers in North and South Wessex Areas - 1 April to 15 October. All other waters - 15 March to 12 October. **Coarse fish and eels:** Rivers, streams, drains, Kennet and Avon Canal, Bridgewater and Taunton Canal - 16 June to 14 March. Enclosed waters, no close season.

North and South Wessex Areas
S, Frome and Piddle - 1 March to 31 August. Other rivers - 1 February to 31 August. MT, 15 April to 31 October, NT. Rivers 1 April to 15 October. Reservoirs, lakes and ponds 17 March to 15 October. Rainbow trout - still waters only - no closed season. FF all waters. 16 June to 14 March following year.

NORTH WEST REGION, Richard Fairclough House, Knutsford Road, Warrington WA4 1HG. (Tel: 01925 653999. Fax: 01925 415961).

Principal Fisheries, Recreation, Conservation and Biology Manager: Dr M Diamond. **Pollution reporting:** Tel: 01925 53999.

North Area
Area Fisheries, Ecology and Recreation Manager: N C Durie, Chertsey Hill, London Road, Carlisle CA1 2QX, Tel: 01228 25151.
Rivers controlled: Esk, Liddel, Lyne, Irthing, Petteril, Wampool, Caldew, Ellen, Derwent, Eamont, Eden, Cocker, Ehen, Irt, Esk, Brathay, Duddon, Crake, Rothay, Leven, Kent, and their tributaries. Lakes Derwentwater, Thirlmere, Ullswater, Haweswater, Bassenthwaite, Windermere, Wastwater, Coniston Water, Esthwaite Water, Grasmere, Rydal Water.

Central Area
Area Fisheries, Ecology and Recreation Manager: Jonathan Shatwell, Lostock House, Holme Road, Bamber Bridge, PR5 6RE, Tel: 01772 39882.
Rivers controlled: Ribble, Hodder, Lune, Wyre, Calder, Crossens, Yarrow, Douglas, Alt, Keer and their tributaries.

South Area
Area Fisheries, Ecology and Recreation Manager: A R Lee, Carrington Lane, Sale M33 5NL, 0161 973 2237.
Rivers controlled: Roch, Irwell, Tame, Etherow, Mersey, Goyt, Bollin, Dean, Weaver, Dane, Gowey, and their tributaries.

Close seasons: Salmon, 1 November to 31 January, except R. Eden system - 15 October to 14 January. Migratory trout, 16 October to 30 April, except rivers Annas, Bleng, Esk, Mite, Irt, Calder, Ehen and all tributaries - 1 November to 30 April. Trout, 1 October to 14 March. Coarse Fish, 15 March to 15 June (no close season for coarse fish in enclosed waters).

NORTH EAST REGION, Rivers House, 21 Park Square South, Leeds LS1 2QG. (Tel: 0113 244 0191, fax: 246 1889.)

FRCN Co-ordinator: Steven Bailey, tel: 0113 2440191.

Northumbria Area

Disabled anglers go afloat in Llys-y-Fran Reservoir, Dyfed, for an international competition. *Photo: Al Mogridge.*

Ecology and Recreation Manager: Godfrey Williams, Tel: 0191 2034000.
Rivers controlled: Aln, Coquet, Fant, Wansbeck, Blyth, Tyne, Wear, Tees, Derwent.

Close seasons: S - 1 November to 31 January. MT - 1 November to 2 April. NT - 1 October to 21 March, excluding Kielder Water, Broomlee Lough, Craglough Loch, Greenlee Lough, Derwent Reservoir, and East and West Hallington where the close season is 1 Nov to 30 Apr.

Dales Area
Principal Fisheries and Recreation Manager: Liz Chalk, Tel: 01904 692296.

Rivers controlled (together with South Yorkshire Area): Tees, Swale, Ure, Esk, Derwent, Wharfe, Nidd, Ouse, Aire, Calder, Rother, Don, Dearne and Hull system.

Close seasons: for River Tees and tributaries northward as per Northumbria Area. For Staithes Beck, River Esk and tributaries of the Ouse and Humber, as per Southern Yorkshire Area.

Southern Yorkshire Area
Ecology and Recreation Manager: Dr John Pygott, Tel: 0113 2440191.
Close seasons: S - 1 Nov to 5 April. MT - 1 Nov to 5 April. NT - 1 October to 24 March.

The use of gaffs is prohibited throughout the Region at all times. Bait restrictions apply in Southern Yorkshire Area and part of Dales Area during freshwater fish close season.

ANGLIAN REGION, Kingfisher House, Goldhay Way, Orton Goldhay, Peterborough PE2 51ZR. (Tel: 01733 371811, fax: 231 840).

Regional Fisheries Manager: John Adams.
Regional Recreation, Conservation and Navigation Manager: Peter Barham.

Northern Area: Acqua Harvey Street Lincoln LN1 1TF. (Tel: 01522 513100).
Fisheries, Recreation, Conservation and Navigation Manager: Irven Forbes.

Central Area: Bromholme Lane, Brampton, Huntingdon PE18 8NE. (Tel: 01480 414581).
Fisheries, Recreation, Conservation and Navigation Manager: Mike Evans.

Eastern Area: Cobham Road, Ipswich, Suffolk IP3 9JE (Tel: 01473 727712).
Fisheries, Recreation, Conservation and Navigation Manager: Dr Charles Beardall.

Close Seasons: S and MT 29 September-last day of February. T 30 October-31 March. Rainbow T; no close season on enclosed waters, otherwise 30 October-31 March. FF 15 March-15 June on rivers, streams, drains, all waters in Broads area, and some SSSI's.

Emergencies: A 24 hour service is provided at Regional Headquarters, Tel: 01733 371811. Emergency hotline: 0800 807060.

MIDLANDS REGION, Sapphire East, 550 Streetsbrook Road, Solihull B91 1QT. (Tel: 0121 711 2324, Fax: 0121 711 5824).

Fisheries, Ecology, and Recreation Manager, Midlands: Martin Stark

Area Fisheries, Recreation and **Conservation Manager**: A S Churchward, Lower Severn Area EA, Riversmeet House, Newtown Industrial Estate, Northway Lane, Tewkesbury, Glos GL20 8JG. Tel: 01684 850951.
Rivers controlled: Severn, Warwickshire Avon, and all other tributary streams in the Severn south of Worcester and all other canals and pools. The Agency also owns or rents water on the Avon and Severn.
Area Fisheries, Recreation, Conservation and Navigation Manager: Dr J V Woolland, Upper Severn Area EA, Hafren House, Welshpool Road, Shelton, Shrewsbury SY3 8BB. Tel: 01743 272828.
Rivers controlled: Severn and tributaries north of Worcester, Teme, Vyrnwy, Tanet, Banwy, Tern, Roden, Mease, Perry and all other canals and pools.

Trent Area
Area Fisheries, Recreation and Conservation Manager: M L Stark, Lower Trent Area EA. Trentside Offices, Scarrington Road, West Bridgford, Nottingham NG2 5FA. Tel: 0115 9455722.

Rivers controlled: Trent, east of Dove confluence, Soar, Derbyshire Derwent and their tributaries, all canals and pools.
Area Fisheries, Recreation and Conservation Manager: M J Cooper, Upper Trent Area EA, Sentinel House, Wellington Crescent, Fradley Park, Lichfield, Staffs WS13 8RR. Tel: 01543 444141.
Rivers controlled: Trent west of Dove confluence, Tame, Dove, Manifold, Churnet and their tributaries, all canals and pools.
Close seasons: Brown trout: 8 October to 17 March inclusive. Rainbow trout: 8 October to 17 March inclusive in all rivers, drains and canals. In reservoirs, lakes and ponds, this may vary from region to region. Salmon: 8 October to 31 January inclusive. Freshwater fish: 15 March to 15 June inclusive in all rivers, streams, drains, ponds and canals. Eels: 15 March to 15 June inclusive in all rivers, streams, drains, ponds and canals, unless using a hook with a gape of not less than 12.7 mm.
Pollution reports: Please report any pollution or dead fish to the following Freephone number: 0800 807060.

THAMES REGION, Kings Meadow House, Kings Meadow Road, Reading, RG1 8DQ. (Tel: 0118 953 5000, Fax: 950 0388.)

Fisheries & Conservation Manager: Dr R A Sweeting, tel: 0118 953 5502.
Area Fisheries and Conservation Manager (West): J Sutton, Lambourne House, Howbery Park, Wallingford, Oxon OX10 4BD, tel: 0118 953 3353. River Thames (source to Hurley); Rivers Churn, Coln, Windrush, Evenlode, Cherwell, Ray, Cole, Ock, Thame, Wye, Oxford Canal; Kennet, Kennet and Avon Canal, Lambourne, Pang, Leach, Enborme.
Area Fisheries and Conservation Manager (North East): Mark W Pilcher, 2 Bishops Square, Business Park, St Albans West, Hatfield, Herts AN10 9EX. Rivers Lee, Stort, Rib, Ash (Herts), Mimram, Beane and tributaries, Roding, Rom, Beam, Ingrebourne and tributaries, Colne, Colnebrook, Ver, Misbourne, Gade Chess and tributaries. Grand Union Canal, Slough Arm, Paddington Arm. Brent, Crane and Duke of Northumberlands River.
Area Fisheries and Conservation Manager (South East): Dr A Butterworth, Ladymead, By-pass Road, Guildford, GU1 1BZ, tel: 01483 577655, Extn 3529. Rivers Thames (Wargrave to Yantlet), Loddon, Blackwater, Wey, Mole, Wandle and 5 London tributaries. Canals: Basingstoke and parts of Grand Union and Regents.
River Pollution, Fish Mortality and Disease: Reports by Members of the Public: phone FREEFONE RIVER POLLUTION. This number covers the whole of the Thames Region catchment 24 hours a day, 7 days a week; or phone 0800 807060.

Seasons: Salmon and Trout (excluding rainbow trout): 1 April to 30 September; enclosed waters: 1 April to 29 October. Rainbow trout: 1 April to 30 September (does not apply to enclosed waters). Freshwater fish: 16 June to 14 March.

Please report salmon or sea trout captures to Reading Office, tel: 0118 953 5511.

WELSH REGION, Rivers House/Plas-yr-Afon, St Mellons Business Park, Cardiff CF3 0LT. (Tel: 01222 770088, Fax: 01222 798555).

Regional Fisheries, Conservation, Recreation, Navigation Manager: Dr David Clarke.

DIVISIONS OF THE AGENCY
Northern Area: Ffordd Penlan, Parc Menai, Bangor, Gwynedd LL5 2EF, tel: 01248 670770.
Area Fisheries, Ecology and Recreation Officer: A J Winstone.
Enforcement Officer: Mark Chapman.

Rivers controlled: Dee (Welsh) Clwyd, Elwy, Alwen, Alyn, Ceiriog, Ceirw, Lliw, Tryweryn, Twrch, Bala Lake and their feeders. Also waters in an area bounded by watersheds of rivers (including their tributaries and all lakes) running into the sea between the eastern boundary of the Division's area at Old Gwyrch, Denbighshire, and the southern extremity at Upper Borth, Cardiganshire: Dulas, Conway, Lledr, Llugwy (with Lakes Elsi, Crafnant, Cowlyd, Eigiau, Conway, Melynllyn, Dulyn), Aber, Ogwen (with Lakes Anafon, Ogwen, Idwal, Ffynnon, Loer), all waters in Anglesey, Seiont, Gwyrfai, Llyfni (with Lakes Padarn, Cwellyn, Gader, Nantlle), Erch, Soch, Rhydhir, Afon Wen, Dwyfawr, Dwyfach (with Lake Cwmystradlyn), Glaslyn, Dwyryd, Prysor (with Lakes Dinas, Gwynant, Llagi Adar, Trawsfynydd, Gamallt, Morwynion, Cwmorthin), Glyn, Eisingrug (with Lakes Techwyn Isaf,

Techwyn Uchaf, Artro, Mawddach, Eden, Wnion (with Lakes Cwm Bychan, Bodlyn, Gwernan, Gregennen), Dysynny, Dovey, Dulas, Twmyn (with Lake Tal-y-Llyn).

South West Area: Glan Tawe, 154 St Helens Road, Swansea, West Glamorgan. (Tel: 01792 645300).
Area Fisheries, Ecology and Recreation Officer: P V Varallo.
Enforcement Officer: Steve Williams

Rivers controlled: Neath, Afan, Kenfig, Ogmore, Ewenny, Llynfi, Tawe, Afan, Kenfig, Gwendraeth Fawr, Gwendraeth Fach and Loughor. Towy, Teifi, Taf, Eastern and Western Cleddau, Gwaun, Nevern, Aeron, Clarach, Rheidol, Ystwyth, Wyre, and the tributaries of these rivers.

South East Area: Rivers House, St Mellons Business Park, Cardiff CF3 0LT. (Tel: 01222 770088).
Area Fisheries, Ecology and Recreation Officer: J Gregory.
Enforcement Officer: Steve Barker.

Rivers controlled: Thaw, Ely, Taff, Rhymney, Usk and tributaries, including Cilienni, Honddu, Yscir, Bran, Cray, Senni, Tarrell, Cynrig, Crawnon, Rhiangoll, Gwryne-fawr, Grwynefechan, Olway, Afon Lwyd and Ebbw and tributary Sirhowy. Wye and all rivers and brooks of the Wye watershed including Monnow, Trothy, Lugg, Arrow, Ithon and Irfon.

24-hour pollution emergency freephone: 0800 807060.

A Sport for the Mature

ENGLISH FISHING STATIONS

Main catchments are given in alphabetical order, fishing stations listed in mouth to source order, first main river, then tributaries. Where national borders are crossed - e.g. Wye and Border Esk - allocation has been arbitrary. Some small streams have been grouped in counties rather than catchments.

Environment Agency rod licences are now required almost everywhere in England and Wales for all freshwater fishing. Details appear on pages 14-19. A list of fishing clubs appears at the end of each national section. 'Free fishing' means only that a riparian owner is reputed to allow fishing without making a charge. It does not imply a right and such information should be checked locally before an attempt to fish is made. All charges shown are exclusive of VAT unless otherwise stated. Reduced charges to juniors, the disabled, pensioners, and in some instances to ladies, are now quite commonplace. In many instances, they are specified. Where they are not, they may nevertheless be in force. If in doubt, ask when booking.

ADUR

(For close seasons, licences, etc, see Southern Region Environment Agency, p16).

Rises SW of Horsham and flows into the English Channel at Shoreham. Sea trout, trout, and very good coarse fishing, with match weights in excess of 70lb.

Shoreham (W Sussex). Bass, codling, flats, eels, mullet from harbour and shore.

Upper Beeding (W Sussex). Chub, bream, perch, rudd, roach, dace, eels and pike. CALPAC fishes 3,000 yds of prolific tidal stretch. Dt £4, conc, from bailiff on bank. No night fishing. Open 15 Jun-15 Mar.

Bramber and **Steyning** (W Sussex). Bream, roach, chub, dace, pike and carp. Pulborough AS has 3m from Bramber Bridge upstream to Streatham Old Railway Bridge. On tidal water, low water best. Dt £4 (£2.50, conc). River also has run of sea trout. Dt from Hyde Square News, Hyde Square, Upper Beeding, or Prime Angling, 74 Brighton Rd, Worthing.

Henfield (W Sussex). Henfield & Dist AS has fishing rights on 7m of Mid and Upper Adur, from Streatham Bridge to Wineham, with sea trout, brown trout, very large pike, carp, perch, eels, and other coarse species, and coarse fishing in lakes and ponds, with large carp. No dt, membership £40, conc for juv, OAP. Apply to Hon Sec. Worthing & Dist Piscatorial S has two stretches of Adur fishing in vicinity, with bream, carp, chub, pike, perch, gudgeon, roach, rudd, tench; Patching Pond, 4m west of Worthing; Laybrook Fishery, 2m from Ashington. Dt £5-£2.50 from Worthing and Littlehampton tackle shops. Society is affiliated with Sussex Anglers Consultative Association. Tackle shops: Ken Dunman, 2 Marine Place; Prime Angling, 74 Brighton Rd, both Worthing.

Shermanbury Place. Stocked coarse fishing lakes, also 1½m of river, with trout. Carp run to 22lb, tench to 6lb, roach over 1lb. St, dt. Lake fishing Summer only. Parking facilities, no night fishing. Phone Partridge Green 710280 for details.

ALDE

(For licences, etc, see Anglian Region Environment Agency, p19)

A small Suffolk stream, rising near Saxmundham and flowing into the North Sea at Orford Haven, 6½m NE of Felixstowe. Sea fish.

Aldeburgh (Suffolk). Bass, codling, flatfish, etc, can be taken in estuary from jetty and boat; cod and whiting from beach; October and November best months. Hotels: Brudenell, White Lion, Wentworth, East Suffolk *(see also Suffolk, Sea Fishing Stations).*

Snape (Suffolk). River tidal. Mullet, bass, eels below sluice. Fishing free. Other free fishing at Thorpness Mere, nr Leiston. Tackle shop: Saxmundham Angling Centre, Market Place, Saxmundham, tel: 01728 603443: day tickets, details of local lake fishing for carp, tench, perch, bream, rudd and pike, and details of local fishing clubs. Hotels: White Hart, Bell.

ALN

(For close seasons, etc, see North East Region Environment Agency, p17)

Short Northumberland river, flowing into North Sea at Alnmouth. Trout and sea trout, occasional salmon; usually a late run river.

Alnwick (Northumberland). Aln AA water (owned by the Duke of Northumberland), 7-9 miles of trout, sea trout and salmon. Stocked yearly with 500 brown trout, av 1¼lb. Portion running through grounds at Lesbury House private. Visitors (excl Sundays) mt £40, wt £25, dt £8, under 12 free, with adult, from Murraysport, Narrowgate, Alnwick, and Leslie Jobson, Tower Showrooms during business hours. Coquet and Till within easy reach. Hotels: White Swan and Hotspur, Alnwick; Schooner, Alnmouth.

ANCHOLME

(For close seasons, etc, see Anglian Region Environment Agency, p19)

This river, in South Humberside and Lincolnshire, with its tributaries drains about 240 square miles of country. Falls into the Humber at **South Ferriby**, where there is a sluice and tidal lock. The lower part is embanked for about 19 miles and is owned by Anglian Water. The fishing rights are leased to Scunthorpe and District Angling Association. Temporary membership day permits are obtainable from their bailiffs on the bankside or local tackle shop, Dan's, tel: 01724 281877. The river is abundantly stocked with coarse fish, especially roach and bream, and recently perch. Winter shoals found mainly at **Brigg**. Other choice sections at **Broughton, Snitterby, Horkstow** areas. Fishing accesses: South Ferriby Sluice, 4m from Barton upon Humber: **Saxby Bridge**, 6m from Barton upon Humber: Broughton, Castlethorpe, **Cadney** and **Hibaldstow Bridges** near Brigg through which town river passes; Brandy Wharf, Snitterby, **Bishop Bridge**, 6m from **Market Rasen**. Improvement work recently completed at Scabcroft, Broughton and Brigg. Disabled fishing stands at Brigg and at Hibaldstow Bridge. At Barton upon Humber are **Barton Broads** mixed coarse fishery, 6½ acres, Malt Kiln Lane. For tickets, *see Goole*; **Pasture House Fishery**, 20 acres, and Hoe Hill Lake, on banks of Humber, 9 acres with roach, rudd, carp, bream, tench, chub. Dt £2.50 from Mrs K Smith, Barton upon Humber, tel: 01652 635119; **Winter Brothers Pond**, East Halton, 21 acre coarse lake, dt £1. Mr Winter, Marsh Lane, East Halton, tel: 01469 40238; Tackle Shop, Boyalls, High St, Barton upon Humber.

ARUN

(For close seasons, etc, see Southern Region Environment Agency, p16).

Rises on NW border of Sussex, flows past Horsham and enters English Channel at Littlehampton. Noted coarse-fish river, largely controlled by clubs. Some sea trout; May to October.

Littlehampton (Sussex). *See under Sea Fishing Stations.* HQ of Littlehampton and Dist AC is at Arun View Hotel, right by river. Billingshurst AS has R Arun fishing at Pallingham, and three lakes.

Arundel (W Sussex). River tidal and mainly mud-bottomed. Roach and dace run large; bream, perch, pike, chub and occasional sea trout. Bass and mullet taken in fair numbers June, July, August between Ford railway bridge and Arundel, where fishing is free. Leger best method when tide running; trotting down successful in slack water. Victoria AC has 5m of bank north of Arundel town, with roach, dace, bream to 6lb, mullet and bass in summer months. Dt £2 from Black Rabbit, Offham; George and Dragon, Burpham; or Tropicana, 6 Pier Rd, Littlehampton. Castle Trout Pond, Mill Rd, Arundel, open June to Sept, tel: 01903 8837427. Hotels: Norfolk Arms;

Keep the banks clean

Several clubs have stopped issuing tickets to visitors because of the state of the banks after they have left. Spend a few moments clearing up, this includes lengths of broken nylon. If discarded, serious injuries can be caused to wild birds and to livestock.

Swan; Howards.

Chalk Springs Fishery, Park Bottom, Arundel, West Sussex, BN18 0AA. Four lakes, clear water, stocked with brown and rainbow trout of 2-20lb. Dt £27.50. Part-day £17.50, £16.50, £22.00. Refreshments, lodge on lakes, tuition, tackle for hire and sale. Tel: 01903 883742.

Amberley (W Sussex). Chub, bream, roach, dace, rudd, eel, perch, pike. Worthing Piscatorial Society, Rother AC and Bognor Freshwater AC (member of Hants and Sussex Anglers Alliance, 24 stillwater and river fisheries, some dt) have stretches on the Arun here and at **Greatham** and **Bury Ferry**. The Central Association of London and Provincial Angling Clubs hold both banks downstream of Houghton Bridge to South Stoke, tidal water. Railway station 2 mins walk from fishery. Dt £4, conc, from bailiff on bank. No night fishing on CALPAC water. This area to Stopham involved in Sussex RD improvement scheme.

Pulborough (W Sussex). Pike, bream, roach, chub, dace, perch, rudd. Central Association of London and Provincial ACs leases tidal stretch at Swan Meadow. Station is 7 mins walk from fishery. Dt £4, conc, from bailiffs. No night fishing on CALPAC water. Pulborough and District AS has fishing on the tidal Arun from Pulborough to Greatham Bridge, approx 3m, 1m on **Rother**, 3m on **Adur**, **Duncans Lake**, Pulborough (good for young anglers) and 6 small lakes near **Ashington**, coarse fish. St £39, conc, from Sec S Marshall, 17 Mill Way, Billinghurst. Dt £4 (£2.50 conc) for Adur only, see Bramber and Steyning. At **Wisborough Green** Crawley AS has water; dt. At **Horsham** is Newells Pond Carp fishery, two lakes of 4.2 acres each. St only, from Tim Cotton, Newells Pond House, Newells Lane, Lower Beeding RH13 6LN.

Rudgwick (W Sussex). Roach, bream, chub, perch, pike, carp, large eels. Southern Anglers fish ½m non-tidal river at Bucks Green, u/s of road bridge. Tickets for members guests, £5-£4; also exchange tickets with four other clubs for several Sussex and Hampshire waters. Annual subscription £40, conc. Rudgwick AS fishes from Slinfold to Gibbons Mill. Tackle shops: Tropicana, Littlehampton; Prime Angling, 74 Brighton Rd, Worthing; Cowfold Angling Centre, Cowfold. Hotel: Arun Hotel, Lower street.

Tributaries of the Arun.

WESTERN ROTHER:

Petworth (W Sussex). Pike, perch, roach, dace, chub, few trout and sea trout. Leconfield Estate operate a commercial fishery, and let trout rods on their section of the Rother. Contact Smiths Gore, Estate Office, Petworth. Hants and Sussex AA has 5½m in all, limited dt; also stretch downstream from Coultershaw Mill to Shopham Bridge, and 1m (N bank only) from Shopham Bridge. Then both banks for 1m from Fittleworth Bridge. St £21 + £10 joining fee, dt £2.50, from Sec. Contact Richard Etherington, South Dean, Tillington, Petworth GU28 0RE, tel: 01798 343111, for 1½m stocked fly fishing on Rother for browns and rainbows, 3 miles from Petworth. **Burton Mill Pond** holds good pike, perch, roach, rudd, carp, tench. **Duncton Mill**, Petworth, GU28 0LF. 9 acres, brown brook tiger trout and rainbow trout, average bags 3 fish, 7½lb total; st £720, ft £376, wt £196.

Selham (W Sussex). Pitshill Fly Fishing Waters: 1½m part double bank downstream from Lods Bridge; also ½m of tributary. R Etherington, South Dean, Tillington, Petworth, tel: 01798 343111. Stocked with b and r trout.

Midhurst (W Sussex). Rother AC has 5 stretches of river and three lakes; coarse fish incl dace, roach, rudd, bream, tench, perch, carp, pike, eels. Tickets for Rother £3, Rotherfield Pond £5 conc, from Backshalls Garage, Dodsley Lane, Easebourne, Midhurst. Membership from Treasurer.

Chithurst (W Sussex). Petersfield & Dist AC is affiliated to the Hants and Sussex Anglers Alliance who have fishing on the Arun, **Rother**, and eleven stillwaters. Fishing is predominately coarse with most species. Permits for Heath Lake, 22 acres (with carp to 27lb), Petersfield, from local tackle shop. Enquiries to Hon Sec. Tel: 01730 66793. Southern Anglers have water on Rother at Habins Bridge, **Rogate**, approx ½m d/s of pumping station, north bank only, with trout, grayling, chub and dace; also Stepstones Lakes, Dumpford, nr Rogate, 3 small lakes containing carp, tench, roach, rudd, and large eels. Dt on river, £4, from club Committee members, or Sec, Mr B Smith, tel: 01705 472110. Tackle shop: Rods and Reels, 418 Havant Rd, Farlington.

AVON (Bristol)

(For close seasons, licences, etc, see South West Region Environment Agency, p16).

Coarse fishing now excellent in places. Large chub, barbel, pike, bream, roach. Trout in weir pools, including exceptional specimens occasionally, and in some tributaries. Much of Avon and tributaries controlled by Bristol, Bath and Wiltshire Anglers, a merger of eleven clubs know as "the Amalgamation". Fishing includes many stretches of Bristol Avon, Somerset Frome, Bristol Frome, stretches on Brue and Axe, and coarse lakes. Membership costs £25 (concessions for ladies, juniors and pensioners), obtainable from tackle shops in the main Avon centres or Hon Sec. Dt waters.

Bristol. On Avon and Frome and in Somerset. Some free fishing on Environment Agency licence from Netham Weir u/s to Hanham, towpath only. Good sport with trout on **Blagdon Lake, Chew Valley** and **Barrow Reservoirs** *(See Somerset streams, lakes and reservoirs)*. Among coarse fishing lakes in area are **Bowood** (2m W of Calne, dt at waterside); **Longleat** apply Nick Robbins, Bailiff, Swancombe Cottage, Crockerton, Warminster (Tel: 844496); dt £4 bottom and middle lake, £5 top (carp). B & B from Mrs Crossman, Stalls Farm, Longleat BA12 7NE, (01985 844323). **Bitterwell Lake** (N of Bristol) excellent bream, roach, rudd, a few common, mirror and crucian carp, perch. Tuck shop and tackle sold. Dt on bank, £3 per rod, £1.50 conc and after 4pm, from Mrs M Reid, The Chalet, Bitterwell Lake, Ram Hill, Coalpit Heath, Bristol BS17 2UF, tel: 01454 778960. **Henleaze Lake** (north of Bristol, dt June-Sep from R W Steel, 63 Hill View, Henleaze, Bristol). City Council runs **Abbots Pool**, Abbots Leigh. Tackle shops: Fish and Field, 60 Broad St, Chipping Sodbury; Scotts, 42 Soundwell Road, Staple Hill; S Shipp, 7 Victoria St, Staple Hill; Avon Angling Centre, 348 Whitewell Road, St George; Bristol Angling Centre, 12 Doncaster Road, Southmead.

Keynsham (Avon). Chub, perch, eels, roach and dace. Free fishing on Environment Agency licence at R **Chew** confluence, end of recreation ground, left bank; also R Chew in Keynsham Park. Keynsham AA has water extending from Compton Dando to Wollard (trout), Chewton Place, Durley Lane, and Willsbridge to Swineford, also Century Pond, carp roach, bream, tench, £2 dt. All waters members only. Special facilities for young anglers. St £10, dt £4 from Keynsham Pet and Garden, 5 Bath Hill, Keynsham, or Veals, Old Market, Bristol BS2 0EJ (0117 9260790). Bristol & West of England Federation has water here. BB&WAA has six stretches of river here and one at **Willsbridge**.

Saltford (Avon). BB&WAA has stretch at Swineford. Bathampton AA has 2½m; most coarse fish, including carp and tench, few large trout. St £15, dt £2 from local tackle shops and Hon Sec.

Bath (Avon). Coarse fish; barbel present from here to Limpley Stoke; few large trout. Some free fishing at Pulteney Weir d/s to Newbridge, along towpath; Bathampton Weir u/s to car park, most of footpath. Bath AA are part of Bristol, Bath and Wiltshire AA. and have water at Kensington meadows and from Bathampton to city weirs. Good trout fishing in tributary streams, all preserved. **Kennet and Avon Canal** to Limpley Stoke aqueduct preserved by Bathampton AA. Assn also fishes on Newton Park, Hunstrete and Woodborough Lakes, Box Brook nr Bathford on A4, fly only, are permit waters. Contact K Rippin, The Grove, Langridge, Bath. Tackle shop: I M Crudgington, 37 Broad Street (information and tickets for Bath AA and Bathampton AA waters).

Batheaston (Avon). BB&WAA has two fields here.

Bathampton (Avon). All-round fishing. BB&WAA and Bathampton AA have water; dt. Bathampton AA also has water at **Kelston, Newton St Loe, Newbridge, Saltford**, and on **Kennet and Avon Canal, Hunstrete, Newton Park** and **Woodborough Lakes** (good carp, tench), Lydes Farm, and **Box Brook**. St £15, conc £3-£4, dt £2 for some waters, from Hon Sec. and local tackle shops.

Claverton (Avon). Bathampton AA has

2m; very good chub, few trout.

Warleigh (Avon). Bathampton AA has four meadows here: (as Claverton above). BB&WAA has five meadows.

Limpley Stoke (Wilts). Good all-round fishing; large carp, with tench, chub, roach bream and trout; fly-fishing on **River Frome** at Freshford and **Midford Brook** at Midford; preserved by Avon and Tributaries AA. Bathampton AA holds **Kennet and Avon Canal** from Limpley Stoke to confluence with Avon at Bath (5½m): dt from Hon Sec, tackle shops. BB&WAA controls 3m from Limpley Stoke down to Kensington, coarse fish and trout; tickets from Hon Sec, two stretches.

Midford (Avon). **Midford Brook**; trout only; preserved and stocked by the Avon and Tributaries AA.

Freshford (Avon). BB&WAA has water on Avon here; dt issued. **Frome**: trout, coarse fish, stocked and preserved by Avon and Tributaries AA (annual sub £90); from Avon up to Farleigh Hungerford. Limited dt for members' guests. Association also has part of Avon, Freshford to Avoncliffe, fly only water on **Midford, Wellow** and **Cam Brooks**.

Bradford-on-Avon (Wilts). Coarse fish, including pike, few trout. **Kennet and Avon Canal**; coarse fish. Some miles of Avon and canal preserved by Bradford-on-Avon and Dist AA. Dt from Hon Sec or tackle shops Wests, Roundstone Street; Smith and Ford, Fore St (all Trowbridge) and Top Gun and Rod, Treenwood Trading Estate, Bradford-on-Avon. Accommodation with 700 yds private coarse fishing for specimen barbel and other species, Avonvilla, Avoncliff BA15 2DH, tel: 01225 863867.

Melksham (Wilts). Coarse fish, few trout. BB&WAA has Lacock stretch 1m from Melksham: excellent barbel. Avon AC has waters at **Waddon**. St £6, dt £1 from Hon Sec or tackle shops. RD licences from Hon Sec and Avon Angling & Sports Centre (tackle shop), 13 Bath Road. Baits from Gogoozler, Marina. Lavington AC has water on **Semington Brook** at Lavington Mill and Baldham Mill. Leech Pool Farm has coarse fishing at **Broughton Gifford**.

Lacock (Wilts). BB&WAA have water here. Tickets from Coles, Market Place, Chippenham. Dt on site for **Silverlands Lake**. Carp and tench. Isis AC has water

Once confined to east-flowing rivers, barbel are now caught throughout England. This fine specimen - 10lbs. 6ozs. - came from the Avonvilla water on the Bristol Avon. *Photo: Robin Chalk.*

at **Pewsham**.

Chippenham (Wilts). Chub, barbel, bream, perch, roach, carp, pike. Chippenham AA has water; st £19.50, wt £10, dt £3.50 from Rob's Tackle, 22 Marshfield Road, who also have dt for **Sword Lake**, coarse, and **Sabre Lake**, coarse with carp. BB&WAA has about 1½m between here and **Lacock**. Isis AC has water on Avon at **Sutton Benger**, members only. Calne AA have **River Marden**, st £16, dt £3, from Robs Tackle. **Devizes AA waters: 15m of Kennet and Avon Canal**, 1m of Avon at Beanacre, Melksham, various coarse, dt £3.50, conc. Melksham AC have Avon from Beanacre to Whaddon, st £10, dt £2. These and others from Rob's Tackle. Other tickets from T K Tackle, 123a London Rd. Mill Farm Trout Lakes, Worton, Nr Devizes, tel: 01380 813138, 2 dt lakes, 3½ acres. Bill Coleman. Ivy House Lakes, nr Swindon, all species, carp to 20lbs. Dt £3, conc. P and J Warner, tel: 01666 510368. Lakeside Caravan Park, coarse lake, dt £4, P and S Gleed, tel: 01380 722767. Pearmoor Lake, nr Swindon, coarse fishing dt £3, conc, from House of Angling, 59/60 Commercial Rd, Swindon SN1 5NX.

Christian Malford (Wilts). Several fields controlled by BB&WAA here, and at **Sutton Benger** Isis AC has 4m including 2 weirs and backwater; further water near **Seagry Mill**. Calne AA has two meadows on church side. For tickets, *see Chippenham*. Somerfords FA has water upstream from Seagry to Kingsmead Mill (part of it, from Dauntsey road bridge, is trout water) and 2m above Kingsmead Mill on left bank and 1m on right bank. Good chub and perch. Assn also has water on **Frome**. Dt for trout and coarse fishing issued. Golden Valley FC has water at Seagry.

Malmesbury (Wilts). Bristol, Bath and Wiltshire AA have fishing here, members only; trout and coarse fish; also Burton Hill Lake. Membership £25, conc. RD licences from Sports and Leisure, 36 High Street.

Lower Moor Fishery, Oaksey Malmesbury, Wiltshire SN16 9TW. Tel: 01666 860232. Forty acres of excellent trout fishing on two lakes: Mallard Lake (34 acres), any kind of fly fishing, stocked rainbow and brown; Cottage Lake (8 acres) confined to nymph and dry fly on floating line. Dt £20 or £12 (4 and 2 fish limits). Fine fly hatch, exceptional mayfly and damsel. Open end of Mar to New Years Day.

Tributaries of the Avon (Bristol)

FROME (Bristol). Rises near Chipping Sodbury and joins Avon estuary near Bristol. Small tributaries upstream provide ideal conditions for trout. Fishing on **Mells River**, **Whatley** and **Nunney Brooks**. Coarse species are barbel, bream, carp, eel, perch, roach, tench, chub and grayling. BB&WAA have water at **Stapleton**.

Frampton Cotterell (Glos). Most of lower Frome controlled by Bristol, Bath and Wiltshire Anglers.

Yate (Glos). Frome Vale AC has water from Moorend Weir to viaduct. Dodington Park Lake, 6m; carp, perch; preserved. Tanhouse Farm, Yate Rocks, has coarse fishing lake.

CHEW: From Confluence to Compton Dando, coarse fish; thereafter, trout.

Keynsham (Avon). Keynsham AA has fishing *(see Avon)*.

Malmesbury (Wilts). Free fishing on Environment Agency licence at Sherston Avon u/s of Cascade at Silk Mills; Tetbury Avon u/s Station Yard Weir, Fire Station, left bank. Club also has long stretch of **Woodbridge Brook**.

Chewton Keynsham (Avon). Water held

Check before you go

*While every effort has been made to ensure that the information given in **Where to Fish** is correct, the position is continually changing, and anglers are urged, in their own interests, to make enquiries before travelling to selected venues. This is especially important with reference to prices quoted. Anglers attention is also drawn to the fact that hotels mentioned under the various fishing stations do not necessarily have water of their own. Any amendments or further data for inclusion in subsequent editions, and any comments, will be welcome.*

by BB&WAA. Keynsham AA also has water; dt issued for fly and coarse fishing. Stretch in Keynsham Park free to licence holders.

Compton Dando (Avon). Mainly trout, grayling and dace. Keynsham AA has water here from above Woollard Weir some way downstream; no dt.

Pensford (Avon). Trout and coarse fish. Lakes: **Hunstrete Park Lake**; carp, tench, bream, roach, perch; Bathampton AA; members only.

Stanton Drew, Chew Magna, Chew Stoke (Avon). Trout dominant; some roach and dace. No spinning. Dt from local inns and Bristol tackle shops from June 15 to Sept 30 (Mon-Fri only). **Emborough Pond**; carp, tench, roach, perch; dt (limited) from bailiff. *(For Chew Reservoirs, see Somerset (lakes and streams)).*

BOYD BROOK: Trout in upper reaches, coarse fish, **Golden Valley FC has stretch above and below Bitton.**

CAM BROOK: Trout. Avon and Tributaries AA has water (members only). Cameley Trout Lakes are at Temple Cloud. St and dt, apply to J Harris, tel: Temple Cloud 52790/52423.

BYE (BOX) BROOK: Trout, coarse fish. Bathampton AA has water at Shockerwick (Som) and **Box** (Wilts); st £15, dt £2. By Brook Fly FC and Two Mills Flyfishers have water for members. Manor House Hotel, Castle Combe, has ½m of good trout fishing in grounds.

SEMINGTON BROOK: Trout, coarse fish. Lavington AC has Bulkington Brook. St £15 and st £3. Concessions for juniors. Members only. Tel: 01380 830425. For **Erlestoke Lake**, D Hampton, Longwater, Erlestoke, Devizes, Wilts SN10 5UE. Coarse fish, carp to 24lb. Members, limited dt. St £70, wt £30, dt £7. Juv £15, £3. Ban on nut baits and keepnets. Tackle shop: Steve's, 26 High St, Warminster.

FROME: Coarse fish, trout.

Frome (Som). Frome and Dist AA has twelve miles above and below town, and coarse fishing lakes at Berkley and Marston, both 3m from Frome. Regular matches. Membership £10 pa, conc, dt £2, conc. Information from R Lee, tel: 01373 461433. Dt from Frome Angling Centre, 11 Church St, Frome; tel: 467143; Haines Angling, Christchurch St West, Frome, tel 466406. BB&WAA have fishing at **Beckington**. Witham Friary Lake coarse fishing open all year, Witham Hall Farm, Witham Friary, Nr Frome, tel: 01373 836239. Other tackle shop: Haines Tackle, Christchurch St West. Hotel: George, Market Place.

Wolverton (Avon). Trout, coarse fish.

MARDEN: Coarse fish, trout.

Calne (Wilts). Trout, barbel, chub, rudd, carp, tench, pike, perch, roach, dace, bream; 6m held by Calne AA: at Christian Malford, dt; at Spye Park, members only. Isis AC has stretch at Newleaze Farm; members only. Above Calne is preserved dry fly water. **Bowood Lake**, large pike (to 26lb), perch, carp, tench, roach; Details from Bowood Estate, Calne, Wilts SN11 0LZ, tel: 01249 812102, who issue st £99-88, jun conc. Waiting list. North end of lake private. *Note: access to lake only at Pillars Lodge entrance on Calne - Melksham road.* Tickets for Sabre Lake, nr Calne, and other local waters, from tackle shops: TK Tackle 123a London Road.

AVON (Hampshire)

(For close seasons, licences, etc, see South West Region Environment Agency p16)

In years gone by the most famous mixed fishery in England. In its upper reaches, the Avon is a typical chalk stream, populated by free-rising trout and grayling. A decline in the coarse fishing which set in thirty years ago has been the subject of investigation and there are now signs of improvement.

Christchurch (Dorset). Avon and Stour. Excellent sea and coarse fishing in Christchurch Harbour, which is leased to Christchurch AC. Bass, mullet, flounders and (higher up) dace, roach, bream and eels. Other Club waters include several stretches of Dorset Stour from Christchurch Harbour to Wimborne, lakes and gravel pits with large carp and pike. Membership £80 per annum. Dt for these waters and the Royalty Fishery on the Avon (excluding Parlour and Bridge Pool) can be obtained from Mr G K Pepler, Davis Tackle Shop, 75 Bargates, Christchurch, tel: 01202 485169. June 16 to Mar 14 inclusive. The Royalty Fishery price structure ranges between £30 per day for salmon, sea trout and coarse fishing, to double rod £75, and £9.50 single rod for coarse and sea trout fishing, with concessions. Davis will supply brochure on receipt of request and SAE. Top Weir Compound, Parlour and Bridge Pool (best sea trout pool), permits from Fishery Manager: advance bookings only, except 1 Nov-14 Mar, when coarse dt are obtainable for Parlour and Compound. No advance bookings on Main River. Limit 2 salmon except Parlour Pool, one per day. Permits for fishings on Stour and in Christchurch Harbour also obtainable from Davis Tackle Shop *(see also Stour (Dorset)* and Pro Fishing Tackle. For other salmon and sea trout fishing apply early in writing to the Royalty Fisheries Manager, Bournemouth and West Hants Water Plc, George Jessel House, Francis Avenue, Bournemouth BH11 8NB. Dt also from Head Bailiff, 2 Avon Buildinngs, Christchurch. Small coarse fisheries in vicinity: Gold Oak Farm, seven lakes with carp and tench, Hare Lane, Nr Cranborne, tel: 01725 517275; Beeches Brook Fishery, Forest Rd, Burley, tel: 01425 402373; Turf Croft Farm, Forest Rd, Burley, tel: 01425 403743; **Hordle Lakes**, Golden Hill, Ashley Lane, **New Milton**, tel: 01590 672300: coarse fishery on seven lakes. Dt on site. Good sea fishing at Mudeford; boats. Tackle shops: Davis, 75 Bargates; Pro Fishing Tackle, 258 Barrack Rd. Both open 7.30 am, 7 days a week. Hotel: Belvedere, 59 Barrack Road.

Winkton (Dorset). Davis Fishing Tackle, 75 Bargates, Christchurch now sole agents for coarse fishing on this fishery. Season is June 16 to Mar 14; good roach, large chub and barbel, pike; also dace, perch. Dt £5. Salmon fishing is offered, March 15 to June 15 only. Details from Davis Tackle, tel: 01202 485169. Hotel: Fishermans Haunt.

Ringwood (Hants). Ringwood & Dist AA has fishing on rivers as follows: **Avon**; Breamore, 1½m (barbel, chub), Fordingbridge (trout), Ibsley, 2m (S and specimen coarse fish), side streams at Ibsley, Ringwood, 2m (coarse fish), East Mills, 1½m (coarse fish), Fordingbridge Park, ¼m (coarse fish); **Stour**; twelve stretches totalling more than 12m (coarse fish); **Test**; over 2m at Broadlands Est. (members only); also nine still waters totalling over 120 acres. Dt for much of the water from tackle shops. Dt £5 from Ringwood Tackle for ¾m both banks above Ringwood; 1¼m E. bank below and several coarse fishing lakes, dt £4. **Beeches Brook**, Forest Rd, Burley, BH24 4DQ (tel: 01425 402373) is dt coarse lake off A31 to Southampton. Dt £5, advance booking advisable. **High Town**, Ringwood: 23 acre pit containing most coarse species. Tickets from Ringwood and Christchurch tackle shops. Other dt waters: river at Lifelands Fishery; Martins Farm Carp Lake, Woodlands, tel: 01202 822335; Hurst Pond. Tackle shops: Ringwood Tackle, 5 The Bridges, West Street, Ringwood BH24 1EA. Tel: 01425 475155; Hales Tackle; Davis, Christchurch. Hotels: Crown, Star Inn, Fish Inn, Nag's Head, White Hart.

Fordingbridge (Hants). Trout, grayling, perch, pike and roach. Park Recreation Ground has fishing, dt from Council grounds staff, Sept to Mar. Burgate Manor Farm Fishery let to Wimborne AC. Albany Hotel has short river frontage (licences obtainable). Few dt for Bickton Estate water from river bailiff, 2 New Cottages, **Bickton**; St (trout streams) £300, st (coarse) £35, st (salmon) £60, dt (trout streams) £12. No licence needed as block licence purchased. Tackle shop on premises. East Mills Manor, Shepherds Spring Restaurant has 1½m of river and lake. Dt water. Two excellent stillwater fisheries in the vicinity. **Damerham** and **Lapsley's Fishery** (ex Allens Farm). Hotel: Ashburn.

Breamore (Hants). Bat and Ball Hotel has 2m of salmon, trout and coarse fish on dt basis, from £2.50. Phone Breamore 252.

Salisbury (Wilts). Avon, Wylye and Bourne; trout, grayling, coarse fish; preserved. Salisbury and Dist AC has water on Avon as follows: 3m within city boundary, incl Fisherton Recreation Ground; 3m at **Durnford**, 2m at **West Amesbury, Countess Fishery** on Upper Avon; plus **R Wylye** at **Stapleford**, dry fly fishing, grayling in late Autumn and winter, **R Bourne** at **Hurdcott**, the same; **Burgate Mill Stream**. Excellent trout, grayling, roach, etc, in all waters. Dt for some waters from Brabans Newsagents, Wilton Rd, Salisbury. Membership £92 game, £62 course. The Piscatorial Society has Avon fishing nr **Amesbury**, members only. Other local clubs: Tisbury AC, Downton AA. Langford Fisheries, 22 acre trout lakes at Duck St, **Steeple Langford**. Good dry fly fishing, catch and release, boats and permits on site.

Fishing includes 1m of R Wylye. Tel: 01722 790770. London AA has **Britford Fishery**; excellent coarse fishing, good sport with trout, some salmon. Members only; no dt. Humberts, 8 Rollestone Street, may know of annual rods to let. For **Avon Springs Fisheries**, Salisbury, tel: 01980 53557. Waldens Coarse Fishery, Walden Estate, **West Grinstead** SP5 3RJ (01722 710480), has coarse fishing on 5 lakes, total 7.5 acres. Tackle shops: John Eadie, 20 Catherine Street; Reids Tackle, Kingsway House, Wilton. Hotels: County, White Hart; Red Lion; Grasmere; Old Mill, Harnham; Lamb, Hinton; Bell, South Newton.

Netheravon (Wilts). Trout, grayling; preserved. The 6m from **Enford** to **Bulford** is The Services Dry Fly FA (Salisbury Plain) water; strictly members only, no tickets.

AVON (Hampshire) tributaries

BOURNE: Enters near Salisbury. Trout, grayling, coarse fish. Fishing stations: **Porton** and **Salisbury** (Wilts).

EBBLE: Joins Avon below Salisbury; good trout fishing, but mostly private.

WYLYE: Trout, grayling.

Wilton (Wilts). 6 miles preserved by Wilton Fly Fishing Club, full-time keeper, club room, wild brown trout (stocked with fry and fingerlings), grayling. Closed membership of forty five, no dt. Wyle Fly FC has stretches at **Steeple Langford**, **Quidhampton**, and elsewhere. Members and their guests only.

Stapleford (Wilts). Salisbury AC has fishing here; members only. (*See Salisbury*.)

Warminster (Wilts). Hunters Moon Lodge, Henford Marsh BA12 9PA has fishing for guests and club members. Tel: 01985 219977 or 212481. **Longleat** Estate owns just over 2m of upper river. Excellent coarse fishing in three lakes in Longleat Park, carp included. Tickets are issued by Bailiff, Parkhill Cottage, Longleat Estate or directly from Estate (Maiden Bradley 551). St £50, dt £2.50-£4. The Sutton Veny Estate, Eastleigh Farm, Bishopstrow, Warminster BA12 7BE, tel: 01985 212325, lets rods, part rods and quarter-rods on 4m of Wylye, chalk stream dry fly and upstream nymph only, brown trout Autumn nymph fishing for grayling. Not less than £395 per season. Occasional dt, £35. Enquiries to Mr and Mr Walker. at about telephone number.

NADDER: Tributary of Wylye. Trout, grayling, roach, dace, chub. Mostly preserved by landowners. Fishing stations: **Wilton, Tisbury**. Tisbury AC has 3m, dt and wt from Arundell Arms. exchanges with Warminster and Salisbury clubs. Club also has lake at Old Wardour and Dinton Lakes; carp, roach tench. St £20 plus £4 joining, conc. Tackle shop: Reid's Tackle, Wilton, Nr Salisbury.

AXE

(For close seasons, licences, etc, see S W Region Environment Agency, p16)

Rises in Dorset and flows south to the English Channel at Axemouth. Trout, sea trout and salmon. Fishing difficult to come by, but one or two hotels can provide facilities.

Seaton (Devon). Trout, salmon. Some sea trout fishing from L Burrough, Lower Abbey Farm, Axminster, and from Ackermans. Axe estuary fishable (for bass, mullet, flounders, etc), on £2 dt from harbour filling station, Axemouth. Tackle and licences: F Ackerman & Co Ltd, Fore Street *(see Sea Fishing Stations)*. Hotel: Pole Arms. Sea trout, rainbow and wild brown trout fishing at **Colyton**: dt £3 from Mrs E Pady, Higher Cownhayne Farm, Colyton, EX13 6HD, tel: 01297 552267. Two farmhouse holiday apartments to let, on weekly or weekend basis.

Axminster (Devon). Axe, Yarty; trout and salmon. Trouting good especially in April and May. Taunton Fly Fishing Club has beats on the Axe at Chard, Tytherleigh, Musbury. Hotels: Cavalier, Bear Inn, Colyton.

Crewkerne (Som). Axe (3m off); trout. Parret (1m off); trout, roach, dace. Stoke-sub-Hamdon AA has trout fishing from Bow Mills to Creedy Bridge on **Parret**; members only. Fees, £6, £3. Wt also. Yeovil AA has trout and coarse fishing on **Yeo** and tributaries; st £6, dt £3 from Hon Sec and C.R. Tackle & Bait. Trout fishing in **Sutton Bingham Reservoir**, near Yeovil. Tackle shop: Yeovil Angling Centre, Forest Hill.

BLACKWATER

(For close seasons, licences, etc, see Anglian Region Environment Agency, p19)

Rises in NW of county, flows by Braintree to Maldon and empties into North Sea through large estuary. Coarse fish include pike, chub, rudd and some carp.

Maldon (Essex). Maldon AS has river, canal and pond fishing in Maldon area; three stretches totalling 1½ of **R Blackwater**, **Chelmer Navigation Canal**, Longford. All coarse, carp over 45lb, tench, roach, rudd, bream, dace, gudgeon, perch, pike. Membership £45, conc. Dt for Chelmer and Blackwater canal sections only, from bailiff on bank or tackle shop. Leisure sport **Chigborough** gravel pits of 8½ acres at **Drapers Farm**. Coarse fish, tench, bream, crucian, etc. St £20, conc. £10. Dt £1.50, jun conc, from bailiff on bank. LSA, RMC House, High Street, Feltham, Middlesex TW13 4HD, tel: 0181 8931168. Tackle shop: East Essex Angling Centre, 48 The Street, Heybridge, Maldon. Hotels: Swan, White Hart, King's Head.

Chigboro Fisheries, Maldon, Essex CM9 7RE tel: 01621 857368. Home Water: sixteen acre lake with brown and rainbow trout of average weight 2lb 6oz, fly only. Lake record, 19¼lb. 4 boats. St from £145. Dt £23(full limit), or £14.50 (half limit). Slough House Water: four acres, stocked brown and rainbow, average 2½lb. Record 16¼lb. St £320, dt £32, 4 fish, combined water ticket, £27. No boats, rod and tuition. Coarse fishing: four lakes, twenty acres total, large carp and other species, incl catfish. St £100-£60, dt £9-£5.

Witham (Essex). Blackwater and **Brain**. Coarse fish. Kelvedon and Dist AA has 7½m from here to **Braintree**; members only. **Witham Lake**, 5½ acres; **Bovingdon Mere**, **Hatfield Peverel**; 4 acre lake coarse fishery, Colchester APS waters. Tackle shop: E & J Tackle, 16 Church St.

Kelvedon (Essex). Kelvedon and Dist AA has various stretches as well as water on Suffolk **Stour**, reservoir and three pits at Tiptree, **Silver End Pits**, 6 acres each, and two 2 acre pits at **Layer Marney**. St £30, conc, dt £3.50 from M Murton, 189 High Street, Kelvedon. Tench, crucian carp, rudd, roach. Club organises sea-fishing boat trips. Maldon AS has water here and at **Feering** and **Braxted**; members only *(see Witham, Coggeshall and Maldon)*. Tackle shop: E & J Tackle, Church St, Witham.

Coggeshall (Essex). Coarse fish. Kelvedon and Dist AA has water here; members only, *(see Witham and Kelvedon)*. Colchester APS fish Houchins Reservoirs, *(see Colchester)*.

Braintree (Essex). Braintree and Bocking AS owns most of water on main river, banks, from Shalford to Bradwell Village and on **Pant**. Well stocked with roach, perch, rudd, dace, and chub. St £17, Juv £6, OAP £2 from subscription Sec D Clack, tel: 01376 44201. *For Gosfield and Sparrows Lakes see Essex (Streams and Lakes).* Hotels: Horne, White Horse, Nag's Head.

CHELMER and CAN: Coarse fish:

Chelmsford (Essex). River stocked: roach, dace, bream, tench, carp, pike, perch. Public fishing in town parks. Dt £3 for towpath between Brown's Wharf and Ricketts Lock, and for **Heybridge Canal** from Beeleigh to Hall Bridge from bailiff on bank. Chelmsford AA has 15m east bank of Blackwater from Back Lake to Appleford Bridge, with bream to 5lbs and chub to 4lbs, also 18 lakes, two carp only, the rest mixed coarse, with trout fly fishing only on one lake near Danbury. All excellent fishing. Membership is open, £38, with concessions. Dt £3 on six of these waters. Leisure sport gravel pit at **Boreham** offers good carp fishing. St £20, conc. £10. contact RMC House, High Street, Feltham, Middlesex TW13 4HD, tel: 0181 8931168, for details. Blasford Hill Fisheries, Little Waltham, nr Chelmsford (01245 357689): lakes stocked with carp, tench, roach, and other species. Dt £5, conc, on bank or from Edwards Tackle, 16 Broomfield Rd (01245 357689). Other tackle shop: Ronnie Crowe, Maldon Road, Gt Baddow. Hotels: County, South Lodge.

BLYTH (Northumberland)

(For close seasons, licences, etc, see North East Region Environment Agency, p17)

Rises near Throckington and flows 20m to North Sea at Blyth. Trout and grayling with coarse fish (especially roach) in lower reaches. All stretches controlled by Bedlington and Blagdon AA, members only, no tickets.

BRUE

(For close seasons, licences, etc, see South West Region Environment Agency, p16).

Rises in Mendips and flows to Bristol Channel at Burnham. Coarse fish throughout. From West Lydford to Glastonbury, a number of weirs provide deep water in which coarse fish predominate. A good late season river, contains numbers of most coarse species.

Highbridge (Som). Roach, bream, etc. North Somerset AA has some of best waters. Club also has Rivers **Kenn, Axe, Apex Pit**, between Highbridge and Burnham, (match record 35lb 11oz), Newtown Pond, Highbridge (carp to 20lb), South and North Drains. Permits for these and local fishings, and club information from tackle shops P & J Thyer, 1A Church Street, Highbridge TA9 3AE, or Richards Angling Centre, 12 Regents Street, Burnham on Sea. Highbridge AA is part of N. Somerset AA, and holds junior matches, and other events. Further information from Hon Sec. Huntspill River, King Sedgemoor Drain and Cripps River are Bridgwater AA waters *(see Bridgwater - Parret)*. BB&WAA has water on Brue and **Axe** at **Wedmore**, as well as Pawlett Ponds and other lakes. Hotels: Highbridge; The George (clubs accommodated). Lamb Guest House, Church St, is recommended locally, for visiting anglers.

Bason Bridge (Som). Area around milk factory noted for carp; fish run up to 16lb or so. Also roach, chub, tench, perch and pike.

Mark (Som). Carp, pike, perch, roach, chub, tench. N Somerset AA has 2½m on river and 3 to 4m on North Drain; dt and wt from Hon Sec. Highbridge AA also has water on North Drain. Inn: Pack Horse.

Westhay (Som). Glaston Manor AA has stretch from Lydford to below Westhay.

Glastonbury (Som). Roach, bream, chub, etc, in lower stretches of River Brue. Glaston Manor AA has water. Dt from Hon Sec. Fishing extends for 7m from White House, Westhay, to Fosseway Bridge, West Lydford (trout av ½lb). No dt. Windmill AC has coarse ponds at Butleigh Rd, nr Street, senior members only, £15 per annum. Apply to Sec. Tackle shop: Street Angling Centre, 160 High Street, Street.

BUDE RIVER AND CANAL

(For close seasons, licences, etc, see South West Region Environment Agency, p16)

Bude Canal has 1¼ miles of wider than average canal with good banks and full variety of coarse fish. Apply to Hon Sec, Bude AA.

Bude (Cornwall). Bass from beaches, breakwater and rocks; bass and mullet in estuary of Bude River. Details from Hon Sec Bude & Dist SAA. Bude Angling Association has fishing on a total of 6½m of banks of **Tamar** and **Claw** from near Bude to half way to Launceston. Wild brown trout and some dace in downstream beats. Membership £5, wt £5, dt £3. Membership enquiries (with 50p if map req.) to Hon Sec, Bude AA. **Tamar Lake** and **Crowdy** (trout reservoir) controlled by SW Water *(see Cornwall lakes, etc)*. **Bude Canal** (roach, bream, eels, dace, perch, carp to 25lb and tench) 1m from town centre towards Marhamchurch leased by Bude Canal AA; wt £15, dt £3, £1.50 jun and OAP, on bank. Tackle shop: Bude Angling Supplies, 6 Queen St, Bude.

BURE

(see Norfolk and Suffolk Broads)

CAMEL

(For close seasons, licences etc, see South West Region Environment Agency, p16)

A spate river, rising on Bodmin Moor near Davidstow, flowing about 30m to enter the Atlantic between Pentire and Stepper Points. Salmon, sea trout and small brown trout.

Salmon enter from April; grilse from June, with the main runs in October, November and December. Sea trout from May to Sept. Best brown trout fishing in tributaries Allen and De Lank. Salmon fishing in upper reaches dependent on heavy rainfall. There is a voluntary restriction in operation covering the whole river. No fishing in April and a limit of 2 salmon per day and 4 per week, and 4 sea trout per day; also no selling of fish and no maggots. Salmon season ends 15 Dec.

Wadebridge (Cornwall). Trout, sea trout, salmon; good mullet fishing in tidal reaches; estuary is now a bass nursery area, prohibiting fishing for bass. Approx 6m held by Wadebridge and Dist AA at Pencarrow, Grogley, Wenford, and **River Allen** above Sladesbridge, 5½m. Membership of Wadebridge & Dist, via a year long list, is £40. Dt on all waters except Grogley, £15, wt £45, conc, from Marcus Watts, The Bait Bunker, Polmorla Rd, Wadebridge. Hotels: Molesworth Arms, Bridge-on-Wool, Swan, Lanarth, and Country Club, St Kew. *(For sea fishing see Padstow.)*

Bodmin (Cornwall). A few miles from the Camel and Fowey, where Bodmin AA issues visitor permits (ten per day) on some 12 miles of the best water. Details from Hon Sec. Wt £40, dt £12 from May 1-Sept 30. Dt £25, Oct-Nov. No permits in Dec. St, wt and dt from Hon Sec. Concessions for jun and OAP. Free maps and licences from Hon Sec R Burrows, 26 Meadow Place, Bodmin, tel: 01208 75513, on receipt of sae. Also, Mr D Odgers, Gwendreath, Dunmere, Bodmin PL31 2RD, has Bodmin AA permits. Mr T Jackson, Butterwell, Nanstallon, Bodmin, PL30 5LQ has 1½m salmon and sea trout fishing, occasional day permits with preference given to residents, fly only, June-Aug. Self-catering cottage and limited b and b. Tel: 01208 831515. For Fenwick Trout Fishery, Dunmere, Bodmin, 2 acres, phone 01208 78296. Lakeview Park Holiday Village, **Lanivet**, has 3 coarse fishing lakes, 6 acres, stocked; specimen carp, bream, tench. Dt £4, conc. Tel: 01208 831808. Temple Trout Fishery, tel: 01208 850250; gravel pit with rainbow trout, 5m from Bodmin; fish from 1½lb to 15lb; dt £19.50, booking reqd in winter months, tackle and tuition on site. Innis Moore Trout Fishery, 7 acres. Contact tackle shop: Roger, Stan Mays Garage, Higher Bore St., Bodmin. 01208 72659 (closed Wednesday). They also issue tickets for Fowey (Lostwithiel AA waters) and Camel (Bodmin AA waters). Tackle, tickets and local fishing information from Roger's Tackle Shop, c/o Stan May's Filling Station, Higher Bore St, Bodmin PL31 1DZ, tel: 01208 72659. Hotel: Penhallow Manor, Launceston PL15 7SJ.

CHESHIRE (Lakes/Reservoirs)

APPLETON RESERVOIR, nr **Warrington**. Trout fishery controlled by Warrington AA. Members only, membership is by annual subscription plus joining fee, with generous concessions. This is one of the larger fishing clubs of Great Britain, controlling approximately sixty fisheries on rivers, lakes, reservoirs, canals and pools. The club keeps a coarse fishing close season between 15 Mar-15 Jun. *See club list*, for address.

BLACKSHAW FARM LAKES, **Leek**. 4 acre coarse fishery; carp, tench, bream, roach. Prince Albert AS water, members only.

BOSLEY RESERVOIR. Fishing station: **Bosley**. Roach (good), bream, pike, perch, carp. Prince Albert AS water, members only.

BOTTOMS RESERVOIR. High Peak, Cheshire. £2 coarse dt on bank. Information from D Blackburn, Woodhead Rd, Tintwistle, Hyde, Cheshire SK14 7HS.

BOTTOMS RESERVOIR. Macclesfield, Cheshire. Prince Albert AC.

CAPESTHORNE POOLS. Fishing station: **Siddington**. Large carp, tench, bream, roach, rudd and pike. Stock pond has excellent carp and tench. Dt £6, ½

Keep the banks clean

Several clubs have stopped issuing tickets to visitors because of the state of the banks after they have left. Spend a few moments clearing up. This includes lengths of broken nylon. If discarded, serious injuries can be caused to wild birds and to livestock.

day £4 from A Bradley, East Lodge Capesthorne (Tel: Chelford 861584). Park and Garden pools controlled by Stoke-on-Trent AS. No tickets.

DOVE MERE, SAND MERE, Allostock, Knutsford. Prince Albert AS waters, members only. Heavily stocked, including large carp. St £55; waiting list.

GREAT BUDWORTH MERE. Nr. **Northwich**, 50-acre lake holding good bream, pike, etc. Northwich AA; tickets from Hon Sec, st only, £20 plus £20 joining fee, conc. **Pickmere** and **Petty Pool** are assn waters nearby.

HORSECOPPICE RESERVOIR, Macclesfield. Trout fishing leased to Dystelegh Fly FC, Hon Sec, G F Grime, 4 Lostock Avenue, Hazel Grove, Stockport. Members only, no permits. Owned by North West Water Ltd, Woodhead Road, Tintwhistle, Hadfield via Hyde, Cheshire SK14 7HR, tel: 01457 864187.

LANGLEY BOTTOMS and **LAMALOAD RESERVOIRS**. Nr **Macclesfield**. Langley Bottoms now coarse fishing, Prince Albert AS, members only. Lamaload, Good fly fishing for trout. Prince Albert AS. Limited dt £8 from Barlows Tackle, 47 Bond St, Macclesfield. Further information, contact Peter Sharples, Conservation, Access and Recreation Manager, North West Water Ltd. (*See Horsecoppice*.)

LEADBEATERS RESERVOIR. Bollington and Royal Oak AC, T Woolley, 51 Palmerston St, Bollington SK10 5PW. Dt from Barlows, Bond St, and Bobs Fishing Tackle, Buxton Road, both Macclesfield.

LYMM DAM, Lymm, beside A56. 15 acre lake, good all year round fishing with big carp and pike. Lymm AC water, 50 pegs, bookable for matches. Contact Hon Sec for this and seven other dt waters. Membership £27 per annum.

MILL LODGE, BOLLINGTON. 3 acres. Large carp. Prince Albert AS, members only.

OULTON MILL POOL. Fishing station: Tarporley. Well stocked with good carp, bream, tench and pike. Dt from Mill Office.

RIDGEGATE RESERVOIR, Macclesfield. Macclesfield Fly FC, dt £12, from D J Harrop, School House, Macclesfield Forest, Macclesfield SK11 0AR. More information from Peter Sharples, Conservation, Access and Recreation Manager, North West Water Ltd. (*See Horsecoppice*.)

ROMAN LAKES LEISURE PARK, Marple, nr Stockport SK6 7HB, tel: 0161 427 2039. Roach, perch, bream, carp to 30lbs, pike to 20lbs. Dt £3.75, with concessions from Lakeside Cafe.

ROSSMERE LAKE. 6 acres. Fishing station: **Wilmslow**. Heavily stocked. 80 match pegs. Prince Albert AS, members only.

TEGGNOSE RESERVOIR, Macclesfield. Trout, Macclesfield Waltonian AC. Dt from The Cycle Shop, Sunderland St, Macclesfield; Barlows Tackle Shop, 47 Bond St, Macclesfield. Information, Peter Sharples, Conservation, Access and Recreation Manager, North West Water Ltd. (*See Horsecoppice*.)

THORNEYCROFT HALL LAKES, Gawsworth. Prince Albert AS water, members only. Carp, tench, roach, pike.

COLNE (Essex)

(For close seasons, licences, etc, see Anglian Region Environment Agency, p19)

Rises in north of county and flows to North Sea via Colchester. Improving as coarse fishery.

Colchester (Essex). Colchester APS controls two short stretches, with roach, chub, perch, pike, bream, dace; no tickets. The society's other waters, with excellent catfish, carp and pike fishing, include **Layer Pit**; pike, perch, bream, roach, rudd, tench, carp; Houchins Reservoirs, Coggeshall, coarse, large catfish; water on **Stour**, Hatfield Peverell Lakes; Witham Lake; Olivers Lake at Witham; Preston Lake, 20 acre mixed coarse fishery, and Bovingdon Lakes, good carp. Members only. St £43, conc to jun, OAP, disabled. Colchester Piscatorial Society has water on Langham Ponds, Stour and Colne; members only. ½m of Colne fished by Kelvedon AA. Tackle shops: W E Wass, 24 Long Wyre Street; K D Radcliffe, 150 High St. Witham tackle shop: E & J Tackle, 16 Church St. Hotels: George, Red Lion.

Aldham (Essex). Colnes AS has water at Fordham and Aldham, three stretches of Stour near Bures, three reservoirs, one lake and two ponds, and Blackwater stretch. Most species. Improved access for disabled. Members only, £20, conc, from Sec P Emson, Emson & Son Tackle Shop, 88 High St, Earls Colne, Colchester CO6 2QX.

Halstead (Essex). Coarse fish, including tench. **Gosfield Lake Resort** (45 acres), Church Rd, Gosfield, tel: 01787 475043; well stocked carp, with perch, roach, tench, pike, rudd; dt £4.50, evening £2.75. Also **Sparrows Pond**, Gosfield; coarse fish including carp and tench; Halstead and Hedingham AC (members only, st £12) has several miles of Pant, stretch of Colne, from Yeldham to Halstead, 2 reservoirs and pits. Membership from P Emson, *see above*. Tackle shop: E McDowell, High Street.

COQUET

(For close seasons, licences, etc, see North East Region Environment Agency, p17)

Rises in Cheviots and enters North Sea near Warkworth. Salmon, sea trout and trout. Sport still very good. Facilities for visitors. Good run of spring salmon.

Warkworth (Northumberland). Trout, sea trout; salmon from Feb onwards to late summer and autumn. Duke of Northumberland leases large part of his water to Northumbrian Anglers Federation. St £55 salmon, £35 trout. Concessions for OAP. Applications to Head Bailiff, Thirston Mill, Felton, Morpeth NE65 9EH, tel: 01670 787663, or tackle dealers for trout permits only. Additional permit for tidal section. Permits for 2m beat, situated 1m d/s from Weldon Bridge, Longframlington, £16 or £11, from Murraysport, Narrowgate, Alnwick.

Acklington (Northumberland). Trout, sea trout and salmon. Northumbrian AF water on Coquet and tributary, Thirston Burn.

Felton (Northumberland).Salmon, sea trout (spring and autumn), trout. Northumbrian AF; trout permits from Post Office *(see Warkworth).*

Weldon Bridge (Northumberland). Nearest station: Morpeth, 9½m. Trout (sea trout and salmon, late summer and autumn). Anglers Arms Hotel, Weldon Bridge, Morpeth NE65 8AL, has fishing, maximum 3 rods, on 1m north bank. Free for residents, otherwise £10 dt. Tel: 01665 570655/570271.

Rothbury (Northumberland). A late salmon run and excellent sea trout fishing in June and Oct. Brown trout, including fish to 3lb. Northumbrian AF has 4m of Coquet *(see Warkworth)*. Tickets for 6m stretch from Whitton Farm House Hotel. Thropton & Rothbury AC has 1½m on Coquet around Rothbury, 2-3m on tributaries. Main runs of salmon and sea trout, Sept and Oct. Non members welcome, dt £7, conc, from Thropton P O, and Morpeth tackle shop. **Fontburn Reservoir**, Ewesley, nr Rothbury, trout fishery of 87 acres stocked with rainbow and American brook trout, fly or worm permitted. Record rainbow, 20lb 14oz. Dt £11, £9 conc, 6 fish. Tel: 01669 621368. Hotel: Whitton Farm House.

Holystone (Northumberland). Salmon (late), trout; mostly private. Holystone Burn, trout; Grasslees Burn, trout. Inn: Salmon, where particulars may be had.

Harbottle (Northumberland). Good trout and some late salmon fishing on Coquet and Alwin. Upper Coquetdale AC has extensive parts of upper river; members only.

CORNWALL (streams, lakes, etc)

(For close seasons, licences, etc, see South West Region Environment Agency p16)

ARGAL and **COLLEGE RESERVOIRS**. (3m W of) SWW fisheries. **Argal**, nr

Penryn: 65 acres, fly only for rainbow trout. Season: Apr 1-Oct 31 incl. Dt £12, evening £10, conc, from self-service at Argal Barn. Full st £375, conc. Boats £7.50 per day, bookable in advance. Ranger, tel: 01579 342366. **College**, nr **Falmouth**: 38 acres coarse fishing with carp over 30lb, large perch, pike, bream, tench, eels. St £100-£65; dt £4, conc; open all year, 24 hr day. Permits from Newtown Angling Centre, Germoe, TR20 9AF, tel: 01736 763721.

BOSCATHNOE RESERVOIR, **Penzance**; 4 acre, stocked SWW coarse fishery, with bream, roach, tench, crucian carp, gudgeon, eels. Permits £4, conc, st £100 or £65, with conc, from Newtown Angling Centre, Newtown, Germoe, Penzance (01736 763721), or Atlantic Fishing Tackle, 36 Wendron St, Helston, or H Symons, Ironmonger, Market Place, St Ives.

BUSSOW RESERVOIR St Ives. SWW coarse fishery, with carp, tench, bream, roach, rudd, perch, crucian carp, eels. Open all year, 24 hour day. Permits £3.50 from Newtown Angling Centre, Newtown, Germoe, Penzance (01736 763721), or Atlantic Fishing Tackle, 36 Wendron St, Helston, or H Symons, Ironmonger, Market Place, St Ives TR26 1RZ (01736 796200). Symons have tickets several small coarse fisheries in locality

STITHIANS RESERVOIR, Redruth. 247 acres. SWW brown and rainbow trout fishery; fly, spinning, bait fishing zoned. Season Mar 15-Oct 12. Full st £90, dt £7, conc. Limited boats, bookable 24 hrs in advance. Permits from Londis Supply Store, Stithians (01209 860301); Peninsula Watersports Centre, Stithians (01209 860409).

PORTH RESERVOIR, **Newquay**. 40 acres, SWW fishery, bream, rudd, tench, roach, perch, eels, and carp. Open all year, 24 hour day, permits £4, conc, from self-service unit at car park.

CROWDY RESERVOIR, **Camelford**. 115 acre SWW trout fishery, stocked with brown trout fry, supplemented with rainbows. Fly, spinning and bait fishing zoned. Season Mar 15-Oct 12. Full st £95, dt £7, conc, from Spar Shop, Camelford PL32 9PA (01840 212356).

SIBLYBACK LAKE, Liskeard. 140 acres. Fly only SWW fishery, with stocked rainbow trout. Season Mar 24-Oct 31. Permits £7 from self-service kiosk, St £110, conc, Watersports Centre, Siblyback, Common Moor, Liskeard. Ranger, tel: 01579 342366.

COLLIFORD LAKE, **Liskeard**. 900 acres. SWW fly fishery, with natural brown trout. Full st £110, dt £7, conc. No boats. Open 15 Mar-12 Oct. Permits from Jamaica Inn, off A30 at Bolventor.

CONSTANTINE BROOK. Fishing station; **Constantine**, ns Penryn WR, 6m. Trout. Constantine joins estuary of **Helford River**. Sea fishing off Helford Mouth *(see Falmouth)*. Ashton, near **Helston, Wheal Grey Pool**; stocked coarse fishery with large carp.

DRIFT RESERVOIR. Near **Penzance** (3m); sixty-five acres in quiet valley. Wild brown and stocked rainbow trout (fly only). Limit, 3 rainbows per day, no limit on wild browns. wt £20 and dt £6, £4 (half price junior), from warden on reservoir, by car park, or Mr Terry Shorland, Driftway, Drift Dam, Penzance (01736 363869). 7m from Penzance are 3 carp pools at **Tindeen Fishery**, carp to 25lbs, dt £3. J Laity, Bostrase, Millpool, Goldsithney TR20 9JG, tel: 01736 763486. **St Buryan Lake** carp pool, tel: St Buryan 220.

GWITHIAN BROOK. Fishing station: **Camborne**. No longer recommended for trout fishing. Several course lakes in area, also very good beach and rock fishing. Camborne AA is sea fishing club. Tackle, baits and tickets from The County Angler, 39 Cross Street TR14 8ES. Hotels: Regal, Tyack's.

HAYLE. Fishing stations: **Relubbus**, **Hayle Causeway** and **Gwinear**. Trout and sea trout. Good beach fishing near Hayle, and estuary fishing very good, particularly for bass, mullet and flats; plenty of natural bait. Marazion AC has three coarse pools in St Erth, nr Hayle, tickets from The County Angler, *see above*. Tackle shop: Angoves Sports, Copperhouse, Hayle.

WEST LOOE RIVER. Approx 7 miles in length, runs to Herodsfoot. Runs of sea trout, occasional Salmon. Liskeard & District AC has water. Shark fishing annual festival: details from Sec, The Quay, East Looe. **Shilla Mill Lakes**, 4 lakes, 6m west of Looe on B3359. Carp, tench, roach. Club house facilities. J Facey, tel: 01503 220271. Hotels: Punch Bowl, Jubilee. Good sea fishing. Tackle and tickets from Looe Tropicals and Pets, Buller St, tel: 01503 326535.

LYNHER. Short spate with runs of sea

trout (Apr onwards) and salmon (best Aug-Oct). No brown trout. Grilse run in July-Oct. Liskeard and District AC have fishing rights on many stretches, also on **Fowey, Camel, Seaton** and **West Looe**, and **Inny Rivers**; 26 miles single/double bank fishing. Weekly/day tickets from tackle shops in local towns. Membership £45, application to Trevor Sobey, Trevartha Farm, Liskeard. Waiting list. Siblyback and Colliford Lakes are near. Royal Albert Bridge AC have 2 acre coarse fishing lake at **St Germans**.

LUXULYAN RIVER. Fishing station: **Par**. Heavily polluted, but tributary **Redmoor River** has good head of trout. Sandeels at Par Sands, mackerel from the bay, pollack by Gribben Head and near harbour, and bass between harbour and Shorthorne Beach. Boats for hire at Par and Polkerris. Hotels: Royal, Par; Carlyon Bay, St Austell.

MELANHYL. Newquay. Brown trout and occasional sea trout. Contact. Sec, St Mawgan AC or The Merrymoor Inn, Mawgan Porth for tickets.

OLD MILL RESERVOIR, Dartmouth. 4 acre SWW coarse fishery with carp, roach, rudd, bream, tench, eels. Open all year, 24 hour day. Season ticket only, on application to South West Water Peninsula Fisheries, Higher Coombepark, Lewdowne Okehampton Devon EX20 4QT, tel: 01837 871565..

PETHERICK WATER. Fishing station: **Padstow**. Small trout. Estuary now a bass nursery area, prohibiting fishing for bass. Other species scarce.

RETALLACK WATERS. St Columb, TR9 6DE, tel: 01637 880974. 20 acres of water, with separate coarse and specimen lakes; carp and pike to 25lb, roach, rudd, tench, eels. Dt £5, tackle and bait from 'The Tackle Cabin' on site. Open seven days a week. Meadowside Coarse Fishery, Winnards Perch, St Columb; three lakes with carp and mixed coarse fish. Dt £3.50, £4.50 2 rods, conc. Mrs Holmes, tel: 01637 880544. Rosewater Lakes, 3 acres, carp, and mixed coarse. Dt £3, conc. Holiday cottages to let. Nr Perranporth, tel: 01872 573040, or 573992.

ST ALLEN RIVER. Fishing Station: **Truro**. St Allen and **Kenwyn** Rivers at Truro; **Tresillian** River (3m from Truro on St Austell road); **Kennel** or **Perranarworthal** River (5m from Truro); trout very small; a few sea trout run into **Lower Tresillian** River. Gwarnick Mill Fly Fishing Lake, St Allen, tel: 0187254 4871; lake of 1½ acres fed by St Allen River, with rainbow trout av 2lb, and wild browns; dt £16 for 4 fish, £10 for 2 fish. At **Perranporth**, nr Redruth, Bolingey Coarse Fishing Lake, coarse fish. Dt £5. Contact John and Maddy, tel: Truro 572388. Hotel: The Morgans, Perranporth *(see also Sea Fishing Stations)*

ST AUSTELL. Roche (St Austell) AC has club waters in area at St Dennis, Rosevean, St Blazey, Bugle and Glynn. Coarse fishing for perch, roach, rudd, carp, tench, eels and pike. Members only. Tackle and information from The Bait Bunker, Polmorla Rd, Wadebridge.

SEATON RIVER. Seaton rises N of Liskeard, runs 1m E of the town and to the sea in 9m. Good trout stream, though bushed over. Liskeard and Dist AC has considerable stretch.

TAMAR LAKE (UPPER), Bude. 81 acres, SWW coarse fishery with carp, bream, tench, roach, rudd, eels. Dt £4, £3.50 conc, from ranger on site.

TAMAR LAKE (LOWER), Bude. 81 acres, SWW fishery with brown and rainbow trout. Fly only, season Mar 15 - Oct 12. St &0, dt £5, 4 fish limit, conc. Bank fishing mainly, limited boat option, bookable in advance (Ranger, tel: 01288 32262).

TIDDY. Fishing station: **St Germans**. Sea trout to Tideford, trout elsewhere.

VALENCY. Fishing station: **Boscastle**. Valency is 4m long; holds small trout and few sea trout. Hotels: Wellington, in Boscastle (Environment Agency licences); Eliot Arms, Tregadillet 15m. Sea fishing good for bass, mackerel, pollack, etc.

WHITEACRES COUNTRY PARK, White Cross, **Newquay**, TR8 4LW. Four stocked coarse fishing lakes in 28 acres. Carp to 25lb, tench 7lb, large bream and roach. Night fishing, matches and competitions. Tel: 01726 860220.

CUCKMERE

(For close seasons, licences, etc, see Southern Region Environment Agency, p16).

Formed by two tributaries, which join at Hellingly, and enters sea at Cuckmere Haven, west of Beachy Head. Mainly coarse fish, roach, bream, chub, carp, perch, dace and pike.

Alfriston (E Sussex). Fishing controlled by the Southdown AA, membership from The Polegate Angling Centre or any Eastbourne tackle shop. Dt £5 for several club fisheries. Below Alfriston Lock the river is salt and tidal, being open to mouth at Cuckmere Haven. In summer grey mullet are plentiful near Exceat Bridge (Eastbourne-Seaford road); also bass and occasionally sea trout. Cuckmere is tidal to ½m upstream from Alfriston. At **Berwick**, Langley AC has coarse fishing on Batbrooks Pond; club also fishes **Langney Haven**, **Hurst Haven**, **Kentland Fleet**. Tickets from Tony's Tackle, Eastbourne.

Hailsham (E Sussex). Cuckmere 2m. Southdown AA (formed 1997 from merger of Hailsham AA and Compleat Anglers FC) has extensive fishing on Cuckmere between Alfreston and Horsebridge (Hailsham); **Wallers Haven**; **Pevensey Haven**; **Abbotts Wood**, lake 3½ acres, and other waters. Membership £40, conc, dt £5 on some fisheries from Hon Sec or tackle shops: Hailsham Bait & Tackle, Battle Rd, Hailsham; Polegate Angling Centre; Tony's Tackle, both Eastbourne; Anglers Den, Pevensey Bay; Battle Angling, Battle; Tight Lines, Bexhill.

CUMBRIA (lakes)

(See English Lake District)

CUMBRIA (streams)

(For close seasons, licences, etc, see NW Region Environment Agency, p17, unless otherwise stated).

ANNAS. Fishing station: **Bootle**. Small trout; good sea trout and salmon; late. Millom AA has fishing, also water on **Esk**, **Lickle**, **Irt**, **Duddon**, **Devoke Water**, **Black Beck** and **Lazy**. St £70 + £10 entrance from Hon Sec Millom & Dist AA. Dt £15 from Duddon Sports. Environment Agency licences from Waberthwaithe P O, Haverigg P O, Millom P O.

BLACK BECK. Fishing station: **Green Road**. This stream rises on Thwaites Fell, and in 7½m reaches Duddon Estuary. Millom AA has water, entrance, Race Grove, The Green, Nr Millom. Tickets from secretary.

CALDER. Empties into Irish Sea some 150 yards from mouth of Ehen. Salmon, sea trout, a few brown trout. Sea trout run large; 10lb and more. Best June onwards: good salmon fishing, July-Oct.

EHEN. Outflow of Ennerdale Water. Flows into Irish Sea on west coast of Cumberland. Salmon, sea trout (June to Oct) and brown trout. At Egremont, Anglers' Assn has good salmon and sea trout fishing to Sellafield; st £30, wt £30; May 1-Oct 31 apply Hon Sec or tackle shop. Hotels: Black Beck, Egremont and Sea Cote (St Bees); Scawfell, Seascale. Good fishing in upper reaches held by Wath Brow and Ennerdale AA; st and wt. Tackle shop: W Holmes, 45 Main Street, Egremont, tel: 01946 820368, has permits for Ehen, Ennerdale Lake and other local fishing.

ELLEN. Rises on Great Lingy Hill and flows into the Solway Firth at Maryport. Salmon and sea trout runs increasing; best late July onwards. Good brown trout fishing (Mar-June best).

Aspatria (Cumbria). Trout; sea trout, and salmon from July. Hotels: Grapes, Sun.

ESK. Rises near Scawfell and flows into Irish Sea near Ravenglass. Good runs of salmon, sea trout, July onwards.

Ravenglass (Cumbria). Salmon, sea trout. Rivers Mite and Irt here join Esk estuary *(see also Irt)*. Ravenglass; Millom AA has three stretches, 620 yds south bank on Esk. St £70. Wt and dt from Sec. Outward Bound School, Eskdale Green, has brown and rainbow trout fishing in private tarn (also perch). Limited to specific days. Enquiries to Bursar (Eskdale 281). May and June are best for trout; June, July, Aug for sea trout; Sept, Oct for salmon. Hotel: Pennington Arms where licences are sold and help given in arranging fishing locally.

Eskdale (Cumbria); trout; sea trout, salmon; various private owners. Millom & Dist AA fishes Dalegarth Estate water, two beats at Gill Force and Beckfoot; good fly fishing, and worming; also stretch at Brantrake, with sea trout from June, salmon from July, Sept-Oct best months. Contact hon sec. Inexpensive fishing on **Wastwater** and **Burnmoor**

Tarn. Good sea fishing for bass within five miles.

IRT. Outflow of Wastwater, joining Esk in tidal water. **Bleng** is main tributary. Runs of salmon and sea trout July onwards, some heavy fish taken.

Holmrook (Cumbria). Salmon, sea trout, brown trout. Short free stretch in village. Enquire at hotel. Lutwidge Arms Hotel is sole agent for supply of permits for 1½m of Sporting Tribune water, limit of 6 rods. Wt £50, dt £11. Tel: 0194672 4230. Millom AA holds two stretches, apprx 1200 yds, Holme Bridge and Drigg Village; tickets (*for prices see DUDDON*) from Duddon Sports and Leisure, Millom; Holmrook Garage; Waberthwaithe and Haverigg POs. Tackle shop: E W Mitchell & Son.

Netherwastdale (Cumbria). On **Wastwater Lake**; trout, permits *(see English Lake District)*. Greendale Tarn and Low Tarn feed Wastwater. Sport is good in May and June.

MITE. Flows south for short course from slopes near Eskdale to join estuary of Irt and Esk at **Ravenglass**. A late river. Sea trout, good brown trout, occasional small salmon later on, but few opportunities for visitors.

POAKA BECK. Barrow AA, J R Jones, 69 Prince St, Dalton in Furness LA15 8ET. Dt from secretary.

WAMPOOL. Fishing stations: **Wigton** and **Curthwaite**. Wampool, under the name of Chalk Beck, rises on Broad Moor. Sea trout in lower reaches mostly free.

WAVER. Trout stream, flowing into the Solway Firth. Some water free, but most subject to agreement by farmers and landowners. Environment Agency licences may be obtained from Saundersons (Ironmongers), 11-13 King Street, **Wigton** CA7 9EB. Waver has run of sea trout and herling, particularly in its lower reaches.

Wigton (Cumbria). Wiza Beck, Wampool, 2m N. Waver, 2m W. Ellen, 8m SW. Lakes: Moorhouse Tarn, 2m N (private). Tackle shop: Saunderson (Ironmongers), 11-13 King Street. Hotels: Royal Oak and Kildare.

CRUMMOCK BECK (tributary of Waver). Flows into Holm Dub, tributary of Waver. Free, but difficult to fish. *(For licences see Waver).*

Leegate (Cumbria). Waver, 1m E.

WHICHAM BECK. Fishing Station: **Sile Croft**. After a course of 6m runs into Haverigg Pool, which joins Duddon estuary at Haverigg (NWW).

DARENT

(For close seasons, licences, etc, see Southern Region Environment Agency, p16).

Rises by Westerham and enters Thames estuary at Dartford. Water retention has been improved by weirs. Modest trout fishing in upper reaches, coarse fishing downstream, roach, dace, chub.

Dartford (Kent). Dartford and Dist A & PS have lakes along river valley which hold coarse fish, (Brooklands, *see Kent*) plus stretches of Medway, Beult and L Tiesse, members only, Long waiting list. LSA have three gravel pits at Sutton-at-Hone, with carp, tench and other species. St £40, conc. *See Chertsey.* Tackle shops: Bob Morris, 1 Lincolnshire Terrace, Lane End; Angling Centre, 84 Lowfield St; Tackle Box, Sutton-at-Hone.

Shoreham (Kent). Trout, chub, roach, dace. Darent Valley Trout Fishers have good 2½m stretch of water between Shoreham and Eynsford; strictly members only (waiting list). Sepham Trout Fishery is nearby, at Sepham Farm, Filstone Lane, Shoreham, TN14 5JT. Tel: 019592 2774.

Sevenoaks (Kent). River preserved. For **Chipstead Lakes** contact Holmesdale AS. Tickets for friends from tackle shop: Manklows Kit & Tackle, 44 Seal Road. Manklows will supply useful general information about local fishing. Bromley AS has fishing in area. **Longford Lake**: Holmesdale AS, coarse fishery of more than 100 swims, with carp to 30lbs and most other species. Joining fee £15, annual subscription £35. Society also fishes two smaller lakes in Montreal Park nr **Riverhead**, Sevenoaks.

Keep the banks clean

Several clubs have stopped issuing tickets to visitors because of the state of the banks after they have left. Spend a few moments clearing up. This includes lengths of broken nylon. If discarded, serious injuries can be caused to wild birds and to livestock.

Tributary of the Darent

CRAY: Coarse fish.

Crayford (Kent). Thameside Works AS, (members of Rother Fisheries Association) has Cray; bream, roach, perch, rudd, pike, carp, tench; members only. They also have a lake at Northfleet and Shorne Country Park lakes. Coarse fish. Dt for Shorne only, £2.50, £1.50 jun. from bailiff. Membership from R Graham, 186 Waterdales, Northfleet DA11 8JW. SAE, please. **Ruxley Pits, Orpington**, coarse fish; Orpington AA has lakes in a Nature Reserve. No dt. Waiting list for membership. Tackle shop: Orpington Angling Suppliers, 304 High Street, St Mary Cray; A & I Fishing Tackle, 33 High St, Green St Green.

DART

(For close seasons, licences, etc, see, South West Region Environment Agency p16)

The East and the West Dart rise two miles apart on Dartmoor. East Dart runs to Postbridge and thence to Dartmeet, where it unites with West Dart which flows through Two Bridges. The West Dart above Dartmeet (with the exception of the right bank from Huccaby Bridge to Dartmeet), and the East Dart above Dartmeet (with the exception of the left bank from Wallabrook Junction to Dartmeet), belong to Duchy of Cornwall. The river has runs of salmon and peal (sea trout). Best months for salmon are March April and Sept in the lower reaches and August to Sept higher up. For peal July to Sept are favoured in the main river, and tidal water of Totnes Weir Pool in May and June. Wild brown trout are mainly small.

Dartmouth (Devon). In river, fishing for ray, bass, whiting, mackerel, garfish, mullet, and pouting. Coastline for dogfish, bull huss, bass, wrasse, whiting, dad, plaice, turbot, conger. Boats effective in river and sea. Skerrie banks and wrecks popular venues. Flatfish off sand. Club: Dartmouth & Dist AA, clubroom open at weekends. Salmon, peal and trout fishing in Dart on Dart AA water *(see Totnes, Buckfastleigh)* and a trout reservoir. Lake; Slapton Ley; pike, rudd, etc, 8m *(see Devonshire, small streams and lakes)*. Also, **Old Mill**, SWW carp pool, dt. Tackle and frozen baits from Sport 'n' Fish, Fairfax Place. Hotel: Victoria, Victoria Rd.

Totnes (Devon). Salmon, peal, trout. Dart AA controls Dart from Staverton Weir to Austins Bridge, left bank only; Totnes Weir Salmon av 10lb; peal 2lb in May-June and about 1lb thereafter. 4lb and 5lb peal not rare. School peal run from late June to mid-Aug. Nearly all peal caught after dark in normal conditions; Aug usually best. Fly only for peal and trout. Newhouse Fishery, Moreleigh, Totnes TQ9 7JS, tel: 01548 821426, has 4 acre trout lake open all year. Dt £16, 4 fish. Half day £10, 2 fish. New Barn Angling Centre, Totnes Rd, Paignton, has coarse and trout ponds. Tel Paignton 553602. Hotels: Seymour, Royal Seven Stars and Cott Inn (at Darlington). At Staverton, near Totnes, is the Sea Trout Inn, close to the river. Old Mill, Harberton, has ½m trout fishing on **River Harbourne**.

Buckfastleigh (Devon). Salmon, peal, trout. SWW Plc has fishery, ¼m Dart, Austins Bridge to Nursery Pool; salmon, sea trout. St £45, 16 rods. Tel: 01392 219666. Holne Chase Hotel, near Ashburton TQ13 7NS, tel: 01364 631471 (fax 631453) has about 1m right bank upstream from bridge, with seven pools; ghillies and tuition if required. End of season tally was 62 sea trout, 2-8lbs, 22 brown trout and 26 salmon to 12lbs. Hotel can arrange fishing on the Moor with Duchy permit, and a further 7m through the Dart Anglers' Association. Permits also from Watercress Farm, Kerwells, Chudleigh, N Abbot TQ13 0DW. Fishing is near Ashburton

Princetown (Devon). Permits for salmon and trout fishing on main river, **East** and **West Dart**, **Wallabrook**, **Swincombe** and **Cherrybrook** from most tackle shops in S Devon; also the Prince Hall Hotel, Two Bridges Hotel, both Princetown; Mabin's News, Fore St, Buckfastleigh; and Princetown Post Office. Salmon best May-Sept. Charges: S and MT, st £125, wt £70, dt £20; T, st £55, wt £15, dt £4. Hotel: Prince Hall, Yelverton PL20 6SA, tel: 01822 890 403, will advise on local fishing and tuition.

Hexworthy (Devon); Salmon, sea trout (peal), brown trout. Hotel: Forest Inn, Hexworthy PL20 6SD, tel: 01364 631211; dt, wt or st, at hotel, for Duchy of Cornwall water. Ghillie, instruction; Inn buys catch. Good centre for E and W Dart and Cherrybrook.

DEBEN

(For close seasons, licences, etc see Anglian Region Environment Agency, p19)

Short Suffolk river (about 30 miles long) rising near Debenham and flowing to North Sea near Felixstowe. Coarse fishing.

Woodbridge (Suffolk). Tidal. Roach, pike, tench, perch above town. Club: Woodbridge and Dist AC, who also have Loam Pond, Sutton, and Holton Pit; st £12, dt £2, from tackle shop or Saxmundham Angling Centre or Anglia Photographics, Halesworth. Other club with Deben fishing, Framlington & Dist AC, tel: 01728 860123. Hotels: Bull, Crown.

Wickham Market (Suffolk). Roach, perch, pike. Woodbridge AC has river and Wickham Market Reservoir.

DERWENT (Cumbria)

(For close seasons, licences, etc, see South West Region Environment Agency p16)

Rises on north side of Scafell and flows through Borrowdale, Derwentwater and Bassenthwaite Lakes to the Solway Firth at Workington. Salmon and trout practically throughout length. A late river. Best months for salmon, July to October. Trout fishing on some stretches excellent. River also holds pike and perch.

Cockermouth to **Workington** (Cumbria). Salmon, sea trout, brown trout. Trout and salmon fishing may occasionally be permitted on dt. Enquiries to fishery Manager, Cockermouth Castle. Permit charges under review. Permits for **Cocker** also (limited). Waters through town can be fished on permit from Tourist Information Office by residents and visitors staying locally on weekly basis. Cockermouth AA has water on Cocker (members only) but issues dt £5.50 for **Cogra Moss**. **Mockerkin Tarn**, stocked with carp. Fishing within reach on Bassenthwaite, Loweswater, Crummock and Buttermere. Tackle shop: N H Temple, 11 Station Street, Keswick; both issue licences and permits, and will give information. Workington tackle shop: Graham's Guns Sports Services, 17 Fisher Street. Hotels: Trout, Globe, Cockermouth Pheasant, Bassenthwaite Lake, Sun, Bassenthwaite.

Brigham (Cumbria). Trout, sea trout, salmon. Broughton Working Men's AA has about 1m from here to Broughton Cross. Permits to local working men only.

Bassenthwaite (Cumbria). Derwent, 1m N; trout, salmon; private. Lakes: Bassenthwaite; pike, perch, trout, occasional salmon *(see English Lake District - Bassenthwaite)*. Hotels: Swan, Pheasant, Armathwaite Hall.

Keswick (Cumbria). For rivers Derwent and Greta. Salmon, trout (average ¼lb), pike, perch, eels; mid August onwards for salmon. Portinscale to ½ mile above Bassenthwaite Lake, Keswick AA water. Assn stocks Derwentwater and Rivers Derwent and Greta with 1,000 12" browns each year. Visitors salmon wt £75, dt £20. Trout permit includes Derwentwater, wt £25, dt £5 (reductions for juniors on all fishing) from Field and

Stream, 79 Main Street, or Keswick P O (017687 72269). Visitors st by application to Sec. Tickets issued for Derwent cover Greta also. For full details of water controlled by Keswick AA, write to secretary, enclosing sae, or contact local tackle shop or main post office. Hotels: Hazeldene, Queen's Royal Oak, Lake, George, County King's Arms. The Derwentwater Hotel. Permit charges subject to annual review.

Borrowdale (Cumbria). Trout, salmon; gin-clear as a rule and best fished after dark. Lakes: Derwentwater; trout, perch, pike; small charge for fishing. Watendlath Tarn 2m S; Blea Tarn, 4m S; trout. Hotels: Scafell; Borrowdale; Stakis Keswick Lodore, CA12 5UX, (017687 77285), free trout permits for patrons, mid-week only.

Tributaries of the Derwent (Cumbria)

COCKER: Salmon, sea trout, trout. July to October best for migratory fish. Mostly private, but dt for Cockermouth AA water (and for **Loweswater, Buttermere** and **Crummock Water**).

Scalehill (Cumbria). Cockermouth. 7m Cocker: Salmon, sea trout, trout. Private. National Trust lakes. Hotel: Scale Hill.

Cogra Moss. 40 acre trout reservoir 8m S of Cockermouth. Browns and rainbows. Contact Cockermouth AA.

NEWLANDS BECK: not worth fishing.

GRETA: Trout (av ¼lb); salmon.

Threlkeld (Cumbria). Keswick AA have fishing here *(tickets see Keswick)*. Best months for salmon Sept and Oct; mostly spinning and worm fishing. Glenderamackin Beck; trout; fishable throughout length, but very narrow and fish few and far between.

DEVONSHIRE (streams and lakes)

(For close seasons, licences, etc, see SW Region Environment Agency, p16)

AVON. Rises on Dartmoor and flows 22m SE, entering English Channel near Thurlestone via long, twisting estuary. Tide flows to Aveton Gifford. Trout (3 or 4lb), sea trout, salmon.

Thurlestone (Devon). Near mouth of Avon estuary. Capital bass fishing off Bantham Sands at mouth.

Aveton Gifford (Devon). Sea trout (end of May onwards), some salmon; good dry-fly trout water (3 to the lb). Banks heavily wooded; good wading. Mt, ft, wt, from post office at Loddiswell, and P O'Neil, 55 Church Street, Kingsbridge.

Loddiswell. Brown trout, salmon, sea trout; Avon FA has a total of 14½m. Full membership £155, no day tickets. Capital bass and pollack in Kingsbridge estuary. Tackle shop: Perrott Bros, 26 Fore Street. Hotels: King's Arms; Buttville; Torcross (for Slapton Ley).

Brent (Devon). Salmon, trout, sea trout. Mrs J Theobald, Little Aish Riding Stables, South Brent, issues dt for stretch of Aish Woods. Red Brook, 2m N; trout. Black Brook, 2m S; trout. Hotel: Anchor.

AVON DAM (8m NE of Totnes). SWW, brown trout fishery, zoned worm, spinning and fly fishing free to Environment Agency licence holders. No boats. Season March 15-Oct 12. Reservoir is about 1½m beyond **Shipley Bridge**, car parking on site.

BELLBROOK VALLEY TROUT FISHERY, Oakford, Tiverton EX16 9EX, tel/fax: 01398 351292. Set in picturesque Devon valley. Three specimen lakes, min stock 3lb, and three normal fishing lakes; specimen fishing, dt £37, 4 fish, various other permits obtainable. Record 1995, 21lb 12oz. Tuition. Corporate party days. Accommodation at fishery farmhouse.

BLAKEWELL FISHERY, Old Mill, Blakewell Lane. 1m N. Barnstaple. Brown and rb. trout av. 2¼ lb. Various day permits from £20, 5 fish, to £12, 2 fish, from fishery. This establishment also runs a commercial fish farm. Richard or John Nickell. Tel: 01271 44533.

BURRATOR RESERVOIR, Yelverton. 150 acres, South West Water. Zoned fly fishing and spinning for brown and rainbow trout. Open Mar 15-Sept 30. Dt £7, st £95 (concessions), from Burrator Inn, Dousland, Yelverton (01822 853121).

CRAFTHOLE, nr **Torpoint**. A popular little SWW fishery of 2 acres, dammed, stocked with carp and tench, open all year 24 hour day. Contact South West Water Peninsula Fisheries, Higher Coombepark, Lewdowne Okehampton Devon EX20 4QT, tel: 01837 871565.

DARRACOTT, Torrington. 3 acre coarse fishery run by South West Water, with carp, tench, bream, roach, rudd, perch, eel. Open all year, 24 hour day. St £65, dt £4, conc, from N Laws, Summerfields Tackle, 3 Golflinks Rd, Westward Ho! (01237 471291), or The Kingfisher, 22 Castle St, Barnstaple (01271 44919).

ERME. Rises on Dartmoor and flows 14m S to Bigbury Bay. Trout.

FERNWORTHY RESERVOIR, near **Chagford**, on Dartmoor. South West Water. 76 acres, natural brown trout fishing, largest 4lb 2oz. Open May 1-Oct 12. Dt £7, concessions. Self-service unit by Boathouse.

JENNETTS RESERVOIR, Bideford. 8 acres, South West Water coarse fishery, with carp principally, to 23lb, as well as tench, bream, roach, perch, eels. Open all year, 6.30am to 10.00pm. Permit, £4, £3.50, conc, from N Laws, Summerfields Tackle, 3 Golflinks Rd, Westward Ho! (01237 471291).

KENNICK RESERVOIR, Christow. A SWW Dartmoor fishery, with stocked rainbow trout. Boats on first come first serve basis, Allenard Wheelie Boat for disabled. Permits from self-service kiosk, £13 per day, full season £375, conc. Open 28 Mar-31 Oct.

MELBURY RESERVOIR, Bideford. 12 acre SWW reservoir, open all year, 6.30am to 10.30pm. Carp, bream, roach, perch, eels. Permits £4, £3.50, conc, from N Laws, Summerfields Tackle, 3 Golflinks Rd, Westward Ho! (01237 471291).

MELDON RESERVOIR (3m SE of Okehampton). 54 acres, natural brown and stocked rainbow trout. Spinning, bait and fly fishing, SWW fishery, free to Environment Agency licence holders. Season Mar 15-Oct 12.

LYN, near **Lynmouth** (Devon). This beautiful river has good run of salmon, July onwards. Also sea trout and brown trout; latter small. Environment Agency **Watersmeet** and **Glenthorne** fisheries: Limits, 2 salmon, 6 sea trout, 8 trout. Restricted season and methods. Salmon and sea trout: wt £35, dt £13.50. Trout: st £27.50, wt £10, dt £3, from Brendon House Hotel, Brendon; Tourist Information Centre, Town Hall, Lynton; Lynmouth PO. Season March 1-Sept 30. Mrs Lester, Glebe House, Brendon, issues dt for 3m (both banks) of East Lyn. Other contacts for East Lyn fishing are Simpkins, Rockford Inn, Brendon; Rising Sun Hotel, Harbourside, Lynmouth EX35 6EQ; Doone Valley Riding Stables, Brendon. Tackle shops: D & M Woolgrove, 13 The Parade, Minehead. *(See also Sea Fishing Stations).*

PLYM. Devon trout stream which rises above Lee Moor and flows south-west to Plymouth, skirts the east of the town to enter the Sound on the south side.

Plymouth (Devon). Good runs of sea trout on Plym and Tavy. Salmon run late on Plym, Oct to 15 Dec. Plymouth and Dist Freshwater AA has R Plym from Plymbridge upstream for about 3m, and Tavy, north of Tavistock. Annual subscription £80, from Hon Sec D L Owen, tel: 01752 705033. Dt for first mile from D K Sports, or from Parkes Weston Supplies (Snowbee), Parkway Ind. Estate, Plympton. Length above Bickleigh Bridge, controlled by Tavy, Walkham and Plym FC. Club issues tickets (salmon, sea trout, brown trout) for its water, here and on Tavy, Meavy and Walkham. Salmon st £100, dt £15, brown trout st £40, mt £20, wt £15. *(see Tamar - Tavy).* Sea fishing excellent. Tackle shops: D K Sports, 88 Vauxhall St; Osborne & Cragg, 37 Bretonside.

MEAVY. Tributary of the Plym, on which Burrator Reservoir blocks salmon migration. Joins main river at Shaugh Bridge. Fishing governed by overspill when Burrator is full. Fishing stations: **Shaugh** and Clearbrook. Tavy, Walkham and Plym FC have water (*see above, and Tavy*).

OAREWATER, Brendon. Trout.

ROADFORD FISHERY, nr **Okehampton**. SWW fishery, with wild brown trout. More than 700 acres, catch and release policy, barbless hooks. Permits £13.50, conc, from Angling and Watersports Centre, Lower Goodacre. Open 24 Mar-12 Oct. Enquiries, tel: 01409 211507.

SID, Sidmouth. Trout.

SLADE RESERVOIRS, Ilfracombe. South West Water fisheries. **Upper Slade** now closed to public owing to dangerous banks, **Lower Slade,** coarse fishing for carp, tench, bream, roach, rudd, gudgeon and perch. St £65-£100, conc £38.50-£30; dt £4, conc £3.25, from Slade Post Office, 80 Slade Rd, EX34 8LQ, or Variety Sports, 23 Broad St, Ilfracombe (01271 862039).

SLAPTON LEY, Dartmouth 7m. Pike, rudd, roach, eel and perch. Part of National Nature Reserve, boats only, bank fishing prohibited. For day tickets only,

Big carp, traditionally the quarry of the ultra-specialist, are now among the most sought-after fish in England and Wales. Enterprising stocking and fisheries development has helped. This 11½lb. "mirror" carp, seen with its captor, Mr. Aaron Heighton, came from Slade Reservoir, North Devon.

£6-£10, £9-£15, £12-£20, for one, two or three anglers, apply Field Centre, Slapton, Kingsbridge, TQ7 2QP (Kingsbridge 580685). Life-jackets on site, compulsory for anglers under 18 years of age. Excellent sea fishing for bass, turbot, plaice, brill and large whiting. Tackle shops: Sport and Fish, 16 Fairfax Place, Dartmouth; Anchor Sports Cabin, Bridge St, Kingsbridge. Hotels: The Torcross and (in Slapton) the Tower Inn. Many guest houses.

SQUABMOOR RESERVOIR. E Budleigh. Bait fishing for coarse fish, with carp to 25lbs, tench, bream, roach, rudd, eels. St £100-£65, conc, dt £3.50, conc, from Exeter Angling Centre, Smythen St, Exeter; Knowle Garage, Knowle, or Tackle Shop, 20 The Strand, Exmouth. **Hogsbrook Lake**, 2½ acres, at Woodbury Salterton is dt coarse fishery nearby. Contact F W S Carter, Greenshill Barton, Woodbury Salterton, tel: 01395 33340/68183.

STAFFORD MOOR FISHERY, Winkleigh EX19 8PP, tel: 01805 804360. Two lakes of fourteen acres and eight acres; regularly stocked with rainbow trout, av. weight over 2lb. Tackle, over 400 patterns of flies, on sale. Dt £17, £15, £13, 5-3 fish. Beginners pond. Tel: 018054 360.

TRENCHFORD RESERVOIR (8m NE of **Newton Abbot**). SWW fishery coarse of 45 acres, pike to 30lb. Open Oct 1-Mar 14. Dt £3.50, conc, from self service kiosk.

VENFORD RESERVOIR, Ashburton. Brown and rainbow trout. Spinning and bubble-float fishing, free to Environment Agency licence-holders. Season: March 15-Oct 12.

WISTLANDPOUND RESERVOIR, South Molton. SWW natural brown trout fishery. Fly only, open Mar 15 1-Oct 12. Dt £7, Conc, from Post Office, Challacombe; The Kingfisher, Coombe Martin; Variety Sports, Ilfracombe.

YEALM. Rises on southern heights of Dartmoor and flows 12m south and west to English Channel, which it enters by a long estuary. Trout, sea trout, occasional late salmon. Fishing private. Estuary is now a bass nursery, bass fishing prohibited.

Newton Ferrers (Devon). On estuary. One of finest deep-sea fishing stations in south-west. Hotel: River Yealm, tel: 01752 872419, has its own harbour frontage and jetty.

DORSET (streams)

(For close seasons licences, etc, see South West Region Environment Agency, p16)

BRIT and **ASKER**. Fishing station: **Bridport**. Trout. Rivers mostly private or over-grown, but Civil Service Sports Council has stretch of Brit for members only. 7/8 Buckingham Place, Bellfield Rd, High Wycombe HP13 5HW. Also **Radipole Lakes**; dt for latter: coarse fish. Tickets from Weymouth tackle shops. Dt for **Osmington Mills Lake** (carp and tench) on site only. Trout fishing at **Watermill Lake**, well stocked with rainbows. Mangerton Mill, Mangerton, Bridport, tel: 0130885 224.

CHAR. Fishing station: **Charmouth**. Char is some 7m long; trout, private. General sea fishing. Hotels: Queen's Arms, Hammons Mead.

CORFE. Rises 1m W of Corfe Castle and runs into Poole Harbour 5m down. Coarse fishing sometimes permitted by landowners. Dt can be obtained for Arfleet Lake at Corfe Castle.

DURHAM (reservoirs)

DERWENT. Edmundbyers. 1,000 acre trout water. Hotel: Lord Crewe Arms. *Reservoir also partly in Northumberland.*

SMIDDY SHAW, and **WASKERLEY**. Good trouting, preserved by North-West Durham AA. Dt £3, Waskerley only, in the hut by the reservoir. Season April 1-Sept 30. Nearest towns: **Wolsingham**, **Consett** and **Stanhope**. Hotel: Royal Derwent at Allensford.

EDEN

(For close season licences, etc, see North West Region Environment Agency, p17)

Rises south of Kirkby Stephen and empties into Solway Firth 5m NW of Carlisle. Salmon, sea trout, brown trout. Still some spring fish, but now more a back-end river. Sea trout in lower and middle reaches and tributaries from June onwards. Trouting best in middle and upper reaches, fish run to good average size for north. Chub and grayling in parts.

Carlisle (Cumbria). Salmon in spring and autumn, sea trout and herling in July and August, brown trout fair, some chub and dace. Carlisle AA has 7m on Eden, permits from Murrays, *below*. **Lough Trout Fishery**, Thurstonfield CA5 6HB; 25 acres, dt £17, boat £5, 4 fish limit. ½ day and evening tickets, self-catering accom, tel: 01228 576552. Three lakes of 25 acres with trout and coarse fishing, and salmon and sea trout in adjacent rivers, at Oakbank Lakes Country Park, Longtown, CA6 5NA. St £60 and dt £8, conc, tel: 01228 791108. Tackle shop: Murrays 5/6 Lowther Arcade, CA3 8LX (01228 23816), permits and tuition. Hotels: Crown and Mitre; Central; Hilltop.

Wetheral (Cumbria). Salmon and sea trout preserved for 3m, both banks from Warwick Bridge upstream, by the Yorkshire Fly-fishers' Club here and at Great Corby; Cairn Beck, 2m, Irthing, 3m N. Scotby Beck, 2m W at Scotby. Hotel: Crown.

Armathwaite (Cumbria). Salmon, trout, grayling. Croglin Waters, 3m E.

Lazonby (Cumbria). Salmon, trout and grayling. Mixed fishery at Crossfield Farm, Kirkoswald, Penrith. Record ide caught, 1993, 3lbs 4½ ozs. Special match tickets on offer. Trout limit 2 fish. Disabled facilities. Holiday accom. on site. Tel: 01768 896275.

Great Salkeld (Cumbria). Fetherston Arms Hotel, Kirkoswald, has 2½m (Lazonby 284). High Drove Inn has salmon and trout fishing; salmon 75p day, trout 50p.

Langwathby (Cumbria). Salmon, trout; preserved by Yorkshire FFC.

Culgaith (Cumbria). Trout; preserved by Yorkshire FFC from Culgaith to below Langwathby apart from vicinity of Watersmeet. Winderwath, left bank. Hotels: Black Swan, Culgaith, King's Arms, Temple Sowerby.

Temple Sowerby (Cumbria). Salmon, trout, grayling; preserved (with some miles of Eamont) by Yorkshire FFC; members only. Penrith AA (with 45m of fishing in all) has Powis House Water above Bolton Village; water upstream of Oustenstand Island. Wt and st issued at various prices for different stretches. *(See Penrith.)* King's Arms Hotel has trout fishing for guests on 1½m of Eden; licences and tickets at hotel; trout average 1lb.

Kirkby Thore (Cumbria). Salmon, trout and grayling. Penrith AA preserves 2m brown trout fishing on main river and Kirkby Thore Beck near Long Marton.

Appleby (Cumbria). Eden trout are very free risers, averaging about ¾lb with better fish to 3 and even 4lb. Tufton Arms can arrange Eden fishing and instruction for guests. Tel: 017683 51593/52761. Sandford Arms, Sandford CA16 6NR, tel: 017683 51121, has private fly fishing for guests on 5m double bank, 15 Mar-30 Sept. Dt when obtainable, £8. Tackle and permits from H Pigney & Son, Chapel St Appleby (017683 51200).

Kirkby Stephen (Cumbria). Kirkby Stephen and Dist AA has about 15m on main river and becks, fly only. *(See Belah and Scandal Tributaries).* Visitors' st £70, joining fee £15, from Hon Sec. Dt £15 from Robinson, Market Street. Fly fishing ponds at Bessy Beck Trout, tel: 015396 23303. For Eden Valley Trout Lake, Little Musgrave, a secluded fishery with brown and rainbow to 8lbs, contact Bearsett, Rowgate CA17 4SR, Tel: 017683 71489/51428. H Parr, 280 Park Rd, Blackpool, runs local fishing courses and holidays. Licences from Mounsey, Newsagent, 46 Market St. Tackle and tickets from H S Robinson, 2 Market St. Hotels: Kings Arms; Pennine; Black Bull, White Lion, Croglin Castle.

Tributaries of the Eden

PETTERIL joins Eden at Carlisle. Good trout fishing, but lower half mostly private.

Plumpton (Cumbria). Trout.

IRTHING. Rises on Grey Fell Common and joins Eden east of Carlisle. Salmon, trout, grayling and few sea trout.

Brampton (Cumbria). Irthing; 1m N; Gelt, 1m S; trout, grayling, chub. Brampton AS preserves; st (£16), wt (£12), dt (£4) and Environment Agency licence from Sports Haus, Front St. Trout average ½ to ¾lb, early months best. Tackle shops: Sporting Guns and Fishing Tackle, 2 Market Place; W Warwick, Front Street. Hotels: White Lion; Scotch Arms; Sand House;

Howard Arms.

Gilsland (Cumbria). Haltwhistle & Dist AA fishes 14m, brown trout only. Visitors welcome, dt £20, wt £50, from Haltwhistle tackle shops *(see Haltwhistle)*.

EAMONT flows from Ullswater Lake. Penrith AA has most of this water. Lake Ullswater good trout fishing; free, but Environment Agency licence required.

Penrith (Cumbria). Eamont, 1m S; trout. Upper portion (trout only) preserved by Penrith AA (fly fishing only for visitors) from Pooley Bridge on both banks to Stainton; also on **Eden**, **Lowther** and on becks. Visitors ticket covering a variety of fishings, from Sykes Tackle Shop *(see below)*. Trout fishing at **Blencarn Lake**, 15 acres, from Mr and Mrs J K Stamper, Blencarn Hall CA10 1TX. Dt £16-£10, 4 and 2 fish, fly only. Tel: 0176 888284. Yorkshire Flyfishers preserve left bank of Eamont from Brougham Castle down to Barrack Bank and then on left bank only to below Udford; members only. Other water on Eamont private. Coarse fish at Whins Pond, **Edenhall**; Mrs Siddle, tel 862671. Sockbridge Mill Trout Farm, tel 01768 865338, off B5320, is suitable family venue, fishing dt £1.50 + £1.65 per lb caught. **Haweswater**, 10m SE; currently, no permit is required *(see Westmorland lakes)*. Crown & Mitre Hotel, Bampton Grange, has 3m of trout fishing on Lowther to residents. Other hotels: Crown, George, Gloucester Arms, Kings Arms, Edenhall, near Langwathby. Tackle shop: Sykes, 4 Great Dockray, tel: 01768 862418.

Pooley Bridge (Cumbria). Eamont; trout. Penrith AA water.

Patterdale (Cumbria). The becks Goldrill, Grizedale, Deepdale and Hartsop; free. Aira Force below NT property (3m) free. N Hawes and Riggindale Becks, permits N West Water. Blea Tarn and Smallwater, N West Water. **Ullswater**. Trout numerous, average three to pound. Evening rise during May and June yields heavy baskets; six brace of trout in evening quite common. Day fishing also good; and heavier fish begin to move about middle of May. Numerous boats. Angle Tarn, permits. Greenside Reservoir, Red Tarn, Grizedale Tarn, free. Hotels: Ullswater, Patterdale; White Lion, Brotherswater; Glenridding (boats).

LOWTHER (tributary of Eamont). Salmon and trout. Abstraction affecting salmon sport, autumn run now very late. Sport with trout remains good (av ¾lb). Crown and Mitre Hotel, **Bampton** (via Penrith), has more than 3m fishing for guests (trout and late salmon) including Haweswater Beck; a good centre, only 100 yds from river. Penrith AA holds substantial stretches of good fly water on river; other assn water on Eden and Eamont. Environment Agency licences from hotel or Penrith tackle shops.

LYVENNET. Good trout stream; runs in a few miles below Temple Sowerby. Leave from farmers in some parts. 1m preserved for Yorkshire Flyfishers' Club.

BELAH. Flows from Pennine fells to join Eden 2m below Kirkby Stephen. Lower reaches, from Brough Sowerby, rented by Kirkby Stephen and Dist AA; members only.

SCANDAL BECK, Smardale (Cumbria) and **Crosby Garrett** (Cumbria). Kirkby Stephen & Dist AA has water. *(See Kirkby Stephen under Eden.)*

ENGLISH LAKE DISTRICT

(For close seasons, licences, etc, see North West Region Environment Agency, p17)

BASSENTHWAITE, 5m Cockermouth; 8m Keswick. Long famous for its pike, also perch and some brown trout. Hotels: Pheasant Inn, Swan, Armathwaite Hall.

BIGLAND WATERS, Bigland Hall Estate, **Backbarrow** LA12 8PB. 13 acre coarse fishery and 16 acre fly only trout lake (barbless hooks only), plus beginners lake. Trout dt £15, 4 fish, £10, 6 hours, 2 fish; coarse dt £4, conc. Contact the Fisheries Manager, tel: 015395 31728.

BLEA TARN. About 2m above Watendlath Tarn; perch; some trout. National Trust. Free fishing.

BLELHAM TARN. Ns **Windermere**. Pike, perch, some trout, tickets from Hawkshead P O.

BORRANS RESERVOIR South Lakeland. Managed by North Tynseide M.B.C., Educational Dept, High Borrans, Outdoor Pursuit Centre, Windermere.

BROTHERSWATER. Good trout and pike. National Trust, fishing free.

BUTTERMERE. National Trust lake. Char, trout, pike, perch. Permits (wt £10, dt £3) which cover Crummock and Loweswater, too, from Mr & Mrs Parker, Dalegarth Guest House, Buttermere,

Cockermouth CA13 9XA, tel: 017687 70233.

CLEABARROW TARN, Windermere. WADAA fishery, 2 acres, 20 pegs. No close season. Well stocked, carp (15lb), tench (5lb), roach, rudd, golden rudd, gudgeon. Dt £3.00, conc, from Tourist Information Centres, and local tackle shops. Night fishing is strictly prohibited.

CODALE TARN, 4m from **Grasmere**. Perch, some trout; free. Hotels: *(see Grasmere).*

CONISTON. Trout, char, perch, pike. Free, licence needed. Boats from Coniston Boating Centre, Lake Rd, Coniston, tel: 015394 41366. Tackle and licences from David Wilson, Tackle and Sports Shop, Tilberthwaite Ave, or Sun Hotel, both Coniston. Local club is Coniston and Torver DAA, which has fishing on Yew Tree Tarn, fly only, dt £6, conc. Hotels: Sun, Black Bull, Crown, Ship Inn.

CRUMMOCK WATER. National Trust lake. Pike, trout, char, perch; salmon and sea trout from Cocker sometimes caught by trolling. Fishes best June and July. Dt £1.5 (covering also Buttermere and Loweswater) from Mr & Mrs McKenzie, Woodhouse, Buttermere, tel: 017687 70208. Rowing boats for hire, £5-£15. Best periods for Crummock, Buttermere and Loweswater are: trout, late May and early June (good mayfly hatch); char, July and August (special technique required: trolling 60 to 90 feet down). *(For hotels see Buttermere).*

DERWENTWATER. Keswick. Trout very good size, are best fished for from a boat in mayfly season. Stocked annually with 1,000 12" browns by Keswick AA. Good sized perch and pike, salmon present but rarely taken. Wt £25, dt £5 (which includes all KAA waters) from Field and Stream, Keswick, or Keswick P O. Boats may be hired from Nicoll End, and Keswick landings. Many hotels and guest houses.

DEVOKE WATER near **Ravenglass** (5m E). Moorland tarn offering sport with fair sized trout. Millom AA holds rights. Membership obtainable. Dt £15 from Sec, or Duddon Sports, Millom; Haverigg P O; Bridge Garage, Holmerook; Waberthwaite PO.

DRUNKEN DUCK TARNS, Ambleside. Brown trout to 4½lb, rainbow to 6lb. Wt £60, dt £12 (reductions for ½ day and evenings), from Drunken Duck Hotel; early booking necessary. Six rods, incl two for Grizedale AC. Guided days on Windermere May/June; boat, food incl.

DUBBS TROUT FISHERY, Windermere. A quiet upland reservoir, controlled by WADAA, open 15th March - 31st Dec inclusive. Stocked rainbow and brown trout to 10lb, fly only, 2 fish limit. Dt £8.50 from Ings Filling Station (A591), Tourist Information Centres, local fishing tackle shops.

EASEDALE TARN, 3m from **Grasmere**. Good perch, few trout. Free fishing. Managed by National Trust, The Hollens, Grasmere, Cumbria LA22 9QZ, tel: 015394 35599.

ENNERDALE, ns **Whitehaven**. Trout, char; controlled by Ennerdale Lake fisheries formed by Egremont Anglers, Wath Brow and Ennerdale Anglers; St £10 and wt £5 from Wath Brow Post Office, Cleator Moor, or W N Holmes, Main St, Egremont. Enquiries to D Crellin (Hon Sec.) 01946 823 337.

ESTHWAITE WATER (nr **Hawkshead**, Lancashire). 280 acres stocked trout fishing. Rainbows to 16lb 3oz, browns to 7lb 4oz. spinning, worming or fly. Boats with o/b. Dt from The Boathouse, Ridding Wood, Hawkshead LA22 0QF, tel: 015394 36541, or from Hawkshead P O. Accommodation plentiful.

FISHER TARN, ns **Kendal**, 3m. Kendal's water supply. Trout. Fisher Tarn Anglers, A Moore, 65 Waterside, Kendal, Cumbria. Dt from Sec or D Bird, 1 Rydal Mount, Kendal, Cumbria.

GRASMERE, ns **Windermere**. Summer fishing, pike over 20lb regularly caught, perch, eels, roach, trout; WADAA water, open 16th June - 14th March inclusive. Live-baiting with fish is strictly prohibited, dead baiting and lure fishing are the most productive methods. Find underwater drop-offs for the best sport. Boat fishing can be good, boats from boathouse at northern end of lake. Dt £3.50 (Juv/OAP £2.00), wt £10.00 (Juv/OAP £5.00). St £30.00 (Juv/OAP £15.00). This permit also allows fishing on Rydal Water, River Rothay, River Brathay, High Arnside Tarn, Moss Eccles Tarn, School Knott Tarn & Hayswater. Permits from: Tourist Information Centres, local fishing tackle shops, Barney's News Box, Grasmere (6.00 am. - 5.30 p.m.)

GREAT RUNDALE TARN, ns **Long Marton**, 5m. Seamore Tarn and Little Rundale Tarn are in the vicinity. Small trout.

GHYLL HEAD TROUT FISHERY, Windermere. 11 acre WADAA stocked fishery, fly only. Open 15th March - 31st Dec. Rainbow and brown trout, 2 fish limit. Dt £8.50 from Beech Hill Hotel (A592 Bowness - Newby Bridge road), Tourist Information Centres, local tackle shops.

HARLOCK RESERVOIR, South Lakeland. Trout water managed by Barrow AA, Hon Sec J R Jones, 69 Prince St, Dalton in Furness, Cumbria LA15 8ET.

HAWESWATER, ns **Penrith** or **Shap**. A good head of wild brown trout, char, gwyniad and perch. Bank fishing, fly only, free to all holders of Environment Agency licence. No maggot or loose feeding.

HAYESWATER RESERVOIR, Patterdale. WADAA water, 34 acres, 9m north of Ambleside, open 15th March - 30th Sept. Brown trout, fly only, stocked annually. Dt £3.50 (Juv/OAP £2.00), wt £10.00 (Juv/OAP £5.00), st £30.00 (Juv/OAP £15.00). This permit also allows fishing on Grasmere, Rydal Water, High Arnside Tarn, Moss Eccles Tarn, School Knott Tarn & Rivers Rothay and Brathay. Permits from: Tourist Information Centres, local fishing tackle shops.

HIGH ARNSIDE TARN, Ambleside; SCHOOL KNOTT TARN, Windermere; MOSS ECCLES TARN, Hawkeshead. Three small fly fisheries stocked by WADAA, open 15 March-30 Sept. Dt £3.50, juv/OAP, £2, wt £10-£5, st £30-£15, from TICs, local tackle shops, Coniston Sports.

HIGH NEWTON TROUT FISHERY, High Newton. WADAA trout fishery, 10.8 acres, open 15th March - 31st Dec, rainbow and brown trout. Dt £8.00. The reservoir is very well stocked with rainbow trout on a regular basis and, in addition, for the 1997 season the Association has introduced a large stocking of bigger rainbow trout between 3 - 10lb which are all tagged and dye marked. These are sport fish and must be returned if captured before the 1st September. The tagged fish are in addition to normal stockings which will continue as usual. All anglers must use barbless hooks (squashed barbs) and the use of buoyant lures or boobys on sunken lines is prohibited.

HOLEHIRD TARN, Windermere, 3 acre WADAA water, open 16th June - 14th March. Carp (16lb), crucian carp (1lb), tench (5lb), roach (2lb), bream (6lb), rudd, chub (5lb), gudgeon. Dt £3.00 (Juv £1.50). The number of anglers permitted at Holehird is limited to ten at any one time, consequently a peaceful day is usually guaranteed. Four day permits are sold per day and only from Go Fishing, Gillys Landing, Glebe Road, Bowness-on-Windermere (tel: 015394 47086). Permits may be obtained in advance of fishing from either of these shops or by sending a cheque made out to WADAA with s.a.e to Mr. C. J. Sodo, Ecclerigg Court, Ecclerigg, Windermere, Cumbria LA23 1LQ (tel: 015394 45083). Fishing is permitted from one hour before sunrise to one hour after sunset. Overnight parking or night fishing is strictly prohibited.

KILLINGTON RESERVOIR, ns **Oxenholme**, 3m. Trout, pike, perch. Leased to Kent AA. St £11, wt £4.50, dt £2 from Kendal tackle shops or Keeper at reservoir. Concession st to jun. Parties should book in advance through Kent AA Sec.

KNOTT END TARN: Birkby, Ravenglass. Regular stocking of brown trout to 6lb. Dry fly and nymph (barbless hook) only. fly casting instruction, also suitable for handicapped anglers. Day tickets, 8 a.m.- 5 p.m., £12. Evenings: £12. Bookings to W Arnold, tel: 01229 717255. Tackle and information from Esso Garage, Holmrook.

Check before you go

While every effort has been made to ensure that the information given in **Where to Fish** *is correct, the position is continually changing, and anglers are urged, in their own interests, to make preliminary enquiries before travelling to selected venues. This is especially important with reference to prices quoted. Inevitably the rate of inflation is affecting stability in this quarter. Anglers' attention is also drawn to the fact that the hotels mentioned under the various fishing stations do not necessarily have water of their own. Any amendments or further data for inclusion in subsequent editions, and any comments, will be welcome.*

LOUGHRIGG TARN, nr **Ambleside**. Pike and perch; apply to M A Murphy, Tarn Foot Farm, Loughrigg, Nr Ambleside.

LONGLANDS LAKE. Cleator, West Cumbria. Wath Brow and Ennerdale Anglers, stocked monthly. Day tickets from Farrens Family Store, Cleator, or Wath Brow GPO.

LOWESWATER. National Trust lake. Pike, perch, trout (av 1½-2lb but hard to catch; fly only up to June 16); no fishing from Oct 31-Mar 15. For dt £5-£6 apply to Mr and Mrs Leck, Water End Farm, Loweswater, tel: 01946 861465.

MEADLEY RESERVOIR. Cleator Moor, West Cumbria. Brown trout and rainbow. Permits from E G & J Littlefair, Wath Brow Stores & PO, 121/2 Ennerdale Road, Wath Brow, Cleator Moor, Cumbria CA25 5LP.

MOCKERKIN, near Loweswater. Tarn stocked with carp by Haigh AA, Whitehaven.

OVER WATER, near Keswick. 30 acre brown trout fishery, fly fishing by boat, float tubing permitted. Stocked regularly. Mrs Richardson, Fold Head Farm, Watendlath, Keswick, tel: 017687 77293.

PENNINGTON RESERVOIR, South Lakeland. Trout fishing, Barrow AA, J R Jones, 69 Prince St, Dalton in Furness. Dt water. For further information contact Paul Phillips, Team Leader, NWW Ltd, Woodland Office, Thirlmere Keswick, Cumbria (017687 72334).

RATHERHEATH TARN, Kendal. 5 acre WADAA coarse fishery, open all year. Carp (10lb), tench (4lb), roach (2lb), bream (6lb), rudd, crucian carp, perch, gudgeon. Dt £3.00 (Juv £1.50) from: Plantation Bridge Filling Station, A591 (Open 7.00 am. - 9.00 p.m.), Tourist Information Centres, local tackle shops. A special platform for disabled anglers stands just inside the entrance gate ten metres from the car park. Fishing is permitted from one hour before sunrise to one hour after sunset. Overnight parking or night fishing is strictly prohibited.

RYDAL WATER, Ambleside. WADAA water, open 16th June - 14th March. Pike, perch, eels, trout. Rydal Water offers similar fishing to Grasmere and is a popular pike fishery producing fish to the mid-twenty pound mark. Parking is at White Moss Common or Rydal Village. Most pike are caught near underwater features around the islands and off the various points. Boat fishing is not permitted. The Association wants to conserve pike stocks in all fisheries so please use adequate tackle and have unhooking gear at hand. Dt £3.50 (Juv/OAP £2.00), wt £10.00-£5, st £30.00-£15.00). NB. This permit also allows fishing on Grasmere, River Rothay, River Brathay, High Arneside Tarn, Moss Eccles Tarn, School Knott Tarn & Hayswater. Permits from: Tourist Information Centres, local tackle shops, Barney's News Box, Grasmere (7.00 a.m. - 6 p.m.)

SKELSMERGH, ns **Kendal**, 3m. Now privately owned, with large tench and perch regularly caught. Dt £5 on bank.

SPRINKLING TARN. Right up Stye Head Pass. Trout. Good on a favourable day until July.

STYE HEAD TARN. Same information as Sprinkling Tarn.

THIRLMERE. Perch, pike, trout. Free fishing to Environment Agency licence holders. No maggots, live baits or loose-feeding. For further information contact Paul Phillips, Team Leader, NWW Ltd, Woodland Office, Thirlmere Keswick, Cumbria (017687 72334).

ULLSWATER, ns **Penrith**. Covers 2,200 acres. Free, with licence. Pike, perch, brown trout. Rowing boats only. Hotels: Ullswater, Patterdale, White Lion, Glenridding, Waterfoot, Waternook, Sharrow Bay, Rampsbeck, Brackenrigg, Howtown, Crown, Sun (last two Pooley Bridge). Boats.

WATENDLATH TARN. Keswick 3m. Brown and rainbow trout fishery, fly only, stocked weekly; boats. Apply to Mrs Richardson, Fold Head Farm, Watendlath, Keswick, tel: 017687 77293. Charges on request.

WINDERMERE, nr **Windermere**. Largest English lake, 10½m long and nearly 1m wide. Good pike and perch, also eels, char and trout (trout best March-June), and roach now caught in numbers. Fishing free, apart from Environment Agency licence. Big fish taken by trolling. Boats from Bowness Bay, Waterhead Bay and Fell Foot NT Park. Local club, Windermere, Ambleside & Dist AA, have special corporate membership arrangement with sixty hotels, which give residents two rods per day on WADAA fisheries. These include **Grasmere, Rydal Water**, Rivers **Rothay, Brathay**, six tarns, Ghyll head and Dubbs Trout Fisheries, High Newton Reservoir, Grange-over-Sands. Details are elsewhere in text. **Rather-**

All smiles on Windermere. The girl was the captor of this shapely 22 pounder. *Photo: Ghillie, Barry Tennant.*

heath and **Cleabarrow** Tarns are now coarse fisheries, dt £3, from local tackle shops: Allsports Ltd, Victoria Buildings, Royal Square, Bowness-on-Windermere, Carlson Tackle Shop, 64/66 Kirkland, Kendal. Hotels: Lonsdale, Lake Rd; Cragwood Country House; Applegarth; Oakthorpe. Ambleside: Skelwith Bridge; Langdale Chase; Fisherbeck. All these offer free fishing on WADAA waters. Boat fishing trips on Lake Windermere with all bait and tackle supplied, may be had from tel: Windermere 88027/45780 daytime, 88348 evenings. Fishing boat trips with expert ghillie from north east shore, also full and half-day boat hire: Low Wood Activity Centre, Windermere, LA23 1LP, tel: 015394 34004/47113.

YEW TREE TARN, near **Coniston**. Rainbow and brown trout; apply Coniston and Torver AC, Nicholson Sports, Tilberthwaite Ave, or Sun Hotel, both Coniston.

ESK (Border)

(Esk in England is under North West Region Environment Agency; close seasons, licences, etc, see p17. For statutory close season in Scotland, see Fishing in Scotland; no licence needed).

Rises in Dumfriesshire and flows into the Solway Firth but is classed as an English river. Upper reaches of Esk and main tributary, Liddle Water, good for brown trout but rivers are primarily sea trout and salmon waters from Langholm and Newcastleton to the mouth. Heavy run of sea trout and herling from July to September. Salmon in late autumn, September and October being best months. Chub and dace in lower reaches provide good sport in winter.

Canonbie (Dumfries and Galloway). Salmon, sea trout, herling, trout; The Buccleugh Estates Esk and Liddle Fisheries issue permits: St £44 to £328, wt £8 to £110, dt £6 to £35. Up to 28 May ½ price. From G Graham, River-watcher, Hagg on Esk, Canonbie DG14 0XE. Six private beats are let on weekly basis to parties of three rods, directly by Buccleugh Estates Ltd, Ewesbank (013873 80202). Liddle tickets from J D Ewart, Douglas Square, and Mrs B Elliott, Thistlesyke, both Newcastleton. Also contact Stevenson and Johnstone, Bank of Scotland Buildings, Langholm, Dumfriesshire DG13 0AD. No licence needed. Hotels: Cross Keys, Canonbie.

Langholm (Dumfries and Galloway). Salmon, sea trout, herling, brown trout. Certain stretches of Esk and its tributary the Liddle, are under the control of Esk and Liddle Fisheries (*see above*). Netherby Estate, Longtown, issues permits for salmon and sea trout fishing at **Netherby**, through Edwin Thompson & Co, Bute House, Rosehill, Carlisle CA1 2RW. No Sunday fishing and restricted night fishing. There are also restrictions on spinning and worm fishing. Full particulars from secretary. Tackle shop: Patties of Dumfries. Hotels: Eskdale, Douglas or Cross Keys (Canonbie).

Westerkirk (Dumfries and Galloway). Salmon, sea trout, herling, trout.

Tributaries of the Border Esk

LIDDLE: Salmon, sea trout, herling, brown trout.

Newcastleton (Roxburgh). Salmon, sea trout, herling, brown trout. Esk and Liddle Fisheries have much water. Tickets for 5m stretch. (*See Canonbie*). Bailey Mill Farm Holidays and Trekking Centre, Bailey TD9 0TR (016977 48617), offer fishing holidays on 7m of Liddle, with accommodation, also 12m of Esk nr **Longtown**.

LYNE: Lyne rises on Bewcastle Fells and joins Esk ½m above Metal Bridge. Salmon, sea trout, herling, trout.

SARK: Trout stream about 10m long, forming for a short distance boundary between England and Scotland, and emptying into Solway at **Gretna**.

KIRTLE WATER: Stream which empties into the Solway at Kirtlefoot. Sea trout, herling, trout. Rigg and Kirtleside farm, Rigg.

Kirtlebridge (Dumfries and Galloway). Sea trout and trout; short free length. Winterhope Burn. Penoben Burn. Annan, 3m SW. Well-stocked reservoir 3m off, **Middlebie Dam**, fishable by permit; trouting very good.

Kirkpatrick (Dumfries and Galloway). Trout.

ESK (Yorkshire)

(For close seasons, licences, etc, see North East Region Environment Agency, p17)

Rises on Westerdale Moor and runs into sea at Whitby. Salmon, sea trout, trout and grayling. River was stocked in 1868 with salmon ova from the Tees. It was recently restocked with salmon in an effort to increase diminishing numbers. Good runs of sea trout, river has twice held British record, 1994 was highest ever total; brown trout plentiful in places, 2-3lb, heaviest in 1994, 4¼lb. River largely controlled by Esk Fishery Association, but some free stretches.

Whitby (Yorks). Salmon, sea trout, trout, grayling, eels; largely preserved by the Esk FA from Whitby to beyond Glaisdale. Visitors' tickets from Mr Sims, Ruswarp Boat Landing, Whitby. No maggot fishing is allowed. fishing from Iburndale Beck down to Ruswarp Dam. St, dt. Salmon, sea trout and brown trout. Tackle shop: Whitby Angling Supplies, 65/67 Haggersgate, Whitby. Hotels: Wheatsheaf; Horseshoe.

RUSWARP (Yorks). Salmon, sea trout, trout, grayling, eels; preserved for 2m by Esk Fishery Association. Tickets from Mr Sims, Ruswarp Boat Landing, Whitby.

Sleights (Yorks). Salmon, sea trout, trout, grayling, eels; preserved by Esk Fishery Association. Tickets from Boatyard, Ruswarp.

Goathland (Yorks). Murk Esk; trout. Goathland FC water.

Grosmont (Yorks). Trout, salmon; preserved by the Esk FA above to Glaisdale, and below to Whitby.

Egton Bridge (N Yorks). Salmon, trout; some water preserved by the Esk FA. Other water (1¼m both banks) owned by Egton Estates Co, Estate Office, Egton Bridge, nr Whitby YO21 1UY. Tickets issued throughout season, 3 rods per day. Trout fishing in **Scaling Dam** (worm and fly). Hotels: Horse Shoe; Wheatsheaf Inn; Station.

Glaisdale (N Yorks). Salmon, sea trout, trout; preserved below by the Esk FA *(see Whitby)*. Hotel: Angler's Rest. Esk FA bailiff, D J Swales, Rosedene, Priory Park, Grosmont, Whitby YO22 5QQ (01947 895488). Dt from Yorkshire Water.

Danby (N Yorks). Salmon, sea trout, brown trout, grayling, preserved by landowners and Danby AC. Danby AC has about 8m of water stocked each year with approx 800 11" brown trout, also between Castleton and Leaholm; st (limited) £12, dt £3, (£6 Oct), from Duke of Wellington (Danby); Post Offices, Castleton and Danby; F Farrow, 11 Dale End, Danby (Club bailiff). Restrictions on method according to date. Accommodation, licences, tickets, at Duke of Wellington.

Tributaries of the Esk (Yorkshire)

MURK ESK: Salmon and trout. Tributaries are: Little Beck, Brocka Beck, Eller Beck, Little Eller Beck. Fishing station: **Grosmont.**

COMMONDALE BROOK: **Commondale** (Yorks). Trout: preserved by the owners.

ESSEX (streams, lakes and reservoirs)

(For close seasons, licences, etc, see Anglian Region Environment Agency, p19)

ARDLEIGH RESERVOIR, nr **Colchester**. Off the A 137, stocked with rainbow trout (20,000 in season). Fly only reservoir season: Mar 15 to Oct 31. Any legal method, trout and coarse season. Coarse fishing allowed from Oct-Feb, excellent pike fishing. Wick Lane Ponds open all year, coarse fishing. 22 rowing boats, outboards allowed. Tackle and flies sold on site, tuition obtainable when required. St £460-£360, dt £13.75, beginners £4. Boats £9-£5.50. Enq to Fisheries & Estate Officer, Ardleigh Reservoir, Nr Colchester, Essex CO7 7PT, with sae, tel: 01206 230642.

BERWICK PONDS, Rainham. Operated by Berwick Ponds, 105 Suttons Avenue, Hornchurch RM12 4LZ. Tench, roach, bream, pike, carp. Dt £3.50, £1.50 extra rods; OAP £1.50, jun £2.50 from bailiff on bank. Night fishing £5.50, 24 hours £7.

CONNAUGHT WATERS, Chingford. Roach, bream, carp; free.

EPPING FOREST PONDS. Fishing permitted in most ponds except where prohibited by notices, namely Alexandra Lake, Eagle Pond, Shoulder of Mutton Pond. Charges apply to the following: Ornamental Water, Perch Pond, Hollow Pond, Connaught Water, Highams Park Lake, Wake Valley Pond, pay bailiff on site. The remaining are free. Further information from Forest Information Centre, 0181 508 0028, or Superintendent of Epping Forest, The Warren, Loughton, Essex IG10 4RW.

FISHERS GREEN, Waltham Abbey. Pike, tench, bream, roach, barbel, chub, perch, eels. A Leisure Sport restricted permit fishery of 68 and 65 acre gravel pits, 3,900m of R Lea, 3,160 of Lea Relief Channel. St £40, no dt. Concessions for jun, OAP, dis. Applications to LSA, RMC House, High Street, Feltham, Middlesex TW13 4HD, tel: 0181 8931168.

GOSFIELD LAKE, Halstead (Essex). 45 acres; well-stocked with carp, perch, roach, tench, pike. Inquire C W Turp, Gosfield Lake Ltd, Church Road, Gosfield. Dt (7.30 am - 7.30 pm) £4, concessions to jun, obtainable from the shop.

HANNINGFIELD RESERVOIR. Near **Chelmsford**. Excellent rainbow trout fishery, average weight 2lb, good numbers of fish to 18lb 9oz. Regular stocking. Bank and boat fishing, incl boats for disabled. Season: Apr 1-Oct 31. Full St: £415; Mon-Fri: £350; named week-day: £245; Sat and Sun £320, weekend one named day £270. Dt, 6 fish, £14.50. Motor Boats £18 per day, rowing boats £10.50. Part day and evening boats also for hire. All prices include VAT. Car parks and fishing lodge. Total catch around 50,000, average weight 2lb, Enquiries to Fisheries Officer, Essex & Suffolk Water, Hall Street, Chelmsford, CM2 0HH, tel: 01245 491234, or Fishing Lodge, Giffords Lane, South Hanningford CM3 8HX (01268 710101).

HATFIELD FOREST LAKE. Near Hatfield Broad Oak and Bishop's Stortford. National Trust property.

HOOKS MARSH. 40 acre Leisure Sport gravel pit nr **Waltham Abbey**. Bream, tench, roach, perch and pike. Dt £3, conc, from Hall's Tackle, 44 Highbridge St, Waltham Abbey EN9 1BS, or on bank. Hall's also sell tickets for two coarse fisheries with carp, at **Clavershambury**.

LAYER PITS. 6m S of **Colchester**; controlled by Colchester APS; coarse fish; members only.

NAZEING MEADS, Meadgate Lane, Nazeing, Essex. Fours gravel pits totalling 125 acres. Pike are main species, with large carp, bream, roach, tench, eels. By written application only, to Lee Valley Regional Park Authority, Abbey Gardens, Waltham Abbey, Essex EN9 1XQ, tel: 01992 713838 (fax: 787533).

STAMBRIDGE STARR FISHERIES, Great Stambridge, Essex, one stocked trout lake, one coarse lake. Dt £3. per 3 hours plus £2.25 per lb fish caught. Coarse dt £5, night fishing. Casting instruction and rod hire. Barbless hooks only. Tel: 01702 258274.

STANFORD-LE-HOPE. Two Leisure Sport gravel pits, 13 acres. Large carp, crucian, perch, pike, roach, tench. St £24, concessions to Jun, OAP, Dis. No dt. Applications to LSA, RMC House, High Street, Feltham, Middlesex TW13 4HD, tel: 0181 8931168.

MARDYKE: Fishing stations: **Purfleet** and **Ockendon**. Rises by East Horndon and flows 12m to Thames at Purfleet. There are some club lengths. Moor Hall & Belhus AS have two members only coarse fisheries at South Ockendon, st on application to Sec.

PANT. Bocking. Upper part of R Blackwater *(see Blackwater in main list)*.

ONGAR. Coarse fish; good chub, roach, dace and perch. Practically whole of fishable Roding controlled by clubs, principally Ongar and Dist AS (members only; river and pit), Collier Row AS. Fishing showing considerable improvement.

PASSINGFORD BRIDGE. Roach, chub, pike; bream, carp, tench. Barkingside and Dist AS has 1½m downstream; bailiff on water. Dt from bailiffs on bank for ¾m upstream of bridge. Woodford AS has 1½m north of bridge; Elm Park AS has water;

Fishing available?

*If you own, manage, or know of first-class fishing available to the public which should be considered for inclusion in **Where to Fish,** please apply to the publishers (address in the front of the book) for a form for submission, on completion, to the editor. (Inclusion is at the sole discretion of the editor). There is no charge for inclusion.*

dt from bailiff. Tackle shop: Edko Sports, 136 North Street, **Romford**.

SCRUBBS LAKE, Hadleigh (Essex). Good perch, roach, rudd, etc; dt.

SHOEBURY PARK LAKE, Shoeburyness (Essex). Coarse fish; dt issued.

SOUTH WEALD LAKES. Weald, Thorndon, South Belhus Woods and Danbury Country Parks all have fishing run by Essex County Council. Usual freshwater fish, esp. carp. St £60 (Weald and Thorndon only), dt £3.20, £1.60 jun, OAP; on lakeside or from Weald Office, Weald Country Park, South Weald, Brentwood, Essex CM14 5QS; tel:01277 216297.

THE CHASE, Dagenham (Essex). White Hart Anglers' water; gravel pit; roach, bream, tench (excellent), carp (common, mirror and crucian), rudd, pike, perch; no night fishing; hempseed banned; dt from bailiff.

WANSTEAD & WOODFORD LAKES AND PONDS. **Eagle Pond, Snaresbrook** (roach, perch, carp); **Knighton Wood Pond, Woodford**; **Hollow Pond, Whipps Cross**; all free.

OTHER TICKET WATERS. Priory Lakes, Priory Park, **Southend**; Eastwood Pit, **Rayleigh**; Essex Carp Fishery (crucian carp, bream) at Mollands Lane, **South Ockendon**; Old Hall Lake, **Herongate**; Moor Hall Farm Fishery, **Aveley**; Raphael Park Lake, **Romford**; Danbury Park Lakes, near **Chelmsford**; Harwood Hall at Corbets Tey, and Parklands Lake, both near **Upminster**; Warren Pond, **Chingford**; carp, bream. Tickets mostly from bailiffs on site. Essex tackle shops: Essex Angling & Sport, 5 Broadway Parade, Elm Park; Avenue Angling, 22A Woodford Avenue, Ilford; Angling Centre, 226 Hornchurch Rd, Hornchurch.

For Walthamstow reservoirs, see under London.

EXE

(For close seasons, licences, etc, see South West Region Environment Agency p16)

Rises in Somerset on Exmoor and runs south through Devon to Exmouth. Salmon and trout, with grayling and coarse fish in lower reaches. At several points on upper reaches trout fishing (moorland) and salmon fishing may be had by hotel guests.

Exeter (Devon). Bream, carp, dace, gudgeon, pike, perch, roach, rudd, tench and eels. **Exeter Ship** and **Tiverton Grand Western** Canals contain bream, carp, pike, perch, rudd, roach, tench, eels and dace. Better part of Exeter canal from Broadwater (lime Kilns) to Turf (where canal enters Exe estuary). Hotels on canal banks: Double Locks, Turf. Exeter & Dist AA (amalgamation of local clubs) has coarse fishing rights on R Exe, on **Culm** and **Creedy**, from City Basin to Turf Basin on Exeter Ship Canal, and on ponds at Kingsteignton, Sampford Peveril, Feneck. St, visitors wt, dt. For fishing on Tiverton Canal contact Tiverton AC, tel: 01884 256721 or tackle shops. At Exwick right bank visitors may fish for ½m, and from Exwick Mills d/s 400 yds below Exwick Rd Bridge. Environment Agency has 3m of salmon fishing on lower Exe in Cowley and Countess Wear areas. Dt £4, st £60, fly or spinning, from Feb 14 to Sept 30, from tackle shops in Exeter, Taunton, Tiverton. Apply Exeter AC, Smythen Street. Dt £2.50, wt £7 for Exeter & Dist AA waters from tackle shops. South View Farm Fishery, Shillingford St George, Exeter EX2 9UP, 6 acres coarse, with carp to 20lb, tench and other coarse; £4 dt on bank. Tel: 01392 832278. 2m W of city, **Haldon Ponds** trout fishery, stocked with rainbows to 10lb, b to 7lb. Wt £35, dt £6, evening £3. Rods limited. Boats. Phone Exeter 32967. One permit a day for salmon fishing (weekdays only) from Exeter Angling Centre, Smythen Street; Brailey's Field Sports Centre, Market St.

Brampford Speke (Devon). Salmon, trout, dace, roach, chub; preserved. Pynes Water, from here down to Cowley Weir (2½m) fished by local syndicate. Exeter & Dist AA water towards Stoke Canon (see Culm).

Silverton (Devon). Trout, chub, roach, dace, pike, perch; preserved. Exeter & Dist AA has coarse fishing on Culm here *(see Exeter and Culm)*.

Bickleigh (Devon). Trout, salmon. Fisherman's Cot Hotel has a short stretch adjoining hotel for salmon and/or trout. Mainly for residents, but a few £12 dt on offer.

Tiverton (Devon). Exe, Lowman and Little Dart; trout, salmon. **Tiverton Canal**; bream, pike, perch, roach, tench. Tiverton & Dist AC has river, canal and lake fishing in vicinity. Canal dt from tackle shops, other waters, members only. Exe preserved for 2m both above and below town (trout and grayling) by Tiverton FFC, fly only. St £12 for residents only. River walk in Tiverton, ½m, free trout fishing to juv. Hotels: Bark House at Oakford Bridge; Fisherman's Cot, Bickleigh (beat on Exe). Tackle shops: Exe Valley Angling; Country Sports, 9 William St.

Dulverton (Som). Salmon, trout, grayling. Usually good run of salmon (May onwards and autumn) to Dulverton and beyond, depending on water conditions. Trout fishing good on Exe and **Barle** (four to lb). For 540m single bank, contact Lance Nicholson *(see below)*. Grayling less plentiful. Guests at Carnarvon Arms *(see advt)* may fish on 5m of Exe and Barle; individual beats, ghillie service, and instruction on site. Wt £100-£130 (S). Dt (S) £12-£25. Trout dt £7-£12. A few day tickets sometimes for non-residents. Some free fishing for guests at Lion Hotel. Royal Oak, Winsford, issues permits. **Exe Valley Fishery**, Exebridge, Dulverton TA22 9AY, tel: 01398 323328 (324079, fax). One large and two small lakes stocked with rainbows averaging 2lb+. Dt £5.50 (£3.50 per kl caught extra) on site throughout year. Limit: 2½ brace. At **Broford**, 5m double bank, with wild brown trout, fly only. Dt £10, from tackle shop: Lance Nicholson, High St, TA22 9HB (01398 323409). Accom. at Anchor Inn, Exebridge, Dulverton.

Tributaries of the Exe

CREEDY: Trout, coarse fish.

Cowley Bridge (Exeter). Coarse fish. Exeter and Dist AA has rights, left bank only (*see Exeter*).

Crediton (Devon). Trout; preserved by owners. Yeo 3m; trout; leave from farmers. Crediton FFC has over 5m, mainly double bank, on Creedy and Yeo, also 1½m on R Taw at Tawbridge. Limited dt £8 (Mon-Fri) Fly only. Contact Sec Crediton FFC. Fly only. Tackle shop: Ladd's Sports. Hotels: Ship, White Hart.

CULM: Trout, coarse fish, few grayling.

Stoke Canon, Rewe and **Silverton** (Devon). Dace, chub, roach, perch and occasional grayling. Exeter and Dist AA has water.

Hemyock (Devon). Trout, small and few. Lower water preserved and stocked by Hemyock-Culmstock syndicate.

Clayhidon (Devon). Upper Culm FA preserves about 4m in this district (see Hemyock). No Sunday fishing. Hotel: Half Moon.

Killerton (Devon). National Trust controls coarse fishing on Killerton Estate; tickets from tackle shops for Exeter AA water.

BARLE. Runs through beautifully wooded valley and holds salmon (av 7-10lb) and trout (av 8-10 in).

Tarr Steps (Som). Salmon, trout. Tarr Steps Hotel, Hawkridge TA22 9PY, has 6m of salmon and brown trout fishing, fly only. Non-residents welcome, dt salmon from £20, trout from £10. Tel: 01643 851293, fax: 01643 851218.

Simonsbath (Som). Exmoor Forest Hotel has rights on approx 1m of Barle, commencing 1½m below Simonsbath Bridge, free to hotel guests. St £50 to dt £3.50, for non-residents. E.A. licences at hotel. Spinning for salmon allowed. Convenient for **Wimbleball Reservoir**.

FAL

(For close seasons, licences, etc, see South West Region Environment Agency, p16)

Rises near Roche and flows about 23 miles, due south, past Grampound and Tregony to the English Channel at Falmouth.

Falmouth (Cornwall). Trout fishing in Argal Reservoir, coarse fishing in College Reservoir: large pike and carp. Trout in some of the small streams flowing into creeks around Falmouth. 2 acres coarse fishing at Tory Farm, Ponsanooth (01209 861272), speciality, carp. Dt on site. Mylor Trout Fishery, Mylor, also dt on site. Tackle shop: The Bait Box, Arwenack St.

Tregony (Cornwall). Trout, 2m off runs Polglaze Brook, 4m long; trout.

FOWEY

(For close seasons, licences, etc, see South West Region Environment Agency p16)

Rises on Bodmin Moor and enters English Channel by estuary at Fowey. Noted sea trout and salmon river. Sea trout run from May to Sept, grilse July-Oct, salmon, Aug-Dec. A spate river with middle and upper reaches fishing best after heavy rain.

Fowey (Cornwall). Capital sea fishing *(see Sea Fishing section)*. Boat hire for estuary fishing from Fowey Diving Services, 21 Station Rd, Fowey. Tackle shops: Leisure Time, 10 The Esplanade; Fowey Marine Services, 23/27 Station Rd. Hotels: Fowey, Riverside, Ship, Fowey Hall, Marina.

Lostwithiel (Cornwall). Sea trout, salmon, no brown trout. Fishing for rod and line below Lostwithiel Bridge free. Liskeard and Dist AA have spinning and bait fishing on middle and upper reaches, 1 Apr-30 Sept, wt £35 from Rogers Tackle Shop, Higher Bore St, Bodmin. Lostwithiel AC has 2m double bank upstream of town road bridge. Limited tickets from J H Hooper, 4 Reed's Park, Lostwithiel. Dt £10, wt £30, st £55, conc, from Rogers or Angling Centre, Parade Square.

Respryn Bridge (Cornwall). Most water above the bridge is in the hands of Lanhydrock AA, NT Cornwall Regional Office, **Lanhydrock Park**, PL30 4DE. St £40 (waiting list), wt £25, dt £10. Artificial bait only. Free fishing on section between Respryn Bridge and footbridge. Hotels: Royal Talbot, King's Arms, Earl of Chatham, Royal Oak, Globe, Trevone Guest House and Restormel Lodge.

Liskeard (Cornwall). Sea trout, salmon, no brown trout. Liskeard and Dist AC has rights on some 26m of single and double bank of **Fowey**, **Lynher**, and on minor rivers, West Looe, Seaton and Inny. Restricted membership from T Sobey, Trevartha Farm, Liskeard.

FROME AND PIDDLE (Dorset)

(For close seasons, licences, etc, see South West Region Environment Agency, p16)

Frome rises above Hooke in West Dorset and flows into the English Channel at Poole Harbour near Wareham. Piddle rises in a mill pond 1 mile north of Piddletrenthide and enters Poole Harbour near mouth of Frome near Wareham. Both are chalk streams and closely preserved but sport may sometimes be had. Some very good sea trout have been caught in the Frome, which also receives a run of heavy salmon. Trout in both rivers plentiful and good. Bass run up to where the river enters Poole Harbour. Piddle carries very small stock of heavy salmon.

Wareham (Dorset). On Frome and Piddle; salmon, sea trout, trout, grayling, pike, roach and dace. Free coarse fishing on towpath side of R Frome, from Wareham South Bridge downstream. E.A. licence required. Salmon and trout preserved. Morden Estate Office, Charborough Park, Wareham, sometimes has rods for entire season (never for day or week) as follows: salmon, Frome and Piddle; trout, Piddle and Bere Stream, and River Stour, coarse fishing. Environment Agency lets 14 rods for the season (on the basis of two per day) for fishery on Piddle; salmon, sea trout (details from Area Conservation Officer). South Drain nr Poole Harbour is Wareham & Dist AS water. Club has 22 local waters, membership £24, £5 jun. Hotels: Red Lion and Black Bear. Tackle shop and bait: G Elmes & Son, St John's

Hill; Guns & Sports, 24 South Street.

Wool (Dorset). Frome: Salmon, sea trout. Spring salmon scarce, summer and autumn fish plentiful in Frome. Woolbridge Manor (100 yards from river) has 1¼m; fly and spinning. Salmon run large, fish over 20lb not rare. Summer run of grilse 6 to 10lb. Season 1 Mar to 31 Aug. St £200, dt £25, approx. For details write to Mr Bowerman, Morden Estate Office, Charbourgh Park, Wimborne, Dorset. Nr **Puddletown, Pallington Lakes, Tincleton**, one trout, one coarse, one carp and tench only. Daily stocking. Trout dt £19; four fish limit. Coarse fishing £4, conc. Records include salmon 19lb, r trout 11lb 12oz and carp 22½lb. Tel: 01305 848141. At Tolpuddle, **Wessex Fly Fishing**, Lawrences Farm, tel: 01305 848460, 7m from Dorchester. Rivers, lakes and pools, accommodation (self catering and B&B), and tuition (Reffis member). Rivers are chalk streams in a natural state, with a good head of wild-bred brown trout. Improving from over-abstraction. Catch and release on rivers, 10 fish limit, barbless hooks. Lake dt £23, ½ day £19, evening £14; rivers, from £17 to £49, depending on season and beat. Tackle shop, B & B and cottage accom. on site.

Dorchester (Dorset). Frome: brown trout and grayling; Dorchester FC has 6½m water in vicinity of Dorchester. U/s dry fly or nymph fishing. Limited dt £20, from J Aplin (*see below*). Rest of river preserved by landowners. Dt and licences from tackle shop. Other society: Dorchester and Dist AS (coarse fishing only) who issue dt for short stretch of **Stour**. At **Kingcombe**, Higher Kingcombe Farm. 8 ponds - coarse fishing; Paul Crocker 01300 320537, St £75, £3 full day, £2 evenings, £5 night. **Rawlsbury Waters**, 4 small trout lakes, tel: 01258 817446. **Flowers Farm Lakes**, Hilfield, Dorchester, Dorset DT2 7BA, tel/fax: 01300 341351; trout fishery of 5 lakes, brown and rainbow. Dt £18, £14, £10.50. Limit, full day limit 4 fish. Open all year. Tickets for Luckfield Lake Fishery, 1½ acres, Broadmayne, with carp, and for R Frome fishing, from Tackle shop: John Aplin, Specialist Angling Supplies, 1 Athelstan Road, Dorchester DT1 1NR, tel: 01305 266500. Hotel: King's Arms.

GIPPING (Orwell)

(For close seasons, licences, etc, see Anglian Region Environment Agency, p19)

Rises between Stowmarket and Bury St Edmunds, and flows into the North Sea by an estuary near Ipswich. Coarse fish.

Ipswich (Suffolk). Most coarse fish. From Yarmouth Rd Bridge to Norwich Railway Bridge, 1m, dt on bank. 2m stretch from Railway Bridge to Sproughton Bridge, dt from tackle shops. Town section, st or dt on bank. Gipping APS controls 10m between Stowmarket and Ipswich, and issues dt for small section of river from Sproughton to Ipswich, from Ipswich tackle shops; members only on other fishings, which include several coarse lakes in vicinity. **Alton Water**, 350 acre coarse fish reservoir at Anglian Water Services Ltd, Holbrook Rd, Stutton, Ipswich, IP9 2RY, tel: 01473 327398, under control of AW, with bream to 7lb and pike to 25lb, plus roach and perch. St £25, dt £2.50, conc, on site or from local tackle shops. Tackle shops: Breakway Tackle, Bramford Rd; Viscount Tackle, Clapgate Lane; R Markham, Woodbridge Road East; Bosmere Tackle, 57 High Street, Needham Market.

Stowmarket (Suffolk). Permits to fish Green Meadow stretch from Bosmere Tackle, see below. Stowmarket and Dist AA has short stretch of **Rattle**; members only. Gipping Valley AC fishes river here, and at **Needham Market** and **Claydon**; also **Needham Lake**, 10 acres: most coarse fish stocked. Membership £17, conc, from Bosmere Tackle, 57 High St, Needham Market.

GLOUCESTERSHIRE (streams)

BIDEFORD BROOK. Fishing station: **Awre**. Rises in Abbot's Wood and flows 7m to Severn estuary; coarse fish; preserved. **Blackpool Brook** enters at Awre; Forest of Dean AC; members only.

CONE. fishing station: **Woolaston**. Cone rises by Hewelsfield, and is 5m long. Eels and flounders.

FROME. Rises near Cheltenham and flows into Severn estuary. Coarse fish; a few trout higher up. Fishing stations: **Stonehouse** (Glos), coarse fish, and **Stroud** (Glos), a few trout and coarse fish. Several brooks in vicinity. Pike and coarse fishing in Stroudwater Canal. Stroud AA controls 2m Thames at Lechlade and 1m at Newbridge. Stroud tackle shop: Batemans Sports, Kendrick Street, GL5 1AB, tel: 01453 764320, issue st £10, £3.50 juv, for local club waters, including Frome at **Eastington** and **Whitminster**, canal from Stroud to Thrupp, tickets for gravel pits, a total of 21 different venues.

NAILSWORTH BROOK (tributary of Frome). Fishing stations: **Nailsworth** (Glos) and **Woodchester** (Glos). Brook reported polluted in parts. Lakes: Longfords Lake, pike, carp. Woodchester Park lakes: pike, perch, roach, tench, brown and rainbow trout; now preserved.

HOPE BROOK. Fishing station: **Westbury-on-Severn**, ns Grange Court, 1½m. Hope Brook rises 2m above Longhope, runs 5m to Westbury and Severn estuary (1m). Coarse fish, mostly preserved. Inn: Red Lion.

LITTLE AVON: Small Gloucestershire stream flowing into Severn estuary.

Berkeley (Glos). Coarse fish, trout, Waterley Brook. Fishing below Charfield preserved. Close by station rises Billow Brook, which runs thence 3m to estuary. Clubs have water on **Gloucester and Berkeley Canal**; 16m Sharpness to Gloucester.

LYD. Chub, roach, perch. Fishing station: **Lydney**. Lydney AA holds stretch from railway station to Tufts Junction. Club also has **Lydney Lake** (carp, roach and perch). **Lydney Canal** and a dam.

GREATER MANCHESTER RESERVOIRS

These are trout fisheries, unless otherwise stated. More information may be obtained from Peter Sharples, Team Leader, North West Water Ltd, Woodhead Road, Tintwhistle, Hadfield via Hyde, Cheshire SK14 7HR, tel: 01457 864187; Team Leader Phil Luff, NWW Ltd, Rivington Water Treatment Works, Horwich, Bolton BL6 7RN, tel: 01204 696118.

BOLLINHURST RESERVOIR, Disley. Leased by Dystelegh Fly FC. Contact G F Grime, 4 Lostock Avenue, Hazel Grove, Stockport. Members only, no permits.

BUCKLEY WOOD RESERVOIR, Rochdale. Rochdale Waltonian Anglers, (*see club list*).

CASTLESHAW (LOWER) RESERVOIR, Oldham. Oldham United Anglers, J K Lees, 10, Packwood Chase, Oldham.

GORTON (LOWER) RESERVOIR. Coarse permits on bank, suitable for disabled anglers.

GORTON (UPPER) RESERVOIR, 'Lawrence Scott Arm'. Coarse fishing permits on bank. Further details from Manchester City Council, Rec Services Dept, Belle Vue Athletics, Pink Bank Lane, Manchester M12 5QN.

HOLLINGWORTH LAKE, Rochdale. Contact Chief Warden, Information Centre, Hollingworth Lake Country Park, Rakewood Rd, Littleborough, Lancs. Tickets from Visitors' Centre on bank.

JUMBLES RESERVOIR, Bolton. Free fishing to licence holders. Contact Team Leader, Paul Phillips, NNW Ltd (*see Thirlmere*).

KITCLIFFE RESERVOIR, Rochdale. Oldham United Anglers, *see Castleshaw*.

LITTLE SEA RESERVOIR, Oldham. Oldham & Dist Amalgamated AA. B Boff, 369 Shaw Rd, Oldham.

LUDWORTH RESERVOIR, Stockport. Crossland's AC, Mr L Donaldson, 57 The Ridgeway, Romiley, Stockport SK6 3HA. Dt for members guests only, from Stockport Angling Centre, 145 Welling-

POLLUTION

Anglers are united in deploring pollution. To combat it, urgent action may be called for at any time, from anyone of us. If numbers of fish are found dead, dying, or seriously distressed, take samples of both fish and water, and contact the officer responsible for pollution at the appropriate Environment Agency office. For hot-line, see Environment Agency section at front of book.

ton Rd North, Stockport SK4 2PF.

OGDEN RESERVOIR, Rochdale. Oldham United Anglers, *see Castleshaw*.

PIETHORNE, Oldham. Oldham Fly FC, R Henshall, tel: 0161 6885510. Tickets from Gilders Fishing Tackle, tel: 0161 6812538.

RUMWORTH LODGE, Bolton. Royal Ashton AC, D T Dobson, 1 Parkway, Westhoughton. Dt water.

WALKERWOOD RESERVOIR, Tameside. Walkerwood Trout Fishery. Fly only, all browns to be returned. Best brown 7lb, best rainbow 14lb 8oz. Dt £15, 4 fish, at Car Park. A range of season tickets on offer. Tel: 0421 619399.

WATERGROVE RESERVOIR, Rochdale. Dt from warden on site at the sailboard club, or from Hollingworth Lake.

HAMPSHIRE (Streams, lakes and canal)

(For close seasons, licences, etc, see Southern Region Environment Agency, p16).

BASINGSTOKE CANAL. Fishing stations: **Greywell, North Warnborough, Odiham, Winchfield, Crookham, Fleet, Farnborough, Aldershot, Ash Vale**. Pike, carp, roach, good tench, perch; fishing from towpath only; dt for 17m of Hampshire section from Greywell Tunnel to Ash Lock from tackle shop Noels Tackle, 314 Fernhill Rd, Cove. Andover AC has fishing. Further enquiries about Basingstoke Canal to BCAA Sec, R Jenkins, 26 Tintern Close, Basingstoke RG24 9HE. Farnborough AS also has rights on **Whitewater** at **Heckfield, Loddon** at **Winnersh, Ash Vale Lake**, 5 acres, **Shawfields Lake**, 3 acres, mixed, and gravel pits. St £13 from Raisons, tackle shops, Park Road, Farnborough for **Willow Park Fisheries**, Ash Vale, three lakes stocked with carp, tench and other coarse fish. Bait and refreshments on site. Dt on site £1 and £1.50, concession for jun. Four Leisure Sport gravel pits at **Frimley**. Carp, crucian carp, bream, perch, tench, perch, rudd, eel and pike. Large specimens recorded. No night fishing, no dt. St £24, ½ price conc, from LSA, RMC House, High Street, Feltham, Middlesex TW13 4HD, tel: 0181 8931168. Tackle shops: Two Guys, 27 Burnby Close, Basingstoke; Raison's, 2 Park Road, Farnborough; Tackle Up, 151 Fleet Road, Fleet: The Creel, 36 Station Road, Aldershot. **Ewhurst Lake** (6m N); pike, perch, roach, strictly limited st £30; inquire of Estate Office.

BEAULIEU. The Beaulieu River is approx 14 miles long. Tickets for tidal stretch, Bailey's Hard to Needs Ore (bass, mullet), st £17, dt £2.50, from Harbour Master, Buckler's Hard (tel: 01590 616200) or Resident Land Agent, John Montagu Building, Beaulieu (tel: 01590 612345). Access from Bailey's Hard and Buckler's Hard. Coarse fishing on **Hatchett Pond** and **Cadmans Pool** (Forestry Commission); bream, carp, tench and pike; tickets from Forestry Commission, Queen's House, Lyndhurst SO43 7NH (01703 283141), campsite offices during camping season and local tackle shops (st £60, wt £9, dt £5, VAT incl, jun conc, barbless hooks only). Children may fish free on two adjacent ponds. Hotel: Montagu Arms. Accommodation at Newhouse Farm, 01590 612297.

DAMERHAM TROUT LAKES, Fordingbridge (3m). Six lakes, and river for St holders. R and b trout. Open March 15 until October 31. Advance bookings only. St £1050, half £525, quarter £350. Corporate rates on application. Bed and breakfast in annex to 16th C. thatched cottage. Tel: 07253 446.

FLEET POND. Fishing station: **Fleet**. Cove AS water. No tickets. Tackle shop: Fleet S C, 182 Fleet Road.

HAMBLE. Sea trout and trout. **Bishop's Waltham**. Fishing mostly private.

HOLBURY TROUT LAKES, Lockerley, Near **Romsey**, Hants SO52 0JR, tel: 01794 341619. Recently improved fishery of four lakes, stocked with rainbow and blue trout (average caught 3lb, largest 7lb 2oz), and ⅔m of River Dun, both banks, stocked brown trout. Dry fly and nymph only on river, wet and dry fly on lakes. No catch and release. Full dt for lakes and river £40, full season £675, limit 4 fish per day; half day £23, half season £350. Lakes only: dt £28-£16, st £600-£300. Full facilities on site, and tuition if required.

LYMINGTON RIVER. Fishing station: Lymington. Sea trout (2-11lb), brown trout (¾ to 1lb). Sea trout best June to Sept. Fishing improved by Brockenhurst Manor FFC; private. Mixed fishery at Sway Lakes, Barrows Lane, Sway Lymington, tel: 01590 682010. Carp over

20lbs. Dt on bank. Tackle and bait from Loni's Angling Centre, Gore Rd, New Milton.

MEON. Trout; sea trout in lower reaches. Fishing station: **East Meon**; Hants and Sussex Alliance has water; inquire Hon Sec. Portsmouth Services FFA has 5 miles on Meon and 2¼ miles on Itchen below Winchester. Membership is immediately obtainable for serving personnel, those retired may have to wait 2 years. Serving members £80, retired £160, guests £16 per day. Portsmouth and Dist AS hold some twenty coarse ponds and lakes around **Portsmouth** and across Hampshire and W Sussex, plus river trout and coarse fishing on Arun, Rother, Ember, and Wallington. Dt on some waters. membership £47, £15 joining fee. Enquiries to Hon Sec. Staunton Country Park, Havant PO9 5HB (01705 453405): 3 acre lake with carp, bream roach, dt in advance. Meon Springs Fly Fishery, Whitewood Farm, East Meon, Petersfield GU32 1HW, (01730 823249): two small lakes between East and West Meon. River Farm Lake, Funtley, Fareham (01329 841215: trout and carp fishing. Chiphall Lake Trout Fishery, 5 acres: Northfields Farm, Wickham. Wintershill Lake, trout fishing on 3½ acres at Durley, Bishop's Waltham. Full and half season rods, contact Lake Bailiff, tel: 01703 601421. Tackle shops: Rover's, 178B West St, Fareham; Coombs Tackle Centre, 165 New Rd, Coptnor, Portsmouth.

SANDLEHEATH. Six lakes and three chalk stream beats at **Rockbourne Trout Fishery**, Sandleheath, Fordingbridge, Hampshire SP6 1QG. Excellent fishing for rainbow trout in lakes and brown trout and grayling in streams, fly only, various period terms from dt £32, limit 5 fish, ½ day £28, 4 fish. Special winter tickets, also. Blocks of tickets at discount. Concessions for juv. Tuition, tackle hire, licensed cafeteria. Tel: 01725 518603.

WAGGONERS' WELLS, near **Haslemere**. Three lakes; National Trust waters, now managed by Greyshott AC. Coarse fishing; carp, roach, tench, gudgeon, a few trout. Dt from Greyshott Tackle, Crossway Road, Greyshott, Hindhead, or bailiff on bank. Hotel: Punchbowl Hotel, Hindhead.

WARBURN. Dace, trout, salmon; preserved; leave sometimes from landowners; joins sea at **Key Haven**.

HERTS AND GREATER LONDON (reservoirs and lakes)

(see also London Reservoirs)

ALDENHAM (Herts). **Aldenham Country Park Reservoir**. Managed by Herts CC. Coarse fishing, incl. tench, pike to 37lb, carp to 39lb, plus very good roach and bream. No night fishing. Dt £3 (jun, OAP £1.50), punt £6-£4. Dis free. From bailiff on site or from Park Manager, Park Office, Dagger Lane, Elstree, Herts WD6 3AT. Tel: 0181-953 1259; or 01831 837446, bailiff's mobile phone.

Shepperton (Middx); **Ashmere Fisheries**, Felix Lane, Shepperton TW17 8NN. Four lakes, total 20 acres, stocked with rainbow trout. Boats. Annual membership only, £350-£585. Apply Mrs Jean Howman, Ashmere Fisheries, Felix Lane, Shepperton, tel: 01932 225445(253793 fax).

STANSTEAD ABBOTS. Leisure Sport coarse fisheries consisting of 5 gravel pits with carp over 40lb, mill stream and part of main river. Other species include roach, tench, dace, pike, barbel. Season tickets £30. Concessions to jun, OAP, dis. No dt. Applications to LSA, RMC House, High Street, Feltham, Middlesex TW13 4HD, tel: 0181 8931168.

TRING (Herts). Four large reservoirs: **Marsworth, Startops End** and **Wilstone** (2m from Tring) main feeders for Grand Union Canal. Good fishing for specimen hunters. Bream over 10lb, former British record tench 12½lb, pike to 26lb, many large roach, British record catfish, 43½lb. Sunday fishing now permitted. St £80 (including night fishing), conc, dt £3.50, conc £2.50, evening £2.50. Tickets obtainable on bank from bailiff, B C Double, Watery Lane, Marsworth or tel: 822379. The fourth reservoir is a private trout fishery. The Tring Anglers have extensive fishing on Grand Union Canal and Arms, **R Thame** at Chearsley and Shabbington Island, Thames at Eynsham, **R Ouzel** nr Newport Pagnell and Stoke Hammond, **R Ivel** at Shefford, plus lakes and ponds which include an excellent bream fishery. Club also fishes Oxford & Dist AA waters on Thames and elsewhere, and Reading & Dist AA waters incl Kennet. Tackle shop: Amersham Outdoor Sports, Station Rd, Amersham. Hotels: Anglers' Retreat, Startops End, Rose and Crown.

HULL

(For close seasons, licences, etc, see North East Region Environment Agency, p17)

Tidal river between Hempholme and Hull is free of any permit charge and is popularly fished by an increasing number of coarse anglers. Upstream of Beverley first-class sport may be had with roach, dace, pike, chub, bream, etc. West Beck is an excellent but preserved trout fishery of chalk-stream character.

Hull (North Humberside). River polluted. Drains giving good coarse fishing. Free fishing on E.A. licence from North Frodingham to Hull. Hull & Dist AA has water on **Derwent** at **Breighton, Wressle** and **Newton**; on the **Rye** at **Butterwick** and **Swinton**; and on the **Trent** at **Carlton**. Also the **Brandsburton Ponds** (open all the year), Tilery Lake, the Broomfleet, Motorway, and other ponds, 9m of **Market Weighton Canal**, 17m from Hull, mixed coarse fishery held jointly with Goole AA, 1m of **R Foulness**, north bank. Membership is unrestricted, st £21. Stone Creek and Patrington Haven hold flounders. Good sea fishing. Burstwick Watersports have coarse fishing nr **Burstwick**; dt £2 or £1.50. Contact P Hall, tel: 01482 26455. Rush Lyvars Lake, coarse fishery at **Hedon**, dt £1.20. Tel: 01482 898970. **Pickering Park Lake** owned by City Council, fine pike. Coarse dt £1.10. Tel: 01482 222693. Tackle shops: Fishing Basket, 470 Beverley Road; Everett's Fishing Tackle, 691 Holderness Rd; G W Hutchinson & Co, 27 Anlaby Rd; B B Fishing Tackle, 567 Holderness Rd.

Beverley (N Humberside). Tidal River Hull and drains give good coarse fishing; from Hull Bridge upstream through **Arram, Aike Wilfholme, Baswicke** and **Hempholme** to Frodingham Beck: North East Region Environment Agency, for enquiries; weedy June to Nov. **Beverley Beck**, canalised stream, 1m long, 60 pegs, good access for disabled. Stocked with most coarse species, but mainly roach to 2lb, bream 7lb, tench and chub. Dt £2.50, jun 50p, from Total Petrol Sta-

A fine specimen roach from Hempholme Lock on the River Hull. *Photo: Bruno Broughton.*

tion, Waterside Rd, Beverley. Further information: Paul Caygill, tel: 01964 542677. Dt £2 for 2 coarse ponds in Lakeminster Park, tel: 01482 882655. **Leven Canal** (6m): course fish, Hull AA water except for 250 yds to right of bridge, Trailer and Marina Ltd, tel: 01482 896879. Fine tench. Dt from Minster Tackle, 3 Flemingate, Everett's Fishing Tackle, Beverley, Leven Marina, and 11 The Meadows, Leven. Hotel: Beverley Arms.

Brandesburton (N Humberside). River Hull 3m W, excellent coarse fishing in gravel pits *(see Hull).*

Wansford (N Humberside). Free left bank below Lock Dow to Brigham. **Driffield Canal Fishery**, from Town Lock, Driffield along B1249 to Snake Holme Lock, ½m west of Wansford. Trout, both bait and fly. Controlled by Tony Harrison on behalf of E Yorkshire CA. Tel: 01377 44152. **West Beck** preserved by Golden Hill AS and West Beck PS; members only. Fishponds Farm and Fishery, Woldgate, Boynton, Nr **Bridlington** YO16 4XE, has 3 ponds coarse fishing ponds. Dt £3, 2 rods. Barbless hooks, no groundbait, no keepnets. Tel: 01262 605873.

Tributaries of the Hull

FOSTON BECK (or **KELK** or **FRODINGHAM BECK**):

North Frodingham, **Foston-on-the-Wolds** and **Lowthorpe** (N Humberside). Rises in Yorkshire wolds; true chalk stream containing brown trout averaging well over the pound. Preserved.

Driffield Beck:

Driffield (N Humberside). Provides chalk stream fishing for trout and grayling of high order. Driffield AA. Kellythorpe Trout Lake now in private hands. For **Pickering Trout Lake**, Newbridge Rd, Pickering, N Yorks, tel: 01715 474219.

ISLE OF MAN

The geographical nature of the Isle of Man tends to dictate the type of river, fish and hence fishing one may encounter when angling in the Island. Being a relatively mountainous place, rivers and streams are small, swift flowing and very clear. There are very few coarse fish on the Isle of Man but nevertheless excellent sport can be had in the numerous trout streams where the art of approach to the river bank and the gentle and accurate cast of the true angler becomes vital.

There are very few preserved stretches of river in the Island and a well chosen word with the land owner is often all that is required to enable an angler to fish in peace. Approx one

DRY FLIES
SILVER MARCH BROWN
DRY SEDGE
SECRET WEAPON
HELEN'S FANCY
COACHMAN
BLACK DOLL
GREENWELL'S GLORY
MAYFLY
STICK FLY
BLACK SPIDER
LUNN'S PARTICULAR
ORANGE NYMPH
PHEASANT TAIL
RED TAG
BLACK PENSIONER
GREY DUSTER
LIGHT PENSIONER
MALLARD & CLARET
BLUE DUN
RED SPINNER
DADDY - LONG - LEGS
ALDER

WET FLIES AND NYMPHS
PETER ROSS
CINNAMON & GOLD
SAWYER'S KILLER BUG
MIDGE PUPA BL
BUTCHER
GREENWELL'S GLORY
PHEASANT TAIL NYMPH
MIDGE PUPA GI
MARCH BROWN
BLACK SPIDER
OLIVE NYMPH
MIDGE PUPA GRI
BLUE ZULU
PARTRIDGE & ORANGE
HARE'S EAR NYMPH
MIDGE PUPA OR
SOLDIER PALMER
SNIPE & PURPLE
PINK SHRIMP
MIDGE PUPA CLA
INVICTA
BLACK & PEACOCK
IRON BLUE NYMPH
HATCHING SEDG
GREEN
BLACK PENNELL
CHURCH PHEASANT TAIL
LIME GREEN
HATCHING SEDG
BROWN
MALLARD & CLARET
CHURCH PHEASANT TAIL
ORANGE
MAYFLY NYMPH

half mile of the River Douglas through the Nunnery Estate is exclusively reserved for the Manx Game FC. Small sections of the rivers Dhoo and Glass can only be fished under permit from the Douglas and District Angling Club. Applications for membership should be sent to Sue McCoubrey, 47 Hildesley Road, Douglas (628460). Subscriptions are now £15, £6 junior. Natural baits (worms, bread, cheese) and artificial baits are allowed on the Island's rivers, ponds and streams but anglers are reminded that only artificial baits are allowed when reservoir fishing (except Eairy Dam). Further details of all freshwater angling can be obtained from the Freshwater Fishery Inspector, Cornaa, Maughold. Anglers must abide by the regulations wherever they fish. (1) Not to use or carry a gaff or tailer. (2) Not to use a line the diameter of which exceeds 0.033 cm, excepting that a fly line used solely for fly fishing may exceed 0.033 cm diameter, provided the leader exceeds five feet in length and does at no point exceed 0.033 cm in diameter. (0.033 cm diameter is approximately equivalent to 10lb breaking strain). (3) Not use more than one hook on a line unless (a) Pennel or Stewart tackles are being used for bait fishing; (b) a 'point with two droppers' is being used for fly fishing only; (c) a spinner is being used for spinning only. (4) Not to use a hook larger than No 6 Redditch scale, unless the hook is comprised in an artificial fly. (5) Return to the water all fish foul hooked. (6) Return to the water unharmed any freshwater fish hooked which is less than 18 cm in length overall. (7) Chest waders prohibited.

The river fishing season commences on 1 April, and finishes on the 30 September for trout and 31 October for salmon. The reservoir season begins on 10 March and continues until 31 October. A freshwater fishing licence is required to fish any river or pond, and a separate licence required to fish a reservoir.

Salmon fishing takes place mainly in the Autumn as the Island does not enjoy a spring run. Salmon and sea trout are usually taken during or after spate conditions. There is a bag limit for the rivers of 6 trout or salmon, of which no more than 2 may be migratory fish in any one day. Fish are small and rarely if ever exceed 20lb -- a more reasonable average would be 5-10lb.

The Department of Agriculture, Fisheries and Forestry pursues a continual stocking programme of rivers, ponds and reservoirs.

At present there are six reservoirs open for fishing. They are: (a) The West Baldwin Reservoir is near the centre of the Island. A main road goes along its side. There is an infrequent bus service to West Baldwin village 1⅓ miles from the reservoir. (b) Clypse and Kerrowdhoo Reservoirs lie, one beyond the other, about 1½ miles north of Onchan Village. A private road runs, off the road to Grange Farm, to the Attendants house where there is room to park cars. (c) Ballure Reservoir is just south of Ramsey. Access is by a private road branching off the main road to Douglas, on the Douglas side of the MER crossing near the town boundary. (d) Cringle Reservoir is just north of the road from Ronague to Foxdale and is on the south slopes of South Barrule. Cars can be parked on the reservoir land. (e) Sulby Reservoir is close to the A14 Sulby-Snaefell road. (f) Eairy Dam is alongside the A24 Douglas to Foxdale road. It is not a water supply and restrictions on the use of live bait do not apply. Reservoirs are stocked on a weekly basis with browns and rainbows up to double figures. There is a limit of four fish.

Fishing Licences

Freshwater fishing licences - needed before fishing commences - cost about: St rivers £25, reservoirs £75. (Jun £9 and £25 respectively.) Wt (to Sep 30) rivers: £9, reservoirs: £25, jun £5 and £9 respectively.) Only st after 30 Sept.

They are obtained from: I.O.M. Department of Agriculture, Fisheries and Forestry, Mount Havelock, Douglas, tel: 01624 685857; from Department of Tourism & Leisure, Information Bureau, Sea Terminal, Douglas, from local Commissioners offices in Onchan and Laxey, and from most Post Offices.

No licence required for sea fishing, which from pier, rocks or boat is excellent, especially for pollack - locally called callig - mackerel, cod and codling, whiting and plaice. Chief bait for ground fish is mackerel, but lugworm, sand-eels and shellfish also found. Jigging with white and coloured feathers and artificial sand-eel for pollack, mackerel and cod is successful. Good centres for most species are Peel, Port Erin, Port St Mary and Ramsey. Department of Tourism & Leisure, Douglas, issues useful booklet on sea and river fishing. Principal rivers as follows:

COLBY RIVER. Trout. This stream is 4m long; preserved in lower reaches.

DOUGLAS RIVER. Salmon, sea trout, trout. Douglas formed by junction of Dhoo and Glass, half a mile above the town of **Douglas**. Fishing on Glass River and lower part of Dhoo preserved, but free above **Union Mills**. Glass largely rented by Douglas AC. Manx Game FC has fishing on these rivers, residents only, no guest tickets.

GLEN MOOR BURN, 3m long. Trout; fishing free, but not very good. Fishing station: **Kirk Michael**.

LAXEY RIVER. Trout; free but poor. This stream is 5m long. 1m above junction with sea at Laxey, Glen River (trout), 3m long, joins on right bank. Fishing station: **Laxey**.

NEB. Trout; mostly free and good; salmon from Aug. Neb (sometimes called Peel River) rises above **Little London** and Blabae and runs 3m to **Glen Helen** (Hotel: Glen Helen). It then runs 4m to **St John's**. Here **Foxdale River**, 6m long, joins on left bank. Hence to **Peel** is 3m. 3m S is **Glen Maye River** 4m long; sea trout below waterfall, trout above.

SANTON BURN. 6m long; trout; mostly preserved, but poor; salmon from Aug. Fishing station: **Santon**.

SILVER BURN. Trout, sea trout; free. This stream rises on the slopes of South Barrule, runs 5m to **Ballasalla**, where Awin Ruy, 4m long, joins on left bank. Silver Burn runs 3m to the sea at **Castletown**. Best sport downstream for about 1m to Castletown.

SULBY. Salmon (from Aug), sea trout; free; moderate in lower reaches only, upstream from Claddaghs, poor. Five miles S is **Cornaa River**, 5m long, which runs into sea at Port Cornaa, the site of the Fishery Department's hatchery. Good for salmon and sea trout in lower portion (Sept, Oct).

WYLLIN BURN. 4m long; trout; free; fishing poor. Near **Kirk Michael**.

(For further information about sea fishing on the Island, see under Sea Fishing Stations)

ISLE OF WIGHT

(For close seasons, licences, etc, see Southern Region Environment Agency, p 16).

Freshwater fishing on the Island is better than is generally appreciated. The **Yar** from St Helens, Bembridge, to Alverstone holds fair numbers of roach, dace and rudd, with perch, carp and bream to 7lb in some stretches. Isle of Wight Freshwater AA has coarse fishing for dace, roach, carp, bream, perch, tench, pike and others at Yarbridge and Alverstone on Yar, dt on bank for Alverstone only; **Gunville Pond**, Newport, Merstone Fishery, 3 coarse lakes (both members only), **Somerton Reservoir**, Cowes, dt from bailiff. IWFAA membership £25, conc £10. At Morton Farm, Brading, tel 01983 406132, is coarse fishing on small lake and R Yar. Hale Manor Lakes are both 1 acre, carp and mixed coarse. Hale Manor, Arreton, tel: 01983 865204. Ideal junior coarse ponds at Jolliffes Farm, Whitewell, 01983 730783. Gillees Pond, Stag Lane, Newport: carp, rudd, roach, bream. Dt £2 from Scotties, *below*. Tackle shops: The Sport and Model Shop, 9 Union Street, Ryde; N R Young, The Sports Shop, 74 Regent Street, Shanklin; W Bates & Son, 5 Springhill, Ventnor; The Sports & Model Shop, Ryde; David's Food Market, Lane End Court, Bembridge; 'Scotties', 11 Lugley St, Newport and 22 Fitzroy St, Sandown. Light sea fishing, for which freshwater tackle may be employed, at Whippingham (River Medina), Fishbourne (Wootton Creek) and in Bembridge Harbour; mullet, bass, flatfish, etc.

ITCHEN

(For close seasons licences, etc, see Southern Region Environment Agency, p16).

Rises some miles north-west of Petersfield and flows via Winchester into Southampton Water at Southampton. Famous Hampshire chalk stream. Trout fishing excellent, but strictly preserved for most part. Some salmon and sea trout lower down, but also preserved. Principal tributaries are **Arle** and **Candover Brook**; both strictly preserved.

Southampton (Hants). Itchen and Test estuaries. Pout, whiting and eels in Southampton Water; and whiting, bass, grey mullet from the piers and quays. Free coarse fishing from public footpath between Woodmill and Mansbridge. **Lower**

Itchen Fishery, Gaters Mill, Mansbridge, west End, offers salmon, brown trout and night sea trout fishing on season basis, and some dt. Contact Embley Ridge, Gardeners Lane, Romsey, Hants, or tel: 0585 175540. **Leominstead Trout Fishery**, Emery Down, **Lyndhurst** SO43 7GA has 8 acres of trout and coarse fishing, trout dt £25, 5 fish limit. Coarse dt £5, jun £2.50. Tel: 01703 282610. Mopley Farm Trout Fishery, Blackfield, 3 acres, fly only, open 3 Apr to 31 Oct. Tel: South. 891616. For Holbury Manor Pond, with tench, carp, pike, roach, contact Gang Warily Recreation and Community Centre, Newlands Rd, Fawley SO45 1GA, tel: 01703 893603. Tackle shop: Bells Sports, 9 New Rd, Hythe, Southampton.

Eastleigh (Hants) Trout, salmon and grayling; preserved. Eastleigh & Dist AC has various game and coarse fishing, incl 3 stretches of river, Upper and Lower Itchen Navigation, and 12 lakes. Dt £4, conc, for one of these, Lakeside Park, Eastleigh, from tackle shops. Membership £47 pa, joining fee £6. Bishopstoke FC has water, which affords excellent sport. Water holds large trout. Salmon run right up to Brambridge. Some sea trout also come up; private. Junior st from Borough Council for Bishopstoke Riverside Rd stretch. Marwell Manor Farm Trout Fishery, Fishers Pond, Eastleigh, has 3.5 acre lake, dt on site. Tackle shop: Eastleigh Angling Centre, 325 Market Street.

Bishopstoke (Hants), ns Eastleigh. Salmon, trout and grayling; preserved by Bishopstoke FC and other owners.

Winchester (Hants). Trout above city; trout and grayling below. Free fishing on E.A.licence between the city weirs, and the left bank of the **Itchen Navigation**, between Blackbridge and St Catherine's Lock. Portsmouth Services FFA has 1¾ miles below town; terms of club membership are described under R Meon entry. The Rod Box, London Road, King's Worthy, Winchester S023 7QN, tel: 01962 883600, offers dry fly fishing on st and dt basis and other rods on celebrated private stretches of the **Test** and on the **Itchen, Arle Anton, Bourne** and **Whitewater**, and on lakes. Charges on request. Tackle shop: The Rod Box, Kings Worthy.

Itchen Abbas (Hants). Trout; preserved by riparian owners. **Avington Trout Fishery**, three lakes plus stretch of R Itchen, provide excellent trout fishing. Open all year, stocked daily. Limit 2 brace. St and dt. British rainbow record broken there several times. (Tel: 01962 779 312.) Tackle Shop: The Rod Box, Kingsworthy, Winchester. Many hotels.

Arlesford (Hants). **Candover Brook, Alre, Itchen**; trout; preserved by riparian owners. Grange Lakes, Alresford Pond; coarse fish; preserved.

KENT (lakes and streams)

BEWL WATER: 770 acre SW fly-only trout fishery nr. **Lamberhurst**. St (full) £432, 6 fish daily. (Mon-Fri) £340. Dt £12.40. Evenings, £9.30, 4 fish. Concessions for beginners and jun, with reduced limits. Motor and pulling boats, £18 and £10.80; evenings: £12.10 and £7.20. Season: April 3-0ct 31. Enquiries: Fishing Lodge, tel: 01892 890352 (out of season) 890661.

BROOKLANDS LAKES. Dartford. 20 acres, Dartford and Dist APS, variety of coarse fish, carp to 26lb, tench 7lb, bream 7lb; dt £3, conc, from bailiffs on bank.

BOUGH BEECH RESERVOIR. Near **Tonbridge**. 226 acres, trout fishing on season ticket only, dt for pike and coarse. Trout fishing Apr-Jun, coarse Jul-Mar, pike in Oct. Tickets from Mr E Crow, Honeycroft Farm, Three Elm Lane, Golden Green, Tonbridge TN11 0BS, tel: 01732 851544.

BURNHAM RESERVOIR (3m north of **Maidstone**). Coarse fishery of 12 acres; carp to 30lbs, 100lb bags of bream, good roach and chub. No day tickets, but membership offered. £43 pa, joining fee £15, conc. Contact Medway Victory Angling and Medway Preservation Society, 33 Hackney Rd, Maidstone, Kent ME16 8LN.

CHIDDINGSTONE CASTLE LAKE Good coarse fishing, especially carp. No night fishing. Prepaid booking advisable at weekends. Dt £8 from Custodian. One onlooker only, per fisherman, £3.50. Apply to the Administrator, Chiddingstone Castle, near **Edenbridge**. TN8 7AD. Tel: 01892 870347.

LARKFIELD LAKES. Three pits of 47, 20, 27 acres. Carp, tench, pike, bream, eels, roach, perch. St £32. Concessions

A $7\frac{1}{2}$lb Bewl rainbow - a fine example of the productivity of Southern waters.

on all for jun, OAP, dis. No dt. Applications to LSA, RMC House, High Street, Feltham, Middlesex TW13 4HD, tel: 0181 8931168.

LONGFORD LAKE. Sevenoaks. Private water of Holmesdale AS, who also have junior water Montreal Park Lake; st £10, £50. Dt £3 for guests of members only, from Hon Sec, or from Manklow Tackle Shop, 44 Seal Rd, Sevenoaks; A & I Tackle, Green St, Orpington.

LULLINGSTONE LAKE, near **Eynsford**. Trout. Kingfisher APS; no tickets.

MID KENT FISHERIES, Chilham Water Mill, Ashford Rd, **Chilham** CT4 8EE, tel: 01227 730668 (738894 fax). Coarse fishing on 16 lakes, from 26 to 3 acres, well stocked with all species. Catches include Kent record carp 49lb 15oz, large bream, perch, rudd, tench, and pike to 27lb. Purpose built match fishing lake with 104 pegs. St £80, half price concessions for OAP, juv, dis. A £5 dt is offered on one lake, with same conc. Trout fishing on river, £35 per day.

MOTE PARK LAKE. Maidstone *(see Medway)*. Coarse fishery of 26 acres; large carp, roach, tench, bream; no day tickets, but membership is open, contact Medway Victory Angling and Medway Preservation Society, 33 Hackney Rd, Maidstone, Kent ME16 8LN.

PETT POOLS. Fishing stations: **Winchelsea**, 2m; Rye, 4m. 25 acres, coarse fish; dt £4 (limited) from T G King, Market Stores, Pett Level, Nr Hastings TN35 4EH.

ROMNEY MARSH. Much good fishing on marsh, especially in main drains to Rother; best in summer (large bream shoals); water on low side in winter. Clubs with water here are: Ashford and Dist APS; Cinque Ports AS; Clive Vale AC (who fish Jury's Gap Sewer; Clive Vale reservoirs (carp), Ecclesbourne Reservoir, Hastings), Hastings, Bexhill and Dist AA (members only); Rye and Dist AS; Tenterden and Dist APS; Linesmen AC (also waters on **Medway, Beult** and **Stour**; details: Hon Sec). Tackle shops; Romney Tackle, The Avenue, New Romney; Point Tackle Shop, Dungeness, and Hastings tackle shops: Steve's, White Rock; Angling Centre, The Bourne.

ROYAL MILITARY CANAL. Summer fishing only; level partially lowered in winter for drainage. Stations: **Hythe** and **Ashford**. Cinque Ports AS has 7m from Seabrook outfall to Giggers Green; carp, bream, roach, rudd, tench, eels, tench, perch, pike; most sections have dt from bailiff or tackle shops. West Hythe Ballast Pit is members only. Rother FA fishes 3m from Appledore Dam to Iden Lock. Dt £3 from John Rees, 18 Lyndhurst Rd, Dymchurch, TN29 0TE. Spurringbrook Sewer, nr Appledore, is CALPAC water, and may be fished from Mock Hill Farm to Arrow Head Bridge. Tackle shops: Ashford Angling Centre, 3B Stanhope Sq; Hythe Angling, Dymchurch Rd.

SCHOOL POOL. At Oare, 1½m N of **Faversham**. Controlled by Faversham AC; large pool containing carp (30lb plus), tench, bream, roach, rudd and pike. Dt £4 in advance from Mr and Mrs Kennett, 14 Millfield, Faversham, tel: 01795 534516. Tackle shop: Ashford Tackle, St Marys Rd, Faversham.

LANCASHIRE AND CUMBRIA (Westmorland) streams

(For close seasons, licences, etc, see North West Region Environment Agency, p17 unless otherwise stated)

BELA. Cumbrian trout stream, flowing from Lily Mere to estuary of Kent at Milnthorpe. Much of its course is through low-lying country with heavy water. Size of fish better than in some northern streams; many dry-fly reaches. Salmon and sea trout below Beetham Mills private. One of the earliest of northern streams; fishing starts March 3.

Milnthorpe (Cumbria). Trout. Preserved by Milnthorpe AA and confined to members and guests. Association also preserves St Sunday's Beck from Deepthwaite Bridge and Peasey Beck from Farleton Beck downwards and thence, from confluence of these streams, to Beetham Mills, which is as far as salmon run. Fishing below mills private. Sport very good in March, April, May and Aug. Licences and tackle from Kendal Sports, Stramongate, Kendal. Hotels at Milnthorpe: Cross Keys, Bull's Head, Coach and Horses; Wheatsheaf at Beetham.

Oxenholme (Cumbria). Bela, 2m E. Beehive Beck, 1m E. Old Hutton Beck, 3m SE. **Killington Reservoir**; large area of water, 3m E. Pike, perch and some big trout. Now privately fished. *(See Kendal).*

CONDOR. Fishing station: Galgate. Brown trout and sea trout.

DUDDON. Fishing station: **Broughton-in-Furness**. Sea trout, salmon. Millom & Dist AA has rights to 366 yds of north bank from Duddon Bridge downstream, and Hall Bridge Dunnerdale stretch; dt £15. Assn also has water on **Esk, Lickle, Annas, Irt, Lazy, Devoke Water** (salmon, sea trout, trout); **Black Beck**; also **Baystone Bank**, Copeland (poor access). Close to Broughton-in-Furness, **River Lickle** joins Duddon on left bank. River rented by Millom AA. Membership £80 plus £10 joining. Day tickets for ass waters from Duddon Sports, Millom, or Haverigg PO, Millom. Applications for membership to Hon Sec.

Ulpha (Cumbria). Good sea trout and salmon, few brown trout. All river below down to Ulpha Bridge private. **Devoke Water** (large trout) may also be fished from here. Millom AA has rights, wt and dt, limit six fish. Applications for membership to Hon Sec. Below this point Duddon runs into estuary. Hotel: Old King's Head.

KENT. Fast-flowing salmon and trout stream running into Morecambe Bay. Fishing reported much improved following pollution and drainage schemes. Salmon, sea trout, trout.

Kendal (Cumbria). Salmon, sea trout, trout. A few spring salmon with main run and sea trout moving up about June; fairly plentiful Aug onwards. Fishing for the public at Lower Levens Farm: st £85, day permits £5 and B&B £10 per night from Mrs Parsons, Olde Peat Cotes, Sampool Lane, Levens, Near Kendal LA8 8EH, tel: 015395 60096. South of the town to Basinghyll Bridge (both banks) held by Kent AA, membership subject to waiting list, wt from £20; dt from £7. Tickets and licences from Kendal Sports (see below). Kendal Corporation owns Fisher Tarn; now privately leased. Kendal & Dist AC fishes pond at Old Hutton, and both river and pond fishing nr Grange-over-Sands. St £20, joining fee £6. **Killington Reservoir** (ns Oxenholme), is property of British Waterways; pike, perch and trout. Fishing rights leased to Kent AA, wt £4.50, dt £2. Tackle shops: Carlsons Fishing Tackle, 64 Kirkland, Kendal; Kendal Sports, 28-30, Stramondgate, who issue licences. Hotels: County, Woolpack, Globe.

Staveley (Cumbria). Trout, salmon and sea trout in Sept and Oct. Staveley and Dist AA has 4m of local Kent and Gowan fishing. Tickets from D & H Woof, 22 Main Street, Staveley. Hotels: Eagle and Child, Duke William, Railway.

MINT (tributary of Kent). Best fished from Kendal. Joins Kent about 1m above town; holds good head of small trout. Kent AA has lowest water *(see Kendal).*

SPRINT (tributary of Kent). Joins Kent at Burneside. Burneside AA (see Burnside) has about 1m of fishing from junction with Kent. Kent AA has ½m (L bank only). Salmon and sea trout from Aug; brown trout small; banks much wooded.

KEER. Rises 4m above Borwick, runs into Morecambe Bay 3m below **Carnforth**. Good sea trout and brown trout (no coarse fish). Carnforth AA has water; wt and dt on application to Hon Sec. Whorleys Moss Fishery, Nether Kellet, Carnforth, has small pond with b and r trout from 3lb. Dt £13.50, 3 fish. ½ day and evening tickets also. Tel: 01524 420300.

LEVEN: Drains Windermere, and is joined by River Crake (from Coniston Water) at Greenodd, near Ulverston, before flowing into Morecambe Bay. Salmon, sea trout, trout. Ulverston AA has members only fishing on R Crake.

Ulverston (Cumbria). Salmon, sea trout, trout. Ulverston AA has members only salmon and sea trout fishing on **R Crake, Knottallow Tarn**, brown trout, and coarse on **Ulverston Canal**, 1¼m long, specimen tench, carp, etc; restocked; dt £2.50, wt £6 and st £20, conc, from Canal Tavern Inn; Angling and Hiking Centre, Rawlinson St, Barrow-in-Furness, Coopers, White Hart Yard, Ulverston. Match permits from AA Sec. Lakes: **Knottallow Tarn**, (brown trout fishing, on associate membership to visitors). Hotels: Armadale, Sun, Queen's, King's, Bay Horse, Lonsdale House.

Lake Side (Cumbria). Salmon, trout, pike, perch, trout. Some free fishing; other sections of the shore private; inquire locally.

TORVER BECK (tributary of Coniston lake), Torver (Cumbria). Lakes: Coniston, 1m E; pike, perch and trout, Goat's Water, 3m NE. Beacon Tarn, 5m S. Hotel: Church House Inn.

CRAKE (tributary of Leven):

Greenodd (Cumbria). Crake; salmon, sea trout, trout. From Sparks Bridge to Little

Dicks Bridge, Ulveston AA, members only. Assn. offers £2.50 dt on bank for **Ulverston Canal** fishing: coarse fish. **Rusland Pool River**, tributary of Leven. Forestry Commission, Satterthwaite issues tickets. Tackle from Coopers of Ulveston, I White Hart Yard.

Coniston (Cumbria). Yewdale Beck, Torver Beck, 2½m S. Crake; salmon, sea trout. Duddon, 8m; salmon, sea trout, (Millom & Dist AA water). Lakes: Coniston; pike, perch, char, trout and eels. Goat's Water, 2m W; Low Tarn, 3m NE. Esthwaite Lake, 4m; pike and perch *(see Hawkshead)*. Char fishing in Coniston Lake very good from May to October. Lake free to holders of E.A. licence. For boats and tackle, *see Coniston, English Lake District.*

GRIZEDALE BECK (tributary of Leven): **Hawkshead** (Cumbria). Forestry Commission, small brown trout, low population at present, let to Grizedale AC. Contact Mr Grant, via The Theatre in the Forest, Hawkshead LA22 0QJ.

RIVERS ROTHAY & BRATHAY, Ambleside. Windermere & Ambleside DAA fisheries. Open, brown trout 15th March - 30th Sept, migratory trout 15th March - 14th Oct. These rivers are the main feeders to Windermere and offer small river fishing for brown trout, sea-trout and the very occasional salmon. They are best fished when above normal level using worm or fly. Maggots, cheese and offal baits are prohibited. The Association does not control all the fishing on these rivers and anglers should ascertain where angling is permitted. The large pool near the head of Windermere contains pike and perch as well as trout. Autumn fishing is usually best when lake trout and sea trout take up residence in the river prior to spawning. At this time of year very large trout can be caught. Dt £3.50 (Juv/OAP £2), wt £10-£5, st £30-£15, from Tourist Information Centre, local fishing tackle shops. NB. This permit also allows fishing on Grasmere, Rydal Water, High Arnside Tarn, Moss Eccles Tarn, School Knott Tarn & Hayswater.

TROUTBECK (trib of L Windermere).

Scandal Beck, Ambleside; trout, preserved.

WINSTER. Parallel with Windermere for 6m. Joins the sea by **Grange-over-Sands**. Sea trout, brown trout, eels. Kendal & Dist AC has R Winster fishing at **Meathop**, nr Grange-over-Sands, stocked with coarse fish. Other club waters nearby include Witherslack Hall Tarn, roach, perch, eels, pike. Membership open. Tickets for Wigan & Dist AA fishing on both banks of R Winster nr A590 road, and second single bank stretch, from K Hogg, 95 Holme Terrace, Wigan.

LANCASHIRE (lakes and reservoirs)

(see North West Region Environment Agency, p17, unless otherwise stated)

ANGLEZARKE RESERVOIR, Wigan. Trout, Ribble & Wyre FA. Dt from bailiff, £1-£1.20. For further information contact P Luff, NNW Ltd (*see above*).

BARROW-IN-FURNESS RESERVOIRS. Barrow AA has trout fishing in five reservoirs. No tickets. Furness FA (Game section) issues day tickets for stocked waters. Coarse section fishes 5 waters, 3m from Barrow-in-Furness, Ormsgill Reservoir.

BARNSFOLD WATERS. 7m NE of **Preston**. Two trout lakes, 22 acres, fly only. St and dt £17 to £6. Boats £5 to £10. F J Casson, Barnsfold Waters, Barns Lane, Goosnargh, Preston PR3 2NJ. Tel: 01995 61583. Tackle shop on premises.

BLACKMOSS RESERVOIR, Pendle. Trout dt from Barley Information Centre. For further information contact Blackmoss FA, R Hudson, 61 Barnoldswick Road, Higherford, Nelson, Lancs BB9 6BQ.

BUCKLEY WOOD RESERVOIR, Rochdale. Leased by NWW to Rochdale Walton AS. Inquire Hon Sec *(see also Mersey and Rochdale)*.

BROWNHILL RESERVOIR. Between Colne and **Foulridge**. Feeder for Leeds and Liverpool Canal. Holds brown trout; preserved by Colne AA, tickets for members' guests only.

CANT CLOUGH RESERVOIR, Burnley. For information contact Team Leader, Paul Phillips, NNW Ltd (*see Thirlmere*). (*see above*).

CHURN CLOUGH RESERVOIR, Pendle. Possibly to be re-let. For further information contact Team Leader, Paul Phillips, NNW Ltd (*see Thirlmere*). (*see above*).

CLOWBRIDGE RESERVOIR, Rossen-

dale. Coarse dt on site at Rossendale Valley Water Park Shop. For further information contact Phil Luff, NNW Ltd (*see above*).

COLDWELL (LOWER) RESERVOIR, Pendle. Nelson AA. Trout day ticket from Coldwell Inn Activity Centre. For further information, NNW Ltd (*see above*).

DEAN CLOUGH RESERVOIR, Hyndburn. Brown and Rainbow trout, fly only, Lancashire FFA water, who issue dt £10, 2 fish limit, from Hyndburn Angling Centre, 71 Abbey Street, Accrington (tel: Acc. 397612). For further information contact NNW Ltd (*see above*).

DILWORTH (UPPER) RESERVOIR, Ribble Valley. Trout, Ribchester and Dist AA, D Harwood, Ribblesdale House, Blackburn Road, Ribchester, Preston PR3 3ZQ. Dt from Happy Shopper, Higher Rd, Longridge. For further information contact Paul Phillips, Team Leader, NNW Ltd (*see above*).

DINGLE RESERVOIR, Blackburn. Dingle Fly Fishing Club. Dt £10-£7 from Bungalow sited on reservoir, and the Black Dog Hotel, Belmont. For further information contact Phil Luff, NNW Ltd (*see above*).

EARNSDALE RESERVOIR, Darwen. Brown and rainbow trout. Darwen AA has rights on reservoir; good fly water, dt £10, 2 fish, from Anglers Den, Darwen. For further information contact Phil Luff, NNW Ltd (*see above*).

ENTWHISTLE RESERVOIR, Blackburn. Entwhistle Flyfishers, I A Rigby, 10 Wayoh Croft, Edgeworth, Bolton BL7 0DF. Dt £14. For further information contact Phil Luff, NNW Ltd (*see above*).

GRIZEDALE LEA RESERVOIR. 9m south of Lancaster. Rainbow trout, 1 Apr-30 Nov; Kirkham and Dist FFC water, fly only, limit 3. Membership £150 plus £150 joining fee. Dt (limited), from Hon Sec, or from A Helme, The Veterinary Surgery, 13-17 Freckleton St, Kirkham, Preston; or from K Curwen, 59 Broadwood Drive, Fulwood, Preston.

HEAPY RESERVOIRS. Chorley. Reservoirs 1,2,3 and 6, roach, carp, perch, bream, tench. Wigan and Dist AA water. St £16, juv £2. Map books £1.25 + SAE from K Hogg, 95 Holme Terrace, Wigan WN1 2HF or from bailiffs.

HODDLESDEN, Blackburn. Trout, Darwen Loyal Anglers, T Berry, 5 Springvale, Garden Village, Darwen BB3 2HJ. Dt from County Sports, Duckworth St, Darwen.

LANESHAW RESERVOIR, Pendle. Trout fishing dt from The Sweet Treat, 51 Keighley Rd. For further information contact NNW Ltd (*see above*).

MITCHELS HOUSE RESERVOIRS, Higher Baxenden. Accrington & Dist FC waters; stocked fortnightly with 14" rainbows. Dt £8, 2 fish limit. Membership is open.

OGDEN RESERVOIR, Rossendale. Haslingden and Dist Fly FC; dt £14.50, contact W Monk, 6 Ryde Close, Haslingden. For further information contact Phil Luff, NNW Ltd (*see above*).

PARSONAGE RESERVOIR, Hyndburn. Trout fishing, Bowland Game FA, B Hoggart, 1 Moorfield Rd, Leyland, Preston PR5 3AR, dt from Roe Tackle Box, 336 Whalley New Rd, Blackburn, tel: 01254 676977.

PENNINGTON FLASH, Leigh. Good coarse fishing. Pennington Flash AA issues st £2.50 and dt 50p. Inquiries to G Unsworth, 142 Chestnut Drive S, Leigh, Lancs.

LOWER RIVINGTON RESERVOIR. Managed and stocked by First Organisation, St Thomas Centre, Ardwick Green, N Manchester M12 6F2. Permits. For further information contact Phil Luff, NNW Ltd (*see above*).

UPPER RODDLESWORTH RESERVOIR. This water is managed by Horwich Fly Fishers Club. Day ticket £8 from The Black Dog Inn, Belmont, tel: 01254 705373. For further information contact Coin Wilson, Horwich FFC sec, tel: 01204 307636. NWW Ltd owned reservoir.

LOWER RODDLESWORTH and **RAKE BROOK RESERVOIRS, Chorley**. Coarse fisheries with pike to 30lbs, managed by Withnell AC. Dt from Brinscall Post Office, School Lane, Brinscall. NNW Ltd. For further information contact Withnell AC sec, B Wren, 1 Belmont Close, Brinscall, tel: 830935 01254.

SABDEN RESERVOIR. Whalley Rd, **Sabden**. Accrington and Dist FC trout water. Members only.

STOCKS RESERVOIR. Slaidburn. 320 acre trout fishery, brown, and rainbow up to 11lb. Fly only, there is a close season. 20 boats and tackle in site, outboard an optional extra. St, wt, dt. 3 and 2 fish limit. Mrs Dobson, Bank House, Low Mill, Caton LA2 9HX. Tickets from

Stocks Fly Fishery, Catlow Rd, Slaidburn BB7 3AQ, tel: 01200 446602.

SWINDEN RESERVOIR, Burnley. Trout fishing, Burnley Anglers, D Thornton, 13 Church St, Briercliffe, Nr Burnley BB10 2HU. Dt from Halstead and Hartley, 1 Cow Lane, Burnley. For further information contact NNW Ltd (*see above*).

WALVERDEN RESERVOIR, Pendle. Coarse fishing on Walverden Reservoir, **Lower Foulridge Reservoir, Colne**, and **Ballgrove Lake**, Colne; large perch, tench, pike, eels, carp, roach. Dt and st from bailiffs on site. Further information from Pendle Leisure Services, Outdoor Recreation, Guy Syke, Colne, Lancs BB8 0QX, tel: 01282 661230.

WITHNELL RESERVOIRS. Withnell Fisheries Ltd, 11 Kearsley Drive, Bolton BL3 2PG manage three reservoirs fishable with season ticket, £32. Waiting list, which restricts fishing to local anglers.

WORTHINGTON RESERVOIRS. Wigan. 39 Acres, 3 reservoirs, one trout, two coarse fish. Wigan & Dist AA water. Assn waters also include several miles of **Ribble** and **Wyre**, part of **Winster** at Grange, whole of **Rufford Canal**, plus numerous ponds, lakes and flashes. Enquiries to K Hogg, Card Secretary, 95 Holme Terrace, Wigan WN1 2HF. Tackle shops: Angling Centre, 15 Orrel Rd, Orrel, Wigan: Lake View Tackle, 38 Lodge Rd, Orrel, Wigan; and many others in Chorley, Westhoughton, Blackburn, Leyland, and Preston.

LEE or LEA

(For close seasons, licences, etc, see Thames Region Environment Agency, p20).

Walton's river; flows through Bedfordshire and Hertfordshire then along boundary between Essex and Middlesex to join Thames near Blackwall; 46m long. Urban development and canalization have largely removed its charm, but still holds good quantities of barbel, and large bream, carp, pike, chub, perch. Very little free fishing, but permits are obtainable from bailiffs on most stretches.

Tottenham (London). Fishing controlled by Lee Anglers' Consortium, tel: 0181 524 0869. St £20, dt 2.50. Good access points are at Lea Bridge Rd, Hackney Marshes, Carpenters Rd, Dace Rd. Dt from bailiffs. Picketts Lock and Stonebridge Lock are popular fisheries, used for matches, with good roach and bream. TW reservoirs close to Tottenham Hale (roach, perch, carp, bream, pike; or stocked with brown and rainbow trout) (*see under London*). D/s of Enfield Lock, **Ponders End** is a good venue with large shoals of bream and roach. Tackle shop: Don's, 239 Fore Street, Edmonton.

Enfield Lock (Middx). Plenty of roach, perch, bream, tench and pike. Day tickets. Controlled by Lee AC, T Mansbridge, tel: 0181 524 0869.

Waltham Abbey (Herts): **Lee Relief Channel** from Hooks Marsh to Highbridge St, Waltham Abbey: 1½m of bank, mixed coarse fishing, with large barbel, chub, tench, bream and carp. This fishery is run by LVRPA (*see Hoddesdon, below*). Tackle shops: P & B Hall, 44 Highbridge Rd; A1 Angling, 176 High Rd, Woodford Green.

Cheshunt (Herts). Good chub, roach, bream fishing, controlled by Lee AC. (*See Tottenham*). Red Spinner AS has Cheshunt South Reservoir; carp and roach. Members only. Annual subscription £220, plus £100 joining fee. Kings Arms and Cheshunt AS run Brookfield Lake, with carp, tench, bream, perch; dt £3 one rod, £5, two rods, from Simpsons *below*. Other society waters include local rivers, lakes and gravel pits. Matches, outings, newsletter organised, new members welcome. **North Met Pit**, gravel pit of 58 acres, various coarse species incl large carp, pike, tench; LVPMF dt water; also **Bowyers Water**, 35 acre gravel pit, with carp and pike, st only, contact LVPMF, *see Hoddesdon*. Tackle shop: Simpsons, Nunsbury Drive, Turnford EN10 6AQ, tel: 01992 468799.

Wormley (Herts). The famous **King's Weir Fishery** (½m R Lee, both banks, and ½m of bank at Langridge Lake), fishable on st £35 + £4 key payment, £15 conc. Large carp (30lb) and pike. Dt £7 for 9 swims on Wier Pool. Contact Kings Weir House. Tel: Hoddesdon 468394 for bookings. **Snipe Lane Pits**, 25 acres of gravel pits with tench, bream, carp, pike, catfish. Dt on bank. Run by LVPMF (*see Hoddesdon*).

Broxbourne (Herts). **Redlands Carthagena Fishery**; consisting of weir pool, 2 lakes (one with carp to 27lb); ¾m of Old R Lee, 1m of Lee Navigation, bream, tench, carp, chub, roach, rudd. St only, £30-£50, juv, OAP £15, from P Brill, Carthagena Lock. Tel: 01992 463656. Towpath from Nazeing New Rd to Dobbs Lock, £2.50-£1.50, from bailiff on bank. **Old Mill and Meadows Fishery**, Mill Lane, Weirpool, Lee Navigation, with roach, chub, pike, perch, run by LVRPA (*see Hoddesdon, below*). Day tickets from bailiff on bank.

Hoddesdon (Herts), ns Rye House or Broxbourne. On Lee, Stort and New River Lee: Dobbs' Weir Fishery, Essex Rd; roach, pike, chub, carp, barbel. Dt from bailiffs. Admirals Walk Lake, 25 acre gravel pit at Conker lane, pike, tench, bream, roach, carp; both fisheries run by Lee Valley Regional Park Authority, Abbey Gardens, Waltham Abbey, Essex EN9 1XQ, tel: 01992 713838 (fax: 787533). For coarse fishing at Crown Fishery, Dobbs Weir Rd, with very large carp, catfish, roach, etc, st £350, dt £5, contact 10/11 Pleasant Place, West Hyde, Rickmansworth WD3 2XZ. Tackle shop: C J Ross, 2 Amwell Street. Hotel: Fish and Eels.

Rye House (Herts). Roach, chub, dace, bream, pike, perch, tench. Rye House Bridge to October Hole is London AA water; West Ham AC controls east bank and Lee AC, west bank, at Fieldes Weir. Dt from bailiff. Hotel: Ye Olde Rye House.

St Margaret's (Herts). Old River Lee. River fishing from towing-path. Lee AC (*see Tottenham*).

Ware (Herts). River Lee Navigation, controlled by Lee AC, tel: 0181 524 0869. Ware AC have members only carp ponds. Membership £14, concessions. Rib Valley Fishing Lake, Westmill Farm, Ware (01920 484913) 13 acres, rainbow trout from 2lbs. Dt £26, 4 fish, to £16, 2 fish. Tackle shop: Ware Angling, High Street, Ware.

Hertford (Herts). For **Lee**, **Mimram**, **Beane**, **Rib** and **New River**. Lee Anglers' Consortium (*see Tottenham*) controls the Lee angling from Hertford to Stort Confluence at Feildes Weir. Very good course fishing. Access points at Folly Bridge, Mill Rd, Marshgate Drive. London AA has stretch from Town Mill gate to junction with Lee Navigation (¾m); members only. For Hertford AC contact C Bite, tel: 01992 467585. for Ware AC contact D Bridgeman, tel: 01920 461054; both clubs have local fishing. Tackle shop: Pro-Angling, Ware Rd, Hertford. Hotels: Salisbury Arms, Dimsdale Arms, White Hart, Station.

Hatfield (Herts). Hatfield and Dist AS has rights on river from Mill Green to Essendon (about 2½m); including seven-acre Broadwater (large carp and bream). Members only.

Luton (Beds). Tring Reservoirs (10m); Grand Union Canal (10m); Great Ouse (20m). Clubs: Milton Keynes AC leases **Milton Keynes Lakes** from AW; Leighton Buzzard AC (01582 28114), Ampthill & Dist AC (01525 715457). Vauxhall AC. Tackle shops: Anglers & Pets Cabin, 61 High Town Rd; Leslies, 89 Park St; Dixons, 95 Tavistock St, Bedford.

Tributaries of the Lee

STORT: Preserved from source to Bishops Stortford.

Roydon (Essex). Roach, dace, perch, pike, chub, bream, carp, rudd, gudgeon, eels, bleak, pope. Globe AS fishes Stort and backwaters here, with the species listed. Members only, £35 fee, conc. Water between road bridge and railway bridge is Two Bridges AS fishing; Hon Sec B Bird, 8 Ducketts Mead, Roydon. Global Enterprises Ltd, Roydon Mill Park, Roydon, Essex (tel: 01279 792777) have 2m fishing for guests camping or caravanning. This includes well stocked weir pool. No Dt, residents only. Lychnobite AS leases Temple Farm Fishery, (about 2m of fishing) with Dt from bailiff on water. Two Leisure Sport gravel pits of 16 acres plus 160 mtrs R Stort at **Ryemeads**, offering large pike, chub, dace, tench, bream and roach. No day tickets, St £22, concessions for jun, OAP, dis. Applications to LSA, RMC House, High Street, Feltham, Middlesex TW13 4HD, tel: 0181 8931168.

Harlow (Essex). Coarse fish. Harlow DC has town nine waters including Rye Mead and Harlow Town Park. Inquiries to Leisure Services, Town Hall. London AA has water here and at Spellbrook and Thorley. LAA grants facilities for Harlow residents on its water. Inquiries to Hon Sec. Tackle shop: Harlow Angling Centre, 5 Long House, Bush Fair.

Sawbridgeworth (Herts). Good head of all coarse fish with many large roach; fishes best Sept onwards. Sawbridgeworth AS has from confluence at Spellbrook to confluence of Little Hallingbury Brook, left hand bank; pike fishing (after Oct 1). Visiting parties welcome; apply Hon Sec for reservation. Mixed lake fishery ½m from Sawbridgeworth Station, on Little Hallingbury Rd. Members only, £3 per rod.

Bishop's Stortford (Herts). Navigational stretch opened by British Waterways. Bishop's Stortford and Dist AS has coarse fishing to Spellbrook Lock (tickets), a length at Harlow, Cam at Clayhithe, lakes, 10 acre gravel pit. Tackle shop: Anglers Corner, 40A Hockerill St. Hotels: Foxley, George.

ASH. Fishing stations: **Widford** (Herts) and **Hadham** (Essex); a few trout, pike, etc; preserved.

RIB: Trout, coarse fish. For Rib Valley Fishing Lake, *see Ware*.

BEANE: This once-excellent trout stream has been largely ruined by abstraction. Some stretches still hold good fish, however. No public fishing except at Hartham Common, Herts.

MIMRAM: Trout, preserved.

LINCOLNSHIRE (small streams)

(For close seasons, licences, etc, see Anglian Region Environment Agency, p19)

GREAT EAU or **WITHERN**. Rises above Aby and flows some 12m to sea at Saltfleet; coarse fish; much free water; fishes best in autumn.

Saltfleet (Lincs), ns Saltfleet, 3m. Grayfleet, South Eau, and Mar Dyke; coarse fish; some free water. At Saltfleetby St Peters is pond on which fishing is permitted by dt, purchased from shop near pond; no Sunday fishing. Sea trout in Haven in Sept; also flounders.

Louth (Lincs). Great Eau private above bridge on main Louth-**Mablethorpe** road, including Calceby Brook, Aby and South Ormesby Park; free below to licence holders as far as Gayton lugs, thence ½m private to members of Mablethorpe, Sutton-on-Sea Dist AC (also another ¾m stretch). Louth Crown & Woolpack AC has small coarse pond at Charles St, good tench, membership £10. **Theddlethorpe** (Mablethorpe Dist AC),

Tench, once they start to feed, can seem insatiable. The sport is then fastand furious. This fine catch was made on the Redlands Fishery at Deeping St. James, Lincolnshire

and free below Cloves Bridge. Altogether 10m free fishing to licence holders; coarse fish, including good roach, bream, perch. pike, rainbow trout (few and mostly small) and grayling. **Lud** generally free below Louth to Alvingham. Coarse fishing in ponds at **Louth, North** and **South Somercotes, Fulstow, Saltfleetby, Legbourne, West Ashby, Hogsthorpe, Chapel St Leonards, Skegness, Wainfleet, Authorpe, Addlethorpe, Alford, Farlesthorpe, Spilsby**, all on dt from local tackle shops. Sutton Brick Pits, Alfred Rd, **Sutton-on-Sea**; dt at adjacent houses. Hatton Lake, trout, tel: Wragby 858682. **Louth Canal** from **Alvingham** to sea outlet at **Tetney** controlled by Witham and Dist. JAF; coarse fish. Tackle shops: Castaline, 18/20 Upgate, Louth (01507 602149); Belas, 54-56 High Street, Mablethorpe. Hotels: Kings Head, Lincolnshire Poacher, both Louth.

STEEPING. Rises 5m above **Spilsby** (1m off on left bank), runs thence to **Wainfleet** and joins the sea 4m below near **Skegness**; coarse fish; Croft AC has stretch at Haven House; tickets. Witham and Dist. JAF controls 20m from Wainfleet upstream, and **Wainfleet Relief Channel**. £1.30 temporary members ticket from Storr's Shop, Market Place, Wainfleet. Spilsby AA has **Ereby Canal**; good bream, tench, Perch, etc; members only; confined to 13m radius; st and dt from Hon Sec or Higgs Bros Tackle Shop, Spilsby, who also issue licences.

LINCOLNSHIRE (small lakes and ponds)

Ashby Park Fisheries, Horncastle LN9 5PP, tel: 01507 527966. 6 lakes, mixed coarse fishing with carp to 21lb 9oz, bream to 9¾lb, and most other species, incl eels to 5¾lb. Dt £4 and bait on site.

Baston Fen Fishery, Baston, Bourne. Mixed coarse and specimen lakes with some very large bream. Mrs Wyman, tel: 01778 560607.

Belleau Bridge Lake, Belleau Bridge Farm, **Alford**. 6 acre coarse fishery, dt from Mr Harrop, tel: 01507 480225.

Brickyard Fishery, South Rd, **South Somercoates**, Louth LN11 7PY, tel: 01507 358331. 4 acre coarse fishing water, dt £4 on site.

Belleau Bridge Farm Lake, Alford. 6 acre coarse fishery. Dt from Mr Harrop, tel: 01507 480225.

Charles Street Pond, Louth. 1 acre lake with crucian carp and tench. St only, from local tackle shops, open all year.

Fish Pond Farm, Usselby, **Market Rasen**, LU8 3YU, tel: 01673 828219. 2 lakes, mixed coarse fishing, dt on site, £3, B&B & meals.

Goltho Lake, Goltho Wragby LN3 5JD, tel: 01673 858358/858907. Lincoln, 10m. 2 acre mixed coarse fishery, dt £2 on site.

Grange Farm Leisure, Mablethorpe. 4 coarse lakes, 1 trout and 1 carp lake. Dt only, sold on site. Also tackle and bait shop, and cafe. Tel: 01507 472814.

Grimsthorpe Lake, Grimsthorpe and Drummond Castle Trust, tel: 01778 591205. 36 acres, mixed coarse fishing.

Hartsholme Country Park Lake, Skellingthorpe Rd, LN6 0EY, tel: 01522 686264; 27 acre lake, mixed coarse fishery, permits on site, st £16.50, dt £2.50.

Lake Helen, near Sutterton. Mixed coarse fishery of 2.75 acres; contact H Greeves, 01205 460681, or Anglian Region EA.

Hill View Lakes, Skegness Rd, **Hogsthorpe**, Chapel St Leonards, tel: 01754 872979. Three lakes, two mixed coarse, one carp. Barbless hooks only.

Hollands Park, Wedland Lane, **Thorpe St Peter**, tel: 01754 880576. Coarse fishing lake, dt £250 on site.

Hatton Trout Lake, Hatton, Nr Wragby, tel: 01673 858682. Dt on site, £7.50-£5.

Lakeside Leisure Ltd, Chapel St Leonards, PE24 5TU, tel: 01754 872631. Three mixed coarse lakes, one with 10 species, the others 20 and 24 species respectively, dt on site, £3.20, £4.50 double.

Mill Road Fishing Lakes, Skegness. Two small lakes with common and mirror carp, roach, bream, tench. Information from P Cumberworth, Mill Road, Addlethorpe, Skegness (01754 767586).

North Kelsey Park, North Kelsey LN7 6QH, tel: 01831 132819. Large lake, mixed coarse fishery, dt on site.

North Thoresby Fisheries, Fen Lane, North Thoresby. 3 lakes, 2 fishable on dt. 1 acre trout, 4½ acre coarse, mostly carp. Contact J Casswell, 01472 812518.

Oham Lake, Alford. 2 acre coarse fishery, with tackle shop and other facilities on site. Contact C Beckenham, Maltby le Marsh, Alford (01507 450623).

Olsten Fishery, Mill Lane, **Legbourne**, Louth LN11 8LT, tel: 01507 607432;

coarse fishing in lake, trout in chalk stream. Trout dt £12-£5, coarse £3.50, on site.

Pelican Pond, Barton-on-Humber, tel: 01652 33600. 80 acre coarse fishery with large stocks of roach, tench, pike, eels, bream. St only, on bank. Contact North Lincs Sailing Club, Pasture Rd.

Redlands Pits, Lolham Level Crossing, West Deeping. Three lakes with tench and rudd fishing. Deeping St James AC, tel: 01778 346355.

Rossways Water, 189 London Rd, **Wyberton** PE21 7HG, tel: 01205 361643. Two lakes mixed coarse fishing, carp to 30lb, large bream and tench. Dt £3, subject to availability. Barbless hooks only. Caravans to let on site.

Skegness Water Leisure Park, Walls Lane, Ingoldmells. 7 acre lake with tench, perch, bream, golden orfe, and carp. Dt from manager's office. Tel: 01754 76019.

Starmers Pit, Tritton Rd, **Lincoln**, tel: 01522 534174. Lincoln AA water; 7 acre lake, mixed coarse fishery with large pike, eels, carp, bream and tench. Dt on site.

Sycamore Lakes, Skegness Rd, **Burgh-le-Marsh**, PE24 5LN; tel: 01754 811411. 5 acre mixed coarse fishery of four lakes, with carp to 32lb, tench, rudd, roach, perch, orfe; Woodland Lake stocked with smaller fish, ideal for matches; dt £3.50, conc, at lakeside. Tackle and bait shop, lakeside cafe, holiday cottages to let on site.

Tattershall Leisure Park, Sleaford Rd, tel: 01526 343315. 7 lakes, mixed coarse fishing, dt on site, £2.

Toft Newton Trout Fishery, Toft-next-Newton, **Market Rasen** LN8 3NE, Lodge tel: 01673 878453. 40 acre reservoir, bank and boat fly only fishing, stocked twice weekly, mainly rainbow, some brown trout. Season varies, usually 1 Mar-15 Dec. Dt £14, 6 fish, £78, 2 fish. Boat £9, £5 ½ day, disabled boat and facilities. Tackle hire and tuition on site.

Thorpe Le Vale Fishery, Louth. 5 acre trout fishery, brown and rainbow. Fly only. Dt from G Wildsmith, Thorpe le Vale, Ludford, Louth, tel: 01472 398978. Season, Mar-Dec.

Vickers Pond, Main Road, Saltfleetby, Louth. 1.5 acre lake with tench, bream, carp and grass carp. Dt on site. No groundbait, and carp not to be kept in nets.

Warren Pond, Warren Rd, **North Somercotes**. Small pond with carp, rudd, perch and bream. Mr Lowis, tel: 01507 358350.

White House Fishery, Crossroads, Baston Fen, Nr Market Deeping, tel: 01778 342 155. Two lakes with rainbow, brown and brook trout. Tickets £6.50, 2 fish. Coarse lake, carp to 15lbs: tickets £5-£3.

Willow Lakes, Grantham. 5 lakes, 1 carp, 4 mixed coarse, dt on site. Contact Mr Chilton, Newark Rd, Foston, Grantham, tel: 01400 282190.

Woodlands Fishery, Ashby Rd, **Spilsby**, tel: 01709 754252. Three coarse lakes with mixed species, best carp 15lb 1oz, tench over 5lb, roach 2lb, best mixed bag 1997 31lb. dt £3.50, £5 two rods, conc. Tackle and refreshments on site.

LONDON (Thames Water Reservoirs)

Most of the waters referred to below are in the area termed Greater London. All are easily accessible from Central London. A number are rented by angling clubs and reserved for members, but at others fishing is offered to the general public at modest charges on season or day ticket basis.

It seems appropriate to mention here two important angling bodies:- first, the **London Anglers' Association**, which has water on many miles on rivers, streams and lakes (125 fisheries in all). The Association now has about 5,000 full members through 160 affiliated clubs. It has offices at Izaak Walton House, 2A Hervey Park Road, Walthamstow, London E17 6LJ (telephone number: 0181-520 7477). For a brochure and application form please send a stamped addressed envelope to the above address. Annual membership (associate) £21.50. Jun, OAP, regd disabled £8.50.

The Central Association of London and Provincial Angling Clubs (CALPAC) has about 120 affiliated clubs and fisheries on rivers, canals and lakes in the South of England. Day tickets issued for many fisheries. Full details from Hon Sec.

Among tackle shops in Central London are: Hardy Bros, of 61 Pall Mall; C Farlow & Co Ltd, 5b Pall Mall *(see advt)*. Tackle dealers in the suburbs are too numerous to list. Tackle shops in Metropolitan area listed under individual centres.

Thames Water Reservoirs where fishing rights are let to clubs include the following: **Banbury, Walthamstow** to Civil Service Sports Council.
Cheshunt (South) to Red Spinner AS, members only, no day tickets.

Reservoirs open to the public for game fishing (stocked with rainbow or brown trout).

Walthamstow Nos 4 & 5 are stocked with brown and rainbow trout. Bank fishing, fly only on **5**.

East Warwick, fly only. Ferry Lane, Tottenham. Tel: 0181-808 1527.

Reservoirs open to the public for coarse fishing.

King George North & South Reservoirs, Chingford; coarse fishing, st only, from gatehouse, Ferry Lane, opp. Ferry Boat Inn. **West Warwick Reservoir, Lockwood Reservoir, Walthamstow Nos 1, 2 & 3, High** and **Low Maynard, Coppermill Stream**. Dt on all except West Warwick and Lockwood, st only. Best catches to date include carp 34lb, pike 29lb, bream 13lb, perch 4lb 10oz, plus large roach, barbel, chub and dace.

LUNE

(For close seasons, licences, etc, see North West Region Environment Agency, p17)

Rises on Ravenstonedale Common (Westmorland) and flows through beautiful valley into Irish Sea near Lancaster. Excellent sport with salmon, sea trout and brown Lower reaches also well-stocked with coarse fish. August to October best for salmon and sea trout.

Lancaster (Lancs). Salmon, sea trout, trout, coarse fish. Environment Agency has Halton and Skerton fisheries. Salmon, Feb 1 to Oct 31, sea trout, May 1 to Oct 15. Brown trout Mar 15 to Sept 30. Coarse fishing June 16 to Mar 14. Permits for Halton fishery from Halton Stores, 9 St Wilfreds Park, Halton. Permits for sea trout at Skerton fishery from Greenup Cottage, Hornby Rd, Caton. Lansil Sports and Social Club has 1½m both banks just above tidal stretch, with additional coarse fishing for usual species plus specimen bream (12lb+). Salmon st £55 + £25 joining fee, other fishing, £25, conc. Littledale Fishery, Nr Caton, mixed coarse; tickets from Morecambe Angling Centre only (01524 832332). Lonsdale AC fishes **Lancaster Canal**, northern stretch, tench, pike, mixed fishery; two lakes, and Upper Swantley mixed fishery. Open membership and dt, from tackle shops: Charlton and Bagnall, 3/5 Damside St, tel: 01524 63043; Gunsmiths & Fishing Tackle, 7 Great John Street, tel: 01524 32033, who supply licences and specialist information on Lune, Greta, Wyre and Wenning; Gerry's of Morecambe, 5-7 Parliament St, Morecambe; Morecambe Angling Centre.

Halton (Lancs). Lune; salmon, sea trout, trout, coarse fish. Permits for Halton top and bottom beats, and other stretches, and limited amount of tackle from Halton Stores, 9 St Wilfreds Park, St Wilfreds Park, Halton, tel: 01524 811507. Permits for Environment Agency water from Mrs Curwen, Greenup Cottage, Hornby Rd, Caton LA2 9JB.

Caton (Lancs). Lancaster and Dist AA has fishing over 6 bank miles divided into three sections. Dt is sold for one section only, 1½m both banks. Fourteen year waiting list for membership. Permits £10 to £20 depending on season, weekdays only, from Mrs Curwen, Greenup Cottage, Hornby Rd, Caton LA2 9JB. No dt Saturdays and Sundays, though Sunday fishing is allowed to members. Fly only when water level 1ft 6in or below, Worm prohibited in October, except at water level of 3 ft. No maggot, shrimp, prawn

POLLUTION

Anglers are united in deploring pollution. To combat it, urgent action may be called for at any time, from anyone of us. If numbers of fish are found dead, dying, or seriously distressed, take samples of both fish and water, and contact the officer responsible for pollution at the appropriate Environment Agency office. For hot-line, see Environment Agency section at front of book.

or grub fishing. No boat fishing, no dogs. Prince Albert AS also have water, and at **Killington**. Bank House Fly Fishery, Low Mill, Caton LA2 9HX, has 2 acres stocked brown and rainbow trout fishing. Day and half-day tickets obtainable. Contact Mrs J Dobson, Low Mill, Lancaster Rd, Caton LA2 9HX, tel: 01524 770412.

Hornby (Lancs). Salmon, sea trout, trout. Lancaster AA has Claughton stretch *(see Caton)*. No dt. From Wenning Foot (North) for ¾m, Southport Fly Fishers, members only.

Whittington (Lancs). Salmon, sea trout and brown trout. Apply to H G Mackereth & Son, Whittington Farm, tel: Kirkby Lonsdale 71286/72375.

Kirkby Lonsdale (Cumbria). Salmon, sea trout, trout. Trout and sea trout fishing are very good; average 1½lb; sea trout up to 8lb. Kirby Lonsdale AA has approx 4m of water, upstream and downstream of town. Limited 5 day visitors permit (except Oct) from Tourist Information Centre, 24 Main St, LA6 2EA. Below Kirkby Lonsdale & Dist AA water, Lancaster & Dist AA has water. Lancashire FFA has fishing here and at Tebay. Redwell Carp and Coarse Lakes: four lakes of stocked fishing. Kirkby Lonsdale Rd, Arkholme LA6 1BQ (015242 21979). Hotels: Royal; Red Dragon; King's Arms; Sun; Orange Tree. Pheasant Hotel at Casterton, 1m upstream, is convenient for association waters. Salmon (best August, September); sea trout (June onwards), trout.

Barbon (Cumbria). Lune, 1m W Barbon Beck. Barbon is good centre for Kirkby Lonsdale AA water. Hotel: Barbon Inn.

Sedbergh (Cumbria). Sedbergh AA has approx 3m on Lune and tributaries, 9m **Rawthey**, from source to Lune, 2m **Dee** and 1m **Clough**. Brown trout; salmon and sea trout from July. Visitors st from visitors Hon Sec; dt, £10, wt £50, st £150, and dt from Lowis' Country Wear Ltd, 25 Main Street, (015396 20446). Mr Metcalfe, Holme Farm, Sedbergh (015396 20654) has stretch of R Rawthey. Hotels: The Bull, The Dalesman.

Low Gill (Cumbria). Trout, sea trout and salmon (salmon and sea trout best at back end); about 2½m both banks preserved by A Barnes, Nettlepot, Firbank, Cumbria LA10 5EG, tel: 015396 20204. Dt £10 or £15. Blackburn AA also has water.

Tebay (Cumbria). Salmon and sea trout (August onwards best), trout (average 3 to lb). Telbay and Dist has 15m of good water; wt £30, OAP £25, Oct £45. Juv £5. Limited dt from Cross Keys Inn. Other club, Lancashire FFA has water. Hotel: Cross Keys.

Orton (Cumbria). Trout (all season), salmon, sea trout. Pinfold Lake, **Raisbeck**; r trout, dt £14 (4 fish) from tackle shop J Pape, Market Place, Appleby. Accommodation at George Hotel. Licences: Davies, 8 North Terrace, Tebay.

Tributaries of the Lune

RAWTHEY. Trout, with sea trout and occasional salmon late in season. Sedbergh AA has virtually whole of river from its source at Fell End down to Lune, and tributaries Dee 2m, and Clough, 1m; visitor's st £150, wt £50, dt £10.

WENNING. Sea trout (good), brown trout, few salmon (late). Best latter part of season. Fishing station: **Bentham** (Yorks). Bentham AA has about 3½m of water; fast stream, good sport; visitors' tickets: st, wt, dt (jun ½) from Hon Sec. Ingleborough Estate holds 5m. St £20, wt £6 (limited); apply Estate Office, Clapham via Lancaster LA2 8DR, tel: 015242 51302; trout run 3 to 1lb. Accrington FC has Hazel Hall Farm fishing, near Clapham, stocked with 11" browns. Bait fishing, spinning and fly, members only. Barnoldswick AC have two stretches of Wenning, upstream from Farrars Viaduct, downstream from Clintsfield Viaduct. Hotels: The Coach House, Black Bull. Punch Bowl Hotel also has ¾m private trout and sea trout fishing and issues dt £5.

GRETA. Trout (4 to 1b) and late run of salmon and sea trout. Fishing stations: **Ingleton** and **Burton-in-Lonsdale** (Yorks). Trout. Ingleton AA controls 6m of unbroken water on Greta, **Twiss** and **Doe**; st £30, wt £20, dt £7 (½ price jun) from Village Pet Supplies, High Bentham; Denbeighs, Main St, Ingleton, and Hon Sec. Sunday fishing on approx 3m, maps issued with permits. Accrington FC has 2m, Burton, Wrayton and Cantsfield, stocked with 11" browns, members only. Hotel: Punch Bowl, Burton-in-Lonsdale (licences).

Boy holding splendid Bartley Mill 4 pounder glows with obvious pleasure. Small wonder! *Photo: Adam Whittle.*

MEDWAY

(For close seasons, licences, etc, see Southern Region Environment Agency, p16).

Kentish river joining estuary of Thames at Sheerness through estuary of its own. Coarse fish (abundant bream, record barbel, 1993) with few trout in upper reaches.

Maidstone (Kent). Free on E.A. licence from Maidstone to East Farleigh, North Bank, except new mooring area. Maidstone Victory Angling and Medway PS have first class fishing from Yalding down to Maidstone, **R Rother** and **R Beult** fishing, and various stillwaters. Membership £43 pa, £15 joining fee, conc, from Hon Sec and local tackle shops. Free fishing on Brookland Lake, Snodland Council, 01634 240228. **Monk Lake**, Riverfield Carp Farm, Marden, mixed coarse fishery, dt £6. Chris Davis, tel: 01580 890120. **Johnsons Lakes**, Larkfield; large bream, carp and pike. Temporary membership from bailiff on bank. Mallaras Way Lake, details from Len Valley A & PS. **Abbeycourt Lake**, Sandling; coarse fishing, dt. Tel: 01622 690318 after 6 pm. Tackle shops: Maidstone Angling Centre, 15 Perryfield St; Nicks Tackle, Knightrider St; Mid Kent Tackle, Milton St; all Maidstone. Medway Bait and Tackle, 64B St Johns Road,

Check before you go

While every effort has been made to ensure that the information given in **Where to Fish** *is correct, the position is continually changing, and anglers are urged, in their own interests, to make preliminary enquiries before travelling to selected venues. This is especially important with reference to prices quoted. Inevitably the rate of inflation is affecting stability in this quarter. Anglers' attention is also drawn to the fact that the hotels mentioned under the various fishing stations do not necessarily have water of their own. Any amendments or further data for inclusion in subsequent editions, and any comments, will be welcome.*

Gillingham. Inns: Medway; West Kent; Rose and Crown; Queen's Head.

East Farleigh (Kent). Free fishing as described under Maidstone; thence mostly Maidstone Victory Angling and Medway Preservation Soc water; weekday dt from Maidstone tackle shops. Inn: Victory.

Wateringbury (Kent). Large carp and tench, chub, bream, roach. Maidstone Victory Angling and Medway Pres Soc has most of towpath bank here and at **Teston**, incl. Teston Bridge Picnic site, dt. Medway Wharf Marina, Bow Bridge, has fishing for boat and caravan owners using their services. Dt £4. Tel: Maidstone 813927. Barking AS has a meadow; members only but open to visiting clubs. Inn: King's Head.

Yalding (Kent). Chub, bream, perch, rudd, dace, roach, eels, and pike. Free fishing on E.A. licence u/s from Yalding Sluice 200m, south bank. Maidstone Victory Angling and Medway Preservation Soc has towpath bank downstream of Railway Inn, also Medway at **Nettlehead**, **Teston**, **Barming** and Unicumes Lane, weekday tickets from tackle shops, on bank for Teston fishing. Yalding AS has water; dt (weekdays only). Central Assoc of London and Prov AC has one meadow at junction of Medway and **Beult**; members only, membership open. Other CALPAC stretch, 1,200 yds Yalding Medway, dt £4, conc, from bailiff on bank. No night fishing on CALPAC water. Inns: Railway (tackle, but no accommodation); George; Anchor (boats).

Tonbridge (Kent). Tonbridge and Dist A & FPS has 9m of Medway, 1½m of Eden and gravel pits of 4 to 8 acres. Dt for parts of Medway and one pit, only. Contact Sec for details. Vacancies for membership; £20 + £5 joining fee, concessions for OAP. Paddock Wood AC offer dt for **Gedges Lake**, coarse fishing. Tel: 01892 832730. **Mousehole Lake**, 3 acre fly only trout fishery, on B2015 at Nettleshead Green. Dt on site all year. Tackle shops: Tonbridge Rod and Line, 17a Priory Road; Medway Tackle, 103 Shipbourne Road.

Tunbridge Wells (Kent). Royal Tunbridge Wells AS has coarse fishery at **Ashurst** and **Fordcombe**, trout waters on **Medway** from Withyham to Ashurst, and coarse fishing from Ashurst to Poundsbridge (4m), also on **Teise** below Finchlock's Bridge to Hope Mill, **Goudhurst**. Grayling and barbel in places. Fishing on three ponds also. Membership limited. Annual subscription £60, joining fee £15, concessions for married couples and jun. Coarse fishing dt for Court Lodge Down, Neville Golf Course. Pembury 2388. Crowborough AA have a dozen ponds and lakes local to **Crowborough**, with large pike, carp, tench, bream; st £40, conc, from tackle shop Tackle shop: Crowborough Tackle, White Hill Rd, Crowborough, E Sussex. Other tackle shops: MA Wickham, 4 Middle Row, E Grinstead; Wadhurst Rod & Line, Highbury Place, Wadhurst.

Ashurst (Kent). Coarse fish, some trout, grayling, barbel to 12lb. Tunbridge Wells AS has water *(see above)*. Limited tickets for members' guests only.

Fordcombe (Kent). Trout, coarse fish, barbel to 16¼lb, large carp. Tunbridge Wells AS has water, limited tickets for members' guests.

Tributaries of the Medway

BEULT: Excellent coarse fishing; lower reaches noted for chub, bream and tench; trout higher. Gravesend Kingfisher A & PA (stretches at **Smarden**, **Hunton**, **Headcorn** and **Staplehurst**; members only); London AA has water at **Hunton** and **Linton**; members only. Dartford AA has fishing. CALPAC has 400 yds at Medway junction, members only. ACT Fisheries Ltd issue tickets for fishing between Linton and **Yalding**. 170 Sydenham Road, London SE26. Coarse fishing dt for Brogues Wood, Biddenden from 015806 4851.

EDEN: Coarse fish.

Penshurst (Kent). On Eden and Medway; coarse fish. Penshurst AS has rights from Ensfield Bridge to Pounds Bridge and from The Point on Medway to weir on Eden; members only. No dt.

Edenbridge (Kent). Coarse fish. 8m controlled by Edenbridge AS (members only) also a mile at Penshurst. Short stretches rented by Holland AS, also Crawley AS.

TEISE: Joins Medway at Yalding. Trout, coarse fish.

Laddingford (Kent). London AA has water for members only at Mileham Farm and Hunton Bridge right bank.

Goudhurst (Kent). Teise Anglers' and Owners' Association holds water from Goudhurst to Marden; brown and rainbow trout; mainly fly only, and winter grayling fishing. Members only (£175 sub, joining fee £50). Ass. also has stocked farm reservoir for trout fishing at Marden. Apply to B Wait, 101 Stanhope Grove, Beckenham, Kent. Season, April 3 to Sept 30.

Lamberhurst (Kent). Tunbridge Wells AS has trout and course fishing water d/s of the Chequers Hotel for approx 4½m; members and guests only. Tackle shop: Glyn Hopper Angling, High St.

MERSEY

(For close seasons, licences, etc, see North West Region Environment Agency, p17)

Forms Liverpool Channel and seaport. Main river polluted and of no account for fishing except in higher reaches. Some tributaries contain trout.

Liverpool (Merseyside). Liverpool and Dist AA has stretch on **Leeds & Liverpool Canal**. Northern AA has stretches on **R Dee** at **Worthenbury, Ribble** at **Salmesbury**; Worthenbury and Emral Brooks; and also fishes Bridgewater and Macclesfield Canals and **R Weaver** at **Vale Royal, R Glaze** at Glazebrook. Dt £2.50 on rivers, £2 canals, conc. For **Shropshire Union Canal**, see *English Canal Fishing*. Tackle shops: Johnsons', 469 Rice Lane; Taskers Tackle, 25 Utting Avenue, Liverpool 4; Hoppys, 14 Sefton Street, Litherland 21.

Wirral (Cheshire). Assn of Wirral Angling Clubs comprises thirteen clubs, and actively promotes lake and pond fishing on Wirral. Club coarse fishing waters include Birkenhead Park Upper and Lower Lakes; Central Park Lake, Wallasey; Arrow Country Park Lake. Annual and monthly permits from bailiffs and tackle shops: Gary Bonner, Parkes Angling, 119 Duke St, Birkenhead; Wirral Angling Centre, 207 Church Road, Tranmere Birkenhead; Fishermans Cove, 118 New Chester St, New Ferry.

St Helens (Merseyside). Two NNW coarse fisheries in vicinity: **Leg O' Mutton Dam**, controlled by St Helens AA and **Paddock Dam**, Holme Rd, Eccleston, with bream, roach, tench, perch, carp, pike. St Helens Ramblers AS, Hon Sec, Alec Twiss, 47 Exeter St, St Helens, WA10 4HS. Good carp, roach, chub, tench and dace in **St Helen's Canal** (Church Street length) and in Blackbrook stretch. Lymm AC offer dt on Sankey St Helens Canal at Halton and Warrington. St Helens Tackle shops: Star Angling, 101 Duke St (01744 738605); Angling Centre, 196 Islands Brow.

Stockport (Cheshire). Stockport County Anglers have private water at Davenport; four pools; carp up to 10lb. Stockport Waltonians AA also has private waters; coarse fish and trout. Tackle shop: Edgeley Sports & Fishing, 145/7 Castle St.

Whaley Bridge (Derbyshire). River here known as Goyt; polluted. Dt (not Sundays), for one bank only. **Cote Lodge Reservoir**, High Peak. Trout water, Old Glossop AC, dt obtainable. **Errwood Reservoir**, High Peak, Trout water, Errwood Flyfishing Club. Dt from tackle shops in Whalley Bridge, Buxton and Stockport. For further information on both these waters contact Peter Sharples, Team Leader, NW Water Ltd, Woodhead Rd, Tintwhistle, Hadfield via Hyde, Cheshire SK14 7HR, tel: 01457 864187. Dt 25p for **Bosley Reservoir**, near Macclesfield, from Harrington Arms on Macclesfield-Leek Road, and Mr J Arnold at 1 Lakeside Estate, Bosley. Both waters hold roach, perch, bream, carp, pike, gudgeon *(see also Weaver)*. **Peak Forest Canal** starts here; coarse, sport patchy. Lock pools at **Marple** stocked with carp and tench. Canal to Ashton Junction being opened and dredged. Tackle shops: J Hallam & Sons, Market St.

Tributaries of the Mersey

NEWTON BROOK (tributary of Sankey Brook):

BOLLIN:

Heatley (Cheshire). Occasional trout, roach, dace, pike. Lymm AC has several lengths of Bollin at Reddish and Little Heatley, near Lymm, part double bank, mostly single. Club also controls a large number of fisheries on Severn, Vyrnwy, Dane, Sankey St Helens Canal, and many lakes and ponds about the north of Cheshire with trout and coarse fishing. Some of these are dt waters, membership costs £27 per annum, joining fee £12, conc, apply to N Jupp, Secretary, (01925 411774).

Ashley (Cheshire). Bollin, 1m N; trout, roach, dace, pike; Bollin and Birkin AA; private.

BIRKIN (tributary of Bollin):

Knutsford (Cheshire). Birkin, 4m; Bollin and Birkin AA has water; private. **Tabley Mere**, 3m, is let to Lymm AC; no permits. Toft Hall Pool, 1½m S; occasional permits. **Tatton Mere**, Knutsford, coarse fishing; let to Lymm AC. Dt on bank. **Redesmere** and **Capesthorne Lakes** (6m S of Wilmslow on A34 road); Stoke AS waters. Capesthorne Hall stock pond: very good carp and roach fishing, dt £6-£4 on bank, or from Keith Walley, Bailiff, East Lodge, Capesthorne Hall, Macclesfield SK11 9JY (tel: 01625 861584). Tackle shop: Naylor's Sports, 2 Minshall Street; Trevor Allen, 16 Altringham Rd, Wilmslow.

IRWELL:

Manchester. River polluted, but some waters have been leased to clubs. At **Poynton**, 10m out, Stockport & Dist FA has pool. St only. 18m from Manchester, at Northwich, is coarse fishing in Weaver *(see Weaver)*. Bolton & Dist AA has **Manchester, Bolton & Bury Canal,** from Hall Lane to Blue Wall length, 6 reservoirs, R Wyre, R Ribble nr Longridge, and other fisheries. No day tickets, but st from tackle shops in district. Warrington AA has a twenty mile stretch of **Bridgewater Canal** as well as water on Dee, **Ribble**, **Severn** and tributaries and **Dane**, reservoirs, meres, etc. Apply Hon Sec. St £20 plus £20 joining fee, concessions for ladies, juniors etc. Macclesfield Prince Albert AS has rights on canal from Buxton Road Bridge to Bosley Aqueduct (about 6m). Tickets from Barlows Tackle, Bond St, or Brians Tackle, Buxton Rd, both Macclesfield. Macclesfield Victoria AC controls **Turks Head Reservoir**, members only. Moss Side AS has water *(see Whaley Bridge)*. Tackle shops: Arrowsmiths, 1a Gorton Lane, West Gorton; David Marsh Tackle, 79 Long Street, Middleton; Trafford Angling Supplies, 34 Moss Rd, Stretford; Kear's, 1 Market St, Droylsden. **Bolton** tackle shops: V Smith, Highfield Road, Farnworth; Anglers Corner, Haliwell Road.

ROCH:

Bury (G. Manchester). Brooks polluted. Accrington and Dist AA has water on **Ribble, Greta, Wenning** and **Calder**. Dt fishing. Bury and Dist AS and has stretches of R Irwell, several small ponds and reservoirs including **Elton**; mostly coarse fishing. Bury AS mem £15 + £5 joining fee, concessions. Trout fishing at Entwistle (Entwistle FFC) and Dingle (Dingle FFC). **Haggs Reservoir**, Hyndburn Rd, Accrington, Accrington FC water. Tackle shop: Fishing Tackle, 12-14 Southworth Street, **Blackburn**.

Rochdale (G. Manchester). Rochdale Walton AS. **Buckley Wood**, 1m N (coarse and trout), also Healey Dell Lodge, dt only on application to Hon Sec. Rochdale and Dist AS has trout and coarse fishing at Castleton (dt 50p; visitors must be accompanied by member), and coarse fishing on **Rochdale Canal**, 3m from town; st, dt from tackle shops. Length of canal also held by Dunlop Cotton Mill Social Club; tickets from local tackle shop. **Hollingsworth Lakes**, Littleborough; coarse fish; dt from tackle shops: Towers of Rochdale, 52 Whitworth Road; Kay's, 18 St Marys Gate; Angling Centre, 204 Yorkshire Street OL16 2DW, who issues tickets for fly-only trout fishery (fish to 12lb) and for coarse fishing in **Calderbrook Dam**. *For Rochdale Canal see also Calder (Yorks) - Hebden.*

TAME:

Ashton-under-Lyne (G. Manchester). River polluted. NWW reservoir **Walker Wood**, 2m NE; trout. Tackle shop: Pet Man, 142 Stamford Street.

COMBS RESERVOIR:

Chapel-en-le-Frith (Derby). **Combs Reservoir**, 2m W; 57 acres, a variety of coarse fish including pike to 27lb, carp to 20lb, roach, bream, tench, perch; dt £3.50; Bailiff collects on bank; enquiries to C N Farley, Lakeside, Combs Rd, Chapel-en-le-Frith, tel: 01298 812186.

MIDLANDS (reservoirs and lakes)

BARKER'S LAKE, Ringstead, 25 acre stocked with carp to 20lb, bream to 6lb, good pike in winter. Wellingborough Nene AC water, membership £14, conc. £4.

BLENHEIM LAKE. Woodstock, Oxon;

excellent tench, perch, roach in summer; pike winter. Boat fishing only for visitors. Apply to the Estate Office, Blenheim Palace, Woodstock, Oxon 0X20 1PS for details of current charges. Tel: (during normal office hours) 01993 811432 (813108 Fax).

CASTLE ASHBY LAKES. Northampton 7m. Coarse fishing in three lakes, two carp and one mixed coarse, leased to Mr M Hewlett, 176 Birchfield Rd East, Abington, NN3 2HG, 01604 712346. Dt waters. **Menagerie Pond** (specimen carp fishery). St £130; Details from Estate Office, Castle Ashby, Northampton NN7 1LJ, tel: 01604 696232.

CLAYDON LAKES. Buckingham, 6m. Upper and Middle Lakes at Middle Claydon, near Winslow, are Leighton Buzzard AC water; Danubian catfish, pike-perch, big carp. Members only.

CARSINGTON WATER, nr **Ashbourne**, Derbyshire. Owned by Severn Trent Water Ltd, 2297 Coventry Rd, B'ham B26 3PU, tel: 0121 722 4000. Opened as brown trout fishery in 1994. Season 3 Apr-26 Oct. Up to 10,000 browns stocked during 1997. Day and part-day tickets for bank and boats, plus concessionary for bank only; dt £11.50, 5 hours £8. Boats £8.00 day, £5.50, 5 hours. Electric outboards £14.50. Disabled boat and facilities and catering on site. Enquiries to the Fishery Office, Carsington Water, Ashbourne, Derbys DE6 1ST. Tel: 01629 540478.

CLATTERCOTE RESERVOIR, Banbury (Oxon). 20 acres, principally carp to 20lb, roach perch tench. Dt £5, night fishing permitted. match bookings welcome, tel 01442 278717. 24 hour information line: 0113 281 6895. Night fishing by arrangement, 01295 255158. Fisheries and Environmental Manager, British Waterways, Southern Region, Brindley House, Corner Hall, Lawn Lane, Hemel Hempstead HP3 9YT.

CLUMBER PARK LAKE. National Trust property, 4½m from **Worksop**; coarse fish (including pike); st £40, dt £3 (jun and dis £1.50) from bailiff on bank.

COSGROVE LEISURE PARK Milton Keynes, 2m (Bucks). Coarse fishing on 10 lakes from 2 to 25 acres, and Rivers Tove and Great Ouse. 2 lakes members only, otherwise dt £3 , £1.50 juv from Manager, Cosgrove Leisure Park, Milton Keynes MK19 7JP, tel: 01908 563360 Tackle and bait shop on site, food and refreshments, camping, caravan site.

CORNBURY PARK. Charlbury, Nr Oxford. Rainbow trout fishing over three beautiful marl lakes set in an historic deer park. Day tickets over two lakes, membership only on remaining water. For further details and day ticket prices contact Cornbury Park Fishery, Southill Lodge, Cornbury Park, Charlbury, Oxon OX7 3EH. Tel/Fax: 01608 811509. Instruction on site. Accom at The Plough, Finstock.

CRANFLEET CANAL. Roach, perch, gudgeon. Trent Lock held by Long Eaton Victoria AS, also Erewash Canal, Long Eaton Lock to Trent Lock. Membership £13, concessions.

DENTON RESERVOIR. Denton (Lincs). Excellent mixed coarse fishing with large carp; held by Grantham AA; st £15, conc, from Hon Sec (tel: 01476 575628), bailiffs and tackle shops. No day tickets.

DRAYCOTE WATER, near **Rugby** (Warks) 600 acre reservoir, brown and rainbow trout. Owned by Severn Trent Water Ltd, 2297 Coventry Rd, B'ham B26 3PU, tel: 0121 722 4000. 46,000 rainbows stocked weekly, Apr-Sept, Season 31 Mar-26 Oct. Dt £13, 8 fish limit; Evenings £9, 5 fish limit. OAP, jun, dis, £8.50. Boats £11, motor boats £19, evening £12.50. Bank anglers limited to 300. Disabled facilities, catering and courses. Optional catch and release. Information from Fishing Lodge (tel: 01788 812018).

DRAYTON RESERVOIR, Daventry. 18 acres, principally carp to 6 lbs, also roach, perch and tench. Average catches, 50lb plus, with 200lb per day often recorded, record 304lbs. Permits £5 per day from patrolling bailiff, £3, conc. Match bookings welcome, 120 pegs, food on site. Tel: 01442 278717. 24 hour information line: 0113 281 6895. Fisheries and Environmental Manager, British Waterways, Southern Region, Brindley House, Corner Hall, Lawn Lane, Hemel Hempstead HP3 9YT.

DUKERIES LAKES, Worksop. Welbeck Estate fisheries controlled by Welbeck Estate Office. Clumber Lakes are fished by Worksop & District AA, members only. The Association has rights on **Sandhills Lake** and **Harthill Reservoir**, being renegotiated Oct 97.

EYEBROOK RESERVOIR. Caldecott (Leicestershire), off A6003 Uppingham to Corby Rd, south of Caldecott village, follow AA signs. 400 acres of excellent trout fishing. Well-stocked water, mostly

rainbows, a few browns and occasional brook trout. Fly only, good bank and boat fishing. Season 27 Mar-1 Nov. Season and day tickets and E.A. licences obtainable from new, purpose-built fishing lodge with disabled access. (Rockingham 770264). All bookings and inquiries to Fishing Lodge, Eyebrook Reservoir, Great Easton Road, Leics LE16 8RP, tel: 01536 770256. Hotels: Falcon, High St East, Uppingham, tel: 01572 823535; Vaults, Uppingham, 5m N; Strakis Carlton Manor, Corby. B&B at Mrs J Wainwright, Homestead House, Melbourne LE16 8DL (01858 565724).

FOREMARK RESERVOIR. Nr **Repton**, Derbys. 230 acres, owned by Severn Trent Water Ltd (*See Draycote*). Season 27 Mar-15 Oct. 25,000 rainbows stocked throughout season. Dt £11, 8 fish, evening £5.30, 4 fish. Conc, £7.25, 4 fish. Rowing boats £9.50 to £4. Motor boats £17.50 to £8. Disabled facilities, catering and courses. Permits on site from Fishing lodge, tel: 01283 703202.

GRAFHAM WATER. **St Neots** (Hunts). 1,560-acre reservoir stocked with brown and rainbow trout. Now managed by Anglian Water Services from the lodge at Mander Car Park, West Perry PE18 0BX. Records include b trout 19lb 12oz, r 13lb 13oz. Full st £519, mid-week £435. Dt £14, 8 fish limit, evening £9, 4 fish. Beginners dt £4, 1 fish. Motor boats £9 to £18. It is advisable to book these in advance. New fishing lodge being built for '98 season with tackle shop, restaurant, access for disabled. Tel: 01480 810531; Fax 01480 812488.

GRIMSBURY RESERVOIR. **Banbury** (Oxon). Coarse fishery leased to Banbury AA. Dt £4 for non members, concessions for juniors, from local tackle shops (*see Banbury*).

HARLESTHORPE DAM. **Clowne**, Derbys. Trout, coarse fish, with pike to 22lb, carp to 32lb. St £70, dt £4 on site; night fishing £7 by arrangement, also tackle and bait. Tel; 01246 810231.

LADYBOWER RESERVOIR, Ashopton Rd **Bamford**, S33 0AZ (Derbyshire). Season 6 mar-31 Oct. St £220, weekday £180. Dt £9.60, 6 fish, evening £6, concessionary £5.80. Limit, 4 fish up to May 31, thereafter 6 fish. Evening 3 and 4. Boats £8.50 to £5.70. Disabled facilities. Limited permits from warden for fly fishing on R Derwent below Ladybower Dam. All prices include VAT. Enquiries to Fishery Office, tel: 01433 651254.

LINACRE RESERVOIRS, near **Chesterfield**. 43 acres in well wooded valley, 3 reservoirs, 2 stocked r trout, one wild b. St £95, from G Nixon, Netherthorpe, Staveley, Chesterfield. Dt £6.50 (4 fish) from The Angling Centre, Chester St, Chesterfield; Peacock Hotel, Cutthorpe, or at water.

NASEBY RESERVOIR, **Northants**. 85 acres. Carp to 19lb, tench to 5lb, rudd. Leased by BW to Naseby Water AC, sec I A McNeil, Bufton, Walcote, Nr Leicester LE17 4JS.

NANPANTAN RESERVOIR. 2m S of **Loughborough**. 8-acre coarse fishery.

OGSTON RESERVOIR, near **Chesterfield**, Derbyshire. 203-acre trout fly fishery owned by Severn-Trent Water Plc, and fished by Derbyshire County AC, guest tickets are obtainable. Membership £180, annual subscription £132.

PACKINGTON FISHERIES, **Meriden** (Warks). Excellent trout fishing on 100 acres of pool, 2½m of river. Dt £16, boats £6.50. Dt for 2 in a boat, £38.50. Flexi 5 hour ticket £11. Fishing on **Somers** fishery for carp, tench, roach, perch, pike, bream and rudd. St £140-£70, dt £6.50-£3. Concessions for juniors and OAP. Reduced rates for evenings. Details from Packington Fisheries, Broadwater, Maxstoke Lane, Meriden, nr Coventry CV7 7HR (01676 22754).

PATSHULL PARK FISHERIES, Nr Pattingham, **Wolverhampton** WV6 7HY. 75 acre lake, well stocked with b and r trout; fly only. St £180, incl boat hire, dt £12 incl 2 fish, other fish £2 each. Afternoon £8, inc 1 fish. Boats £5, £3. Conc. Permits from Fishing Lodge. Regular fly fishing contests held. Pike fishing is allowed during winter months. Small stocked coarse pool. Tel: 01902 700774.

PITSFORD RESERVOIR, **Northampton** 5m. 750 acres, owned and managed by Anglian Water Services. Rainbow and brown trout, fly only, 42,000 fish released during season. Good fly hatches all season. Dt (8 fish) £14, conc £10. Evening £9 (4 fish). Beginners £4. Boats £18 to £9. Pike fishing in Nov. Permits from Pitsford Lodge, Brixworth Rd, Holcot NN6 9SJ, tel: 01604 781350.

RAVENSTHORPE RESERVOIR, **Northampton** 8m. 100 acres, owned and managed by Anglian Water. Brown and rainbow trout, fly only. 18,000 fish released in season. 1996 av catch, 2.8. Best rainbow, 12lb.5oz. Dt £14 (6 fish limit),n£10 conc, evenings: £9 (3 fish). Beginners £4. Boats £10, £8-£6 eve. Apply to Pitsford Fishing Lodge, Brixworth Rd, Holcot NN6 9SJ, tel: 01604 781350. Accom, White Swan Inn, Holcot; Poplars Hotel, Moulton.

RUTLAND WATER, Leics. **Stamford** & A1 5m, **Oakham** 3m; managed by Anglian Water Services; Normanton Fishing Lodge, Rutland Water South Shore, Edith Weston, Oakham, LE15 8HD, tel: 01780 86770. 3,100 acres, 17m of fishing bank, largest stocked trout fishery in Britain. Browns to 15 lbs and rainbows to 13 lbs, 130,000 released per season. Pike fishing in late Oct-early Nov. 65 motor boats. Competition facilities, accommodation list. St £475 full, mid week £435, 8 fish limit, conc £260. Dt £14, £10 conc, boat hire £18-£11. Full restaurant facilities, and tackle shop on site.

SHELSWELL LAKE, Buckingham 7m. Tench, perch, roach and pike, winter best; st £8, conc £3, from Hon Sec, Bicester AS and Allmonds Sports, Market Square, Bicester; boat at no extra charge. Bicester AS also has two stretches on **River Ray**; coarse fish; no tickets.

SHUSTOKE RESERVOIR. Shustoke; Coleshill 3m. Leased to Shustoke fly fishers by STW. St £255 to £305, dt £12, 5 fish limit, £7 for 4 hours, 2 fish, boat £3; t on site from 12 Apr. Tel: 01675 81702.

SULBY RESERVOIR. 1m **Welford**, 14m **Northampton**. Coarse fishing; exclusive syndicate fishery of 100 anglers, with specimen carp to around 35lb. Limited st only, £150. Contact MEM Fisheries Management Ltd, Bufton House, Walcote Lutterworth, Leics LE17 4JS.

STAUNTON HAROLD RESERVOIR, near **Melbourne**, Derbys. Severn-Trent W coarse fishery, 209 acres, leased to Swadlincote AC. Tackle shop, Melbourne Tackle and Gun, 52/54 High St, Melbourne. Tel: Derby 862091

SYWELL RESERVOIR. Northampton 6m. Now a County Park. Tench to 10lb, pike (over 20lb), perch, roach and carp; members of Wellingborough and Dist Nene AC only. St £14, conc £4, dt £5, apply Hon Sec, warden or tackle shops for details.

THORNTON RESERVOIR. Leicester 3m S of junction 22 on the M1. 76 acres. Trout, annual stocking of 15,000, fly only, Mar to Nov. Leased to Cambrian fisheries by STW. St £300 and £160, dt £12, ½ day £8. Boats £6.50 and £4.50. Bag limits, 6 and 2. Tickets on site. Tel: 01530 230807.

TITTESWORTH RESERVOIR, near **Leek**, (Staffs). 184-acre trout water now leased by STW to Tittesworth Fly Fishers Ltd. St, long waiting list. Dt £8.75-£6.25, and boats £7.75-£4.75, 6-4 fish limit, advance bookings from fishing lodge at reservoir, tel: 01538 300389, Dave Naylor, Karl Humphries. Concessions to jun, OAP and regd disabled.

TRIMPLEY RESERVOIR, near **Bewdley**, Worcs. Trout, fly only, from early March-July 31. Aug 1-Oct 15, mixed fishery; then coarse fishing until Feb 28. St £110 weekday, £75 weekend; mixed £40; coarse £15. There is a £15 joining fee. Dt for guests of members only. Write for details to sec, Trimpley AA.

WELFORD RESERVOIR, near **Welford**, Northants, 20-acre coarse fishery. Many specimen bream, pike, carp, tench, perch and roach. St £30 to fish 2 rods, (Jun half price) from BW or bailiff W Williams, Welford Grange Farm, Welford, Northants.

NENE

(For close seasons, licences, etc, see Anglian Region Environment Agency, p19)

Rises in West Northamptonshire and flows to Wash. Good, all-round coarse fishery slow-running for most part. Roach and bream predominate, the bream in particular running to a good average size. Excellent sport with carp in Peterborough and Northampton areas. Trout Fishery in upper reaches,

Wisbech (Cambs). Centre of intricate system of rivers and drains, including the Nene-Ouse Navigation Link; all waters well stocked with pike, bream, roach, perch and some good tench. Fenland Assn of Anglers is centred in Wisbech. Wisbech and Dist AA sub hires sections of **Pophams Eau, Sixteen Foot River** and **Middle Level Main Drain** (12 miles of fishing). Assn wt required. **Great Ouse Relief Channel** provides 11m of good fishing from Downham to King's

Lynn. Algethi Guest House, 136 Lynn Rd, caters for anglers. Tel: 01945 582278. Tackle shops: Brian Lakey, 12 Hill St; Mark One Tackle, 32 Norwich Rd. Hotels: Queens, Rose and Crown, Marmion House.

Peterborough. Excellent centre for roach, bream, chub, tench, carp, rudd, eels and pike. Peterborough AA now controls most of the N bank of the Nene from **Wansford** to the Dog in a Doublet and some fishings on the S bank in the same area. The Association also has water on the **Welland** from **Spalding** to u/s of Crowland. St £16, dt £3, conc. Dt **Ferry Meadows Lakes**, £3, from bailiffs. Whittlesey AA has local fishing on Nene and Twenty Foot, bream to 7lb, bags to 130lb, with dt £2 on bank. Contact Hon Sec for details. Wansford AC waters now members only. At **Wansford** A1 road bridge, Stamford Welland AAA have ½m of south bank, downstream. First-class sport in fen drains and brick pits, but many pits being filled in. For Yarwell Mill, mixed coarse and carp lake nr Wansford, K Usher, tel: 01780 221860. Licences, st, wt and dt from tackle shop Webbs (*below*), for North Bank Trout Fishery (£12, 6 fish), and local coarse fisheries **Gerards Pit** at **Maxey**, **Werrington Lakes**, **Tallington Lakes**. Sibson Fisheries, New Lane, Stibbington, PE8 6LW, have coarse lakes with large carp, tench, bream. Dt usually in advance. Tel: 01780 782621. Tackle shops: Webbs, 196 Newark Avenue PE1 4NP(01733 566466), information and permits on various local waters; C Shelton & Sons, tel: 65287; K. Wade, 65159; Peterborough; Nobby's, 57 Manor Way, Deeping St James. Hotel: Newark.

Cotterstock (Northants). One mile of excellent fishing for roach, chub, bream, perch, tench, dace and pike held by Cotterstock AA here and at **Tansor**. St £5, conc, and dt £2 from B Wing, Manor Farm Cottage. Jun, OAP, clubs welcome. Deeping St James AC has Nene fishing here, also water at Kings Cliffe known as Willow Brook. All dt £3.50.

Elton (Northants). Leicester and Dist Amal Soc of Anglers has extensive stretches here and at **Nassington** and **Fotheringhay**. Dt from Hon Sec or bailiffs. Coventry AA has 55 pegs at Fotheringhay. Good head of tench, roach and bream. Dt £2.50.

Warmington (Northants). Warmington AC has several stretches, including backwaters, members only. £10 pa, no dt. Bluebell Lakes and Country Park, Warmington, is controlled by Church Pit FPAA, T Bridgefoot, Bluebell Cottage, Walpole St, Peter, Wisbech PE14 7PE, tel: 01945 780309. Fishery consists of Kingfisher, Swan and Bluebell Lakes, 1½m stretch of Nene, and Willow Creek, a backwater of 750 yds. Good coarse fishing with large carp, chub, bream, tench and pike. Deeping St James AC fishes two stretches of Nene and coarse lake at **Stibbington**.

Oundle (Northants). Roach, bream, carp, tench, dace, etc. Oundle AA has water on both banks; limited st £10, dt £2. OAP free. Oundle AA has local Nene fishing. Coventry AA has 70 peg stretch with good head of tench and bream and roach, also large carp. St £7, night st £11. Wellingborough Nene AC has 3m at Barnwell, just upstream of Oundle and 2 acre gravel pit (tench, pike, perch and rudd). Members only. Elinor Trout Fishery, Aldwincle, 36 acre lake stocked with browns and rainbows, fly only. Dt £12.50 (6 fish), evening £8, (3 fish), boats £4.50 or £6.50. Conc. Full st £370. Inquiries to E Foster, Lowick Rd, Aldwincle, Kettering. Tel: 01832 720786. Coarse lake also on site, with tench, bream and roach. Perio Mill, tel: 018326 241/376, has trout stream stretch of 1 km, fly only, £30, 4 fish limit. Wadenhoe Mill Stream Trout Fishery: river fishing on backwater of Nene, 900 yds well stocked, dt £9.50, 4 fish, evening £5.50 2 fish. Permits from Aldwincle PO, or Kings Head, Wadenhoe. Hotels: Talbot, caters for anglers, 01832 273621; Ship; Chequered Skipper, Ashton (Oundle HQ).

Thrapston (Northants). Roach, dace, perch. Wellingborough Nene AC control backwater from Thrapston to Denton. (*See Wellingborough.*) Kettering and Thrapston AA has **Aldwinkle Pits**. Tackle shop: W Jaques, High Street.

Rushden, **Higham Ferrers** and **Irchester** (Northants). Coarse fish. With new sewage works completed, fishing now showing marked improvement. Rushden, Higham Ferrers AC have water at **Bletsoe** and **Turvey** on Ouse: barbel and chub. Information, tackle and Rushden club cards (membership £10 pa) from Dave Walker, 26 Church St, Rushden and Webster, Corn merchant, Irthlingborough. **Ditchford Lakes** in the vicinity, well stocked and with improved banks; excellent trout fishery at **Ringstead Grange**, Kettering NN14 4OT; 36 acres, well-stocked with large fish. Record brown 10lb 6oz, record rainbow, 14lb 4oz. Dt £12.50, boat for two £6.50 extra, evening, OAP and junior tickets. Limit 6 fish, full day. Tel: 01933 622960. Irthlingborough AC has several gravel pits. St £12. No dt. Tackle shop: D Walker, 26 Church St, Rushden. Hotels: Rilton; Westward, both Rushden.

Wellingborough (Northants). Wellingborough Nene AC from Ditchford Weir to one meadow below Hardwater Crossing, plus seven other Nene stretches. Other club waters: **Great Ouse** at Harrold, **Sywell Country Park Reservoir**, Ditchford, good tench fishing, **Barker's Lakes**, ponds, and backwaters at Barnwell, Ringstead, Denford and Ditchford. These fisheries contain many large carp, chub, bream, pike, etc. Membership £15, conc £5, from Hon Sec. Kettering and Thrapston AA has Nene fishing between Denford and Pilton, also **Islip Lake**, mixed coarse fishing, and **Aldwinkle Pits** nr Thrapston. Northampton Nene AC has from Doddington up to paper mills, excluding Earls Barton AC water (1m) and water at **Billing** *(see Castle Asby, Billing and Northampton)*. Tackle shops: Ron's Tackle, 5 Church Way; Colin's Creel, 26A Hill St, Raunds, Wellingborough.

Castle Ashby (Northants). Pike, perch, bream, tench, roach; preserved for most part by Northampton Nene AC, which issues dt. Lakes on **Castle Ashby Estate** (1¼m S); pike, bream, tench, perch, roach; dt from bailiff at waterside or estate office. *(See also Midlands Reservoirs)*. Hotel: Falcon.

Billing (Northants). Pike, roach, perch, bream, tench, chub: preserved by Northampton Nene AC (01604 757589), which issues dt for 1½m on both banks of river and Ecton Gravel Pits off A45. Good coarse fishing at Billing Aquadrome. Seven lakes open from June 16 to Oct 16. St £15, wt £4, dt £1. All on site. Tel: Northampton 408181 or 01933 679985. At Earls Barton, Hardwater Lake, large mixed coarse gravel pit. Earls Barton AC, tel: 01604 812059, or 812433.

Northampton (Northants). Pike, perch, bream, chub, roach, carp, etc; Nene AC controls north bank from Weston Mill to Clifford Hill Lock. Castle AA fishing includes Nene at Victoria Park, Barnes Meadow (north bank), Midsummer Meadow, Becket's Park, and lakes at Canons Ashby. Membership £18, conc, dt on some waters. Northampton good centre for lake and reservoir fishing. **Heyford Fishery**, Weedon Rd, Nether Heyford, tel: 01327 340002: a purpose-built match fishery, 1,200m long, 127 pegs, with annual stocking of 800lbs of carp, roach, bream, and other coarse species. Dt £5, conc, on bank. Long Buckby AC has Nene fishing at Nether Heyford. Towcester and Dist AA has water on Nene at Kislingbury. Northampton Britannia AC controls much local canal fishing, members only. Affiliated with Leicester & Dist ASA, cards from local tackle shops: Gilders, 250/2 Wellingborough Road; Angling Centre, 85 St Leonards Rd; Sportsmans Lodge, 44 Kingsthorpe St; Trinders, 221 Birchfield Rd East.

Weedon (Northants). Pike, perch, bream, roach. **Grand Union Canal**. Northampton Nene AC has rights from Weedon to Yardley Gobion (16m); dt. At **Fawsley Park** are two lakes with pike, roach, rudd, etc; dt from Nene AC. Nene and Ouse licences needed for canal. **Hollowell Reservoir**, 140 acres, pike to 35lb, large roach and rudd. St £55, dt £5, conc. The Fishery Warden, c/o Pitsford Water, Holcot, NN6 9SJ, tel: 01604 781350.

Tributaries of the Nene

OLD RIVER NENE:

March (Cambs). Pike, perch, bream, rudd, roach, tench. Fen drains. **Old River Nene** mostly free to licence-holders. **Reed Fen** (south bank) is now private fishing. **Twenty Foot** controlled by March and Dis AA (tickets). **Popham's Eau**, and **Middle Level** are Wisbech AA waters. **Forty Foot** is now leased by Chatteris WMC. Dt £1 are sold on bank. **Mortens Leam**, 5m from March, 7m of river fishing from Rings End to Whittlesey. Wide variety of coarse fish. Dt on bank. Tackle shop: Mill View fishing Tackle, 3 Nene Parade, March. Hotels: Griffen, Wades, Temperance.

Ramsey (Hunts). Pike, perch, bream, etc. Ramsey AS has fishing on **Forty Foot Drain**, and **Old River Nene** at Ramsey St Mary's and Benwick: roach, bream, perch, tench, pike, zander. Dt waters. Contact Mr P E Aldred, 9 Blackmill Road, Chatteris PE16 6SR, tel: 01354 2232. To the east and north of **Sawtry**, Holme and Dist AA have fishing on both banks of **Kings Dyke, Yaxley Lode, New Dyke, Monks Lode** and **Great Ravely Drain**. Contact Mr K Burt, 55 Windsor Rd, Yaxley, Peterborough, tel: 01733 241119. Tackle shop: H R Wade, Great Whyte, Ramsey.

WILLOW BROOK: Trout, coarse fish; preserved.

King's Cliffe (Northants). Willow Brook. Welland, 3m NW.

ISE:

Kettering (Northants). **Cransley Reservoir**; roach, perch and tench. For st and dt on **Wicksteed Lake**, also preserved water on Nene at **Thrapston**, apply Kettering and Thrapston AA. Tackle and licences from Alans Angling Mart, 86 Rockingham Rd, Corby, Northants NN17 1AE, tel: 01536 202900.

Geddington (Northants). Preserved to Warkton.

STRECK:

Crick (Northants). Streck, 2m S. Dunsland Reservoirs (pike, perch, etc) 3m SW; private.

Daventry (Northants). **Daventry Reservoir**, Daventry Country Park, Northern Way, Daventry NN11 5JB, tel: 01327 877193. Coarse fishery, good pike fishing in winter, bream in late summer and autumn. Dt on bank. **Drayton Reservoir**, see *Midlands reservoirs and lakes*. Hellidon Lakes Hotel, Hellidon NN11 6LN has fishing, tel: Daventry 262550. Tackle shop, Trinders Tackle, Vicar Lane, NN11 5AG.

NORFOLK AND SUFFOLK BROADS

(Rivers Bure, Waveney and Yare)

(For close seasons, licences, etc, see Anglian Region Environment Agency, p19)

Rivers Bure, Waveney and Yare, their tributaries and Broads are among the finest coarse fisheries in England. They contain pike, perch, roach, dace and large chub. Some banks of tidal water which may be fished free. For details, contact Environment Agency Fisheries, tel: 01603 662800. Some Broads are preserved and can be fished on payment. Rivers and most Broads very busy with boating traffic in summer, so early morning and late evening fishing advised. Best sport in autumn and winter. Boats are essential.

BURE

Strong current from Yarmouth to little above Acle; upper reaches gentle and ideal for float fishing. The river contains a good head of coarse fish. Excellent roach, bream and pike etc, at Thurne Mouth, St Benets, Horning, Wroxham. Several Broads are connected and can be fished as well as tributaries Thurne and Ant.

Stokesby (Norfolk). Bream, roach, pike, perch. Strong tides and sometimes brackish; legering best; free.

Acle (Norfolk). Bream, roach, pike, perch. Tides often strong. River traffic heavy in summer. Acle and Burgh Marshes free fishing on E.A. licence. Inns: East Norwich Inn, Old Rd, Acle; Travel Lodge, A47 By Pass, Acle (tel: 01493 751112).

S Walsham and **Upton**. 3¾m R bank below **Ant** mouth, and 1m right bank from S Walsham Broad to Bure confluence free to licence-holders.

St Benets Abbey, bream and roach. North bank from Ant d/s, Norwich & Dist AA. Dt £1 for St Benets abbey and Cold Harbour from A T Thrower & Son, Ludham PO NR29 5QQ. Accommodation at Holly Farm, and Olde Post Office.

Horning (Norfolk); ns Wroxham, 3½m. Good coarse fishing; free to licence holders; boat almost essential; roach, rudd, bream, perch, pike, tench; river very busy in summer, hence early morning and late evening fishing gives best results. At **Woodbastwick** Environment Agency has ¾m of right bank, tidal; free to licence-holders. Broads: **Ranworth** (tickets for Inner Ranworth from store on Staithe); **Decoy** (club water), **Salhouse** (dt issued); and **Wroxham**, small charge, upstream. Tackle shop: Granary Stores, The Staithe, Ranworth. Several boat yards. Hotels: Swan, Kepplegate and Petersfield House Hotel.

Wroxham (Norfolk). Roach, rudd, bream,

pike, perch, tench; good pike and bream in winter; boats only. Much river traffic, summer. Broads: **Bridge Broad**, boats only. **Salhouse Broad**, right bank, dt issued. **Alderfen Broad**, specimen tench. Boats £5 per day from Wroxham Angling Centre, Station Rd, Hoveton. Hotels: Broads; Hotel Wroxham.

Coltishall (Norfolk). Boats in vicinity. Hotels: King's Head; Risings; Norfolk Mead.

Buxton Lamas (Norfolk). All banks now private.

Abbots Hall (Norfolk). Ingworth. Brown trout, stocked 4 times during season. 1m both banks, dry fly, or upstream nymph only, open to Salmon and Trout Assn members. Applications to Simon Dodsworth, The National Trust, Blickling, Norfolk (01263 733471).

Bure Valley Lakes, nr **Aylsham** NR1 16NW, tel: 0126358 7666. Three lakes of 3, 2 and 5 acres with trout to 15lbs, fly only, carp to 30lbs, roch and tench. Dt £12.50, trout, £5 coarse, £7.50 two rods. Instruction on site.

Blickling (Norfolk). Trout upstream from Ingworth Bridge. Abbots Hall, R Bure at Ingworth, 1m both banks, Salmon and Trout Assn members fishing. Tel: 01603 620551. Dt for **Blickling Lake** (20 acres), from bailiff at 1 Park Gates, Blickling NR11 6NJ; £3.50, conc. No night fishing. Tickets on bank in summer. Pike season Oct 1 to Mar 14.

Tributaries of the Bure

THURNE: Slow-flowing, typical Broadland river; tidal below Potter Heigham. Coarse fish, good bream and roach. Environment Agency water at **Potter Heigham, Martham, Thurne Marshes**.

Thurne Mouth (Norfolk). Good roach, bream, perch and eels. Hedera House, tel: 01692 670242, has ½m of river, with fishing for guests at self-catering chalets. Contact Miss C Delf.

Potter Heigham (Norfolk). Popular centre; good roach and bream; fair-sized eels. Bure. 3m, S. Broads: **Womack**, 1½m; **Hickling Broad** and **Heigham Sound** (tench, bream, roach, perch). Approx 3½m left bank, Martham to Repps and 4½m right bank Martham to Coldharbour free to licence-holders. Access points at Ferry Rd, Martham; Potter Heigham Bridge and Repp's Staithe. Hotels: Broads Haven, Cringles, Broadland House. Boats from Whispering Reeds Boatyard, Hickling, tel: Hickling 314; Arthur Walch, Nurses House, Martham. Licences, tackle, etc. from Q/D Tackle, Bridge Road, Potter Heigham.

Martham (Norfolk). Rudd, tench, bream, roach, perch, pike; good bank fishing; **Heigham Sound** 1m free on E.A. licence. Dt £3 for 24 hours on **Martham Pits**, 3½ acres good coarse fishing, from Mollys Sweet Shop, Martham. Local club is Martham and Dist. AC. Boats: Beale, The Staithe, Hickling; and Whispering Reeds Boatyard, Hickling. Accommodation at Mustard Hyrn Farm.

ANT:

Ludham. Roach, bream, eels, perch, pike. 2¼m of the river, upstream and downstream of Ludham Bridge, free to licence-holders.

Irstead and **Neatishead** (Norfolk). Good bream, perch, rudd, pike; also tench and roach. Fishing free.

Stalham (Norfolk). River clear, slow-running and weedy in summer; roach, rudd, bream, perch, pike and few tench. Broads: **Barton**, 1m; bream, roach, eels, perch and big pike; free fishing. Boats from Barton Angler Country Inn, Neatishead NR12 8XP, or Cox, Barton Turf Staithe. **Hickling**, 3m by road; good pike, bream, etc. Sutton Broad overgrown. Tackle shop: Broadland Angling and Pet Centre, 24-26 High Street NR12 9AN. Hotel: Sutton Staithe Hotel and Kingfisher.

Wayford Bridge (Norfolk). Upper Ant; head of navigation; fishing free to licence-holders; roach, rudd, perch, pike, tench, bream; boat advisable; river is narrow and fairly busy at times in summer; weedy and clear. Bait and tackle from Stalham. Good fishing also above the head of Ant Navigation in Dilham and North Walsham Canal, navigable to rowing boats as far as Honing Lock. Caravan site and food at Wood Farm Inn. Houseboat accom. from George Mixer & Co Ltd, Catfield, Gt Yarmouth, tel: 01692 580355, who reserve ½m downstream. tel: 01692 650491.

North Walsham (Norfolk). Several coarse fisheries in locality. Gimmingham Lakes, with carp to 30lbs, Roughton, with carp, tench bream, roach, and perch; Felming-

Part of the angler's library and tackle. *Photo: Arthur Oglesby*

ton, with roach, perch, tench, carp. Dt £3 on all of these, and other local tickets and information from tackle shop Country Pursuits, 49 Market Place. Tel: 01692 403162. Inns; Ockley House; Toll Barn.

SAW MILL LAKE: Fishing station: **Gunton** (Norfolk) near Cromer. 16 acre lake in Gunton Park, 3m; coarse fish; dt £3.50, from bailiff, on bank. Jun, OAP £1.50.

Horning (Norfolk). **Salhouse Broad**; too much traffic in summer, but good fishing in early mornings and from Oct to March. Dt issued. **Ranworth Broad** (tickets for Inner Ranworth from store on Staithe). **Malthouse Broad**; free. **Decoy Broad**; now open only to clubs. Tackle, licences, bait at Post Office.

Ormesby, Rollesby and **Filby**. Fishing by boat only, from Filby and Eels Foot Inn, or Kingfishers, Rollesby, tel: 01493 748724. These Broads are connected and undisturbed by motor cruisers and yachts, but electric outboards may be used. Fishing good everywhere. Excellent pike in winter. Wt £27.50. **Little Ormesby Broad**, free fishing by boat only, from Mr French, tel: 01493 732173.

Salhouse (Norfolk). Salhouse Broad, 1m NE; few pike in winter.

Broads connected with the Bure

Wroxham Broad, 1m N; *(see Wroxham);* Information and boat-hire from Wroxham Angling Centre, tel: Norwich 782453. **Decoy** or **Woodbastwick Broad**, 2m NE; fishing on payment. **Little Ranworth Broad**, 3m E; good for bream. These three are controlled by Norwich & Dist AA. **South Walsham Broad**, 5m E; private; good bream and pike fishing.

Wroxham (Norfolk). **Wroxham Broad,** boat fishing only. Dt from Tom Boulton, 175 Drayton Rd, Norwich, 01603 426834, and Norwich Angling Centre, 476 Sprowston Rd, Norwich. **Bridge Broad**, boat fishing only. **Salhouse Broad**, right bank, 2m SE. **Alderfen Broad**, has specimen tench and bream; dt £5 from Wroxham Angling Centre, Station Rd.

Broads connected with the Thurne and Ant

Potter Heigham (Norfolk). **Heigham Sounds**; fine fishing in summer; pike fishing, roach and bream in winter (free). Pike fishing on Horsey (no live-baiting). Womack Water dredged and cleared of weed, and may be fished from quay below. *(For hotels, boats, etc, see entry under Thurne.)*

Hickling (Norfolk). **Horsey, Barton** and **Hickling Broads**, bream, roach, pike, perch. All free except Horsey: dt from keepers. Licences from Post Office and stores; boats for hire.

Martham (Norfolk). R Thurne. Bream.

WAVENEY

Flows along Norfolk-Suffolk border. Fishing from tidal limit at Ellingham. Between Geldeston Lock and St Olaves, the tidal river gives some wonderful sport with bream in summer, winter roach at Beccles Quay.

Lowestoft (Suffolk). Oulton Broad and Waveney, which connects with Broad; bream, perch, roach, pike, etc; boats at Broad. Flounders and smelts in harbour. Good sea fishing in Oct, Nov and Dec from boats and beach for whiting, cod and flatfish. Several Broads within easy reach. Much of **River Hundred** is Kessingland AC water. **Oulton Broad** (Suffolk). Broad gives good sport with eels to 5lb, bream, roach, etc, but crowded with boats in summer. Bank fishing from Nicholas Everitt Park. Waveney near; 2m of free fishing at Puddingmoor Lane, **Barsham**; 170 yds at **Worlingham**; best from boat. Good perch and pike (best Oct-March); roach (good all season, best Jan, Feb, Mar), bream (moderate, best June-Nov); dace. **North Cove**; 400 yards with bream to 7lb, big pike, st from Post Office. **Oulton Dyke** (north side only); bream (excellent Aug, Sept, Oct); perch, roach, eels. Club: Oulton Broad Piscatorial Society. Tackle shops: Ted Bean, 175 London Rd; P & J Fishing Tackle, 52 High St, Kessingland. Hotels: Wherry; George Borrow; Broadlands.

Haddiscoe (Norfolk). **New Cut**: good coarse fishing; free. **Fritton Lake**, Countryworld, Fritton, Gt Yarmouth NR31 9HA, tel: 01493 488288. 163 acres, perch, pike, roach, rudd, tench, bream, eel, carp. Open Apr-Sept, 10 am to 5 pm.

Worlingham (Suffolk). 170 yds of Suffolk bank free fishing via Marsh Lane.

Beccles (Suffolk). Good roach, bream, pike, etc; best early or late in summer but especially good Oct onwards, when river traffic eases off. Free fishing from Beccles Quay. Beccles AC has 31 pegs at Barsham Drain, half mile out of Beccles off Bungay Rd, and Haddiscoe Lake, 5m away. Various coarse species. St £15 from tackle shop. 400 yds stretch at **Aldeby** is George Prior AC water. **Aldeby Pits** coarse fishery is 5m from Beccles, on Waveney. Tackle shop *(see below)* is helpful, and issue st and dt for waters belonging to Beccles, Bungay Cherry Tree, and Harleston and Wortwell clubs, on river and lakes. Charges range from st £17 to £5; dt from £1.50 to 50p. Tackle shop: Beccles Angling Centre, 27 Blyburgate. Hotels: King's Head; Waveney House; Ship House.

Geldeston (Norfolk). Good pike, roach, perch, bream, etc; free. Inns: Wherry (licences) and Geldeston Lock. Tackle shop in Beccles (3m).

Barsham (Suffolk). 2m free fishing on Suffolk bank from Puddingmoor Lane.

Bungay (Suffolk). Good roach, chub, bream, perch, pike and tench; fishes best at back end. Bungay Cherry Tree AC has from Earsham to Geldeston, 2m between Wainford and Ellingham, mostly roach, and **Ditchingham Pits**, all members only; also **Broome Pits**, dt £2.50 on bank, tel: 01986 895188. Club Hon Sec, Mr Gosling, tel: 01986 892982. Membership £24, conc, from Bungay Angling Centre, Outney Meadow Caravan Park, who also offer fishing on private stretch of river. Suffolk County AAA has Bungay Common stretch, dt from Angling Centre. Tackle and bait from N R Sports Shop, 4A Market Place. Accommodation at White Lion, Earsham St, Bungay NR35 1AF. **Homersfield** (Suffolk). Pike, perch, roach (large), dace, tench. Licences from Black Swan Hotel, Harleston IP20 0ET for 300 yds of free fishing. There is also excellent specimen carp fishing locally here and at **Wortwell** Leisure Sport gravel pit.

Harleston (Norfolk). Waveney, 1m S; coarse fish. Harleston, Wortwell and Dist AC has fishing on Weybread Pits, 6 lakes stocked with most coarse species. Waveney Valley Lakes, tel: 01986 788676; Highfield Fishery, 3 lakes coarse, tel; 01986 874869, dt on site; Mendham Trout Lakes, fish to 15lb, tel: 01379 852328. Dts and information on all these local waters from Waveney Angling, 5 London Road, Harleston IP20 9BH, tel: 01379 853034.

Eye (Suffolk). **Dove Brook**; large dace. Fishing in Waveney at Hoxne, 3m. **Weybread Pits,** permits from Mr Bowman, tel: 01379 852248.

Diss (Norfolk). **Waveney** and **Dove**. Diss & Dist AC has good quality stocked water on Waveney at Scole, Billingford, Hoxne, Brockdish, 6m total, best end Sept onwards; Dove at Oakley, d/s of bridge, roach, rudd, bream, pike, tench; **Diss Mere**, 5 acres, mirror carp, tench, roach and crucian carp. No dt. St £17.50, conc £8.50, for all fisheries from P Peg, Tackle shop, 133 Victoria Rd, Diss ID22 3JN. Hotel: Saracens Head.

YARE

Rises few miles from East Dereham and flows through Norwich to Yarmouth. Tidal, still one of the best Broads rivers for roach and bream, the main species; specially good for roach in middle reaches, bream in lower.

Great Yarmouth (Norfolk). Broads and rivers. Rivers Yare, Bure and Waveney fall into **Breydon Water** (Bure joined in upper reaches by Thurne and Ant). In all, some 200 miles of rivers well suited to boat and bank angling are within easy reach; some Broads are landlocked, strictly reserved for angling and free from river traffic; others connected to rivers, but mostly best fished from boat. Many Broads easily accessible; also rivers **Bure, Thurne, Ant** and **Waveney**. Trout in Bure. Also good sea fishing. Tackle shops: Dave Docwra, 79 Churchill Rd; Pownell and Son, 74 Regent Rd; Greensteads Tackle, 73 High Street, Gorleston-on-Sea; Dyble & Williamson, Scratby Rd, Scratby, Great Yarmouth NR29 3PQ (01493 731305).

Reedham (Norfolk). Strong tide; legering best; roach, perch, bream, eels; free at Langley on E.A. licence. Hotel: Ship.

Cantley (Norfolk). Roach, bream, perch; bream and perch plentiful; fishing free to licence-holders; mostly by leger. Inn: Red House.

Buckenham (Norfolk). Bream, roach, perch; pike; fishing free to licence-holders here and at Claxton, Rockland and Langley, 2,900 yds left bank and 5,200 right bank. Mouth of Hassingham Dyke is good spot. Lakes Strumpshaw Broad, 1m NW. Buckenham Broad and Hassingham Broad, 1m SE; preserved. Rockland Broad, 1½m SW on other bank of river; free.

Brundall (Norfolk). Roach, bream, perch in Yare. Several reaches between Coldham Hall and Surlingham Ferry can be fished by boat. Surlingham Broad belongs to National Trust; fishing only fair in summer; water shallow and weedy; pike in winter.

Norwich (Norfolk). Free fishing at Earlham Bridge to Cringleford Bridge, 2m of left bank, with dace, roach, chub, bream, pike. **Wensum** above city holds fine roach, perch, dace, chub and pike. Good roach and bream fishing at **Rockland Broad**; 7m from Norwich; but poor ac-

LURES AND SALMON FLIES

TANDEM MUDDLER
HITE MARABOU
BLACK MARABOU
UDDLER MINNOW
ELLOW MUDDLER
ABBOT
NAILER
ISKY FLY

ELIZABETH OF GLAMIS
LEPRECHAUN
SWEENY TODD
BOWLER HAT
BEARDED DOLL
BABY DOLL
PINK DOLL
ORANGE DOLL
LIME DOLL

MUNRO KILLER
STOATS TAIL
ORANGE SHRIMP
MACKENZIE GREEN
TEAL, BLUE, & SILVER
BOURACH
GENERAL PRACTITIONER
ELIZABETH OF GLAMIS

BROWN MARABOU
SHREDGE
MACLAREN
MURDOCH'S BUTCHER
DOG NOBBLERS.

cess to banks. 10m from Norwich, Haveringland Lake Caravan Park, Cawston NR10 4PN, has excellent coarse fishing lake, open most of year on wt or dt, from site office. Tel: 01603 871302 for details. Norwich AA has water on **Bure, Thurne, Ant** and **Yare, Ranworth Inner Broad** and **Woodbastwick Decoy** (fishing by boat only on last two waters); dt from Hon Sec and tackle shops. AW coarse fishery: **Taverham Mills**, Fishing Lodge, Norwich NR8 6TA, tel: 01603 861014 (fax 262082). Tackle shops: Norwich Angling Centre, 476 Sprowston Rd (01603 100757); Gallyons Country Clothing and Fishing Tackle, 7 Bedford St NR2 1AN; John's Tackle Den, 16 Bridewell Alley; Tom Boulton, 173 Drayton Rd. Hotel: Maid's Head.

Tributaries of the Yare

CHET:

Loddon (Norfolk). Free coarse fishing in Chet at Loddon Staithe: roach, bream. This water now navigable and fishes best in autumn and winter when traffic finishes. Hardley Marshes, coarse dt £1. Licences, river and sea bait and tackle from C Nicholls, 14, The Market Place and P Clemence, 22 High St, Loddon. Hotels: Swan, and Angel Inn, Loddon; White Horse, Chedgrave.

WENSUM: Coarse fish (good chub and barbel).

Norwich (Norfolk). Tidal. Riverside Rd, Oak St and Hellesdon Mill controlled by City Amenities Dept. Free fishing at Fye Bridge Steps, Cow Tower, Bishop Bridge, Yacht Station and d/s of Foundry Bridge to apprx 100yds d/s of Carrow Bridge.

Costessey (Norfolk). Chub, roach, dace, bream and pike. Norwich & Dist AA have 600 yds u/s of Costessey Mill. Membership from local tackle shops. At **Taverham**, 5 gravel pits known as the Ringland Pits, large carp, pike, roach, bream, and 480m R Wensum. St, conc. ½ price, from Leisure Sport, RMC House, High Street, Feltham, Middlesex TW13 4HD, tel: 0181 8931168. Dt from bailiff at lakes. **Costessey Pits**, 100 acres AW coarse fishery, dt from Norwich tackle shops, or tel: 01603 262082. Shallowbrook Lake, 2¼ acres, coarse fish, st water, Martin Green, tel: 01603 747667/1741123.

Drayton (Norfolk). Free fishing at Drayton Green Lane for half mile, with roach, chub, bream, dace and pike.

Attlebridge (Norfolk). Good trout fishing here, some miles of water being preserved. Tud, 4m S; private. Reepham Fishery, Beck Farm, Norwich Road, **Reepham** NR10 4NR: 3½ acre lake, with carp to 28lb, tench to 6lb, roach, rudd. Dt £3 from bailiff on bank.

Lenwade (Norfolk). Fishing in three old gravel pits set in 25 acres, administered by the trustees of two Great Witchingham charities. There is a lake with carp to 20 lbs. plus mixed coarse fishing. Permits £4 day, £8 night (conc. jun, OAP) from bailiff. Enquiries to Mrs D M Carvin, Blessings, The Street, Lenwade, Norwich NR9 5SD, tel: 01603 872399.

Swanton Morley (Norfolk). Dereham & Dist AC has water, *see Lyng, below*. Swanton Morley Fishery, bream roach, rudd, tench, perch, pike, carp, tel: 01362 692975. Permits and information from F W Myhill & Sons, Church St, East Dereham. **Whinburgh Trout Lakes**, East Dereham, 4 acres of stocked b and r trout fishing. Tel: 01362 850201, Mr Potter. Accommodation: J Carrick, Park Farm, Swanton Morley, tel: 01362 637457. Fishing and shooting parties welcome at Wensum Valley Golf Club, Beech Avenue, Taverham, Norwich NR8 6HP (01603 261012).

Hellesdon (Norfolk). Roach, chub, dace, carp, pike. Free fishing from Mill Pool to New Mills.

Lyng (Norfolk). Fine roach, dace and some trout. Dereham and Dist AC has Wensum here, at **Swanton Morley** and at **Worthing**; **Lyng Pit**, tench, bream, pike, roach; **Worthing Pit**, specimen bream, tench, pike, **Billinford Pit**, tench, bream, crucians, roach; five pits at Swanton Morley with pike, bream, tench, roach and others, and stretch of **Blackwater**, coarse fish. Membership £30, £15 conc, from Myhills Tackle Shop, Church St. Other tackle shop: Churchills, 24 Norwich St, both Dereham. London AA has water for members only. Accom, Park Farm, Swanton Morley, 01362 637457.

Elsing (Norfolk). Environment Agency has 1,270 yards of right bank.

North Elmham (Norfolk). Fishing in Wensum for pike, roach, perch, dace and few trout. Fakenham AC has Railway Lake, 1 acre, mixed coarse, members only. **Roosting Hills**, 6 acre lake at Beetley. For details of fishing contact P Green, Two Oaks, Fakenham Rd, Beetley, tel: 01362 860219.

Fakenham (Norfolk). Trout, dace, roach, perch, gudgeon, eels. Fakenham AC has 2m, dt only for trout, £5 from Dave's Fishing Tackle, Millars Walk, tel: 01328 862543. Several coarse lakes in area: **Willsmore Lake**, Hayes Lane, Fakenham AC water, members only.

TASS or **TAES:**

Swainsthorpe (Norfolk). Yare, 3m N. **Taswood Lakes**, good carp and other coarse fish. Dt £4, night £4.50, conc. Tel: 01508 470919.

BASS:

Wymondham (Norfolk). Yare, 4m N at Barford and 6m N at Marlingford; roach. Club: Wymondham AC. Season tickets £5 from Sec, or Myhills Tackle, Queens Square, Attleborough. Tackle shop: F W Myhill & Son, Fairland St (branches at Swaftham, Dereham and Thetford). Hotel: Abbey.

BLACKWATER: Trout; preserved.

Booton (Norfolk). Booton Clay Pit, with carp to 30lb, bream to 10lb and large roach, tench, etc; stocked by Cawston Angling Club. 24 hour dt £3.50 from bailiff on bank. Under 16, 50p. For further details contact S Brownsell, 3 Purdy Way, Aylsham NR11 6DH, tel: 01263 732263.

Broads connected with the Yare

Buckenham. Rockland Broad, 1½m SW; good roach fishing and pike fishing in winter. R Dye, The Kilns Boatyard or tel: 015088 251/301, has some boats for hire. Bed & breakfast nr Broad.

Brundall. Belongs to National Trust; shallow water grown up in summer, but good for pike in winter.

NORFOLK (small streams)

(For close seasons, licences, etc, see Anglian Regional Environment Agency, p19, unless otherwise stated.)

BABINGLEY RIVER. Fishing station: **Castle Rising**, ns North Wootton, 2m. Rises in the lake at Hillington Hall, and is 9m long. King's Lynn AA has water; no tickets. *See King's Lynn - Ouse (Great).*

GLAVEN. Rises 3m E of **Holt** and joins sea at **Cley**, 6m down. 1m at Cley. Fishing now held privately. No permits. There are several small coarse lakes in this area. **Letheringsett, Booton** at **Cawston, Selbrigg** at **Hemstead**; dt on bank, £2.50. **Felbrigg Park Lake**, NT fishery, dt £2.50 in advance, tel: 0126375 444.

NAR. Rises above **Narborough** to enter the Wash at **King's Lynn**. Chalk stream brown trout fishing. 1m both banks below Narborough Mill, stocked, fish 11" upwards, dry fly and upstream nymph fishing only, reserved for Salmon and Trout Assn members. Dt for out-of-area members in advance only from David Burrows, Apple Tree Lodge, Squires Hill, Upper Marham PE33 9PJ, tel: 01760 337222. At Narborough, five trout lakes. Enq to Narborough Mill, tel 01760 338005.

TASS. Rises N of **Wacton**, 11m S of **Norwich**, to enter Yare on outskirts of city.

OTTER

(For close seasons, licences, etc, see South West Region Environment Agency, p16)

Noted Devonshire trout stream flowing into English Channel immediately east of Exe. Mullet in estuary and some sea trout, with brown trout of good average size for West Country higher up, where hotels have some excellent dry-fly water.

Budleigh Salterton (Devon). Tidal. Free fishing from river mouth to Clamour Bridge (about 1½m, both banks) to visitors staying in East Budleigh or Budleigh Salterton. Sea trout, brown trout, grey mullet plentiful but difficult to catch. Fishing on both banks from Clamour Bridge to Newton Poppleford. Sea fishing; bass, flatfish, etc, from extensive beach. *(see Sea Fishing Stations under Sidmouth).*

Ottery St Mary (Devon). Some good trout water in vicinity.

Honiton (Devon). Deer Park Hotel, Buckerell Village EX14 0PG, tel: 01404 41266, has 3m (both banks) of wild brown trout fishing; trout up to 2lb, average 1lb. Dt £30, £25 after 4pm, at hotel. Hotel also has 2 acre lake. 3 lakes with rainbow trout at Otter Falls, Rawbridge, nr Honiton. Otter Inn, **Warton**, has trout fishing on 100 yds of Otter, tel: 01404 2594. Coarse fishing on 3 acre lake at Fishponds House, Dunkeswell EX14 0SH, tel; 01404 891358. Carp, rudd, tench.

OUSE (Great)

(For close seasons, licences, etc, see Anglian Region Environment Agency, p19)

Rises in Buckinghamshire and flows north-east through Northamptonshire, Bedfordshire, Cambridgeshire, Huntingdonshire and Norfolk, entering the North Sea by The Wash. Coarse fishing throughout. Slow, winding river for most part. Roach and dace are to be found in quantity, together with barbel and bream. Between Newport Pagnell and Bedford there are large roach and chub.

King's Lynn (Norfolk). Coarse fish of all kinds except barbel. King's Lynn AA has water on the Ouse from Modney Court to Denver Sluice east bank; Denver Sluice to Danby's Drove, west bank; on the Wissey, From Dereham Belt to R Ouse; on the **Relief Channel Drain**, King's Lynn to Denver Sluice; on the **Middle Level Drain** from St Germans to aqueduct, 8m; Engine Drain, Ten Mile Bank, and pits. St £20, wt £10, dt £3.50, conc, from bailiffs. Gatton Water, Hillington, coarse fishing in 8 acre lake, for visiting campers, and caravans. Tel: 01485 600643, Mr Donaldson. Willow Lakes Trout Fishery, Ash Farm, Chediston, Halesworth. Two lakes of total 4 acres stocked, fly only, brown and rainbow trout fishing, dt £15, 4 fish limit, half day £8.50. Tel Mr Pat Gregory, on 0198 6785392. Woodlakes Holiday Park, Holme Rd, Stow Bridge, PE34 3PX, tel: 01553 810414, 8m south of King's Lynn, coarse fishing on five lakes, the largest 12 and 10 acres. St and dt. Swaffham AC has Bradmoor lakes, Narborough, stocked with carp, bream, etc. St £16.50, conc. Tackle shops: Anglers Corner, 55 London Rd; Geoff's Tackle Box, 38 Tower St, King's Lynn. Hotel: Park View.

Downham Market (Norfolk). Coarse fish, sea trout; tidal.

Hilgay (Norfolk). King's Lynn AA water on Ouse and **Wissey** *(see King's Lynn)*. London AA has water on Ouse; dt from bailiffs.

Littleport (Cambs). Ouse and **Lark**; coarse fish, except barbel, good pike and bream, with roach, perch, zander. Littleport AC has fishing on Ouse: Littleport A10 Bridge u/s to Sandhills Bridge, both banks, except Boat Haven on west bank. Bream to 7lb, roach, rudd, perch, eels, pike, zander, carp. Permits £3 from bailiff on bank or £2 from tackle shop in village. Full membership £8, conc. London AA controls 14m of water from Littleport Bridge to Southery (Norfolk), both banks. Dt from bailiffs. Ely Beet Sports and Social Club has fishing on both banks of Ouse and Lark, at confluence. Contact Mr R J Oakman, tel: 01353 649451. Tackle shop: Coleby's Tackle, Granby St.

Ely (Cambs). Free fishing from Lincoln Boatyard upstream to Newmarket Railway Bridge. Ely Highflyers have about 5m downstream from this and last mile of River Lark (Queen Adelaide stretch). Cambridgeshire and Isle of Ely Federation of Anglers: a body with has no water under its own jurisdiction, but is comprised of some 24 angling clubs and societies. See club list for address. Rosewell pits hired by Ely Beet Sugar Factory FC; dt on bank. Dt for Borrow Pit from Cambridge FPS. Tackle shop: Ely Trophy Shop; Thornton's, Broad Street. Hotel: Lamb.

Earith (Hunts). Histon & Dist AC has apprx 1m opposite village, members only st £25. **Old West River**. Earith Bridge to Pope's Corner (Cambs); partly hired by Cambridge Albion AS; good coarse fishing. **Old Bedford River** from Earith to Welches Dam and **New Bedford Level** or **Hundred Foot** (tidal) from Sutton Gault to Ox Willow Lode controlled by Cambridge Albion AS and Shefford AS; members only but dt issued by Hon Sec for Ivel. Ploughman's Pit (good carp, bream, pike; dt also from Airman public house) and lake at Oldfield Farm. St obtainable at local inns near the waters and Cambridge tackle shops. The Hundred Foot (Earith to Sutton Gault), rented by

Cambridge FPS, tidal; practically all coarse fish, except barbel; **Borrow Pit** nr Ely, coarse fish, dt £1.50, in advance, from Hon Sec or local inns for Cambridge FPS water. Cambridge Albion AS has stretch on **Delph** from Welches Dam to Chequers, Purls bridge. Great Ouse Fishery Consultative Association rents water on **Counterwash Drain, Old Bedford River, Pingles Pit** (Mepal) and the **Hundred Foot**. Affiliated clubs have rights. Members of Sheffield AAS may fish these waters, the **Delph** at Manea (Manea AC water) and the **Bedford River** from Purls Bridge to **Welches Dam**.

Over and **Swavesey** (Cambs). Bream, perch, chub, rudd, tench, pike, dace and zander. Sea trout runs up to the locks; fish over 12lb taken. Occasional salmon. St from Cambridge tackle shops.

Holywell Ferry (Hunts). Hotel: Ferry Boat. Pike, bream, roach, rudd, chub, etc; free; boats; good fishing, especially roach.

St Ives (Hunts). All coarse fish, bream, dace, perch, chub, gudgeon in quantity; also carp, barbel, rudd and tench. Ample bank fishing, but boats for hire. St Ives FP & AS has 3m water; st £12, dt £2, conc, from tackle shop. Adjoining water held by London AA. Histon & Dist AS has Holywell stretch. Tackle shop: St Ives Angling Centre, 5 Crown St PE17 4EB. Hotels: Golden Lion, Slepe Hall, Firs.

Godmanchester (Hunts). Good bream, roach, chub and chance of carp. Godmanchester A & FPS has about 10m. Tickets from Hon Sec or tackle shop. St £6, dt £1. London AA has Portholme Meadow, Berry Lane Meadows and 1¼m Old West River at Stretham (members only). Boats from Huntingdon; no free fishing. Tackle shop: Stanjay Sports, who manage **Woolpack Fishery**, Cow Lane, 60 acres of well stocked coarse fishing. St £35, £20 jun, OAP. Dt £2.50. Hotels: Black Bull, Exhibition, Bridge and George.

Huntingdon (Cambs). Chub, bream, roach and tench; good when boat traffic declines. Huntingdon AS has water from Town Bridge to Hartford Church. St £8, wt £4, dt £2, juv st £2.50, from tackle shops. London AA *(see Clubs)* has 4½m of Ouse, stretch of **Alconbury Brook, Brampton Mill Pool** and millstream, and other water at **Brampton**; members only. Tickets issued for some waters. Brampton AS has two stretches of Ouse, 4 brooks and 4 lakes. Mainly st (£15) but dt on river and one lake. Tackle shops: Kellys Discount Angling Centre, 188 High St; Sports & Fashion, 51 High St; Webbs, 88 High St; Stanjay Fishing Tackle, 7 Old Court Wall, Godmanchester; Ouse Valley Angling, 25/31 Huntingdon St, St Neots.

Offord Cluny (Hunts). Stocked by Environment Agency. Chub, roach, bream, tench, carp, barbel, catfish. Offord and Buckden AS has 3½m of Great Ouse between St Neots and Huntingdon, incl two weir pools; dt £3, conc, from bank by car park. Several sections are free of boat traffic at all times. Coach-party enquiries from E Blowfield, 4 Monks Cottages, Huntingdon. 01480-810166.

St Neots (Hunts). St Neots and Dist Angling & FPS has six sections from Nuffield down to Wray House, Chawston Lake, carp over 20lbs, Wilden Reservoir; good tench, chub to 7lbs, bream, roach and big carp. St £25 from tackle shops. Dt £3, conc, on most of R Ouse fishing, from bailiffs. Letchworth and Dist AA has water at **Offord D'Arcy**. No dt, membership £33 conc. London AA has water at **Tempsford** and **Blunham** *(see Ivel)*. 30 acres of lake and ¼m of Ouse at **Little Paxton**, from OWR/Redland. 3 pits open. St £15, wt £8, dt £2. Permits from Fishery Manager, Mrs M R May, 5 Hayling Avenue, Little Paxton. Tel: Huntingdon 212059. Tackle shops: Ouse Valley Angling, 25/31 Huntingdon St; St Neots Angling Centre, Eynesbury, St Neots.

Biggleswade (Beds). Ouse, Ivel, Biggleswade, Hitchin & Dis. AC AA has 7m on mid Ouse at Wyboston, and 15 acre lake at Eaton Socon with large carp, tench, rudd, bream. St £18, conc, from sec of local tackle shops. Blue Lagoon, **Arlesey** (4m S); large coarse lake, Letchworth and dist AA. No dt, membership £33, conc. Tackle shop: Rods Tackle, Arlesey.

Bedford (Beds). Approx 4m water in town centre and above, free to E.A. rod licence-holders. Council controls three lakes at Priory Country Park, dt £2 on bank. Bedford AC has fishing and issues limited dt at £3, st £22, conc, tickets from Dixon Bros. Vauxhall AC controls Radwell complex, 6m of Ouse, and local stillwaters, members only st £25, conc. At **Kempston**, Vauxhall AC lease west bank, Kempston AC has 2½m on Biddenham side, dt from Bleak Hall Sports or on bank. Ampthill FPS fish Ampthill Reservoir, and Marston Pits, membership £18.

Hotels: Embankment, Swan, Lion. Tackle shops: Bleak Hall Sports; Dixon Bros. 95 Tavistock Street.

Felmersham (7m N of Bedford) Ampthill FPS stretch here, at Pavenham and at Goldington Storm Drain. Membership, £18. Concessions. Vauxhall AC fish here and at **Willington**, membership £22. Letchworth and dist AA has left bank d/s of road bridge. No dt, membership £33, conc.

Sharnbrook (Beds). Wellingborough & Dist Nene AC has ¾m upstream of **Harrold**. Leighton Buzzard AC has water on left bank here. Ampthill AC has 1½m stretch on river at Dairy Farm, Renhold, with Gadsey Brook and Westminster Pool, and Stafford Bridge stretch. St £18, (½ price conc.) for Leisure Sport **Harrold Fishery** (1,500m Ouse, 1,200m Ivel and Lower Caldecott), with carp, chub, roach, dace, pike, catfish, barbel. No dt. Apply LSA, RMC House, High Street, Feltham, Middlesex TW13 4HD, tel: 0181 8931168.

Newton Blossomville (Bucks). Coarse fish. Northampton Nene AC has water; strictly limited dt £2 from Hon Sec.

Olney (Bucks), Coarse fish, good bream. Leighton Buzzard AC has ¾m stretch at **Stoke Goldington**, from Gayhurst Spinney to brook, st £14.50; jun, OAP £4.

Newport Pagnell (Bucks). Good barbel, roach, bream, chub, perch. Stretch fishes well in winter. Leisure Sport has 3m of river above town at Tyringham Estate, offering large barbel, chub, bream, roach and dace. St £20, conc, from LSA, tel: 0181 8931168. Newport Pagnell AA leases Newport Pagnell Lakes from AW. At **Great Linford** there is a complex of gravel pits holding bream, roach, tench and pike on which the fishing rights are now held by ARC. **Vicarage Spinney** is 8 acre trout fishery at **Little Linford**, stocked with large r, 11lb to 18lb. St £200, dt £10, 4 fish, and boats £5. 6 acre b trout lake, large fish. Tel: 01908 614969. Tackle shop: Angling Centre, Newport Pagnell, tel: 01908 216711. Hotel: Bull Inn (club HQ).

Stony Stratford (Bucks). Deanshanger and Stony Stratford AA has 6m of Ouse, bream, roach, perch, chub and pike, plus Grand Union Canal at **Castlethorpe**, st £15, dt £4 on bank, or £4 from Lake Bros, Church St, Wolverton, Milton Keynes. Milton Keynes AC also has fishing here, and between Wolverton and Haversham. **Cosgrove Lodge** lakes at Cosgrove (Northants): noted for roach, tench, bream, pike; dt on water. Kingfisher Sporting Club, Deanshanger, has lakes of 36 acres. Trout, fly only. Dt £25.60 or £17.40 (non members), £18.40 to £10.25 (members), 4 fish and 2 fish. Tel; 01908 562332. Hotels: Cock; Bull.

Buckingham (Bucks). Chub, roach, perch, dace, pike. Buckingham and Dist AA has water on Ouse and tributaries, and stillwaters, with good coarse fishing, best Nov-Mar, depending on rainfall. Assn records include carp 38lb 1oz, pike 27lb 4oz, bream, chub and tench over 7lb. Joining fee £10, st £30, dt £3, conc, from Tight Lines, 9A Market Sq, Winslow; Jakeman Sport, 5 Bourbon St, Aylesbury. Leighton Buzzard AA, Claydon Lakes, 6m; no dt. At **Mursley**, Church Hill Fishery, Swanbourne Rd, MK17 0RS: 3 lakes of 15 acres stocked with r and b trout. Dt £25, evening £15, 4 and 2 fish. Tel: 0129672 0524.

Tributaries of the Ouse (Great)

WISSEY:

Hilgay (Norfolk). King's Lynn AA have 2m of both banks down to Ouse. St £14, wt £5, dt £2.50. London AA issues dt for Five Mile House Farm.

LITTLE OUSE: Good bream and roach.

Brandon (Suffolk). The above species, plus dace, perch, pike (good), a few chub and zander. Brandon and Dist AC has 2 ponds and ¾m river at Recreation Park, and 1½m L Ouse at Weeting, Norfolk. No dt, membership £11 annually with concessions, from Recreation Centre. Thetford and Breckland AC has water above bridge. Hotel: The Ram.

Thetford (Norfolk). Little Ouse and Thet. Roach, rudd, tench, chub and pike; and dace to specimen size. Fishing free for 7 miles through town centre out to Santon Downham.

LARK: Trout and coarse fish.

Mildenhall (Suffolk). Trout, carp, rudd, roach, perch, tench, bream, pike, dace, gudgeon, eels, chub, bream. Mildenhall AC has several stretches excellent coarse fishing on Lark at Mildenhall, u/s and d/d at Isleham Lock, and West Row Drains, around West Row village. For £10 st, contact Hon Sec, tel: 01638 718205. From Bury St Edmunds to Lackford controlled by Bury St Edmund's AA; trout water; no permits. Lark APS has water between Lackford Bridge and West Row, with 5 mile coarse section containing roach, rudd, carp, pike, bream, eels, perch. Trout membership £100, coarse £12, conc £3-£1 from Hon Sec. Disabled facilities at Barton Mills and Mildenhall. Tackle shops: Colbys, Littleport; Little Downham Tackle; Matthews Garden Centre, Lakenheath. Hotels: White Hart, High St; Riverside, Mill St.

Bury St Edmunds (Suffolk). Coarse fish. Club: Bury St Edmunds AA, who have L Ouse, Blackbourne and Stour stretches, and lakes at Rougham and West Stow Country Park, mainly carp. St £15, jun £6, OAP £1, from sec N Bruton, tel: Bury 766074, or tackle shop: R Nunn, Tackle Up, 49a St John's Street, IP33 1SP. Other tackle shop: Anglia Arms, Risbygate St.

CAM: Excellent fishery, with good roach and pike. Best catches between Baitsbite Lock and Clayhithe Bridge.

Waterbeach (Cambs). Waterbeach AC has fishing on both banks here, and on Bottisham and Swaffham Bulbeck Lodes. Contact H Reynolds, tel: 01223 351696. Cambridge FP & AS has Reach, Burwell and Wicken Lodes.

Cambridge. Roach, chub, dace. Some good stretches of free fishing on common land, but disallowed on college property. Cam from near Pike and Eel Pub, Chesterton, d/s through Baitsbite Lock to Clayhith Bridge, Cambridge FP & AS; st £15, dt £2 from Hon Sec or Coopers (*below*). Concessions to OAP, juniors and disabled. Society also has about 4m of the **Hundred Foot River** from Earith Bridge to Sutton Gault and sole rights on whole of **Burwell Lode** and **Reach Lode**, stretch of **Great Ouse** at **Great Barford**, 1m of **Lark** below **Prickwillow Bridge**; and lakes; inquire Hon Sec for permits. Waterbeach AC controls Cam, Baitside Lock area, also **Swaffham Bulbeck Lode**, and **Old Bedford River** nr Manea. Cambridge Albion AS controls Cam at Wicken and other local fishing, dt £3. Agrevo ASC controls **Drayton Fen**, 80 acres, with good carp, tench, pike, also Holywell and Swavesey Lakes and Gt Ouse. Permits from Coopers (*below*). London AA has water for members only at **Swaffham Prior**. Cambridge Albion AS has two stretches at Wicken Fen, and Dimmocks Cote, also **Barnwell Lake**, Barnwell Bridge. **Cam** and **Granta** offer some free fishing to licence-holders. Tackle shops: Cooper & Son, 12 Milton Rd; Farrington, 2/4 Ferry Lane; Beecrofts, 207 Cherry Hinton Rd, Cambridge.

OLD WEST RIVER: Good stock of coarse fish. **Milton Lake**. Large carp and other coarse fish.

IVEL: Dace, roach and perch.

Tempsford (Beds). Ouse and Ivel. Biggleswade AC, now merged with Hitchin and District AA, has water on both rivers. London AA has several miles on Ouse here and at Blunham; members only.

Blunham (Beds). Ouse (1m W). Blunham AC controls local fishing. Below Blunham Bridge to Ouse held by Biggleswade and District AC. Club also has right bank of Ivel from Langford Mill to Broom Mill; no dt. Shefford AC has left bank. **Lower Caldecote** (Beds). Leisure sport has ¾m stretch, with trout, dace, chub, mirror carp and barbel to 3lb.

Langford (Beds). Letchworth and dist AA has fishing opposite garden centre, and at Langford Mill. No dt, membership £33, conc. Assn fishes most of Ivel through its membership of the Ivel Protection Society.

Henlow (Beds). Letchworth and dist AA fishes Henlow complex, 4 lakes and river

Check before you go

While every effort has been made to ensure that the information given in **Where to Fish** *is correct, the position is continually changing, and anglers are urged, in their own interests, to make preliminary enquiries before travelling to selected venues. This is especially important with reference to prices quoted. Inevitably the rate of inflation is affecting stability in this quarter. Anglers' attention is also drawn to the fact that the hotels mentioned under the various fishing stations do not necessarily have water of their own. Any amendments or further data for inclusion in subsequent editions, and any comments, will be welcome.*

at Henlow Village, entry via Park Lane.

HIZ (tributary of Ivel). Controlled by Biggleswade, Hitchin and District AA who have 15 acre coarse fishery nearby, and 7m increase of water on Middle Ouse. Membership £25 pa, specimen perch, etc. Club also has water on **Ouse**, River **Oughton** (trout, few chub, restocking under consideration; members only), and fishes waters of Great Ouse FCA and Ivel Protection Assn. St £25. Tackle shop: Alan Brown, Nightingale Road, **Hitchin**.

OUZEL: Coarse fish.

Leighton Buzzard (Beds). Leighton Buzzard AC preserves various stretches above Leighton Buzzard and at Stoke Hammond, Water Eaton, Bletchley and Newport Pagnell. Club also has several stretches on **Gt Ouse** (three at **Emberton** and others at **Stoke Goldington**), five on **Thame Shabbington**, 3m of **Oxford Canal** and 3m of **Grand Union Canal**. Also **Claydon Lakes, Tiddenfoot** and other pits. Annual membership £14.50. Concessions to jun & OAP. Leisure Sport has three gravel pits stocked with large pike, carp and catfish. St £32 (conc. ½ price). Phone 0181 8931168 for details. Tackle shop: Leighton Tackle Centre, 18 Peacock Market LU7 8JH.

RELIEF CHANNEL: not strictly a tributary but included here because of its traditional status as an excellent coarse fishery in its own right, now re-established as such, after a difficult period with zander, by an intensive programme of investigation and re-stocking by AWA. Now rented to Wisbech & Dist AA which issues dt.

TOVE: Coarse fish.

OUSE (Sussex)

(For close seasons, licences, etc, see Southern Region Environment Agency, p16).

Rises few miles south-east of Horsham and flows for 33 miles to enter English Channel at Newhaven. Tidal for 12 miles from mouth to point 4m upstream of Lewes. Coarse fish and trout, but notable for run of big sea trout.

Lewes and **Barcombe Mills** (E Sussex). Sea trout (good), barbel, perch, bream, roach, dace, chub, carp and pike. Ouse APS has west bank from Hamsey to Barcombe Mills (about 4m) and certain stretches of non tidal water above the mills. Sea trout from May to Oct, but June to August best, given rain. Annual permits at £30, jun £10, limited dt £5. Contact E W McLening, Old Barn Cottage, Peak Lane, East Preston BN16 1RN (01903 773104). Barcombe Mills Pool and side streams reserved for sea-trout fishing and open to permit holders at £3 a day (two rods daily) bookable in advance from Bailiff Jim Smith (01825 750366). Old Mill Farm, Barcombe, has Ouse fishing. Dt at farm. Swanborough Lake: coarse fishing on three lakes at Ilford. Tel: 01273 472232. Tackle shop: Percy's, 9 Cliffe High Street; Uckfield Angling Centre, 212A High St. Hotels: Shelleys; White Hart; Crown (all Lewes). for Barcombe Mills: Angler's Rest, Anchor Inn.

Isfield (E Sussex). Coarse fish, trout and sea trout. Isfield and Dist AC has sections of Ouse at Isfield Club also has stretches of **Cuckmere** at Upper Dicker, **Uck** at **Uckfield**. and lakes around **E Grinstead, Uckfield, Horsted Keynes** and elsewhere, twenty four fisheries in all. Large carp, tench, bream, perch, eels and pike. St £40 plus £10 joining fee, conc, from Memb Sec (sae). No dt. Exchange ticket system with other clubs. Free fishing on Piltdown Pond, 2m west of Uckfield, which is owned by golf club. Hotels: Laughing Fish, Isfield (club HQ); Maiden's Head, Uckfield. *(Tackle see Lewes).*

Haywards Heath (W Sussex). Coarse fish and trout. Haywards Heath & Dist AS has 11½m bank of **Ouse** from **Linfield** down to **Newick**, and several lakes, including **Balcombe Lake, Slaugham Mill Pond, Valebridge Mill Pond**. Fishing coarse mainly, trout in river, and is for members only. Membership open to approved applicants, with concessions. Tackle shops: Sporting Chance, 29 Boltro Rd; Angling Centre, 143 Church Rd, Burgess Hill.

UCK: mainly coarse fishing below Uckfield with occasional sea trout. Joins Ouse at Isfield.

Isfield (E Sussex). Coarse fish and trout. Isfield and Dist AC has water from here to **Uckfield** (members only), with excellent course fishing and trout to 3lb. **Colin Godman's Trouting**, Furners Green, TN22 3RR, tel: 01825 74 322; 3 lakes, 7 acres, browns and rainbows to 4lb, members only.

OUSE (Yorkshire)

(For close seasons, licences, etc, see Noth East Region Environment Agency, p17)

Forms with Trent the estuary of the Humber. Coarse fish, with some trout. Dunsforth, Beningbrough and Poppleton reaches noted for barbel and chub. Large bream present but difficult to catch. Most water held by Leeds and York clubs. Tributaries give excellent trout and coarse fishing.

Goole (N Humberside). Don enters Ouse here. Goole AA has stretch of **Derwent** from Wressle to Breighton; good roach, chub, pike, dace, few trout. No dt. Club also has water on **Selby Canal**, **Market Weighton Canal**, and local ponds. Memberships (£16, concessionary £5 pa) from Barry's of Goole Ltd, 25 Westfield Avenue, Goole DN14 6JY, tel: 01405 720231. Barry's own Barton Broad, Maltkiln Rd, **Barton upon Humber** (not to be confused with Barton Broad, Norfolk), 6½ acre mixed coarse, dt £4 on bank; also Staddlethorpe Pond, Broad Lane, Gilberdyke, **Brough**, 2½ acres coarse, dt £5 from Barry's. Carlton AC has dt £1.25 for several fishings around Selby and Goole, including R Derwent at Bubwith, West Haddlesey Lake, and Selby Canal, from local tackle shops. Selby Miners Welfare AC offers dt £2.50 on bank at Selby Canal between Brayton and Burn Bridges, with roach, chub, carp, dace and other species. Selby tackle shops: Selby Angling Centre, 69 Brook St; Field Sports, 24/26 New St, Selby N Yorks YO8 0PT.

Acaster (N Yorks). Coarse fishing. Controlled by the Leeds Amalgamation. Tickets at Blacksmith's Arms, Naburn, and Manor Guest House, Acaster Maibis. Castleford Anglers fish on 150 yds below old salmon hut. Dt £1. Fish include barbel; above dam, trout and coarse fish. Accommodation: Manor Guest House.

Naburn (N Yorks). Below dam, right bank to old salmon hut, York Amalgamated. Left bank, tickets £3 from lock keeper, or tackle dealer G E Hill, of York.

York (N Yorks). Coarse fish; some free fishing on public waters. On left bank nearly all free except 8m from Rawcliffe Ings and Clifton Ings up to Aldwark. York Amalgamation has fishing on 80m of **Ouse**, **Derwent**, **Nidd**, **Rye**, **Seven**, and several still waters. St £25, conc, dt £3 from local tackle shop for lower Nidd. 4m on Rivers Rye and Seven; very good grayling and trout; ½m on Derwent, all three fisheries members only. Tackle shops: G E Hill, 40 Clarence Street; Anglers Corner, 41 Huby Court, Walgate.

Poppleton and **Newton** (N Yorks). Good barbel, pike, etc. York and Leeds Amalgamations have extensive stretches. Dt from Fox Inn, Nether Poppleton, and Post Office.

Aldwark (N Yorks). Coarse fish. York Amal have 2½m above and ½m below Aldwark Bridge with exception of short stretch. Hotels: Three Horseshoes and Crown, Great Ouseburn; Bay Horse, Aldwark.

Low Dunsforth. from Low Dunsforth to Aldwark Bridge (about 4m right bank) fishing is in hands of Leeds Amal. Dt from Angler Inn, Low Dunsforth. Leeds Amal also has good length at **Hunterslodge** on opposite side below Aldwark bridge (left bank). Tickets as above.

Tributaries of the Ouse (Yorkshire)

DON. Rises on Wike Head and flows through Sheffield and Doncaster to the estuary of the Ouse; after 150 years of pollution from the Sheffield steel industry, this river is once more fishable. The NRA-Environment Agency has stocked over past twelve years, and 30lb nets of roach have been caught. Hemp and tares are best summer baits, maggots and casters in winter.

Doncaster (S Yorks). Doncaster & Dist AA has much widespread coarse fishing, including water on the canalised Don and **South Yorkshire Navigation Canal** at **Sprotsborough**, 4m d/s to and Doncaster Prison; 5m of **Idle** from Newington to Idle Stop; 10m of the **Torne**; the 6m of **New Junction Canal** from Barnaby Dun to the **Aire & Calder** junction; 5m **Warping Drain**; **also BW Southfield Reservoirs, Cowick**, 110 acres total, 40lb bags of roach and bream. Dt on the banks at many of these fisheries. **Thrybergh Reservoir**, 34 acres, near **Rotherham**; Rotherham MBC trout fishery. Permits on site. Rotherham MBC also has **Fitzwilliam Canal**, Rotherham 1m, dt. Tinsley & dist AA offer £2 dt for canal fishing in the area. Tel 01709 366142. BW Castleford Anglers have **Woodnook Reservoir**. St from Assn HQ and tackle shops. Barnby Dun Social AC have dt £1 on bank at S Yorkshire Navigation Canal between **Barnby Dun** and Kirk Sandall, with chub, roach, perch, bream, gudgeon. Tel: 01302 886024 for match bookings. Tackle shops: Anglers Supplies, 148 High St, Bentley, Doncaster; R & R Sports, 40 High St, Bawtry; Doncaster Angling Centre, 207 Carrhouse Rd.

Sheffield (S Yorks). **Damflask**, YW reservoir, 5m W; trout. **Underbank**, corporation reservoir, coarse fishing and a few large trout. Tickets from attendant's office. Further information under *'Yorkshire Lakes'*. Sheffield Amal AS (membership books from Lord Nelson, Arundel Street) has three waters on Trent, at Besthorpe, Girton and North and South Clifton. Dt from bailiff on bank. Sheffield and Dist AA has water on Rivers **Trent**, trout fishing at Thurgoland on **Don**, and **Chesterfield Canal** from A631 to Trent junction. Dt issued for most waters. **Stainforth and Keadby Canal** controlled by joint committee including Rotherham, Doncaster, Sheffield Amal, and British Railways clubs. Dt on bank. At **Staveley** Urban District Council have five acre lake stocked annually with coarse fish; dt and st. Also **Foxtone Dam**; dt. Chapeltown & Dist AA fish **Westwood** and **Howbrook Reservoirs**, and ponds, various coarse species. St £9, dt £2, from G Hamstead, Tackle Shop, Station Rd, Chapeltown, or bailiffs. Tackle shops: Terry & John's, 297 Buchanan Rd; Concord Fishing, 283 Hatfield House Lane; Kerfoot Fishing Tackle, 6 Southey Green Rd; Bennett's, 1 Stanley Street, Sheffield; Ernest Stamford, 419 Attercliffe Common; W G Dawson, 70 Holme Lane; Park Angling Centre 181 Middlewood Rd; Gunnies, 279 Buchanan Rd; M J Tackle, 85 Doncaster Rd, Rotherham; Fishermans Supplies, 131 Sheffield Rd; Angling Centre, 34 Chester St, Brampton, both Chesterfield.

DEARNE (tributary of Don):

Barnsley (S Yorks). Dearne; Free fishing on length within Hoyle Mill Country Park. Mainly free, between here and **Dar-**

field, and through common near Wombwell. Stocked at **Haigh**, where Wakefield AC has water. Club also has lakes near **Wakefield**, fishing on R Calder, and Calder & Hebble Navigation. Membership £12, conc, from Wakefield tackle shops. Barnsley MBC control six lakes and ponds, dt from 50p to £3. Barnsley Trout Canal fishes **Scout Dike Reservoir**; trout av ¾lb; bait restrictions, dt on site. **Wintersett Reservoir**; coarse fish; dt from bailiff. Barnsley & Dist AAS fishes for all species of coarse at Fiskerton on Trent, ½m Brampton Canal nr Wombwell, **Worsbrough Reservoir**; dt £2 on bank. Tackle shops: Tackle Box, 7, Doncaster Rd; Wombwell Angling Centre, 25 Barnsley Rd.

Claycross (Derby). Lakes: Williamthorpe Ponds, 2m NE. Wingerworth Hall Lakes (two), 2½m NW. Great Dam, 3½m NW.

ROTHER (tributary of Don):

Killamarsh (Derby). Short Brook. Lakes: Woodhall Moor Dams, 2m E. Barlborough Hall Lake, 3m SE. Pebley Dam, 3m SE. Harthill Reservoir, 3m E. Woodhall Pond, 3m E.

AIRE: Issues from ground at Aire Head, half a mile south of Malham village. Its upper reaches contain quality trout and grayling, which give place to coarse fish between Steeton and Keighley. Marsden Star AS has stretch at Keighley with trout, chub, roach, pike, plus other fishing on ponds and 3m Leeds & Liverpool Canal; st £18, dt £2, conc. Tackle shop in Keighley. Lower reaches and others near large towns polluted. *(For Malham Tarn-see Ribble-Settle).*

Leeds (W Yorks). Polluted. Adel Beck and Dam (private). **Roundhay Park Lakes**, 4m NE. Leeds and Dist ASA have fishing; dt from local tackle shops. Larger lake (Waterloo) contains pike, perch, roach. tench, carp, etc; small lake stocked with carp, bream and roach. Leeds Amal has extensive fishing on Ouse and tributaries, canals and lakes, dt for many waters; full details from Hon Sec. Also trout at Pool and Arthington *(see Ouse (Yorks)-Wharfe).* Castleford & Dist SA fish Fairburn Ings and Fairburn Cut. Dt £1 on site. At **Swinsty** and **Fewston**, 7m from **Otley**, are YWS reservoirs, containing trout; visitors' dt can be had at Reservoir Lodge, Fewston. Minnow and fly only. Tackle shops: Abbey Match Anglers, 38 Commercial Rd; Kirkgate Anglers, 95 Kirkgate; Bob's Tackle Shop, 1A Chapel Lane, Garforth; Headingly Angling Centre, 58 North Lane.

Bradford (W Yorks). Aire, 7m N. Bradford City AA has extensive rights here and on water on the canals at **Apperley Bridge** and near Skipton; on **Wharfe, Ure** and **Swale**, reservoirs and lakes. Assc shares Saltaires length of **Leeds and Liverpool Canal** with Bradford No 1 AA. Bradford No 1 AA has water on Wharfe, **Aire, Swale, Ure, Nidd, Derwent**, and reservoirs. Membership £24, entrance £18, conc. Addingham AA have water on **Wharfe** (Addingham, 2m; Denton and Ben Rhydding, 2½m; trout to 3lb (av 1½lb) and grayling) and three reservoirs holding trout and perch. Members only st £85. Waiting list. Tackle shops:Watercraft Products, 899 Harrogate Rd; Westgate Anglers, 63 Westgate; Wibsey Angling Centre, 208 High St, Wibsey, Bradford; Richmonds, 110 Morley St.

Bingley, Saltaire (W Yorks). Trout, coarse fish; Bingley AC has 1m through Bingley coarse fish; restocked annually with trout; 2m of Leeds and Liverpool Canal, with large carp and others. St £17 and dt £2, from tackle shop. Club has good trout fishing on **Sunnydale Reservoir**, Eastmorton; trout and coarse fish, dt £3.50; also two dams and beck. Trout waters are for members only. Bradford No 1 AA has two lengths, left bank, along Bingley Cricket and Football Fields, d/s. Members only. Excellent trout preserve in **Myrtle Park**; water restocked; dt 75p. Dt £1 for **Leeds & Liverpool Canal**. Saltaire AA (HQ Ring of Bells, Bradford Rd, Shipley) Saltaire AA has 4m stretch of Aire, mixed fishery, dt water, best match bag 1997, 29lbs chub; and **Tong Park Dam**, brown and rainbow trout, dt £4 from Shipley Angling Centre. From Bankfield Hotel downstream to Baildon Bridge (both banks, except Roberts Park) is Bradford No 1 water.

Keighley (W Yorks). Trout, grayling, coarse fish, chub plentiful. Sport improved after restocking. Keighley AC has 14m; st £17 (concessions to ladies, juniors, OAP) dt £2 for R Aire only. Trout to 5 lbs; best May-June and Sept. Club also has fishing on the **Leeds-Liverpool Canal, Whitefields Reservoir**, stocked with carp, tench, roach and perch, and, for members only, **Roberts Pond** (large tench, carp, pike), **Sugden End Reservoir**, Crossroads, (large trout, roach, perch, and tench, dt £3.50) and the **R**

Worth, trout. *(See also Yorkshire lakes, reservoirs, etc)*. Club also has water at Stockbridge and at Riddlesden, dt £2. Tackle shops: K & L Tackle, 131 Mornington St; Willis Walker, 109 Cavendish Street, Keighley.

Cononley (W Yorks). Trout, perch, chub, roach, dace, bream, grayling; dt after June 1, for Bradford City AA water, dt £2 from Post Office or tackle shops from 16 June. Dt from tackle shops.

Skipton (N Yorks). Trout, grayling, pike, chub, roach, perch, dace and bream. At Skipton, Skipton AA has three miles of fishing, mainly both banks; st £40 (entrance fee £15), dt £3, from Hon Sec. or tackle shops. Association also has rights on **Embsay Reservoir** (trout), **Whinnygill Reservoirs** (trout and coarse fish) dt, and beck fishing on Eller Beck at Skipton. Bradford City AA water begins on both banks below Skipton water; about 7m in all. Near Skipton at **Kilnsey Park**, are two trout lakes of 3 acres. Tel: 01756 752150. Dt £13, £9.50. Bradford No 1 AA has **Bradley**, **Broughton** and **Sandbeds** fisheries, left bank. Members only. Hotels: Highfield, Devonshire.

Bellbusk (N Yorks). Trout; preserved by owners. Lakes: **Conniston House**; trout. **Eshton Tarn**, 2m NE; pike. **Malham Tarn**, 8m N; trout and perch; tickets *(see Ribble-Settle)*

CALDER (tributary of Aire): Good coarse fishing from Brighouse to Sowerby Bridge.

Halifax (W Yorks). Calder 2m S. Clubs: Halifax and Dist AC (dams); Dean Clough & Ryburn AS have fishing on Calder, **Calder And Hebble Navigation**, and elsewhere. Dt from Jewsons (*below*). Other societies: Brighouse AA; Friendly AC, The Friendly Inn, Ovenden. Ripponden Flyfishers have good trout fishing in **Ryburn Reservoir**, Ripponden. Brighouse AA and Bradford No 1 AA control 14m on Calder above and below **Brighouse**; heavily restocked and now provides sport with good-quality roach. St £24 + £18 joining fee from D B Arnett, 49 Templars Way, Bradford. No dt. Brighouse AA also has water on canal and gravel pits. Tackle shop: A J Jewson, 1 Westgate, HX1 1DJ, has tickets and membership for local assc waters. Hotels: Imperial Crown; Calder & Hebble Inn; Black Horse Inn, Brighouse.

Hebden (W Yorks). At **Todmorden**

(Yorks, postal address Lancs), The Todmorden AS has mixed coarse fishing which includes the **Rochdale Canal**, within the Todmorden boundary, **New Mill Dam, Grove Lodge, R Calder, Chatham Reservoir**, Croft Head Fishery, **Littleborough**; all waters members only, except Clivinger Fishponds, dt £3 from Clivinger Petrol Station, and Grove Lodge, dt £2 from Round House Newsagents, Littleborough. Annual membership, £20, plus £10, conc, from Tackle dealers (*below*), or those in Burnley and Rochdale. **Calder and Hebble Navigation**: from Salterhebble Top Lock, through Brighouse, Lower Hopton Bridge, Thornhill, to upstream of Ganny Lock, the following clubs have water: Dean Clough & Ryburn AS (2½m, dt), Mackintosh AC, Brighouse AA, Bradford No. 1, Thornhill C & BC, Unity AC. Unity AC also have fishing on R Aire and R Calder, members only on most waters, but dt for good coarse fishing on **Leeds and Liverpool Canal**, £2, conc. Tackle shop: Todmorden Angling Services, 10 Union Street South, Todmorden. Hotel: Queen.

COLNE (tributary of Calder):

Huddersfield (W Yorks). Holme Valley PA fishes **R Calder** from Battyeford to Mirfield, Magdale Dam and pond at Holmfirth. Dt on river and pond from tackle shops. Facilities for the disabled. **Hill Top, Sparth**, and **Longwood Compensation Reservoirs, Huddersfield Narrow Canal**, all Slaithwaite & Dist AC waters, dt obtainable. Tickets from Chris Roberts, 98 Northgate; Angling Centre, 22 Chapel Hill; Woodys, 13 Britannia Road, Slaithewaite; Hotel: Huddersfield and many others.

Slaithwaite (W Yorks). Slaithwaite and Dist AC has fly only trout fishery from Marsden to Slaithwaite, no fishing in village centre, then east stretch from Linthwaithe Steps, all members only, no dt; **Narrow Canal**, Slaithwaite to Bargate and three other stretches, three reservoirs, dams and ponds; trout, coarse fish; st £18 + £5 joining, conc, enquiries to D Rushforth, 122 Longwood Gate, Longwood, Hudds. Tackle shop: Chris Roberts, 22 Chapel Hill, Huddersfield.

HOLME (tributary of Colne);

Holmfirth (W Yorks). Holme Valley Piscatorials have water from Holmfirth to steps Mill, Honley, except 50 yard stretch by old Robinson Mill Dam. Membership £15, conc, dt on some club waters. Slaithwaite & Dist AC fishes most of stretch from Holmebridge to Bottoms Dam, river is extremely shallow and overhung, with many small wild trout. Members only. **Holmstyes Reservoir**; trout (Huddersfield 8m) preserved by Huddersfield AA. St £38. **Boshaw Reservoir** (Huddersfield 8m); preserved as above.

DERWENT: Rises in high moors and flows almost to coast near Scarborough where it turns south and enters estuary of Ouse. Its upper reaches, most easily reached from Scarborough, are trout and grayling waters *(see Ayton)*. Lower down coarse fish predominate, barbel included.

Wressle (N Humberside). Coarse fish free, some access.

Breighton (N Humberside); ns Wressle 1m. Bubwith 1m. Chub, dace, pike, etc; fishing free.

Bubwith (N Humberside). Coarse fish; Howden and Dist AC: 4m controlled by Mike Redman, 2 Meadowfield, Breighton Rd, Bubwith YO8 7DZ, 01757 288891.

Ellerton; roach, perch, dace, bream, chub, eels and pike; flatfish lower down. For Ellerton Landing, 2m, Aughton, 1m, Bubwith, 1m, dt from White Swan Inn; V G Shop; Mike Redman, 2 Meadowfield, all bubwith, or Boot and Shoe, Ellerton.

East Cottingwith (N Yorks); ns High Field, 4m. Coarse fish (pike and chub very good). York AA controls East Cottingwith Water (2m) and 10m of good coarse fishing on **Pocklington Canal**. Dt from secretary. At **Thorganby**, on other side of Derwent, Ferry Boat Inn has day tickets for approximately 1½m of river. Very good pike fishing.

Pocklington (N Yorks). **Pocklington Canal**; Well stocked with bream, roach, perch, pike, etc. York AA water. Dt from Canal Head; College Arms, Beilby; Melbourne Arms, Melbourne; and The Cottage at Coats Bridge.

Ellerton Landing (N Yorks). Mixed fishing Hotel: White Swan, Bubwith.

Kexby (N Yorks). Pike, chub, etc. York and Leeds Amalgamated Societies have water; members only.

Low Catton (N Yorks). Coarse fish. Bradford No 1 AA has good length of water on left bank; members only.

Stamford Bridge (N Yorks). Excellent for roach, pike, chub, dace. York and Dist Amal has fishing on good length down to Kexby Brickworks and length at Stamford Bridge Bottom, acquired from Leeds

ASA; also pits. Dt at cafes in Stamford Bridge.

Howsham (N Yorks). Coarse fishing. York and Dist AA has water on Derwent and Barton Hill Beck; Bradford No 1 AA has left bank at Howsham Wood; members only.

Kirkham Abbey (N Yorks). Coarse fish, some trout. Leeds and York Amalgamations have water; members only. Scarborough Mere AC has approx 1,300 yds north bank u/s from bridge. Members only.

Castle Howard (N Yorks). **Castle Howard Great Lake** contains specimen coarse fish, including pike, perch, tench, bream, roach and bank fishing only. For further details, see *'Yorkshire Lakes.'*

Huttons Ambo (Yorks). Roach, pike, dace, eels, gudgeon, grayling, perch and few trout. South bank, 1m down and 1m up, held by Malton and Norton AC, no dt, membership £15 pa. North bank held by Huttons Ambo AC for 2m down and 2m up; membership, for people resident within 10m Malton, £5 pa. Dt £1.50 from village post office. 1,500 lbs bream stocked in Nov 1996, 1lb-6lb. Upper derwent Preservation Society stocked 3,000 6"-10" roach in April 1997 and intend to repeat this over the next few years.

Malton (Yorks). Coarse fish, mainly roach. Malton and Norton AC. Waters extend to 1m below Huttons Ambo. Membership discretionary, st £15, wt £3.50, dt 75p issued by Hon Sec, and N & C Swift, Castlegate, Malton. York and Dist AA has 5½m at Old Malton to Ryemouth; st £18, dt £1.80. Contact John Lane, 39 Lowfields Drive, Acomb, York YO2 3DQ, tel: 01904 783178. Good deal of free water on Derwent and Rye. Tackle shops: J Anderson & Son, Market Place; and C Swift, Castlegate (tickets for Malton & Norton AC waters). Hotel: Green Man.

Rillington (Yorks). Derwent, 1m N. Coarse fish; Leeds Amal water, st £21, dt £1.50. Scampston Beck, 1m E, private. Rye, 2m N. Costa Beck, 3m N.

Yedingham (Yorks). Coarse fish. Dt at Providence Inn for Leeds Amal waters. Inn also has private stretch. Foul Bridge Farm issue dt.

Ganton (Yorks). Chub, pike, dace, grayling; dt for 1m each way from Hay Bridge, from Mr and Mrs Seller, Bogg Hall Farm, at first house across railway crossing at Ganton. Ruston Beck, 2m W. Dt waters at **Seamer** (Malton Rd), from house by stream.

Ayton (Yorks). Some good trout water, Scarborough Mere AC has **Scarborough Mere**, just outside town; coarse fish; dt £2; mere restocked regularly. About 2m trout fishing from Ayton towards Ganton controlled by Leeds Amal; no tickets.

Hackness (Yorks). Derwent AC, controls 10m of trout (brown and rainbow) and grayling fishing down to **East Ayton**, for part of which dt at £20 are obtainable from July 1 to Sept 30. Farther up, above Langdale End Bridge (3m both banks), dt at £8 from April 1 to Sept 30. Fishing one fly only, wet or dry, is club rule on all water. Tickets from Grange Hotel (rod for residents on 8m of Derwent). Sunday fishing reserved for members and guests on lower club water, and all fishing between Hilla Green bridge and Langdale End bridge exclusively reserved to members and guests. Size limit for trout 10 in; limited two brace per day. Wading allowed.

FOSS BECK (tributary of Derwent). Fishing station: **Fangfoss** (Yorks); fishing private.

SPITTLE BECK (tributary of Derwent)

Barton Hill (Yorks). Derwent, 2m E. Whitecarr Beck, 4m SE. Loppington Beck, 4m SE. Swallowpits Beck, 5m SE at Scrayingham. York and Dist AA have trout water **Barton Hill Beck**.

RYE (tributary of Derwent): Trout, grayling, other coarse fish.

Ryton (Yorks). Scarborough Mere AC has 5 fields at Ryton Bridge: trout, grayling and coarse fish, including barbel. Members only.

Newsham Bridge (Yorks). Approx 1½/2m from Great Habton, u/s right bank, and 1m d/s both banks, Bradford No 1 AA water, members only.

Butterwick (Yorks). Trout, coarse fish. Scarborough Mere AC has stretch, members only.

PICKERING BECK (tributary of Rye) and Costa Beck (chalk stream). Trout, grayling.

Pickering (Yorks). About 1m of free fishing in town; private above, preserved below (3m) by Pickering FA; fly only; membership limited to 120. Water also on **Costa Beck** and **Oxfold Becks**, trout and grayling, and Duchy of Lancaster water, **Newbridge**. Two trout lakes. Dt for members' guests only. Club HQ: Bay Horse Hotel. Brown trout fishing at Hazelhead

Lake, Newgate Foot, Saltersgate, Pickering YO18 7NR, tel: 01751 460215; tickets from farmhouse B & B. Pickering Trout Lake, Newbridge Rd, Pickering YO18 8JJ, tel: 01751 474219: open all year, dt from £4. Tackle shop and flies on site. Scarborough Mere AC has 6m on **Rye** near Pickering and Bradford No 1 have **Newsham Bridge** fishing on Rye, near Great Habton. Hotels: White Swan, Black Swan, Forest and Vale, Crossways.

SEVEN (tributary of Rye): Trout, grayling; some coarse fish.

Newsham Bridge (Yorks). York and Dist AA has water on Seven and Rye; no dt.

Marton (Yorks). Private from mill to Marton; below Marton some free water; grayling, pike, chub, dace and a few trout. Tackle shop in Malton, 12m.

Sinnington (Yorks). Seven AC has 2½m downstream from the main road; brown, rainbow trout, some grayling; members only, long waiting list. Coarse fishing mainly below large weir and bottom farm.

WATH BECK (tributary of Rye):

Slingsby (Yorks). Trout; preserved. Rye, NE.

DOVE-IN-FARNDALE (tributary of Rye):

Kirby Moorside (N Yorks). Dove-in-Farndale, 1m E; trout; private. Dt for stretches downstream of Kirby Moorside from some of the farms. Hodge Beck, in Sleightholme Dale, 1m W, trout only. Hotel: King's Head.

THORNTON BECK (tributary of Derwent):

Thornton-le-Dale (N Yorks). Trout and grayling; preserved. Pickering Beck, 3m W. Derwent, 3m S. Hotels: The Hall; The Buck; all Thornton-le-Dale.

WHARFE: Rises on Cam Fell and flows 60m south-east to join Ouse near Cawood. Trout in upper reaches, with coarse fish downstream.

Ryther (N Yorks); ns Ulleskelf, 3m. Castleford and Dis ASA has water; mainly coarse fish. Hotel: Ryther Arms.

Ulleskelf (N Yorks). Coarse fish; preserved by Leeds Amal; dt £1.50 and B&B from Ulleskelf Arms LS24 9DW (01937 832136).

Tadcaster (N Yorks). Trout, chub and dace, good head of barbel perch and bream; preserved by Tadcaster Angling and Preservation Association on both banks downstream from road bridge, ¾m east bank, and 1½m west bank Grimston Park; st £15; dt £2, jun 50%. Tickets from Hon Sec; The Bay Horse; Newsagent; or Pet and Aquatic Centre.

Boston Spa (W Yorks). Trout, grayling other coarse fish (chub, barbel and pike good; bream introduced) Most rights held by Boston Spa AC. Dt £2 from Lower Wharfe Anglers, Boston Spa. Club members (who must live within 3m of Boston Spa Post Office) allowed guests at current cost of dt and guest must fish with member on non-ticket waters. Club stocks water with trout and grayling of 12 in or over. Limit two trout, one grayling, or vice-versa; trout 12 in. May best month for trout and August for barbel and chub.

Wetherby (W Yorks). Wetherby and Dist AC water (stocked with trout and coarse fish) extends from Collingham Beck to Wetherby Weir, south bank (about 350 yards in Collingham Wood, south bank is private). Club also has four fields between golf course and playing fields, north bank. This water is open for visitors on st (above weir), and dt. Members only below and on weir, but visitors may fish if accompanied by a member. Same charge as above. Dt from: The Paper Shop, Market Place, Wetherby; Star Garage, Collingham Bridge. No legitimate bait or lure barred. Trout limit 11 in. Tackle shops: J R Country & Pet Supplies, & Horsefair; Lower Wharfe Ang-

Check before you go

While every effort has been made to ensure that the information given in **Where to Fish** *is correct, the position is continually changing, and anglers are urged, in their own interests, to make preliminary enquiries before travelling to selected venues. This is especially important with reference to prices quoted. Inevitably the rate of inflation is affecting stability in this quarter. Anglers' attention is also drawn to the fact that the hotels mentioned under the various fishing stations do not necessarily have water of their own. Any amendments or further data for inclusion in subsequent editions, and any comments, will be welcome.*

ling Centre, 236 High St, Boston Spa.

Collingham (W Yorks). Wetherby AC has water here; trout and coarse fish including barbel, grayling and good dace.

Pool (W Yorks). Trout, dace, chub; preserved by the Leeds and Dist ASA which has 5m of fishing from River **Washburn** to Castley Beck on left bank. Dt £2.50 from Leeds and Otley tackle shops. Members of Leeds AA, small private club, may fish Harewood Estate preserves, 3m right bank, 2m left bank.

Otley (W Yorks). Otley AC hold 2m left bank and 2½m right bank below Otley Bridge. Fishing for members only, no dt. Bradford No 1 AA fish two lengths on left and right bank, members only. Dt £2.50 for Leeds & Dist ASA **Knotford Lagoon**, near Otley; large carp and other coarse fish; stocked. Also some r trout. Bradford No 1 AA has second Knotford Lagoon. At Yeadon (6m) Airboro' and Dist AA has **Yeadon Tarn**, Cemetery Rd; Good catches of roach, perch, carp, tench. Dt £1.50 from newsagent in same road. Tackle shop in Otley: Angling and Country Sports, 36 Cross Green, Pool Road, Otley, tel: Otley 462770.

Burley and **Askwith** (W Yorks). Trout, grayling, chub, dace. Bradford clubs have rights for members only.

Addingham (W Yorks). Trout, grayling; Bradford City AA has water here. Bradford No 1 AA has four lengths on left and right bank, and Steven Bank Fishery, no dt obtainable. Bradford Waltonians have water at **Denton** and **Ben Rhydding**; also 4 reservoirs including **Chelker Reservoir** near here. Tickets £8 to members' guests, only; membership £205, subscription £205. Bradford No 1 AA has some left bank at Denton and right bank at Ben Rhydding, members only. Keighley AC has water; dt from Hon Sec. Addingham AA has both banks u/s from High Mill at Addingham to Farfield Cottages on left bank, and right bank of Kexgill Beck, with trout and grayling. Dt £6 from Addingham PO. Waiting list for membership, apply Hon Sec.

Ilkley (W Yorks). Ilkley and Dist AA have water from Old Bridge to Stepping Stones, both banks, with trout, grayling dace and chub. Dt £6.50 (April 15-Sept 30 inc) from Tourist Information Centre, Station Rd, Ilkley LS29 8HA, or Runnymead News Agency, 297 Leeds Rd, Ben Rhydding, Ilkley. Membership: st £39 + £39 joining, jun, OAP ½, some vacancies. Club also has two coarse ponds. Hotels: Riverside, Craiglands, Cow and Calf.

Bolton Abbey (N Yorks). Trout and grayling. 5 miles stretch (both banks) on R Wharfe, fly only. Bailiffed, concentrating on wild trout fishery, light stocking only. Trout April 1-Sept 30. Grayling if caught to be released. St £230, wt £60, dt £14.50. Limit 2 fish of not less than 10 ins. Fishing not recommended on Sundays and Bank Holidays. Apply Estate Office, Bolton Abbey, Skipton, BD23 6EX, tel: 01756 710227. Hotel, Devonshire Arms, Bolton Abbey.

Burnsall (N Yorks). Trout (av ½lb-1lb; many large fish), grayling; preserved by Appletreewick, Barden and Burnsall AC from Linton Stepping Stones, below Grassington, to Barden Bridge, some 7m. Dt for trout, June-Sept (excluding June and Sept week-ends) £18; wt £90, fly only; limit three brace; grayling dt £10 Nov-Jan (fly only). Waters re-stocked regularly with trout from ½ to 1lb and over. Tickets from Red Lion Hotel and Fell Hotel, Burnsall, and Burnsall Village Store. For special juvenile ticket, apply to River watcher, Bob Mason, Conistone House, Main Street, Burnsall, Skipton BD23 6BU, tel: 01756 720650. Bradford City AA has water at **Appletreewick**; members only.

Grassington (N Yorks). Trout (av ¾lb), grayling (av ¾lb); preserved by Linton, Threshfield and Grassington AC for 2½m both banks (also in Captain Beck and Linton and Threshfield Becks until August 31); wt £50, dt £12 for fly-fishing only. Long waiting list for membership. No night or Sunday fishing. No canoeing. Trout season: April 1 to Sept 30 inclusive. Grayling only from Oct 1 to Feb 28; st £20, dt £5; fly only during Oct. Fly only tickets £16, excl Sunday, from Dales Book Centre, 33 Main St, or Black Horse Hotel, Grassington. Saltaire AA also has left bank at **Linton**, no dt. Fishing best in May. **Eller Beck**, **Hebden Beck**, 2m E. Lakes: **Blea Beck** dams 4m NE. Hotels: Black Horse (Saltaire AA HQ), and others.

Kilnsey (N Yorks). Brown trout. Preserved by Kilnsey AC of 65 members, from Beckamonds to Yockenthwaite and from 1m above Starbotton down to Netherside 2m below Kilnsey; artificial fly only, limit three brace over 10". St £420 + £75 entrance fee, from Hon Sec; wt £100, dt

£20, daily, between 9am and 10am (number limited, and none on Sundays or Bank Holidays), from Keeper, C S Nesbitt, Tennant Arms, Kilnsey, via Skipton BD23 5PS, tel: 01756 752310. Hotels: Tennant Arms, Falcon.

Buckden (N Yorks). Trout. Bradford City AA has 2m; dt £3.45 from Dalesgarth Holiday Cott. Other fishing for guests at Buck Inn; dt issued.

SKIRFARE (tributary of Wharfe); well stocked with brown trout, average 1lb.

Arncliffe (N Yorks). Some Skirfare Fishing preserved by Kilnsey AC, dt water *(see Kilnsey)*. 2½m on Skirfare and 1½m on **Cowside Beck** open to guests at Falcon Inn *(see advt)*. Dt £7, no Sunday fishing.

FOSS (tributary of Ouse): Trout.

Earswick (N Yorks). Free fishing on right bank. Owners are Joseph Rowntree Trust.

Strensall (N Yorks). Foss Navigation Cut, 1m NE. **Whitecar Beck**, 1m NE. York and Dist Amal has coarse fishing here and at **Towthorpe**; members only.

NIDD: Trout and grayling, with coarse fish from Birstwith downstream in increasing numbers.

Nun Monkton (N Yorks). Coarse fish. Bradford No 1 AA has 1m good coarse fishing here on left bank, both banks at **Ramsgill** and left bank at **Summerbridge**, for members only.

Moor Monkton (N Yorks). Leeds ASA has 1m mixed fishery, members only.

Kirk Hammerton (N Yorks). Coarse fish. Following on Harrogate AA water *(see Goldsborough)* almost all fishing downstream to where Nidd joins the Ouse controlled by Leeds and York Amalgamations. York Amal holds York side of river from Skip Bridge on Boroughbridge Road upstream for about 2m and also for about 1m above Hammerton Mill dam. Tickets from York tackle shops; and Aykroyd, Skip Bridge Filling Station, Green Hammerton.

Cowthorpe (N Yorks). Coarse fish. Stretch of 1m, one bank, belongs to Old Oak Inn, tickets issued; Sunday fishing. Licences and tackle sold in Wetherby.

Goldsborough (N Yorks). Trout, grayling and mixed coarse fishing, including pike and barbel. Left hand bank at Goldsborough, Knaresborough Piscatorials. From Little Ribston downstream through Walshford Bridge to first meadow below Cattall Bridge belongs to Harrogate AA. Association also has both banks of **Crimple Beck** from confluence with Nidd above Walshford Bridge up to Spofforth. Waiting list for membership. Dt issued by Hon Sec to members' guests only. Water otherwise strictly preserved.

Knaresborough (N Yorks). Trout, grayling and coarse fish, including barbel. Practically all fishing in vicinity controlled by Knaresborough AC and Knaresborough Piscatorials. Former issues st £25 and dt £3 for good stretch upstream from Little Ribston village. Club also owns fly only trout lake in Knaresborough area, members only. Full membership £110. Knaresborough Piscatorials fish 8 miles of Nidd, plus various stretches of Wharfe, Ure, Ouse, and Swale, mostly in Knaresborough area. Trout, chub, barbel, roach, bream, perch, rudd, dace, pike, may be caught in club waters. Fees, £55 pa, conc. York Amal has good stretches here. Tickets from M H & C Johnson, 2 Briggate HG5 8BH (01423 863065); also from C J Fishing Tackle *(see Harrogate)*. **Farmire Trout Fishery**, 12 acres, at Farmire House, Stang Lane, Farnham, Kna-

Weirpools concentrate fish and have generated their own techniques for catching them. These anglers on the Nidd at Knaresborough might be offering silkweed in small clumps (and the small invertebrates harboured there) scraped from the sill with the hook thus baited. *Photo: Arthur Oglesby.*

resborough HG5 9JW, tel: 01423 866417, has b and r trout fishing. Dt £18 4 fish, £12 2 fish, boats £10.

Ripley, Nidd Bridge (N Yorks). Trout, grayling and coarse fish. On right bank from about 300 yds below Harrogate-Ripon road bridge to Killinghall and downstream to Sewerage Works, about 2½m, held by Harrogate and Claro Anglers. Downstream for 2m river privately owned. Knaresborough AC holds left bank d/s to Scotton, fly only, members only.

Birstwith (N Yorks). Trout and grayling above Birstwith Dam upstream to upper reaches of Nidd. Below Dam there are also coarse fish. Knaresborough AC has about 1,000 yd of right bank downstream from Hampsthwaite Bridge. Members and their guests only.

Darley (N Yorks). Trout and grayling water, preserved by Harrogate Fly Fishers. No tickets.

Pateley Bridge (N Yorks). Trout and grayling. From 1½m above Pateley Bridge down to **Summerbridge**, 11m total, owned and rented by Nidderdale AC, who hold nearly all water, both banks, except short pieces here and there which are private; also Scar House Reservoir. Dt £8, £6 Scar House only (conc for juv), at Royal Oak, Dacre Banks, or local post offices in Lofthouse, Pateley Bridge, Glasshouses and Summerbridge. Anglers must obtain tickets before fishing.

Gouthwaite (N Yorks). River enters **Gouthwaite Reservoir**, privately owned and fished; no permits. Below reservoir Nidd private.

CRIMPLE (tributary of Nidd). This river is now private fishing.

Harrogate (N Yorks). Trout and coarse fishing, within easy reach of town in Nidd, Wharfe and Ure, and stillwaters. Information, club yearbooks and tickets from C J Fishing Tackle, tel: 01423 525000 (*see below*). Harrogate & Claro CAA run matches, visitors welcome. Harrogate Flyfishers preserve excellent trout and grayling water at Darley. Coarse fishing at Newby Hall, **Skelton-on-Ure**, st £23, dt £2. Tel: 322583. Hotels: Crown, Majestic, Old Swan, St George, Cairn, Prospect. Tackle shops: C J Fishing Tackle, 182 Kings Road; Linsley Bros, 55 Tower St; Orvis, 17 Parliament St, all Harrogate.

KYLE: Coarse fish.

Tollerton (N Yorks). Coarse fishing free down to Alne. Ouse at Aldwark, 4m W, and Linton Lock, 3m S and 7m NE, at Stillington.

URE (or **YORE**): Noted for grayling, but also holds good trout. Coarse fish from Middleham downstream.

Boroughbridge (N Yorks). Fine coarse fishing (especially chub and roach, bream increasing); few trout and grayling; Boroughbridge and Dist AC, issues dt £2 (weekdays only, from June 1-Feb 27) sold at Post Office and Horsefair Grocers. At **Aldborough** Bradford City AA has 6m (roach, perch, dace, pike, chub); no dt, limited privilege tickets for members only. Bradford No 1 AA also has Langthorpe stretch, left bank. Harrogate and Claro CAC have Ure water at Boroughbridge, with chub, dace and pike. Dt £3, from tackle shops in Boroughbridge, Harrogate and Knaresborough. Unity AC has water here, no dt, st £10, conc, from Wibsey Angling Centre, Main St, Wibsey; or Richmonds, Morley St, Bradford. Hotel: Boroughbridge Social Club.

Ripon (N Yorks). Trout, dace, pike, perch, chub, barbel, roach; preserved for 6m both banks by Ripon Piscatorial Assn. Association also has Racecourse Lake and 6m on **R Laver**. Visitors dt £4, wt £12, st £45. Ripon AC has **R Skell** at Ripon and 1m on Ure above city. Limited dt £5. These and Piscatorial Assn tickets from Ripon Angling Centre. **Ripon Canal**, coarse fishing dt £2, conc, from Angling Centre. Lakes: Queen Mary's Ponds; coarse fish; Bradford No 1 AA. Roger's Pond, coarse dt £4 from Angling Centre. **Leighton Reservoir**, Swinton Estate, Ripon, tel: 01765 89224 or 89713; 100 acre trout fishery, dt £12-£6, from fishing hut. Tackle shop: Ripon Angling Centre, 58/9 North Street, HE4 1EN.

Tanfield (N Yorks). Trout, grayling; preserved for about 5m, mostly both banks, by Tanfield AC. Guests must be accompanied by member. Full time bailiff employed. Long waiting list. Two trout fisheries at West Tanfield: Bellflask, brown and rainbow, dt £20, 4 fish. Run as fishery and nature reserve, barbless hooks. Michael Moreland, tel: 01677 470716; Tanfield Lake, brown and rainbow, 11½ acres, disabled access. Dt £9-£4, tel: 01677 470385.

Masham (N Yorks). Trout (stocked), grayling. 6½m west bank belongs to Swinton Estate. Limited st. Details from Estate Office, Swinton, Masham. Well stocked 2½m stretch of Swinton water fished by Masham AC; brown trout and grayling; waiting list. St £125 + £30 Joining. Jun conc. Apply to Mr A R Proud, River Keeper, Park St, Masham; tel: 01765 689361. Yorkshire Flyfishers hold Clifton Castle water (about 2m left bank) above Masham. No tickets. Tackle, information, and large selection of flies, from A Plumpton, Hairdresser, Silver St. Hotel: King's Head. **Leighton Reservoir** near here. *See Yorkshire Lakes.*

Cover Bridge (N Yorks). Trout, grayling. East Witton Estate issue dt on **R Cover** from Hullo Bridge to Cover Bridge. Mostly both banks, fly only, £2. Tickets from Cover Bridge Inn, Middleham.

Middleham (N Yorks). Trout, chub, grayling. Bradford No 1 AA has right bank here, and left bank at **Langthorpe**, members only. Fishing may be had in Leeds ASA waters at Middleham Deeps and 1m upstream from Middleham Bridge both banks by dt from Old Horn Inn, Spennithorne. Excellent barbel, chub and grayling; few large trout; odd salmon. Dt £1 from Cover Bridge Inn for trout and grayling fishing on Cover. White Swan, Middleham, has tickets.

Leyburn (N Yorks). Grayling, trout, coarse fish. Two dt from Blue Lion, E Witton, for E Witton Estate water on Ure from Ulshaw Bridge to Harker Beck, 1¾m S bank, fly only. Tackle shops: Wray Bros, Town Hall (also licences). Hotels: Bolton Arms, Golden Lion.

Redmire (N Yorks). Trout, grayling; preserved. Restocked; fly only. All fishing now by st only (£150); numbers limited; apply Estate Office, Leyburn DL8 5EW. Trout best April, May and June; grayling Oct and Nov. Hotels: King's Arms, Redmire; White Swan, Middleham; Rose and Crown, Bainbridge; Wensleydale Heifer, Westwittom.

Aysgarth (N Yorks). Trout, grayling. Bradford AA has approx 2m from footbridge, both banks, 3¾m both banks at **Worton Bridge**; Palmer Flatt Hotel has short stretch. Wensleydale AA water extends from 2m west of Hawes to Worton Bridge, plus ¾m beyond on north bank only. Tickets are obtainable, £6, conc. HQ, Rose and Crown Hotel, Bainbridge.

Askrigg (N Yorks). Trout, grayling; preserved by Wensleydale AA, *see above*. Tickets from King's Arms or Victoria Arms, Worton. Hotel: King's Arms.

Bainbridge (N Yorks); Wensleydale AA water includes 6m on Ure, all 2m on west bank of **R Bain**, and first mile from confluence with R Ure on east bank. For permits, *see above*.

Hawes (N Yorks). Trout, grayling; preserved with tributaries, from headwaters to 2m downstream of Hawes, by Hawes and High Abbotside AA. The fishing is pleasant, peaceful and not crowded. Sunday fishing, no ground bait. Tickets from Visitors st £40, wt £24, dt £8, conc, from Hon Sec; from Lowis Country Wear, Riverside House, Bridge End, Hawes DL8 3NM; The Gift Shop; or Board Hotel Main St. Assn also has rights on Cotterdale, Hardraw, Duerley and Snaizeholme Becks, all both banks, trout and grayling. Below Hawes Wensleydale AA has several miles of excellent water. Disabled anglers may fish Widdale Beck at Apperset, near Hawes. Hotel: White Hart.

SWALE: Good chub and barbel water. Trouting best in upper reaches, water improving..

Helperby (N Yorks). Coarse fish; right bank from Swing Bridge to Myton Plantation controlled by Leeds Amal. Helperby & Brafferton AC have left bank from footbridge d/s for ¾m, also **Fawdington Fishery**, from ½m above Thornton Bridge, approx 1½m u/s to Fawdington Beck mouth. Chub, barbel, dace, pike, roach, perch. Dt for both these waters, 16 Jun-14 March, £2.50 from Plowman-Render Groceries, Main St; or Oak Tree Inn, Helperby. Hotel: The Farmers Inn.

Topcliffe (N Yorks). Noted coarse fishing centre; especially good for chub and barbel. Thirsk AC has Skipton and Baldersby fishing, dt from Thirsk Anglers Centre, Town End, Thirsk. Bradford No 1 AA has 900 yds at **Catton**, and further water at Topcliffe, members only. Black Bull Hotel, Topcliffe YO7 3PB has water. Assn of Teeside and Dist Acs has 1½m at **Sand Hutton**; members only **Cod Beck**; trout; preserved by Bradford City AA; apply Hon Sec for permits.

Pickhill (N. Yorks). Coarse fish; trout. Bradford No 1 AA fishes 1,800 yards at Scarborough farm, right bank. Members only. Leeds Amalgamation has a ¾m stretch at **Ainderby**.

Maunby (N Yorks). Bradford No 1 AA has two lengths left bank, members only.

Gatenby (N Yorks). Bradford No 1 AA has three stretches of right bank here, and at Old Hall Farm. Members only.

Morton-on-Swale (N Yorks). Roach, roach, chub, dace, barbel; fishing good. Northallerton AC has 2½m left bank downstream from A684 road bridge, for which dt £3 can be had from Mrs Grainger, Morton-on-Swale.

Great Langton (N Yorks). Trout, grayling, coarse fish; Kirkby Fleetham AC has both banks for 2m downstream from Langton Bridge, linking up with Northallerton AC's water at Bramper Farm; fly only; no tickets. Membership limited, with preference given to local residents.

Catterick (N Yorks). Good mixed fishing; trout, grayling, dace, chub, barbel, few roach and pike. Trout from 8oz to 1lb; fast takers. Richmond & Dist AS has 14m of water on both banks, Richmond being the centre. Ferryhill AC also has 1½m trout and coarse fishing above and below village, good barbel, chub, grayling, no dt. Hotels: Farmers' Arms; Angel Inn.

Richmond (N Yorks). Richmond and Dist AS preserves 14 miles above and below town centre, stocked with trout, plus most coarse species. St £25, wt £15, dt £5, conc. From tackle shop, 5 Market Place or Richmond Angling Centre, 8 Temple Square, Graven Gate, Richmond.

Reeth (N Yorks). Swale; trout. Black Bull Hotel has water for residents £1 day.

Muker (N Yorks). Trout; strictly preserved. Muker Beck; trout; Thwaite Beck, 1m W; trout; free. Summer Lodge Beck, 5m E; trout; preserved.

Keld (N Yorks). Trout; plentiful but small; preserved.

GUN BECK (tributary of Swale):

Husthwaite (N Yorks). Centre for good trout fishing on **Husthwaite Beck**; dt from York tackle shops.

Coxwold (N Yorks). Hole Beck and Gun Beck preserved.

BEDALE BECK (tributary of Swale):

Leeming (N Yorks). Swale, 2m NE; preserved by Black Ox AC from A1 road to confluence with Swale, excepting only two small fields above Leeming Bridge. Trout and coarse fish. St £5 from R M Wright, 5 Lascelles Lane, Northallerton.

COD BECK (tributary of Swale); good trout water, but recent pollution of lower reaches has affected sport.

Thirsk (N Yorks). Good local fishing for barbel and chub. Thirsk AC has water on Swale and Cod Beck; dt from tackle dealer. York and Dist AA have 5½ acre lake at **Sand Hutton**, Park View. Hotels: Royal Oak, Three Tuns. Tackle shop: Thirsk Anglers Centre, 7 Sowerby Rd YO7 1HR, have river and stillwater tickets, for coarse and trout fishing, also instruction in fly fishing and fly tying. Free information on a variety of day ticket waters.

Sessay (N Yorks). Cod Beck, 2m W; Thirsk AC, Swale, 2m SW; Bradford club now has fishing on P J Till's farm (The Heights). The Oaks Fishery, nr Thirsk, three lakes with carp and other coarse species. Disabled access. David and Michael Kay, tel: 01845 501321. Inn: Railway, Dalton.

Brawith (N Yorks). Trout; preserved.

Topcliffe (N Yorks). Bradford City AA has water here, and on **Cod Beck**.

WISKE (tributary of Swale): River still troubled by pollution.

Otterington (N Yorks). Cod Beck, 2m E. Broad Beck. Sorrow Beck, 4m E.

Northallerton (N Yorks). Roach, dace, chub pike; preserved: fishing good. Northallerton AC has fishing on Wiske (members only) and on several miles of water on the Swale at Morton Bridge. *See also Morton-on-Swale.*

PARRETT

(For close seasons, licences, etc, see South West Region Environment Agency, p16)

Rises in hills on border of Somerset and Dorset, and flows into Bristol Channel near Bridgwater. Roach, bream and dace predominate. Thorney-Middle Chinnock stretch and some of tributaries hold trout. Occasional salmon and sea trout run through into Tone.

Bridgwater (Som). River tidal here. Now a Marina. **King's Sedgemoor Drain** is preserved by Bridgwater AA which has fishing ¾m above Greylake Bridge, where 18ft Rhyne enters Cary River to A38 Road bridge at Dunball. Good roach, rudd, pike, tench, bream, carp and perch. St £20, wt £8, dt £3, from tackle shops in area or Hon Sec. Other Bridgwater AA fisheries: Rivers **Parrett**, **Isle**, **Hunstspill** and **Cripps** Rivers, **North Drain** (jointly held with North Somerset AA), **South Drain** (jointly held with Glaston Manor AA), **18ft Rhyne**, **Langacre Rhyne**, **Bridgwater and Taunton Canal**, **Dunwear**, **Screech Owl**, **Combwich** and **Walrow** Lakes (carp, bream, roach, rudd, tench, perch). Season, weekly and day tickets, with concessions for jun, OAP. Permits cover all waters. Pocket maps from Hon Sec. **South Drain**, lower part, is held by North Somerset AA. Day/night coarse fishing on Westhay Lake, 3½ acres, large tench and carp. Tel: 01278 456429. Tackle shops: Somerset Angling, 74 Bath Rd; Angling Centre, Unit 1, Wye Avenue; Waynes Tackle, 61 Eastover; Enterprise Angling, Taunton Rd. Accommodation with special facilities for anglers: Admiral Blake Guest House, 58/60 Monmouth St; Brickyard Farmhouse, River Rd, Pawlett TA6 4SE. Hotels: Brookland; Friars Court.

Langport (Som). Parret; pike to 30lbs, large perch, carp, bream, roach, hybrids, tench, chub, rudd, eels. Langport AA has rights to 6½m, members of Wessex Fed, ticket holders may fish Fed waters on Parret and Isle. Ass also owns 2 acre Coombe Lake, stocked with carp, bream and others. St £10, wt £5 and dt £3, conc, obtainable from tackle shop. Stoke-sub-Hamdon AA has stretches at **West Chin-**

nock and **Thorney**. Thorney Lakes, Muchelney, Langport TA10 0DW, tel: 01458 25011, has coarse fishing, with carp to 21lb, and other species, dt £4. Tackle shop: Langport Angling Shop, North St, Langport TA10 9RP (01458 253665). Accommodation at Dolphin Hotel, Bow St (01458 250200).

Crewkerne (Som). Trout, coarse fish. Stoke-sub-Hamdon AA has trout fishing (with restocking) from Bow Mills to Hurdle Pool (trout av ¾lb); members only; coarse fishing, 12 different species including 3 types of carp, from Hurdle Pool to Thorney Mill. St £4, concessions to jun & OAP, from local tackle shops and committee members.

TONE: Trout and coarse fish above Taunton, below, most species of coarse. Weedy in summer below **Taunton** but provides first-class coarse fishing in winter.

Taunton (Som). Good coarse fishing free on town stretch. Taunton Fly Fishing Club has water on the Tone, trout and grayling, fly only. St £50 and dt for restricted areas of Tone from Topp Tackle. Taunton AA has water on **Bridgwater Canal** at Taunton; **West Sedgemoor Drain** from Pincombe Bridge, Stathe; **R Tone** fast stretch at Taunton, Creech and Ham; Ponds at Walton, Norton and Wych Lodge. St £17, wt £10, dt £4, conc, from tackle shops, *below*. Quantock Fishery, Stream Farm, Bloomfield TA5 2EN (01823 451367): 2 acre stocked rainbow trout, av 2lb. Viaduct Fishery, Cary Valley, Somerton, TA11 6LJ, (01458 74022), has trout fly fishing in 25 acre site, dt £19, 5 fish. Additional coarse fishing, dt £3. Enterprise Angling have tickets £3.50 for British Telecom pond, nr Taunton, carp, roach, skimmers. No night fishing. Tackle shops: Topp Tackle, 63 Station Rd, TA1 1PA, tel: 01823 282518; Enterprise Angling, I Grays Rd, Taunton TA1 3BA, tel: 01823 282623. Hotels: Castle (which advises visiting anglers on local facilities); County.

Hillfarrance Brook (a Tone tributary, from Hillfarrance to confluence with Tone). Trout, grayling, fly only, Taunton FFC water, members only. Axe (Chard Junction) ¾m single bank fishing below the village, fly only, Taunton FFC, members only. Axe (Axminster) ½m single bank fishing both sides of Cloakham Bridge, fly only, Taunton FFC members only. Annual subscription £50. Tickets for restricted areas from Topp Tackle.

Wellington (Som). Trout, roach, dace; trout average ½lb. Wellington AA has water from Fox Bros' works 2m up stream, and ¾m below, brown trout, grayling, roach, dace. Members only. Thereafter preserved by owners through Bradford to Taunton FFC water. Dt £2 for trout and coarse on R Tone at **Nynehead**: Mr R E Darby, Hornshay Farm, Nynehead, Wellington. Langford Lakes, Langford Budville, Wellington, tel: 01823 663166: four stocked coarse fishing ponds. Tackle, tickets and licences from Wellington Country Sports, 5 Lancer Court, High Street TA21 8SG (tel: 01823 662120).

Wiveliscombe (Som). Tone, Milverton Brook and Norton Brook; trout; banks bushed.

NORTON BROOK (tributary of Tone):

Bishops Lydeard (Som). Trout; banks overgrown.

MILVERTON BROOK (tributary of Tone).

Milverton (Som). Trout; private; banks bushed.

YEO: Coarse fish, some trout.

Long Load (Som). Good coarse fishing.

Ilchester (Som). Mainly roach, dace, good chub fishing. St and wt for 6m stretch u/s and d/s of Ilchester, plus Long Lode Drain, from A D Goddard (*see Yeovil*). Club: Ilchester AC, who have fishing on **Yeo** and **Cam** above Ilchester. Viaduct Fishery, Somerton, 2 lakes, 4 acres, mixed coarse, dt on site. Tel: 01458 74022.

Yeovil (Som). Roach, dace, chub. Yeovil and Sherborne AA have water downstream of **Sherborne Lake, Sutton Bingham Stream** from Filter Station to Yeovil Junction and R Wriggle from Yetminster to R Yeo; trout. Tackle shop A D Goddard, 27/29 Forest Hill (01935 476777) has tickets for local river and stillwater fisheries. Hotels: Mermaid; Manor; The Choughs.

ISLE: Prolific chub water; also roach, dace, etc. First ½ mile from junction with Parrett held by Wessex Federation of Anglers.

Isle Brewers (Som). Roach, chub, dace, some trout from Fivehead Road to Hambridge; Newton Abbott FA has R Ilse at Hambridge, and many coarse lakes and ponds. *See Newton Abbot*. **Ilminster** (Som). Roach, chub, dace. Chard & Dist AA water, members only, £10 membership from Chard Angling Centre. From below Ilminster to just above Fivehead River, Ilminster AA water; dt £2.50 from Hon Sec or Chard Angling Centre, 2 Holyrood St, Chard. Bathampton AA obtain fishing through exchange tickets. Contact Hon Sec.

RIBBLE

(For close seasons, licences, etc, see North West Region Environment Agency, p17)

Rises in the Pennines and flows 56 miles into the Irish Sea between St Anne's and Southport. Good coarse fishing lower down, between Great Mitton and Preston. Also coarse fishing in Church Deeps. Best salmon, sea trout, brown trout and grayling fishing is between Settle and Great Mitton. Tributary Hodder has good salmon, sea trout and brown trout fishing throughout length but much affected by water abstraction. Upper waters impounded in Stocks Reservoir. Its main tributary, the Loud, also provides good trout and sea trout fishing.

Preston (Lancs). Coarse fish, few salmon and sea trout. 2m Preston Federated Anglers water through town; st £8.50, dt £1.50, including other waters on **Ribble** and **Wyre**, and **Rufford Canal**. **Twin Lakes Trout Fishery, Croston**, 12 acres, stocked fly only rainbow and brown trout, best rainbow 15¼lb. Dt £19.50 (4 fish), ½ day £11.50 (2 fish), boats from £3.50. Tel: 01772 601093. Other local fishing: Greenhalgh Lodge Fishery, Greenhalgh Lane, Nr Kirkham PR4 3HL, tel: 01253 836348. 36 pegs coarse fishing with carp. Dt £4, one rod only; Hudson's Farm, Rawcliffe Rd, St Michaels PR3 0UH, mixed coarse fishery of 2 ponds and 2 lakes, large carp, bream tench. Further information from tackle shops in Preston: Ted Carter, 85/88 Church Street. R Crossens, 1m from Southport, fished by Southport & Dist AA. Dt from Robinsons Tackle Shop, 71 Sussex Road, Southport.

Samlesbury (Lancs). Coarse fish, few salmon and sea trout. Several miles preserved by Ribble and Wyre FA, dt from Hon Sec. Members only. Assn also has stretch of R Wyre at St Michaels on Wyre. Northern AA have water, dt £2.50 from bailiffs or tackle shops.

Balderstone (Lancs). Northern AA have 2¼m at Balderstone Hall Farm to Lower House Farm. Fishing 4 am to 11 pm. Coarse, with game fish (Mar 15-Jun 15). Dt £2.50 on bank, conc. 30p, OAP, juv.

Longridge (Lancs). Ribble, 3m SE. Hodder, 5m NE. Salmon, sea trout and trout. Loud 2m N. Most of right bank preserved by Loud and Hodder AA. Visitors' tickets issued if accompanied by member. Bolton & Dist AA have two stretches near here. No dt, but st £13, conc. £4.50, from any tackle shop in district. Prince Albert AS, Macclesfield, own several miles above M6 bridge. Warrington AA has short stretch at **Hurst Green**.

Ribchester (Yorks). Lancashire FFA have 4m here, and water at **Gisburn**; also **Hodder** at **Newton and Chaigley, Lune** at Kirkby Lonsdale and Tebay; **Irt** at Santon Bridge, all with salmon, sea trout, some browns. Tickets only to members' guests. Other local bodies are Ribchester AC, Ribchester Arms, Ribchester; Ribble Fisheries Assn, C J Heap, Moorland Rd, Langho BB6 8HA. Dt £4 for good barbel fishing at Ribchester from Spar shop or White Bull.

Mitton (Yorks); ns Whalley, 2m. Salmon, sea trout, trout and coarse fish. Environment Agency controls left bank d/s from Mitton Bridge. Salmon fishing open Feb 1-Oct 31; brown trout Mar 15-Sept 30; coarse, June 16-Mar 14. Permits Mrs Haynes, Mitton Hall Farm, Mitton Rd, Mitton, Nr Whalley, Clitheroe BB7 9PQ, tel: 01254 826002.

Clitheroe (Lancs). Trout, salmon, sea trout. Clitheroe AA Ltd fishes 3m of Ribble, mostly double bank, and 1m of **Lune**, at **Kirkby Lonsdale**. Members only, no dt. The Inn at Whitewell, in the Forest of Bowland, offers fishing to guests. By the A59 between Clitheroe and Accrington, Pine Lodge Coarse Fishery, dt £6-£5 on bank. Phone 0125 4822211 for details. Blackburn and Dist AA have several miles on Ribble and other fisheries on **Lune, Wenning, Aire, Gilpin** and reservoirs. Some dt; apply Hon Sec. Commercial Services Dept, Ribble Valley Borough Council, issues st £25 to residents for water at Brungerley and below Edisford Bridge. Wt £17 for visitors, also dt £7 for Edisford alone, from T I Centre, Market Place, Clitheroe. Tickets on offer, tel: 01200 22010. Two rods on Hodder for residents of Red Pump Hotel, Bashall Eaves; dt issued. Tackle shops: Ken Varey's Outdoor World, 4 Newmarket St,

Clitheroe; Fishing Tackle, 12-14 Southworth Street, Blackburn. Hotels: Inn at Whitewell, Old Post House; Calf's Head, Swan and Royal; Victoria.

Chatburn (Lancs). **Ribble**, 1m W; good trout, occasional salmon and sea trout. Several miles of river preserved by Clitheroe AA; limited visitors' tickets through members only. Hotels: Pendle; Manor House Cottage.

Sawley (N Yorks). On Ribble. Salmon, sea trout, trout and grayling. Trout and salmon fishing good. Several miles preserved by Yorkshire FFC (visitors' tickets through members only). Inn: Spread Eagle.

Gisburn (N Yorks). Trout, salmon. Lancashire FFA have water at Ribchester and Gisburn. Fly fishing for members only. Hotels: Park House; Stirk House.

Long Preston (N Yorks). Ribble, 1m W. Trout, grayling, odd salmon, coarse fish. Left bank is preserve of Padiham & Dist AS. Members only. Staincliffe AC also have water, members plus 5 tickets for their guests. Hotels: Boar's Head; Maypole.

Settle (N Yorks). Settle AA has 7½m of good trout and grayling fishing in Ribble between Langcliffe, Settle and vicinity of Long Preston. Wt, dt at Royal Oak Hotel, tel: 01729 822561, during licensing hours. Fly only; limit 1½ brace. Water stocked yearly. **Malham Tarn** is 6m from Settle and holds large trout. Dt water *(see Yorkshire lakes, reservoirs, etc)*. Further north are Manchester AA's waters. Licences from post offices. Other hotels at Settle: Falcon Manor and Golden Lion.

Horton in Ribblesdale (N Yorks). Trout; preserved from source to Helwith Bridge, including all tributaries, by Manchester AA. Assn also has **Newhouses Tarn** (fly only); stocked b and r trout. No tickets.

Tributaries of the Ribble

HODDER: Good salmon and trout water.

Higher Hodder Bridge (Lancs and Yorks). Salmon, sea trout, trout, grayling and coarse fish.

Chipping (Lancs). Hodder, 1½m E. Salmon, sea trout and grayling. Loud, 1m SE. Trout and sea trout. About ½m of Hodder below Doeford Bridge on right bank and several miles of **River Loud** are preserved by Loud and Hodder AA; tickets if accompanied by member. Hotel: Derby Arms.

Whitewell (Lancs). Salmon, sea trout, trout, grayling. The Inn at Whitewell, Forest of Bowland BB7 3AT, has four rods for residents on 7m of Whitewell FA water. Dt £6 Nov-Mar, £12.50 15 Mar-31 Jul, £28 Aug-Oct incl. Tel: 012008 222 for details. The Red Pump Hotel, Bashall Eaves, has two rods 8m further down the river.

Newton (Lancs); Lancashire FFA have water downstream from Newton to Dunsop Bridge. At **Chaigley**, Southport FF have water, and Edisford Hall Estate; contact Townson Bros, Pendle Trading Estate, Chatburn, Clitheroe BB7 3LJ. Also at Chaigley, Hodder Bridge Hotel has 100 yds right bank u/s of Hodder Higher Bridge.

Slaidburn (Lancs); ns Clitheroe, 8½m. Hodder; salmon, sea trout and trout. Tickets for several miles of Hodder from The Jam Pot Cafe, Slaidburn. Stocks Reservoir in vicinity. Hotel: Bounty.

CALDER: Coarse fishing. Some club water.

Elland (Yorks). Bradford No 1 AA fishery extends u/s of Elland Road Bridge for approx 1,800 yds. Members only.

Whalley (Lancs). West Calder. Ribble, 2m W; salmon, sea trout and coarse fish. Hodder, 2m W; salmon, sea trout and trout. Accrington FC have fishing on three stretches of Calder, members only. Contact Non Sec.

Barrowford (Lancs). Pendle Water; trout. Colne Water (polluted) and Pendle join near Barrowford to form Calder (polluted). **Leeds and Liverpool Canal** from Barnoldswick to East Marton (10m), and 3½m at Keighley leased to Marsden Star AS. Dt £2.

Burnley (Lancs). Local waters mostly polluted. Burnley AS leases **Lea Green Reservoir**, at Hapton but tickets only to local ratepayers; trout. **Hapton Lodges Reservoir** at Hapton stocked with rainbow trout; Blythe A C. Marsden Star AS fishes Gawthorpe Hall Pool at Padiham, members only, tench, carp, roach, perch fishing. Tackle shop: Macks Tackle, 33a Parliament Street.

COLNE (tributary of Calder). Much pollution but holds some trout and coarse fish.

Colne (Lancs). Colne; trout. Water held by Colne Water AS. **Leeds and Liverpool Canal** held by Marsden Star AS (10m from Barnoldswick to Bank Newton, and 3½m Howden to Morton); pike, trout, tench, bream, roach, rudd, carp and perch; st and dt for waters held by both clubs. Marsden Star AS also fishes Knotts Lane Ponds at Colne, coarse fish, members only. Tackle shops: Anglers All, Colne; Jackson's Fishing Tackle, 27 Albion Street, Earby; Boyces, 44 Manchester Road, and Fly and Tackle, 59 Cross Street, both Nelson.

Foulridge (Lancs). Four British Waterways reservoirs: **Lower** (or **Burwains**), **Upper**, **Slipperhill**, **White Moor**. Let to clubs: members only.

ROTHER

(For close seasons, licences, etc, see Southern Region Environment Agency, p16).

Rises near Rotherfield and reaches the sea at Rye Bay. Mostly coarse fish, with trout in upper reaches and tributaries but runs of sea trout increasing. Mullet and bass in estuary.

Rye (E Sussex). Near mouth of Rother; coarse fish. Free fishing from roadside bank between Iden and Scots Float, nr Rye. Clive Vale AC has 1m of **Tillingham River** above Rye and **Rother** at Wittersham to Iden Bridge; south bank footpath for 2 fields on **Royal Military Canal** at Winchelsea. Romney Marsh is close by. Several clubs have water, including Hastings, Bexhill and Dist Freshwater AA; st £35, dt £5, conc.

Wittersham (Kent). Roach, chub, bream, perch, pike, tench, bleak, eels, and other species. Rother Fisheries Association has 7m of Rother, accessible at Robertsbridge, Salehurst, Udiam, Bodiam, Newenden, Potmans Corner and Blackwell Bridge at Wittersham, also 3m of Royal Military Canal from Iden Lock to Appledore. Membership open to clubs, not individuals. Mostly members only, but £3 dt on canal from Bailiff John Rees, 18 Lyndurst Roade, Dymchurch TN29 0TE (01303 872160). Clive Vale AC have 2 good stretches at Blackwall Bridge and Otter Channel junction. Dt £3, only in advance, from Hon Sec or Hastings tackle shops. Hastings, Bexhill and Dist FAA has **Rother and Hexden Channel** between Rolveden and Wittersham. St £35, with concessions.

Newenden (E Sussex). Large bream, chub and roach; Rother Fishery Assn has fishing rights, terms described under *Wittersham*. Maidstone Victory Angling & Medway PS fish Rother here and at **Blackwell and Salehurst**. Membership on application.

Bodiam (E Sussex). Trout (small), coarse fish. Maidstone Victory Angling & Medway PS fish Rother here. Hastings, Bexhill & Dist FAA has 500 yds fishing on south bank with prime chub and dace, membership £35, conc. Hotels: Castle, Justins.

Etchingham (E Sussex). Hastings, Bexhill and Dist FAA has many miles of dykes and drains noted for pike, bream, tench and rudd on **Romney Marsh** between **Gulderford** and **Appledore**, **Wishing Tree Reservoir**, lakes and ponds, dt £5, conc, on some waters from Hon Sec or local tackle shops. CALPAC controls **Speringbrook Sewer**, Snargate, nr

Keep the banks clean

Several Clubs have stopped issuing tickets to visitors because the state of the banks after they have left. Spend a few moments clearing up.

Appledore, fen-like fishing of about 2,000 yds, with chub, roach, bream, dace, perch, pike. Dt £4 at Arrowhead Bungalow, £4, conc. No night fishing on CALPAC water. At **Burwash** is **Lakedown Trout Fishery**, 4 lakes, 5 acres each, b and r trout from 1½lb to 16lb. Dt £28.50, 5 fish, ½ day £23.50, 3 fish. May_Aug evenings, £14.50. Contact A Bristow, Lakedown Fishery, Broad Oak, Heathfield TN21 8UX; tel: 01435 883449.

Stonegate (E Sussex). Wadhurst AS has trout water; dt to members' guests only. Hotel: Bridge.

Tenterden (Kent). Tackle & Gun, 3 Eastwell Parade, High St, TN30 6AH, have tickets for a large number of local fisheries. These include Rother FA (*see Wittersham*), Tenterden AC (incl various ponds, Dowels Sewer, Hexden Channel, Rother at Potmans Heath); Northiam AC (carp lakes and several miles of Rother); Rye AC (R Tillingham and R Brede, good coarse fishing); Headcorn AC (carp ponds in Biddenden area); also tickets for **Hawkhurst Fishery** (01580 754420), 11 lakes, with trout and coarse fishing; Tenderden Trout Waters (01580 763201), 3 lakes of 5 acres total, brown and rainbows.

BREDE: Rother tributary. Coarse fish, a few small trout; approx 6 miles controlled by Clive Vale AC. Members only, st £23, from Hon Sec or local tackle shops. Fishing station **Rye, Winchelsea**.

SEVERN

(For close seasons, licences, etc, see Midlands Region Environment Agency, p19)

Longest river in England. Rises in Wales (N Powys) and flows 180m into Bristol Channel. Fair salmon river, with commercial fisheries near mouth; spring salmon in January/April and May. Average size good. Some trout and grayling in upper reaches, but river noted chiefly for coarse fishing, especially for chub in the upper reaches and barbel in the middle river. Shad run up river in May and are taken on rod and line, principally at Tewkesbury Weir.

Sharpness (Glos). Coarse fishing in the **Gloucester and Berkeley Canal** from Severn Bridge to Hempstead Bridge, Gloucester (about 16m); bank licence from any bridge house.

Gloucester (Glos). Gloucester United AA controls several miles of Severn from Hawbridge u/s and d/s, and Stank Lane. Dt £2, from bailiffs. (Assn also has water from **Lower Lode** to **Deerhurst**, on gravel pit at **Saul** and on **Gloucester Sharpness Canal**). Red Lion Inn, Wainlode Hill, Norton, has Severn fishing with facilities for disabled. Tel: 01452 730251. **Witcombe Reservoirs**: three lakes of 12, 9, and 5 acres, fly only; stocked rainbow trout. St £445-£185, dt £20-£12, depending on limit. Boats bookable in advance. Mr and Mrs M Hicks Beach, Witcombe Farm, Great Witcombe GL3 4TR, tel: 01452 863591. Staunton Court, tel: 01452 840230: Pleck Pool, 25 acres, coarse fishing with carp and tench. Tickets on site. Tackle shops: Allsports, 126/128 Eastgate Street (dt for Wye salmon fishing); Rod & Gun, 67 Alvin St; Tredworth Tackle, High St, Tredworth; D & J Sports, 75 Cricklade Street, Cirencester; Ian Coley 442/444 High St, both Cheltenham. Hotels: New County, Fleece, New Inn.

Tewkesbury (Glos). Salmon, twait and coarse fish. Avon: coarse fish. Below weir shoals of big bream. Birmingham AA has 38 stretches on Severn including those at Bushley, Ripple, Uckinghall, Severn Stoke, Deerhurst, Chaceley, Apperley (2 pools at Apperley, also) and Maisemore; also Church End Trout Fishery. Tewkesbury Popular AA has 80 pegs on Severn from mouth of Avon to Lower Load, with bream, chub, barbel, eels, gudgeon, pike and bleak, and salmon, and **Avon** from Healings Mill to abbey Mill Ham side; bream, roach, chub, skimmer, bleak, gudgeon. Membership £14, conc, from R Danter. Only limited number of salmon permits issued each year. Gloucester United AA have water at Drirhurst and Lower Lode. Dt from bailiff, tackle shops and Hon Sec. Trout fly fishing at Witcombe Waters, Great Witcombe, tel: 01452 863591. Tackle shop: R Danter, Tackle Shop, 31 Barton Street GL20 5PR. Hotels: Abbey; Malvern View; many others.

Ripple (Worcs). Bream, pike, perch, chub, dace, roach. Environment Agency fishery, 1900 yds free to licence holders, is on east bank, at M50 viaduct. Birmingham AA has 2 meadows and Uckingham pool, Ripple.

Upton-on-Severn (Worcs). Chub, barbel, bream, roach, dace, perch and pike. 1200 yds of west bank above old railway embankment is free to E.A. licence holders. Upton-upon-Severn AA has 15 pegs at Hanley Rd, 42 pegs at Upper Ham. Free parking. Dt £2 from G Shinn, tackle shop, 21/3 Old Street. Birmingham AA has 7 meadows, members only. Hotels: King's Head, Swan, Star.

Worcester (Worcs). Barbel, bream, chub, roach. Free fishing behind cricket ground. Worcester & Dist United AA has stretches at Kempsey below Worcester, 350m l bank; Pixham Ferry, 800m r bank; West Diglis, 900m r bank; East Diglis, 350m l bank; Pitchcroft, 800m l bank. Assc also has stretches of **Avon**, and 2,500m l bank **Teme** at Knightwick. Dt through Hon Sec (01905 424505) or through tackle shop (*below*). Dt on bank for 12 pegs at Bevere Lock (01905 640275). Birmingham AA has stretches at Severn Stoke, Hallow, Kempsey, Grimley and Holt Fleet, rights on Worcester and Birmingham Canal from King's Norton to Blackpole (near Worcester); bream, roach, perch, pike. Bank House Hotel Lake, 40 acres, has carp fishing. Tel: 01886 833557. Tackle shop: Alan Reynolds, Worcester, tel: 01905 422107, has tickets for Evesbatch Fisheries, two lakes with carp and roach.

Lincombe and **Holt** (Worcs). Wharf Inn (01905 620289) has section at Holt Fleet, 19 pegs with carp and bream. Disabled access, dt from inn. Holt Fleet Restaurant (01905 620286) has 550m r bank with barbel and chub. Dt on bank. Dt for Lincombe Lock, 180m l bank, from keeper on site. Tel: 01299 822887.

Stourport-on-Severn (Worcs). At confluence of Severn and Stour: barbel, chub and large roach; also **Staffordshire and Worcestershire Canal**: coarse fish. Lyttelton AA has 80 pegs right bank u/s of Stourport. Tickets from Mark Lewis only. Birmingham AA has ½m both banks. Hampstall hotel (01299 822600) has 225m r bank, perch and roach. Tackle shop: Mark Lewis, Raven Street, where Lyttelton AA tickets are sold. 1¼m both banks downstream of **Cilcewydd Bridge** is Environment Agency fishery, free to licence holders.

Bewdley (Worcs). Chub, roach, dace, barbel. Kidderminster AA has 125 stretches, 2m ¾m of water above and below town, 70 pegs below Stourport at **Winnalls**, and water at **Buildwas** and **Alveley**. Members only, st £17, conc, from all local tackle shops. Telford AA has 2,000m l bank, dt from Rod & Gun, Dawley, information from Hon Sec (01952 590605). Harbour Inn, Arley (01299 401204), has two meadows. Dt from bailiff. Birmingham AA has six stretches in vicinity. Cards for both clubs from Stan Lewis, (*see below*). Stan Lewis also runs riverside guest-house and clubroom and issues tickets for 1½m Severn at Bewdley and 9 local pools under his own supervision. Various coarse fish, dt £2. Tackle shops; Stan Lewis, 1-4 Sevenside South, tel: 01299 403358; Bill Heavesley, Severn side North: both Bewley; Mal Storey, Sutton Rd, Kidderminster; Mark Lewis, Raven St, Stourport.

Upper Arley (Worcs). Salmon, trout, grayling, chub, dace, pike, etc. Dowles Brook, 3m S. Birmingham AA has stretches at **Arley Stanley**, **Arley Kinlet**, **Arley**, **Aveley** and **Rhea Hall**. Hotels: Valentia, Harbour and Unicorn (last two issue dt).

Hampton Loade (Salop). Barbel, roach. Dt on bank for 1,875m l bank at Hampton Lock; contact Wolverhampton AA (01902 457906). 350m, r bank, dt on bank, or from Caravan Site, Old Forge House, Hampton Loade. Birmingham AA has extensive fishing here, on both banks, and at **Alveley**.

Bridgnorth (Salop). Barbel, roach. Ship Inn (01746 861219) has 270m west bank, dt on bank. Birmingham AA has stretches at **Knowle Sands**, **Danery**, **Quatford** and **Eardington**. **Willey Park Pools** at **Broseley** (5m) and pools at **Ticklerton** are also on club card; rainbow, brown and some American brook trout. Membership limited. Boldings Pools, six lakes with carp and tench, dt on bank. Tel: 01746 763255. **Poole Hall**, nr Kidderminster, five coarse lakes with carp and other species. Dt on bank. Tel: 012997 861458. **Shatterford Lakes**, Bridgenorth Rd, tel: 01299 861597: two trout lakes; "Masters", catch and kill or catch and release; "Knight's Folly", catch and kill; dt £14 4 fish, £9 2 fish, extra trout £2.30 each. Catch and release dt £7.50; OAP conc, Mondays; also eight coarse lakes with carp, catfish, dt on site. 100 pegs at Townsend Fisheries, tel: 01746 780551; carp and roach, tickets on bank. 20 pools with bream and carp at **Kingsnordley**; tel: 01746 780247. Tickets on bank. For details of **Underton Trout Lakes**, fly fishing, tel: 0174635 254. Astbury Falls Fish Farm, tel: 01746 766797, has £10 dt, 5 hours, 2 trout, £15 full day, 3 trout, also coarse dt £5, large carp. Fishing holidays at Bandon Arms, Mill St, 01746 763135. Accommodation with facilities for anglers at The Woodberry Down, Victoria Rd, tel: 01746 76236. Kidderminster tackle shops: Siviter Sports, 2 Tower Building, Blackwell St; Storey's Angling Centre, 129 Sutton Rd. Hotels: Severn Arms; Falcon; Croft; Kings Head.

Coalport (Salop). Chub, barbel, pike, etc, fewer roach and dace than are found farther downstream. Some free water. Rowley Regis and Dist AS has stretch on right bank. No tickets.

Ironbridge (Salop). Barbel, chub, roach, perch, etc. Birmingham AA has ¼m. 600 yds of fishing on left bank free to E.A. licence-holders. Dawley AS has right bank d/s from power station fence to Free Bridge, also pools at **Telford, Broseley** and **Dawley**. Dt £2.50, conc, on all waters from bailiffs. Telford AA (01952 590605) has Sweeneycliffe House fishery near Dawley, 700m l bank. Dt on bank, or from Rod & Gun. Queens Arms AC (01952 592602) has 3 stretches, total 51 pegs u/s and d/s of Free Bridge. Dt from bailiff on bank. Little Dawley Pools: three pools with carp, roach, bream, carp, tel: 01952 590605; dt on bank or from tackle shop, Rod & Gun, High St, Dawley. Hotel: Tontine.

Atcham (Salop). Barbel, chub. Environment Agency has 2,895m r bank, dt from Atcham Post Office. Macclesfield Prince Albert AS has members only fisheries here, at **Bicton, Melverley, Longnor, Royal Hill, The Isle, Welshpool** and **Newton**. Also fishings on the rivers **Gam, Vyrnwy** and **Banwy**.

Shrewsbury (Salop). Chub, roach, barbel. Town waters, 1,800m both banks, dt on bank or from all tackle shops. Wingfield Arms Inn (01743 850750) has 1,125m at Montford Bridge with barbel and eels. Montford Bridge to Bicton Farm, 1,125m with barbel, chub; Wolverhampton AA (01902 457906), dt on bank. Seven Oaks Log Cabin Park (01743 884271) has 350m, dt from warden on site. **Weir** fishery controlled by council, tel: 01743 231456 for fishery; 356046 for bailiff. St £29.60 to £26.64, salmon; £14.30 to £6.60 course. Old LMS SC has fine stretches at **Emstry**, with fords and runs. Dt from all local tackle shops. St Helens Ramblers AS, Hon Sec, Alec Twiss, 47 Exeter St, St Helens, have two stretch at Shrewsbury. Permits. Birmingham AA has stretches at **Underdale, Pool Quay** and **Buttington Bridge**. Warrington AA has **Severn** at **Loton Park**, Alberbury. Lymm AC has dt water at Atcham and Rossall (Nr Montford Bridge) with very large chub and barbel, members only. Tackle shops: Ebrall Bros, Smithfield Road; Kingfisher Angling Centre, 8 New St; Sundorne Fishing Tackle, 1 Sundorne Avenue; Shrewsbury Bait Centre, Whitchurch Rd.

Melverley (Salop). Two meadows on left bank, about 500 yds, free to E.A.licence holders. Chester AA has 800yds immediately d/s of Environment Agency stretch.

Llandrinio (Montgomery). Chub, dace, trout, barbel, salmon; leave from farmers. Lymm AC has water on Severn and Vyrnwy, members only. Montgomery AA has 2,290 yds left bank, upstream from bridge to Lower Farm. Cheshire AA has Haughton Farm and Pentre stretches. St £10. Canal; coarse fish, tickets *(see Welshpool)*. **Maerdy Brook**, 2m SW. Arddleen Brook, excellent trout, dace and chub. Hotel: Golden Lion.

Welshpool (Powys). Salmon, trout, coarse fish (inc grayling). Trout small in streams, few but big in river. Welshpool and Dist AC now in Montgomeryshire AA which has 60m of coarse and game fishing in **Severn, Camlad, Vyrnwy, Banwy**. Also **Shropshire Union Canal** (coarse fishing). Their 2 Welshpool stretches are at **Coed-y-Dinas** and **Lower Leighton**, 750m and 1,500m.Dt from tackle shops in Welshpool. Black Pools trout fishery, fly only, is 1m from Welshpool on Llanfair Rd; Montgomery AA water, dt £10, 4 fish, from A E Bond. Some permits are sold for **Maesmawr Pool** (5m NW). Bank and boat fishing (dt £9 and £4) on Marton Pool, Marton, 5m SE. Good coarse fishing. Apply to Site Manager, Marton Pool Caravan Park. Warrington AA has Hope Farm stretch, Welshpool. Tackle, permits and licences from A E Bond, 9 Hall Street. Hotels: Westwood Park, Salop Rd, Welshpool, who have Montgomery AA tickets; Bear, Newton; Black Lion, Llanfair Caereinion.

Forden (Powys). Montgomery, 3m. Trout, salmon, chub, dace, etc. Birmingham AA has 3m. Camlad; trout, grayling. Montgomeryshire AA and Cheshire AA have water on river; tickets.

Montgomery (Powys). Severn, 2m; trout, salmon, grayling, chub, pike and perch. Lion Hotel, Caerhowell has 400 yards of Severn; st £25 dt £1.50. **Camlad**, 2m N; good trout, grayling, chub. Montgomeryshire AA has water; tickets. Warrington AA has waters at Caerhowell Hall, **Dolwen, Fron** and **Llanidloes**. Also **Vyrnwy, Dee**, canals and pools. Herbert Arms, Cherbury, has 1½m; dt. Caerhowel Cottage (01686 668598) has dt for 80m r bank, mixed coarse. Tackle shops in Welshpool and Newtown.

Abermule (Powys). **Severn** and **Mule**; salmon, trout, grayling, coarse fish; mostly private but dt for some lengths. Water not always fishable in summer. Montgomeryshire AA has 1¼m of Severn and water at Mule junction; dt from Hon Sec. Warrington AA has stretch; Lymm AC has 1,000 yds, members only, trout and grayling.

Newtown (Powys). Salmon, trout, grayling, pike, chub, dace. Environment Agency has free fisheries: ½m, mainly north bank, beginning at municipal car park; 500 yds north bank beside sewage farm at Penarth. Newtown and Dist FC, Llanfair Caerinion FC and Welshpool AC form Montgomeryshire AA, who have waters here as follows: the old free stretch from above Halfpenny Bridge, both banks; Newtown recreation ground; **Vaynor Estate**; **Penstrowed** and **Dolwerw**; also **Fachwen Pool**, fly only r trout fishing. St and dt from Mikes Tackle, and M Cakebread's Garage, Pool Rd, Newtown. Severnside AC has extensive Severn fishing at Newtown, Penstrowydd, Vaynor, Glan Hafren Hall, Dolerw Park, also 4 meadows at **Abermule**, and pools. Membership £15, £3 dt, conc, from Severn Angling (*see below*). Prince Albert AS has stretch here. Penllwyn Lodges (tel: 01686 640269) offers self-catering log cabins with fishing in 1m of canal plus small lake; tench, chub, carp. Tackle shop has dt £1.50 for canal at **Abermule** and **Nettershiem Trout Lake**, 4½ acres, £10. Tackle shops: Severn Angling, Railway Terrace, Old Kerry Rd, Newtown SY16 1BH; Mid Wales Angling, Unit 2E6, Lion Works, Pool Rd. Hotels: Elephant and Castle, Maesmawr Hall, Dolforwyn Hall.

Caersws (Powys). Maesmawr Hall Hotel has 3½m on Severn free to guests. Trout, coarse fish, some salmon. Caersws AA has water 2m above and below village with good brown trout and grayling; fly, spinning and worm. St £60, dt £6 for good trout and grayling, (also covers Llandinam fishery) from Spar supermarket or Buck Hotel, Main St, Caersws SY17 5EL.

Llandinam (Powys). 4m of trout and grayling fishing on both banks. Dt £4, OAP, jun £2 from Lion Hotel, Llandinam. Caersws AA controls Llandinam fishery, 1m above, 2m below village, fly only, dt £5; from Llandinam P O. Hotel: Lion.

Llanidloes (Montgomery). Trout, salmon, pike, chub, dace, grayling. Llanidloes AA has about 20m fishing on upper **Severn**, **Afon Clywedog** and other tributaries. St and dt from Hon Sec. Warrington AA has Dolwen Bridge to Llanidloes. Upper Penrhyddlan, 1,125m r bank, grayling fishing, dt on bank. Tel: 01686 412584 for information. Environment Agency has ½m on south bank beginning at sewage works, which is free fishing to licence holders. O S Evans, Dol Llys Farm, SY18 6JA has 300 yds right bank, tel 015512 2694. Warrington AA, has water downstream. At **Trefeglwys** (4m N) is caravan park with of fishing (trout and coarse) on **Trannon**. Best months for trout April-July. Llyn Ebyr, 30 acre coarse lake with perch, pike, tickets from J Williams, Llyn Ebyr, tel: 01686 430236. Hotels: Lloyds, Unicorn, Queen's Head, Angel, Temperance, Royal Oak, Red Lion.

Tributaries of the Severn.

LEADON: Trout, coarse fish (some barbel introduced).

Ledbury (Hereford). Ledbury AA has trout water, no dt. Castlemorton Lake; coarse fishing; free, but licence necessary. Three Counties Fisheries have 25 peg carp pool here, with roach, tench and rudd. Management also runs pool fishing at **Bromsberrow, Grandison** and **Leominster**. Contact Field Cottage, Ryton, Nr Dymock, Glos GL18 2DH, tel: 0531 890455. Hotel: Royal Oak, The Southend, tel: 0531 632110, caters for anglers.

AVON: The principal tributary of the lower Severn. Roach, chub, dace and perch dominate higher reaches; bream and pike,

The old bridge at Eckington, on the lower Warwickshire Avon. *Photo: S R Spencer.*

the latter patchily distributed.

Tewkesbury (Glos). Confluence of Avon and Severn, connected also by 'Mill Avon'. Weirs and weir-pool fishing, including twaite shad during the spawning run. Cheltenham AC controls 2m of Avon at Corpus Christi by **Strensham** village. Good coarse fishing, chub, roach, bream, perch, pike included. Membership £11, dt £2, conc, (Mon to Sun only) from Hon Sec, Cheltenham tackle shops or the Bell Inn, Eckington. Mythe Pool, Tewkesbury: 10 acre coarse lake with bream, roach; tickets from Alan Reynolds Tackle Shop, Worcester, tel: 01905 422107

Twyning (Glos). Chub, dace, roach, pike, perch, bream. Birmingham AA has ½m stretch.

Eckington (Worcs). Most species of coarse fish, principally bream, big head of roach. For Solihull AC, contact G Gill, tel: 013867 50538. Bailiff for Lower Avon, S R Spencer, Butchers Shop, Eckington, Pershore WR10 3AW, tel: 013867 50235. Hotel: Bell Inn, ¼m from river.

Pershore (Worcs). Roach bream. Worcester & Dist United AA has 900m at Burlington, and 1,000m at Pensham. Information from Assc, tel: 01905 424505; dt from Alan Reynolds Tackle Shop, Worcester. Fox Inn AC has water 1½m below Pershore, tel: 0121 458 2797 or 0121 327 3113. Birmingham AA has water here, both banks and at Pensham, Birlingham, **Nafford, Eckington, Bredon, Twyning, Bredons Hardwick** and at Mythe Farm. Some free water in recreation ground. Tackle shop: Rochelle Country Sports, 32 Bridge St; Hotel: Angel.

Evesham (Worcs). Pike, perch, bream, roach, dace, gudgeon, chub, bleak. Evesham AA has 60 pegs in town, and 26 pegs behind football club, dt £2.80 from bailiff on bank. Club has free fishing for jun and disabled at Workman Gardens, Waterside. Dt on bank for Crown Corp Meadows, 57 pegs: C Thompson (01386 458800). At **Hampton Ferry**: S M Raphael, E W Huxley & Son, has 104 pegs. Dt £3 (incl car park) from bailiffs or Raphael's Restaurant. Hampton Ferry, WR11 4BP, tel: 01386 442458. Anchor Meadows, **Harvington**: 500m right bank with barbel and chub, dt on bank, or The Bungalow, Anchor Meadows (01386

48065). Birmingham AA has fisheries at Swifts, **Wood Norton**, **Chadbury**, **Charlton**, **Cropthorne**, **Fladbury**, **Lower Moor** and **Wick**. Manor Farm Leisure (caravan holidays), Anchor Lane, Harvington, 01386 870039, has 1200m coarse fishing on Avon. Waterside and Workman Gardens (overnight only), reserved for local and disabled anglers. Twyford Farm, Evesham, has 1,000m right bank, chub, roach, tickets on bank. Tel: 01386 446108. Licences from post office. At Twyford Farm, Evesham WR11 4TP, 1½m R Avon, and coarse fishing lake, with carp, bream, etc. Dt £3 river, £3.50 carp pool, conc, Contact May Vince, tel: 01386 446108, day, 01789 778365 evening. **The Lenches Lakes**, Hill Barn Orchard, Church Lench, Evesham WR11 4UB, (01386 871035), stocked rainbow trout fly fishing on two lakes of 3 and 4 acres; fish from 1lb to 9lb 8oz; dt £26, 6 fish, £16 3 fish, conc. Tackle shops: Bait Box, High St; Woof's, Mill Bank. Alcester tackle shop: Sports and Tackle, 3A High St, Alcester.

Stratford-upon-Avon (Warwick). A stretch of the Avon preserved by District Council, Elizabeth House, Church St, CV37 6HX, tel: 01789 267575. Royal Leamington Spa AA has Lido and Recreation Ground fishing, dt £2; reservoir and two pools at Snitterfield, River Avon and pool at Wasperton, members only. Local club, Stratford-upon-Avon AA has 500 pegs on R Avon from Hampton Lucy to Luddington, and **R Stour** at Preston-on-Stour, with good variety of coarse fish in both; also 12m fishing in **South Stratford Canal**, Stratford to Wilmcote, and Grand Union Canal, **Hatton**; membership £17, conc, dt £2.50 from tackle shops. Worcester & Dist United AA has Alveston Hill fishery, 1,500m both banks, with roach, chub. Tickets from Reynolds Tackle Shop, Worcester. Birmingham AA has stretches at **Avon Meadows**, **Welford**, **Barton**, **Bidford**, **Marlcliff**, **Cleeve Prior** and **Salford Priors**. Good chub and dace and also water on **Stour** (2m S). Alveston Village AC has 17 pegs on Avon at **Alveston**, with chub, bream, roach, carp, barbel. Dt £3 from secretary. At **Moreton in Marsh**, Lemington Lakes: four small pools with carp, rudd, roach, tench, bream, dt water, tel: 01608 650872. Park Farm, Compton Verney, 20 acre coarse fishery with bream, tench, dt on bank; tel: 01926 6402415. Tackle shop: Stratford Angling Centre, 17 Evesham Rd. Hotels: Welcombe, Falcon, Arden and many others.

Leamington (Warwick). Bream, chub, dace, roach, pike, perch. Avon at **Wasperton** and **Stratford** Lido and Recreation Ground preserved by Royal Leamington Spa AA.Assn, also has 12½m in Grand Union Canal, Warwick to Napton, coarse fish (good carp and tench in June, July, Aug); R **Leam, Offchurch** to outfall of Avon, several ponds. Dt £2, conc, for most of these at Stratford from Frosts or Nickards, tackle shops. Annual membership £17.50, conc. **Chesterton Mill Pool**, Chesterton Green, **Harbury** CU33 9NL, tel: 0831 137277, has dts £19 to £11 on site, for 4½ acres fly only, brown and rainbow trout. 1 Mar-30 Nov. **Bishops Bowl Lakes**, 14 acres, 6 lakes with carp and tench. Dt on bank. Tel: 01926 614194. Tackle shops: Frosts, Bath St; Nickards Tackle Cellar, Russell Terrace; Baileys, 30 Emscote Rd, Warwick.

Rugby (Warwick). Coarse fish. Environment Agency have free fishery at Avon Mill, 640m north bank beside B4112 road. Avon Ho AC have water on Oxford Canal nr Barby. Club also has 3 pools at Kings Newsham and stretch of upper Avon. Membership from Banks and Burr (*below*). Aces AC have water on North Oxford Canal, contact C Bower (01788 656422). Foxholes Fishery at Crick, close to M1, 4 st pools and 1 dt pool. All species stocked. One lake is specialist water with carp to 30lbs. Contact R Chaplin (01788 823967). Barby Mill Pool is fishable on dt, good carp and all species, contact R Bubb (01788 579521). Spring Pools are three pools close to Rugby at Newton. All species, dt on bank, or tel: 0467 834873. Clifton Lakes on A5 offer 8 pools and 1 lake plus length of R Avon. Dt on bank. Contact Barry Entwhistle (0956 634079). **Newbold Quarry**, old established water for good tench and roach fishing, run by Severn Trent. Water close by Dunchurch, dt from lodge on site. **Stemborough Mill**, Stemborough Lane, Leire, nr **Lutterworth**, Leics LE17 5EY, tel: 01455 209624. 4 acre trout fishery on upper reaches or Soar. Dt £15-£12 (and refreshments) from bankside self-service. Tackle shops: Banks & Burr, 25/27 Claremont Road, CV21 3NA (01788 576782); Donalds, 155A Bilton Rd. Hotels: Grosvenor; Three Horseshoes, both Rugby; Post House, Crick.

ARROW joined by the **Alne** at Alcester; flows into Avon at Salford Priors: Coarse fish, some trout.

Salford Priors (Worcs). Arrow and Avon; coarse fish. Birmingham AA has ¾m.

Wixford (Warwick). Pike, perch, roach, dace, chub and bream; dt for about 1m of water from Fish Inn. Dt £2.50 for water L bank above bridge from public house. Lakes: Ragley Park, 1m NW.

Redditch (Worcs). Redditch & Dist FA are local federation, who fish **Arrow Valley Lake**, with carp to 25lb, large roach and other coarse fish. Dt £2.80 on site, Avon at Wick nr **Pershore** and **Birmingham - Stratford Canal**. Contact S Mousey, tel: 01527 854160. 3m SW of town, Powell's Fishery on 3½ acre **Norgrove Pool**. R trout to 6lb, av 1½lb. Dt £8 + £2 per fish, 5 fish limit. Barbless hooks, no tandem lures. 12 rods per day. Contact Powell's *(see below)*. Good fishing in **Lodge Pool**, tench and carp. Tackle shops: Powell's, 28 Mount Pleasant, tel: 62669; Corn Stores, Headless Cross. Hotels: Royal, Southcrest.

Alvechurch (Worcs). Barnt Green FC has rights on **Upper and Lower Bittell Reservoirs, Arrow Pools** and **Canal feeder**. **Lower Bittell** and **Mill Shrub** trout (fly only), remainder coarse fish. Fishing for members and their guests.

STOUR (tributary of Avon): Coarse fish, trout, mostly preserved.

Shipston (Warwick). Shipston-on-Stour AC has water; members only. Birmingham AA has Stour fishing at Milcote. Hotel: George.

LEAM (tributary of Avon): Coarse fish.

Eathorpe (Warwick). Coventry Godiva AS has fishery here; coarse fish. Good winter fishing; st. Dt for fishing at Newbold Common, Avon confluence, from Frosts, Bath St, Leamington. Red Lion waters, **Hunningham**, from Red Lion, 01926 632715. Warwick DC (01926 450000) has 750m at Pump Room Gardens, Leamington Spa. Dt on bank; and Leamington Mill Gardens, 350m l bank; both with roach, perch.

HAM BROOK (tributary of Leam): Coarse fish.

Fenny Compton (Warwick): Good pike, bream, tench, roach in **Oxford Canal**. **Claydon**. Stoneton House Lake, 2½m NE.

SOWE (tributary of Avon): few fish.

Coventry (W Midlands). Excellent trout and coarse fishing on **Packington Estate**. **Meriden**. More than five miles of river fishing and 160 acres of lakes. Rainbow and brown trout; also coarse fishery 2m off. *(For details see Midlands (reservoirs and lakes))*. Coventry AA has extensive fishing on rivers, canals and reservoirs and coarse fishing in **Trent** and **Soar** at Thrumpton, **Ouse** at Turvey, **Nene, Thames** and **Anker**, 30 acres of coarse pools nr **Atherstone**; day tickets for some of this fishing may be had from tackle shops in Coventry area or Hon Sec. Canal waters include stretches on **Coventry Canal** and **Oxford Canal**. Dt £5 from bailiffs for Assn's **Napton Reservoirs**, noted bream, carp (to 29lb), tench and roach water, also pike to 22lb. 6m from town, Hopsford Hall Fishery, Shilton Lane, nr Withybrook. Carp to 20lb and other coarse species. Good access for disabled. Dt from bailiff on bank. Royal Leamington Spa AA control Jubilee Pools, at Ryton-on-Dunsmore. For membership, *see Leamington*. Tackle shops: W H Lane & Son, 31/35 London Road, Coventry CV1 2JP, tel: 01203 223316 (assn cards); Tusses Fishing Tackle, 360 Aldermans Green Rd. Brandon Hall Hotel, Brandon (01203 542571) offers details and instruction on local angling.

TEME: Trout and coarse fish, with a few salmon; grayling. Very large barbel, strong tackle recommended. Trout in upper reaches.

Worcester (Worcs). Barbel, chub. St John's AS (01905 358263) has 1500m right bank at Powick Hams. Worcester and Dist UAS has 2,500m l bank at Knightwick. Dt for both from Reynolds Tackle, Worcester. Talbot Hotel (018868 21235) has 135m both banks.

Leigh (Worcs). Trout, chub, dace, grayling, pike, perch, salmon. Bransford AS and local clubs rent Leigh to Powick; members only.

Broadwas (Worcs). Trout, grayling, chub, dace. Birmingham AA has stretch of left bank here and at Eardiston, 1¼m.

Knightwick (Worcs). Salmon, trout, barbel. Permits for one mile from Stan Lewis, 1-4 Sevenside South, Bewley, tel: 01299 403358.

Tenbury (Worcs). Barbel, chub. Peacock Waters (01584 881411) has 900m l bank, tickets on bank. Tickets for Little Hereford, 500m right bank d/s of bridge, A Jones, Westbrook Farm, 01584 711280.

Tenbury FA has approx 4m of Teme above and below town and 1m of **Ledwyche Brook**, trout, salmon and grayling, and barbel, chub, pike etc. Membership £80. Dt £7 game, £3 coarse; from Hon Sec, or from Mr Bill Drew, Oak Tree cottage, Berrington Rd, Tenbury Wells WR15 8BB. Tackle shop: Moby Dick, Market St. Hotels: Crow; Royal Oak; Swan.

Stourport on Severn (Worcs). Barbel, chub. Ham Bridge fishing, 1,500m 1 bank, dt from Ham Bridge Farm (01866 812228), or Grinnals Tackle Shop, Stourport (01299 822212).

Ludlow (Salop). Chub, dace. Ludlow AC (01584 873577) has 1,000m right bank u/s of Dinham Weir; Saltmore fishery, 500m below bridges, r bank dt from Ludlow tackle shops. Birmingham AA has 1m here, Ashford Carbonnel, Eastham and Lindridge. Delbury Hall Trout Fishery, Diddlebury SY7 9DH, tel: 01584 841267: dt £18, 2 fish limit. Tackle shop: Ludlow Tackle, Bromfield Rd SY8 1DW, (01584 875886), controls 5 stretches of dt water with good coarse fishing on Severn and on Teme, and local stillwaters. **Walcot West Lake**, 18 acres with bream and tench; tickets from Powys Arms Public House, or Ludlow tackle shops. Hotels: The Feathers, Angel, Bull, Bull Ring Tavern, Charlton Arms, and Exchange.

Knighton (Powys). Trout; preserved except for 1m free to licence-holders. Accom. with fishing, Red Lion, Llanfair Waterdine, on Teme (tel: 528214). For brown and rainbow trout, fly fishing pool nr **Llangunllo**, G Morgan, Gefnsuran, Llangunllo LD7 1SL, tel: 01547 550219. Farmhouse accom on site. Permits for **Elan Valley** fishing from Mr R Potts, 19 Station Rd. Hotels: Swan, Norton Arms.

ONNY: Good trout, chub, etc.

Plowden (Salop). Trout, chub; private water. Plowden Club has 4m trout fishing at Plowden Estate, members and guests only, no dt. Occasional membership, £120 plus joining fee.

Craven Arms (Salop). Water owned by Border Holidays (UK). Quinney and Byne Brooks, preserved and strictly keepered by Midland Flyfishers; trout, grayling; members only; no tickets; club also has water from Stokesay Castle Bridge to Bromfield. Stokesay Pool; pike, chub. Bache Pool, Bache Farm; carp; dt from farm. Dt for trout and grayling fishing on 150 yards of Onny from Mrs Maund, 1 Onny Cottage, The Grove.

SALWARPE: Trout, coarse fish. Birmingham AA has 1,300 yds at **Claines**.

Droitwich (Worcs). Trout above, coarse fish below. Severn 6m W. Droitwich and District AS has water at **Holt Fleet**; dt from Hon Sec to members' guests only. Noted chub waters. Society also has **Heriotts Pool** (large carp). Dt 80p on site. Two sections of Droitwich Canal at Porters Mill: 36 pegs, stocked with carp, chub, roach and rudd: dt £2.50 on bank; match bookings and other enquiries, tel: 01562 754809/630355. Astwood Fishery: 2 acre pool with carp and bream; dt on bank. Tel: 01905 770092. Tackle shop: Droitwich Fishing Tackle, 27 High St.

Bromsgrove (Worcs). Tardebigge Reservoir rented to Bourneville Club (messrs Cadburys) for many years. Limited st for local anglers. Upper and Lower Bittel Reservoirs owned by Barnt Green FC; members only *(see also Arrow-Alvechurch)*. Hewell Grange Lake; permits for local clubs. (See also Worcester and Birmingham Canal). Upton Warren Lake, 18 acres with carp and roach. Dt on bank; contact County Youth Sailing Centre (01527 861426), Tackle shops; Bromsgrove Angling, 54 Broad St, Sidemoor; Roy Huin, 138 Worcester Rd.

STOUR: Once heavily polluted, but fish now returning in some areas, principally lower river.

Stourbridge (Worcs). **Staffordshire and Worcestershire Canal**; coarse fish. Tackle shop: Riley's, Lower High Street (see also canal).

POLLUTION

Anglers are united in deploring pollution. To combat it, urgent action may be called for at any time, from any one of us. If numbers of fish are found dead, dying, or seriously distressed, take samples of both fish and water, and contact the officer responsible for pollution at the appropriate Environment Agency. (Emergency Hotline for reporting all environmental incidents relating to air, land and water: Tel. 0800 80 70 60).

Brierley Hill (W Midlands). Stour, 3m S, polluted. Clubs: Brierley Hill AC (no water) and various works clubs. Tackle shop: Black Country Tackle, 51 High St.

Dudley (W Midlands). Lakes: Pensnett Grove Pool, Middle Pool, Fenns Pool, 3m SW *(see Brierley Hill)*. **Netherton Reservoir**; Himley Park Lakes (01902 324093); 16 acres good coarse fishing with carp and tench, dt on bank. Plenty of fishing in canals within 6m radius. Lodge Farm Reservoir; Dudley Corporation. At Parkes Hall, **Coseley**, 2½m away, is good pool for which dt can be had; coarse fish (Dudley Corporation). Some local clubs are: Dudley AS, 01384 831924; Cross Keys AC, 01384 259147. Licences from Val's Pets, 100 Childs Avenue, Sedgley. Tackle from Hingley's, 46 Wolverhampton St, Dudley.

SMESTOW (tributary of Stour): Polluted.

Wolverhampton (W Midlands). Smestow, 2m W; polluted. Some fishing in **Penk** at Penkridge. Most local water on Severn held by Birmingham AA; permits from tackle shops. Patshull Park, nr Pattingham, trout and coarse, dt at lodge; Pool Hall, Compton, carp and other coarse, dt on bank. Lakes at Himley Park have dt. Swan Pool, **West Bromwich**, tel: 0121 553 0220: 20 acres with carp and pike, tickets on bank. **Staffordshire Worcester Canal** is Wolverhamton AA water. Tickets from local tackle shops: Fenwicks, Pitt Street, tel: 01902 24607; Catchers Angling, 386 Bilston Rd; Fenwick's, Pitt St.

TERN: Coarse fish, some trout.

Telford (Salop). Tickets from Telford Angling Centre, Church St, St Georges TF2 9JU (01952 610497), for Telford AA and other local clubs, including a good stretch at Ironbridge for barbel, pools, flashes and lakes. Raby Estate Waters, 9,000m one side, 3,000m other, tickets on bank or from Uppingham Estate Office (01952 740223). Baylis Pool, 10 acres with carp, bream. Dt on bank. Tel: 01952 460530.

Crudgington (Salop). A few trout and coarse fish. Cheshire AA have ¾m.

Hodnet (Salop). Tern. 1m E; a few trout and coarse fish. Strine Brook, 2m E. Lakes: Rose Hill Ponds, 4m NE. **Hawkstone Park Lake**, 3½m; excellent tench and carp water (40lb bags not uncommon) and large roach, rudd, pike and eels; private preserve of Wem AC, membership closed.

Market Drayton (Shrops/Staffs). Trout and coarse fish. Environment Agency has free fishery of 1,200 yds on right bank, mainly d/s of Walkmill Bridge, above sewage works. For stocked section, Tern Fisheries Ltd, Broomhall Grange, M Drayton TF9 2PA, tel: 01630 653222 (fax 657444). Dt £20, 5 fish, ½ day £10, 2 fish, eve £6, 1 fish. At **Great Sowdley**, 7m SE, are canal reservoirs; Stoke AS; perch, pike, roach, tench, carp. Market Drayton AC fishes Shropshire Union Canal at Knighton, Bridges 45-47, dt £1.50 on bank. Stoke City & Dist AA controls Sutton Lake, brown and rainbow trout, Tyrley Pool, coarse, both Market Drayton, and **Roden** at **Shawbury**, u/s and d/s of Poynton Bridge; also stretch of Shropshire Union Canal. No dt, membership from Stoke tackle shops or Hon Sec.

MEESE (tributary of Tern); Trout, coarse fish.

Newport (Salop). Meese, 1m N; trout; private. Lakes: Chetwynd Park Pond, 1m N. Minton's, Limekiln and Wildmoor Pools, 3m S. Moss Pool, 1½m NE. Park AC has good coarse fishing water on Grand Union Canal, with carp to 20lb, bream to 5lb, perch to 4lb: dt £2 on bank. Tackle shop, Newport Tackle, 91A High St. Hotels: Bridge Inn; Fox & Duck.

REA: Trout, grayling; preserved.

Minsterley (Salop). Trout, grayling, Minsterley Brook. Habberley Brook, 3m SE. Lake: Marton Pool, 7m SW. **Lea Cross**; Warrington AA fishes on 1,000 yds stretch.

SHELL BROOK (tributary of Roden):

Ellesmere (Salop). Shell Brook, 2m NW; preserved. Halghton Brook, 4m N. Roden, 6m SE. Lakes: **Ellesmere Meres**, noted for bream (12lb plus). Ellesmere AC (st £10), issues wt £5, dt £1.50 for **Whitemere** and **Blakemere** (bank fishing only). Sunday fishing is allowed. Boats on most assn waters for members only. Ellesmere AC members may fish 4m stretch of **Shropshire Union Canal**; coarse fish. Hotels: Black Lion, Bridgewater, Red Lion (Ellesmere AC HQ); tickets *(see also Shropshire lakes)*.

PERRY: Trout, preserved.

Ruyton Eleven Towns (Salop). 300m stretch on 1 bank with chub and pike; dt from Bridge Inn (01939 260651).

VYRNWY; Provides sport with trout, grayling, coarse fish and salmon.

Llanymynech (Salop). Trout, salmon, grayling, roach, perch, pike, eels, chub, barbel, etc. Oswestry AC has water here, members only, £10 st, conc. For Lord Bradford's water at Lower House Farm inquire of agent, Llanymynech. Phoenix AC has ¾m at Domgay Farm; **R Lugg** at Moreton, and Kidderminster Captains Pool, coarse fishing; dt £2. Contact Hon Sec. Tackle shop: Brian's Tackle, North Rd, Canalside, tel: 01691 830027, which supplies Montgomery AA tickets. Other hotels: Bradford Arms, Cross Keys, Dolphin. Good trout fishing at **Lake Vrynwy** *(see lakes in Welsh section).*

Llansantffraid (Powys). Warrington AA has water here on Vyrnwy and **R Cain**, on Vrynwy at **Four Crosses**, and **Cross Keys**. Cheshire AA has Myliniog Farm stretch.

Meiford (Powys). Montgomeryshire AA (01938 553867) has 750m l bank at Great Dufford Farm, with barbel and chub. Dt from Welshpool tackle shops.

MORDA (tributary of Vyrnwy): mostly trout, but some coarse fish in lower reaches.

Oswestry (Salop). Most river fishing preserved. Lloran Ganol Farm, **Llansilin** (tel: 01691 70286/7) offers accommodation with fishing; also Woran Isaf, **Llansilin** SY10 7QX, with trout lake (tel: 01691 70253). Oswestry AS has coarse fishing pools, st £10. Fawnog Fishing Lake, **Porthywaen**, well stocked with r and b trout. Tel: 01691 828474. Turfmoor Fishery, mixed, **Edgerley**; tel: 0174381 512. Trewalyn Fly Lakes, Deythaur, Llansantffraid (01691 828147): trout fishing. Stoke on Trent AS controls **Colemere**, 70 acre coarse lake nr Welshampton, with roach, bream. Tickets from D Sharpe, 30 Postland st, Hanley, Stoke on Trent. Westlake, 2½ acres, stocked r and b trout fishing, fly only. Dt £17, 2 acre coarse lake, dt £4. Domgay Rd, Four Crosses, **Llandrinio** SY22 6SJ, tel: 01691 831475. B & B, tearoom and tackle on site. Tackle shops: Guns and Angling Centre, G & A Building, Beatrice St (01691 653761); Brians Angling Supplies, North Rd, Llanymynech. Accom. with fishing: Hand Hotel, Llanarmon, tel: 01691 76666. Five coarse fishing ponds with accommodation: Sontley Farm Cottages, Middle Sontley, Wrexham LL13 0YP (01978 840088).

TANAT (tributary of Vyrnwy): Trout (good average size), chub and grayling.

Llan-y-Blodwel (Salop). Horseshoe Inn has 1½m (dt £3), 3 rods per day, fly only, and Green Inn, Llangedwyn, has short stretch; dt issued (3 rods only); fly only.

Llanrhaiadr-y-Mochnant (Powys); trout; free. Tanat, 1m; trout, grayling, chub, etc; 6m from Llangedwyn to Llangynog strictly preserved. No dt.

CAIN (tributary of Vyrnwy): Trout, coarse fish.

Llansantffraid (Powys). Trout. Warrington AA has two stretches.

BANWY (tributary of Vyrnwy): Trout, grayling, chub, pike, dace and chance of salmon here and there.

Llanfair-Caereinion (Powys). Montgomeryshire AA has right bank downstream from town bridge to boundary fence; mainly trout, some chub and dace. At **Cyffronydd** Warrington AA has 610 yds. 700 yds right bank at **Neuadd Bridge**; dt from Mr Edwards, Neuadd Bridge Farm, Caereinion. Hotel: Wynnstay Arms.

Llangadfan (Powys). Trout; Montgomeryshire AA has good stretch; dt from Hon Sec.

SHROPSHIRE LAKES

ELLESMERE LAKES. Fishing station: **Ellesmere**. Excellent coarse fishing in Ellesmere (noted for bream), **Crosemere**, **Newton Mere**, **Blakemere**, **Whitemere** (bream of 12lb 4oz taken). Controlled by Ellesmere AC who issue dt £1, bank fishing only, on **Blakemere**. Dt also for **Hardwick Pool** (1m) noted tench water from Clay, 5a Scotland Street.

WALCOT LAKES. Lydbury North, 3m NE of Clun. Two extensive lakes, one controlled by Birmingham Anglers' Assn. Tench, pike and other coarse fish.

SOMERSET (streams, lakes and reservoirs)

(For close seasons, licences, etc, see South West Region Environment Agency, p16)

AXE. Rises on Mendips and flows 25m NW to Bristol Channel near Weston-super-Mare. A few trout in upper reaches and tributaries, but essentially a coarse fish river, containing a mixture of the usual species, with roach now predominating.

Weston-super-Mare and Bleadon (Som). Weston-super-Mare & Dist AA fishes

A good day at Blagdon draws to a close. *Photo: J Wilshaw.*

Old R Axe, Bleadon, R Axe nr Weston, South and North Drains. Assn waters contain roach, bream, carp, perch, rudd, pike, eels. No night fishing. Active junior section. St £13, conc, wt and dt from Thyers Tackle, and Weston Angling Centre. North Somerset AA has water on **Brue** near **Highbridge, Old River Kenn (Blind Yeo), Congresbury Yeo**, and **North Drain**, Newtown and Apex Lakes, and Walrow Pond (jointly with Bridgwater AA), together with some smaller rivers. Membership £16, conc. Clevedon & Dist Freshwater AC fish Old River Kenn and R Kenn (Blind Yeo) at **Clevedon**, also Congresbury Yeo in Congresbury. Mainly bream, roach, tench, pike, a few trout. Dt £3 from tackle shops. Wessex Federation have **Parrett** from Thorney to Yeo, and below Langport. Tackle shops: Thyers Tackle, Church St, Highbridge; Richards Angling, Regent St, Burnham-on-Sea; Clevedon Angling Supplies, Old Market Hall, Alexandra Rd; Tackle Box, 15 Station Rd; both Clevedon.

BRICKYARD PONDS: **Pawlett.** BB&WAA tench fishery. St from Hon Sec or tackle shops *(see Bristol).*

BRISTOL RESERVOIRS:

Chew Valley, Blagdon and **Barrow** reservoirs provide some of the best lake trout fishing in Europe, with a total annual catch of 46,000 fish of high average size. Season and day tickets obtainable. All fishing is fly only. Limits are four brace per day, two brace per evening bank permit. Details as follows:

Barrow Reservoirs - Barrow Gurney; brown and rainbow trout; from Bristol Water *(see Chew Valley Lake),* bank fishing, fly only, No. 1 brown trout only.

Blagdon Lake - Blagdon; noted brown and rainbow trout water, bank fishing and rowing boats only.

Chew Valley Lake - Chew Stoke. Open April to November; noted brown and rainbow trout water where fish run large. For all waters apply to: Bristol Water Plc, Recreations Department, Woodford Lodge, Chew Stoke, Bristol BS18 8XH (01275 332339). Bank dt and part dt from self-service kiosk. Motor boats from Woodford Lodge office (advance booking recommended). Season tickets are priced as follows: all waters, £487; Chew £394; Barrows, £271. Day tickets: all waters, £8, Chew £7, Barrows, £4. Boats, £20.50 per rod; Chew £5.50. Concessions for jun (under 17), OAP and registered disabled. Tackle shops at Woodford and Blagdon Lodges, breakfasts at Woodford Lodge. Tackle hire and tuition arranged.

Cheddar Reservoir, Cheddar. Coarse fishery managed by Cheddar AC. Season and day permits, £24 and £12, from Broadway House Caravan Park, on A371 between Cheddar and Axbridge. No permits at water.

WESSEX WATER RESERVOIRS: Grosvenor House, The Square, Lower Bristol Road, Bath BA2 3EZ. Brochure enquiries, tel: 0345 300600. St from above address; dt from dispensing units at reservoirs. There is a season ticket covering Clatworthy, Sutton Bingham, Hawkridge: £310, £249 conc. Dt £11, conc £9. Boat £10 (2 anglers max). Limits: 4 fish on st, 5 fish on dt, 2 fish on evening ticket. Concessions for jun and OAP.

Clatworthy Reservoir. 12m from **Taunton** in Brendon Hills; 130 acres brown and rainbow trout; fly only; 2¼m bank fishing. Season Mar 25-Oct 18. Tel: 01984 623549.

Durleigh Reservoir. 2m W of **Bridgwater**. 80 acres; coarse fishing, carp, roach, bream, pike. Biggest recently, pike 27lb, carp 18lb, bream 7lb. Dt £4, eve £2.50. Tel: 01278 424786 for more information.

Hawkridge Reservoir. 7m W of Bridgwater. 32 acres. Brown and rainbow trout; fly only. Season Mar 18-Oct 11. Boat or bank. Tel: 01278 671840.

Otterhead Lakes. About 1m from **Churchingford** nr Taunton. Two lakes of 2¾ and 2 acres; brown and rainbow trout; fly only; no boats. Season Mar 18-Oct 11.

Sutton Bingham Reservoir. 3m S of **Yeovil**. 142 acres. Brown and rainbow trout; average 1¼lb; fly only, bank or boat; season Mar 18-Oct 11. Tel: 01935 872389.

CHARGOT WATER, Luxborough. 3 ponds. Trout; fly only.

DONIFORD STREAM (Swill River at Doniford) and **WASHFORD RIVER, Taunton**. Trout; preserved.

HORNER WATER. On National Trust Holnicote Estate, Selworthy TA24 8TJ; upstream from Packhorse Bridge, Horner, to Pool Bridge, approx 2½m; fly fishing, small wild trout. Dt £1 from Horner Tea Garden.

WIMBLEBALL LAKE, Dulverton. 374 acres. SWW, fly only, well-known stocked rainbow trout fishery. Season Apr 1-Oct 31, boats from May 1. Dt £13, boats £7.50, (Allenard boat for disabled), conc, from self-service kiosk at Hill Farm Barn. Wimbleball Flyfishers Club obtains discount permits for members. Tackle shop: L Nicholson, High St, Dulverton TA22 9HB. Hotel: Carnarvon Arms.

YEO. Fishing station: **Congresbury**. Tidal, good fly water for trout; a few coarse fish. Somerset AA has various short stretches in area. Clevedon & Dist Freshwater AC fish here, roach, bream, a few trout. Dt £3 from Clevedon tackle shops (*see Weston*).

STOUR (Dorset)

(For close seasons, licences, etc, see South West Region Environment Agency, p16)

Rises in Wiltshire Downs and flows through Dorset, joining Hampshire Avon at its mouth at Christchurch. Noted coarse fishery throughout year (large barbel, chub, roach, dace and pike are common).

Christchurch (Dorset). Avon and Stour. Pike, perch, chub, roach, tench, dace. Christchurch AC has many miles of Stour, Avon, plus numerous gravel pits, lakes and ponds. Limited dt for lower Stour and harbour, and Lifelands stretch of Hants Avon, Ringwood, from Davis (*address below*). Club membership, £80 pa, conc, juv and OAP. **Hordle Lakes**, 1m from New Milton; 5 lakes of total 5 acres, coarse fishing. Dt £2-£6 from Davis (*below*). Coarse fishing can be had on Royalty Fishery waters *(see Avon)*, and Winkton Fishery. Sea fishing from Mudeford in Christchurch Bay is fair. Tackle shops: Pro Fishing Tackle, 258 Barrack Road; Davis Fishing Tackle, 75 Bargates; Yesterday Tackle, 42 Clingan. Hotel: King's Arms, Christchurch.

Throop (Dorset). Throop fisheries; 5½m of top quality coarse fishing; preserved. Carp to 26lb 6oz, pike to 27lb, barbel to 12lb 9oz, chub to 6½lb, roach to 3lb in 1995. Also a mill pool stocked with roach, bream, carp and tench. Coarse fishing: st £92, ft £46, wt £25.80, dt £5.75 (reduced rates for OAP and juv; special rates for clubs: booking essential). Throop Fisheries own holiday cottage for family summer lets, overlooking river.

Disabled facilities. Tackle and bait shop open throughout season. For tickets, licences and all inquiries apply to Glenn Sutcliffe, Manager, South Lodge, Holdenhurst Village, Bournemouth. Tel 01202 35532, fax 01202 395532.

Hurn Bridge (Dorset). Stour and Moors; no angling. Preserved now as a bird sanctuary.

STOUR (Dorset) - Tributaries

Wimborne (Dorset). Good chub, roach, bream, barbel, dace and pike. Some trout in Stour, also in R Allen. Small runs of salmon and sea trout. Red Spinner AS has water at Barford and Eyebridge; about 9m in all; members only. Wimborne & Dist AC has approx 10m of Stour in Wimborne, Longham to Child Okeford; eight coarse and six trout lakes, and stretch of Avon at Fordingbridge. Membership £50 pa, contact Sec (tel: 01202 382123). Environment Agency own Little Canford Ponds, Wimborne, coarse fishery with good access for disabled. Leaflet from Conservation Officer. Tackle shops: Minster Sports, Wimborne; Wessex Angling Centre 321 Wimborne Rd, Oakdale, Poole. Hotels: King's Head, Three Lions, Greyhound.

Sturminster Marshall (Dorset). Southampton PS has about 2m here. Coarse, a few trout; dt £3 from Minster Sports, Wimborn Minster; ten venues on offer. The Old Mill Guest House, Corfe Mullen, now lets to Wimborne AC, day tickets £5 from local tackle shops. Dt on site for Dorset Springs, Sturminster Marshall, 01258 857653, 3 acre stocked coarse fishery.

Shapwick (Dorset). Coarse fish. Southampton PS has several miles of fishing here; dt £3, conc, from Minster Sports, Wimborne Minster.

Blandford Forum (Dorset). Fine roach, chub, dace, perch, bream, carp and pike; good all year. Some tench. Durweston AS has fishing. St £20, dt £5, from C Light, 4 Water Lane, Durweston, Blandford. Dt from Durweston Stores. Blandford and Dist AC have most fishing from **Durweston** Bridge to **Crawford** Bridge (tickets for Bryanston school stretch £3, £1 conc) and 2 coarse lakes at **Buckland Newton**. St £19, dt £2 (lakes) from Hon Sec or A Conyers (tackle shop), West Street. Also club membership forms and licences (Tel: 012584 2307). Other clubs with fishing in area: Durweston AC, Ringwood AC.

Sturminster Newton (Dorset). Chub, roach, dace, pike, perch, tench, bream; fishing good. Sturminster and Hinton AA has 7m above and below town; 2 lakes at Stoke Wake, with tench; lake at Okeford Fitzpaine, mixed fishery, members only, St £15. For wt £10 and dt £3 apply to Harts Garden Centre, or Kens Autos, both Sturminster Newton. Gillingham 7 Dist AA has 5 lake complex at Mappowder, nr Sturminster Newton, dt £4 from Kings Stag Garage or Gillingham tackle shop. Tackle and baits from Harts. Hotel: White Hart.

Stalbridge (Dorset). Chub, roach, tench, dace, pike. Stalbridge AS (membership £15 pa) has 2m of Stour, 2m on **Lydden** and 2 lakes for members only at **Buckland Newton**. Wt £15, dt £3 (jun ½ price) from Corner Cottage Tackle Shop, High St.

Gillingham (Dorset). Trout and coarse fish. Gillingham and Dist AA has fishing from Mere to Stalbridge, dt £4 from tackle shop or club treasurer; **Turner's Paddock Lake**, coarse dt £5; Loddon Lakes, members only. Tackle shop: D & D Angling, High St. Hotel: Royal (01747 822305).

Stourton (Wilts). **Stourhead New Lake** on Stourhead (Western) Estate at Stourton, near Mere. Now a fly fishing syndicate water. Rods from April to September. Contact Malcolm Bullen, tel: 01747 840624.

MOORS:

Verwood (Dorset). Trout in parts, otherwise mainly roach; Ringwood club has water.

STOUR (Kent)

(For close seasons, licences etc, see Thames Region Environment Agency, p20).

Rises in two arms north-west and south-east of Ashford, where they join. From junction river flows about 30m north-east and east to sea beyond Sandwich. Below Canterbury, good roach fishing with fish to 2lb common, bream to 6lb and pike over 20lb. Trout fishing restricted to club members in upper reaches.

Sandwich (Kent). River fast-flowing from Minster to Sandwich (Vigo Sluice); good fishing for bream and roach; few perch and tench; sea trout and grey mullet. Free fishing from quay and from Ropewalk, carp, tench, roach. Private fishing from Richborough Road, upstream. Sandwich and Dist AA has Reed Pond and Swallowbrook Water; **Stonar Lake** (stocked, carp and rudd), dt £5 from tackle shop. and North and South Streams, **Lydden**. Tackle shop: Brian Bayliss, Sandwich Bait and Tackle, 13 The Chain. Hotel: Bell.

Grove Ferry. Stour and Little Stour. Betteshanger Colliery Welfare AS has 6m on Stour from **Plucks' Gutter** to **Stonar**. Roach, bream and mullet (Red Lion stretch, June-Aug). Society also has stretch at **Minster**. Tickets from Hon Sec, Red Lion or bailiff on bank.

Canterbury (Kent). Trout, tench, bream, roach, rudd, pike, etc. Free within city boundary, except for municipal gardens stretch. Canterbury & Dist AA hold water from city boundary d/s to Plucks Gutter, 9 both banks, dt £3 from Grove Ferry to Plucks Gutter, from bailiff on bank; also Fordwich Lakes, Stour Lake (trout pool), Trentley Lake, Royal Military Canal from Appledore Dam to Kennardington Bridge (dt £3 on bank). Assc st £36, ½ price conc. Chilham Mill AC controls 12 lakes and 2 stretches of river, coarse and trout fishing, at Chilham. Limited dt on some waters. Fly fishing is £35-£18 per day, strictly in advance. Contact Mid Kent Fisheries, Chilham Water Mill, Ashford Rd, Chilham CT4 8EE, tel: 01227 730668. Stour and Trenchley Lakes, fine coarse fishing, and **Fordwich Lake**, members only. **Honeycroft Fisheries**, 7 acre coarse lake, large carp. Tel 01732 851544. Tackle shop: Greenfield's Rod and Gun Store, 4/5 Upper Bridge Street. Hotels: County; Falstaff; George and Dragon.

Ashford (Kent). Ashford AS holds **River Stour** between **Ashford** and **Wye** (members only). Cinque Ports AS controls 4½m of Royal Military Canal from Seabrook Outfall, Hythe, to Giggers Green, Ashford. St £15 (+ entrance fee £7.50, conc), dt £2, conc 50p, from bailiff. Ashford Working Men's Club has a pit; good tench, carp, rudd; members only; no dt. Chequer Tree Trout Fishery is at **Bethersden**, tel: 01233 820383. Dt £15 to £6.50. Licences, tuition, tackle hire and camping facilities on site. Coarse dt £2. Tackle shops: Ashford Angling Centre, 36 Stanhope Square; Denn's Tackle, Dymchurch Rd, Hythe. Hotels: County, Kent Arms.

LITTLE STOUR: Same fish as main river but overgrown in places. Most fishing now private.

WANTSUM. Carp, tench, bream, perch, roach, rudd, gudgeon. Wantsum AA has water from sea wall between Reculver and Minnis Bay to Chambers Wall Farm at St Nicholas-at-Wade, and 2m on Stour at **Minster**. Left of car park at R Wantsum members only, otherwise dt £2, conc, on bank. Membership £17 plus £5 enrolment, conc £5. Tackle shop: Kingfisheries, 34 King Street, Margate.

STOUR (Suffolk)

(For close seasons, licences etc, see Thames Region Environment Agency, p20).

Coarse fish river forming border between Suffolk and Essex. Enters sea at Harwich via large estuary. Some sea trout in semi-tidal waters below Flatford.

Harwich (Essex). Harwich AC has several coarse fisheries in area: Dock River; Oakley Lodge Reservoirs, Great Oakley; The Dykes, Harwich, with roach, rudd, pike, perch, carp, eels, bream. Members only; weekly membership sold at Dovercourt Aquatics and Angling Centre, Main Rd, Dovercourt, Harwich.

Manningtree (Essex). Tidal; roach, dace, perch, pike and occasional sea trout (fish of 9lb caught). Lawford AC has stretch at **Cattewade** (A137 bridge). Tickets. Dt from bailiff for Elm Park, Hornchurch and Dist AS stretch between club notices at **Flatford Mill**. Hotel: White Hart.

Nayland (Suffolk). Bream, chub, dace, perch, pike, roach, tench. Colchester APS has water here and at **Wiston**, **Boxted**, **Langham** and **Stratford St Mary**. New membership £43 incl £4 entry, to Box 1286, Colchester CO2 8PG. No dt. Colnes AS has stretches at **Little Horkesley**. Dt from P Emsom, Tackle Shop, Earls Colne.

Bures (Essex). Colnes AC has stretch. Dt from Emson, Tackle Shop, Earls Colne. London AA controls a good deal of water here and in **Clare, Cavendish** and **Sudbury** areas. Also **Bures Lake**; members only, but some waters open to associates at Bures. Moor Hall and Belhus AS has 2 excellent coarse lakes of 5 and 7 acres at Hill Farm Fishery and Little Belhus Pits, **South Ockenden**. Members only, details on application.

Henny Bridge (Essex). Great Cornard AC fishes from Henny Bridge to Henny Weir. Book a month in advance, dt £1.50.

Sudbury (Suffolk). Bream, roach, chub, dace, tench, carp, perch, pike, gudgeon. Eight stretches around Sudbury, and 4 large lakes incl. Rushbrook and Donylands (Snake Pit), controlled by Sudbury & Dist AA. Donylands Lake contains large carp, also sizeable tench. Membership £30, conc. Tickets from bailiff on most waters, or from tackle shops. Hadleigh & Dist AS have various stretches on Stour, R Brett and 6 local stillwaters. restricted membership £24, concessions. D R Warner, 5 Churchill Ave, Hadleigh, IP7 6BT. Tackle shops: Sudbury Angling, No 1, Unit 2, Acton Square CO10 6HG; Stour Valley Tackle, East St, both Sudbury.

Haverhill (Suffolk). Haverhill Angling Centre, 2A Primrose Hill, Camps Rd, Haverhill CB9 9LF (01440 705011), has tickets for R Stour and numerous lakes controlled by Haverhill AA.

SURREY (lakes)

BURY HILL FISHERIES. Nr. Dorking. Well known coarse fishery of three lakes, the largest of which is 12½ acres. Particularly known for its tench, roach, carp, bream, pike and zander fishing, all of which run to specimen size. Also good stocks of rudd, perch and crucian carp. Open all year, bank and boat fishing, full facilities include sit down cafe, all of which are suitable for disabled anglers. Dt £8, one rod, second rod £4 extra. Boat: £4 per person. Evening £4 per rod. Concessions to jun, OAP. Match bookings and corporate days organised. Further details from Fishery Manager, Estate Office, Old Bury Hill, Surrey RH4 3TY, tel: 01306 883621/877540.

ENTON LAKES. Witley, Nr Godalming. Trout fishery of two lakes total 16 acres, bank and boat fishing. Dt £25 (4 fish), boat £5 per person extra. Steven Hillbery, Enton Lakes, Petworth Rd, Witley, GU8 5LZ, tel: 01428 682620.Chalet accommodation on site.

FRENSHAM PONDS. Farnham (4m). 60 acres and 30 acres. Farnham AS has rights on Great Pond, and Little Pond, leased from NT; coarse fishing; members of Farnham AS only.

FRIMLEY, nr **Camberley**. 4 Leisure Sport lakes totalling 47 acres stocked with large carp and all other coarse species. St £24, £12 conc. (*See below*).

RIPLEY. Papercourt fishery, Sendmarsh. Pike, bream, tench, chub, perch, eels, roach. A Leisure Sport restricted permit fishery. St £24, ½ price conc. No day ticket. Applications to LSA, RMC House, High Street, Feltham, Middlesex TW13 4HD, tel: 0181 8931168.

SOUTH LAKE, Yateley. 8 acre lake heavily stocked with carp to 30lbs. Dt only, £6 or £10. From Yateley Angling Centre, 16 the Parade (01252 861955) A Leisure Sports fishery.

TRILAKES. Sandhurst (Berks). Mixed fishery; well stocked with tench, very large carp (common and crucian, ghost), bream, rudd, roach, perch, pike, eels, trout. Open 8am to 7,30 pm or sunset if earlier. Purchase dt on entry, £7. Car park, licensed cafe, access for disabled: (Tel 01252 873191).

VIRGINIA WATER. Virginia Water, Johnson Pond and Obelisk Pond, Windsor Great Park fishable by season ticket only; coarse fish; st £35 (incl VAT). Early application advised in writing, to Crown Estate Office, The Great Park, Windsor, Berks SL4 2HT (sae).

WILLOW PARK, Ash Vale, nr Aldershot. Three lakes of 15 acres, mixed fishery stocked with a variety of species. Dt £6, £12 double rod, from bailiff. Night permit £15 from fishery, Youngs Drive, Shawfields Rd; tel: 01252 25867.

WINKWORTH LAKES. Winkworth, nr Godalming. National Trust property. Trout fishery (fly fishing and boats only) managed by Godalming AS. St £160, waiting list. Details from Hon Sec.

WIREMILL POOL. Nr **Lingfield**. Coarse fish include tench up to 6lb, bream up to 7lb, roach up to 3lb, carp up to 6lb.

YATELEY. Nr Camberley. Thirteen Leisure Sport lakes totalling 73 acres

A brace of 20 pounders caught at Ardingly Reservoir during the winter. *Photo: N Roberts*

stocked with pike, carp, tench, roach and perch, bream, rudd, catfish, crucian carp. Large specimens recorded, carp to 46lb. A restricted permit fishery. St £34, day and night £60. No dt. Concessions to jun, OAP, dis. Applications to LSA, RMC House, High Street, Feltham, Middlesex TW13 4HD, tel: 0181 8931168.

SUSSEX (lakes and streams)

ARDINGLY RESERVOIR. Ardingly, nr Haywards Heath. 198 acre coarse fishery; coarse season 1st June-1st June; 16 June; pike season 1 Oct-1 May, dt 1 Nov-31 Mar. (Only very experienced specialist pike anglers allowed, 18+.) Enq to The Lodge, Ardingly Reservoir, Ardingly, W Sussex RH17 6SQ. Tel: 01444 892591.

ARLINGTON RESERVOIR, South East Water, Fishing Lodge, Berwick, Polegate, BN26 6TF, tel: 01323 870810. Fly fishing for rainbow trout. Information from Fishing Lodge. Dt in advance.

BARCOMBE RESERVOIR, Nr Lewes. 40 acres, South East Water, fly fishing for rainbow trout only. Information from Fishing Lodge (01273 814819). Dt in advance.

BUXTED. Uckfield. Buxted Oast Farm, TN22 4AU, coarse pond, Mr Greenland, tel: 01825 733446. Cyprus Wood Trout Fishery, Tallanmoor Cottage, Howbourne Lane TN22 4QD, contact Mr & Mrs Cottenham, tel: 01825 733455. Tackle, B & B on site. Boringwheel Trout Fishery, **Nutley**, tel: 01825 712629.

CHICHESTER CANAL. Chichester (W Sussex). Chichester Canal Society has 2½m from Chichester to Donnington Bridge, with roach, rudd, perch, carp, tench, bream, pike, eels, chub and dace. No fish to be removed. St £21, dt £2.40, conc, from bailiffs on bank. Southern Anglers have 1¾m south from A27 road, with tench, carp, roach, perch, pike. 24 hr fishing. Annual subscription £39, conc. Mixed fishery at Lakeside Village, tel: 01243 787715. Tackle shops: Southern Leisure Centre, Vinnestrow Rd; Southern Angling Specialists, 2 Stockbridge Place. Selsey tackle shop: Raycrafts, 119 High Street Selsey (01243 606039), sells canal angling tickets.

DARWELL WATER. At Mountfield, **Robertsbridge** (Tel: 01580 880407); brown and rainbow trout to 6lb; 180 acres; leased from Southern Water by Hastings Flyfishers Club Ltd; membership £220, st £250, dt £13.50, self-vending service at fishing lodge; boats £10 day extra, to be booked 48 hrs in advance from bailiff. Fly only; limit 6 fish; season Apr 3-Oct 31. Take precise care over approach route down small lanes.

FRAMFIELD PARK FISHERY, Brookhouse Rd, Framfield, Nr Uckfield TN22 5QJ, tel: 01825 890948. Three coarse fishing lakes totalling over 17 acres. Good match weights, with large tench, bream and carp. Shop on site. Bailiff will give instruction, free to juniors.

FURNACE BROOK TROUT FISHERY Nr. Herstmonceux. Brown and rainbow trout from 2lbs up. Dt £10. St water. Phone 01435 830298 or 830151 for details.

POWDERMILL WATER. Sedlescombe. 52 acres, brown and rainbow trout to 6lb. Hastings Flyfishers Club Ltd. (*See Darwell Water.*) Bookings, tel: 01424 870498, between 8.30 and 9.30 am.

MILTON MOUNT LAKE. Three Bridges (W Sussex). Crawley AS water (st £20); mostly carp; dt, Crawley AS also has Titternus Lake (pike, tench, carp, roach, perch) and **Sandford Brook** (trout; fly only) in Tilgate Forest; Roffey Park Lake, near Colgate (carp, roach, tench, perch, gudgeon); New Pond, Pease Pottage (carp and crucian carp, tench), the Mill Pond, Gossops Green, and Furnace Lake, Felbridge (carp and crucian carp). These are for members and guests only. At **Buchan Park** nr Crawley, Crawley AS has lakes; dt £2 from Hon Sec; carp pike, etc.

CLIVE VALE RESERVOIRS. Harold Road: mixed coarse fishery, Clive Vale AC; st £23, junior £10; dt £4.50, junior £2.50.

ECCLESBOURNE RESERVOIR. Hastings. Good carp, tench, roach, bream pike and rudd. Tickets issued by Clive Vale AC. St £23 from Hon Sec. Dt £5 on bank, or from local tackle shops, which include Redfearns, Castle St, Hastings; Tight Lines, Station Rd, Bexhill.

PEVENSEY LEVELS. Marshland drained by various streams into **Pevensey Haven** and **Wallers Haven**; good coarse fishing on large streams (pike, roach, rudd, perch, bream, carp and tench), most of best waters rented by clubs. Fishing stations: **Eastbourne, Hailsham, Pevensey.**

Southdown AA has major stretches of Pevensey Haven between Pevensey and Rickney, also Railland's Ditch and Chilley Stream (tench, bream, rudd, perch, carp and eels); both banks of Wallers Haven (renowned pike, tench and bream); water on **R Cuckmere** on both banks between Horsebridge and Alfriston, Abbots Wood and three other small lakes at Arlington, stocked with large carp, and other species. Tickets, st £25, dt £3 from Hon Sec at Polegate Angling Centre, 101 Station Rd, Polegate BN26 6EB; or from Anglers Den, 6 North Rd, Pevensey Bay.

SCARLETTS LAKE. 3 acres, between E Grinstead and **Tunbridge Wells**. Good coarse fishing, carp incl (Free st offered to any angler beating record carp, 23lb 4oz). Dt £5 at lakeside. St £50 from lakeside or Jackson, Scarletts Lake, Furnace Lane, Cowden, Edenbridge, Kent TN8 7JJ. (Tel: 01342 850414). F/t students, OAP, jun, dis, unemployed, 50%.

WEIR WOOD RESERVOIR. Forest Row (W Sussex), 1½m; **East Grinstead**, 4m; 280 acres. Re-stocked with trout for 1986 season, after some years as a coarse fishery. Fly only April 2-Oct 31, thereafter any legal rod & line method. St £325, 25 visits £135 (3 fish per visit), dt £6.50 to £11, full 6-fish limit, conc. Enquiries to The Lodge, Weir Wood Reservoir, Forest Row, Sussex, tel: 01342 822731 (24 hour). Tackle shop: Mike Wickams Fishing Tackle, 4 Middle Row, E Grinstead.

TAMAR

(For close seasons, licences etc, see South West Region Environment Agency, p16)

Rises in Cornwall and follows boundary between Devon and Cornwall for good part of course, emptying finally into Plymouth Sound. Holds salmon, sea trout, brown trout to the pound not uncommon.

Milton Abbot (Devon). Endsleigh FC has 9m, salmon and sea trout. Limited wt and dt (£140-£322 and £20-£48) for guests at the historic Endsleigh House, PL19 0PQ, tel: 01822 870248. Average salmon catch 230; 90% taken on fly. Good car access to pools. Tuition on site. Apply to Manager for accommodation details, and to J

8lb Rainbow - Chew Lake. Caught by Mr A Reynolds from a boat *Villice Bay* on Worm Fly. *Photo: Bristol Water Fisheries.*

Medd, 52 Strode Rd, Fulham, London SW6 6BN (0171 610 1982) for fishing.

Lifton (Devon). Tamar, **Lyd, Thrushel, Carey, Wolf** and **Ottery**; trout, sea trout (late June to end Sept), salmon (May, to mid-October). Hotel: Arundell Arms, Lifton, Devon PL16 0AA, tel: 01566 784666 (fax 784494), has 20m of excellent water in lovely surroundings; 23 individual beats, also 3-acre trout lake, brown and rainbow trout to 9lb. Licences and tackle at hotel, fly fishing courses (beginners and semi-advanced) by two resident instructors. Dt (when there are vacancies) for S & ST £15.50-£25, according to date; lake trout £17, brown trout £16. *(See advt).*

Launceston (Cornwall). Salmon, sea trout, trout. Permits can be obtained for seven miles of Tamar, also **Ottery, Kensey, Inney** and **Carey** from Launceston AA, which has about 16m of fishing in all. Lakes and ponds: **Stone Lake**, 4½ acres coarse fishing, tel: 0183786 253. **Tredidon Barton Lake**, dt £2, tel: 0156686 288. **Alder Quarry Pond**, Lewdown, Okehampton EX20 4PJ, tel: 01566 783444, 4½ acres, coarse, dt water. **Dutson Water**, coarse fishing, tel: 01566 2607. Hotels: White Hart; Eagle House; Race Horse Inn, North Hill. Launceston Publicity Committee issues booklet listing accommodation.

Bridgerule (Devon). **Tamar Lakes** here: SWW waters for which tickets are issued, *(See Cornwall lakes).* Hotel: Court Barn, Clawton, Holsworthy.

Tributaries of the Tamar

TAVY: A moorland spate river, rises in Cranmere Pool on Dartmoor and flows about 17m before entering Tamar estuary at Bere Ferrers. Excellent salmon and sea-trout river.

Tavistock (Devon). Tavy, Walkham and Plym FC; limited membership. Salmon, sea trout and brown trout permits for visitors on main river, **Meavy, Plym** and **Walkham**. Spinning allowed but no natural baits. Salmon and sea trout st £100, dt £15. Brown trout st £40, mt £20, wt £15, dt £5, from Barkells, 15 Duke Street, Tavistock PL19 0BA; DK Sports, The Barbican, Plymouth. **Tavistock Trout Fishery** (01822 618886): on A386 towards Oakhampton; fishing on four lakes beside R Tavy, holder of 30lb 12oz record for cultivated rainbow. Full wt £36, 5 fish per day. Dt £23.50, 3 fish. Fishery owns Trout 'n' Tipple Hotel (01822 61886). Other Hotel: Bedford (salmon and trout fishing on Tamar and Tavy); Endsleigh.

Mary Tavy (Devon). Brown trout; late run of salmon and sea trout. Fishing mostly privately owned. Plymouth & Dist Freshwater AA has rights at **Peter Tavy** (members only, st £80 from D L Owen, tel: 01752 705033).

Yelverton (Devon). Good centre for Tavy, Walkham and Plym FC waters. Salmon, sea trout. Ticket suppliers listed under Tavistock. Hotels: Moorland Links; Rock.

WALKHAM (tributary of Tavy): rises north-west of Princetown, and joins the Tavy below Tavistock. Upper reaches rocky and overhung, but downstream from Horrabridge there are many fishable pools. Peal run from July onwards.

INNY: Trout, sea trout.

LYD: Trout, sea trout, some salmon.

Lifton (Devon). Arundell Arms *(see advt)* has fishing for salmon, sea trout and brown trout, also on main river and other tributaries.

TAW

(For close seasons, licences etc, see South West Region Environment Agency, p16)

Rises on Dartmoor and flows 50m to Barnstaple Bay, where it forms estuary. Salmon with sea trout (peal) from May onwards. Excellent brown trout always available and good coarse fishing in places.

Barnstaple (Devon). Bass and mullet in estuary. Salmon, trout, peal, roach and dace. Salmon best March, April, May; peal July, August. Barnstaple and Dist AA has water immediately below New Bridge (d/s of this, 300 yds free water), on **Yeo** (trout and sea trout), and on pond at **Lake Venn** (carp, tench, bream, rudd, perch). Visitors' tickets for salmon, trout and coarse fisheries from local tackle shop or Hon Sec. Visitors may become assn members which entitles them to coarse fishing in ponds (Mon-Fri only). Tickets limited and not weekends or Bank Holidays. Riverton House and Lakes, Swimbridge, EX32 0QX, tel: 01271 830009, has coarse fishing on two 2 acre lakes, carp, bream, tench, roach, perch, rudd. Night fishing by prior arrangement. Dt £4.50, evening £3.50, £2. Self-catering cottages on site. **Braunton,** has coarse fishing with carp over 20lbs. Dt £5-£3. Tel: 01271 812414. Self catering and B & B. C L and Mrs Hartnell, Little Bray House, **Brayford,** have about 1m (both banks) of Bray; small trout only; dt £2. For other trout fishing see tributary Yeo. East and West Lyns, Badgeworthy Water and Heddon are accessible, as well as fishing on Wistlandpound and Slade Reservoirs. Tackle shop: The Kingfisher, 22 Castle St, supplies local tickets and information.

Chapelton (Devon). Salmon, peal, trout, dace. Taw mostly private down to New Bridge. Barnstaple and Dist AC water below *(see Barnstaple).*

Umberleigh (Devon). Salmon, peal, trout; preserved. Rising Sun has almost 4m of water (eight beats) for which dt are issued when not required for residents; fly only after April 30. Sunday fishing is allowed; salmon best March, April, May, August and September; sea trout June, July, August and September. Brochure, giving charges, etc, on request. Dt £25 non-residents, £21.50 residents only. Other hotel: Northcote Manor, Burrington.

South Molton (Devon). Oaktree Carp Farm and Fishery, Yeo Mill, EX36 3PU, tel: 01398 341568. three lakes: two match, one specimen, large carp, tench, roach, open all year.

Eggesford, Chulmleigh (Devon). Fox and Hounds Hotel has 7m of private salmon, sea trout and brown trout fishing on Taw. Spinning March to May. Fly only from May 1. No fishing in Feb. St £600-£350, wt £100, dt £18.50 and £10. Salmon fishing March-April. Full details from hotel.

Coldridge (Devon). Taw Fishing Club has water from Brushford Bridge to Hawkridge Bridge; very good trout fishing; complimentary for members' guests only. St £40 + joining fee £40. Limited to 30.

Chenson (Devon). Chenson Fishery, salmon from 1 Mar, sea trout from Apr, trout. St only, £150-£250. Contact M Nicholson, Schoolmasters Cottage, Chenson, Chulmleigh.

North Tawton (Devon). Trout. Burton Hall Hotel has about 4m of water here; trout; occasional sea trout and salmon. Free to guests; dt issued subject to hotel bookings. K Dunn, The Barton, also issues dt for about 1m.

Sticklepath (Devon). Trout. Dt £1 from Mr & Mrs P A Herriman, Davencourt, Taw Green, S Tawton for ½m downstream. Accommodation: Taw River Inn.

YEO (Barnstaple): Sea and brown trout. Barnstaple and Dist AA has water on Yeo, wt and dt from Barnstaple tackle shop. *(See Barnstaple).*

BRAY (tributary of Mole):

South Molton (Devon). South Molton AC has right bank from Brayly Bridge u/s to Newton Bridge, with salmon, trout and peal, fly only; £5 dt issued, from Hon Sec. Tackle shop: Sports Centre, 130 East St, South Molton, EX36 3BU. Hotels: The George; The Tiverton.

North Molton (Devon). Trout, sea trout, few salmon; ns South Molton, 2m. Poltimore Arms Hotel has 2m of fishing on Bray; fishing good. Cdr R H Dean, Little Bray House, **Brayford**, issues dt for about 1m of river.

TEES

(For close seasons, licences etc, see North East Region Environment Agency, p17)

Rises below Cross Fell in Pennines, flows eastward between Durham and Yorkshire and empties into North Sea near Middlesbrough. The Tees Barrage was completed in June 1995, and has already created a much cleaner river, upstream. Fish are being caught throughout all previously tidal stretches, from the new Princess of Wales Bridge to Thornaby and above. Well stocked from Middleton-on-Tees down to Croft.

Middlesbrough (Cleveland). NW reservoirs **Lockwood** and **Scaling Dam** in vicinity. Stocked with trout; dt on site. Middlesbrough AA have R Tees at Over Dinsdale, trout and usual coarse fish, 8 stretches of **R Swale** at Ainderby, Gatenby, Maunby, Skipton, Wiske, Danotty Hall, Holme and Baldersby, Marske Reservoir (stocked with carp) and ponds, all good coarse fishing. Local tackle shops: Anglers Choice, 53 Clive Rd, who has st £20 (+ £10 entry), conc, for Middlesbrough AA waters, and tickets for Middlesbrough stillwaters; Cleveland Angling Centre, Thornaby.

Stockton (Cleveland). Trout; grayling, coarse fish on one of best stretches of river. Stockton AA has over 10m at **Gainford**, **Winston**, **Dinsdale**, **Middleton-on-Row**, nr Darlington, **Aislaby**, nr Yarm, and on **Swale**, nr **Ainderby** (Moreton-on-Swale) and above Great Langton, lower reaches of Tees and Swale fishinngs. **Hartlepool Reservoir** is coarse fishery run by Hartlepool & Dist AC. Contact Mr J Hartland, 7 Chillingham Ct, Billingham, Teeside. Tackle shop: F Flynn, 12 Varo Terrace, Stockton; Tackle Box, Station Rd, Billingham, Stockton. Stockton Tees permits are sold at Anglers Choice, 53 Clive Rd, Middlesbrough TS5 6BH.

Eaglescliff, (Cleveland). Yorkshire bank in Yarm free fishing. **Leven** joins just below Yarm. Trout and coarse fish. Middlesbrough AA to falls; Thornaby and Yarm AA together up to Hutton Rudby. Excellent brown trout fishing; occasional sea trout.

Yarm (Cleveland). Tidal good coarse fishing; chub, dace, roach, occasional trout. Some free fishing inside of loop surrounding town, ½m, on E.A. licence. Mixed fishery, deep, slow moving water. Yarm AA, strong team club with 15m of Tees fishing at Low Middleton, Yarm, Over Dinsdale, Sockburn and Piercebridge; members of Assn. of Teeside & Dist Angling Clubs, with 10m water; st £29, dt £1.50; limited dt from Yarm AA headquarters, 4 Blenavon Court, Yarm, tel: 0164278 6444.

Neasham (Durham). Free fishing for 300 yards behind Fox and Hounds pub (mixed fishery).

Sockburn (Durham). Chub, dace, roach. Approx 3m controlled by Assc of Tesside & Dist Angling Clubs, which consists of Thornaby AA, Yarm AA, Darlington Brown Trout Anglers and Stockton Anglers.

Croft (Durham). Fair head of trout, grayling and coarse fish. Free fishing for 200 yds upstream of road bridge. Several miles controlled by Thornaby Anglers, members only, application forms from W P Adams *(see Darlington)*.

Darlington (Durham). Trout, grayling, coarse fish. Council water free to residents. Darlington AC fish 10½m between Croft, Darlington and High Coniscliffe, and 1m of **Clow Beck**, 3m S of Darlington; north bank. Strictly for members only. Darlington Brown Trout AA has water between Middleton and Croft, also on **Swale**. Dt for members' guests only. Stockton AA has water at **Winston**. At **Whorlton**, T J Richardson, Whorlton Farm, issues limited permits for stretch. Woodland Lakes, Carlton Miniott, nr Thirsk, tel: 01845 522827, has good carp fishing in 5 lakes. Dt £5. Tackle shops: W P Adams Fishing Tackle & Guns, 42 Duke Street, DL3 7AJ, tel: 01325 468069, (has permits for several small coarse ponds in vicinity, and for R Tees fishing); Darlington Angling Centre, 341 North Rd, DL1 3BL.

Piercebridge (Durham). Trout, grayling, dace, chub, gudgeon. Tickets for Raby Estates water, £32 trout, £23 coarse; Estate Office, Staindrop, Darlington DL2 3NF, tel: 01833 660207. Otherwise preserved. Forcett Park Lake, 8m SW; pike, perch; private, occasional winter permits. Hotel: George.

Gainford (Durham). Trout, grayling, coarse fish. Up to Winston, most of the water held by Stockton AA. No tickets. Alwent Beck, 1m W; trout; private. Langton Beck, 2m N.

Barnard Castle (Durham). Trout, grayling. Free fishing on south bank d/s from stone bridge to Thorngate footbridge. Taking of salmon prohibited. M Hutchinson, Thorngate Mill, has fishing offered. Barnard Castle FFC has from Tees Viaduct to Baxton Gill, near **Cotherstone**, private club water, and stretch above Abbey Bridge to beyond Tees Viaduct on south bank. Barnard Castle AC has from a point below Abbey Bridge to Tees Viaduct on north bank; private club water, but some dt to visitors staying locally. Darlington FFC has 2½m above and below Abbey Bridge, 1m below Barnard Castle. Water holds trout and grayling; members only. Grassholme, Selset, Balderhead, Blackton and Hury reservoirs, 5m NW; dt obtainable *(see Tees Valley Reservoirs)*. Two small trout fisheries nr **Barningham**: at Moorcock Farm, Barningham (01833 621351), 4 acre pool stocked with rainbows, dt £8-£15; Langlands Lake fly fishing, Langlands Farm, Barningham DL11 7ED (01833 621317), rainbow trout, dt £5-£9, joint father and son dt £12. All local permits from R T Oliver, 40 Horsemarket, Barnard Castle DL12 8NA. Hotel: King's Head, Market Place.

Mickleton (Durham). Trout. St £15, wt £6, dt £3 for S bank between Cronkley Bridge and Lune Fort from Cleveland Arms; J Raine & Son 25 Market Place; both Middleton-in-Teesdale.

Middleton-in-Teesdale (Durham). Trout (plentiful but small), a few late salmon. Several miles open to dt on Raby Estate water, tel: 01833 40209 (office hours). Teesdale Hotel (01833 40264) offers dt on several miles of south bank. Strathmore Estate water, 7m north bank, fly only, dt £7.50, wt £20, st £50, salmon £100. Contact J Raine & Son, 25 Market Place, Middleton-in-Teesdale DL12 0QA (01833 640406).

GRETA: Trout.

Bowes (Durham). All private fishing.

TEIGN

(For close seasons, licences etc, see South West Region Environment Agency, p16)

Rises from two sources high on Dartmoor, which form the North and South Teign, joining west of Chagford while still small streams. Between Chagford and Steps Bridge river runs through a wooded gorge, which is best fished above Fingle bridge. Upper Teign contains trout, sea trout and salmon. Principal tributary is Bovey. Salmon, sea trout (peal) and brown trout. Teign usually fishes best for salmon from late May to September. River flows to sea through an estuary beginning below Newton Abbot

Newton Abbot (Devon). Salmon, sea trout, trout; preserved by Lower Teign FA from Sowton Weir to Teignbridge (stretch from New Bridge to Preston Footbridge members only). Three separate beats. Dt (3 per beat) £10, valid for 24 hrs from sunrise. Spinning by day, at night fly only. Assn also has 3m on Bovey, members only *(see Bovey)*. Tickets from Drum Sports *(see below)*. Newton Abbot FA has six lakes at **Rackerhayes**, five at **Kingsteignton**, two ponds at **Coombe-in-Teignhead**, two at **Chudleigh**, newly acquired pond beside Stover Canal, and **R Isle** at **Hambridge**. Fisheries contain carp to 36lbs, pike to 20lbs, large tench, roach, rudd, perch, bream. Dt £4, conc, on some of these waters. Full membership £30, conc. Coarse fish, including carp. **Watercress Farm**, 4 acres trout fishing, tel: 01626 852168. **Trago Mills** has 600 yds coarse fishing, dt £3, OAP, jun £2. G Mole, tel: 01626 821111. Decoy Lake, small coarse lake open all year, stocked. Tackle shop: Drum Sports, 47a Courtenay Street.

Chudleigh (Devon). Salmon, sea trout, trout; Lower Teign FA has water (*see Newton Abbot*). Dt £17 for 1m of Teign from Mrs C Thatcher, Ryecroft, Christow, tel: 01647 52805. 2½ acre coarse lake at Finlake Woodland Village. Open 31 Mar to 31 Oct. Newton Abbot FA has two ponds here.

Chagford (Devon). Trout, sea trout, Upper Teign FA preserves about 14m in all, on left and right bank, fly only before June 1 on some parts and whole season elsewhere; size limit 8in. Full annual sub £135, trout membership £45. Brown trout tickets from Bowdens, The Square, Chagford, also limited sea trout dt on 2 short stretches, Chagford Weir, £6. Limited non-members salmon and sea trout tickets £15, from Anglers Rest, Fingle Bridge, Drewsteignton EX6 6PW (01647 281287). Halfstone Sporting Agency offers salmon and sea trout fishing and instruction; 6 Hescane Park, Cheriton Bishop EX6 6SP, tel: 01647 24643. Fernworthy Reservoir, 3½m.

Tributary of the Teign.

BOVEY: Salmon, sea trout, trout.

Bovey (Devon). On Bovey and Teign. Fishing above Bovey preserved by landowners and below by Lower Teign FA. No tickets. Lakes: Tottiford and Kennick Reservoirs; trout (*see Devon lakes, streams, etc*). Hotels: Manor House, one mile from North Bovey (water on Bovey and Bowden, and salmon and trout fisheries on Teign); Glebe House, North Bovey.

TEST

(For close seasons, licences etc, see Southern Region Environment Agency, p16).

Rises from springs in the chalk near Overton, above Whitchurch and flows via Stockbridge and Romsey to enter Southampton Water. Brown and rainbow trout, salmon run as far as Romsey. The Test and Itchen Association represents virtually all riparian owners and many who wish to fish these rivers and their tributaries. The secretary maintains a register of rods to let. (*See clubs list.*) Roxton Bailey Robinson let beats on a daily, weekly and seasonal basis. 25 High St, Hungerford, RG17 0NF, tel: 01488 683222, fax: 01488 682977. Test Valley Angling Club has various lakes and river stretches of 600yds to 2m. Tickets from Tight Lines Angling Centre, 1A Rumbridge St, Southampton, tel: 01703 86068.

Romsey (Hants). Trout and grayling fishing good; salmon fishing good below the town, all preserved by the different landowners. **Broadlands Estates** has salmon fishing on 3 beats of ¾m each, and trout fishing on three ¾m beats of Test and on 3m carrier stream. Average season salmon catch, 35 fish, average weight 6lb. Salmon rods and ½ rods, a named day per week for two for £925 and a named day for two per fortnight for £465. Trout fishing st for one rod (1 day per week) is £1,235 and £640 (1 day per fortnight), 2 brace, dry fly only. Trout fishing in carrier stream, st £1,005. There is also an excellent stillwater coarse fishery with large carp, roach, bream, tench. Enquiries: Estate Office, Broadlands, Romsey S051 9ZE. Tel: 01794 518885. Fisheries Manager, John Dennis, 01703 739438. Dt for residents from Council Offices, Duttons Road, for Romsey Memorial Park; limited to two rods daily. Salmon, few small trout, grayling, coarse fish. Good trout fishing at **Two Lakes**, near Romsey (**see Hampshire, streams, lakes, etc**); John O'Gaunt Lake, Kings Somborne, two lakes of 8 and 4 acres with trout fishing, contact K Purse (01794 388130).

Stockbridge (Hants). Greyhound Hotel has water stocked with brown and rainbow trout; Dry fly and nymph only. Fish average 3lb. St (2 rods) (one day per month) £425. Dt £50 May/June, £40 otherwise; 4 fish limit. Instruction, £30 per day. Early booking advisable as rods are limited. Special fishing/accommodation package can be arranged. Roy Gumbrell, tel: 01264 810833. Greyhound Hotel can also offer fishing on a further stretch of Test, and 1½m of **R Dever**. Tackle from Orvis, High St.

Awbridge (Hants). The Parsonage, Awbridge: Full rod £1350 (one day per week, plus 4 guest days), half rod £725 (one day a fortnight, plus two guest days), quarter rod £425 (one day in 4 weeks, plus one guest day) dt £100-£85 for trout, grayling and occasional salmon, from Fishing Breaks Ltd, 16 Bickerton Rd, London N19 5JR, tel 0171 281 6737, fax: 0171 281 8151. Fishing Breaks also offers rods on **R Itchen, Avon** above **Amesbury**, and **Dever**.

Houghton (Hants). Bossington Estate, Stockbridge SO20 6LT lets rods by season. (Tel 01794-388265; waiting list.)

Fullerton Bridge (Hants). Trout (av 2lb 8oz). Season mid-April to end of Sept.

Tributaries of the Test

ANTON: Trout, grayling.

Andover (Hants). Anton joins Test at Testcombe Bridge. Trout and grayling; all preserved. At **Rooksbury Mill**, Rooksbury Road, a first-class trout fishery (two lakes and river fishing), st £375, dt £28 (5 fish), river £36. Boats on Mill Lake. Well stocked game fishing tackle shop on site. Tel: 01264 352921 (333449 fax) for full details. Andover AC owns Foxcotte Lake at **Charlton**, 50 to 60 pegs approx. Usual coarse species; also has access to Broadlands at **Romsey** and **Basingstoke Canal**. Dt from tackle shop John Eadies, 5b Union St or Charlton PO. **Dever Springs Trout Fishery**, 2 lakes, 7 acres and river: contact tel: 0126472 592. Other Tackle shop: Cole & Son, 67 High Street, who also supply st £18, which includes Broadlands Lake fishing. Hotels: Star and Garter, White Hart, Junction, George, Anton Arms, Globe Central.

PILL HILL BROOK: Trout, grayling.

Amport and Monxton (Hants). Trout and grayling. Nearly as long as Anton, but pure chalk-stream. Monxton Mill reach greatly improved and contains full head of locally bred brown trout averaging 14oz, with occasional heavier fish. Fishing preserved by landowners. Dry-fly only.

DEVER: Trout, grayling. Dever joins Test at Newton Stacey.

Bullington (Hants). Trout and grayling fishing. Dt £85 for trout and grayling, from Fishing Breaks Ltd, 16 Bickerton Rd, Upper Holloway, London N19 5JR, tel 0171 281 6737, fax: 0171 281 8151.

BOURNE:

St Mary Bourne (Hants). Strictly preserved. Bourne joins Test above Longparish.

THAMES

(For close seasons, licences, etc, see Thames Region Environment Agency, p20).

Second longest river in England. Tidal reaches much recovered from pollution and fish returning in considerable numbers. The occasional salmon and sea trout in river, together with dace, roach, flounder, bream, perch, carp and smelt; rainbow trout are caught quite regularly in the freshwater tideway. River worth fishing from Southwark Bridge upstream. Downstream of this point, estuarine species such as eel, flounder, bass and even whiting may be caught. Above Teddington Lock boat traffic largely spoils sport in summer, except in weir pools, but fishing can be good early and late. River fishes well from October to March. Holds good stock of coarse fish, with excellent bream and barbel in some stretches. Perch seem to be making a welcome return to the river throughout its length. However, the tremendous dace fishing of recent years has declined. Bream, roach and perch now dominate the lower river, above Teddington, with chub becoming more numerous the further up the river one goes. Among famous tributaries are Kennet, which comes in at Reading and is one of best mixed fisheries in England. Trout and coarse fish run large. Higher up, Coln, Evenlode and Windrush are noted trout streams, but for most part are very strictly preserved and fishing difficult to obtain. Fishing on Thames open up to City Stone at Staines. Above, permission often necessary and lock-keepers and local tackle shops should be consulted. Thames Environment Agency issues permits on seventeen locks, and these are entered below, in the appropriate section of the text. The Thames Angling Preservation Society, founded in 1838, has restocked seven tributaries - now keeps close watch on water quality and fish stocks in whole Thames basin. It is not a fishing club, but a fishery preservation society supported by anglers, membership details from secretary, A E Hodges, The Pines, 32 Tile Kiln Lane, Bexley, Kent DA5 2BB. London Anglers Association (LAA) HQ, Izaak Walton House, 2A Hervey Park Road, London E17 6LJ, has numerous fishings on Thams and elsewhere. Permits issued for some waters. Several reservoirs in which fishing is allowed (coarse fish and trout). *(See London - Reservoirs, etc)*.

London Docklands. Redevelopment has led to increased angling facilities at **Shadwell, Millwall, Royal Docks** and **Southwark**, each locality with its own angling society. Details from Docklands Watersports Club, Unit 1, Royal Victoria Dock, Mill Rd, E1 6XX, tel: 0171 511 7000.

Isleworth to **London Bridge** (G London). Tidal. Dace, flounder, eel, roach, perch, with some carp and bream. Juvenile bass common at seaward end of this stretch; free from towpath or boats and foreshore throughout Central London 2 hrs each side of low tide. Fly-fishing for dace on shallows when tide is down. Reach down past Chiswick Eyot can be good for roach, dace; towpath only; free. Tackle shops: Hounslow Angling Centre, Bath Road also Colne-Wraysbury).

Richmond (G London). Tidal below Teddington Lock, non-tidal above. Down to Isleworth is fishing for roach, dace, bream, perch, eel, the odd chub; free from towpath or boats. Barnes and Mortlake APS are local club, with water on Grand Union Canal from Thames at Brentford to Clitheroe Lock (dt on bank), and members only coarse lakes at Barn Elms, Barnes, and Bedfont Country Park, st £25. In Richmond Park **Pen Ponds** hold perch, carp, bream, roach and pike. Open 16 jun-14 Mar. St £11, conc £5.50 (I.D. required). Apply to Park Superintendent at Holly Lodge, Richmond Park, Richmond, TW10 5HS (enclose sae). Tickets on bank day and night for coarse fishing in Potoma Lake, Gunnersbury Park. Tackle shop: Ron's Tackle, 465 Upper Richmond Rd West, East Sheen SW14 7PU.

Twickenham (G London). Coarse fishing; free from boats and towpath. Deeps hold barbel, roach, bream, eel, carp. Corporation allow fishing from Radnor, Orleans and Terrace Gardens. Syon Park Trout Fishery, Brentwood, managed by Albury Estate Fisheries, Estate Office, Albury, Guildford GU5 9AF, tel: 01483 202323. Tackle shop: T & S Angling, 150 Heath Rd; Guns and Tackle, 81 High Street, Whitton. Hotels: Bird's Nest, White Swan.

Teddington (G London). Thames holds dace, roach, bream, eel, perch; free fishing from towpath. Molesley Lock on Environment Agency permit, tel: 0181 979 4482. Hotels: Anglers', Clarence, Railway.

Kingston (G London). Canbury Gardens is very popular stretch and has yielded large carp, bream, perch and roach.

Hampton Court (G London). Thames, Mole; coarse fish. Environment Agency fishery at Molesey Lock, Surrey KT8 9AW, tel: 0181 979 4482. Barge Walk, left bank, requires a Royal Parks permit. Gardens and Estate Manager, Hampton Court Palace Gardens, Surrey KT8 9AU, tel: 0181 781 9610, issues permits for Hampton Court: Long Water and Rick Pond, also Bushy Park: Diana Pond, Heron Pond and Leg of Mutton Pond. Coarse fish. St £12, conc £6. No night fishing. Tackle shops: E C Cheeseman, 11 Bridge Road, East Molesey.

Hampton (G London). Hampton Deeps hold bream, pike, perch and sometimes a good trout; free fishing from towpath and boats.

Sunbury (Surrey). Excellent for all-round angling; free. Fine weir and weir shallows fishable on Environment Agency permit, tel: 019327 82089; barbel, chub, dace, bream and occasional trout may be taken. Tackle shop: Tackle Up, 357 Staines Rd West, Ashford Common TW15 1RP, sells tickets for local fisheries, trout and coarse. Hotel: Magpie.

Walton-on-Thames (Surrey). Bream, perch, dace, chub, carp and pike; perch and pike in backwater. Weybridge AC fishes Broadwater Lake. Dt from bailiffs.

Shepperton (Surrey). Pike, barbel, perch, bream and carp; free; boats for hire. Shepperton Lock Environment Agency fishery, tel: 01932 221840. Ashmere Fisheries, *see Herts and Greater London*. Two Leisure Sport gravel pits, 16 acres, coarse fishing for carp, roach, chub, pike, eels, etc. No night fishing. St £20, ½ price conc. No dt. For full details phone 0181 8931168. Hotel: Anchor.

Weybridge (Surrey). There is local free fishing in Thames and **R Mole**. Members of Weybridge AC and other clubs have fishing on 6 sections of **Wey Navigation** Canal between Town Lock and Walsham Lock and have formed Wey Navigation Angling Amalgamation; dt £1.50 from bailiff. Weybridge AC also fishes 1,000 yards d/s and 1,000 yards u/s of Wey Bridge on R Wey. Tackle Shop: Weybridge Guns & Tackle, 137 Oatlands Drive, Weybridge KT13 9LB, has £2 dt for R Wey at Thames Meadow. Hotels: Ship, Thames St; Lincoln Arms, Thames Street; Oatlands Parks; Blue Anchor.

Chertsey (Surrey). Pike, perch, chub, roach, bream, occasional trout; free fishing from boats and towpath. LSA, RMC House, High Street, Feltham, Middlesex TW13 4HD, tel: 0181 8931168, have 4½ acre gravel pit and 1,000m of River Bourne. Excellent tench, bream, carp, roach and pike in pit, chub, roach, dace and perch in river. St £24, ½ price jun, OAP, dis. Club: Addlestone AA, which has water at **New Haw, Wey** and **Bourne** and a gravel pit at Laleham; dt to members' guests only. Leisure Sport have two stretches of Wey at **Addlestone**, 600m total, with pike, barbel, chub, carp, roach, bream, dace, perch. St only, £20. Several boat yards. Hotels: Cricketers, Bridge.

Staines (Surrey). Good coarse fishing; free from boats and towpath. Environment Agency fisheries at Penton Hook Lock, tel: 01784 452657, and Bell Weir Lock, **Egham**, tel: 01784 432333. Club: Staines AS, stretch opposite Runnymede; members only. Tackle shop: Davies Angling, 47/9 Church St.

Wraysbury (Bucks). LSA **Kingsmead Fishery**, 2 lakes of 80 and 6 acres with pike to 38lbs, and other coarse species. St £24. LSA also has fishery at **Horton** nr Wraysbury; syndicate membership, specimen carp, bream, tench and catfish; and Wraysbury One Fishery, 120 acre specimen carp fishery which holds current British record carp 55lbs 13oz. Applications to LSA, *see Chertsey*. Berkshire Fisheries Assoc. has Slough Arm of G Union Canal from **Cowley** to Slough Basin, approx 5m, excellent fishery in summer, very little boat traffic. Specimen tench and other species, and good pike fishing in winter; dt from bailiff. Tackle shop: Stows Tackle, Wexford Rd, Slough.

Windsor (Berks). Chub, barbel, bream, roach, dace, perch, pike. Fishing from south bank below Windsor Bridge and north bank to Eton-Windsor road bridge, by E.A. licence only. Dt issued for club waters near Maidenhead; enq tackle shops. Salt Hill AC has Clewer Meadow, Windsor, dt on bank. Old Windsor AC has Romney Island and Meadow fishing to east of Windsor, and Albert Bridge, Datchet, all river species; also Bray Lake, off A308, large bream and carp. Tickets £3 at Romney and Albert Bridge on bank, from Windsor Angling Centre, or Maidenhead Baits, 11-13 Station Parade, Station Hill, Cookham. Free public fishing on right bank from Victoria Bridge u/s to railway bridge. Royal Berkshire Fishery, North St, Winkfield, tel: 01344 891101: 3 small lakes with coarse fish. Dt on bank. Fishing can be had in Windsor Great Park ponds and Virginia Water *(see Surrey lakes)*. Tackle shop: Windsor Angling Centre, 153 St Leonard's Rd, Windsor tel: 01753 867210.

Boveney (Bucks). Coarse fish. Backwater good for pike, and weir pool for trout and barbel. Towpath free. LAA Eton Wick fishery here. Hotels: Clarence, Royal Windsor.

Bray (Berks). Weir pool good for trout, and free from boat or punt. Bray Mill tail from 1m above lock to lock cut private. Towpath free. Monkey Island Hotel caters for anglers. Tel: 01628 23400. Environment Agency fishery at Bray Lock, tel: 01628 21650.

Maidenhead (Berks). Roach, pike, perch, barbel, dace, chance of trout. Some free fishing right bank, Maidenhead Bridge to Boulter's Lock. Hurley Lock, Environment Agency fishery, tel: 0162882 4334. Maidenhead and District AS has Left bank u/s from Boveney Lock to gardens at Dorney Reach. Permits from Hon Sec. Dt for clubs stretch from My Lady Ferry to gardens at Maidenhead from bailiff. Boats: Bushnell Ltd. Tackle shops: Kings, 18 Ray St; Jack Smith, 4 High Street.

Cookham (Berks). Cookham & Dist AC has right bank u/s of Cookham Bridge to Railway Bridge. London AA has water at Spade Oak Ferry, members only. Hotels: Ferry, Royal Exchange, King's Arms, Bell and Dragon, Crown.

Bourne End (Bucks). Wide, open water with some shallow stretches, good for fly fishing. London AA has water here. Stretch also open to associates.

Marlow (Bucks). Usual coarse fish, including barbel. Free fishing d/s from Marlow Lock to end of Riverside Drive, ½m stretch. Marlow AC has water from Riverswood Drive to opp. first islands and left bank u/s from Marlow Bridge opp. Temple Island, and pits; tickets from Kings Tackle, 1 Ray St, Maidenhead. The Compleat Angler Hotel, Marlow Bridge, SL7 1RG, has fishing from grounds, free for residents, non-residents at hotel's discretion. Tel: 01628 486388.

Hurley (Berks). London AA has fisheries at Frogmill Farm and Hurley Flats. Dt issued for 1½m. Members and associates only. Hurley Lock Environment Agency fishery, tel: 01628 824334.

Henley (Oxon). Pike, roach, perch, tench, bream, eels. Free fishing u/s from Promenade to Cold Bath Ditch. Environment Agency fishery at Marsh Lock, tel: 01491 572992. Oxon and Bucks bank water controlled by society for members only. Also from end of Henley Promenade upstream to Marsh Lock, bridges and meadows upstream from Marsh Lock. London AA has stretches for members. Reading & Dist AA has Aston Ferry fishing, about 4m d/s of Henley, 25 swims stretching nearly to Hambledon Lock. Tackle shops: Alf Parrot, 15 Thameside; Sports Centre, Greys Rd. Boats: Hobbs, Parrott. Good accommodation for anglers at Flower Pot Hotel, Aston, RG9 3DG.

Wargrave (Berks). Thames and Loddon; good coarse fishing.

Sonning (Berks). Much fishing from **Shiplake** to Sonning Bridge on Oxfordshire bank controlled by Shiplake and Binfield Heath AS; members only. Guests at White Hart can fish private stretch of ½m on Berkshire bank towards Shiplake. London AA has water for members only at Shiplake, Lowfield and Mapledurham. Reading & Dist AA has Sonning Eye fishery (lake and river). Members only. Environment Agency fishery at Shiplake Lock, tel: 01734 403350.

Reading (Berks). Most coarse fish. Reading Borough Council controls length from opposite Caversham Court Gazebo to 1½m u/s of Caversham Bridge. The fishing from Thames-side Promenade to Scours Lane is controlled by Thames Water. There is some free water on the **Kennet** from Horseshoe Bridge to County Weir (adjacent to Inner Distribution Road). Reading and District AA, comprising about forty affiliated clubs, control twenty eight miles of river and canal, plus fourteen lakes in Berkshire and Oxfordshire. Subscription £30, with concessions. £3 dt offered for Wylies Lake, stocked, with good tench and bream fishing in Reading vicinity. Farnborough AS has good trout and coarse fishing on **Whitewater** at Heckfield (8m), also 2m fly only stretch. St £30, joining fee £10. dt £4, conc. Countryside Club, 109 Upper Woodcote Road, Caversham Heights, Reading, has trout and carp fishing let on a family st basis; At Bradfield, **Pang Valley trout lake**, approx 6 acres, stocked with rainbow trout. Dt £25, 4 fish limit £15 2 fish, from tackle shop T Turner *(see below)*. Leisure Sport has coarse fisheries on permit at **St Patrick's Stream, Twyford** and **Theale** (52 acres), apply LSA, RMC House, High Street, Feltham, Middlesex TW13 4HD, tel: 0181 8931168. Tackle shops: Reading Angling Centre, 69 North'land Avenue; Tadley Angling, Padworth Rd, Padworth; T Turner & Son Ltd, 21 Whitley Street, RG2 0EG. Hotels: Thameside; Thames House; Pennyfarthings, Swallowfield.

Tilehurst (Berks). Reading and District AA control the fishing at Purley, and on the Oxfordshire bank. Free fishing from towpath to Caversham *(see restrictions under Reading)*. Beethoven Hotel has private stretch on south bank. Tackle shop: Thames Valley Angling, 258 Kentwood Hill, Tilehurst.

Goring (Oxon). Pike, bream, roach, chub, perch and (in weir pool especially) barbel and a few trout; weir pool Environment Agency fishery, tel: 01491 872687. Other fishing can be had from towpath above and below lock. London AA has R bank from Beetle & Wedge Hotel to Cleeve Lock; Gatehampton Farm fishery. Members only, but ¾m open to associates. Hotel: Leathern Bottle.

Pangbourne and **Whitchurch** (Berks). Thames and **Pang**. Trout, perch, pike, roach, bream, chub, dace. River fishes well in winter; free fishing 1½m above and below Whitchurch Bridge; good coarse fishing; boats for hire. Weir pool private. Pang holds trout, especially near Tidmarsh, but is strictly preserved; trout at its mouth. Pangbourne and Whitchurch AS is affiliated with Reading & Dist AA, and fishes in a number of localities, including 3m of R Kennet with good chub, barbel, roach and dace. St £23 from Hon Sec.

Moulsford (Berks). All coarse fish. London AA has water here; members only. Hotel: Beetle.

South Stoke (Oxon). London AA controls the water from footbridge above railway bridge down to Beetle and Wedge ferry and second meadow below the ferry down to Runsford Hole; members only.

Wallingford (Oxon). Reading & Dist AA has Severals Farm fishing: two sections above Bensons Lock, with barbel, chub, roach, perch. Local club: Jolly Anglers, who have four stretches (good bream in summer. chub in winter); st £10, wt £7, dt £3 (concessions for juniors), from Rides on Air, 45 St Mary's Street and Wallingford Sports Shop, 71 High Street.

Cleeve (Oxon). Usual coarse fish. Landlord of Leathern Bottle issues dt for 1m upstream of Cleeve Lock, including ferry.

Benson (Oxon). Usual coarse fish. Club: Benson AS. Wt £5, dt £2 from E Bond, 5 Sands Way, Benson OX10 6NG, from Benson Marina or from Hon Sec. Sundays reserved for matches. Benson Lock is Environment Agency lock and weir fishery, tel: 01491 35255.

Shillingford (Oxon). Wallingford AA has water upstream; dt from Hon Sec. Shillingford Bridge Hotel nr Wallingford OX10 8LZ, tel: 01865 858567(fax 858636), has good pike fishing with trout, tench, dace, etc, on ¼m (both banks) reserved for guests and members of High Wycombe AC.

Little Wittenham (Oxon). Thame comes in here.

Clifton Hampden (Oxon). Oxford & Dist AA has water here, d/s from the scenic bridge for nine fields. Bream, chub and roach, also large barbel. Dt on part of this water from tackle shops only, no night fishing. The Tring Anglers have water here *(See Tring)*. Clifton Lock is Environment Agency fishery, tel: 0186 730 7821. Inn: The Barley Mow.

Appleford (Berks). London AA controls from just above the railway bridge down to beginning of Clifton Hampden cutting; both banks, then a short stretch on R bank only; members only.

Culham (Oxon). All water except weir pools controlled by Abingdon & Dist ARA. Other clubs: Culham AC and Sutton Courtenay AC has pits. No day tickets.

Abingdon (Oxon). Bream, chub, pike and barbel good. Free fishing for residents. Tickets from Town Clerk's office for the 1½m controlled by Council, from Nuneham railway bridge to notice-board 200 yds u/s from Culham footbridge. Details from Stratton Lodge, 52 Bath Street, Abingdon. Fishery includes weir, but must be fished from bank. Abingdon & Oxford Anglers Alliance has much local fishing. The Alliance trout section has lake at **Standlake**, Oxon, st £50, entrance fee £15. Members and their guests only: R H Williams, 2 Holyoake Rd, Oxford, 0X3 8AE. Millets Farm Trout Fishery, Kingston Rd, **Frilford**, OX13 5HB, tel: 01865 391394, has 2 lakes in 7 acres, stocked with b and r trout and freshwater raised Atlantic salmon. St, dt, conc for OAP, dis: Orchard Way, Fyfield, Oxon, tel: 01865 391394. Tackle shop: The Right Angle, Wootton Rd.

Sandford-on-Thames (Oxon). Pike, bream, roach, perch, etc. Oxford & Dist AA has water here on both banks d/s of weir to the main river, with roach, chub, dace, barbel and pike. Abingdon A & RA have water; R Pitson, tel: 01235 25140. Environment Agency lock and weir fishery at Sandford Lock, tel: 01865 775889.

Iffley (Oxon). Thames (or Isis). From Botley Road Bridge d/s to Folly Bridge is Oxford & Dist AS water. Large shoals of roach, perch and chub. Dt from tackle shops. Inn: Isis Tavern.

Oxford (Oxon). Thames (Isis), **Cherwell** and **Oxford Canal**. All coarse fish. N Oxford AS has water on Thames, at **Godstow** and **Carrot's Ham**, Cherwell, canal, and carp and tench fishing in **Dukes Lake**. Their best water is **Seacourt Stream** at Carrot's Ham, with many species. Club offers dt on water between Godstow and Seacourt Overspill, and Seacourt Stream from Overspill to A420. Rose Revived Hotel, Newbridge, tel: 0186 731 221 has tickets for 2 fields d/s on left bank at Newbridge and from road bridge to confluence with left hand bank R Windrush. The Tring Anglers fish at **Eynsham**. **Donnington** and **Iffley** water held by Oxford & Dist AA. Good roach fishing, also chub. Heavy boat traffic here. Assn is an affiliation of clubs local to Oxford. It has excellent coarse fishing on Thames at **Medley**, **Kennington**, **Newbridge**, and elsewhere, with dt £2.50 from tackle shops only. (4½m W of Oxford, **Farmoor Reservoirs**, Cumnor Rd, Farmoor OX2 9NS. No.1 leased by Farmoor Flyfishers. Members only. Tel: 01235 850619. Reservoir No. 2, Cumnor Rd, is 240 acre trout fishery, stocked with brown and rainbow, fly only from boat or bank. Dt and st from gatehouse. Facilities for disabled. Phone 01865 863033 for advance bookings. Day tickets for **Adderbury Lakes** coarse fishing from Old Bake House Stores, High St, Adderbury. Shimano-Linear Fisheries have five pools near **Stanton Harcourt** on B4449 road. Fishery records incl pike to 27lbs, carp to 40lbs. Contact Fishery Manager, 10A Rackstaw Grove, Old Farm Park, Milton Keynes MK7 8PZ (01908 645135). Tackle shops: North Oxford Tackle, 95 Islip Rd; Dells of Oxford, 136 Oxford Rd, Cowley; State Tackle, 19 Fettiplace Rd, Witney OX8 5AP; Catch 1, 14 The Parade, Kidlington; and others. Hotels: Cherwell, Oxford; Swan, Islip; Prince of Wales, Cowley Rd (APS HQ).

Eynsham (Oxon). Good coarse fishing; large bream. Oxford Angling and Pres Soc has water *(see Oxford)*. Eynsham Lock fishing open to holders of Environment Agency lock permits (tel: 01865 881324). Hotels: Ye Talbot Inn, Railway, Red Lion.

Bablock Hythe (Oxon). Ferryman Inn issues dt for 1½m on north bank downstream. Special fishing mini-break for two persons, any two nights, £70. Tel: 01865 880028. Water upstream on north bank (and some on south bank) is Appleton and Tubney AS as far as Oxford APS water.

Newbridge (Oxon). Near Witney. Good coarse fishing (bream increasing), few trout in the **Windrush**. Shifford Lock is one of Environment Agency's fisheries, tel: 0136787 247. Newland AC has water from **Shifford** to within 600 yds of Newbridge, Steadies Lane, Stanton Harcourt and Heyford Lakes, Standlake, with specimen fish. St, dt for lakes only. Non-locals membership by approval of committee, only. Shifford Lock is Environment Agency fishery, tel: 0136 787 247. Hotels: Rose Revived (¾m water on Thames and Windrush; good coarse fish, some trout) and May Bush (½m water on Thames). Witney AS have Thames fishing here, R Windrush, trout only, and coarse pits; members only, £20 per annum, conc. Stroud AA have 1m of Thames (dt Batemans Sports, Stroud. Tel: 4320). Tackle shop: State Fishing Tackle, 19 Fettiplace Rd, Witney, tel: 01993 702587, who can give further information.

Tadpole Bridge, Buckland (Berks). Coventry & Dist AA has Rushey Wier fishery. Good chub and barbel; pike in weir-pool.

Radcot (Berks). Thames trout; bream, chub barbel and roach. Radcot AC has 5m. St £7, mt £4, wt £3, dt £1.50. Apply Hon Sec or Swan Hotel. Clanfield AC also has left bank, Old Man's Bridge to Rushey Lock. Clubs catered for. Three Environment Agency lock fisheries, at Radcot, tel: 01367 20676; Grafton Lock, tel: 0136781 251; and Buscot Lock, tel: 01367 52434. Permits for stretch from **Buscot** to Graf-

Keep the banks clean

Several Clubs have stopped issuing tickets to visitors because the state of the banks after they have left. Spend a few moments clearing up.

ton Lock, Turner's Tackle, Faringdon, tel: 01367 21044.

Lechlade (Glos). For Thames, Coln and Leach. Stroud AA controls 2m of Thames at Lechlade upstream from Trout Inn to Murdoch Ditch. Permits from Trout Inn or from Batemans Sports, Stroud. St £7.50. For Highworth AC water between Lechlade and Buscot, contact M Mills, 58 Croft Rd, Swindon.

Cricklade (Wilts). Thames known here a Isis. Isis AC has water on main river, tributaries **Ray** and **Churn**. Isis No 1 Lake at **South Cerney** (Glos), carp to 30lb. Membership £27, dt £5 from tackle shops. South Cerney AC has five lakes in Cotswold area, membership £25, conc, from House of Angling 59/60 Commercial Rd, Swindon SN1 5NX.

Tributaries of the Thames

MOLE: Coarse fish.

Esher (Surrey). Pike, roach, perch the odd big chub. Feltham Piscatorials has 'The Ledges'. Epsom AS has ½m at Wayne Flete and ½m on Wey at **Weybridge**. St £10, conc £4, from Hon Sec. Tackle shop: Weybridge Guns & Tackle, 137 Oatlands Drive, Weybridge KT13 9LB.

Cobham (Surrey). Central Association of London and Provincial Angling Clubs (CALPAC) has 1½m of Mole here, various coarse species, and Manor Pond, holding pike, carp, roach, tench and bream. Members only. Further CALPAC stretch, 1½ miles at **Hersham**, chub, perch, roach, dace, eels, pike, dt £4, conc, sold on bank. Cobham Court AC have water adjacent and above: large chub, pike, very big perch and eels. Some rainbows stocked.

Leatherhead (Surrey). Leatherhead & Dist AS have waters above A246 road bridge. Sunmead AS has water at Norbury Park, Leatherhead, with chub, roach, dace, perch, together with carp and pike to double figures. Dt £3 on bank. Tackle shops: Fullers Tackle, South St, Dorking; F.U. Tackle, Cock Lane, Leatherhead. Hotel: Bull.

Dorking (Surrey). Coarse fish. Dorking AS has about 4m of Mole and four lakes; large stocks of carp, tench, bream, roach, rudd, orfe. Members only except Fourwent Pond, South Holywood, dt on bank or from tackle shop. Leisure Sport Angling has two gravel pits at **Newdigate** heavily stocked with carp, pike, roach, rudd, crucian carp; St £24, ½ price conc. Full details from LSA, *see Chertsey*. Furze Farm Fishery, Knowle Lane, Nr Cranleigh, 3½ acre mixed fishery. Dt £6 on bankside. Contact Stone Cottage, Ridgeway Rd, Dorking RH4 3EY. Tackle shop: S C Fuller, 28 South Street, Dorking. Hotels: White Horse, Bell, Arundel.

Brockham (Surrey). Chub, roach, carp and bream. Brockham AS water.

Betchworth (Surrey). Chub dominate below weir, anything can, and does appear above weir. Carshalton and Dist AS has water; members only.

Sidlow (Surrey). Roach dominate, together with perch, carp, chub. Horley P S fish much of this water.

WEY: Coarse fish, trout higher up.

Weybridge (Surrey). Wey Amalgamation have water here *(see Thames),* St £12.50, dt £1.50, jun, OAP, 50%; from bailiff. **Woking** (Surrey). Roach, chub, pike, etc. Woking and Dist AS has rights on 23 miles of river bank and two ponds (perch, carp and tench) at Send; dt for members' guests only. New members welcome; details from Hon Sec.

Wisley (Surrey); ns Ripley. Ponds: Wisley Mere, Hut Pond, and several other ponds on Ripley Common and Ockham Common; carp, pike, perch, roach.

Guildford (Surrey). Guildford AS has about 9½m R Wey; lakes at Broad Street and Whitmoor Common (carp to 19lb in Britton Pond). CALPAC fishes Stoke Park Farm stretch of Wey, 1½ miles nr Guildford. Dt £4, conc, on bank or from Guildford Angling Centre. At Shamley Green **Willinghurst Trout Fishery**, 2 acre lake, also 6 coarse lakes, tickets on bank. Tel: 01483 271005. **Albury Estate Fisheries**, Estate Office, Albury, Guildford GU5 9AF, tel: 01483 202323; 8 lakes, totalling 16 acres, of brown and rainbow trout fishing; 3 dt waters: Powdermills (4lbs av), Weston (2½lbs) and Vale End (1lb 14oz); one syndicated: Park (2lbs av), membership £750-£305, waiting list; dt waters £24-£16 per day. Limits 2-5 fish, depending on venue. One lake of 6 acres, rainbow trout dt £27, 4 fish. Instruction, if required. Tackle shops: S R Jeffrey & Son, 134 High St; Guildford; Peter Cockwill Game Angling, 32 Meadrow, Godalming. Accommodation: Drummond Arms, Albury.

Shalford (Surrey). Wey; bream, roach, pike, etc. **Tillingbourne**; trout; preserved. Inns: Parrot, Victoria, Sea Horse, Percy Arms, Chilworth.

Godalming (Surrey). Godalming AS has Wey from Eashing Bridge (Stag Inn) to Broadford Bridge (about 8m); coarse fish, some grayling and trout. Society also has Broadwater Lake (10 acres) which holds carp, roach, tench and perch. Busbridge Lake, Enton Lake and Bramley Park Lake: st £38, long waiting list except for residents. Dt for lower river £4, wt £10, from A & G Allchorne (*below*). Peper Harow Flyfishers have 2m of Wey and three ponds (brown and rainbow trout); rods limited; st only. **Wintershall Waters**, Bramley, is 3 acre trout fishery. St only. Tel: 01483 275019. Tackle shop in **Farncombe**: Peter Cockwill Game Angling, 32 Meadrow, tickets and information. Tackle shop in Godalming: A & G Allchorne, 42 Bridge Street GU7 1HL. Hotels: Farncombe Manor, Lake, King's Arms (Godalming AS HQ).

Frensham (Surrey). Farnham AS has trout water below Frensham Mill, **Frensham, Great and Little Ponds,** roach, perch, carp, etc; open membership for coarse fishing. St £45 (joining fee £20), conc, from The Creel, Station Rd, Aldershot.

Haslemere (Surrey). Coarse fish. Surrey Trout Farm is at Rake. At St Patricks Lane, **Liss**, is coarse fishing on 2 lakes, plus 5 ponds at **Rake** for matches only. For dt, contact MBK Leisure, Petersfield Angling Centre, 34 Dragon St, Petersfield GU31 4JJ (01730 266999).

Farnham (Surrey). Farnham AS offers extensive local fishing, for members only. Club coarse fishing waters include 1m R Wey at **Dockenfield, Basingstoke Canal** (through canal assc), with carp, roach, pike etc, **Frensham Ponds, Badshot Lea Ponds, Lodge Pond, Stockbridge Pond** at **Tilford, Loddon** at **Aborfield**, lakes at **Yateley**, 1m of **R Blackwater**, Farnborough (excellent roach), **R Whitewater** near Heckfield Heath, small stream with chub, dace and roach. No day tickets; st £45, joining fee £20, conc, apply Hon Sec for details. Note: All waters heavily fished early in season.

COLNE: Coarse fish, some trout. Information about the river is obtainable from the Colne Valley Anglers Consultative, Mr R McNab, 136 Braybourne Close, Uxbridge UB8 1UL.

Wraysbury (Bucks). Blenheim AS has **Colne Brook** from Wraysbury Rd to Hythe End Bridge; coarse fish and occasional trout. Also Cargill Lake, Silver Wings Lake, and Watts Pool, members only. Twickenham PS and Staines AC have gravel pits; no tickets.

West Drayton (G London). Trout, pike, perch, bream, dace, roach, tench, chub. Grand Union Canal is near.

Uxbridge (G London). Pike, perch, roach, dace and bream. Fishing free on Uxbridge Moor. London AA holds long stretches of **Grand Union Canal**, on which dt £1.50 is issued. National Trust **Osterley Park Lake** holds bream, tench, pike, roach. St £20, conc. No night fishing. Enquiries to Head Gardener, Osterley Park, Jersey Rd, Isleworth, Middx TW7 4RB. **Farlows Pit, Iver**, holds roach, tench, carp, bream, pike; limited number of st.

Denham (Bucks). Colne; coarse fish. Blenheim AS has 6½m of **Grand Union Canal**; dt on Rickmansworth stretch, £2.50, from bailiff on bank.

Harefield (G London). **Savay Lake**, Moorhall Road. A 52 acre gravel pit stocked with specimen coarse fish. St £40, conc, from P Broxup, Fishery Manager, 309 Shirland Road, London W9, tel: 0181 969 6980; dt £4, £2 conc, from newsagents, Peverills, Harefield, or Balfours, Denham. Concessions for junior and OAP. Bowmans Lakes, **London Colney**, three lakes, two of which have 60 and 100 pegs, with large bream, carp and pike. St £50, dt £7-£5, enquiries to 10/11 Pleasant Place, West Hyde, Rickmansworth WD3 2XZ, tel: 01895 824455. Tackle shop: Harefield Tackle, 9 Park Lane.

Rickmansworth (Herts). Trout, chub, dace, roach, pike, perch. Blenheim AS has 1½m of **Grand Union Canal**; good roach and bream; dt £2.50 from bailiff on water. Limited st from Harefield Tackle. (Note: no dt on section between Springwell Lock No 83 and Black Jays Lock No 85.) Watford Piscators have 1½m canal and 2 lakes at Aquadrome, good carp and other species, dt from bailiff. **Batchworth Lake** and **Bury Lake**; dt on site. Club has 12 to 16 jun. section. **Croxley Hall** Trout Fishery, Rickmansworth WD3 3BQ; four lakes in 20 acres: trout, fly only. Tel: 01923 778290. **Gade**; Watford Piscators AS have upper and lower Gade fishing, with barbel, large roach, shoals of bream and chub, good perch. **Chess**; trout, preserved. North Harrow Waltonians have water in river and lake; members only. Tackle shops: Tudor Tackle, Money Hill Parade; Tackle Corner, 157 St Albans Rd, Watford.

Watford (Herts). **Gade** at Cassiobury is free fishing for approx 1m. Ticket waters: Elstree and Tring reservoirs and Grand Union Canal. London AA issues dt for canal from Hunton Bridge to Tring. Free fishing in Gade in Cassiobury Park. Watford Piscators AS have fishing in Rivers Gade and Colne, large roach, chub; and lakes, incl. Tolpits Complex, Castles and Thurlows, and Broadacres; all with good stocks of large carp, trench, bream, and others, also Grand Union Canal fishing. Membership £20, plus annual fee of £75, conc. Further information from Hon Sec. Tackle shop: The Tackle Carrier, St Alban's Road Hotels: Maldon, Clarendon, Rose and Crown.

CHESS: Brown and rainbow trout - one of few British streams where rainbows spawn naturally. There is free public fishing at Scotts Bridge Playing Fields, Rickmansworth.

Chorleywood (Bucks). Chess; trout.

Latimer (Bucks). Upper river and two lakes (12 acres in all) open for trout fishing; brown and rainbow; average 2lb 12oz; daily restocking; boat for hire. Fly only. Season: Mar to Oct. St £565 to £165. Dt £25, short day £18, evenings £14. Advance booking essential. Details from Latimer Park Lakes Chesham, Bucks HP5 1TT, tel: 01494 766333(766555 fax).

GADE: coarse fish.

Boxmoor (Herts). Boxmoor and Dist AS has private water at Westbrook, and Berkhamsted AS now controls Pixies Meres; members only; no tickets. Boxmoor Trout Fishery, 3 acres of converted water cress farm. St £350 to £160 on flexible basis. Inquiries to R Hands, 23 Sebright Rd, Boxmoor, Hemel Hempstead, tel: 01442 393381 or to Fishery, 81 Marlowes, Hemel Hempstead.

Berkhamsted (Herts). Visitors can fish London AA water on Grand Union Canal; coarse fish, dt £1.50 from bailiff. No free water. Hotels: King's Arms (Trust House), Crown, Swan.

LODDON: coarse fish, barbel improving, trout scarce.

Twyford (Berks). Three pits, 100 acres, with carp, bream, tench, pike, chub, dace, eels at Twyford, plus Charvil and St Patrick's stream (fine barbel), held by Leisure Sport Angling. St £22, concessions to jun, OAP, dis. Applications to LSA, *see Chertsey*.

Arborfield Cross (Berks). Farnham AS has a stretch here, and 1½m at Stanford End; coarse fish, barbel in faster stretches *(see Wey - Farnham)*. Cove AS also has water near here at **Shinfield** and on **Hart** and **Whitewater**; members only *(see also Fleet)*. Farnborough AS has 2½m R Loddon at **Winnersh**, 4m R Whitewater at Heckfield, Basingstoke Canal and Shawfields Lake and Hollybush Pits. Fine mixed coarse fishing, fly fishing, membership £30 + £10 joining fee. At **Binfield** is Felix Farm Trout Fishery, Howe lane RG42 5QL; tel: 01734 345527. 10 acres, stocked with b and r between 2-10 lb. Dt £24, 4 fish, ½ day £18, 3 fish, evening £13, 2 fish. Boats for hire. Contact Martin Suddards at fishery for more details.

KENNET: One of England's finest mixed coarse fisheries; upper reaches noted for trout and grayling.

Theale (Berks), Water west of point 1m upstream of Bridge House (Wide Mead Lock) strictly preserved; few trout and coarse fish. Englefield Lake, 2m. Pike, and fine tench and carp (private). Reading and Dist AA has much water on lower **Kennet** at Theale, Rushey Meadow, Calcot, Lower and Upper Benyons, Ufton, Padworth Mill and elsewhere, the **Holybrook** and backwaters, together with 9 local gravel pits, 120 acres. No dt. Blenheim AS fishes Kennet and Holybrook at Southcote. Barbel, roach, dace, chub, perch. Members only, £45 pa, £10 joining fee, conc. At **Burghfield**, three Leisure Sport lakes with big carp and other species, and 1m R Kennet, large chub and barbel. St £26, ½ price conc. *For LSA See Chertsey.*

Aldermaston (Berks). Coarse fish and few trout. Old Mill, Aldermaston RG7 4LB, tel 0118 9712365, issues permits for about 1m of water; dt £8, club bookings £115 inc. CALPAC has 750 yard stretch of Kennet at **Padworth**, with large barbel, tench, bream, pike, etc. Members only, membership £26, conc. London AA has 2m on **Fisherman's Brook**; coarse fish; members only.

Thatcham (Berks). Fishing between Reading and Thatcham controlled chiefly by Reading & Dist AA. Members only on river and Hambridge Lake, but £3 dt on site for Whylies Lake, Thatcham. Details from Hon Sec *(see club list)*. Thatcham AA has water on canal, R Kennet plus lakes. Members only, £52.50 per annum. Tackle shops: Thatcham Angling Centre, 156 Sagecroft Rd; Berkshire Angling Centre, Turnpike Garden Centre.

Newbury (Berks). On Rivers Kennet and **Lambourn** and **Kennet and Avon Canal**; trout and coarse fishing. Newbury & Dist AA, Thatcham AA and Reading & Dist AA hold water in this area. Kintbury AC fish Reading AA waters, plus own canal and river fishing. St £34. Contact Field and Stream. CALPAC has Kennet fishery at Bulls Lock, with large barbel and other coarse species. Some brown and rainbow trout have been caught. Members only. Tackle shops: Field and Stream, 109 Bartholomew Street (01635 43186), and Nobby's, Kingsbridge Road. Foley Lodge Hotel (0635 528770) and Millwaters (0635 528838) both cater for anglers.

Hungerford (Berks). Kennet and **Dunn**; trout, grayling; preserved. **Hungerford Canal** fishing in hands of Hungerford Canal AA (3m). CALPAC has fishery at **Sulhampstead**, 750 yds of river, followed by 700 yds of canal, with large barbel and other coarse species. No night fishing. Dt £4, conc, from Canal Cottage or on bank. Accommodation at Red Lion, Three Swans, Bear, Lamb Hotel (Canal AA HQ).

Lockinge (Oxon). 2m E of Wantage, **Lockinge Trout Fishery**. Av brown and rainbow, 2lb. St £515. Enquiries to John Haigh, Orpwood, Ardington, Wantage OX12 8PN, tel 01235 821116 (820950 fax). Tackle shop: Didcot Angling Centre, 36 Wantage Rd, Didcot.

Marlborough (Wilts). Trout at Axford, Marlborough and District AA has fishing rights in **Kennet and Avon Canal** from Milkhouse Water to Burbage Wharf and Bruce Tunnel to Little Bedwyn. St £12 + £2 entry, conc. **Wroughton Reservoir**, Overtown Hill, Wroughton, Swindon. Coarse fishing, Wroughton AC: Mr Hammond, tel: 01793 81231. Bristol, Bath and Wilts AA has **Tockenham Reservoir**, near Swindon, members only, st £25 from House of Angling *(below)*. Tackle shop: Leathercraft, High Street. Tackle shops in Swindon: Cotswold Angling, Hyde Road, Kingsdown; Angling Centre, 5 Sheppard Street; House of Angling, 60 Commercial Road. Hotels: Aylesbury Arms, Savernake, Castle and Ball, Crown (Marlborough AA HQ).

THAME: Coarse fish.

Dorchester (Oxon). Thames and Thame. Coarse fish; good chub and dace, and carp quite numerous. Dorchester AA has water; dt from Hon Sec or Fleur-de-Lys.

Thame (Oxon). Roach, bream, perch, chub. Leighton Buzzard AC has stretches at **Shabbington**, **Worminghall**, **Ickford** and **Waterperry**.

Eythrope (Bucks). Roach, bream, perch, chub, good dace. Aylesbury Dist and Izaak Walton AA has water (4m from Aylesbury), members and friends only. Blenheim AS has water at Shabbington and Cuddington and backwaters, with roach, dace, chub, perch. Members only, annual sub £45, £10 entrance, usual conc.

CHERWELL: Coarse fish.

Islip (Oxon). Cherwell and Ray; good chub, roach, perch and pike fishing may be had in the Cherwell. Preserved by Oxford Angling and Preservation Society, st £8.50, dt £1.50. The Bicester AS has 1½m on Cherwell Northbrook, and ½ acre carp pool, 2m Bicester. St £12 from tackle shops. Oxford & Dist AA has Cherwell at Enslow and Northbrook; wt from tackle shops. Bicester AA has Kirtlington water. Ft from Allmond Tackle Shop. Other Bicester tackle shop: J & K Tackle, 8/9 Wesley Precinct. Inns: Red Lion, Swan.

Heyford (Oxon). Preserved by Banbury and Dist AA; members only. Oxford & Dist AA has South Oxford Canal from Enslow Bridge to Heyford Wharf. Dt £2.50 from Oxford tackle shops.

Banbury (Oxon). Banbury AA has much local R Medway and canal fishing, incl stretches at Cropedy, Nell Bridge, Clifton, Somerton, Heyford and Bletchington, also **Clattercote** and **Grimsbury Reservoirs**. Dt £4, conc, for reservoirs only from tackle shops. Coventry AA hold stretch 8m of **Oxford Canal**, with large carp, amongst other species. Dt on bank, £2. Farnborough Hall Lake is leased to Banbury AA. Coarse fishing at Butler Hill Farm, Gt Rollright, OX7 5SJ, tel: 01608 684430. Carp to 25lbs, large rudd, chub, bream. Obtain ticket at commencement of fishing. Rye Hill, Milcombe, and Chacombe Fishery, carp bream, tench, etc, dt for these and others from Castaway, *see below*. Cheyney Manor Fishery, Manor House, **Barford St Michael**; 5 acres, rainbow trout are fly fished in trout pond, brown trout in river. The moat contains carp, and fishpond has rudd, roach, tench, perch. Tickets from bailiff. Tel: 01869 38207. Castle AA fishes two lakes, 6 acres, at **Canons Ashby**: carp to 22lb, bream and roach. Tackle shops: Banbury Angling Centre, 12B South St, OX16 7LN; Castaway, 86 Warwick Rd OX16 7AJ; Banbury Gunsmiths, 47A Broad St, OX16 8BT. Chipping Norton tackle shop: K & M, 23 west Rd.

EVENLODE: Trout, coarse fish (roach and dace especially).

Long Hanborough (Oxon). Red Spinner AS rents 10 to 12m of the Evenlode; trout (re-stocked annually), dace, roach, chub, pike; members only. Good fishing on **Blenheim Park Lakes**. Excellent tench, perch and roach, with pike in winter. Boat fishing only. *(See Midlands lakes, reservoirs, etc)*. **Salford Trout Lakes**; 5 and 3½ acres stocked with r and b trout. Dt £18 (4 fish limit), ½ dt £13. St also offered. E A Colston, Rectory Farm, Salford, Chipping Norton OX7 5YZ. Tel: 01608 643209.

WINDRUSH: Trout, grayling, coarse fish (dace up to 1lb and 2lb roach not rare).

Witney (Oxon). Large trout; preserved below; leave must be obtained from the Proprietors; good hatch of mayfly. Witney AS (HQ Eagle Vaults) has water. No dt and membership £15 pa restricted to county as a rule, but outside applications considered; apply Hon Sec. Club now has water on gravel pits at **Stanton Harcourt** (carp, tench, etc). Newland AC have stretch of backstream from Hardwick Village downstream, and Heyford Lakes Fishery, dt £2.50. Tackle shop: Derek State, Tackle, 19 Fettiplace Rd.

Minster Lovell (Oxon). Cotswold Flyfishers have 10m at **Swinbrook** and **Stanton Harcourt**; trout (restocked yearly), fly only; membership limited; no dt. Whitney AA has water on Windrush at **Worsham** (1m above village; trout restocked yearly) and Thames at **Newbridge** and **Standlake**; trout, grayling, coarse fish; fishing much improved. **Linch Hill Leisure Park**, Stanton Harcourt; Willow Pool stocked with specialist carp; Stoneacres Lake mixed trout and coarse fishing. 10 acre Christchurch lake, carp. St £25, dt £2.50 to £5.50, depending on which pool fished. Concessions. Boats for hire. Tel: 01865 882215. Hotel: Old Swan Inn.

Burford (Oxon). Burford AC holds water in vicinity; trout and coarse fish. St from J Swallow, 8 Meadow End, Fulbrook, Burford, Oxon. Dt from Carpenters Arms, Fulbrook. Hotels: Cotswold Gateway, Lamb, Bay Tree, Bull, Winters Tale.

COLN: notable dry fly fishing for trout of good average size; grayling.

Fairford (Glos). Trout; excellent; April 1 to Sept 30. Grayling Oct-Mar. Dry fly only upstream. Not stocked. Tickets can be had for 1½m from Bull Hotel, Market Place, GL7 4AA. Catch/return; trout of 1-1½lb plentiful. Dt £20, half day £12 (reduction for residents). Whelford Pools, coarse fishery, off A417; dt on site, £5, £6 specimen lake, conc. Tel: 01285 713649. Nearest tackle shop at Lechlade, 4m.

Bibury (Glos). Coln: trout. Swan Hotel GL7 5NW, tel: 01285 740695 has 300 yds facing hotel, day tickets from hotel: dry fly only, 3 rods on offer.

TORRIDGE

(For close seasons, licences, etc, see South West Region Environment Agency p16)

Rises on Cornwall Devonshire border, but is also fed from Dartmoor via a tributary, the River Okement. It flows into Bideford/Barnstaple Estuary. Salmon, sea trout, peal and brown trout.

Bideford (Devon). River for 2m on east side, and two reservoirs, at **Gammaton**, stocked with brown and rainbow trout, leased by Torridge Fly Fishing Club; st £100 from Hon Sec, written application only; dt £7 from Summerlands Tackle, 3 Golf Links Rd, Westward Ho!, tel: 01237 471291. **Weare Giffard**, 1m right bank, salmon, sea trout, brown trout; dt £15 from E Ellison, Riversdale Guest House, Weare Giffard, tel: 01237 423676. Torridge Valley Trout Farm, Halspill, Weare Giffard EX39 4RA tel: 01237 475797: rainbow trout dt £3.50, plus catch weight. Hotels: Royal, New Inn, Tanton's.

Torrington (Devon). Salmon, sea trout, brown trout. Fishing lodge and occasional day rods on **Beaford** stretch; contact Group Capt P Norton-Smith, Little Warham, Beaford, Winkleigh EX19 8AB; tel: 0180 5603317. Coarse fishing at **Darracott Reservoir**, Torrington; 3 acres, Peninsula Coarse Fishery open all the year, 24 hr day, dt £3.50 from Summerlands Tackle, *see above*. Tackle shop: The Kingfisher, 22 Castle St, Barnstaple.

Shebbear (Devon). Devil's Stone Inn, EX21 54RU, tel: 01409 281210, has an arrangement with local farmers for 2½m of salmon, sea trout and brown trout fishing on Torridge; fly and spinning; excellent dry-fly trout water. Nearest beat 1m. Licences, tackle, and angling instruction on site. Dt sometimes issued to non-residents.

Sheepwash (Devon). Half Moon Inn, EX21 5NE (01409 231376), has 10m of private salmon, sea trout and brown trout fishing on Torridge. Season 1 Mar-30 Sept, spinning allowed in Mar, otherwise fly only; Also 6 acre lake stocked with rainbow trout. Dt £18, salmon, £12 sea trout, £8, b trout. Brochure on request from Charles Inniss. Tackle shop at hotel, also tackle for hire.

Hatherleigh (Devon). Torridge, Lew, Okement; salmon, sea trout, brown trout. Highhampton Trout Lakes, 6 acres, fly only, rainbow trout: Mrs S Thomas, Greenacres, Highhampton, tel: 01409 231376 for bookings. 4 coarse lakes at **Halwill**, 'Anglers Eldorado'. Specimen fish: carp, golden tench, golden orfe, golden rudd, koi, grass carp, all on £4 dt. Z Gregorek, The Gables, Winsford, Beaworthy EX21 5XT, tel: 01409 221559. Anglers Paradise Holidays, 11 lakes, with less usual species of coarse fish, fishing for residents only. Address: Z Gregorek, *above*. Tackle shops: D.I.Y. Centre, 25 The Square. Holsworthy. Hotel: New Inn, Meeth (½m on Torridge; dts for salmon and trout).

A grilse in the net on the Little Warham Fishery on the Torridge. *Photo: Captain P Norton-Smith.*

Tributaries of the Torridge

LEW: Sea trout, trout.

OKEMENT:

Okehampton (Devon). Trout fishing on 1,870 yards of single bank, st £10, from Hill Barton Farm, tel: 01837 52454. **Mill Leat Fishery**, Thornbury, Holsworthy and **Highampton Trout Fishery** are accessible from Oakhampton.

TRENT

(For close seasons, licences, etc, see Midlands Region Environment Agency, p19)

Largest river system in England. Rising in Staffordshire, Trent drains much of Derbyshire, Nottinghamshire and Lincolnshire, and empties into Humber. A hundred years ago, one of England's principal fisheries; now recovering its status following massive effort at water quality improvement. The tidal water, in particular, now fishing excellently. Some famous trout-holding tributaries, notably Dove, Wye and Derwent.

Gainsborough (Lincoln). Pike, perch, roach, carp, barbel, chub. There are a few fish to 3m below Gainsborough. Tidal. Scunthorpe AA has ¾m, Coates to N. Leverton. Dt on bank. Lincoln AA has water south of Gainsborough, and at North Clifton and Laughterton. Membership £20, dt £2.50. Good local carp fishery: Daiwa Gull Pool, nr Scunthorpe, 53 acre complex. Contact N J Fickling, 27 Lodge Lane, Upton, Gainsborough DN21 5NW. Tackle shop: Tackle shop, Kings Court, Bridge Rd.

Marton (Lincoln). Tidal water. Free fishing at Littleborough. Excellent catches of roach. Doncaster and Dist AA has sole fishing rights on the land owned by Mr H R Tindale, and 4m on the Osburton Estate at Littleborough, members only, on both stretches. Lincoln & Dist AA has stretch here. Tickets from bailiff, Mr P Robinson, 37 Lincoln Rd, Fenton LN1 2EP. South of Marton, Retford & Dist AA, left bank.

Torksey (Lincoln). Chub, roach. South of Laneham Waterski Zone, Lincoln & Dist AA fish right bank. White Swan AC has 15 pegs of natural bank and 15 pegs off platforms, between Lincoln and Gainsborough. Dt £2 on bank. B&B at White Swan Hotel, 400yds from bank. Scunthorpe & Dist AA (01652 655849) has 1,125m at North Leverton. Dt on bank. Worksop District AA (01909 486350) fishes 25 pegs of Torksey Arm, with chub, roach; dt on bank.

Dunham (Notts). Sheffield and Dist AA have a lake and left bank of Trent u/s and d/s. Rotherham and Dist AA offers dt for its fishing on right bank, u/s and d/s of Dunham.

High Marnham (Notts). Mansfield & Dist AA has 50 pegs here. Dt on bank. Worksop and Dist AA has water above Mansfield, including High Marnham Boat Club (12 pegs) and **Normanton-on-Trent**, 85 pegs. Dt on bank, £2,50, conc. Sheffield & Dist AA also has 40 pegs on left bank at Normanton, dt £2.50, before commencement of fishing

Sutton-on-Trent (Notts). Tidal water. Pike, roach, dace, chub. Sheffield AA has Sutton left bank. Dt from Lord Nelson, Sutton-on-Trent. Sheffield Amalgamated AS has sole right of Newcastle Fishery, about 6m. Heavily match-fished. Lincoln & Dist AA has fishing at **North Clifton** and **Laughterton**. Tickets £.2.50 from tackle shops in Lincoln and Gainsborough. Sheffield ASA has **South Clifton** fishing, dt on bank

Carlton-on-Trent (Notts). Retford AA has 650 yds with barbel, bream, chub, roach, perch and gudgeon. Dt £2 on bank. Sheffield & Dist AA has right bank at **Girton**. Dt from Bridge Garage, Dunham.

Collingham (Notts). Club water. Trent 2m W; pike, carp, barbel, roach, dace, chub, perch, bream. Collingham AA has 4m from Cromwell Weir to Besthorpe parish boundary; dt £2.50 from bailiff on bank. All round coarse fishing. Between Holme and **Winthorpe** are several waters of Worksop AAA. At Besthorpe Wharf is Newcastle Fishery; dt 50p. Sheffield AAA. Hotels: Royal Oak, King's Head, Grey Horse.

Muskham (Notts). Nottingham Piscatorial Society preserves from Fir Tree Corner (Kelham boundary) to Crankley Point, both sides, including gravel pits; members only.

Averham, Kelham (Notts). Very good coarse fishing; preserved by Nottingham Piscatorial Society for members only - roach, dace, chub (excellent fly water) - from weirs as Staythorpe to South Muskham boundary on both sides of the river.

Newark-on-Trent (Notts). Roach, dace, pike, chub, bream, barbel, gudgeon, perch, eels. Newark and Dist Piscatorial Federation (01636 702962) has 540m on Trent at **Winthrope**, and 1,260m at Redbridge. Sheffield Amal AS, 6m at **Besthorpe, Girton** and **South Clifton**, dt on bank or from HQ Lord Nelson, Arundel St, Sheffield. Mansfield & Dist AA have Besthorpe and High Marnham fishing, dt for latter on bank. Sheffield & Dist AA has left bank at **Cromwell**, right bank and lake at **Winthrope**. Dt from Level Crossing Cottage, Winthrope. Nottingham AA fishes from Farndon Ferry to Newark Dyke. Dt from bailiff on bank. Other dt stretches: Cromwell Lock and Winthrope Lake to Winthrope Crossing, 225 pegs; Ness Farm, 40 pegs; Footits Marsh 25 pegs; Worksop & Dist AA, dt on bank £2.50, conc. Holme Marsh fishing: 185 pegs n bank, dt on bank, and 40 pegs at Winthrope Crossing, contact Three Rivers (01909 485176). **Hazelford Ferry, Bleasby**, Mrs Mitchell, tel: 01636 813014; Trent Lane, **Collingham**, Collingham AA. Tickets on bank. Tackle shop: Angling Centre, 29 Albert Rd, Newark.

Farndon (Notts). Nottingham Piscatorial Society has north bank (tickets as Rolleston), south bank let to Nottingham AA; dt issued.

Rolleston (Notts). Nottingham Piscatorial Society water from Greet mouth (Fiskerton) to Farndon, (excluding members field and car park); good roach, barbel and chub; dt £3 from Hon Sec (01623 759589), Nottingham tackle shops and Pa Li Chuang, Fiskerton Rd, Rolleston, Newark (01636 812141). No permits on bank. Newark & Dist PF have fishing here, dt £3. Greet, trout; preserved. Nottingham AA has water at **Farndon Ferry** (opp Rolleston); dt from bailiff; matches can be arranged in advance. Sheffield & Dist AA has left bank at **Normanton**, dt.

Fiskerton (Notts). Good roach and chub fishing. Barnsley Anglers have one mile of left bank. Dt £2.50 from bailiffs. Concessionary st. The Greet enters Trent at Fiskerton; trout; preserved.

Hazleford (Nott). Nottingham FAS has dt water on both banks. Nottingham AA has water south, on left bank towards Hoveringham, dt.

Hoveringham (Notts). Dt £2 for Nottingham AA stretch from Star and Garter 1¾m u/s. Midland AS has stretch to Caythorpe, barbel, roach, chub, bream, gudgeon, etc. 134 pegs, dt £2.40, conc, on bank, also 144 pegs d/s on **Dover Beck**. Dt £2 for Nottingham AA stretch from Hazelford Ferry hotel.

Gunthorpe (Notts). Good coarse fishing; roach, dace, chub. Nottingham FAS has water, dt.

Burton Joyce (Notts). Chub, roach (mainly), dace. Nottingham and Dist Fedn has good stretch for which dt issued (matches arranged, booked in advance after Nov 1 for following season); tickets from bailiff, Stoke Ferry Boat Inn, Lord Nelson.

Shelford (Notts). Stoke Weir to Cherry Orchard and Gunthorpe Bridge to Boatyard, Nottingham AA water. Dt on bank.

Radcliffe-on-Trent (Notts). Roach, chub, dace and gudgeon, with perch, pike and tench in Lily Ponds. North Bank from Stoke Weir down to **Gunthorpe**, Nottingham AA; dt. From Stoke Weir up to Radcliffe Ferry, including Lily Ponds, Nottingham Fedn; dt. Fedn also holds from Radcliffe Ferry upstream (members only) and water below Radcliffe railway bridge *(see Burton Joyce)*.

Colwick (Notts). Nottingham AA has from Viaduct downstream for one field. Other fishing, Eastwood Anglers, dt, Nottingham City Council, dt.

Nottingham (Notts). Good mixed fishing. Several miles in city free. Nottingham AA (0115 9708080) has **Clifton**, south bank; for 1,500m Clifton north bank, Royal Ordnance AS (0115 9279241). **Holme Pit Frontage**; **Colwick**, viaduct d/s 600 yds; **East Bridgford**, 180 yds below weir, d/s for 1,350 yds. Dt £3 from bailiff. Nottingham Piscatorial Society has fishing at **Rolleston**, **Fiskerton** and **Farndon**; dt from tackle shops only. Long Eaton Victoria AS has 30 pegs below Colwick sluices, left bank; dt £1.50. Raleigh AC have dt at Clifton Bridge, other clubs with Trent fishing near town are Nottingham Waltonians (right bank north of Clifton), Nottingham AA, (several stretches on both banks, south of town). Nottingham and District Federation of Angling Societies comprises upwards of 68 clubs, with water at **Burton Joyce, Thrumpton, Gunthorpe, Carlton, Hazelford, Clifton Grove, Holme Pierrepont, Colwick, Flintham,** also **R Derwent** at **Borrowash**. Coventry AA also has R Trent fishing at Thrumpton, dt on bank, £3.50. Midland AS (0115 9634487) has 144 pegs at **Hoveringham**

and **Caythorpe**; dt on bank. Earl Manvers AC (0115 9879994) has dt on bank for 27 pegs at **Long Higgin**, and **West Bridgford** fishing. Parkside AC (0115 9787350) has Long Higgin fishing; 67 pegs s bank, dt on bank. Lake in **Wollaton Park** may be fished by dt from Parks Superintendent, Wollaton Park. **Sutton Lake** (not to be confused with Sutton Lake, Shropshire): 17 acre trout fly water, fished by Derbyshire County AC. Guest tickets obtainable. **Colwick Park**, Mile End Rd, Colwick, NG4 2DW, operated by Nottingham City Council, includes a 65 acre trout fishery, and coarse waters on River Trent and lake. Permits and information from Fishing Lodge, tel: 0115 9870785. Council also runs Newstead Abbey Park fishing. Long Eaton Victoria AS has left bank below sluice at Colwick; dt £1.50 on bank. National Watersports Centre, Holme Pierrepont, tel: 0115 9821212, offer angling on 62 acre coarse lake with roach, perch, dt on bank. Tackle shops: Meadows and Netherfield, Bunbury St, Junction Tackle, 210 Tamworth Rd; Gerry's, 96/100 Radford Boulevard, and many others.

Ilkeston (Notts). Cotmanhay AC has Manor Floods Fishery: roach, tench, chub, carp, bream; dt £1.75, conc, on bank or from Taylor's Tackle. Tackle shops: Tom C Saville Ltd (mail order specialists) Unit 7, Salisbury Square, off Ilkeston Road. Walkers, 9-15 Nottingham Road, Trowell; T Watson, 1 Oak Street, Carrington; Toni Bridge, 25 Clayfield Close NG6 8DG; Taylors Tackle, 136 Cotmanhay Rd, Ilkeston. Hotels: Nottingham Moat House; Queens; St George.

Wilford (Notts). Rivermead to Wilford footbridge, Nottingham AA; dt on bank. Club also has Ironmongers Pond, dt on bank. Clifton Grove is Nottingham FA water.

Beeston (Notts). Chub, roach, dace, bleak, gudgeon; preserved by Nottingham AA. Dt for stretch from N Bank Lock from bailiff. Assn also has water on **Beeston Canal**. Tackle shop: Beeston Angling Centre, 33 Humber Rd; Supertackle, 192 Station Rd. Hotels: Brackley House; Hylands.

Thrumpton and Long Eaton (Notts). Roach, bream, dace, chub, perch, barbel. Long Eaton Victoria AS has 2 meadows d/s of Cranfleet Lock. Full membership £13, conc. Coventry & Dist AA also has water here with large barbel and carp, dt £3.50 for Ferry Farm on bank, and for sections above weir. Soldiers and Sailors have Trent Lock, dt £1.50 on bank. **Erewash Canal**. Roach, gudgeon, bream, carp, perch, chub. Dt at Sandiacre, £1 on bank, or from West End AC. Long Eaton Victoria AS has **Soar**, at Kegworth, Radcliffe, dt £1.50; canal fishing, on Cranfleet Canal (Trent Lock), Erewash Canal, (Long Eaton Loch to Trent Lock), also ponds in Long Eaton, members only. Long Eaton and Dist AF has water on Trent at Long Eaton, and **Erewash Canal** fishing. Tackle shops: Wainwrights, Bridge Tackle, 30 Derby Rd; Junction Tackle, 210 Tamworth Rd, Sawley. Hotels; Elms; Europa; Sleep Inn.

Sawley (Notts). Above moorings, Olympic AC offer day tickets, purchased in advance. Pride of Derby AA has fishing on both banks above and below M1 motorway bridge, from Marina down to R Derwent, and 7m between Swarkeston and Willington on Melbourne bank. St £30, conc.

Barrow-upon-Trent (Derbys). Derby AA controls 1,500m both banks, Swarkestone Inglesby, Twyford and Chelaston. Dt from Bridge Guest House, Swarkestone, and local tackle shops.

Burton-upon-Trent (Staffs). Free fishing for Burton residents, at R Dove confluence on right bank, (left bank Swadlincote and Warrington Assns), and on right bank above and below Burton Bridge up to Stapenhill. Burton Mutual AA have fishing which includes **Dove** at **Tutbury** to confluence with Trent, Trent at **Walton** and **Kings Bromley**, and Branstone Water Park; members only. Warrington AA has **Claymills** river fishery. Wychnor Manor Stables (01283 791056) have dt for 100m north bank, with barbel and chub. **Hartshorne Dams**, 2 coarse lakes, are 2 min off A50 at Woodville. Dt from Rooney Inn or Manor Farm, both Hartshorne. Wetmore Hall has 450m, dt from the Lodge (01283 536041). Ripley & Dist AC has 1m left bank of Dove at **Scropton**; mixed fishery, members only. Tickets for canals, various stretches on the R Trent and eight local trout and coarse venues from tackle shop Mullarkey, 184 Waterloo Street. Other tackle shop: Burton Angling Supplies, 30 Borough Rd. Hotels: Queen's, Station and Midland.

Alrewas (Staffs). Chub, dace, roach. Prince

Albert AS has fishing on both banks, north of Alrewas, below Alrewas AC water on right bank. Birmingham AA has water here, **Wychnor, Kings Bromley** and at **Yoxall. Trent and Mersey Canal,** dt from keeper. All three clubs, members only. Catton Park fishing: 1,500m, and 10 acre pool with carp and roach; dt on bank. Tel: 01283 716876.

Rugeley (Staffs). Usual species. Rugeley and Brereton AS has about 1m on Trent and water on **Trent and Mersey Canal** from Armitage to Wolseley Bridge. From here to Colwich held by British Waterways (dt from them); roach, pike, perch. **Blithfield Reservoir,** 4m NE; trout; Blithfield Anglers Ltd allows fishing on season permit only. Inquiries to Fishery Office, Blithfield Reservoir, Abbots Bromley, Staffs.

Stone (Staffs). Stone & Dist AS (01785 819035) fishes 750m Trent left bank here. Tickets from Dales (*below*). Cookston AC fishes right bank at Weston, and Hanley AS has a stretch of double bank between Sandon and Burston. Heronbrook Fisheries, Slindon, nr Eccleshall, 2 lakes stocked with carp and other coarse species. Dt on bank. Crown AC has pools at Eccleshall and Market Drayton, as well as Shropshire Union Canal. Dt £1.50 from tackle shops: Dales Tackle, Albert St, Stone ST15 8HQ, tel: 01785 813708; Cooper Sports, Queen St, Market Drayton.

Stoke-on-Trent (Staffs). Stoke City & Dist AA has Longwaste fishing on **R Tern, R Roden** at Poynton Bridge, **R Meece** at Norton Bridge, **Trent & Mersey Canal,** from Aston Lock to Burston and in city between Wieldon and Etruria Road Bridges; **Shropshire Union Canal** (200-peg match venue, enq invited) and **Knighton Reservoir, Cheswardine.** Also pools at Stoke, Market Drayton and Eccleshall. Coarse fish, members only on all waters. Subscription £20, conc. £9, for ladies, jun, OAP, from mem sec D Deaville, 1 Churston Place, Sneyd Green. Tel: 267081. Club also has 6 and 4 acre trout lakes, 36 rod syndicate, extra cost. apply to Hon Sec. Fenton & Dist AS has fishing on **R Dove** (barbel, chub and grayling), **R Churnet,** trout and coarse, **R Blithe,** Stoke Overflow, with large carp, Trent & Mersey and Caldon Canal fishing, Sutton Brook, and pools in area, st £20, conc, dt £2 for Trent & Mersey Canal stretch only, from Dolphin Discount, Mellors, and elsewhere. At **Newcastle-under-Lyme,** Cudmore Fishery, six pools with carp, barbel, bream, tench, chub, incl specimen pool; tickets from the Lodge (01782 680919). Tackle shops: Abbey Pet Stores, 1493 Leek Road, Abbey Hulton; Dolphin Discount, Old Whieldon Road, Stoke; Mellors Tackle, 30/32 Brunswick st, Hanley ST1 1DR; Horsley's 63/7 Church St, Audley; and many others.

Trentham (Staffs). Lake in Trentham Gardens; area about 70 acres. Village about 3m from Stoke-on-Trent on main road London to Manchester. Fishing tickets at Lodge Gate. Trentham Hotel 1m. Catering offered in Trentham Gardens, caravan site.

Weston-on-Trent (Staffs). Coarse fishing in **Trent and Mersey Canal**; chub, roach, bream, perch.

Tributaries of the Trent

IDLE: Excellent coarse fishing in parts, with bream, roach, chub, predominating.

Misterton (Notts). Worksop & Dist AA has Cornley Lane to Stockwith pumping station; 4,250m l bank, dt on bank. Scunthorpe & Dist AA (01652 655849) has 2,200m from Haxey Gate to Trent confluence. Dt on bank. Gate Inn AC (01427 891106) has 1,500m at Haxey Gate, dt from Gate Inn public house. Dt on bank for 6,375m north bank at West Stockwith. Contact Three Rivers (01909 485176).

Misson (Notts). Doncaster and Dist AA has from Newington to Idlestop, about 10m on the Misson side. Good roach, bream, perch, pike; st and dt from tackle dealers. Assn also has Warping Drain and R Idle and ponds at Idle Stop, with carp, pike, tench, roach, eels. Dt on bank.

Bawtry (Notts). Environment Agency has 500 yds of left bank free to licence holders. Doncaster & Dist AA has 100 pegs at Newington, both banks; Idlestop, 170 pegs, both banks; Cornley Lane, 2,200m both banks; dt on bank.

Retford (Notts). Poulter, 4m S. Meden, 4m S. Maun, 4m S. Idle above Retford private. Derbyshire County AC has 6½m, Lound to East Retford, with chub, roach, dace, bream, pike. Membership £180, annual sub, £132. Apply to Autosport, 2 Mansfield Rd, Creswell, Worksop, tel:

01909 721322. Club also controls coarse section of R Idle, and trout fishing on Dove, Manifold, and Ogston Reservoir. Worksop AA controls a stretch of the **Chesterfield Canal** from Drakeholes Basin to West Retford bridge, 10½m, famous for chub, match weights up to 50lb. Limited membership. dt £2 on bank, conc. Retford & Dist AA fishes 5½m Chesterfield Canal at Retford, **R Trent** at Fledborough (1200yds), and **Carlton,** also 2m **R Till, Saxilby,** various coarse species. Woodside Lake, Lound, further Retford AA coarse fishery. **Daneshill Lakes,** 30 acres with carp and pike, tickets on bank or from local newsagents. Information from Daneshill Lakes (01909 770917). Hallcroft Coarse Fisheries, tel: 017777 10448; four lakes total 16 acres with bream, roach, carp. Tickets at fishery reception.

TORNE and NEW IDLE. Doncaster and Dist AA has 10m from Candy Farm to Pilfrey Bridge and water on **Stainforth and Keadby Canal**; dt from Doncaster and Bawtry tackle shops.

Althorpe (S Humberside). **Stainforth & Keadby Canal;** coarse fish; about 14m of water above and down to Trent; good fishing; rights held by Sheffield, Rotherham, Doncaster, Scunthorpe and British Rail associations. Other fishing stations for canal are **Thorne** and **Crowle. Lindholme Lakes, Sandtoft,** Doncaster, S Yorks, mixed fishery on 3 lakes, 1 trout, 1 carp and a general coarse lake. Dt water, tel: 01427 872015/872905.

Crowle (S Humberside). Excellent centre for coarse fishing. **Stainforth and Keadby Canal,** and **Torne** are ½m from Crowle Central Station; Doncaster AA; roach, tench, bream, perch, carp, pike. Three Drains on A18; Sheffield and Dist AA; roach, perch, tench, carp. Licences, association books and dt from hotels or Hon Sec (enclose s/a envelope). Tackle shop: Thorne Pet & Angling, 5 The Green; also many in Doncaster and Scunthorpe. Hotels: South Yorkshire, Crowle; Friendship Inn, Keadby. Tackle shops in Doncaster (17m) or Scunthorpe (10m).

RYTON (tributary of Idle); Coarse fish.

Scrooby (Notts). Ryton. From Bramshall's farm to junction with Idle, 2m; dt from Pilgrim Fathers and the garage, Scrooby.

Worksop (Notts). On Ryton and **Chesterfield Canal**; coarse fish. Worksop and Dist AA has 10½m of canal from W Retford Bridge to Drakeholes Basin. Dt £2 from bailiffs on bank. Assc also fishes Trent at various locations, Coronation Channel, Spalding, 350 yds **River Till, Clumber Park Lake** (National Trust), where dt and st can be had; Woodsetts Quarry Pond, 8 acres, and **Sandhill Lake**; coarse fish. Grafton AA fishes 4m of Chesterfield Canal in vicinity of town, with 150 pegs; large bream, chub, tench, carp, eels, plenty of roach. St £7, conc, Dt £1, contact Sec G D Williams (01909 474940). For **Langold Lakes,** 14 acres with bream and carp, north of Worksop, contact Site Office, tel: 01909 730189 or Bassetlaw Leisure Centre, Eastgate, Worksop, tel: 01909 480164. Tackle shops: Angling Supplies, 49 Retford Rd; Ken Ward Sports, Carlton Rd.

MAUN (tributary of Idle): Polluted, but fish returning in some parts.

Mansfield (Notts). Field Mill Dam; coarse fish, dt. Vicar Water, Clipstone; coarse fish, dt. Kings Mill Reservoir, Sutton Rd: Nottingham AA water, with carp, roach, bream, dt £2 on bank. Mansfield & Dist AA has water at High Marnham on **Trent,** and Bleasby Gravel Pits; st £18, conc; dt £2 for from Hon Sec and tackle shops. Permits for local coarse ponds also from Forest Town Angling, 113 Clipstone Road NG19 0BT; Mansfield Angling, 20 Byron Street NG18 5PR.

Sutton-in-Ashfield (Notts). Lakes: Lawn, Dam. King's Mill Reservoir, 1m NE; tickets on bank. Hardwick Lakes, Hardwick Hall, are 6m W. Tackle shop: H Burrows, 91 Outram Street NG17 4AQ, tel: 01623 557816. Hotels: Nag's Head, Denman's Head.

DEVON: Coarse fish.

Bottesford (Notts). Smite, 3m NW at Orston. Car Dyke, 5m NW. Bottesford AA preserves 5m of **Grantham Canal** at Bottesford, Muston and Woolsthorpe-by-Belvoir; st and dt from Bull Inn and Rutland Arms, Woolsthorpe-by-Belvoir (on canal bank); and from Hon Sec and from bailiffs on bank. Good coarse fishing, with pike over 20lb.

Belvoir Castle (Leics). Between Melton Mowbray and Grantham, Belvoir Lakes and Knipton Reservoir (coarse fish); open 1 Jun-31 Mar; st £50, ½ st £30, dt £4.50 (£6 on bank), conc £3.50, from Estate Office, Belvoir Castle, Grantham NG32 1PD, tel: 01476 870262 (fax 870443), also from Knipton Shop, or Keepers Cottage, Knipton Reservoir. **Nottingham and Grantham Canal**: Bottesford and District AA has water. Other stations on canal are **Long Clawson**, **Harby**, **Hose** and **Stathern**.

GREET: Trout; coarse fish; preserved.

Southwell (Notts). River private. Trent, 3m SE at Fiskerton. At Oxton, 5m SW, Nottingham Fly Fishers' Club has a trout lake at Gibsmere; strictly members only, long waiting list. Greet FC, too, has trout fishing. Cromwell Fly Fishers, 20 Norwood Gardens, Southwell, has a lake north of Cromwell.

NUT BROOK no longer a fishery.

West Hallam (Derby). Lakes: **Mapperley Reservoir**, 2m N, **Shipley Park Lakes**, **Lescoe Dam** and stretch of Erewash Canal all NCB waters. St £12. jun, dis, £3 from D Allsop, 27 Hardy Barn, Shipley, Derbys. Dt £1 from park rangers.

SOAR: Very popular coarse fishery with anglers in the Leicester area. Environment Agency fishery at **Thurmaston**, nearly 1.000 yds right bank free to licence holders, west of A46 road.

Radcliffe (Derby); Good coarse fishing. Long Eaton & Dist AF administrate between Kegworth and Radcliffe Flood Locks, and 1m Trent, Trent Lock, south bank. Dt £2 from tackle dealers. Soldiers and Sailors AC have water, dt £1.50, also Trent Lock fishing. Contact W Walker, tel: 0115 9721478.

Kegworth (Derby). Roach, dace, bream, tench, chub, perch. Confluence with R Trent upstream approx 75 pegs, Zingari AC. Dt from bailiff on bank. Two meadow u/s of Kegworth Bridge held by Long Eaton Victoria AS. Dt and st. Nottingham AA has from notice board below Kegworth Bridge to Kingston Dyke (members only). Long Eaton AF has good 2m stretch down to Radcliffe. Dt from tackle shops. Soar AS has water here. Kegworth AS has approx 400 mtrs.

Normanton-on-Soar (Leics), Good coarse fishing. Loughborough Soar AS water.

Loughborough (Leics). Loughborough Soar AC (01509 813384) has fishing near here with large carp, chub, bream, roach, perch, plus dace and barbel on two stretches. Dt in advance from tackle shop: Soar Valley Tackle, 7 Woodbrook Rd LE11 3QB (01509 231817). Proctor's Pleasure Park, Barrow-on-Soar LE12 8QF, lake and river fishing, mainly carp, bream, tench, perch. Dt £1.50 from machine on site. Tel: 0150 9412434. Charnwood Leisure Centre: 11 acre lake with carp, pike. Tickets on bank, or from All Seasons Angling (01509 269566). Tackle shop: Bennetts, 9 Market Place, Mountsorrel. Hotels: King's Head and Railway Inn.

Quorn (Leics). Roach, bream. Quorn AS has rights on stretches of river and 1m of canal; they now have joint ticket with Leicester & Dist AS, st £6, jun £2.50; inquire Hon Sec. River fishes best in autumn and winter.

Barrow-upon-Soar (Leics). About 3m river and canal fishing; good roach and bream; recently restocked. Fishes best autumn and winter. Loughborough Soar AS has water. (*See Loughborough*), also Quorn AC.

Leicester (Leics). Coarse fish. 6,000m between Leicester and Barrow on Soar, towpath side held by Leicester and Dist Amal Soc of Anglers (0116 2666911); also 4,500 l bank **Wreake** at **Melton Mowbray, Nene,** and canals. Membership £7. St and dt from bailiffs or Lakeside Marina, 0116 2640222. Leicester AC: Soar and canal; dt and st. **Leicester Canal**; some good coarse fish but boat traffic ruins summer sport. Very high quality coarse fishing in five lakes totalling 22 acres in **Mallory Park**, 8m from Leicester. St £180, conc, (covering all five lakes) from Marks and Marlow, address below. The Pool, Groby, 5m NW; bream, tench, roach, pike; dt from house at pool. Broome AS fishes Birstall Park Lakes, 50 acres, **Birstall**; good tench and bream fishing; also 4 coarse lakes at Asfordby, and stretches of Welland and Soar. Membership, £30 per annum, conc, from Mr G Taylor, 100 New Romnet Cres, Leicester, tel: 0116 2417018. Baxters Garden Farm Lake, **Hinckley**: 2 acres, carp and roach. Tel: 01445 291193. Tackle shops: Marks & Marlow, 39 Tudor Road LE3 5JF (0116 2537714); The Angling Man, 228 Melton Road; J C Townsend, 394 Humberstone Road; Cooper's 225 Saffron Rd; Match Catch, Syston; Bob Berry, 8 Dunton St, S Wigston. Hotels: Grand, Royal, Hermitage (Oadby).

Narborough (Leics). Hinckley and Dist AA has water here containing trout and grayling; permits from permits sec. Broome AS has a stretch here and at **Wanlip**, roach, perch, chub, barbel.

WREAKE (tributary of Soar): An attractive coarse fishery on which Leicester and Dist ASA has extensive coarse fishing rights between Thrussington and Mel-

A nice bag of fine winter grayling taken on trotted redworm, caught from a small tributary of the Derbyshire Derwent. But grayling are found in fast-flowing clean rivers in most parts of Great Britain, south of the Scottish Highlands. *Photo: Bruno Broughton,* who also caught the fish.

ton Mowbray; dt.

Asfordby (Leics). Roach, perch, dace, pike, chub. Mostly Leicester ASA water; dt £1.50 from E Edwards, G Rainbow, bailiffs. Asfordby SOA has water on Wreake and pits at **Frisby** (1m). Members only, no dt. Dt for **Holwell Works Reservoir** from E Madden, The Limes, Ashford-by-Valley.

Melton Mowbray (Leics). Leicester and Dist AS has water at Brokesby, Hoby, Frisby on the Wreake, Pig Sties. Dt from bailiff. Local clubs: Melton AS; Asfordby AS. **Knipton Reservoir**, 8m N, at Branston. Tackle shop: Arbon & Watts, 39 Sherrard St LE13 1XH.

DERWENT: Noted trout and grayling water in upper reaches; downstream coarse fish come into their own.

Sawley (Derby). Coarse fish. Pride of Derby AC has from Wilne Weir to mouth of Derwent (south bank), 750 yd stretch on north bank, and both banks of **Trent** above confluence to Red House on one bank and Sutton's Eaves on other. Also canal from Derwent Lock to Trent and Trent to Sawley Lock; 12m between Derwentmouth Lock and Eggington, excl stretch at weston-on-Trent; and further water on Trent below Sawley Weir towards lock house, including the island and several ponds. Members only (st £30, conc, applications to Hon Sec). Long Eaton & Dist AF has 1m south bank of Trent at Sawley, very good fishing, dt £2. Soldiers and Sailors AC has Derwent fishing nearby at **Draycott**, members only. Contact W Walker, tel: 0115 9721478. Inn: Harrington Arms, Old Sawley, Long Eaton (permits for local waters).

Borrowash (Derby). Coarse fish. Earl of Harrington AC waters *(see Derby)*. Derbyshire County AC has 5m from Borrowash to Sawley, mainly double bank, with barbel, chub, roach, bream, carp, tench, perch and pike. Membership £180, annual subscription £132. Apply to secretary. Nottingham and Dist FAS has fishing rights at Riverside Farm Estates, on Derwent, mill streams and lake. Strictly members only.

Spondon (Derby). Coarse fish; preserved by Earl of Harrington AC. Chaddesden Brook, 1m NW, and Locko Park, 2m N. Private.

Derby (Derby). Coarse fish, Earl of Harrington AC has Derwent from Borrowash Road Bridge u/s to Darley Park, st £12.50, conc, and from Borrowash u/s to Railway Bridge, dt £2, from Hon Sec and tackle shops. Derby City Council issues dt ½ conc, for Derwent from Darley Abbey to Derby Railway Station. Council also issues tickets for coarse fishing at **Alvaston Lake, Markeaton Park Lake, Allestree Park Lake** and **Derwent** in **Darley Abbey Park** (dts from keeper). DCC, Leisure Services Dept, Council House, Corporation St DE1 2XJ. Locko Park Lake and Chaddesden Brook private, Other clubs: Pride of Derby AA *(see Sawley)*; Derby RIFC (water on Derwent, **Trent**, **Dove**, **Ecclesbourne**; canals). Earl of Harrington AC (Derwent, 1m of **Big Shrine** at Borrowash, canal, dt).

Duffield (Derby). Coarse fish, trout and grayling. Derbyshire Angling Federation has 3m from Milford Bridge to Little Eaton, trout and coarse fish, also R Ecclesbourne from Duffield to Derwent confluence. St £20, conc, from Hendersons Tackle (*see Belper*).

Belper (Derby). Chub, roach, bream, perch, barbel, pike, occasional grayling, trout; Belper AC: 6m covered by st, £25, conc, incl 2½ acre Wyver Lane Pond, large carp etc. 2m covered by dt £5, conc, from Hendersons Quality Tackle, 37 Bridge Street.

Ambergate (Derby). Few trout, pike, coarse fish. Alderwasley Ponds, 2m NW.

Check before you go

While every effort has been made to ensure that the information given in **Where to Fish** *is correct, the position is continually changing, and anglers are urged, in their own interests, to make preliminary enquiries before travelling to selected venues. This is especially important with reference to prices quoted. Inevitably the rate of inflation is affecting stability in this quarter. Anglers' attention is also drawn to the fact that the hotels mentioned under the various fishing stations do not necessarily have water of their own. Any amendments or further data for inclusion in subsequent editions, and any comments, will be welcome.*

Butterley Reservoir and **Codnor Park Reservoir**; roach, bream, tench, carp, pike; Ripley and Dist AA waters, st £18, dt £2 from Hon Sec, bailiffs and tackle shops. Loscoe Dam; dt from keeper. Hotel: Hurt Arms.

Whatstandwell (Derby). Mostly grayling and trout, with former predominant and some large chub. Dt £2 from Derwent Hotel, Derby Rd, Whatstandwell, Matlock DE4 5HG, which has ¼m fishing; rather overhung with trees, but plenty of fish and good wading in low water. Free fishing to hotel guests. At **Hartlington**, Charles Cotton Hotel has 1m double bank, dt £15, 4 fish limit, fly only. Tel: 01298 84229.

Cromford (Derby). Trout; fly only; preserved below road bridge (both banks), as far as and including Homesford Meadows, by Cromford Fly Fishers; members only, no tickets. St £100 + £200 entrance fee; 4 year waiting list. Above bridge, Derbyshire County AC water. No tickets. Hotel: Greyhound.

Matlock (Derby). Trout (some rainbows), grayling and coarse fish. Matlock AC issue wt and dt; dt from Midland Hotel (Matlock Bath); water at Matlock and Matlock Bath; trout and coarse; about 1m. Tackle shop: Lathkill Tackle, Unity Complex, Dale Rd North, Matlock DE4 2HX.

Rowsley (Derby). Haddon Estate owns **River Wye** from Rowsley to just north of Bakewell, together with Rivers Lathkill and **Bradford** for most of their length. Wye has pure wild rainbows and fine head of natural browns. Dt £25, fly only. Grayling fishing is open in the winter. For information contact Head River Keeper I Ross, tel: 01629 636255. Two day tickets are obtainable from the Peacock Hotel, Rowsley, to residents and non-residents. Warrington AA has fishing at Darley Abbey.

Baslow (Derby); nr Bakewell, 4m. The Cavendish Hotel, originally the famous Peacock, has 6 rods on the Chatsworth Fishery (brown and rainbow trout, grayling), and Monsal Dale Fishery (brown and rainbow trout), by courtesy of Chatsworth Estate. 4½m of the **Derwent,** 4½m of the **Wye**. Residents only. For full details, phone 01246 582311. For annual membership of Chatsworth and Monsal Dale Fisheries apply to Estate Office, Edensor, Bakewell DE45 1PJ.

Hathersage (Derby). Trout, grayling; preserved by the Derwent FFC; also at Bamford and Grindleford (members only).

Bamford (Derby). Trout, grayling. Derwent FFC has water below Bamford Mill; and from Bamford Mill to Yorkshire Bridge; members only. Peak Forest AC has **River Noe** upstream from Derwent confluence to Jaggers Clough in Edale; fly fishing for brown and rainbow trout and grayling. Members only; subscriptions £350. Tel: 01433 621613.

Ladybower. Centre for **Ladybower and Derwent Reservoirs;** trout; fly only *(see Midlands reservoirs and lakes).* Hotels: Ladybower Inn, Yorkshire Bridge Inn, Ye Derwent Hotel, Bamford (1m), Anglers' Rest (1m), Marquis of Granby, Bamford (2m), Rising Sun, Bamford (2m).

AMBER (tributary of Derwent): trout, coarse fish.

Alfreton (Derby). St £18. dt £2 from Ripley AC for reservoirs at **Butterley** and **Codnor Park**: pike, perch, roach, tench, bream, and carp; dt also from keepers. Sheffield Trout Anglers have water on Amber at Wingfield. Tackle shop: Alfreton Angling, 77 Mansfield Rd. Hotels: George, Castle. Also fair fishing in Derwent at Ambergate, 5m SW.

WYE (tributary of Derwent): One of few rivers in which rainbow trout breed. Also holds good brown trout.

Bakewell (Derby). Trout. Fishing preserved by Haddon Hall Estate. Details are to be found under **Rowsley**, above.

Monsal Dale (Derby). The Chatsworth Estate has excellent trout fishing on ¾m double bank. 4 rods per day only. Apply for day tickets at £20 to Fisheries Secretary, Estate Office, Edensor, Bakewell, Derbys DE45 1PJ.

Buxton (Derby). River private. Brown and rainbow trout fishing in **Lightwood** and **Stanley Moor reservoirs**; Buxton FFC: dt £8, conc, from Buckingham Hotel, Buxton, tel: 01298 70481. Tackle shop: Peak Aquatics, 4 Fairfield Rd, Buxton.

DOVE. Dovedale waters, where Izaak Walton and Chas Cotton fished, are preserved, no tickets. Good sport with trout and grayling elsewhere. In lower reaches, where polluted Churnet enters Dove, angling is improving. Stretches below Uttoxeter, Doveridge, Marchington, Sudbury, etc, also improving: barbel, chub, grayling, pike present. Very limited opportunities for day tickets.

Uttoxeter (Staffs). Trout, grayling. Uttoxer AA preserves good deal of water between Rocester and Uttoxeter; no permits. Leek and Moorlands FC has water here. Membership £30. 3,000m 1 bank, dt on bank, or from Doveridge Sporting Club, nr Uttoxeter (01889 565986).

Rocester (Staffs). Trout, grayling. ¼m single bank, dt £8, contact Mr Appleby (01889 590347). Churnet; fishing spoilt by pollution, but improving; private.

Ashbourne (Derby). Several miles of **R Henmore** and **Bentley Brook**, both tributaries stocked with trout and grayling, and two small lakes controlled by Ashbourne Fly Fishers' Club. St only; no dt. In **Dovedale** 3m of good trout and grayling fishing can be had by guests at Izaak Walton Hotel. Yeaveley Estate nr Ashbourne has coarse fishing on 1 acre lake, open all year. Tel: 01335 330247. Tackle shop: Fosters of Ashbourne Ltd, Compton Bridge DE6 1BX, publish guide to all local day ticket waters. Hotel in Ashbourne; Green Man; hotel at Mayfield, 2m SW (Staffs); Royal Oak.

Hartington (Derby). Trout. Charles Cotton Hotel has about 250 yds of the River Dove; residents only. Proprietor will give data about stretches permitted by farmers.

CHURNET (tributary of Dove): Mixed fishery spoilt by pollution for some years, but improving.

Leek (Staffs). Trout, coarse fish; preserved above Leek town by landowners. Fishing improving as pollution decreases. Leek and Moorlands FC has local fishing on canal, pools, **R Dove**, **R Churnett**; tickets for Deep Hayes Country Park from John Morgan, see below. Membership £30. **Turners Pool**, Swythamley, nr Rushton Spencer; coarse fish, dt £4. Mr Wilshaw, tel: 01260 227225. Springfield Fishery, Onecote: r and b trout, 4 fish dt £7.50. Tel: 01538 300 223/452. Freshwater Trout Farm, Macclesfield Rd, tel: 01538 33684. Dt £1.41 plus charge for fish caught. **Rudyard Lake** is 3m NW, 170 acre reservoir; very good bream, with roach, perch, and pike to 30lb; dt £2.50-£1.50, depending on season. Punts on half and full day from water bailiff Lake House, Rudyard, near Leek or from BW. Match lengths pegged. Basford Coarse Fishery, Turners Croft, **Basford** ST13 7ER; carp and other coarse fish, dt £3.50, conc, at poolside. **Tittesworth Reservoir**: 189-acre Severn-Trent W trout fishery. *(See Midlands reservoirs and lakes).* Tackle shops: John Morgan, Albion Mill, Albion St; Leek Pet and Fishing Centre, 36 St Edward St.

MANIFOLD (tributary of Dove): Offers visitors few opportunities.

Longnor (Staffs). Buxton, 7m; trout. Dove, 1m E; trout, grayling. Crewe and Harpur Arms stretch now acquired by Derbyshire County AC; members only. Part of Hoo Brook and Manifold is National Trust property; trout restocked.

MEASE. Coarse fish. Fishing stations are: **Measham** (Leics); **Snarestone** (Leics); and **Ashby-de-la-Zouch** (Leics); **Netherseal** (Derby); **Edingale** and **Harlaston** (Staffs); Birmingham AA has water at last three. Hazeldine AA has Clifton Campville fishing, membership £10, conc. Hotels: Queen's Head, Royal.

SEAL BROOK (tributary of Mease): a small watercourse with few fish.

Over Seal (Leics). Lakes: Ashby Wolds Reservoir, 1m N.

TAME: After a long history of pollution, much recovered under the care of the Severn-Trent W. Fish now present in many stretches. Further improvement scheduled.

Tamworth (Staffs). Tributary Anker holds roach, pike and perch. Town waters are all let to clubs, tickets from Tamworth Tackle. 500m double bank in castle grounds may be fished through Dosthill Cosmopolitan AC, 69 High St, Dosthill, Tamworth, tel: 01827 280024. Chub, barbel, roach, dace, perch. Dt on bank. Birmingham AA has approx 1,300 yds here. Hazeldine AA also has stretch. Dt from Warren Farm, **Amington**. Mease; roach, chub, dace; Haunton, **Harleston**; dt from W T Ward and Harleston Mill. Local clubs: Lamb AC; Fazeley Victory AC; Birch Coppice AC; Tamworth WMC, Polesworth AC; which fishes Coventry and Birmingham Canals; some tickets on offer. Tackle shops: Tamworth Fishing Tackle, 23 Lichfield St; Hambry's Fishing Tackle, The Square, Polesworth.

Kingsbury (Warwicks). Kingsbury Water Park, nr B'ham. 2m from Junction 9 of M42. 40 acres, with specimen carp to 32lb, tench to 8lb, large bream and pike. Dt from machine at lodge; information from Visitors Centre, Kingsbury Water Park, Bodymoor Heath Lane, Sutton Coldfield, B76 0DY, tel: 01827 872660.

Sutton Coldfield (W Midlands). Lakes at Visitors Centre, Sutton Park, Park Rd,

Sutton Coldfield B74 2YT, tel 0121 3556370: Bracebridge Pool, Blackroot Pool, Powell's Pool. Fishing includes carp to 30lb, bream, roach, pike, and other species. Dt £2.50 (£1.05 jun) on bank. Local club: Sutton Coldfield AC has fishing on rivers and lakes. Tackle shop: Fosters, Kingstanding Rd, B'ham 44, 021 344 3333.

ANKER (tributary of Tame): coarse fish; best sport in winter.

Amington (Warwick). Hazeldine AA has 30 pegs here, coarse fish, members only, membership £10, conc.

Polesworth (Warwick). Coventry AA has 2m plus Alvecott Pools; good head of tench and chub in river, large carp and bream in pools. Dt £2.50 on bank. St from Hon Sec. Assn also has 7m on canal; dt from Assn, bailiffs and tackle shops.

SENCE (tributary of Anker): small stream, but good trout and grayling in places, as well as chub, roach and dace.

BOSWORTH BROOK (tributary of Sence): Trout; preserved.

Market Bosworth (Leics). Bosworth Brook, 1m North; trout; preserved by owner of Bosworth Hall. Sence, 3m W. Tweed, 3m SW.. Lakes: The Duckery, Bosworth Park, 1m S; pike, etc. Gabriel Pool, 3m NE.

BOURNE BROOK (tributary of Bourne). Fishing station: Plough Inn, **Shustoke**, Warwicks. Trout fishing in Avon Division STW Shustoke Reservoir.

BLYTH (tributary of Tame): Coarse fish. Centres: **Coleshill** (Warwicks). Chub, perch, pike, roach. **Hampton-in-Arden** (Warwicks). Chub, dace, roach. **Solihull** (Warwicks). Earlswood Lakes, 6m SW; ticket for three coarse lakes on bank from bailiff. **Olton Mere** coarse fishing; apply to sec, Olton Mere Club.

REA (tributary of Tame): Polluted and fishless.

Birmingham (W Midlands). Birmingham AA, formed from a number of local clubs, controls extensive water on river, canal and lake throughout the Midlands and into Wales. The club-card gives details of all fishing rights, which include numerous fisheries on **Severn and tributaries, Trent and tributaries, Wye and tributaries,** canals, lakes and ponds. A detailed guide with excellent maps is issued from Assn HQ, *see clubs list*. White Swan Piscatorials own or rent waters on the **Severn, Avon, Teme, Mease, Tern, Rea, Lugg, Ithon, Herefordshire Arrow** and numerous pools. St £32 + £32 entrance fee; limited. Day permits to members' guests only. Reservoir at **Edgbaston** fishable on permit. **Park Lakes**: coarse fishing on 14 lakes and pools in city. Dt from park keepers. Special st for pensioners. Tackle shops: William Powell, 35 Carrs Lane, City Centre; Triplex Angling, 213 Monyhullhall Rd, Kings Norton; Barry's, 4 School Rd, Hall Green; West Heath Tackle, 36 The Fordrough, W Heath; John's, 42 Kitsland Rd, Shard End; Jim's Tackle, 11 Hollyfield Rd South, Sutton Coldfield; and many others. Many hotels.

Lifford (Birmingham). Lifford Reservoir. Good coarse fishing. Dt from park keeper. Tackle shop: Clissets, Pershore Rd, Cotteridge.

FORD BROOK (tributary of Tame). Fishing stations : **Pelsall** and **Walsall** (W Midlands). Brook polluted. Lake: Hatherton Lake; pike. Swan AC leases **Sneyd Pool,** Bloxwich, Essington Wyrley and Shropshire Union Canals, coarse fishing. Dt £2 on bank. Match booking. Walsall and Dist AS has **Hatherton Canal**. **Park Lime Pits**; carp, bream, roach, perch, pike; dt and st for small charge. **Aboretum Lake**; bream, tench, roach, perch, pike; dt. Tackle shop: Bentley Bait Box, 197 Wolverhampton Rd.

SOWE: Coarse fish, some trout.

Stafford (Staffs). Upstream of town; perch, pike, dace, roach, chub. Downstream; perch, roach, bream, chub, occasional trout. Free for about ¼m upstream of town on left bank only; remainder preserved by Izaak Walton (Stafford) AA. This association has fisheries on the Sowe, the **Penk, Trent & Mersey Canal, Shropshire Union Canal** and **Hopton Pools**, carp, tench and other coarse fish. Apply Hon Sec for annual membership, wt and dt. White Eagle Anglers have North End Pool, on B5066. Carp to 20lb, st £8, conc. Hotels: Swan, Station, Vine, Royal Oak, Garth, Tillington Hall.

Great Bridgford (Staffs). Sowe. Izaak Walton (Stafford) AA has about 1½m (see Stafford).

Eccleshall (Staffs); Trout; preserved. Stoke City & Dist AA fishes Garmelow Pool, 4 rods per day; bookings to E Gardner, tel: Stoke-on-Trent 818380. Stone & Dist AS fishes Ellenhall Pools. Dt water.

PENK (tributary of Sowe):

Penkridge (Staffs). Coarse fish. **Staffordshire and Worcestershire Canal**. Stafford AA has water *(see Stafford)*. Radford Bridge (Staffs). Izaak Walton (Stafford) AA has water here. **Gailey Upper Reservoir**, Cannock, 34 acres, trout fishery managed by Tern Fisheries, Broomhall Grange, Market Drayton. Stocked rainbows, browns, American brook trout; open all year, pike fishing Nov-Mar. Apply to Gailey Fishing, Gailey Lea Lane, Penkridge, Staffs ST19 5PT, tel: 01785 715848, or booking, 01384 836955. Tackle shop: Tight Lines, Market Place, Penkridge.

TYNE

(For close seasons, licences, etc, see North East Region Environment Agency p17)

Formed by junction of North and South Tyne at Hexham, and empties into North Sea at Tynemouth (Northumberland). Since recovery from pollution this river is considered by some to be the best salmon river in England; trout fishing fair. Pike are increasing in lower reaches (below Hexham) and dace in the North and South Tyne.

Newcastle upon Tyne (North'land). **Whittle Dene Reservoirs**, nr Stamfordham, trout fishery of 68 acres, leased to Westwater Angling. Dt £16 from fishing hut at reservoir, 6 fish limit, self service. Tel: 01434 681 405. George Hotel has fishing at **Chollerford**. Free fishing at Killingworth Pond, N Tyneside. **Killingworth Lake** is dt coarse fishery, tel: 0191 266 8673. Westwater A has 125 acre trout fishery on 4 lakes. Tel: 01434 681 405. Tackle shops: Angling Centre, 123/5 Clayton St West; J Robertson, 101 Percy Street; Bagnall & Kirkwood, 52 Grey Street. Whitley Bay tackle shop: W Temple, 43 Ocean View (0191 252 6017).

Ryton (Tyne and Wear). Occasional salmon; trout, coarse fish. Federation water. Ferryhill AC have 1½m stretch, which can be reached via Heddon on the Hall.

Wylam (North'land). Federation water. Salmon; trout, coarse fish.

Prudhoe (North'land). Trout, coarse fish; occasional salmon; water here and at **Ovingham** and **Wylam** preserved by the Northumbrian Anglers' Federation; also Coquet at Warkworth, Felton and Rothbury. St £55 salmon from Head Bailiff, Thirston Mill, Felton NE65 9EH, tel: 01670 787663; £35 trout, from most Newcastle tackle shops and Alto Outdoors, 72A Front St, Prudhoe.

Mickley (North'land). Trout, coarse fish; occasional salmon; Federation water *(See Prudhoe)*. Lakes: Whittle Dene Reservoirs, 5m N.

Bywell (North'land). Salmon, sea trout. Limited day rods for 3m double bank from Reeltime Fishing Services, Stocksfield NE43 7HP, tel: 01661 843799.

Corbridge (North'land). Trout and dace; trout plentiful but small with runs of sea trout and salmon. Corbridge Riverside Sports Club has 3m on south bank; membership restricted to persons living locally; dt to members' guests only.

Hexham (North'land). Trout (av ¾lb), coarse fish; salmon improving. Tynedale Council, Prospect House, Hexham NE46 3NH, tel: 01434 652200, owns ½m on south bank off Tyne Green from Hexham bridge upstream. St £24, dt £4.80, conc for residents, OAP, etc, from Hexham House, Gilesgate, Hexham, or Tourist I.C. All other salmon water preserved. Langley Dam, 8m west of Hexham: 14 acre lake stocked weekly with r trout. Fly only. Dt £19, 7 fish; £14, 5 fish. NWW Derwent Reservoir, 10m east, 1,000 acres; dt for brown and rainbow trout, £10, conc, 6 fish. eve £6. Dam and north bank fly only, south bank fly and worm. Tel: 01207 255250. Club: Hexham AA has water; no tickets. 4 miles south, Linnelwood Lake, fly only trout lake of 4½ acres. Dt £20, 4 fish. Tel: 01434 609725. Licences from Blair, Post Office, Allendale.

Tributaries of the Tyne

DERWENT: Stocked brown trout, average about 1lb, with fish to 3lb, some grayling.

Swalwell (Durham). Derwent Haugh to Lintzford is now pollution free, held by Axwell Park and Derwent Valley AA; dt for b and r trout, fly only until June 1, then limited worm. Enquiries to PO Box 12, Blaydon NE1 25TQ.

Shotley Bridge (Durham). Derwent, 1m W; trout and grayling. Derwent AA preserves about 14m of river from Lintzford to **Derwent Reservoir** *(see Durham* *reservoirs)* and one bank above reservoir to Baybridge; worming allowed after July 1, except one bank above reservoir to Bay Bridge, fly only. Open membership, £35. Dt £5 from Royal Derwent Hotel, Allensford. Licences from Post Office, Shotley Bridge. Hotels: Crown; Cross Swords.

NORTH TYNE: trout water, with one or two salmon.

Chollerford (North'land). Trout, coarse fish. The George Hotel, Chollerford NE46 4EW, tel: 01434 681611, has ¾m bank fishing upstream of bridge for residents and non-residents. Trout average ½lb. Dt £4.80 £2.40, conc, free to guests.

Bellingham (North'land). Trout, salmon sea trout; best July-Oct. Bellingham AC has 5m water above and below town; runs have improved since 1965; memberbership limited. Ferryhill AC have 800 yds d/s from Burn, dt £5 from Town & Country Shop in town centre. Riverdale Hall Hotel, NE48 2JT, tel: 01434 220254, has 3m salmon and trout fishing for residents, on Tyne (3 beats) and Rede. Licences; Bellingham Hardware, Park Side Place. Hotels: Rose and Crown, Cheviot, Black Bull, Riverdale Hall.

Falstone (North'land). Forest Enterprise offers dt £3, wt £12 for stretch between **Butteryhaugh** and **Deadwater**. The permit also covers Akenshaw, Lewis, Kielder and Ridge End Burns, and is sold at Kielder Castle Forest Centre, tel: 01434 250209. Falstone FC issues permits for 2m of North Tyne, £10 per day, £75 per season, from Blackcock Inn, tel: 01434 240200, or from A Banks, 5 Hawkhope Rd, Falstone.

Kielder (North'land). Major NW reservoir of 2,700 acres. Stocked with browns and rainbows, also contains a good head of wild brown trout. Dt £8 and £6 conc, motor boats for hire. Fly, trolling and worm. Tickets on site. Tel: 01434 240398. Hotels: Riverdale Hall, Bellingham; Percy Arms, Otterburn.

REDE: Trout and pike, with few autumn salmon.

Otterburn (North'land). Otterburn Tower Hotel, NE19 1NS, tel: 01830 520620, has 3½m on Rede, south of Mill Bridge. Trout dt £10. **Sweethope Lake**, Lough House, Sweethope, **Harle** NE19 2PN, tel: 01830 540349: trout fishing for natural b, stocked r; dt £19, 6 fish, boat £8 extra. Dt for **Fontburn Reservoir**, 87 acres, with stocked rainbow and brook trout, on site. Linn Heads Lake, r trout fishing 4m w of Kirkwhelpington: tel: 01830 40349. Otterburn Towers Hotel distributes licences. Other hotel, Percy Arms. Self-catering accom from Ray Demesne Office, Kirkwhelpington NE19 2RG, tel: 01830 540341.

SOUTH TYNE: A spate river, usually fishes well by September. One or two clubs issue tickets for trout and salmon fishing.

Fourstones (North'land). Trout and occasional salmon. Newbrough and Fourstones AA has 2½m of north bank only; no visitors' tickets.

Haydon Bridge (North'land). Trout and occasional late salmon. South Tyne AA preserves 5m of water. Enquiries to Clarke Newsagents, Church St, tel: 01434 684303. Hadrian Lodge Trout Fishery, North Rd, Haydon Bridge, NE47 6NF (01434 688688); 1½ acre upland water, rainbow and browns 1-6lbs; no booking reqd; £10 permit, 2 fish. Hotel: Anchor, adjoins river.

Haltwhistle (North'land), Brown trout, sea trout, salmon. Haltwhistle and Dist AA has visitors wt £50, conc, for 7m around Haltwhistle, sold at Four Seasons Shop, and Greggs Sports, both Main St. Hotels: Railway, Vallum Lodge, Manor House, Wallace Arms.

Alston (Cumbria). Salmon, sea trout, trout. Alston & Dist AA has 10m of water with wt £30 to £70 and dt £5 to £17.50, ½ price conc, from Sandra Harrison, Newsagents, Front Street, tel: 01434 381462.

EAST ALLEN: Allendale AA stocks river with brown trout, and issues wt £5, dt £1 for 6m stretch. Jun ½ price. From Allendale Post Office, tel: 01434 683201.

WANSBECK

(For close seasons, licences, etc, see North East Region Environment Agency p17)

Northumberland trout stream which fishes well under favourable conditions of water, but opportunities for visitors are few.

Morpeth (North'land). Brown trout; preserved by Wansbeck AA for 5m; members only, st £10 + joining £10. Water in town free to E.A. licence holder-

s. Licences obtainable from D Bell, 9 Biltons Court, Morpeth. Tackle shops: 112 McDermotts Fishing Tackle, Station Rd, Ashington; Tackle and Game Supplies, Black Rigg, Morpeth; Chevy Sports, PO Box 1. Hotels: Waterford Lodge, Queen's Head, Angler's Arms, Weldon Bridge.

Tributary of the Wansbeck

BROOKER BURN:

Longhirst (North'land). Wansbeck, 2m S; trout. Lyne, 2m N.

WAVENEY

(see Norfolk and Suffolk Broads)

WEAR

(For close seasons, licences, etc, see North East Region Environment Agency p17)

Rises on Kilhope Moors in extreme west of Co Durham and enters North Sea at Wearmouth. After history of pollution, river now contains salmon, sea trout, brown trout, dace, chub, roach and barbel, perch and bream. Tributaries Browney and Rookhope are improving. Bedburn preserved.

Chester-le-Street (Durham). Sea trout, brown trout (stocked by club) excellent coarse fish. Chester-le-Street AC has 12m good water with the above species plus salmon, dace, chub, barbel, eels, roach. St £44 + £10 joining, conc, dt £1.25, from O'Briens, North Burns. Dunelm AA fishes Chester Moor and Frankland stretches. Contact G Hedley tel: 0191 386 4603. Tackle shop: Sports and Photographs, 139 Front Street.

Durham (Durham). Trout, sea trout. Free fishing on E. A. licence from Ice Rink to Sewage Works, also Ice Rink to Kepies Farm Boundary. Last stretch to Orchard Wall is strictly private. Durham City AC

Not just a sport for men. Miss Tricia King prepares to return a 24lb. common carp alive and well to the water. *Photo: Bruno Broughton.*

has more than 1½m on river, and stillwater fisheries stocked with coarse fish. St £34, conc. Dt for guests of members only. Enquiries to M J Hall, 21 Northumbria Place, Stanley, Co Durham, tel: 01207 232401. Grange AC has water from Belmont Dragonville Flyover to Old Railway Viaduct. Sea trout, salmon and coarse fish. Membership and dt from Anglers Services (*below*). Bear Park, Cornsay and New Branspeth Assns all have water on **Browney**, 4m W of Durham; limited dt; restocking. Ferryhill & Dist AC have Wear fishing, also Browney, both banks to Wear junction, and R Gaunless, 1½m from West Auckland, with brown trout. Tackle shop: Anglers Services, 45 Claypath, tel: 0191 384 7584.

Willington (Durham). Willington & Dist AC has fishing at Sunnybrow to Page Bank. Dt from Bonds Tackle Shop, tel: 01388 746273.

Bishop Auckland (Durham). Sea trout, brown trout, grayling, salmon. Bishop Auckland & Dist AC controls some 20m of water on Wear, between Witton le Wear and Croxdale. Also Witton Castle Lakes, trout stillwater. Dt at lakes or tackle shop. Dt £5 for grayling fishing, 1 Nov-31 Jan, from Windrow Sports, Fore Bondgate; hotels, post offices and other tackle shops in the area. Further details from Hon Sec. Ferryhill & Dist AC has fishing at **Croxdale, Tudhoe, Witworth Estates; Byers Green** and **Old Durham** fisheries, also **Newfield** and **Page Bank**. Club waters also include Rivers **Browney, Tees, Swale, Skern, Gaunless** and various coarse fishing ponds. Hotel: Manor House, West Auckland.

Witton le Wear (Durham). Bishop Auckland AC, see above.

Wolsingham (Durham). Trout, sea trout (good). Wolsingham AA has water; members only (limited st £29 + £10 joining, for visitors). Long waiting list. No dt. At Hagbridge, **Eastgate** (about 8m W), Northumbrian Environment Agency has stretch; dt water. North-West Durham AA has trout fishing on **Hisehope, Waskerley** and **Smiddy Shaw Reservoirs**. Contact Gordon Byers, tel: 010207 501237. **Tunstall** a NWW fishery.

Frosterley (Durham). Trout, sea trout. About 1½m water belongs to Frosterley AC; members only, who must reside in area.

Stanhope (Durham). Trout, sea trout and salmon. About 2m water (both banks) belongs to Stanhope AA; limited st for visitors, £15. local st £6, conc, from Hon Sec. Sea trout June onwards. Northumbrian Water has 2m. Dt (limited) from West End Filling Station. Tackle from Ian Fisher, Market Place. Hotels: King's Arms, Phoenix. For **Eastgate** fishing: Miss Bell, tel: 01388 528414.

Upper Weardale (Durham). Trout, sea trout (Sept and Oct). Upper Weardale AA has 6m in total of Wear and tributaries from Westgate to Cowshill; st £30, wt £10 (not open Sept/Oct), dt £5 (Sept/Oct £7), jun 50%, from The Bluebell Inn, St John's Chapel (01388 537256). Water restocked annually with fish up to 12in. Hotels: Cowshill, Cowshill; Golden Lion, St John's Chapel.

Tributary of the Wear

BROWNEY: now free of pollution; trout and sea trout.

Langley Park (Durham). Langley Park AA lease river here. Assn. also has R Wear at Durham, trout and coarse, and coarse ponds.

Burn Hill (Durham). Waskerley, Tunstall Hisehope and Smiddy Shaw Reservoirs close together on moors between Stanhope and Consett. *(See above and under Durham Reservoirs).*

WEAVER

(For close seasons, licences, etc, see North West Region Environment Agency, p17)

Rises south-west of Cheshire and flows into Mersey estuary. Most species of coarse fish, trout in the upper reaches. British Waterways have a cooperative scheme, the Weaver Waiters, which invites fishing clubs to partake in the management of the River Weaver Navigation between Saltisford and Weston, and represents a long-term strategy of improvement and development of the lower reaches of the river. Contact Regional Manager for further details (*See English Canal Fishing*).

Northwich (Cheshire). Good coarse fishing held by Northwich AA. Water on **Weaver, Dane, Trent and Mersey Canal** (about 17m); **Billinge Green Pools; Great Budworth Mere; Petty Pool Mere** (limited access); **Pickmere Lake**. Comprehensive st (all waters); St £15, wt £5. Exceptional concessions to OAP and regd disabled, from Box 18, Northwich. No tickets sold on bank. Tackle shop: Scotts of Northwich, 185/7 Witton St, tel: 01606 46543. Hotels: Moulton Crow Inn, Moulton; Mayfield Guest House, London Rd.

Winsford (Cheshire). Roach, bream, carp. Winsford & Dist AA have stretch from New Bridge upstream to Church Minshull, several pools around Winsford and R Dane at Middlewhich. St £20, conc, dt £2.50 on bank for Dane, Mon-Fri and Weaver, Newbridge to Bottom Flash. Stockport & Dist AF has water on Rochdale Canal, Weaver and the lake in Drinkwater Park. Dt on bank. Crewe LMR Sports AS has Sandhole Pool (coarse fish) and good tench water at **Warmingham** (½m); some permits *(see Crewe)*. Tackle shop: Weaverside Angling Centre, Wharton Road, Winsford.

Crewe (Cheshire). Weaver 2½m W. No fishing in Crewe, but Crewe LMR Sports AS has 3m of Weaver near Nantwich (4m away) on Batherton Estate. **Sandhole Pool** (1m), and **Doddington Hall Pool** (5m), rights on **Shropshire Union Canal** and stretches of **Severn, Weaver** and **Dane**, as well as good bream, tench and pike fishing on **Hortons Flash**. Guest tickets are not issued for any of these waters. Dt for Macclesfield Canal; coarse fish *(see also Congleton)*. Tackle shops: Tilleys Tackle Shop, 10 Edleston Road.

Nantwich (Cheshire). Trout, grayling, dace, roach, chub, Nantwich AS controls nearly all Weaver near Nantwich; st only; water starts on Reaseheath Estate and stretches SE of town for 7m mainly on both banks, broken at Batherton Mill. Society also has stretch on **Severn** at Trewern. Other clubs with water near Nantwich are Pioneer AA, Amalgamated Anglers and LMR Sports (all Crewe) and Wyche Anglers; Winsford and District AA control **Dane**, (Croxton Lane to King Street), **Weaver**, from Newbridge to Church Minshull; flashes; pools; st from Hon Sec. These 4 clubs are members of Cheshire AA. Winsford Club's pools contain fine tench, carp, bream and pike. Weaver is chalk stream here; well stocked with roach, dace and chub. **Shropshire Union Canal** controlled by BW: dt from bank ranger; st from tackle shop. Other waters within 10m of Nantwich are: Big Mere, Osmere, Blakemere (boats), Combermere (boats). Hotels: Lamb, Crown, Three Pigeons.

Audlem (Cheshire). Adderley Brook. Birchall Brook, 2m NE. Lake: Woolfall Pool, 2m NE. Hotels: Lamb, Crown. *(for club water see Nantwich)*.

Wrenbury (Cheshire). Nantwich AS has water in area; no tickets. Marbury Brook. Sale Brook, 2m S. Baddiley Brook, 2m N. Hotel: Combermere Arms, Burleydam, Whitchurch.

Tributaries of the Weaver

DANE: Trout in upper reaches, but difficult to come by. Coarse fishing, with odd trout and grayling lower down.

Northwich (Cheshire). Chub, dace and roach. Northwich AA have fishing, dt offered.

Davenham (Cheshire). Trout, barbel, roach. Davenham AC have fishing, members only, Davenham to Leftwich.

Middlewich (Cheshire). Trout, dace, roach, chub. Winsford and Dist AA have fishing from Croxton Lane to King St, dt water, also right bank d/s to Bulls Wood. Middlewich Joint Anglers have canal, pool and river fishing, which includes R Dane, left bank u/s from Byley Bridge, approx 2m; right bank u/s approx ½m, both banks between Byley and Ravenscroft Bridge; also **R Wheelock**, right bank u/s from R Dane confluence, and left bank d/s to Bullswood, Bostock, approx 4m. Chub, dace, roach, gudgeon, barbel, and other species. Dt £3, on bank or from tackle shop: Dave's, 67 Wheelock St, Middlewich.

Congleton (Cheshire). Dace, roach, chub, gudgeon and occasional grayling and perch. 5m of prolific water in and around Congleton controlled by Congleton AS, plus excellent carp and coarse fishing in Goodwins Pool. Membership obtainable. Dt £2 for members guests only, from Sec, or tackle shop. From Radnor Bridge towards Holmes Chapel partly controlled by Prince Albert AS, Cheshire AA, Grove and Whitnall AA and Warrington

AA. St for Cheshire AA stretch at **Somerfordbooths** from secretary or Crewe tackle shops. Assn also has water on Severn. Buglawton Trout Club have fly only water from Eaton to Congleton Park, and at Holmes Chapel, Saltersford. Dt, mainly coarse fish. Moreton Coarse Fisheries, New Rd, Astbury, Nr Congleton, (01260 272839): fishing on 3 lakes, dt from bailiff. Carp to 28lb, large bream and tench. Barbless hooks only, bays for disabled. Westlow Mere Trout Fisheries, Giantswood Lane, 01260 270012. **Macclesfield Canal**: Corbridge AS; roach, perch, tench, bream, pike; recently dredged; st and dt at small charge from bailiff; Congleton AS (*see above*). Winsford AA and Lymm AC also have stretches of Dane. Tackle shop: Terry's of Congleton, 47A Lawton St, tel: 01260 273770; Johns Tackle, High St, Biddulph.

Bosley nr **Macclesfield** (Cheshire). Roach, chub, carp, bream, pike; private. Lake: **Bosley Reservoir**; Prince Albert AS water, members only.

Macclesfield (Cheshire). Extensive fishing controlled by Prince Albert AS, a nationally famous club with many rivers, lakes and reservoirs in the NW of England and in Wales. These include stretches on the R Dane, the **Severn**, the **Ribble**, **Wye**, **Towy**, **Teifi**, **Cothi**, **Banwy**, **Twymyn**, **Trent**, **Dove**, **Winster**, **Vyrnwy**, **Lledr**, **Dulas**, **Dysinni**, **Dee**, **Dovey**, **Mawddach** and **Lune**; **Marbury Mere**, Whitchurch, **Isle Lake**, Shrewsbury, **Langley Bottoms and Lamaload Reservoirs**, Macclesfield and others. St £55 + £60, long waiting list. Dt issued for a few of their waters. Danebridge Fisheries has small trout lake at Wincle, fish to 16lb, dt £14-£9, 3 or 2 fish limit; instruction on site. Tel: 01260 227293. Marton Heath Trout Pools, Pikelow Farm, School Lane, Marton SK11 9DH, tel: 01260 224231; coarse pool on site, and tackle. Macclesfield Waltonian AS has **Teggsnose Reservoir**, coarse fish, carp to 20lb; dt £5-£3 from Barlows (*below*). Other clubs: Macclesfield Fly-fishers' Club (12m on Dane and **Clough**, preserved; no tickets), and Macclesfield and District Amalgamated Society of Anglers. **Macclesfield Canal**; good carp, pike, roach, etc. Prince Albert AS has approx 6m. Dt from Barlows (*below*). Macclesfield Waltonians also fish stretch, at Buglawton, dt from Maccl. Tile Centre, Windmill St. **Redesmere** and **Capesthorne**; roach, bream, tench, perch, pike, mirror and crucian carp; dt from bailiff. East Lodge, Capesthorne *(see Cheshire lakes, meres, etc)*. Other waters in area: **South Park Pool**; carp, roach, perch, pike; dt. **Knypersley Reservoir** controlled by Cheshire AA; dt from bailiff. No night fishing. Tackle shop: Barlows Tackle, Bond St, Macclesfield.

WHEELOCK (tributary of Dane):

Sandbach (Cheshire). Clubs with fishing in vicinity are Northwich AA, Winsford & Dist AA, Middlewich AS.

WELLAND

(For close seasons, licences, etc, see Anglian Region Environment Agency, p19)

Rises near Market Harborough and flows through Lincolnshire Fens to The Wash. Coarse fishing very good, much of it controlled by clubs.Upstream of Market Deeping river is renowned for large winter catches of chub and roach. Downstream, river is much wider, with regular banks and excellent access, and slow flowing with bream, roach, tench and eels, also a popular match and pike venue. Fen Drains hold roach, bream, tench and pike, North and South Drove Drains improving, especially in winter.

Spalding (Lincs). Welland, from Spalding to The Deepings, provides 12m of good fishing for pike, perch, chub, roach, dace, bream and tench; controlled by Peterborough AA to Crowland. Dt £2 from D T Ball. **Lincolnshire Drains**; good coarse fishing. At South Holland Drain, Foreman's Bridge Caravan Park, Sutton Rd, Sutton St James PE12 0HU (01945 440344), has permits for Holbeach & Dist AC water in South Holland and Little Holland Main Drains. Spalding FC preserves Counter, North, South and Vernatts Drains; pike, perch, roach, carp, rudd, bream, tench; also **River Glen** from Guthram Gowt to Surfleet village bridge and **New River** from Spalding to Crowland. **Coronation Channel** also fishable (east bank reserved for matches). Worksop and Dist AA lease 2½m, both banks, at Spalding. Tickets on bank.

Cowbit (Lincs). Pike, perch, dace. Spalding

FC water *(see Spalding)*.

Crowland (Lincs). Pike, perch, dace. Nene, 2m SE at Black Horse Mills. New River from Spalding to Crowland preserved by Spalding FC; pike, roach, perch, dace, rudd, bream, tench; tickets from D T Ball, or M Tidwells *(see Spalding)*.

Deeping St James (Lincs). Chub, dace, roach, bream, rudd, pike. Deeping St James AC controls much water in vicinity, including Several Fishery, above town at junction of old river and Mill Stream; Greatford Cut, also Welland at Market Deeping and **Tallington**; Folly Bridge Peakirk, National Grid waters, Bainton; **Nene** fishing; the **Bourne Eau**; **R Glen**; **Redlands Lakes**, with good access for disabled. All mixed fisheries, dt obtainable. Tackle shop: Deeping Angling Centre, 57 Manor Way.

Market Deeping (Lincs). Several Fishery controlled by Deeping St James AC. It extends 6½m from Market Deeping to Kennulph's Stone, on Deeping high bank. Notice boards erected. Dt £3.50 on most club waters, from bailiffs or Deeping St James tackle shop. Accom at Broughtons B & B, 44 Halfleet.

Stamford (Lincs). Chub, dace, roach, pike, perch; fishing free to licence holders on N bank between Town and Broadeng Bridges; approx 1¼m. Elsewhere preserved by Stamford Welland AAA. Approx 18m of water, stretching from Barrowden to confluence of R Gwash and w bank of **Gwash** to Newstead road bridge, eight stretches in all. Chub to 5lb, bream to 7lb. St £13, jun £3, OAP free, from Hon Sec or tackle shop. Other local assn, Stamford & Dist AA. **Burghley Park Lake**, 1m SE (bream an tench, some rudd), Monday to Saturdays; dt £5 to fish island side of Burghley Lake from Burghley Estate Office, St Martins, Stamford, tel: 01780 52075. Tackle shop: Bob's Tackle, 13A Foundry Road.

Ketton (Leics). Oakham AS has water here and on **River Chater**; members only; coarse fish. Broome AS has 1m at **Duddington**, with roach, chub, perch, bream, dace. St £30, half price for juv, OAP, etc, from Mem Sec Mr G Taylor, 100 New Romney Cres, Leicester, tel: 0116 2417018. One year waiting list.

Rockingham (Northants). 400 acre Eyebrook Reservoir is only 2m distant, just south of Caldecott; good trout fishing *(see Midlands reservoirs and lakes)*. At **Corby**, District Council runs coarse fishery on Corby Boating Lake, with specimen carp. Tel: 01536 402551. Hotels: Falcon, High St East, Uppingham, tel: 01572 823535; Vaults, Uppingham, 5m N; Strakis Carlton Manor, Corby. B&B at Mrs J Wainwright, Homestead House, Melbourne LE16 8DL (01858 565724).

Market Harborough (Leics). **Saddington Reservoir** is Saddington AA water. Enquiries to Hon Sec. Broughton and Dunton AC has **Grand Union Canal** stretch, and members only lake at Liere. Dt for canal, £2.50, on bank. Market Harborough and District Society of Anglers has about 1½m of **Grand Union Canal**, good for tench, bream, carp early in season; roach Nov-March, also local Folly Pond, with roach, tench, bream, roach, rudd, carp. Membership cards £14, dt £4-£2, conc, from tackle shop or bailiffs on bank. 1½ acre coarse lake with carp, roach, tench and other coarse fish, in grounds of Welland Lodge Public House, Market Harborough. Dt £5 on bank, conc £3; Nick Bale (01858 433067). At Leire, near Lutterworth is **Stemborough Mill Trout Farm**, well stocked with r trout. Dt £12 6 fish, £10 4 fish. Open all year. Tel: Leir 209624. Tackle shop: Bait Box, Nelson St. Hotels: Angel, Grove.

Tributaries of the Welland

GLEN: River free from Surfleet village to reservoir, coarse fish; trout above Bourne.

Surfleet (Lincs). Glen free below village. Preserved above by Spalding FC.

Pinchbeck (Lincs). Permits issued by Welland and Nene RD. River Welland, 2m SE at Spalding; also Coronation Channel.

Counter Drain (Lincs). Counter Drain; coarse fish; Spalding FC.

Bourne (Lincs). Glen holds trout upstream.

GWASH: Fair trout and grayling stream. Private fishing. Stamford Welland AA have confluence with Welland to Newstead road bridge, west bank.

CHATER:

Ketton (Leics). Roach and dace. Stamford Welland AA has stretch from junction with Welland to Ketton road bridge, both banks.

EYE BROOK: Good head of roach, dace and chub; trout upstream.

WITHAM

(For close seasons, licences, etc, see Anglian Region Environment Agency, p19)

Rises south of Grantham and flows northward to Lincoln, then south-eastward to Boston, where it enters the Wash. Above Grantham noted mainly for trout and grayling, mainly private. Between Grantham and Lincoln it is a good mixed coarse fishery, with chub, dace and barbel, mainly private clubs. Winter areas include Kirkstead and Tattershall Bridge sections. From Lincoln to Boston it is entirely embanked with excellent roach and bream fishing. The fishing rights for the majority of this length are leased to the Witham and District Joint Anglers' Federation. Members of affiliated associations have free fishing. Otherwise, temporary members, day-permits from their bailiffs on the bankside or local tackle shops. Main fishing accesses are **Washingborough, Bardney, Southrey, Stixwold, Kirkstead Bridge** to **Tattershall Bridge** (road alongside), **Chapel Hill, Langrick Bridge** and **Boston. Woodhall Spa** is another good centre for Witham angling, with several hotels catering for anglers, including Kings Arms, Kirkstead Bridge, LN10 6XZ, tel: 01526 352633, who also sell local permits; Railway, 01526 352580.

Boston (Lincs). Angling facilities exceptionally good; at least 100 miles of good coarse fishing (pike, perch, dace, tench, roach and bream) in Witham; Witham and Dist JAF holds 30m between Lincoln and Boston, also tributaries. **South Forty Foot Drain, Sibsey Trader, Bargate Drain** (Horncastle Rd) and **East and West Fen Catchwaters** are Boston & Dist AA waters within easy reach. Dt £2; **River Bain** at **Coningsby**, members only. Tackle shops: Don Whites, 122/4 West Street; Vanguard Fishing Tackle, 25 Wide Bargate. For Boston AA waters to Hon Sec. Accom. with fishing at Moon Cottage, Cowbridge PE22 7BA, tel: 01205 350478.

Lincoln (Lincs). Good coarse fishing. Witham fishes best from Aug-Oct with bream predominant. Lincoln is HQ for Lincolnshire Anglers Fedn and Lincolnshire Rivers Anglers Consultative Assn. Witham and Dist JAF has Witham from Stamp End Lock to Boston West on right bank, with exception of a few short stretches, Witham left bank, Lincoln 1,500 yds d/s of Stamp End Lock to Bardney, with exception of 1,200 yds in Willingh Fen, Witham at Stixwould to Kirkstead Bridge; **Sincil Drain/South Delph** between Stamp End Lock and point 630 yds u/s of Bardney Lock; **North Delph, Branston Delph, Sandhill Beck, Timberland Delph, Billinghay Skerth, Kyme Eau**. Dt £1.75 from bailiffs, local inns or Secretary. Lincoln AA has excellent coarse fishing on **Trent**; 5m **Upper River Witham** to R Brant confluence; **Till** at Lincoln, **Saxilby** and **Sturton by Stow**; drains, dykes, **Boulton Park** and **Hartsholme Lakes** (good bream, eels, pike, carp and others species). Membership books £20 from tackle shops, concessions to jun, OAP. 11m **Fossdyke Canal** between Torksey and Lincoln, mainly roach and bream; BW managed: address in Canal section. **North Hykeham; Richmond Lakes**, 40 acres, coarse; dt £1.50, on bank. Tel: Lincoln 681329. **Butterley Aggregates Lake**; 200 acre coarse; dt 80p on site. Lincoln tackle shops: South End Pet Stores, 447 High Street LN5 8HZ; G Harrison, 55 Croft Street, LN2 5AZ; Boundary Pet Stores, 6 Bunkers Hill LN3 4QP; J Wheater, 9 Tentecroft Street LN5 7DB; Newport Tackle Shop, 85 Newport, Lincoln LN1 3DW; Feed'n'Weed, 22 Birchwood Centre LN6 0QQ. Hotels: Barbican; Brickmakers Arms; Branston Hall; Red Lion, many others.

Grantham (Lincs). Grantham AA has good coarse fishing on Witham, **Grantham Canal** and **Denton Reservoir**; dt £3 for canal from local tackle shops. Note: Grantham AA is a member of the federation of Midlands clubs, which includes Peterborough, Wreake, Boston, Oakham, Newark, Asfordby and Deeping St James Clubs, and has been established to protect fisheries in area and leases waters on **Bourne Eau** and the **Glen**. Tackle shops: Arbon & Watts, 96 Westgate, tel: 01476 63419, has many local permits; Gun Shop, Westgate, Grantham.

Long Bennington (Lincs). Chub, roach, perch, grayling, etc. No dt. Trout lakes at Lakeside Farm, Caythorpe (0400 72758). Pickworth Hall, Folkingham, has fishery, tel: 015297 257.

Tributaries of the Witham

SOUTH FORTY FOOT DRAIN:
Good coarse fishing. From Boston to Hubbert's Bridge, and from Swineshead Bridge to Donington, Boston and Dist AA. Matches booked through Hon Sec, Mrs Jill Sawyer, tel: 01205 350088. Centres are **Boston, Wyberton, Hubberts Bridge, Swineshead, Donington**.

RIVER BAIN:

Horncastle (Lincs). Rivers Bain and Waring; trout, roach; preserved. Some good chub water, free fishing. Tupholme Brook 7m NW. Horncastle AA has Bell Yard Pit and about 1½m on Horncastle Canal; st £8, conc, from Hon Sec. **Revesby Reservoir**, 35 acres, coarse fish; contains big pike, roach, tench, bream, perch, eels; apply to Estate Office, Revesby, Bolton; tel: 01507 568395. Other water on site, the Wong, 4 acres, syndicate water with carp. Tickets for local fishing from tackle shop: F & D Grantham, Synchro Sports, Market Place. Hotels: Bull, Red Lion, Rodney.

FOSSDYKE NAVIGATION: Fossdyke held by BW. Centres: **Lincoln, Saxilby** and **Torksey**. Good coarse fishing, especially noted for bream. Match bookings to BW, tel: 01522 530762, dt on bank from patrolling bailiff.

HOBHOLE DRAIN, EAST AND WEST FEN DRAINS: All canalised lengths of river forming part of fen drainage system. Hold good stock of coarse fish (bream, roach, perch, pike, tench), and include following waters: **Maud Foster, Sibsey Trader, East Fen Catchwater drains, West Fen, Kelsey** and **Bellwater drains**. St £5 and dt £1 from Boston tackle shops and D G Wootton, Myyorn, Hall Lane, Spilsby, Lincs PE23 4BJ. Match pegs 80p. Hobhole and West Fen drains may be fished free on E. A. licence only. St covers also fishing on **Witham, Steeping, Steeping Relief Channel, Glen, Bourne Eau** and **South Forty Foot**.

SLEA: Rises west of Sleaford and enters Witham at Chapel Hill. Trout in upper reaches. Coarse fish, particularly roach, elsewhere. Private fishing throughout length. Tackle shop: Slingsby. Hotel: Carr Arms.

WYE

(For close seasons, licences, etc, see Welsh Region Environment Agency, p20).

Most famous of English salmon rivers. Rises on south side of Plynlimmon near source of Severn and enters estuary of Severn 2m south of Chepstow. Most of rod fishing in private hands, but there are several hotels and one or two associations with rights on river. Sea trout fishing is of no account, but coarse fishing in middle and lower reaches exceptionally good. No free fishing. Licences may be obtained from main post offices and have usually to be produced when obtaining tickets or other permits to fish. Good brown trout fishing in Upper Wye and tributaries, very little trout fishing in Middle Wye. There is a Wye Salmon Fishery Owners Association: Secretary, C E J Bastin, Hill Cottage, Symonds Yat West, Ross-on-Wye HR9 6BL. Carter Jonas of Hereford have more than 30m of river under management.

Tintern (Gwent). Tidal; mostly eels and flatfish, though salmon sometimes taken. Contact J Jones, The Rock, Tintern, Gwent. Rose and Crown Inn.

Redbrook (Gwent). Chub, dace, pike, perch, salmon. Contact the Post Office, Redbrook. For Whitebrook fishing, V Cullimore, Tump Farm, Whitebrook, Gwent. At Fairoak Fishery, The Cot, St Arvans, Chepstow, Monmouth NP6 6HQ, tel: 01291 689711, fly only fishing for trout. Various tickets on site, incl £28, 5 fish, £15, 2 fish.

Monmouth (Gwent). Wye holds salmon, pike, trout, grayling, chub, dace; preserved. Town water is fishable on day, week and annual permit, coarse and salmon, from Council Offices, Monmouth. Monmouth Dist AS own or rent 7m of three rivers: Wye, coarse fishing during salmon close season, on both banks from Wye Bridge downstream; **Monnow**, with trout, grayling, chub, dace, carp, 3m of single or double bank trout fly fishing; **Troddi** at Dinglestow, over 5m of single or double bank trout fishing, all methods. Contact Hon Sec (016001 71382). Skenfrith AS also has local water, members only, details from Bob Forrest-Webb, 1 Trelasdee Cottages, St Weonards, Hereford HR2 8PU, tel: 01981 580497. Trothy, trout; preserved. Brockweir to Livox Quarries, trout and coarse fish; St £20, dt £6 from Information Bureau,

Agincourt Sq, Monmouth.

Symonds Yat (Hereford). Salmon, trout and coarse fishing all preserved. 1½m both banks between **Goodrich** and Symonds Yat controlled by Newport AA. Good S water; members only. For Lower Lydbrook, contact G H Crouch, Greenway Cottage, Stowefield Rd, Lower Lydbrook, Glos,. Tel: 01594 60048.

Kerne Bridge (Hereford). Chub, dace, pike, perch, salmon, trout; preserved. Castle Brook, Garron, 2m; trout. Luke Brook, 2m. Lammerch Brook, 5m.

Ross (Hereford). Salmon, trout, barbel, bleak, carp, bream, roach, large pike, chub and good dace. Ross-on-Wye AC has fishing on town water, Weir End, Netherton and Benhall. Permits for town water on bank or from G B Sports, 10 Broad Street, Ross HR9 7NY. Salmon dt £10, for town and Netherton, coarse dt £4. Ebbw Vale Welfare AC has 2½m at **Foy**, with chub, dace, roach, barbel. Members only, membership open to application. Hotels: Royal, Radcliffe Guest House. Ross-on-Wye AC will be pleased to help visitors; send sae if writing. Foy Bridge Fishery, Lyndor has 250 metres double bank, spinning and fly fishing. Boats for hire. Tel: 01989 63833. Wye Lea County Manor, **Bridstow**, HR9 6PZ, tel: 01989 562880 (768881 fax), has 1m single bank from Backney to Wye Lea. Salmon (4 rods), mixed coarse, ghillie, boat and tackle on site. Hartleton Trout Lake, 14 acres, tel: 01989 63723. Licences from G B Sports, 10 Broad St.

Hereford (Hereford). Salmon, trout, grayling, other coarse fish incl big chub, and more recently barbel. Hereford and Dist AA holds 11½m bank on Wye and 8½m **Lugg**, intended as brown trout fishery, with £12 dt; in addition, three stillwater fisheries with trout and coarse fish. Three types of membership offered: salmon, £80-£75; trout £55, trout and coarse fish £37, conc. Salmon members may fish some 18 named pools, fishable at various heights. Salmon dt obtainable, coarse dt £3.50. Membership applications to Hereford & Dist AA, PO Box 35, Hereford, or tackle shops. 40 pegs at Monte Bishop, 12 Old Eign Hill, HR1 1TU, tel: 01432 342665. Permits from Mordiford PO. Letton Court, Hereford HR3 6DJ, has salmon fishing on 1½m of Wye, dt £20-£25; also coarse fishing on 1½m of river and two lakes with chub, tench, carp, pike, dt £5. Ghillie, R F Pennington, tel: 01544 327294, day, 01497 831665, evening. Birmingham AA has water on Lugg at Dinmore and Moreton. Longworth Hall Hotel, **Tidnor**, has coarse fishing on Wye, and a short stretch on the Lugg. For other fishing inquire Garnons Estate Office, Bridge Sollars, who sometimes have salmon dt, in advance only, also coarse dt; phone bailiff on 01981 590270. W Jones, Carrier Cottage, Whitney-on-Wye; and Red Lion, Bredwardine. Local tackle shops: Hattons (also fishery agent, pleased to give information), 64 St Owen Street, tel: 272317; Perkins of Hereford Ltd, 23 Commercial Road HR1 2BD, tel: 274152, who have information about several mixed fisheries and carp pools. Hotels: City Arms, Green Dragon, Kerry Arms, Booth Hall. Red House Farm, Eaton Bishop, caters for anglers.

Bredwardine (Hereford). Red Lion Hotel HR3 6BU, tel: 01981 500303, has tickets for 8m, salmon, trout, coarse fishing.

Hay-on-Wye (Hereford). Salmon, trout, pike, perch, chub. Hay-on-Wye Fishermans Assn has local fishing, with trout, grayling and coarse, not salmon. Waiting list for membership, tel: 01497 820545. E. A. licences from post office. Tackle and permits (£25 to £3) for Hay Town Council water from H R Grant & Son, 6 Castle Street. Swan at Hay Hotel, Church St HR3 5DQ, tel: 01497 821188, has permits for fishing on Wye, £25 non-residents, £15 residents. For R Llynfi and Ford Fawr, Wye confluence, contact Mrs Lloyd, Bridgend Cottage, Glasbury-on-Wye, tel: 01497 847227. **Llangorse Lake** can be fished from here. Other fishing in area belongs to Sportsmail Ltd, Cardiff. Griffin Inn, Ilyswen, Brecon, has 7½ miles u/s from Hay-on-Wye. Tackle shop: Sportfish, Winforton, Nr Hay-on-Wye HR3 6EB.

Glasbury-on-Wye (Hereford). Salmon, trout, chub, dace, grayling, pike. Fishing in Wye and Llynfi preserved. Llangorse lake is accessible.

Builth Wells (Powys). Salmon (best April, May, June and Oct); wild brown trout declining. Groe Park & Irfon AC has 2m on Wye incl ½m double bank, 1m on Irfon, incl ½m double bank, with 9 salmon catches on Wye and 4 late season catches on **Irfon**. Best S 38½lb, b trout 5½lb. Club stocks heavily with 14oz rainbows. 3-day salmon permit £25, trout £18, trout dt £9, juv £3, coarse dt £4, from N J Guns; Park Hotel; Mrs Morgan, 23

Garth Rd, Builth. No keep nets for grayling on club waters, prawn and shrimp for salmon banned. Lake fishing at Llyn Alarch, 1½ acres, nr Builth, stocked rainbows and browns. Access for disabled anglers. 4 fish limit, dt £13, conc, from Mrs Morgan (*above*), **Elan Estate Reservoirs** accessible *(see Rhayader)*. Cueiddon, Duhonw, Baili and Edw preserved. Tackle shop: N J Guns, High St, Builth.

Hotels: Park Hotel; Lion; Caer Beris Manor Hotel.

Newbridge-on-Wye (Powys). Salmon, trout, grayling, chub, dace, pike, roach; preserved, Ithon; trout; preserved. Accommodation with fishing at Disserth Farm, tel: 277; Mr Philips, Laundry Cottage, tel: 237/208.

Rhayader (Powys). Wye; trout (av ½lb; Wye record, 10½lb, caught at Rhayader Bridge), salmon. Rhayader AA has 4m on Wye, 3m on Marteg to St Harmon, 1.5m on R Elan, and 16-acre **Llyngwyn** at Nant Glas, rainbow trout to 6lbs; fly only. River dt £4, lake dt £12, st £90, conc, from Nant-y-Mynach Farm, nr Llyngwyn, or D Powell, newsagent, Rhyader. Brown trout fishing in **Elan Valley**, (Caban Coch, Garreg Ddu, Pen-y-Garreg and Craig Goch), all fly only, st £55, dt £7, conc, from Visitors' Centre below Caban Coch dam (10 am-6 pm), and Mrs Powell, Newsagent, West St. Rhayader. Dt £4 for local Wye stretch. **Llngwyn Fishery**. Dt £10, st £65, conc, from J and L Price, Nant Y Mynach Farm, Nantmel, tel: 01597 810491. Tickets also from Newsagents. Spinning on Craig Goch; other waters fly only. Elan Valley AA (01597 811099) fish **Dolymynach Reservoir (3-6m W) Claerwen Reservoir** (650 acres), controlled by WW. Hotels which cater for anglers: Elan; Elan Valley who issue permits *(see advt);* Lion Royal, Crown Inn. Accommodation for anglers on Wye, 3m south of Rhayader: Mr and Mrs C Easton, Glanrhos, Llanwrthwl, Llandridod Wells LD1 6NT, (01597 810277): m single bank of Wye, plentiful trout and grayling, salmon late season. Dt £8 by arrangement.

Tributaries of the Wye

TROTHY: Trout, some assn water.

Dingestow (Gwent). Trout; preserved. Glamorgan AC, Cardiff, has 6m fishing. Inquiries to the Hon Sec. Monmouth and Dist AS has 4m, mostly double bank. Trout and eels, excellent mayfly. St £20, dt £6 from Information Bureau, Agincourt Sq, Monmouth.

MONNOW: Good trout and grayling stream. The Game Fishers' Club has water on **Lugg, Rea, Monnow** and several brooks. Trout and grayling. Day permits to members' guests only. Annual membership £100, entrance fee, £75, conc. Monmouth & Dist AS has 3m of Monnow, *see Monmouth.*

Skenfrith (Hereford). Trout, chub, dace. Birmingham AA has fly fishing here. The Priory Hotel has 300 yards; free to guests.

Pontrilas (Hereford). Trout, grayling; preserved by owner of Kentchurch to 3m below here, thence by private owners to within 1m of Monmouth.

Pandy (Gwent). Trout, grayling; preserved. Honddu: trout; preserved. Hotel: Pandy Inn.

HONDDU (tributary of Monnow): Trout.

Llanfihangel Crucorney (Gwent). Trout only, preserved. No tickets issued.

Llanthony. Fishing for trout in unstocked

water can sometimes be arranged at Abbey Hotel; variable charge, not expensive.

LUGG: Trout and grayling, with coarse fish in some stretches.

Mordiford (Hereford). Trout, grayling, etc; Birmingham AA has good stretch here, also water at Tidnor, Lugg Mill, Bodenham, Dinmore, Marden and Moreton. Tickets for Wye at The Moon Inn. Tickets for Sufton Estate fishing, both banks between Mordiford Bridge and Wye junction, also for Wye fishing, from Post Office & Stores, Mordiford HR1 4LN (01432 870235).

Longworth (Hereford). Longworth Hall Hotel has trout and coarse fishing, and on **Wye**, outside salmon season. Mt £34, wt £9, dt £1.50. Advance booking recommended.

Lugwardine (Hereford). 8½m preserved by Hereford and District AA. Dt for right bank d/s starting some 150 yds below the Worcester Rd.

Leominster (Hereford). Trout, grayling, pike, perch, dace. Above town Lugg preserved by landowners. White Swan Piscatorials also have water; otherwise preserved by landowners. **Pinsley Brook**; trout, grayling; landowners sometimes give permission. Coarse pools at Docklow: Mrs Brooke, tel: 0156882 269, dt £3; Mr Bozwood, tel: 0156882 256, dt £3.50. Hotels: Royal Oak (where fishing can be arranged for guests); Talbot.

Kingsland (Hereford). Lugg. Arrow, and Pinsley Brook; trout, grayling. Fishing generally preserved by landowners. 2m from Kingsland is River Arrow at Eardisland. Accommodation: Angel and Mortimer Cross.

Presteigne (Powys). Lugg, Arrow and Teme afford excellent trout and grayling fishing, generally dry fly; preserved. The Gamefishers Club has Lugg here, as well as Monnow, Honddu, Rea, and Severn tributaries Tanat and Cound Brook, Salop, 13m in all, fly only. Subscription £100 + £75 entrance: J H Andrews, Meadow View, Dinedor, Hereford, HR2 6LQ, tel: 01432 870301. At **Walton**, fly fishing for trout in 4-acre lake reserved for tenants of holiday flat, boat for hire. Wt £50, children usually fish free of charge. Details from Mrs A Goodwin, Hindwell Farm, Walton, Presteigne. Tel: 0154421 350252.

FROME (tributary of Lugg). Trout, preserved.

Ashperton (Hereford). Frome, 2½m Leddon, 2½m. Devereux Park Lakes, 4m.

ARROW (tributary of Lugg): Trout, grayling, dace; but few opportunities for visitors.

Pembridge (Hereford). Trout, grayling, dace; preserved by landowners. White Swan Piscatorials have a stretch at Ivington. No tickets. Inn: New Inn.

Kington (Hereford). Trout; preserved. Inns: Swan, Royal Oak.

LLYNFI: Trout, grayling, etc; preserved.

Glasbury-on-Wye (Hereford). Lynfi enters Wye here. Trout, grayling, chub. Fishing good, but mostly preserved. Hotel: Maesllwch Arms, tel/fax 01497 847637, located on R Wye, has day tickets for local fishing.

Talgarth (Powys). Llynfi. Dulais brook. Rhiangoll; trout. Treffrwd, 2m. **Llangorse Lake** (pike, perch) can be fished from here (4m); boats for hire. Hotel: Castle. Visitors' tickets from local association.

IRFON: limited salmon, trout few unless stocked; good grayling.

Llangammarch Wells (Powys). Lake Country House Hotel, LD4 4BS, tel: 01591 620202 (620457 fax) has about 5m of Irfon and nearby streams (**Garth Dulas, Chwefri**, etc), and some rods for salmon fishing on Wye negotiated each year and charged accordingly. Also 2½ acre trout lake (brown and rainbow; fish to 3½lb) in grounds. Lake and rivers restocked annually. Fly only, wt and dt offered. Salmon dt £20, trout £15. Neuadd Farm Caravan Park, LB4 4BY, tel: 01591 620 465 has ¾m fishing on Irfon, fly only £3.50 per rod per day.

Llanwrtyd Wells (Powys). Trout. 3m of Association water. Lakes. Riverside Guest house has accom. with fishing, tel: 429. Victoria Wells Mountain Centre has accom. with fishing, tel: 334. Hotel: Neuadd Arms has 1½m of fishing.

ITHON: Trout, chub, few salmon. Good hotel and assn water.

Llandrindod Wells (Powys). Trout, grayling, chub, some eels and salmon. Llandrindod Wells AA controls 5m of trout fishing close to town, mainly between Disserth and Llanyre Bridges. Limit 2 brace per day. Sunday fishing; no spinning for trout allowed, 9" size limit; waders essential. Open to visitors on st £25, wt £15, dt £5, conc, from Wayfarers, Ddole Rd Enterprise Park (01597 825100). Hotel: The Bell, Llanyre.

Penybont (Powys). Trout, chub, grayling, dace, eels, pike. Hotel: Severn Arms LD1 5UA, tel: 01597 851224/344, which has 6m of trout fishing (on Ithon) free to residents. Dt £3 for non residents. Fish run 3 to lb average. Licences at post office in village, tackle from Wayfarers, Llandridod Wells.

Llanbadarn Fynydd (Powys). Upper Ithon. New Inn, LD1 6YA, tel: 01597 840378, has 3½m trout fishing; free to guests (fly only).

WYRE

(For close seasons, licences, etc, see North West Region Environment Agency, p17).

From Churchtown downstream coarse fish and brown trout. Above Churchtown limited amount of salmon, sea trout and brown trout fishing.

Fleetwood (Lancs). Sport in estuary improving as pollution lessens; flatfish mostly. Bolton AA have water, st £13, £4.50 conc, from tackle shops. Licences and sea baits from Langhornes, 80 Poulton Road, tel: 01253 872653.

St Michael's (Lancs). Mainly brown trout and coarse fish. Ribble and Wyre FA have fishing at St Michaels, some sea trout. Hotel: Grapes.

Churchtown (Lancs). Salmon, sea trout, trout and coarse fish. Warrington AA has fishing here.

Garstang (Lancs). Salmon, sea trout, trout and coarse fish. Garstang AA preserves 3m both banks. Fly only. No dt, members only. Wt for temporary residents in area from tackle shop. Tackle shop: Garstang Fishing and Shooting, 6 Pringle Court, has information on several local trout and coarse day ticket waters. Hotels: Royal Oak, Eagle and Child, Crown.

Scorton (Lancs). Salmon, sea trout, trout, coarse fish. Wyresdale Anglers have 7m water; no tickets.

YARE

(See Norfolk and Suffolk Broads)

YORKSHIRE (lakes, reservoirs, canals and streams)

(For close seasons, licences, etc, see North East Region Environment Agency p17)

BRANDESBURTON PONDS. Several ponds offering varied sport to leisure anglers and specialists. Hull and District AAA, membership from local tackle shop or Secretary. No dt.

CASTLE HOWARD GREAT LAKE. Near **Malton**. 78 acres, noted for specimen pike over 40lb, perch, tench to 10lb, bream to 14lb, roach, and eels to 8lb+. Fishing 6am to sunset. Ground bait allowed in moderation. Peat and leam banned. Maggots, groundbait and tackle on sale from bailiff. Dt £3, OAP and children £1.50 from Richard Callan, Head Bailiff, North Lodge, Castle Howard, York YO6 7DH, tel: 01653 684331. Close season 1 Apr-31 May. Sunday fishing.

CHELKER, SILSDEN, LEESHAW and WINTERBURN RESERVOIRS. Trout; let to Bradford Waltonians; no tickets. Waiting list. Near Silsden and Ilkley.

CONSTABLE BURTON LAKES. At caravan park in grounds of Constable Burton Hall; excellent coarse fishing for roach, bream, perch, tench, carp and pike. St £27.50, mt £14, wt £7 from Warden, Old Lodge, Sproatley, nr Hull. 25 acres of fishing. Season 1 Mar-31 Oct.

DAMFLASK and UNDERBANK RESERVOIRS. YW Services Ltd. Damflask, 5m from Sheffield. Underbank Stocksbridge, 10m. Both coarse fisheries. Dt £2.60 sold from machines at reservoirs. Tel: 01274 372751/5.

DOE PARK RESERVOIR, Denholme. 20 acres. Trout, coarse fish; let to Bradford City AA; dt £5, Mon-Fri incl, 7 am (8.30 weekends) until 1 hour after sunset.

EMBSAY, and WHINNYGILL RESERVOIRS. Let by YW to Skipton AA, jointly with Barnoldswick AC. St £40 + £15 entrance fee. Dt £6 (Embsay, trout), £3.95 (Whinnygill, Trout, roach, bream and perch). £2 Winter coarse fishing. Assn also has fishing on R Aire, dt £3.50. Tickets obtainable from Paper Shop, Embsay, and Earby tackle shops.

FEWSTON and SWINSTY RESERVOIRS. YWS Ltd trout fishery, 153 acres each, fly only, barbless hooks. Regular stocking, 1lb 6oz av, 3lb rainbows. Dt (limit 4/2 fish), from machine at Fishing Office at Swinsty Moor Plantation. Area for disabled only, at Swinsty Lagoon where worm or fly may be used. Av catches for 1994, 2 fish per rod. Near **Harrogate** and **Otley**.

HORNSEA MERE. Hornsea HU18 1AX. Yorkshire's largest inland water (350 acres). Very good pike, carp, bream, rudd, perch, roach, tench. Hornsea Mere Marine Co (Tel: 01964 533277). Dt £2, evening and junior £1, punts £7 day (limited boat and bank fishing).

LEEMING RESERVOIR. Fishing station: **Oxenhope**. 20 acres; good trout fishing, brown and rainbow. Bradford City AA; dt £3, Mon-Fri.

LEIGHTON RESERVOIR. Masham, N Yorks. 105 acre water-supply reservoir on the Swinton Estate stocked with rainbow trout (some very large) for season and day ticket fishing. Barbless hooks. Dt £12, (4 fish), evening £6, (2 fish), concessions, from fishing hut in carp park. Catch and return allowed after limit reached. Estate Office, Swinton, N Yorks HG4 4JH. Phone 01765 689224 for further details.

LEVEN CANAL. Beverley 6m. 3m of good coarse fishing.

LINDHOLME LAKE FISHERIES, Sandtoft. 4 acre fly only trout lake, 16 acre coarse lake and 1½ acre carp pool. Trout dt: £15, 4 fish, £12, 3 fish, £10, 2 fish. £4 dt, coarse. Enquiries to Lindholme Leisure Lakes Ltd, West Hale Farm, Epworth, Doncaster DN9 1LF. Tel: 01427 872015.

MALHAM TARN. 6m from **Settle**. A Nature Reserve owned by the National Trust. Boat fishing only, for trout with fly, and for perch with worm. Barbless hooks only. Fish may run large. Dt £7 boat, £6 rod. Weekends, £12 boat, £6 rod. ½ price conc, except weekends and public holidays. No outboard motors allowed. Bookings and detailed information from Warden or Secretary (01729 830331). Phone bookings recommended. Seasons May 1 to Sept 30 for trout. Accommodation locally.

MARKET WEIGHTON CANAL. Fishing stations: **Newport** and **Broomfleet**. 6m long; bream, perch, roach, pike. Match fishing leased from Environment Agency. Dt sold locally.

MORE HALL RESERVOIR. Sheffield 7m. YW Services Ltd. Trout, fly only; dt £9 from machine at reservoir (limit 4 fish). Tel: 01274 372751/5.

NOSTELL PRIORY LAKES. Foulby, nr Wakefield. Well-stocked with perch, pike, eels, large carp, bream, tench and roach. St £35, dt £4, ½ day £2.25. Various concessions. Details from Fisheries Office, Foulby Lodge. Tel/fax: 01924 863562. Open from 7.00 daily.

SCOUT DIKE, Penistone. 16m from Sheffield. YW (Southern Division). Trout, 2 fish limit; st £17.50. Dt £3.50 sold from machine at reservoir.

SHIPTON LAKE. Shipton-by-Beningbrough. Tench, perch, roach, trout, pike. Bradford City AA, members only.

STAINFORTH AND KEADBY CANAL. Controlled by joint committee including following clubs: Rotherham, Doncaster, Sheffield Amal, Scunthorpe AA and British Railways. Usual Coarse fish.

THORNTON STEWARD RESERVOIR, Bedale. 35 acre YW trout fishery, fly only, barbless hooks. Regularly stocked, 1lb 6oz av, together with many 3lb rainbows. Season: Mar 25 to Nov 30. 4 or 2 fish limit. Dt from Joan Hainsworth, Hargill House, Finghall, Leyburn DL8 5ND, (01677 450245).

TILERY LAKE, Faxfleet, nr Goole. 60 acres of water with carp to 30lb, bream, pike and roach. Controlled by Hull AA, st from Hon Sec or tackle shops in Hull and Goole locality. No night fishing without special permit, from Night Permit Sec.

ULLEY COUNTRY PARK, nr **Sheffield**. Rotherham MBC. 33 acre coarse fishery with bream, roach, perch, pike, rudd. Disabled access. Season: June 1 to Feb 27. St £37, conc. Dt £3, conc, from ticket machine at fishery. Enquiries to Ulley C P, Pleasley Road, Ulley S31 0YL. Tel: 01709 365332.

WORSBROUGH RESERVOIR, Barnsley. Coarse fish, all species, open all year. Barnsley AS has rights and on ½m of canal. St £15, ladies, juniors, disabled £8. Dt £2 from bailiffs walking the bank. Sunday fishing to assn members only; hempseed and bloodworm barred, no keep nets.

NORTHUMBERLAND, Co DURHAM, and CLEVELAND RESERVOIRS. These groups of reservoirs, managed or leased by Northumbrian Water, include both stocked and wild trout fishing. **Burnhope, Grassholme** (140 acres) Cow Green, **Scaling** (105 acres), **Blackton** (66 acres), **Hury** (125 acres), **Lockwood Beck**. Fly only on Lockwood Beck,

Blackton and **Tunstall** (66 acres). For **Kielder**, *see North Tyne*. Prices are as follows: Elite Permit, covering all waters, £450, £360 conc; Select Permit, excluding fly only waters, £400, £320 conc. "Favourite Fishery" permit from £420 to £270, depending on water chosen. Dt from £13 to £8, conc £10 to £6. Rowing boats £12-£9; motor boat (Kielder) £20. For information: Kielder: 01434 240398; Fontburn: 01669 621368; Grassholme, Blackton and Hury: 01833 650204; Tunstall: 01388 527293; Scaling Dam: 01287 640214. Lockwood Beck, Burnhope, Cow Green (all leased): (0191 383 2222).

Tring anglers on the Grand Union Canal at Marsworth

ENGLISH CANAL FISHING

British Waterways own 1100 miles of canal, and 92 operational supply reservoirs. The large majority of these fisheries are leased to fishing clubs, but the Board retains direct control of fishing on a number of canal sections, and several reservoirs (shown below) or in the appropriate geographical section of the book, with season or day tickets easily obtainable.

100,000 anglers over the age of 12 fish British Waterways fisheries regularly. They form an important part of the coarse fishing on offer in England and Wales. Roach, perch, bream, gudgeon, eels, pike, dace, chub, and other coarse fish are to be found. Carp to 38lb have been reported from Middlewich Branch Canal, and in some Grand Union stretches, a good head of tench, larger bream and crucian carp. Stocking levels are extremely good and surpass the E.E.C. designated standard. The fishing is governed, as elsewhere, by water quality and natural food supply. Facilities for anglers in wheelchairs have been introduced in places; competitions can be arranged on directly controlled waters on application to the Fisheries Manager. The North West Region has introduced both the Waterways Anglers Scheme, by which a number of fishing clubs share the leasing of 43m of Shropshire Union Canal, 40m of Llangollen Canal, 45m of Leeds and Liverpool Canal, 55m of Lancaster Canal, and a further 30m on eight additional waterways: clubs participating are able to fish all waters for a year at less than half the day ticket charge; also the Waterway Wanderers permit on the same fisheries. The latter is offered as a £10 season, or £1.50 day ticket, with concessions, and covers all fishing under the scheme. A further permit is the Waterways Permit, offered on monthly basis, and income from it is used for restocking. The Weaver Waiters scheme invites fishing clubs to partake in the management of the River Weaver Navigation for 10m between Saltisford Locks and Weston Point, and represents a long-term strategy of improvement, development and restocking of the lower reaches of the river. Over 10,000 carp, bream, chub and barbel were introduced in 1996. Contact Regional Manager for further details. **Anglers should take special care to avoid overhead power lines above rural canals**.

There are at present three administrative areas of British Waterways Fisheries: North West Region, Navigation Road, Northwich, Cheshire CW8 1BH (tel: 01606 723800, fax: 01606 871471); North East and Midlands Regions, Peel's Wharf, Lichfield Street, Fazeley, Tamworth, Staffordshire B78 3QZ (tel: 01827 252000, fax: 01827 288071); Southern Region, Brindley House, Corner Hall, Lawn Lane, Hemel Hempstead, Hertfordshire HP3 9YT (tel: 01442 235400, fax 01442 234932). Some of the fishing clubs mentioned below are, for reasons of space, not in the club lists of this edition. The Regional Fisheries Manager at the appropriate office will supply addresses and other information.

SOUTHERN REGION:

Grand Union Canal; Osterley Lock to Hayes leased by London AA. Hayes to West Drayton, Central Assn of London & Prov AC. West Drayton to Denham, London AA. Denham to Batchworth, Blenheim AS. Sabeys Pool and part of R Chess, West Hampstead AS. Batchworth to Lot Mead Lock, Sceptre AC. Lot Mead to Cassionbury Park, Watford Piscators, and to Hunton Bridge, Kings Langley AS. Hunton Bridge to Tring, London AA. Tring to Cheddington, Tring Anglers. Cheddington to Stoke Hammond. Luton

Check before you go

While every effort has been made to ensure that the information given in **Where to Fish** *is correct, the position is continually changing, and anglers are urged, in their own interests, to make preliminary enquiries before travelling to selected venues. This is especially important with reference to prices quoted. Inevitably the rate of inflation is affecting stability in this quarter. Anglers' attention is also drawn to the fact that the hotels mentioned under the various fishing stations do not necessarily have water of their own. Any amendments or further data for inclusion in subsequent editions, and any comments, will be welcome.*

AC. R Ouzel at Three Locks. From Stoke Hammond to Great Linford, Milton Keynes AA. Milton Keynes Marina, Milton Keynes Marina Ltd. Great Linford to Wolverton Bridge, North Bucks Div. SE Midlands, CIU Ltd. Old Wolverton to R Ouse Aqueduct, Galleon AC. 400m Canal and Broadwater at Cosgrove, Mr & Mrs M Palmer, Lock House, Cosgrove. Cosgrove to Castlethorpe, Deanshanger & Old Stratford AA. Castlethorpe to Yardley Gobion, Britannia AC. Yardley Gobion to Dodford, Northampton Nene AC. Brockhall to Watling Street Bridge, Daventry AC. Norton Junction to southern end of Braunston Tunnel, AM-PRO UK Ltd AC.

Grand Union: Arms and Branches:

Paddington Arm; Bulls Bridge Junction to Lock Bridge at Paddington, London AA. **Paddington Basin**; Westminster AC.

Regents Canal; Little Venice to Islington, Raven AC. Islington to Mile End, London AA. Mile End Lock to Commercial Road, Brunswick Brothers AS. **Hertford Union Canal**; Junction with Regents Canal nr Victoria Park to Lee Navigation at Old Ford, London AA. **Slough Arm**; Whole of Arm from junction with Main Line at Cowley to Slough, Gerrards Cross & Uxbridge AC. **Wendover Arm**; Main Line to Tringford Pumping Station, Tring Anglers. **Aylesbury Arm**; Main Line to Red House Lock, Tring A. Red House Lock nr Aston Clinton to u/s of Aylesbury Basin, Aylesbury & Dist AF. To the Basin Terminus, Aylesbury Canal Society. **Northampton Arm**; Main Line to Milton Malsor, Northampton Britannia AC. Milton Malsor, Northampton Castle AA. Milton Malsor to Hardingstone, and Hardingstone to Duston Mill Lane, Northampton Castle AA. Bridges 13 to 14, Glebe AC, Bridges 14 to 18, Northampton Castle AA. Gayton Marina, Gayton AC. **Leicester Branch**; Norton Junction to Crick Tunnel, Towcester & Dist AA. North end of Crick Tunnel to Bridge 20, Knightley AC. Bridges 20 to 22 at Yelverton, Eldon Sports and SC. Bridges 31 to 33, Lutterworth AC. Bridges 34 to 37, and 39 to 41, White Hart Match Group. Bridges 37 to 39, Bostrom AC. Bridges 41 to 45, Brixworth AC. North Kilworth to southern end of Bosworth Tunnel, White Hart Match Group. To Bridge 47, Broughton & Dunton AC. Bridges 47 to 51, Desborough AC. Bridges 54 to 60, Broughton & Dunton AC. Whole of **Welford Arm**, Bostrom AC.

River Lee Navigation; Limehouse Basin to Blackwell Tunnel, Brunswick Brothers AS. Bow Lock stretch, Lee Anglers Consortium. Cheshunt, off-side bank plus Cadmore Lane Gravel Pit, Metrop Police AS. West bank Old R Lee, Kings Weir, W E Newton, Slipe Lane, Wormley. Carthegena Lock, Mr P Brill, Carthagena Lock, Broxbourne, Herts. Above Kings Weir to below Aqueduct Lock, London AA. Dodds Wier, L.V.R.P.A. Wier Pool at Feildes Weir, and Feildes Weir Lock to Rye House Station Bridge, plus stretch ½m u/s of Ryehouse Bridge, Lee Anglers Consortium. Ryehouse Bridge for 1020 metres, London AA. Offside Bank between Hardemeade and Stanstead Locks, Ware AC.

Oxford Canal (South); Dukes Cut, Wolvercote Pool, Hythe Bridge Street to Kidlington Green Lock, North Oxford AS. Kidlington Green Lock to Bullers Bridge, N. Oxford AS. Bullers Bridge to Langford Lane, Kidlington AS. Langford Lane to Bridge 221, Tring Anglers. Bridge 221 to end of moorings at Thrupp, Thrupp Canal Cruising Club. Thrupp to Bridge 216, Tring Anglers. Bridges 216 to Lower Heyford, plus River Cherwell at Enslow, Kirtlington, and Northbrook, Oxford & Dist AA. Lower Heyford to Aynho, Banbury & Dist AA. Aynho to Banbury, Coventry & Dist AA. Banbury to Cropredy, Banbury & Dist AA. Cropredy Lock to Bridge 148, Standard-Triumph Recreation C. Bridge 148 to Claydon, Sphinx C. Claydon to Fenny Compton, Ford (Leamington) AC. Fenny Compton Marina to Bridge 136, Cowroast Marina AC. Folly Bridge to Napton Junction, Leamington Liberal AC. Napton Junction to Bridge 103, and Bridges 101 to 102, Coventry & Dist AA. Bridge 102 to Bridge 103, Northampton Castle AA.

River Stort; From junction with Lee Navigation to Lower Lock, Lee Anglers Cosortium. From Road Bridge 6 to Railway Bridge 7, Roydon, Two Bridges AS. To Hunsdon Mill Lock, Globe AS. Stort and Stort Navigation at Burnt Mill, Harlow FA. Burnt Mill Lock to Parndon Lock, Stort Valley AA. Spellbrook Backwater, O J Smith, Spellbrook Lane East, Bishops Stortford. Bishops Stortford and to Spellbrook Lock, Bishops Stortford & Dist

AS. Further stretch to Sawbridgeworth AS.

Oxford Canal (North); Bridges 101 to 97, Warwick & Dist AA. Bridges 97 to 85, Willoughby, Braunston Turn and Braunston Tunnel, Braunston AC. Willoughby Wharf Bridge to Bridge 83, George AC. Bridges 80 to 77, Avon Ho AC. Bridge 76 to Hillmorton Top Lock, Avon Ho AC. Hillmorton Bottom Lock to Bridge 9, Aces AC.

Bridgwater and Taunton Canal; Bridgwater to Durston, Bridgwater AA. Durston to Taunton, Taunton AA.

Gloucester and Sharpness & Stroudwater Canals; Hempsted Bridge, Gloucester, to Sharpness, leased to Gloucester Canal Angling on the towpath side. Frontage of Borrow Silos (150 yds), Babcock AC. Tanker Bay Area, MEB AC. Offside bank at Two Mile Bend, nr Gloucester, and Rea Bridge to north of Sellars Bridge, Gloucester United AA. Stroudwater Canal; Walk Bridge to 'Feeders', Frampton & Dist AA, also from Ryalls Farm to 'Stone' near Frampton. Walk Bridge to Whitminster, Whitbread AC.

Kennet and Avon Canal; Eight stretches from Bear Wharf, Reading, to Kennet Junction, Reading & Dist AA, with the exception of stretch near Sulhampstead Lock, Central Assn of London & Prov AC. Woolhampton Lock to Heales Lock and stretch near Oxlease Swing Bridge to Heales Lock, Glendale AC. Heales Lock to Midgham Bridge, Reading & Dist AA. Junction with Kennet at Northcroft, Two stretches at Midgham Lock, Reed Thatcham AA. Thatcham to Widmead Lock, Thatcham AA. Bulls Lock to Ham Lock, Newbury AA. Ham Mill (offside bank) I Fidler, Ham Mill, London Road, Newbury. Whitehouse Turnover Bridge to Greenham Lock, Twickenham PS. Greenham Lock to Greenham Island, Newbury, and Northcroft to Guyers Bridge, Newbury AA. Two sections at Kintbury (560 yds), Civil Service AS. Ladies Bridge near Wilcote to Milkhouse Water Bridge, Pewsey and District AA. Ladies Bridge to Semington Bridge, Devizes AA. Semington Bridge to Avoncliffe Aqueduct, and Bradford Lock to Winsley Bridge, Bradford on Avon Dist AA. Winsley Bridge to Limpley Stoke Bridge, Kingswood Disabled AC. Limpley Stoke Bridge to R Avon confluence, Bathampton AA.

Monmouthshire and Brecon Canal; from Pontypool to Brecon, BW directly controlled fishery. Goytre Marina, Red Line Boats. Cattle Upper Bridge to Llanfoist Bridge, Cwmcelyn AC. Stretch nr Llanfoist, Mr R Tod, Boat House, Llanfoist, Abergavenny. Auckland Bridge to Haunted House Bridge, Gilwern & Dist AC. Haunted House Bridge to Penpedair Heal Bridge, Gwent Avengers. Workhouse Bridge to Fro Bridge, Ebbw Vale Welfare AC. Brynich Lock to Canal Terminus at Brecon, BW directly controlled. **River Usk**; at Llanfrynach and Brynich, private fishing.

River Severn Navigation; Island bank at Upper Lode Lock, Diglis, BW directly controlled. Belvere Lock, G H Drake, 30 Dunstans Close, Worcester. Cock Island, left bank 350 yds d/s, Shoulton AC. East bank at Diglis, Punchbowl AC. Bevere Lock, Mrs M E Smith, Bevere Lock, Grimley. Holt Lock u/s and d/s, A S Portman, Holt Lock, Holt Heath, near Worcester. Salmon rights, Lincomb Lock, P Gough, Courtnay House, Feiashill Road, Trysull, WV5 7HT. Coarse rights, B Turner, Lincomb Lock, Stourport. West bank, Lincomb Lock, Carter Jones, 20 St Owen St, Hereford. (Severn Valley Sand & Gravel Ltd).

MIDLAND REGION:

Ashby Canal; Stretches leased by Birchmoor AC, Shackerstone & Dist AC, Measham AC.

Birmingham and Fazeley Canal; Tyburn to Curdworth Tunnel, Fosters of Birmingham, Dams and Lock AC, BRS (Midlands) AC, Stirrup Cup AC. Curdworth Tunnel to Whittington is Birmingham AA, Fazeley Victory AC, Lamb AC and Hope and Anchor AC. Whittington Bridge to Huddlesford Junction, Whittington Social AC.

Birmingham Canal Navigation (BCN), Wyreley and Essington Canal; Cannock Extension; Yates AC, Chase Social AC. **BCN Rushall and Daw End Branch Canal;** leased to Pelshall Social AC, Trident AC, Fletchers Tackle AC, Hawkins AC, WMTS AC, Conex AC. **BCN Soho Loop**, Fisherman of England AC.

Coventry Canal; Coventry to Polesworth, Coventry & Dist AA. The remaining sections leased by Birchmoor AC, Amington AC, Tamworth Progressive AC, Weddington Social Club AS, Dordon AC. Huddlesford Junction to Fradley Junction, Lamb AC, Lichfield Marina AC, Pirelli AC, Drayton Manor AC, Belgrave AS.

Grand Union Canal, Main Line; North Napton Junction, through Calcutt Bottom Lock to Junction Bridge, Warwick, Royal Leamington Spa AA. Junction Bridge to Ugly Bridge, Warwick & Dist AA. **Saltisford Arm**; Saltisford Canal (Trading) Ltd. Hatton Top Lock to south end of Shrewley Tunnel, Stratford upon Avon AA. Shrewley Tunnel to Rowington, Tunnel Barn AC. Rowington to Chessets Wood and Small Arm at Kingswood Junction, Massey Ferguson Recreation C. Knowle, Civil Service AC. Knowle Top Lock to Birmingham, Tavern AC, Crown Leisure AC, Wild Manufacturing AC, Hay Mills AC, Lode Mill AC.

Staffordshire and Worcester Canal, South; York Street Stourport to Botterham Lock, Birmingham AA. Botterham Lock to Dimmingsdale Lock, Wolverhampton AA. **Stratford-upon-Avon Canal**; leased by Olton AC, Raven AC, Redditch FA, Solihull AC. **South Stratford Canal**; Stratford AA, Evesham AA, Alcester AC, Studley Rd AC. **Worcester and Birmingham Canal**; Diglis Basin to Blackpole Bridge, Worcester UA. Blackpole Bridge to Kings Norton Tunnel, Birmingham AA.

Staffordshire and Worcester Canal, Northern Section; stretches held by Lilleshall & Dist AS, Marston Palmer AS, Goodyear AS, New Invertion WMC, Littleton & Mid-Cannock AC, Union Locks Anglers, Staffs Co Council AC, Four Ashes FC, Whitmore Reans CAA. Roseford Bridge to Milford Aqueduct, Izaac Walton (Staffs) AA. Milford Aqueduct to Great Haywood Junction, Potteries AS.

Trent and Mersey Canal; Derwent Mouth to Weston-upon-Trent, Pride of Derby AA. Weston-upon-Trent, Derby Railway AC. Weston-on-Trent to Clay Mills, Pride of Derby AA. Clay Mills Bridge to Wychnor Lock, Burton Mutual AA. Findern Crossing Pond, Derby RAC. Wychnor Lock - south west, Alrewas AC. Section to Woodend Turn, Woodside Caravan Park AC. Handsacre Bridge to Wolseley Bridge, Rugeley & Brereton AS. Wolseley Bridge to Colwich Lock, Norton Lido AC. Three stretches between Great Haywood Lock and Ingestre Bridge, Evode AC. Ingestre Bridge to Weston Lock, Cadbury AC. Next beat, Hazeldine AA to Salt Bridge. Salt Bridge to Sandon Lock, Universal Sports C. Sandon Lock to Flute Meadow Bridge, Olditch AC. Flute Meadow Bridge to Long Meadow Bridge, Stone AS. Section to Aston Lock, Stoke City & Dist AA. Aston Lock to Meaford Lock, Dove Valley AA. Meaford to Stoke-on-Trent, Fenton & Dist AC.

Shropshire Union Canal; in Wolverhampton area Wolverhampton AA have section, also Post Office AC, Dawley AC, then British Rail AC, George Carter Ltd AC. Further sections leased by Codsall Legionnaires AC, Penkridge Anglers; section to Stretton Aqueduct, Swan AC. Stretton, Brewood AC. Next two sections are leased by Hazeldine AA. Section to Cowley Tunnel, Izaac Walton (Stafford) AA. To Gnossal, Marston Palmer AS. The leased sections to Tyreley are held by the following clubs: Market Drayton AC, Fusileer AC, Park AC, Stafford Hospital AC, Hodnet WMC AC, Palesthorpes AS, Crown AC. Tyreley Locks to Audlem, Crewe Pioneers AC. Audlem Bottom Lock to Ellesmere Port is BW managed. *See introduction*.

NORTH EAST REGION:

Chesterfield Canal; Stockwith to Drakeholes Low Wharf, Sheffield & Dist AA, Clayworth Church Lane Bridge to Retsford Bridge, Worksop & Dist. AAA. West Retford Bridge to Chequer House Bridge, Retford & Dist AA. Chequer House to Bracebridge Lock, Worksop United AA. Bracebridge Lock to High Grounds Farm Bridge, Grafton AA.

Erewash Canal; Trent Lock to Long Eaton Lock, Long Eaton Victoria AS, also **Cranfleet Canal**. Long Eaton Lock to Sandiacre Lock, Long Eaton & Dist FA. Sandiacre Lock to B5010 Bridge, West End AC. B5010 to Pasture Lock, Lace Webb Spring Co Sports & SC. Pasture Lock to Stanton Lock, Draycott AC. Stanton Lock to Greens Lock, and on to A6096, Middleton WMC. A6096 to Common Bottom Lock, Durham Ox FC. Common Bottom Lock to Shipley Lock, Cotmanhay AC. Shipley Lock to Langley Mill Lock, NCB No 5 Area FC. **Grantham Canal**; Grantham to Woolsthorpe-by-Belvoir, Grantham AA. Lady Day Bridge to Gamston Bridge, Matchman Supplies AC. Other sections, Nottingham AA. Very little of this canal is fishable. **River Soar Navigation**; Sections at Thurmaston and Wreake Junction, Leicester & Dist ASA. Barrow Shallow to

Kegworth Old Lock, Loughborough Soar AS. 400 metres at Lock Island, Kegworth AS. Kegworth Flood Lock to Ratcliffe Lock, Long Eaton & Dist AF. Canal in Loughborough, Quorn AS. **River Trent**; Hazelford Island, BW directly managed. Lenton, Raleigh FC. Beeston Canal, Nottingham AA. Trent at Gunthorpe, Nottingham & Dist FAS. These are small fisheries.

Grand Union Canal: Arms and Branches; Market Harborough Arm; Junction, Foxton Boats Ltd. Foxton to Mkt Harborough, Tungstone FC, Desborough and Rothwell AC, Mkt Harborough AC. Foxton to Leicester, Wigston AS.

Huddersfield Broad Canal; section from Apsley Basin entrance, Holme Valley PA. Red Doles Lock to Deighton Mill, Huddersfield Broad Canal Alliance. **Pocklington Canal**; Pocklington to Derwent junction, East Cottingwith, York & Dist AA. **Ripon Canal**; terminal to R Ure junction, Ripon Canal Fisheries (T Welbourne, 116 Stonebridgegate, Ripon). **Selby Canal**; wide commercial waterway. Selby Basin to Bawtry Road bridge, Wheatsheaf AC. Bawtry Bridge to Brayton Bridge, Knottingley Conservative Club AS. Brayton Bridge to Burn Bridge, Selby AA. Burn Bridge to Paperhouse Bridge, Goole & Dist AA. Paperhouse Bridge to Tankards bridge, Carlton AC.

Sheffield and South Yorkshire Navigation (Stainforth and Keadby Canal); Keadby Lock to Mauds Bridge, Stainforth & Keadby Joint AC. M18 to Dunston Hill Bridge, Hatfield Colliery AC. Dunston Hill to Stainforth High Bridge, Stainforth AA. Bramwith Lock to Barnby Dun Swing Bridge, Northfield Bridge to aqueduct on New Junction Canal, and on past Sykehouse Lock, Doncaster & Dist AA.

Sheffield and South Yorkshire Navigation; wide commercial section. Barnby Dun to Kirk Sandal, Barnby Dun SAC. Kirk Sandal to Railway Bridge, Pilkington (Kirk Sandal) Rec C. Rotherham to Sprotborough (9 miles) all Rotherham AA, except short lengths controlled by Group 35 AC, Conisborough AC, E Hemingthorpe S & SC, and Guest & Chrimes Ltd AS. Sprotborough to Kirk Sandall (6 miles) all Doncaster AA.

Remainder Length; Tinsley & Dist ACA have two sections; Tinsley Canal junction with R Don, and R Don to Holmes Lock. Tinsley Wire Sports & SC have two basins, as do Firth-Derihon (Tinsley) FC.

Canals are often narrow and sheltered waters, making less dramatic venue than rivers. Not so the Aire & Calder canal near Selby. *Photo: L Rogers.*

Broughton Lane to Tinsley, BSC (Tinsley) Sports & SC. To Coleridge Road, Tuffnells AC. Between bridges at Coleridge Road and Darnall Road, Fox House Social Club AS. Darnall Road to Shirland Road, Ranmoor Dept AC. Shirland Rd to Staniforth Rd, Firth Park WMC. Staniforth Road to Bacon Lane, Stocks AC. Bacon Lane to Bernard Road, Hogs Head AC. Bernard Road to Cadman Street, Woodseats WMC. **River Ure**; Ure and Milby Cut at Boroughbridge, Plus Milby Lock to Tinkers Lane; Harrogate & Claro Conservative AA. Also on Ure and Milby Cut at Boroughbridge, Unity AC.

NORTH WEST REGION:

Caldon Canal; very good water quality. Bedford St Double Lock to Planet Lock no 3, Waterway Wanderers and Adderley Green AC. Planet Lock no 3 to Lichfield St Bridge, Fenton & Dist AS. Lichfield St Bridge to Abbey Rd Bridge 15, Waterway Wanderers. Abbey Rd Bridge 15 to Foxley Lift Bridge 172, Corbridge Coronation CIUC. Foxley Lift Bridge 17 to Stockton Brook Bridge 25, Waterway Wanderers. Stanley Rd Bridge to Post Bridge 28, Abbey Hulton Suburban AS. To Hazlehurst Junction, and from Hazlehurst Bottom Lock to Cheddleton Top Lock Bridge 43, Waterway Wanderers. From Cheddleton Top Lock Bridge 43 to Consall Forge Bridge 49, Embreys Bakeries AC; Basford Bridge 44 to Bridge 47, Stoke Telephone AG. Bridges 49 to 53, Waterway Wanderers. 53 to 54, TBJ AC. Froghall Tunnel Bridge to Bridge 55, Stoke on Trent Disabled AC. Bridge 55 to terminus, Frognall Wharf. **Leek Branch**; Hazlehurst to Horse Bridge, Waterway Wanderers. Horse Bridge to end, Leek, Leek & Moorlands FC.

Llangollen Canal; Hurleston Locks to Little Mill Bridge 55, Rubery Owen AC and Waterway Wanderers. Ellesmere to Tetchill, Oswestry Dist AC. Tetchill to Prices Bridge 68, and Nicholas Bridge 2 to Kings Bridge 49A, Waterway Wanderers.

Macclesfield Canal; Hardingswood Junction to Hall Green Stop Lock, Kidsgrove & Dist AA. Five sections to Watery Lane Aqueduct, Burslem Surburban AC, Warrington AA, Middleport WMC, Warrington AA, Victoria AC. To Henshalls Bridge 80, Warrington AA. From Henshalls Bridge to Lamberts Lane Bridge 77, Victoria and Biddulph AS. To Lamberts Bridge, Bridges 72 to 77, Warrington AA. Porters Farm Bridge to Buxton Road Bridge, Congleton, Macclesfield Waltonian AS. To Congleton Bridge 61, Waterway Wanderers.

Montgomery Canal; Burgedin Locks to Bridge 106, incl Wern Clay Pits, Churchstoke AC. Bridges 131 to 133, Waterway Wanderers. Bridge 134 To Tan-y-Fron Bridge 136, Penllwyn Lodges AC. Tan-y-Fron to Bridge 142, Waterway Wanderers. Bridge 142 to Glanhafren Bridge, Lymm AC. 143 to 144, Montgomery AA. Bridges 143 to 147, Waterway Wanderers. Bridges 147 to Bridge 147A, Severnside AC. Bridges 147A to 153, Waterway Wanderers. **River Severn** at Penarth Weir, Potteries AS. Penllwyn AC have stretch at Tan-y-fron. R Severn at Penarth Weir, Potteries AS. **Peak Forest Canal**; Dukinfield Junction to Whaley Bridge Terminus, Stockport & Dist AF.

Trent and Mersey Canal; Trentham Lock to Stoke Basin, Fenton & Dist AS. Whieldon Road Bridge to Stoke Summit Lock, Stoke City & Dist AA. To Longport, Middleport WMC. Longport to Tunstall, Red Lion A. Tunstall to S end of Harecastle Tunnel, Waterway Wanderers. N end of Harecastle Tunnel to Red Bull Bottom Lock 46, Waterway Wanderers. Church Lawton to Lawton Lock 50, Royal Doulton AC. Lawton Lock to Rode Heath Bridge, Waterway Wanderers. Rode Heath Bridges 138-139, Knutten British Steel AC. 139-141, Waterway Wanderers. 141 to Middlewich Junction, Cheshire AA. Rookery Bridge to Booth Lane Top Lock, Middlewich Joint A. Rookery Bridge to Booth Lane Top Lock, Cheshire AA. Middlewich Junction to Preston Brook Tunnel, Trent & Mersey Canal AA.

Middlewhich Branch Canal; From Bar-

Keep the banks clean

Several clubs have stopped issuing tickets to visitors because of the state of the banks after they have left. Spend a few moments clearing up, this includes lengths of broken nylon. If discarded, serious injuries can be caused to wild birds and to livestock.

bridge Junction to Cholmondeston Lock, Waterway Wanderers. Cholmondeston Lock to Railway Bridge 5A, Venetian Marine AC. Railway Bridge 5A to Bridge 22 Clive, Waterway Wanderers. Bridge 22 Clive to Bridge 32, Middlewich Junction, Middlewich Joint Anglers.

River **Weaver**; at Eaton Bank Pool and Witton Brook, Northwich AA. At Saltersford, Sutton, Sutton Pool, Warrington AA.

Weaver Navigation; various sections between Winsford and Newbridge, Winsford & Dist AA. Between Newbridge and Bostock Works, Meadowbank Sports and Social C AS. Newbridge to Saltersford leased by Northwich AA. Saltersford to Sutton Weaver, Weaver Waiters.

Ashton Canal; Junction Street Bridge to Ancoats Lock No 1, and Ancoats Lock No 3 to Ashton New Bridge 10, Waterway Wanderers. Ashton New Bridge 10 to Clayton Bridge 11, Ciba Clayton AS. Clayton Lane Bridge 11 to Fairfield Bottom Lock, Waterway Wanderers. Fairfield Bottom Lock to Top Lock, Water Sports Adventure Centre. Fairfield Top Lock to Guide Bridge 26, Stockport & Dist AF. Guide Bridge 26 to Bridge 28, Tootal AC. Bridge 28 to Whitelands Rd, Stockport & Dist AF.

Huddersfield Narrow Canal; water tends to acidity, but contains trout. Bayley St, Stalybridge to Lock no 1, Stalybridge Fox AS. Bayley St to Caroline St, Waterway Wanderers. Scout Tunnel to Mottram Rd, Stalybridge, Waterway Wanderers. Mossley to Scout Tunnel, Border Anglers and Naturalists. Greenfield to Mossley, Medlock Bridge AC. Saddleworth to Greenfield, Diggle AC. Diggle to Saddleworth, Saddleworth & Dist AS. Saddleworth to Huddersfield, Waterway Wanderers and Slaithwaite & Dist AC, except stretch from Lock 25 to 28, Sefton Hall Piscatorials AC, and from Lock 23 to Lock 25, Colne Valley match Group AC.

Lancaster Canal; Stocks Bridge, Preston to Stainton, Waterway Wanderers.

Leeds and Liverpool Canal (East); Bank Newton Top Lock to Milking Hill Swing Bridge 184, Waterway Wanderers. Milking Hill Swing Bridge 184 to Brunthwaite Bridge 192, Keighley AC. Brunthwaite Bridge 192 to Swine Lane Bridge, Marsden Star AS. Swine Lane to Dowley Gap Top Lock, Bingley AC. To Bridge 210, Saltaire AC. Bridge 210 to Field Lock, Thackley, Waterway Wanderers. Thackley to Idle Swing Bridge 212, Unity AC. Idle Swing Bridge to Thornhill Bridge, Idle and Thackley AA. Thornhill Bridge 215 to Calveley Lodge Swing Bridge 215, Waterway Wanderers. Bridges 215 to 216A, Listerhill Old Boys AA. Horseforth Rd Bridge 216A to Rodley Swing Bridge, Rodley Boats AC. 219 to Newley Lock, Leeds & Dist ASA. To Redcote Bridge 224, Waterway Wanderers. 224 to Spring Garden lock 6, Leeds & Dist ASA. To Bridge 225H, Waterway Wanderers.

Leeds and Liverpool Canal (West); Liverpool to Halshall Bridge 24, Liverpool & Dist AA. Halsall to Moss Lane, Wigan & Dist AA. Johnson's Hillock Bottom Lock to Jacksons Bridge 87, Waterway Wanderers. From Jacksons Bridge to Bridge 89, Deane AC. Bridge 89 through Foulridge Tunnel to Park Bridge 151A, Waterway Wanderers. Park Bridge 151A to Long Ings Bridge 152, Marsden Star AS. **Leigh Branch**; Dover Lock to Plank Lane Bridge, Ashton & Dist Centre Northern AA. To Leigh Wharf, Leigh & Dist AA.

Manchester, Bolton and Bury Canal; Canal Wharf Bury to Ladyshore Road Bridge, Waterway Wanderers. To Canal End at Paper Mill, Tonge AC. Hall Lane to Nob End, Bolton & Dist AA. Road Bridge to Ringley Lock, Prestolee, and Park House Road to Canal End, Agecraft, Waterway Wanderers.

St Helens Canal; Section leased by St Helens AA; Carr Mill End to Old Double Locks.

RESERVOIRS AND LAKES in **English canal system:**

Halton Reservoir, Wendover. Coarse fishery leased from BW by Prestwood & Dist AC. Enquiries to Hon Sec.

Wormleighton Reservoir, near **Banbury**. Tench to 9lb. Contact Mr Roe (01926 853533).

Gayton Pool, Gayton, near Northampton. Carp fishery; Gayton AC members only.

Tardebigge Reservoir, Bromsgrove, now BW directly controlled, season ticket only.

Upper and **Lower Bittell Reservoirs** (near **Bromsgrove**). Rights owned by Barnt Green FC, who stock Lower Bittell and adjacent Arrow Pools with trout; other pools hold coarse fish, including pike and bream. Tickets for coarse fishing to members' personal guests only *(see also*

Arrow tributary of Warwickshire Avon).

Lifford Reservoir. Birmingham Parks. Dt from park keeper.

Earlswood Lakes. BW direct managed fishery. Three Lakes totalling 85 acres stocked with roach, perch, bream, pike; carp and tench in two. Large eels. Dt on bank from bailiff. Match booking enquiries to Mr J Howells, tel: 021 783 4233.

Stockton Reservoir. Excellent coarse fishery, tickets from Blue Lias public house, near site.

Sneyd Pool, Walsall. Excellent carp and tench fishing, leased by Swan AC. Dt on bank.

Harthill, near **Worksop**. Coarse fishing leased by Worksop & Dist AA.

Gailey Lower Reservoir, near **Wolverhampton**. 64 acre coarse fishery. Management under review, fishing temporarily closed.

Calf Heath Reservoir, nr **Wolverhampton**. Good coarse fishery with carp, tench, big bream. Leased to Blackford Progressive AS.

Lodge Farm Reservoir, Dudley. Coarse fishery. Enquiries to Dudley Corporation.

Himley Hall Lake, Himley. Trout, coarse fish. Enquiries to Dudley Corporation.

Trench Pool, Telford. 16 acres, coarse fishing. Leased to Telford AA.

Elton Reservoir, Greater Manchester. Leased to Bury AA.

Wern Clay Pits, Montgomery. Leased by Mid-Wales Glass AC.

Stanley Reservoir, Stoke-on-Trent. Coarse fishery leased by Stoke-on-Trent AS.

Sulby Reservoir, Northants. Specimen carp to 32lb, numerous 20lb fish. Limited dt. Unique platforms designed exclusively for carp fishing. Contact Southern Region, tel: 01442 278717. Annual permits only.

Huddersfield Narrow Canal Reservoirs. Brunclough, Saddleworth & Dist AS water; **Tunnel End**, vacant; **Redbrook**, Cairo Anglers; **March Haigh**, vacant; **Black Moss**, vacant; **Swellands, vacant; Slaithwaithe** and **Sparth**, Slaithwaite & Dist AS waters. **Diggle**, Pennine Shooting and sports AS.

Welford Reservoir, Northants. Bream, tench and pike to 20lb plus. Permits from Mr Williams (01858 575394).

Lower Foulridge Reservoir, Borough of Pendle Council, Town Hall Pendle BB8 0AQ (0282 865500).

ENGLISH SEA FISHING STATIONS

In the following list the principal stations are arranged in order from north-east to south-west and then to north-west. Sea fishing can, of course, be had at many other places, but most of those mentioned cater especially for the sea angler. Clubs secretaries and tackle shops are usually willing to help visiting anglers either personally or by post on receipt of a stamped and addressed envelope. Details of accommodation, etc, can generally be had from the local authority amenities officer or information bureau of the town concerned. Those fishing the Devon and Cornwall estuaries should be aware of prohibitions on the taking of bass in some areas.

Seaham (Co Durham). Cod, whiting, flounder (winter); coalfish, flounder, plaice, dab, mackerel, cod (summer). Excellent fishing from North and South Piers, open only to members of Seaham SAC, Clifford House, South Terrace. Club has 300 members, and well equipped HQ; promotes annual competitions and active junior section. Membership £11, conc. Further information from G Hope, tel: 0191 5810321. Tackle shop: Bait Box, 5 North Terrace, Seaham, (0191 5819585).

Sunderland (Co Durham). Cod and codling (best Oct-April), whiting (best Sept-Oct), mackerel (June-Aug), coalfish, flounders, dabs, plaice, throughout year. Roker Pier provides good sport with cod and flatfish. North Pier is free of charge to anglers. Several small-boat owners at North Dock will arrange fishing parties, but there are also good beaches. R Wear banks at entrance good for flounders throughout year. Bait can be dug in Whitburn Bay and bought from tackle shops. Clubs: Sunderland Sea AA. Ryhope Sea AA (both affiliated to Assn of Wearside Angling Clubs). Tackle shop: Rutherfords, 125 Roker Ave. Hotels: Parkside, 2 park Ave; Parkview, 25 Park Ave.

Saltburn (Cleveland). Flatfish, coalfish, codling, whiting, mackerel, gurnard, some bass in summer and haddock late autumn. Float-fishing from pier in summer gives good sport; good codling fishing Oct to March. Club: Saltburn and Dist AA.

Redcar (Cleveland). Five miles of fishing off rock and sand. Principal fish caught: Jan-April, codling; April-June, flatfish; summer months, coalfish (billet), whiting, mackerel, gurnard. Larger codling arrive latter part of August and remain all winter. South Gare breakwater (4m away); good fishing, but hard on tackle, spinning for mackerel successful. Good fishing from beach two hours before and after low tide. Competitions every month. Tackle shops: Redcar Angling Centre, 159 High St, Redcar TS10 3AH; Anglers Services, 27 Park Rd, Hartlepool.

Whitby (N Yorks). A popular centre for boat fishing about wrecks, with charter boats travelling up to 30 miles from Whitby. Cod taken from boats, British record cod, 58lb 6oz caught here, as well as catches of haddock, coalfish, whiting, flatfish, sea bream, catfish, ling, mackerel, etc. Boat festival in July. West Pier: fishing only from lower part of pier extension. Mainly sandy bottom, but weeds and rock towards end. Billet, codling, flatfish, mackerel and whiting in season. East Pier: mainly on rocky bottom, weed off pier extension. More and bigger codling off this pier. Beach fishing from the sands either to Sandsend or Saltwick: billet, codling, flatfish, whiting, mackerel, a few bass. Small area at end of New Quay Rd for children only. No fishing allowed in harbour entrance. Best baits are lugworm, mussel, peeler crab. Local assn: Whitby Sea Anglers, meets in winter only, at Pier Inn, Pier Rd. Boat Club: Whitby Charter Skippers Assn, Tony Stevens, 01609 780412. Boats to accommodate 8 to 12 persons on hire at quays: Achates, tel: 01947 820320; Enterprise, tel: 01609 780412; Mermaid, tel: 01947 603200, and others. For boats, accom, rod hire, contact John Brennan, 01947 820320. Tackle shop: Whitby Angling Supplies, 65 Haggersgate, tel: 01947 603855.

Scarborough (N Yorks). Sea fishing good from boat or harbour piers most of year. Autumn whiting very good in bay. West Pier fishes on sandy bottom, East Pier on rock, with better chances of bigger codling. Marine Drive good all year round cod fishing. Codling most plentiful Aug onwards. Winter codling fishing from First or Second Points to south of Scarborough and the Marine Drive. Mackerel,

June-Sept, float or spinning. Various boats take out parties; bags of 3-4,000lb of cod in 12hr sessions sometimes taken. Many over 20lb, ling also, 20lb plus from wrecks. Festival in Sept. Clubs: Scarborough Rock AC; South Cliff AC. Tackle shops: at 56 Eastborough, and Buckley's Angling Supplies; 6 Leading Post Street, YO11 1NP, tel: 01723 363202 (who issue dt for the Mere; coarse fish). Charter boats for hire, taking 8-12 anglers. Charge: approx £2.50 per person for 4 hrs but longer trips to fish reefs and wrecks now popular. Valhalla, (01723 362083); Wandering Star (01723 374885); Sea Fisher, (01723 364640); Linda Maria, (01482 823644); Eva Anne, (01723 352381).

Filey (N Humberside). Cod, coalfish, ling, mackerel, flatfish, bass, pollack. Famous Filey Brigg, ridge of rocks from which baits can be cast into deep water, is fishable in most weathers and tides. Ledgering with crab and mussel baits (summer), worm and mussel (winter) can produce good catches of cod, coalfish and wrasse. Use of a sliding float with mussel, and mackerel bait is effective technique for coalfish, pollack and mackerel (Jul-Sept). At Reighton Sands, ledgering with mussel, rag, lug and mackerel baits can produce flounders, some dabs, and occasional plaice or bass. Preferred method for bass is spinning. Local bait digging prohibited, good supplies from local tackle shop. No boat charters, but ideal launching site for small privately owned boats. Local clubs: Filey Brigg AS (st £3) organises fishing festival every year (first week of Sept), with 6 boating and 8 shore events. Filey Boat AC. Good flyfishing for coalfish (billet) from Brigg. Tackle and bait from Filey Fishing Tackle, 12 Hope St YO14 9DL (01723 513732). Hotel: White Lodge, The Crescent YO14 9JX.

Bridlington (N Humberside). South Pier may be fished free all year and North Pier in winter only. Sport in summer only fair - small whiting, billet, flatfish mainly - but good codling from Dec-March. Launches and cobles sail daily from Harbour at 0630, 0930, 1330, 1800 during summer. They operate from 3 to 60 mile radius around **Flamborough Head**, or wrecks. Catches include cod, haddock, plaice, ling and skate. Rock fishing from shore at Thornwick Bay. Bait: lugworm may be dug in South Bay and small sand eels caught by raking and digging on edge of tide. Sea angling festival Sept 18-23. Boats: I Taylor, 679434, (British record ling caught from this vessel); J Jarvis, 604750; D Brown, 676949. Cobles: R Emerson, 850575. Tackle shop: Linford's, 12 Hilderthorpe Road. Hotels: Windsor, Lonsborough and others.

Hornsea (N Humberside). Tope, skate, flounders, occasional bass from shore; cod, haddock, plaice, dabs, tope, skate from boats. May to Oct. Whiting, dabs, codling, Oct to May.

Grimsby (NE Lincs). Sea fishing along Humber bank free, and along foreshore to Tetney Lock; plaice, codling, dabs, flounders, eels. West Pier: st from Dock Office. Boat fishing: 12 hour trips, mainly around oil rigs. Tel: 01472 885649 or 72422. All boats and persons in charge of boats must be licensed by N.E. Lincolnshire Council. Enquiries to Municipal Office, Town Hall Square DN32 7AU, (01472 324770, 324785, fax). Good centre for fens and broads. Clubs: Humber SAC, Cromwell Social Club (SA section). Tourist Information: National Fishing Heritage Centre, Alexandra Dock, DN31 1UZ (01472 323222, 323223 fax). Tackle shops: Fred's Fishing Tackle, 413 Weelsby St; Grimsby Angling Centre, 18 Wellowgate; Lightwoods, 172 Cleethorpe Rd; Garden & Pet Centre, 25 Louth Rd; Sparks Bros, 43 Cromwell Rd; M.T.S. Tackle, 168E Sutcliffe Ave, all Grimsby; Tight Lines, 51 Cambridge St, Cleethorpes. Many hotels and B&B.

Mablethorpe (Lincs). Good sea fishing from Mablethorpe to Sutton-on-Sea. Beach all sand; mainly flatfish, but some bass, skate, mackerel, tope from boats. Cod in winter. Sept-Dec best. Boat fishing limited by surf and open beach. Good flounders in Saltfleet Haven; also sea trout in Sept. Local club: Mablethorpe, Sutton-on-Sea and Dist AC (water on Great Eau for members only). Tackle shop: Bela's, 54-56 High Street. Hotels at Mablethorpe, Trusthorpe, Sutton-on-Sea.

Skegness (Lincs). Beach fishing for cod, dab and whiting in winter; silver eels, dabs and bass in summer; whiting and dab in Sept and Oct. Chapel Point, Huttoft Bank and Ingoldmells the best beaches in winter, 3 hrs before high tide until 2 hours after. Lugworm best bait. No charter boats operate in Lincolnshire.

Club: Skegness SAC. Tackle and bait from Skegness Fishing Tackle, 155 Roman Bank; Palmers, 11 High St (01754 764404).

Salthouse, near **Sheringham** (Norfolk). Sea here is deep quite close in shore, and fishing considered good. Good flatfish, Oct-Jan. Occasional bass and mackerel in summer. Guest house: Salthouse Hall.

Sheringham (Norfolk). Flatfish all year; cod autumn and winter, mackerel June-Sept. Beaches good all year, best months April and May. Best sport west of lifeboat shed towards Weybourne or extreme east towards Cromer. Centre beaches too crowded in season. Bait can be ordered from tackle shops. Boat fishing best well off shore. Tope to 40lb and thornbacks to 20lb; plenty of mackerel. Tackle shop: Fiddy's Fishing Tackle, 28 Beeston Road. Club: Sheringham Sea AC. Blakeney: good launching ramps, boat hire from R Bishop, 01263 740200.

Cromer (Norfolk). Good all-year fishing; mainly cod (Sept-April), whiting and dabs, with odd tope (summer); skate and bass (summer) from pier (50p) and beaches. Around the third breakwater east of the pier the water is deeper, last three hours of flood tide best time. Occasional mackerel from end of pier. Boat fishing in calm weather (beach-launching). Club: Holt Sea AC. Fresh lugworm baits, and dt for local coarse fishing, obtainable from tackle shop: Marine Sports Shop, 21 New St, Cromer, NR27 9HP, (01263 513676); open Sundays. Hotels: Cliftonville; Red Lion; Hotel de Paris; Cliff House; Western House, recommended for anglers.

Great Yarmouth, (Norfolk). All styles of sea fishing catered for, including two piers, several miles of perfect shore line for beach angler, two miles of well-wharved river from harbour's mouth to Haven Bridge, and boat angling. To north are Caister, Scratby, Hemsby, Winterton, Horsey, Sea Palling, Weybourne etc, and to south, Gorleston-on-Sea and Corton. The riverside at Gorleston from the lifeboat shed leading to the harbour entrance, and Gorleston Pier are popular venues. Sport very similar in all these places; Sept-Jan, whiting, dabs, flounders, eels, cod from latter end of Oct. From Apr-Sept, Winterton known for good bass fishing. Most successful baits are lugworm, herring or mackerel; lug, peeler crab and squid for bass, flatfish etc, Apr-Sept. Boats: Bishops, tel: 01493 664739; Dybles: (*below*). Tackle shops: Dave Docwra, 79 Churchill Rd; Gorleston Tackle Centre, 7/8 Pier Walk; Dyble & Williamson, Scratby Rd, Scratby, NR29 3PQ, (01493 731305).

Gorleston-on-Sea (Norfolk). Whiting, cod, dabs and flounders from beaches and in estuary (best Oct to March); good skate Aug and Sept. Sport good in these periods from boats, pier or at Harbour Bend in river and on beaches. Baits: lugworm, crab and ragworm. Freshwater fishing (coarse fish) within easy reach on rivers and broads. Boats: Bishop Boat Services, 48 Warren Rd, tel: 664739. Tackle shops: Gorleston Tackle Centre, 7/8 Pier Walk; Greenstead Tackle Centre, 72 High St.

Lowestoft (Suffolk). Noted centre for cod, autumn-May. Also whiting, flatfish, pollack and coalfish, with bass, tope, ray from charter boats and mullet in warmer months. Lugworm best bait. Good sloping beaches to north and south. Hopton, Pakefield, Kessingland are best. North best on flood, south on ebb. Club: Lowestoft SA. Baits from tackle shop: Ted Bean, 175 London Road N. Further information from Tourist IC, The Esplanade; tel: 523000.

Southwold (Suffolk); ns Halesworth. Good codling, whiting, bass, plaice, flounder, dab, pollack, mackerel, mullet fishing from beach, October to March. Bass main species in summer from harbour or shore; soles and silver eels also provide sport May to Sept. Reydon Lakes are local freshwater fishery. Licences from Purdy's Newsagents, High St. Hotels: Swan, Crown, Red Lion, Avondale.

Felixstowe (Suffolk). Fishing in autumn and winter for cod and whiting. Excellent bass fishing in recent years, with fish well into double figures from sea front and Rivers Orwell and Deben; garfish from the pier by day and sole at night, and with eels in the estuaries; flounders from Oct-Jan from the Orwell towards Ipswich. Skate fishing good in May, June and July, especially in harbour. Good sport from boats and Town Pier (constructed 1906). Good fishing in evenings from Manor Terrace to Landguard Point, Sept onwards. Wrecking trips obtainable locally. Felixstowe SAS organise matches, beach festivals, and cater for the needs of boat anglers, with a compound of 50 dinghies adjacent to club HQ. Tackle shop: Castaway, 20 Undercliff

Road.

Harwich and **Dovercourt** (Essex). Bass, mullet, eels, garfish, flatfish, sting-ray, thornback, skate, soles (all May to Sept), whiting, pouting, codling (Sept to March). Best fishing from boats, but Stone Breakwater, Dovercourt is good. Several good boat marks in estuary of Stour and Orwell and in harbour approaches. Best baits: lug, king rag, soft and peeler crabs. Boats: Bartons Marina, 8 West St, 01255 503552, or V Caunter, 01255 552855. Club: Harwich AC (freshwater). Devonshire Arms Sea Angling Club. Tackle shop: Dovercourt Aquatics and Angling Centre, Main Rd, Dovercourt, Harwich. Copy of Borough Guide supplied by Town Clerk on request.

Walton (Essex). Cod, skate, mullet and dab are species most commonly caught, best fishing is from pier, Frinton Wall and Frinton Sea Front. Cod fishing begins about second week in Sept and runs to end of March. Club: Walton-on-Naze Sea AC. Boats may be chartered in Walton: S Murphy, tel: 01255 674274. Tackle shop: J Metcalfe, 15 Newgate St. Hotels: Elmos; Queens.

Clacton (Essex). Mainly autumn and winter fishing for whiting and cod. Summer fishing from beach, pier and boats for dabs, plaice, bass, eels, thornback, dogfish, tope, sting ray to 50lb (Walton-on-Naze). Matches arranged by Clacton Sea AC, membership £7 p.a. Tackle shop: Brian Dean, 43 Pallister Road, tel: 01255 425992; baits, permits and information. Hotels: Frandon, Kingscliff, many others, from Tendring T.I., Clacton, tel: 01255 423400.

Southend-on-Sea (Essex). Mullet, bass, mackerel, scad, garfish, plaice and flounders are the main catches from the pier during the summer, with cod, codling and large flounders in the winter. A fleet of registered charter boats operate from the Pierhead, but prior booking is essential. Thornback, stingray, smoothhound, bass, tope, plaice and cod can be expected. Pier: st £36, dt £2.35. Application form from Southend Council, Directorate of Leisure Services, Civic Centre, Victoria Ave, SS1 3PY. Off season shore fishing in vicinity, with all year round facilities at the Thorpe Bay and Westcliff bastions, also the river Crouch. Numerous open, pier, shore and boat events organised. Tackle shops: Jetty Anglers. Essex Angling Centre (Westcliff).

Sheerness (Kent). Venue of British Open in Nov. Popular marks around Sheerness are Bartons Point; New Sea Wall, Garison; East Church Gap; cod and whiting plentiful from beaches in autumn. Local Club: I of Sheppey AC. Tackle shop: Island Bait & Tackle Shop, 57 High St, (01795 668506). Fresh baits always obtainable.

Whitstable and **Tankerton** (Kent). Good fishing in spring and summer on shore between Swale and Whitstable. Dabs, plaice, bass, skate, flounders, eels, etc. Lugworm and white ragworm are to be found in shallow areas. Peeler crabs are plentiful in Swale estuary. Cod in winter from Tankerton beach. Boats for hire. Freshwater fishing on Seasalter Marshes, near Whitstable; roach, rudd, tench, pike, eels. T I Centre: Horsebridge, Whitstable.

Herne Bay (Kent). Excellent spring fishing for flounders, bass and eels, bags of up to 20lb may be expected on peeler crab bait, which can be collected locally or bought at tackle shops in April and May. In June, bass move into the shallow warm water of the estuary. These may be caught with the last of the peeler crab, ragworm, and by spinning. In July and August bass are plentiful, black bream, lesser spotted dog, smoothound and stingray may be caught with ragworm on beaches between Bishopstone and Reculver. Local record stingray, over 40lb. Whiting in autumn and winter on main beaches: just after dark is the best time to fish for them. Excellent facilities for anglers with own dinghies to launch and recover from new slipway. Local information on best marks, etc, from tackle shops. Club: Herne Bay AA, HQ 59/60 Central Parade. Tackle, bait and licences: Ron Edwards, 50 High Street; Herne Bay Angling, 224 High St. Hotels: Victoria, Adelaide and Beauville Guest Houses, all Central Parade.

Margate (Kent). Noted for mixed catches. Fine bass often taken from shore on paternoster, and boat by spinning. Stone pier good for cod and whiting in winter. Bass and cod from rocks at low water. Cod best Nov to May; fish up to 20lb. April and May mixed bags of bass and eels. Most popular rock marks are at Foreness, Botany Bay, Kingsgate, Dumpton Gap. Skate at Minnis Bay, Birchington. Tope fishing from boat from June on through summer. Also dogfish and conger. Clubs: Margate Fishing Club; Old Centrals AC (130 Grosvenor Place). Tackle shop: Kingfisheries, 34 King Street.

Broadstairs (Kent). Bass, plaice, flounders eels, from beaches or stone jetty. Best in winter months. Lugworm usual bait, dug in Pegwell Bay. T I Centre: Pierremont Hall, High St.

Ramsgate (Kent). Good sport along 2m of shore, harbour piers (free fishing), and Eastern and Western Chines. East Pier gives ample scope, best in winter. Beaches crowded in summer, so night fishing best. In spring and summer good bass fishing (from shore), also soles, flounders, dabs and thornbacks. In autumn and winter; cod in large quantities, whiting. Pegwell Bay Foreness and Dumpton Gap are good boat marks for mackerel, bass and pollack. Upwards of twenty boats operate at Harbour. Goodwin Sands produce skate, bass, dogfish, spurdog, tope and plaice. The Elbow and Hole in the Wall, also marks for boat fishing. Lugworm may be dug in Pegwell Bay. Licences, baits, fishing trips and freshwater angling information from tackle shop: Fisherman's Corner, 6 Kent Place. Hotels in Thanet too many to list.

Sandwich (Kent). Bass at the mouth of the haven; sea trout and mullet run up the river; flounders, grey mullet, plaice, dabs, codling and pouting more seaward. Entry to Sandwich Bay by toll road, 9am to 5pm. For winter cod fishing, deep water off yacht club end of bay is best. Local club: Sandwich and Dist AS. Hotels: Bell, Haven Guest House. *For freshwater fishing see Stour (Kent).*

Deal and **Walmer** (Kent). Excellent sea fishing throughout the year from beaches and Deal Pier, open 8 am to 10 pm, all night Saturday. Winter cod fishing, from Sandown Castle, Deal Castle, Walmer Castle. Charter boats take anglers to the Goodwin Sands and outside Dover Harbour. Cod and whiting in winter, plaice, dabs, sole, mackerel, eels, flounders, mullet and garfish. Strong tidal currents. Tables from local tackle shops. Deal & Walmer Inshore Fishermen's Assn supplies list of boats: Tony Robinson, tel: 01304 361850. T I Centre: Town Hall, Deal. Clubs: Deal and Walmer AA. Deal 1919 AC. Tackle shops: Channel Angling, Beach St; The Foc'sle 33 Beach St; The Downs Tackle Centre, 29 The Strand, Walmer. B & B: Admiral Penn; Lobster Pot; Dunkerleys. Hotel: Royal.

Dover (Kent). Excellent boat and beach fishing in the area; cod taken from wrecks and sand banks; good fishing for bass, codling, whiting and flatfish. Good beach fishing from Shakespeare Beach. Prince of Wales Pier suitable for all anglers, incl junior and handicapped. Admiralty Pier controlled by Dover Sea AA: open 8 am to 4 pm, and 6 am to 9 pm Fri and Sat. £2.50 dt, conc. Access to Sandwich Bay is by toll road, £2.50. Boat trip (Dover Motor Boat Co, tel: 01304 206809) to fish Southern Breakwater departs 9 am from Dump Head, Wellington Dock, £3 + £3.50 fishing charge. Tackle shops: Bill's Bait & Tackle, 121 Snargate St; Brazils, 162 Snargate St (01304 201457). Hotels: Ardmore, Beaufort; many others.

Folkestone (Kent). Good boat, beach and pier fishing. Conger, cod, bass, bream, flatfish, whiting, pouting and pollack, with mackerel in mid-summer. Pier open to anglers, £2 per day. Cod caught from boats on the Varne Bank all through the year, but from the shore, Oct-Feb only. Beach fishing best dusk onwards for bass and conger. The Warren produces good catches of cod in winter and bass in summer. Good sport from pier. Some good offshore marks. Popular rock spots are Rotunda Beach, Mermaid Point, Sandgate Riviera. For tickets, boats and bait apply: Garry's Tackle Shop, 12 Tontine Street, (01303 253881). Tourist Information Centre, Harbour St CT20 1QN (01303 258594, 259754 fax). Hotels: Burlington, Windsor and others.

Sandgate (Kent). Very good fishing from beach and boats. There is a ridge of rock extending for over a mile 20 yds out from low-water mark. Bass good July-October; codling, whiting, pouting, conger March-May, August-Nov; good plaice taken May-June, especially from boats. Best months for boat fishing, Sept-Nov. Hotel: Channel View Guest House, 4 Wellington Terrace.

Hythe (Kent). Fishing from boat and shore for bass, codling, pouting, whiting, conger and flats. Princes Parade, Seabrook, is popular for cod fishing, between Sept and Jan, lugworm is the best bait. Open storm beach, giving pouting, whiting, mackerel, sole, dab and flounder in summer and cod (up to 25lb), whiting and pouting in winter. Few bass. Clubs: Seabrook Sea AS; Sandgate Sea AS; Castaways Sea AS. Tackle shops: Hythe

Angling, 1 Thirstane Terrace; Romney Tackle, 19 Littlestone Rd, Littlestone,(01797 363990). Hotels: Nyanza Lodge, 87 Seabrook Rd; Romney Bay House, New Romney.

Dungeness (Kent). Cod fishing around the lighthouse, with whiting, and dab in winter, pout, bass, dab, eels and sole in summer. Best baits in winter are black or yellowtail lugworm. Denge Marsh is a top venue for sole, marks are at Diamond and towards Galloways, ragworm and lugworm for bait. Best months: May to Oct for boat fishing; Oct to Feb for shore fishing. Club: Brett Marine AC.

Hastings (Sussex). Sea fishing from pier and boats. Tope, bass, conger, plaice, codling, whiting, etc. Boats from local fishermen. Hastings and St Leonards SAA has its own boats on beach opposite headquarters; club boundary, Beachy head to R Rother at Rye. Guests £1 per day in boats. Winching facilities. Association also has clubroom on Hastings Pier. Annual International Sea Angling Festival in October. Bait, tackle: S.H. Tackle, Bohemia Rd; Steve's Tackle Shop, 1/5 Palace Chamber, White Rock; Redfearn's, 8 Castle Street, who have good knowledge of local course fishing, and have dt.

St Leonards (Sussex). Good sea fishing all the year round from boats and beach for flatfish, bass, mackerel, conger, tope, whiting, cod, bull huss, turbot. Boats and boatmen from Warrior Square slipway. St Leonards Sea Anglers' club house at 16 Grand Parade. Competitions run throughout the year, boats and beach. Annual subscription £9 + £2 joining fee. Concessionary £4.

Bexhill (Sussex). Boat and shore fishing. Cod, conger, whiting (Sept to end Dec). Dabs, plaice, mackerel, tope (July-Sept). Bass, best months May, June and July. Club: Bexhill AC (hon sec will help visitors, enclose sae). Freshwater fishing in Pevensey Sluice, Pevensey Haven and dykes; coarse fish. Tackle shop: Tight Lines. Hotel: Granville.

Eastbourne (Sussex). Boat, pier and shore fishing. Dabs, huss, pouting and conger (all year), cod in winter and skate (May to Dec). Best for plaice and bream from June to Nov. Also soles, whiting, flounders, mullet. Good bass and mullet in warmer months. Notable tope centre, many around 40lb; June and July best. Some of the best beach fishing for bass around Beachy Head (up to 17lb). Pollack from rocks. Flatfish off Langney Point and from landing stages of pier. Best marks for beach fishing are on east side of pier. West side can be rocky in places. Club: Eastbourne AA, Club House, Royal Parade, tel: 723442. Membership £32 p.a. Boats available to members, £42 p.a. Tackle shops: Anglers Den, Pevensey Bay; Tony's, 211 Seaside.

Seaford (Sussex). Beach and boat fishing. Bass, cod, codling, conger, flats, huss, mackerel and few ling and pollack. Good catches of tope few miles offshore. Seaford AC has freshwater fishing on five local waters, members only, tel: 01323 897723. Tackle shop: Peacehaven Angler, Coast Rd, Peacehaven.

Newhaven (Sussex). Centre for deep sea fishing. Beach fishing for bass excellent May-Oct. Flounders from Tide Mills Beach. Good cod fishing from beaches between Seaford Head and Newhaven's East Pier, late Oct to early March. Breakwater gives good all-round sport, with bass, and cod all running large. Boat fishing excellent for cod in winter, large Channel whiting also give good sport. Monkfish off Beachy Head late August and Sept. Boats from Harbour Tackle Shop, Fort Rd (tel 514441). Other tackle shops: Dennis's, 107 Fort Road; Book & Bacca, 8 Bridge Street. Hotel: Sheffield.

Brighton and Hove (Sussex). Very good bass fishing from boats, trolling with variety of plug baits, Apr-Oct. Charter boats operate from Shoreham, Newhaven and Brighton Marina, for deep sea and wreck fishing. In spring and summer boat fishing produces bream, bass, conger, tope, plaice and dabs; shore fishing: mackerel off marina wall, bass at night or l/w surf, mullet. Winter boat fishing for large cod, whiting, bull huss; shore for whiting, flounders and cod. Most dealers supply bait. Hove Deep Sea AC members launch boats from beach, and generally fish inshore marks. Membership £35 pa plus £30 joining, allows free use of boats, equipment, car park. Active social club. Tel: 01273 413000 for details. Marina arms for mackerel, garfish, pollack, occasional bass, fishing fee, £1.50 per rod per day. Tackle shops: Brighton Angler, 1/2 Madeira Drive, BN2 1PS (01273 671398); Jack Ball, Edward St.

Shoreham and Southwick (Sussex). Boat and harbour fishing. Bass (July and August); grey mullet, skate and huss (June to

Sept); cod and whiting (Sept to Dec); dabs, plaice, pouting, black bream, mackerel and flounders (May onwards). Mullet fishing in River Adur near Lancing College very good July-August; light paternoster tackle and red ragworm recommended. Baits: white rag, red rag and lugworms may be dug from beach and mud banks of river. Mussels and other baits can also be obtained.

Worthing (Sussex). Beach and pier fishing. Flounder, bass, whiting, codling, plaice, mullet, eels. Mixed catches from boats. River Adur, east of Worthing, noted for flounders, mullet and eels. Bait digging in Adur restricted to between toll bridge and harbour. Local association: Worthing Sea AA (HQ, Worthing Pier). Tackle shops: Ken Dunman, 2 Marine Place BN11 3DN, (01903 239802), opp Pier entrance; Prime Angling, 74 Brighton Rd, Worthing, tel: 01903 821594. Boats from harbours at Shoreham and Littlehampton. Popular one day pier festival held in early September. Reduced fee to OAP and juniors.

Littlehampton (Sussex). Noted for black bream, which are taken in large numbers during May and early June, but wide variety, including skate, smoothound (spring), whiting and cod (winter best) and plaice. Mid channel wrecking for cod, pollack, ling and conger (spring onwards). Well known marks are Kingmere Rocks for black bream, West Ditch for smoothound, Hooe Bank for conger. A large fleet of boats caters for sea anglers, and there is good fishing from beaches and in harbour. Boats from M Pratt, (01798 342370); S Hipgrave, (01903 691697); F Durrent (01243 262616); P Heaslewood (01903 730229) and others, full list from Harbour Master, Harbour Office, Pier Rd, BN17 5LR (01903 721215). Tackle shop: Tropicana, 5 Pier Rd. B&B: Quayside, Pier Rd; Bunkhouse, Pier Rd.

Bognor Regis (Sussex). Good sea fishing at several marks off Bognor. Tope, bass, pollack, mackerel, whiting, wrasse. From May to July bream are plentiful. The conger, skate and sole fishing is very good. Grey mullet abound in the shallow water between Felpham and Littlehampton Harbour. Good cod fishing between September and November. Bass weighing 5-10lb and more caught from pier and shore. Good shore fishing for bass, mackerel, cod, smooth hounds off East and West Beaches at **Selsey**. Club: Selsey Angling & Tope Club. Tackle shops: Suttons, 7 Shore Rd, East Wittering; Raycrafts Angling Centre, 119 High St, Selsey (01243 606039), who has tickets for Chichester Canal fishing.

Hayling Island (Hants). From the South Beach of Hayling Island good fishing can be had with a rod and line for bass, plaice, flounders, dabs, whiting, etc, according to season. Fishing from boats in Hayling Bay for tope, skate, bass, mackerel, etc, is popular and a much favoured area is in the vicinity of the Church Rocks and in Chichester Harbour. Portsmouth AS has coarse lake in area. Tackle shop: Paige's Fishing Tackle, 36 Station Rd, Hayling Island.

Southsea (Hants). Over 4m of beach from Eastney to Portsmouth Harbour provide good sport all year. Bass fishing especially good from spring to September. Flatfish and rays numerous, large mackerel shoals in midsummer. Best sport from boats. Boom defence line from Southsea to IoW, although navigational hazard, is probably one of the best bass fishing marks on the South Coast. Vicinity of forts yields good bags of pollack, bass, black bream, skate, etc. Tope fishing good during summer. Portsmouth, Langstone and Chichester within easy reach and provide good sheltered water in rough weather. Boats can be hired from Portsmouth boatmen. Tackle shops: Pier Tackle, South Parade Pier; A & S Fishing Tackle, 147 Winter Rd, Southsea PO4 8DR (01705 739116); Allan's Marine, 143 Twyford Ave, Portsmouth.

Southampton (Hants). Fishing in Southampton Water really estuary fishing; thus not so varied as at some coastal stations. However, flounders abound (float and/or baited spoon fishing recommended), and whiting, pouting, silver eels, conger, bass, grey mullet, soles, dogfish, thornback, skate, stingray, plaice, dabs, scad, shad, mackerel have all been caught. At the entrance to Southampton Water, in Stokes Bay and the Solent generally, excellent tope fishing may be had. Angling from Hythe Pier, and from Netley and Hamble shores, but best fishing from boats. Southampton Water is rarely unfishable. Good sport in power station outflow. Tackle shops: Eastleigh Angling Centre, 325 Market St, Eastleigh, (01703 653540); Angling Centre of Woolston, 6 Portsmouth Rd, Woolston, (01703

A good day off West Bay, Bridport, Dorset. 14 year-old Danny Clarke displays a dozen plaice to 4lbs. *Photo: Skipper of 'Leo One.'*

422299). Rovers, 135A High St, Lee on Solent.

Lymington (Hants). Tope, sting-ray in Lymington and Beaulieu rivers. Facilities through Lymington & Dist Sea AC. Hurst Castle area good beach spot for cod and large bass. Hurst and Pennington-Lymington Marshes, boat and shore. Mackerel and bass are caught, spinning in Solent from small boats. Flatfish on all beaches from Hurst Castle westwards to Mudeford. Boat fishing from Keyhaven around Needles area: tel 01590 622923 and 01831 460977; 'Lady M' and 'Star Bird'. At **Beaulieu**, fishing from a well located private beach into Solent water, for mullet, bass, flounder and others. St £17, dt £3, from Harbour Master, Bucklers Hard (01590 616200), or Estate Office, John Montegue Building, Beaulieu (01590 612345). Tackle shops: Smiths Sports, 25 Queen Street; Sea Angling Centre, Quay St, Lymington; Spreadbury's, 28 High St, Milford on Sea.

Mudeford (Dorset). Christchurch Harbour at Stanpit is good for bass and grey mullet. All-round sea fishing in Christchurch and Poole Bay, the vicinity of the Ledge Rocks and farther afield on the Dolphin Banks. Fishing is free below Royalty Fishery boundary (a line of yellow buoys across harbour). Tope, dogfish, conger, bream, pout, pollack, whiting and good sport spinning for mackerel and bass. Plaice off Southbourne; flounders, dabs, skate and sole off beaches at Highcliffe, Barton and Southbourne; flatfish, bass, whiting, etc, from quay, beach, groyne or shore at Hengistbury Head; large tope, stingray, skate and occasional thresher shark off The Dolphins. Fairly good cod fishing in winter, Needles-Christchurch Ledge, Pout Hole and Avon Beach (off Hengistbury Head). Whole squid favourite bait, but large baited spoons and jigs also successful. Good sole from Taddiford and Highcliffe Castle (best after dark). Groyne at Hengistbury good for bass in summer; sand eels by day and squid by night. Best months for general sport, mid-June to mid- or late Sept. Most local fishermen now take parties out mackerel fishing in summer. Flounders, eels, bass and mullet taken inside the harbour. Boats from R A Stride, The Watch House, Coastguards Way, Mudeford. Hotels: Avonmouth, Waterford Lodge, The Pines Guest House. For tackle shops and freshwater fishing, see Christchurch under Avon (Wiltshire) and Stour (Dorset).

Bournemouth (Dorset). Fishing good at times from the pier yielding bass, grey mullet, plaice, dabs, etc. Excellent catches of plaice, dabs, codling, silver whiting, mackerel (spinning), tope up to 40lb, conger, skate, from boats. Shore fishing, when sea is suitable, for bass and other usual sea fish. Bait supplies fairly good. Club: Christchurch & Dist FC. Tackle shops: Christchurch Angling Centre, 7 Castle Parade, Iford Bridge, Bournemouth. Good accommodation for anglers at Edelweiss Guest House, 32 Drummon Rd, and Malvern Guest House, 7 Hamilton Rd, Boscombe (angling proprietor); Bournemouth Fishing Lodge, 904 Wimborne Rd, Moordown. For freshwater fishing, *see Avon (Wiltshire) and Stour (Dorset).*

Poole (Dorset). Boat, beach and quay fishing in vast natural harbour. Great variety of fish, but now noted for deep-sea boat angling and bass fishing. Conger, tope, bream, etc, are caught within three miles of the shore. Bass, plaice, flounders, etc, caught inside the harbour at Sandbanks and Hamworthy Park in their seasons. Local tackle shops should be consulted for up-to-the-minute information. Boat fishing facilities largely controlled by Poole Sea Angling Centre (tel 676597), who has over twenty boats for hire. Sea Fishing (Poole) Ltd, Fisherman's Dock, The Quay BH15 1HJ, also cater for bass and deep-sea angling (01202 679666). Baits favoured locally: mackerel, squid, sand eel and ragworm. Tackle shops: Poole Sea Angling Centre, 5 High Street; Dicks Fishing Tackle, 66a High Street; Sea Fishing Poole, Fisherman's Dock, The Quay.

Swanage (Dorset). Double high tide in Swanage and Poole Harbour. Species taken from pier and beach incl bass, mullet, pollack, mackerel, flounder, wrasse and pouting. Beach here too crowded for daytime fishing, but boat fishing is very good, with skate, conger, bream, huss, dogfish, pollack, large wrasse, tope and other species. Good cod fishing in winter, a few miles offshore, and boats are on hire at Poole and Weymouth. In summer, boats operate from Swanage Angling Centre, just off quay, or from Angling Club House, Peveril Boat Park. Local knowledge is essential, as tides and races are very dangerous for small boats. Several open angling competitions are held each year. Swanage T I Centre is at The White House, Shore Rd, Swanage BH19 1LB. Tackle and boat hire from Swanage Angling & Chandlery Shop, 6 High St. Many hotels.

Weymouth (Dorset). Centre for the famous Chesil Beach, Shambles Bank, Portland and Lulworth Ledges. The steeply sloping Chesil Beach provides year-round sport for many species, but autumn and winter best for mackerel, codling, whiting, bream and dogfish; beach fishes best at night; fairly heavy tackle required. Good conger fishing at the Chesil Cove end, Ringstead Bay, Redcliffe and round the piers. Piers yield good sport with grey mullet. Good bass from Greenhill beach in heavy surf, with variety of flatfish at most times. Ferrybridge and the Fleet noted for bass, mullet and flounders. Boat fishing: In the area around Portland Bill some big skate and stingray give good sport, while the notable Shambles Bank continues to yield turbot and skate, etc. Lulworth Ledges have a large variety of fish including tope, blue shark, conger, skate, dogfish, black bream, pollack, whiting, etc. Best baits are lugworm, ragworm, soft crab, mackerel and squid. No boats from Chesil Bank, but 16 boatmen operate from Weymouth throughout year. Angling Society booklet from Weymouth Publicity Office, Weymouth Corporation and hon sec. Tackle shops: Anglers' Tackle Store, 56 Park Street; Denning Tackle & Guns, 114 Portland Road, Wyke Regis.

Portland (Dorset). Good bass fishing in harbour; live prawns for bait. Mullet, mackerel, whiting and conger are plentiful. Boats from fishermen at Castletown (for the harbour), Church Ope, The Bill and on the beach. Near the breakwater is a good spot, where refuse from the warships drifts up.

Bridport (Dorset). Beach fishing yields bass, pouting, flatfish, thornback rays and conger, with whiting and cod in winter and large numbers of mackerel in summer. From boats: black bream, conger, pollock, whiting, pout, dogfish, bull huss, rays, cod and wrasse, West Bay the angling centre. Burton Bradstock, Cogden, West Bexington and Abbotsbury are popular venues on Chesil Beach. Eype and Seatown favoured to west. Bait: lugworm, ragworm, squid, mackerel favoured. Boat hire from West Bay: Duchess II, (01308 425494); licensed for offshore wreck fishing trips. Club: West Bay Sea AC, has thriving junior section with special competitions, etc. Tackle shops: West Bay Water Sports, 10A, West Bay, DT6 4EL (01308 421800), boat fishing trips arranged; The Tackle Shop, Clarence House. Hotel: The George, West Bay.

Lyme Regis (Dorset). Bass may be caught from the shore. Best baits are live sand eel, fresh mackerel, (sometimes obtainable from motorboats in harbour), or ragworm from tackle shop. Mackerel may be caught from May to October. Pollack plentiful in spring months. Conger and skate can be caught from boats about 2m from shore. Deep sea day and half day trips from Charter boats bookable. Information from Harbour Master, The Cobb, Lyme Regis, DT7 3JJ, (01297 442137). Tackle shop: Chris Payne, The Tackle Box, Marine Parade (01297 443373).

Seaton (Devon). Boat fishing. Pollack, pouting, conger, wrasse (March to Sept), bass (virtually all year, but best Sept-Nov), bream, mackerel, dabs, skate, plaice, dogfish. Axe estuary good for bass, mullet and sea trout: dt from Harbour Services Filling Station, Seaton. Local Club: Beer and Dist Sea AC, c/o V Bartlett, 9 Underleys, Beer, Devon EX12 3LX. Tackle shop: Royal Clarence Sports, Harbour Rd, Seaton EX12 2LX; (tel/fax: 01297 22276) Hotels: Anchor, (01297 20386); Mariners, (01297 20506); Seaton Heights (01297 20932).

Sidmouth (Devon). Sea fishing in Sidmouth Bay. Mackerel (May to Oct), pollack (excellent sport spring and summer east and west of town), bass (to 13lb in surf at Jacob's Ladder beach during summer), wrasse, large winter whiting (July-Oct on rocky bottom), skate to 105lb and conger to 44lb have been taken; bull huss to 19lb, and tope. Also plaice, dabs, flounders and occasional turbot. Club: Sidmouth SAC. At **Budleigh Salterton**, a few grey mullet in river, but fairly uncatchable; beach best fished at night for flat-fish.

Exmouth (Devon). Main species caught here in summer are pollack, wrasse, pout whiting, garfish and Mackerel. Favourite baits are lugworm, ragworm, peeler crab and sand eel. Pollack are caught on artificial sand eels. Popular places are: car park near Beach Hotel, docks area, estuary beaches, where flounders are caught, mid Sept to Jan. Deep Sea fishing trips can be booked, with chances of big conger eel, or small cuckoo wrasse, from W Means, skipper of Cormorant. Details from tackle shop: Exmouth Tackle & Sport, 20 The Strand. Other charter boats: Foxey Lady, (01404 822181); Trinitas, (01626 865768), Pioneer, (01404 822183).

Dawlish (Devon). Dabs and whiting in bay off Parson and Clerk Rock and between Smugglers' Gap and Sprey Point. Mackerel good in summer. Conger eels and dogfish about ¾m from shore between Parson and Clerk Rock and Shell Cove. Good fishing sometimes off breakwater by station and from wall of Boat Cove. Boats from Boat Cove. Good trout fishing at Chagford and Moretonhampstead.

Teignmouth (Devon). Sea fishing ideal (especially for light spool casting with sandeels for bass). Bass, pollack, flounders in estuary. Mackerel, dabs and whiting in the bay. Good flounder fishing from the shore. Deep sea, wreck and offshore trips are possible. The town has an annual sea fishing festival. Club: Teignmouth SAS (HQ, River Beach). Fisherman's & Waterman's Assc, J Trout, 18 Haldon Ave, Teignmouth (776079). Tackle shop: McGeary Newsagents, Northumberland Place (bait for sea angling; information). Boats and bait obtainable on river beach. Details of accommodation from Tourist Information Centre, The Den. It should be noted that the estuary is a bass nursery area between May and October.

Torcross; nr **Kingsbridge** (Devon). Hotel: Torcross Apartment Hotel, offering both self-catering facilities and high-class catering beside the Slapton Ley nature reserve and coarse fishery. Slapton Sands; ns Kingsbridge. The sea fishing is very good, especially the bass fishing. Hotel can make arrangements. For coarse fishing *see Slapton Ley*.

Torquay (Devon). Excellent centre for sea fishing, most species found. Base for famous Skerries Bank and Torbay wrecks; conger, cod, pollack, turbot, flatfish, whiting, etc. Hope's Nose peninsula provides best venue for shore angler, with bass and plaice mainly sought. Other species caught are dabs, wrasse, mullet, flounder, gurnard. Babbacombe Pier good for mackerel. Bass and pollack off the rocks. Natural bait hard to come by, but tackle dealers can supply. Local association: Torbay and Babbacombe ASA (membership £10, jun £3). Tackle shops: Quay Stores, Vaughn Parade. Details of accommodation from Local Authority Publicity Dept, 9 Vaughan Parade. *For freshwater fishing, including Torquay Corporation reservoirs, see Teign and Dart.*

Paignton (Devon). Summer and autumn best. Bass, mackerel and garfish can be taken from beaches between Preston and Broadsands and from harbour, promenade and pier respectively. Mullet also present, but very shy. Fishing from rock marks, too. Club: Paignton Sea AA, who have information service and social centre for anglers at HQ at Ravenswood, 26 Cliff Road, The Harbour (open 7.30 pm onwards); annual membership £6; Mr Holman (553118). Wreck fishing, Our Jenny (857890); Simon Pedley (551504); Sea Spray II (851328); Gemini (851766). Tackle shops: The Sportsman, 7 Dartmouth Rd; H Cove Clark, 45-47 Torbay Road; S.W. Tackle Development, Unit 16, Oak Tree Yard, Upper Manor Rd. Venture Sports, 371 Torquay Rd, Preston. Details of accommodation from Tourist IC, Esplanade TQ4 6BN. Trout fishing 2½m away at New Barn Angling Centre, a series of lakes and pools, £3 per day, fish caught extra, tel: 553602.

Brixham (Devon). Boat fishing in bay for plaice, dabs, mackerel. Good pollack off East and West Cod rocks of Berry Head. Neap tides best; baits: worms or prawn. Farther out is Mudstone Ridge, a deep area, strong tide run, but good general fishing with big conger. Local boats take visitors out to deep water marks (wreck fishing) or to Skerries Bank, off Dartmouth, for turbot, plaice, etc; advance bookings (at harbour) advisable. Charter boats: Tight Lines, (01308 851185); Sea Spray II, Vic Evans, (851328). Shore fishing: bass, pollack, wrasse, conger, mackerel from Fishcombe Point, Shoalstone and the long Breakwater. Grey mullet abound in the harbour area (bait, bread or whiting flesh). Bass from St Mary's Beach (best after dark) and south side of Berry Head (bottom of cliffs) for flat fishing. Sharkham Point good for mackerel and bass (float with mackerel, strip bait or prawn for bass). Mansands Point good for bass and pollack (float). Night fishing from Elbury or Broadsands beach for bass, flatfish or conger (use thigh boots). Club: Brixham SAA, Mr Hall (855821). Quayside Hotel has boats.

Tackle shop: Angling Centre, 42 Middle St; Quay Stores, 10 The Quay.

Dartmouth (Devon). River holds large conger, record around 60lb; thornback ray to 15lb: best bait, prawn; also dabs, flounder, mullet, pollack, pouting. Baits, squid, ragworm, peeler crab. Shore angling is best from late Sept. Good marks are rocks at castle and compass: wrasse, bass, garfish; Eastern Black Stone: conger, wrasse, pollack, bull huss; plaice, gurnard, bass off sand. Charter boats: Steve Parker, (01803 329414); Lloyd Sanders, (01803 554341). Association Club House is at 5 Oxford St. Tackle shops: Sport 'n' Fish, 16 Fairfax Place, Dartmouth TQ6 9AB; Sea Haven, Newcomen Road. Hotels: Castle, Victoria, Dart Marina. *For freshwater fishing, see Dart.*

Salcombe (Devon). Mackerel June to Sept and turbot, dabs, flounders, plaice, skate and rays rest of year. Entire estuary is a bass nursery area, and it is illegal to land boat caught bass between April-December. Plenty of natural bait. Beaches crowded in summer, but fishable in winter. Wreck fishing for conger, bream, etc. June-Oct. Turbot numerous. Boats: Whitestrand Boat Hire, Whitestrand Quay TQ8 8ET (01548 843818); Tuckers Boat Hire, Victoria Quay. Both sell tackle and bait. Club: Salcombe and Dist SAA (HQ: Fortesque Inn, Union St.); annual membership £6 (jun £3); annual festival, four weeks from mid August; special prizes and trophies for visitors throughout season.

Newton Ferrers (Devon). Noted station on Yealm Estuary. All-year bottom fishing; bass, flounders, pollack (from rocks), with mullet, conger, mackerel and flat fish from boats; shark June-Oct. Good base for trips to Eddystone. Boats from D Hockaday (Tel: 359); L Carter (Tel: 210). Abundant bait in estuary. Hotels: River Yealm, Family, Anglers, Yachtsmen.

Plymouth (Devon). One of finest stations in country for off-shore deep water fishing at such marks as East & West Rutts, Hands Deep and, of course, famous Eddystone Reef. Specimen pollack, conger, ling, whiting, pouting, cod, bream and mackerel plentiful. Fishing vessels for charter are Decca and Sounder equipped - fast exploring numerous wrecks within easy steaming of port; outstanding specimens taken. Inshore fishing for same species off Stoke Point, The Mewstone, Penlee, Rame and The Ledges. Sheltered boat and shore fishing in deep water harbour and extensive estuary network - at its best in autumn for bass, pollack, flounders, thornback and mullet. Shore fishing from rocks at Hilsea, Stoke, Gara Point, Rame Head, Penlee and Queeners for bass, pollack and wrasse, etc. Beach (surf) fishing at Whitsands and sand bar estuaries of Yealm, Erme and Avon rivers for bass, flounder and ray. All angling associations in city - British Conger Club (affiliated with ninety seven sea angling clubs), Plymouth Federation Sea AC and Plymouth SAC - now under one roof, on waterfront, at Plymouth Sea Angling Centre, Vauxhall Quay. Visiting anglers cordially welcomed. Tackle shops: D K Sports Ltd, 88 Vauxhall Street; Osborne & Cragg, 37 Bretonside; Clive's Tackle and Bait, 182 Exeter St. Charter boats are all moored on Sea Angling Centre Marina, Vauxhall Quay, and ownership is as follows; D Brett, (551548); G Hannaford, (500531); Mac, (666141); R Street, (768892); D Booker, (666576); R Strevens, (812871), G Andrews, (338967). Plymouth Angling Boatman's Assn, (01752 666576).

Looe (Cornwall). Important centre for all-round sport. Bass, pollack and mullet from 'Banjo Pier' breakwater, October to March. Excellent bass fishing in Looe River when fish are running, and mullet. Good rock fishing from White Rock, Hannafore, and westwards to Talland Bay, where pollack, bass, conger and wrasse can be taken. Eastwards, flatfish from beaches at Millendreath, Downderry and Whitsand Bay. Bass, flounders, eels, pollack and mullet from river at quayside and upriver. Excellent sport from boats on deep-sea marks; porbeagle, mako, blue and some thresher shark taken, and wide variety of other fish. Clubs: Looe is HQ of Shark AC of Gt Britain, tel/fax: 01503 262642, and is official weighing-in station for British Conger Club. Looe Sea AA, information from hon sec, Dave Snell. Information also from Looe Information Bureau, tel: 01503 262072. Deep sea boats and information from Harry Barnett, The Tackle Shop, Fish Quay, East Looe (tel: 01503 263218, shop freephone: 01800 074 3554); Pearns Chandlery, West Looe, and Boards, on the Quay. Boat charges are as follows: shark, £23 per head; bottom fishing, from £20 per head. Inshore, from £6.

Polperro (Cornwall). Few boats, shore fishing weedy. Bass, whiting, pollack, mackerel are most likely catches. Hotels: Claremont, Noughts & Crosses, Ship, Three Pilchards; also farm accommodation.

Fowey (Cornwall). Excellent sport with bass (June to Oct) in estuary and local bays from Udder to Cannis. Pollack numerous and heavy (20lb and more). Good bream, cod, conger, dogfish, ling, mullet, mackerel, wrasse, whiting and flatfish (big flounders and turbot). Bass, mullet and flounders taken from river. Par Beach to west also good for bass. Rock fishing at Polruan, Gribben Head and Pencarrow. Sand-eel, rag and lugworm obtainable. Clubs: Polruan Sea AC, 9 Greenbank, Polruan; Foye Tightliners SAC, 20 Polvillion Rd, Fowey. Boats: Fowey Town Quay, Troy Chandlers, (0172 683 3265). Tackle shops: Leisure Time, 10 Esplanade; Fowey Marine Services, 21/27 Station Rd.

Mevagissey (Cornwall). Excellent sea fishing, boat and shore, especially in summer. Shark boats are based here (local club affiliated to the Shark AC of Great Britain). Shark Centre & Tackle Box will make arrangements for shark and deep-sea trips. £17 per day, £9 half day. Shore fishing quite productive, especially bass from beach. Good pollack off Dodman Point and from marks out to sea. Bass in large numbers were at one time taken at the Gwinges, but few have been caught in recent years. Excellent sport with large mackerel at Gwinges and close to Dodman from late Aug. Sport from the pier can be very good at times, especially with mullet. Boatmen can be contacted through The Tackle Box, 4 Market Sq, (01726 843513). Club: Mevagissey SAC (HQ, The Ship Inn, Pentewan; visitors welcome). Annual sub £3.

Gorran Haven (Cornwall). Same marks fished as at Mevagissey. Rock fishing in area. Bass from sand beach. The Gorran Haven fishermen offer some facilities for visitors wishing a day's fishing. Excellent pollack fishing from boat with rubber sand-eel off Dodman Point. Limited accommodation at the Barley Sheaf (1½m); also Llawnroc Country Club and houses.

Falmouth (Cornwall). Excellent estuary, harbour (pier, shore and boat) and offshore fishing, especially over Manacles Rocks. Noted for big bass and pollack, latter taken off wreck and rock marks. Pendennis Point for wrasse and pollack; St Anthonys Head for wrasse, black bream at night in autumn. Porthallow for coalfish and conger; Lizard for wrasse, mackerel, and conger at night. Bait in estuary or from tackle shops. For boat fishing: Blue Minstrel (01326 250352); from Helford Passage, deep water wrecks; Gamgy Lady (01326 375458); K&S Cruises (01326 211056), MV Seaspray from Prince of Wales Pier; 2½ hr or 4 hr wreck fishing trips. Boats in St Mawes: M E Balcombe, (01209 214901). Club Falmouth and Penryn AA (festival each autumn). Tackle shops: Tackle Box, Arwenack St; AB Harvey, Market Strand. For wreck and shark fishing apply: Frank Vinnicombe, West Winds, Mylor Bridge, near Falmouth (Falmouth 372775). Charter-rates per rod £20, Per boat £140. Details of hotel accommodation from Town Information Bureau, Killigrew Street. *For freshwater fishing, see River Fal.*

Porthleven (Cornwall). Bass are to be taken from the rocks in Mount's Bay. Best bass fishing from Loe Bar, 1½m E. Good pollack and mackerel fishing outside the rocks. Nearly all fishing is done from the Mount's Bay type of boat in deep water. For charter boats, contact Harbourmaster. Hotel: Tye Rock.

Penzance (Cornwall). Excellent boat, pier, rock and shore fishing for pollack, mackerel, mullet and bass. Marazion beaches offer flatfish and ray. Pier at Lamorna, turbot, gurnard and dogfish. Breakwater at Sennen, the same. Boat trips can be arranged with The Shell Shop, tel: 68565. Shark fishing also possible. Best months: June-Nov. Club: Mount's Bay AS (headquarters: Dolphin Inn, Newlyn). Annual fishing festival, five weeks, Aug-Sept. Tackle shop: Newtown Angling Centre, Newton Germoe.

Mousehole, via **Penzance** (Cornwall). Good station for fishing Mount's Bay. Excellent mackerel, bream, pollack, conger, whiting, bass close to harbour according to season. Sheltered from west. Rock fishing in rough weather. Bell Rock between Newlyn and Mousehole has produced record catches. Between Mousehole and Lamorna, Penza Point, Kemyell Point and Carn Dhu are marks. Charter boat: Talisman, contact S Farley, tel: 01736 731895/731154. Best grounds: Longships and Runnel Stone. Good results with sharks. Hotels: The Ship; Old Coastguards; The Lobster Pot.

Isles of Scilly. From shores and small boats around islands, wrasse, pollack, mackerel, conger and plaice; farther off in deep sea, particularly on The Powl, south-west of St Agnes, big catches made of cod, ling, conger, pollack, etc. Mullet pay periodical visits inshore, but usually caught by net; bass rare in these waters. Some shark fishing, but visitors advised to take own tackle. Peninnis Head and Deep Point on St Mary's are good rock marks for pollack, wrasse and mackerel. Boating can be dangerous, so experience essential. Accommodation limited, early bookings advisable between May and Sept. Full information from Tourist IC, Porthcressa, St Mary's TR21 0JL, tel: 01720 422536, fax: 01720 422049. For boats inquire of St Mary's Boating Assn, "Karenza", Ennor Close, St Mary's. Several shops stock tackle.

St Ives (Cornwall). Bass, flounder, turbot, plaice, mackerel and garfish plentiful in St Ives area. Surf fishing from shore, especially from island, Aire Point, Cape Cornwall, Portheras, Besigrau, Man's Head, Clodgy Point; Godrevy Point offers mackerel, pollack and wrasse, which are also found at Navax Point. Chapel Porth good for ray and turbot. Boat fishing gives sport with mackerel (summer months) and large pollack (off reef from Godrevy Island). For boats contact Harbourmaster, tel: 01736 795081. Bass, tope, mullet, flatfish and occasional sea trout taken in Hayle river estuary. Trout fishing on Drift Reservoir, Penzance and St Erth Stream (4m). Symons of Market Place, TR26 1RZ, sells tackle and bait, also local coarse permits. Tel: 01736 796200. Hotels: Dunmar; Demelza; St Margarets, and many others.

Newquay (Cornwall). Boat, beach; rock and estuary fishing. Mackerel (April to Oct); school bass (June-Sept); larger fish July onwards, including winter; pollack (May-Nov); flatfish, wrasse (May-Sept); whiting in winter. Mullet good from June-Sept. Beach fishing at Perranporth, Holywell Bay, Crantock and Watergate Bay: ray, turbot and plaice. Off-peak times only. Shark and deep sea fishing possible. Club: Treninnick Tavern AC, HQ the Tavern, holds monthly competitions. Tackle hire, F Bickers, Fore St; Fishing Centre, 2 Beach St. For boats, contact Boatmans Assn. (01637 876352/871886); Anchor Sea Angling Centre, (01637 877613/874570), or Dolphin Booking Office, (01637 878696/877048). Trout fishing in Porth Reservoir. Sea trout and brown trout in Gannel estuary. Tackle Shop: Beach Rd; Goin Fishin, 32 Fore St. Numerous hotels.

Padstow (Cornwall). Trevose Head, Park Head and Stepper Point are good marks in summer for float fishing and spinning for mackerel, pollack, garfish, bass, wrasse, rays, dog fish, plaice, turbot, occ. tope, and in winter for whiting, codling, dogfish, conger. The beaches at Trevone, Harlyn, Mother Ivys, Boobys, Constantine, Treyarnon, Porthcothan, Mawgan Porth, provide surf casting for bass, plaice, turbot, rays. The estuary has good flounder fishing in winter. Clubs are Padstow AC, Social Club, Padstow; St Columb Club, The Red Lion, St Columb; Glenville Fishing Club, Social Club, St Dennis; or contact Treyarnon Angling Centre (Ed Schliffke), Treyarnon Bay, St Merryn, Padstow PL28 8JN, tel: 01841 521157. Tackle shop: Treyarnon Angling Centre, provides shore fishing guide. Hotel: Treyarnon Bay.

Bude (Cornwall). Codling, flatfish, mackerel, whiting and dogfish from breakwater and Crackington Haven. Northcott Mouth Crooklets, Maer, good for skate and flatfish. Widemouth Bay is good venue. Rays may be taken from shore in late

Check before you go

While every effort has been made to ensure that the information given in **Where to Fish** *is correct, the position is continually changing, and anglers are urged, in their own interests, to make preliminary enquiries before travelling to selected venues. This is especially important with reference to prices quoted. Inevitably the rate of inflation is affecting stability in this quarter. Anglers' attention is also drawn to the fact that the hotels mentioned under the various fishing stations do not necessarily have water of their own. Any amendments or further data for inclusion in subsequent editions, and any comments, will be welcome.*

summer and autumn. Good rock fishing is to be had from Upton, Wanson and Millock. Several boats work from Port Isaac in summer. Tackle shop, Vennings, Fore St, Tintagel. Club: Bude and Dist SAC.

Hartland (Devon); ns Barnstaple, 24m. Good all-round sea fishing, especially for bass at times with india-rubber sand-eel, prawn or limpet from beach or rocks according to tide (bass up to 11½lb have been caught); whiting, mullet, conger and pouting also taken. Hotels: Hartland Quay, New Inn, King's Arms.

Lundy (Bristol Channel). Good mackerel, conger, pollack and wrasse inshore. Ray, plaice, dabs, tope and bass at East Bank. 1¼ to 2½m E. Good anchorage at Lundy, but no harbour. Boats occasionally on hire for 8 persons fishing. For accommodation write to The Agent, Lundy, Bristol Channel, N Devon EX39 2LY.

Clovelly (Devon); W of Bideford. Whiting, cod, conger, bull huss, dogfish and the occasional plaice caught all the year round; ray in spring, bass and mackerel in summer. Few inshore boats; fishing from the breakwater forbidden from 9 am to 6 pm in summer. Tackle shops: see Bideford. Hotels: New Inn; Red Lion.

Appledore. N of Bideford in Torridge estuary. In summer, good bass fishing from rocks. Greysands and boats. Cod, some over 20lb, and whiting in winter. Lugworm beds at Appledore and Instow. Few boats. Tackle shop: B & K Angling Supplies, 14 The Quay.

Bideford (Devon). Bass (from the bridge, in summer) flounders, mullet higher up the river. 2m miles away at Westward Ho, extensive beach and rocks from which bass, dogfish, smooth-hounds, bull huss, tope and mackerel may be taken in summer; cod in winter.

Ilfracombe (Devon). From pier: conger, pollack, whiting, dabs; Capstone Point, bass, wrasse; key from Willy's (*below*). Capstone Rocks, similar species; Watermouth Cove, mixed bag. pollack, coalfish, wrasse, bass, a few flatfish. From boat, conger, skate, ray; mackerel Jun-Sept. Cod Dec-Feb. Bait: mackerel, squid, sand eel. Boat hire: (863460), (864625), (863849), or (01271 867947). Club: Ilfracombe and District AA, c/o Variety Sports, or Willy's (*below*). Reservoir trout fishing *(see freshwater section).* Hotel: Royal Britannia. Details of other accommodation from The Manager, Tourist Information Centre, The Promenade EX34 9HN (01271). Tackle and bait from Willy's Tackle Shop, Portland St, or Variety Sports, 23 Broad St EX34 9EE (01271 862039).

Lynmouth (Devon). Good harbour and boat fishing. Grey mullet and bass from harbour arm. Drift fishing for pollack and mackerel. Tope, skate and conger in Lynmouth Bay and off Sand Ridge, 1m. For motor boats with skipper, (015987 53207). Best months: June to Oct. Several hotels in Lynton and Lynmouth; details from Exmoor National Park Visitor Centre, The Esplanade, Lynmouth EX35 6EQ, (01598 752509), Easter-Oct. *(For freshwater fishing see Lyn).*

Minehead (Som). Beach, boat and rock fishing, principally for tope, skate, ling, thornback ray, conger, cod, bass and flatfish (Dunster to Porlock good for bass from beaches). Dogfish in bay. Mackerel in summer. Harbour and promenade walls provide sport with mullet, codling and some bass. Boats: through the tackle shop named below, all year round. Bait from sands at low water. Club: Minehead and Dist SAC. Tackle shop: Minehead Sports, 55 The Avenue. For further information and for boats contact Information Centre, Market House, The Parade.

Watchet (Som). Watchet and Dist Sea Angling Society fishes all the year round, covering coast from St Audries Bay to Porlock Wier. Monthly competitions from piers and shore. Codling, bass, whiting, conger and skate, according to season. Good boat fishing. New members welcomed by AS.

Weston-super-Mare (Avon). Record list of the Weston-super-Mare Sea AA includes conger at 25lb, sole at 2lb 8oz, bass, 13lb, skate 16lb 8oz, cod at 22lb, silver eel at 4lb, whiting and flounder at 2lb. Best venues 2 hours either side of low tide are Brean Down, conger, skate; Weston Beach, whiting, flatfish; Knightstone, the same. Woodspring is fishable throughout year, best at autumn. Boat fishing, tel: 01934 418033, or through Weston Angling Centre. For baits, beds of lugworms are to be found along the low water mark of the town beach and off Kewstoke Rocks. Also from Tackle shop: Weston Angling Centre, 25A Locking Rd, Weston-s-Mare BS23 3BY, (01634 631140).

Southport (Merseyside). Dabs and flounders, with whiting and codling in winter, chief fish caught here; also skate, mullet, dogfish, sole, plaice, conger, gurnard and some bass. Shore flat and sandy, and fishing mainly from pier. Local clubs: Southport SAS. Good coarse fishing on River Crossens run by Southport AS. Tackle shops: Robinsons, 71 Sussex Road.

Blackpool (Lancs). Seven miles of beach, and fishing from North Pier, but boat fishing is the best option at Blackpool. Boat trips from P Atkinson, Harvester Sea Charter, 78 Belvedere Rd, Thornton FY5 5DG, tel: 01253 825217. Tidal parts of R Wyre may be fished without a licence. Tickets for certain parts of Wyre from tackle shops. Coarse fishing in Stanley Park Lake. Dt. Tackle shop: Howarth, 128 Watson Rd. Many hotels.

Morecambe and **Heysham** (Lancs). Beach and stone jetty fishing throughout year. Beaches yield plaice, flounders, dabs, bass and eels from June to October, and dabs, codling, whiting and flounders in winter. Estuary catches up to 100 flounders to 2lb weight at Arnside. Stone Jetty has been extended, angling free; good catches of plaice, flounders, codling, whiting. At Heysham Harbour and North Wall whiting, cod, flounders, dabs, pouting, conger and mullet can be taken. Storm Groynes is producing good flatfish. Club: Heysham AC. Tackle shops: Morecambe Angling Centre, Thornton Rd, Morecambe; Charlton & Bagnall, 3/5 Damside St, Lancaster.

Fleetwood (Lancs). Plaice, whiting, skate, codling, tope, etc, from boats and shore. Club: Fleetwood and District AC. Sea baits from tackle shop: Langhorne's, 80 Poulton Road, tel: 01253 872653. Boats: C B Bird, 25 Upper Lune Street, Tel: 01253 873494; Viking Princess, tel: 01253 873045, Harvester, *see Blackpool*.

Barrow-in-Furness (Cumbria). Boat and shore fishing for tope, bass, cod, plaice, whiting, skate. Good marks include Foulney Island, Roa Island, Piel Island, Scarth Hole and Black Tower (Walney Island) and Roanhead. Good beach areas are Priory Point to Canal Foot, bait may be dug here, also, and Greenodd from sea wall alongside A590 and from car park.

ISLE OF WIGHT

The Island provides a wealth of shore and boat fishing, and sheltered conditions can always be found, Bass are the main quarry for beach anglers, but pollack, conger, mackerel, pouting, thornback rays, flatfish and wrasse, with occasional tope, are also taken. Black bream, skate and shark are caught by boat anglers as well as the species already mentioned. Cod run regularly to 20lb in autumn. Due to strong tides on the north coast and lack of harbours on the south coast, the visiting angler would be best advised to arrange boat trips with one of the local charter skippers working out of Yarmouth or Bembridge. Strong tides also mean heavy leads and sometimes, wire line. There are a large number of fishing clubs on the island. T I centres provide information about them.

Alum Bay. This necessitates a steep descent from the car park down the steps provided. From March to October there is a chair lift in operation. Fishes well after dark for large conger, bass, rays and sole, especially when rough. From the old pier remains to the white cliffs is the main area, although the rocks to the east, towards Totland, make a good station from which to spin for bass in the tide race, or to light leger with squid or mackerel. Deep water at all states of tide.

Atherfield. A number of record fish have been taken from this stretch. The beach is of shingle with scattered rock, easily reached via path alongside holiday camp. Bass, rays, pout, etc after dark, to mackerel, squid and cuttle baits. Crab bait produces smooth hounds. Ragworm fished over the drying ledge to the left of this mark produces large wrasse and bass, day or night. Large cod in late autumn.

Bembridge. Species to be caught include bass, pout, conger, ling, bream, dogfish, turbot, brill, pollock, skate and ray. The shore from Whitecliff to Bembridge is mainly rock formation with stretches of shingle and is good ground for bass and conger although not fished a great deal. Bass, mullet, eels, among the rocks. Here, the beach turns to fine flat sand and flatfish and bass are taken. Bembridge Harbour is a wide inlet with St Helens on the opposite bank. Shark fishing, July-August, drifting from St Catherines Light to Nab Tower. Boats and bait obtainable on shore. A sand gully near the 'Crab and Lobster' can be fished from the rocks. Fine bream may be taken from boats on Bembridge Ledge, early May to June, plenty of mackerel, also. A good number of fish are taken in the harbour: flounders, eels, bass. Many large mullet can be seen but are seldom fished for. Very strong tide in narrowest part of entrance. Kingrag and lugworm are good baits for ledgering and small mud ragworm on light float tackle is successful. Baited spoon or wander tackle works well for flounder and plaice. Sea wall at St Helens is a convenient place to park and fish over the top of the tide. Club: Bembridge AC, holds 12 competitions p.a. Membership £12 annually.

Bonchurch. Bass, conger, wrasse and pout from beach. Good fishing in gulleys between the extensive rocks at flood tide, after dark, especially after a south westerly gale.

Brooke. A shallow water mark that fishes well when the sea is coloured. Expect conger, bass, pout, plus cod in late autumn. One good spot is to be found in front of easy cliff path, 200 yds to left of point.

Chale. Best beach for rays on island, reached by steep cliff path. Specimen small eyed rays are taken on frozen sand eel, day or night, from Mar-Sept, when sea is coloured after a storm. Some bass and conger, plus mackerel in summer.

Colwell Bay. A shallow sandy beach with easy access. Bass, sole, wrasse after dark, when crowds have gone home.

Totland Bay. Next to Colwell Bay, deeper water. More chance of bass, especially when rough. It's possible to fish straight from a car on the sea wall. Fishing is good beside the disused pier.

Compton Bay. 1m west of Brooke. Long flat sandy beach with patches of flat rock. Occasional bass when the sea is rough. Avoid the rocks under the cliff at the west end, where there is a danger of major cliff falls.

Cowes. The River Medina runs from Newport to Cowes Harbour and offers flounder fishing throughout the year with the best sport from the late summer to autumn. The shoals move about the river with the tide and location is often a matter of local knowledge. As a general guide the fish may be expected further upstream on the stronger spring tides. Weights average up to a pound. Bass also move into the river and have been taken to 4lbs, often on flounder tackle. Rowing boats may be launched from the Folly Inn on the East bank, reached by turning off the main Newport to East Cowes road. Kingston power station about a mile down from Folly is a good boat mark for

Hastings and St. Leonards SAC offers fine offshore fishing. This is one day's catch of conger.

school bass, plaice, sole. Mullet and silver eels may be caught anywhere. Ragworm is usually used in preference to lugworm..

Cowes Harbour. Bass, flounder, plaice and sole may be taken by the boat angler from either side of the fairway above and below the floating bridge and during the summer there are many large mullet within the harbour. Inside the breakwater to the east, flounder and plaice are taken on the bottom from along the edge of the hovercraft channel to inshore towards the East Cowes Esplanade. Flounder and plaice are also taken from the mud-flats outside the East Cowes breakwater.

West Cowes Esplanade to **Gurnard**. Float fishing and spinning from the slipways and jetties for bass and mullet. Along the Princes Green to Egypt Light, bass and conger can be found and in late summer bass often venture close in under the walls in search of prawns and may be taken by trailing a worm over the balustrade and walking it quietly along. At Egypt Light, the shingle slopes steeply so long casting is unnecessary, and tope have occasionally been landed here as well as bass to 8lb, and cod to 20lb in late autumn. The sandy patches among the rocks may yield sole and plaice in season. Free car parking here.

Freshwater Bay. Pouting, bass, small pollack and few conger. Fish from middle of beach when rough. Survey at low tide, then fish after dark. Very easy access.

Newport. Nearest sea fishing in River Medina; flounders, school bass, mullet, plaice, eels. Tackle/ boat hire from Scotties, branch at 11 Lugley St, tel 522115.

Newtown. Bass and flounders in Newtown River. Clamerkin reach is best, using light gear and ragworm. Limited access, as large area is nature reserve.

Ventnor to **St Catherines**. Series of rocky ledges and gullies, best surveyed at low water. Bass, conger, pout, wrasse etc after dark and some mullet during calm days.

Yarmouth. Flounder and mullet and school bass in harbour. Bass, rays and mackerel from pier in summer. Notable cod venue in late autumn but strong tides prevail.

Ryde. A very shallow, sandy beech, popular with holiday makers. Bass, small pollock, plaice, flounders, eels, bream and grey mullet from pier. Conger, dogfish, dabs, skate, mackerel from deep water marks, and plaice, flounder, bass and sole fishing inshore. Cod up to 24lb taken in autumn. Sheltered resort giving ideal fishing conditions all year. All beaches fishable. King rag and lugworm plentiful. Vectis Boating and Fishing Club offers annual membership. Details from hon sec (enclose sae). Boats can be hired along shore.

Sandown. Fishing from end of pier (daytime only) produces plaice, rays, bass and bream on sandy ground. Float fishing produces mackerel, scad, small pollack and mullet. Local club: Sandown and Lake AS, organising frequent open competitions. Visitors welcome. Boat hire and tackle, Scotties, 22 Fitzroy Street.

Seaview. From St Helens to Seaview the coast is a mixture of rocks and sand and shingle. Priory Bay is reached by boat and provides very good mackerel and bass fishing. Plaice may be taken to 3lb from early April, with lugworm. During the summer months bream can also be taken from this spot. From June onwards, bass and mackerel are shoaling and large catches from boats are common. Cod are also taken late in the year.

Shanklin. Pier has been demolished. Various other venues exist which fish well for specific species, such as sting ray, but require very detailed directions re access, times to fish, etc. Contact Scotties of Newport for such details, and to obtain a wide variety of suitable baits. Norfolk House Hotel, The Esplanade, PO37 6BN, offers fishing holidays of two or three nights, for experienced angler and novice, with two full days at sea with all bait and tackle supplied. Contact Alan Davis, tel: 01983 863023.

Totland. Bass off shingle bank from boat. Bass, conger from shore. Fishing also from pier. Boats from Fair Deal Amusements, The Pier. Hotels: Chalet, Sentry Mead.

Ventnor. The western end of the beach is good for bass, skate, pout and conger and the sea wall in front of the canoe lake is a good bass spot. Boat (from Blakes) for pollack and mackerel. Club: Ventnor AC (associate members welcome). Tackle and bait: Bates & Son, 5 Spring Hill; J Chiverton 70 High St. Beach fishing *(see also Bonchurch)*.

Wootton. School bass and flounders.

Yarmouth. Bass, small pollack; pier fishing.

CHANNEL ISLANDS

Wide variety of sport from beaches, rocky headlands and boats. Many specimen fish landed from deep-sea marks. Shark fishing growing in popularity. Boats easy to come by.

Guernsey. No fewer than 52 different species are recorded in Bailiwick of Guernsey rod-caught record list. Guernsey is 15 miles from the Hurd Deep, near major shipping lanes, and hundreds of wrecks yield high catches. Inshore, many headlands offer first-class spinning, and a flat, sandy, west coast gives good surf-casting for bass and a few flatfish. Several Guernsey fish accepted as new British records. The most common species are bass, bream, conger, dogfish, garfish, mackerel, mullet, plaice, pollack and wrasse. Anglers may fish anywhere from the shore except for marinas, the fishermans quay, and the land reclamation to the south of St Sampson's Harbour. Bottom fishing is productive in spring, late autumn and winter; spinning in summer. Long casting is no advantage, on westerly rocks. Baits: ragworm is found in the rocky bays on west coast, Grand Havre, Bordeaux North, to Beaucette Marina, Bellgreve Bay; lugworm in sandy bays, especially, Grand Havre, Cobo and Vazon. Crabs, prawns and white rag can also be obtained. In north east, Fort Doyle is one of the best marks; south east, Soldiers Bay. South west cliffs are fishable but dangerous. There are nine different fishing competitions between June and December. Boat charter; D Lane, "Midnight Express", Mon Desir, Les Hautes Mielles, L'Ancress, Vale GY3 5JU; (01481 45444); Brian Blondel (04481 101288); R Taylor, (37959). Local clubs: Guernsey SAC; Guernsey Freshwater AC; Guernsey Mullet Club; Castaways AC, and others. Tackle shops: North Quay Marine, St Sampson's Harbour (46561); Tackle & Accessories Centre, The Market, (723225); Marquand Bros, North Quay, **St Peter Port**, (01481 720962). Baits, rod hire; Boatworks & Castle Emplacement, St Peter Port, (726071). For further information about Guernsey fisheries contact States of Guernsey Department of Fisheries, Raymond Falla House, PO Box 459, Longue Rue, St Martins, Guernsey GY1 6AF, tel: 01481 35741 (35015 fax). Tourist Information publishes official sea angling guide, £1, widely obtainable.

Jersey. Winter fishing yields pollack, ray and other flatfish, conger, a few bass, cod fishing poor. Spring: garfish, early mackerel off such points as Sorel and La Moye; grey mullet, porbeagle, blue shark and other species. Summer is good for all forms of fishing, by boat on offshore reefs, which is 80% of charter angling. Excellent fishing for bream commences in May and continues to Oct, fish up to 5lb. Rays (incl blonde rays, over 30lb) are caught in good quantities on inshore sandbanks, as well as brill and turbot, especially early and late season. In autumn, whitebait concentrates at places such as Belle Hougue bring in large mackerel and bass, and flatfish move into shallow waters in the Islands bays. Venues: St Helier's harbour heads; Noirmont Point; St Brelade's Bay; La Corbiere; L'Etacq; Plemont; Greve de Lecq; Bonne Nuit Bay harbour; Bouley Bay harbour; Rozel Bay harbour; St Catherine's breakwater; St Aubin's Bay. Charter boats: 'Anna II', from St Helier Marina, contact A Heart, Highview Farm, Rue de la Hauteur, Trinity, tel: 0860 863507; 'Theseus', D Nuth, tel: 0860 740316. Local club: Jersey SFC. Tackle shops: PJN Fishing Tackle, 7 Beresford Market, JE3 4WN, tel: 01534 74875; I S Marine, 15/16 Commercial Buildings; J F S Sport, Green St; all St Helier.

ISLE OF MAN

The Island's coastline is extremely varied. The long, flat, surf beaches of the North contrast sharply with the sheer faces of the South. Similarly, its fishing methods and species of fish are equally diverse. Despite the Island's location, coastline and clean waters, salt-water angling from both shore and boat remains unexploited and largely undiscovered. Information is obtainable from Isle of Man Tourist and Leisure Department, Information Bureau, Sea Terminal, Douglas, tel: 01624 686766.

Castletown. Conger, pollack, cod, wrasse, tope, flatfish from beach and boat; best months, June to Oct. Big skate from boats 600 yds off Langness; best Aug-Sept Boats for hire locally.

Douglas. Plaice, sole (British record lemon

sole), coalfish, pollack, flounder from Victoria Pier; best months, May to Oct, coalfish, wrasse, cod, plaice, dabs, sole from boats in Douglas Bay. Rock fishing off Douglas Head; float or spinner (good for pollack). Cod, wrasse, red gurnard, plaice, Little Ness Head to Douglas Head; skate from boats 2m out, and large tope, conger, cod, etc. Club: Douglas (IOM) and District AC, annual membership fee £12 (£4 discount before 28 Feb), jun £3 (membership includes trout fishing rights in **R Glass**). Club sec/treasurer, Mrs Sue McCoubrey, 47 Hildesley Rd, Douglas, takes applications for membership. Tackle shops: Hobbytime, Castle St; Intersport, 58 Duke St. Also, Tackle Bow, at Foxdale.

Kirk Michael. Beach fishing from here to Point of Ayre is excellent for bass, flatfish, dogfish.

Laxey. Plaice, dabs and bass from March to Oct from beach. Cod, mackerel, flat-fish, offshore from boats at Garwick Bay. Clubs: Garwick Sailing and Fishing Club.

Peel. Breakwater: cod, coalfish, dogfish plentiful all year round; mackerel, dogfish, coalfish, plaice, flounder, dabs (July to Oct). Beach: similar. Rock fishing: from Castle rocks and headlands plenty of pollack. Sand eel best bait all season. Limited lugworm on beach. Boat fishing, but hire limited: cod and haddock in winter. In spring and summer spur dogfish common. Rock fishing off St Patrick's Isle for mackerel, wrasse, coalfish; float and spinner. Local club; Peel Angling Club.

Port Erin. Good sport from pier and breakwater for pollack, mackerel, wrasse, grey mullet, coalfish, angler fish and conger. The bay yields flatfish and mackerel, with cod in the colder months. Tackle shop: Henry Crellin, IOM Sea Sports Ltd, Strand Road. Hotels: Balmoral; Falcons Nest.

Port St Mary. Probably best centre on island. Pollack, coalfish, wrasse from rocks, pier, boats (most of year). Flatfish and mackerel offshore and pier during herring season. Tope, skate, cod, conger, ling from boats. Boats from J Williams, Beach Cliff, Bay View Rd and W Halsall, Lime Street PSM. Several competitions. Inquiries to hon sec, Southern AC. Visitors welcome. Tackle shop: The Tackle Box, Foxdale. Hotels: Station; Albert.

Ramsey. From pier, dogfish, codling, whiting, flounder, dab, coalfish, plaice, mackerel, rockling; from Ramsey beach to Point of Ayre, same as pier, plus bass (Aug-Sept). Pollack also taken by spinning with artificial sand-eel. For help with bait and boats, contact officials of Ramsey AC, annual membership fee £8, conc 50p. Tackle shop: The Ramsey Warehouse, 37 Parliament Street.

FISHING CLUBS & ASSOCIATIONS IN ENGLAND

The English fishing clubs and associations listed below are by no means the total number of those existing. Club secretaries retire or change address, often after a comparatively short term of office, making it all too probable that the address list is out of date by the time it is issued. This regrettable fact also applies to the club lists in the others national sections of the book. Please advise the publishers (address at the front of the book) of any changed details for the next edition. The names and addresses of countless more fishing clubs and associations may be obtained from the various regional offices of the Environment Agency, from British Waterways, and from such federated bodies as the British Conger Club, *see below*.

NATIONAL BODIES

Anglers' Conservation Association
Jane James, Director
5H Alford Dairy
Aldermaston
Berks RE7 4NB
Tel: 01476 61008 Fax: 01476 60900

Angling Foundation
Federation House
National Agriculture Centre
Stoneleigh Park
Warwickshire CV8 2RF
Tel: 01203 414 999
Fax: 01203 414 990
http://www.british-sports.co.uk

Atlantic Salmon Trust
Director:
J B D Read
Moulin, Pitlochry
Perthshire Phl6 5JQ
tel: 01796 473439
Fax: 01796 473554

Association of Professional Game Angling Instructors
Michael Evans, Secretary
Little Saxbys Farm
Cowden, Kent TN8 7DX
Tel: 01342 850765.
Fax: 01342 850926.

Association of Stillwater Game Fishery Managers
Packington Fisheries
Meriden, Coventry
West Midlands CV7 7HR
Tel: 01676 522754
Fax: 01676 523399

British Conger Club
Tom Matchett
112 Bearsdown Road
Eggbuckland
Plymouth, Devon PL6 5TT
Tel: 01752 769262
HQ: Sea Angling Centre,
Vauxhall Quay, Sutton Harbour,
Plymouth,
Devon
Affiliated with ninety seven sea angling clubs

British Record (rod-caught) Fish Committee
David Rowe, Acting Secretary
c/o National Federation of Sea Anglers
51A Queen Street
Newton Abbot
Devon TQ12 2QJ
Tel & Fax: 01626 331330

British Waterways
All Fishery enquiries to
Fisheries Manager:
Brindley House, Corner Hall
Lawn Lane, Hemel Hempstead
Hertfordshire HP3 9YT
Tel: 01442 278717.
Fax: 01442 234932.

Countryside Alliance
Robin Hanbury-Tenison
59 Kennington Road
London SEI 7PZ
Tel: 0171-928 4742
Fax: 0171 793 8484 (8899)

Freshwater Biological Association
The Director
The Ferry House
Far Sawrey, Ambleside
Cumbria LA22 OLP
Tel: 015394 42468
Fax: 015394 46914
http://wiua.nwi.ac.uk/idm/fba.html
e-mail: CSR@wpo.nerc.ac.uk

Grayling Society
R Cullum-Kenyon
Hazelwood
The Green

Fairford
Glos. GL7 4HU
Tel: 01285 712530
Fax: 01285 713636

International Fly Fishing Association
Ian Campbell, Secretary and Treasurer
2 Golf View
Bearsden
Glasgow G61 4HJ

Marine Biological Association of the United Kingdom
The Secretary
The Laboratory
Citadel Hill
Plymouth PLI 2PB
Tel: 01752 633100
Fax: 669762/633102

National Federation of Anglers
Halliday House
Egginton Junction
Nr Hilton
Derbyshire DE65 6GU

National Federation of Sea Anglers
D Rowe
NFSA Development Officer
NFSA Office,
51A Queen Street
Newton Abbot,
Devon TQl2 2QJ
Tel & Fax: 01626 331330

Salmon and Trout Association
C W Poupard, Director
Fishmongers' Hall
London Bridge
London EC4R 9EL
Tel: 0171-283 5838
Fax: 0171 9291389

Shark Angling Club of Great Britain
Linda Reynolds
The Quay, East Looe
Cornwall PL13 IDX
Tel/Fax: 01503 262642

CLUBS

Abbey Cross Angling Club
P Jourdan
12 Burnside
Hertford
SG12 2AW

Accrington and District Fishing Club
A Balderstone
42 Townley Avenue
Huncoat, Lancashire
BB5 6LP

Addingham Angling Association
H D Sutherland
51 Moor Park Drive
Addingham
Ilkley LS29 0PU

Aln Angling Association
L Jobson
Tower Showrooms
Alnwick, Northumberland

Alveston Village Association Angling Club
M A Pitcher
6 Ferry Lane, Alveston
Stratford upon Avon CV37 7QX

Ampthill and District Angling Club
R Ward
15 Kingfisher Road
Flitwick
Bedfordshire
MK45 1RA

Appletreewick Barden and Burnsall Angling Club
J G H Mackrell
Mouldgreave
Oxenhope
N Keighley, West Yorks BD22 9RT

Ashmere Fisheries
Mr & Mrs K Howman
Felix Lane
Shepperton, Middlesex

Avon Fishing Association (Devon)
J E Coombes
19 Stella Road, Preston
Paignton
South Devon TQ3 1BH

Aylsham and District Angling Club
K Sutton
17 Town Lane
Aylsham
Norfolk NR11 6HH

Banbury and District Angling Association
G V Bradbeer
7 Bentley Close
Banbury, Oxon OX16 7PB

Barnes and Mortlake Angling and Preservation Society
G M Nolan
109 Samuel Lewis Trust Estate
Lisgar Terrace
West Kensington
London W14 8SF
Barnes
London SW13 0AE

Barnsley and District Amalgamated Anglers' Society
T Eaton
60 Walton Street

Gawber, Barnsley
Yorkshire S75 2PD

Barnstaple and District Angling Association
S Toms
1 Maysleary Cottages
Filleigh, N Devon
EX32 7TJ

Barnt Green Fishing Club
Mrs J Lunt
Square Cottage
Cherry Hill Drive
Barnt Green
Worcs B45 8JY

Basingstoke Canal Angling Association
R Jenkins
26 Tinern Close
Basingstoke, Hampshire
RG24 9HE

Bathampton Angling Association
D Crookes
25 Otago Terrace
Larkhall
Bath, Avon BA1 6SX

Beccles Angling Club
A W J Crane
27 Rigbourne Hill
Suffolk

Bedford Angling Club
Mrs M E Appleton
18 Moriston Road
Bedford MK41 7UG

Bedlington and Blagdon Angling Association
S Symons
8 Moorland Drive
Bedlington
Northumberland
NE22 7HB

Belper and District Angling Club
P Smith
11 Lander Lane
Belper
Derbys

Bembridge (IOW) Angling Club
P Knight
Berrylands
Heathfield Road
Bembridge IOW
PO35 5UW

Bexhill Sea Angling Club
J Boston
17 St James Street
Bexhill-on-Sea, Sussex

Bicester Angling Society
W H Bunce
Tel: Bicester 44653

Bideford and District Angling Club
Mrs Joan Ash
42 Clovelly Street
Bideford, N Devon

Billingshurst Angling Society
J Hitchin
12 West Lark Lake
Goring-by-Sea
Worthing

Birmingham Anglers' Association Ltd
J Williams
100 Icknield Port Road
Rotton Park, Birmingham B16 0AP

Bishop Auckland and District Angling Club
J Winter
7 Royal Grove
Crook, Co Durham DL15 9ER

Blenheim Angling Society
F W Lancaster
Briarwood, Burtons Lane
Chalfont St Giles
Buckinghamshire HP8 4BB

Blunham Angling Club
G Palmer
5 Brockwell
Oakley
Bedfordshire

Bodmin Anglers' Association
R Burrows
26 Meadow Place
Bodmin, Cornwall PL31 1JD

Bolton and District Angling Association
Terence A McKee
1 Lever Edge Lane
Great Lever
Bolton, Lancs BL3 3BU

Boston and District Angling Association
Mrs Jill Sawyer
Hatfield,
Wyberton West Road
Boston
Lincolnshire PE21 7LQ

Fishing Clubs

When you appoint a new Hon. Secretary, do not forget to give us details of the change. Write to the Publishers (address in the front of the book). Thank you!

Boston Spa Angling Club
A Waddington
The Cottage
17 The Village
Thorp Arch
Wetherby, Yorkshire
LS23 7AR

Bradford No 1 Angling Association
H M Foster
6 Moorclose Lane
Queensbury
Bradford BD13 2BP
Tickets and licences
D B Arnett
49 Templars Way
Bradford BD8 0LW

Bradford Waltonians' Angling Club
H J B Swarbrick
43 Hawksworth Drive
Menston, Ilkley
West Yorkshire LS29 6HP

Brampton (Cambs) Angling Society
Kevin Medlock
1 Stanch Hill Rd
Sawtry, Huntingdon
Cambs PE17 5XG

Brandon and District Angling Club
P Cooper
16 High Street
Feltwell, Thetford
Norfolk IP26 4AF

Bridgwater Angling Association
Mrs Carol Howe
£ Cedar Close
Bridgwater
Somerset TA6 5DP

Bristol, Bath and Wiltshire Anglers Amalgamation
Jeff Parker
16 Lansdown View
Kingswood,
Bristol BS15 4AW

Bristol and West of England Federation of Anglers2
B Williams
157 Whiteway Road
Bristol BS5 7RH

Brixham Sea Anglers' Society
Clubhouse at 16a Castor Road
Brixham

Bromley and District Anglers' Society
M Sale
13A Charlesfield Road
Horley Road
Horley
Surrey RH6 8BJ

Broome Angling Society
A Smith
10 Lords Avenue
Benskins Croft
Leicester LE4 2HX

Brunswick Brothers Angling Society
Terry Taylor
40 St Andrews Road
Cranbrook
Ilford IG1 3PF

Buckingham and District Angling Association
Mrs J Begley
20 Vicarage Close
Steeple Claydon
Buckingham
MK18 2PU

Bude Angling Association
Mrs P Casson
29 West Park Road
Bude, Cornwall EX23 0NA

Bude Canal Angling Association
K M Harris
9 Quarry Close
Bude
Cornwall

Bungay Cherry Tree Angling Club
I Gosling
37 St Mary's Terrace
Flixton Road
Bungay, Suffolk
NR35 1DW

Burton-on-Trent Mutual Angling Association
D J Clark
7 Denton Rise
Burton-on-Trent,
Staffordshire DE13 0QB

Caersws Angling Association
R Davies
1 Broneirion Cottages
Llandinam
Powys

Calne Angling Association
Miss J M Knowler
123A London Road
Calne, Wiltshire SN11 0AQ

Cambridge Albion Angling Society
R Gentle
34 Ramsden Square
Cambridge CB4 2BL

Cambridge Izaak Walton Society
T J Sawyer
6 Pump Lane
Hardwick
Cambs CB3 7QW

Cambridge Fish Preservation and Angling Society
G Tweed
27A Villa Road
Impington
Cambridge

Cambs
Cambridge Izaak Walton Society
T Sawyer
6 Pump Lane
Hardwick
Cambridge CB3 7SW
Canterbury and District Angling Association
R Barton
14 Mill Road
Sturry, Canterbury
Kent CT2 0AF
Castaways Angling Club
P Dunne
Dieu Donne
La Bellieuse
St Martins
Guernsey
Central Association of London and Provincial Angling Clubs
A J Jenkinson
68 Taynton Drive
Merstham, Surrey
RH1 3PT
Cheddar Angling Association
A T Lane
P O Box 1183
Cheddar,
Somerset BS27 3LT
Chelmsford Angling Association
Membership Secretary
61 Readers Court
Great Baddow
Chelmsford
Essex CM2 8EX
or
Irene Lewis
60 Delamere Road
Chelmsford CM1 2TG
Cheshire Anglers Association
Graham Tompkinson
31 Wareham Drive
Crewe, Cheshire
CW1 3XA
Chester-le-Street and District Angling Club
G Curry
62 Newcastle Road
Chester-le-Street
Co Durham
DH3 3UF
Chichester And District Angling Society
Mrs C Luffham
17 Arun Road
Bognor Regis
W Sussex
Chichester Canal Society
Edward Hill
9 Marden Avenue
Chichester
West Sussex
PO19 2QZ
Chippenham Angling Club
J Duffield
95 Malmesbury Road
Chippenham
Wilts SN15 1PY
Club HQ
Liberal Club
Gladstone Road
Chippenham
Christchurch Angling Club
Mr Andrews
4 Marley Close
New Milton
Hants BH25 5LL
Clevedon and District Freshwater Angling Club
R L Purchase
28 The Tynings, Yeo Park
Clevedon, Avon BS21 7YP
Clitheroe Angling Association
B Jacques
24 Rylstone Drive
Barnoldswick
Lancs BB8 5RG
Clive Vale Angling Club
J Greenhalf
33 Hollington Park Road
St Leonards-on-Sea
E Sussex TN38 0SE
Cockermouth Angling Association
Ken Simpson
36 High Rigg
Brigham
Cockermouth
Cumbria
Colchester Angling Preservation Society
M K Turner
29 Lodge Road
Braintree, Essex CM7 1JA
Colchester Piscatorial Society
R J Moore
66 The Willows
Colchester
Essex CO2 8PX
Collingham Angling Association
P Thomas
61 station Road
Collingham
Nottinghamshire NG24 7RA
Colnes Angling Society
P Empson
16 Station Road
Colne Engain,
Colchester, Essex
CO6 2ES
Suffolk Stour

Compleat Angler Fishing Club
T Lelliott
Polegate Angling Centre
101 Polegate Road
Polegate, E Sussex
BN26 6EB

Congleton Angling Society
N J Bours
8 Norfolk Road
Congleton, Cheshire
CW12 1NY

Coquet Angling Club
J Engles
80 Castle Terrace
Ashington, Northumberland

Cotterstock Angling Association
Mrs Joan E Popplewell
40 North Street
Oundle, Peterborough PE8 4AL

Coventry and District Angling Association
A J Hyde
1 Oak Tree Avenue
Green Lane
Coventry CV3 6DG

Danby Angling Club
F Farrow
11 Dale End, Danby
Whitby, N Yorkshire Y021 2JF

Darlington Anglers Club
I Ablott
58 Swaledale Avenue
Darlington DL3 9AL

Darlington Brown Trout Angling Association
G Coulson
5 Grange Avenue, Hurworth Place
Darlington

Darlington Fly Fishers Club
W D Holmes
39 Barrett Road
Darlington DL3 8LA

Dartmouth and District Angling Association
L Berry, Chairman
c/o Club HQ
5 Oxford Street
Dartmouth,
Devon

Darwen Anglers' Association
F W Kendall
45 Holden Fold
Darwen
Lancashire BB3 3AU

Dawley Angling Society
Mike Tuff
18 New Road
Dawley, Telford
Shropshire TF4 3LJ

Deal and Walmer Inshore Fishermen's Association
A J C Robinson
4 Tormore Park
Deal Kent
CT14 9UY

Dean Clough and Ryburn Angling Society
T Hooson
4 Chester Terrace
Boothtown, Halifax
W Yorks HX3 6LT

Deanshanger and Stratford Angling Association
T Valentine
34 Mallets Close
Stony Stratford
Milton Keynes MK11 1DQ

Deeping St James Angling Club
Derek L Bailey
11 Lime Tree Avenue
Towngate West
Market Deeping
Peterborough
Lincs PE6 8DQ

Derbyshire Angling Federation
S W Clifton
14 Highfield Road
Little Eaton
Derbys

Derbyshire County Angling Club
O W Handley
Osprey House, Ogston
Higham, Alfreton
Derby DE55 6EL

Dereham and District Angling Club
D Appleby
6 Rump Close
Swanton Morley
Norfolk NR20 4NH

Diss and District Angling Club
Mr D Gladwell
5 Martin Road
Diss
Suffolk IP22 3HR

Fishing Clubs

When you appoint a new Hon. Secretary, do not forget to give us details of the change. Write to the Publishers (address in the front of the book). Thank you!

Doncaster and District Angling Association
W Sams
28 Pipering Lane
Scawthorpe
Doncaster DN5 9NY

Dorchester Fishing Club
J Grindle
36 Cowleaze
Martinstown
Dorchester, Dorset DT2 9TD

Droitwich and District (Talbot) Angling Society
c/o Talbot Hotel, High Street
Droitwich, Worcestershire

Durham City Angling Club
M J Hall
21 Northumbria Place
Co Durham, DH9 0UB

Earl Manvers Angling Association
G R Dennis, 11 First Avenue
Carlton
Nottingham NG4 1PH

Eastbourne Angling Association
The Club House
Royal Parade
Eastbourne, Sussex
BN22 7AA

Eastfield Angling Association
J Ford
3 Newby Court
Eastfield
Northampton

Eastleigh and District Angling Club
J Remington
121 Desborough Road
Eastborough
Hants SO5 5NP

Edenbridge Angling Club
Mr Fishlock
3 Locks Meadow
Dormansland
Surrey

Egremont Angling Association
Clive Fisher
69 North Road
Egremont, Cumbria
CA22 2PR

Ennerdale Lake Fisheries
D Crellin
3 Parklands Drive
Egremont
Cumbria CA22 2JL

Evesham and District Angling Association
C Leeming
44 Coronation street
Evesham, Worcs
WR11 5BD

Exeter and District Angling Association
D Cornish
9 Denmark Road
Exeter EX1 1SL

Fakenham Angling Club
G Twite
16 Back Street
Hempton, Fakenham
Norfolk NR21 7LR

Farnham Angling Society
Mr Borra
The Creel
Station Road
Aldershot
Hants

Faversham Angling Club
N Prior
Flat 1C
St Nicholas Road
Faversham
Kent ME13 7PG

Felixstowe Sea Angling Association
End Manor Terrace
Felixstowe, Suffolk
IP11 8EL
Secretary:
K M Tompkins
11 High Road East
Felixstowe
Suffolk IP11 9JU

Fenton and District Angling Society
C Yates
The Puzzels
5 Gatley Grove
Meir Park
Stoke-on-Trent
Staffs ST3 7SH

Ferryhill and District Angling Club
Financial Secretary
R Staff
19 Opal Avenue
Chilton, Ferryhill
Durham
DL17 0QW
Secretary
B Hignett
74 Grasmere Road
Garden Farm Estate
Chester-le-Street
Co Durham

Filey Boat Angling Club
H Cammish
11 Ravine Top
Filey
N Yorks YO14 9HA

Filey Brigg Angling Society
Mrs K Marshall
87 Scarborough Road
Filey

N Yorks Y014 9NQ,
Flyfishers' Club
Commander T H Boycott OBE RN
69 Brook Street
London WIY 2ER
Private members club, no fishery.
Framlington and District Angling Club
D Smith
11 Lake Rise
Martlesham Village
Ipswich IP5 7SA
Frome and District Angling Association
R J Lee
Marvic, Keyford Terrace
Frome
Somerset BA11 1JL
Gamefishers Club
J H Andrews
Meadow View, Dinedor
Hereford HR2 6LQ
Gillingham and District Angling Association
Treasurer
Paul J G Stone
The Timepiece
Newbury (High Street)
Gillingham
Dorset SP8 4HZ
Gipping Angling Preservation Society
George Alderson
19 Clover Close
Chantry, Ipswich,
Suffolk IP2 0PW
Gipping. Tickets
Gipping Valley Angling Club
W Cook
36 Stowmarket Road
Needham Market
Suffolk IP6 8DS
Glebe Angling Club
C Broome
2 Crockett Close
Links View Estate
Northampton
Godalming Angling Society
M R Richardson
87 Summers Road
Farncombe, Godalming
Surrey GU7 3BE
Goole and District Angling Association
L Rogers
39 Clifton Gardens
Goole
North Humberside DN14 6AR
Grafton Angling Association
G D Williams
9 Edward Street
Worksop
Notts S80 1QP
Grantham Angling Association
W J C Hutchins
28 Cottesmore Close
Grantham, Lincolnshire NG31 9JL
Great Cornard Angling Club
P Franklin
48 Queensway, Gt Cornard
Suffolk
Great Yarmouth and Norfolk County Angling Association
K Ford
2 Parana Close
Sprowston
Norwich
Grenville Sea Angling Club
Social Club
St Dennis
Padstow
Cornwall
Groe Park and Irfon Angling Club
H G Lloyd
Dolrhedyn
Irfon Road
Builth Wells, Powys LD2 3DE
Guernsey Freshwater Anglers Society
A Bradley
Les Tracheries Cottage
Les Tracheries
L'Islet
Guernsey
Guernsey Mullet Club
M Weyson
La Cachette
6 Clos des Caches
St Martins
Guernsey
Guernsey Sea Anglers Club
P Le Lacheur
Santa Ana
Les Emrais Estate, Castel
Guernsey
Hadleigh and District Angling Society
D R Warner
5 Churchill Avenue
Hadleigh, Ipswich
Suffolk IP7 6BT
Haltwhistle and District Angling Association
Chris Wilson
Melkridge House, Melkridge
Haltwhistle, Northumberland
NE49 0LT
Harleston, Wortwell and District Angling Club
P Brown
15 Pine Close
Harleston, Norfolk
Harrogate and Claro Conservative Angling Association

M G Cooke
1 Kirkham Road,
Bilton
Harrogate
Yorkshire HG1 4EL

Harwich Angling Club
G Shields
5 Gordon Way
Dovercourt
Harwich
Essex CO12 3TW

Hastings and St Leonards Sea Angling Association
Marine Parade
Hastings
Sussex TN34 3AG

Hastings, Bexhill and District Freshwater Angling Association
P T Maclean
37 Colliers Road
Hastings TN34 3JR

Hastings Flyfishers' Club Ltd
D E Tack
23 Wealden Way
Little Common
Nr Bexhill-on-Sea
E. Sussex TN39 4NZ

Hawes and High Abbotside Angling Association
G Phillips
Holmlands, Appersett
Hawes, North Yorks
DL8 3LN

Hawkshead Angling Club
J L Locke
Flat 1 The Croft
Hawkshead, Ambleside
Cumbria LA22 0NX
Limited to 100 members

Hay-on-Wye Fishermans' Association
B Wigington
Flat 2, Pembertons,
4 High Town
Hay-on-Wye
Herefords HR3 5AE

Haywards Heath and District Angling Society
J Kenward
60 Franklyn Road
Haywards Heath
RH16 4DH

Hazeldine Anglers Association
J W Hazeldine
8 Dudley Road
Sedgley
Dudley, Staffs DY3 1SX

Helperby and Brafferton Angling Club
F Marrison
Gardeners Cottage
York Road
Helperby, York
North Yorkshire
YO6 2PJ

Herne Bay Angling Association
Honorary Secretary
c/o HQ, 59 Central Parade
Herne Bay, Kent

Heron Angling Society (Herne Bay)
Red Shelter
Spa Esplanade
Herne Bay, Kent

Histon and District Angling Club
Colin Dodd
122 Rampton Road
Willingham, Cambs
CB4 5JF

Holmesdale Angling Society
Mrs E M Divall
Windmill Farm, Chevening Road
Chipstead
Sevenoaks, Kent
TN13 2SA

Holme Valley Piscatorial Association
P Budd
39 Derwent Road
Honley, Huddersfield
Yorkshire HD7 2EL
Membership secretary:
I R McCullie
199 Bourne View Road
Netherton
Huddersfield HD4 7JS

Horizon Angling Club
P Bradbury
The Bungalow
12A Petworth Road
Milton, Portsmouth
PO3 6DH
Angling opportunities for registered disabled.

Horncastle Angling Association
G Alder
The Cottage
Sandy Lane
Woodhall Spa
Lincs LN10 6UR

Horsham and District Angling Association
PO Box 22
Horsham
West Sussex RH12 5LN

Hull and District Angling Association
P O Box 188
Hull HU9 1AN

Huntingdon Angling and Fish Preservation Society
Mrs A Wallis
8 Clayton's Way

Huntingdon
Cambridgeshire
PE18 7UT

Huttons Ambo Angling Club
Paul Thompson
Firby Hall
Firby, Yorks
YO6 7LH

Idle and Thackley Angling Association
Charles Taylor Hardaker
24 Park Avenue
Thackley
Bradford
West Yorkshire
BD2 4LP

Isle of Man Fly Fishing Association
Ray Caley
Caley's Stores
Sulby
Isle of Man

Isle of Wight Freshwater Angling Association
Ian de Gruchy
66 Merrie Gardens
Lake, Sandown
Isle of Wight

Jersey Rodbenders Sea Angling Club
E Read
3 Clos Des Pas
Green Street
St Helier
Jersey

Jersey Sea Fishing Club
T Jones
9 Valley Close
St Saviour, Jersey

Keighley Angling Club
Dennis Freeman
62 Eelholme View Street
Beechcliffe
Keighley
West Yorks
BD20 6AY

Kelvedon Angling Association
B Pike
11 Keene Way
Galleywood
CM2 8NT

Kempston Angling Club
K Green
24 The Elms
Kempston, Beds MK42 7JW

Keswick Angling Association
J D Thompson
15 Low Mill
Greta Side
Keswick, Cumbria
GA12 5LL

Kettering and Thrapston Angling Association
L R Garret
10 Naseby Road
Kettering
Northants

Keynsham Angling Association
K N Jerrom
21 St Georges Road
Keynsham
Bristol
Avon BS18 2HU
Chew, Avon. Tickets

Kidderminster and District Angling Association
M Millinchip
246 Marpol Lane,
Kidderminster
Worcestershire
DY11 5DD

Kings Arms and Cheshunt Angling Society
Roger Glindon
P.O. Box 13
Waltham Cross
Herts EN7 5QT

King's Lynn Angling Association
M R Grief
67 Peckover Way
South Woonton
King's Lynn
Norfolk PE30 3UE

Kirkby Fleetham Angling Club
M L Smith
26 Eden Grove
Newton Aycliffe
Co Durham DL5 7JG

Kirkby Lonsdale and District Angling Association
D E Halton
Briglands
Wennington Road
Wray
Lancashire LA2 8QH

Kirkham and District Fly Fishers' Club
D Wardman
65 Longhouse Lane
Poulton-le-Fylde
Lancashire FY6 8DE

Knaresborough Piscatorials
P Davies
26 Kendal Road
Harrogate HG1 4SH
Membership Secretary
M Johnson
2 Briggate
Knaresborough

Lancashire Fly Fishing Association
J Winnard
Manor House, Grunsagill
Torside, Skipton
Yorks

Langport and District Angling Association
c/o The Tackle Shop
Old Market Square
North Street
Langport
Somerset TA10 9RP

Lancashire Fly-Fishing Association
J Winnard
Manor House, Grunsagill
Tosside, Skipton
N Yorks

Lanhydrock Angling Association
B Muelaner
The National Trust Estate Office
Lanhydrock Park
Bodmin
Cornwall PL30 4DE

Lark Angling Preservation Society
E T West
8 Arrowhead Drive
Lakenheath, Suffolk IP27 9JN

Lee Anglers' Consortium
T Mansbridge
7 Warren Road
Chingford
London E4 6QR

Leeds and District Amalgamated Anglers Association
Derek Taylor
75 Stoney Rock Lane
Beckett Street
Leeds
West Yorkshire
LS29 7TB

Leek and Moorlands Angling Club
Roy Birch-Machin
53 Novi Lane
Leek, Staffs
ST13 6NX

Leicester District Angling Society
c/o Justin Mould
tel; 01780 782789

Leigh and District Angling Association
C Hibbs
417 Nabchester Road
Lewigh
Lancashire
WN7 2ND

Leighton Buzzard Angling Society
H Holliday
54 Pebble Moor
Eddlesborough
Leighton Buzzard
Beds LU7 8EF

Letchworth and District Angling Association
P N Jones
79 Howard Drive
Letchworth
Herts S96 2BO

Lewisham Piscatorials Association
D J Head
75 Riverview Park
Catford
London SE6 4PL

Lincoln and District Angling Association
Colin W Parker
4 Pottergate Close
Waddington
Lincoln LN5 9LY

Liskeard and District Angling Club
W E Eliot
64 Portbyhan Road
West Looe, Cornwall
PL13 2QN

Littleport Angling Club
David Yardy
168 High Barns
Ely, Cambs

Liverpool and District Angling Association
James Browne
33 Eleanor Road
Bootle
Liverpool
Merseyside
L20 6BP

Llandrindod Wells Angling Association
B D Price
The Cedars
Llanyre
Llandrindod Wells
Powys LD1 6DY

London Anglers' Association
A E Hedges
Isaak Walton House
2A Hervey Park Road
Walthamstow,
London E17 6LJ
(LAA offices)

Long Buckby Angling Club
M Hill
33 South Close
Long Buckby
Northants NN6 7PX

Long Eaton and District Angling Federation
E Ainsworth
37 Dovecote Lane
Beaston
Notts NG9 1HR

Long Eaton Victoria Angling Society
D L Kent
2 Edge Hill Court
Fields Farm
Long Eaton
Notts, NG10 1PQ

Looe and District Sea Angling Association
c/o Cotton's Tackle Shop
The Quay, E Looe, Cornwall
PL13 1AQ

Lostwithiel Fishing Association
J H Hooper
4 Reeds Park
Lostwithiel, Cornwall
PL22 0HF

Luton and District Angling Club
Mrs B A Bunnage
33 Kingsdown Avenue
Luton
Beds LU25 7BU

Lymm Angling Club
Neil Jupp
P O Box 350
Warrington WA2 9FB

Macclesfield Flyfishers' Club
W F Williams
1 Westwood Drive
Brooklands, Sale
Cheshire M33 3QW

Macclesfield Waltonian Angling Society
Michael E Bowyer
7 Ullswater
Macclesfield
Cheshire SK11 7YN

Maidstone Victory Angling and Medway Preservation Society
J Perkins
33 Hackney Road
Maidstone
Kent ME16 8LN

Maldon Angling Society
T Lazell
14 Barn View Road
Coggeshall
Essex CO6 1RF

Malton and Norton Angling Club
M Foggins
123 Wellram Road
Norton, Malton
Yorks

Manchester and District Angling Association
c/o 1 Chapel Lane
Horton in Ribblesdale
N Yorks

Mansfield and District Angling Association
A Quick
158 Huthwaite Road
Sutton-in-Ashfield
Nottinghamshire NG17 2GX

Manx Game Fishing Club
P O Box 95
2A Lord Street
Douglas, Isle of Man

Marazion Angling Club
Tickets from
County Angler
39 Cross Street
Camborne
Cornwall TR14 8ES

Market Harborough and District Society of Anglers
N Bale
27 Rainsborough Gardens
Market Harborough
Leicestershire
LE16 9LN

Marsden Star Angling Society
Jeff Hartley
3 Duerden Street
Nelson
Lancs BB9 9BJ

Martham and District Angling Club
Ian Bradford
15 Repps road
Martham
Norfolk NR29 4TJ

Melksham and District Angling Association
D Branton
16 Ingram Road
Melksham

Mevagissey Sea Angling Club
The Ship Inn
Pentowan
Cornwall

Middlesbrough Angling Club
R Thompson
25 Endsleigh Drive
Acklam, Middlesbrough
Cleveland TS5 4RG

Middlewich Joint Anglers
C Bratt
13 Elm Road
Middlewich, Cheshire
CW10 0AX

Mildenhall Angling Club
M Hampshire
63 Downing Close
Mildenhall, Suffolk
IP28 7PB

Millom and District Angling Association
D Dixon
1 Churchill Drive
Millom, Cumbria
LA18 5DD

Milton Keynes Angling Association
c/o 52 Jenkinson Road
Towcester
NN12 7AW
Montgomeryshire Angling Association
P Hulme
306 Heol-y-Coleg
Vaynor Estate, Newtown
Powys SY16 1RA
Moor Hall and Belhus Angling Society
M Tilbrook
46 Mill Road
Aveley, South Ockendon
Essex RM15 4SL
Nelson Angling Association
H Hargreaves
171 Reedley Road
Briarfield
Nelson, Lancs
Nene and Welland Angling Consultative Association
G Bibby
5 Ermine Way
Sawtry
Cambs
Newark and District Piscatorial Federation
J N Garland
58 Riverside Road
Newark, Notts NG24 4RJ
Newport Pagnell Angling Association
R Dorrill
7 Bury Road
Newport Pagnell
Milton Keynes MK16 0DS
Newton Abbot Fishing Association
David Horder
Mistlemead, Woodlands
Higher Sandygate
Newton Abbot
Devon TQ12 3QN
Nidderdale Angling Club
T Harpham
P O Box 7
Pateley Bridge, nr Harrogate
North Yorks, HG3 5XB
Norfolk and Suffolk Flyfishers Club
E A Fenn
White Horse House
White Horse Common
North Walsham, Norfolk
Northampton Britannia Angling Club
G H Richmond
34 Ilex Close
Hardingstone
Northampton NN4 6SD
Northampton Nene Angling Club
Mrs P Walsh
363 Kettering Road
Northampton NN3 6QT
Northern Anglers' Association
A G R Brown
10 Dale Road
Golborne
Warrington WA3 3PN
North Oxford Angling Society
L Ballard
70 Blackbird Leys Road
Cowley
Oxford 0X4 5HR
North Somerset Association of Anglers (Embracing Highbridge and Clevedon clubs)
R Newton
64 Clevedon Road
Tickenham
Cleveden,
Somerset BS21 6RD
Northumbrian Anglers' Federation
P A Hall
3A Ridley Place
Newcastle upon Tyne
Northumberland NE1 8LF
Northwich Anglers Association
J Clithero
High Acres
Hartford Bridge, Hartford
Northwich
Cheshire CW8 1PP
Northwich, Cheshire
Norwich Anglers Association
C Wigg
3 Coppice Avenue
Norwich NR6 5RB
Nottingham Anglers' Association
I Foulds
95 Ilkeston Road
Nottingham
Nottingham and District Federation of Angling Societies
W Belshaw
17 Spring Green
Clifton Estate, Nottingham
Nottingham Piscatorial Society
P F Olko
63 Forest Road
Annesley Woodhouse
Nottingham NG17 9HA
Offord and Buckden Angling Society
John Astell
154 Eastrea Road
Whittlesey
Cambs
PE7 2AJ
Old Glossop Angling Club
R North
1 Morpeth Close
Ashton-under-Lyne

Lancs OL7 9SH
Old Windsor Angling Club
A Beaven
88 St Andrews Way
Slough, Berks SL1 5LJ
Orpington and District Angling Club
PO Box 682
Bexley
Kent DA5 3YA
Oswestry Angling Club
L Allen
30 Brookfields
Weston Rhyn
Oswestry
Shropshire
Oundle Angling Association
D Laxton
31 St Peters Street
Oundle
Peterborough
Ouse Angling Preservation Society
Permit secretary
Keith Potter
3 Orchard mews
Heighton Road
Denton, Newhaven
W Sussex BN9 0RB
Over and Swaverley District Anglers Society
D Cook
75 Willingham Road
Over
Cambs CB4 5PE
Oxford and District Anglers Association
Secretary
D H Witham
15 Broad Close
Botley, Oxford OX2 9DR
Padstow Sea Angling Club
Social Club
Padstow
Cornwall
Paignton Sea Anglers' Association
26 Cliff Rd
The Harbour
Paignton, Devon
Parkside Fishing Club
D Fallows
27 Woodstock Avenue
Radford
Nottingham NG7 5QP
Peak Forest Angling Club (Derbyshire)
Colin Jones
Greenwood
Edale Road
Hope Valley
Derbys S33 6ZF
Penrith Angling Association
Mrs P Studholme
39 Brougham Street
Penrith, Cumbria CA11 8DH
Peterborough Angling Club
R Warr
24 Whitmore Court
Whittesley
Cambs
Petersfield and District Angling Club
Ash Girdler
3 Chase Plain Cottages
Portsmouth Road
Hindhead, Surrey
GU26 6BZ
Petworth Angling Club
R Haenaire
25 Station Road
Petworth
GU28 0EX
Phoenix Angling Club
J A Mobley
155 Greenhill Road
Halesowen
West Midlands B62 8EZ
Plowden Fishing Club
S J Finnegan
The Old School
Brimfield
Salop SY8 4NZ
Plymouth and District Freshwater Angling Association
D L Owen
39 Burnett Road
Crownhill
Plymouth PL6 5BH
City of Plymouth Sea Angling Club
c/o Osborne and Cragg Fishing Tackle
37 Bretonside
Plymouth
Devon PL4 0BB
Portsmouth and District Angling Society
R Snook
86 Caernarvon Road
Copnor
Portsmouth PO2 7NL
Portsmouth Services Fly Fishing Association
Captain F Hefford OBE, DSC, AFC, RN (Retired)
20 Stoatley Rise
Haslemere,
Surrey GU27 1AF
Pride of Derby Angling Association
A Miller
16 Mercia Drive
Willington, Derby
DE65 6DA
Prince Albert Angling Society
J A Turner
15 Pexhill Drive

Carp specialist, John Aplin, with a 40lb 6oz. common carp.

Macclesfield
or
Queens Hotel
Waters Green
Macclesfield

Ramsey Angling Club (Cambs)
P E Aldred
9 Blackmill Street
Chatteris
Cambs PE16 6SR

Ramsey Angling Club (I.O.M.)
Chris Culshaw
see Isle of Man Angling Federation

Reading and District Angling Association
W Brown Lee
47 Calbourne Drive
The Orchard, Calcot
Reading RG3 7DB

Red Spinner Angling Society
K Stabler
9 Marlborough Road
London N9 9PT

Retford and District Angling Association
H Wells
31 Ainsdale Green
Ordsall, Retford
Nottinghamshire DN22 7NQ

Rhayader Angling Association
Alan Lewis
Crown Inn
Rhayader, Powys
LD6 5BT

Ribble and Wyre Fisheries Association
S A Gray
10 Lord Street, Wigan
Lancs WN1 2BN

Richmond (Yorks) and District Angling Society
P Bennett
Tel: 01748 824894.

Ripon Angling Club
Roger Trees
43 College Road
Ripon
N Yorks HG4 2HE

Ripon Fly Fishers
C Clarke
9 Moorside Avenue
Ripon
N Yorks HG4 1TA

Ripon Piscatorial Association
S Looney
Cornerstones
2 Hellwath Grove
Redwell Heath
HG4 2JT

Rochdale Walton Angling Society
R Pealin
723 Whitworth Road
Rochdale

Rochford Angling Club
L Dorey
231 Kents Hill Road
Benfleet
Essex SS7 5PF

Ross-on-Wye Angling Club
T Gibson
10 Redwood Close
Ross-on-Wye
Herefordshire

Rother Angling Club
C Boxall
Innisfree
Ashfield Road
Midhurst
West Sussex GU29 9JX

Rother Fishery Association
Steve Crowley
9 Haydens Close
Orpington, Kent
BR5 4JE

Royal Leamington Spa Angling Association
E G Archer
9 Southway
Leamington Spa,
Warwickshire CV31 2PG

Royston and District Angling Club
P R Harrow
46 Greengage Rise
Melbourne
Herts SG8 6DS

Rudgwick Angling Society
C Wood
16 Waldy Rise
Cranleigh
Surrey GU6 7DF

Rushden and Higham Ferrers Angling Association
D Parkin
31 Mountfield Road
Irthlingborough
Northants

Saddleworth and District Angling Society
John Cox
3 Rhodes Avenue
Uppermill
Saddleworth
Oldham OL3 6ED

St Helens Angling Association
Leslie Bromilow
4 Bassenthwaite Avenue
Moss Bank
St Helens
Merseyside
WA11 7AB

St Ives and District Fish Preservation and Angling Society
H Pace
48 Fairfields
St Ives, Cambs
PE17 4QF

St Leonards Sea Anglers
HQ, 16 Grand Parade
St Leonards, Sussex

St Mawgan Angling Club
T J Trevenna
Lanvean House
St Mawgan, Newquay
Cornwall TR8 4EY

St Neots and District Angling and Fish Preservation Society
Mrs D Linger
Skewbridge Cottage
Great Paxton
Huntingdon
Cambs PE19 4RA

Salcombe and District Sea Anglers' Association
Headquarters
Victoria Inn
Fore Street
Salcombe, Devon TQ8 8BT

Saltaire Angling Association
Alan D'Arcy
68 Grosvenor Road
Tarporley
Cheshire
CW6 9UW

Sawbridgeworth Angling Society
Miss D Barnes
10 The Crescent
Old Harlow
Essex CM17 0HN

Saxmundham Angling Club
A Firman
46 Barhams Way
Wickham Market
Woodbridge
Suffolk IP13 0SR

Scunthorpe and District Angling
M Storey
74 Appleby Lane
Brougham, Brigg
South Humberside
Association

Sedbergh and District Angling Association
G Bainbridge
El Kantara, Frostrow
Sedbergh
Cumbria LA10 5JL

Selsey Angling and Tope Club
Mike Bell
166 Littlefield Close
Selsey
west Sussex

Services Dry Fly Fishing Association (Salisbury Plain)
Major (Retd) C D Taylor
c/o G2 Regional Headquarters
3rd (United Kingdom) Division
Picton Barracks
Bulford Camp
Salisbury SP4 9NY

Seven Angling Club
Mrs B J Stansfield
Sun Seven
Sinnington, Yorkshire
YO6 6RZ

Seven Stars Angling Club
The Seven Stars
Birchfield Road
Headless Cross, Redditch
Worcs

Severnside Angling Club
H Rodway
Fairview
Bryn Gardens
Newtown, Powys
SY16 1NP

Sheffield Amalgamated Anglers' Society
A D Baynes
HQ Lord Nelson
166/8 Arundel Street
Sheffield

Sheffield and District Anglers' Association
142/4 Princess Street
Sheffield S4 7UW
or
G Woods
I Everingham Road
Longley
Sheffield S5 7LA

Sheffield Piscatorial Society
Mr Anderson
Farm House
Retford
Notts

Shefford and District Angling Association
J Leath
3 Ivel Close
Shefford
Beds SG17 5JX

Shropshire Anglers Federation
Ian Moorhouse
22 Pendle Way
Shrewsbury
Salop SY3 9QN

Slaithwaite and District Angling Club
D Rushforth
122 Longwood Gate

Longwood
Huddersfield
HD3 4US
or
S K Makin
1 Weldon Drive
Outlane
Huddersfield
HD3 3FZ

Southern Anglers
B D Smith
3 Cheriton Close
Havant, Hants
PO9 4PU
or
T Irons
7 Nelson Crescent
Horndean, Portsmouth PO8 9LZ

Stalybridge (Fox) Angling Society
I S Warton
17 Coneymead
Stalybridge
Cheshire SK15 2LJ

Stamford Welland Amalgamated Anglers Association
G E Bates
16a Austin Street
Stamford, Lincs PE9 2QP

Stanhope Angling Association
J J Lee
1 Eastcroft, Stanhope
Co Durham

Stockport and District Anglers Federation
H Ollerenshaw
133 Manchester Road
Hyde
Cheshire SK14 2BK

Stoke City and District Anglers Association
P Johansen
31 East Crescent, Sneyd Green
Stoke-on-Trent ST1 6ES

Stoke on Trent Angling Society
A Perkins
Muirhearlich
Fowlers Lane
Light Oaks
Stoke on Trent
ST2 7NB

Stratford-upon-Avon Angling Association
A Bruce
Lower Lodge Farm
Bishopton Lane
Stratford-upon-Avon
Warwickshire
CV37 0RJ

Sturminster and Hinton Angling Association
S Dimmer
38 Grosvenor Rd
Stalbridge
Sturminster Newton
Dorset DT10 2PN

Sudbury and District Angling Society
T R Fairless
39 Pot Kiln Road
Gt Cornard
Sudbury, Suffolk
CO10 0DG

Sunmead Angling Society
P Tanner
24 Ryebrook Road
Leatherhead
Surrey KT22 7QG

Swan Angling Club
J Stanhope
4 High Road
Lane Head
Willenhall, West Midlands
WV12 4JQ

Swanage and District Angling Club
Peveril Slipway
Swanage, Dorset

Taunton Angling Association
M Hewitson
56 Parkfield Road
Taunton, Somerset
Tone, Taunton Canal, Drains

Taunton Fly-Fishing Club
J Greene
2 Old Vicarage
Bradford on Tone
Taunton TA4 1HG

Tavy, Walkham and Plym Fishing Club
Ian H Parker
Oakhaven
36 Upland Drive
Derriford, Plymouth
Devon PL6 6BD

Taw Fishing Club
J D V Michie
Wheel Barton
Broadwoodkelly
Winkleigh, Devon
EX19 8ED

Teignmouth Sea Angling Society
Mrs L Hexter
1 Headway Rise
Teignmouth
Devon TQ14 9UL
or
D Lawer
19 Inverteign Drive
Teignmouth
Devon

Tenbury Fishing Association
Mrs L M Rickett
The Post House
Berrington Road
Tenbury Wells, Worcestershire
WR15 8EN

Test and Itchen Association Ltd
Jim Glasspool
West Haye, Itchen Abbas
Winchester SO21 1AX

Tewkesbury Popular Angling Association
Terry Smith
25 Milne Pastures
Ashchurch
Tewkesbury
Gloucestershire
GL20 8SG

Thetford and Breckland Angling Club
S J Armes
Kings Croft
Shropham Road
Great Hockham
Thetford
Norfolk IP24 1NJ

Tisbury Angling Club
Match Secretary:
B Ricketts
26 St Martins Close
Barford St Martin
Salisbury
Wilts SP3 4AX
Treasurer:
E J Stevens
Knapp Cottage
Fovant
Salisbury SP3 5JW

Tiverton and District Angling Club
R Retallick
21 Alstone Road
Canal Hill, Tiverton
Devon EX16 4LH

Todmorden Angling Society
R Barber
12 Grisedale Drive
Burnley, Lancs
BB12 8AR

Torbay And Babbacombe Association of Sea Anglers
Mrs C Wilden
100 St Marychurch Road
Torquay
Devon TQ1 3HL

Towcester and District Angling Club
Mr Pannet
30 Bickerstaff Road
Towcester, Northants

Trent and District Anglers Consultative Association
N Walsh
5 Derby Road
Homesford
Matlock

The Tring Anglers
P Welling
PO Box 1947
Tring, Herts HP23 5IZ

Ulverston Angling Association
J A Baldwin
24 Springfield Park Road
Ulverston, Cumbria
LA12 0EQ

Unity Angling Club
E K Mann
19 Busfield Street
Bradford, Yorks BD4 7QX

Upper Teign Fishing Association
J Getliff
22 The Square
Chagford, Devon
TQ13 8AB

Upper Tanat Fishing Club
R R Hall
Melyniog
Llansantffraid
Powys SY22 6AX

Upper Thames Fisheries Consultative Association
R Knowles
360 Banbury Road
Oxford OX2 7PP

Upper Weardale Angling Association
H C Lee
7 Westfall
Wearhead, Bishop Auckland
Co Durham DL13 1BP

Uttoxeter Angling Association
I E Davies
Three Oaks
Hollington Lane
Stramshall
Uttoxeter, Staffordshire
ST14 5AJ

Vauxhall Angling Club
R W Poulton

Fishing Clubs

When you appoint a new Hon. Secretary, do not forget to give us details of the change. Write to the Publishers (address in the front of the book). Thank you!

20 Leeches Way
Cheddington
Beds LU7 0SJ

Victoria Angling Club
John Rowley
98 Franklin Road
Penkhull
Stoke on trent
Staffordshire
ST4 5DS

Victoria and Biddulph Angling Society
Philip R Moston
4 Stile Close
Brown Lees, Biddulph
Stoke on Trent
Staffordshire
ST8 6NL

Wadebridge Angling Association
A Gill
Jasmine Cottage
Kelly Park
St Mabyn
Bodmin, Cornwall, PL30 3BL

Walkham, Tavy and Plym Fishing Club
I H Parker
36 Upland Drive
Derriford
Plymouth PL6 6BD

Wansford, Yarwell, Nassington and District Angling Club
S Longfoot
2 Dovecote Close
Yarwell, Peterborough
PE8 6PE

Warmington Angling Club
R Bosworth
2 Buntings Lane
Warmington
Peterborough
PE8 6TT

Warrington Anglers' Association
F Lythgoe
Smithy Cottage
Preston Brook
Warrington
Cheshire WA7 3AQ
Lancashire

Waterbeach Angling Club
H Reynolds
3 Crosskeys Court
Cottenham
Cambs BB4 4UW

Wath Brow and Ennerdale Angling Association
D F Whelan
11 Crossing Close
Cleator Moor, Cumberland

Watford Piscators
J A Dickinson
51 Gallows Hill
Kings Langley
Herts WD4 8LX

Wellingborough and District Nene Angling Club
R Blenkharn
66 Redland Drive
Kingsthorpe
Northampton NN10 8TU

Wellington Angling Association
M Cave
60 Sylvan Road
Wellington
Somerset TA21 8EH

Wensleydale Angling Association
Mrs P A Thorpe
Grange Farm
High Birstwith
Harrogate HG3 2ST

Wessex Fèderation of Angling Clubs
J J Mathrick
Perham Farmhouse
Wick, Langport
Somerset TA10 0NN

West Bay Sea Angling Club
A Neal
116 Gerrards Green
Beaminster
Dorset

Weston-super-Mare and District Angling Association
K Tucker
26 Coniston Crescent
Weston-super-Mare
Somerset BS23 3RX

Westwater Angling
3 Crossways
East Boldon
Tyne & Wear NE36 0LP

Weybridge Angling Club
Mrs M Colclough
137 Oatlands Drive
Oatlands Village
Weybridge, Surrey
KT13 9LB

Wey Navigation Angling Amalgamation
Secretary
c/o Village Hall
Byfleet
Surrey

Weymouth Angling Society
S Atkinson
Angling Centre
Commercial Road
Weymouth, Dorset

White Eagle Anglers
R A M Skelton

339B Stone Road
Stafford
Staffs ST16 1LB

White Swan Angling Club
N Barratt
Three Trees
Newark Road
Torksey, Lock
Lincoln LN1 2EJ

Whittlesey Angling Association
P Frost
80 Mayfield Road
Eastrea
Whittlesey
Cambs

Wigan and District Angling Association
G Wilson
11 Guildford Avenue
Chorley
Lancs PR6 8TG

Wimbleball Fly Fishers Club
A D Ridgeway
13 Glen Drive
Taunton, Somerset
TA2 7RG

Wimborne and District Angling Club
G E Pipet
12 Seatown Close
Canford Heath
Poole
Dorset BH17 8BJ

Windermere, Ambleside and District Angling Association
Hon Secretary
J R Newton
Brackenthwaithe House
Black Beck Wood
Storrs Park
Windermere
Cumbria LA23 3LF
Hon Treasurer
C J Sodo
Ecclerigg Court
Ecclerigg
Windermere
Cumbria LA23 1LQ

Winsford and District Angling Association
J Stewart Bailey
22 Plover Avenue
Winsford CW7 1LA

Association of Wirral Angling Clubs
Chairman
D Billing
2 Patterdale Road
Bebington
Wirral
Secretary
S Ross
17 Greenville Road
Bebington
Wirral

Wisbech and District Angling Association
B Lakey
28 Hill Street, Wisbech
Cambridgeshire

Witby Sea Anglers Association
D Johnson
14 Runswick Avenue
Whitby YO21 3UB

Witham and District Joint Anglers Federation
Stewart Oxborough
6 Ormsby Close
Cleethorpes
South Humberside
DN35 9PE

Woodbridge and District Angling Club
D N Abbott
17 Prospect Place
Leiston, Suffolk

Worksop and District Anglers Association
D Brown
4 Dove Close
Worksop
Notts S81 7LG

Wroxham and District Anglers Association
R Westgate
31 The Paddocks
Old Catton
Norwich
Norfolk NR6 7HF

Yarm Angling Association
c/o 4 Blenavon Court
Yarm
Co Durham

York and District Angling Association
John Lane
39 Lowfields Drive
Acomb
York YO2 3DQ

WELSH FISHING STATIONS

In the pages that follow, the catchment areas of Wales, are given in alphabetical order, being interspersed with the streams and the lakes under headings such as 'Powys (streams)'; 'Gwynedd (lakes)', etc. The rivers of each catchment area are arranged in the manner described under the heading 'English Fishing Stations', on p.21 and the other notes given there apply equally to Wales. The whole of the Wye and the Severn, it should be remembered, are included in the section on England, while the whole of the Dee is listed among the Welsh rivers.

Note: *Sea trout are commonly referred to as 'sewin' in Wales although some associations define sewin as immature sea trout returning to the river for the first time.*

AERON

(For close seasons, licences, etc, see Welsh Region Environment Agency, p20)

Rises in Llyn Eiddwen, 7m north-west of Tregaron, and flows about 17m to sea at Aberaeron. Excellent run of sewin from June onwards with smaller salmon run. Brown trout plentiful but small.

Aberaeron (Dyfed). Salmon, sea trout and brown trout. Aberaeron Town AC has a 2½m stretch on R Aeron; 3m on **Arth**, a stream to the north, which holds fine brown trout and has an excellent run of sea trout; and 3 stretches on **Teifi**, north of Lampeter. Permits from Ceilee Sports, Bridge St. Tackle shop: F K Moulton & Son, Aeron Sports & Fishing Tackle, Bridge St, Aberaeron, tel: 01545 571209.

ANGLESEY (streams)

(For close seasons, licences, etc, see Welsh Region Environment Agency, p20)

ALAW. Llanfachraeth (Anglesey). Rises above Cors y Bol bog and flows some 7m to sea beyond Llanfachraeth, opposite Holyhead. Fishes well (trout) for first three months of season and again in September when good run of small sea trout expected; usually too low in summer. Permission of farmers.

BRAINT. Llangeinwen (Anglesey). Small stream which flows almost whole width of the island, parallel with Menai Straits, to sea at Aber Menai, beyond Llangeinwen. Trout, some sea trout, but usually fishable only first three months of season. Permission of farmers.

CEFNI. Llangefni (Anglesey). Rises above Llangwyllog, flows through Llyn Frogwy, on to Llangefni and Cefni Reservoir, and then to sea in 6m. Lower reaches canalised. Only fair-sized river in island. Brown trout and chance of late salmon or sea trout. Permission of farmers.

CEINT. Pentraeth (Anglesey). Small stream entering sea at Red Wharf Bay; some trout; permission of farmers; summer conditions difficult.

FFRAW or GWNA. Bodorgan (Anglesey). Under the name of Gwna rises 4m above Bodorgan and waters Llyn Coron just below village. Stream then takes name of Ffraw and runs to sea at Aberffraw in 2m. Little more than brook. One or two pools fishable early on, but overgrown June onwards. Trout, some sea trout.

WYGYR. Cemaes (Anglesey). Small stream falling into sea at Cemaes Bay. Trout; restocked. Wygyr FA has about 2m (both banks); permits from Treasurer. Good sea fishing in bay. Hotel: Harbour, Cemaes Bay; Cefn Glas Inn, Llanfechell.

ANGLESEY (lakes)

Bodafon Lake. Llanallgo (Anglesey). Rudd and tench; contact Trescawen Estate, Anglesey, Gwynedd.

Cefni Reservoir. Llangefni (Anglesey). 172 acres. Brown and rainbow trout; fly only; good wading; boats. Leased by Welsh Water plc to Cefni AA. Permits from D G Evans (Treasurer), Wenllys, Capel Coch, Llangefni; dt and wt from Ken Johnson, Tackle and Guns, Devon House, Water St, Menai Bridge and Peter Rowe, Jewellers, Llangefni. Hotels: Nant yr Odyn Country; Tre Ysgawen Hall.

Cwn Reservoir. Holyhead (Anglesey).

Coarse fishing on 2 acre reservoir; carp, rudd, bream, roach and tench; open all year round. Dt from Tackle Bar Shop, William St, Holyhead.

Llyn Alaw. Llantrisant (Anglesey). Situated in open lowland countryside this productive 777 acre reservoir offers fly fishing, spinning and worming, for brown and rainbow trout. Season 20 Mar - 17 Oct for brown. 20 Mar - 31 Oct for rainbow. Dt £10, evening £8, st £320, from Visitor Centre at reservoir (dt and evening from machine in car park). Concessions to OAPs, juniors and disabled. Boats (rowing or with engine) for hire. Boat for disabled at no extra charge. Worms, flies, line, weights, spinners and a wide variety of other tackle for sale at Visitor Centre. Further information from Llyn Alaw Visitor Centre, Llantrisant, Holyhead, Anglesey, Gwynedd LL65 4TW, tel: 01407 730762. Accommodation: caravans and camping, and bed and breakfast at Bodnolwyn Wen Farm, Llantrisant, Holyhead, Anglesey LL65 4TW, tel: 01407 730298; and caravans and camping, plus meals, at The Ring (Public House), Rhosgoch, Anglesey LL66 0AB, tel: 01407 830720.

Llyn Bryntirion. Dwyran (Anglesey). Carp and perch fishing on 3 ponds (3 acres of water); season Mar-Oct; no barbed hooks or keepnets; only one rod per angler. Dt from J Naylor, Bryntirion Working Farm, Dwyran, Anglesey LL61 6BY, tel: 01248 430232.

Llyn Coron. Bodorgan (Anglesey). Trout, sea trout; fly only. St £90, wt £30, dt £6 and evening tickets £5. St and rod licences from Bodorgan Estate Office, Gwynedd LL62 5LP; other tickets at lake.

Llyn Dewi. Llandeusant (Anglesey). Coarse fishing on 1 acre lake; carp, roach and rudd; open all year. Dt from Mr & Mrs Hughes Fferam Uchaf Farm, Llandeusant, Anglesey, tel: 01407 730425.

Llyn Jane. Llandegfan (Anglesey). Trout fishing on 4 small, man-made lakes including pool for juniors. Contact Dewi & Linda Owen, Llyn Jane, Llandegfan.

Llyn Llwydiarth Fawr. Llanerchymedd (Anglesey). Coarse and game fishing on 1½ acre lake; rudd and brown trout. Fishing is only available for guests at Llwydiarth Fawr (guest house); contact R & M L Hughes, Llwydiarth Fawr, Llanerchymedd, Anglesey LL71 8DF, tel: 01248 470321.

Llyn Maelog. Rhosneigr (Anglesey). Roach, perch, rudd, bream, eels. Permission to fish from various landowners. Information, licences and tackle (not bait) from K D Highfield, 7 Marine Terrace, Rhosneigr. Hotels: Maelog Lake, Cefn Dref, and Glan Neigr.

Llyn y Gors. Llandegfan (Anglesey). 5 acres coarse fishery, two lakes. Mixed lake with carp, tench, roach, rudd and perch ; and carp lake with carp to 25lb. Permits, tackle and bait on site. Self-catering cottages. Further information from Llyn y Gors, Llandegfan, Menai Bridge, Anglesey, LL59 5PN, tel: 01248 713410, fax: 01248 716324.

Llywenan Lake. Bodedern (Anglesey). Brown trout. Apply to H T Radcliffe, Bryn Adfed, Bodedern.

Parc Newydd Trout Fishery. Llanerchymedd (Anglesey). Llyn Edna is 5 acre, man-made lake; stocked with brown and rainbow trout. Accommodation in self-catering cottages. For further information contact Andrew Gannon, Parc Newydd, Nr Llanerchymedd LL71 7BT, tel: 01248 470700.

Plas-y-Nant Trout Fishery. Mynydd Mechell (Anglesey). Fishing on 2½ acre lake; American brook, rainbow and brown trout; fly only, max fly size 10 and no boobys are allowed. Fishing hut and 4-5 berth caravans for hire. Also tuition and tackle hire. Permits from Plas-y-Nant Fishery, Mynydd Mechell, Amlwch, Anglesey LL68 0TH.

Ty Hen Lake. Rhosneigr (Anglesey). 1½ acres of natural spring water (Ph 7.8, nitrate 0.01) for specimen carp, tench, roach and rudd. Dt £5 at lake. All fish to be returned to water. Cottage and caravan self-catering family holidays with fishing. Further information from Mr Bernard Summerfield, Ty Hen Farm, Station Road, Rhosneigr, Anglesey LL64 5QZ, tel: 01407 810331 or mobile: 0831 535583. Tackle shop: Tackle Bar, 23 Williams St, Holyhead, Anglesey LL65 1RN. Hotel: Maelog.

Tyddyn Sargent. Benllech (Anglesey). Coarse fishing on 1½ acre lake; common carp, ghost carp, crucian carp, roach, rudd, tench and bream; barbless hooks only. Fishing by appointment only; contact K Twist, Tyddyn Sargent, Tynygongl, Nr Benllech, Anglesey, tel: 01248 853024.

CLEDDAU (Eastern and Western)

(For close seasons, licences, etc, see Welsh Region Environment Agency, p20)

East Cleddau rises on the east side of Prescelly Mountains and flows 15m south-west, partly along old Carmarthenshire border, to north branch of Milford Haven. West Cleddau rises in the hills and valleys south-west of Mathry and flows east towards Castle Morris. It is joined by streams such as the Afon Cleddau and Nant-y-Bugail and then flows south-east to Wolf's Castle. Here it is joined by the Afon Anghof and Afon Glan Rhyd. It then flows south to Haverfordwest and on to join the E Cleddau in a creek in the Haven. Fishing for sewin and trout is mainly in June, July and August; for salmon in August.

WESTERN CLEDDAU: Salmon, sewin and trout.

Haverfordwest (Pembrokeshire). Pembrokeshire AA has 15m stretch from Wolf's Castle to Haverfordwest; salmon, sea trout, brown trout; st £40, wt £40, dt £10: permits from County Sports, 3 Old Bridge, Harvordfordwest, Pembrokeshire; facilities for disabled in field at Nan-y-Coy. Accommodation: The Rising Sun Inn, St David's Road, Haverfordwest. Hamdden Ltd manages 2 reservoirs in the area on behalf of Welsh Water plc. **Llys-y-Fran Reservoir** (212 acres), rainbow trout reared on in cages within the reservoir and brown trout. Season Mar - 31 Oct; limited winter fishing only until mid Dec; catch limit 6 fish (half-day 3 fish); size limit 10"; boats; permits and tackle from Visitor Centre Shop. **Rosebush Reservoir** (33 acres) brown trout fishery in Prescelly Hills. Now operated by local syndicate but bank and boat rods from Llys-y-Fran Reservoir; advanced booking advisable. For further information contact J Waddington, Visitor Centre, Llys-y-Fran Reservoir, Clarbeston Road, Nr Haverfordwest, Pembs SA63 4RR, tel: 01437 532732/532694. **Hayscastle Trout Fishery**, 3 acre, stocked trout lake; fly only. Booking advisable. Permits from Hayscastle Trout Fishery, Upper Hayscastle Farm, Hayscastle, Dyfed, tel: 01348 840393. Riparian owners may give permission elsewhere. Sewin fishing good June to August. Tackle shop: County Sports, Bridge Street. Hotels: Mariners.

EASTERN CLEDDAU. Trout in all rivers and tributaries in E Cleddau area; stocks mostly small fish under 7½". Trout, sewin and salmon in **Syfynwy**, a tributary of E Cleddau.

Llanycefn (Dyfed). Fishing in E Cleddau controlled by individual syndicates as far as the ford at Llandissilio; day tickets are sold at Langwm Farm, Llanycefn SA66 7LN; for other tickets contact T & P J Murphy, tel: 01437 563604. Upstream seek farmers permission. Downstream it is difficult and expensive to join syndicates. Glancleddau Farm, Felinfach and Landre Egremont have holiday caravan parks where visitors enjoy some of the best fishing in the area. Rod licences from Post Office, Felinfach.

CLWYD

(For close seasons, licences, etc, see Welsh Region Environment Agency, p20)

A celebrated sea trout and salmon river which has its source in the high ground to the north of Corwen and runs down through Ruthin, passes Denbigh, St Asaph and Rhuddlan and finally enters the Irish Sea at Rhyl.

Best fished for sea trout from June onwards as these fish tend to run during latter part of the month. The native brown trout population is composed of small fish, though stocking of larger specimens is undertaken annually by most of the angling clubs. There are no coarse fish species in this area.

Rhyl (Clwyd). Salmon, sea trout, brown trout. No permits needed for stretch from sea to railway bridge, however, no holding pools therefore salmon and sea trout tend to run straight through; for salmon, trout and eels, rod licence needed; close season 30 Sept-31 May. Rhyl and District AA is one of the oldest fishing clubs in the Vale of Clwyd; the majority of its waters are rented, but the club is fortunate in owning the fishing rights on 2 substantial stretches on the **R Elwy** known as Maes Elwy and Pont y Ddol; it rents 2 further stretches at Dolganed and Bron Heulog; all beats on the **R Clwyd** (Bryn Clwyd, Wern Ddu and Bryn Polyn, and Bodfair) are rented. All stretches contain pools which give good fishing, holding salmon, sea trout and trout. Members only. St £75 + £100 joining fee; apply to Hon Sec. Waiting list approx 1 year. No day tickets. Concessions for juveniles. **Llyn Aled Isaf** is a Chester AA water; assn also has private fishing on **Rough Hill Farm Lake. Tan-y-Mynydd Lake**, rainbow, brown and brook trout from 1½ to 10lb; purpose-built trout lakes, total 4 acres. Permits from A Jones, Moelfre, Abergele, Clwyd. Self-catering cottages also available. Tackle shops: Wm Roberts Ltd, 131 High St.

St Asaph (Clwyd). Salmon, sea trout and brown trout. St Asaph AA has excellent and various fishing: 6 beats on Clwyd; 3 beats on **Elwy**, 4m in St Asaph area; a beat on **Aled**, 1½m double bank at **Llansannan**; and an excellent beat on **Conwy** at Bettws-y-Coed. St £60 (OAP £38, jun £22, family £82) + £60 joining fee (no joining fee for juniors). Day permits for Elwy; and dt £10 on Gypsy Lane beat (limited rods), from Foxon's Tackle. Tackle shop: Foxon's Tackle Shop, Penrhewl, St Asaph, tel: 01745 583583, which, in addition to a comprehensive range of tackle, offers expert advise on all aspects of fishing both game and coarse. Hotel: Oriel House.

Denbigh (Clwyd). Clwyd, 2m E; salmon, sea trout, brown trout. Denbigh & Clwyd AC has extensive water on Clwyd, **Ystrad, Elwy, Wheeler**, and also on small stocked trout lake; members only. Tickets from Hon Sec. **Llyn Brenig** and **Alwen Reservoir**, 11m SW; trout. **Llyn Aled**, 11m SW; coarse. Permits for Llyn Brenig, Alwen Reservoir and Llyn Aled; from Llyn Brenig Visitor Centre, Cerrigdrudion, Corwen, Conwy LL21 9TT, tel: 01490 420 463. Coarse fishing at **Lleweni Parc**, Mold Road, Denbigh. Hotel: Fron Haul.

Ruthin (Clwyd). Trout, salmon, sea trout. Denbigh & Clwyd AC has water on Clwyd and on **River Clywedog**; members only. Hotel: Ruthin Castle.

Tributaries of the Clwyd

ELWY: Brown trout, sea trout (June onwards), salmon. No coarse fish.

St Asaph (Clwyd). St Asaph AA has Gypsy Lane Waters: dt £10 from Foxon's Tackle, Penrhewl, St Asaph. Capenhurst AC has water; salmon and trout; member only.

Bodelwyddan (Denbighshire). Bodelwyddan Angling Club has two small beats on the Elwy; day tickets for small beat on lower Elwy; permits from Foxon's Tackle, Penrhewl, St Asaph. **Felin y Gors Fisheries**, stocked brown and rainbow trout; 4 lakes; 10½acres; fly only. Day ticket fishery with various prices from £6 to £17 (full-day). Children's bait fishing on 3 separate waters. Tuition, tackle hire, tackle shop and self-contained accommodation. Bookings in advance from Robert Monshin, St Asaph Road, Bodelwyddan, Denbighshire LL18 5UY, tel: 01352 720965 (day), 01745 584044 (evening).

Llansannan (Clwyd). St Asaph AA has 1½m double bank on **Aled**. **Dolwen** and **Plas Uchaf Reservoirs**, a few miles SW of St Asaph; well stocked with brown and rainbow trout; fly, spinning and worming; 6 fish limit. Season 14 Mar - 31 Oct. Permits from D & J Davies, Newsagents, 12 Church View, Bodelwyddan, St Asaph, tel: 01745 582206. Booking advised as rods limited to 16. Concession OAP and jun.

WHEELER: Trout.

Afonwen (Clwyd). Denbigh & Clwyd AC has 2m; some fly only. Mold Trout A has 1¼m. Mold Kingfishers AC has fishing on Wheeler and on lake at Afonwen.

CLYWEDOG: Salmon and sea trout (very late), trout. All water strictly preserved.

Ruthin (Clwyd). Denbigh & Clwyd AC has

Check before you go

While every effort has been made to ensure that the information given in ***Where to Fish*** *is correct, the position is continually changing, and anglers are urged, in their own interests, to make enquiries before travelling to selected venues. This is especially important with reference to prices quoted. Anglers attention is also drawn to the fact that hotels mentioned under the various fishing stations do not necessarily have water of their own. Any amendments or further data for inclusion in subsequent editions, and any comments, will be welcome.*

stretch from confluence with Clwyd to Rhewl; and has water in Bontuchel and Llanrhaeadr areas; member only. Capenhurst AC has stretch at Bontuchel; salmon, sea trout and trout; members only. Members children (under 18) may fish free of charge, but must be accompanied by adult.

CONWY

(For close seasons, licences, etc, see Welsh Region Environment Agency, p20)

Rises on Migneint, in the County of Conwy and flows between the old Caernarvonshire and Denbighshire boundaries for much of its course, emptying into the Irish Sea near Conwy. The upper part of its valley is noted for its beauty. Spate river with salmon runs throughout season (May and June usually best); grilse early July; sea trout late June to September.

Conwy (Gwynedd). Tidal; sea fishing only. Codling, dabs, plaice, bass and mullet above and below suspension bridge. Boats for hire. Salmon and sea trout; Prince Albert AS has ½m on Conwy, 6m from Conwy. **Llyn Gwern Engan**, a small lake on Sychnant Pass Common; rudd, tench, carp, gudgeon; also free fishing, contact Snowdonia National Park Committee, Penrhydeudraeth, Gwynedd. **Llyn Nant-y-Cerrig**, Brynymaen, 1½ acres; carp, bream, tench, perch; tickets at lakeside or local tackle shops. For further information contact N Roberts, Goleugell, Eglwysbach, Colwyn Bay, Clwyd LL28 5UH, tel: 01492 650314. **Clobryn Pool**, Clobryn Rd, Colwyn Bay; tench, crucian carp, roach, rudd, perch. **Glas Coed Pools**, Bodelwyddan, set in grounds of Bodelwyddan Castle, carp, tench, roach, rudd. **Trefant Pool**, newly opened; stocked with tench, carp, roach, rudd and perch. Permits for Llyn Nant-y-Cerrig, Clobryn Pool, Glas Coed Pools and Trefant Pool from The Tackle Box, 17 Greenfield Rd, Colwyn Bay LL29 8EL, tel: 01492 531104; the shop offers a full list of trout, coarse and specialist waters in the area and the proprietor (a previous Welsh bass champion) can also advise on all aspects of local sea fishing. Other tackle shops: North Wales Bait Supplies, 4 Parc Ffynnon, Llysfaen; and Llandudno Fishing Tackle, 14 Mostyn Ave, Llandudno.

Dolgarrog (Gwynedd). Salmon, sea trout and brown trout; deep tidal pools. Dolgarrog FC has tidal water. Club also has rainbow and brown trout fishing on **Llyn Coedty**; and trout fishing on **Llyn Eigiau**. Permits from Hon Sec. **Llyn Melynllyn**, 5m E; **Llyn Dulyn**, 6m E; **Llyn Cowlyd** (5m W Llanwrst); all trout reservoirs belonging to Welsh Water plc; free to licence holders. Enquiries to Dwr Cymru, Conwy Unit Office, Cefndy Road, Rhyl, Clwyd LL18 2HG.

Llanrwst (Gwynedd). Salmon and good sea trout; brown trout poor. Llanrwst AC has various beats on R Conwy at Llanrwst and Trefriw; some sections members only. Limited wt £45 (to 12 Sept only) and dt £15 from Hon Sec and The Old Library Tackle Shop, Bridge St. Sunday fishing allowed. Permits from Forestry Commission, Gwydyr Uchaf, for left bank of **Machno** from junction with Conwy and portion of right bank. Dt 60p, from P Haveland, Manchester House, Penmachno, Betws-y-Coed LL24 0UD, tel: 01690 760337. Tackle shop: Gwen Booth, The Square. Hotels: Maenan Abbey Hotel and Victoria Hotel (both have salmon and trout); and Eagles Hotel, Bridge St.

Betws-y-Coed (Conwy). Salmon, sea trout, brown trout. Betws-y-Coed AC has 4½m of salmon, sea trout and brown trout fishing on Conwy and **Llugwy**; on the Conwy, from the Waterloo Bridge (left bank) downstream to the confluence of the **Llugwy**. The club also three trout lakes: **Elsi Lake**, stocked with some American brook trout and brown trout; **Llyn Goddionduon**, stocked with brown trout; and **Llyn Bychan**. St £135 (£65 for partially disabled) from Hon Sec; dt £30 and £18 (river), and £15 (lake) from Mr G Parry, Tan Lan Café (nr Post Office). Concessions juniors. St AsaphAA has

Keep the banks clean

Several clubs have stopped issuing tickets to visitors because of the state of the banks after they have left. Spend a few moments clearing up. This includes lengths of broken nylon. If discarded, serious injuries can be caused to wild birds and to livestock.

¾m stretch. Gwydyr Hotel has 8m of salmon and sea trout fishing; season 20 Mar - 17 Oct; tickets for residents only. For further information contact Owen Wainwright, Gwydyr Hotel, Bangor Road, Betws-y-Coed LL24 0AB, tel: 01690 710777. Tackle at hotel. Bryn Trych Hotel has salmon, trout and sea trout fishing on Conwy, tributaries and lakes. Other hotels: Craig-y-Dderwen Country House; Waterloo.

Ysbyty Ifan (Conwy). Brown trout. National Trust has stretch at Ysbyty Ifan and Dinas Water on upper Conwy; fly, worm and spinning. Permits from National Trust, Trinity Square, Llandudno, Conwy LL30 2DE; National Trust, Estate Office, Dinas, Nr Betws-y-Coed, Gwynedd LL24 0HF; and R Ellis, Bron Ryffydd, Padog, Betws-y-Coed, Conwy LL24 0HF, tel: 01690 710567. For holiday cottages contact The National Trust Holiday Booking Office, PO Box 536, Melksham, Wiltshire SN12 8SX, tel: 01225 791199.

Tributaries of the Conwy

ROE: Trout.

Rowen (Gwynedd). Fly fishing impossible on lower reaches. **Conwyn Valley Fisheries**, 2 acre, spring fed lake, rainbow trout, fly only, all year round. Tackle is for hire and fly fishing lessons can be arranged. Shop stocks flies and accessories. Accommodation at Glyn Isa in 4 self-contained cottages with free fishing on Conwy Valley Fisheries. Contact Conwyn Valley Fisheries, Glyn Isa, Rowen, Nr Conwy LL32 8PT, tel: 01492 650063.

DDU: Trout.

Pont Dolgarrog (Gwynedd). Trout. Ddu enters Conwy ½m below village; drains Llyn Cowlyd. **Llyn Cowlyd**, brown trout and Arctic char; fly only; free permits from Welsh Water plc, Conwy Unit Office, Cefndy Road, Rhyl, Clwyd LL18 2HG, tel: 01244 550015.

CRAFNANT: Trout.

Trefriw (Gwynedd). Trout fishing on Llyn Crafnant, one of the most beautiful lakes in Wales, 63 acres, stocked rainbow trout supplementing wild brown trout. Sunday fishing. Day tickets, rod licences, boats, cafe, self-catering accommodation, toilets, car parking and information from Mr & Mrs J Collins, Lakeside Café, Llyn Crafnant, Trefriw, LL27 0JZ, tel: 01492 640818. Hotel: Princes Arms; and Fairy Falls.

LLEDR: Trout, sewin, salmon.

Dolwyddelan (Gwynedd). Plas Hall Hotel has stretch, salmon and sea trout; for residents and limited number of day tickets. Permits from Plas Hall Hotel, Pont-y-Pant, Dolwyddelan LL25 0PJ. Dolwyddelan FA fishing on River Lledr both above and below the village; salmon, brown trout and sea trout; good late season salmon runs; sea trout from 1st July. Wt (Mon-Fri) and dt for visitors, although wt only for visitors resident in village. Permits and tackle, including locally tied flies, from Post Office, Dolwyddelan, Gwynedd LL25 0NJ, tel: 01690 750201. Prince Albert AS has stretch here; enquire Hon Sec. Hotel: Elen's Castle Hotel, Dolwyddelan.

LLUGWY: Salmon, sea trout, brown trout.

Betws-y-Coed (Conwy). Betws-y-Coed AC has a stretch, both bank, from Swallow Falls downstream to the confluence of Conwy on right bank and to railway bridge on left bank. Permits from Tan Lan Café, Betws-y-Coed, tel: 01690 710232.

MACHNO: Trout.

Penmachno (Conwy). National Trust has water on Machno; no salmon fishing above Conwy Falls; brown trout only. Permits from National Trust, Trinity Square, Llandudno, Conwy LL30 2DE; National Trust, Estate Office, Dinas, Nr Betws-y-Coed, Conwy LL24 0HF; and Robin Ellis, Bron Ryffydd, Padog, Betws-y-Coed, Conwy LL24 0HF, tel: 01690 710567.

DEE (Welsh)

(For close seasons, licences, etc, see Welsh Region Environment Agency, p20)

Usually has a spring run of fish up to 30lb. Grilse enter in June and there is a run of grilse and summer fish until the end of the season as a rule. In spring most fish are taken from Bangor to Corwen. Trout from Bangor upstream and grayling above Llangollen. Coarse fish predominate downstream of Bangor. River holds good bream, roach, dace, perch and pike.

Holywell (Clwyd). Holywell A has fishing on **Llyn Helyg**; carp, tench, pike, roach, rudd; members only. Rainbow and brown trout fishing at **Forest Hill Trout Farm**, Mostyn, Nr Holywell, CH8 9EQ, tel: 01745 560151; 2 shaded peaceful lakes fed by spring water, stocked with home reared rainbow and brown trout, fly or bait. **Seven Springs Trout Farm and Fisheries**, Caerwys, Nr Mold, Flintshire CH7 5EZ, tel: 01352 721051; 3 pools over 1 acre, containing rainbow trout; fly and bait; tackle hire and tuition; anglers room, toilet and gutting room; tickets at fisheries (bookings taken). Coarse fishing at **Gyrn Castle Fishery**, Llanasa, Holywell, Flintshire CH8 9BG; 2 lakes, 3 acres and 1 acre; well stocked with carp, rudd and tench; heaviest carp to date - 30 lbs; barbless hooks only. Fishermen's hut with tea and coffee-making facilities. Closed 30 Sept - 31 Jan. Dt £15; only 8 permits per day allowed. Permits from Mrs Ellis, Gyrn Castle Estate, South Lodge, Glan-yr-Afon, tel: 01745 561677. Greenfield Valley Trust AC issue permits for **Flour Mill Pool**; 4 acre fishery situated in Greenfield Valley Heritage Park; rudd, crucian carp, tench, perch, bream, ghost carp, gudgeon, common and mirror carp, roach; permits from bailiff on bankside.

Connah's Quay (Clwyd). Connah's Quay and Dist AC has 2m trout fishing at **Wepre Brook**; 2½m trout and coarse fishing on **River Alyn**; no dt. Club also has coarse fishing at **Wepre Pool, Swan Lake** and **Cymau Pools**; st and dt from Deeside Tackle & Sport, Chester Road, Shotton, Deeside. Tackle shop: Mrs I M Williams, 316 High Street, Connah's Quay.

Chester (Cheshire). Coarse fish. Little permit-free fishing. No licence for coarse fishing in tidal waters. Most fishing on River Dee controlled by Chester AA. Assn also has fishing on **River Vyrnwy, River Severn**, and **Llyn Aled Isaf**. No day tickets. St £10 (OAP and jun £4) for trout and coarse fishing only from Hon Sec or Chester area tackle shops. Free fishing from Mon to Fri, on Eaton Estate from public footpath that adjoins river; beat can be booked through V J Hedley, 12 Marlston Avenue, Lache Lane, Chester CH4 8HF, tel: 01244 671796. **River Gowy**, which runs into Mersey, passing by Mickle Trafford about 3m from Chester; Warrington AA has water. **Meadow Fishery**, Mickle Trafford, tel: 0124 300 236, rainbow trout; 5 acres; st and dt. Tackle shops: Henry Monk (Gunmaker) Ltd, 8 Queen Street (tel. 01244 320988; David Gibson, Upper Northgate St; Jones Fishing Tackle & Pet Foods, 39 Vernon Rd; Hoole Angling Centre, 17 Hoole Rd, Hoole.

Holt (Clwyd). Salmon, trout, pike, bream. Holt and Farndon AA has stretch at Holt; bream, dace, roach, perch; st and dt from Hon Sec. Dee AA rent approx 10m of Dee from Chester AA in the Farndon and Sutton Green area. Maps can be obtained from Hon Sec, price 50p plus SAE. Assn issues salmon permits (limited) for Sutton Green stretch; separate trout and coarse fish permits. Permits from local tackle shops and B W Roberts, 23 Alpraham Crescent, Upton, Chester, tel: 01244 381193. All waters in the Chester area and downstream to Queensferry controlled by the Chester AA; match permits and membership cards from B W Roberts; no day tickets issued for these waters. Maghull and Lydiate AC has stretch on Dee at Lower Hall; roach, bream, chub, perch, sea trout, salmon, trout and gudgeon; members only. Instruction for juniors and competitive events for all members. Warrington AA has Shocklach Water and stretch at Almere; members only, but visiting anglers accommodated, providing they supply date of visit in advance. Lavister AC has 1m stretch (left bank) upstream from Almere Ferry; bream, dace, roach, perch, pike; members only. Kirkdale AA has 2m at Holt; members only. Cheshire AA has 1m on Dee upstream of Farndon Bridge, south bank. Waters on the **Grosvenor Estates** at Churton and Aldford downstream to Chester; free freelance fishing but matches must be booked with H Barter, Eaton Estate Office, Eccleston, Chester.

Bangor-on-Dee (Clwyd). Salmon, trout, coarse fish. Bangor-on-Dee Salmon AA has 2 stretches; one downstream from town, the other near Shocklach; member only but membership available (£55 + £25 joining fee); dt £5 (coarse) and £12 (salmon). Permits from Hon Sec. Northern A has stretches on **Dee** and **Worthenbury Brook**; club also has fishing on **Shropshire Union Canal** and **River Alyn**; members only. Warrington AA has water on Worthenbury Brook. Hotel: The Buck Hotel.

Overton (Clwyd). Bryn-y-Pys AA has 7m

on R Dee between Overton Bridge and Bangor-on-Dee; rainbow and brown trout, grayling and coarse fish. St £30, £21 (OAP) and £15 (junior); entrance fee £10. Dt £8 (trout season) and £4, from Deggy's Fishing Tackle, 2 Ruabon Road, Wrexham. Boat Inn, Erbistock, has salmon and trout beat. **Trench Fisheries** have 4 pools (3 acres) with carp, tench, rudd and crucian carp; day tickets only; contact Mr & Mrs M A Huntbach, Trench Farm, Redhall Lane, Penley, Wrexham LL13 0NA, tel: 01978 710098.

Cefn Mawr (Clwyd). Trout, salmon, coarse fish (including pike and grayling). Maelor AA has water. Coarse fishing good September onwards. Tickets from Hon Sec. Newbridge AA has Wynnstay Estate Waters from Newbridge Old Bridge downstream on wooded bank, approx 3m; salmon, trout, grayling, dace and pike fishing; members only, except for salmon rods on top beat; members to reside within local radius of 5m. Salmon permits from Hon Sec. Tackle shop: Derek's Fishing Tackle, London House, Well St. Hotel: Wynnstay Arms, Ruabon.

Llangollen (Denbighshire). Salmon, sea trout, brown trout, grayling. Llangollen AA has 12m of bank fishing around the town. All waters have good access and parking provided. Downstream from Horseshoe Falls, all methods for salmon and trout; above Horseshoe Falls, all methods for salmon, fly only for trout and grayling. Trout water stocked with 5,500 trout per season, averaging 12" with larger fish up to 3lbs. Both trout and grayling fishing excellent and near best on River Dee. Salmon fishing good from May to end of season, average catch for club is 65 fish. St £70 + £30 joining fee (S) and £50 + £10 joining fee (T), wt £40 (S) and £25 (T), dt £15 (S) and £6 (T). No waiting list for trout membership. Permits from Hughes Newsagents, 12 Chapel Street, Llangollen, Denbighshire LL20 8NN, tel: 01978 860155, where fishing tackle and information on ghillies are also available. **Abbey Fishery**, a trout farm 1½m from Llangollen; 2 bait ponds, 1 fly pond and ½m on River Dee. Accommodation in log cabins. Contact David and Margaret Penman, Penvale Lodges, Abbey Fishery, Llangollen, Denbighshire LL20 8DD, tel: 01978 860266. Northern A has stretch on **Shropshire Union Canal** from Hurleston Junction to Llantysilio; members only. Hand Hotel, Bridge St, Llangollen, Denbighshire LL20 8PL, tel: 01978 860303, has own stretch of water below the bridge on right bank; fishing on hotel stretch of river for hotel residents only; fishing is free to residents; permits for non-residents and tackle from Hughes Newsagents, 12 Chapel St, Llangollen, tel: 01978 860155. Liverpool & Dist AA has salmon and trout fishing at Chain Bridge; st and dt. Hotels: Royal; Bryn Howell.

Glyndyfrdwy (Denbighshire). Salmon, trout and grayling. Corwen and Dist AC has 1½m (mainly single bank) on Berwyn Arms Water; 5 named salmon pools; salmon, trout and grayling. Midland Flyfishers has 3m of salmon and trout fishing on the Dee from Groeslwyd to Glyndyfrdwy; and trout fishing on **River Onny**, **Quinney Brook**, **Byne Brook**, **River Lugg** and a trout pool. Fly fishing for trout and grayling only. Salmon fishing is prohibited except to full members. Membership is strictly limited to applicants supported by two existing members; apply to T J P Lea, Keepers Cottage, Hill Lane, Elmley Castle, Nr Pershore, Worcs WR0 3JA. Dt £6, from Post Office, Glyndyfrdwy; Bob Jones-Roberts, Coedial, Glyndyfrdwy; Hughes Newsagents, 12 Chapel Street, Llangollen, Denbighshire LL20 8NN.

Corwen (Clwyd). Corwen and Dist AC has **Rhug Estate Water**, approx 4m mostly double bank, trout and grayling, fly only except winter grayling; ¼m stretch at **Cynwyd** including large holding pool, salmon, trout and grayling; ¾m stretch at **Carrog**, 3 named pools and runs, salmon, trout and grayling; 1½m stretch at Glyndyfrdwy; 2 stretches, 1m (double bank) and ¾m (double bank), between Cynwyd and Llandrillo, salmon, trout and grayling; and Chain Pool at Bonwn. Club also has several miles of water on **Rivers Alwen** and **Ceirw** at Bettws Gwerfil Goch and Maerdy; salmon and sea trout, mid to late season; and good trout early and late. No dt; members only. Application for membership welcome with concessions for juniors and OAPs. Capenhurst AC has stretch downstream of Carrog Bridge, Carrog; salmon, sea trout and trout; members only. **Gwyddelwern Pool**, Corwen, ¾ acre lake, stocked with coarse fish (large carp and tench); permits from D M Lewis, Maes-y-Llyn, Gwyddelwern, Corwen, Clwyd LL21 9DU, tel: 01490 412761. Rod licences from Corwen Post Office. Hotel: Owain Glyndwr.

Cynwyd (Clwyd). Trout, grayling, salmon. Corwen and Dist AC has stretch on Dee from Glascoed to Cynwyd Bridge; plus ¾m double bank (salmon, trout and grayling) above Cynwyd Bridge; and trout fishing on **Cynwyd Reservoir**; Sunday fishing, fly only. Members only.

Llandrillo (Clwyd). Salmon, trout, grayling, perch and pike. Strictly preserved by executors of Duke of Westminster's Pale Estate. Tyddyn Llan Country Hotel arranges fishing for guests; tuition and equipment. Rod licences from Tyddyn Llan Country House Hotel & Restaurant.

Llandderfel (Gwynedd). Salmon, trout, grayling. Pale Hall Country House Hotel, Llandderfel, Nr Bala, Gwynedd LL23 7PS, tel: 01678 530285, has prime salmon and trout fishing during game season. Excellent grayling fishing provides ideal winter sport with specimens reaching 3lbs. Fishing is based on 6m of **River Dee** with access to brown trout in mountain lake. Coarse fishing on **Bala Lake** included in permit. Permits from D Evans, Yr Eryr Sports & Tackle, 31-33 High Street, Bala LL23 7AF; and Bryntirion Inn, Llandderfel.

Bala (Gwynedd). Salmon, trout, perch, pike and grayling. Bala AA has water, including from confluence with Tryweryn to Bala Lake; and fishing on Bala Lake (members only). Assn also has water on **Rivers Tryweryn, Lliw,** and **Llafar** (dt); **Cwm Prysor Lake** (trout, fly only, dt); **Llyn Celyn** (brown trout). Sunday fishing allowed. Concessions for juniors. Instruction and competitions for juniors. Permits from tackle shop and J A Jones, Post Office, Frongoch, Nr Bala. **Bala Lake** (Llyn Tegid); trout, roach, perch, pike, grayling, eel; owned by County Council. Permits from tackle shops and Lake Warden, Warden's Office, 24 Ffordd Pensarn, Bala, tel: Bala 520626. Tackle shop: D Evans, Yr Eryr Sports & Tackle, 31-33 High Street, Bala LL23 7AF. Hotels and accommodation: White Lion Royal; Plas Coch; Mrs Shirley Pugh, 4 Castle St; Mr T G Jones, Fronderw Private Hotel, Stryd-y-Fron, Bala, Gwynedd LL23 7YD; Penbryn Farm Guesthouse, Sarnau (coarse fishing).

Llanuwchllyn (Gwynedd). Trout and grayling. Prince Albert AS has trout and grayling fishing on Little Dee, Twrch and Lliw; members only; waiting list. Hendre Mawr Farm Caravan Park has fishing; tuition and equipment.

Tributaries of the Dee

ALYN: Trout. Drains hills to west of Clwydian Range, runs past Mold towards Wrexham and finally opens into lower part of Dee on Cheshire Plains near Farndon at Almere.

Rossett (Clwyd). Trout. Rossett and Gresford FF has brown trout fishing on 2m stretch (both banks) on well maintained and stocked section of R Alwyn between Rossett and Gresford, nr Wrexham; and stretch at Cefn-y-Bedd. Members only; fly only; bag limit. St £35 and £5 (juniors). Permits from Hon Sec. Warrington AA have water lower down and stretch on Dee, at Almere. Hotel: Trevor Arms Hotel, Marford, Wrexham, tel: 01244 570436.

Gresford (Clwyd). Trout. Griffin AC has three stretches; members only.

Wrexham (Clwyd). Wrexham and Dist AA has water on Alyn; trout fishing, fly only. Permits issued to guests of members only. Dee Valley Services PLC, Packsaddle, Wrexham Rd, Rhostyllen, Wrexham, Clwyd LL14 4DS, tel: 01978 846946, manage 3 local reservoirs: **Ty Mawr Reservoir** (20 acres), **Penycae Upper Reservoir** (7 acres) and **Penycae Lower Reservoir** (5 acres). The fishing is quiet and secluded with very clear water; possible to locate and stalk individual fish (stocked up to 6 lbs). Brown and rainbow trout; fly fishing only. St £228, dt £16-£11 (Penycae) and £15-£10

(Ty Mawr). At least 12 hrs notice must be given in order to reserve a rod. Number of rods limited. Contact the bailiff, tel: 01978 840116. Ponciau AS has **Ponciau Pool**, 2½m from Wrexham; roach, bream, tench, carp; members only. Rhostyllen AC has coarse fishing at pool near Sontley; club also has access to extensive game and coarse fisheries on **Dee**, **Vyrnwy** and **Shropshire Union Canal**. Tackle shops: Deggy's Fishing Tackle, 2 Ruabon Rd, tel: 01978 351815; and Morrison's Fishing Tackle, York Street, Wrexham. Hotel: Trevor Arms Hotel, Marford, Wrexham.

Llay (Clwyd). Llay AA has good coarse fishing on **Llay Reservoir** (tench, carp, rudd, perch, pike); and **Cymau Pool** (carp, rudd, tench, perch, roach, crucian carp and gudgeon) at Caergwrle. Members only. St £8.50 (jun £3.50 and OAP £1) from Hon Sec, local shops or bailiff on bank. Hotels: Crown Inn; and Mount Pleasant.

Hope (Clwyd). Wrexham and Dist AA has trout fishing from Llong railway bridge to Pont y Delyn; fly only; permits issued to members' guests only. Caergwrle AC has 3m; stocked regularly with brown and rainbow trout; wet and dry fly and worming; spinning prohibited. Permits from Hon Sec; dt from June 1 only. Brown and rainbow trout fishing at **Tree Tops Fly Fishery**; ten lakes - nine lakes stocked with rainbow trout and tenth with brown trout. Rods to hire and basic tuition by arrangement. Cafe, tackle shop and accommodation. For further details contact Joy & Peter Price, Tree Tops Fly Fishery, Llanfynydd, Nr Wrexham, Flintshire LL11 5HR, tel: 01352 770648.

Mold (Clwyd). Mold TA has 5m on Alyn and 2m on **R Wheeler**; and fishing on **New Lake**, Rhydymwyn. All fisheries stocked with brown and rainbow trout. Permits from Grosvenor Pet and Garden Centre, Grosvenor St, tel: 01352 754264. Mold Fly Fishers have trout fishing on **Pistyll Pool** at **Nercwys**, 1½ acres (stocked brown and rainbow trout) and 1½m of **R Terrig** at Nercwys (brown trout); members only; day tickets if accompanied by member. Concessions for juniors. Mold Kingfishers AC has stretch on **R Wheeler** and lake at Afonwen; also coarse fishing at **Hendre Tilcon Quarry Pool** and **Lloyds Gravel Quarries**. Northern A has stretch near Llanferres; members only. Buckley AA has **Trap Pool**, a good mixed fishery; permits from Lionel's Tackle Shop, Ashgrove, Pentre Lane, Buckley, Flintshire CH7 3PA, tel: 01244 343181. Alltami AC has coarse fishing on **Alltami Clay Pits**; carp, tench, bream, roach; no dt, details from Lionel's Tackle Shop. Mixed fishery at **Gweryd Lakes**, Gweryd Lodge, Plas Lane, Llanarmon-yn-Lal, nr Mold, Denbighshire CH7 4QJ. Accommodation: Old Mill Guest House.

Cilcain (Clwyd). Cilcain FFA has four trout reservoirs nearby; stocked with rainbow trout; fly only. Permits from H Williams, Treasurer, 20 Maes Cilan, tel: 01352 740924. **Nant-y-Gain Fishery**, 2 pools stocked with brown and rainbow trout, fly only. Access and facilities for disabled anglers. Tickets and refreshments available on site. Contact Glyn and Judy Jones, Nant-y-Gain Fishery, Cilcain, Flintshire CH7 5PE, tel: 01352 740936.

Nannerch (Clwyd). **Sarn Mill Trout Fishery**, Sam Mill, Nannerch, Nr Mold, tel: 01352 720323, 5 pools; one pool wild brown trout; 2 pools stocked with brown trout and rainbow trout; 2 pools stocked with brown trout, rainbow trout, roach, rudd, tench and carp. Bait for sale, fishing tackle for hire and camp site for tents and caravans. **Wal Goch Fly Fishing**; 2 lakes (2½ and ½ acre); brown and rainbow trout. Open all year; fly only; max 20 rods; floodlights, catch-and-release, trickle stocked. Contact Philip Robinson, Wal Goch Fly Fishing, Wal Goch Farm, CH7 5RP, tel: 01352 741378.

CEIRIOG: Trout.

Chirk (Clwyd). Ceirog Fly Fishers have 6½m, both banks, from Dee Junction to Ladies Bridge and from Chirk Aquaduct to Pontfadog Village; good fishing, trout and grayling; fly only; keepered and stocked. No tickets; strictly members and guests only. St £150 from to Hon Sec. Hotel: The Hand Hotel.

Glyn Ceiriog (Clwyd). Glyn Ceiriog FC has trout fishing on **River Teirw** at Pandy, nr Glyn Ceiriog; permits from Golden Pheasant Hotel, Glyn Ceiriog, Nr Llangollen LL20 7BB, tel: 01691 718281.

Llanarmon Dyffryn Ceiriog (Clwyd). Ceiriog, 2½m, brown trout. West Arms Hotel has 1½m (both banks) trout fishing; shallow clear water with some deep pools. Free to hotel residents; dt for non-residents. Limit 2 rods per day; fly only. Hand Hotel has trout and coarse fishing for guests (both hotels issue rod licences).

ALWEN: Flows out of large reservoir (trout, perch) on Denbigh Moors and enters Dee near Corwen. Very good trout fishing and some salmon.

Cerrig-y-Drudion (Clywd). Cerrig-y-Drudion AA has river fishing on Alwen and on **R Ceirw**, parallel with A5 road; members only. Membership from Hon Sec. Crown Inn, Llanfihangel Glyn Myfyr, has trout fishing; fly and worm; permits (free to hotel residents). Welsh Water plc manage three reservoirs north of town. **Llyn Brenig**, 919-acre reservoir amid heather moorland and forest. Fly only, brown and rainbow trout. Llyn Brenig was the venue for 1990 World Fly Fishing Championship and regular Home Fly Fishing Internationals. St £340, dt £10.50, evening £8.50, boats £17 per day. Season: Mar-Nov. Concessions OAP & jun; block bookings offered. **Alwen Reservoir** (368 acre), moorland reservoir stocked with rainbow and brown trout, although also natural population of brown trout and perch; dt £7.50. Fly fishing, spinning and worming permitted; catch limit 6 trout. Season Mar-Nov. **Llyn Aled Reservoir** (110 acres), holds large numbers of roach, perch and pike and is a good match venue; occasional wild brown trout. No close season for coarse fish. Concessions OAP and jun. Tickets and further information from Llyn Brenig Visitor Centre, Cerrigdrudion, Corwen, Conwy LL21 9TT, tel: 01490 420 463; where there is also a café and well-stocked tackle shop. Coarse fishing at **Tyddyn Farm Field Centre**, Cefn Brith, Cerrig-y-Drudion, Corwen LL21 9TS. Fly fishing at **Dragonfly Fisheries**, On the A5, Cerrig-y-Drudion, Corwen, Clwyd, tel: 01490 420530; American brook, rainbow and brown trout; dt.

TRYWERYN: Joins Dee below Lake Bala. Good trout fishing.

Bala (Gwynedd). Bala AA has 2 stretches on Tryweryn, **Llyn Celyn** and mountain lake **Cwm Prysor**. Tickets from E W Evans, Sports & Tackle Shop, 31-33 High St, LL23 7AF.

DYFI (DOVEY)

(For close seasons, licences, etc, see Welsh Region Environment Agency, p20)

Rises on east side of Aran Fawddwy and flows 30m south and south-west to Cardigan Bay at Aberdovey. Has long estuary and provides splendid sport with sewin (sea trout) and salmon. Many large sea trout taken. Salmon run in from May to October; sea trout from May on. Best months: July, August, September. Small tributaries hold some little trout, and permission can generally be obtained from owners.

Aberdyfi (Gwynedd). At estuary mouth; surf and estuary fishing. Free trout fishing in Happy Valley on permission of farmers; stream; trout small.

Machynlleth (Powys). Sea trout and salmon. New Dovey Fishery Association controls 15m (both banks) of river between Llyfnant stream and Nant Ty-Mawr and left bank, from opposite Llyfnant mouth to Abergwybedyn brook. Season rods available £55 when vacancies occur (long waiting list - contact Hon Sec). Upper reaches st £150 from Hon Sec. Limited visitors wt £95 from T A Hughes, Newsagent, Penrallt St, Machynlleth, Powys SY20 8AG, tel: 01654 702495; D G Evans, Garage, Cemmaes Road, Machynlleth, Powys SY20 8JZ; and Hon Sec, tel/fax: 01654 702721. Dt £10 for upper reaches. No Sunday fishing. Permission from farmers for **Pennal Stream**; rapid water; trout small. Corris AC controls 7m of **N Dulas**. St £15, wt £7.50 and dt £5. Concessions for juveniles and OAPs. Permits from Hon Sec; Hughes Newsagents, Machynlleth; and Maelor Stores, Corris. Llugwy Hotel, Pennal, has ½m on **S Dulas** free to guests. Tackle shop: Greenstiles. Hotels: Wynnstay Arms, White Lion.

Cemmaes (Powys). Trout, sea trout, salmon. New Dovey Fishery Association water.

Llanbrynmair (Powys). On **River Twymyn**, a tributary of **Dyfi**; sewin, salmon. Llanbrynmair and Dist AC has water on Twymyn from village to confluence with Dyfi (apart from one stretch held by Prince Albert AS); and wild brown trout fishing on **Lakes Gwyddlor** and **Coch-Hwyad**, both lakes 25 acres with a boat on each. Best months Jul-Oct. Permits from Mrs D R Lewis, Bryn-Llugwy Llanbrynmair, Powys SY19 7AA, tel: 01650 521 385. Prince Albert AS control 3m of Twymyn; enquiries to Hon Sec.

Dinas Mawddwy (Gwynedd). Sewin, salmon, trout; fishing good. Brigands Inn, Mallwyd, has some of the best pools on upper reaches and stretch on **Cleifion**; day tickets for guests only. Buckley Arms Hotel has water from the Cowarch down to hotel, for residents only. Sea trout runs (water permitting) May, July, Sept; best July to October. The Dolbrodmaeth Inn, Dinas Mawddwy, Machynlleth, Powys SY20 9LP, tel: 01650 531333, has ½m stretch on Dyfi in grounds of hotel; sewin, salmon, trout; reserved for guests. The hotel also issues tickets for 12m of Rivers Mawddach and Wnion, and Lake Cynwch (all in vicinity of Dolgellau). Prince Albert AS has 2½m stretch of Dyfi at Gwastad Coed, Gwerhefin.

DWYRYD

(For close seasons, licences, etc, see Welsh Region Environment Agency, p20)

Rises in small, nameless pool 3m above Tanygrisiau and flows into Cardigan Bay through estuary north of Harlech. A classic spate river with deep pools which hold good numbers of fish following a spate. Sea trout enter the river towards the end of May: these tend to be large fish with the 1-3lbs following in June. Fresh sea trout still enter the river in October. The first run of salmon appear in July with increasing numbers in August, September and October.

Maentwrog (Gwynedd). Dwyryd Anglers Ltd has fishing at **Tan-y-Bwlch Fishery** on River Dwryrd (north bank only), 1¾m downstream from Maentwrog Bridge. St £40 (limited), wt £20 (any 7 consecutive days) and dt £7. Concessions for juniors and OAPs. Permits from Gareth Price, Tackle Shop, Hafan, Fford Peniel, Ffestiniog, Gwynedd, tel: 01766 762451. Dwyryd Anglers Ltd also has 3½m (double bank) of private water on Dwyryd; a very limited number of season rods may become available, contact G. Price for information.

Blaenau Ffestiniog (Gwynedd). Principal trout lakes controlled by Cambrian AA as follows: **Dubach**, well stocked with brown trout; **Manod**, fishing rather rough due to rocky shore conditions, holds plenty of fish; **Morwynion**, most easily accessible, average weight 12ozs; **Cwmorthin**, well stocked with brown trout 8-9ozs. Other Cambrian AA lakes: **Dubach-y-Bont**, **Barlwyd**, **Cwm Foel** and **Cwm Corsiog**. Concession for juniors. **Tanygrisiau Reservoir** (2m NW), 95 acres, stocked with brown and rainbow trout; controlled by local syndicate. Spinning and bait fishing allowed. Permits for Cambrian AA waters and for Tanygrisiau from F W Roberts, Fishing Tackle, 32 Church Street, Blaenau Ffestiniog, Gwynedd LL41 3HD, tel: 01766 830607. Hotels: Pengwern Arms, Ffestiniog. Fly casting tuition from D Pritchard, 13 Tyn-y-Nams, Ffestiniog, Gwynedd LL41 4NW.

Tributaries of the Dwyryd

PRYSOR:

Trawsfynydd (Gwynedd). Prysor AA controls 5m on **Prysor River**; provides good fishing towards the end of the season when lake trout run upstream. Season 1 Mar - 30 Sep. Also 3m on upper **Eden**: salmon and sea trout July onwards. Assn also manages **Trawsfynydd Lake**, 1200 acres; brown and rainbow trout (average 1½lb), also perch and rudd. Season: rainbow trout 1 Feb - 31 Dec; brown trout 1 Mar - 30 Sept; coarse fish 1 Feb - 31 Dec. Fly fishing, bottom fishing and spinning. Boats with motors for daily hire; fly only from boats. St £170, wt £50 and dt £8. Boats with motors per day £30 (pair) and £20 (single). Concessions for OAP. Fly only from boats. Regular trout stocking. Membership and permit enquiries to Hon Sec or to M P Atherton, Newsagent, Manchester House, Trawsfynydd, tel: 01766 540234. Hotels: Cross Foxes and White Lion, Trawsfynydd; Grapes and Oakely Arms, Maentwrog; Abbey Arms and Pengwern Arms, Ffestiniog. Accommodation at Fron Oleu Farm, Trawsfynydd and in self-catering chalets at Trawsfynydd Holiday Village.

DYSYNNI

(For close seasons, licences, etc, see Welsh Region Environment Agency, p20)

Rises in Llyn Cau, on steep southern side of Cader Idris, then falls rather rapidly via Dol-y-Cau. Falls into Talyllyn Valley about half a mile above well known Talyllyn Lake. Emerging from lake, flows westwards as typical upland stream to Abergynolwyn where, joined by the Gwernol, it turns north through narrow valley until it enters upper end of broad Dysynni Valley. At Peniarth it becomes deep and sluggish and finally enters Cardigan Bay 1½m north of Tywyn. Trout along whole length and tributaries, and sea trout (sewin) and salmon travel beyond Talyllyn Lake and up to Dolgoch on Afon Fathew. In lower reaches good sport may be had, early and late in season, with trout and sewin; August generally best. Also excellent grey mullet and bass in estuary.

Tywyn (Gwynedd). Salmon, sewin, trout, eels, with grey mullet in tidal parts and excellent bass fishing at mouth and from adjacent beaches. Rod licence only needed for fishing on estuary. Tywyn Post Office issues permits for several beats on River Dysynni; **Penowern Water**, ½m left bank from confluence with Afon Fathew; Peniarth Estate, Llanegryn, Tywyn, Gwynedd LL36 9LG, has 3 beats, permits for 1 beat and north bank of Afon Fathew (st £49, wt £18, dt 7.50); and Estimaner AA water at Abergynolwyn. Middle Peniarth Estate beat is private. Prince Albert AA has Upper Peniarth Estate beat; members only. **Peniarth Uchaf Fishery**, 2½m both banks, held by Hamdden Ltd; permits from Tynycornel Hotel, Talyllyn.

Abergynolwyn (Gwynedd). Salmon, sea trout, brown trout. Estimaner AA has 3m on Dysynni; stocking at intervals during seasons. Membership for local residents only. Visitors permits: st £25, wt £12, dt £6 (concessions for jun). Contact Hon Sec, tel: 01654 782 632.

Talyllyn (Gwynedd). Salmon, sea trout, brown trout. Tynycornel Hotel issues permits for **River Dysynni**, 3½m of mostly double bank fishing; **Talyllyn Lake**, 220 acre; and **Llyn Bugeilyn**, 45 acres. Brown trout fishing second to none. Tackle shop, ghillies, fishing tuition, boat hire (with engine) and tackle hire. Boat hire priority given to hotel residents but day tickets for boat and bank fishing invariably available. Permits from The Fishery Manager, Tynycornel Hotel, Talyllyn, Tywyn, Gwynedd LL36 9AJ, tel: 01654 782282 for permit availability).

Keep the banks clean

Several clubs have stopped issuing tickets to visitors because of the state of the banks after they have left. Spend a few moments clearing up. This includes lengths of broken nylon. If discarded, serious injuries can be caused to wild birds and to livestock.

GLASLYN

(For close seasons, licences, etc, see Welsh Region Environment Agency, p20)

Rises in Llyn Glaslyn, 3m south-west of Pen-y-Gwyrd, and flows through three lakes to Beddgelert then along Pass of Aberglaslyn to lower reaches and Porthmadog, where it enters the sea. Noted sea trout river and efforts are being made to increase salmon run. Best trout fishing in upper reaches, mountain lakes and tributaries. Best spots for salmon and sewin are: Glaslyn Hotel Bridge; Verlas; and above the pass.

Porthmadog (Gwynedd). Glaslyn AA has most of both banks of R Glaslyn and far bank of **Dinas Lake**; trout, sea trout and salmon; no prawn fishing; no ground bait; no boat fishing. St £50, wt £25 and dt £10; concessions for OAPs, disabled and juniors. Tickets from Y Pysgotwr, High St, Porthmadog; K Owen, Llyndu Farm, Nantgwynant, Beddgelert, Gwynedd; Penrhyn Guns, High St, Penrhyndeudraeth, Gwynedd. **Llyn Cwmystradllyn**, Caernarfon Rd, wild brown trout fishery, 95 acres, 6 bag limit. **Llyn Glan Morfa Mawr**, Morfa Bychan, 8 acre lake, rainbow trout, 6 bag limit. **Bron Eifion Fisheries**, Criccieth, Gwynedd, fly-only lake and bait lake; 6 fish limit. Permits from The Fisherman, Central Buildings, High St, Porthmadog, Gwynedd LL49 9LR, tel: 01766 512464, open 7 days a week, fresh bait sold; Penryn Guns, High St, Penrhyndeudraeth. Hotels: Royal Sportsman, High St; Madog Hotel, Tremadog.

Beddgelert (Gwynedd). Sea trout and salmon. Best for sea trout mid-May to early Sept; salmon May-Oct. Glaslyn AA has Glaslyn from Beddgelert to Porthmadog; and **Llyn Dinas**, 2m NE, sea trout and salmon. Permits - Mon to Fri; left bank (only) on Llyn Dinas, no boats, one day. Concessions jun & OAP. Permits from Beddgelert Post Office, Beddgelert, Caernarfon, Gwynedd, tel: 01766 890201.

GWYNEDD (rivers and streams)

(For close seasons, licences, etc, see Welsh Region Environment Agency, p20)

ABER. Aber, nr **Llanfairfechan** (Gwynedd). Aber rises in Llyn Anafon, runs to Aber and sea in 2m. Trout (average 7-8 in). Now a Nature Reserve. No fishing.

ARTRO. Rises in Llyn Cwm Bychan, 6m E of Harlech, and enters sea 1m below Llanbedr. Good bass fishing in tidal waters. Noted for night fishing for sea trout. Good fly pools below village and above Dol-y-Bebin.

Llanbedr (Gwynedd). Artro and Talsarnau FA has salmon and sea trout fishing on Artro. Assn also has water on **River Nantcol**, brown trout; **Cooke's Dam**, rainbow trout; **Llyn Tecwyn Uchaf** (brown trout) and **Llyn Tecwyn Isaf** (stocked with carp, roach, rudd, tench, perch) at Talsarnau; **River Glyn** at Talsarnau, sea trout and salmon; and **Llyn Fedw** at Harlech, brown trout. St £45, wt £20, dt £6. Concessions for OAP and junior. Permits from Newsagent, Llanbedr; Post Office, Talsarnau; Seafarer Fishing Tackle, Church St, Barmouth; and tackle shops in Penrhyndeudraeth and Porthmadog. Hotels: Victoria; Ty-Mawr.

DARON. Aberdaron (Gwynedd). Daron and Cyll-y-Felin run down two valleys and join at Aberdaron; restocked and hold good sized trout. Sea fishing for mackerel, pollack, lobster, crab, etc., from rocks or boat. Tackle and licences from R G Jones, Eleri Stores, Aberdaron LL53 8BG.

DWYFAWR. Best part of river lies 1m W of Criccieth, where there is length of 12m unobstructed and good for fly fishing. Salmon fishing has greatly improved owing to restrictions on netting. Sewin very good; late June to Oct; night fishing best.

Criccieth (Gwynedd). Sea trout and salmon. Criccieth, Llanystumdwy and Dist AA controls about 10m both banks. Assn also has about 2m on **Dwyfach**; shorter river than Dwyfawr (about 10m) and rather heavily wooded. Permits from Hon Sec; and R T Pritchard & Son, Sheffield House, High Street, Criccieth, Gwynedd LL52 0EY, tel: 01766 522116. Rod licences from Post Office. Good sea fishing in this area. Hotels: Glyn y Coed; Lion; Marine; George; Caerwylan.

ERCH. Pwllheli (Gwynedd). Pwllheli and Dist AA has brown trout, sea trout and salmon fishing on **Rivers Erch** and **Rhydhir**. Assn also has brown trout fishing on **Llyn Cwmystradllyn**; approx

10m NW; 95-acre lake holding wild and stocked brown trout; an upland fishery, situated in the heart of the rugged foothills of Snowdonia. Bag limit 6 brown trout per day. Weekly and daily tickets. Concessions for juniors and OAPs. Permits from D & E Hughes, Walsall Stores, 24 Penlan St, LL53 5DE, tel: 01758 613291.

GEIRCH. Nefyn (Gwynedd). Geirch, 2m W, 5m long; good sea fishing at Morfa Nefyn. Tackle shop: Bryn Raur Sports Shop, Morfa Nefyn, Pwllheli, Gwynedd.

GWYRFAI. Issues from Llyn Cwellyn, near Snowdon, and flows into Menai Strait through Betws Garmon and Llanwnda. Salmon, sea trout, trout.

Betws Garmon (Gwynedd). Seiont, Gwyrfai and Llyfni AS controls much of Gwyrfai; salmon, sea trout and brown trout. Wt £50, dt £12. Permits from Post Office, Betws Garmon; and Post Bach, Pool St, Caernarfon. Castell Cidwm Hotel water; permits which include use of boat, from Mr & Mrs D Roberts, Castell Cidwm Hotel, Betws Garmon, Nr Caernarfon. Preference given to hotel guests. **Bontnewydd Fishery**, salmon, sea and brown trout; dt from G J M Wills, Bryn Mafon, Caethro, Caernarfon, tel: 01286 673379 - after 6pm).

Rhyd-Ddu (Gwynedd). Seiont, Gwyrfai and Llyfni AS offers boat and bank fishing on **Llyn Gadair**, brown trout; **Llyn Cwellyn**, brown trout, char, salmon and sea trout; **Llyn-y-Dywarchen**, regularly restocked with rainbow and brown trout, fly only, bag limit 4. Wt £50, dt £12 (Llyn Cwellyn £7 and Llyn-y-Dywarchen £8). Permits from Cwellyn Arms. Boat packages available, enquiries to Hon Sec, tel: 01248 670666.

LLYFNI. Penygroes (Gwynedd). Rises in Drws-y-Coed, 4m E of town and runs through Nantlle Lake; salmon, sea trout (good), trout. Seiont, Gwyrfai and Llyfni AS controls most of river; wt £50, dt £12; permits from A D Griffiths, Newsagent, Snowdon St. Club also has fishing on **Llyn Nantlle**; boat only for salmon and trout; apply to Hon Sec, tel: 01248 670666.

SOCH. Llangian (Gwynedd). Trout and rudd; an early stream; dry fly useful; weeds troublesome later; some sewin, late; plenty of sea fishing, bass, pollack, whiting, flatfish, at Abersoch, from which this stream can be fished. Hotels: Rhydolion (Soch runs on boundary of farm, equipment available); Coed-y-Llyn, Sarn Bach Rd, Abersoch.

YSGETHIN. River rises in **Llyn Bodlyn**. Brown trout, Arctic char.

GWYNEDD (lakes)

(For close seasons, licences, etc, see Welsh Region Environment Agency, p20)

Bala Lake or Llyn Tegid. **Bala** (Gwynedd). Owned by Gwynedd County Council, Caernarfon. Permits from Lake Warden, Warden's Office, 24 Ffordd Pensarn, Bala, tel: Bala 520626, and tackle shop. Salmon may sometimes be taken and trout early in season. Pike, perch, roach, grayling, eels. Bala is largest natural lake in Wales, 4m long, 1m wide. Here, too, is found that rare and interesting fish called the gwyniad, a land-locked whitefish. Coarse fishermen will find all their wants more than provided for; pike up to 25lb; perch and good roach. Rod licence required. Tackle shop: Eryr Sports & Tackle, 31 High St, tel: Bala 520370.

Llyn Celyn. Bala (Gwynedd). Situated in the Snowdonia National Park at the foot of the Arenig Mountains; rainbow trout are stocked to supplement wild brown trout. Reservoir managed under licence by Bala AA; permits from D Evans, Tackle Shop, 31-33 High Street. Concessions for jun and OAP. Sunday fishing.

Hafod-y-Llyn. Llanbedr (Gwynedd). Roach, perch, eels. Permits from Lewis Bros, Tyddyn Ddu, Llanfair, Nr Harlech.

Cwm Bychan Lake. Llanbedr (Gwynedd). Trout and sewin; good fishing. For permission to fish, apply to Farm Manager, Cwm Bychan Farm, Cwn Bychan. For **Gloywlyn Lake** apply Cwmrafon Farm. **Llyn Perfeddau**, trout, good fishing;

Keep the banks clean

Several Clubs have stopped issuing tickets to visitors because the state of the banks after they have left. Spend a few moments clearing up.

free.

Maentwrog (Gwynedd). **Y-Garnedd**, 1m N (trout) and **Hafod-y-Llyn**, 1m NW (pike, coarse fish) are both private. Cambrian AA lakes in area: **Morwynion, Cwmorthin, Manod, Barlwyd, Dubach, Dubach-y-Bont, Cwm Foel, Cwm Corsiog**. Permits from F W Roberts, 32 Church St, Blaenau Ffestiniog, Gwynedd LL41 3HD, tel: 01766 830607.

Talsarnau (Gwynedd). Artro and Talsarnau FA has water on **Llyn Tecwyn Uchaf** and **Llyn Tecwyn Isaf**, brown trout; and on **River Glyn**, sea trout and salmon. St £45, wt £20, dt £6. Permits from Post Office. Hotels: Ship Aground; Motel.

LLWCHWR (or LOUGHOR)

(For close seasons, licences, etc, see Welsh Region Environment Agency, p20)

Rises some 3m east of Llandybie on Taircarn Mountain and flows 15m south-west through Ammanford and Pontardulais to Burry Inlet, north of Gower Peninsula. Fishing very good for sewin, and some brown trout and salmon (Apr-July; Aug-Oct best). Salmon and sewin runs reported to be increasing. Most fishing controlled by clubs, from whom tickets are available.

Llanelli (Carmarthenshire). Carmarthenshire County Council controls fishing on **Upper** and **Lower Lliedi Reservoirs**; season 20 Mar - 30 Oct; both reservoirs stocked with brown and rainbow trout. Fly only on Upper Lliedi. Boat for hire to members on Upper Lliedi; £6 per day. The council also has fishing at **Furnace Pond** and **Old Castle Pond** (carp, bream and pike), and at **Gwellian Pool** (trout, sewin and salmon), nr Kidwelly. Permits on site at Furnace Pond. Permits for all other sites from council offices and Anglers Corner, 80 Station Rd, tel: 01554 773981). For further information, contact Leisure Services, Ty Elwyn, Llanelli, Carmarthenshire SA15 3AP, tel: 01554 741100.

Llangennech (Dyfed). Llangennech AC has 4m on **River Gwendraeth Fach** between Llandyfaelog and Llangendeirne Bridge near Kidwelly; and 2m on **River Morlais,** a tributary of R Loughor, from the road bridge at Llangennech upstream. Season 1 Apr - 17 Oct. Mainly brown trout with good runs of sea trout in both rivers. Waters stocked with average 12" brown trout at intervals during the season. Bag limit 4 fish. St £20 plus £15 joining fee. Concessions for juniors, OAPs and disabled. Season members only, application forms from Hon Sec or Anglers Corner, 80 Station Rd, Llanelli, tel: 01554 773981. Club offers fresh water and some sea fishing competitions; and, during the close season, runs fly-tying classes.

Pontardulais (Glamorgan). Trout and a run of sea trout; some salmon. Pontardulais and Dist AA has 6m good fishing; permits from Bridge Café. Concessions for OAP and jun. Llangyfelach AA also has water. **White Springs Lakes**; 2 trout lakes and 2 coarse lakes; night-fishing and tents allowed on coarse lakes. Lakeside parking. Tickets on site in shop; also maggots, ground bait, tackle and rods for sale. Accommodation in holiday apartments. For further information contact White Springs Lakes, Holiday Complex, Garnswllt Rd, Pontardulais, Swansea SA4 1QG, tel: 01792 885699.

Ammanford (Dyfed). Ammanford & Dist AA has water on middle and upper reaches of Llwchwr and tributaries. Boat for club members at **Llys-y-Fran Reservoir**, much improved sea trout run, biggest fish 16½lb. Permits for these and other local waters from Tightlines Direct, 72-74 Wind St, Ammanford, Carmarthenshire SA18 3DR, tel: 01269 595858. Hotel: Glynhir Mansion, Llandybie, Carmarthenshire SA18 2TD, tel: 01269 850438.

Tributaries of the Llwchwr

AMMAN. Trout, sewin, few salmon. Very fast running; fishes well in spate.

Ammanford (Dyfed). Ammanford & Dist AA has water on **Llwchwr**, 5m; **Amman**, 3m; **Lash**, 3m; **Marlais**, 3m; **Cennen**, ½m; **Gwili**, 1½m. Sea trout run from May onwards. Concessions for juniors, youths and ladies. Instruction, fly-tying classes and competitions. Club boat based on Usk Reservoir, £5 to members. Permits from Tightlines Direct, 72-74 Wind St, Ammanford, Carmarthenshire SA18 3DR, tel: 01269 595858; and John Jones, 8 Florence St, Ammanford, tel:

01269 595770. Hotel: Glynhir Mansion.

MARLAIS BROOK. Llandybie (Dyfed). Sewin, July onwards. **Llwchwr**, 3m. **Gwendraeth Fawr**, 5m W. **Llyn Lechowen**, 5m W.

MAWDDACH

(For close seasons, licences, etc, see Welsh Region Environment Agency, p20)

Rises in hills between Bala and Trawsfynydd Lakes and flows 10m south to confluence with Wnion, 2m below Dolgellau, and thence through long estuary to sea at Barmouth. River holds salmon, sea trout and brown trout and is all preserved, although permits can be had for some stretches. Successful stocking with locally hatched salmon and sea trout. Salmon and sea trout may be taken up to Pistyll Mawddach.

Barmouth (Gwynedd). Rivers Mawddach and **Wnion**; trout, sea trout and salmon. Run of sea trout and salmon is from beginning of June to end of season. Trout fishing on **Cregennan Lakes** at Arthog; 2 natural lakes owned by the National Trust, situated on northern slopes of Cader Idris overlooking beautiful Mawddach Estuary. Large lake with island, 27 acres, wild brown trout only, fly spin or worm; dt £7.50 and evening £5. Small lake, 13 acres, regularly stocked with rainbows, plus a good head of wild brown trout, fly only; dt £12 and evening £6. Boat for hire but booking advisable. Permits from Emlyn Lloyd, Fridd Boedel Farm, Arthog, Nr Fairbourne, tel: 01341 250426. **Penmaenpool** (Gwynedd). Salmon, sea trout. George III Hotel, Penmaenpool, Dolgellau, Gwynedd LL40 1YD, tel: 01341 422525, has access to Dolgellau AA permits on all waters; salmon and sea trout fishing on lower beats of Mawddach near hotel; free fishing for residents.

Ganllwyd (Gwynedd). Salmon, sea trout. Dolgellau AA has left bank of upper beat from Ganllwyd to Tyn-y-Groes Pool. Hotels: Tyn-y-Groes, Ganllwyd, (1½m salmon and sea trout fishing on river); Dolmelynllyn Hall, Ganllwyd (1½m salmon and sea trout fishing on Mawddach, priority given to guests).

Tributaries of Mawddach.

WNION: Salmon, sewin, sea trout. The Rivers Mawddach and Wnion are well known for the excellent salmon and sea trout fishing. Dry weather only effects the upper reaches of the two rivers, as lower beats cover tidal waters.

Dolgellau (Gwynedd). Salmon and sea trout. Wnion runs by Dolgellau and joins Mawddach 2m below town. Best months for salmon and sea trout: May-Oct. Sewin fishing: Jul-Oct. Dolgellau AA owns fishing rights on 13m of Mawddach and Wnion. Stocked with salmon and sea trout from Mawddach Trust Hatchery. Assn also has wild brown trout and rainbow trout fishing on **Llyn Cynwch**, near well-known Precipice Walk. Annual Family Fishing Competition held on Llyn Cynwch early in August; contact Hon Sec for further details. St £52, wt £30, dt £11 (rivers) and dt £8 (lake). Concessions for juniors. Permits from W D Pugh & Son, Garage & Motel, Ardd Fawr, Dolgellau, tel: 01341 422681; and Fish Tails (Fishing Tackle Shop), Link House, Bridge St, Dolgellau, tel: 01341 421080. Hotels: Fronolau Farm Hotel, Dolgellau, tel: 01341 422361; Dolmelynllyn Hall, Ganllwyd, Dolgellau, Gwynedd LL40 2HP; Dolbrawdmaeth, Dinas Mawddwy, Machynlleth, Powys; George III Hotel, Penmaenpool, Dolgellau. These hotels can arrange fishing holidays for residents on all Dolgellau AA waters.

OGWEN

(For close seasons, licences, etc, see Welsh Region Environment Agency, p20)

Rises in Ogwen Lake, halfway between Bethesda and Capel Curig, with tributaries running in from Ffynnon Lloer and Bochlwyd Lakes, and runs from lake to outlet at Menai Straits, near Bangor, about 10m in all. Excellent trout fishing; leased by Ogwen Valley AA from Penrhyn Estate. Trout, sea trout (sewin) and salmon. Autumn good for salmon.

Bangor (Gwynedd). **Ogwen**, 2m E; salmon, sewin, trout. Sea trout run starts about mid-June. Salmon best Aug-Oct. Parts of river leased by Ogwen Valley AA. Tackle shop: Bangor Angling Supply Stores, 21 The High St, Bangor, Gwynedd LL57 1NP, tel: 01248 355518. Hotels: Waverly; British; Castle; Railway.

Bethesda (Gwynedd). Ogwen Valley AA has approx 5m of River Ogwen and tributaries near Bethesda; sea trout and salmon from July onwards. Assn also has brown trout fishing on four lakes: **Ogwen, Idwal, Ffynon Lloer** and **Bochlwyd**. Lake Ogwen stocked annually. Wt £25 and dt £10. Concessions for juniors. Permits from W Edwin (Grocer), opp Victoria Hotel, High St, Bethesda; The Post Office, Tregarth, nr Bethesda; The Post Office, Bangor; and Ogwen Bank Caravan Park, Bethesda.

POWYS (lakes)

Llyn Clywedog. Llanidloes (Powys). NW 3m; 615 acres; Llanidloes and Dist AA. Reservoir shared with sailing club; western half is fishery area, but fishing also permitted in much of eastern half by arrangement with sailing club. Well stocked with brown and rainbow trout averaging 1¾lb. Fly only. Boat hire. Permits from Hon Sec and Mrs Gough, Traveller Rest Restaurant, Longbridge Street, Llanidloes, tel: 01686 412329. Rod licence required. **Dol-llys Farm** has free fishing for their caravan users; contact O S Evans, Dol-llys Farm, Llanidloes, Powys SY18 6JA, tel: 01686 412694. Hotels: Mount Inn; Unicorn; Lloyds; Trewythen Arms.

Llangorse Lake. Llangorse (Powys). Holds good pike, good bream, perch, roach, eels. Fishing from boats only; can be hired. Permit needed to launch privately owned boats. Caravans for hire from Apr-Oct. Permits and boats from Ray Davies, Lakeside Caravan and Camping Park, Llangorse Lake, Brecon, Powys LD3 7TR, tel: 01874 658226. Accommodation and fishing at Trewalter Farm, LD3 0PS; equipment for hire. Llynfi runs from lake to Wye at Glasbury and holds a few trout; overgrown in places; requires short rod. Hotel: Red Lion.

Talybont Reservoir. Brecon (Powys). Reservoir in Brecon Beacons National Park, 318 acres, good wild brown trout fishery. Season 20 Mar - 17 Oct; fly only; catch limit 6 fish; size limit 9 inches. Permits from machine at Llwyn-On treatment works. Further information from C Hatch, Area Manager, Hamdden Ltd, Sluvad Treatment Works, Llandegfedd Reservoir, New Inn, Pontypool, Gwent NP4 0TA, tel: 01495 769281.

Lake Vyrnwy. Llanwddyn (Powys). Lake (1100 acres) stocked with rainbow and brown trout. Annual catch 3000 to 3500 averaging 1lb. Fly only. Ghillies and instructors can be arranged together with hire of rods. Apply to Lake Vyrnwy Hotel *(see advt)*, Llanwddyn, via Oswestry, Shropshire SY10 0LY, tel: 01691 870692.

SEIONT

(For close seasons, licences, etc, see Welsh Region Environment Agency, p18)

Rises in two tarns in Cwm-glas, under crest of Snowdon, and runs to Llanberis, 3m, where it enters the Llanberis Lakes, Llyn

Peris and Llyn Padarn. Flows thence into Menai Straits at Caernarfon. Attractive river with long flats, nice runs and excellent pools holding salmon (May onwards), sea trout (June onwards), and brown trout. Trout rather small, but in faster water can give good account of themselves.

Caernarfon (Gwynedd). Salmon, sea trout, trout. Seiont, Gwyrfai and Llyfni AS has 40m of salmon, sea trout and brown trout fishing on **Rivers Seiont, Gwyrfai** and **Llyfni**. Assn also has boat and bank fishing on **Llyn Padarn**, brown trout, char, salmon, sea trout; **Llyn Cwellyn**, brown trout, char, salmon, sea trout; **Llyn Gadair**, brown trout; **Llyn-y-Dwarchen**, 35 acres, rainbow trout and brown trout, fly only. Season ticket on application only. Wt £50, dt £12 (£7 Llyn Padarn and Llyn Cwellyn; £8 Llyn-y-Dywarchen), from Post Bach, Pool St; A D Griffiths, Newsagent, Penygroes; Garth Maelog Pet Centre, 51 High St, Llanberis, tel: 01286 870840, which stocks tackle and bait; Cwellyn Arms, Rhyd-Ddu; Post Office, Betws Garmon (also sells some fishing tackle and rod licences out of PO hours). Maps and information from Hon Sec, tel: 01248 670666. Seiont Manor Hotel, Llanrug, Caernarfon, Gwynedd, tel: 01286 673366, offers free fishing for guests on all club waters including use of boats on all lakes. Hotels: Royal; Black Boy Inn; Minffordd Guest House, Bethel, Caernarfon; Pantiau Farm, Rhosgadfan.

Llanberis (Gwynedd). Brown trout, Arctic char, salmon, sea trout. Seiont, Gwyrfai and Llyfai AS has bank and boat fishing on almost the whole of **Llyn Padarn**; dt £7 from A C Philips at Boat Hire Jetty, tel: 01286 870717, on lake, with special rates for boats for fishing. Permits, tackle and bait from Garth Maelog Pet Centre, 51 High St, tel: 01286 870840. Hotels: Lake View, tel: 01286 870 422; Dolbadarn, tel: 01286 870 277.

SOUTH EAST WALES

(For close seasons, licences, etc, see Welsh Region Environment Agency, p20)

AFAN. Aberavon (West Glamorgan). Small trout stream (with sewin on lower reaches) on which Afan Valley AC has water from Aberavon to Cymmer. Assn has improved sport; 3 salmon caught in 1991 season; tremendous runs of sewin in last few years; regular stocking. Fly only in March; worming allowed rest of season; spinning July-Sept at certain water levels. Permits, rod licences and tackle from Paddywacks, Aberavon Shopping Centre, Port Talbot. **River Nedd** 4m away; trout, sewin. Hotels: The Twelve Knights; Aberavon Hotel; Grand Hotel, Beach.

CADOXTON STREAM. Cadoxton (South Glamorgan). Cadoxton Stream rises 6½m from Cardiff and enters the sea 2m below Cadoxton. Small trout; permission from farmers (Glamorgan RD).

Eglwys Nunydd Reservoir. Margam (West Glamorgan). British Steel plc (Port Talbot) reservoir. Excellent trout fishing, brown and rainbow. Season: 3 Mar - 31 Oct. Very high stocking levels. Special terms for working and retired employees, and families. 4 boats for members. Fishing lodge for anglers. Apply Sports Club, British Steel plc, Groes, Margam, Port Talbot, tel: Port Talbot 871111 Ext 3368 during day.

NEATH. Rises in the Brecon Beacons and flows 27m to sea. Salmon, sewin, brown trout. Tributaries of the Neath are **Dulais** and **Pyrddin**.

Neath (West Glamorgan). Neath and Dulais AA has fishing on **River Neath** from Rehola to the estuary except for a short private beat; both banks; trout, sea trout and salmon. Assn also has both banks on **River Dulais** above Aberdulais Falls to the treatment works at Crynant. St £55 and dt £10; from Gary Davies, 6 Martins Ave, Seven Sisters, Neath, tel: 01639 701828. Limit of 100 members out of area. Concessions for juniors and OAPs. Skewen Coarse AC has fishing on: **Tennant Canal**, Aberdulais to Jersey Marine (all species); **Neath Canal**, Tonna to Briton Ferry (all species except pike); **Square Pond** at Briton Ferry (carp, roach, rudd, tench, bream, perch, eels, grass carp); and **Lower Reservoir** at Briton Ferry (carp, roach, rudd, perch, trout, bream). Close season in force on both canals but not on other waters. 2 rods only on all waters except Square Pond where 3 rods allowed. Permits available from Membership Secretary, tel: 01639 639657; Tackle and Bait, Stockholms Corner, Neath; and Mainwarings, Sketty, Swansea, tel: 01792 202245. Hotel:

Castle.

Glynneath (West Glamorgan). Glynneath and Dist AA has salmon, sea trout and brown trout waters on Neath and its tributaries, **Pyrddin, Nedd Fach, Mellte, Hepste** and **Sychryd**. Fly, worm and spinning from June only. Junior (under 12s) competition in June. Membership £20 + £10 joining fee, wt £10 and dt £5 (concessions for OAP, disabled and juniors). Coarse fishing on canal, between Tonna and Neath, also from Assn. Daily and weekly permits from Hon Sec; Dave Pitman's Hair-Stylist, 3 Avenue Buildings, Heathfield Avenue, Glynneath, tel (home): 01639 720127, which also sells a large selection of fishing tackle; and White Horse Inn, Pontneddfechan. Rhigos Fishing Club has a small coarse fishing pond; carp up to 20lb, roach, rudd; further information from Alex Greenow, tel: 01685 810037, or Dave Pitman's Hair-Stylists. Pyrddin AS (10m from Neath) has water; trout, salmon, sea trout; permits from Hon Sec. In headwaters of the Neath is Ystradfellte Reservoir.

OGMORE.

Porthcawl (Mid Glamorgan). Porthcawl SAA has coarse fishing on **Wilderness Lake** and **Pwll-y-Waem Lake**; carp, bream, tench, roach, perch and eels. Concessions for juniors. Permits from Porthcawl Angling, Dock St; and Ewenny Tackle Shop, Bridgend. Hotel: Brentwood, St Mary St.

Bridgend (Mid Glamorgan). Ogmore AA has 15m of Ogmore and tributaries **Ewenny, Llynfi** and **Garw**; salmon, sea trout and brown trout. Membership is restricted but weekly tickets are available from secretary. Concessions for juniors. Competitions for juniors; and fly-tying and casting lessons. Ogwr Borough AA has water on Ogmore and Garw. Membership restricted to residents but weekly tickets for visitors. Concessions for juniors and OAPs. Tackle shops: Ewenny Angling, Bridgend; Keens, Marine and Angling Superstore, 117-119 Bridgend Rd, Aberkenfig, Bridgend, Mid Glamorgan CF32 9AP, tel: 01656 722448. Hotel: Heronstone.

Maesteg (Mid Glamorgan). **River Llynfi**, a tributary of Ogmore; trout and sea trout. Llynfi Valley AA has 8m (Maesteg to Tondu); trout, sea trout and salmon. Fly-fishing-only stretch and no spinning until

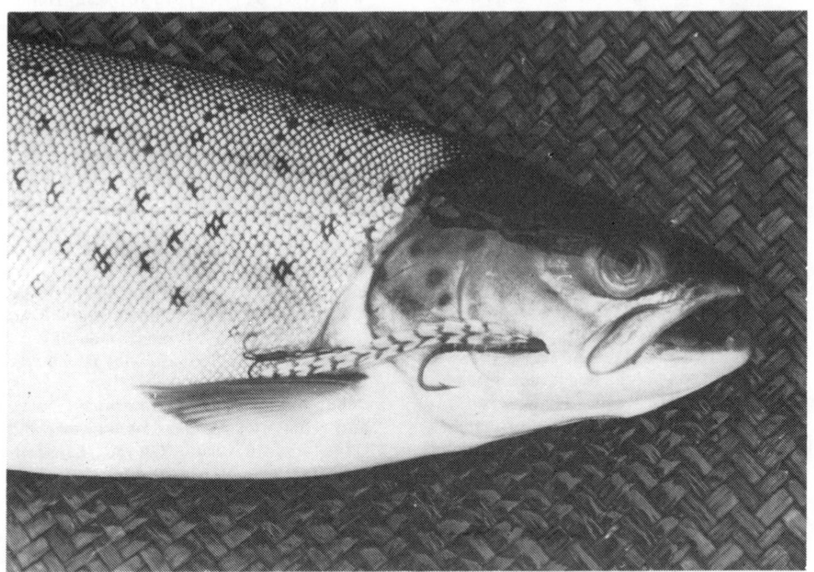

Importance is attached by Welsh sea trout fishers to the fly having a 'life.' This one appears to have possessed that attribute. *Photo: Moc Morgan.*

1 Jul. Members only. St £25 + £20 joining fee from Hon Sec.

RHYMNEY. Rhymney (Mid Glam). About 30m long, rises above town. Excellent grayling, chub, roach and dace fishing run by Caerphilly AC; further information from Green's Fishing Tackle. Rhymney and Dist AS has rights on two reservoirs: **Butetown** and **Rhos-Las**. Both well stocked with coarse fish of all usual species; pike in Rhos-las. All coarse fish, except pike, to be returned to water. Matches run most Saturdays for juniors and Sundays for seniors Jun-Aug, plus aggregate awards. St £12 first year then £10 (jun £6), dt £3 (jun £2) for both reservoirs from Hon Sec; Cal White, 39 The Square, Pontlottyn, Mid Glamorgan CF8 9PD, tel: 01685 841 245; Greens Fishing Tackle, Bryn Road, Pontllanfraith, Blackwood, Gwent NP2 2BU; and T Draper, Tackle Shop, Tredegar, Gwent. Coarse fishing at **Cwm-Darren Lake**, a modern fishery lake with excellent camping and caravanning facilities, predominantly carp with some other coarse fish; **Pembrith Pond**, a small water stocked with carp, chub, bream, roach, perch, tench; and a stretch on **Brecon-Pontypool Canal**. Day tickets from Cal White.

TAWE. Lower tidal reach now impounded by a barrage. Salmon and sewin runs have increased in recent years and they can be caught from Abercraf to Morriston. Upper reaches noted for scenery. Fishing controlled by clubs in all but tidal reaches.

Swansea (West Glamorgan). Swansea Amateur AA has salmon and sea trout fishing on the upper reaches of **Cothi** and a section of **Towy** at Llnwrda. Assn is a private company with a limited membership with a limited allocation of tickets for members' guests. Swansea AC has coarse fishing at Gower on **Fairwood Lake**, pike, bream, carp, perch, tench, roach, rudd, eels; and **Werganrows**, bream, carp, perch, tench, roach, rudd, eels. Members only. No day tickets. Concessions for juniors; also junior matches and match league coaching. City and County of Swansea has coarse fishing on 3 lakes. **Singleton Boating Lake**, Singleton Park, 2 acres; carp, tench, rudd, perch, crucian carp, eels; angling permitted when boats not in use. **Clyne Valley Pond**, small, very deep lake; perch, rudd, eels, trout. **Pluck Pond**, Lower Swansea Valley, 1 acres; perch, rudd. City and County of Swansea and Brynmill DAC have coarse fishing in **Morriston**, located on Swansea's Enterprise Zone; at **Fendrod Lake**, a large water with fairly good head of fish from carp up to 26lb and bream up to 7lb with an added bonus of wonderful surroundings; and at **Half Round Pond**, 2 small adjoining ponds; rudd, perch, tench. Permits from Leisure Services Dept, The Guildhall, Swansea SA1 4PE, tel: 01792 635411. **Shimano Felindre Trout Fishery**; rainbow, brown and golden trout; fly only. Tackle for sale and hire; casting lessons. Contact Jud Hamblin, Manager, Shimano Felindre Trout Fishery, Blaen-Nant Ddu, Felindre, Swansea SA5 7ND, tel: 01792 796584; accommodation for anglers 2m from fishery at Ganol Guest Houses, contact Frank Jones, tel: 01269 595640. Riverside Caravan Park has stretch on Tawe; bungalow accommodation and touring caravan park with all facilities. For further information contact Riverside Caravan Park, Ynysforgan Farm, Morriston, Swansea SA6 6QL. Tackle shops: Mainwaring's Angling Centre, 44 Vivian Road, Sketty, Swansea, tel: 01792 202245; Hook, Line & Sinker, James Court, Swansea Enterprise Zone, Winchwen, tel: 01792 701190; Kingfisher Sports, 25 High St, Swansea SA1 1LG; Siop-y-Pentref, Ynystawe, Swansea.

Pontardawe (West Glamorgan). Pontardawe and Swansea AS has stretch on R Tawe from Pontardawe to Morriston; brown trout, sea trout and salmon; st £50 and dt £10; concessions for OAP, disabled and juniors; tickets available by post from secretary or from tackle shops in Swansea. Llangyfelach and Dist AA has water on **River Llan**; sewin, brown trout; permits from B I Thomas, 1321 Carmarthen Rd, Fforestfach, Swansea, tel: 01792 427449; Mainwaring's Angling Centre, 44 Vivian Road, Sketty, Swansea, tel: 01792 202245; or County Stores, Gowerton.

Ystradgynlais (West Glamorgan). Tawe and Tributaries AA has 25m on **Tawe** and tributaries **Twrch**, **Gwys**, **Llynfell**, **Giedd**, **Lech**, **Gurlais** and **Cwn Du**, above Pontardawe; salmon, sea trout, brown trout and eels; trout stocked regularly up to 3lbs. Assn runs its own brown trout hatchery and rearing pond complex (during 1997, stocked waters with over 15,000 brown trout measuring from 9-18in). Membership restricted to local residents but permits available to non members. St £55 and dt £15. Concessions for juniors and OAPs. Junior river competition held annually. Fly-tying and casting tuition during close season. Permits from John Glynne Davies, Fieldsports, Station Road, Ystradgynlais, tel: 01639 843194; Pet, Garden and Sports Centre, Ystradgynlais, tel: 01639 843194; and Turners Newsagents, Capital Buildings, Ystalyfera. Hotels: Copper Beech Hotel, Abercrave; and Gwyn Arms Public House, Craig y Nos, Swansea Valley.

SOUTH WEST WALES (lakes)

Lake Berwyn. Tregaron (Ceredigion), 4m SE. Liming has taken place and as a result it holds excellent brown trout up to 1-2lbs. Stocked periodically. Tregaron AA hold fishing rights; permits from Medical Hall, Tregaron; Post Office, Pontrhydfendigaid; W Rees, London House, Llanddewi Brefi; Post Office, Llanfair Clydogau; and Alan Williams, 57 Bridge St, Lampeter.

Devil's Bridge (Ceredigion). Aberystwyth AA has the Penrhyncoch lakes in the hills between Devil's Bridge and Nant-y-Moch Reservoir (**Llyn Craig-y-Pistyll, Llyn Rhosgoch, Llyn Syfydrin, Llyn Blaenmelindwr** and **Llyn Pendam**); the Trisant Lakes 2m SW of Devil's Bridge, (**Llyn Frongoch and Llyn Rhosrhydd**); and part ownership of **Bray's Pool** and **Llyn Glandwgan**. Some are stocked, others self-stocking. Several contain trout up to 3lb. Fly only on Rhosgoch, Frongoch and Rhosrhydd; spinning and fly only on Craig-y-Pistyll. Permits from Aber Fishing Tackle and Gun Shop, 3 Terrace Road; and Mrs Dee, Erwyd Garage, Ponterwyd, Aberystwyth (who sells small amounts of fishing tackle and has fresh live worms for sale). Hotel: Hafod Arms.

Nant-y-Moch and **Dinas Reservoirs. Ponterwyd** (Ceredigion). These waters are set in the hills 12m E of Aberystwyth. Dinas, 38 acres, stocked weekly with brown and rainbow trout; fly, spinning and worming. Nant-y-Moch, 600 acres, native and stocked brown trout, fly only. Boats for hire on lake. **Cwm Rheidol Dam**, native and stocked brown trout, salmon and sea trout. Boats for hire on lake. Fly spinning and worming. Permits from Mrs Dee, Erwyd Garage, Ponterwyd, Aberystwyth, Dyfed SY23 3LA, tel: 01970 890664. Permits for Cwm Rheidol Dam also from PowerGen Visitors Centre and Fish Farm at the Power Station, Capel Bangor.

Pembroke (Pembrokeshire). Pembroke Town Mill Pool; mullet, bass, flatfish; also trout and sewin higher up. Hotel: Milton Manor.

Talybont (Ceredigion). Talybont AA has exclusive rights on **Llyn Conach, Llyn Dwfn, Llyn Nantycagal** and **Llyn Penrhaeadr**. Lakes some 7-9m into hills from village; 3 lakes stocked with brook trout; native wild brown in Penrhaeadr. Fly only on all lakes except Nantycagal. Boat hire on all lakes for holders of season tickets. Assn also has fishing rights on Forestry Commission land; 1m, both banks, on **River Leri** from Talybont to Dolybont; trout, sea trout and salmon. St £35 (junior £10) and dt £10 (bank only). Permits from Spar Store, Talybont; The White and Black Lion Hotels in Talybont; Mrs Hubbard, Compton Gift Shop, Borth, Ceredigion SY24 5JD (information and tackle also available); and Flymail Tackle Shop, Aberystwyth.

Teifi Lakes. Pontrhydfendigaid (Ceredigion). Lakes at headwaters of Teifi. Permits from Post Office, Pontrhydfendigaid.

SOUTH WEST WALES (rivers and streams)

(For close seasons, licences, etc, see Welsh Region Environment Agency, p20)

ALUN. St David's (Pembrokeshire). 6m long; 4m suitable for fishing, mostly on private property with owners permission; trout good quality but small. Boat trips and fishing tackle from R O Evans, High Street, St David's. Rod licences from Post Office, 13 New Dew St.

BRAWDY BROOK. Brawdy (Pembrokeshire). Small trout. Brook, 7m long, is mostly on private property. Licences can be purchased at Post Office, 13 New Dew Street, St David's.

CARNE. Loveston (Pembrokeshire). Carne rises 1½m W of Templeton, runs 3m to Loveston, and 1m down is joined on left bank by **Langden Brook**. Little or no rod fishing interest; fishing wiped out in 1993 with agricultural pollution; although an important spawning area for salmon and sea trout. Possible sea trout late in season, if adequate flows and no pollution. From confluence of Carne and Langden Brook into Cresswell, fishing controlled by Cresselly Estate. Coarse fishing reservoir at **Roadside Farm**; common, crucian and mirror carp, bream and roach; well stocked; tranquil surroundings and ample parking. Day, week and year permits. Contact D A Crowley, Roadside Farm, Templeton, Narberth, Dyfed SA67 8DA, tel: 01834 891283. Carp fishing at West Atherton near Narberth. Tackle shop: Bay Fishing, High Street, Saundersfoot, Dyfed.

CAREW BROOK. Carew (Pembrokeshire). This river, which rises by Redberth, is 4m long, joining sea water at Carew which is an inlet from Milford Haven. Although there is an element of rod fishing effort put into this river and its tributaries, the controlling interest is the farmer and the catchment is prone to agricultural pollution. The river does support a very small number of sea trout which only seem to appear in the close season.

CLARACH. Good numbers of sea trout can be found in the river late July onwards.

Aberystwyth (Ceredigion). Enters sea 1m N of Aberystwyth. Holds trout, sewin and occasional salmon; preserved. Permission from farmers.

GWAUN. Fishguard (Pembrokeshire). This 8-9m trout stream rises on lower slopes of Prescelly Mountains, and runs through a beautiful wooded valley. Trout not large but provide excellent sport with fly, and sewin also caught in season. A few salmon. **Yet-y-Gors Fishery** has two adjoining lakes covering 3 acres, well stocked with rainbow trout and brownies for fly fishing. Also coarse fishing pond with common and mirror carp, bream, tench, rudd and roach. Tackle for sale or hire. Facilities for disabled. Tickets available on site. Further information from Colleen and Hans Verhart, Yet-y-Gors Fishery, Manorowen, Fishguard, Pembrokeshire SA65 9RE, tel: 01348 873497. Tackle shop: Thomas & Howells, Dyfed Sport, 21 West St. Hotel: Glanmoy Country House.

GWENDRAETH FACH. Kidwelly (Carmarthenshire). Carmarthen and Dist AC has 5m; very good trout fishing; occasional sea trout in lower reaches. Llangennech AC has 4m stretch from Llandyfaelog to Llangendeirne Bridge, brown trout and sea trout. **Gwendraeth Fawr** runs 1m E from Kidwelly; trouting fair. Hotel: White Lion; Pen-y-Bac Farm (river fishing for trout, sewin and salmon; tuition and equipment).

LLANDILO BROOK. Maenclochog (Pembrokeshire). Small trout. Electrofishing surveys show very few fish of takeable size. No angling clubs. Seek permission from farmers to fish.

LLETHI. Llanarth (Ceredigion). Llethi Gido rises 3m above Llanarth, and 2m down is joined on left bank by brook 4m long. Llethi runs to Llanina and sea. One mile NE runs Drowy to sea, 4m long. Small trout. **Nine Oaks Fishery**, fly and coarse fishing, 2m inland between Newquay and Aberaeron; rainbow and brown trout in four pools; carp, tench and bream in coarse fishing lake. Tackle hire, beginners tuition and accommodation. Permits from Tony Evans, Nine Oaks Trout and Coarse Fishery, Oakford, Nr Aberaeron, SA47 0RW, tel: 01545 580 482.

MARLAIS. Narberth (Pembrokeshire). Gwaithnoak, 2m. Eastern Cleddau, 2m. Taf, 5m. Small trout. Rod licences from: Salmon & Son, Narberth Ltd, 28 High St; S H Davies, 1 St James St.

MULLOCK BROOK. St Ishmael's (Pembrokeshire). Small trout, 6m long, joining the sea at Dale Road.

NEVERN: Nevern (Pembrokeshire). River rises near Crymych and flows to sea at Newport; fast-flowing, densely wooded, deep holding pools. Nevern AA has salmon, sea trout and brown trout fishing; 6m on **Nevern**, nr Newport; and ¾m on **Teifi**, nr Llechryd. St £45 from Hon Sec. Wt £20 and dt £10 from Trewern Arms, Nevern; Y Siop Lyfrau (Bookshop), Newport; The Reel Thing, Market Stall, Cardigan; and Castaways, Cardigan. Concessions for juniors. Coaching for beginners and juniors (fly only). There are also club outings and fly-tying lessons. Hotels: Trewern Arms; Cnapan, Newport; Salutation Inn, Felindre Farchog.

PERIS. Llanon (Ceredigion). Peris is 6m long. Llanon, 4m long, runs ½m. Small trout. Hotel: Plas Morfa.

RHEIDOL. Aberystwyth (Ceredigion). Salmon, sea trout. Hydro-electric scheme governs flow. River almost entirely Aberystwyth AA water. Assn also has 2m stretch on **River Ystwyth**; and trout fishing on 9 lakes. Permits from Aber Fishing Tackle and Gun Shop, 3 Terrace Road; Mrs Lee, Erwyd Garage, Ponterwyd, Aberystwyth; and Richard Rendell, Blaenplwyf Post Office, Nr Aberystwyth, Ceredigion, tel: 01970 612499. Assn has 2 caravans (6-berth) to let at **Frongoch Lake**, approx £120 per week; includes week's fishing on the whole fishery and exclusive use boat for 4 days of the week. Coarse fishing at **Cwm Nant Nursery**; 2½ acre pond; carp, roach and tench. Permits from Mr W Evans, Cwm Nant Nursery, Capel Bangor, Aberystwyth SY23 3LL. Coarse fishing at **Tair Llyn Coarse Fishery**; privately owned 9-acre lake; carp, bream, roach, tench, rudd and perch. Permits from Mrs Ruth Jones, Tair Llyn, Cwm Rheidol, Aberystwyth. Hotels: Conrah; Chancery; Bay.

WYRE. Llanrhystyd (Ceredigion). Trout (small), some salmon and sometimes good for sewin. Fishing controlled by a number of riparian owners.

YSTWYTH. Aberystwyth (Ceredigion). Llanilar AA has 15m sea trout and salmon fishing on stretch of Ystwyth from Aberystwyth to Pontrhydygroes; some brown trout in Llanilar area. Best fishing is by fly at night, spinning in high water and with quill minnow as water clears; fly is also effective during the day when there is a touch of colour in the water. Concessions for OAP and junior. Competitions for locals on river and local lakes. Permits from Hon Sec; Fly Mail (Leather Shop), 3 Terrace Rd, Aberystwyth; Post Office, Crosswood; The Garage, Llanilar; Richard Rendell, Blaenplwyf Post Office, Nr Aberystwyth, Ceredigion, tel: 01970 612499. **Trawscoed Estate Fishery** has over 3m stretch on the central reaches of R Ystwyth, sea trout from June onwards; **Birchgrove Reservoir** situated in Forestry Commission woodlands, 1½ acres, carp fishing; and **Maesllyn Lake**, 5 acres, stocked with rainbow and brown trout, boat available. For further information contact Mr P Bowen, No 1 Estate Cottage, Trawscoed Mansion, Trawscoed, Aberystwyth SY23 4HT, tel: 01974 261 405; or Mick and Nikki Skevington, Post Office Trawscoed, Aberystwyth, tel: 01974 261 201. Accommodation can be arranged; and permits, rod licences and fishing tackle, including locally produced flies, are available at the Post Office.

TÂF

(For close seasons, licences, etc, see Welsh Region Environment Agency, p20)

Rises on Prescelly Mountains and flows about 25m south-west and south-east to Carmarthen Bay at mouth of Towy. Has good runs of salmon most years. Brown trout fishing excellent upstream of Whitland. Sewin can be caught most seasons from late March onwards.

St Clears (Dyfed). Good salmon and sewin; brown trout fair. April, May, Sept best for salmon. Sewin mid-June onwards. Carmarthen and Dist AC have water on Tâf and stretch on **Dewi Fawr**. St Clears and District AA has 5m on Tâf, from St Clears to Llanddowror; salmon, sea trout and brown trout. Assn also has salmon, sea trout and brown trout fishing on **R Ginning**, 3m; **R Dewi Fawr**, 1½m; **R Cowin**, 1½m. Concessions for juveniles and OAPs. Permits from Hon Sec; and The Pharmacy, Pentre Road. Other waters on these rivers by permission of farmers. Hotels: Black Lion; Gardde House; Picton House, Llanddowror, St Clears. Caravan sites at St Clears and Laugharne.

Whitland (Carmarthenshire). Salmon, sewin, brown trout. Whitland AA has 6m of fishing. St £55, wt £22 and dt £6 from Ithel Parri-Roberts, Swyddfa'r Post Office, Hendygwyn-ar-daf; Iorry Griffiths, The Garage, St Mary's St, Whitland, Carmarthenshire, tel: 01994 240753; and Chwareon Gog Sports, St Johns Street,

Fishing available?

*If you own, manage, or know of first-class fishing available to the public which should be considered for inclusion in **Where to Fish** please apply to the publishers (address in the front of the book) for a form for submission, on completion, to the Editor. (Inclusion is at the sole discretion of the Editor). No charge is made for editorial inclusion.*

Something comparatively new in Welsh angling - specimen coarse fish in farm ponds. This fish, a mirror carp from Dderw Farm, Llyswen, Brecon. *Photo: Mrs J Eckley.*

Whitland. Fly fishing at **White House Mill Trout Fishery**; contact White House Mill, Whitland, tel: 01834 831304. Coarse fishing on **Llyn Carfan**; stocked with carp, tench, roach and rudd. Rods and tackle for hire. Contact Llyn Carfan, Whitland, Dyfed SA34 0ND, tel: 01994 240819.

TAFF and ELY

(For close seasons, licences, etc, see Welsh Region Environment Agency, p20)

Taff has its source in two headstreams on the Brecon Beacons and flows about 40m south-east to enter the Severn Estuary at Cardiff. A short and steep river, heavily polluted since the 19th century by local iron, coal and steel industries. However, by the early 1980's there had been major improvements in the water quality due to economic recession and improved pollution control; and sea trout and some salmon were again entering lower reaches of river. Since then, the Welsh Water Authority, and subsequently the National Rivers Authority, have been successfully carrying out a strategy for rehabilitating salmon in the Taff; through pollution control, building fish passes, transporting adult fish upstream, artificial propagation and control of exploitation. In the 1990s, the Taff has become a prolific salmon and sea trout river in the lower reaches; these fish can now travel as far as Pontypridd. The Lower Taff, from Cardiff to Pontypridd is also a good coarse fishery, the main species being chub, dace, roach, gudgeon and barbel. Now, that the polluted legacy of the past has largely disappeared, the remainder of the Taff catchment supports good brown trout. The River Ely joins the mouth of Taff at Penarth. There are good roach in the lower reaches of the Ely; and an improvement in trout fishing throughout; salmon and sea trout have also been making a steady return since the late 1980s.

Cardiff (Glamorgan). Brown trout (stocked) and run of sea trout and salmon. Glamorgan AC has fishing on **River Taff** (chub, dace, eels, roach, salmon, sea trout, barbel, pike, perch and brown trout); 2 stretches on **River Wye**, at Monmouth (chub, dace, perch, pike, roach, bleak, gudgeon, eels and barbel) and at Clifford (chub, dace, roach, perch, pike, barbel, bleak and grayling); **River Usk** near Abergavenny (chub, dace, brown trout, salmon and sea trout); **East Dock** (roach, perch, chub, dace, carp and eels); **River Ely** at St Fagans (roach, chub and trout); **River Trothy** near Monmouth (chub, dace, trout, grayling, roach and pike); **Troes Pond** at Troes near Bridgend (bream, tench, perch, carp, roach and rudd); **Pysgodlyn Mawr** (bream, carp, roach, perch, rudd and tench); **Warren Mill** (carp, roach, bream, tench, rudd and perch); **Llantrythyd Lake** (carp, bream, roach, rudd, tench, perch and eels); and **St-y-Nyll Ponds** (pike, rudd, tench, perch and carp). For membership contact Chris Peters, 24 Llaleston Close, Barry, S Glamorgan. Bute AS, Birchgrove (Cardiff) AS and Glamorgan AC share lease of approx 3m fishing on R Taff in city limits; coarse (chub, roach, dace, gudgeon with barbel introduced recently); and game (salmon, sewin and brown trout) under auspices of combined Cardiff clubs known as Taff Fisheries. Day tickets from Gary Evans, 105 Whitchurch Rd, Heath, Cardiff, and A E Bales & Son, 3 Frederick St, Cardiff CF1 4DB. Bute AS has fixture list fishing on **R Wye** at Builth Wells and **R Usk** at Monmouth, and on a private lake within Cardiff's city limits; all venues hold roach, dace, gudgeon, bleak; members only; club membership from secretary. Birchgrove AS has fishing on **Rivers Ely** and **Taff**; salmon, sea trout, chub, dace, grayling, roach and barbel. Through kindness of riparian owners, the society also has coarse fishing on prime stretches on **R Wye** between Glasbury and Built; chub, dace, eels, grayling, pike, roach and perch. Fishing on Wye for members only. Permits from A E Bale & Son, 3 Frederick St. **Roath Park Lake** (Cardiff Corporation) holds rudd, roach, carp, tench. **Llanishen** (59 acres) and **Lisvane** (19 acres) **Reservoirs**, located within Cardiff City boundary, approach via B4562 road; leased to Cardiff Fly Fishing Club; day tickets sold at reservoirs. Tackle shop: A Bale & Son, 3 Frederick Street, Cardiff CF1 4DB (information, bait, licences); Gary Evans, 105 Whitchurch Road, Heath, Cardiff; Anglers Supplies, 172 Penarth Rd, Cardiff; Ely Angling Suppliers, 572 Cowbridge Rd East, Ely Bridge, Cardiff. Hotels: Angel; Cardiff International; Clare Court; Glenmor.

Merthyr Tydfil (Glamorgan). Merthyr Tydfil AA offers a large variety of waters from wild brown trout fishing on the Upper Neuadd Reservoir in the heart of the Brecon Beacons to salmon fishing on the Usk, with ponds and reservoirs for the coarse fishing enthusiast. The assn has 17m on **Taff** and **Taf Fechan** at Merthyr Tydfil from Pontsticill Reservoir to Quaker's Yard, brown trout, regularly stocked, size limit 10", bag limit 6 fish;

Upper Neuadd Reservoir, wild brown trout, very lightly stocked, fly only; **Taf Fechan Reservoirs**, trout (20 Mar - 17 Oct) and coarse (16 Jun - 17 Mar), no pike or other coarse fish to be removed; **Penywern Ponds**, coarse fish including carp in excess of 10lb, dt. Permits from Cefn Coed Tackle, High St, Cefn Coed, tel: 01685 379809; A Rees, 13 Alexandra Avenue, tel: 01685 723520; N Morgan, 20 James St, Twynyrodyn. Assn also has 2 stretches of salmon and trout fishing on **Usk** at **Mardy Fishery**, 1¼m; and **Kemeys Commander Fishery**, ¾m. Day tickets for Usk from A Rees and N Morgan (*see above*). Reservoirs in Taf Fawr Valley managed by Hamdden Ltd: **Beacons Reservoir** (52 acres) brown trout fly only; **Cantref Reservoir** (42 acres) rainbow and brown trout, fly only; **Llwyn-On Reservoir** (150 acres) rainbow and brown trout, fly, worm and spinner. All located in Brecon Beacons National Park adjacent to A470 (T) road, 3m north of Merthyr Tydfil and 15m south of Brecon. Cater for disabled. Private boats permitted. Dt from machine at Llwyn-On water treatment works. For further information contact C Hatch, Area Manager, Hamdden Ltd, Sluvad Treatment Works, Llandegfedd Reservoir, New Inn, Pontypool, Gwent NP4 0TA, tel: 01495 769281. Tackle shops: Cefn Coed Tackle, High St, Cefn Coed.

Tributaries of Taff

RHONDDA FAWR and RHONDDA FACH:

Pontypridd (Mid Glamorgan). At Junction of Rhondda Fawr and Fach, and Taff.

Tonypandy (Mid Glamorgan). Glyncornel AA has trout fishing on Rhondda; restocked annually with brown and rainbow trout. St £22 and wt £8. Concessions for juniors. Competitions for adults and juniors. Club also holds rights on very good coarse fishing at **Darran Lake**; carp, bream, tench, rudd, perch and silver bream; st £16 and wt £5. Permits from Top Line Anglers, Porth; Four Seasons Fishing Shop, Penygraig; Four Seasons Fishing Shop, Tonypandy; and Valley Fishing, Treorchy.

Ferndale (Glamorgan). Maerdy and Ferndale AC has water on River Rhondda Fach; and on **Lluest Wen** and **Castell Nos Reservoirs** at Maerdy. All water are trickle-stocked throughout the season. Fly only on Lluest Wen. Season and day permits from Top Line Angling, 7 Cemertary Rd, Porth, Rhondda; and day permits from David Hughes, North Road Motors, North Road, Ferndale.

ELY: Roach, chub, trout.

Ely (Glamorgan). Glamorgan AC has trout fishing on River Ely at St Fagans and coarse fishing in **St-y-Nyll Ponds** at St Brides-super-Ely.

Llantrisant (Glamorgan). **Seven Oaks Trout Fishery** has mainly rainbow trout on a put-and-take basis; and brown trout for sport. Tackle hire and some tackle sold on site. Contact Seven Oak Fishery, Cowbridge Road, Nr Pontyclun, Mid Glam CF7 9JU, tel: 01446 775474.

TEIFI

(For close seasons, licences, etc, see Welsh Region Environment Agency, p20)

Rises in Llyn Teifi, near Strata Florida, in NE Dyfed, flows south-west and then west, entering Cardigan Bay below Cardigan Town. Association water provides salmon, sea trout (sewin) and brown trout fishing. April and May are the best months for spring salmon; summer salmon fishing through to October can also be lucrative given reasonable water levels. Sea trout run from May onwards. Coracle and draft nets come off 1 September. Main salmon run September onwards.

Cardigan (Dyfed). Salmon, sewin, trout. Bass, mullet and flounders below bridge to sea, 2m; boats for hire. Teifi Trout Assn has fishing for salmon, sea trout and brown trout on 20m stretch of lower River Teifi, from a few miles above Cardigan to just beyond Newcastle Emlyn, including fishing at Cenarth. Assn also has stretch, ¾m, above Henllan (salmon, sea trout and brown trout). St £125 plus £20 joining fee from Membership Secretary. Surcharge of £40 on Cenarth waters. Concessions for OAPs, disabled and junior. Wt £60-£70 and dt £15-£20 (junior £3) from The Reel Thing, Lower Market, Cardigan SA43 2JR; Thomas Sports Shop, Newcastle Emlyn; Old Post House, Cilgerran; The Salmon

Leap and Cenarth Falls Holiday Park, Cenarth; and Afon Teifi Caravan Park, Pentrecagal.

Llechryd (Dyfed). Salmon, sea trout. Castle Malgwyn Hotel has 2½m of salmon, trout and sea trout fishing on the lower reaches of Teifi; best time for salmon July and Aug; reserved for guest of hotel; special rates for parties. Nevern AA has ¾m stretch on R Teifi, nr Llechryd. Teifi Trout Assn water.

Cenarth (Dyfed). Salmon, sewin, trout. Famous falls. Teifi Trout Assn water; surcharge for Cenarth Fishery. Permits from The Salmon Leap, Cenarth, Newcastle Emlyn, Dyfed SA38 9JP, tel: 01239 711242, where there is also a comprehensive range of fishing tackle and bait for sale; and Cenarth Caravan Park. West Wales School of Fly Fishing has its own private fisheries (clients only) on **R Cych** and **R Gwili**, and teaching beats on **R Teifi**; wild brown trout, sea trout and salmon. It also has 2 lakes stocked with brown and rainbow trout. The school runs courses for beginners and for those keen to improve their skills; free flyfishing lessons for young people in school summer holidays. Contact Pat O'Reilly, Senior Instructor, West Wales School of Fly Fishing, Ffoshelyg, Llancych, Boncath, Pembrokeshire SA37 0LJ, tel: 01239 698678.

Newcastle Emlyn (Dyfed). Salmon and sea trout. Good centre for Teifi. Teifi Trout Assn has water; permits from Thomas Sports Shop, Newcastle Emlyn. Riverside cottages with exclusive private fishing on an adjoining ¾m stretch of Teifi, salmon, sea trout and brown trout; for further information contact Dr D Rowe, Dôlhaidd Isaf, Newcastle Emlyn, Dyfed SA38 9HU, tel: 01559 370084. Rod licences from Chwaraeon Andrew Sports, 7 Sycamore St; and Dr D Rowe, Dôlhaidd Isaf. Hotels: Emlyn Arms.

Llandysul (Dyfed). Salmon, sewin, brown trout. Popular centre: fishing good. Best April-May and Aug-Sept for salmon; sewin July onwards. Llandysul AA has 28m of Middle Teifi. Wt and dt from Gwilym Jones, The Alma Store, Wind St, Llandysul SA44 6HB, tel: 01559 363322, and Alan Williams, Lampeter Angling, 57 Bridge St, Lampeter, tel: 01570 422985. Free instruction for children by qualified instructors from the West Wales School of Fly Fishing every Fri through Aug, including for non-members. Cross Hand and District AA has stretch on R Teifi, nr Llandysul; salmon and sea trout. Rainbow trout fishing on a 2-acre lake at **Rhydlewis Trout Farm**; stocked daily; fly only. Lakeside parking, toilets, tea & coffee-making facilities, smokery and smokery shop. For further details contact Doug & Jacky Quilgley, Ryd-yr-Onnen, Rhydlewis, Llandysul, Dyfed SA44 5QS, tel: 01239 851224. Hotels: Kings Arms; Castle Howell; Henllan Falls, Henllan, Llandysul; Porth and County Gate, Llanfihangel-ar-Arth, Pencader.

Llanybydder (Carmarthenshire). Salmon, sewin, brown trout. Llanybydder AA has approx 5m of Middle Teifi, both banks, above and below Llanybydder Bridge. St £45, wt £31.50 and £36.50, dt £8.50 and £12.50. Concessions for jun. Instruction, and challenge cup for best junior angler. Permits from Hon Sec and David Morgan, Siop-y-Bont, Llanybydder. Hotels: Crosshands; Black Lion; Grannell Arms, Llannwnen, Ceredigion.

Lampeter (Dyfed). Salmon, April onwards; sewin, late June, July, August onwards; brown trout, both dry and wet fly. Both Llandysul AA and Tregaron AA have water on Teifi around Lampeter. **Hendre Pools**, rainbow trout; permits from O G Thomas, Hendre, Cilcennin, Nr Lampeter SA48 8RF. **Troed-y-Bryn Fisheries**, rainbow and brown trout, privately owned lakes, 3½ acres, fly only; permits from Mrs E E Edwards, Troed-y-Bryn, Cribyn, Lampeter. Rod licences from Post Office, Cribyn. Tackle shop: Alan Williams, 57 Bridge St, Lampeter, Dyfed SA48 7AB, tel: 01570 422985.

Tregaron (Dyfed). Good fly fishing for brown trout. Salmon fishing also good when conditions right. Tregaron AA has 17m of **R Teifi** from Pontrhydfendigaid to Tregaron and down river to Cellan; **Teifi Pools**, 3 lakes, wild brown trout; and **Llyn Berwyn**, 50 acres. St £40 and dt £6. Concessions for juniors. Permits from Medical Hall Newsagent, The Square, Tregaron; Post Office, Pontrhydfendigaid; W Rees, London House, Llanddewi Brefi; Post Office, Llanfair Clydogau, Lampeter, Dyfed SA48 8LA; and Alan Williams, 57 Bridge St, Lampeter. Permits for **Teifi Pools**; dt £5; from Newsagent, Tregaron; Post Office at Pontrhydfendigaid; and farm on road to fishery. Other good fishing on Aeron, 6m. Hotel: Talbot. Accommodation: Brynawel and Aberdwr Guest Houses.

TOWY (or TYWI)

(For close seasons, licences, etc, see Welsh Region Environment Agency, p20)

Lower reaches near Carmarthen are tidal holding trout, salmon and sewin in season (May, June and July best); association waters. Above this Towy mostly preserved, but some fishing by leave, ticket or from hotels. Salmon average 12lb and sea trout up to 8lb are taken; brown trout generally small.

Carmarthen (Dyfed). Salmon, sewin, trout. April and May usually good for large sewin. Tidal up to Carmarthen and 3m above. Carmarthen Amateur AA has 14m on **Towy** at Nantgaredig, White Mill and Abergwili; sewin and salmon. Assn arranges 6 competitions a year and has 5 private car parks. Weekly permits from Outdoor Pursuits, Jackson's Lane, Carmarthen; or the secretary. Carmarthen and Dist AC has water on **Rivers Towy** (tidal and non-tidal), **Cothi, Gwili, Taf** and **Gwendraeth Fach**; all these waters are within 5-10 miles of Carmarthen. Membership £60; dt £20 and £5 (junior). Permits are available from Hon Sec and Fishfinder, Jackson's Lane, Carmarthen. Hotel: Golden Groves Arms, Llanathne, Carmarthen SA32 8JU. Accommodation: Farm Retreats, Capel Dewi Uchaf Farm, Capel Dewi Road, Capel Dewi, Carmarthen, Carmarthenshire SA32 8AY, tel: 01267 290799; and Old Priory Guest House, Carmarthen.

Nantgaredig (Dyfed). Salmon and sea trout fishing on the Abercothi Estate; 3 beats on **Towy** and 1 beat on **Cothi**. Weekly letting on Towy for parties of up to 5 rods; seasonal letting on Cothi. Contact Hamdden Ltd, Plas y Ffynnon, Cambrian Way, Brecon, Powys LD3 7HP, tel: 01874 614657 and fax: 01874 614526. Carmarthen Amateur AA has water on **Cothi** and **Gwili**. Cross Hand and District AA has stretches on R Towy and R Cothi in area; salmon and trout. Rod licences from Post Office Dolgoed, Station Rd. Tackle shop: The Armourers Shop, Ye Olde Post Office, Felingwm Uchaf.

Llandeilo (Dyfed). Salmon, sea trout, brown trout. Llandeilo AA preserves 4½m on Towy, about 1½m on **Lower Dulais** and about 3m on **Lower Cennen**. Season tickets, members only (waiting list), from Hon Sec; weekly and day tickets from Hon Sec and Towy Sports, 9 King St, tel: 01558 822637. Concessions for jun. Fishing good when water in condition. Salmon and sea trout fishing on Golden Grove Estate; 10m stretch on **Towy** from Llandeilo to Llanegwad, mainly double bank; best months Jun-Aug. Self-catering accommodation for anglers at Sannan Court, Llanfyndd. For further information on Golden Grove fishery and Sannan Court, contact Hamdden Ltd, Plas y Ffynnon, Cambrian Way, Brecon, Powys LD3 7HP, tel: 01874 614657 and fax: 01874 614526. Black Lion Inn, Llansawel, has 2½m on Towy; rods also on **Teifi** and **Cothi**. **Cennen** good trout stream. Hotels: Cawdor Arms; Castle; Edwinsford Arms; Plough Inn; White Hart; Cottage Inn; Ty-Isaf Fishing Lodge and Country Cottages, Trapp, Llandeilo (game fishing on rivers and reservoirs; tuition).

Llangadog (Dyfed). Salmon, sewin, trout. Llangadog AA have water. Wt, dt and limited night-fishing tickets issued.

Llanwrda (Dyfed). Salmon and sea trout. Swansea Amateur AA rents 1m (both banks), on an annual basis; access south of railway station; fly only. Members and guests only. Concessions for juniors. Glanrannell Park Country House Hotel, Crugybar, Llanwrda, Nr Llandovery, Carmarthenshire SA19 8SA, tel: 01558 685230, has agreements with a number of private owners on **Rivers Cothi, Towy** and **Teifi;** and tickets for assn waters are obtainable from nearby towns, Llandeilo and Lampeter. Hotel keeps some tackle for hire and basic instruction in fly fishing is from Dai Davies, the hotel's resident proprietor. Fishing at **Harford Fishery**: 2½-acre trout lake and 2-acre coarse lake. Fishing tackle. Contact Harford Fishery, Llanwrda, Dyfed, tel: 01558 650505.

Llandovery (Dyfed). Salmon, sewin (best June-Sept), trout. Llandovery AA waters 7m on **Towy**, excellent fly water below Llandovery, holding pools with fish (sewin) up to 14lbs, and salmon and grilse in Aug-Sep; and 10m on tributaries **R Gwydderig** and **R Bran**, good head of natural trout and sewin from July onwards. Tickets from secretary and The Carmarthen & Pumpsaint Co-operative Store at Main Car Park, Llandovery. Hotels: Castle Hotel, Llandovery;

Llwyncelin Guest House, Llandovery; and Cwmgwyn Farmhouse (B&B) which over looks R Towy, tel: 01550 720150.

Tributaries of the Towy

GWILI. Small river of 12ft to 16ft in width which joins Towy 1m north of Carmarthen. Sea trout (sewin), fish running from early June onwards, averaging 2lb and attaining 6lb. Brown trout fishing poor. A few salmon caught on Gwili, especially at the end of year.

Llanpumsaint (Dyfed). Sewin, trout, occasional salmon. Carmarthen Amateur AA and Carmarthen and Dist AC both have stretches on Gwili. Hotel: Fferm-y-Felin (18th century farmhouse with 15 acres of countryside for fishing and bird watching, tuition and equipment for hire).

COTHI. The largest tributary of the Towy, noted for its sewin which run in late summer and early autumn. Salmon, sewin and brown trout.

Carmarthen (Dyfed). Carmarthen Amateur AA and Carmarthen & Dist AC both have stretches on Cothi. The Cothi Bridge Hotel, Nantgaredig, Carmarthen, Dyfed SA32 7NG, tel: 01267 290251, has a short stretch of salmon fishing and has arrangements for guests to fish on other private and club waters; special rates for fishermen. Tackle shop: M Lewis, Fishing & Shooting Supplies, 33 King St.

Brechfa (Dyfed). Salmon and sea trout. Swansea Amateur AA has 2m (both banks), between Abergorlech and Brechfa. Members and guests only. Hotels: Ty Mawr.

Pumpsaint (Dyfed). **Cothi** and **Twrch**. Trout, sea trout (June onwards); salmon from early July. Dolaucothi Arms, Pumpsaint, Llanwrda, Dyfed SA19 8UW, tel: 01558 650547, has approx 8m of fishing, made up of 12 rods. Season starts from July to August when the salmon come up. Permits from pub; and bed and breakfast. Glanrannell Park Country House Hotel, Crugybar, Llanwdra, Nr Llandovery, Carmarthenshire SA19 8SA, has salmon, sea trout and trout fishing on Teifi, Cothi and Twrch.

SAWDDE. Llanddeusant (Dyfed). Trout. Accommodation and fishing at Cross Inn and Black Mountain Caravan and Camping Park, Llanddeusant, Nr Llangadog, Dyfed SA19 9YG, tel: 01550 740621; rainbow and brown trout fishing on **Usk Reservoir** (3m), also on Sawdde (3m) and Towy (6m).

USK and EBBW

(For close seasons, licences, etc, see Welsh Region Environment Agency, p20)

The River Usk is a good salmon river and first rate for trout. Geological formation is red sandstone, merging into limestone in lower reaches. Trout average from about ¾lb in the lower reaches to ¼lb towards the source. Some tributaries also afford good trout fishing: Afon Llwyd, Honddu, Grwyne, Yscir and Bran. Salmon fishing mostly private, but several opportunities for trout. The River Ebbw flows into the Severn Estuary between the mouths of the River Rhymney and the River Usk. The Ebbw has recently experienced great improvements in water quality which has been reflected in the fishery improvements, with very good trout and reports of sea trout. The Sirhowy, a tributary of Ebbw, also has good trout fishing.

Newport (Gwent). Newport AA has stretch of **Monmouthshire and Brecon Canal**, **Woodstock Pool**, **Morgans Pool**, **Liswerry Pond** and **Spytty Lake**; all providing good coarse fishing, including roach, perch, bream, carp and tench. Assn also has coarse fishing on **R Wye** at Symonds Yat; roach, dace, chub. Day tickets from bailiffs at lakes. Islwyn & Dist AC have trout fishing on Ebbw, **Sirhowy** and **Penyfan Pond**. Membership from Mrs J Meller, Membership Secretary, 7 Penllwyn Street, Cwmfelinfach. Day tickets from Pontllanfraith Leisure Centre, Pontllanfraith, Blackwood, Gwent, tel: 01495 224562. Newport Reservoir Fly Fishing A has fishing on **Ysyfro Reservoir**, High Cross, nr Newport; rainbow and brown trout. Day permits (£11) for non members can be purchased from hut at reservoir. Trout fishing at **Wentwood Lake**, 40 acres; fly only; tel: 01291 425158. Rainbow and brown trout fishing on **Cefn Mably Lakes**, a complex of 5 spring-fed waters on farm land lying beside the River Rhymney; one 6½ acre lake, fly only; others any method; all stocked. Apply to

An Usk trout brought to the net by Grace Oglesby. If there is a finer trout stream in Wales, few know of it.

John and Maggie Jones, Cefn Mably Lakes, Nr Castleton, Newport, tel: 01633 681101. **Hendre Lake**, 10-acre coarse fishery at St Mellons; an excellent lake, especially in hot and cold weather when other lakes are struggling; permits from Garry Evans, Fishing Tackle. Tackle shops: Garry Evans, Fishing Tackle, 29 Redland St, tel: 01633 855086; Dave Richards, 73 Church Road, tel: 01633 254910; Pill Angling Centre, 160 Commercial Rd, tel: 01633 267211; Richards Tackle, Duckpool Rd. Hotels: Rising Sun, High Cross, Nr Newport, Gwent; Tredagar Arms, Bassaleg, Nr Newport, Gwent; Tredegar Arms, Risca Road, Nr Newport, Gwent.

Pontypool (Gwent). Usk private. Tributary **Afon Llwyd**, good trout fishing and regularly stocked by local clubs. Subject to periodic pollution but soon recovers due to exceptionally fast flow. Pontypool AA and Cwmbran AA have stretches. Pontypool AA also has **Allway Brook**, nr Usk, trout, dace and chub: and coarse fishing on **Monmouthshire & Brecon Canal** at Pontypool (Bridges 55 to 57), roach, perch, bream, carp and tench. Permits from Pill Angling, Orsbourne Road. **Llandegfedd Reservoir** (429 acres) owned by Welsh Water plc is a major boat fishery; well stocked with brown and rainbow trout; season 20 Mar-31 Oct (rainbow), 20 Mar-17 Oct (brown). Fly only; catch limit 6 fish (part day, 4 fish). Permits from Sluvad Treatment Works, Llandegfedd Reservoir, Panteg, Pontypool, tel: 01495 755122; and vending machines on site. Forty boats for hire, pre-booking is recommended. Cwmbran AA has coarse fishing on **Monmouthshire & Brecon Canal**; average depth 4ft; stocked with bream, tench, crucian carp, roach, perch, good eels in parts; strict control on litter. Assn also has coarse fishing, for members only, at **Llantarnam Industrial Estates Ponds** (3 ponds stocked with roach, perch and dace, and one stocked with rudd and bream); and excellent mixed fishing on **River Monnow**, trout, grayling, bream, roach, perch, dace, chub and carp. Night fishing on canal and Monnow. Permits from Cwmbran Pet Stores and Angling Supplies, 23 Commercial St, Old Cwmbran. No day tickets on Llantarnam Ponds; members only.

Usk (Gwent). Usk Town Water Fishery Association holds about 2m, mostly above Usk Bridge. Trout fishing only. Rod licence required. Wading advisable. Merthyr Tydfil AA has water at **Kemeys Commander**. Permits, tackle and licences from Sweet's Fishing Tackle, 14 Porthycarne Street, Usk, Gwent NP5 1RY, tel: 01291 672552. Hotels: Three Salmons; Castle; Cross Keys; Glen-yr-Avon; Kings Head; Chain Bridge, Nr Usk; Bridge Inn.

Abergavenny (Gwent). Salmon, trout. Monmouth DC holds town waters, both banks from Llanfoist Bridge to Sewer Bridge. Tickets from Bridge Inn, Llanfoist and PM Fishing Tackle. Crucorney Trout Farm, on **River Honddu**; small river fishing with lots of cover; stocked with 1-2lb rainbows, wild browns; fly only; permits from farm shop. Advance booking essential, tel: 01873 890545. Merthyr Tydfil AA has rights to **Mardy Fishery**, 1¼m above town. Tickets for various waters from PM Fishing Tackle. Tackle shops: PM Fishing Tackle, 12 Monk Street; Fussells Sports, 53 Cross Street, both Abergavenny; Brutens, Market Street, Ebbw Vale. Hotel: Wenallt; Penpergwm House.

Glangrwyney (Powys). Salmon, sea trout, brown trout. Bell Hotel has water here and issues tickets to residents and non-residents for salmon and trout fishing. Hotel stocks Usk flies.

Crickhowell (Powys). Salmon, sea trout, wild brown trout. Gliffaes Country House Hotel, NP8 1RH, tel: 01874 730371 *(see advt)*, has 1m on Usk adjacent to hotel and a further 1½m upstream. Excellent wild brown trout water; salmon improving and some sea trout. Primarily hotel guests but outside rods if space. Bridge End Inn has short length below bridge. **Trecastle** and **Talybont Reservoirs** are within reach. Hotel: Stables.

Brecon (Powys). Brecon AS has water on R Usk from Llanfaes Bridge to Boat House; salmon and trout. Left bank (Llanfaes side) members only. Promenade bank (right bank) dt £1 from S Richardson, Newsagent, Struen, Brecon; Mrs Lindsey Wilding, Post Office, Llanfaes, Brecon, tel: 01874 622739; and H.M. Supplies Ltd, Watton, Brecon, tel: 01874 622148. Brecon Borough Council has stretch on Usk from boathouse to promenade at Watton. Salmon and trout fishing on Wye and Usk in the Brecon and Builth Wells area; day tickets from Woosnam & Taylor (Chartered Surveyors & Land Agents), Dolgarreg, North Road, Builth Wells, Powys LD2 3DD, tel: 01982 553248. Brecon FA has 1m both banks below Llanfaes Bridge; trout; fly only. Coarse fishing in pools on **Dderw Farm**; carp (to 20lbs), roach, tench; self-catering studios; fishing inclusive for residents; permits from Mrs J Eckley, Dderw Farm, Llyswen, Brecon LD3 0UT, tel: 01874 754224. **Llangorse Lake**, 6m from Brecon; pike, perch, roach and bream; no permits required only rod licence. Boats and caravans from Mr Davies at Waterside. Hotels: Griffin Inn, Llyswen, Brecon; Castle of Brecon; Nythfa, Uskview GH.

Sennybridge (Powys). Rods on **Crai Reservoir** (100 acres) owned by Cnewr Estate Ltd, Sennybridge, Brecon LD3 8SP, tel: 01874 636207. Wild trout; fly fishing from bank only. Day tickets from reservoir keeper. Self-catering accommodation is usually with the fishing. Hotels: Tir y Graig Uchaf.

Trecastle (Powys). **Usk Reservoir** (280 acres), one of the best trout fisheries in Wales, well stocked with rainbow and brown trout supplementing natural production. Fly fishing, spinning and worming. Catch limit 6 fish; size limit 9 inches. Anglers are permitted to use their own boats by prior arrangement. Caters for disabled. Permits from machine on site. For further information contact C Hatch, Area Manager, Hamdden Ltd, Sluvad Treatment Works, Llandegfedd Reservoir, New Inn, Pontypool, Gwent NP4 0TA, tel: 01495 769281. Hotel: Castle.

Ebbw Vale (Gwent). Ebbw Vale Welfare AC has coarse fishing on **River Wye** at Foy, nr Ross-on-Wye, 2½m (chub, dace, roach and barbel); **Monmouthshire & Brecon Canal**, nr Crickhowell, ½m (roach, perch, bream); **Machine Pond** at Brynmawr, 5 acres (carp, roach, perch); and 10 ponds in the Ebbw Vale area (carp, pike, roach, perch and gudgeon). Members only. Membership open to all; from Hon Sec and local pet shop. Contact Hon Sec for season tickets for people on holiday. Concessions for juniors. Tackle shops: J Williams & Son, Bethcar St; Petsville, Bethcar St.

WYE

(For close seasons, licences, etc, see Welsh Region Environment Agency, p20)

The whole of the river Wye is included in the section on England, although it also flows through Monmouthshire and Powys.

WELSH SEA FISHING STATIONS

Those given in the following list are arranged from south to north. Sea fishing is available at other places also, but those mentioned are included because they cater specially for the sea angler. Further information may be had from the tackle shops and club secretaries (whose addresses will be found in the club list). When writing, please enclose stamped addressed envelope for reply. Local tourist information offices will help with accommodation.

Newport (Newport). Newport and District Sea Anglers operate in Magor, Redwick, Goldcliff, St Brides, Cardiff and Barry, with rover matches from Severn Bridge to Gower in West Wales; matches held every weekend; and, during the summer, Docks Summer League every Wed for 16 weeks. Tackle shops: Dave Richards, 73 Church Road, tel: 01633 254910; Pill Angling Centre, 160 Commercial Rd, tel: 01633 267211. Hotel: Kings Head.

Swansea (Swansea). Bass, flatfish from beaches and rocks (Worm's Head). Fish baits cast from Llanmadoc take conger, tope, thornbacks and monkfish. Mackerel caught in warmer months. Bass, mullet and flounders in estuary at Loughor Bridge. Excellent boat fishing in Carmarthen Bay and off Worm's Head. Welsh Tope, Skate and Conger Club charters boats leaving Swansea riverside quays and fishing the bay and Pwlldu. All booking for boats and bait (which is difficult) can be obtained by Mainwaring Angling Centre, 44 Vivian Rd, Sketty, Swansea, tel: 017921 202245. Club membership made through qualifying fish. HQ: Rock and Fountain Inn, Skewen. Small bass, mullet, flatfish and mackerel off Mumbles Pier; no night fishing. Docks permit required for Queens Dock breakwater; good for cod in winter. Bait can be dug in Swansea Bay and estuary; squid, herring, sprats and mackerel from Swansea Market. Tackle shops: Mainwaring Angling Centre, 44 Vivian Rd, Sketty, Swansea, tel: 017921 202245; Hook, Line & Sinker, Fishing Tackle Shop, Viking Way, Enterprise Park, Winchwen; The Pilot House, Marina Maritime Quarter, Pilots Wharf; Sea Angling Centre, Pilot House Wharf, Maritime Quarter; Kingfisher Sports, 25 High St, Swansea SA1 1LG.

Tenby (Pembrokeshire). Good sport from Old Pier; whiting, pollack, bass, codling and grey mullet; good bass fishing from south and north sandy beaches, and spinning from rocks. Fine mackerel fishing most seasons, and tope off Caldey Island. For boats enquire tackle shop. Shark trips also arranged. Tackle shop: Morris Bros, Troy House, St Julian Street.

Milford Haven and **Pembroke** (Pembrokeshire). Fine surf-fishing and spinning from rocks for bass from Freshwater West and Broad Haven (Bosherton); best late summer and autumn. Kilpaison good for bass, flatfish early on; also codling and coalfish. Stone piers and jetties inside Haven provide deep water sport for pollack, skate, rays, whiting, codling, dogfish and coalfish. Hobbs Point (Pembroke Dock) excellent for conger and skate. Mackerel from rocks and boats (Stackpole Quay good). Tope from boats in Barafundle Bay and mackerel and bass from rocks. Other useful venues are Nab Head, Martins Haven and Angle Bay, Thorn, Rat and Sheep Islands and Harbour Rock. Mackerel from boats at harbour entrance. Lugworm and razor fish may be dug in several places, especially mud-flats at Kilpaison and Angle Bay. Pennar Gut and Pembroke River. Brindley John Ayers, "Antique Fishing Tackle", 8 Bay View Drive, Hakin, Milford Haven SA73 3RJ, tel: 01646 698359, is a mail orders business that collects and specialises in used high quality fishing tackle; visitors are welcome; and bed and breakfast is available. Tackle shops: Penfro Fishing Tackle, Pembroke Dock.

Fishguard (Pembrokeshire). Main captures from shore and breakwaters are flatfish, codling, conger, pouting, mackerel, bass, pollack, whiting and some tope. Sea trout and mullet near mouth of Gwaun. Tope, mackerel, conger, skate, etc. from boats. Boats from Fishguard Yacht & Boat Co, Main Street, Goodwick, tel: Fishguard 873377, and Brooks, Lower Town. Tackle shop: Thomas and Howells, Dyfed Sports, 21 West Street. Hotel: Beach House, Fishguard Bay, Goodwick, Dyfed SA64 0DH (sea fishing trips and packed lunches plus freezer for keeping

Porbeagle sharks of 140lbs. and 145lbs. caught off Aberystwyth. *Photo: Vic Haigh.*

catch).

Aberystwyth (Ceredigion). From the shore, May to November, bass (especially on soft crab bait), pollack, painted ray, mullet, huss, conger, wrasse. From October to January, whiting; July to September, mackerel. Dogfish, dabs and flounder throughout the year. Fish caught off the rocks, off storm beaches, from the harbour and stone jetty. Borth beach and Leri estuary specially good for flounders; Tan-y-Bwlch beach particularly good for whiting. Bull huss and thornback ray form the backbone of the boat fishing, but dogfish, dabs, gurnard, pollack, tope, bream, turbot, monkfish and porbeagle shark are taken in their seasons. Boat trips are run from the harbour ranging from 2-hour sessions for mackerel to 12 hours out at sea. There are many well-equipped boats commanded by highly experienced skippers. Endeavour Deep Sea Angling Club operates from St Davids Wharfe, Aberystwyth; instruction and tackle hire; specimen competitions all year. Annual membership £5 (individual) and £10 (affiliated club); visiting membership £1. Contact club for fully equipped offshore boat; skipper with 30 years experience; operating in 20m radius on day-to-day basis; long range wreck-fishing on suitable neap tides. Tackle shops: Aber Fishing Tackle & Gun Shop, 13 Terrace Road. Accommodation: Mr & Mrs Elwill, Shoreline Guest House, 6 South Marine Terrace.

Barmouth (Gwynedd). Bass (large), flatfish, mullet in Mawddach estuary and from nearby beaches; also codling, mackerel, flatfish, and even tope and skate from boats. Ynys-y-Brawd island good for bass and flounders from shore and boats. Charter boat, The Viking, operates Apr-Oct; 8-hour deep sea or 2-hour short fishing, pleasure trips; licenced by the Dept of Trade for up to 60 passengers; full safety equipment and fishing tackle provided. Bookings can be made at Seafarer Fishing Tackle, Church St, Barmouth, Gwynedd LL42 1EH, tel: 01341 280978.

Porthmadog (Gwynedd). Mackerel fishing trips (2 hrs) and deep sea fishing trips (8 hrs, 10 hrs, 20 hrs); bookings from The Fisherman, Central Buildings, High St, Porthmadog, Gwynedd LL49 9LR, tel: 01766 512464.

Pwllheli and **Criccieth** (Gwynedd). Improved bass fishing April-October with new size limit to protect small bass; dogfish, dabs, plaice, skate, pollack and a few sole the year round; mackerel, tope and monkfish from June to September and black bream now on the increase. October to January; whiting and coalfish. Boats and bait available. Tackle shops: D & E Hughes, Walsall Stores, 24 Penlan Street, Pwllheli LL53 5DE; R T Pritchard & Son, Sheffield House, High Street, Criccieth LL52 0EY, tel: 01766 522116.

Bangor (Gwynedd). Centre for Menai Straits and Anglesey. Excellent bass and plaice in Menai Straits. Best beaches on Anglesey. Good rock marks abound for wrasse, pollack, thornback, smooth hound, mackerel, herring and bull huss. Good cod fishing in winter. Boats, for parties and clubs, apply A J Regan, 106 Orme Road, tel: 01248 364590. Tackle shops: BASS Fishing Tackle, Unit 2, Plaza Buildings, High St.

Deganwy (Conwy). Wide variety of fish taken from boats in Gt Orme, Menai Straits and Puffin Island areas. Bass in estuary and off Benarth, Bodlondeb and Deganwy Points and Beacon Light. Wreck fishing. Bait from shore and estuary. Sea fishing trips (wreck fishing a speciality); and tackle for sale or hire; from Meurig Davies, Pen-y-Berllan, Pentywyn Road, Deganwy LL31 9TL, tel: 01492 581983.

Llandudno (Conwy). Skate, cod, codling, pollack, bass, mackerel, plaice, whiting, conger, coalfish, etc. Rocky beach at corner of Little Orme good for bass; so is west shore, especially Black Rocks area. Bait plentiful. Fishing from pier, beach, rocks and boats. Tope and mackerel taken by boat fishers. Tackle shop: Llandudno Fishing Tackle, 41a Victoria St, Craig-y-Don. Hotel: Epperstone (fishing can be organised from hotel).

Colwyn Bay (Conwy). Bass off Rhos Point and Penmaenhead. Whiting, codling in winter from beach. Dabs, whiting, some plaice from pier (dt available all year). Tope and skate from boats. For sea fishing contact Rhos-on-Sea Fishing, Rhos-on-Sea Harbour, Rhos-on-Sea, Colwyn Bay, tel: 01492 544 829. Tackle shops: Duttons, 52 Sea View Road (bait); and R D Pickering, 60 Abergele Road. Hotel: Ashmount Hotel, College Avenue, Rhos-on-Sea, Colwyn Bay LL28 4NT (a variety of activities available including sea fishing trips); Stanton House, Rhos-on-Sea (sea fishing organised by hotel).

Rhyl (Denbighshire). Skate, dabs, codling, whiting, plaice, gurnard, dog-fish, tope. From Foryd Harbour at Rhyl, east towards Dee Estuary at Prestayn, no licence or permit to fish is required, providing tackle and bait used are for sea fishing and not game fishing. Several boats, fully licensed to take fishing parties and charter booking, are available at Foryd Harbour from Blue Shark Fishing Trips, The Harbour, Quay Street, tel: 01745 350267.

ANGLESEY

Holyhead and **Holy Island** (Anglesey). Fishing off Holyhead Breakwater, 1¾m long, good on any tide; summer and winter fishing, many species caught. Very good fishing also on Stanley Embankment, at Cymyran, Rhoscolyn, Trearddur Bay, Porthdafarch and Holyhead Mountain. Bull huss, dogfish, pollack, wrasse, mullet, cod, plaice, dab, flounder, conger, whiting, codling, thornback ray and bass all taken in season from the various shore-marks. Boat-fishing, possible in all but the worst of weather, yields also shark, tope, ling and smooth-hound. Bait readily available. Excellent boat fishing; thornbacks, tope, etc. Bait in harbour or from tackle shop: Thos Owen, 19/20 Cybi Street. Hotel: Bull.

Amlwch (Anglesey). Tope taken to 40lb, skate, conger, herring, mackerel, etc, from boats; obtainable at Amlwch Port and at Bull Bay (1½m). Tackle shop: The Pilot Store and Fishing Tackle, 66 Machine St, Amlwch Port, Anglesey LL68 9HA, tel: 01407 831 771; maggots, fresh and frozen bait, and rod hire available with flexible opening times to suit anglers. Hotel: Bryn Arfor, Amlwch Port. Hotels: Lastra Farm, Trees.

Beaumaris (Anglesey). Big bass, tope, pollack, mullet and mackerel opposite Beaumaris and along the Straits. Between Menai and The Tubular Bridge fair-sized bass and conger are caught. For boat fishing contact Stan Zalot, Starida Boats, Little Bryn, off Rosemary Lane, tel: 01248 810251, and Dave Jones, Beaumaris Marine Services, The Anchorage, Rosemary Lane, tel: 01248 810746. Tackle shop: Anglesey Boat Co, The Shop, Gallows Point, tel: 01248 810359; Ken Johnson, Menai Bridge, tel: 01248 714508. Hotels: Ye Olde Bulls Head Inn; Bulkeley; Bishopsgate.

FISHING CLUBS & ASSOCIATIONS IN WALES

Included in this list of fishing clubs and associations in Wales are some organisations which have their water on the upper reaches of the Wye or Severn, details of which are contained in the English section of **Where to Fish**. Further information can usually be had from the Secretaries and a courtesy which is appreciated is the inclusion of a stamped addressed envelope with postal inquiries. Please advise the publishers (address at the front of the book) of any changed details for the next edition.

NATIONAL BODIES

Wales Tourist Board
Davis Street
Cardiff CF1 2FU
Tel: 01222 499909

Welsh Federation of Coarse Anglers
Mrs A Mayers
6 Biddulph Rise
Tupsley
Hereford HR1 1RA

Welsh Federation of Sea Anglers
G H Jones, M.B.E.
8 Moreton Road
Holyhead
Gwynedd LL65 2BG
Tel: 01407 763821

Welsh Salmon and Trout Association
M J Morgan
Swyn Teifi
Pontrhydfendigaid
Ystrad
Meurig, Dyfed SY25 6EF

Welsh Tope, Skate and Conger Club
Colin Delfosse
25 Mill Place
Ely, Cardiff CF5 4AJ

CLUBS

Aberaeron Town Angling Club
D S Rees
10 North Road
Aberaeron, Dyfed SA46 0JF

Aberaeron Angling Club
Nigel R Davies
Wenallt
16 Belle Vue Terrace
Aberaeron
Dyfed SA46 0HB

Abergwili Angling Club
Eric Thomas
60 Abergwili Road
Carmarthen, Dyfed

Aberystwyth Angling Association Ltd
P W Eklund
42 Erwgoch
Waunfawr
Aberystwyth
Dyfed SY23 3AZ

Afan Valley Angling Club
M Reynolds
8 Newlands
Baglan
Port Talbot
W Glamorgan

Alltami Angling Club
A Price
69 Circular Drive
Ewloe, Clywd

Ammanford and District Angling Association
Ron Woodland
2 Pontardulais Road
Llangennech
Llanelli
Dyfed SA14 8YF

Artro and Talsarnau Fishing Association
B Powell
3 Glandwr

Fishing Clubs

When you appoint a new Hon Secretary, do not forget to give us details of the change. Write to the publishers (address at front of the book). Thank you!

Llanbedr
Gwynedd LL45 2PB

Bala and District Angling Association
David Gumbley
Llwyn Ffynnon
17 Mawnog Fach
Bala
Gwynedd LL23 7YY

Bangor City Angling Club
Mrs Pat Thomas
21 Lon-y-Glyder
Bangor
Gwynedd

Bangor-on-Dee Salmon Angling Association
P Edwards
13 Ludlow Road
Bangor-on-Dee
Wrexham LL13 0JG

Betws-y-Coed Anglers' Club
Melfyn Hughes
Cae Garw
Betws-y-Coed LL24 0BY

Birchgrove (Cardiff) Angling Association
J S Wilmot
4 Clydesmuir Rd
Tremorfa, Cardiff CF2 2QA

Bradley Angling Club
M Harper
6 Yorke Avenue
Marchwiel
Wrexham, Clwyd

Brecon Angling Society
D D Harris
66 Coryton Close
Brecon
Powys LD3 9HP

Brynmill and District Angling Club
C Tonner
14 Notts Gardens
Uplands
Swansea SA2 0RU

Bryn-y-Pys Angling Association
Mrs A Phillips
2 Ruabon Road
Wrexham LL13 7PB

Buckley Angling Association
R W Jones
Cresta
35 Bryn Awelon
Mold, Clwyd CH7 1LT

Bute Angling Society
S G Allen
37 Aberporth Road
Gabalfa, Cardiff CF4 2RX

Caergwrle Angling Club
Mrs E Lewis
Bronwlfa
Hawarden Road
Caergwrle
Nr Wrexham, Clwyd LL12 9BB

Capenhurst Angling Club
A T Howdon
24 Saughall Hey
Saughall
Chester, Cheshire CH1 6EJ

Carmarthen Amateur Angling Association
Ron Ratti
Rhydal Mount
The Parade
Carmarthen SA31 1LZ

Camarthen and District Angling Club
Herbert Evans
25 Maple Crescent
Carmarthen SA31 3PS

Carmarthen Fishermen's Federation
Garth Roberts
Talrhyn
Tresaith Road
Aberporth
Dyfed SA43 2EB

Cefni Angling Association
G R Williams
Tyn Lon, Gaerwen
Pentre Berw
Anglesey

Ceiriog Fly Fishers
Alan Hudson
Kingfisher
96 Crogen
Lodgevale Park
Chirk
Wrexham LL14 5BJ

Cerrig-y-Drudion Angling Association
W M Roberts
4 Cae Lwydd
Cerrig-y-Drudion
Clwyd

Cheshire Anglers Association
Graham Tomkinson
31 Wareham Drive
Crewe
Cheshire CW1 3XA

Chester Association of Anglers
B W Roberts
23 Alpraham Crescent
Upton Cross
Chester CH2 1QX

Cilcain Fly Fishing Association
A E Williams
Gwynfryn
Caerwys Hill
Caerwys, Mold
Clwyd

Connah's Quay and District Angling Club
Paul Roberts

118 Wepre Park
Connah's Quay
Clwyd CH5 4HW

Connah's Quay Angling Association
R W Ambrose
25 Pinewood Avenue
Connah's Quay, Clwyd

Conway Valley Fisheries' Association
Gareth Hughes
Golygfa'r Graig
Betws Road
Llanrwst
Gwynedd LL25 0PT

Corris and District Angling Association
Jeremy Thomas
Foamation Products
Era Works
Ceinws, Machynlleth
Powys SY20 9HA

Corwen and District Angling Club
Gordon H Smith
Llais-yr-Afon
Bontuchel
Ruthin
Denbighshire LL15 2DE

Criccieth, Llanystumdwy and District Angling Association
Gordon Hamilton
Morawel
Llanystumdwy
Criccieth, Gwynedd LL52 0SF

Crickhowell Angling Club
Tom Probert
Crickhowell
Powys

Cross Hands and District Angling Association
Pat Kieran
48 Waterloo Road
Penygroes
Llanelli
Carmarthenshire SA14 7NS

Cwmbran Angling Association
P M Gulliford
305 Llantarnam Rd
Cwmbran, Gwent NP44 3BJ

Cwmcelyn Angling Club
P Hunt
East Pentwyn Farm
Blaina, Gwent NP3 3HX

Cwmllynfell Fly Fishing Club
D Lloyd
73 Bryn Road
Bryn Villas
Cwmllynfell
West Glamorgan

Cymdeithas Bysgota Talybont Angling Association
I Jones
Wern
Talybont
Ceredigion SY24 5ER

Dee Anglers Association
A Hogg
6 Llwynon Close
Bryn-y-Baal
Mold
Clwyd CH7 6TN

Denbigh and Clwyd Angling Club
C P Harness
8 Llwyn Menlli
Ruthin, Clwyd LL15 1RG

Dolgarrog Fishing Club
Peter Jones
12 Hillside Cottages
Dolgarrog
Gwynedd LL32

Dolgellau Angling Association
E M Davies
Maescaled, Dolgellau
Gwynedd LL40 1UF

Dolwyddelan Fishing Association
D E Foster
The Post Office
Dolwyddelan
Gwynedd LL25 0NJ

Dwyryd Anglers Ltd
Gareth Ffestin Price
Hafan
Ffordd Peniel
Ffestiniog
Gwynedd LL41 4LP

Ebbw Vale Welfare Angling Club
R Satterley
8 Pen-y-lan
Ebbw Vale
Gwent NP3 5LS

Elan Valley Angling Club
Noel Hughes
25 Brynheulog
Rhayader
Powys LD6 5EF

The Endeavour Deep Sea Angling Club
B Haigh
Ty-Llyn
Cwm-Rheidol
Aberystwyth
Dyfed SY23 3NB

Estimaner Angling Association
John Baxter
11 Tan y Fedw
Abergynolwyn, Tywyn
Gwynedd LL36 9YU

Felindre Angling Club
M Randall
77 Water Street
Kidwelly, Dyfed

Gilwern and District Angling Club
H R Lewis
27 Brynglas, Gilwern
Nr Abergavenny
Gwent NP7 0BP

Glamorgan Anglers' Club
Jon Taylor
23 Adenfield Way
Rhoose
S Glamorgan CF62 3EA

Glaslyn Angling Association
J Daniel Hughes
Berthlwyd
Penrhyndeudraeth
Gwynedd LL48 6RL

Glyncornel Angling Association
John M Evans
126 Ystrad Road
Ystrad, Rhondda
Mid Glamorgan CF41 7PS

Glynneath and District Angling Association
Gareth Evans
21 Godfrey Avenue
Glynneath, Neath
West Glamorgan SA11 5HF

Clwb Godre Mynydd Du
203 Cwmamman Road
Glanamman
Dyfed

Greenfield Valley Angling Club
Chris Hallmark, Head Bailiff
Greenfield Valley Heritage Park
Greenfield
Holywell
Flintshire CH8 7BQ

Griffin Angling Club
A Pickles
Green Pastures
Pont-y-Capel
Gresford
Wrexham, Clwyd

Gro Park and Irfon Angling Club
Dolshedyn
15 Irfon Road
Builth Wells
Powys LD2 3DE

Gwaun-Cae-Gurwen Angling Association
P E Edwards
32 Heol Cae, Gurwen
Gwaun-Cae-Gurwen
Amman Valley
West Glamorgan

Gwent Avengers
R Dalling
3 The Spinney
Malpas Park
Newport, Gwent

Holt and Farndon Angling Association
R Williams
4 The Cross
Holt, Wrexham
Clywd

Isca Angling Club
P Facey
357 Pilton Vale
Newport
Gwent NP9 6LU

Islwyn and District Anglers
Mrs J Meller
7 Penllwyn Street
Cwmfelinfach, Gwent NP1 7HE

Kingfishers Angling Club
M Howells
97 Bwllfa Road
Cwmdas, Aberdare
Mid Glamorgan

Kirkdale Angling Association
A C Hoer
61 Baythorne Road
Liverpool L4 9TJ

Lavister Angling Club
G Watkins
Rathgillan
Lache Hall Crescent
Chester
Cheshire CH4 7NE

Llanbrynmair and District Angling Club
M Jones
Craig-y-Gronfa
Mallwyd
Machynlleth, Powys

Llandeilo Angling Association
28a Rhosmaen St
Llandeilo
Dyfed

Llandovery Angling Association
Michael Davies
Cwmrhuddan Lodge
Llandovery
Carmarthenshire SA20 0DX

Llandybie Angling Association
R Jones
9 Margaret Rd

Fishing Clubs

When you appoint a new Hon Secretary, do not forget to give us details of the change. Write to the publishers (address at front of the book). Thank you!

Llandybie
Dyfed SA18 3YB

Llandysul Angling Association
Artie Jones
Glas-y-Dorlan
Llyn-y-Fran Road
Llandysul, Dyfed SA44 4JW

Llanelli Angling Association
D Watkins
60 Llwyn Hendy
Llanelli, Dyfed

Llangadog Angling Association
Hafan Las
Llangadog
Dyfed

Llangennech Angling Club
D A Owen
99 Hendre Road
Llangennech
Llanelli
Carmarthenshire SA14 8TH

Llangollen Angling Association
W N Elbourn
Bwthyn Bach
2 Green Lane
Llangollen
Denbighshire LL20 8TB

Llangyfelach and District Angling Association
R L Griffiths
Cefn Cottage
Cilibion
Llanrhidian
Swansea SA3 1ED

Llangynidr Service Station Angling Club
T B Williams
Llangynidr Service Station
Llangynidr
Crickhowell, Powys NP8 1LU

Llanidloes and District Angling Association
J Dallas Davies
Dresden House
Great Oak Street
Llanidloes, Powys SY18 6BU

Llanilar Angling Association
John H Astill
Dryslwyn, Llanafan
Aberystwyth
Ceredigion SY23 4AX

Llanrwst Anglers' Club
David W P Hughes
36 Station Road
Llanrwst
Gwynedd LL26 0AD

Llanybydder Angling Association
William Wilkins
Maes-y-Fedw
Llanybydder
Dyfed SA40 9UG

Llay Angling Association
John Preston
20 Mold Road Estate
Gwersyllt, Wrexham
Clwyd LL11 4AA

Llynfi Valley Angling Association
G Thomas
39 Darren View
Llangynwyd
Maesteg
Mid Glamorgan

Llysyfran Angling Club
Peter J Eaton
18 Mount Pleasant Way
Milford Haven
Pembrokeshire SA73 1AB

Maelor Angling Association
K Bathers
Sunnyside, Hill Street
Cefn Mawr, Wrexham
Clwyd

Maerdy and Ferndale Angling Club
Terry Pain
16 Highfield
Ferndale, Rhondda
Mid Glamorgan CF43 4TA

Merthyr Tydfil Angling Association
Nigel Morgan
20 James Street
Twynyrodyn
Merthyr Tydfil
Mid Glamorgan

Midland Flyfishers
Paul T Stafford
5 Deansway
Worcester WR1 2JG

Mold Fly Fishers
A T Allcock
3 Highfield Avenue
Mynydd Isa
Mold, Flintshire CH7 6XY

Mold Kingfishers Angling Club
R W Ambrose
25 Pinewood Avenue
Connah's Quay, Clwyd

Mold Trout Anglers
Alun Powell
Makuti
Sunny Ridge
Mold
Flintshire CH7 1RU

Montgomeryshire Angling Association (including Llanfair Caereinion FC, Welshpool AC)
Lionel Whitley
18 Adelaide Drive
Welshpool
Powys

…nd Dulais Angling Association
…r J Jones
… Bryndulais Row
Seven Sisters
Neath SA10 9EB
Nevern Angling Association
Mrs Nica Prichard
Spring Gardens
Parrog Road
Newport
Pembrokeshire SA42 0RJ
Newbridge Angling Association
Kerry F R Clutton
28 Worsley Avenue
Johnstown
Nr Wrexham
Clwyd LL14 2TD
New Dovey Fishery Association (1929) Ltd
Ian C Rees
Leeds House
20 Maengwyn Street
Machynlleth
Powys SY20 8DT
Newport Angling Association
L J Clarke
14 Allt-yr-yn Ave
Newport
South Wales NP9 5DB
Newport and District Sea Anglers
Joe Guscott (Secretary)
51 Monnow Walk
Bettws Estate
Newport
Monmouthshire NP9 6SS
or
Joe Crowley (Chairman)
55 Moore Crest
Newport
Monmouthshire
Newport Reservoir Fly Fishing Association
W G C Jones
74 Greenfield
Newbridge
Gwent NP1 4QZ
New Quay Angling Club
H Davies
Min-yr-Afon
Abergorlech
Dyfed SA32 7SN
Ogmore Angling Association
W A Protheroe
Henllan
Coychurch Road
Pencoed, Bridgend
Mid Glamorgan CF35 5LY
Ogwen Valley Angling Association
Bryn Evans
Tan y Coed
Bron Arfon
Llanllechid, Bangor
Gwynedd LL57 3LW
Ogwr Borough Angling Association
T J Hughes
20 Heol Glannant
Bettws, Bridgend
Mid Glamorgan CF32 8SP
Pembroke and District Angling Club
Mrs T Lustig
10 Deer Park
Stackpole
Pembrokeshire
Pembrokeshire Anglers Association
Mrs B E Summers
72 City Road
Haverfordwest
Pembrokeshire SA61 2RR
Pembrokeshire Fly Fishers
Captain & Mrs Oliver
Red House
Llawhaden
Narberth
Pembrokeshire
Pencoed and District Angling Club
Dr G M Gwilliam
5 Velindre Road
Pencoed, Bridgend
Mid Glamorgan
Penllwyn Lodges Angling Club
Derek Thomas Field
Penllwyn
Garthmyl
Powys SY15 6SB
Picton Waters Angling Club
I Richards
North Pines
Wiston
Haverfordwest, Dyfed
Ponciau Angling Society
D K Valentine
Bryn-yr-Owen
Ponciau
Wrexham, Clwyd
Pontardawe and Swansea Angling Association
R H Lockyer
8 Bwllfa Road
Ynystawe
Swansea SA6 5AL
Pontardulais and District Angling Association
J Gabe
20 James Street
Pontardulais, Swansea
West Glamorgan SA4 1HY
Pontypool Angling Association
B J Jones

79 Robertson Way
Woodlands
Malpas, Newport
Gwent NP9 6QQ

Porthcawl Sea Angling Association
(Freshwater Section)
J Lock
67 West Road
Nottage
Porthcawl, Mid Glamorgan

Prince Albert Angling Society
J A Turner
15 Pexhill Drive
Macclesfield
Cheshire SK10 3LP

Prysor Angling Association
Idwal W Williams
8 Pantycelyn
Trawsfynydd
Gwynedd LL41 4UH

Pwllheli and District Angling Association
R G Jones
18 Lleyn Street
Pwllheli
Gwynedd

Pyrddin Angling Society
Robert Browning
91 Main Road
Duffryn Cellwen
Nr Neath, West Glamorgan

Pysgotwyr Maesnant
D P Higgins
90 Maesceinion
Waunfawr
Aberystwyth SY23 3QQ

Ridgeway Angling Club
R Martin
Hillcroft
Bethlehem
Cardigan Road
Haverfordwest, Dyfed

Rhayader Angling Association
G H Roberts
Belmullet, Rhayader
Powys LD6 5BY

Rhostyllen Angling Club
J R Williams
57 West Grove
Rhostyllen
Wrexham
Clwyd LL14 4NB

Rhyl and District Angling Association
Martin Fowell
Bon-Amie
28 Ffordd Tanrallt
Meliden
Prestatyn
Denbighshire LL19 8PS

Rhymney and District Angling Society
J Pugh
12 Castle Field
Rhymney
Gwent

Rossett and Gresford Fly Fishers
Brian Harper
7 Hawthorn Road
Marford
Wrexham LL12 8XJ

St Asaph Angling Association
W J P Staines
Delamere
Coed Esgob Lane
St Asaph
Denbighshire LL17 0LH

St Clears Angling Association
David J Bryan
Madras Cottage
Laugharne
Carmarthen, Dyfed SA33 4NU

Seiont, Gwyrfai and Llyfni Anglers' Society
H P Hughes
Llugwy, Ystad Eryri
Bethel, Caernarfon
Gwynedd LL55 1BX

Severnside and Newtown Angling Club
Michael John Thomas
253 Measyrhandir
Newtown, Powys SY16 1LB

Skewen Angling Club
Mike Doyle
58 The Highlands
Skewen, Neath
West Glamorgan SA10 6PD

Swansea Amateur Angling Association Ltd
J B Wolfe
147 St Helen's Road
Swansea SA1 4DB

Swansea Angling Club
Paul Cannin
9 Heol Ceri
Waunarlwydd
Swansea SA5 4QU

Talsarnau and District Angling Association
I Owen
Eryri Llanfair
Harlech
Gwynedd

Tawe and Tributaries Angling Association
Michael Matthews
32 Farm Road
Briton Ferry
Neath
West Glamorgan SA11 2TA

oled Fishers' Association
ale
ow Bank
ston
Swansea SA2 7LD

eifi Trout Association
W Bishop
Greenacres
Pentrecagal
Newcastle Emlyn
Carmarthenshire SA38 9HT
or
Mike Evans (Membership Secretary)
Llysycoed
Llandygwydd
Llechryd
Cardigan
Ceredigion

Tenby and District Angling Club
Mr Bird
Primrose Villa
Narbeth Road
Tenby
Pembrokeshire

Tregaron Angling Association
Moc Morgan
Swyn Teifi
Pontrhydfendigaid
Aberystwyth
Ceredigion

Warrington Angling Association
Frank Lythgoe, Secretary
P O Box 71
Warrington WA1 1LR
Headquarters
52 Parker Street
Warrington
(Open every Friday 7pm - 9.30pm)

Wentwood Reservoir Fly Fishing Association
D G P Jones
123 Castle Lea
Caldicot, Gwent

Whitland Angling Association
Ithel Parri-Roberts
Swyddfa'r Post Office
Hendygwyn-ar-Daf
Whitland
Dyfed SA34 0AA

Wirral Game Fishing Club
D Jones
31 Meadway
Upton, Wirral
Cheshire

Wrexham and District Angling Association
J E Tattum
Llys Athro, King Street
Leeswood, Mold
Clwyd CH7 4SB

Wygyr Fishing Association
J M Fraser (Treasurer)
Crug Mor Farm
Rhydwyn
Llanfaethlu
Anglesey

Jonathon Hughes with a 20lb pollack and a 22 pdr. The larger fish became a Welsh record for the species when caught in 1993. The fish were caught over the wreck of a ship sunk in the Irish Sea in 1917. *Photo: Vic Haigh.*

FISHING IN SCOTLAND

SCOTTISH ENVIRONMENTAL PROTECTION AGENCY

The Scottish Environmental Protection Agency (SEPA) is the body entrusted by the Secretary of State for Scotland with the task of protecting and improving the quality of the water environment. The present structure dates from 1996, under new arrangements contained in the Environment Act 1995, but Scotland has benefitted from independent control over water pollution by the Authorities since the 1950s. SEPA's powers derive primarily from the Control of Pollution Act 1974. Its main job is to monitor discharges, to see that the necessary standards are maintained, and to be fully aware of the general conditions of Scotland's waters. As a consequence of its vigilance and that of its predecessors the River Purification Boards, pollution has been considerably reduced in such river systems as the Tweed, the Solway, the Clyde, the Tay, and the Forth, and salmon have returned to the Clyde after an absence of more than 80 years. Cases of pollution should be reported to the appropriate office.

SEPA Regional Addresses

East Region

Clearwater House
Heriot Watt Research Park
Avenue North
Edinburgh EH14 4AP
Tel: 031 449 7296
Fax: 0131 449 7277
Perth Office
1 South Street
Perth PH2 8NJ
Tel: 01738 627989
Fax: 01738 630997
Galashiels Office
Burnmae
Mossilee Road
Galashiels TD1 1NF
tel: 01896 754797
Fax: 01896 754412

West Region

Rivers House
Murray Road
East Kilbride G75 0LA
Tel: 013552 38181/6
Fax: 013355 26432
Dumfries Office
Rivers house
Irongray Road
Newbridge
Dumfries DG1 0JE
Tel: 01387 720502
Fax: 01387 721154

North Region

Graesser House
Fodderty Way
Dingwall Business Park
Dingwall IV15 9XB
tel: 01349 862021
Fax: 01349 863987
Aberdeen Office
Greyhope House
Greyhope Road
Aberdeen AB1 3RD
tel: 01224 248338
Fax: 01224 248591
Orkney Office
58a Junction Road
Kirkwall KW15 1NY
(01856 3535)
Shetland Office
O.I.L. Building
Gremista
Lerwick ZE1 0PY
tel: 01595 696926
Fax: 01595 696946
Western Isles Office
1 Quay street
Stornaway HS1 2XX
tel: 01851 706477
Fax: 01851 703510

District Boards and Close Season for Salmon and Trout

Fishing in Scotland is under the general jurisdiction of the Scottish Office Agriculture, Environment and Fisheries Department, Pentland House, 47 Robb's Loan, Edinburgh, EH14 1TW.

The annual close season for **trout** in Scotland extends from October 7 to March 14, both days included. Trout may not be sold between the end of August and the beginning of April, nor at any time if the fish are less than 8 in long.

Visiting anglers are reminded that on Scottish rivers and lochs the owner of the fishing is the riparian proprietor, whose permission to fish should be obtained. The only public right of fishing for brown trout is in those portions of the rivers which are both tidal and navigable, but the right must not be exercised so as to interfere with salmon or sea-trout fishing and can be exercised only where there is a right of access to the water from a boat or from the banks. A number of rivers in Scotland including the Aberdeenshire Don are subject to Protection Orders granted by the Secretary of State for Scotland. On rivers where a Protection Order is in force, it is an offence to fish for any freshwater species without the owner's permission.

Salmon. Provision is made in the Salmon Act, 1986, for the formation and amalgamation of District Boards, composed of representatives of proprietors of salmon fisheries in each district. These boards, the addresses of which are given on pages below, are responsible for the administration and protection of the salmon fisheries in their districts, and boards have been formed for practically all the important salmon rivers. More recently, the Boards have become increasingly involved in management, research and stock enhancement, as well as the more traditional function. During the 1995 fishing season, the Dee District Board asked all proprietors (rod and net) to observe a voluntary extension of the Annual Close Time until 1 March. This was unheld by virtually all proprietors. The Board has now submitted an application to the Secretary of State for Scotland for an Order in terms of the Salmon Act 1986 extending the annual Close Time until 1 March. If this is not granted, the Board will again promote a voluntary closure during February 1996. In districts in which boards have not been formed, the salmon fisheries, of which sea-trout fisheries are legally part, are under the direct control of the proprietors.

In the following list, the days fixing the start and finish of the annual close time for net fishing and for rod fishing respectively are in all cases inclusive, and, as in the case of the Add, the first river in the list, the first pair of dates are the limits of the net season and the second pair apply to rod fishing.

Add. Annual close time for net-fishing: From Sept 1 to Feb 15, both dates inclusive. Annual close time for rod-fishing: From Nov 1 to Feb 15, both days inclusive.

Ailort. Aug 27 to Feb 10; Nov 1 to Feb 10.

Aline. Aug 27 to Feb 10; Nov 1 to Feb 10.

Alness. Aug 27 to Feb 10; Nov 1 to Feb 10.

Annan. Sept 10 to Feb 24; Nov 16 to Feb 24.

Applecross. Aug 27 to Feb 10; Nov 1 to Feb 10.

Arnisdale. Aug 27 to Feb 10; Nov 1 to Feb 10.

Awe. Aug 27 to Feb 10; 16 Oct to Feb 10.

Ayr. Aug 27 to Feb 10; Nov 1 to Feb 10.

Baa and Goladoir. Aug 27 to Feb 10; Nov 1 to Feb 10.

Badachro and Kerry. Aug 27 to Feb 10; Nov 1 to Feb 10.

Balgay and Shieldaig. Aug 27 to Feb 10; Nov 1 to Feb 10.

Beauly. Aug 27 to Feb 10; Oct 16 to Feb 10.

Berriedale. Aug 27 to Feb 10; Nov 1 to Feb 10.

Bervie. Sept 10 to Feb 24; Nov 1 to Feb 24.

Bladnoch. Aug 27 to Feb 10; Nov 1 to Feb 10.

Broom. Aug 27 to Feb 10; Nov 1 to Feb 10.

Brora. Aug 27 to Feb 10; Oct 16 to Jan 31.

Carradale. Sept 10 to Feb 24; Nov 1 to Feb 24.

Carron. Aug 27 to Feb 10; Nov 1 to Feb 10.

Clayburn. Sept 10 to Feb 24; Nov 1 to Feb 24.

Clyde and Leven. Aug 27 to Feb 10; Nov 1 to Feb 10.

…ug 27 to Feb 10; Oct 1 to Jan

…e. Aug 27 to Feb 10; Nov 1 to Feb

…ree. Sept 14 to Feb 28; Oct 15 to Feb 28.
Creran (Loch Creran). Aug 27 to Feb 10; Nov 1 to Feb 10.
Crowe and Shiel (Loch Duich). Aug 27 to Feb 10; Nov 1 to Feb 10.
Dee (Aberdeenshire). Aug 27 to Feb 10; Oct 1 to Jan 31.
Dee (Kirkcudbrightshire). Aug 27 to Feb 10; Nov 1 to Feb 10.
Deveron. Aug 27 to Feb 10; Nov 1 to Feb 10.
Don. Aug 27 to Feb 10; Nov 1 to Feb 10.
Doon. Aug 27 to Feb 10; Nov 1 to Feb 10.
Drummachloy (Bute). Sept 1 to Feb 15; Oct 16 to Feb 15.
Dunbeath. Aug 27 to Feb 10; Oct 16 to Feb 10.
Eachaig. Sept 1 to Apr 30; Nov 1 to Apr 30.
East Lewis. Aug 27 to Feb 10; Oct 17 to Feb 10.
Esk, North. Sept 1 to Feb 15; Nov 1 to Feb 15.
Esk, South. Sept 1 to Feb 15; Nov 1 to Feb 15.
Ewe. Aug 27 to Feb 10; Nov 1 to Feb 10.
Fincastle. Sept 10 to Feb 24; Nov 1 to Feb 24.
Findhorn. Aug 27 to Feb 10; Oct 7 to Feb 10.
Fleet (Kirkcudbrightshire). Sept 10 to Feb 24; Nov 1 to Feb 24.
Fleet (Sutherlandshire). Sept 10 to Feb 24; Nov 1 to Feb 24.
Forss. Aug 27 to Feb 10; Nov 1 to Feb 10.
Forth. Aug 27 to Feb 10; Nov 1 to Jan 31.
Fyne, Shira and Aray. Sept 1 to Feb 15; Nov 1 to Feb 15.
Garnock. Sept 10 to Feb 24; Nov 1 to Feb 24.
Girvan. Sept 10 to Feb 24; Nov 1 to Feb 24.
Glenelg. Aug 27 to Feb 10; Nov 1 to Feb 10.
Gour. Aug 27 to Feb 10; Nov 1 to Feb 10.
Grudie or **Dionard**. Aug 27 to Feb 10; Nov 1 to Feb 10.
Gruinard and Little Gruinard. Aug 27 to Feb 10; Nov 1 to Feb 10.
Halladale. Aug 27 to Feb 10; Oct 1 to Jan 11.
Helmsdale. Aug 27 to Feb 10; Oct 1 to Jan 10.
Hope and Polla. Aug 27 to Feb 10; Oct 1 to Jan 11.
Howmore. Sept 10 to Feb 24; Nov 1 to Feb 24.
Inchard. Aug 27 to Feb 10; Nov 1 to Feb 10.
Inner (Jura). Sept 10 to Feb 24; Nov 1 to Feb 24.
Inver. Aug 27 to Feb 10; Nov 1 to Feb 10.
Iorsa (Arran). Sept 10 to Feb 24; Nov 1 to Feb 24.
Irvine. Sept 10 to Feb 24; Nov 16 to Feb 24.
Kannaird. Aug 27 to Feb 10; Nov 1 to Feb 10.
Kilchoan. (Loch Nevis). Aug 27 to Feb 10; Nov 1 to Feb 10.
Kinloch (Kyle of Tongue). Aug 27 to Feb 10; Nov 1 to Feb 10.
Kirkaig. Aug 27 to Feb 10; Nov 1 to Feb 10.
Kishorn. Aug 27 to Feb 10; Nov 1 to Feb 10.
Kyle of Sutherland. Aug 27 to Feb 10; Oct 1 to Jan 10.
Laggan and **Sorn** (Islay). Sept 10 to Feb 24; Nov 1 to Feb 24.
Laxford. Aug 27 to Feb 10; Nov 1 to Feb 10.
Leven. Aug 27 to Feb 10; Nov 1 to Feb 10.
Little Loch Broom. Aug 27 to Feb 10; Nov 1 to Feb 10.
Loch Long. Aug 27 to Feb 10; Nov 1 to Feb 10.
Loch Roag. Aug 27 to Feb 10; Oct 17 to Feb 10.
Loch Sunart. Aug 27 to Feb 10; Nov 1 to Feb 10.
Lochy. Aug 27 to Feb 10; Nov 1 to Feb 10.
Lossie. Aug 27 to Feb 24; Nov 1 to Feb 24.
Luce. Sept 10 to Feb 24; Nov 1 to Feb 24.
Lussa (Mull). Aug 27 to Feb 10; Nov 1 to Feb 10.
Moidart. Aug 27 to Feb 10; Nov 1 to Feb 10.
Morar. Aug 27 to Feb 10; Nov 1 to Feb 10.
Mullanageren. Sept 10 to Feb 24; Nov 1 to Feb 24.
Nairn. Aug 27 to Feb 10; Oct 8 to Feb 10.
Naver and **Borgie**. Aug 27 to Feb 10; Oct 1 to Jan 11.
Nell, Feochan and **Euchar**. Aug 27 to Feb 10; Nov 1 to Feb 10.
Ness. Aug 27 to Feb 10; Oct 16 to Jan 14.
Nith. Sept 10 to Feb 24; Dec 1 to Feb 24.
Orkney Islands. Sept 10 to Feb 24; Nov 1 to Feb 24.

Ormsary. Aug 27 to Feb 10; Nov 1 to Feb 10.
Pennygowan and **Aros** (Mull). Aug 27 to Feb 10; Nov 1 to Feb 10.
Resort. Aug 27 to Feb 10; Nov 1 to Feb 10.
Ruel. Sept 1 to Feb 15; Nov 1 to Feb 15.
Sanda. Aug 27 to Feb 10; Nov 1 to Feb 10.
Scaddle. Aug 27 to Feb 10; Nov 1 to Feb 10.
Shetland Islands. Sept 10 to Feb 24; Nov 1 to Feb 24.
Shiel (Loch Shiel). Aug 27 to Feb 10; Nov 1 to Feb 10.
Sligachan (Skye). Aug 27 to Feb 10; Nov 1 to Feb 10.
Snizort (Skye). Aug 27 to Feb 10; Nov 1 to Feb 10.
Spey. Aug 27 to Feb 10; Oct 1 to Feb 10.
Stinchar. Sept 10 to Feb 24; Nov 1 to Feb 24.
Strathy. Aug 27 to Feb 10; Oct 1 to Jan 11.
Tay. Aug 21 to Feb 4; Oct 16 to Jan 14.
Thurso. Aug 27 to Feb 10; Oct 6 to Jan 10.
Torridon. Aug 27 to Feb 10; Nov 1 to Feb 10.
Tweed. Sept 15 to Feb 14; Dec 1 to Jan 31.
Ugie. Sept 10 to Feb 24; Nov 1 to Feb 9.
Ullapool (Loch Broom). Aug 27 to Feb 10; Nov 1 to Feb 10.
Urr. Sept 10 to Feb 24; Dec 1 to Feb 24.
Wick. Aug 27 to Feb 10; Nov 1 to Feb 10.
Ythan. Sept 10 to Feb 24; Nov 1 to Feb 10.

DISTRICT SALMON FISHERY BOARDS

The names, addresses and telephone numbers of the clerks of the various salmon district fishery boards in Scotland are as follows: Please note that their duties are purely to operate the Acts and that they do not have fishing to let.

Alness District Salmon Fishery Board. J H S Stewart, 57 Culduthel Rd, Inverness IV1 1HQ (Tel: 01463 714477)

Annan District Salmon Fishery Board. Ms C A K Rafferty, Messrs McJerrow and Stevenson, Solicitors, 55 High Street, Lockerbie, Dumfriesshire DG11 2JJ (Tel: 015762 202123/4).

Awe District Salmon Fishery Board. T C McNair, Messrs MacArthur, Stewart & Co, Solicitors, Boswell House, Argyll Square, Oban, Argyllshire PA34 4BD (Tel: 01631 562215).

Ayr District Salmon Fishery Board. F M Watson, D W Shaw & Company, 34a Sandgate, Ayr KA7 1BG (Tel: 01292 265033).

Beauly District Salmon Fishery Board. J Wotherspoon, MacAndrew & Jenkins WS, Solicitors and Estate Agents, 5 Drummond Street, Inverness, IV1 1QF (Tel: 01463 233001)

Bladnoch District Salmon Fishery Board. Peter M Murray, Messrs A B & A Matthews, Bank of Scotland Buildings, Newton Stewart, Wigtownshire DG8 6EG (Tel: 01671 3013).

Broom District Salmon Fishery Board. Messrs Middleton, Ross and Arnot, Solicitors, PO Box 8, Mansfield House, Dingwall, Ross-shire IV15 9HJ (Tel: 01349 862214).

Brora District Salmon Fishery Board. C J Whealing, Sutherland Estates Office, Duke Street, Golspie, Sutherland, KW10 6RR (Tel: 01408 633268).

Caithness District Salmon Fishery Board. P J W Blackwood, Estate Office, Thurso East, Thurso, Caithness KW14 8HW (Tel: 01847 63134).

Conon District Salmon Fishery Board. Miles Larby, Finlayson Hughes, 45 Church Street, Inverness IV1 1DR (Tel: 01463 224343).

Clayburn District Salmon Fishery Board. *see Fincastle*.

Cree District Salmon Fishery Board. Peter M Murray, Messrs A B & A Matthews, Solicitors, Bank of Scotland Buildings, Newton Stewart, Wigtownshire DG8 6EG (Tel: 01671 3013).

Creran District Salmon Fishery Board. Lady Stewart, Salachail, Appin, Argyll PA38 4BJ.

Crowe and Shiel (Loch Duich) Salmon Fishery Board. Lord Burton (Chairman), Dochfour Estate Office, Dochgarroch, Inverness IV3 6JP.

Dee (Aberdeen) District Salmon Fishery Board. George Alpine, Messrs Paull & Williamson, Solicitors, Investment House, 6 Union Row, Aberdeen AB9 8DQ (Tel: 01224

621621).

Dee (Kirkcudbrightshire) District Salmon Fishery Board. G S Scott, Messrs Gillespie, Gifford & Brown, 27 St Cuthbert Street, Kirkcudbrightshire DG6 4DJ. (Tel: 01557 330539).

Deveron District Salmon Fishery Board. John A Christie, Murdoch, McMath and Mitchell, Solicitors, 27-29 Duke Street, Huntly AB54 5DP (Tel: 01466 792291).

Don Distinct Board. George Alpine, Messrs Paull & Williamson, Solicitors, Investment House, 6 Union Row, Aberdeen AB9 8DQ (Tel: 01224 621621).

Doon District Salmon Fishery Board. A M Thomson, 23 Wellington Square, Ayr KA7 2HG (Tel: 01292 266900).

Eachaig District Salmon Fishery Board, Robert C G Teasdale, Quarry Cottage, Rashfield, By Dunoon, Argyll PA23 8QT (Tel: 01369 84510)

East Lewis District Salmon Fishery Board. George H MacDonald, Estate Office, North Uist Estate, Lochmaddy, North Uist HS6 5AA (Tel: 01876 500428)

Esk District Salmon Fishery Board. John Scott, Scott Alexander, 113 High Street, Montrose, Angus DD10 8QR (Tel: 01674 671477)

Ewe District Salmon Fishery Board. G C Muirden, Messrs Middleton, Ross and Arnot, Solicitors, PO Box 8, Mansfield House, Dingwall, Ross-shire IV15 9HJ (Tel: 01349 62214).

Findhorn District Salmon Fishery Board. Sir William Gordon Cumming, Altyre House, Altyre, By Forres, Moray

Fleet (Kirkcudbrightshire) District Salmon Fishery Board. C R Graves, Pinnacle, Gatehouse of Fleet, Castle Douglas DG7 2HH (Tel: 01557 814 610).

Forth District Salmon Fishery Board. T Mackenzie, 12 Charles Street, Dunblane FK15 9BY. (Tel: 01786 825544)

Girvan District Salmon Fishery Board. S B Sheddon, Messrs Smith & Valentine, Solicitors and Estate Agents, 16 Hamilton Street, Girvan, Ayrshire KA26 9EY (Tel: 01465 713476)

Grudie or **Dionard District Salmon Fishery Board**. A MacKenzie, Redwood, 19 Culduthel Road, Inverness IV2 4AA (Tel: 01463 235353).

The islands of Loch Maree. *Photo: D W Roxburgh.*

Gruinard District Salmon Fishery Board. Messrs. Middleton, Ross and Arnot, Solicitors, P O Box 8, Mansfield House, Dingwall, Ross-shire IV15 9HJ (Tel: 01349 862214).

Halladale District Salmon Fishery Board. G D Robertson, 29 Traill Street, Thurso, Caithness KW14 8EQ (Tel: 01847 893247)

Harris District Salmon Fishery Board. G A Macdonald, The Estate Office, Lochmaddy, North Uist HS6 5AA (Tel: 01876 500428

Helmsdale District Salmon Fishery Board. N Wright, Arthur and Carmichael, Cathedral Square, Durnoch (Tel: 01862 810202)

Hope and Polla District Salmon Fishery Board. Messrs Middleton, Ross and Arnot, Solicitors, PO Box 8, Mansfield House, Dingwall, Ross-shire IV15 9HJ (Tel: 01349 862214).

Iorsa (Arran) District Salmon Fishery Board. J W Perkins, Ramera, Sannox, Isle of Arran (Tel: 01770 810671).

Inver District Salmon Fishery Board. D L Laird, Thornton Oliver WS, Solicitors and Estate Agents, 53 East High Street, Forfar, Angus DD8 2EL (Tel: 01307 66886).

Kanaird District Salmon Fishery Board. J Bramell, Drummond Road Stafford ST16 3HJ.

Kirkaig District Salmon Fishery Board. D L Laird, Thornton Oliver WS, Solicitors, 53 East High Street, Forfar, Angus DD8 2EL (Tel 01307 66886).

Kinloch District Salmon Fishery Board. A Sykes, Messrs Brodies WS, 15 Atholl Crescent, Edinburgh EH3 8HA (Tel: 0131 228 4111).

Kyle of Sutherland District Salmon Fishery Board. J Mason, Bell Ingram Ltd, Estates Office, Bonar Bridge, Sutherland IV24 3EA.

Laggan & Sorn District Salmon Fishery Board, R I G Ferguson, Messrs Stewart, Balfour & Sutherland, 2 Castlehill, Campeltown, Argyll PA28 6AW (Tel: 01586 552871).

Laxford District Salmon Fishery Board. A R Whitefield, The Estate Office, Achfary, by Lairg, Sutherland IV27 4PQ (Tel: 01971 500221).

Leven District Salmon Fishery Board. Alister M Sutherland, Burness WS, Solicitors, 242 West George Street, Glasgow G2 4QY (Tel: 0141 248 4933).

Loch Fyne District Salmon Fishery Board. Robert N Macpherson, Messrs Stewart & Bennet, Solicitors, 82 Argyll Street, Dunoon, PA23 7NE (Tel: 01369 702885).

Loch Inchard District Salmon Fishery Board. J C Drysdale, Anderson Strathern, W.S., 48 Castle Street, Edinburgh, EH2 3LX (Tel: 0131 220 2345).

Loch Shiel District Salmon Fishery Board. E T Cameron Kennedy, Robertson Paul, 95 Bothwell Street, Glasgow G2 7JH (Tel: 0141 204 1231).

Lochy District Salmon Fishery Board. D Macphee, Messrs MacArthur, Stewart & Co, Solicitors, Gordon Square, Fort William, Inverness-shire (Tel: 01397 701000).

Lossie District Salmon Fishery Board. Messrs Andrew McCartan, Solicitors, 145 High Street, Forres, Moray.

Luce District Salmon Fishery Board. E A Fleming-Smith, Stair Estates, Estate Office, Rephad, Stranraer, Wigtownshire DG9 8BX (Tel: 01776 2024).

Morar District Salmon Fishery Board. M H Spence, 2 Gray's Inn Square, Gray's Inn, London WC1R 5JH (Tel: 0171 242 4986).

Mullanagearan District Salmon Fishery Board. The Clerk, Estate Office, Lochmaddy, Isle of North Uist PA82 5AA (Tel: 01876 3324).

Nairn District Salmon Fishery Board. E M B Larby, Finlayson Hughes, 45 Church Street, Inverness IV4 1DR.

Naver and Borgie District Salmon Fishery Board. N Wright, Arthur and Carmichael, Cathedral Square, Dornoch, Sutherland IV25 3SW.

Ness District Salmon Fishery Board. F Kelly, Messrs Anderson, Shaw & Gilbert, Solicitors, York House, 20 Church Street, Inverness IV1 1ED (Tel: 01463 236123).

Nith District Salmon Fishery Board. R Styles, Walker and Sharp, Solicitors, 37 George Street, Dumfries DG1 1EB (Tel: 01387 67222).

Ruel District Salmon Fishery Board. J Ferguson, 6 The Strand, Rye, E Sussex TN31 7DB.

Skye District Salmon Fishery Board. Mr P R A Butler, Mile End House, Glen Hinnisdal, Snizort, Portree, Isle of Skye IV51 9UX (Tel: 0147 042 331).

Spey District Salmon Fishery Board. C D R Whittle, Messrs R & R Urquhart, 121 High Street, Forres, Morayshire IV36 0AB (Tel: 01309 72216).

Stinchar District Salmon Fishery Board. Mrs A McGinnis, 6 The Avenue, Barr, Nr Girvan, Ayrshire KA26 9TX

Tay District Salmon Fishery Board. R P J Blake, Messrs Condies, Solicitors, 2 Tay Street, Perth PH1 5LJ (Tel: 01738 440088).

Tweed District Salmon Fishery Board. Mrs J Nicol, River Tweed Commissioners, North Court, Drygrange Steading, By Melrose, Roxburghshire TD6 9DJ (Tel: 01896 848 294/277(fax))

Ugie District Salmon Fishery Board. B Milton, Masson & Glennie, Solicitors, Broad House, Broad Street, Peterhead AB42 6JA (Tel: 01779 74271).

Ythan District Salmon Fishery Board. M H T Andrew, Estate Office, Mains of Haddo, Tarves, Ellon, Aberdeenshire AB41 0LD (Tel: 01651 851664).

Note. Anglers visiting Scotland to fish for coarse fish should note that it is not, in certain districts, lawful to fish with two or more rods simultaneously. The rule is one rod only.

SCOTTISH FISHING STATIONS

The nature of Scotland with its many rivers and lochs, especially on the west coast, makes it impracticable in some cases to deal with each river's catchment area separately. Thus some fisheries on the west coast, north of the Firth of Clyde are group under the heading 'West Coast Rivers and Lochs'.

The need again arises to decide whether a river should be included in England or Scotland. The Border Esk is dealt with in the English section, together with the Kirtle and the Sark, which happen to fall within the Esk's catchment area on the map. The Tweed and *all* its tributaries are included in this Scottish section. All the Scottish Islands, including Shetland and Orkney, are considered as within one watershed, viz, 'The Islands', in which, for convenience, Kintyre is included. The exact position in the book of any river or fishing station can, of course, readily be found by reference to the index.

ALNESS and GLASS

Alness drains **Loch Morie**, then flows 12 miles to enter Cromarty Firth at Alness. Glass drains Loch Glass then flows into Cromarty Firth near Evanton.

Alness (Ross-shire). Salmon, sea trout, grilse and brown trout. Alness AC has water on R Alness, salmon, sea trout, brown trout; and on Loch Morie, brown trout and Arctic char. Good bank fishing on Loch Morie; worm or fly only. Permits from Hon Sec. Novar Estate, Evanton, also issues permits for fishing on R Alness; salmon, sea trout, grilse and brown trout.

Evanton (Ross-shire). Brown trout fishing on R Glass and **Loch Glass**; bank fishing on loch. Permits from Factor, Novar Estates Office, tel: 01349 830208. Salmon, sea trout and brown trout fishing on Rivers Glass and **Skiach**; and brown trout fishing on Loch Glass. Sea trout fishing on shore of Cromarty Firth. Permits from A & M Alcock, Newsagent, 16 Balconie St, tel: 01349 830672. Local club, Evanton A C.

ANNAN

Rises in Moffat Hills and flows about 30 miles to Solway Firth. Strong tidal river. Several good pools on river N of Annan. Some spring salmon, excellent sea trout in June and July, and excellent salmon in late autumn, Oct-Nov; a few brown trout in spring and summer.

Annan (Dumfriesshire). Warmanbie Hotel has stretch; salmon, sea trout and brown trout, free to residents. Hotel also has access to many other waters, including on **Rivers Nith** and **Eden**, plus access to Sunday trout fishing. Rod and tackle hire, bait, tuition and ghillie can be arranged. Hotel also stocks a range of tackle for sale. For further information contact Warmanbie Hotel, Annan DG12 5LL, tel: 01461 204015.

Ecclefechan (Dumfries & Galloway). Annan, 2m SW; salmon, herling (late July onwards), brown trout. Hoddom & Kinmount Estates, Estate Office, Hoddom, Lockerbie DG11 1BE, tel: 01576 300244, have Hoddom Castle Water, over 2m stretch on Annan. Salmon; grilse late July onwards; sea trout, May-Aug. Dt £8-£14; limited to 15 rods per day. Fly only, except when river height is above white line on Hoddom Bridge when spinning is permitted. Hoddom & Kinmount Estates also have trout fishing on **Purdomstone Reservoir**; and coarse fishing on **Kelhead Quarry** and **Kinmount Lake**, which has first rate pike fishing. Purdomstone Reservoir, brown trout; 2 boats; 2 rods per boat; dt £8 per boat. Kelhead Quarry; brown and rainbow trout, perch, roach, bream, carp, pike, tench, eels; dt £3.50-£4.50; suitable for disabled. Permits for Hoddom Estates waters may be booked from Water Bailiff, Estate Office, Hoddom, Lockerbie DG11 1BE, tel: 0157 300417; Kelhead Quarry permits, from Water Bailiff, Kinmount Bungalows, Kinmount, Annan, tel: 01461 700344.

Lockerbie (Dumfriesshire). R Annan 1½m W; salmon, sea trout, brown trout. Castle Milk Estate has two beats on R Annan and a beat on **River Milk**. **Castle Milk Water**; salmon and sea trout, brown trout; 1¾m, left bank; fly only. Limited dt £20 (early season) and £30 (late season). **Royal Four Towns Water**; salmon, sea trout, brown trout, herling, chub, grilse; 3¾m, both banks. Dt £10 (early season) and £12 (late season), also st, £35-£55. River Milk at Scroggs Bridge; sea trout and brown trout; fly only. Permits and bookable holiday cottages from Anthony Steel, Kirkwood, Lockerbie, tel: 01576 510200. **Kirkwood** water: 1⅓m single bank with good salmon and sea trout fishing. Wt from £50-£170. **Jardine Hall** water: 2½m, some double bank, good sea trout, and late salmon. Wt from £50-£200. Contact Anthony Steele, *above*. **Halleaths Water**, west bank of Annan, near Lockerbie and Lochmaben; salmon and trout, fly only. Three tickets per week in the season, 25 Feb - 15 Nov. Permits from McJerrow and Stevenson, Solicitors, 55 High St, Lockerbie DG11 2JJ. **Black Esk Reservoir**: bank fishing; fly and spinner only. Salmon and sea trout fishing on **River White Esk**, 6m, both banks, with a number of named pools, 12m from Langholm. Salmon and sea trout run from late July. Upper Annandale AA has 4m salmon, trout fishing on Applegarth Estate, this includes stretches on R Annan, **Kinnel Water** and **Dryfe Water**. Grayling and chub, which are also caught on this beat, may only be fished in salmon season. Permits from Video Sports, 48 High St, or A Dickson, secretary of Upper Annandale AA, tel: 01683 300592.

Lochmaben (Dumfries & Galloway). Salmon, sea trout, brown trout, chub (good). Royal Four Towns Water, Hightae. Salmon season, Feb 25 to Nov 15; trout, March 15 to Oct 6. No Sunday fishing. Permits from Clerk, Mrs Kathleen Ratcliffe, Jay-Ar, Preston House Road, Hightae, Lockerbie DG11 1JR, tel: 01387 810 220. From Sept-Nov advance booking advisable. Brown trout fishing on **Water of Ae** in Forest of Ae; fly, worm and spinning: Forest Enterprise, Ae Village, Dumfries DG1 1QB. Permits from Hart Manor Hotel, Eskdalemuir, Lockerbie 013873 73217. Coarse fishing on **Castle Loch**; permits from Warden, Lochfield, Lochmaben. **Hightae Mill Loch**, bream, carp, perch, tench, rudd, chub and roach; boat fishing only. Permits from J Wildman, Annandale Cottage, Greenhill, Lockerbie. Hotels: Balcastle; Royal Four Towns, Hightae.

Wamphray (Dumfriesshire). Two beats of R Annan controlled by Upper Annandale AA. Permits for these, and 1 beat of Annandale FC, totalling 13m in all, from Red House Hotel, Wamphray, nr Moffat DG10 9NF, tel: 01576 470470, who have been catering for anglers for 40 years.

Moffat (Dumfries & Galloway). Upper Annandale AA has 4m on Upper **Annan** and 1m on **Moffat Water**; salmon, brown trout, sea trout, herling. Wt £25-£45, dt £8, conc. No day tickets after 15 Sept. Permits from Helen Smith, Gentlemen's Hairdressers, Well St; Esso Petrol Station, Moffat.

AWE and LOCH AWE and LOCH ETIVE

A short river, but one of best-known salmon streams of west coast. Connects Loch Awe to sea by way of Loch Etive, which it enters at Bonawe. River fishes best from July onwards.

Taynuilt (Argyll). Salmon, sea trout, trout. Inverawe Fisheries, Taynuilt, Argyll PA35 1HU (01866 822446), has ½m on River Awe, salmon and sea trout; and three lochs stocked daily with rainbow trout. Fly only. Wt and dt, with half-day and father/son concessions. Tuition, tackle for hire and refreshments on site. Salmon and trout fishing also from A R Nelson, Muckairn, Taynuilt, who has a stretch on R Awe. Loch Etive, brown, sea, rainbow trout and sea fish; no permit required. Hotel: Polfearn Hotel. Inverawe Holiday Cottages on estate.

LOCH AWE. Protected and controlled by Loch Awe Improvement Association, and fished by permit only. Salmon, sea trout, wild browns (av. half pound), char, occasional large rainbows, perch and pike. British record brown trout caught in 1996, 25lb 6oz, and 20lb pike not uncommon. There is a road right round loch. Salmon are most often caught by trolling. Sea trout are rarely caught and only at north end. Trout can be caught anywhere and average just under ½lb; best months Mar, Apr, May, Jun and Sep. Char are caught on a very deep sunk line. Pike and perch can be taken on a spun lure but are rarely fished for. Boats may be hired at Loch Aweside Marine, Dalavich,or Loch Awe Boats, Ardbreckinish, from £30 with motor, to £10 without, half-day.

Lochawe (Argyll). The Loch Awe IA is open to all who buy season tickets £36, but also sells weekly (£12), 3 day (£6), and daily (£3) tickets. Assn also has trout and pike fishing on **River Avich** and **Loch Avich**. Concessions for OAPs and juniors. Permits from D Wilson, Ardbrecknish House, Dalmally; Lochawe Stores, Lochawe, Dalmally, PA33 1AQ; and many other sales points including tackle shops throughout Scotland (a full list is issued by Assn).

Kilchrenan (Argyll). Taychreggan Hotel, on lochside, has pike, trout and salmon fishing on Loch Awe. Fish run to good size. 2 boats with outboard engines. Ghillie can be arranged. Fishing also on River Awe (salmon), and Loch Etive (sea trout). Good sea fishing. Hotel has own jetty and it is possible to arrive by seaplane from Glasgow. Permits and further information from Mrs Annie Paul, Taychreggan Hotel, Kilchrenan, By Taynuilt, Argyll PA35 1HQ (tel: 01866 833211, fax: 01866 244). Cuil-na-Sithe Hotel, tel: 01866 833234, has boats on Loch Awe, and launching from private jetty; fishing for salmon, sea trout, browns and rainbows free to residents. Brown trout fishing on **L Nant** (two mile walk); Oban & Lorn AC permits from Trading Post.

Portsonachan (Argyll). Portsonachan Hotel on shore of Loch Awe has fishing in loch; trout, salmon, sea trout, perch pike. Boats for hotel guests. Salmon fishing and fishing on hill lochs also arranged. Sonachan House, also on shore of Loch Awe, issues permits for boat fishing on Loch Awe. Self-catering accommodation in flats, chalets and caravans for anglers. Lures for sale. Apply to Jonathan and Jane Soar, Sonachan House, Portsonachan, By Dalmally, Argyll PA33 1BN (01866 833240).

Dalavich (Argyll). Forestry Commission has fishing on Loch Awe (brown trout, rainbow trout, char, perch, pike), **Loch Avich** (brown trout) and **River Avich** (salmon and brown trout). Dt £2.50. Permits, boat hire and rod hire, from N D Clark, 11 Dalavich, By Taynuilt (01866 844209).

Ford (Argyll). **Cam** and other hill lochs: brown trout, bank fishing, dt £3. Permits for hill lochs and also for Loch Awe (dt 2.50) from D Murray, Ford Hotel.

Tributaries of the Awe

ORCHY: Good salmon.

Dalmally (Argyll). River flows into Loch Awe here, excellent salmon fishing in May, June, Sept and Oct. Permits for several beats on Orchy, and pike and trout permits for **Loch Awe** and **Loch Avich**, from Loch Awe stores, Loch Awe (01838 200200), who can also supply fishing tackle for sale or hire. Hotels: Glenorchy Lodge; Orchy Bank; Craig Villa. Self-catering and B & B accommodation in area.

Bridge of Orchy (Argyll). Inveroran Hotel has 2m stretch on **Orchy** and also brown trout fishing on **Loch Tulla**, fly only. Permits from Inveroran Hotel, Black Mount, Bridge of Orchy (tel: Tyndrum 220); and Alan Church, Croggan Crafts, Dalmally.

AYR

Rises in Glenbuck and flows into Firth of Clyde through town of Ayr opposite south end of Isle of Arran. Good brown trout river (av ½lb) with fair runs of salmon and sea trout.

Ayr (Ayrshire). Mostly preserved, but tickets can be had for ¾m Cragie stretch at Ayr (no Sunday fishing) from the Director of Strategic Services, South Ayrshire Council, Burns House, Burns Statue Square, Ayr KA7 1UT, (01292 612270), and from Gamesport (*see below*). Ayr AC has stretch on River Ayr at Ayr and near Annbank (salmon, sea trout, brown trout); and on **Loch Shankston** and **Loch Spallander** (rainbow and brown trout). Members only. Wading essential for good sport. Water restocked with brown trout. Membership from Gamesport (*below*). Troon AC has fishing on **Collenan Reservoir**, rainbow and brown trout. Dt £13 from Torbets (*below*), and the Spar shop, Barassie. Prestwick AC has fishing on **Raith Waters**, rainbow trout. Dt £7, 4 fish limit, conc for juv and OAPs, from Gamesport (*below*); Newall's Newsagent, Monkton; Wallace's Shoe Repairer, Prestwick; and from Torbet's Outdoor Leisure, Portland Street, Troon. Block bookings (outings etc.), R McFarlane, tel: 01292 520150. **Belston Loch** at **Sinclairston**, a small rainbow trout fishery, 6m from Ayr. Four other fisheries: Springwater, tel: 01292 560343, 3m from Ayr; Dalvenan Sports; Burns Fishery, Tarbolton; Coyle Water; all stocked and 5m from Ayr; for further information contact Gamesport of Ayr, 60 Sandgate, Ayr, from whom tickets for town and other waters on Rivers Ayr and **Doon** can be obtained, and for coarse fishing lochs. Hotel: Manor Park, Monkton.

Mauchline (Ayrshire). Salmon, sea trout and brown trout fishing on Rivers **Ayr**, **Cessock** and **Lugar**; and brown and rainbow trout fishing on **Loch Belston** at Sinclairston. Boats on Loch Belston. Permits from Linwood & Johnstone, Newsagent, The Cross.

Muirkirk (Ayrshire). Fish pass has been built at Catrine Dam, allowing fish to run to headwaters at Muirkirk. Muirkirk AA has approx 6m on River Ayr, both banks; salmon, sea trout, brown trout, grayling. Assn also has fishing on **Greenock Water**; salmon and sea trout fishing allowed until end of September. Brown trout restocking program. Limited season tickets sold but membership full. Dt £6, Mon-Fri, limited to 6 per day. Wt £18. Apply to Mr Scott Davidson, President, 3 Lapraik Avenue, Muirkirk (01290 661800). Concessions and 3 competitions per year for juveniles. Hotel: Black Bull.

Tributaries of the Ayr

COYLE. Sea trout, trout, grayling, few salmon.

Drongan (Ayrshire). Drongan Youth Group AC issues permits for **River Coyle** and **Snipe Loch;** brown and rainbow trout stocked weekly; fish up to 11lb are being caught. Permits from H Lees, 2 Reid Place, and Snipe Loch.

BEAULY

Beauly is approximately 9m long, and flows from the junction of Glass and Farrar into Beauly Firth and thence into Moray Firth. Salmon, sea trout good from beginning of season. Main grilse runs in July/August. Plentiful food supply in Beauly Firth, hence the presence of bottlenose dolphins, porpoises and seals.

Beauly (Inverness-shire). Salmon, sea trout, occasional brown trout. Beauly AA has water below Lovat Bridge, and river mouth to Coulmore Bay, north shore, and **Bunchrew Burn** on south shore (sea trout and occasional bass). Strictly fly only from Lovat bridge to Wester lovat. Permits £10, conc, for assn water and for sea trout fishing on Beauly Firth from Morison's, Ironmonger, Westend, Beauly IV4 7BT. Members only, Thursdays and Saturdays. Sea trout fishing on Beauly Firth at Clachnaharry and North Kessock; permits from Grahams, 37 Castle St, Inverness, tel: 0463 233178; Kessock PO, North Kessock, tel: 01463 731470. Good sea trout from the beginning of the season. **Loch Aigas**, brown trout and stocked rainbow trout (up to 5lb). Fly fishing from boats only. Permits £18 and £10 from Aigas Field Centre, By Beauly IV4 7AD, tel: 01463 782443 (782097 fax). Tackle may be hired, flies sold at Estate Office. **Loch Ruthven**, trout fly fishing by boat, 12m from Inverness; **Tarvie Lochs**, rainbow trout, fly and boat only, 25m from Inverness; **Loch Ashie** and **Loch Duntelchaig**, fly and spinning, 10m from Inverness. Tickets for these, for 3m double bank of **R Ness**, and 9m on **R Nairn**, from J Graham, *above*. Hotels: Lovat, Priory, Caledonian, all Beauly.

Check before you go

*While every effort has been made to ensure that the information given in **Where to Fish** is correct, the position is continually changing, and anglers are urged, in their own interests, to make enquiries before travelling to selected venues. This is especially important with reference to prices quoted. Anglers attention is also drawn to the fact that hotels mentioned under the various fishing stations do not necessarily have water of their own. Any amendments or further data for inclusion in subsequent editions, and any comments, will be welcome.*

Tributaries of the Beauly.

FARRAR and GLASS:

Struy (Inverness-shire). Permits from Mr & Mrs F R Doyle, Kerrow House, Cannich, Strathglass, Inverness-shire IV4 7NA (01456 415 243), for 3½m of brown trout fishing on River Glass (fly only). Special rates for guests of Kerrow House (B&B and self-catering). Fly fishing on **R Farrar** and **Glass**. Dt £15-£40 (salmon) and £10 (trout); from F Spencer-Nairn, Culligran House, Glen Strathfarrar, Struy, Nr Beauly, tel/fax: 01463 761285. Priority given to guests of Culligran Cottages (self-catering), brochure issued. Hotels: Cnoc; Chisholm Stone House, Kerrow House.

Tomich (Inverness-shire). Tomich Hotel, Tomich, Strathglass, By Beauly IV4 7LY, has fishing in **Guisachan Hill Lochs**; brown and rainbow trout. Season: 1 May - 6 Oct.

CANNICH.

Tributary of the Glass.

Cannich (Inverness-shire). At confluence of Cannich and Glass. Glen Affric Hotel issues permits for brown trout fishing on **River Cannich, Loch Benevean, Loch Monar, Loch Beannacharan, Loch Mullardoch, Loch A-Bhana** and **Knockfin Forestry Hill Lochs**. Also salmon fishing on 1½m of **River Glass**. Permits for Loch Benevean, Loch Mullardoch and Knockfin Hill Lochs only if not required by hotel guests. Pike and eel fishing can also be arranged after 15 Oct. Reservations direct to Glen Affric Hotel, Cannich, by Beauly (01456 415 214). Fishing from boat. Fly only. No Sunday fishing. Glen Affric Hotel, in conjunction with Caledonian Hotel, Beauly, offers a special trout fishing package; seven nights DBB, boat on a different loch every day (including engine and petrol), £330 per person subject to 2 persons sharing a boat.

BERVIE

Rises on Glen Farquhar Estate and flows 14m to North Sea near Inverbervie. Essentially an autumn river for finnock, sea trout and salmon although also good for brown trout.

Inverbervie (Kincardineshire). Finnock, sea trout, salmon (best Sept-Oct). Free tickets for foreshore for fortnightly periods (restricted; advance booking advised), bookable from Joseph Johnston & Sons, 3 America Street, Angus DD10 8DR (01674 72666). For fishing upstream from Donald's Hole; dt £2 from Aberdeen Council, Area Officer, Church St, Inverbervie, Montrose DD10 0RU, or Leisure Centre, Kirkburn, Inverbervie.

BRORA

After being joined by tributaries Blackwater and Skinsdale, Brora flows through Loch Brora and into sea at Brora.

Brora (Sutherland). **Loch Brora**; salmon, sea trout and brown trout. Permits and boats on Loch Brora can be hired from Rob Wilson's Tackle Shop, Fountain Square (tel: Brora 621373). Hotel: Royal Marine.

CARRON (Grampian)

Rises in Glenbervie and flows about 9m to the North Sea at Stonehaven. Trout.

Stonehaven (Kincardineshire). About 2½m brown trout fishing offered to visitors by Stonehaven and Dist AA. Permits also issued for **River Cowie** (about 1¼m), sea trout, salmon and brown trout. Best July, August and Sept. Permits from David's Sports Shop, 31 Market Sq. Good sea fishing. Hotels: Eldergrove, Arduthie House.

Keep the banks clean

Several clubs have stopped issuing tickets to visitors because of the state of the banks after they have left. Spend a few moments clearing up. This includes lengths of broken nylon. If discarded, serious injuries can be caused to wild birds and to livestock.

CLYDE

Rises near watershed of Tweed and Annan, and flows about 50m to the Atlantic by way of Glasgow. Once a famous salmon river, then spoiled by pollution. Now, river has improved, with salmon and sea trout returning annually. Controls are in force, to conserve stocks. Trout and grayling fishing, especially in higher reaches. The Clyde's most famous tributary, the Leven, which connects with Loch Lomond, has run of salmon and sea trout. In north-west corner of Renfrewshire is Loch Thom, linked by water spill with Loch Compensation, which, when water is high, drains into River Kip in Shielhill Burn. United Clyde Angling Protective Association Ltd, controls much of Clyde and tributaries upstream of Motherwell Bridge to Daer Reservoir, in three sections, the Upper, Middle and Lower Reaches, and restocks annually. Permits are prices as follows: annual £15, day £3, grayling £2, OAP free, juv conc. These are obtainable from various tackle dealers and sports shops in Lanarkshire and Glasgow. Avon AC, Stonehouse, Lanarkshire, controls some leases on Avon.

Greenock (Strathclyde). On the estuary of Clyde. Greenock & Dist AC preserves **Loch Thom** (365 acres, trout - three to the pound), and has rights on **Yetts, No. 8 and No. 6** (Spring Dam), good trout. Permits from Brian Peterson, The Fishing Shop, *below*, or Jean Caskie, Garvocks Farm. Club membership restricted to persons resident in Greenock and district, but permits sold to visitors; Sunday fishing; no parties. Fly only. Bank fishing only. Tickets for trout fisheries in vicinity; Lawfield, Houston Rd, Kilmacolm (01505 87 4182); Fairlie Moor (10 acres), Dalry Moor Rd, Fairly (01850 162543); Pine Wood, Kilmacolm (01589 033403); and Haylie (3 acres), Largs, (01475 676005), Ardgowan Fly Fishery (dt £9-£20, boats extra), Daff Bait Fishery (7 fish £15), and Kip River, (dt £13) from The Fishing Shop, 24 Union Street, tel: 01475 888085. Good sea fishing for cod, skate, dogfish, conger, haddock and plaice. Hotel, Tontine, 6 Ardgowan Square.

Glasgow (Strathclyde). Glasgow has excellent trout, sea trout and salmon fishing within a radius of 60m. Lochs Lomond, Dochart, Awe, Tay, Ard, Leven, Lubnaig, Venachar, Lake of Menteith, etc, and Rivers Annan, Goil, Cur (head of Loch Eck), Clyde (trout and grayling only), Teith, Tweed, Allan, Dochart, Leven, Kinglass etc, all accessible from here. Coarse fishing on whole of **Forth and Clyde Canal**; pike, perch, roach, tench, rudd and bream. No close season. Canal is leased by K-Mac AC; dt £1. Permits from J B Angling, Kirkintilloch. For further details apply to British Waterways, I Applecross St, Glasgow G4 9SP, tel: 0141 332 6963. Free coarse fishing in 5m radius of Glasgow at **Auchenstarry Pond**, Kilsyth (tench, roach, perch and rudd); **Kilmadinny Loch**, Bearsden; **Bardowie Loch**, Balmore; **Mugdock Park Pond**, Milgavie; **Tench Pool**, Milgavie; **Carp Pond**, Seafar; and **Hogganfield Loch**, Glasgow. For further information contact Milton Coarse AC. United Clyde Angling Protective Association, issues annual tickets for stretches on Clyde and **R Douglas** near Motherwell, Lanark, Carstairs, Roberton and Thankerton; brown trout and grayling fishing. Permits from Hon Sec or tackle shops. Tackle shops: Cafaro Bros, Queen's; Tackle & Guns, 920 Pollokshaws Rd (0141 632 2005); Anglers Rendezvous, 74-78 Saltmarket; William Robertson & Co Ltd, 61 Miller St; J B Angling, Kirkintilloch.

Coatbridge (Lanarkshire). **Lochend Loch** is Monklands Dist water; pike, perch, brown and rainbow trout. Permits from waterside. Monklands District Coarse AC now manages **Monklands Canal**, west of Coatbridge; bream, 2lb-6lb, perch, gudgeon, common and mirror carp, dace, rudd and tench. St £12 and dt £1, conc. Day tickets on bank, fishing is allowed during close season, all anglers are welcome. Hotel: Georgian.

Airdrie (Lanarkshire). Airdrie AC has **Hillend Reservoir**; brown and rainbow trout 1lb-5lb, 1,000 stocked each month, pike

Fishing Clubs

When you appoint a new Hon Secretary, do not forget to give us details of the change. Write to the publishers (address at front of the book). Thank you!

and perch. All legal methods. Bag limit 6 fish. Boat and bank fishing, good access for disabled. No ground bait. Permits at water £4, 4 fish limit, St £50. Clarkston Independent AC has **Lilly Loch** at Calderdruix; rainbow and brown trout. Season 15 Mar - 6 Oct. Any legal method (fly only from boats). Dt £3 (£2 OAPs & juniors). Tickets from bailiffs on site. Hotel: Old Truff Inn, Caldercruix, By Airdrie.

Motherwell (Lanarkshire). United Clyde APA has water on **Clyde** and **Douglas**; brown trout and grayling. Permits from local tackle shops. Coarse fishing on **Strathclyde Country Park Loch** and adjacent R Clyde; carp, bream, roach, pike, perch and dace. No close season. No fly fishing. Lead free weights recommended. Also trout and grayling fishing; 15 Mar-29 Sept. Permits from Booking Office, Strathclyde Country Park, 366 Hamilton Rd, Motherwell. Tackle shop: Macleod's Tackle Shop, 176 High St, Newarthill, Motherwell.

Strathaven (Lanarkshire). Avon; trout and grayling. United Clyde Angling Protective Assn has water on Clyde; permits from tackle shops in Glasgow and Lanarkshire.

Lanark (Lanarkshire). Trout and grayling. United Clyde APA water on Clyde and **Douglas**; permits from local tackle shops. Coarse fishing on **Lanark Loch**; carp and tench. No close season. Hotel: Cartland Bridge.

Carstairs (Strathclyde). Trout and grayling. United Clyde APA water on Clyde and **Douglas**; permits from local tackle shops.

Thankerton (Strathclyde). Lamington AIA has 9m of water from Thankerton to Roberton; trout and grayling. St £20, wt £15, dt £5. Grayling season, 7 Oct - 14 Mar; st £5 and dt £2. Permits from Hon Sec or Bryden Newsagent, Biggar. Concessions for OAP and junior. No Sunday fishing. United Clyde APA water below Thankerton.

Biggar (Lanarkshire). Lamington AIA fish from Roberton Burn mouth to Thankerton boat bridge, approx 9m, both banks, with brown trout and grayling. 2,000 9-10" browns were stocked in 1997. Good wading. Permits from tackle shop, O'-Hara, Grocers, Mill Rd, Thankerton, or from Hon Sec, £5 daily, £15 weekly, st £20; grayling dt £2, st £5. Night ticket, £3. Conc. Hotels: Hartree Country House; Shieldhill. Tackle shop: Bryden, Newsagent, High Street.

Abington (Lanarkshire). Trout and grayling; UCAPA (United Clyde) water. Other assn water at **Crawford** and **Elvanford**. Hotel: Abington.

Tributaries of the Clyde

LEVEN and **LOCH LOMOND**: Salmon, trout, pike and perch.

Loch Lomond (Strathclyde). Loch is the largest area of inland water in Britain, being 22.8 miles long and up to 5 miles wide, and has over forty islands on it. The powan, a freshwater herring, is unique to its waters, the loch holds the record for Britain's largest pike, and there are 17 other species present. Good trout, sea trout and salmon fishing (also perch and pike) can be had from various centres on loch. Under control of Loch Lomond Angling Improvement Assn, c/o R A Clements & Co, 29 St Vincent Place, Glasgow G1 2DT (0141 221 0068). Fishing reserved for full members only on **Fruin**, **Blane** and some stretches of **Endrick**. Dt are issued for Leven and Loch Lomond at all local tackle shops, boat hirers and hotels. St and children's permits also obtainable for Leven. No Sunday fishing. Late April and May earliest for fly on Loch Lomond (sea trout and salmon). Tickets for three trout fisheries from The Tackle Box: Carman Reservoir, Killearn House, and Blairmore. Tackle shops: McFarlane & Son, The Boatyard, Balmaha (boats for hire); and Balloch Tourist Information Centre, Balloch.

Rowardennan, By Drymen (Stirlingshire). Convenient for Loch Lomond; permits and boats. Hotel: Rowardennan.

Balloch (Dumbartonshire). Trout, good sea trout and salmon fishing on River Leven and Loch Lomond; large perch and pike in loch; fishing controlled by Loch Lomond AIA. Vale of Leven & Dist AC issues permits for brown trout fishing on **Loch Sloy**. Fly only. Dt £2.50. Apply to Hon Sec. Hotel: Balloch, Tullichewan. Also Tullichewan Caravan Park.

FRUIN: (tributary of Loch Lomond).

Helensburgh (Strathclyde). Salmon, sea trout and brown trout. Fly only. Permits issued by Loch Lomond AIA. Full members only.

Ardlui (Dumbartonshire). Trout, sea trout

and salmon fishing in Loch Lomond. Hotel: Ardlui.

ENDRICK: (tributary of Loch Lomond).

Killearn (Stirling). Good trout, sea trout and salmon fishing. Loch Lomond AIA has water. No worm fishing; spinning restricted. No Sunday fishing. Accommodation arranged. Ghillie and boat hire. Full members only.

GRYFE (or GRYFFE): Brown trout, salmon, sea trout.

Bridge of Weir (Strathclyde). Bridge of Weir River AC has 3m of water. Trout: 15 Mar - 6 Oct. Salmon: 15 Mar - 31 Oct. St (locals only) from Hon Sec. Day tickets from M Duncan, Newsagent, Main St; Mon-Fri only.

Kilmacolm (Strathclyde). Strathgryfe AA has water on R Gryfe and tributaries **Green Water, Black Water** and **Burnbank Water**; approx. 25m in all, with brown trout and grayling. St £15 plus £10 entrance, with concessions. Permits from Hon Sec, or from Cross Cafe, Kilmacolm. No day tickets on a Sunday. Two fisheries with rainbow trout in Kilmacolm area: Lawfield and Pinewoods. Enquire M Duncan, Newsagents (*see Bridge of Weir*).

CALDER and BLACK CART:

Lochwinnoch (Strathclyde). St Winnoch AC has stretch of Calder (brown trout); and **Castle Semple Loch**, pike, perch, roach and eels. St £6 and dt £1-£3. Concessions for juniors. Permits from Hon Sec or A&G (Leisure) Ltd, 48 McDowall St, Johnstone. Also from Rangers Centre at loch.

AVON:

Strathhaven (Lanarks). Avon AC fishes approx 14m of excellent brown trout and grayling water, with additional salmon and sea trout, near Strathhaven Stonehouse and Larkhall. Restocked annually. Members only, membership £12 p.a., £16 salmon and sea trout, with concessions, from Sportsman Emporium, Hamilton; Gibson, Union St, Larkhall; Paper Shop, Stonehouse; or from bailiffs.

CONON (including Blackwater)

Drains Loch Luichart and is joined by Orrin and Blackwater before entering the Moray Firth and North Sea by way of Cromarty Firth. Spring fishing has declined and main salmon runs now take place from July to September. Sport then among best in Highlands.

Dingwall (Ross-shire). Salmon, sea trout and brown trout. Dingwall & District AC has lower beat on R Conon. Fly only, for salmon, sea trout and brown trout. Thigh waders only. Season: Jan 26 to Sept 30, best months May, Aug and Sept. Dt £7-£10 from H C Furlong, Sports & Model Shop, High Street, Dingwall IV15 9RY. Permit also covers **Loch Chuilin** and **Loch Achanalt**. At **Brahan** there are 3 beats of brown trout fishing on **R Conon** and a stocked, brown trout pond. Coarse fishing on **Loch Ussie**, pike and eels. Permits from Seaforth Highland Estates, Brahan, by Dingwall (01349 861150). Tackle shop: Maclean Sport, High St. Hotels: Conon at Conon Bridge; Craigdarroch and Coul House, both Contin.

Strathpeffer (Ross-shire). **R Conon**, above Loch Achonachie, salmon and brown trout; fly or spinning. **River Blackwater** above Rogie Falls, salmon, brown trout and pike. **Loch Achonachie**, brown trout, perch and occasional salmon; bank and boat fishing; use of a boat produce best results; fly or spinning. **Loch Meig**, brown trout; boat and bank fishing; fly only. Permits East Lodge Hotel, Strathconon (019977 222). Coul House Hotel issues permits for beats on Rivers Conon, **Blackwater** and **Beauly** (salmon, sea trout, brown trout); and for **Lochs Tarvie** (rainbow trout), **Achonachie** (brown trout) and **Meig** (brown trout). Apply to Coul House Hotel, Contin, by Strathpeffer IV14 9EY (01997 421487). Hotel provides full angling service, including rod racks, rod and reel hire, small tackle shop, guest freezer, drying room and fish-smoking arranged.

Garve (Ross-shire). Garve Hotel (01997 414205) has excellent fishing on **Loch Garve**, which holds large trout (fish up to 12lb taken) also pike to 30lb and perch; and brown trout fishing on $1\frac{1}{2}$m of **River Blackwater** within hotel grounds. Free fishing for hotel patrons. **Loch an Eich Bhain (The Tarvie Loch),** 25 acres, Ross-shire's only troutmaster water; stocked with rainbow trout to 15lbs and brown trout to 4lbs; fly only. Fishing exclusively by boat. **Loch Ruith a Phuill**, 12 acres; wild brown trout, stocked rainbow to 6lbs; coarse and fly fishing tackle

A salmon well hooked on the Boat Pool, Upper Fairburn beat, River Conon. *Photo: Eric Chalker.*

allowed. Permits from Tarvie Lochs Trout Fishery, Tarvie, by Strathpeffer, tel: 01997 421250; Morison, Ironmonger, Beauly; Sports & Model Shop, Tulloch St, Dingwall; J Graham & Co, 37/39 Castle St, Inverness, and Urray PO, Marybank. **Loch Glascarnoch**, brown trout, pike and perch; fly only. Contact Aultguish Inn, by Garve, tel: 019975 254).

CREE and BLADNOCH

Cree drains Loch Moan and flows about 25m to sea at Wigtown Bay. Runs of salmon and sea trout in summer and early autumn. **Minnoch**, tributary of Cree, is also a salmon river, joining Cree about six miles from Newton Stewart. Bladnoch, a strong tidal river, flows into Cree Estuary at Wigtown. Salmon in season. Good pools.

Newton Stewart (Wigtownshire). Salmon, sea trout; best early in season. Newton Stewart AA has fishing on Cree, salmon and sea trout; **Bladnoch**, salmon; and **Bruntis Loch**, brown and rainbow trout, bank fishing only; **Kirriereoch Loch**, brown trout, bank fishing, fly only, **Clatteringshaws Loch**, browns, pike and perch, plus other waters. Assn spends between £10,000-£15,000 annually, restocking 4 stillwaters with trout. Permits £2-£10, salmon weekly, £65, from A J Dickinson, Galloway Guns & Tackle, 36a Arthur St, Newton Stewart DG8 6DE (01671 403404), who supply all game, coarse and sea fishing tackle together with frozen and live bait. Forestry Commission has fishing on **R Palnure**, salmon, sea trout, brown trout; **R Minnoch**, brown trout (Mar-Jun) and salmon (Jul-

Oct); **Black Loch,** brown trout, stocked, fly only until 1 July; **Loch of Lowes**, brown trout, fly only; **Lilies Loch,** brown trout; **Lochs Spectacle** and **Garwachie**, pike, perch, tench, roach, rudd; **Loch Eldrig**, pike, perch, roach. Permits from Forest Enterprises, Newton Stewart Forest District, Creebridge, Newton Stewart DG8 6PJ (01671 2420); and Galloway Wildlife Museum. Creebridge House Hotel, Newton Stewart DG8 6NP, tel: 01671 402121, offers fishing on **R Bladnoch**, good spring run of grilse, Feb-Oct, 2m for up to 4 rods; **R Minnoch**, a tributary of Cree fed by Glentrool Loch, 4m for up to 12 rods, spawning pools; 2 beats offered, 22 pools in all. Hotel has excellent food and accommodation, can store rods in a lockable room and has freezer and drying facilities. Permits from £15-£25, only from A J Dickinson, *above.* **Upper Cree**, at Bargrennan, 2m salmon fishing: also assn water on stretch of Cree which runs through town to estuary mouth. Corsemalzie House Hotel, Port William, DG8 9RL *(see advt.)*, has salmon and trout fishing on **Bladnoch** and **Tarf**, 5m on each, dt £18, wt £80; trout fishing on **Malzie Burn**; and coarse fishing in nearby lochs. Ghillie for hire. Salmon, brown trout and pike fishing on Tarf; pike and perch fishing on **Whitefield Loch;** and trout and coarse fish on **Torwood Lochs**. Permits from David Canning, Torwood House Hotel, Glenluce, Newton Stewart. Trout fishing on **Black Loch**, and mixed coarse and pike fishing on **Lochs Heron** and **Ronald**; permit and boat hire from A Brown, Three Lochs Caravan Park, Nr Kirkcowan, Newton Stewart DG8 0EP (0167183 304). Castlewigg Hotel, nr Whithorn, 19m S of Wigtown, can arrange salmon and trout fishing in local lochs and rivers; and sea angling from Port Patrick and Isle of Whithorn. Tel: 0198 85-213. Permits for salmon and trout fishing on River Bladnoch **Torhousekie** (6 rods) and **Low Malzie** (2 rods) fisheries, also 6 acre trout loch, from Bladnoch Inn, Wigtown DG8 9AB (01988 402200). River beats have salmon and wild browns. Fishing holidays at inn, ghillie on site, £20 per day (10 am to 4 pm.) Local tackle shops have drying and freezing facilities. Cree and Bladnoch fishing holidays are arranged on private waters by J Haley, Mochrum Park, Kirkcowan, tel: 01671 830471.

Barrhill (Ayrshire). Drumlamford Estate Fisheries comprising 1m of salmon and trout fishing on **River Cree**; three stocked trout lochs; and **Loch Dornal**, a coarse fish loch. Boats, permits.

CROSS WATER OF LUCE

Dependent on flood water for good salmon fishing, but very good for sea trout after dark. Best July onwards.

Stranraer (Wigtownshire). Excellent centre for river, loch and sea fishing. Stranraer & Dist AA has **Soulseat Loch**, rainbow and brown trout, fly and bait; **Dindinnie Reservoir**, brown and rainbow trout, fly only; **Knockquassan Reservoir**, brown and rainbow trout, fly only; and **Penwhirn Reservoir**, brown trout, fly only. All these waters are near Stranraer. Permits, £10, £50 weekly, from The Sports Shop, 86 George St DG9 7JS (01776 702705); and Rogersports,

Charlotte St. Cross Water of Luce administered by J V Greenhill, Leswalt, Stranraer. Torwood House Hotel issues permits for **Torwood Lochs,** trout, bream, tench, carp, roach, rudd, perch; and **Whitefield Loch**, pike and perch. Apply to R Goodship, Cock Inn, Auchenmalg, Glenluce (01581 500224). Durskey Estates, Port Patrick, Strantaer, has 2 lochs with stocked brown and rainbow trout. Contact P Hoyle, tel: 01776 810346. Sea fishing in **Loch Ryan**, Irish Sea and Luce Bay. Charter boats and bait obtainable locally. Hotel: Ruddicot.

DEE (Aberdeenshire)

Second most famous salmon river of Scotland; for fly fishing probably the best. Also holds sea trout and brown trout. Rises in Cairngorms and flows into North Sea at Aberdeen. Best months for salmon: February to mid-June. Best for finnock (small sea trout) mid-August to end of September.

Aberdeen. Salmon, sea trout, brown trout; sea fishing. Many owners let for whole or part of season, but some good stretches held by hotels. Some hotel waters free to guests during summer. Lower reaches give good finnock fishing. Sea fishing is good in vicinity of Aberdeen. Hotels: Bucksburn Moat House; Cults; Dee Motel.

Banchory (Kincardineshire). Salmon and sea trout. Banchory Lodge Hotel by river can arrange salmon and trout fishing on Dee for five rods, bait fishing to April 15, fly only after. Ghillies and tuition on site. Apply to Mr & Mrs Dugald Jaffray, Banchory Lodge Hotel, Banchory AB31 3HS (0133 082 2625). Feughside Inn, Strachan, by Banchory, issues Aberdeen Dist AA permits for 1½m on **River Feugh**, salmon and sea trout, dt £30. Salmon and sea trout fishing on Dee at Blairs; apply to Salar Properties UK Ltd, 60 Castle St, Edinburgh EH2 3NA. Tor-na-Coille Country House Hotel *(see advt.)* also provides fishing. Other hotels: Invery House, Raemoir House.

Aboyne (Aberdeenshire). Dee, salmon and sea trout; and **Aboyne Loch**, rainbow trout, stocked. Fly only. No Sunday fishing on Dee. Permits from Glen Tanar Estate, Brooks House, Glen Tanar AB34 5EU (013398 86451). Coarse fishing on Aboyne Loch; pike and perch; permits from the Office, Aboyne Loch Caravan Park AB34 5BR, (013398 86244). **Tillypronie Loch,** brown trout, fly only. Permits hourly or daily, tel: 013398 81332. Hotels: Birse Lodge; Huntly Arms.

Ballater (Aberdeenshire). Balmoral, Mar, Glenmuick and Invercauld Estates preserve most of Upper River Dee salmon fishings. **River Gairn,** brown trout, fly only. St £9, wt £5, dt £1.50; from tackle shop. Ballater AA has fishing on **Loch Vrotichan,** brown trout, fly only. Permits from Hon Sec and tackle shop. Tackle shop: Countrywear, 15 & 35 Bridge St, Ballater (013397 55453). Hotels: Gairnshiel Lodge.

Braemar (Aberdeenshire). Salmon fishing: Invercauld Estate lets Crathie, Lower Invercauld and Monaltrie beats, 20m in all, details from The Factor, Invercauld Estates Office, Braemar, By Ballater AB3 5TR (013397 41224). Brown trout fishing on **Rivers Gairn** and **Clunie**. Permits from Invercauld Estates Office; Tourist Office, Braemar. **Lochs Bainnie** and **Nan**

Ean, brown trout, fly only; permits from Invercauld Estates Office and the keeper, Mr J Cruickshanks (01250 885206). Hotels: Invercauld Arms; Braemar Lodge.

DEE (Kirkcudbrightshire), (including Lochs Dee and Ken)

Flows through Loch Ken about 16m to Solway. Salmon, sea trout and brown trout. Netting reduced and river stocked with salmon fry. An area in which acidification problems have been reported. Some lochs affected.

Castle Douglas (Kirkcudbrightshire). Forestry Commission has fishing on **R Dee**, trout; and **Stroan Loch,** mainly pike but also perch, roach and trout. Dt £1, from dispenser at Raider's Road entrance. **Woodhall Loch,** best known as pike water but also roach, perch and large trout; good winter venue with big pike catches, including 20lb plus fish. Dt £1.50 from Mossdale Shop. Castle Douglas & Dist AA has 7m stretch on **River Urr**; salmon, sea trout and brown trout; re-stocked annually; good runs of sea trout and grilse starting in June. Dt £5 and £15 (Sept, Oct, Nov). Assn also has brown and rainbow trout fishing on **Loch Roan**; 4 boats. Dt £25 per boat for 2 rods. Permits from Tommy's Sports, 178 King Street, tel: 01556 502851. **Loch Ken**, pike and perch; open all year for coarse fish. Permits from local hotels and shops. Brown trout fishing on **Lairdmannoch Loch** at Twynholm; boat fishing only. Permits from G M Thompson & Co Ltd, 27 King St; self-catering accommodation. Other tackle shop: McGowan's, King St. Hotels: Douglas Arms; Imperial; Urr Valley Country House.

Crossmichael (Kirkcudbrightshire). Boats for **Loch Ken** from Crossmichael Marina, which has been recently upgraded and re-equipped, boats for hire all year round. Loch Ken, pike, perch, roach, brown trout, rainbow trout, sea trout, salmon, some bream, eels. Hotel: Culgruff House Hotel.

New Galloway (Kirkcudbrightshire). Dee private. Forest Enterprise controls fishing on eleven lochs, trout, coarse, or mixed, including **Loch Dee**, stocked brown trout; **Lillies Loch**, wild browns (ideal for beginners), and **Stroan Loch**, pike and perch, and stretches of Rivers **Palnure** and **Minnoch**, with salmon and sea trout. Weekly permits £25, with concessions, from Forest Enterprise, 21 King

Tailing a salmon from the Canary Pool, Middle Blackhall beat. *Photo: Eric Chalker.*

St, Castle Douglas DG7 1AA (01556 503626); and Clatteringshaws Forest Wildlife Centre, New Galloway DG7 3SQ (01644 420285). New Galloway AA controls stretch of **River Ken**, brown trout, salmon, pike, roach, perch; stretch of **Loch Ken**, brown trout, pike, perch, and salmon run through loch during season; **Blackwater of Dee** (N bank only), brown trout, salmon, pike; **Mossdale Loch,** native brown trout and stocked rainbow trout, fly only; and **Clatteringshaws Reservoir**, brown trout, pike, perch, roach. Fishing on Clatteringshaws Reservoir shared with Newton Stewart AA. Visitors permits, for all except Loch Ken and Mossdale Loch, £2 per rod per day or £10 per week; Loch Ken, dt £2 plus 50p surcharge if permit bought from bailiffs; Mossdale Loch, dt £12 per boat (1 rod) per day, from Mossdale shop. Permits from hotels in town; Ken Bridge Hotel; Mr Hopkins, Grocer, High St; Post Office, Mossdale; and Kenmure Hotel: Concession for jun. Ken Bridge Hotel has own stretch on R Ken (wt £10, dt £2). **Barscobe Loch;** brown trout; dt (incl boat) £5 from Lady Wontner, Barscobe, Balmaclellan, Castle Douglas. Tackle shop: Gun & Tackle.

Dalry (Kirkcudbrightshire). Dalry AA has fishing on **River Ken** from Dalry; good stocks of brown trout and occasional salmon; fly spinning and worm, bank fishing only. Assn also has water on **Carsfad Loch,** brown and rainbow trout, bank fishing only; **Earlstoun Loch**, brown trout, fly only, two boats. No Sunday fishing. Visitors tickets sold from 15 Mar - 30 Sept, dt £4-£5, wt £16 from N W Newton (Grocers), 17 Main St, Castle Douglas DG7 3UP. Milton Park Hotel (Tel Dalry 286), rainbow and brown trout fishing on **Lochs Moss, Roddick, Brack** nd **Barscobe**, boats for hire. All waters stocked with trout. Tickets for non-residents but guests have priority. Lochinvar Hotel can arrange fishing in rivers, lochs and reservoirs (salmon, trout, pike and perch). Permits from Duchrae Farm for **Lochinvar Loch;** wild brown trout, no shore fishing, fly only. Hotel: De Croft.

DEVERON

Rises in Cabrach and flows some 45m into the Moray Firth at Banff. A salmon river, but has a reputation for its brown trout fishing. There are also some large sea trout, many of 8-10lb. Sea trout run June to September; finnock spring months.

Banff (Banffshire). Salmon, sea trout, brown trout. Fife Lodge Hotel, Banff Springs and County Hotel can sometimes arrange fishings. Early bookings advisable as best beats are heavily booked. Best months: salmon, March to Oct; sea trout June to Aug; brown trout, April, May and Sept. Sea trout improving. Banff and Macduff AA has about 1m, left bank only, of tidal. St £10 restricted to residents within 5m of Banff; wt £10 and dt £4, Mon-Fri fishing only, from Jay-Tee Sports, Low Street, Banff. Sea trout fishing (July onwards) in **Boyne Burn**, 6m away. Tickets from Seafield Estate, Cullen (no charge, but limited).

Turriff (Aberdeenshire). Turriff AA has salmon, sea trout and brown trout fishing on Deveron. Wt £80 Jun-Aug, £100 Sept-Oct, Mon-Fri. Day tickets Feb-May only, £5; 6 rods per day limit. Permits from tackle shop. Fly only when level falls below 6in on gauge. Best months July, August and Sept; also a fishery on opposite bank, dt £5. Bognie, Mountblairy and Frendraught Group, has salmon, grilse, sea trout and brown trout fishing on Bognie Pool, Upper and Lower Mountblairy, 4m (part double bank), salmon, grilse, sea trout, brown trout. 11 Feb to 31 Oct. Wt £50-£250 depending on time of year. Fishing is open to all, usually on a weekly basis along with holiday cottages. Day permits only up until May, from Mrs Joanne McRae, BMF Group, Estate Office, Frendraught House, Forgue, Huntly

AB54 6EB (tel: 01464 871331, fax: 01464 871333). Enquiries to Bell Ingram, 7 Walker Street, Edinburgh for **Beldorney Castle Water**. £55 per rod per week. Tackle shop: Ian Masson, Fishing Tackle, 6 Castle St. Hotels: Union; White Heather. Bed and breakfast accommodation suitable for anglers, from Mrs Beattie, Colp Farm, Turriff (01888 56278); and Jenny Rae, Silverwells, St Mary's Well, Turrif AB53 8BS (01888 562469).

Huntly (Aberdeenshire). Salmon, sea trout, brown trout. Permits for **Deveron, Bogie** and **Isla**; st £60, mt £40, wt £30, dt £15 from Clerk, Huntly Fishings Committee, 27 Duke Street, Huntly AB54 5DP. Only 10 day tickets per day and none on Saturdays or Public Holidays. Castle Hotel has Castle Beat of ½m double bank fishing, 1 mile from Huntly, with salmon and sea trout, open to residents. An extensive improvement scheme carried out in early 1991 has improved and restored a number of croys to form new lies and pools. Wt £80. Hotel offers first class catering and facilities for anglers, including rod room, freezer space, picnics. Forbes Arms Hotel at Rotheimay issue permits for Deveron; salmon, sea trout and brown trout; fly fishing and spinning. The Old Manse of Marnoch Hotel, on the banks of the Deveron, caters for anglers with ample freezer and drying space; although the hotel does not sell permits these are sold locally on a daily and weekly basis. Apply to Patrick and Keren Carter, The Old Manse of Marnoch, Bridge of Marnoch, By Huntly, Aberdeenshire AB54 5RS. Tackle from Iain Forbes, Huntly.

DIGHTY

Drains some small lochs and falls into the Firth of Tay not far from Dundee. Banks built up on lower reaches. Now clear of pollution. Trout, odd sea trout and salmon. Badly weeded and difficult to fish in summer.

Dundee (Angus). Trout with occasional sea trout; free. 10m east, **Monikie** and **Crombie Reservoirs** leased to Monikie AC, stocked browns and rainbows. Boats £24-£12, with concessions, via bailiff (01382 370300). **Lintrathen Reservoir** leased to Lintrathen AC. Good trout fishing; boats for hire; catch limit 15 fish (over 10") per boat. Club bookings from Dr Parratt, 91 Strathern Road, Broughty Ferry, Dundee, tel: 01382 77305. **Loch Fitty** near Dunfermline also with in easy reach. Tackle shop: Shotcast Ltd, 8 Whitehall Crescent. Hotel: Northern.

DON (Aberdeenshire)

Rises near Ben Avon and flows for nearly 80m to North Sea at Aberdeen. Long famed as a dry fly trout water, the river is also becoming known for its salmon, which run from April to October. Sea trout numbers are on the increase.

Kintore (Aberdeenshire). Salmon and trout fishing on both banks of River Don; 2½m on right bank and 3½m on left bank. Permits from Sloans of Inverurie, 125-129 High St, Inverurie AB51 3QJ (01467 625181). No Sunday fishing.

Inverurie (Aberdeenshire). **River Don** (2½ miles) and **River Urie** (3½ miles) salmon, brown trout and occasional sea trout. No Sunday fishing on Don. Salmon best March, April, May and Sept-Oct. Permits from Sloans of Inverurie, 125-129 High St, Inverurie AB51 3QJ (01467 625181).

Kemnay (Aberdeenshire). Salmon, sea trout, brown trout. Mrs F J Milton, Kemnay House, AB51 9LH (01467 642220), issues limited permits for one beat on Don at Kemnay; wt £90, dt £15 and £6 (trout). Booking essential. Hotel: Parkhill Lodge.

Alford (Aberdeenshire). 25m from Aberdeen. Salmon, brown trout and some sea trout. Forbes Arms Hotel, Bridge of Alford AB33 8QJ (019755 62108), has 3¼m of Don for guests and also issues permits. Wt £45-£85, dt £8-£17. Preference given to guests. Some good trout burns (free) in vicinity.

Kildrummy (Aberdeenshire). Kildrummy Castle Hotel has good stretch of salmon and brown trout fishing. Trout best early, salmon late.

Glenkindie (Aberdeenshire). Glenkindie Arms Hotel issue permits for salmon and trout fishing. No Sunday fishing; 4 rod limit.

Strathdon (Aberdeenshire). Colquhonnie Hotel, AB36 8UN, tel: 019756 51210, has 9m of salmon and trout fishing. Permits for salmon fishing also from Glenkindie Arms Hotel; and Kildrummy Castle Hotel, Kildrummy.

DOON

Drains Loch Doon on the Firth of Clyde watershed and flows right through the old County of Ayr to the Firth of Clyde, near Ayr Town. Good salmon, sea trout and brown trout water.

Ayr (Ayrshire). On Rivers Doon and Ayr. Salmon and sea trout July onwards. Brig o' Doon Hotel, Alloway (01292 442466), has water on Doon. Salmon and sea trout fishing on 2 beats at Skeldon Estate, with self-catering accommodation, from Mr Campbell, Skeldon Estate, Dalrymple (01292 560656). District Council issues permits for **Ayr**. Club membership and permits for various club waters issued by Gamesport of Ayr, 60 Sandgate, Ayr KA7 1BX (01292 263822). Hotel: Parson's Lodge, 15 Main St, Patna.

Dalmellington (Ayrshire). Good salmon and sea trout (July onwards). **Loch Doon**, 6m; plenty of small brown trout and occasional salmon and char; fishing free; boats for hire. Craigengillan Estate KA6 7PZ (01292 550237) has both banks of River Doon from Loch Doon to the Straiton Road Bridge, and coarse fishing from bank at Bogton Loch. Tickets from keeper. Brown trout and occasional salmon and sea trout. Apply Farm, Craigengillan (Tel: Dalmellington 550 366).

EDEN (Fife)

Rises in Ochil Hills not far from Loch Leven and falls into North Sea in St Andrews Bay. Provides some very fair trout fishing. Slow-flowing stream suitable for dry-fly fishing. Some sea trout below Cupar.

St Andrews (Fife). **Cameron Reservoir**, brown trout; stocked by St Andrews AC (trout av 1¼lb). Fly only. Sunday fishing. Boat and bank fishing. Boat hire (3 rods per boat) £23 per session. Bank permit £8 per session. Permits sold at reservoir. Tackle shop: J Wilson & Son, 169-171 South St, St Andrews KY16 9EE (01334 72477).

Cupar (Fife). Salmon, sea trout and brown trout fishing on Eden; permits £7 from J Caldwell, Newsagent & Fishing Tackle, Main St, Methihill, Fife. Clatto and Stratheden AA has brown trout fishing on **Clatto Reservoir**. Dt £5, evening £6; from Waterman's Cottage at reservoir. Boats, £4.

Ladybank (Fife). Fine dry-fly fishing; trout. Some free, but mostly preserved. **Lindores Loch**, near **Newburgh** (7m NW), holds brown and rainbow trout; fly only; no bank fishing. Permits from F G A Hamilton, The Byre, Kindrochet, St Fillans, Perthshire PH6 2JZ (01764 685 337).

ESK (North)

Formed by junction of Lee and Mark, near Loch Lee, and flows for nearly 30m to North Sea near Montrose. Good river for salmon and sea trout.

Montrose (Angus). Salmon, sea trout, finnock (whitling) and brown trout. Joseph Johnston & Sons Ltd, 3 America Street, Montrose DD10 8DR, issue permits for salmon fishing on the Gallery and Canterland beats, charges varying from £6 to £50, according to time of year. Spring and Autumn best fishing. North esk tickets from Post Office, Marykirk. For Mill of Criggie trout fishery, Mr McVicar, St Cyrus, nr Montrose. Montrose AC fishes **South Esk**. 4m south of Montrose is **Lunan River**, salmon, sea trout, brown trout. Tackle shops: The Gun Shop, 180 High Street; Cobsport, 7 Castle Place DD10 8AL. Hotels: Carlton, George, Hillside, Marykirk.

Edzell (Angus). Salmon and sea trout. Dalhousie Estates, Brechin DD9 6SG, has boats to hire for trout fishing on **Loch Lee** in Glen Esk; no bank fishing, and fly only. Permits from Mrs Taylor, Kirktown of Invermark, Slenesk, by Brechin (01356 670208); also salmon beats to let by the week on North Esk at Edzell, dt when no weekly lets; 2 beats at Millden, 4 and 3 rods, salmon and sea trout; mill dam at Edzell stocked with browns, fishable on day permit; details from Dalhousie Estates. Panmure Arms Hotel has

1m of fishing on **West Water** (trout, sea trout and occasional salmon); and can arrange fishing on North Esk and Loch Lee. Hotels: Glenesk and Central. Self-catering cottages through Dalhousie Estates Office.

ESK (South)

Rises in Glen Clova and flows some 49m to North Sea near Montrose. Good salmon river with plentiful runs of sea trout. Best months for salmon are February, March and April. Good autumn river (mid-September onwards), sea trout May-July.

Brechin (Angus). Good centre for North and South Esk. Salmon and sea trout; fishing good, but mostly reserved. South Esk Estates Office, Brechin, let beats on 2½m, usually by the week or longer periods, but very limited. Brechin AC has fishing on **Loch Saugh** near Fettercairn, brown trout, fly only; and **River West Water**, brown trout, salmon and sea trout. Permits for **L Saugh** from Drumtochty Arms Hotel, Auchenblae; and Ramsay Arms Hotel, Fettercairn. Carroll-s Tackle Shop, Church St, Brechin, issues limited dt for West Water.

Kirriemuir (Angus). Kirriemuir AC has approx 7m on South Esk. Salmon, sea trout, a few brown trout. Permits from Hon Sec (01575 73456). Some fly only water, but much of it unrestricted. Concessions to jun. No Sunday fishing and no permits on Saturdays. Strathmore AIA has rights on lower **Isla** and **Dean**; permits from tackle shops in Dundee, Blairgowrie and Forfar.

EWE

This river has good runs of salmon (best May onwards) and sea trout (end June onwards) up to Loch Maree. Fishing again excellent, after problems caused by disease. Owned by Inveran Estate.

Aultbea (Ross-shire). Bank fishing for wild brown trout on **Aultbea Hill Lochs**. Permits from Bridgend Stores, Aultbea, Achnasheen, Ross-shire IV22 2JA (01445 731204); Woodcraft Shop, Drumchork, Aultbea; Post Office, Laide. Bridgend Stores, as well as issuing permits, has a comprehensive range of tackle. Hotels: Aultbea; Drumchork Lodge; Ocean View, Laide.

Poolewe (Ross-shire). Salmon, sea trout, brown trout. The National Trust for Scotland, Inverewe Estate, Visitors' Centre (01445 781299), offers trout fishing on several lochs: **Kernsary, Tournaig, Na Dailthean** and **A'bhaid**, Luachraigh, either by part ownership, or on behalf of owners. Dt £4.50, boat £3. No Sunday fishing. Reduction for members.

LOCH MAREE (Ross & Cromarty). Spring salmon fishing from April until June. Sea trout from June until Oct. Also brown trout fishing.

Talladale (Ross-shire). Salmon, sea trout, brown trout. Loch Maree Hotel has fishing. Heavy demand for sea-trout season so early booking advised. Hotel owned by anglers' syndicate which provides excellent facilities. Boat fishing only. Apply to Loch Maree Hotel, Talladale, By Achnasheen, Wester Ross IV22 2HL. Gairloch Angling Club has brown trout fishing in many hill lochs, including **Bad na Scalaig, Tollie, Garbhaig**. Membership closed but permits £2-£10 from K Gunn, Strath Square, Gairloch.

Kinlochewe (Ross-shire). Salmon and sea trout fishing on loch. Boats for hire. Permits from Kinlochewe Hotel (01445 760253) and Kinlochewe Holiday Chalets (0144584 234). Brown trout, char and sea trout fishing on **Loch Bharranch**; and brown trout, pike and perch fishing on **Loch a'Chroisg**. Permits from Glendocherty Craft Shop. **Loch (A'chroisg) Rosque**, ¼m from village; pike, perch, brown trout; permits from Ledgowan Lodge Hotel, Achnasheen, Ross-shire IV22 2EJ (01445 720252). Hotel is HQ of Achnasheen AC.

FINDHORN

Rises in Monadhliath Mountains and flows over 60m to Moray Firth. Good salmon river with many rock pools, mostly preserved by owners. Also sea trout and brown trout. Best months: May/June and August/Sept. Recent native hardwood regeneration schemes along substantial lengths of the river have enhanced the quality of the spawning beds; and helped to limit erosion previously caused by livestock.

Drynachan (Nairnshire). Cawdor Estate has fly only salmon fishing on Findhorn, 4 beats with 2 rods per beat; and trout fishing on **Loch of Boath** (brown). Excellent accommodation is bookable on Estate at Drynachan Lodge. Contact the Factor, Cawdor Estate Office, Cawdor, Nairn IV12 5RE (tel: 01667 404666, fax: 01667 404787). Good trout fishing on nearby lochs; **Loch of Blairs, Loch Lochindorb**. Tickets for 7m stretch of **R Nairn** with sea trout and salmon, from tackle shop: Pat Fraser, 41 High St, Nairn. Permits for Lochindorb from J Mitchell, Tackle Shop, 96D High St, Forres.

Forres (Moray). Broom of Moy beat, 1½m double bank, with salmon and sea trout. Fly, spinning, worming permitted. Permits from J Mitchell, Springbank, Findhorn, Forres IV36 0YN, or J Munro, South St, Elgin. Permits for **Loch of Blairs**, from Ian Grant, Tackle Shop, High St, Forres.

FLEET (Kirkcudbrightshire)

Formed by junction of Big and Little Water, empties into the Solway Firth at Gatehouse. Good sea trout and herling, and few grilse and salmon; best months July and August.

Gatehouse-of-Fleet (Dumfries and Galloway). Murray Arms Hotel, Gatehouse-of-Fleet DG7 2HY (01557 814207), issue permits for Rusko and Cally Estate waters on River Fleet. Sea trout and herling with some grilse and salmon. No sunday fishing. Gatehouse and Kirkcudbright AA has **Loch Whinyeon**, 120 acres, 3½m from town, brown trout, stocked and wild; fly only. Two boats; bank or boat fishing. Assn also controls **Loch Lochenbreck**, 40 acres, 3m from Lauriston, rainbow and brown trout. Fly only. Bank or boat fishing. Permits £10, boats £3, from Watson McKinnel, 15 St Cuthbert St, Kirkcudbright. Hotels: Angel; Selkirk Arms, Kirkcudbright.

FORTH (including Loch Leven and Water of Leith)

Formed from junction of Avendhu and Duchray not far from Aberfoyle, and thence flows about 80m to its firth at Alloa, opening into North Sea. Principal tributaries, Teith and Allan, flow above Stirling. A large salmon river, which at times, and especially on upper reaches, provides some good sport. Good run in lower reaches during February and March, as a rule. This river and Teith, Balvaig, Leny Water and Allan Water being extensively restocked with salmon and sea trout by Forth District Salmon Fishery Board. Trouting in upper reaches and tributaries, particularly in lochs, where salmon also taken.

Dunfermline (Fife). **Loch Fitty**, good trout water. Bank and boat fishing, 30 boats, tackle shop and restaurant to which visitors are welcome. Boats, including outboard motor, for 3 anglers, day (10am-5pm) £30; evening (5.30pm-dark) £32 with reductions during Apr, Aug, Sept; bank permits £13 per session; boats for single anglers, £16; 'father and son/daughter', £17; OAP, (Tues and Thurs) £21. Apply to Fife Angling Centre, The Lodge, Loch Fitty, Kingseat, by Dunfermline, Fife (01383 620666). Halfway House Hotel by Loch Fitty welcomes anglers and can arrange fishing for guests. Apply to Ann and Vic Pegg, Halfway House Hotel, Kingseat, Dunfermline KY12 0TJ (01383 731661). Civil Service SA has brown trout fishing on **Loch Glow** in Cleish Hills near Kelty; fly, bait and spinning. Regularly stocked. Permits from Mr Balfour, Lochornie Cottage, Kelty; and tackle shops in Dunfermline, Cowdenbeath, Kelty and Kinross. Permits for **River Devon**, trout, £3 from D W Black, The Hobby and Model Shop, 10-12 New Row, tel: 01383 722582. Other tackle shops: Gamesport, St Andrews St, Dunfermline; Fife Tackle Centre, 56 High St, Cowdenbeath; Alex Constable, 39a High St, Kirkcaldy; Aladdin's Cave, 259 High St, Leslie. Hotels: Abbey Park House, Auld Toll Tavern, King Malcolm Thistle. B & B, Loch Fitty Cottage, tel: 01383 831081.

Stirling (Stirlingshire). Forth, **Allan** and **Teith** may be fished from here. Herling in Forth in spring and autumn. Salmon fishing from Lands of Hood to mouth of Teith (7½m) including Cruive Dykes is controlled by District Council. Good run in lower reaches, March and Aug-Sept. Permits for Forth and Teith; salmon, sea trout and brown trout; from D Crockart & Son, 47 King St, Stirling FK8 1AY (01786 473443). **North Third Trout Fishery**, Greathill, Cambusbarron, FK7 9QS (01786 471967): rainbow and brown trout (record rainbow, 19lb 2oz; brown, 9lb 14oz); fly only; 23 boats and bank fishing, tuition by appointment. Permits and season tickets from fishery. Tackle shop: J Henderson, Country Pursuits, Henderson St, Bridge of Allan (01786 834495).

Aberfoyle (Perthshire). Trout; a few salmon taken. Aberfoyle APA has brown trout fishing on **Loch Ard**; fly only; stocked with young brown trout. Dt £2.50. Boats for hire; £10 per day. Boats and permits from Addison's, Newsagent, Main St; Altskeith Hotel, Kinlochard; and Forest Hills Hotel, Kinlochard. Free fishing for residents of Altskeith and Inverard Hotels; apply to hotels for details of package. Brown trout fishing on **Loch Arklet, Loch Katrine** and **Glen Finglas**; permits now issued by Trossachs Fishings, Loch Vennacher, by Callander. Forest Enterprise controls fishing for brown trout, pike and perch on River Forth and **Loch Chon**, brown trout on **Lochs Drunkie**, **Achray**, and **Lochan Reodhte**, and salmon, sea trout and brown trout on **Loch Lubnaig**. Bank fishing only. Permits from £5.50 to £2.50 from Forest Enterprise, Aberfoyle District Office FK8 3UX (01877 382383); and Queen Elizabeth Forest Park Visitor Centre, Aberfoyle (01877 382258) (open Easter to Oct). Access to Loch Drunkie via Forest Drive; no vehicle access after Oct. Among other accessible waters is **Lake of Menteith**, brown and rainbow trout, fly only. Permits from Lake Menteith Fisheries Ltd, Port of Menteith, Stirling (01877 385 664). Tackle shops: D Crockart & Son, King St, Stirling; James Bayne, 76 Main St, Callander. Hotel: Inverard.

Tributaries of Forth

ALMOND. West of Edinburgh the river flows into the Firth of Forth at Cramond.

Cramond (West Lothian). Cramond AC has fishing leases on most of River Almond and tributaries. Salmon, sea trout and brown trout. Permits from Post Office, Cramond.

Livingston (West Lothian). River Almond

The Lake of Mentieth (the only 'lake' in Scotland?). *Photo: Lake of Mentieth Fisheries.*

AA has ½m of Almond with salmon and sea trout, and 2m with brown trout. Permits from Hon Sec; Livingston Sports, Almondvale Centre; Country Life, Balgreen Rd, Edinburgh; Shooting Lines, Roseburn Terrace & Hope Park Terrace, Edinburgh. **Crosswood Reservoir**, 30 acres; stocked brown trout. Fly only. 3 boats. No bank fishing. Bag limit: 6 trout. Permits from Lothian Regional Council, Dept of Water and Drainage, Lomond House, Beveridge Square, Livingston (tel: Livingston 414004). **Morton Fishery**, brown and rainbow trout; fly only; bag limits 3-6 fish. Advanced bookings. Permits from Morton Fishery, Morton Reservoir, Mid Calder, West Lothian.

NORTH ESK and **SOUTH ESK**. These two rivers are fed by Lothian regional reservoirs and join near Dalkeith to form the River Esk. The Esk flows a short way down to enter the Firth of Forth at Musselburgh. Simpsons of Edinburgh offer salmon fishing on the North Esk Burn beat. Cost is between £40 per rod day, spring, and £810 per three rod week, autumn. Bookable cottage sleeps six. Contact Simpsons, 28/30 West Preston St, Edinburgh EH8 9PZ, tel: 0131 667 3058, fax: 0131 662 0642.

Musselburgh (East Lothian). Musselburgh and District AA has salmon, sea trout and brown trout fishing on Esk, from estuary, 2m upstream of Musselburgh; permits from Musselburgh Pet Centre, 81 High St; Mike's Tackle, 41 High St, Portobello. No Sunday fishing.

Penicuik (Midlothian). Esk Valley AIA has rainbow and brown trout fishing on North and South Esk; fly rod and reel only to be used. Permits from Hon Sec. **Glencorse** and **Gladhouse Reservoirs**. Brown and rainbow trout; fly only; boat only. Permits from Lothian Regional Council, Pentland Hills Regional Park, Boghall Farm, Biggar Rd, Edinburgh EH10 2DX, tel: 0131 445 5969. **Rosebery Reservoir**; 52 acres; brown and rainbow trout, pike, perch.

West Linton (Peeblesshire). Brown trout fishing on **West Water Reservoir**; 93 acres; fly only. 2 boats. No bank fishing. Permits from Lothian Regional Council, Pentland Hills Regional Park, Boghall Farm, Biggar Rd, Edinburgh EH10 2DX, tel: 0131 445 5969; and Slipperfield Estate, c/o Romano Inn, Romano Bridge, Peeblesshire (01968 60781).

DEVON: Fair brown trout stream; sea trout and salmon lower down.

Alloa (Clackmannanshire). Devon AA has salmon, sea trout and brown trout fishing on nine beats of Devon, from Glendevon to Devonside. Assn also has brown trout fishing on **Glenquey Reservoir**, near Muckhart; fly only on all waters to mid-April, no spinning; bank fishing only. Sunday fishing permitted on reservoir, prohibited on river. Season tickets for sea trout and salmon are only obtainable from Hon Sec (postal application only). Permits for brown trout fishing from Scobbie Sports, 2-4 Primrose St, Alloa FK10 1JG (01259 722661); D Crockart & Son, 47 King St, Stirling; Hobby & Model Shop, 10 New Row, Dunfermline; McCutcheons Newsagents, Bridge St, Dollar; and Marco Palmieri, The Inn, Crook of Devon KY13 7UR; Muckhart PO; and Mrs Small, Riverside Caravan Park, Dollar, FK14 7LX (01259 742896). **Gartmorn Dam Fishery**, stocked brown trout, fly and spinning, artificials only; bank and boat fishing, Wheelyboat for disabled. Permits (from st £80 to boat dt £25, bank dt £6, conc,) from Gartmorn Dam Country Park, by Sauchie (Alloa 214319); and Clackmannan District Council, Leisure Services Dept (Alloa 213131). Fife Regional Council control **Upper** and **Lower Glendevon Reservoirs**, and **Castlehill Reservoir**; brown trout; fly only. No Sunday fishing on **Glendevon Reservoirs**. Permits from Fife Regional Council, Craig Mitchell House, Flemington Rd, Glenrothes; and from The Boathouse, Castlehill Reservoir, Muckhart. Fife Regional Council also lease out a number of reservoirs to local clubs; **Cameron Reservoir** to St Andrews AC; **Craigluscar Reservoirs** to Dunfermline Artisan AC, rainbow trout dt £10 for 5 fish, conc, from bailiff's hut; **Glenquey Reservoir** to Devon AA; **Lochmill Reservoir** to Newburgh AC; **Stenhouse Reservoir** to Burntisland AC; **Upper Carriston Reservoir** to Methilhaven & District AC (01592 713008). Hotels: Castle Campbell, Dollar; Castle Craig, Tillicoultry; Tormaukin, Glendevon.

Gleneagles (Perthshire). The Gleneagles Hotel, Auchterarder PH3 1NF, has access to Lower Scone and Almondmouth beats on **River Tay**; salmon, grilse and sea trout. Trout fishing on **Fordoun Loch**; and also on **Laich Loch**, in hotel grounds. Costs range from £80-£495 per rod for salmon fishing (includes ghillie and tackle). Trout fishing costs £80 per rod and £40 for hire of a ghillie. Should venues be fully booked hotel will arrange alternative fishing on **River Tay** at **Upper Kinnaird**. Apply to The Country Club, The Gleneagles Hotel (01764 662231).

AVON: Flows 18m to estuary of Forth near Grangemouth. Lower reaches polluted; good brown trout elsewhere (av ½lb with few around 2lb). River fishes best in late June, July and Aug.

Linlithgow (West Lothian). Linlithgow AC (01506 842832) has stretch of Avon north of Muiravonside Country Park, with trout, pike, perch, carp, roach. Permits obtainable. Avon Valley AC offer excellent value season tickets on a lengthy stretch in Avonbridge area. Muiravonside Country Park, The Loan, by Whitecross (01506 845311): brown trout and coarse tickets, £3, conc. **Union Canal** from Edinburgh to Falkirk: pike, perch, roach, carp and tench; no close season. Permits from British Waterways, Canal House, 1 Applecross Street, Glasgow G4 9SP, tel: 0141 332 6936.

Slamannan (Stirlingshire). Slamannan Angling Club offers brown trout day permits, £3, conc, from Fit o' the Toon Bar, Slamannan.

CARRON:

Larbert (West Lothian). Larbert & Stenhousemuir AC issue permits for **Loch Coulter**, near Carronbridge; brown and rainbow trout. Fly only. No Sunday fishing. Outlets: Scrimgeou Fishing Tackle, 28 Newmarket St, Falkirk (01324 24581); Paton's newsagent, Larbert; This 'n That, Denny.

Denny (Stirlings). East of Scotland Water controls **Carron Valley Reservoir**, together with sixteen other trout fisheries in various localities. No bank fishing at Carron Valley, and fly only. On the day booking; apply Environmental Manager, Pentland Gait, 597 Calder Road, Edinburgh, EH11 4HJ, tel: 01786 458705. **Drumbowie Reservoir**, fly only brown trout permits from Bonnybridge AC (01324 813136), £5, visitors accompanied by member, st £25. **Little Denny Reservoir**, Little Denny AC (01324 823365), members only, brown trout fishing. Waiting list. Club also controls stretch of Carron, dt £1 from This n' That, Denny.

TEITH: Noted salmon and brown trout fishery, with good sea trout in summer.

Callander (Perthshire). Stirling District Council controls part of Teith, in which excellent salmon, sea trout and brown trout. Brown trout average ¾lb. Fishing open to visitors; st £80, dt £28. Conc for residents, OAP & jun, from Baynes Fishing Tackle (**below**). **Loch Venachar** controlled by the Town Council; sea trout and brown trout fishing: trout average 1lb; fishing from bank permitted on parts of loch; st £35, dt £8, with concessions to OAP and juniors; boats for hire. Permits also for **River Leny**, 1m from town, salmon, fly and spinning; **River Balvaig**, 10m north, trout fishing, any method; **Loch Lubnaig**, 2m north, trout, perch, char; and Loch Venachar, from James Bayne, (*below*). **Loch Drunkie** (brown trout), **Loch Achray** (brown trout, perch, pike) and **Lochan Reoidhte** (brown trout, fly only), boat hire on Lochan Reoidhte; permits £6 from Queen Elizabeth Forest Park Visitors' Centre, Aberfoyle; and James Bayne, Fishing Tackle, 76 Main St FK17 88D, (01877 330218).

BALVAIG and CALAIR (Tributaries of Teith): salmon and brown trout.

Balquhidder (Perthshire). Salmon and brown trout fishing on **R Balvaig, Loch Voil** and **Loch Doine**; from Kings House Hotel, Balquhidder, Perthshire FK19 8NY (01877 384646). Boat hire and ghillie can be arranged. Dt £3 for Loch Voil trout fishing also from Baynes Fishing Tackle (*see Callander*). Rod and tackle hire, and tuition from Craigruie Sporting Estate, Balquidder, Perthshire FK19 8PQ (01877 384262).

Strathyre (Perthshire). Salmon and brown trout fishing from Munro Hotel: Season 1 Feb-1 Oct. No boats.

Loch Leven

Famous Kinross-shire loch which produces quick-growing trout. Loch is nowhere deep so feed is good, and practically whole area is fishing water. Under efficient management, this has become one of the most notable trout fishing lochs of Scotland.

Kinross (Kinross-shire). Loch Leven Fisheries is a predominantly brown trout loch which boasts the famous Loch Leven trout. These average over 1lb pound with many specimen of 3-4lbs being taken. It is also stocked each year with high quality rainbow trout. Fly fishing by boat only. The pier is ¼m out of Kinross. Boats are bookable by letter or phone. For full information on charges and booking conditions, apply to the Manageress, The Pier, Kinross, Tayside KY13 7UF (01577 863407). Tackle can be bought at the pier. Top quality trout fishing on **Heatheryford**; brown and rainbow trout; bank fishing. Permits from office on site (01577 64212). Tackle shop: James Philip, The Pier. Hotel: Green.

Ballingry (Fife). Rainbow and brown trout fishing on **Loch Ore**; bank and boat. Permits from Lochore Meadows Country Park, Crosshill, Balligry, Fife KY5 8BA (01592 414312).

Glenrothes (Fife). Permits may be had from Fife Regional Council for reservoir trout fishing on **Holl**, **Castlehill**, **Glenfarg**, **Upper Glendevon** and **Lower Glendevon Reservoirs**. Morning and evening sessions. Boats (2 rods) £10. Bank (Lower Glendevon and Castlehill only) £3. Concessions for jun. Permits from Fife Regional Council, Water Division, Craig Mitchell House, Flemington Road, Glenrothes.

Water of Leith

Local people who know river well get fair numbers of trout.

Edinburgh (Mid Lothian). Water of Leith, running through the city, is stocked annually with brown trout. Permits issued free of charge. Permits for trout, boat fishing at **Gladhouse, Glencorse, Clubbiedean, and Crosswood**, and **West Water Reservoirs** from Lothian Regional Council, Pentland Hills Regional Park, Boghall Farm, Biggar Rd, Edinburgh EH10 2DX, tel: 0131 445 5969. Bank permits for **Harperrig** from ticket machine on site. **Rosebery Reservoir**, brown and rainbow trout, pike, perch; permits from Mrs Grant, Keeper's Cottage (01875 830353). **Talla** and **Fruid Reservoirs**, brown trout; permits from Crook Inn, Tweedsmuir, Biggar, Lanarkshire ML12 6QN (0189 880272). Permits for **Whiteadder Reservoir** from Goblin Ha' Hotel, Gifford (01620 810244), or Cranshaws Smiddy Tea Room, Duns, Berwickshire TD11 3SL (01361 820277). Permits for **Hopes Reservoir** from Alderston House, Haddington (0162 0182 6422). Coarse fishing on **Duddingston Loch**; carp and perch. Loch situated in a bird sanctuary, therefore a restricted area. Bank fishing. No lead weights. No close season. Permits from Historic Scotland, Royal Park Constabulary, Holyrood Park, Edinburgh EH8 8AZ (0131 556 3407). **Union Canal** from Edinburgh to Falkirk; pike, perch, roach, carp and tench; no close season. Permits from British Waterways (*see Linlithgow*). Tackle shops: John Dickson & Son, 21 Frederick Street; Shooting Lines Ltd, 18 Hope Park Terrace and 23 Roseburn Terrace; F & D Simpson, 28/30 West Preston Street; Countrylife, 299 Balgreen Rd; Mike's Tackle Shop, 48 Portobello High St.

Balerno (Edinburgh). Trout fishing on Water of Leith; permits from Balerno PO, 36 Main St; and Colinton PO. Brown and rainbow trout fishing on **Threipmuir** and **Harlaw Reservoirs**. Fly fishing only. Bank fishing only. Season tickets are balloted for, contact The Factor, Dalmeny Estate Office, Dalmeny Estate, South Queensferry, West Lothian EH3O 9TQ (0131 331 4804). Day tickets from Flemings Grocery Shop, 42 Main Street, Balerno (0131 449 3833). Concessions for OAP and jun. Cobbinshaw AA has fishing on Top Loch, **Cobbinshaw Reservoir**, leased from BWT. Permits from keeper at reservoir. **Harperrig Reservoir**, 237 acres; brown trout. Fly only, bank fishing. Permits from machine at reservoir (coins required).

GIRVAN

Drains small loch called Girvan Eye and thence runs 25 miles to the Atlantic at Girvan. Good salmon and sea trout; fair brown trout. Salmon run March onwards; sea trout from June.

Girvan (Ayrshire). Salmon, sea trout, brown trout. Carrick AC issues permits, from Gilmour, Knockushan St, Girvan KA26 9AG (01465 712122). **Penwhapple Reservoir**, near Barr, stocked with brown trout; Penwhapple AC water. Fly only. Dt £6 and evenings £4; boats £5 (9-5) and £3 (5-10), apply Mrs Stewart, Lane Farm, Barr (½m beyond reservoir). Hotels: King's Arms, Ailsa Craig.

Straiton (Ayrshire). Salmon (late), sea trout, brown trout. Blairquhan Estate water, fly only. Permits from D Galbraith, The Kennels, Blairquhan Estate, Straiton. Forestry Commission controls fishing in Galloway Forest Park, with brown trout fishing on **Lochs Bradan**, (boats), **Skelloch**, (boat), **Loch Dee**, **Black Loch**, and **Loch of the Lowes**; all stocked waters. Unstocked: **Loch Brecbowie**, **Lilies Loch**, and **Dhu Loch**. Pike and perch fishing, with other coarse on **Linfern Loch**, **Spectacle**, **Garwachie**, **Eldrig**, and **Stroan**. Permits £6.50 to £3, conc, from Robin Heaney, Tallaminnoch, Straiton (016557 617); and Forestry Commission Office, Straiton (016557 637).

HALLADALE

Rises on north slope of Helmsdale watershed and empties into sea at Melvich Bay. Early salmon March onwards, 10-16lbs. Grilse run from June, 5-7lbs.

Melvich (Sutherland). Melvich Hotel, Melvich, By Thurso, Sutherland KW14 7YJ (016413 206), 18m from Thurso, offers trout fishing on several lochs, one of which has a boat. Fly only. Dt £7.50 for bank fishing and £15 for boat fishing.

Forsinard (Sutherland). Salmon sport good, especially after freshets. For salmon beats on Halladale from Forsinard to Melvich Bay: contact Mrs J Atkinson, Factor, 8 Sinclair Street, Thurso, Caithness (01847 63291). Accommodation; self catering in Lodge. Forsinard Hotel has salmon fishing on River Halladale, 2½m stretch from Forsinain bridge to junction with River Dyke; and on **River Strathy**; both fly only. Hotel also has trout fishing on 6 lochs exclusively for guests and on 14 lochs open to non-residents. Apply to Forsinard Hotel, Forsinard KW13 6YT (016417 221).

HELMSDALE RIVER

Formed by two headstreams near Kinbrace, this river flows 20m southeast through Strathullie to sea. Excellent salmon river, where there is now no netting.

Helmsdale (Sutherland). Salmon and sea trout. Salmon beat lettings from Roxton Bailey Robinson, Fishing Agents, 25 High St, Hungerford, Berks RG17 0NF (01488 683222). Lower Helmsdale only: permits from Strathullie Crafts, Dunrobin St (01431 821343). Information from J A Douglas Menzies, Mounteagle, Fearn, Ross-shire. Navidale House Hotel KW8 6JS, tel: 01431 821 258, has limited salmon fishing on river from Jan-March, and arranges brown trout fishing on six lochs, fly only on all but one. Hotel has permits for Lower Helmsdale. Other hotels: Bridge: Belgrave Arms.

INVER (including Kirkaig and Loch Assynt)

Draining Loch Assynt, this river flows into a sea loch on the west coast of Sutherland known as Lochinver (village and loch having the same name), a little north of the old Ross-shire border. Holds salmon and sea trout but fishing is hard to come by.

Lochinver (Sutherland). Inver Lodge Hotel has salmon fishing three beats of River Inver, the upper of which is bookable. The hotel has further fishing on **River Kirkaig**, 3½m S of Lochinver, and brown trout fishing on **Loch Culag**, **Fionn Loch** and numerous other hill lochs. Apply to Inver Lodge Hotel, Lochinver IV27 4LU (01571 844496). Assynt AC controls twenty seven hill lochs and lochans with brown trout fishing to the north and east of Lochinver, and two beside the Achiltibuie road, lying south of Loch Kirkaig. 7 boats are for hire, at £10 per day. Permits are mostly £5, but cost £6 on three waters, and obtainable from Tourist Office, or Simpsons Newsagents, Lochinver. In 1993 the Assynt Crofters bought the North Assynt Estate. Through the Trust, anglers may fish a large number of hill lochs, in a landscape of great natural beauty, including **Loch Poll**, the biggest, which contains large trout, also char, **Loch Drumbeg**, with two boats, **Lochs Roe, Manse, Tuirk**, which can produce excellent sea trout runs, and many others. 10 boats are for hire, £6-£10, and £5 permits may be bought at Stoer and Drumbeg Post Offices, and Lochinver Tourist Office and Newsagents. Inchnadamph Hotel (01571 822202) has fishing on **Loch Assynt**. Kylesku Hotel, Via Lairg IV27 4HW (01971 502231) is conveniently placed for free fishing in Reay forest lochs. Hotel hires equipment, and can provide knowledgeable guides and tuition.

Ledmore (Sutherland). The Alt Bar and Motel, 20m N of Ullapool, has brown trout and char fishing on **Loch Borralan**. Boat £18 and bank £3 per day. Also, 12m of double bank salmon and sea trout fishing from Rosehall to Bonar Bridge on the Kyle of Sutherland at £15 per day. Bed and breakfast, and self-catering accommodation. Further information from Bruce and Alba Ward, The Alt Bar and Motel, The Altnacealgach, Nr Ledmore Junction, By Lairg, Sutherland IV27 4HF (01854 666220).

Loch Assynt

Inchnadamph (Sutherland). Salmon fishing (fair) from June on upper end of Loch Assynt. Inchnadamph Hotel (01571 822202) has fishing on loch, also celebrated **Gillaroo Loch** and **Loch Awe** (£6 per rod plus £15 for boat, 8 boats for hire). Season: salmon from May 15 till Oct 15, trout, 15 Mar to 6 Oct.

IRVINE (including Annick, Garnock and Lugton)

Rises near Loudonhill and flows about 20m to Firth of Clyde at Irvine Town. Main tributaries are Cessnock Water, Kilmarnock Water and Annick. Fishing controlled largely by clubs. Salmon and sea trout July onwards; brown trout average ½lb; early season best.

Irvine (Ayrshire). Salmon, sea trout, trout; Irvine and Dist AA issues permits for 2m on Irvine and 3m Annick (no dt Saturdays). Irvine Water runs from estuary to Red Bridge, Dreghorn, on north bank and to Bogie Bridge on south bank. Annick

'Spring' fishing for salmon on the River Helmsdale. *Photo: Eric Chalker.*

Water is from confluence with Irvine to northern boundary of Annick Lodge Estate, except for one private stretch.

Dreghorn (Ayrshire). Salmon, sea trout, trout; Dreghorn AC issues wt and dt for 12m water on both banks of Irvine and Annick; apply Hon Sec or R W Gillespie, 16 Marble Ave or Alyson's Flowers, 10 Bank St, Irvine. Applications for new associate membership must be made in writing to Hon Sec. July to Sept best for salmon and sea trout. Brown trout average ½lb.

Kilmarnock (Ayrshire). Salmon, sea trout, trout. Permits for stretches on Irvine at Hurlford and Crookedholm from P & R Torbet, 15 Strand St.

Galston (Ayrshire). Good sport with salmon and brown trout. Aug to Oct for salmon. Galston AC has salmon and trout fishing on Irvine and **Cessock**. Permits from Hon Sec; P & R Torbet, 15 Strand St, Kilmarnock.

GARNOCK: Trout, sea trout, salmon.

Kilwinning (Ayrshire). Garnock and Irvine join in tidal water and have common mouth. Salmon, sea trout, brown trout. Kilwinning Eglinton AC has 9m on Garnock and **River Lugton**. No Saturday or Sunday fishing. Permits from Craft Shop, 42 Main St.

Kilbirnie (Ayrshire). Kilbirnie AC has water on river Garnock and **Kilbirnie Loch** (brown and rainbow trout) and two reservoirs. Yearly stocking of brown trout; monthly stocking of rainbow trout. Kilbirnie Loch best trout: brown 9lb 2oz. Kilbirnie Loch, any legal method. St £15; wt £7, dt £5. Club has excellent brown trout fishing on **Camphill Reservoir**; fly and boat only. Season holders £5 per boat per day and non-holders £12 per boat per day. Permits from Hon Sec; R T Cycles, Glengarnock, Beith KA14 3AA (01505 682191); and Glengarnock PO. Tackle from R T Cycles. For other trout fisheries in vicinity, *see Greenock*.

ANNICK: Brown trout; small runs of salmon and sea trout Sept-Oct.

Irvine (Ayrshire). Dreghorn AC issues permits for 12m of water on Irvine and Annick. Permits from Hon Sec.

Kilmaurs (Ayrshire). Kilmaurs AC has fishing on Annick and **Glazert**; sea trout and brown trout, with salmon in autumn. Other fishing: North Craig Reservoir, Kilmaurs: Burnfoot Reservoir, Fenwick; Loch Gow, Eaglesham. Permits £6, conc, from Spar supermarket, Kilmaurs. St £25 (membership £20) from J Graham, 99 East Park Drive, Kilmaurs.

Stewarton (Ayrshire). Stewarton AC has water on Annick and tributaries, and **White Loch;** permits from Hon Sec and John Gordon, 6 Main Street KA3 5AE, tel: 01560 48207.

THE ISLANDS

The term 'The Islands' includes the Inner and Outer Hebrides, the Orkney and Shetland Islands and, for convenience, Kintyre.

ARRAN: In the rivers, brown trout are generally small, although brown trout up to 1lb have been recorded. In Aug, Sept and Oct there is often a good run of sea trout, especially in post spate conditions, along with good salmon catches, particularly in **Sliddery**, **Kilmory**, **Sannox** and **Cloy**. **Benlister** and **Monamore** are also worth fishing under spate conditions. The Tourist Office at Brodick pier provides a free Information Sheet detailing all the main freshwater fishing opportunities on Arran, with charges. It also issues day and 6-day permits for various Arran AA waters. These include Kilmory (from above the bridge at Lagg Hotel), Cloy, Benlister, Monamore, Sannox, **Ashdale**, Sliddery Water and **Loch Garbad** (stocked with sizable brown trout).

Machrie. Machrie Fishings consistently record excellent sea trout and salmon returns. A fine spate river which has numerous named pools extending from the sea pool for approx 3 miles. Fly water, but worming area for 2 rods. Season, 6 Jun-15 Oct, 6 rods maximum (2 per beat), enquiries should be made to Mrs Margo Wilson, 10 Leysmill, by Arbroath, Angus DD11 4RR, tel/fax: 01241 828755, 9am-5pm), or to the Water Bailiff, Riverside Cottage, Machrie 840241. No Sunday fishing.

Dougarie. The **Iorsa River** has two beats, the upper beat includes **Loch Iorsa** (with boat). A spate sea trout river, with occasional salmon. The lower beat stretches from Gorge Pool to sea. Fishing is fly only and let by the week, from £105 (June) to £125 (July-Aug), and £135 Sept-Oct). Enquiries should be directed to The Estate Office, Dougarie, Isle of Arran KA27 8EB (01770 840259).

Blackwaterfoot. Blackwater offers good sea trout catches and also salmon under suitable conditions; permits are obtainable from the General Store, Blackwaterfoot. Port-na-Lochan Fishery, Kilpatrick (01770 860444), is a small lochan of 2 acres, with good quality rainbow trout fishing. 4 hours (2 fish limit), £10.50. Tickets and tackle at reception desk, Kinloch Hotel, Blackwaterfoot.

Brodick. The **Rosaburn** is now let to a local syndicate.

BENBECULA: Lies between N and S Uist. Numerous lochs, giving good sea and brown trout fishing.

Balivanich. South Uist AC has brown trout fishing on many lochs in South Uist and Benbecula. Bank and boat fishing. Permits from Colin Campbell Sports. Creagorry Hotel, Creagorry, tel: 01870 602024, has fishing for guests on fifteen lochs and three sea pools; boats on some waters; waders useful; trout to 1lb; all within five miles of hotel. June-Sept best for brown trout and August-Sept for sea trout. Sea trout up to 8lb in sea pools.

BUTE: 5m from Ayrshire coast; 16m long and 3-5m wide. Trout and coarse fish.

Rothesay. Loch Ascog, 1½m pike, perch and roach. **Loch Quien**, 5m first-class trout fly fishing (fish averaging 1lb). Fishes best early and late in season for brown trout. Applications to Bute Art and Tackle, Rothesay (01700 503598), or The Tackle Shop, Deanhood Place, (01700 502346). **Loch Fad**, 175 acres, rainbow and brown trout fishing. Boat and bank fishing. 25 boats; booking advisable. Permits from bailiff's hut at Loch (01700 504871). All information from Isle of Bute Trout Co Ltd, Ardmaleish, Isle of Bute PA20 0QJ (01700 502451). Hotel: Palmyra (01700) 502929, Ardbeg Lodge 505448, Port Royal, 505073. B & B: Commodore 502178, Tigh-na-Camus 502782, Carleol 502716, Vanetzia 502203. Sea fishing: from rocky shore popular and good; by boat from Rothesay pier.

Tighnabruaich. Kyles of Bute AC has fishing on **Loch Asgog**, brown and rainbow trout, fly only; on **Upper** and **Lower Powder Dams**, brown and rainbow trout, fly and bait only; and on **Tighnabruaich Reservoir**, brown trout. Permits £5, conc, from Kames Post Office, Spar supermarket, and Glendaruel Hotel. Hotels: Kames, Royal, Kyles of Bute.

COLONSAY: Reached by car ferry from Oban. Colonsay Fly Fishing Association has been formed to protect the Colonsay loch fishing. In recent years the fishing has been abused by the use of coarse fishing methods, bubble floats and even nets; fishing has continued late into the season and affected breeding fish, and a large number of fish (many undersized) have been taken from the island.

Scalasaig. Colonsay FFA control most of the loch fishing on the island, including brown trout fishing on **Lochs West Fada, Mid Fada, East Fada, na Sgoltaire** and **Turamin**. Best months, May, June and Sept; fish average 10-16oz; fly only. Boats for hire. Permits covering all waters £10 from Isle of Colonsay Hotel and shop at Scalasaig. Further information from Kevin Byrne, Isle of Colonsay Hotel, Argyll PA61 7YP (tel 01951 200316).

CUMBRAE: Small islands lying between Bute and Ayr coast. Largs is nearest mainland town, approx 30m from Glasgow.

Millport. Cumbrae AC has trout fishing on two reservoirs, **Top Dam** and **Bottom Dam**. Club restricted to 30 members only. Juveniles must be accompanied by an adult and be over 12 years; dams are too steep and could be dangerous. Sea fishing good from shore or boats. Tackle shops: Mapes; Masties, Main St, Largs. Hotel: Royal George.

HARRIS: Southern part of the island of Lewis and Harris, comprising the two distinct areas of North and South Harris. Accessible by car ferry from Ullapool, Isle of Skye, and North Uist. Daily flights from Inverness and Glasgow to Stornoway. Most of the trout, salmon and sea trout fishing in North Harris belongs to the North Harris Estate and is centred around Amhuinnsuidhe Castle, which is let along with the fishing on a weekly basis. There are six river systems with lochs, which all contain salmon and sea trout. Enquiries to the Estate Office, Lochmaddy, North Uist, HS6 4AA, tel: 01876 500329 (fax 500428). For dt £70, incl boat, on Saturdays and unlet weeks, contact Roddy Macleod, Head Keeper, Amhuinnsuidhe (01859 560232).

South Harris, Good fishing for salmon and sea trout; brown trout lochs and lochans. Near Tarbert, salmon and brown trout fishing at Ceann an Ora Fishery, on **Lochs Sgeiregan Mor, A'Mhorghain** and **Na Ciste**. Fly and bank fishing only.

Further information from The Anchorage, Ardhasaig, Isle of Harris HS3 3AJ (01859 2009). Accommodation at Macleod Motel, HS3 3DG, tel: 01859 502364, with waterfront location, and sea angling competitions arranged by Harris Sea AC. Borve Lodge, Scarista, 7m west of Tarbert, has fishing on sea trout lochs. Day tickets sometimes obtainable. Enquire Tony Scherr, Factor, Borve Lodge Estate Fisheries, Isle of Harris HS3 3HT (01859 550202). Finsbay Fishing, 4 Ardslave, HS3 3EY, tel: 01859 530318, has accommodation with over 100 lochs for salmon, sea trout and brown trout fly fishing. For Rodel Estates salmon and sea trout fishing, contact R Coles, 5 Lever Terrace, Leverburgh, Harris, tel: 01859 520426.

ISLAY: Most southern island of Inner Hebrides. Lies on west side of Sound of Islay, in Argyllshire. Greatest length is 25m and greatest breadth 19m. Sport with salmon, sea trout and trout. Hotel: Harris.

Bridgend. Salmon and sea trout fishing on **Rivers Sorn, Laggan** and **Grey River**; all within 2m of Bridgend; fly only. Brown trout fishing on **Lochs Gorm, Finlaggan, Skerrols** and **Ardnahoe**, with boats. Also trout fishing on numerous hill lochs without boats. Permits and self-catering accommodation from B Wiles, Headkeeper, Head Gamekeeper's House, Islay House Square, Bridgend, Isle of Islay, Argyll PA44 7NZ (0149 681 293).

Port Askaig. Port Askaig Hotel has trout fishing nearby in **Lochs Lossit, Ballygrant** and **Allan**. Dt (boat) from Post Office. Sport on other lochs by arrangement. Salmon fishing in **River Laggan**. Best months: May, June and Sept.

Port Ellen. Machrie Hotel has salmon and sea trout fishing on **R Machrie**, and **Kinnabus Loch**. Apply to Machrie Hotel, Port Ellen, Isle of Islay, Argyll PA42 7AN.

KINTYRE: This peninsula is part of Argyll and lies between Islay and Arran.

Campbeltown (Argyll). Campbeltown AC has brown trout fishing on **Lochs Lussa, Knockruan**, and **Aucha Lochy**; fly only, permits from McGrory *below*. Carradale AC has fishing on **Tangy Loch**, 60 acres, trout to 2lb. Access road to waters edge. Permits from tackle shop. Sea fishing in harbour and **Firth of Clyde**. Permits from A P McGrory, Electrical Hardware, 16-20 Main Street (01586 552132). Hotel: White Hart.

Carradale (Argyll). Excellent salmon and sea-trout fishing may be had on **Carradale Water**, a small spate river. Carradale Estate lease the water to Carradale AC. Bait and spinner under certain conditions, otherwise fly only. Assn also has brown trout fishing on **Tangy Loch**. St £30, ft £21, wt £16, dt £5. Apply Hon Sec, Mr D Paterson, Tormhor, Carradale; J Semple, The Garage; D Oman & Co, The Pier; Mr William Shaw, Westhill, Carradale (River Keeper); A P McGrory, Fishing Tackle, Main St, Campbeltown. Hotel: Carradale.

Crinan (Argyll). Near west end of Crinan Canal. Brown trout lochs controlled by Lochgilphead Dist AC. Canal (trout).

Lochgilphead (Mid Argyll). At east end of Crinan Canal. Lochgilphead and Dist AC has rights on nine lochs located in the hills above Cairnbaan; brown trout; wt £18, dt £5 from tackle shop. Forest Enterprise, White Gates, Lochgilphead PA31 8RS, has leased fishing on **Loch Coille Bhar, Cam Loch, Loch An Add, Daill Loch, Seafield Loch, Lochs Glashan, Blackmill** and **Bealach Ghearran** to Lochgilphead AC; brown trout, fly only. Permits from Fyne Tackle, 22 Argyll St, Lochgiphead PA31 8NE (tel; 01546 606878). Stag Hotel can arrange fishing on **River Add** and various lochs. Salmon and sea trout in river, brown trout in lochs. Six holiday cottages with fishing on 5m of the River Add from Kilmichael Bridge to tidal pools, fly only, mid June-mid Sept: normally, 2 or 3 day permits for non-residents, £15, £75 weekly, from Robin Malcolm, Poltalloch Estate Office, Duntrune Castle, Kilmartin, by Lochgilphead, Argyll (01546 510283).

LEWIS: Some salmon and sea trout, much trout fishing on a large number of lochs.

Stornoway. Permits for salmon and sea trout fishing in **River Creed** and **Lochs Clachan** and **An Ois**, approx 5m from town, cost £10-£12, £20-£22 with boat. For more details enquire of the Factor, Stornoway Trust Estate Office, 20 Cromwell St, Stornoway (0185 702002). Stornoway AA is local association. Permits from Sportsworld, 1-3 Francis St (01851 705464). Soval AA has brown trout fishing on several lochs within easy distance of Stornoway. Wt £5 if staying in Soval area and £10 if not, dt £2, from Hon Sec; and N Mackenzie, Treasurer, Tabhaigh,

Keose, Lochs (01851 830 242). **Loch Keose**, a beautiful 90 acre loch with plentiful wild brown trout. Permits and information brochure from Murdo Morrison, Handa Guest House, 18 Keose Glebe, Lochs, Isle of Lewis HS2 9JX (01851 83334). Hotels: Caberfeidh, Caledonian. Tackle and waterproof clothing from Lewis Crofters Ltd, Island Rd, tel: 01851 702350.

Garynahine. The **Grimersta** belongs to Grimersta Estate Ltd, who occasionally have salmon, sea trout and brown trout fishing for individuals or small parties in April, May and early June. Accommodation at the estate. For Garynahine Estate fishing, contact M Macphail, Head Keeper, tel: 01851 621383 (home).

Uig. Salmon, sea trout and brown trout fishing on Scaliscro and North Eishen Estates including **Loch Langavat**. Bank and boat fishing. Also sea angling trips in **West Loch Roag**. Permits, boat and tackle hire, and ghillies; apply to Estate Office, Scaliscro Lodge, Uig, Isle of Lewis PA86 9ER (01851 672325). Uig and Hamanavay Estate, 10 Ardroil, Uig HS2 9EW, tel: 01851 672421, offers fly only salmon and sea trout fishing, with self-catering accommodation, on the **Hamanavay** and **Red River** systems, also Lochs Cro Criosdaig, Benisval, Cragach and Fuaroil with sea trout and the occasional salmon. For details contact Estate Manager on the above tel. number. The estate allows Stornoway AC to fish **Loch Langavat**. For information contact Sportsworld Stornoway (*see above*). For Uig Lodge Estate fishing, contact K A Mackay, Head Keeper, tel: 01851 672250.

Kintarvie. The Aline Estate, on the march of Lewis and North Harris, has one salmon fishery, **Loch Tiorsdam**, plus 12 brown trout lochs and numerous lochans. Boat and bank fishing for both salmon and trout on **Loch Langavat** and trout lochs. Wild browns to 10lb have been caught in recent years, salmon are mostly grilse, Arctic char taken every year in Loch Langavat. Cottage and lodge to let. Boat and ghillie. Contact The Aline Estate, Lochs HS2 9JL (01859 502006). Further fishing contacts on Lewis are: Barvas Estate, D Macdonald, Keeper, 01851 840267; Soval Estate, J Macleod, Keeper, tel: 01851 830223; Mike Reed, 23 Gravir, South Lochs, Lewis HS2 9QX, tel/fax: 01851 880233.

MULL:

Tobermory. Salmon and sea trout fishing on **Rivers Aros** and **Bellart**. No Sunday fishing. Salmon, sea trout and brown trout fishing on **Loch Squabain**; boat fishing only. Fishing on **Torr Loch**, sea trout, wild browns; no Sunday fishing; 2 boats; banks clear. Bank fishing on **Loch Frisa**. Permits from Tackle & Books, 10 Main St (01688 302336). Tobermory AA has fishing on **Mishnish Lochs**, well stocked, native brown trout only, 3 boats for hire on daily basis; and **Aros Loch**, open all year for rainbow. Dt £10 and wt £30. Boat hire (01688 302020): £5 for 4 hrs and £12 all day. Permits from A Brown & Son, General Merchants, 21 Main Street PA75 6NX (01688 302020). Fishing on **Loch Frisa**, good brown trout, some salmon and sea trout; and River Lussa. Apply to Forest Enterprise, Mull Office, Aros (01680 300346). List of hotels from Tourist Office, tel: 01688 302182.

Bunessan. Argyll Arms Hotel has good salmon, sea trout and brown trout fishing on **Loch Assapol**. Fly and spinner only. No Sunday fishing.

RAASAY:
The Isle of Raasay is near Skye. Free trout fishing in lochs and streams; waders should be taken.
RUM:
The fishing in the burns and lochs of the Isle of Rum is all owned and managed by Scottish National Heritage, The White House, Rum National Nature Reserve, Isle of Rum PH43 4RR, tel: 01687 462026. Permits to fish are required, and SNH reserves the right to restrict fishing over certain areas in the interests of successful ornithological conservation, most particularly, red throated divers. There are always fishing opportunities, however.
NORTH UIST: Island in Outer Hebrides, 17m long and 3-13m broad. More water than land with over 400 named lochs and lochans, and many more unnamed, some probably unfished. Plenty of lochs by road-side for elderly or infirm anglers.
Lochmaddy. Fishing on North Uist is controlled by the North Uist estate, Lochmaddy HS6 5AA, tel; 01876 500 329, fax: 01876 500 428. This covers all the salmon and sea trout systems on North Uist, and comprises sixteen brown trout lochs, most of which are provided with a boat, and eleven salmon and sea trout lochs, six of which have a boat. Visitors' charges range between £38 per day, two rods, salmon and sea trout, to £6 per day, brown trout. Salmon and sea trout fishing is available to guests staying at the Lochmaddy Hotel (01876 500331) *(see advt)* or the Langass Lodge Hotel (01876 580285); residents have the first option. Non residents day tickets cost £35 per rod per day, when obtainable. Brown trout fishing costs visitors £20, weekly, or £6 daily, bank only, plus £15 per day boat hire. All permits from the Lochmaddy Hotel. North Uist AC offers brown trout permits for the Newton Estate waters, comprising numerous lochs with boats on 3 of them, st £35, wt £15 and dt £4, from J Matheson, Clachan stores, Clachan. Other North Uist accommodation: Lochportain House, Lochmaddy HS6 5AS, tel: 0131 447 9911, self catering; Sealladh Traigh, Claddach Kirkibost, tel: 01876 580248.

SOUTH UIST:
Bornish. South Uist AC has trout fishing on many lochs in South Uist and **Benbecula**. Bank and boat fishing; boats on 12 lochs: Secretary, W P Felton, tel: 01870, 610325. Permits from Mrs Kennedy, Bornish Stores. For South Uist Estates fishing, Captain J Kennedy, tel: 01878 700332 (Hotel).
Lochboisdale. Lochboisdale Hotel issues permits for brown trout fishing on many lochs; sea trout and salmon fishing may also be open. Boats on several lochs. Fly only. Contact John Kennedy, Lochboisdale Hotel (01878 700332) *(see advt.)*.

ORKNEY

While sea fishing for skate, ling, halibut (British record), haddock, cod, etc, is general in waters about Orkney, good fun may be had in the evenings with saithe comparatively close to the shores.

Trout fishing is prolific, there are a multitude of lochs which hold excellent stocks of wild brown trout, and sea trout also are plentiful. **Loch of Harray** is the

most famous and will produce fish from the first day of the season to the last, with May, June and July the best months. **Boardhouse Loch** in Birsay is ideal for the visiting angler as there are no skerries and the fish average three quarters of a pound. The best months to fish at Boardhouse are May, June, and early July. **Loch of Swanney**, again in Birsay, is another favourite with visiting local anglers, with the best months being May and June. The **Loch of Stenness** is a challenge, connected to the sea, it is partly tidal. Native brown trout and sea trout thrive in this environment, growing big and strong on the abundant marine life. The **Loch of Skaill** in Sandwick should also be mentioned as it holds specimen trout, with fish averaging two pounds. The lochs on the islands of Sanday and Westray also contain a number of very large trout.

The Orkney Trout Fishing Association is a non-profit making voluntary body, dedicated to the preservation and enhancement of game fishing throughout the islands of Orkney. The Association operates a trout hatchery. Restocking has yielded excellent results, notably in the Loch of Swanney. Membership is £16, visitors season £13, OAP & jun season £6, invalid season £3. Membership entitles anglers to use assn facilities, which include access to fishing on **Loch of Skaill**. Subscriptions are accepted at **Orkney Tourist Board Office, Kirkwall;** Barony Hotel, Birsay; J I Harcus, Bridge St, Kirkwall; Merkister Hotel, Harray; The Longship, Broad St, Kirkwall; W S Sinclair, Tackle Shop, Stromness; E Kemp, Bridge St, Kirkwall.

There is good quality accommodation throughout Orkney and there are taxi services to fishing waters. The Merkister Hotel, Harray, is close to Loch of Harray (now the best of the Orkney Lochs) and offers excellent loch fishing: boats, outboards, ghillies; tel: 01856 771 366. The Standing Stones Hotel, Stenness, is fully licensed, and can provide boats, outboards, ghillies. The hotel is situated on the shores of Loch of Stenness and is also convenient for the Loch of Harray, while Smithfield Hotel (01856 771 215) and The Barony (01856 721 327), are convenient for the Lochs of Boardhouse, Hundland and Swanney.

SHETLAND

Shetland was formerly renowned for its sea trout fishing, but for a variety of reasons this fishing has now drastically declined and anglers are recommended to concentrate on the excellent wild brown trout fishing in over three hundred lochs containing trout up to five pounds in weight.

Taking the Shetland Islands as a group, the majority of the fishing is controlled by the Shetland Anglers Association, who charge a fee of £15 for unlimited fishing, juniors free. Boats are bookable at a weekly cost of £20. Details of all fishing and permits are obtainable from Rod and Line Tackle shop, Harbour Street, Lerwick, and also from the Association secretary, Alec Miller, 55 Burgh Road, Lerwick,Shetland ZE1 0HJ, tel: 01595 695903 day, 01595 696025 evening, fax: 01595 696568. The association publishes a comprehensive local guide covering over two hundred trout lochs. There are now several hotels specialising in catering for anglers, and among the best are Hildasay Guest House, Scalloway; Herrislea

Hotel, Tingwall, Westings Hotel, Whiteness, Baltasound Hotel, Baltasound, Unst.

SKYE

Trout and salmon fishing generally preserved. Sea trout especially good in places. Excellent sea fishing.

Dunvegan. Numerous streams in area can be very good for sea trout in May and June. Hotels: Atholl House; Misty Isle.

Sleat. Brown trout and sea trout fishing on a number of small rivers and lochs in the South of Skye. Permits from Fearann Eilean Iarmain, An t-Eilean, Sgiathanach (01471 833266). Tackle shop: Dunvegan Boats and Fishing Tackle, Main Rd, Dunvegan; The Gun & Tackle Room, Uiginish Lodge, Dunvegan.

Portree. Lochs Fada and **Leathan** have good brown trout (average 1lb, occasionally 5lb). **Storr Lochs** are 4m away. Bank fishing; 10 boats. Mid-May to mid-June and early Sept best. Permits for these and other hill lochs from Anderson, MacArthur & Co, Somerled Sq. There is also salmon fishing in **Staffin**, **Lealt** and **Kilmuluag** rivers. Sea trout in **Brogaig** and numerous small brown trout lochs in the north of the island. St and dt for these fishings. Enquiries to Hon Sec, Portree AA. Also sea fishing, for pollack and saithe in harbour. Sea trips from Portree daily, apply Tourist Office. Portree AA permits from tackle shop: Jansport, Wentworth Sq. Hotel: Cuillin Hills.

Skeabost. Skeabost House Hotel, Skeabost Bridge, Isle of Skye IV51 9NP (0147 532202) has salmon and sea trout fishing (8m double bank) on **River Snizort**, reputed to be the best salmon river on Skye, and trout fishing; discounts for residents.

Sligachan. Sligachan Hotel currently issues permits at £15 for salmon and sea trout fishing in 2m **Sligachan River** and brown trout fishing in **Loch na-Caiplaich** free for guests; salmon few, sea trout quite plentiful; best months, mid-July to end Sept. Brown trout fishing by arrangement in Storr Lochs (15m); boats for hire; season, May to end Sept. No permit is required for brown trout fishing in **Loch Marsco**.

Broadford. Sea trout and salmon in the **Broadford River**. 1½m south bank, fishing permits £5 from Broadford Hotel (01471 822204). **Loch Sguabaidh** and **Lochan Stratha Mhor**, brown trout, sea trout, occasional salmon, permits £5 from Mrs Anderson, Torrin Post Office (01471 822232).

Staffin. Salmon, sea trout, brown trout. Portree AA hold the fishing rights. Tickets from D Burd, College of Agriculture, Portree.

Struan. Ullinish Lodge Hotel, IV56 8FD (01470 572214) has salmon, sea trout and brown trout fishing in three lochs (Connan, Duagrich and Ravag) and on **Rivers Ose** and **Snizort**. Special rates for residents of hotel; trout free, salmon fishing charges adjusted according to water conditions. Residents only on Loch Ravag.

Uig. Uig Hotel, IV51 9YE (01470 542205/ 542308 (fax)) can arrange fishing on north bank **River Hinnisdale** and **Storr Lochs:** also on various hill lochs on which Portree AA has rights. River Hinnisdale is run by angling club. Permits £15 daily, £40 weekly, for salmon and trout fishing on **Rivers Rha**, **Connan** and north bank R Hinnisdale from MacKay's Building Supplies, Uig.

LOCHY (including Nevis and Coe)

Drains Loch Lochy and, after joining the Spean at Mucomir, flows about 8m to salt water in Loch Linnhe close to Fort William. Very good salmon and sea trout river but affected by hydro works at Falls of Mucomir. Best months: July, August and Sept. Whole river is on weekly lets only. Further information from River Lochy Association, c/o Mr J A Douglas-Menzies, Mounteagle, Fearn, Ross-shire.

Tributaries of the Lochy

SPEAN: Flows from Loch Laggan. A rocky river with good holding pools. Good fishing for salmon and sea trout from May to October. For lettings and permits enquire at Rod & Gun Shop, 18 High Street, Fort William.

Spean Bridge (Inverness-shire). Beats open on dt for left bank only, also for **Lochs Arkaig** and **Lochy**. Enquire at Spean Bridge Hotel.

ROY (tributary of Spean): Salmon. A spate river; fishes best July onwards.

Roy Bridge (Inverness-shire). Lower half

Spinning the Sligachan River, Skye, with the Cuillins in the background. *Photo: Eric Chalker.*

let to Roy Bridge AC; and Glenspean Lodge. Permits from Roy Bridge Hotel and Stronlossit Hotel: Upper half owned by Roy Fisheries; permits from Finlayson Hughes, 29 Barossa Pl, Perth (01738 30926) and keeper, Braeroy Estate. Roy Bridge AC has fishing on **Loch na Turk**; stocked rainbow trout; apply to Hon Sec.

NEVIS: A short river flowing around south side of Ben Nevis and entering Loch Linnhe at Fort William, not far from mouth of Lochy. Very good salmon and sea trout fishing.

Fort William (Inverness-shire). River Nevis; salmon, grilse, sea trout. Fort William AA has about 6m; dt from tackle shop after 9am on day required. No spinning; best June onwards. Good brown trout fishing on **Loch Lundavra** 6m from town. Dt £12.50, boat and £3, bank; from Mrs A MacCallum, Lundavra Farm, Fort William PH33 6SZ (01397 702582). For **Loch Arkaig** and **Loch Lochy**, sea trout and brown trout; bank fishing only. Permits from West Highland Estates Office, 33 High St. Tackle shop: Rod & Gun Shop, 18 High St (licences and permits for town beat on River Lochy). Hotels: Imperial, Grand, Alexandra, West End, Milton.

COE. River flows through Glen Coe to enter **Loch Leven** and from there into **Loch Linnhe**. Salmon, sea trout and brown trout.

Glencoe (Argyll). Salmon and sea trout fishing on 1½m stretch; May until Oct; fly, spinning and worm permitted. Apply to H S J MacColl (018552 256). Brown trout and salmon fishing on Coe; permits and information from The National Trust for Scotland, Glencoe Visitor's Centre, Glencoe, Argyll PA39 4HX (01855 811729). Brown and rainbow trout fishing on **Loch Achtriochtan**. Rainbow trout fishing on **Hospital Lochan**; managed by Forest Enterprise. Permits from Scorrybreac Guest House, adjacent to the lochan, or from Forest Enterprise Camp, outside village. Hotels: Clachaig Inn; Mamore Lodge, Kinlochleven.

LOSSIE

Drains Loch Trevie and flows about 25m to the Moray Firth at Lossiemouth. A good trout stream; salmon runs improving, July onwards. Provides good sport with sea trout from June onwards, especially near estuary.

Lossiemouth (Moray). Salmon, sea trout. Elgin and Dist AA, has water; estuary and sea; salmon, sea trout and finnock. Permits and information on other fishings from Hon Sec and tackle shops in Elgin and Lossiemouth. Hotels: Stotfield, Huntly House.

Elgin (Moray). Elgin AA has water on Lossie at Elgin (salmon, sea trout and brown trout) and **Loch Park** fishings (brown trout). Permits from The Angling Centre, Moss St (01343 547615). For membership apply to Membership Secretary, A F Garrow, 8 School Walk, New Elgin, Elgin, Moray (01343 546168), enclosing £1 to cover administrative costs. Trout fishing can be had on the Town Council's Millbuies Estate: **Glenlatterach Reservoir**, brown trout, boats on site; **Loch of Blairs**, stocked rainbows, boat fishing only, and **Millbuies Loch**, mainly rainbow trout, also boat fishing only. Permits for Millbuies and Glenlatterach from The Warden, Millbuies Lochs, Longmorn, Elgin (0134386 234); for Blairs: Fishing Tackle Shop, 79d High St, Forres (01309 72936). Information from Moray District Council, Dept of Leisure and Libraries, High St, Elgin IV30 1BX (01343 543451). Hotels: Braelossie; Mansefield House; Mansion House.

LUNAN

Rises near Forfar and flows about 13m to North Sea between Arbroath and Montrose. Some good trout, dry fly good. Sea trout and finnock in autumn. A protection order now in force requiring all anglers to be in possession of proper permits.

Arbroath (Angus). Lunan and its tributary, the **Vinney**, about 8m of water, leased to Arbroath AC by riparian owners; restocked each year, holds good head of brown trout, also sea trout and occasional salmon. Bag limit 6 fish. River mouth, sea trout and salmon. Upstream, st £15 and dt £3; river mouth, dt £3. Concession for OAPs and juniors. Permits from Arbroath Cycle & Tackle Centre, 274 High Street, Arbroath DD11 1JE (01241 73467). Good sea fishing. Local sea angling trips daily.

Forfar (Angus). **Rescobie Loch**, 200 acres, 3m E of Forfar; fly fishing for large trout (brown and rainbow). Bank and boat fishing; full dt £9, 6 fish limit; boat £25 per day, evening £20 (includes permits) from Mr Jack Yule, South Lodge, Reswallie, Forfar. Tel: 01307 818384. Special rates for all disabled anglers. Canmore AC (members of Strathmore Angling Improvement Association) has trout fishing on **River Dean**, fly only; **Cruick Water; R Kerbet**, fly only; R Lunan; **R Lemno; R Airneyfoul**; Rescobie Loch; **Den of Ogil Reservoir**, fly only, no Sunday fishing; **R Isla**; and **Forfar Loch**. Permits for Lunan and Isla from C Kerr, 1 West High St. For other permits contact Hon Sec.

NAIRN

Rises in Monadhliath Hills and flows about 36m to Moray Firth at Nairn. Salmon, sea trout, finnock and yellow trout.

Nairn (Nairn). Tickets for the lower reaches (estuary to Cantray Bridge 8m, barring one stretch at Holmrose Bridge) can be had from Nairn AA; salmon and sea trout. Best months: July to September for salmon. Tuition for club juniors. Wt £38 and dt £12. Permits from Pat Fraser, Radio, TV and Sports Shop, 41 High Street. Clava Lodge Holiday Homes, Culloden Moor, By Inverness IV12 2EJ (01463 790228), also issues permits for a stretch on Nairn. **Lochs Lochindorb, Allan**, and **Loch-an-Tutach** privately owned; brown trout; dt and boat. Other tackle shop: Sportscene, Harbour St. Other hotels: Meallmore Lodge, Daviot (private stretch of river); Newton (river and loch fishing by arrangement).

NAVER (including Borgie and Loch Hope)

Drains Loch Naver and flows about 24m to north coast at Naver Bay. The Borgie, which also debouches into Naver Bay, drains Loch Slaim and has course of about 7m. Both are good salmon and sea trout rivers; all preserved, but beats can be arranged, usually for weekly periods.

Altnaharra (Sutherland). Altnaharra Hotel, By Larg, Sutherland IV27 4UE (tel/fax: 0154 411 222), which specializes in catering for fishermen, provides salmon fishing in **Loch Naver** and **River Mudale**; sea trout fishing in **Loch Hope** and brown trout fishing in a number of lochs; all lochs have boats and are close to the road. Some are open to non-residents. Dt £18 to £30. Excellent sea trout water; also holds salmon. No bank fishing; fly only. Hotel has fully stocked tackle shop; and provides outboard motors, tuition and accommodation.

Tongue (Sutherland). Limited day tickets for quality salmon fishing on River Naver from Bettyhill TIC. Salmon and sea trout fishing on **Loch Hope**; approx £100 per week. Early booking advisable. Contact Ian MacDonald, Keeper (0184756 272). Tongue Dist AA (HQ at Ben Loyal Hotel) has brown trout fishing on 8 lochs; fly only. Boats on **Lochs Loyal, Cormach**, and **Craggie**, and **Lochan Hakel**. Ghillie by arrangement. St £20, wt £12 and dt £3; from hotel: Drying room and freezer space at hotel: Kyle of Tongue estuary also assn water; excellent sea trout when shoals are running; fly or spinner. **R Borgie**, stretch from Borgie Lodge Hotel to sea; dt £15 from David Crichton, Water Bailiff (01641 521231). Private beats on Borgie; Mar-Sept; fly only; contact Mather Jamie, Rectory Pl, Loughborough, Leics (01509 233433), or Borgie Lodge Hotel, Skerray, Tongue KW14 7TH (tel/fax: 01641 521332). Hotel has brown trout fishing on 20 lochs, with salmon in three, boats on three at £10 hire, and runs fishing packages with ghillie, and all other facilities. Hotel is HQ of Borgie Angling Club. **River Naver** permits from Bettyhill Tourist Office.

NESS

Drains Loch Ness and flows to North Sea close to Inverness. Notable salmon and sea trout river. Best July to October.

Inverness (Inverness-shire). Salmon, sea trout, brown trout. Inverness AC has stretch from estuary upstream for about 3¾m, both banks. No day tickets on Saturdays; no Sunday fishing. Permits from the River Watcher, to be found on left bank above Infirmary Bridge, June onwards, from 8 am, Mon-Sat; from tackle shops, or Tourist information. **Loch Ruthven**, brown trout; fly only; boat only; permits from J Graham & Co; and R Humfrey, Balvoulin, Aberarder. Sunday fishing permitted. **Loch Choire**, brown trout; fly only; permits from R Humfrey, Balvoulin, Aberarder. Sea trout fishing on North Kessock sea shore; permits from North Kessock PO; and J Graham & Co. Tourist Office: Castle Wynd, IV2 3BJ (01463 234353), issues permits and local fishing information. Tackle shops: J Graham & Co, 37-39 Castle St (01463 233178); Frasers, 15 Market Arcade IV1 1PG (01463 710929; Ormiston & Co., 20 Market Brae Steps (01463 222757). Hotels: Glen Mhor; Loch Ness House; Haughdale.

LOCH NESS: Sea trout at Dochfour and Aldourie; salmon, especially out from Fort Augustus and where **Rivers Moriston**, **Enrick** and **Foyers** enter the loch. Brown trout all round the margins. Boats and boatmen from hotels at Fort Augustus, Drumnadrochit, Foyers, Lewiston and Whitbridge.

Dochgarroch (Inverness-shire). Dochfour Estate has brown trout fishing on **Loch Ness** and **Loch Dochfour**; north bank only. No Sunday fishing. Permits from Dochfour Estate Office, Dochgarroch, Inverness IV3 6JY (01463 86218/fax: 01463 861366).

Drumnadrochit (Inverness). Salmon and brown trout. **River Enrick**, which enters loch here; best months, April, May, June. **Loch Meiklie**, brown trout; fly only. Permits for Enrick and Loch Meiklie from Mrs Taylor, Kilmartin Hall, Glenurquhart.

Foyers (Inverness). Foyers Hotel has salmon and brown trout fishing on Loch Ness. Boats and ghillie service. Several other lochs may also be fished, including **Lochs Bran**, **Garth**, **Farraline** and **Killin**.

Invermoriston (Inverness). **River Moriston** enters Loch Ness here. Permits for River Moriston; trout fishing on hill lochs on Glenmoriston Lodge Estate; and salmon fishing by boat on **Loch Ness**; from Headkeeper, Levishie House, Glenmoriston (01320 51219).

Fort Augustus (Inverness). Salmon and brown trout. Salmon season opens Jan 15. Trout season, March 15. Dt for **River Oich** £15-£20 salmon, £2.20 trout, from A D McDonald, Craigphadric, Fort Augustus (01320 6230). Brown trout fishing on **Loch Quoich**; permits and boats from Lovat Arms Hotel. Other hotels: Caledonian, Brae, Inchnacardoch.

Tributaries of Loch Ness

FOYERS. Free brown trout fishing.

Foyers (Inverness-shire). **Loch Mhor**, 18m from Inverness, is 4m long by ½m broad, and contains trout averaging ½lb. Outlet from loch enters Loch Ness via River Foyers. Accommodation ½m from loch at the Old Manse Guest House, Gorthleck and 2½m from loch at Whitebridge Hotel, Whitebridge, Inverness IV1 2UN (01456 486226). Tackle for purchase or hire, and boats (£12 per day); from Whitebridge Hotel: **Loch Ruthven** can be fished, also **Loch Bran** and **River Fechlin**.

Whitebridge (Inverness). Whitebridge Hotel has boats for use of guests on **Loch Knockie** and **Loch Bran**; brown trout; fly only. Arrangements also made for guests wishing to troll on Loch Ness. River and burns dried out in course of hydro-electric development. Other hotel: Knockie Lodge.

MORISTON: Salmon, brown trout.

Glenmoriston (Inverness-shire). Glenmoriston Lodge Estate, Invermoriston, IV3 3YA, has fishing rights on Loch Ness, salmon and brown trout; R Moriston, salmon and brown trout; and **Glenmoriston hill lochs**, brown trout. Permits from Headkeeper, Levishie House (01320 51219). **Loch Cluanie**, brown trout. No Sunday fishing. Permits and boats from Colin Campbell, Stalker, Cluanie Lodge, Glenmoriston.

OICH and GARRY: Garry rises in loch SW of Loch Quoich and runs into that loch at western end, thence to Lochs Poulary, Inchlaggan and Garry. Good salmon and trout river. Outlet to Loch Garry dammed by North of Scotland Hydro-Electric Board. At Loch Poulary are fish traps; at Invergarry, a hatchery.

Invergarry (Inverness). Glen Garry FC controls fishing on the whole of Upper Garry (both banks), **Lochs Quoich**, **Poulary**, **Inchlaggan** and **Garry**. Loch

Quoich holds brown trout record and Loch Garry holds Arctic char record; both lochs hold char. Salmon only good July onwards, closing mid-Oct. Boats on all lochs and some of pools of Upper Garry. Permits from Tomdoun Hotel (018092 218) and Garry Gualach, Glengarry (018092 230). Garry Gualach also issues permits for Loch Inchlaggan; fly only. Tomdoun Hotel issues permits for **Lochs Quoich**, **Poulary**, **Inchlaggan**, **Garry** and **Loyne**, and Upper River Garry; trout, salmon, char and pike (no salmon in Quoich and Loyne, and no pike in Quoich). Upper Garry reserved for hotel guests. Boat fishing only on Quoich. Bank fishing only on Loyne. Boats from hotel for all waters except Loyne. Apply to G F Heath, Tomdoun Hotel, Invergarry, Inverness-shire PH35 4HS (018092 218/244). Bed and breakfast accommodation plus a self-catering chalet from Mrs P A Buswell, who can arrange fishing holidays and operates a small mini bus to collect and transport clients who have no transport. Apply to Mrs P A Buswell, Nursery Cottages, Invergarry, Inverness-shire PH35 4HL (01809 501 297).

NITH

Rises on south side of Ayr watershed and flows south and east to Solway, which it enters by an estuary with Dumfries at its head. Is the largest and best known river in the Dumfries and Galloway region and has established a reputation for the quality of its salmon and sea trout which continue to improve. Carries a good head of small trout.

New Abbey (Kirkcudbrightshire). New Abbey AA has 2m on a small tributary of Nith; occasional salmon, good sea trout and herling, and stocked with brown trout and rainbow trout. Visitor's st £12 and dt £3. Concession for jun. Permits from Hon Sec; The Shop, The Square; and Criffel Inn, The Square. Hotels: Abbey Arms; Criffel Inn.

Dumfries (Dumfries & Galloway). Dumfries Common Good Fishing, 3m on Nith, 1½m on **Cairn** (tributary); salmon, sea trout, brown trout and grayling; best, March-May and Sept-Nov. St £170, wt £75, dt £30 (cheaper dt and wt prior to 30 June). Juveniles half price. Permits from Director of Finance, Nithsdale DC, Municipal Chambers, Buccleuch St, Dumfries DG1 2AD (01387 53166 - ext 230). Dumfries and Galloway AA has 3m on Nith and 16m on Cairn; salmon, sea trout and brown trout. Fly fishing anytime; spinning and bait fishing restricted to water level. Daily and weekly tickets; no daily tickets on Saturday. Concessions for juniors. Permits from D McMillan, Fishing Tackle Specialists. **Glenkiln Reservoir** (trout) controlled by Dumfries and Galloway Regional Council, Director of Water and Sewage, Marchmount House, Marchmount, Dumfries DG1 1PW. St £20, wt £10, dt (bank) £2.75. Boats on site. Bank fishing free to OAP and disabled residents. **Jericho Loch**, rainbow and brown trout; fly only; bank fishing only. Permits from Mousewald Caravan Park, Mousewald, By Dumfries; Thistle Stores, Locharbriggs, Dumfries. **Barony College Sports Fishery** has rainbow and brown trout fishing, contact Barony College, Parkgate (01387 86251). Tackle shops: D McMillan, 6 Friar's Vennel (01387 52075); Malcolm Pattie, 109 Queensberry Street.

Thornhill (Dumfriesshire). Mid Nithsdale AA has 3½m on Nith and tributary **Scaur**; salmon, sea trout and brown trout. No permits on Saturdays. Assn also has brown and rainbow trout fishing on **Kettleton Loch** 4m NE of Thornhill, 40 acres. Advanced booking for autumn fishing. Permits from Hon Sec. Drumlanrig Castle Fishing on the Queensberry Estate offers salmon and sea trout fishing on River Nith, 7m, both banks, 4 beats; **Morton Castle Loch** and **Starburn Loch**, rainbow and brown trout; and **Morton Pond** and **Dabton Loch**, coarse fish. Accommodation at Auchenknight Cottage on estate. Apply to The Factor, The Buccleuch Estates Ltd, Drumlanrig Mains, Thornhill, Dumfriesshire DG3 4AG (018486 283). Barjarg Estate has stretch on Nith; salmon, grilse, sea trout, brown trout and grayling. Daily or weekly permits until end August; normally weekly from Sept to end Nov. Self-catering accommodation. Apply to Andrew Hunter-Arundel, Newhall, Auldgirth, Dumfriesshire DG2 0TN (01848 331342). **Loch Ettrick** near Closeburn, rainbow and brown trout; apply to Gilchristland Estate Office, Closeburn, Thornhill DG3 5HN (01848 30827). Hotels: Buccleuch, George, Elmarglen.

Sanquhar (Dumfries & Galloway). Upper Nithsdale AC has approx 11m of Nith; and stretches on tributaries **Kello, Crawick, Euchan** and **Mennock**. Salmon, sea trout, brown trout and grayling. No Sunday fishing. No Saturday day tickets. Reduced membership charge for resident juveniles; and Forsyth Shield presented each year in Jan to resident boy for heaviest fish caught. Permits from K McLean Esq, Solicitor, 61 High Street, Sanquhar (01659 50241). Day tickets for grayling fishing, Jan and Feb, from W Laidlow, Water Bailiff, 22 Renwick Place. Tackle shop: Alex Stenhouse, Ironmongers, High St. Hotels: Nithsdale; Glendyne; Mennockfoot Lodge; Blackaddie House.

New Cumnock (Ayrshire). New Cumnock AA has brown trout fishing on River Nith, **Afton Water** and **Afton Reservoir**; and on parts of **Rivers Deugh** and **Ken**, and **Carsphairn Lane Burn**. Club also has grayling fishing on River Nith and rainbow trout fishing on **Creoch Loch**. Creoch Loch open all year. Permits from Hon Sec; and Stanleys and Lapwing. Hotels: Lochside House, Crown.

OYKEL (including Carron, Cassley, Shin and Loch Ailsh)

Rises at Benmore Assynt, flows through Loch Ailsh and thence 14m to enter the Kyle of Sutherland at Rosehall. Excellent salmon and sea trout fishing. The Lower Oykel has produced an average catch of over 780 salmon in recent years.

Oykel Bridge (Ross-shire). Lower reaches fish very well for salmon early on and good grilse and sea trout run usually begins in the latter half of June. Loch Ailsh. Good sea and brown trout fishing with occasional salmon. Best months **Lower Oykel**, March to September. **Upper Oykel** and **Loch Ailsh**, mid-June to September. Inver Lodge Hotel has salmon and trout fishing on Oykel. Contact Inver Lodge Hotel, Lochinver IV27 4LU.

CASSLEY: Some 10m long, river is divided at Rosehall into upper and lower Cassley by Achness Falls. Below falls fishing starts early. Upper Cassley fishes well from May to Sept. Sea trout July and Aug.

Rosehall (Sutherland). Rods let by week (av £200) on both banks. Sole agents: Bell Ingram, Estate Office, Bonar Bridge, Sutherland IV24 3AE. Hotel: Achness House.

SHIN (Loch Shin and Kyle of Sutherland): Loch Shin is largest fresh water loch in Sutherland, 16m long. Brown trout in loch av ½lb, but very large fish taken early in season. Outlet from Loch Shin controlled by hydro-electric works. River flows about 7m and empties into Kyle of Sutherland at Invershin. Salmon fishing privately let.

Lairg (Sutherland). Lairg AC has trout fishing in Loch Shin and hill lochs, including **Loch Beannach** (brown trout, 5m from Lairg, 1m walk). Loch Shin, brown trout including ferox up to 12lbs. Loch Craggie, members only. Competitions held on Loch Shin throughout the season - details from club hut at loch side. St £10 from Hon Sec; wt £15 for L Shin, and dt £5 from local tackle shop. Concessions for juveniles. Boats for hire. Bookings from Hon Sec (01549 402010). Best mid-May to end of July. No Sunday fishing. Sutherland Arms Hotel, Lairg, IV27 4AT, can arrange salmon fishing on River Shin; and trout fishing on Loch Shin and hill lochs (01549 2291). Overscaig Hotel, on shore of **Loch Shin**, has boats on loch and others on **Lochs A' Ghriama** and **Merkland** with many hill lochs within walking distance. There are usually facilities for sea trout and salmon fishing on **Lochs Stack** and **More**. Hotel ghillies, advice and instruction. Large brown trout caught on hotel waters in recent years. Fishing free to residents. Boats with ob motors. For further information contact Overscaig Lochside Hotel, Loch Shin, by Lairg IV27 4NY. Tackle shops: Messrs R Ross (prop. D Keniston), New Buildings, Main St. Sutherland Sporting Co. Main St.

DORNOCH FIRTH:

Dornoch (Sutherland). At entrance to Firth. Permits from Dornoch AA for sea trout at **Little Ferry**; wt £6, dt £2 and brown trout on **Lochs Lannsaidh, Buidhe, Laoigh, Lagain, Laro** and **Cracail Mor**, boat, £12 per day and bank on Buidhe, Laoigh and Lagain £5. Assn has recently acquired salmon, sea trout and brown trout fishing on **Loch Brora**; boat only, £15 per day. Fly only on lochs. Spinning allowed on Little Ferry. No Sunday fishing. Permits from W A MacDonald, Hardware Store, Castle St. Hotels: Burghfield House; Castle.

KYLE OF DURNESS

Durness (Sutherland). Simpsons of Edinburgh offer fishing on the first six beats of **River Dionard**, from the sea pools. Sport best after heavy rain. This fishing also includes four trout lochs, and costs £30 per day salmon, £12 trout. Ghillie hire, £12. Fishing with accommodation, £670 per week double, £345 single. Contact Simpsons, 28/30 West Preston St, Edinburgh EH8 9PZ, tel: 0131 667 3058, fax: 0131 662 0642. Cape Wrath Hotel at Keoldale has good salmon and sea trout fishing on Rivers Dionard **Grudie** and **Dall**, and the Kyle of Durness. Best for salmon and sea trout mid-June to mid Sept. Big brown trout in **Lochs Calladale, Crosspool, Lanlish,** and **Borralaidh** - well-conditioned fish of 8lbs in weight have been taken - and there are several lochs, three with boats. Lochs and rivers stocked with salmon, sea trout, brown trout fry. Hotel open throughout year. Enquiries to Cape Wrath Hotel, Keoldale, by Lairg, Sutherland.

SCOURIE (including Laxford River and Lochs Stack and More)

Scourie (Sutherland). Excellent centre for sea trout, brown trout and salmon fishing. About 200 trout lochs. Scourie Hotel has extensive fishing rights on over 100; four with salmon and sea trout. Boats on many. Ghillies may also be hired. Dt varies between £15 and £40, depending on season. Days on **Loch Stack** and **Loch More** open to guests during July, Aug and Sept. Salmon, sea trout (good), brown trout. For further information apply to Ian A S Hay, Scourie Hotel, Scourie, By Lairg IV27 4SX (01971 502396). Laxford River is preserved. Scourie & Dist AC has rights on 33 lochs to N of village and 2 lochs S; trout around ½lb mark, but some larger fish. Wt £12 and dt £4 (boat £3 extra) from D Ross, Post Office. Tackle for hire.

SHIEL (Argyll/Inverness-shire) (including Moidart and Loch Shiel)

Short salmon river, only about 3m long, draining Loch Shiel. Moidart is a good spate river with excellent holding pools. Loch Shiel is fed by four major rivers, **Slatach, Finnan, Callop** and **Alladale**, which all tend to be spate rivers. Fishing in the loch has been poor of late.

Acharacle (Argyll). River preserved. **Loch Shiel**, 17m long, holds salmon and sea trout, and a few brown trout. No bank fishing. Boats and permits for Loch Shiel from D Macaulay, Dalilea Farm (0196 431 253); Fergie MacDonald, Clanranald Hotel; and Loch Shiel Hotel: Also apply to Fergie MacDonald, Clanranald Hotel, for salmon and sea trout fishing on **Rivers Carnoch, Strontian** and **Moidart**; boats. Fly fishing on the Ardnamurchan Peninsular in **Lochs Mudle** and **Mhadaidh**; wild brown trout, sea trout and the occasional salmon. Permits from Nick Peake, Sithean Mor, Achnaha, Nr Kilchoan, By Acharacle, Argyll PH36 4LW (01972 510212). Fly fishing tuition, tackle and boat hire, accommodation, sea fishing from Nick Peake. Permits for fresh water fishing sold at Kilchoan Tourist Office (01972 510333); and Natural History and Visitors Centre, Glenmore. Some tackle can be bought at the Post Office. Hotels: Sonachan (01972 510211); Kilchoan House (01972 510200). Self catering accommodation at

Ardnamurchan Estate (01972 510208).
Glenfinnan (Inverness-shire). **Loch Shiel**: fishing now sub-standard and not recommended.

SPEY

One of the largest rivers in Scotland, from its source Loch Spey, it flows 97 miles to Moray Firth, emptying between Banff and Elgin. The total catchment area is 1,154 sq miles. The Spey is an alpine river, with melting snow supplementing flow well into spring. The waters are low in nutrients, and have remained fairly free from pollution. The main river is also relatively free from obstructions. Historically, one of the great salmon rivers, net fishing ceased at the end of the 1993 season, and there is now no commercial netting for salmon within the Spey district.

Fochabers (Morayshire). Extensive salmon fishings are let by the Factor, Estate Office, Gordon Castle IV32 7PQ (01343 820244). Fochabers AA lease a stretch of 1¾m, from May to Aug; resident members only; four visitor permits on a daily basis. Permits from Fochabers Tackle & Guns, 91 High St, Fochabers, Moray IV32 7DH (01343 820327). Gordon Arms Hotel, High St IV32 7DH, (01343 820508/9) and Mill House Hotel, Tynet, By Buckie, Banffshire AB56 2HJ, cater for fishermen and fishing parties.

Craigellachie (Banffshire). Salmon, sea trout, trout. Craigellachie Hotel, Craigellachie, Speyside, Banffshire AB38 9SR (013940 881204), arranges salmon fishing on Spey and brown trout fishing on local lochs for residents.

Aberlour (Banffshire). Salmon, sea trout. Aberlour Association water. Six tickets per day on first-come-first-served basis. Hotels Dowans and Aberlour have 3 bookable tickets for residents. Dt £15 and wt £75. No day tickets issued on Saturdays. Permits from J A J Munro, Fishing Tackle, 93-95 High St, Aberlour, Banffshire AB38 9PB (01340 871428). Season 11 Feb - 30 Sept. Best season usually March till June but can be very good in July and August too. J A J Munro is a specialist supplier of hand-tied salmon flies, also re-felting wader soles with traditional felt with studded heels.

Grantown-on-Spey (Moray). Salmon and sea trout. Strathspey Angling Improvement Association has 7m on **Spey**, and 12m on **Dulnain**; salmon, sea trout and brown trout. Permits offered to visitors resident in Grantown, Cromdale, Duthill, Carrbridge, Dulnain Bridge and Nethy Bridge areas. Permits from tackle shop. Trout fishing on **Avielochan**, bank fishing only; **Loch Dallas**, fly only; **Loch Mor**, fly only; and **Loch Vaa**, boat fishing only. Permits from tackle shop. Arthur Oglesby runs occasional game angling courses at the Seafield Lodge Hotel; for dates and information apply to Alasdair Buchanan, The Seafield Lodge Hotel, PH26 3JN (01479 2152). *(see advt)* Tackle shop: Mortimer's, High St.

Nethy Bridge (Inverness-shire). Salmon, trout. Best months, May, June, July. Permits for Abernethy AIA water on River Spey and **River Nethy** from Allen's Tackle Shop, Boat of Garten. Hotels: Nethy Bridge.

Boat of Garten (Inverness-shire). Salmon, sea trout, brown trout. Abernethy Angling Improvement Assn issues tickets for Abernethy Beat, 6 mile stretch of Spey, both banks, 15 named pools (owned by

Barratts Timeshare); and Broomhill Pool. No Sunday fishing. Certain stretches restricted to fly only when river below certain level, otherwise spinning and worming allowed; no prawn or shrimp allowed at any time. Brown trout fishing - fly only at all times. Permit only for those staying locally, 6-day ticket £90, dt £28; from A J Allen, Allen's, Tackle Shop, Deshar Rd, Boat of Garten PH24 3BN (01479 831372). Hotels: The Boat; Craigard; Nethy Bridge, Nethy Bridge.

Aviemore (Inverness-shire). The principal Spey Valley tourist centre. Kinara Estate has salmon and trout fishing on Spey; apply to Kinara Estate Office, Aviemore. Trout and pike fishing on Rothiemurchus Estate; apply to Rothiemurchus Fish Farm Shop, Aviemore PH22 1QH (01479 810703). Ghillie service and instruction on site. Trout fishing on **Loch Morlich** at Glenmore. Permits from Warden's Office, Glenmore Forest Camping and Caravan Park, Glenmore, by Aviemore. Permits 3½m single bank of Spey, £22 day, £65 weekly, conc, from Allens, Boat of Garten *above*. Permits for **Avielochan**, 10 acres stocked rainbow trout fishing just outside Aviemore, from Mrs G A McDonald, Lochside, Avielochan (01479 810847).

Kingussie (Inverness-shire). Alvie Estate has fishing on Spey, salmon and trout; **Loch Alvie**, brown trout and pike; and **Loch Insh**, salmon, sea trout, brown trout, pike and Arctic char. Fly fishing or spinning. Apply to Alvie Estate Office, Kincraig, by Kingussie PH21 1NE (01540 651255); and Dalraddy Caravan Park, Aviemore PH22 1QB (01479 810330). Loch Insh Watersports & Skiing Centre, Inch Hall, Kincraig PH21 1NU, also has fishing on loch; boats for hire, and tuition on site; tel: 01540 651272. Badenoch AA has fishing on River Spey from Spey Dam down to Kingussie, Loch Ericht at Dalwhinnie, and Loch Laggan on the Fort William Road. All brown trout fishing, stocked monthly, very few salmon. Spey Dam has 2 boats, fly only, the other waters allow worm and spinning. Permits £6 for all waters, boat £6, from Hamish Cromarty Fishing Tackle, Kingussie, and local hotels. Ossian Hotel has private fishing; salmon and brown trout. Permits from Ossian Hotel, Kincraig, By Kingussie PH21 1NA (01540 651 242). Tuition from Jock Dallas, Castwell, Fishing Instruction School, Kingussie. Tackle shop: Spey Tackle, 25 High St, PH21 1HZ (01540 661565).

Newtonmore (Inverness-shire). Badenoch AA has trout fishing on Upper Spey, **Loch Laggan, Loch Quoich** and **Spey Dam**. Boat and permits: Mains Hotel.

Tributaries of the Spey

AVON: Main tributary of Spey.

Ballindalloch (Banffshire). Ballindalloch Estate owns 5m stretch on Avon from junction with Spey; salmon and sea trout. Weekly and daily permits. Special rates for guests staying at Delnashaugh Inn, AB37 9AS (01807 550 255/(389 fax)). Permits from The Estate Office, Ballindalloch, Banffshire AB37 9BS (01807 500 205).

Tomintoul (Banffshire). Sea trout, grilse and salmon. Gordon Arms Hotel guests can fish 2m of Avon and 1m of Livet. Price varies depending on duration of stay. Fishing only open to residents of hotel.

The Stinchar is not one of Scotland's most famous rivers. Those familiar with it often wonder why. Its brown trout may offer early summer fishing as memorable as that in autumn for its salmon. *Photo: Arthur Oglesby.*

STINCHAR

One of west coast streams, rising on western slope of Doon watershed and flowing about 30m to Atlantic at Ballantrae. Has a late run of salmon, and fishes best from mid August till late October. Yearly catch is normally over 1,200 salmon. Also good sea trout and brown trout.

Colmonell (Ayrshire). River rises and falls rapidly after rain. Salmon and sea trout. Boar's Head Hotel, 4 Main St, KA26 0RY (01465 881371), can arrange fishings on river. Permits for Kirkholm Farm from W Marshall, 01465 831297. For Knockdolian (best beat): Estate Office, Colmonell, Ballantrae (01465 881 237), or A Boag, 881254. For Kirkhall Water: Mrs Shankland, 881220. Badrochet Estate: Bob Anderson, 881202. Hallow Chapel fishing: David Telfer, 881249. Almont: D Love, 841637. Dalreogh Estate: David Overend, 881214. These are the main beats on the river, of which majority are fly only, prices range between £15 and £60 per day, depending on season. Queen's Hotel, 21 Main St KA26

0RY (01465 881213) can supply information to visiting anglers.

TAY

A great salmon river. Tay proper runs out of Loch Tay, but its feeder, the Dochart, at head of loch, takes its head water from slopes of Ben More. After a course of some 120m it empties into North Sea at Dundee, by a long firth. River fished mainly from boats, but certain beats provide spinning and fly fishing from banks. Notable in particular for run of spring fish, though autumn fishing often gives good results. Netting has been substantially reduced in recent years and is now only carried out in the estuary below Perth. At least half a dozen of its tributaries are salmon rivers of slightly less repute than main stream. An excellent run of sea trout, big brown trout (less often fished for), grayling, and coarse fish (scarcely fished at all). Loch Tay itself has been improving over recent years as a salmon fishery, the largest taken being a little over 40lbs. For fishing hotels on loch, *see Killin*.

Perth (Perthshire). Scone Estate offers salmon fishing on two beats of Tay. Daily lets in spring, and weekly, sometimes daily in July and August. Stormont AC has salmon fishing on Tay, 3 beats; and on **R Almond**, 2 beats. Members only (c. 550). Permits for 3 beats of brown trout and coarse fishing on Tay and Almond, from tackle shops. Perth & Dist AA has various leases for brown trout and salmon fishing on Tay. Assn also has fishing on **Black Loch**, rainbow trout; **Loch Horn**, rainbow and brown trout; and **Balthatock Loch**, brown trout. All game fishing members only. Brown trout on Tay permits from P D Malloch. Permits for Perth Town Water; salmon, trout, grilse and also coarse fish; from Perth and Kinross District Council, Leisure & Recreation Dept, 3 High St, Perth PH1 5JU; and Tourist Information Centre, 45 High St, Perth PH1 5TJ (Saturday only). Advisable to book in advance; only 20 permits per day and only 2 permits in advance by any one person. Tackle shops: P D Malloch, 259 Old High St; and Perthshire Field Sports, 13 Charlotte St. Hotels: Royal George; Tayside, Stanley.

Stanley (Perthshire). Stanley & Dist AC has brown trout and grayling fishing at Luncarty, Upper Redgorton, Stanley Taymount, Burnmouth and Meikleour. A limited number of permits are offered at £2 per day, from Stanley PO (Mon-Fri). Tayside Hotel PH1 4NL (tel; 01738 828249, fax: 827216), offers permits for salmon and sea trout during the summer lettings (May to July) on Linn Pool, Burnmouth, Catholes, Pitlichrie, Benchil, and Luncarty. Special rates to residents. Hotel has tackle for sale, and special anglers' facilities. Ballathie House Hotel (01250 883268) has a 6 rod beat of 1¼m, for residents. Permits from Estate Office, Ballathie (01250 883250), for Ballathie salmon beat.

Dunkeld (Perthshire). Dunkeld & Birnam AA and Perth & Dist AA have trout fishing on **Tay**. Wt £10; dt £2 and £1, respectively. Permits are also issued for grayling, mostly in the trout close season. Coarse fishing on **Loch Clunie**; dt £2. Concessions for OAP & jun. Permits from Kettles of Dunkeld, Atholl St, Dunkeld PH8 0AR (013502 727 556). Dunkeld & Birnam AA also has brown trout fishing on **River Braan**; and **Loch Freuchie** at Amulree, trout and pike, bank fishing only. Permits for R Braan from Kettles and for L Freuchie from Amulree PO. Stakis Dunkeld House Hotel has salmon and trout fishing on Tay; 2 boats with 2 rods; 8 bank rods; experienced ghillies; no salmon fishing on Sundays. **Butterstone Loch**, put and take rainbow and brown trout; fly only. 17 boats on water. Permits (day and evening) from Butterstone Loch Fishings, Butterstone, by Dunkeld PH8 0HH (01350 724238).

Dalguise (Perthshire). Perth and Dist AA fishes Dalguise and Newtyle beats, permits £1 from Kettles, Atholl St, Dunkeld; also Kinnaird-Balnaguard fishing, north bank, from Ballinluig Post Office (01796 482220). Permits, with boat and ghillie from Finlayson Hughes, 29 Barossa Place, Perth (01738 630926/625134). £22-£50 per rod per day, depending on season.

Grandtully (Perthshire). Permits for Tay from Grandtully Hotel (01887 840207); salmon, brown trout and grayling; fly, bait or spinning. Boat and ghillie on site. Booking advisable. Permits for Sketewan fishing from Mrs Garbutt, Sketewan Farm, Grandtully (01796 482207. Salmon, £10, trout £3. For Tay at Edradynate and Upper Grandtully, permits from Robert Cairns (01887 840228). Boat, ghillie and tuition offered. From Grandtully Bridge to Tulliepowrie Burn, permits from Mr Welding, Tulliepowrie House, Strathtay (01887 840337).

Aberfeldy (Perthshire). Salmon and brown trout fishing on Tay. Grayling tickets no longer issued, owing to out-of-season trout fishing. Permits from Jamiesons Sports Shop, 41 Dunkeld St. Weem Hotel, Weem, By Aberfeldy, Perthshire PH15 2LD (01887 820 381) has trout and salmon fishing open to guests on River Tay, salmon, trout sea trout; Loch Tay, salmon, and trout; and various hill lochs, including coarse fish and wild brown trout. Permits also issued to non-residents. Special fishing breaks with accommodation either serviced or self-catering. Full ghillie service, tuition and tackle hire on request. Brown trout permit from R Kennedy, Borlick Farm (01887 820463).

Kenmore (Perthshire). Tay leaves **Loch Tay** at Kenmore. Salmon and trout fishing on river and loch for guests at The Kenmore Hotel, Kenmore PH15 2NU (01887 830 205); boats. Permits for non-residents from hotel or Post Office.

Killin (Perthshire). Killin & Breadalbane AC has fishing on **Loch Tay, River Dochart, River Lochay**, and part of **Lochan an Laraig**; salmon, brown trout, rainbow trout, perch, pike and char. Stocking policy includes annual stocking with mature brown trout. Salmon of up to 30lbs are caught; rainbows of 5-6lbs. An excellent venue for visiting anglers who are made very welcome. Rods for hire. Permits £4 for these waters, with concessions, from J R, News, Newsagent & Tackle Shop, Main St.

Crianlarich (Perthshire). GPOCS AA has trout fishing on **Loch Dochart** (good early in the season), **Loch Iubhair** and **River Fillan**, a tributary of Tay. In summer, salmon find their way into loch and up Fillan and tributaries. Best months: May, June, July and Sept. Dt £5. Day tickets for River Fillan from Ben More Lodge Hotel, Crianlarich FK20 8QS (01838 300 210). Permits £5 for Lochs Dochart and Iubhair from Portnellan Lodge Estate FK20 8QS (018383 00284). Boats, tackle, engines and ghillies on site.

Tributaries of the Tay

EARN: Salmon, sea trout, brown trout (av ½lb) and excellent grayling. Loch Earn fishing closed in winter.

Bridge of Earn (Perthshire). Rainbow trout fishing on **Sandyknowes Fishery**, 8 acres; fly only; bank fishing only. Bag limit 4 trout. Permits from E C Christie, The Fishery Office, Sandyknowes, Bridge of Earn (01738 813033).

Auchterarder (Perthshire). Salmon, sea trout, brown trout and grayling fishing from Kerr & Co, James Sq, Crieff (01764 652659). £8 to £15, depending on month. Oct best season. No Sunday fishing. James Haggart, Haugh of Aberuthven, Auchterarder (01738 730206) has fishing for the same at **Lower Aberuthven**: salmon on application, grayling ticket £3. All legal baits allowed. Tickets for **Orchill Loch** trout fishery, from A Bond, *see below*. Dupplin Estate, **Dupplin**, Perth PH2 0PY, tel: 01738 622757, has £4 permit on offer for brown trout and grayling, issued Mon-Fri from estate Office.

Crieff (Perthshire). Crieff AC has Drummond and Upper Strowan beats; brown, sea trout, salmon, dt £5-£20, depending on month. Season 1 Feb-15 Oct; no Saturdays in Oct. Laird Management Ltd has Lochlane and Laggan fishings, with sea trout and salmon, dt £12-£40, 1 Feb-31 Oct. Permits for all these from Crieff Tourist Office, 33 High St PH7 3HU (01764 652578(fax: 655422). Brown trout fishing on **Loch Turret**; fly only; boats for hire. Permits from A Boyd, Newsagents and Tackle, 39 King St, Crieff PH7 3AX (01764 653871). Drummond Fish Farm, **Comrie** (01764 670500), on A85, has three lochans stocked daily with trout, open all year, from 10am.

St Fillans (Perthshire). Trout fishing for visitors in **Loch Earn**. Whole of loch controlled by St Fillans & Lochearn AA. Stocked with brown trout, between 12oz and 2½lb. Permits from Post Office (also tackle), Drummond Arms Hotel, and shops and hotels around the loch.

Lochearnhead (Perthshire). Loch Earn, natural brown trout. St Fillans & Lochearn AA water. Visitors day and season permits are now issued by Drummond Estate Boat Hire, tel: 01567 830 400. Dt £5, wt £12, concessions. Permits also from St Fillans PO, and from Lochearnhead PO, FK19 8PR, tel: 01567 830201.

ISLA: Trout (av ½lb and up to 3lb) and grayling. Pike also in lower reaches.

Dundee (Angus). Permits for brown trout and grayling fishing from Strathmore AIA; and local tackle shops. Assn also issues permits for **Dean Water**, tributary of Isla; brown trout. Cameron Loch, **St Andrews**, brown trout; Lintrathen Loch, **Kirriemuir**, brown trout; Mill of Criggie, **Montrose**; Newton Farm, **Newport on Tay**; Rescobie Loch, **Forfar**; all brown and rainbow; details and permits from tackle shop: John R Gow Ltd, 12 Union St, Dundee DD1 4BH (10382 225427).

ALYTH (tributary of Isla):

Alyth (Perthshire). Several streams in neighbourhood. Isla contains trout and grayling in lower reaches. Above Reekie Linn trout very numerous but small. Alyth Hotel can arrange salmon and trout fishing on River Tay and a number of its tributaries; also trout fishing on a selection of lochs. Both day fishermen and coach parties are catered for. Apply to The Alyth Hotel, Alyth, Perthshire PH11 8AF, tel: 01828 632447.

ERICHT (tributary of Isla):

Blairgowrie (Perthshire). Salmon and brown trout. Blairgowrie, Rattray and Dist AC has fishing on part of Ericht. St £100; dt £15 and £2, trout; from local tackle shops and Tourist Information Centre. Salmon fishing for non-club members on Mon, Wed and Fri. Bridge of Cally Hotel has permits for Glenericht beat. Lowest beat, about 1m both banks plus adjacent stretch of R Isla u/s from junction, salmon dt £15 from Grange of Aberbothrie Farm, tel: 01828 632643. Tributaries **R Ardle**, contact (01250 881224); or Auldchlappie Hotel, Kirkmichael; **R Blackwater, R Shee, R Arle**, permits from tackle shops. **River Isla**: Jim Wilson (01828 627205), Kate Fleming or James Crockart *below*; in Glen Isla, inquire from Mr Maynard (01575 582278). For salmon and trout fishing on Isla and **Dean**, contact Strathmore AIA (01382 668062). Permits from local tackle shops. Loch fishing in area; some lochs hold pike and perch, including **Loch Marlee**, bank fishing only. Also Loch Clunie, enquire at tackle shops; **Butterstone Loch**, boat fishing for brown and rainbow, permit from Bailiff, Lochend Cottage, Butterstone, by Dunkeld (01350 724238); **Monksmyre Loch**, brown and rainbow, permit from Jim Wilson (01828 627205); **Loch Nan Ean** and **Loch Bainnie**, brown trout, fly only, boat on Bainnie, permits from Invercauld Estate Office, Braernas; and others. Tackle shop: Kate Fleming, Shooting and Fishing, 26 Allan St, Blairgowrie PH10 6AD (01250 873990); James Crockart & Son, 28 Allan St, Blairgowrie PH10 6AD, tel: 01250 877056. Other hotels: Bridge of Cally.

Blacklunans (Perthshire). Dalrulzion Hotel, Glenshee, PH10 7LJ (01250 882222), has salmon and trout fishing on **River Blackwater** from hotel grounds. Free to guests. Day permits offered to non-residents. Other fishings in vicinity.

BRAAN: runs from Loch Freuchie.

Dunkeld (Perthshire). Forestry Commission, National Trust and riparian owners have leased water on R Braan to Dunkeld and Birnam AA. Brown trout. Permits for Hermitage beat and beats 1 and 2 from Kettles of Dunkeld, Atholl St. Permits for beat 3 and for assn **Loch Freuchie** fishing (perch, pike, brown trout) from Amulree Post Office. Amulree Hotel, Amulree, by Dunkeld, has private trout fishing on R Braan for hotel residents; fly only. Hotel has boat hire, also.

TUMMEL: Salmon, trout and grayling.

Pitlochry (Perthshire). Pitlochry AC has salmon fishing on R Tummel from marker post below Pitlochry Dam to bottom of Milton of Fonab Caravan Site; south bank only. Spinning, worm or fly only. Dt £6-£30; 3 anglers per day. Advance booking recommended, particularly for Apr-Jun. Recent average annual catch, 93 salmon and grilse. Contact Ross Gardiner, Pitlochry Angling Club (tel: Pitlochry 472157). Club also has fishing on **R Tummel**, brown trout and grayling; and on **Lochs Bhac** and **Kinardochy**, brown trout. Bank and boat fishing on Bhac; boat only on Kinardochy. Fly only. Permits from Mitchells of Pitlochry. Permits for trout fishing on R Tummel also from Tourist Office, Atholl Rd; Milton of Fonab Caravan Site; Ballinluig PO; and Ballinluig Service Station. General advice (by phone, evenings) from Ron Harriman (472484, evenings) or Ross Gardiner (472157, evenings). **Loch Faskally**; salmon, brown trout, pike, perch; any legal lure. Permits, boats and bait from D McLaren, Pitlochry Boating Station, Loch Faskally, Pitlochry PH16 5JX (472919/472759).

GARRY: Good river for about 6m.

Blair Atholl (Perthshire). Blair Atholl has trout fishing on R Garry and **Tilt** (approx 4m); and a stocked rainbow trout loch. Permits from Highland Guns & Tackle. The Highland Shop, Blair Atholl, Perthshire PH18 5SG (01796 481 303). Private salmon fishing on **R Tilt** (3m); and trout and pike fishing on **Errochty Dam**; tickets from Highland Gun & Tackle.

Dalwhinnie (Inverness-shire). **Loch Ericht**, 22 mile long brown trout loch, and rivers; weekly permit £24, day permit £6, from Loch Ericht Hotel, Dalwhinnie, Inverness-shire PH14 1AF (01528 522257). Open all year, boats for hire.

LOCH RANNOCH: Trout, some large but averaging 9lbs; best May to October.

Kinloch Rannoch (Perthshire). Loch Rannoch Conservation Assn has fishing on Loch Rannoch; brown trout, pike and char. Permits from Hon Sec, and local shops and hotels. For **Dunalastair Loch** contact Lassintullich Fisheries (01882 632238); brown trout, 5 boats, no bank fishing, fly only. Moor of Rannoch Hotel, Rannoch Station PH17 2QA, tel: 01882 633238, has trout fishing on **L Laidon, R Gaur** and **Dubh Lochan**, which is stocked with brown trout. Permits £3 per rod, £25 per day with boat and outboard. Rannoch & District AC has fishing on **Loch Eigheach**, 1m from Rannoch Station; brown trout and perch. Fly fishing only. Bank fishing only. June best month. St £15, wt £8, dt £3, from J Brown, The Square, Kinloch Rannoch; Moor of Rannoch Hotel: Rannoch Station tea room. Tackle shop: Country Store, Kinloch Rannoch.

LYON (near Loch Tay): Good salmon and trout river in the magnificently forested Glen Lyon, reputedly the longest glen in Scotland. River runs from two dammed lochs at glen head.

Aberfeldy (Perthshire). Salmon and brown trout fishing on **Lyon**; max 4 rods; no bait fishing. Permits from Coshieville Hotel, by Aberfeldy PH15 2NE (01887 830319). Rods and ghillies for hire.

Fortingall (Perthshire). Fortingall Hotel has 3m on Lyon; dt £20 (salmon) and £5 (trout). Also **River Tay** and **Loch Tay** by arrangement from £20 per day. Special rates for guests. Apply to Alan Schofield, Fortingall Hotel, By Aberfeldy, Perthshire PH15 2NQ (01887 830 367).

Glen Lyon (Perthshire). Brown trout and salmon permits from Post Office House, Bridge of Balgie (01887 886221). North Chesthill Beat: Gregor Cameron, Keeper's Cottage, Chesthill Estate (01887 877207), £10-£15 per day, fly and spinning. Brown trout permits from the following: Mr Walker, Slatich (01887 877221, £2.50 per day, fly only, except in spate; Mr Sinclair, Keepers Cottage, Cashlie (01887 886237), £3-£5 per day, fly only, except in spate; River Lyon and **Loch Archie**, salmon, brown and rainbow trout ticket on application from Mr Drysdale, Keepers House, Innerwick (01887 886218). **Loch Lyon**: brown trout, Mr Bisset, Keepers Cottage, Lubreoch (01887 886244), £1.50 per day, fly only from May 1; **Loch an Daimh**: brown trout permit £2.50 from W Mason, Croc-na-keys (01887 886224). Accommodation at Invervar Lodge, PH15 2PL, tel: 01887 877206.

DOCHART (feeds Loch Tay):

Killin (Perthshire). At confluence of Dochart and Lochay, near head of Loch Tay. Salmon fishing best in July, Aug and Sept. Trout numerous and run to a fair size. Water is very deep and sluggish from Luib to Bovain, but above and as far as Loch Dochart there are some capital streams and pools. Auchlyne & Suie Es-

October on the Garry. *Photo: John Marchington.*

tate Water; trout and salmon. Permits issued by G D Coyne, Keeper's Cottage, Auchlyne, Killin FK21 8RG; Luib Hotel; and Glendochart Caravan Park. Trout fishing best April-May, good run of autumn salmon. Ardeonaig Hotel, South Lochtayside, Perthshire FK21 8SU, has own harbour with 4 boats on **Loch Tay**; salmon, trout and char. Hotel fishing for residents only. Loch Tay Highland Lodges, Milton Morenish, by Killin FK21 8TY, (01567 820 323 (fax: 581)), have salmon and trout fishing on Loch Tay; 18 boats with outboard motors for hire, trolling is the usual method. Hotel is ideally placed for fishing middle and western beats of the loch.

THURSO

A noted salmon river and one of the earliest in Scotland. The spring run has been improving recently, after a period of decline. Water level may be regulated by a weir at Loch More on the upper reaches. The river is entirely preserved.

Thurso (Caithness). Thurso AA has Beat 1 (from River Mouth up to the Geise Burn, including tidal water), which produces 10% of total river catch; members only, but possibility of permit if no members fishing. Salmon fishing (fly only) can be arranged through Thurso Fisheries Ltd, Thurso East, Thurso KW14 8HW (01847 893134). Bookings usually by week, fortnight or month, but day lets arranged. Weekly charges, including accommodation, range from £515 to £900, according to date. Fishing improves progressively from opening on Jan 11 to close on Oct 5. First-class loch, burn and river fishing for trout. Fly only brown trout permits from Harpers; salmon permits (on the day) from Bike and Camping, 35 High St. Brown trout loch fishing in vicinity: **Loch Calder, Lochs Watten, St John's** and **Stemster**; **Loch Hielan; Brubster Lochs, Dunnet Head Lochs**; permits for all these from tackle shop: Harper's Fly Fishing, 57 High St KW14 8AZ, tel/fax: 01847 3179.

Halkirk (Caithness). The Ulbster Arms Hotel has fishing on **Loch Calder** and many other hill lochs; excellent accommodation and fishing, £410-£900 per week. Salmon fishing on **Thurso River**. Information from The Manager, Ulbster Arms Hotel, Halkirk, Caithness KW14 6XY (01847 831 206/641).

Dunnet (Caithness). House of the Northern Gate, Dunnet Estate. 7 Estate lochs for good brown trout. £100 per day inclusive (inc. drinks). Fishing for residents only. Sea fishing from Estate boat. Contact Michael Draper (0184 785 622). St John's Loch AA has fishing on **St John's Loch**; bank and boat fishing. Permits from Northern Sands Hotel.

TWEED

Rises in corner formed by watersheds of Clyde and Annan, and flows over 100m to North Sea at Berwick-upon-Tweed, forming, for some of its course, the boundary between England and Scotland. The Tweed is probably the most popular of large Scottish rivers, partly owing to its proximity to England. It contains over 300 named casts and its salmon harvest is considerable. It has the longest season (1st February to 30 November), and its autumn run is noted for the size and number of salmon caught. There is a good spring run, and sometimes even the most famous beats such as the Junction at Kelso are open for permit fishing, for around £25 per day. Summer fish may be difficult to catch at low water. Ghillies are employed by most beats. The Tweed produces a strain of sea trout, formerly called bull trout, which are remarkable both for size and distance they are known to travel in sea. The best sea trout fishing is on tributaries, the Till and Whiteadder, both of which fish well in summer. The season on the Tweed is the same as for salmon, and the permits are combined.

Over recent years there has been a decline in wild brown trout fishing in the Tweed and Lyne. To combat this, the rivers have been stocked with brown trout. These are marked with a blue spot on the underbelly, and there is a bag limit of 4 stocked fish in force. Further, a policy of catch and release for indigenous trout is in operation. There has been improved brown trout fishing since 1995. There exists a code of conduct with regard mainly to fly fishing for salmon and sea, and full copies may be obtained from River Tweed Commissioners or from most tackle shops and letting agents.

'Tweedline' is a service for fishermen provided by the Tweed Foundation, a charitable trust established by the River Tweed Commissioners to promote the development of salmon and trout stocks in the Tweed river system. It provides information on fishing catches and prospects, tel: 0891 666 410 (T Hunter, Anglers Choice Tackle Shop, Melrose, Roxburghshire); and on river heights at 7am each day, tel: 0891 666 411 (The Scottish Environment Protection Agency, Mossilee Road, Galashiels, Selkirkshire TD1 1NF, tel: 01896 754797, fax: 01896 754412; and on last minute fishing lets, tel: 0891 666 412. J H Leeming, Letting Agents, Stichill House, Kelso, Roxburghshire TD5 7TB, tel 01573 470280, fax: 01573 470259, provide a freephone 24hr information service: 0800 387 675 (from abroad, +44 1573 470322), and the internet information is at: www.scotborders.co.uk/fishing. There is a Borders Angling Guide produced by the local tourist board, which gives comprehensive information on the whole river, cost £1.50 from any Borders T I Centre. For further information write to Tweed Foundation, Dock Rd, Tweedmouth, Berwick-upon-Tweed TD15 1HE.

Berwick-upon-Tweed (Northumberland). Salmon, sea trout, trout, grayling, coarse fish. Tidal Tweed gives free fishing for roach and grayling. Salmon fishing on Tweed offered by J H Leeming, Letting Agents, Stichill House, Kelso, Roxburghshire TD5 7TB; 11 beats between Tweedhill, near Berwick, and Peebles; from £25 to £550, one or two rods per day; early booking advisable. Berwick and Dist AA has brown trout fishing on 8m of **River Whiteadder**, which joins Tweed 1m from Berwick. St £25, wt £10, dt £5 trout, from Game Fair, Marygate; Jobsons, Marygate; and Hoolets Nest, Paxton. Allanton Inn, Main St, Allanton, nr Chirnside TD11 3JZ, tel: 01890 818260, has permits for local clubs, facilities to accommodate anglers, and can arrange salmon fishing on Tweed and Whitewater. **Till** enters Tweed 2½m above Norham, 9m from Berwick. **Coldingham Loch**, near Great North Road, Ayton. Brown and rainbow trout, 4 boats, bank fishing for 4 rods. Permits from Dr E J Wise, West Loch House, Coldingham, Berwickshire (018907 71270), who has chalets and cottages to let. Booking essential. Coldingham is noted for the quality and size of the trout caught there. Tackle shops: Game Fair, 12 Marygate; and Jobsons, Marygate. Hotels: Castle; Kings Arms; Chirnside Hall, Chirnside; Hay Farmhouse, Cornhill-on-Tweed; Coach House, Crookham, Cornhill-on-Tweed. The owner of Wallace Guest House is prepared to arrange early starts and late returns for fishermen and has private parking; apply to J Hoggan, Wallace Guest House, Wallace Green, Berwick upon Tweed (01289 306539).

Horncliffe (Northumberland). Tidal. Salmon, trout, grayling, roach, dace and eel. No permits required for trout and coarse fishing. Salmon fishing on Tweedhill Beat; 3m single bank; 6 rods; 2 ghillies; 2 huts. Obtainable from J H Leeming, Letting Agent, Kelso.

Norham (Northumberland). Salmon, trout. Salmon fishing on Ladykirk and Pedwell Beats from J H Leeming, Letting Agent, Kelso. Ladykirk, 3½m single bank, 4 huts, 5 boats and up to 1-5 ghillies, 6-10 rods; over 3 years average catch 195; also good sea trout water. Pedwell, 1½m single bank for 2 rods with hut, boat and ghillie; Fri and Sat only. Prices range from £25, to £110, 2 rods for 2 days. Ladykirk & Norham AA has fishing from Norham boathouse to Horndean Burn, both banks, brown trout and grayling. Reputed to be one of the best waters along border. St £30, wt £20 and dt £4, concessions OAP, junior free if accompanied. Permits from Mace Shop; Masons Arms Hotel; and Victoria Hotel.

Coldstream (Berwickshire). Tweed; salmon, sea trout. Salmon fishing on The Lees and West Learmouth Beats obtainable from J H Leeming, Letting Agent, Kelso. The Lees is a prime quality spring and autumn beat including the well known Temple Pool; 2m, 4 rods, 2-3 ghillies, 2 huts, 4 boats. Mrs Jane Douglas-Home has rods to let at The Lees, TD12 4LF (tel/fax 01890 882706), £40-£60 per day. West Learmouth is a good spring and autumn beat for 2 rods opposite The Lees; ⅔m of single bank with boat and ghillie. Prices vary tremendously, from £25, to £540, 2 rods for 6 days. Tillmouth Park Hotel, Cornhill-on-Tweed, TD12 4UU, has facilities for anglers. Sale & Partners *(see Fishery Agents)(see advt.)* offer fishing by weekly or daily booking on beats 2 to 7 of Tillmouth Water, **Cornhill-on-Tweed**. Prices range from £300 to £2,000 per week, and from £50 to £90 per day, depending on season. October is the most productive month. All prices include boat, ghillie, and use of fishing huts, plus VAT, Tweed levies and taxes. Head Ghillie: tel/fax: 01289 382443. Hotels: Collingwood Arms; Purves Hall.

Kelso (Roxburghshire). Salmon and sea trout preserved, trout and grayling. Salmon and sea trout fishing can be obtained daily during summer months on some of the best beats of the Tweed. For further information contact James H Leeming, Stichill House, Stichill, By Kelso (01573 470 280). Kelso AA has about 8m of Tweed and **Teviot**, and short stretch on **River Eden**; brown trout and grayling. No Sunday fishing; size limit 10in; restrictions on spinning; trout season, April 1 to Sept 30. Trout fishing good. St £20, wt £10, dt £5. Concessions for OAPs and juniors. Permits from local tackle shops. Brown and rainbow trout fishing on **Wooden Loch** at Eckford. Boat on site. No bank fishing. Advance booking necessary. Apply A H Graham, Gamekeeper's House, Eckford, Kelso. Tackle shops: Forrest & Son, 35 The Square; Intersport, 43 The Square; Tweedside Tackle, 36/38 Bridge St TD5 7JD (01573 225306). Hotels: Cross Keys; Ednam House; Sunlaws House, Heiton, By Kelso.

St Boswells (Roxburghshire). St Boswells & Newtown District AA rent miscellaneous stretches on River Tweed between Ravenswood and Mertown; brown trout; rod limits on 4 stretches. Permits from Agnes Laing, Newsagent; Christine Grant, Newsagent, Newtown St Boswells; Railway Hotel, Newtown St Boswells; and Anglers Choice, 23 Marlet Square, Melrose (01896 8230700). Assn also has rainbow trout fishing on **Eildon Hall Pond**, nr Newtown St Boswells. Permits from Brian Shackleton, Langlands Garage, Newtown St Boswells.

Melrose (Roxburghshire). Salmon fishing on Bemersyde Beat, prime beat superbly set in beautiful wooded gorge; 1m with 6 rods, 1-2 ghillies, 4 boats. Prices range between £25 and £190, 6 days, 2 rods. Apply to J H Leeming, Letting Agent, Kelso. Melrose and Dist AA has several stretches open to visitors for trout and grayling fishing. No Sunday fishing; no spinning or use of natural minnow or maggot permitted. Tickets from Anglers' Choice, High St. Hotel: Burts.

Earlston (Berwickshire). A good centre for Leader and Tweed trout fishing. Earlston AA controls about 5m of **Leader** adjacent to Earlston, with the exception of two small private stretches. St £5 (OAP & jun £1), dt £1, from local hotels and shops; and Anglers Choice, Melrose (*see St Boswells*). No Sunday fishing and saturday fishing for st holders only. 2 day permits at £1 each on River Tweed at Gledswood estate for st holders. Other portions of Tweed are reserved. No salmon or sea-trout fishing is open on trouting portions of Tweed. Hotel: Red Lion; Black Bull; White Swan.

Galashiels (Selkirkshire). Salmon fishing on Fairnlee Beat, good varied autumn beat in lovely scenery; 3m of single bank, 20 small pools; 9 rods; ghillie, huts and full facilities. Prices, from £40 to £100, 1 rod for 6 days, depending on month. Contact J H Leeming, Letting Agent, Kelso. Gala AA has trout fishing on 13m of Tweed; st £16, wt £8, dt £6, schoolboys £1 (no Sunday tickets; no spinning). Tickets from J & A Turnbull, Tackle Shop, 30 Bank St; and Anglers' Choice, Market Square, Melrose. April to Sept provides best daytime sport; Mid-June to Aug best evenings. **Gala Water** is included in permit. Sunderland Hall (01750 21298) has 2 rods let, £46-£394 per rod week, up to 30 Aug. The School of Casting, Salmon and Trout Fishing, offer weekly salmon and trout fly fishing courses throughout the season. Further information from Michael Waller or Margaret Cockburn, The School of Casting, Salmon and Trout Fishing, Station House, Clovenfords, Galashiels, Selkirkshire TD1 3LU (tel/fax: 01896 850293). Hotels: Kings; Clovenfords.

Selkirk (Selkirkshire). Salmon fishing preserved. Good centre for Tweed, **Yarrow** and **Ettrick**, covering 80m of trout fishing. Selkirk and Dist AA has water on Ettrick and Yarrow; restocks annually from own hatchery; size limit 10". Permits from Hon Sec; Gordon Arms; Bridge End PO; Honey Cottage Caravan Site; P & E Scott, 6 High St. Trout average four to the pound and go up to 3lb. No spinning allowed. P & E Scott also have boat fishing permits £12 for Lindean Reservoir, four per day. Hotels: Glen, Heatherlie House, Woodburn, Priory.

Walkerburn (Peeblesshire). Salmon, trout. Tweed Valley Hotel, EH43 6AA, has salmon fishing on hotel's private beat. Peak season spring and autumn. Hotel also has river and loch, trout and grayling fishing on private and Peeblesshire Trout FA

Three splendid springers from the Upper Floors water on the Tweed.

water; open all season. Hotel offers fishing courses at £97.50 one week adult. Tackle hire on site. Season: salmon, 1 Feb-30 Nov; trout, 1 Apr-30 Sep. Reservations direct to hotel: Tel: 01896 870636 (fax 870639). George Hotel (01896 870336) has permits from £40.

Innerleithen (Borders). Salmon, trout. Salmon fishing on Traquair Beat, good late autumn beat in grounds of Scotland's oldest inhabited historic house; 3m with easy casting and access for 10 rods; ghillie. £40 to £55, 3 days, 1 rod. Contact J H Leeming, Letting Agent, Kelso. Peeblesshire Trout FA has trout and grayling fishing on Tweed; tickets sold by Traquair Arms Hotel.

Peebles (Borders). Salmon fishing on approx 1½ miles of River Tweed. Season Feb 21 to Nov 30. Fly fishing only. Tickets (limited in number) issued by Peeblesshire Salmon FA. St £130, apply by Jan 31, to Blackwood & Smith WS, 39 High St, Peebles EH45 8AH. Dt £25 and £35 - 15 Oct to 30 Nov. Permits only from Tweeddale Tackle Centre, 1 Bridgegate, Peebles EH45 8RZ (tel/fax: 01721 720979). Salmon and trout fishing on Town Water and Crown Water. Permits: £44 per 3 day, 16 Sept - 30 Nov; £11 per week, 21 Feb - 14 Sept. Apply to Tweeddale District Council, Rosetta Road, Peebles. Peeblesshire Trout FA has approx 23m on Tweed and 5m on **Lyne**; trout and grayling. Season April 1 to Sept 30. No spinning or float fishing. Fly only April and Sept and all season on upper reaches. Catch and release policy is described under main river heading; waders desirable. Good trout April/May on wet fly then dry best. St £36, wt £24, dt £8. Permits from Hon Sec (01721 720131); Tweeddale Tackle Centre; Peebles Hotel Hydro; and Rosetta Caravan Park. Tweeddale Tackle Centre, 1 Bridgegate (01721 720979), besides issuing permits on the waters above, will arrange fishing on private beats for salmon, sea trout and trout; and also arrange casting tuition by qualified specialists in all fly fishing techniques. Kingsmuir Hotel, Springhill Rd, Peebles EH45 9EP (01721 720151), can arrange salmon and trout fishing on Rivers Tweed, Lyne and tributaries. Gytes Leisure Centre, Walkershaugh (01721 723688) has permits for Town water from old railway bridge to Vennel, and Crown water from Hay Lodge, Vennel, to Manor Bridge. Peebles Angling School, 10 Dean Park (01721 720331), offers private instruction.

Tweedsmuir (Peeblesshire). Crook Inn issues permits for Peeblesshire Trout FA water on Tweed. **Talla Reservoir** (300 acres) and **Fruid Reservoir** (293 acres); wild brown trout. Talla: fly only. Fruid: fly fishing, spinning and worm fishing. 2 boats and bank fishing on each reservoir. Permits from Reservoir Superintendent, Victoria Lodge, Tweedsmuir (018997 209). Hotels: Kingsmuir; Park.

Tributaries of the Tweed

WHITEADDER: Runs from junction with Tweed via Cantys Bridge and Allanton Bridge to source. A good trout stream which is well stocked with both natural fish. Upper waters, from Blanerne Bridge to source, including tributaries, are mainly controlled by Whiteadder AA.

Allanton (Berwickshire). Blackadder joins river here. Waters from ½m above Allanton bridge (including lower Blackadder) down to tide are mainly controlled by Berwick & Dist AA. Tickets are obtainable from local pubs and tackle shops and private salmon and sea trout fishing is offered on a daily basis, apply to Secretary.

Chirnside (Berwickshire). Trout. Chirnside is good centre for Whiteadder. From here to source, except for stretches at Ninewells, Abbey St Bathans Estate, Chirnside Paper Mills and Cumledge Bridge, river is controlled by Whiteadder AA, including all tributaries entering above Chirnside, except **Monynut** above Bankend; **Fasney** above Fasney Bridge; and certain stretches of the **Dye**. Tickets from bailiffs, hotels and public houses. **River Eye**, runs parallel to Whiteadder a few miles to N, entering sea at Eyemouth. Eye Water AC has water on River Eye at town, Ayton and East Reston, 3½m, and **Ale Water**; river stocked annually with brown trout. Tickets from McMurchies, High Street, Eyemouth. Hotels: Ship, Whale, Home Arms, Dolphin, Glenerne.

Duns (Berwickshire). Trout. The following streams are within easy reach: **Blackadder, Whiteadder, Fasney, Bothwell, Dye, Blacksmill, Monynut** and **Watch**. These, except Blackadder, are, with main stream, largely controlled by Whiteadder AA. Tackle shop: R Welsh, 28 Castle Street TD11 3DP (01361 883466) sells tickets for local associations. Hotels: White Swan, Barnikin, Plough, Black Bull, Whip & Saddle.

Longformacus (Borders). 7m from Duns. On Dye, Watch and Blacksmill burns. Permits from R Welsh, *see Duns*. Brown and rainbow trout fishing on **Watch Reservoir**; 119 acres, fly only. Trout mostly ½-¾lb. Permits and refreshments from Bill Renton, the Fishing Lodge, 01361 890331/01289 306028.

Cranshaws (Borders). East of scotland Water manage **Whiteadder Reservoir**; 193 acres, brown trout. Fly only. Bag limit 10 trout, bank fishing only at present. Permits from Mr Whitson, Waterkeeper's House, Hungry Snout, Whiteadder Reservoir (01361 890362, (257, office)).

BLACKADDER (tributary of Whiteadder): Very good for brown trout early in season.

Greenlaw (Borders). About 12m held by Greenlaw AC. Season from 1 April to 6 Oct, very good for brown trout, early in season. St £7 and dt £4, conc for OAP and juniors from Blackadder Mini Market, 20 West High St TD10 6XA, Post Office, The Cafe, and all hotels. Hotel: Blackadder; Castle.

TILL and BREAMISH: Trout, sea trout, salmon, good grayling, some pike and perch.

Milfield (Northumberland). Local beats on River Till all have good seasonal runs of salmon and sea trout with resident stocks of brown trout and grayling. No Sunday fishing. Ford Public Water, 3m stretch; daily, weekly and seasonal tickets sold by Post Office, Milfield; and Post Office, Ford. Ford and Etal Estates fishing, Estate Office, Ford, Berwick on Tweed, tel: 01890 820224, is as follows. Top Beat, 1m u/s of Redscar Bridge: Flodden Beat, 2m d/s to Tileheds: Redscar Beat, 1m stretch; let by day or week, max 3 rods. Upper and Lower Tindal Beats, 3m total; let by day or week, max 4 rods each. Bookings from Brian R Thompson, River Keeper, Redscar Cottage, Milfield, Wooler, Northumberland NE71 6JQ (01668 216223). Prices range from £15 dt to £150 wt per rod.

Wooler (Northumberland). Good centre for Till (2m N) and **Glen**, which join below Wooler, running through Milfield Plain into Tweed, and are open for sea trout and salmon angling from Feb to Nov. Whitling early summer if conditions right; later on large fish numerous. Wooler and Doddington AA preserves 2m of the Till and 1m of **Wooler Water**; limited dt £6 issued to visitors staying locally, but not for Sundays; fixed-spool reels prohibited; no maggot fishing; fly only, Feb-April inclusive and from Sept 14 to Nov 30. Tickets from Hon Sec. Some miles from Wooler, at Bewick Bridge, Breamish becomes Till. Wading in Till dangerous. Fishing on **Bowmont** and **Kale Waters**. Trout (small), grayling, with good sea trout in wet season.

Chatton (Northumberland). Trout, grayling; and some fine roach: preserved by Chatton AA for 6½m. Limited number of associated members' tickets, waiting list 5 years; st apply by Jan 1 to Hon Sec; dt from hotel.

EDEN: Trout

Ednam (Borders). No salmon fishing open to general public. Kelso AA has trout fishing for short stretch. Permits from Kelso tackle shops.

Gordon (Berwickshire). Permits for brown trout fishing from Gordon FC, Hon Sec J H Fairgrieve, Burnbrae, Gordon. £3.50 st, juvenile £1. No spinning. No Sunday fishing.

TEVIOT: First class for trout and grayling.

Roxburgh (Roxburghshire). Kelso AA controls some miles of brown trout fishing on Teviot and Tweed. Visitors tickets from Kelso tackle shops.

Eckford (Borders). Eckford AA issues dt for Teviot; salmon and trout. The Buccleuch Estate has Eckford Beat, 1m: 1½m on **Kale Water**: and **Wooden Loch**. Tickets from Waterkeeper, Keeper's Cottage, Eckford (018355 255). Morebattle & Dist AA has brown trout fishing on Kale Water, **Bowmont Water** and **Oxnam Water**. Permits from Hon Sec; the Garage; and Templehall Hotel.

Hawick (Roxburghshire). Hawick AC has fishing on River Teviot and tributaries **Slitrig**, **Borthwick** and **Ale**; salmon, sea trout, brown trout and grayling. Club also has fishing on **Lochs Alemoor**, pike, perch and brown trout; **Hellmoor**, brown trout, perch and pike; **Acremoor**, brown trout and perch; **Williestruther**, rainbow trout and brown trout; **Acreknowe**, rainbow trout and brown trout; **Synton Mossend**, rainbow trout and brown trout. Day permits £4-£8 from Hon Sec; The Pet

Store, 1 Union Street; Hawick Tourist Office, and Sanford's Country Sports, 6/8 Canongate, Jedburgh. Hotels: Elm House.

Jedburgh (Roxburghshire). Jedforest AA has water on Teviot, salmon, trout and grayling; **River Jed**, trout; **River Oxnam**, trout; and **Hass Loch**, rainbow trout. Concessions for OAP & jun. Visitors permits for salmon from Hon Sec; for Hass Loch from Jedforest Filling Station; for trout from Sanford's Country Sports Shop, 6/8 Canongate, Jedburgh TD8 6AJ (01835 863019), and W Shaw, Canongate. Sandfords also sell Hawick AC tickets. Jedforest Hotel has stretch of Jed Water, which runs by hotel (brown trout). Royal Hotel can arrange fishing in Jed Water and Teviot.

LEADER: Trout (4 to lb).

Lauder (Borders). Lauderdale AA controls 6m of Leader and 20m of tributaries upwards from Whitslaid Bridge to Carfraemill with the exception of waters in Thirlestane Castle policies and Kelphope Burn above Carfraemill. St £4, wt £3, dt £2 from Hon Sec, shops, hotels and Post Office. Earlston AA has water. Hotels: Tower, Oxton; Carfrae Mill (4m from Lauder); Lauderdale; Black Bull.

Oxton (Borders). Lauderdale AA has Leader Water from Carfraemill and tributaries.

GALA WATER: Popular trout water; fish average about 5 to lb.

Stow (Borders). Salmon and trout fishing on Gala Water. No permit required for local trout fishing. Royal Hotel stands on banks of Gala; apply to The Royal Hotel, Townfoot, Stow, Nr Galashiels TD1 2SG (01578 730 226).

ETTRICK and YARROW: Salmon.

Bowhill (Selkirkshire). The Buccleuch Estates Ltd has 12m double bank on Rivers Ettrick and Yarrow; salmon and trout; Tweed rules apply. Dt £20-35. Estate also has brown and rainbow trout fishing on **Bowhill Upper Loch**; fly only; 2 rods, 8 fish limit, and Dt £35 per boat. Permits for loch and salmon fishing from Estate Office, Bowhill, Selkirk TD7 5ES (01750 20753). All trout fishing in Ettrick and Yarrow by ticket; water being restocked with brown trout by Selkirk AA. Permits from Hon Sec; Gordon Arms, Selkirk; Bridge End PO; Honey Cottage Caravan Site, Selkirk; P & E Scott, High St, Selkirk.

Ettrick Bridge (Selkirkshire). Ettrickshaws Hotel, Selkirk (01750 522229), has 1 rod per double room on offer. Non residents on application.

St Mary's Loch (Selkirkshire). East of Scotland Water manage **Megget Reservoir**; 640 acres; stocked brown trout. Fly only. 6 boats and bank fishing. Bag limit: 6 trout. Permits from Tibbie Shiels Inn, St Mary's Loch TD7 5NE (01750 42231). St Mary's Loch AC has fishing on **St Mary's Loch** (500 acres) and **Loch o' the Lowes** (100 acres); brown trout, pike and perch. Season 1 Apr-30 Sept, fly only until 1 May. Boat and bank fishing; fly and spinning; no private boats allowed. Outboard motors are really essential on St Mary's Loch, but they must be supplied by the angler as none are for hire. Permits £4 fly, £6 spinning, junior £1, boats £5 only from Mr Brown, Keeper, Henderland East Cottage, Cappercleuch (01750 42243); Tibbie Shiels Inn; The Glen Cafe, Cappercleuch; Gordon Arms Hotel, Yarrow; Anglers' Choice, Melrose; Tweeddale Tackle Centre, Peebles.

TYNE (Lothian)

Rises on north slopes of Lammermuir Hills and flows about 25m to North Sea a little south of Whitberry Ness, known best as brown trout stream.

Haddington (East Lothian). Brown and sea trout. East Lothian AA controls most of water in county. St £10-£12 from Main & Son, 87 High Street, and East Linton Post Office, High St; also river watchers. No Sunday fishing; no spinning. Concessions OAP & jun. **Markle Fishery** near Dunbar; 3 lochs total 10 acres, stocked with rainbow trout; fly only. All year for rainbow. Permits from Lodge, Markle Fishery, East Linton, East Lothian EH40 3EB. North Berwick AC has no club water but organises 15 outings per year on various waters, for example, Loch Leven, Loch Fitty and North Third Fishery. **Hopes Reservoir**, near Gifford; 35 acre; brown trout. Fly only. Bag limit 6 trout. 2 boats. No bank fishing. Permits from East of Scotland Water, Alderston House, Haddington (0162 082 6422). Tackle from Mike's, 46 High St, Portobello, Edinburgh.

UGIE

A small river entering the sea at Peterhead. Salmon, good sea trout, some brown trout. Salmon and sea trout best from July to October; good run of finnock in February and March.

Peterhead (Aberdeenshire). Permits for approx 13m of fishing leased by Ugie AA. St £125-£150, wt £50-£60, limited dt for tourists only, from Robertson Sports, 1 Kirk Street, Peterhead (01779 472584); and Dick's Sports, 54 Broad Street, Fraserburgh (01346 514120). Concessions OAP & jun. **Crimonmogate Trout Fishery**, Lonmay, Fraserburgh AB43 4UE (0374 224492/01779 471432): fly fishing on two trout lakes. Crimonmogate Lake, 6 acres, wild brown trout and stocked with rainbow. Dt £18, limit 4 fish. **Loch Logie**, newly formed, 5 acres, stocked rainbow trout and wild brown trout. Open all year. Full day £18, limit 4 fish. Half day, £12, 2 fish. Tuition for beginners and tackle hire on site. Permits issued on bank. Hotels: Albert, Waterside Inn.

Tributaries of the Ugie

STRICHEN (or North Ugie):

Strichen (Aberdeenshire). Free trout fishing (subject to permission of riparian owners). Salmon fishing strictly preserved.

URR

Drains Loch Urr and flows to Solway. Late run of salmon; also sea trout, herling and brown trout.

Dalbeattie (Kirkcudbrightshire). Dalbeattie AA has Craignair beat, with salmon, sea trout, and brown trout, best Sept-Nov. Assn also has trout fishing on **Buittle Reservoir**; fly only; stocked monthly with rainbows. Permits for river £17, reservoir £10, juniors half price, from M McCowan & Son, 43 High Street. Castle Douglas AA has about 5m of Urr; brown trout, sea trout and salmon. Assn also has fishing on **Loch Roan**, 60 acres, no bank fishing, 8 fish limit. Permits from Tommy's Sports Goods, 178 King St, Castle Douglas. Carp fishing on **Barend Loch**; by the hour. Rods for hire. Permits from Barend Holiday Villages, Sandyhills, By Dalbeattie (01387 780663).

WEST COAST STREAMS AND LOCHS

Some complex fisheries and one or two smaller - though not necessarily less sporting - streams are grouped here for convenience. Other west coast waters will be found in the main alphabetical list.

AILORT

A short but good sea trout river which drains Loch Eilt and enters sea through saltwater Loch Ailort. One of the few rivers where run of genuine spring sea trout takes place.

Lochailort (Inverness-shire). Salmon and sea trout fishing on **Loch Eilt** and River Ailort; loch is renowned for some of largest sea trout caught in Britain. Fly only. Permits from Lochailort Inn. **Loch Morar**, a few miles north; good brown trout and occasional salmon and sea trout. Fly, spinning and trolling allowed. Boats from A G MacLeod, Morar Hotel, Morar, Mallaig, when not taken by guests. Also from Loch Superintendent, tel: 01687 462388. Permits £4, weekly £20, boats £25 per day, or £2.50-£5 per hour.

LOCH BROOM (including Rivers Broom, Dundonnell, Garvie, Oscaig, Polly and Ullapool)

Achiltibuie (Ross-shire). Sea trout, brown trout and sea fishing. Summer Isles Hotel has much fishing for guests on rivers and lochs in the vicinity. Sea trout and brown trout: **Lochs Oscaig** and **Lurgain**. Boat on Oscaig £24.50 (electric outboard £6); no boats on Lurgain. Brown trout lochs, dt £5. Ghillies can be arranged £20 per day extra. Own boats for sea fishing. Apply to Robert Mark Irvine, Summer Isles Hotel, Achiltibuie, By Ullapool, Ross-shire IV26 2YG (0185 482 282). Inverpolly Estate, Ullapool IV26 2YB (01854 622452) has salmon, sea trout and brown trout fishing, with accommodation, on the following: **River Garvie** (very good little sea trout river which runs from Loch Osgaig); **River Osgaig** (running from Loch Badagyle to Loch Osgaig, fishes best in late season); **River Polly**, mainly below road bridge (numerous lies and pools), **Polly Lochs, Loch Sionascaig** and **Loch Badagyle**; **Black Loch, Green Loch, Loch Lurgainn** and others. Mostly fly only. Loch permits with boat, £10-£14; bank, £5. Accommodation with fishing, £430-£495 weekly.

Ullapool (Ross-shire). **Ullapool River,** sea trout, brown trout and salmon; dt £15 (upper beat) and £5 (lower beat). **Loch Achall**, salmon, sea and brown trout; dt £12 (boat) and £6 (bank). Permits from Ullasport. Salmon and sea trout fishing on **River Kaniard** at Strathkanaird; prices according to time in season. Full details from Ullasport. Ullapool AC has brown trout fishing on Strathkanaird hill lochs: **Lochs Dubh** (brown trout), **Beinn Dearg** (brown and rainbow trout) and **na Moille** (brown trout and char). Membership for residents in area. 2 rainbow limit, no brown trout limit. All lochs fly only except Loch na Moille where under 15's may spin or bait fish. Open annual pike fishing competition on third Sunday in October. Day tickets £10. Permits from Ullasport. Tackle shops: Ullasport, West Argyle St IV26 2TY (01854 612621), who have large range of fly rods, reels and flies; and Lochbroom Hardware, Shore Street (01854 612356). Hotel: Argyle; Arch Inn.

Leckmelm (Ross-shire). Brown trout fishing on Leckmelm Estate lochs; excellent fish up to 4lb. Permits from Leckmelm Holiday Cottages, Loch Broom IV23 2RN (01854 612471).

Inverbroom (Ross-shire). **River Broom** is a spate river sometimes suitable for fly-spinning. Inverlael Lodge has approx 1½m, single bank, including 10 pools. The bottom pool is tidal. Inverlael Lodge also has fishing on **River Lael** and on some hill lochs. Apply to Inverlael Lodge, Loch Broom, by Ullapool (01854 612471).

Dundonnell (Ross-shire). **Dundonnell River;** salmon and sea trout.

LOCH DUICH (including Shiel and Croe)

Glenshiel, by Kyle of Lochalsh (Ross-shire). Salmon and sea trout. Fishing on **River Croe**, a spate-river with late runs. National Trust for Scotland, Morvich Farm House, Inverinate, by Kyle IV40 8HQ, issues £12 permits on alternate days by arrangement with neighbouring estate Reductions for members. Sea fishing on Loch Duich. Hotels: Kintail Lodge; Loch Duich; Cluanie Inn, Loch Clunie.

EACHAIG (including Loch Eck)

Drains Loch Eck and flows about 5m into Atlantic by way of Holy Loch and Firth of Clyde. Salmon and sea trout.

Kilmun (Argyll). On Holy Loch and Firth of Clyde. Eachaig enters sea here. Salmon, sea trout in Loch Eck (5m), where Whistlefield Inn, Loch Eck, has boats for guests: fly best at head of loch where **River Cur** enters. Other hotel: Coylet, Eachaie.

Dunoon (Argyll). Salmon and sea trout; limited weekly lets on River Eachaig from R C G Teasdale, Fishing Agent, Quarry Cottage, Rashfield, Nr Dunoon, Argyll PA23 8QT (01369 840510). Coylet Hotel, Loch Eck (01369 840426) and Whistlefield Inn have salmon (mainly trolling), sea trout and brown trout fishing on **Loch Eck** for guests (preferential terms for residents); st £50, wt £25 and dt £5; boats for hire at hotels. Loch Eck is about 7m long. No good for salmon until early June; best in August, Sept. Apply to Whistlefield Inn, Loch Eck, By Dunoon PA23 8SG (01369 860440). Dunoon & Dist AC has **Rivers Cur**, **Finnart** and **Massan**, salmon and sea trout, any legal lure; **Lochs Tarsan** and **Loskin**, brown trout, fly only; and **Dunoon Reservoir**, rainbow trout, fly only. Permits £6, £7, £10, conc, from Purdies of Argyll, 112 Argyll Street (01369 703232). Permits for River Finnart; sea trout, and occasional salmon; from S Share, Keeper's Cottage, Ardentinny, Argyll PA23 8TS. Glendaruel Hotel at **Glendaruel** (18m) has salmon, sea trout and trout fishing on **River Ruel** (best July to Sept). Permits £10. Hotel: Clifton, Marine Parade PA23 8HJ (01369 702623).

LOCH FYNE (including Rivers Douglas, Fyne, Kinglas, Shira and Garron, and Dubh Loch)

Large sea loch on west coast of Argyll, which provides good sea fishing, moderate and salmon and sea trout in streams. These are spate rivers; best from June to September.

Inveraray (Argyll). Argyll Estates have fishing on Rivers **Aray**, Shira, Douglas and Garron, Dubh Loch, and hill lochs. Weekly lets offered, with accommodation. No Sunday fishing. Apply to The Factor, Argyll Estates Office, Cherry Park, Inveraray PA32 8XE (01499 302203). Salmon and sea trout fishing on R Douglas; fly only. Permits from Argyll Caravan Park.

GAIRLOCH

A sea loch on the west coast of Ross.

Gairloch (Ross-shire). Gairloch AC manages several trout lochs, including Lochs **Bad na Scalaig, Tollie, Garbhaig**. Permits for these from Mr K Gunn, Strath, Gairloch. Gairloch Hotel has sea angling, and trout fishing in hotel's own hill lochs. Permits for **Lochs na h-Oidhche, na Curra**, **Maree** and other fishing, from Post Office, Pier Rd, Gairloch (01445 712175); fishing from mid-June. Salmon and sea trout fishing in **River Kerry**, a spate river; easily accessible; season May-Oct; best Aug-Oct. Permits from Creag Mor Hotel: Shieldaig Lodge Hotel, by Gairloch IV21 2AW (01445 741250), has salmon and trout fishing on **Badachro River** and trout fishing on a dozen hill lochs, boats on most. Priority to guests. Casting instruction for salmon and trout, rod repairs and special fly tying service from D W Roxborough, The Old Police Station, Gairloch (01445 712057). Tackle, ghillie service and boat hire from Chandlers, Pier Rd (01445 72458).

GLENELG

Rises in Glen More and flows about 10m to the sea at **Glenelg**. Salmon and sea-trout fishing preserved by owner of Scallasaig Lodge. Rod occasionally let for the day at owner's discretion.

LOCH LONG (including Rivers Finnart and Goil)

A sea loch opening into the Firth of Clyde. Good sea trout, some salmon in streams. Finnart good in spates.

Ardentinny (Argyll). River Finnart enters Loch Long at Ardentinny. Dunoon and District AC lease both banks of **River Finnart** from Forestry Commission on condition that river is kept open to the public at a low cost. Grilse and sea trout, season July to mid-October. Small brown trout in plenty; wild stock and healthy. Catch and return policy advised for late coloured spawning fish. Spate and high rivers due to wet Argyll climate makes all parts of river fishable - not many permits. Fishing peaceful and enjoyable. Permits for River Finnart and advice on local fishing from S Share, River Warden, Keeper's Cottage, Ardentinny, Argyll PA23 8TS (01369 810228), also Purdies 112 Argyll St, Dunoon.

Arrochar (Dumbartonshire). Cobbler Hotel (tel 013012 238) overlooks Loch Long, where good sea fishing obtainable. Hotel has trout fishing in **Loch Lomond** (1½m).

Carrick (Argyll). Carrick Castle Hotel has salmon, sea trout and brown trout on River and **Loch Goil**, free to guests. Boat on loch.

Lochgoilhead (Argyll). River Goil Angling Club has 15 years lease on **River Goil** salmon and sea trout fishings, and has bought the salmon netting stations on **Loch Goil** with the intention of closing them for good. Club also stocks the river. Membership £120 pa, plus £50 joining fee. Visitors dt £15. Loch Goil (sea fishing) - mackerel, dabs and cod. Strictly limited permits, boat hire and accommodation from J Lamont, Shore House Inn (01301 703340). A tackle shop in village and at Carrick Castle.

FIRTH OF LORN (including Loch Nell)

Forming the strait between Mull and the mainland on the west coast. Lochs Linnhe and Etive open into it. Good sea trout and a few salmon.

Oban (Argyll). Oban & Lorn AC has trout fishing on **Oude Reservoir** and on twenty seven lochs in the Lorn district. Oude Reservoir, stocked with brown trout; club boat often located on this loch; bank fishing can be difficult because of fluctuating water level. **Loch Nell**, salmon, sea trout, brown trout and char; salmon best in summer; sea trout all through season. Other brown trout fishing include **Lochs Nant** and **Avich**, the largest of these waters. No bait fishing and fishing with more than one rod is illegal. Except for Loch Nell and Oude Reservoir, where spinning, bubble and fly are permitted, all lochs are fly only. There is a junior section which has separate outings and competitions; and juniors are given instruction, etc. Annual membership £12, wt £30, dt £10 and boat £8. Permits from tackle shops in Oban; and Cuilfail Hotel, Kilmelford. Forest Enterprise, Lorne Forest D.O., Millpark Rd PA34 4NH (01631 566155) has brown trout fishing on **Glen Dubh Reservoir**. Permits J Lyon, Appin View, Barcaldine, Argyll. Brown trout fishing on **Loch Gleann a'Bhearraidh** at Lerags. Permits from Forest Enterprise, Oban; and The Barn Bar, Lerags, by Oban. Accommodation one mile from loch: Cologin Chalets, Lerags, by Oban PA34 4SE, tel: 01631 564501. **MacKays Loch**, well stocked with rainbows, plus natural browns, fishing from bank or boat, 10 minutes from town centre. Permits for this, and other hill lochs from Anglers Corner. Tackle shops: Anglers Corner, 2 John St, Oban PA34 5NS (01631 566374); David Graham's, 11-15 Combie St, Oban PA34 4HN (01631 562069). Hotel: Ayres; Columba; Manor House.

Kilninver (Argyll). On **Euchar** estuary (10m south of Oban on A816). Good salmon, sea trout and some brown trout fishing may be had from Mrs Mary McCorkindale, Glenann, Kilninver, By Oban (01852 316282). Boat + 2 rods on **Loch Scammadale** £15 per day. Bank and river fishing dt £3. As the Euchar is a spate river, bookings are not accepted more than a week in advance. Price concession for full week booking. Permits for Euchar also from Andrew P Sandilands, Lagganmore, Kilninver; salmon, sea trout and brown trout; fly only; 3 rods per day only; no Sunday fishing.

Knipoch, by Oban (Argyll). **Dubh Loch** (Loch Leven and brown trout) and **Loch Seil**, (sea trout and brown trout); dt £5 with boat. **River Euchar**, salmon and sea trout; dt £5. **Loch Tralaig**, near Kilmelford; trout; bank fishing only. Permits from Mrs J Mellor, Barndromin Farm (01852 316 273/297).

LOCH MELFORT

A sea loch opening into the Firth of Lorn south of Oban. Sea trout, mackerel, flounders, etc.

Kilmelford (Argyll) 15m from Oban. Cuilfail Hotel, Kilmelford, Argyll PA34 4UZ (01852 200274(ext 264)), can arrange fishing on **Lochs nan Drimnean** (10 min walk, trout; March-May, Aug-Sept best; fly only; 10in limit); **a'Phearsain** (15 min walk; trout, char; fly only; April-June, Aug-Sept best); **Avich** (5m by road; trout; May-Oct best); **na Sreinge** (8m by road and 35 min walk; trout; May-Oct best), and **Scammadale** (8m by road; sea trout, salmon; end June-Sept). Melfort (10 min walk; sea trout, mackerel, flounders, skate, etc; June-Aug best), and five hill lochs (hour's walk and climb; trout; June-Oct). Wt £25, dt £5. Membership from Oban & Lorn AC. Season: March 15 to Oct 15.

MORVERN

Lochaline (Argyll). Salmon and sea trout fishing on both **River Aline** and **Loch**

Arienas. Native brown trout in over 16 hill lochs. River fishing £33 per day for 2 rods; loch fishing dt £5. Boats on site. Contact Ardtornish Estate Co Ltd, Morven, By Oban, Argyll PA34 5UZ (01967 421 288). Fishing tackle from Estate Information Centre and Shop; and self-catering accommodation in estate cottages and flats.

LOCH TORRIDON

River Torridon, small salmon and sea trout river, flows into Upper Loch Torridon. Outer Loch Torridon offers excellent sea angling for a wide variety of species.

Torridon (Ross-shire). **Rivers Torridon,** and **Thrail, Lochs an Iascaigh** and **Damph**, and hill lochs. Torridon Hotel, Torridon, By Achnasheen, Wester Ross, IV22 2EY (0144 587 242), can advise on these, and also arrange fishing on Loch Maree, subject to availability. Salmon and sea trout fishing on **River Balgy**, which drains Loch Damph into southern shore of Upper Loch Torridon. Permits on Tue, Thu and Sat; from Tigh an Eilean Hotel, Shieldaig. Hotel guests have priority.

WEST LOTHIAN, (lochs and reservoirs).

Allandale Tarn Fisheries, West Calder (01506 873073): land-locked salmon, brown and rainbow trout, minimum 1½lb to 12lb plus, dt (4 fish limit), £14. Barbless hooks only.

Beecraigs Loch, Beecraigs Country Park, **Linlithgow** (01506 844516). Rainbow, brown trout, fly fishing, 6 boats on site. Limit, 12 fish per boat (2 rods). No bank fishing, conservation area. All facilities, including tackle hire and visitors centre. Advance booking essential.

Bowden Springs Trout Fishery, Carribber, **Linlithgow** EH49 6QE (01506 847269), 2 lochs 5 and 2 acres, plentifully stocked with large rainbows, dt £11, 3 fish limit, open 7 days a week.

Crosswood Reservoir, West Calder (01506 414004), fly fishing for brown, rainbow, American brook trout. Limit 6 fish. 3 boats on site. Tickets from reservoir.

Linlithgow Loch, Linlithgow. Brown and rainbow trout, Mar-Oct, 12 boats, and bank fishing. Limit, 8 fish per rod. Permits from Forth Federation of Anglers, tel: 01831 288921.

Morton Fishery, Morton Reservoir, **Mid Calder** (01506 880087), fly only brown and rainbow trout, 8 boats on site, and bank fishing, limit 3-6 per rod. All facilities, tickets from Fishery.

Parkley Fishery, Edinburgh Rd, **Linlithgow** (01506 842027), fly and bait fishing for rainbow trout. 5 fish limit, £15.

WICK

Salmon, sea trout and brown trout fishing on Wick. Spate river with good holding pools. River controlled by Wick AA. Famous Loch Watten (trout) is 7m from Wick.

Wick (Caithness). Wick AA has fishing on River Wick; salmon, sea trout and brown trout. River well stocked from association's own hatchery. Fly and worm fishing. Tackle specialist Hugo Ross, 56 High St, Wick KW1 4BP (01955 604200), has boat and bank fishing permits on **Lochs Watten, St Johns, Toftingall** and **Calder**; wild brown trout. Fly only on Watten and St Johns; all legal methods on Calder. Bank fishing is open on most other Caithness lochs, including those on the Thrumpster Estate.

Lybster (Caithness). Lybster is 12m S of Wick at mouth of Reisgill Burn. Portland Arms Hotel can usually arrange salmon fishing on **Berriedale River,** also by arrangement on **River Thurso**. Trout fishing on several hill lochs by arrangement, also on **Lochs Watten** and **Calder**. Hotel has a boat on **Loch Sarclet**.

YTHAN

Rises in "Wells of Ythan" and runs some 35m to North Sea at Newburgh. Late salmon river which used to fish best in autumn. River of no great account for brown trout, but noted for sea trout and finnock, which run up from June through to September, with some fish in

October. Ythan has very large estuary for so small a river and is markedly tidal for the lower five miles or so of its course.

Newburgh (Aberdeenshire). Sea trout and finnock and salmon. Fishing on the large estuary controlled by Ythan Fisheries. Sea trout average 2-2½lb run up to 12lb; finnock May onwards with large ones in September. Fly fishing and spinning only; spoons. Ythan Terrors, devons and Sutherland Specials fished on a 7-8ft spinning rod with 8-12lb line as most usual tackle. Worm, maggot, bubble float and other bait not allowed. Lead core lines, sinking lines not allowed. Floating line with sinking tip allowed. Much fishing from bank, but boats for hire. Best months June to September. Limited fishing open from 1 June to 30 Sept. Prices on application to Mr E I Forbes, Fishing Manager, Ythan Fisheries, 3 Lea Cottages, 130 Main Street, Newburgh, Ellon, Aberdeenshire AB41 0BN. (01358 789 297), who also stocks tackle.

Ellon (Aberdeenshire). Buchan Hotel (Ellon 720208) issues permits for Ellon Water on River Ythan.

Methlick (Aberdeenshire). Some spring fish, but main run Sept to Oct. Good early run of finnock; a second, smaller run in the autumn. Sea trout; June-Oct. Fishing on Haddo Estate water; now leased to Haddo House AA. Dt £6-£15. Permits from S French & Son, Methlick. Hotel: Ythanview.

Fyvie (Aberdeenshire). Brown trout, sea trout and salmon. Sept and Oct best months for salmon. Fyvie AA has approx 3m on upper River Ythan, single bank. St £25 and dt £5-£10; obtainable from Vale Hotel or Spar Grocer.

SEA FISHING STATIONS IN SCOTLAND

It is only in recent years that the full sea angling potential of the Scottish coast, indented by innumerable rocky bays and sea lochs, has come to be appreciated. Working in conjunction, tourist organisations and local sea angling clubs smooth the path for the visiting angler. He is well supplied in matters of boats and bait, natural stocks of the latter remaining relatively undepleted in many areas. The Scottish Federation of Sea Anglers can supply information about more than fifty annual sea fishing festivals, championships and competitions, at venues all around the Scottish mainland and islands.

Note: The local name for coalfish is 'saithe' and for pollack 'lythe'.

Kirkcudbright (Dumfries & Galloway). Centre for excellent shore fishing. Rocky points give good fishing for dogfish, with occasional conger, bull huss and thornback. Clear water gives pollack, garfish, mullet. The Dee estuary produces bags of plaice, dabs and flounders. Boats may be launched at harbour, Ross Bay and Brighouse. Baits: lug and ragworm may be dug locally, mackerel and herring are obtainable in town. Tackle from Watson Mckinnel.

Stranraer (Dumfries & Galloway). Loch Ryan, the W coast of Wigtownshire and Luce Bay offer first-class sea fishing, boat and shore. Loch Ryan: codling, whiting, plaice, flounders, dabs, skate, conger, tope and dogfish. Other species found in Luce Bay and off Irish Sea coast include pollack, coalfish, bass, wrasse, mackerel, plaice, dabs, whiting, dogfish, conger. Tackle shop supply blast frozen sea baits, ammodytes and starmers. Boats: Mike Watson, Main St (01776 85 3225). Local club: Lochryan Sea AA, Ray Smith, 24 Millbank Road, Stranraer. Tackle shop: Sports Shop, 86 George St, Stranraer DG9 7JS (01776 702705), has information and tickets for Stranraer AA trout waters.

Girvan (Ayrshire). Pier fishing. Mostly plaice, codling, rays, flounder, pollack and ling, wrasse, mackerel, dogfish, conger, all from boat, pollock, wrasse, dogfish, codling, flounders from shore. Horse Rock is popular local fishing mark, approachable at half tide; nr Stranraer Rd. Lugworm and ragworm may be dug locally. Boat hire: Mark McCrindle, 7 Harbour St KA26 9AJ (01465 713219); Tony Wass, 22 Templand Rd, Dalry (01294 833724). Hotel: Mansefield.

Ayr (Ayrshire). On the estuaries of the Rivers Ayr and Doon. Beach fishing for flounders from Newton Shore, where baits may be dug; flounders and eels in harbour, mullet in tidal stretches of Ayr. Good mackerel and herring fishing from May to October. Good boat fishing for cod, spotted dogs, and other species. Tackle shop: Gamesport, 60 Sandgate.

Saltcoats and **Ardrossan** (Ayrshire). Shore fishing in the South Bay, and around the harbours, for pollack, wrasse, dogfish, eels, cod, saithe, flat fish and herring. Ragworm and lugworm may be obtained locally, at Fairlie Pier and saltcoats Harbour. 3m north, Ardneil Bay, codling. Club: Ardrossan and District SAC.

Brodick and **Lamlash** (Isle of Arran). Brodick: good fishing from Markland Point to Clauchlands Point. Boats from Brodick Boat Hire, The Beach, Brodick. Lamlash is the main centre for sea fishing on Arran, Lamlash Bay, and boat trips off Whiting Bay very popular. Cod, plaice, mackerel, conger, wrasse, pollack, gurnard and flatfish. Boats also from Jim Ritchie (017707 382) or at Whiting Bay. Tackle from local boat hirers. Baits from local shops.

Campbeltown (Argyll). Good sport with cod, haddock, flatfish, etc, in Kildalloig Bay and from The Winkie, causeway between Davaar Island and mainland. Plenty of loch and river trout fishing in vicinity. Details from the Tourist Information Office Mackinnon House, The Pier PA28 6EF (01586 552056). Tackle shop: A P MacGrory & Co, Main Street; Country Sports, Main St, both with permits for Kintyre AC waters.

Oban (Argyll). Best fishing off south and west sides of Kerrera Island. Best shore marks, Salmore Point, North Connel at road bridge. Good mackerel fishing in Oban Bay. Species found from shore and boat: tope, conger, whiting, codling, cod, pollack, coalfish, skate, thornback ray, spurdog, dogfish, mackerel, ling, wrasse and gurnard. Boats from R Campbell, 14 Kenmore Cottages, Bonawe (01631 75213). Tackle shop: Anglers' Corner, 2 John St (01631 66374).

Portree (Isle of Skye). Sheltered harbour, with fishing marks in and around it. Free anchorage. Cod, haddock, whiting, coalfish, pollack and mackerel. For bait, unlimited mussels and cockles in tidal areas. Camastianavaig is a sheltered bay 4m south east of Portree, where heavy bags of skate, cod, whiting, haddock, spurdog, gurnard, pollack may be caught with trace or paternoster. Boat for hire: Greshornish House Hotel (0147082 266).

Kyle of Lochalsh (Ross-shire). Conger, coalfish, pollack and whiting from harbour; from boat, pollack, cod, coalfish, mackerel and whiting. Mussels, clams and cockles are local baits. Tackle shop: Maclennan & Co, Marine Stores (01599 4208).

Shieldaig (Ross-shire). Skate, cod, conger, saithe, ling, huss, dabs, sole and mackerel. Fishing in sea lochs of Shieldaig, Torridon and Upper Torridon; sheltered water nearly always. Outside lochs conditions can be dangerous. D N Cameron, 'Hillcroft', takes boat parties out; boat charter £125 per day, suitable for 10 rods.

Gairloch (Ross-shire). Cod, haddock, mackerel, whiting, pollack, saithe, ling, thornback and flatfish in Loch Gairloch. Boats for sea angling, including skippered cruises, B&B and self-catering accommodation from West Highland Marine Ltd, Chandlers, Pier Rd, Gairloch IV21 2AH (tel: 014458 712458 (712511 fax)). Gairloch Tourist Information: Gairloch IV21 2DN (01445 712130).

Ullapool and **Summer Isles** (Ross-shire). Noted for large skate, fish over 100lb have been landed from boats. Also haddock, whiting, codling, pollack, coalfish, mackerel, gurnard, flatfish, thornback ray, conger, dogfish, turbot and wrasse. Excellent sport inshore from dinghies and in charter boats around the Summer Isles. Good shore fishing at Morefield, Rhu and Achiltibuie. Charter boats from I McLeod, Achiltibuie. Boats and fishing tackle for hire, from Ardmair Point Caravan Site and Boat Centre (tel: 01854 612054). Tackle shop: Lochbroom Hardware, Shore Street, Ullapool.

Lochinver (Sutherland). Cod, halibut, skate, tope, saithe, codling, lythe, mackerel. A large fleet of fishing boats operates from harbour. Tackle from Lochinver Fishselling Co, Culag Sq (015714

Afloat off Orkney: whose seas are the home of many specimen fish. *Photo: Orkney Tourist Board.*

228/258). Hotel: Lochinver.

Stornoway (Isle of Lewis). Cod, conger, pollack, ling, dabs, bluemouth, flounder, dogfish, wrasse, whiting, saithe, skate, etc. Fast-growing centre with local club, Stornoway Sea AC, South Beach Quay, whose secretary will gladly help visiting anglers. Club organises Western Isles Sea Angling Championships in August. Accommodation and information from Western Isles Tourist Board, 26 Cromwell St, Stornoway Isle of Lewis HS1 2DD (01851 703088 (705244, fax)).

Kirkwall (Orkney). Sheltered waters in Scapa Flow hold variety of fish (record skate; halibut over 150lb, ling of 36lb). Also plaice, pollack, coalfish, haddock, mackerel wrasse, from shore or boat. Boats mainly booked by divers, hence hard to obtain. Orkney Tourist Information, Broad Street, Kirkwall KW15 1NX. Tackle shops: E Kemp, 31-33 Bridge St; W.S. Sinclair, 27 John St, Stromness. Hotels: Stromness; Royal Hotel, Stromness.

Lerwick (Shetland). Superb skate fishing: Nearly 200 skate over 100lb taken. Also excellent mixed fishing for ling, cod, tusk, haddock, pollack, etc, and chance of halibut. Area holds British records for tusk, homelyn ray, grey gurnard and Norway haddock. Also Scottish hake record. Tackle shops: J A Manson, 88 Commercial St; Cee & Jays, 5 Commercial Rd. Hotels: Lerwick, Shetland; and Busta House, Brae.

Thurso (Caithness). Conger from harbour walls, and rock fishing. Cod, ling, haddock, conger, pollack, coalfish, dogfish, spurdog, plaice, wrasse, mackerel, dabs, whiting, rays, halibut, porbeagle shark. Thurso Bay and Dunnet head are sheltered areas. Baits: mussel and lugworm at lower water. Most boats are based at **Scrabster**. Tackle shop: Harpers, 57 High St KW14 8AZ (01847 63179).

Wick (Caithness). Mainly rock fishing for conger, pollack, saithe, cod, haddock, mackerel and flatfish. Porbeagle shark off Caithness, and excellent halibut fishing. Good points are: Longberry, Broadhaven, Sandigoe and Helman Head. Excellent cod fishing off Noss Head. Best months: June to Sept. Hotels: Nethercliffe, Mackay's, Mercury Motor Inn, Queen's. Caithness Tourist Board, Whitechapel Road. Caithness Tourist Board is at Whitechapel Rd (01955 2596).

Portmahomack (Ross-shire). The fishing off the Easter Ross coast gives the serious angler and tourist, alike, ample opportunity to catch substantial numbers of cod, ling, pollack, etc. The best of the season runs from April to October, probably peaking in August and September. Good reef and limited wreck fishing. Two charter vessel for parties of up to 20; boats charged at £30 per hour or £160 per day including roads and bait. Accommodation can be arranged. Contact John R MacKenzie, Carn Bhren, Portmahomack, By Tain (tel: 01862 871257). Tackle shop: R McLeod, Tackle Shop, Lamington St (wide and comprehensive stock including bait). Hotels: Caledonian; Castle: and Oystercatcher.

Lossiemouth (Moray). Notable centre for sea-trout fishing off east and west beaches; spinning into breakers provides splendid sport. Also mackerel, saithe, flatfish from beach, pier and boats. Tackle shops: Angling Centre, Moss St, Elgin; The Tackle Shop, High St, Elgin.

Aberdeen (Aberdeenshire). Excellent rock fishing for codling, saithe, mackerel, whiting, haddock and flatfish. Few boats. Hotels: Caledonian, Imperial, Royal.

Stonehaven (Kincardineshire). Rock fishing for haddock, flounder and mackerel very good. Cod, haddock, ling, etc, from boats; available from A Troup (01569 62892), A Mackenzie (01569 63511), W Lawson (01569 63565) and J Lobban (01569 65323). Bait may be ordered from the above. Tackle shops: Davids, Market Square. Hotel: Arduthie House.

Nairn (Nairn). Sea angling on Moray Firth. Most fishing is done from two piers at the entrance to the harbour which is tidal. Boats: one or two privately owned will often take a passenger out. Enquiries should be made at the harbour. Lugworm available on the beach at low water. MacAulay Charters offer sea angling trips for up to 12 anglers; times depend on tides. Tackle shop: Pat Fraser, Radio, TV and Sports shop, 41 High St; issues permits for 7m stretch of R Nairn, with sea trout and salmon, and stillwaters. Hotels: Altonburn; and Greenlawns Guest House.

Dundee (Angus). Fishing from rocks, pier and boats at Broughty Ferry, Easthaven and Carnoustie for mackerel, cod, saithe, lythe and flatfish. Fishing from boats at Arbroath; for bookings apply to Doug Masson, 12 Union St DD1 4BH (01382 225427). Tackle shop: John R Gow Ltd,

12 Union Street, who issue permits for Strathmore AA waters.

Dunbar (Lothian). Excellent rock, pier and boat fishing. Saithe, cod (up to 10lb), codling, dabs, plaice, flounders, eels and, at times, small whiting, gurnard and mackerel can be caught.

FISHING CLUBS & ASSOCIATIONS IN SCOTLAND

Included in the list of fishing clubs and associations in Scotland are those organisations which are in England, but which have water on the Tweed and its tributaries or on the Border Esk. Further information can usually be had from the Secretaries and a courtesy which is appreciated is the inclusion of a stamped addressed envelope with postal inquiries. Please advise the publishers (address at the front of the book) of any changed details for the next edition.

NATIONAL BODIES

Committee for the Promotion of Angling for Disabled People
Scottish Sports Association for Disabled People
Fife Sports Institute
Viewfield Road
Glenrothes
Fife KY6 2RB
Tel: 01592 415700
Fax: 01592 415721

Federation of Highland Angling Clubs
K Macdonald
30 Swanston Avenue
Scorguie
Inverness IV3 6QW
Tel: 01463 240095
Over 30 clubs and associations registered

Fisheries Research Services, Freshwater Fisheries Laboratory
Faskally
Pitlochry
Perthshire PH16 5LB
Tel: 01796 472060
Fax: 01796 473523
http://www.marlab.ac.uk

Forestry Enterprise
Information Office
231 Corstorphine Road
Edinburgh EH12 7AT
Tel: 0131 334 0303

Institute of Aquaculture
University of Stirling
Stirling FK9 4LA
Tel: 01786 473171

Institute of Ecology and Resource Management
University of Edinburgh
Darwin Building
King's Buildings
Mayfield Road
Edinburgh EH9 3JU

Scottish Anglers' National Association
Caledonia House
South Gyle
Edinburgh EH12 9DQ

Scottish Federation of Sea Anglers
Caledonia House
South Gyle
Edinburgh EH12 9DQ
Tel: 0131 317 7192

The Scottish Office Agriculture and Fisheries Department
Marine Laboratory
PO Box 101
Victoria Road
Aberdeen AB9 8DB
Tel: 01224 876544.
Facsimile: 01224 295511

The Scottish Office Agriculture, Environment and Fisheries Department
Pentland House
47 Robb's Loan
Edinburgh EH14 1TY
Tel: 0131 244 6230

Scottish Record Fish Committee (Saltwater)
G T Morris
8 Burt Avenue

Fishing Clubs

When you appoint a new Hon. Secretary, do not forget to give us details of the change. Write to the Publishers (address in the front of the book). Thank you!.

Kinghorn, Fife
Tel: 01592 890055
Aims as for British Record Fish Committee

Scottish Sports Council
Caledonia House
South Gyle
Edinburgh EH12 9DQ
Tel: 0131 317 7200 (7202, fax)

Scottish Tourist Board
23 Ravelston Terrace
Edinburgh EH4 3EU
Tel: 0131-332 2433
Gives information on fishing holidays in Scotland

CLUBS

Aberfeldy Angling Club
G MacDougall
60 Moness Crescent
Aberfeldy
Perthshire PH15

Achnasheen Angling Club
c/o Ledgowan Lodge Hotel
Achnasheen
Ross-shire IV22 2EJ

Airdrie and District Angling Club
J Potter
c/o 12 Sharp Avenue
Coatbridge
Lanarkshire ML5 5RP

Assynt Angling Club
S Taylor
17 Kirk Road
Lochinver
Sutherland IV27 4LM

Avon Angling Club
P Brooks
3 The Neuk
Stonehouse
Lanarkshire ML9 3HP

Badenoch Angling Association
Alexander Bennett
113 High St
Kingussie
Inverness-shire PH21 1JD

Ballater Angling Association
M Holroyd
Golf Road
Ballater
Aberdeenshire

Beauly Angling Club
J Morrison
Mo-Dhachaidh
Windhill, Beauly
Inverness-shire IV4 7AS

Berwick and District Angling Club
D Cowan
129 Etal Road
Tweedmouth
Berwick

Blairgowrie, Rattray and District Angling Association
Walter Matthew
9 Mitchell Square
Blairgowrie
Perthshire PH10 6HR

Brechin Angling Club
W Balfour
9 Cookston Crescent
Brechin, Angus DD9 6BP

Carradale Angling Club
Donald Paterson
21 Tormhor
Carradale
Argyll PA28 6SD

Castle Douglas and District Angling Association
Stanley Kaye
2 Cairnsmore Road
Castle Douglas, Galloway DG7 1BN

Chatton Angling Association
J Douglas
10 Church Hill
Chatton, Alnwick
Northumberland

Central Scotland Anglers' Association
Kevin Burns
53 Fernieside Crescent
Edinburgh EH17 7HS

Coldstream and District Angling Association
H F Bell
12 Priory Hill
Coldstream
Berwickshire

Cramond Angling Club
Craig Campbell
2 Canmore Street
South Queensferry
West Lothian EH30 9ND

Crieff Angling Club
Percy Wilson
Tulliallan
Duchlage Road
Perthshire PH7 3BN

Dalbeattie Angling Association
J Moran
12 Church Crescent
Dalbeattie
Kirkcudbrightshire DG5 4BA

Dalmally Angling Club
I MacIntyre
Glenview
Dalmally
Argyll

Dalry Angling Association
N Harvey
Lochside Cottage
Balmaclellan
Castle Douglas
Kirkcudbrightshire DG7 3QA

Devon Angling Association
R Breingan
33 Redwell Place
Alloa
Clackmannanshire FK10 2BT

Dunfermline Artisan Angling Club
W B Stewart
13 Foresters Lea Cross
Dunfermline
Fife KY12 7TE

Dunkeld and Birnam Angling Association
A Steele
21 Willowbank
Birnam
Dunkeld
Perthshire PH8

Dunoon and District Angling Club
A H Young
Ashgrove
28 Royal Crescent
Dunoon, Argyll PA23 7AH

Earlston Angling Association
D G Stafford
36 Queensway
Earlston, Berwickshire

East Lothian Angling Association
John Crombie
10 St Lawrence
Haddington
East Lothian EH41 3RL

Eckford Angling Association
The Buccleuch Estates Ltd
Bowhill, Selkirk

Elgin and District Angling Association
W E Mulholland
9 Conon Crescent
Elgin, Moray IV30 1SZ

Esk and Liddle Fisheries Association
G L Lewis
Buccleuch Estates Ltd
Ewesbank, Langholme
Dumfriesshire
DG13 0ND

Esk Valley Angling Improvement Association
Kevin Burns
53 Fernieside Crescent
Edinburgh

Evanton Angling Club
P F Cumberlege
Balavoulin
Evanton
IV16 9XW

Eye Water Angling Club
William S Gillie
2 Tod's Court
Eyemouth
Berwickshire TD14 5HW

Federation of Highland Angling Clubs
W Brown
Coruisk
Strathpeffer
Ross-shire IV14 9BD

Fyvie Angling Association
J D Pirie
Prenton
South Road
Oldmeldrum, Inverurie
Aberdeenshire AB51 0AB

Gairloch Angling Club
Mrs L MacKenzie
4 Strath
Gairloch
Ross-shire IV21 2BX

Galashiels Angling Association
S Grzybowski
3 St Andrews Street
Galashiels, Selkirkshire TD1 1EA

Gatehouse and Kirkcudbright Angling Association
Eric Farrer
32 Boreland Rd
Kirkcudbright DG6 4JB

Goil Angling Club
Ian K Given
Bonnyrigg
25 Churchill Drive
Bishopton
Renfrewshire PA7 5HB

Gordon Fishing Club
J Fairgrieve
Burnbrae, Eden Road
Gordon
Berwickshire TD3 6UU

Greenlaw Angling Association
Mr T Waldie
26 East High Street
Greenlaw, Berwickshire
TD10 6UF

Haddo House Angling Association
J French
Kirkton
Methlick
Ellon, Aberdeenshire

Hawick Angling Club
D Smith
Wellogate Bank

Wellogate Brae
Hawick
Roxburghshire

Inverness Angling Club
K Macdonald
30 Swanston Avenue
Inverness IV3 6QW

Jedforest Angling Association
J Tait
9 Boundaries
Jedburgh
Roxburghshire TD8 6EX

Keithick Angling Club
John Carrick
c/o Athole Arms
Coupar Angus

Kelso Angling Association
Euan M Robson
Elmbank
33 Tweedside Park
Kelso
Roxburghshire TD5 7RF

Kilbryde Angling Club
John Cooper
65 Carlisle Road
Crawford ML12 6TP

Killin and Breadalbane Angling Club
Dave Murray
"Clan Alpine"
Main Street
Strathyre
Perthshire FK18 8NA

Kilmaurs Angling Club
Colin Ritchie
48 Hillmoss
Kilmaurs, Ayrshire

Kinlochewe Angling Association
c/o S Condon
Glendocherty Craft Shop
Kinlochewe
Ross-shire IV22 2PA

Kintyre Angling Club
Shore Street
Campbeltown,
Argyll

Kyles of Bute Angling Club
Allen Richardson
Allt Beag
Tighnabruaich, Argyll
PA21 2BE

Ladykirk and Norham Angling Association
R G Wharton
8 St Cuthberts Square
Norham
Berwick-on-Tweed
Northumberland TD15 2LE
(01289 382467)

Lairg Angling Club
J M Ross
St Murie
Church Hill Road
Lairg, Sutherland IV27 4BL

Lamington and District Angling Improvement Association
B Dexter
Red Lees
18 Boghall Park
Biggar, Lanarkshire ML12 6EY

Lauderdale Angling Association
Donald M Milligan
The Torts
Portling
By Dalbeattie
Kirkcudbrightshire DG5 4PZ

Loch Awe Improvement Association
T C Macnair
Macarthur Stewart
Boswell House
Argyll Square
Oban, Argyll PA34 4BD

Lochgilphead and District Angling Club
D MacDougall
23 High Bank Park
Lochgilphead
Argyll PA31 8NL

Loch Lomond Angling Improvement Association
R A Clement & Co,
Chartered Accountants
29 St Vincent Place
Glasgow G1 2DT

Loch Rannoch Conservation Association
E M Beattie
2 Schiehallion Place
Kinloch Rannoch
Perthshire

Melrose and District Angling Association
T McLeish
Planetree Cottage
Newstead
Melrose
Roxburghshire

Monikie Angling Club
I Smith
6 Collier Street
Carnoustie
Angus DD7 7AJ

Monklands District Coarse Angling Club
John McShane
5 Crinian Crescent
Townhead
Coatbridge
Lanarkshire ML5 2LG

Montrose Angling Club
c/o Community Office

George Street
Montrose
Angus
Morebattle Angling Club
D Y Gray
17 Mainsfield Avenue
Morebattle
Kelso
Roxburghshire
Muirkirk Angling Association
J Timmins
38 Hareshaw Crescent
Muirkirk
Ayrshire KA18 3P
Musselburgh and District Angling Association
George Brooks
29 Eskside West
Musselburgh
East Lothian EH21 6PP
Nairn Angling Association
G Young
Earlseat Cottage
Moyness
Nairn
Inverness IV12 5LB
New Galloway Angling Association
Allan Cairnie
4 Carsons Knowe
New Galloway
Castle Douglas
Kirkcudbrightshire DG7 3RY
Newton Stewart Angling Association
Bertie Marr
1 St Coans Place
Newtown Stewart
Wigtownshire
North Berwick Angling Club
Norman M Morrison
Kidlaw Farm
Gifford
East Lothian EH39 4JW
North Uist Angling Club
P Harding
Claddach, Kyles
North Uist HS6 5EW
Oban and Lorne Angling Club
Secretary
8G Colinsay Terrace
Soroba, Oban
Argyll
Orkney Trout Fishing Association
Captain James E Purvis
3 Maitland Place
Finstown
Orkney Isles KW17 2EQ
Peeblesshire Salmon Fishing Association
Messrs Blackwood & Smith, W.S.
39 High Street
Peebles, Peeblesshire EH45 8AH
Peeblesshire Trout Fishing Association
David G Fyfe
Blackwood and Smith, W.S.
39 High Street
Peebles, Peeblesshire EH45 8AH
Portree Angling Association
Neil Cameron
Hillcroft, Treaslane
By Portree
Isle of Skye IV51 9NX
Rannoch and District Angling Club
John Brown
The Square
Kinloch Rannoch
Perthshire PH16 5PN
River Almond Angling Association
H Meikle
23 Glen Terrace
Deans, Livingston
West Lothian LH54 8BU
River Goil Angling Club
See Goil AC
St Andrew's Angling Club
Peter F Malcolm
54 St Nicholas Street
St Andrews
Fife KY16 8BQ
St Fillans and Loch Earn Angling Association
Grant Mackay
37 Alligan Crescent
Crieff
Perthshire PH7 3JT
St Mary's Loch Angling Club
Neil Macintyre
Whincroft
8 Rosetta Road
Peebles
Borders EH45 8JU
Selkirk and District Angling Association
D Heatlie
8 Knowepark
Selkirk
Shetland Anglers' Association
Alec Miller
55 Burgh Road
Lerwick
Shetland Isles ZE1 0HJ
Soval Angling Association
Edward Young
Stile Park
Willowglen Road
Stornoway
Isle of Lewis H51 2EW
Stanley and District Angling Club
S Grant
7 Murray Place

Stanley
Perth PH1 4LX

Stranraer and District Angling Association
D Pride
Almar View
Ochtrelure
Stranraer
or
c/o The sports Shop
86 George Street,
Stranraer DG9 7JS

Stornoway Angling Association
H Fraser
5 Laxdale
Stornoway, Isle of Lewis

Strathgryfe Angling Association
Kingsley Wood & Co, Solicitors
Burnside Chambers
The Cross, Kilmacolm
Renfrewshire PA13 4ET

Strathmore Angling Improvement Association
Mrs M C Milne
1 West Park Gardens
Dundee DD2 1NY

Tobermory Angling Club
W G Anderson
Carna, 7 West Street,
Tobermory
Isle of Mull PA75 6QJ

Thurso Angling Association
N Murray
20 St Magnus Road
Thurso
Caithness
or
T Stitt, President
Horndean
Glengolly
By Thurso KW14 7XP

Turriff Angling Association
R Masson
6 Castle street
Turriff,
Aberdeenshire AB53 7BJ

Ullapool Angling Club
D Taggart
37 Morefield Place
Ullapool
Ross-shire

United Clyde Angling Protective Association
Joseph Quigley
39 Hillfoot Avenue
Branchalwood, Wishaw
Lanarkshire

Upper Annandale Angling Association
A Dickson
Braehead, Woodfoot
Beattock
Dumfriesshire DG10 9PL

Whiteadder Angling Association
Cdr R Baker
Millburn House
Duns
Berwickshire TD11 3TN

FISHING IN NORTHERN IRELAND

Boards of Conservators, Close Seasons, etc.

For game fisher and coarse fisher alike, Northern Ireland is still largely undiscovered country. There is a wealth of lakes, large and small; miles of quiet unpolluted river, plentifully stocked with large, healthy fish, anything but well-educated to anglers and their methods. By the standards of most other parts of Britain, all of it is underfished. In recent years, coarse fishermen have begun to find out what Northern Ireland has to offer, and there is much, too, for the game fisherman. The visitor as yet unfamiliar with the province is recommended to concentrate on the waters owned and managed by the Department of Agriculture, possibly the largest single fishery proprietor in Northern Ireland. They include some of the very best.

The Dept of Agriculture (Fisheries Division, Annexe 5, Castle Grounds, Stormont, Belfast BT4 3PW, tel: 01232 523434 (523121 Fax) is the ultimate authority for fisheries in Northern Ireland. In addition to the Department, and working in co-operation with it, there are two Conservancy Authorities, The Foyle Fisheries Commission; and The Fisheries Conservancy Board for Northern Ireland. They operate in separate areas.

The Department publishes an Angling Guide to the waters under its control, available from Fisheries Division at the above address, and from many tackle shops.

The Foyle Fisheries Commission (8 Victoria Road, Londonderry BT47 2AB, Tel: 01504 42100 (42720 Fax)) act as conservator and issues rod licences in the Foyle area: i.e. the North-Western parts of the province drained by the Foyle/Mourne/Camowen river systems and the rivers Faughan and Roe. The Commission is also responsible for a number of river systems in Co Donegal, R.O.I., including the Finn, Culdaff and Deele. The Foyle Fisheries Commission is controlled jointly by the Governments of Northern Ireland and The Republic of Ireland, including in the total area the former Moville District in the Republic and the former Londonderry District in N.I.

The Fisheries Conservancy Board for Northern Ireland (1 Mahon Road, Portadown, Co Armagh BT62 3EE, Tel: 0762 334666 (338912 Fax)). This board issues licences for the remainder of the province.

The Northern Ireland Tourist Board (St Anne's Court, 59 North Street, Belfast BT1 1NB, (Tel: 01232 246609, fax: 312424) is also involved in angling, concerning itself with development and promotion, and issues literature on travel and accommodation.

Under the provisions of The Fisheries Act (N.I.) 1966, **The Fisheries Conservancy Board** and **The Foyle Fisheries Commission** co-operate with the **Dept of Agriculture** in the development and improvement of fisheries. As a result, there has been in recent years a dramatic improvement in the quantity and quality of angling, game and coarse, available to visitors. The Department's Rivers Agency is also actively engaged in the improvement of fisheries in watercourses under its control. Works include the construction of fishery weirs, groynes and deflectors; restoration of gravel, landscaping of altered watercourses and comprehensive schemes of tree-planting.

Rod Licences. The Fisheries Conservancy Board for Northern Ireland, whose jurisdiction extends to all fisheries in Northern Ireland except the Foyle Fisheries Commission area, requires a rod licence for **ALL** freshwater fishing for each rod and line. A Game Rod Licence covers coarse fishing only *on waters designated as coarse fisheries*. The following licences are available.

Game fishing 1998:
Season game fishing rod licence, £18.85.
8-day game fishing rod licence, £9.35.
1-day game fishing rod licence, £3.35.
Additional amount payable by the holder of a Foyle Fisheries Commission season game fishing rod licence to use a single game rod, £15.

8-day joint licence/DANI permit, £22.85.
1-day joint licence/DANI permit, £11.35.

Coarse Fishing (FCB):

Season coarse fishing rod licence, £7.20.
8-day coarse fishing rod licence, £3.60.
3-day joint coarse fishing rod licence/DANI coarse fishing permit, £6.55.
8-day joint coarse fishing licence/DANI coarse fishing permit, £11.60.

Foyle Fisheries Commission, whose jurisdiction extends to all waters in the Foyle catchment in both the South and the North including the feeders into the Foyle estuary, requires a **Game Fishing** Rod licence for salmon, sea trout, brown and rainbow trout. These are available in the following categories:

Season game fishing rod licence, £18.
14-day game fishing rod licence, £12.20.
1-day game fishing rod licence, £3.20

Under 18 years of age juvenile game fishing rod licence, £9.
Licence endorsements for holders of FCB licences or licences issued in the Republic of Ireland are now £15 and £14.25 respectively (£13.45).

With two like that one, why change the fly? A change in light or temperature, perhaps. *Photo: Eric Chalker.*

FISHING STATIONS IN NORTHERN IRELAND

As in other sections, principal catchment areas are dealt with in alphabetical order, and details of close seasons, licences, etc, will be found on preceding page. Anglers wanting further details of accommodation, etc, should write to the Northern Ireland Tourist Board, St Anne's Court, 59 North Street, Belfast, BT1 2NB, or 11 Berkeley Street, London (0171-493 0601).

BANN (Lower)

(For close seasons, licences, see under Boards)

A mainly sluggish river running approx 30m from where it leaves Lough Neagh to where it enters the sea below Coleraine. River is canalised at upper end. Good coarse fish population; sea trout fishing in the tideway. Salmon stretches are mostly in private hands but some days, on some beats, are open to visitors.

Coleraine (Co Derry). River tidal below Cutts. Good game and coarse fishing above tidal stretches. Bann Systems Ltd, The Cuts, 54 Castleroe Rd, Coleraine BT51 3LR (01265 43343), has beats on some days, but these must be booked by the end of January; and also has salmon fishing open to tourists on **River Bush**; dt £25-£50, depending on season. Coleraine AA allow dt fishing on R Ree, and Ballyinreese Reservoir, obtainable from E Kee, 3 Kings Rd, Coleraine. Agivey AA has 12m stretch on R Agivey plus stretch on **Wee Agivey**, nr **Garvagh**. Permits (£12, £5) from Mrs J McCann, 162 Agivey Rd, Aghadowey. **Ballyrashane Trout Lake**, Creamery Rd: fly only, stocked r trout, dt £10, 4 fish limit, season 1 May to mid-Oct, Contact Council Offices, 41 Portstewart Rd, Coleraine, tel: 01265 52181. For Ballylagan Fishing and Conservation Club water, dt £10, contact Smyth's. Tackle shops: Smyth's Country Sports, 1 Park St BT52 1BD; B Atkins, 67 Coleraine Rd, Garvagh. Hotels: Lodge; Bohill Auto Inn. Brown Trout, Aghadowey.

Kilrea (Co Derry). Pike and perch in local canals and loughs. Trout day tickets on Kilrea & Dist AC waters, from Sean Donaghy, Electric Goods, Kilrea. Salmon and trout tickets for Lower Bann at Portna from J Semplton, 34 Coleraine Rd, Gavagh. Hotel: Portneal Lodge.

Portglenone (Co Antrim). **Clady River** joins Bann below town. Brown trout, late salmon and dollaghan. Dt £5 (1 Mar-30 Sept), £10 (Oct), from Clady & Dist AC, who control whole river and tributaries. Obtainable from Weirs, Clady Rd, or M Cushanan, Main St, both Portglenone. Kingfisher Angling Centre, 24A Hiltonstown Rd, Portglenone, BT44 8EG (01266 821630), has self-catering accommodation and fishing on Upper and Lower Bann, with salmon and trout, and mixed coarse fishing. St £13.80 from Bann Guns & Tackle. Other tackle shop: McGall's, Main St.

Toomebridge (Co Antrim). Here, the Lower Bann leaves L Neagh. Dept of Ag controls **Lower Bann Navigational Canal** at **Toome**, **Portna** and **Movanagher**. Tickets from tackle shops. Bann Systems Ltd, Dundarave, Bushmills BT57 8ST (012657 312150) issues permits for Portna fishing on Lower Bann, all legal methods except maggot. **Lough Neagh**, with an area of 153 sq miles, is the largest inland water in the British Isles. It supports an immense commercial eel fishery, but apart from that, its potential is as yet largely untapped. The bottom-feeding habits of Lough Neagh trout and the exposed conditions on this enormous stretch of water have so far discouraged anglers from trying to exploit it. A principal problem is the absence of sheltered bays.

BANN (Upper)

Flows west and north from its source in the Mourne Mountains to enter Lough Neagh near the middle of its southern shore at a point north of Portadown.

Portadown (Co Armagh). Pike, perch, roach, bream and trout. Dept of Ag has

10m stretch from Portadown to Lough Neagh; a designated coarse fishery which is one of the best in Europe. Licences from Fisheries Conservancy Board; permits from The Field and Stream, Moy (018687 89533). Tackle shop: Tetford's Sport, 28 West St, tel: 01762 338555. Hotels: Carngrove; Seagoe.

Banbridge (Co Down). Late salmon, brown trout and coarse fish for 15 miles from **Rathfriland** to **Moyallen**; controlled by Rathfriland AC u/s from **Katesbridge**. Banbridge AC fishes from Katesbridge to **Lenaderg**, browns and late salmon, and has 76 acre **Corbet Lough**, rainbow trout, 4m from town. Dt £8 lake, £4 river, conc, from tackle shops. Gilford AC fishes from Lenaderg to Moyallen, plus **Kernan Lake**. **Lough Brickland**, 62 acres, Dept of Ag, fly only, b and r trout. **Altnadue Lake**, stocked with rainbows, dt £5 from tackle shops. Coarse fishing: **Newry Canal** (roach, bream, rudd, perch, pike); **Lough Shark**; Lakes **Drummillar**, **Drumaran**, **Drumnavaddy**; **Skillycolban** (Mill Dam, perch, pike, eels); Lakes **Ballyroney**, **Hunshigo**, **Ballyward**, **Ballymagreehan**, pike, perch, F C B coarse licence required. Tackle, licences and permits from Cobürns Ltd, 32 Scarva St, Banbridge, tel: 018206 62207. Hotels: Belmont, Banville, Downshire. Wright Lines, tel: 018206 62126, offers two day Angling Breaks for £43. Mrs J Fleming, Heathmar, 37 Corbet Rd, Banbridge (018206 22348), has accommodation close to Corbet Lough, above. Mrs M Maginn (018206 38090), has accommodation half mile from R Bann.

Hilltown (Co Down). Dept of Ag have four good trout lakes, totalling more than 350 acres in the area: **Spelga**, **Castlewellan**, **Hillsborough**, **Lough Brickland**. Castlewellan and Annsborough AC fish **Ballylough**, **Annsborough**, a few miles north east. Brown and rainbow trout, fly only. Day tickets from Chestnut Inn (*see below*). Shimna AC has **Altnadue Lough**, stocked with rainbows. Dt £5 from The Four Seasons, Newcastle. Tackle shops: J Coburn, 32 Scarva Street Banbridge; W McCammon, Main St, Castlewellan; W R Timble, 25 Downpatrick St, Rathfriland. Hotels: Downshire Arms and Belmont, Banbridge. Chestnut Inn, Lower Square, Castlewellan (013967 782470), offers trout fishing weekends and mid-week breaks on Ballylough.

BLACKWATER

(For close seasons, licences, see under Boards)

The largest of the rivers flowing into L Neagh, rising in S Tyrone to enter the lough at its SW corner. Coarse fish and trout.

Blackwatertown (Co Armagh). Dept of Ag has 1½m, mainly coarse fishing but short stretch of good game fishing. Permits from K Cahoon, 2 Irish St, Dungannon. Ulster Coarse Fishing Federation has water from Bond's Bridge to end of Argory Estate, a mixed fishery with excellent match weights. Individuals may fish free on F C B licence. Three trout lakes near **Dungannon**: Dungannon Park, 12 acres, (018687 27327); **Aughadarragh**, (016625 48320), r trout; **Altmore Fishery**, 5 acres, (018687 58977). **Ballysaggart Lough**: bream, eels, perch, pike, roach, rudd, tench. No permit needed. Contact (018678 22231). Other local fishings include **Lough More**, Clogher, wild browns, **Annaginny Lake**, Dungannon, rainbow trout. Contact Inn on the Park (*below*). Tackle shops: Cahoon Bros; Lakeview Tackle, Tight Lines Tackle, all Dungannon. Inn on the Park, Moy Rd (018687 25151) offers various types of fishing holiday.

Moy (Co Tyrone). Moy AC has coarse fishing on Blackwater at Moy, tickets from tackle shop The Field and Stream, Killyman St, Moy. Hotels: Charlemont House; Tomneys Licensed Inn (018687 84895).

Benburb (Co Tyrone). Trout for 2½m downstream. Armagh & Dist AC leases or owns stretch on river, and seven lakes.

Keep the banks clean

Several clubs have stopped issuing tickets to visitors because of the state of the banks after they have left. Spend a few moments clearing up. This includes lengths of broken nylon. If discarded, serious injuries can be caused to wild birds and to livestock.

The tailer in use on the Blackwater in Ireland. Generally speaking, a much-underemployed item of landing equipment. *Photo: S J Newman.*

Dep of Ag has **Brantry Lough** (brown trout); and **Loughs Creeve** (pike to 35lb) and **Enagh** (pike, perch, bream). Permits from Outdoor World, 46 Molesworth St, Cookstown. Dept of Ag also has coarse fishing on **Clay Lake**, nr **Keady** (Co Armagh); 120 acres, pike rudd and perch, open all year. Hotel, Salmon Leap View offers private fishing on riverbank, at £10 B & B, plus £1.50 fishing.

Clogher, **Augher** and **Aughnacloy**. (Co Tyrone). Local stretch of river has undergone fishery rehabilitation following a major drainage scheme of the Blackwater River. Permits from Aughnacloy AC, Clogher & Dist AC, Augher Dist &

Upper Blackwater AC and landowners. Permission from landowners for tributaries. **Callan, Oona** and **Torrent**. Dept of Ag has rainbow trout fishing on **White Lough**. 4 fish per day, min. size 10 ins. Fly only from boats, otherwise, spinning and worming permitted. Permits from R Morrow, 48 Rehaghey Road, Aughnacloy. Accommodation: Mrs K Hillen, 48 Moore St, Aughnacloy.

Armagh (Co Armagh). Beside **River Callan**, centre for Blackwater and its tributaries, with many fishing lakes in district. Six of these are controlled by Armagh AC, who offer day tickets on three, with brown and rainbow trout. Fly only on **Shaws Lake** and **Seagahan Reservoir**, all legal methods on **Aughnagorgan Lake**. Tackle shop: Armagh Garden and Sports Centre, 48 Dobbin St. Carnwood Lodge Hotel, 61 Castleblaney Rd, Keady (01861 538935), is close to **Keady Trout Lakes**, and caters for anglers.

SMALLER RIVERS EMPTYING INTO LOUGH NEAGH

MAINE (Co Antrim): Flows 25m from source in Glarryford Bogs to enter lough south of Randalstown, Co Antrim. With tributaries **Kellswater, Braid, Clough** and **Glenwherry** provides good fishing for salmon, trout and dollaghan. Gracehill, Galgorm and Dist AC has 3m stretch at **Ballymeda**, brown trout with salmon from July. Dt from Galgorm P O. 6 fish limit. Randalstown AC controls Maine from **Randalstown** Road Bridge to Andraid Ford. Trout, with salmon and dollaghan in season. Dt £3 from C Spence, 32 New Street, Randalstown. Membership £20 p.a, juv £5. Kells and Connor AC has dt £3 or £1 for fishing on Kells and Glenwherry. B and r trout and late salmon run. Apply to Duncan's Filling Station, Kells. Dept of Ag has brown trout fishing on **Dungonnell** and **Killylane Reservoirs**, 70 and 50 acres. Limit 4 fish. Maine AC issues 12 day tickets (£3) on 4 miles of river from above **Cullybackey** to Dunminning Bridge; brown trout and salmon. From Simpsons, 52 Main St, Cullybackey, Ballymena. Tackle shops: Spence Bros, New St; Groggans, 34 Broughshane St, Ballymena. Hotels: Adair Arms; Leighinmore House and Tullyglass House, Ballymena.

SIXMILEWATER: Flows 15m from Ballyclare to enter lough at Antrim, at its NE corner. A heavily-fished but highly productive trout water. Antrim & Dist AC issues £8, £5 and £3 permits for water between **Doagh** and **Antrim**; brown trout, salmon from August; from Templepatrick Supermarket. Mrs Marigold Allen, The Beeches Country House, 10 Dunadry Rd, Muckamore (01849 433161) has accommodation convenient for Sixmilewater between Antrim and Doagh. Dunadry Inn, (018494 32474), has fishing for guests on Sixmilewater. Ballynure AC issues dt £5 Mar-Jul, £8 Aug-Oct, for water between Doagh and **Ballynure**, from Twelve Milestone Petrol Station, Main st, Ballyclare; Doagh Petrol Station, Main St, Doagh. **Potterswalls Reservoir**, off Steeple Rd, nr Antrim, has rainbow trout fishing for members and visitors. Dept of Ag has trout fishing on **Woodburn Reservoirs**, nr **Carrickfergus**. Upper South, 65 acres, Middle South 64 acres, Lower South 22 acres, North, 18 acres. Upper and Lower South, fly only. Lough Mourne, 127 acres, Copeland (Marshallstown) 24 acres. North Woodburn, Rainbow, others, rainbow and brown. Limit 4 fish. Fishing at trout farm nr **Ballycarry**: Mr J Caldwell, 73 Bridgend Rd, Ballycarry, tel: 019603 72209. Tackle shop: Country Sports & Tackle, 9 Rough Lane, off Steeple Rd, Antrim. Hotel: Deer Park, Antrim. Ballyclare accommodation: Five Corners B & B.

CRUMLIN AND **GLENAVY** (Co Antrim): small rivers which flow west

Fishing available?

If you own, manage, or know of first-class fishing available to the public which should be considered for inclusion in ***Where to Fish,*** *please apply to the publishers (address in the front of the book) for a form for submission, on completion, to the editor. (Inclusion is at the sole discretion of the editor). There is no charge for inclusion.*

through these villages to enter lough. Trout fishing near their mouths. Centre: Crumlin. Tackle shop: Fur, Feather and Fin, 3a West Terrace, Mill Rd, tel: 0184 94 53648. Accommodation: Hillvale Farm, 11 Largy Road.

BALLINDERRY: Flows east for approx 30m, through **Cookstown**, to enter lough about midway along west shore. Good fishing for brown trout and dollaghan for 20m up from the mouth. Permission from Cookstown AC and landowners. Moy AC has stretch at Coagh. Tickets from The Field and Stream, Moy. **Lough Fea** is fished by the Mid Ulster AC. Tackle shop: Outdoor World, 46 Molesworth St, Cookstown. Hotels: Glenavon House, Drum Rd, (016487 64949), Angling Breaks - fishing on local river; Greenvale, both Cookstown, Co Tyrone.

MOYOLA (Co Londonderry): Flows east and south from its source in S Derry to enter lough at NW corner. Brown trout in lower reaches and a good run of salmon from July. Fishing rights held by Moyola and Dist AC, dt from G Ewings Confectionary, 41 Main St, Castle Dawson, of tackle shop H Hueston, 55 Main St, Castledawson, Magherafelt, BT45 8AA (01648 468282). Accommodation: Laurel Guest House, 60 Church St, Magherafelt (01648 32238).

BUSH

(For close seasons, licences, see under Boards)

The Bush flows 30m west and north through Bushmills, Co Antrim, to enter the sea near Portballintrae. The fishing rights of the entire catchment (except the stretch from the sea to Bushmills) have been acquired by the Dept of Agriculture primarily as an experimental river for studies into the biology and management of salmon. Within the terms of this programme, salmon angling is maintained at the highest possible level. Trout in the Bush and its tributaries are small but plentiful: there is a modest run of spring salmon and a grilse run for which the river is best known which begins in June or July, according to flow. It is important to report catches of fin-clipped fish. Bush season has been extended to 20 October.

For angling management, the river is divided into the following sections: the *Town Stretch* about 200 yds downstream of the Project Centre at Bushmills; the *Leap Stretch* upstream (approx 600 yds of water); the *New Stretch* (500 yds); and the *Unrestricted Stretch*, the remaining 24m of fishing water. The *Walk Mills* stretch (700 yds), from the top of the salmon leap to Ballyclogh Burn is now open for day tickets. Special daily permits, which may be booked in advance, are required for the Town, Leap and New stretches, as shown under 'Licences, permits and close seasons.' Weekend or Bank Holiday angling must be booked and paid for by 1400 hours on the preceding Friday or normal working day. Half day tickets are sold for the Town and Leap stretches from 1 June to 20 Oct. Tributary: **River Dervock**, flowing through the village of that name, offers 2m of good trout fishing. *(For details of permit charges see under Boards).*

Bushmills (Co Antrim). Salmon, sea trout and brown trout. Dunadarve Estates Ltd, Dundarave, Bushmills BT57 8ST, have excellent salmon fishing stretch from Bushmills to the sea. Dt £25 and £50. Fishing lodge also on site. Dept of Ag has short stretches (Town, New, Leap and Walk Mill) near Bushmills. Dt from The Hatchery, and should be booked in advance. M C McKeever, Bushmills (012657 31577) has accommodation with R Bush fishing. Dept of Ag has 24m stretch (unrestricted). Bank fishing only. Permits from R Bell, 40 Ann St, Ballycastle, tel: 012657 62520. Other Bushmills tackle dealer: Angling Supplies, 39 Main St. Hotels: Bushmills Inn; Antrim Arms, Ballycastle.

Ballymoney (Co Antrim). **Bush River** may be fished for brown trout, as can the Ballymoney Burn. Good coarse fishing on **Movanagher Canal** and **R Bann**. Brown and rainbow trout fishing on **Altnahinch Reservoir**, at head of R Bush. Dept of Ag water, 44 acres, bag limit 4 fish, bank fishing only. Permits from Pollocks Filling Station, Rodeing Foot, also E J Cassell, 43/45 Main St, both Ballymoney.

LOUGH ERNE (Upper and Lower)

(For close seasons, licences, under Boards)

Upper and Lower Lough Erne, with the R Erne and tributaries feeding the loughs, comprise

15,300 hectares of mixed game and coarse fishing owned and annually restocked by the Dept of Agriculture and offering some of the best sport in Europe. The flow is in a NW direction, through the beautiful and largely unspoilt Fermanagh countryside, via Belleek, to where the R Erne reaches the sea at Ballyshannon. Infinitely varied fishing in the lakes, with innumerable secluded bays, inlets and small islands. Rich, unpolluted waters teeming with fish-life, the Erne system is truly an angler's paradise. Centres: Belleek; Kesh; Enniskillen; Bellanaleck; Lisnaskea; Newtownbutler; Derrygonnelly (Tirnavar).

RIVER ERNE. River heavily populated with large bream and roach, pike of record-breaking proportions. Good salmon runs in late summer and autumn. **Belleek**, Co Fermanagh, is a good centre for fishing river and Lower Lough. Dept of Ag has 3¾ miles with brown trout and salmon. Limit, 6 fish; also b and r trout on **Lough Keenaghan**, 38 acres. **Scolban Lough** (171 acres) has pike to 20lb as main quarry, also perch, and is stocked with rainbow trout to 2lb by Dept of Ag. Belleek Angling Centre & Cottages, The Thatch, Belleek BT93 3FX, tel: 013656 58181, offers self-catering accommodation, boats, engines and organisation for lake, river and sea fishing. **LOWER LOUGH ERNE**. The trout fishing areas, in which the fish may run very large, are in the north and west of the lake. Recommended areas are from Roscor Bridge up to the Heron Island, and across to the **Garvary River**. South and east of a dividing line, the lake may be fished on coarse fishing licence and permit only.

TRIBUTARIES FEEDING LOWER LOUGH: Ballinamallard River flows south through the village of Ballinamallard, to enter the lake near St Angelo Airport. Dept of Ag controls 1 mile nr Ballinamallard; brown trout. **Colebrook** and **Tempo** enter lake from the east. 2 miles of Colebrook is Dept of Ag Designated Coarse fishery, nr Lisnaskea: roach, bream, perch, rudd, eels, the occasional pike, trout and salmon. Ballinamallard and Colebrook rivers are currently being stocked with juvenile salmon as part of a cross-border salmon enhancement initiative for the Erne system. Tackle shop: J A Knaggs, Main St, Ballinamallard.

UPPER LOUGH ERNE: Principally coarse fish: pike, eel, perch, rudd, bream, roach, occasional salmon and sea trout. Centres: **Lisnaskea**; **Newtown Butler**; **Enniskillen**. The National Trust at Crom Estate has fishing on Inisherk and Derryvore Islands, with excellent bream and roach. Dt £3 in advance from Sharon Sey, Gate Lodge, Crom Estate, Newtownbutler, Fermanagh, tel: 013657 38825. Stocked pike lake dt £20, very limited. Boats for hire, contact Visitors Centre, tel: 013657 38118. Accommodation at national Trust Holiday Cottages, tel: 01396 881204; Carrybridge Hotel & Marina, 171 Inishmore Rd, Lisbellaw (01365387), is situated on Upper Lough Erne, and has boats on site. **Mill Lough, Bellanaleck**: 100 acres Dept of Ag r and b trout fishery 4 miles from Enniskillen, 4 fish limit. At Castle Coole, **Lough Coole**, National Trust Fishery. B and r trout to 5lbs. ½ dt (boat) £3. **Killyfole Lough**, 56 acres, nr Lisnaskea, has a variety of coarse fish, incl perch and pike. Permits from F Dowler, Main St, Lisnaskea. Tackle shops: J E Richardson, East Bridge Street, Enniskillen (tickets for local fishing); Erne Tackle, Main Street, Lisnaskea; J & K Mullen, Sligo Road, Enniskillen, Co Fermanagh. Hotels: Killyhevlin; Manor House; Railway; all Enniskillen; and Ortine, Lisnaskea. Ely Island Chalets (0136589 777) offer self-catering accommodation with boats and tackle, also private trout lake, with breeding rainbows. Riverside Farm, Gortadrehid, Enniskillen (01365 322725) has accommodation with boats and bait supplied. Derryad Cottages, Lisnaskea (0181 5674487): fishing holidays with motor boats supplied. J & S Reihill (013657 21360), accommodation with fishing on 80 acre **Inniscorkin Island** shoreline. Killyhevlin Hotel, Enniskillen, has chalets on banks of Erne, with fishing stages. Tel: 01365 323481. Other accommodation at Lough Erne Cottages, Bo-

Keep the banks clean

Several clubs have stopped issuing tickets to visitors because of the state of the banks after they have left. Spend a few moments clearing up. This includes lengths of broken nylon. If discarded, serious injuries can be caused to wild birds and to livestock.

lusty, c/o J E Richardson, see above. Boats and engines on site.

TRIBUTARIES FEEDING UPPER LOUGH ERNE: Swanlinbar River flows north from Co Cavan to enter the lough midway on the S side. Coarse fish in lower reaches, trout in upper. Permission from landowners. The **Sillees River** flows from above Derrygonelly to enter the lough between Enniskillen and Lisgoole Abbey. Excellent coarse fishing, some trout. **Arney River** flows from Lower Lough Macnean to Upper Lough Erne (large trout and exceptional pike fishing) to enter Upper L Erne near **Bellanaleck**. Good mixed fishing all the way to **Lough Macnean**. Upper and Lower L Macnean both have coarse fishing on them, notably pike. Permits from tackle shops in Bellanaleck and Enniskillen. Also ten Dept trout lakes of various sizes in the area (5 acres to 100 acres), including the famous **Navar Forest Lakes**, and **Mill Lough** at Bellanaleck which holds trout to 5lb. Dept of Ag permits for Mill Lough and for Navar Forest Lakes from Carlton Park Information and Fishing Centre, Belleek and tackle shops in Enniskillan.

FOYLE

(For close seasons, licences, see under Boards)

The Foyle system is half in Northern Ireland, half in the Republic. It is formed by the **Derg** (draining Lough Derg) and the **Strule**, constituting the **Mourne**, which unites with the **Finn** at Strabane to become the Foyle proper, which enters the sea at Londonderry. That part of the system in Northern Ireland, including the **Faughan** and **Roe**, is the largest salmon and trout fishery in the country. It drains the north and west slopes of the Sperrin Mountains and most of Co Tyrone.

Londonderry. River tidal here, with fishing for salmon in tidal pools from July. Also a run of sea trout. Permits from Foyle Commission. Tackle shops: Rod and Line, 1 Clarendon St, tel: 01504 262877; P McCrystal, Spencer Rd; Fitzpatrick Sports, Spencer Rd; Hills (Derry Ltd), Spencer Rd, all Waterside, Londonderry. Hotels: White Horse Inn, Everglades, Broomhill House.

Strabane (Co Tyrone). Here **Mourne** and **Strule** unite to form Foyle. Salmon and sea trout. Permits from Foyle Commission. Dept of Ag has five lakes in the area. Fir Trees Hotel, Melmount Rd, tel: 01504 382382, offers weekend fishing breaks, £99.

Tributaries of the Foyle

MOURNE: Excellent fishing in the 10m between Strabane and Newtownstewart, but largely private and not open to visitors.

Sion Mills (Co Tyrone), Dept of Ag has 4m stretch managed by Sion Mills AC, salmon, brown and sea trout; 10 dts from T Kee, Mourne Bar, Victoria Bridge; 20 dts from M Gough, 6 New St, Sion Mills. Tackle shop: N M Tackle, 9 Alexander Park.

Newtownstewart (Co Tyrone). The **Owenkillow** and **Glenelly** enter here, offering 30m of ideal game fishing waters noted for their sea trout and salmon. Owenkillen is spate river, only worth fishing in Jun/Oct. For **Gortin** fishing on Owenkillow and Owenrea, contact G Treanor (016626 48543). Blakiston-Houston Estate has fishing on 6m stretch of **Owenkillen** and 3m stretch of **Owenrea**; salmon and sea trout; limited fly only dt, £10, from Gabriel Treanor, 56 Main St, Gortin (016626 48534/48824), or K Fleming, 51 Gorticashel Rd, Gortin. Omagh AA holds most of fishing rights on Mourne, Strule and Owenkillow around this area, (some 28 miles) and offers dt £12. These, also Gaff AC dt (£5) on **Glenelly River** from tackle shop:

Campbell's Mourne Valley Tackle, 50 Main St, Newtonstewart, tel: 016626 61543/61167. Campbell's also offer accommodation with private fishing on Rivers **Mourne** and **Glenelly**: Salmon, brown trout, sea trout. Baronscourt Cottages, tel: 016626 61013, has pike fishing for guests. Weekend break, £54, midweek, £46.50. B & B and self-catering: Anglers Rest, Mr & Mrs D Campbell, 12 Killymore Rd, Newtownstewart

STRULE: Very good trout fishing from Omagh to Newtownstewart.

Omagh (Co Tyrone). Dept of Ag controls the coarse fishing on a stretch of R Strule by arrangement with Omagh AA. Roach and eels. Assn also controls stretches of **Camowen, Owenkillen** and **Drumragh Rivers**. More good fishing upstream of Omagh, to Camowen, but fish smaller. Salmon in season. **Owenragh, Quiggery/Fintona** and **Drumragh** enter near **Omagh**. Dept stillwaters, **Loughs Bradan** and **Lee**, 60 and 37 acres, 5 miles from **Castlederg**; Brown trout fishing, 4 fish limit, per day, min. size 10 ins. Tackle and Permits for Strule from C A Anderson, 64 Market St, Omagh. Omagh hotels: Royal Arms; Silverbirch.

FAIRYWATER: Flows E from Drumquin (trout) to enter **Strule** below Omagh. Remarkably good roach fishing in lower reaches. No permit required. **Burn Dennett River, Dunamanagh**: Small brown trout, occasional salmon and sea trout in season. Fly, spinning and worm. Permit from Burn Dennet AA.

DERG: flows E from Donegal for 50m to enter Mourne N of **Newtownstewart**. Good trout water for 15m to above Castlederg, Co Tyrone, with salmon and occasion sea trout. Permits £15, £20 weekly from Castlederg AA, c/o H Irwin, 5 John St, Castlederg, tel: 016626 71050 (day). Tackle shop: Campbell's Mourne Valley Tackle, 30 Main St, Newtownstewart, tel: 016626 61543. Hotel: Derg Arms, 43 Main St Castlederg (016626 71644, 70202).

FAUGHAN and ROE

(For close seasons, licences, see under Boards)

The Faughan flows N for 20m to enter the Foyle area E of Londonderry city; the Roe flows the same distance in the same general direction to enter the Foyle Estuary N of Limavady, Co Londonderry. Salmon, sea trout and brown trout in Faughan; principally sea trout in Roe, but also salmon from July.

FAUGHAN: River Faughan Anglers Ltd lease the fishing rights of tributaries and main river, a 30 mile stretch of water divided into two sections, approx 2m tidal and 28m freshwater, situated between Londonderry and Claudy. Both sections are productive of sea trout and salmon. Visitors season and daily (24 hr) permits (£40, £15, with concessions) and licences from Club Office, 26A Carlisle Rd, Londonderry, or from Foyle Fisheries Office.

ROE:

Limavady (Co Londonderry). Good fishing for 15m from Limavady to Dungiven. Dept of Ag has 1¼m at **O'Cahan's Rock**, S of Limavady, with salmon and sea trout. Roe AA offers 12 day tickets for most of a 34 mile stretch, both banks, from source to river mouth, from Limavady tackle shops. Dungiven AC controls 6m between Ross' Mill and Bovevagh Bridge, salmon, sea trout, best Sept/Oct. Dt £5 from P McGuigan, 24 Station Rd, Dungiven, and Bovevagh P O. Tackle shops: R Douglas & Son, Rod & Gun, 6 Irish Green St, Limvaday; S J Mitchell, 29 Main St, Limavady, who displays map of all local fishings, issues permits and is a reliable source of local information. Hotels: Gorteen House, Limavady; Alexander Arms; many guest houses.

GLENS OF ANTRIM RIVERS

(For close seasons, licences, see under Boards)

GLENARM: Short privately-owned spate river. A few salmon and sea trout.

GLENARIFF: Small sea trout river which flows into Red Bay at Glenariff. Occasional salmon. Permission from Glens AC.

GLENDUN: enters sea at **Cushendun**. Fair run of late salmon and sea trout. Glens AC; Dt £5, st £20, £10 for Oct, from Mrs M McFettridge, 116 Tromara Rd, Castle

Green, Cushendun, and J O'Neill. Fly, spinning, worm permitted, but no bait digging allowed. Tackle from Red Bay Boats and J O'Neill, Main St, both Cushendall.

MARGY/CAREY/GLENSHESK: a system of small rivers entering the sea at **Ballycastle**. Sea trout, brown trout and salmon. Dept of Ag waters. Tickets from R Bell, 38/40 Ann St, Ballycastle, tel: 012657 62520. Hotels: Antrim Arms, Ballycastle; Thornlea, Cushendun. Tackle shop: R Bell, 40 Ann St, Ballycastle, tel: 012657 62520.

LAGAN

(For close seasons, licences, see under Boards)

A productive river which flows into the **Belfast Lough**. Trout fishing upstream from Magheralin, Co Down, for 12m.

Belfast (Co Antrim). Dept of Ag has 2¼m of coarse fishing on R Lagan. Permits from: Tight Lines, 198/200 Albertbridge Rd, tel: 01232 457357; J Braddell, 11 North St; H D Wolsey, 60 Upper Newtownards Rd. Dundonald AC fishes **Lough Creevy**, Ballylone Rd, nr Saintfield: rainbow trout, pike. Limited dt £10 from Legge Bros, 56 Belmont Rd, Belfast 4.

Lisburn (Co Antrim). Iveagh AC has stretch of 7 miles from Thornyford Bridge, Dromore, to Spencer's Bridge, Flatford. 10 free dt for holders of Dept. of Ag annual game season permit. Tickets from Premier Angling, 17 Queen St, Lurgan. Lisburn & Dist AC fish on 7 miles of **Lagan** between Lisburn and Maira, containing a fair head of b trout, roach, bream; also a stretch of a small tributary, the **Ravarnette**, with b trout to 3lb not uncommon, also roach and bream. This fishing is open to general public with no charge. Club membership is £12 p.a. Dept of Ag has brown and/or rainbow trout lakes, totalling more than 700 acres, in the Lagan Valley area. Near to Belfast, these waters are fished more heavily than

The stones visible a yard beneath the surface. A water typical of the Ards Peninsular, Co. Down.

most in N Ireland. They include: **Stoneyford** and **Leathemstown Reservoirs**, 160 and 28 acres, b and r trout, fly, spinning and worm, 4 fish limit, no boat angling; **Ballykeel Loughherne**, 53 acres, b and r trout, fly only. Abundant coarse fishing on canals and loughs **Henney**, **Begney**, **Aghery**, **Beg**, **Neagh**. All with pike, perch, etc. Tackle shop: Lisburn Sports, 9 Smithfield Square. Hotels: Greenan Lodge, Conway, both Dunmurry.

Lurgan (Co Armagh). Dept of Ag water: **Craigavon City Park Lakes**, 168 acres, South Lake, r trout, fly, spinning, worming, 4 fish limit. North Lake, coarse fishery with pike and roach. Permits from F C Computers & Tackle, 28 High St; Premier Angling, 17 Queen St.

Dromore (Co Down). Dromore AC has 2 miles of river below, and 5 miles above Dromore: good trout water, for wet and dry fly. Season starts 1 March. Dt £3.50, juv £1, from J McCracken's Confectionary, Gallows St, Dromore. 5 miles away at **Hillsborough**, 40 acres r trout fishery, Dept of Ag water, season 1 Feb-31 Dec. Accommodation at Win Staff B & B, Banbridge Rd; Mrs Rhoda Marks, B & B, Milebush Rd, both Dromore.

LOUGH MELVIN

(For close seasons, licences, see under Boards)

A 5,000 acre natural lake, approximately one fifth of which lies in Northern Ireland, (Co Fermanagh). A good spring run of salmon starts in February and a grilse run in June, but the lake is famous chiefly for the variety of its native brown trout. In addition to fish of orthodox appearance, there are dark 'sonaghan' caught over the deeper water and the yellow-bellied 'gillaroo', found in the shallows near the shore. Regarded as the Dept of Agriculture's best game fishery. No coarse fishing. **Garrison**, Co Fermanagh is the centre for fishing the lough and **Lough Macnean**, Upper and Lower, also in the vicinity. (Pike, large trout, general coarse fishing.) Small trout in **L Lattone** may be caught from the roadside between Belcoo and Garrison.

NEWRY RIVER

(For close seasons, licences, see under Boards)

A small system flowing into the head of **Carlingford Lough** at **Newry**, Co Down. 3m of fair brown trout water above Carnbane Industrial Estate. Newry & Dist AC issues dt £4 for **Clanrye River**, **Greenan Lake**, stocked with brown and rainbow trout and **McCourt's Lake**, **Poyntzpass**, brown trout, fly only. Apply to Mrs E McAlinden, 12 Lisgullion Park, Armagh Rd, Newry. 3m from town, Cooper's Lake, fly fishing for brown trout. Two Dept of Agriculture trout lakes in area: **Lough Brickland** and **Glassdrumman**. Tackle shop: J C Smyth, 7/9 Kildare Street, Newry.

NEWRY SHIP CANAL

The first ship canal in British Isles, ceased operation in 1976. The fishable section which runs from Newry to sea locks on Omeath road, 3½m approx, has produced match weights of over 50lb. Summer algae improves roach and bream catches, while large pike are to be caught in winter. Most winter fishing is in Albert Basin. There is free fishing for licence holders.

QUOILE

(For close seasons, licences, see under Boards)

Flows into top of **Strangford Lough** at **Downpatrick**, Co Down. Coarse fish and some trout in lower reaches; fair trout waters between Annacloy Bridge and Kilmore. Dept of Ag has fishing rights on **Quoile Basin** (100 acres) and 7m of Quoile River from Downpatrick to Kilmore; pike, perch, rudd, eels and brown trout; south bank fishing only. No fishing on nature reserve d/s of Steamboat Quay. No wading. Other Dept of Ag fisheries, **Portavoe Reservoir**, nr Donaghadee and Bangor, 31 acres b and r trout, fly only, 20 rods per day, 4 fish limit; **Lough Money**, 53 acre coarse fishery with pike, perch, eels, nr **Downpatrick**. Downpatrick & Dist AA hold fishing rights to **Loughinisland Lake** and **Magheraleggan**

Lake; guests only when accompanied by a member. A new fishery for disabled anglers has been opened at **Marybrook Mill**, nr Ballynahinch. Rainbow trout and coarse fish. Tel: 01396 830173. **Lough Cowey**, 2 miles north of **Portaferry**, natural 70 acres lough with rainbow and brown trout mostly 2lbs plus, fly fishing. Dt and boats on site; contact Manager, The Fishery, Lough Cowey Rd, Portaferry (012477 28946). Tackle shops: H W Kelly & Son, Market Street, Downpatrick; Dairy Fishery, 179 Belfast Rd, Ballynahinch. Hotel: Portaferry, (012477 28231), offers fishing breaks on Lough Cowey.

SHIMNA

(For close seasons, licences, see under Boards)

Small attractive river with deep rocky pools flowing from E slope of Mournes to enter sea at **Newcastle**, Co Down. Sea trout and salmon from July. Dept of Agriculture fishery in forest areas. Bag limit 2 fish. No Sunday fishing. Permits from Forest Office at Tolleymore Forest Park and the Forest Ranger. The rest of the river is controlled by Shimna AC. Wt £25 and dt £7, from Four Season, see below. Fishing is by all legal methods. Dept stillwaters: **Spelga Reservoir**, 148 acres, b trout; **Castlewellan Lake**, 4 miles from Newcastle, 103 acres, b and r trout, 4 fish limit. Fly, spinning and worming. Tackle shop: The Four Seasons, 47 Main Street, Newcastle. Hotels: Slieve Donard; Enniskeen.

WHITEWATER

(For close seasons, licences, see under Boards)

Small attractive sea trout water flowing into sea W of **Kilkeel**, Co Down, 3m of good fishing. Kilkeel AC offers dt £2 for Kilkeel and Whitewater system, from Nicholson's Hardware, The Square, Kilkeen, or tackle shops: J Graham, 66 Greencastle St; McConnell & Hanna, 19 Newcastle St, both Kilkeel. Hotel: Kilmorey Arms, Kilkeel.

Check before you go

While every effort has been made to ensure that the information given in **Where to Fish** *is correct, the position is continually changing, and anglers are urged, in their own interests, to make preliminary enquiries before travelling to selected venues. This is especially important with reference to prices quoted. Inevitably the rate of inflation is affecting stability in this quarter. Anglers' attention is also drawn to the fact that the hotels mentioned under the various fishing stations do not necessarily have water of their own. Any amendments or further data for inclusion in subsequent editions, and any comments, will be welcome.*

SEA FISHING STATIONS IN NORTHERN IRELAND

The popularity of sea fishing in N Ireland has grown immensely in recent years, leading to the discovery of new and exciting possibilities. 300 miles of unpolluted coastline offers fishing for a variety of species from rock and beach alike. Sheltered inlets of which Strangford and Belfast Loughs are the largest and best known, offer protection to the boat angler when the open sea may be unfishable due to adverse weather. Twenty-four species of sea fish are caught regularly, including blue shark, skate, tope, cod, bass and flatfish.

Magilligan (Co Antrim). From point, surf fishing for dogfish, flounder, occasional bass. From strand, where lug and ragworm can be dug, beach fishing for flounder. Other venues are: Benone Strand, Downhill Strand, **Castlerock** beach and breakwater, **Barmouth** pier (spinning for mackerel) and beach; flatfish, coalfish, whiting, occasional mullet and bass.

Portrush (Co Antrim) and **Portstewart** (Co Derry). Near mouths of Lough Foyle and River Bann. Rock, pier and beach fishing for pollack, mackerel, wrasse, dogfish, coalfish, flounder, plaice, conger and bass. Conger fishing in Portrush harbour. Rock fishing from Ramore Head east and west, Blue Pool rocks, and **Dunseverick**. Skerries, 2m off Portrush produce good catches of turbot, plaice, dogfish, dab. Causeway bank off **Giants Causeway** good rock fishing for wrasse, coalfish, pollack, plaice, turbot. Boats for hire: Barracuda, Geoff Farrow, 6 Sunset Park, Portstewart BT55 7EH (01265 836622); experienced skipper for day and evening deep sea angling trips. Club: Portstewart SAC. Tackle shop: Joe Mullan, Sea Angling Specialist, 74 Main Street, Portrush. Hotels: Northern Counties; Magherabuoy House, Eglington, Kiln-an-Oge; all Portrush (and many more).

Ballycastle (Co Antrim). Rock fishing for wrasse, pollack, coalfish, mackerel from Ballintoy. At Ballycastle strand, codling, plaice, small coalfish and whiting. Best in autumn, on evening tides. Spinning or float fishing for cod and pollack. **Rathlin Island**, just off the coast opposite Ballycastle, has wreck fishing for conger in Church Bay; and cod, coalfish, dogfish, plaice, pollack, turbot, haddock, ling, herring, conger eel, spurdog and skate off Bull point. Boats from C McCaughan, 45 Ann St, tel: (012657 62074), and others. Tackle shop: R Bell, 40 Ann St. Hotel: Antrim Arms. Hilsea B & B, 28 North St Ballycastle BT54 6BW (02657 62385) has accommodation with sea fishing trips arranged.

Larne (Co Antrim). No fishing from harbour, but bottom fishing at nearby beach for coalfish, cod, dogfish, wrasse. Lugworm can be dug at Larne, **Glynn** and **Magheramorne** strands or bought at McCluskey's. Local venues are: Glenarm, popular night fishing mark for codling, flatfish; **Murlough Bay**, spinning from rocks for coalfish, mackerel, pollack; Garron point, codling, wrasse, pollack, coalfish, dogfish. Boats available from W Mann, (01574 74547). Club: Larne & Dist SAC. Tackle shops: Larne Angling Centre, 128 Main St, BT40 1RG; S McCluskey, 47 Coastguard Rd (01574 63128). Hotels which cater for anglers: Magheramorne House, Curran Court, Halfway House, Kilwaughter House.

Whitehead and **Carrickfergus** (Co Antrim). Opposite Bangor at entrance to Belfast Lough (Belfast 16m). Pollack, mackerel, coalfish, cod, whiting, from rocks, beach and boats. Wrecks off Blackhead for cod, pollack, coalfish. Local venues are Whitehead Promenade, Carrickfergus Harbour and East pier, Ballycarry Causeway, nr **Islandmagee**. Below Blackhead lighthouse, conger, wrasse, cod, mackerel. Boat trips from Marina, Rogers Quay, (019603 66666), as well as Sailing Club, The Harbour, (019603 51402). Clubs: Woodburn AC and Greenisland AC. Hotels: Dobbins Inn; Coast Road, both Carrickfergus.

Bangor (Co Down). Bangor is on Belfast Lough, 12m from capital. Cod, plaice, turbot, whiting. Lugworm can be dug on beaches at Bangor, ragworm at Kinnegar. Smelt Mill Bay and Orlock point are good summer venues for wrasse, codling, coalfish, dogfish, mackerel. Bangor and **Donaghadee** piers for mackerel, coalfish, flatfish. Boats from Tom Martin (01247 454672), £15 per angler, charter £150.

Tackle shop: Trap & Tackle, 6 Seacliff Rd (2047 458515).

Donaghadee (Co Down). Fishing from pier or rocks for pollack, codling and mackerel. Rigg sandbar (3m off Donaghadee) for cod, whiting, gurnard, coalfish, flatfish, mackerel, rays, dogfish, plaice, pollack. Back of Sandbar for big huss. Boats from Q Nelson, 146 Killaughey Rd, (01247 883403), specialising in wreck and reef drift fishing. Twice daily June-Sept, and weekends Sept-Nov, around the Copeland Islands. All tackle provided for beginners. Club: Donaghadee SAC. Tackle shop: Kennedy's, 1 The Parade.

Strangford Lough (Co Down). Good boat fishing in estuaries and inlets around the lough. Big skate (Aug-Oct), spurdog, huss, thornback. Skate and tope are protected species in lough, and must be returned to the water alive. Codling, turbot, whiting, haddock, mackerel, spurdog and wrasse at deep-water entrance to lough. Best fishing in slack water. Lugworm is plentiful at Island Hill nr Comber and shore at Kircubbin. Wreck fishing for big ling and conger outside lough. Boats in **Portaferry**: D Rogers, (01247 728297). Tackle and bait from Hillview Service Station, 91 High St, Portaferry; Scott's Service Station, 34 Catherine St, Killyleagh; Country Sports, 48a Regent St, both Newtownards.

Kilkeel (Co Down). Harbour fishing for coalfish and mackerel; West strand for flatfish, dogfish. Black Rock, **Ballymartin**, produces mackerel and codling; **Carlingford Lough,** flatfish, dogfish, thornback, a few bass. Good points are Cranfield and Greencastle. Lugworm can be dug in **Newcastle** harbour and **Greencastle**, rag and lug at **Warrenpoint** beach. Boats are available at Newcastle, phone Newcastle Centre, (013967 22222), or Harbourmaster, (013967 22106/22804). Boats are also for hire at Greencastle (016937 62422) and Warrenpoint (72682 or 73776). Tackle shops: J Graham, 47 Greencastle St; McConnell & Hanna, 19 Newcastle St; Four Seasons, 47 Main St, Newcastle.

Keep the banks clean

Several clubs have stopped issuing tickets to visitors because of the state of the banks after they have left. Spend a few moments clearing up. This includes lengths of broken nylon. If discarded, serious injuries can be caused to wild birds and to livestock.

FISHING CLUBS ETC. IN NORTHERN IRELAND

The following is an alphabetical list of fishing clubs and associations who fish in Northern Ireland. Particulars of the waters held by many will be found by reference to the Index, in the section headed 'Fishing Stations in Northern Ireland', and information about the others, which may not have their own water, could be had from the Secretaries. A courtesy they appreciate is the inclusion of a stamped addressed envelope with postal inquiries. Please advise the publishers (address at the front of the book) of any changed details for the next edition.

NATIONAL BODIES

Ulster Coarse Fishing Federation
Robert Buick, Chairman
7 Knockvale Grove
Belfast BT5 6HL

Fisheries Conservancy Board for Northern Ireland
1 Mahon Road
Portadown,
Craigavon
Co Armagh BT62 3EE
Tel: 0762 334666
Fax: 0762 338912

Fisheries Office
Riversdale
Ballinamallard
Co Fermanagh

CLUBS

Agivey Anglers Association
J P McCusker
27 Drumeil Road
Aghadowey
Co Londonderry
BT51 4BB

Antrim and District Angling Association
B McNeill
41 Derry Road
Newtown Abbey BT36 7UF

Ards Fly Fishing Club
James Crothers
c/o Lough Cowey Fishery
Lough Cowey Road
Co Down

Ards & District Sea Angling Club
J Purdy
Ivy Cottage
22 Glenmount Park
Rosehill
Newtownards BT23 4QL

Armagh Angling Club
c/o Armagh Colour Copy Shop
Dobbin Centre
Armagh

Armagh and District Angling Club
Contact
Amagh District Council
The Palace Demesne
Armagh BT60 4EL

Ballylagan Fishing and Conservation Club
c/o Smyths Country Sports
1 Park Street
Coleraine
Co Londonderry BT52 1BD

Ballymoney and District Angling Club
J McKay
15 Pharis Road
Ballymoney

Ballynure Angling Club
John Arneill
17 Collinview Drive
Ballyclare
BT39 9PQ

Banbridge Angling Club
J Curran
2 Ballydown Road
Banbridge
Co Down BT32 4JB

Belfast Anglers' Association
John A Collinson
7 Hawthorne Drive
Belfast BT4 2HG

Blue Circle Angling Club
N Hutchinson
c/o Blue Circle
Sandholes Road
Cookstown

British Legion Angling Club
C McFetridge
c/o British Legion
Burn Road
Cookstown
Co Tyrone

Burn Dennet Angling Association
W O'Neill
Carrickatane Road
Dunamanagh
Co Tyrone

Castlecaldwell Anglers
c/o Leggs Post Office
Fermanagh

Castlederg Anglers Club
R R Harron
36 Ferguson Crescent
Castlederg BT81 7AG
or
c/o H Irwin, Grocer
5 John Street
Castlederg, Co Tyrone

Castlewellan and Annsborough Angling Club
S P Harrison
Garden Cottage
Forest Park
Castlewellan

Clady and District Angling Club
H Doherty
95 Clady Road
Portglenone
Co Antrim BT44 8LB

Clogher Angling Club
Seamus McGirr
016625 48293

Coleraine Angling Club
B Liddell
53 Seapark
Castlerock BT51 4TH

Derg Angling Club
c/o Campbells
50 Main Street
Newtownstewart
Co Tyrone

Dromore Angling Club
R Russell
49 Ravenscroft Avenue
Belfast

Donaghadee Sea Angling Club
Billy Greer
29 Ravenscroft Avenue
Belfast BT5 5BA

Dundonald Angling Club
Peter Grahame
13 Cherryhill Drive
Dundonald
Belfast BT16 OJG

Dundonald Sea Angling Club
Sam Burns
24 Tara Crescent
Newtownards BT23 3DF

Dungiven Anglers Club
Now amalgamated with Roe AA

Enler Fishing Club
Comber
Co Down

River Faughan Anglers Ltd
L F Thompson
17 Rockport Park
Londonderry
BT47 1JH
Office:
26A Carlisle Road
Londonderry
BT48 6JW

Gaff Angling Club
c/o Campbell's Mourne Valley Tackle
50 Main Street
Newtownstewart
Co Tyrone

Galgorm and District Angling Club
N Anderson
56 Ballykennedy Road
Gracehill

Garrison & District Angling Club
Garrison
Fermanagh

Gilford Angling Club
M Magee
Station Road
Scarva Craigavon

Glenravel & Clough Angling Club
D Anderson
6 Old Cushendun Road
Newtowncrommelin
Co Antrim

Glens Angling Club
J McKillop
30 Coast Road
Cushendall
Co Antrim

Gracehill, Galgorm and District Angling Club
Norman Anderson
50a Ballykennedy Rd
Gracehill, Co Antrim

Greenisland Angling Club
W Hinton
18 Glenkeen Drive
Greenisland
Carrickfergus
Holywood Flydressers Guild
A J Kennedy
6 Demesne Park
Holywood BT18 9NE
Holywood Fly Fishing Club
C F Kyle
2 Seymour Park
Crawfordsburn Road
Bangor
Kells and Connor Angling Club
N Wilson
35 Templemoyle
Kells, Ballymena
Co Antrim
Kildress Angling Club
Edgar Thom
3a Killycurrage Road
Cookstown
Co Tyrone
Kilkeen Angling Club
A Kilgore
4 Mill Street
Annalong
Kilrea and District Angling Club
David Laughlin
Bann Road
Kilrea
Co Londonderry
Kingsbridge Angling Club
c/o The Dunleath Bar
Church Street
Cookstown
Kings Road Game Angling Club
c/o 8 Kirn Park
Dundonald, BT5 7GA
Larne and District Sea Angling Club
S Givran
16 McGee Park
Larne BT40 1PP
Lisburn and District Anglers' Club
D Croot
109 Benson Street
Lisburn, Co Antrim
BT28 2AF
Maine Angling Club
Bill McCartney
7 Demesne Manor
Holywood
Co Down BT 18 9NW
Mid-Antrim Angling Club
R Topping
24 Cameron Park
Ballymena
Co Antrim
Mid-Ulster Angling Club
D Boner
57 Molesworth Road
Cookstown
Co Tyrone
Moy Angling Club
D Tomney
10 The Square
Moy, Dungannon
Co Tyrone
Moyola and District Angling Club
T Maguire
3 Graigmore Road
Maghera
Co Londonderry
Newry and District Angling Club
D Kidd
8 Cloneden
Dallan Road
Warrenpoint
Co Down
Omagh Angling Association
c/o D Campbell
Fishing Tackle Shop
Main Street
Newtownstewart
Co Tyrone
Portstewart Sea Angling Club
A McCallion
23 Hillview Park
Cleraine
Co Londonderry BT51 3EH

Randalstown Angling Club
R Magee
67 Muckamore Garden Village
Antrim
BT41 1NB
Rathfriland and District Angling Association
D A Crory
5 Castlewellan Road
Rathfriland, Co Down
Roe Anglers
c/o R Douglas and Sor
6 Irish Green Street
Limavady
Co Londonderry
Shimna Angling Club
P Mornin
84 Bryansford Road
Newcastle, Co Down
BJ33 0LE
Sion Mills Angling Club
Eddie McCrea
35 Main Street
Sion Mills
Co Tyrone

Tullylagan Angling Club
Jim Warnock
133 Dungannon Road
Cookstown
Co Tyrone

Warrenpoint, Rostrevor and District Angling Club
John O'Crey
Springfield Road
Warrenpoint
Co Down

Woodburn Angling Club
W Moore
544 Upper Road
Woodburn
Carrickfergus

Picture opposite: Almost as much fun as the actual fishing. Catching live mayflies for dapping is a common sight on an Irish lough shore - in this case, Lough Arrow.

FISHING IN IRELAND

The Irish Republic is world famous for the quality of its fisheries. Salmon, sea trout, brown trout, pike and other coarse fish, are to be found there at their best. The seas around Ireland contain very good quantities of many varieties of fish which provide excellent sport for visiting and native sea anglers. Where to fish in Ireland is virtually everywhere. Fisheries are administered by a Central Fisheries Board and by seven Regional Fisheries Boards coordinated by the Central Board. The function of each Regional Board is to conserve, protect, develop and promote every aspect of the inland fisheries (salmon, trout, coarse fish, eels), including sea angling, within the Board's fisheries region.

Rod/Line Licences:

Salmon/Sea Trout - Season (All districts) £25
Salmon/Sea Trout (Single District Only) £12
Salmon/Sea Trout Juvenile £8
Salmon/Sea Trout 21-Day £10
Salmon/Sea Trout 1 Day £3
Foyle Area Extension £17

Central/Regional Fisheries Board Permits on trout fisheries

Ordinary (Season) From £5 to £20
Pensioner/Juvenile (Season) From £2 to £10, (Day) from £0.50 to £5

South Western Board Permits

Annual £20. Three week £10. Day £3

Shannon Board Permits

Adult Annual £20. Day £5
Pensioner Annual £20. Day £5
Juvenile Annual £20. Day £1

Share Certificates

There are eight fisheries development societies in the country, and their purpose is to raise funds for the development of coarse and trout fishing. At present the Northern and Upper Shannon regions are the only ones where a share certificate is obligatory. Elsewhere their purchase is voluntary. Annual share certificate costs £12; 21 days: £5; 3 days: £3. They may be obtained from tackle shops.

The modified close seasons now in force for salmon, sea trout and brown trout differ not only as between regions, but also within regions, in a formulation too complex for reproduction here in detail. The general pattern is that seasons for migratory fish tend to open early and close early, while that for brown trout opens early in many places (Feb 15) and does not close until a date in October. There are, however, important exceptions and anglers proposing to visit the Republic, especially early or late in the year, should make careful enquiries with the appropriate Regional Board before making firm plans, whether the intention be to fish for salmon, migratory or brown trout.

There is no annual close season for angling for coarse fish or for sea fish.

Overall responsibility for the country's fisheries rests with the Department of the Marine, Leeson Lane, Dublin 2, tel: 01 678 5444, fax: 01 661 8241.

The Central Fisheries Board consists of the Chairman of the seven Regional Boards and from four to six members nominated by the Minister for the Marine. The functions of the Central Board are prescribed in the Fisheries Act 1980 and include such things as co-ordination and, where necessary, direction of the regional boards in the performance of their functions, which are: management, conservation, protection, development and promotion of inland fisheries and sea angling resources, and the protection of molluscs. Pollution, poaching and environmental incidents should be reported immediately to the appropriate regional board (*addresses below*).

The Central Fisheries Board owns and operates an important commercial and rod salmon fishery on the River Corrib at Galway, Co Galway (inquiries to the Manager, The Fishery, Nun's Island, Galway, Co Galway, tel: 091 562388), and the famous Erriff Fishery in Co Galway. Enquiries for fishing and accommodation here - at Aasleagh Lodge or Cottage - to the Manager, R Erriff Fishery, Aasleagh Lodge, Leenane, Co Galway (tel: 095 42252).

The Electricity Supply Board also holds extensive fishing rights: principal salmon waters are the River Mulcair and the Shannon at Parteen, above Limerick, and at Castleconnell, Co Limerick. The Board preserves and develops the fisheries under its control. Inquiries to Electricity Supply Board, Fisheries Division, Ardnacrusha, Co Clare (tel: 061 345588).

Inquiries about accommodation and general tourist angling information (e.g. leaflets, brochures about local angling resources and amenities throughout the country) should be addressed to **Bord Failte, Baggot Street Bridge, Dublin 2, tel: 01 602 4000, fax: 602 4100** or **The Irish Tourist Board, 150 New Bond Street, London W17 0AQ, tel: 0171 4933201**.

THE REGIONAL BOARDS

The Eastern Regional Fisheries Board. Covers all lakes and river systems entering the sea including coastal waters between Carlingford Lough, Co Louth and Kiln Bay, Co Wexford. Inquiries to: Regional Manager, Balnagowan House, Mobhi Boreen, Glasnevin, Dublin 9 (tel: 01 8379209, fax: 8360060).

The Southern Regional Fisheries Board. Covers all lakes and river systems entering the sea, including coastal waters, between Kiln Bay, Co Wexford and Ballycotton Pier, Co Cork. Inquiries to the Board's Regional Fisheries Manager, Anglesea St, Clonmel, Co Tipperary (tel: 052 23624, fax: 052 23971).

The South Western Regional Fisheries Board. Covers all lakes and river systems entering the sea, including coastal waters, between Ballycotton Pier, Co Cork and Kerry Head, Co Kerry. Inquiries to the Board's Regional Fisheries Manager, Nevilles Terrace, Massey Town, Macroom, Co Cork (tel: 026 41221/2; fax 026 41223).

The Shannon Regional Fisheries Board. Covers the inland fisheries of the Shannon catchment, the River Feale catchment in North Kerry and the rivers of Co Clare flowing westwards to the Atlantic. The coastal boundary stretches from Kerry Head, Co Kerry to Hag's Head, Co Clare. Inquiries to the Board's Regional Fisheries Manager, Thomond Weir, Limerick (tel: 061 455171, fax: 061 326533).

The Western Regional Fisheries Board. Covers all lakes and rivers entering the sea, including coastal waters, between Hag's Head, Co Clare and Pigeon Point, near Westport, Co Mayo. Inquiries to The Board's Regional Fisheries Manager, The Weir Lodge, Earl's Island, Galway City (tel: 091 563118/9, fax: 091 566335).

The North Western Regional Fisheries Board. Covers all lakes and rivers entering the sea, including coastal waters, between Pigeon Point, near Westport, Co Mayo, and Carrickgarve, Co Sligo. Inquiries to the Board's Regional Fisheries Manager, Ardnaree House, Abbey St, Ballina, Co Mayo (tel: 096 22788; fax: 096 70543).

The Northern Regional Fisheries Board. Covers all lakes and rivers entering the sea, including coastal waters, between Carrickgarve, Co Sligo and Malin Head, Co Donegal Inquiries to the Board's Regional Fisheries Manager, Station Road, Ballyshannon, Co Donegal (tel: 072 51435/ 52053; fax: 072 51816).

FISHING STATIONS IN IRELAND

Details of close seasons, licences, etc, for Irish rivers and loughs listed alphabetically here will be found in pages on the previous pages. Anglers wanting further details of accommodation should write to **Bord Failte (Irish Tourist Board), Baggot Street Bridge, Dublin, 2. Tel: 0602 4000, (4100 Fax)**. Anglers in the **Western Fisheries Region** should note the fact that the killing of sea trout is now illegal. **All sea trout must be returned alive to the water.**

BALLYSODARE and LOUGH ARROW

(For close seasons, licences, etc, see The Regional Fisheries Board).

River Ballysodare formed by junction of three rivers, **Unshin** or **Arrow, Owenmore** (not to be confused with Owenmore River, Co Mayo), and **Owenbeg**, near Collooney, flows into Ballysodare Bay. Near mouth of river, at Ballysodare Falls, is earliest salmon ladder erected in Ireland (1852). Salmon, trout, very few sea trout. R Arrow, which runs out of Lough Arrow, contains small stock of brown trout for which fishing is free. The Owenmore has good coarse fishing, especially bream, at Ballymote. Lough Arrow is a rich limestone water of 3,123 acres on the border of Sligo and Roscommon, situated 14 miles from Sligo town and 4 miles from Boyle. It is about 5m long and varies in width from ½m to 1½m. The lough is almost entirely spring-fed and has a place of honour among Ireland's best known mayfly lakes. Nowhere else is the hatch of fly so prolific or the rise so exciting. The brown trout rise to mayfly from late May to mid-June and sport is varied at this time by dapping, wet-fly and dry-fly fishing with green drake and the spent gnat. This is followed soon after (mid-July to mid-Aug) by a late evening rise to big sedge called the Murrough and Green Peter which may give the lucky angler as much fun as mayfly. The lough is regularly stocked with trout. Boats and ghillies may be hired at all seasons and at many centres on lake shore. **Loughs Bo** and **na Súil** are in close proximity, and ideal bank fishing for trout. Coarse fishing may be found nearby at **Lough Haugh, Temple House Lake, Ballanascarrow** (**Ballymote**), and the **Owenmore River**. Salmon may be fished at Ballysadare (10 miles from Lough Arrow). Permits for Loughs Bo and na Súil from Eileen McDonagh, Lough Bo. Boats: J Hargadon, (079 66050); R Acheson, (079 66181); F Dodd, (071 65065); D Grey, (071 65491). For information about Lough Arrow, contact Arrow Community Enterprises Ltd, tel: 071 65765; Lough Arrow Fish Preservation Society, tel: 079 66666/65065, 079 66181/66050; Lough Arrow District AC, tel: 071 65491. Tackle from Brian Flaherty, Boyle; Barton smith, Sligo. Accommodation in Lough Arrow area includes Cromleagh Lodge, Ballindoon, (079 65155); Rockview Hotel, Riverstown (079 66073/66077); Tower Hill B & B, Castlebaldwin, (079 66035).

Collooney (Co Sligo). Best season, May to July. Fishing dependent on sufficient rain. Permission to fish for sea and brown trout sometimes obtainable. Good dry fly. River contains sizeable pike. **Lough Bo** fished from here (*See above*).

Castlebaldwin via **Boyle** (Co Sligo). Trout fishing on L Arrow, free. Season 1 March-30 Sept. Bank fishing not recommended. Boats can be hired on lake shore from Dodd Boats, Ballindoon, and Annaghloy Boat Hire. L Arrow FPS fishes in Loughs **Arrow** and **Augh** (pike, perch, b trout in L Arrow). NWRFB permits required, season £12, £5 conc, daily £3-£1. **Lough Bo**, in hills provides good shore fishing for brown trout. Fly only. Season 1 April-30 Sept. **Lake na Leibe** has rainbow trout stocked by Central Fisheries Board. Season 1 April-30 Sept. Fishing from shore or boat. Good stock of brown trout in **Lough Feenagh**; boats for hire. River fishing on **R Unshin** and **R Feorrish** (above Ballyfarnon); trout. Coarse fishing on **Templehouse Lake** and **Cloonacleigha Lake**; good pike fishing; boats for hire. Coarse and trout fishing on **Lough Key**, 3m east of Arrow. Contact sec of L Arrow FPS (079 66666). Hotels: Cromleach Lodge, Rock View.

Boyle (Co Roscommon). L Arrow, trout, free; contact Fishery Inspector (079 66033) for information. **River Boyle**, a tributary of R Shannon, connects **Loughs Gara** and **Key**. Upstream of town are quality bream, rudd, perch, roach, eels, hybrid and brown trout. Downstream, pike are to be found. A short distance southwest at **Ballaghaderreen**, is the **Lung River** connected to **Breedoge**

Lough, and several other waters, among them **Loughs Cloonagh**, **Urlaur**, and **Cloonacolly**. This area holds some of the best coarse fishing in Ireland, with many species incl pike to 30lbs. Contact J Cogan, Ballaghaderreen AC (0907 60077). **Lough Nasool**, 13m north, contains rainbow trout, dt from Eileen McDonagh, (071 65325), beside lake. Tackle shops: Abbey Marine, Carrick Rd; Christy Wynne, Main St, who supplies live and ground bait; Boyle Tourist Office, (0796 2145); Martin Mitchell, Abbey House, (07962 62385), bait stockist; Michael Rogers, Ballymote. Accommodation for anglers: Mrs Mitchell, Abbey House, (079 62385), situated beside R Boyle, with fine game and coarse fishing within easy reach; Arrow Angling Accommodation, (079 66181/66050); Mrs Kelly, Forest Park, (079 62227); Arrow Lakeside Accommodation; Rockview Hotel, Ballindoon via Boyle, (079 66073).

BANDON

(For close seasons, licences, etc, see The South Western Regional Fisheries Board)

45 miles in length, rises in Sheshy Mountains and drains approx 235 square miles. Salmon fishing extends all the way from **Inishannon** u/s to **Togher Castle**, depending on conditions. An estimated 1,300 salmon are caught each season; about 300 of these are spring fish. Grilse run at end of June. Big run of sea trout from early July to end of Aug, and good stocks of browns. Fishing can be excellent on 4m stretch from Bandon to Innishannon. Ghillies are for hire. Season 15 Feb-30 Sept.

Bandon (Co Cork). About 7m double bank controlled by River Bandon Salmon and Trout AA. Dt £15, wt £75. Bag limit 6 fish, size limit 10in. Tickets from M J O'Regan, Oliver Plunkett St, Bandon (023 41674).

Ballineen (Co Cork). The 4m stretch of river to about 1m above Ballineen Bridge is controlled by Ballineen and Enniskeane AA; salmon and trout. St and dt from Tom Fehilly, Bridge Street, Ballineen. Kicoleman Fishery, Eniskeane, tel: 023 47279 (fax 47408), offers lodge accommodation and private fishing on Bandon with ten named salmon pools, and excellent stocks of wild brown trout. Season Feb 15-Sept 30, spate fishing, mainly fly only. Av salmon catch 103 per annum.

Dunmanway (Co Cork). Above Manch Bridge is Dunmanway Salmon and Trout AA water. Tickets from P MacCarthy, Yew Tree Bar, Dunmanway. River fishable for about 8m. Many small trout loughs in region, incl **Cullenagh** (4½m west), **Coolkeelure** (2¼m north west), **Ballynacarriga**, **Atarriff**, **Chapel Lake**; free fishing, small browns; for **Curraghalickey Lake**, contact P MacCarthy, *see above*.

CAHA RIVER. Joins Bandon 3m north of Dunmanway. Holds good stock of trout to 14 oz, for 3m up from confluence. Free fishing, best in early season, because of weed. Free fishing on **Neaskin Lough**, 3¼m north of Dunmanway. Difficult access, but plenty of 6oz browns.

Clonakilty (Co Cork). **River Argideen**, rises n.w. of Clonakilty, flowing into Courtmacsherry Harbour, rated among best sea trout rivers in SW Ireland, occasional salmon. Lower fishery owned or managed by Argideen AA. Maximum 6 rods per day, bag limit 10 trout, size limit 9in. Permits from Fishery Office, Inchy Bridge. Tackle shop: Jeffersports, South Main St, Bandon.

BARROW (including Suir and Nore)

(For close seasons, licences, etc, see The Southern Regional Fisheries Board)

A limestone river which has been underrated in its potential, and not heavily fished. The second longest in Ireland, it rises well in the centre of the country on the eastern slopes of the Shannon watershed and flows over 120m south to the sea at Waterford Harbour, entering by a long estuary. Upper river from Mountmellick is all game fishing, river south of Monasterevin, through Athy down to Carlow, mainly coarse fishing. Plentiful stocks including bream, rudd, eels, pike, and tench.

Waterford (Co Waterford). Reservoirs managed by SRFB, **Knockaderry** and **Ballyshunnock**: both 70 acres at normal level, with wild brown and stocked rainbow, 6 fish limit. Boats on Knockderry, no bank fishing, fly only, book in advance, (051 84107). All legal methods on Ballyshunnock, bank only, no maggot. Dt from Carrolls Cross Inn, (051 94328). **Mahon River** (15m) holds sea trout and salmon, and mackerel, bass and pollack abound along the coast.

Graighuenamanagh (Co Carlow). Good coarse fishing, with pike and large bream. Local venues are Tinnehinch Lower Weir and Bahanna. Contact J Butler, Tinnahinch, Graighuenamagh.

Carlow (Co Carlow). Bream, rudd, pike. Trout fishing on **Rivers Lerr, Greese, Douglas** and **Burren**, which fish well wet or dry, controlled by Barrow AC and restocked yearly (membership £2 from local tackle shops). Club: Carlow AA. Annual membership £2. Permits for Milford Weir to canal mouth d/s of Milford Bridge from Lock House, **Milford**. Tackle shops: Tully's Sports, Tullow St, Carlow; Byrne & Dawson, Main Street, Tullow. Accommodation: Royal Hotel; Mrs Quinn, Milford, (0503 46261).

Athy (Co Kildare). Trout, bream, rudd, pike. Several tributaries within easy reach. **R Greese**, from Dunlavin to Barbers Bridge, Kilkea, approx 8m, fishable on permit from Greese Anglers. Bream to 8lb are regularly caught in Barrow, as well as pike above 30lbs, perch, rudd and game fish. **Grand Canal** holds good head of tench, pike, perch, rudd and bream. There is some good free dry-fly water on left bank d/s of Athy, known as the Barrow Track. Kilberry & Cloney AC fish 5m **Boherbaun River** from Milltown Bridge to Forth of Dunrally Bridge, Vicarstown, eastside, (natural browns, 1-4lb); **Stradbally River**, 6m away, with trout; permits from Griffin Hawe (*below*). Vicarstown & Dist AC club waters extend on west side of R Barrow from Laois/Kildare border northwards to the Glasha River. Athy & Dis AC fishes Barrow to Maganey Lock. In Sept 1992 club released 20,000 brown trout into Barrow as part of a general improvement program. There are no fishing rights on Barrow, but a club card allows access from landowners. Membership £5 p.a. and accom list from tackle shop: Griffin Hawe, 22 Duke St, tel: 0507 31221 (fax 38885). Self-catering accom: Mrs C Crean, Vicarstown Inn (0502 25159; Mr Jim Crean, Milltown Cottage, tel: 0502 25189, fax: 0502 25652; many B & B in locality.

Portarlington (Co Laois). River at town is easily accessible, and holds some salmon from March. Portarlington AC has approx 6 miles of good dry fly trout fishing on **Upper Barrow**. Best mid-May to mid-Sept. Mountmellick AC has 7m, good trout, a few salmon. Bracknagh AC has approx 5 miles of the **Figile River**, a tributary of the Barrow. Mainly coarse, a few trout around Millgrove Bridge. St £5 for all these waters are readily obtainable from Portarlington AC treasurer Mr Pat Maher; Inchacooley, Monasterevin; or Mick Finlay, publican, Bracklone St. Another tributary, the **Cushina River**, north of **Monasterevin** is fished by Cushina AC: tickets from P Dunne, Clonsast, Rathangan. For general information about local fishing, and tickets, contact Mick Finlay (*above*); Kieran Cullen, Gun and Tackle, Monasterevin, (045 25902/25329); or Donegan, Tackle, Main St Portarlington.

GRAND CANAL (Co Kildare). Much free fishing. Canal runs through **Prosperous** and **Robertston** where it contains bream, rudd, tench, hybrids and some pike. Prosperous Coarse AC fishes on a length of some 20m. At **Edenderry**, Co Offaly, canal has large bream, tench, carp, rudd, roach, perch, eels. Edenberry Coarse AC controls 18m first class coarse angling. Fishing free, membership £10, £2 conc. Contact Pauric Kelly, Tackle Shop, 48 Murphy St, Edenderry, tel: 0405 32071 (home).

GRAND CANAL, BARROW BRANCH (Co Kildare and Co Laois). Fishing for bream, roach, tench, hybrids, rudd and pike, 5 minutes walk from **Rathangan**. Information from M J Conway, Caravan and Camping Park, Rathangan, (045 524331). At **Monasterevin** canal has pike, perch and bream. Contact Pat Cullen, Tackle Shop. At **Vicarstown**, Co Laois, fishing for bream, tench, pike and rudd. For permits, accom and information contact Jim Crean, Vicarstown Inn, Vicarstown (0502 25189). Naas tackle shop: Countryman Angling Ltd. Bait stockists: Griffin Hawe, Athy; Countryman Angling, Haas; Jim Cream.

SUIR

(For close seasons, licences, etc, see The Southern Regional Fisheries Board)

Considered to be one of Europe's finest dry fly trout rivers, with average trout size of ¾lb, and fish up to 3lb often caught. It is fairly shallow with deep glides, and drains large areas of limestone. Runs into the same estuary as Nore and Barrow, reaching sea at Waterford. Fishes best from mid-May to the end of September. Record salmon for Ireland, 57lb, was caught in Suir, in 1874. Salmon fishing opens on 1 March, and in good years large springers up to 25lb are caught. Grilse run usually begins in late May and continues to end of Sept. Late August and Sept often bring bigger fish, over 10lb. There are large stocks of wild brown trout in river, but they not easily caught, and best fished in faster glides, from May to mid-June. Season 1 Mar-30 Sept. A wide network of tributaries, excellent fishing in their own right, includes the Rivers Nire, Tar, and Anner (*see below*).

Carrick-on-Suir (Co Tipperary). Start of tidal water. **Duffcastle** to Carrick-on-Suir is last freshwater section, well stocked with trout. Carrick-on-Suir AA has north bank from Miloko to Duffcastle, also **Coolnamuck Fisheries**, 3 miles south bank, fishing for salmon, trout, twait shad. Tickets and ghillies though J O'Keeffe, *see below*. Free trout fishing on tributary **Lingaun River**, which runs from north into tidal water east of Carrick-on-Suir; landowners consent reqd. Up river there is good trout fishing and occasional sea trout; free for 400m on left bank d/s of **Kilsheelin**. 1½m south bank permits from Mrs Maura Long, Glencastle, Kilnasheelin, (052 33287); salmon and trout, £15, £5. About 4m to south mountain loughs, largest of which are **Coumshingaun** and **Crotty's**, provide very good fishing as also does **Clodiagh River**, which springs from loughs and is close to road for part of way. Good salmon and trout fishing from Carrick to Cashel. Most of river preserved for salmon, but some owners give permission to fish for trout. Tackle shop: O'Keeffe, OK Sports, New St, (051 40626). Hotel: Orchard House.

Clonmel (Co Tipperary). Moderate to good stocks of trout to 30cm. Free fishing between the bridges in town. Clonmel and Dist AC controls water from **Knocklofty Bridge** d/s one mile on south bank, also from Clonmel New Bridge to **Anner River**. Permits from J Carroll, 3 New Quay, Clonmel. Private fishing u/s of Knocklofty Bridge reserved for residents of Knocklofty House Hotel. Fishing on Marlfield Fisheries through Jean Loup Trautner, Marlfield Lodge, Clonmel (052 252340). Clonmel & Dist Salmon and Trout Anglers control fishing rights on both banks from Deerpark to Kilmanahan Castle. Permits from John Kavanagh (*below*). Further trout and salmon fishing in locality may be booked through Eileen Ryan, Clonanav Farm, Ballymacarbry, Clonmel (052 36141). At **Kilsheenan** left bank d/s is free fishing for 400m. 2m private salmon and trout fishing is obtainable from Mrs Maura Long, Glencastle, Kilsheelin (052 33787). Local tributaries of main river are **Nire** (mountain stream with trout av ½lb, to 6lb) **Tar** (lowland stream with exceptional fly life, densely populated with trout av ½lb), **Duag**, **Anner** (fast moving stream with good stocks of trout av ¾lb, very good fishing in early season by u/s nymph method). Andrew Ryan, Clonanav Angling Centre, Ballymacabry, Clonmel, (052 36141), offers accommodation and instruction, and arranges dry fly fishing on these, also Suir, Blackwater, and lakes. Nire Valley AC has 6m of **Nire**, st £5 from Mrs Wall, Hanoras Cottage, Ballymacarbry. Mountain loughs can also be reached from this centre. Tackle shop: Kavanagh's Sports Shop, Westgate, Clonmel. Hotels: Clonmel Arms; Hotel Minella.

Ardfinnan (Co Tipperary). Good numbers of trout to 30cm. Ardfinnan AC has much trout fishing in locality, d/s of Rochestown to Corabella. Permits from John Maher, Green View, Ardfinnan. Limited rods at Cloghardeen Fishery, Clogghardeen Farm.

Cahir (Co Tipperary). Cahir and Dist AA, controls Suir from Suir Castle, to Bakery Weir, and from Swiss Cottage to Carrigatuha. Salmon dt £5 and tackle from Mrs B Morrissey, Castle St; also left bank from Swiss Cottage down to Garnavilla ford. Shamrock Lodge offers permits on a short stretch of good fishing, left bank u/s of Rochestown. Tackle shop: Suirtackle, The Square, Cahir. Hotels: Cahir House, Galtee and Kilcoran Lodge; 8m salmon and trout water. Salmon and brown trout flies from E Heavey, Cahir Park. Hotels: Castle Court, Kilcoran Lodge.

Cashel (Co Tipperary). Brown trout and salmon. Cashel, Tipperary and Golden AA issues visitors' permits for 8m both banks **Suir** from Camas Bridge south to **Ballycarron Bridge**, fly only, wild brown trout to 2lb, dt £5, wt £15 from Mrs Ryan, Tackle Shop, Friar St, Cashel. Dundrum Dist AA fly fishes on **Marl Lake, Dundrum**. Permits from Dundrum House Hotel. Other hotels: Cashel Place; Ardmayle House; Baileys, Cashel, Ryans, and many excellent guest houses and B & Bs.

Thurles (Co Tipperary). Good centre for upper river trout fishing. Thurles, Holycross and Ballycamas AA has water from **Holycross** to Kileen Flats both banks, fly only. Dt £5 from Hayes Hotel. Club also fishes **R Clodiagh** and **R Drish**. Good stocks of trout to 40cms. U/s from Drish Bridge weeded in summer; d/s fishable throughout season, usually. Accommodation and permits: J & T Grene, Farm Guesthouse, Cappamurra House, Dundrum, 062 71127.

Templemore (Co Tipperary). Templemore AA water; visitors' dt for Suir (trout only, av ½lb).

BLACKWATER RIVER (Co Kilkenny). This tributary joins the Suir about 2 miles upstream of Waterford City. It is tidal as far as the weir below **Kilmacow**, and holds good stocks of small trout between Kimacow and **Mullinavat**. Some fishing with landowners consent. Enquire at local tackle shops.

PORTLAW CLODIAGH (Co Waterford). Tributary, which joins **Suir** east of Portlaw. Moderate trout stocks. Fishing rights on entire river owned by the Marquis of Waterford, but fishing is open u/s of **Lowrys Bridge** and d/s of **Portlaw**.

ARA/AHERLOW (Co Tipperary). Tributary joins Suir north of Cahir, flowing from a westerly direction. Significant numbers of trout to 28 cm. Ara AC has trout fishing from **Tipperary Town** to **Kilmyler Bridge**, where R Ara meets R Aherlow; fly, spinning or worming, wt £5, from J Evans, Main St, Tipperary.

NORE

(For close seasons, licences, etc, see The Southern Regional Fisheries Board)

River rises in Co Tipperary, flows east through Borris-in-Ossory and then south through Kilkenny to join River Barrow near New Ross, about 8 miles south of Inistioge. 87 miles long with a total catchment of 977 square miles, Nore is a limestone river with abundant fly life. Because the salmon fishing is good, the trout fishing is somewhat neglected, although trout are plentiful in the river. Mills and weirs are a feature of this river, and long deep stretches provide excellent dry fly fishing even in low water.

Thomastown (Co Kilkenny), Thomastown AA has excellent salmon and trout stretch of Nore and issues temporary cards to visitors. Trout fishing is fly or worm only. Inistioge AC controls 3m both banks both banks at **Inistioge**. Salmon, sea trout, brown trout and eels. Visitors are welcome, salmon dt £5, 1 Feb-30 Sept. Brown Trout dt £3, 1 Mar-30 Sept, from Castle Inn, Inistioge. Tel: 05658 483. Tanguy de Toulgoet, Moyne Estate, Durrow, has fishing here and at Kilkenny, Durrow, Rathdowney, Kells and Callan, with instruction, and his own flies. Dry fly catch and release, permits through local clubs. Tel/Fax: 0502 36578.

Kilkenny (Co Kilkenny). Kilkenny AA has some excellent salmon and trout fishing on **Nore**, left bank from **Dinin R** to **Greenville** weir, and from **Maddockstown** to 1m u/s of **Bennetsbridge**; also **Dinin R**, Dinin Bridge to Nore. Assn issues permits to visitors, from P Campion, Tackle Shop, Kilkenny. Durrow & Dist AC fishes from **Watercastle Bridge** to **Owveg** confluence, and **Erkina R** from **Durrow Castle** to R Nore. Dt from Susan Lawlor, Foodmarket, The Square, Durrow (0502 36437). Rathdowney AC fishes approx 4m of **Erkina R** from local meat factory to **Boston Bridge**, early season best for open fishing, May-Sept for fly. Brown trout from 8oz to 2lb, dt £2 from M White, Moorville, Rathdowney. **Kings River**; good brown trout. Free fishing at Ballinakill Lake: good tench, perch, rudd, pike. New coarse fishery at Grandtown Lake: Mat Doyle, Grandtown, Ballacolla, Portlaoise. Tackle shops: M McGrath, 3 Lower Patrick Street, Kilkenny; Kilkenny Sports Scene,

1 Irishtown, Kilkenny. Hotels: Castel Arms, The Durrow Inn, both Durrow. B & B, James Joyce, The Square, Durrow..

Abbeyleix (Co Laois). Abbeyleix & Dist AC fishes from **Shanahoe Bridge** to **Waterloo Bridge**, dt from V Bowell, Sandymount, Abbeyleix. Self-catering gate lodge and apartments, Mrs Shirley Seale, The Glebe, Attanagh, Portlaoise.

Mountrath (Co Laois). Nore; brown trout, pike, perch, roach, eels. Mountrath & Dist AC stocks and fishes Nore main channel from Nore/**Delour** confluence to New Bridge at **Donore**, and **Whitehorse River**, which runs through town. Permits £4 to £1 tourists from Hon Sec Tom Watkins, 0502 32540. Tackle and salmon permits from Mrs Kelly, Main St. Accommodation: Mrs Geraldine Guilfoyle, Redcastle, 0502 32277; Mrs Fiona Wallis, Coote Terrace, 0502 32756.

KINGS RIVER (Co Kilkenny). Tributary which joins Nore above Thomastown. Callan & Dist AA fishes from Metal Bridge, 2½m u/s of Callan to Newton Bridge, 2½m d/s. Dt from Chris Vaughan, Green St, Callan. Kells AC also has water: permits, enquire locally.

BLACKWATER

(For close seasons, licences, etc, see The Southern Regional Fisheries Board)

Perhaps most famous salmon river in the Republic. Rises west of Killarney Mountains and flows eastward about 70m until it reaches town of Cappoquin, where it becomes tidal and turns sharply south, entering sea by estuary 15m long at Youghal Bay. Salmon (best stretches mainly between Mallow and Lismore), sea trout, brown trout, but large quantities of dace, roach, perch and pike in some parts. Best fishing strictly preserved. Big runs of spring salmon from Feb to April; grilse June to Sept; and often good run of autumn salmon during Aug and Sept. Sea trout in Blackwater and Bride, June onwards.

Youghal (Co Cork). Youghal Sea AC has fishing on main river and tributaries. All arrangements through secretary. At **Castlemartyr** on Cork/Youghal road is **Lough Aderry**, rainbow trout fishery, 6 fish limit, fly, worm and spinning.

Cappoquin (Co Waterford). The freshwater here is backed up by the tide and fishing is best when the water is either rising or falling. Salmon and trout, good coarse fishing for roach and dace throughout year but best autumn and spring. Cappoquin Salmon & Trout AC have 4 miles of water on both sides of town. Day tickets £12-£15, wt £60-£70, depending on season, from tackle shop. Good stocked tench fishing at **Dromana Lake**, south of Cappoquin. Trout fishing on **Rivers Owenshed** and **Finisk** and on R Blackwater downstream of **Lismore Bridge**; permits from Lismore Estate Office, Lismore Castle, Lismore, 058 54424. Lismore Estate now lets two stretches of Blackwater to Lismore Salmon AA. These are 1½m starting d/s from Lismore Bridge, and 1⅓m going u/s from Lismore Weir. Permits may be bought from John O'Gorman's Newsagents, Main St, Lismore. Tackle shop: Tight Lines Tackle & Gift Shop, Main St. Hotels: Richmond House; Ballyrafter House, Lismore, 058 54002. Anglers accommodation: 'The Toby Jug'; Flynn's River View Guesthouse, 058 54073.

Upper Ballyduff (Co Waterford). Ballyduff Trout FAA has approx 3m east of bridge and 3m west, both banks. Restricted to local club members only. Private salmon fishing at Blackwater Lodge Hotel, Upper Ballyduff, tel: 058 60235 (fax 60162) *(see advt)*; a complete service to the visiting angler, with 17 beats covering 40 miles of river, (dt £35-£60), self-catering accommodation, tackle, smokery and ghillies at hotel. Tackle shop: Bolger's, Ballyduff.

Conna (Co Cork). Beats owned by Mrs Green, Ballyvolane House, Castlelyons, Co Cork, and Mrs McCarthy, Elgin Cottage, Ballyduff, Co Waterford (058 60255).

Fermoy (Co Cork). Salmon, brown trout, dace, roach, perch, gudgeon and pike. Four coarse fishing beats are open by courtesy of Fermoy Salmon AA, best being Barnane Walk, Jones Field and Hospital bank. Permits from Toomey's, *see below*. Salmon fishing on R Blackwater at **Careysville Fishery**, 1¾m stretch, both banks with well defined pools. One of the most prolific salmon fisheries in the country. Grilse run in June. Fishing peaks on the lower beats in June and on the rest of river in July. Max 2 to 4 rods per day depending on month. Ghillie price included in fishing charges.

Permits from Careysville House (025 31094) or Lismore Estates Office (058 54424). Stretches near town which hold roach and dace; waters accessible and banks well kept. For information on coarse fishing contact John Mulvihill (Competition Secretary and Live Bait) 3 Casement Row, Fermoy, tel: 025 32425, or Brian Toomey, Sports Shop & Fishing Tackle, 18 McCurtain St, Fermoy, tel: 025 31101. U/s of Fermoy are ten miles of salmon beats owned by Merrie Green, Ballyvolane House, Castlelyons, tel: 025 36349, with beats at Ballyduff, Fermoy, Ballyhooly and Killavullen. Fishing Feb-Apr, May-Sept, spring run Apr/May. Accommodation, tackle, and ghillies. Chest waders recommended. Local facilities for smoking or freezing salmon. **Araglin** holds brown trout; good dry fly. **Funshion (Funcheon)** runs in near Careysville on north bank; trout, dace, rudd. Contact Peter Collins, tel: 022 25205. Hotel: Grand. B & B information from Slatterly Travel, 10 Pearse Sq, Fermoy, tel: 025 31811.

Mallow (Co Cork). Salmon fishing from 1 Feb to end of Sept; trout 15 Feb to end of Sept. Coarse fishing for dace, roach, pike. Mallow Trout Anglers have 4m both banks, salmon, trout, dace and roach. Dt for this and for other private beats from tackle shop; coarse fishing free. Information from the Bridge House Bar. Tackle shop: Pat Hayes, the Spa, Mallow. Hotels; Hibernian; Central.

BRIDE. This tributary of the Blackwater holds salmon and sea trout as well as brown trout, also dace.

Tallow (Co Waterford). River is 500 yds from town. Tallow & Dist AC have 4½m fishing from Mogeely Bridge to Bride Valley Fruit Farm. Brown trout, sea trout; salmon and peal from June onwards. Fly only between Mogeely and Tallow Bridges, otherwise, maggot, worm, etc. There is also coarse fishing for big dace and roach. Visiting anglers welcome. St (£10) and dt (£5) from Treasurer, Alan Sivyer, Bride View Bar, tel: 56522, or tackle shops: John Forde; Dan Delaney, both Main St; Peter Dempster, Conna. Ghillie service: Lonnie Corcoran, Ballyduff. Hotels: Bride View Bar; Devonshire Arms.

AWBEG. Tributary which runs into the Blackwater midway between Mallow and Fermoy. A very good trout stream, especially for dry fly.

BOYNE

(For close seasons, licences, etc, see The Eastern Regional Fisheries Board)

Rises near Edenderry and flows for about 70m, entering the sea near Drogheda north of Dublin. One of Ireland's premier game fisheries, in main channel and tributaries. Good salmon fishing between Navan and Drogheda. Excellent run of sea trout as far up river as Slane Bridge. Superb stocks of brown trout in Boyne and tributaries. Virtually no free fishing, but permits are sold on many club waters. Contact Joint Council of Boyne Anglers, Mrs T Healy, Little Grange, Drogheda, tel: 041 24829. Fishable tributaries include **Rivers Trimblestown** (small browns), **Kells Blackwater** (trout, u/s of Headford Bridge), **Borora** (7m good trout fishing from Corlat d/s to Carlanstown), **Martry** (small stream, trout to 1lb), **Stoneyford** (excellent trout water, Rathkenna Bridge to Shanco Bridge), **Deel** (a few salmon at Riverdale, trout), **Little Boyne** (spring trout fishery, club based at Edenberry), **Nanny** (sea trout up to Julianstown, browns to Balrath Bridge).

Drogheda (Co Louth). Drogheda and District AC has prime salmon and sea trout fishing below Oldbridge and u/s at Donore, and **Nanny**; and also **Reservoirs Killineer** and **Barnattin** which are stocked with brown and rainbow, and Rosehall, a mixed coarse fishery. Permits £10-£6, conc, from Mr Ace, Tackle Shop, 8 Laurence St. Lower parts of Boyne and Mattock preserved. Brown trout in two reservoirs; St from Drogheda Corporation. Hotels: Central, White Horse,

Truly wild fish. The class of trout for which anglers from all over Europe visit Ireland. *Photo: Trout and Salmon.*

Boyne Valley, Rosnaree, Cooper Hill House (Julianstown).

Navan (Co Meath). Salmon and sea trout. Navan Angler's Fishery consists approx 10m of single and double bank fishing on R Boyne and 1m on R Blackwater. Hotels: Central and Russell Arms.

Slane (Co Meath). Slane, Rossin & Dist AC have salmon and sea trout fishing at Oldbridge, also excellent salmon and brown trout below Slane. Dt £10, juv £5, From Sec, Ray Foster, tel: 01 8315406, or Mr Ace, Tackle Shop, *see Drogheda*. Hotel: Conyngham Arms.

Trim (Co Meath). Good trout in main river and tributaries. Trim, Athboy and Dist AA preserves and restocks **Athboy River** and some stretches on Boyne itself; st £16; dt £5. Concessions to jun and OAP, from sec. Deel and Boyne AA has trout and salmon water on tributary **Deel**. Longwood Anglers also have salmon and trout fishing on Boyne. Hotel: Wellington Court; Brogans Guest Accommodation.

Kells (Co Meath). Good trout fishing on **River Blackwater**, a tributary of R Boyne, dry fly. Mayfly fishing good. 15m preserved and restocked by Kells AA; permits from Tom Murray, *below*. Trout up to 7lb may be had in the river, also large pike and salmon, 1½m of free fishing from source. Hotel: Headford Arms. Tackle shop: Tom Murray, Shooting & Fishing, Carrick St.

Virginia (Co Cavan). On headwaters of R Blackwater. Lough Ramor gives good trout fishing and excellent fishing for bream, roach, perch and pike; boats for hire, two tributaries. Ten lakes and four rivers within 5m; trout and coarse fish. Virginia Coarse AC has fishing on **Lough Ramor**, with large bream, pike above 25lbs, 200lbs catches of coarse fish per day recorded. Membership £10 per annum, conc. Other fisheries: **Lisgrea Lake** (all species); and **Rampart River** (roach, perch and bream). **Mullagh Lake** is a popular pike fishery. For further information contact Pat McCabe, Rahardrum (049 47649); Nattie Dogherty, Salmon Lodge, Main St; and Edward Tobin, Mullagh Rd. Accommodation: Mrs McHugho, White House, tel: 049 47515; P & M Geraghty, Knocknagarton, tel: 049 47638, both Virginia. To north east, **Bailieboro** is an ideal centre for coarse fishing, with innumerable lakes within easy reach, incl **Castle, Parker's, Gallincurra, Galboly, Drumkeery, Skeagh, Town, Gallin,** good coarse fishing with pike, perch, roach, bream, tench, rudd, and others, and under-fished. Virginia AC local club. Bailieboro tackle shop: Raymond Lloyd, Main St. Baailieboro hotels include Bailie; Droimlinn, Kells Rd; Hilltop Lodge, Corkish Lane.

BUNDROWES RIVER AND LOUGH MELVIN

(For close seasons, licences, etc, see The Northern Regional Fisheries Board)

About 4m south of Erne, the Bundrowes River carries water of Lough Melvin to sea in Donegal Bay. The entire 6 mile river is open to anglers except for private stretch from Lareen Bay to the Four Masters Bridge. For accommodation and information, contact T Gallagher (*see below under Kinlough entry)*. The lough is 8m by 2m, approx 5,000 acres; part of it is free and part under private ownership. It is renowned for its three different species of trout, these being sonnaghan, gilaroo and ferrox. Good run of big spring salmon in Feb and March; smaller fish arrive in April and May; grilse in late May and run right through to June. Best time for fly fishing for salmon late April to end June. Trolling baits, where permitted, takes place from early Feb.

Bundoran (Co Donegal). Salmon, trout. Bundrowes R, 1½m, and west end L Melvin, 3m. Salmon season 1 Jan-30 Sept (Bundrowes); 1 Feb-30 Sept (Melvin). **Bunduff River**, 3½m from Bundoran, flows 8m to enter Donegal Bay near Castlegal; salmon, brown trout. Best salmon, June to Aug. Brown trout in upper reaches. Bunduff Angling Syndicate has water; dt £12 from Mrs Kathleen McGloin, The Shop, Bunduff Bridge, Co Leitrim. Also Kinlough Anglers, c/o John Fahy, Kinlough. Tackle shops: Mrs McGloin (*above*); Pat Barrett, Main St; Rogans, Bridgend, Ballyshannon, Co Donegal. Hotels: Allingham; Foxes Lair.

Kinlough (Co Leitrim). Salmon, grilse, trout. Season for spring salmon, Jan to Apr; grilse, sea trout, May to Sept. Boats and tickets for **Bundrowes** fishing at Drowes and Lareen Fisheries from Thomas Gallagher, Lareen Angling Centre, Kinlough (072 41208); Thomas Kelly (072 41497). Tackle shop: The

Lough Ramor at sunset. Ten miles of accessible shore-line fishing.*Photo: Marese Callaghan*

Fishery Office, Lareen Park.

Rossinver (Co Leitrim). Salmon, grilse, sonaghan and gillaroo trout. Rossinver Bay, strictly fly only. All legal methods elsewhere. Ghillies in vicinity. Dt £10, boat, engine and 2 rods £28, from Peter Bradley, Rossinver Fishery, Eden Quay (072 54201). Part of Lough Melvin is in Northern Ireland and is served by village of Garrison (Co Fermanagh). Tickets and boats for Garrison AC fishing from Sean Maguire, Tackle shop, Garrison.

CLARE

Flows into **Lough Corrib**, near Galway, and was considered one of best spawning streams for Galway River fish. Best season: Spring salmon, mid-April to mid-May; grilse, third week June to third week July; brown trout, April to June. Holds large trout and suitable for dry fly.

Galway (Co Galway). For lower reaches. 25m W of Galway on coast road is Carraroe Hotel; sea and lake fishing. Permits from WRFB, tel: 091 63112; Mr S Martin, Esso Station, Galway Rd, Tuam, tel: 093 24151; P Balfe, Corofin, tel: 093 41715. The Buckley Family, Spiddal House, Spiddal, tel: 091 83395, controls north bank from Corrib to Kiniska Bridge, and also south bank from 1m above Galway/Headford road to Claregalway village. Corrofin AA and St Colman's AC, both Corofin, have salmon fishing on R Clare. Contact secretaries.

Tuam (Co Galway). For upper waters. Tuam and Dist AA controls Clare River from Gardenfield, several miles u/s of Tuam, to Clonmore Bridge, also left bank d/s at Turloughmartin, for 930 yds past Grange junction. **Castlegrove Lake**; pike, perch, bream, rudd.

Tributaries of the Clare.

ABBERT. Enters from east, 7m south of Tuam. Good trout fishing, with excellent fly hatches. Brown trout of 3lb regularly taken, and salmon in flood conditions. The best angling is at Ballyglunin junction with Clare.

GRANGE. Joins Clare from east, 4m south of Tuam. Brown trout and salmon in lower reaches. U/s of Castlemoyle for a distance of 3m is a very good area for large brown trout. Salmon when in spate.

SINKING. Enters from east, 8m north of Tuam. Salmon may be taken in lower reaches, following flood conditions anytime after the end of May, but primarily a brown trout fishery, the best areas being from Dunmore as far as Cloonmore. Good fly hatches. **DALGAN**. Runs into Sinking. Stocks of brown trout, salmon may be caught from the end of May, depending on water conditions.

Co. CLARE (streams and loughs)

A number of salmon and sea trout rivers and streams run from Co Clare to the Shannon estuary or to the west coast. Most of them offer free fishing, with landowners permission. Trout and coarse fishing lakes abound in the East Clare 'lakeland' and in the south west. The rivers are listed here in their geographical order, westwards from Limerick.

BUNRATTY. Enters Shannon at Bunratty Castle, and holds a small stock of ½lb brown trout; modest grilse and sea trout run, best in June/July, from tide to D'Esterres Bridge, 3m. Free fishing. At source, **Doon Lough** nr Broadford, is a fine coarse fishery with large bream and other species; boats on hire locally. Several other coarse fishing Loughs in region: **Rosroe** and **Fin**, nr Kilmurry: pike over 20lb, from boat; **Cullaun**, 400 acres, 2m from **Kilkishen**, specimen pike and large bream, best from boat; just south, **Stones Lough:** big tench. As well as these, there are other less accessible lakes for the angler to explore. Further north east is another notable group of coarse fishing loughs: **Kilgory**, nr **O'Callaghan's Mills**, with large bream; 4m West of Tulla are **Bridget Lough** and others, with pike, perch, rudd, bream, tench, roach, hybrids; by **Scarriff**, **O'Grady (Canny's Lough),** shallow water, difficult access, but good bream fishing, with pike, tench and big rudd; and **Keel Lough,** inaccessible and unfished, with large tench, bream and rudd. On the **Scarriff River,** shoals of good bream and pike, easily accessible. On **R Graney** is **Lough Graney, Caher,** at 1,000 acres the biggest lake in the county with abundant perch, bream, pike, rudd and eel, boat essential, on hire at Caher and Flagmount. **Tulla** is central to much lake fishing: north are **Loughs Clondanagh** and **Clondoorney**, easily accessible with rudd, with pike and perch. At **Kilkishen** are **Loughs Cullaunyheeda, Avoher, Doon, Rathluby, Clonlea**, and others, with similar species.

RINE (QUIN RIVER). Runs from the lakes of East Clare to the estuary of the **Fergus**. Fishing similar to Bunratty; about 5m fishing from Latoon Bridge u/s to Quin. Permission to fish **Dromoland Castle** water from Rec. Manager, tel: 061 71144. Castle also has 20 acre lough in grounds, stocked trout fishery. Rest of fishing free. A few miles SE of Rine are **Loughs Caherkine, Fin, Ballycar, Rosroe, Teereen, Castle** (at **Kilmurry**) and others, with pike, perch, bream and rudd.

FERGUS. This medium-sized, limestone river with several loughs along its course, rises in Burren region of North Clare and flows southward to join Shannon at Newmarket-on-Fergus. Holds good stocks of brown trout, av ¾lb, with fish to 3½lb. Good dry fly water, both banks fish well for trout, best in Feb-May and Sept. Pike fishing also good. Approx 200 spring salmon and grilse each year, salmon Feb-March, grilse June-Sept, from Ennis u/s. Much free fishing in **Corofin** locality. **Loughs Dromore** and **Ballyline**. 6m east of Ballyline; limestone waters with trout to 5lb. Best March-May and Sept. Free fishing, boat hire, contact M Cleary, Lakefield Lodge, Corofin, tel: 065 37675. **Ballyteige Lough:** 50 acre limestone fishery, trout to 7lb. Best in March/Apr, at dusk in June/July. Boat necessary; contact M Cleary. **Inchiquin Lough,** 280 acres: excellent stock of wild browns, av 1¼lb. Fishes well in early season, and Sept. Boats from Burkes Shop, Main St, Corofin, tel: 065 37677. **Lough Cullaun** (Monanagh Lake): limited stock of big trout; also a good pike fishery. Trolling popular method. **Muckanagh Lough (Tullymacken Lough):** 60 acre shallow lake with good trout and pike. Boat necessary. Boats through M Cleary for both these loughs. **Lough Atedaun**, 1m from Corofin, has excellent fishing for large pike, tench and rudd. Best fished from boat. **Lough Ballycullinan**, 1½m from Corofin, has good stocks of large pike, perch, bream, tench and hybrids. Boat essential. Contact Burke's, Corofin, tel: 065 37677. **Ballyeighter Lough**: a rich limestone water which holds pike, rudd and large tench. On this water in 1994, Mr Nick Parry of Tubber broke Irish record with 7lb 15¼oz tench, then broke his own record with one 8lb 2oz (June 1995).

CLOON. This small river enters north east corner of Clonderalaw Bay. It gets a sea trout run in June/July, and is fishable for 2m d/s of new bridge on secondary road. Free fishing. Nearby trout loughs are **Knockerra**, 50 acres, **Gortglass**, 80 acres, and **Cloonsneaghta**, 30 acres. Boat hire on Gortglass (M Cleary, tel: 065 37674), free fishing on all.

DOONBEG. A better known salmon and sea trout river, rising in Lissycasy, flowing west to the sea at Doonbeg. Small spring salmon run, fair grilse and sea trout from June. Overgrown in places; best fishing on middle and upper reaches. Free with permission. For **Knockerra Lough,** *see Kilrush, under Shannon.*

CREEGH. Small spate river, running to west coast north of the Doonbeg, on which 150 to 200 grilse are taken each season. Small brown trout, and sea trout under the right conditions. Free fishing. Near Kilmihil is **Knockalough**, with good stock of small browns. Boat is helpful; dapping with daddy-long-legs in Aug/Sept. Free fishing.

ANNAGEERAGH. Runs into **Lough Donnell**. Sea trout fishing at dusk for about 1m u/s of lough in June/July. Sea trout fishing and a few grilse in rest of river. **Doo Lough,** 220 acres, a little north west of Glenmore, holds good stock of small browns.

Check before you go

*While every effort has been made to ensure that the information given in **Where to Fish** is correct, the position is continually changing, and anglers are urged, in their own interests, to make enquiries before travelling to selected venues. This is especially important with reference to prices quoted. Anglers attention is also drawn to the fact that hotels mentioned under the various fishing stations do not necessarily have water of their own. Any amendments or further data for inclusion in subsequent editions, and any comments, will be welcome.*

KILDEEMEA. A small spate river which enters sea 2m south west of **Miltown Malbay**. Excellent sea trout, to 3lb. Best June/July, fishable over ½m stretch on south bank from Ballaclugga Bridge u/s. Fly and spinner, fly best at night. Free fishing.

CULLENAGH (INAGH). This river is a good coarse fishery for 8m from Inagh towards sea. Open banks for pike and rudd fishing, easily accessible. Near village, **Inagh Loughs** contain good numbers of small brown trout. Free fishing. 2m west of Inagh, **Lough Caum**, 45 acres, pike fishery, boat fishing only. Contact M Fitzgerald, Fishing Tackle, Strand St, Castlegregory, (066 39133), or Landers Leisure Lines, Courthouse Lane, Tralee, (066 71178).

DEALAGH. Joins sea from north east at Liscannor. Spate river with sea trout and grilse in June/July. Sea trout best at night, between first and fourth bridges u/s from tidal water. Free, with permission. **Lickeen Lough,** 200 acres, 2m south of **Kilfenora**, contains small wild browns and stocked rainbows to 2lb. Boat for hire. Contact John Vaughan, sec of Lickeen Trout AA, tel: 065 71069.

AILLE. Small spate river running from **Lisdoonvarna** to **Doolin**. Stock of 14" browns, moderate grilse and sea trout. Best between Roadford and Lisdoonvarna; access difficult, banks overgrown. Free fishing.

CORK South West (rivers and loughs)

ARGIDEEN. Runs from west, above Clonakilty, and enters sea at **Timoleague**. A sea trout river, most of which is jointly managed by Argideen AA and SWRFB. Best methods are single worm by day, or fly at night. Tickets from P Wolstenholme, tel: 023 46239, or SWRFB, tel: 026 41222. Fishing with accommodation is obtainable from Tim Severin, Argideen River Lodges, Inchy Bridge, Timoleague, tel: 023 46127 (fax 46233). To west of river, **Lough Atariff**, permission from P McCarthy, Dunmanway Salmon & Trout AC, Yew Tree Bar, Dunmanway; and **Curraghalicky Lake**, free fishing. Both with good stock of small wild brown trout.

ILEN. A medium sized spate river about 21 miles long, scenically pretty, rising on watershed of Bantry district and flowing into sea through long estuary, from Skibbereen. Spring salmon from late March. Main salmon runs in Apr-Jun. Average size 10lb. Good grilse run from mid-June. Sea trout begin in February, August is the most prolific month, fish run from ½lb to over 4lb. Fly, spinning and worming are practised. Prawn and shrimp not permitted.

Skibbereen (Co Cork). R Ilen AC has 6m fishing on river, with salmon and sea trout. Tickets (dt £15, wt £60) from Fallons (*below*). 3m east, stocked rainbow and wild brown trout fishing on **Shepperton Lakes**, 35 and 15 acres, with boats; st and dt from E Connolly, Shepperton, Skibbereen (028 33328). West nr Schull is **Schull Reservoir**, 5 acres, small native browns and stocked rainbows. Both these are SWRFB fisheries. 2m north of **Leap**, **Ballin Lough**: wild stock supplemented with brown trout fingerlings and limited number of 2 year-olds, by Ballin Lough AC. Boats and tickets at lough, season 1 Apr-30 Sept. Information from Sec, Jim Maxwell, tel: 028 33266, or HQ, Bee Hive Bar, Connonagh, Leap. 3m south west of Dunmanway is **Garranes Lake**, 25 acres, Stocked rainbows and wild browns. Jointly run by SWRFB and Dunmanway & Drinagh AA. Dt and boats from G Carolan, Filling Station, Garranes, Drimoleague. 3m south of Leap, **Lough Cluhir**, free fishing on small lough for tench, pike and roach. Tackle shop: Fallon's Sports Shop, 20 North Street, Skibbereen. Full range of accommodation, from T.I. Office, North St (028 21766).

Bantry (Co Cork). Bantry Salmon & Trout AC fishes **Lough-Bo-Finne**, or **Bofinne**, 3m east of Bantry, 25 acres, first class rainbow and brown trout fishery, stocked weekly by Fisheries Board. Tickets (st £20, dt £3) from Sports Shop or from Mrs P Spillane, The Bungalow, Lough-Bo-Finne. Tackle shops; Vickery's Store; McCarthy's Sports Shop, all Main St, Bantry. Hotels; West Lodge; Vickry's; Bantry Bay Hotel.

MEALAGH. 1m north of Bantry, salmon and sea trout. Free except for bottom pool below falls.

OUVANE and **COOMHOLA**. Small spate rivers which run into north east Bantry Bay. Salmon and sea trout, the latter declined in Ouvane, better in Coomhola R. Ouvane has four good pools in first mile, and three more below Carriganass Falls. Coomhola has a good supply of brown trout. Coomhola Anglers, O'Brien's Shop, Coomhola Bridge, Bantry, offer permits to fish some 20 pools.

GLENGARRIFF. This small river flows into Bantry Bay at north east end through one of Ireland's most beautiful national parks, and has good salmon fishing when in spate, and trout. Rights are held by Glengarriff AA, who offer dt £7 river, (£5 for loughs, *see below*), conc, from Bernard Harrington, Vintner, Glengarriff. Limited tackle from Shamrock Stores and Maureen's, Glengarriff. Hotels incl Eccles; Caseys.

BEARA PENINSULA. (Co Cork). **Adrigole River** runs into Bantry Bay on north side: 6m long spate river with grilse and sea trout, controlled by Kenmare AA. Contact J O'Hare, 21 Main St, Kenmare, tel: 064 41499. Beara AA has tickets for local lough fishing. Ramor Craigie (027 63522) has tickets for salmon and trout fishing. **Upper** and **Lower Loughs Avaul** contain wild brown trout, and are stocked with rainbows, fish to 17lb being caught. Tickets £5, conc, from Glengarriff AA, c/o M Harrington, Mace Supermarket, Castletownbere, B Harrington, Bar Glengarriff. High in the Caha Mountains, south west of Glengarriff, free fishing on **Loughs Eekenohoolikeaghaun** and **Derreenadovodia**, and **Barley Lake**, 100 acres: small wild brown trout. Other small loughs in area with similar stock: **Glenkeel, Moredoolig, Begboolig, Shanoge** (larger fish, many over 1lb). Best in April/May and Sept. South of **Ardgroom** is **Glenbeg Lough,** leased by Berehaven AA. Big stock of small browns; tickets from Harrington, *see above* Hotel: Ford Rí, Castletownbere (027 70379) has local fishing information.

CORRIB SYSTEM

(For close seasons, licences, etc, see The Western Regional Fisheries Board)

River Corrib drains Lough Corrib and runs 5½m to Galway Bay passing virtually through the city of Galway. Salmon, trout. Salmon fishing very good. For particulars as to present conditions and rods apply Central Fishery Board, Nuns Island, Galway. Best fishing for springers early in season; grilse, May-June. Rods let by the day or by week.

Galway (Co Galway). Salmon fishing at Galway Fishery, situated in City of Galway, less than 1m from sea. Applications to The Manager, Galway Fishery, Nun's Island, Galway, tel: 091 562388. Dt £30 to £16, depending on season. The flow of the river is controlled by a regulating weir and the short stretch down stream of the weir is the salmon angling water. **Kilcolgan River** (10m E) part tidal, salmon and sea trout. WRFB controls 645 yards of north bank in town land of Stradbally East. Dt £3, from WRFB, tel: 091 63118. Tackle shops: Freeney's, 19 High St.

LOUGH CORRIB

This, the largest lough in the Republic is 65 square miles of water, and dotted with islands, around which are shallows that make for good fishing. Specially noted for large brown trout, each season a number of specimen fish are taken, and the record stands at 22lb. The lough is so immense that anglers unfamiliar with it will do best using the services of a local ghillie. Trout fishing opens on Feb 15 and is mainly by trolling until April. Wet fly good in April and early May, but lough best known for dapping with mayfly (beginning in mid-May) and daddy-long-legs (mid-July to end of season). Some dry-fly fishing on summer evenings. Salmon taken mainly by trolling, and in June on wet fly in many of the bays. Also big pike and other coarse fish in Corrib, so that angling of some kind is possible all year. Fishing free, but salmon licence required. Many hotels issue licences. Boats and boatmen at Portacarron,

Keep the banks clean

Several clubs have stopped issuing tickets to visitors because of the state of the banks after they have left. Spend a few moments clearing up, this includes lengths of broken nylon. If discarded, serious injuries can be caused to wild birds and to livestock.

Oughterard, Baurisheen, Derrymoyle, Glan Shore, Cong, Greenfields, Doorus, Carrick, Salthouse, Carey's and Inishmacatreer. A detailed angling map of Lough Corrib may be purchased from WRFB, Weir lodge, Earl's Island, Galway City.

Oughterard (Co Galway). Best fishing is from April to early June. **Owenriff River** flows through Oughterard; good in high water late summer. Local club is Oughterard Anglers Assn. There is additional good fishing for bream and roach on **Moycullen Lakes**, Moycullen, on Galway/Oughterard Rd. Currarevagh House Hotel (09182 313) provides boats, ghillies, outboard motors with fuel and tackle if necessary for a charge of £40 per day, also has boat on top lake of **Screebe** sea trout fishery. Oughterard House (free fishing on Corrib; Private water within 12m; salmon and sea trout); Corrib, Angler's and Egan's Lake. Also new motel: Connemara Gateway (Reservations: Tel: 01-567 3444) and Ross Lake Hotel, Rosscahill (boats and boatmen). Tackle shops: Tucks, Main Street; M Keogh. Galway tackle shop: Freeney's, 19 High St.

Clonbur (Co Galway). Good centre for **Loughs Corrib** and **Mask**. Clonbur AC fishes these waters, **Loughs Coolin, Nafooey** (pike over 36lb) and others, and is affiliated with Corrib Federation. Tackle shop: Ann Kynes, Clonbur, tel: 092 46197. Accommodation: Fair Hill Guest House, Clonbur, tel: 092 46197, caters for anglers, and arranges fishing trips with local boatmen; Noreen Kyne, tel: 092 46169; Ann Lambe, Ballykine House, tel: 092 46150. Self-catering with boats, J O'Donnell, tel: 092 46157.

Headford (Co Galway). Convenient for the east side of Lough Corrib. **Black River** (limestone stream) provides excellent if somewhat difficult dry fly water. Affected by drainage work. Best near village of **Shrule**. A £3 dt is sold by WRFB, Weir Lodge, Galway, tel: 0915 63118. Tackle shop: Kevin Duffy. Accommodation at Angler's Rest Hotel and guest houses.

Greenfields, nr Headford (Co Galway). Trout, salmon and coarse fish. Situated on shore of **L Corrib**. Boatmen in vicinity. Rooms-en-suite, tackle, boats, apply to Michael Walshe, Ower House Guesthouse, Greenfields, Headford, Co Galway (093 35446 (35382 fax).

Cong (Co Mayo), Good for **Lough Mask**, also. Boats from Michael Ryan, River Lodge (092 46057); boats and accommodation. from Mike and Rose Holian, Bayview Angling Centre, Derry Quay, Cross P O, Nr Cong (092 46385), open during winter for pike fishing. Tackle shops: O'-Connors, Cong; T Cheevers, Northgate Street, Athenry.

Tributaries of Lough Corrib.

BLACK RIVER. Fifteen miles in length, it enters lough just north of Greenfields. Access is easy from Shrule, Co Mayo. A rich limestone river with a good stock of brown trout. Best in early season, before weed accumulates.

CREGG RIVER. Rises half mile upstream of old Cregg Millhouse, and flows four miles to Lower Lough Corrib. Upper stretch is nursery for stocking into Corrib, and fishing is not encouraged. Salmon and brown trout angling is permitted on lower stretches.

CLARE RIVER: for this river entering L Corrib at the easternmost end, and its own tributary system, *see Clare*.

LOUGH MASK

Limestone lake of 22,000 acres connected by underground channel with Lough Corrib, holding large ferox trout, pike, eels, perch and a few char. Angling is free. Trout to 15lb are taken by trolling and on dap (5-6lb not uncommon). Mayfly best from mid-May to mid-June; daddy-long legs and grasshopper, late June to Sept; wet fly, Mar-April and July-Sept. Dry fly fishing can be successful from May-Sept. Ballinrobe, **Cong, Clonbur** and **Tourmakeady** are good centres. At Cong is Cong AA; (st £5), at Ballinrobe is Ballinrobe and Dist AA (st £5) and at Tourmakeady is Tourmakeady AC. All are open to visitor-membership. Tackle shops: Fred O'Connor, Cong; Dermot O'Connor, Main Street, Ballinrobe. Boats for hire at Cushlough Pier, Bay of Islands Park, Rosshill Park, Caher Pier. Good accommodation at Ard Aoidhinn Angling Centre (92 44009); Derry Park Lodge Angling Centre (92 44081), both Tourmakeady, catering especially for fishermen; Mask Lodge and Mask Villa on lake shore; Red Door Restaurant, Ballinrobe (092 41263). River fishing on **Finney** and canal joining Mask and Corrib. At Tourmakeady are some good spate rivers, and mountain lake fishing can be had in **Dirk Lakes**; brown trout.

The class of trout - the sort which used to be termed *ferox* - which has been drawing anglers to the West of Ireland for generations. This one, taken from L. Mask on a trolled copper and silver spoon in 1983, weighed 17¾lb. Shown with it is a typical 1¾lb specimen taken on a fly. *Photo: Bord Failte.*

LOUGH CARRA. Connected to Lough Mask, 4,003 acres, limestone, relatively shallow with brown trout which are considered to be freer rising than those in Lough Mask, and average heavier. All are derived entirely from natural population of wild fish. Boats and anglers' accommodation from Roberts Angling Service and Guest House, Lough Bawn, Kilkeeran, Partry, tel: 092 43046; Mrs J Flannery, Keel Bridge, Partry, tel: 092 41706; Mr R O'Grady, Chapel St, Ballinrobe, tel: 092 41142. East of L Carra, **Claremorris** and **Irishtown** are notable centres for little-known coarse lakes, containing large numbers of perch, pike, bream and roach.

Lough Nafooey. Connected to Lough Mask, and contains coarse fish.

Tributaries of Lough Mask.

ROBE RIVER, has brown trout fishing, free, best u/s of Robeen Bridge as far as Clooncormack, from Hollymount u/s to Hollybrook, and from Crossboyne through Castemagarrett Estate as far as the Claremorris/Tuam road. Also d/s from Ballinrobe.

KEEL RIVER. Enters west of Ballinrobe, holds a fair stock of brown trout, and is an ideal dry fly water.

NORTH DONEGAL (streams)

(For close seasons, licences, etc, see The Northern Regional Fisheries Board)

Donegal is mostly salmon and sea trout country. Its waters are generally acid; rocky or stony streams and small lakes in which the brown trout run small - though there are one or two fisheries where they may be taken up to 2lb and more.

LENNON. Rises in Glendowan Mountains and flows through **Garton Lough** and **Lough Fern** before entering **Lough Swilly** at Ramelton. Historically is one of the best salmon rivers in Donegal. It is best known as a spring river and its most famous pool, The Ramelton Pool is privately owned. The rest of the river is a 'free fishery' and only a state licence is required. Season 1 Jan-30 Sept. June to Sept for grilse. Trout fishing equally good on upper and lower reaches; best April to July. Loughs Garton and Fern have stocks of small brown trout, and fishing is free.

Ramelton (Co Donegal). Salmon fishing on lower portion of river at Ramelton owned and fished privately by Ramelton Fishery Ltd. **Lough Fern** is best fished from a boat and produces mostly grilse. Other brown trout loughs in vicinity, Akibbon, Sessigagh, Glen and Keel. Information on these and all other local waters from Anglers Haven Hotel, Kilmacrennan, Co Donegal (074 39015).

SWILLY. Flows into Lough Swilly. Much free salmon and trout fishing of good quality in region. Recently, the river has undergone major development with work being carried out by the Northern Regional Fisheries Board and the Letterkenny and District AA.

Letterkenny (Co Donegal). Letterkenny AA has salmon, sea trout and brown trout fishing on Rivers **Swilly, Lennon, Owencarrow**, and more than 25 lakes; trout av ½lb. Salmon run into Lakes **Glen, Gartan** and **Lough Fern**. Boats on Glen Lake: J Doherty, tel 38057; on Lough Keel: P Cullen, 39015 or W Gallagher, 39233. Membership and permits from A McGrath, Port Rd. Hotel: Mount Errigal.

Churchill (Co Donegal). **Lough Beagh** situated in the heart of the **Glenveagh National Park**; 4m long by ½m wide; salmon, sea trout and brown trout. Best known for quality of sea trout fishing in August and Sept. Boat fishing only; 2 boats for hire. Anglers are requested to respect the bird life on this lake, as there are some rare and interesting species residing. Season 15 July-30 Sept. Dt £20, from The Superintendent, Glenveagh National Park (074 37090).

CRANA. Enters **Lough Swilly** at Buncrana. Primarily a spate river which gets a good run of grilse and sea trout. Access to fishing is excellent.

Buncrana (Co Donegal). Salmon and sea trout. Buncrana AA issues permits. For first week £25 and for each subsequent week £10. Licences from Bertie O'Neill's Fishing Tackle Shop, Bridgend, tel: 077 68157; Seamus Gill, tel: 077 61064. Other waters: **Mill River;** brown trout to ½lb numerous; free. **Inch Lake** (6m): good sea trout; free. **Dunree River** (6m) free; brown trout, occasional salmon and sea trout. **Clonmany River** (5m); salmon sea trout and brown trout fishing; fair sport in good water; best June onwards. Hotel: Lake of Shadows.

CULDAFF. A small spate river on the Malin Peninsula, with brown trout, sea trout from mid-June onwards, and salmon in August and September. Nearest towns, Malin and Carndonagh. Season, 1 April-20 Oct. Fly spinning and worm, no float fishing. Permits from Faulkners, Main St, Culdaff.

DEELE. East Donegal rather than North, a tributary of the Foyle which enters downstream of Strabane. Fished by Deele AC from 3m u/s of Convoy to 4m d/s, for brown trout, sea trout, and grilse from July on. Season 1 Apr-20 Oct, fly, spinning, worm, no floats. Dt £5, st £30 from Billy Vance, Milltown, Convoy, Co Donegal. (074 47290).

WEST DONEGAL (streams)

(For close seasons, licences, etc, see The Northern Regional Fisheries Board)

EANY and **ESKE**. Eany is a spate river which flows for 10m SW from Blue Stack Mountains and enters sea in Inver Bay close to Inver village. Good run of salmon and sea trout and has resident population of small brown trout. The Eany has undergone extensive development in 1992/3 and is now in the ownership of the Regional Fisheries Board. Salmon runs in 1993 were excellent. Salmon 20 April-30 Sept. Trout 20 April-9 Oct. **Eske River** drains **Lough Eske** (900 acres) then runs SW for about 5m to join sea at Donegal Bay. The system gets a good run of salmon and a fair run of sea trout; and has a resident stock of brown trout and char. Salmon 1 March-30 Sept. Trout 1 March-30 Sept. Most fishing is on the lake from boats and the river has a number of good pools. In recent years the system has been getting a declining run of fish but this may be temporary.

Donegal (Co Donegal). Donegal Town & Dist AC controls fishing on Eany. Eske Anglers control fishing on Eske River and Lough Eske. Dt £10 from C Doherty, Tackle Shop, Main St.

GLEN. Flows S for 8m from Slievetooe to enter sea at Teelin Bay beside the town of Carrick. A spate river but has a number of good holding pools. Salmon, sea trout, brown trout. Fishes best in summer after a flood. Slieve League AA has fishing, Donal Ward, Ardcrin, Carrick (073 39004). Also Sliabh Liág AA.

Carrick (Co Donegal). Salmon and trout. Private fishing. Tackle shop: Hugh Cunningham.

LACKARGH (Co Donegal). At Creeslough in extreme north of county, river system has spring salmon run mid-March to Mid-May. Creeslough & Dist Anglers. Contact NRFB.

FINN. Governed by Foyle Fisheries Commission. Flows from Lough Finn nr **Fintown** in an easterly direction until it joins Mourne below **Strabane** and **Lifford**, to form River Foyle. Spring salmon best in March-May, between Lifford Bridge and Salmon Leap at Cloghan, depending on flow. Grilse, main run in May-July, best in middle section between **Liscooley** and **Letterbrick**, and at **Commeen** on **R Reelan**; sea trout, good runs in May-July, best in middle and upper sections. Brown trout and coarse, lower reaches. Foyle Fisheries Commission water, near **Clady**, is best for spring salmon. Finn AC and Glebe AC fish sections from Liscooley Bridge to near Edenmore. Ballybofey and Stranorlar AA fish water from Edenmore

A handsome 24 pdr. from the Cloughan Lodge water on the River Finn. *Photo: Cloghan Lodge Estate.*

to Dooish townland, limited rods. Tickets £10 from Ken Rule, Killygordon. Cloghan Lodge Fisheries, **Cloghan**, tel: 074 33003, has over 30m both banks, from Dooish to Lough Finn, plus tributaries **Reelan, Cummirk, Elatagh**. Excellent fly fishing, spinning and worm also permitted, with spring salmon and grilse, autumn salmon, average take per year, 1,500 (2,500 in 1996). Good sea trout run in May-July. Limited tickets, ghillie service, B & B, by advance booking. Much of this fishing is held jointly with Glenmore Estate. Glenmore Estate, T McCreary, Altnapaste, **Ballybofey**, tel: 074 32075, has fishing on Rivers Reelan and Finn from Glenmore (3½m west of Ballybofey) to Cummirk River (3m west of Brochar). Salmon with good grilse run. Dt on first come first serve basis.

OWENEA AND OWENTOCKER. Short rivers running into head of Loughrosmore Bay near Ardara. Owenea is primarily a spate river with a run of spring fish, grilse, sea trout, and has a resident stock of small brown trout. It has a number of good pools about halfway between Glenties and Ardara, and when in condition is one of the best in the country for salmon. Season 1 Mar-30 Sept.

Ardara and **Glenties** (Co Donegal). Fishing controlled by Northern Regional Fishery Board, Glenties, Co Donegal (075 51141). Fishery has been upgraded and there are additional facilities for anglers. Excellent run of salmon and sea trout from March to Sept. Dt £10; st £20 for Glenties and Ardara Angling Clubs members. Permits from Glenties Hatchery and Mary Kennedy, both Glenties; John McGill, Tackle Shop, Main St, Ardara. Free salmon and sea trout fishing on Rivers Brackey and Doug. Many lakes also free. Hotels: Nesbitt Arms, Ardara; Highlands, Glenties.

GWEEBARRA. Drains **Lough Barra** and flows south-west about 7m to Doochary Bridge, where it becomes tidal and flows hence through long estuary between high hills a further 6m to the Atlantic.

Doochary (Co Donegal). Bridge here marks end of tidal water; several trout lakes in vicinity. Salmon, sea trout. Best season: Spring salmon, Feb-May; grilse and sea trout, end of June to Sept. Fishing belongs to riparian owners, leave obtainable. Salmon and sea trout run into Lough Barra in large numbers and into tributaries.

THE ROSSES. The Rosses Fishery is made up of five salmon and sea trout rivers, including **River Dungloe**, and one hundred and thirty lakes, some of which contain salmon and sea trout, all of which contain brown trout.

Dungloe (Co Donegal). Salmon and sea trout. Rosses Fishery controlled by Rosses AA. **Loughs Meeala, Dungloe, Craghy**, stocked with browns and rainbows. Season 2 Feb-12 Oct. Fly only on all lakes. Prices are: dt £6, boat £5 per angler; with ghillie, £25. Juv free. River prices vary for season on **Crolly River** and **Clady River**. Permits and boat hire from Charles Bonner, Tackle Shop, Bridge End (075 21163); Bill McGarvey, Main St, Dungloe. Hotels: Sweeney's; Ostan na Rosann. Wide range of accommodation.

EAST COASTAL STREAMS

(For close seasons, licences, etc, see The Eastern Regional Fisheries Board)

AVONMORE RIVER. Runs through Rathdrum, Co Wicklow, from **Loughs Tay** and **Dan**, approx 8m north. It joins **River Avonbeg**, runs into the **Avoca** and reaches sea at Arklow. Big stocks of small brown trout. Two clubs have salmon and trout fishing: Rathdrum Trout Anglers, Aughrim Anglers, Vartry Anglers, have fishing for salmon, sea trout, brown and rainbows. Tickets (£2) from Geoghagans, or Tourist Office, Rathdrum.

BROADMEADOW RIVER. Dublin District; trout. Drainage scheme has affected sport. Broadmeadow AC fishes river and **Tonelgee Reservoir**. Contact K Rundle, tel: 01 438178.

DARGLE RIVER. Short river which reaches sea at Bray. Salmon, sea trout. Dargle AC has fishing. Contact Michael Keenan, tel: 01 515540. Tackle from Dargle Tackle, U5 Everett Cntr, Castle St, Bray.

DELVIN RIVER. In Drogheda District. Fair brown trout stream entering sea at Gormanstown; Holds few sea trout. Gormanstown and Dist AA has water. River being stocked and developed with co-operation of landowners and members. Balbriggan is convenient centre. (Hotel: Grand).

DODDER. Dublin District; brown trout (av 9oz, but fish to 2lbs caught), with some sea trout fishing in tidal portion. Dodder AC controls all fishing; contact R O'Hanlon, 82 Braemor Rd, Dublin 14, tel: 01 982112. Fishing on Dublin Corporation's **Bohernabreena** and **Roundwood Reservoirs** (10m from Dublin); by st £10, wt £4, dt £1.50 from Dublin Corporation, Block 1, Floor 3, Civic Offices, Fishamble St, Dublin 8. No boats. Conc for OAP. Members of these clubs are entitled to reduced rates: Dublin Trout AA; Wicklow AA; Dodder AC.

GLENCREE RIVER. In Dublin District. Enniskerry is a centre; small brown trout. Mostly free.

NANNY RIVER. In Drogheda District. River enters sea at Laytown, Co Meath. Fair brown trout fishing; some sea trout in lower reaches. Drogheda and Dist AC has water and issues permits. Club also fishes R Boyne, and three stillwaters. *See Drogheda*.

TOLKA RIVER. In Dublin District. A once excellent trout stream which has suffered from pollution. Best fishing is from Finglas Bridge to Abbotstown Bridge. For fishing information contact secretary, Tolka AC, tel: 01 361730.

VARTRY. Small river which drains **Roundwood (Vartry) Reservoir** and flows into sea near Wicklow, with sea trout from late August, and small brown trout. Vartry AC controls river and Co Wicklow AA controls Roundwood Reservoir, the latter on lease from Dublin Corporation. Tickets. Fishing station: Rathnew (Co Wicklow). Hotels: Hunter's, Tinakilly House.

ERNE

(For close seasons, licences, etc, see The Northern Regional Fisheries Board)

A large hydro-electric scheme has turned the River Erne into two large dams. Sea trout fishing in estuary from June to Sept. Coarse fishing excellent; bream, rudd and perch abundant and roach multiplying following their introduction in recent years.

Ballyshannon (Co Donegal). **Assaroe Lake** is a man-made lake resulting from the Erne Hydro-Electric Generating Scheme. Located above Kathleen Falls Power Station, it acts as a reservoir. Fishing is open, controlled by ESB, and a permit to cover salmon, brown trout and coarse, may be purchased from ESB Fisheries Office, Ardnacrusha, Nr Limerick; ESB Generating Station or ESB Shop, both Ballyshannon; Mr T Kelly, Edenville, Kinlough, Co Leitrim; st £15, dt £5, conc; boats from Jim McWeeney, *see below*. Other ESB waters are Gweedore Fishery: Rivers **Clady** and **Crolly**, st £25, wt £15, dt £5, conc, from ESB Office (*above*); C Bonner, The Bridge, Dungloe, Co Donegal. Tackle shops; Jim McWeeney, Arena, Rossnowlagh Road, Ballyshannon, tel: 072 51165; E McAloon, Newsagent; Pat Barrett's, Main St, Bundoran. Hotels: Creevy Pier, Dorians Imperial.

Belturbet (Co Cavan). Good centre for **Rivers Erne** and **Woodford**, and some thirty seven lakes, with most coarse fish and some trout. **Putighan** and **Derryhoo Lakes** are popular venues, tench to 5lb in L Bunn, to 3lb in L Carn. New developments at Loughs Grilly, Killybandrick, Bunn, Drumlaney, Greenville, Round. Bait, boats and tackle from J McMahon, Bridge St, tel: 049 22400. Anglers accommodation includes Kilduff House, 2m from Belturbet and Fortview House, Cloverhill.

Cavan (Co Cavan). All lakes and rivers in the area hold coarse fish except **Annagh Lake** (100 acres) which holds brown and rainbow trout; fly only, no bank fishing, 6 fish limit. Trout season 1 March-30 Sept. **Lough Oughter**, a maze of lakes fed by **R Erne** and **R Annalee**, holds a wealth of coarse fish; bream, rudd, roach, pike perch, tench. Further details from The Secretary, Cavan Tourist Assn. Tackle shop: Magnet Sports Store, Town Hall. Accommodation catering for anglers: Mrs Myles, Halcyon, Cavan Town; Lakevilla, Blenacup, and Forest Chalets, both Killykeen.

Lough Gowna (Co Cavan). Coarse fishing on Lough Gowna, the source of R Erne. Information from Lough Gowna Tourist Assn. Anglers accommodation can be found at Kilbracken Arms Hotel, Greenville House, both Carrigallen; Lakeview House, Lough Gowna; Mr & Mrs Barry, Farrangarve, Co Cavan.

Cootehill (Co Cavan). A notable fishing centre, with more than thirty coarse fishing lakes within fifteen mile radius, and **Rivers Dromore** and **Annalee**: trout, bream, rudd, tench, pike, hybrids, roach, perch. Fishing free in Dromore and Annalee, permit required for **Bunoe** and **Laragh Rivers**. **Moyduff Lake** is brown trout fishery, controlled by NRFB. Permit at lake. Local clubs are Cootehill AC, Laragh AC, Moyduff AC and Bunnoe AC: contact through Cootehill Tourist Development Assn, Riverside House, Cootehill (tel/fax: 049 5150). Boats from same address. Tackle shop: J J Bait and Tackle, Bridge St. Anglers accommodation: Riverside House; Cabragh Farmhouse; Hillview House, Cootehill.

Clones (Co Monaghan). Coarse fishing. **River Finn**, a sluggish tributary of Upper Lough Erne, excellent bream fishing. There are sixty lakes within 5m of town: pike, perch, rudd, bream, roach, eel, and other species. A Few miles north of **Monaghan** is **Emy Lake Fishery**, Emyvale, 136 acres trout fishing, fly only, 6 fish limit. Tackle shop: T J Hanberry, 3/4 Fermanagh St, Clones. Hotels: Creighton, Lennard Arms.

WOODFORD RIVER. **Ballinamore** (Co Leitrim) is close to river, which produces large catches of bream av 2½lb, roach, perch, pike and other coarse fish. River runs into **L Garadice**, one of 25 fishing lakes in this area. Permits are normally £5. Riversdale Farm Guesthouse (078 44122) caters for anglers, also McAllister's Hotel; Kennedy, Glenview, tel: 078 44157; Price, Ardrum Lodge, tel: 078 44278, all Ballinamore. Tackle from G Owens, High St (Agent for Irish Angling Services).

FANE (including Glyde and Dee)

(For close seasons, licences, etc, see The Eastern Regional Fisheries Board)

Rises in **Lough Muckno** at Castleblaney and flows SE to enter sea at Blackrock, 4m S of Dundalk. Small run of grilse in June, good run of salmon in August, which may be caught in high water, as far up as Lough Ross. Brown trout are to be caught, from ½lb to 2½lb.

Dundalk (Co Louth). Waters from Knockbridge to border (except 1m at Balentra), plus all **Castletown** and **Ballymascanlon** Rivers and tributaries controlled by Dundalk & Dist Brown Trout AA. Assn stocks each year with browns, and there is a good run of sea trout and salmon (Aug-Oct best). Membership £12, dt £3, conc, from tackle shops and tourist office. Tackle shops: Island Tackle, 58 Park St; Mac's Sports, 3 Demense, Dundalk. Hotels: Ballymascanlon, Derryhale.

Inniskeen (Co Monaghan). Waters in Inniskeen area controlled by Inniskeen AC. Trout, fly only. Salmon, fly, spinning, lure or shrimp. Membership from A Campbell, Monvallet, Louth, Co Louth. Dt £5 from Ruddys Filling Station, Dundalk.

Castleblayney (Co Monaghan). Good centre for Rivers Fane, **Clarebane**, **Frankfort** and **Mullaghduff**, brown trout. Several coarse fishing loughs in area; **Lough Muckno**, 325 hectares, with pike, perch, roach, bream, and other species; good fishing from several islands in lough. Permission and access controlled by Lough Muckno Leisure Park. **Lough Egish** (5m), pike, perch and eel. **Dick's Lake**, large roach; **Smith's Lake**, good tench fishing, also bream, roach, perch; **Loughs Na Glack** and **Monalty**, big bream. Castleblayney Trout AA has trout fishing on **Milltown Lough** (3m); stocked annually with 3,000 brown trout; dt from Hon Sec. Tackle shop: J Flanagan, Main Street. Hotels: Glencarn; Central. Fishing accommodation at Hillside, tel: 042 40385, and Hazelwood, tel: 043 46009.

Ballybay (Co Monaghan). Excellent coarse fishing centre for **Dromore River** and loughs, of which there are a large number; some, it is claimed, have never been fished. Boats and ghillies are to be found on the more important local fisheries, including **Bairds Shore, Corries, Convent, Derryvalley, Mullanary, Corkeeran and White Lakes**. There is much free coarse fishing for visiting anglers, and typical weights per day exceed 40lb, mainly bream and roach. Local pike fishing is also very good. Town holds annual coarse angling festival. Local Assn: Corkeeran and Dromore Trout and Coarse AA. Dt £5. Tackle from Martin O'Kane; Mick Harte, both Main St. Accommodation: Riverdale Hotel (042 41188) caters for anglers: boat hire and ghillie service, bait and tackle, special rates for angling packages.

GLYDE: Rises near Kingscourt in Co Cavan and flows E for 35m to join River Dee before entering the sea at Annagassan. Flows through some prime coarse fisheries in upper reaches, notably **Rahans** and **Ballyhoe Lakes**. Small run of spring salmon and fair run of grilse in late summer depending on water levels. Good stock of brown trout. Excellent Mayfly hatch. Due to drainage works some years ago, there are some steep banks on which care should be taken. A Good centre for anglers is **Carrickmacross**, with several fine coarse lakes near to hand with bream, roach, tench, rudd, hybrids, perch, pike, etc, incl **Lisaniske, Capragh** and **Monalty Lakes, Lough Na Glack**, and fishing accommodation: Mrs Haworth, Rose-Linn Lodge, Carrickmacross, tel: 042 61035; Mrs Campbell, Glencoe, tel: 042 67316; Mrs Tinnelly, Corglass, tel: 042 67492, both Kingscourt.

Castlebellingham (Co Louth). Salmon, sea trout, brown trout. Season 1 Feb-30 Sept. Dee & Glyde AC protect and fish river. St £7 and dt £2 from Moonan's Fishing Tackle, Ardee. Hotel: Bellingham Castle.

DEE: Rises above **Whitewood Lake**, near Kilmainham Wood. Flow E for 38m, joining **River Glyde** at **Annagassan**. Fair runs of spring salmon, some grilse and good runs of sea trout to 5lb (May). Lower reaches below **Ardee** and **Drumcar** yield most salmon and sea trout. Brown trout water above Ardee. Due to drainage works some years ago, many banks are steep and dangerous. Weeds can be a problem during dry summers, ruining fishing in many sections. Season 1 Feb-30 Sept.

Dunleer (Co Louth). Salmon, sea trout. Drumcar Fishery has water. St £10 and dt £3, from The Reception, St Mary's, Drumcar House. Permits 9am-5pm only. Sea trout fishing allowed after dark.

Ardee (Co Louth). Dee & Glyde AC has water on Rivers Dee and Glyde. St £7 and dt £2, from Moonan's Tackle Shop. Other tackle shop: Ardee Sports Co, John St. Hotel: The Gables.

Drumconrath (Co Meath). Drumconrath AC issues permits. Dt from Callans, Main St. **Ballyhoe Lakes**, tench fishing, plus bream, roach, perch, pike; coarse fishing in **Lough Mentrim**, (specimen bream and tench), **Lake Balrath**, Corstown. Fishing accommodation at Inis Fail, tel: 041 54161, and Ballyhoe, tel: 041 54400/54104.

Nobber (Co Meath). Nobber AC has stretch from **Whitewood Lake** to Yellow-Ford Bridge. Mainly brown trout, occasional salmon in late autumn, usually during flood water. Weeds can be a problem during low water.

MULLAGHDUFF: Tributary which enters Lough Muckno. A good trout stream, wet fly fishing best from April onwards, dry fly late in season.

FRANKFORT: Short river which connects Milltown Lough with Lough Muckno, stocked by local assoc. Trout to 3lb. Best in May-July.

FEALE

(For close seasons, licences, etc, see The Shannon Regional Fisheries Board)

Rises in North Cork on the southern slopes of Wullaghereick Mountain, then flows west through Abbeyfeale, Listowel, and enters Shannon Estuary south of Ballybunion. Its total length is an estimated 46 miles, and there are eleven main tributaries: the **Gale, Oolagh, Allaghaun, Cahir, Brick, Smearlagh, Tullylease, Owveg, Glashacooncore, Clyddagh** and **Breanagh**. A spate river, with salmon, sea trout and brown trout. Season is from 1 Mar-30 Sept. Sometimes salmon run poor owing to low water. The Feale system is controlled almost entirely by five associations. (*See below.*)

Abbeyfeale (Co Limerick). Best centre for Feale. Waders essential. Abbeyfeale AA has 6m of single and double bank d/s of town, with salmon and sea trout; st £40, plus £25 joining fee and dt £15 from Ryan's, New Street, Abbeyfeale. Brosna AA has 6m upstream; trout permit from S Quinlan, Kilmanahan, Abbeyfeale. Hotel: Leen's. Tackle shops: P Ryan, New Street; Lane (manufacture of the famous 'Lane' artificial minnow) New Street.

Listowel (Co Kerry). North Kerry AA has 8m single and double bank on R Feale and on **River Smearlagh**; salmon and sea trout; wt £70 and dt £15, from Hon Sec or tackle shops. Killocruin/Finuge Club controls 3m d/s of town, best stretch for spring salmon and grilse. Tralee AA has 5m u/s, both banks; dt issued. Fly fishing for salmon quite good from mid-Aug. Brosna/Mountcollins Club has 8m on upper reaches of Feale, with good sea trout fishing from mid Aug to end of Sept. Salmon licences and permits from Mr Jim Horgan, The Square, Listowel. Tackle shops: Halpins; Landers Leisure Lines, Courthouse Lane, Tralee. Hotels: Stack's; Listowel Arms.

GALWAY and MAYO (rivers and smaller loughs)

(For close seasons, licences, etc, see The Western Regional Fisheries Board)

BALLYNAHINCH

An extensive system of lakes, tributaries and connecting rivers draining into Bertaghboy Bay. One of the most important salmon and sea trout fisheries in the west of Ireland.

Recess. Salmon and sea trout. The famous **Ballynahinch Castle Fishery** consists of **Ballynahinch River** (2½m) and **Ballynahinch Lake**; situated at bottom of 25m long system of river and lakes. Salmon best June to Sept. Sea trout best July to Oct. Fly fishing (shrimp fishing for salmon for 2 hrs each day). Dt £30-£60. Max 28 rods. Ghillies £28 per day. Permits for non-residents from The Manager, Ballynahinch Castle Hotel (095 31006). Fishing permits for **Lakes Aleen** and **Tombeola**, from Mrs L Hill, Angler's Rest (095 31091). Lough Inagh Lodge Hotel, Recess, is central to the **Lough Inagh Fishery**, seven beats including two outstanding loughs, **Inagh** and **Derryclare**, and associated rivers; situated at top of Ballynahinch system in heart of Connemara. Dt, boats and Ghillies. Permits from John O'Connor. Lough Inagh Lodge (095 34706); Della MacAuley, Inagh Valley Inn (095 34608). Tackle for sale or hire at fishery office. **Athry Fishery** comprises five loughs on Upper Ballynahinch, including **Lough Athry**. Lower loughs get run of sea trout and occasional salmon, and upper loughs sea trout only. Season mid-July to 12 Oct. Dt £25 (boat and 2 or 3 rods). Max 9 rods. Ghillies £25 per day. Permits from John Prendergast, The Zetland Hotel, Cashel (095 31111). For fishing on **Bealnacarra River** and **Glendollagh Lake**, apply to W Holling and B Gilmore, Recess House. Tackle shops: Ballynahinch Castle Hotel; Percy Stanley, Clifden, Co Galway.

Maam Cross (Co Galway). Salmon and sea trout. Top Waters Ballynahinch Fishery comprises six lakes and part of **Owentooey** and **Recess Rivers**. **Lough Oord**, at top of system, is 2m W of Maam Cross with **Loughs Shannakeela**, **Derryneen** and **Cappahoosh** forming a chain westward. Season mid-June to 12 Oct. Wt (boat) £100, dt (boat) £18 and (bank) £10. Permits and accommodation from Mr L Lyon and Mrs Iris Lyons-Joyce, Tullaboy House (091 82305).

CARROWNISKEY: rises in Sheefry Hills and flows 6m to sea beyond Louisburgh. Spate river, overgrown by trees in parts, making fishing difficult. Lower reaches characterised by long flat stretches. There are runs of salmon and sea trout from June onwards. Roonagh Lough, into which river runs, offers fishing for both, either by fly or dapping. St and wt £50, dt £12 from Charles Gaffney's Pub, Louisberg, tel: 098 66150.

Louisburgh (Co Mayo). Permits for Carrowinsky fishing from Charles Gaffney's Pub (*above*). Salmon and trout in **Altair Lake**. Good shore fishing for bass, pollack, etc; boats at Roonagh and Old Head.

BUNOWEN: spate river with some deep pools, providing excellent lies for salmon and sea trout. Sea trout and salmon, best from mid-June. Season: 1 Apr to 30 Sept. Tagged salmon were introduced into river in 1992, any tagged fish caught should be reported to an officer of WRFB. Permits £50 season and week,

£12 day, for river and **Lough Namucka** from Charles Gaffney's Pub, as above. Tackle shop: Hewetsons, Bridge St, Westport. Hotels: Old Head, Durkans. For sea fishing Bay View Hotel, Clare Island, recommended; boats for hire.

CASHLA: drains a complex system of lakes then flows into Cashla Bay at Costelloe. Good run of salmon up to 22lbs, but it is as a sea trout fishery that it really excels.

Costelloe (Co Galway). Sea trout, salmon. Costelloe and Fermoyle Fishery: Lower fishery includes R Cashla and **Lough Glenicmurrin**, and holds excellent sea trout and good salmon; Upper fishery Loughs **Fermoyle Clogher**, **Carrick** and **Rusheen**, and holds excellent sea trout. Dt £20-£45, £60-£70 with ghillie service. Permits and tackle from Tim Moore, Bridge Cottage, Costelloe (091 572196 (572366 fax)); accommodation may be booked through fishery. Tackle shops: Freeney's, 19 High St; Hugh Duffy, Mainguard St, all Galway, Co Galway; Costelloe and Fermoyle Fishery Office.

DAWROS: drains Kylemore Lakes then flows 5m before entering Ballinakill Harbour. Run of spring salmon, grilse, sea trout. Best July to Sept (sea trout); Aug (salmon).

Kylemore (Co Galway). Salmon, grilse, sea trout. Mrs Nancy Naughton, Kylemore House Hotel, issues permits. Tackle shops: Percy Stanley, Clifden, Co Galway; Hamilton's, Leenane, Co Galway.

DOOHULLA: drains a number of lakes, then runs one mile to Ballyconneely Bay. Holds some summer salmon and sea trout. Best sea trout July to Sept. Best salmon June to Aug.

Ballyconneely (Co Galway). Between Roundstone and Ballyconneely lies the Doohulla Fishery, consisting of The Pool at Callow Bridge, **Doohulla River**, and **Loughs Maumeen**, **Emlaghkeeragh**, **Carrick** and others. Salmon, sea trout, browns. Dt £10 (The Pool) and £5. Hire of boats £10. Permits from N D Tinne, Emlaghmore (095 23529). Clifden tackle shop: Stanley.

ERRIFF AND BUNDORRAGHA: good salmon and sea trout rivers lying short distance north of Ballynahinch country and flowing into Killary Harbour near Leenane.

Erriff Fishery, Leenane (Co Galway). At the east side of Killary Harbour, fishery consists of River Erriff (8m) and **Tawnyard Lough**. Noted for salmon and some sea trout. Fishery acquired by Central Fisheries Board in 1982. Dt £10 from April, £35 from early June. River season 1 Apr-30 Sept. Tawnyard Lough, boat for 2 rods, £50, from 1 July. Accommodation at Aasleagh Lodge. Enquiries to Erriff Fishery Office, Aasleagh Lodge, Leenane, Co Galway (095 42252).

Delphi Fishery, Leenane (Co Galway). On the north side of Killary Harbour, fishery has the following waters: **Bundorragha River** (1m), 4 rods, salmon from 1 Feb-30 Sept, some sea trout from July onwards; **Finlough,** two boats, and **Doolough**, three boats, salmon from March onwards, sea trout from July. **Glencullin** and **Cunnel Loughs**, some trout from July. Fly only, dt with boat to £60. Ghillies, £40. Apply to Fishery Manager, Delphi Lodge, Leenane, Co Galway (095 42211, fax: 095 42296). Accommodation at Delphi Lodge and 4 fishing cottages. Tackle shops: The Fishery Office, Delphi Lodge; Hamilton's Bar, Leenane.

Knock (Co Mayo). Situated in east of county, a notable centre for coarse fishing. Local loughs include **Cloontariff,** pike and perch, **Carrownamallagh**, excellent pike, **Clooncurry**, pike and perch, **Curragh**, bream and pike, **Derrykin**, pike, **Lakehill Pond**, specimen tench, **Nanonagh**, mixed coarse. Boats are available on all lakes. Hotel and B & B accommodation is plentiful locally.

NEWPORT: drains Lough Beltra and runs into Clew Bay, at Newport. River over 7m long and usually fished from banks. Good for salmon and very good sea trout. There are about 20 pools, some for both day and night fishing. Fly only. River known for length of season, 20 March-30 Sept.

Newport (Co Mayo). Salmon and sea trout. Newport House Hotel has fishing on **Newport River, Lough Beltra, East** (fine run of spring fish) and 4m on **River Skerdagh**, a tributary. Fly only, all sea trout to be returned alive. Dt £26, £85 for 2 rods with boat and ghillie, from The Fishery Manager, Newport House (098 41222) *(see advt)*. Newport AC, whose members are free to fish Newport River by concession of Newport House, issue permits for salmon and sea trout fishing (June to Sept) on **Owengarve**, a small spate river near **Mulrany**. Fly only, all sea trout must be returned alive. Dt £10. Various small trout loughs around Newport. Hotel also issues tickets to non-members, when available. A few miles from Newport, boat fishing for salmon and sea trout at **Burrishoole Fishery** which consists of **Loughs Feeagh** and **Furnace** with short tidal stretch of river. Fishery owned and administered by Salmon Research Agency of Ireland; fishing season effectively mid-June to end September. Boats with or without boatmen, package holidays arranged by request incorporating local accommodation of varying grades. Full details from SRAI, Newport, Co Mayo. Tel (98) 41107. Agency also controls **Ballinlough Fishery**, 54 acres, 2m north west of Westport: stocked rainbow and brown trout, £20 per boat per day (2 rods), limit 6 fish.

OWENDUFF: Good for salmon from end of Mar. Grilse and sea trout, mid-June to end of Sept. Provides excellent all-round fishing when water right.

Ballycroy (Co Mayo). Salmon, sea trout. Upper reaches owned by Rock Estates (Newport) Ltd, Rock House, Ballycroy (098 49137), together with **R Bellaveeny** and **L Gall** fishing. For dt apply to John Campbell, tel: 098 49116. Middle reaches owned by Craigie Bros, Finglass, Co Dublin (01 6272671); occasional weekly lettings with accommodation, for up to 16 guests and 8 rods. Lagduff Lodge (lower beat). All privately held, but occasional lettings by lodges named. Lower down, a small beat is owned by Mr Colm O'Brian of New Park, Bray Rd, Foxrock, Dublin 18, tel: 01 2895337. Good accommodation, Shranamanragh Lodge, let with fishing by the week. Good for salmon (April/May), grilse and sea trout (July onwards).

OWENGARVE: Spate river. Salmon, grilse and sea trout, early June to early Oct.

Mulrany (Co Mayo). Most of river controlled by Newport AC, which has mutual agreement with Dr J Healey, Rosturk Castle, Rosturk, Westport, Co Mayo, whereby whole river can be fished. Daily (£2), weekly and monthly rods from club Hon Sec or from Rosturk Castle.

ACHILL ISLAND: Off Mayo coast, has become famous in recent years for its sea fishing *(see Sea Fishing section)*. Excellent sea trout. Good brown trout fishing on four lakes, fish plentiful but small, larger lake with sea trout. Controlled by Achill Sporting Club, permits from sec Roger Gallagher, Valley House, Dugort, Achill. Tackle from P Sweeney, Achill Sound. Hotel: Slievemore, Dugort. Accommodation at Achill Sound, tel: 098 45245, or 45272.

OWENGOWLA and INVERMORE: two short rivers, each draining a complex of lakes. Owengowla flows into Bertraghboy Bay and Invermore flows into Kilkieran Bay. Both are excellent sea trout fisheries.

Cashel (Co Galway). Sea trout. **Gowla Fishery** consists of **R Owengowla**, with holding pools, and about 14 loughs, permits from Fishery Office. **Invermore Fishery** has ten sea trout lakes and an additional brown trout lake. Upper lakes are remote, but accessible by path. Lower lakes fish from mid-June; upper lakes governed by summer rainfall. There are 10 boats on the fishery, and accommodation. Dt (boat) £25 from Mrs Margaret McDonagh, Glenview (095 31054). Ghillies at both fisheries.

OWENMORE: 20m long and principally spate river from Bellacorick Bridge, rises near Ballycastle and flows into Blacksod Bay. Principal tributary is **Oweniny** (Crossmolina AA). River divided among number of owners. Good for spring salmon from April 1, given really high water; good grilse and sea trout from mid-June to end of Sept, if water is right. To the south of river are a number of small loughs with brown trout. Some of these have free fishing, including **Loughs Brack**, **Nambrock**, and **Nalagan**. They are remote, but worth exploring.

Bangor Erris (Co Mayo). Upper and middle reaches owned by syndicate, not for letting. Part of fishery let to Bangor Erris AC. Permits from Seamus Henry, *see below*. Enquiries respecting **Carrowmore Lough,** salmon, sea trout and brown trout, plus 4m of **Owenmore** and **Glenamoy** Rivers, to Seamus Henry, West End Bar, Bangor Erris, Ballina, tel: 097 83487. Bellacorick Fisheries have salmon and trout fishing on **Srahnakilly** and **Oweninny** Rivers. Permits from Musical Bridge Inn, **Bellacorick**, tel: 096 53094.

SCREEBE: drains a group of lakes, including Lakes **Ardery**, **Shindilla**, **Loughanfree**, **Ahalia** and **Screebe**, then flows into Camus Bay at Screebe. Gets good run of grilse and some summer salmon.

Screebe (Co Galway). Salmon and brown trout. Screebe Estate Fishery is professionally managed and includes Screebe River and numerous lakes. It also has its own hatchery. Fly fishing only. Permits from The Manager, Screebe Estates, Camus (091 74110). Hotel: Currarevagh House Hotel, Oughterard, Co Galway (091 552312/3), situated beside L Corrib on NW shore, good centre for local fishing, caters for anglers. Tackle shops: Tommy Tuck (Oughterard AA); M Keogh, both Oughterard, Co Galway.

MAYO North (streams)

Several small sea trout rivers run to the coast in north west of county. **Bunnahowen** is a short river near Belmullet, with free fishing for brown trout (to 1lb), and sea trout. **Glenamoy** and **Muingnabo** both empty into a sea lough at **Broad Haven Bay**, and have salmon and sea trout. Fishing on the Muingnabo R. is free. Near **Ballycastle** are **Glencullin** and **Ballinglen Rivers,** both with sea trout, late run on Glencullin, a few salmon in Ballinglen. Free fishing on both. The **Cloonaghmore River** runs into **Killala Bay**, west of the Moy. It has both salmon and sea trout. Free fishing with permission of local assn. **Leafony** is a small spate river which runs into east side of Killala bay, and has free fishing for salmon and sea trout (late run, Aug-Sept). **Easkey River** runs north from **L Easkey** (brown trout, free), and has salmon and sea trout. Some of this river is preserved, elsewhere free fishing. **Drumcliffe** and

Grange Rivers run into sea loughs north of Sligo. Grange has brown trout, free fishing; Drumcliffe (connected to Glencar Lough) is assn water, with salmon fishing, contact Mr Harold Sibbery, The Waterfall, Glencar, Co Leitrim.

GARAVOGUE and LOUGH GILL

(For close seasons, licences, etc, see The North-Western Regional Fisheries Board)

Garavogue River connects Lough Gill with sea, which it enters in Sligo Bay to south of Donegal Bay and Erne. Salmon, trout, coarse fish. Lough Gill is a fine coarse fishery, with pike to 30lbs and excellent stock of bream at Hazelwood, Dooney, Aughamore and Annagh Bay.

Sligo (Co Sligo). Salmon, trout. **Lough Gill**, a large lake 5m long. Good run of spring salmon; best Feb to March. Northern and eastern shores controlled by Sligo AA. Dt £10, from Barton Smith, Tackle Dealer, Hyde Bridge. Fishing on the rest of the lake is free. Boats £10 per day, from Blue Lagoon, Public House (071 42530/45407), also tackle hire and ghillie service. **Drumcliffe River** and **Glencar Lake**, 6 to 9 miles north of Sligo, controlled by Sligo AA and Manorhamilton Anglers. Small brown trout. Good spring salmon run from mid Feb. Some very large sea trout caught. **Ballisodare River**, 5m south, excellent run of summer salmon. **Lough Colga**, 4m; brown trout; free. Permits from Barton Smith, Tackle Shop, Hyde Bridge (071 42356).

Dromahair (Co Leitrim). **River Bonet** feeds Lough Gill; salmon, trout. Best for salmon in summer. Dromahair AA fishes locally. Permits from McGoldricks Mace Foodmarket. Abbey Hotel has free, all-round fishing for guests. Manorhamilton AA also preserve some water on river and **Glencar Lake**. St £12, dt £5, from A Flynn, Post Office. Manorhamilton (072 55001). Also abundance of coarse fishing in river and **Loughs Belhavel, Glenade** and **Corrigeencor**; all free, with pike and perch. Tackle from Spar, Main St.

Co. KERRY (rivers and loughs)

(For close seasons, licences, etc, see The South Western Regional Fisheries Board)

KENMARE BAY. Several small salmon rivers empty into this bay, which provides excellent sea fishing (large skate, tope, etc). Best season, May to August.

Kenmare (Co Kerry). Salmon, sea trout, small wild brown trout. Kenmare Salmon Angling Ltd owns 1¼m of **Roughty** at Ardtully Castle, 5 miles from Kenmare-Cork Road. Spring salmon, March to June; good grilse runs, June to Aug; fly, spinning, prawning and worming permitted; spring salmon average 9lb, grilse 4lb. Permits (dt £12, wt £35) for visitors staying locally, from John O'Hare, 21 Main St, Kenmare, tel: 064 41499. No Sunday fishing for visitors. **Sheen River** runs in on south shore and is preserved by owner. It produces approx 1,000 salmon and grilse every season. Contact the Manager, Sheen Falls Lodge, Kenmare, tel: 064 41600. **Finnihy River** is overgrown and requires determination, but has grilse run: free fishing. **Lough Barfinnihy** 35 acres, is 6½m from Kenmare, off Killarney Rd. Good brown and stocked rainbows. **Lough Inchiquin**: char, sea trout, salmon, browns. One boat on site. Permits for these and for **Uragh Lough** from J O'Hare, *see above*. **Cloonee Loughs**, on the south shore, have excellent game fishing. Permission and boats from May O'Shea, Lakehouse, Cloonee, tel: 064 84205. For fishermen with taste for mountain climbing there are at least 40 lakes holding brown trout on plateau of **Caha Mountains**, all easily fished from Kenmare. *See also South West Cork.* **Kerry Blackwater** 10m long, drains Lough Brin, spring salmon run, sea trout and browns. Fishing part over 4m long, with about thirty pools. Good fly fishing up near Lough Brin itself. Dt £20 may be obtained from Fishery Manager, SWRFB, Macroom, also from hut on river bank, limit 2 salmon. **Lough Brin**, 10m northwest, trout to 1lb, and sea trout from August, dt £5, boat £6 half day. Both these controlled by SWRFB. **Sneem River**, farther west, is let with holiday cottage: H Cowper, Sneem. run of grilse and sea trout July/August. For trout fishing on SWRFB **Lough Fadda**, contact Monica O'Shea, Tahilla, Sneem, (064 82901), or J O'Sullivan, Hill Top House,

Derryquin, Sneem (064 45306). Hotels: Sheen Falls Lodge (064 41600) permits; Park Hotel; Kenmare Bay; Riversdale; Dunkeron Lodge.

WATERVILLE RIVERS. Waterville River or **Currane**, short river joining **Lough Currane**. Popular with visitors. Salmon, sea trout, brown trout. All migratory fish running to Lough Currane go through this river, which also has spring run of large sea trout. There is a commercial fishery, traps of which are lifted on July 15. Lough Currane: famous for its large sea trout and spring salmon fishing, grilse from June; fishing predominately by boat, free to licence-holders. All sea trout under 12in to be returned alive. Season 17 Jan-30 Sept. Boat hire, Waterville AA, c/o Lobster Bar, Waterville (066 74183), and others.

Cummeragh River, spate river with five upper loughs, **Derriana, Niamona, Cloonaghlin, Na Huisce** and **Coppal**, feeding main river which flows into Lough Currane. All these loughs contain salmon, sea trout and browns, and river has good catches of salmon in summer and autumn. Tickets for all these may be obtained from Tadhg O'Sullivans Fishing Tackle, Waterville, Co Kerry (066 74433/75384). Local hills contain numerous small loughs rarely fished.

Inny River, a fair sized spate river some 15m in length, with good run of salmon and sea trout from June onwards. Salmon fishing on these rivers is from 17 Jan-30 Sept. Spring fish average 11lbs, fish over 15lbs caught, record 32lbs. An unusual feature is that fish may be caught by a small fly on a floating line from opening day, although many are taken on rapallas, toby spoons and other baits. The system is noted for its large sea trout, with over 70% of Irish specimen (6lbs plus) fish taken. Season 14 Feb-30 Sept. Brown trout fishing is from 14 Feb-12 Oct. The bigger fish are caught in Lough Currane and Derriana. Tickets from Tadgh O'Sullivan (*above*). **Waterville House, tel: 0667 4244, lets occasional rods on R Waterville** and R Inny, for 4 hour periods. Spinning allowed in spring, thereafter, fly only. Several other owners have fishing to let on Inny, incl Butler Arms Hotel, Waterville, tel: 0667 4156; J O'Connell, Foildrenagh, Mastergeehy, Killarney (066 74523), lake and river with salmon, sea trout, brown trout, tickets from Butler Arms Hotel; J O'Shea, Killenleigh, Mastergeehy; M J O'Sullivan, tel: 0667 4255. Tackle shops: Tadgh O'Sullivan (*above*); Coomaciste Crafts; Sean O'Shea. Other hotels: Silver Sands, White House.

CARHAN and FERTA: small spate rivers which enter Valentia Harbour. Small run of grilse and sea trout. Carhan is overgrown and worm is the best method. **Kells Lough** is between **Glenbeigh** and **Caherciveen**. Plentiful stock of small browns.

CARAGH: river runs through **Caragh Lake** to sea at Dingle Bay. Salmon, sea trout, trout. Salmon best from May, sea trout late, good fishing at night. Bass and mullet in estuary. Permits for lower river from Mrs Maureen O'Grady, Ferndale Heights, Glenbeigh (066 68228); for upper river from Glencar Hotel, Glencar (066 60102). Immediately to the east of Caragh Lake is a large group of small loughs, incl **L Nakirka**, 20 acres, with good stocks of small wild browns and stocked larger fish. For permit contact SWRFB, 1 Neville Terrace, Macroome, Co Cork (026 41222).

Glenbeigh (Co Kerry). For lower water; wt £26 and dt £6, from Towers Hotel. Hotel also issues permits for 6m of **Laune** (single bank only), 8½m of **Feale**, 3m of **Flesk, Behy** and **Loughs Caragh** and **Currane**. To south west of Glenbeigh is a group of small trout loughs drained by **R Behy**, incl **Coomnacronia** and **Coomaglaslaw**: free fishing on all of them.

Glencar (Co Kerry) Glencar House Hotel *(see advt)* has 7 beats, one rod per beat, reserved for guests only; salmon; best months, Feb to end of June; grilse June onwards; sea trout. Average salmon catch over 10 years, 310 per annum. The hotel also has fishing on **Loughs Cloon, Acoose** and **Reagh**. Many smaller rivers and lakes holding brown trout. Ghillies and boats in vicinity. Tackle and licences at hotel, tel: 066 60102(60167 fax).

MACGILLYCUDDY'S REEKS (Co Kerry). In the Gap of Dunloe, a line of three small lakes drain into **Laune** at Beaufort Bridge: **Black Lake, Cushvalley** and **Auger**. Free fishing for plentiful small brown trout that fight extremely well. Very small fly recommended. At head of Black Valley are **Cummeenduff Loughs** and **Lough Reagh**, which are approached via Gap of Dunloe. Free fishing with spring salmon and good grilse run.

Boats from J O'Donoghue, Black, Valley, Killarney.

DINGLE PENINSULA (Co Kerry). Several small rivers and loughs are fishable in this area; **Rivers Milltown** and **Owenascaul** on south side, free fishing with some sea trout; **Owencashla, Glennahoo, Scarid, Owenmore** on north side: some migratory fish in spate, worth fishing. Mostly free. Owencashla overgrown. Loughs incl **Anascaul**, with sea trout in Aug/Sept; **Gill**, west of **Castlegregory**: free, for small browns; **Adoon**, with sea trout from August, free; and many others worth exploring. **Lough Caum** at Castlegregory is SWRFB trout fishery with small native browns and stocked rainbows. Boats for hire on water.

LAUNE and MAINE (including Killarney Lakes)

(For close seasons, licences, etc, see The South-Western Regional Fisheries Board)

LAUNE: Drains Killarney Lakes and flows 14m NW to Dingle Bay. Salmon, sea trout. Late summer best time for trout. **Muckross Fishery**: visitors permits from Laune Salmon AA fishing (sec T O'Riordan, 50 Oak Park Demesne, Tralee, tel: 066 24690), from O'Sullivan's Foodstore, Beaufort Bridge, Beaufort, Killarney.

Beaufort (Co Kerry). For upper reaches. Permits and light tackle from O'Sullivan's, Beaufort Bridge, Killarney, tel: 064 44397. Self-catering house on banks. Accom at Anglers lodge, Beaufort.

MAINE: Maine and tributaries **Little Maine** and **Brown Flesk** hold salmon, sea trout and brown trout. Salmon fishing fair, after drainage setbacks in 1950s, and Brown Flesk has at least 35 holding pools; over 200 salmon per season, sea and brown trout fishing often good. River is late. Best at medium to low water; good grilse from end of June, sea trout in July. Little Maine has seven or eight salmon pools and good fishing for small browns. Sea trout best at night. Part of this system is free fishing: check with SWRFB.

KILLARNEY LAKES: Consist of three lakes: **Upper Lake, Muckross Lake, Lough Leane**, last being much the largest at 4,500 acres, connected with sea by **R Laune**. Good free trout fishing, excellent stocks of wild browns av 8ozs. Numerous boatmen for hire, £50 per day, two fishing. Boat distributors: Henry Clifden, Ross Castle, Killarney (064 322252); Sean Sweeney (064 44207). **R Flesk** feeds **Lough Leane**. Medium sized spate river, with good grilse run: Saratoga House Hotel, Muckross Rd, Killarney, offers free fishing to guests. Many small mountain lakes; free trout fishing. **Barfinnihy Lake**, 10m away on Sneem Road, is well stocked with brown trout, fishing by permit only, contact O'Neills (*see Killarney*) or J O'Hare (*see Kenmare*).

Killarney (Co Kerry). Salmon fishing best in May/June. Sea trout fishing poor, brown trout excellent, best June, and Sept to mid-Oct. Fishing on R Flesk is open for £10 per week from Lough Leane AA. **Lough Leane** (4,500 acres), largest of Killarney lakes; famous for beauty of scenery; estimated that local fishermen get hundreds of salmon and grilse by trolling baits every season. Free fishing; max rods 40-50. Boats from Harry Clifton, Ross Castle (064 32252); Abbey Boating & Fishing Tours, tel: 064 34351. Tackle shops: O'Neill's, 6 Plunkett St (064 31970 (35689 fax)), supplies tickets for rivers and lakes, ghillies and boats; The Handy Stores, Main St; Harry Clifton. Many hotels and guest houses.

LEE

(For close seasons, licences, etc, see The South-Western Regional Fisheries Board)

Draining **Gougane Barra Lake** and flowing 53m to Cork Harbour, Lee was formerly notable early salmon river (Feb to May) but fishing partly spoilt by hydro-electric schemes; salmon sport restricted to lower 6m. Experimental trout stocking programme is planned. Trout are more plentiful from Leemount Bridge to below Inniscarra Dam. SWRFB Fisheries: **Inniscarra Lake**, River Lee: 530 ha, and over 25 miles of bank side, possibly Ireland's best bream fishing. Bags in excess of 100lb are common. **Inniscarra Salmon Fishery** is a ¾m double bank salmon fishery, below hydro-electric station. Fishable from March, peaks in April-May, mid-June for grilse, brown trout 15 Feb-12 Oct. Permits £12. Tel: 026 41221.

Cork (Co Cork). Salmon fishing on lower R Lee at Inniscarra Dam and below Millbro; season Feb 1 to Sept 30. Fishing is privately owned or leased and controlled mainly by Lee Salmon A and Cork Salmon A (dt £10, from Hon Sec). Salmon fishing licence is required, obtainable from tackle shops. Trout fishing on **R Shournagh, Martin, Bridge** and **Dripsey**; small streams with brown trout; fishing mostly free. For information contact Cork Trout AA, Blarney AA and tackle shops. Lough in Cork City, 10 acres, has large carp (Irish record 22lb) and eels, 2lb to 6lb. Tackle shops: T W Murray & Co, 87 Patrick St; The Tackle Shop, 6 Lavitts Quay. Hotels: Jurys, Metropole, Imperial.

Macroom (Co Cork). Stocked brown trout fishing on **Inniscarra Reservoir**; contact SW Fisheries Board, Macroom, tel: 026 41222. **Carrigohid Reservoir** is good pike fishery, with perch shoals. Other venues for pike are lower **Sullane River, Middle Lee, Lough Allua**. Middle Lee, Rivers Sullane, Laney and Foherish, and **Gougane Barra** lake are good fisheries for small trout. Hotels: Castle, Victoria.

LIFFEY

(For close seasons, licences, etc, see The Eastern Regional Fisheries Board)

Winding river with two reservoirs along its course, rises some 13m SW of Dublin but flows over 80m before entering sea at Islandbridge, Dublin. Subject to hydro-electric floods, it has salmon, brown trout and some sea trout in lower reaches. Recorded salmon run about 3,000 pa with rod catch of 500-800. Mayfly hatch end of May. Best trout fishing from Lucan upstream. Best salmon between Straffan and Islandbridge.

Dublin (Co Dublin). Most water controlled by clubs. Dublin & Dist Salmon AA: Liffey at Islandbridge, Lucan, and below Leixlip Bridge; Dublin Trout AA: about 6m on Upper and Lower Liffey at Ballyward Bridge, Clane, Straffan/Celbridge, **Leixlip**, **Blessington** and **Upper** and **Lower Bohernabreena Reservoirs**; mainly trout fishing, some salmon in Liffey, and pike, also. Dt £5-£2, depending on water. Clane Trout and Salmon AA: approx 4m of excellent brown trout water, best from early May, with moderate salmon after July. Dt £5 (from Wallace's Trophy Shop, Clane, or Hon Sec), fly, bait fishing discouraged, no coarse; North Kildare Trout & Salmon AA: Millicent Bridge to Kilcullen Bridge; Kilcullen Trout and Salmon AA, Kilcullen u/s to Harristown; Ballymore Eustace Salmon and Trout AA, Ballymore Eustace to Harristown; Kilbride AC: Ballyfoyle to Ballysmutton; Lucan AC fishes Lucan stretch. Chapelizod AC has water from Old Mill Race River to Laurence Brook Weir, game and coarse fishing, no dt, membership £20 p.a., conc. Broadmeadow AC fishes **Broadmeadow R** and **Tonelgee Reservoir**. Tickets from tackle shops. Dt £2 for Dublin Trout AA waters from Dan O'Brien, New Rd, Blackhall, Clane, Co Kildare and Sy Gallagher, Reeves, Straffan, Co Kildare. Dublin Corporation controls fishing on **Roundwood Reservoir** (20m) and on **Bohernabreena Reservoir** (8m); the former leased to Co Wicklow AA; fly only; bank fishing; st and dt. **Grand Canal**, which runs alongside Liffey for some distance, holds brown trout, bream, rudd, perch and pike. Coarse fishing also in **Royal Canal**, similar species. Tackle shops: P Cleere &

Son, 5 Bedford Row; Rory's, 17a Temple Bar, Dublin 2 (Dublin 6772351), who sells permits for Dublin Salmon A, Dodder A, North Kildare A, Tolka A.

Naas (Co Kildare). Ballymore Eustace Trout & Salmon AA has fishing on Liffey from **Ballymore Eustace** to **Harristown**, and also **Golden Falls Lake**. St and dt are from Michael Murphy, Publican, The Square, Ballymore Eustace. Kilcullen & Dist Trout and Salmon AA fishes Liffey at Kilcullen, u/s to Harristown. Prosperous Coarse AC fishes 20m of **Grand Canal**, *see Grand Canal*. Tackle shops: Cahills Sports; J Prescott, Pachelli Rd, both Naas; bait from Prescott. Hotel; Ardenode, Ballymore Eustace. Several guest houses.

MOY

(For close seasons, licences, etc, see The North Western Regional Fisheries Board)

Flowing 63m from its source in the Ox Mountains to enter Killala Bay at Ballina, its tributaries drain an area of some 800 square miles. One of Ireland's premier salmon rivers, particularly famous for its grilse and summer salmon. Stretches to suit all forms of angling from fly fishing to spinning to worm fishing. Spring run starts in early Feb; main grilse run starts in May and peaks in June/July.

Ballina (Co Mayo). Salmon fishing on three beats owned by **Moy Fishery**, May to end of Sept. Beat 1, £10 per day, rods limited; beat 2, ghillie and boat of two rods, £65; beat 3, £8 per day, st £20. Apply to Moy Fishery, Ridge Pool Rd, Ballina (096 21332). Moy Fishery can also arrange boats and engines for **Lough Conn** fishing. Ballina Salmon AA issues permits for a stretch downstream of Ridge Pool, apply to local tackle shops. Mount Falcon Castle Hotel has 7½m between Ballina and **Foxford**, including famous Wall Pool. Wt £60, dt £10. Apply to Mrs Aldridge, Mount Falcon Castle tel; 096 21172). Armstrong Fishery has adjoining left bank stretch of about 1m. Contact George Armstrong at fishery, tel: 094 5680. For the next mile up river, left bank, contact Gannons, Post Office, Foxford, tel: 094 56101. Ballina Angling Centre arranges boat fishing trips in Moy Estuary, also on Lough Conn. Tackle shops: M Swartz, Ballina Angling Centre, Dillon Terrace; Ridge Pool Tackle Shop; Boozy O'Brien's Pub, Ballina; John Walkin, Tone St; Vincent Doherty, Bridge St. Hotels: Conn Moy Lodge, Sligo Rd, tel: 096 70736 (caters for anglers), Balleek Castle, The Imperial, Downside.

Foxford (Co Mayo). Pontoon Bridge Hotel offers salmon and trout fishing on 4m of water, including renowned salmon pool at Pontoon Bridge. Tuition from May to Oct. Boats on lake, with or without motor and ghillie £25-£45 per day from hotel or tackle shop; tackle also (094 56120). Other local fisheries on **R Moy** are Foxford Salmon Anglers' Leckee Fishery: 1m both banks south of Foxford, dt £15, conc, tel 094 56731; Clongee Fishery, both banks above and below Lough Cullin: dt £15 from Sean Ruane, Clongee (094 56534); East Mayo AA, two separate beats above Foxford, dt £12: contact Mrs Wills, Ballylahan Bridge, tel: 094 51149; Beal Easa Fishery, Patrick Michael Gannon, (094 56101); Foxford Fishery, Chris Downey, 9 Moy View, Foxford (094 56824); m dt water, £15 per day, from Chris Downey or Maloneys Lodge, Foxford. Permits for most of these fisheries from Tiernan Bros (*below*). Free fishing on **Loughs Conn** and **Cullin**, 2m from town, and on a short

Check before you go

*While every effort has been made to ensure that the information given in **Where to Fish** is correct, the position is continually changing, and anglers are urged, in their own interests, to make enquiries before travelling to selected venues. This is especially important with reference to prices quoted. Anglers attention is also drawn to the fact that hotels mentioned under the various fishing stations do not necessarily have water of their own. Any amendments or further data for inclusion in subsequent editions, and any comments, will be welcome.*

stretch of R Moy downstream of Foxford Bridge. Healys Hotel at **Pontoon** has boats at southern end of Lough Conn and at Lough Cullin. Tackle shops: Tiernan Bros, Main St; Angling Advice Centre (094 56731), both Foxford; J J Connor, Spencer St, Castlebar, Co Mayo.

Crossmolina (Co Mayo). Salmon, grilse, trout. Free fishing on **Lough Conn**. Boats and ghillies from J Moffat, Kilmurry House, Castlehill Crossmolina (096 31227); P Kelly, Cloghans, Ballina. Cloonamoyne Fishery, Enniscoe, Castlehill, Ballina, tel/fax: 096 31851, provides a complete angling service covering brown trout fishing on Loughs Conn and Cullin, and salmon fishing on Loughs Carrownore, Beltra, Furnace and Feeagh; also river fishing for salmon, sea trout, browns, and pike; accommodation and transport arranged. Tackle shop: Philip Munnelly, Main St (096 31314). Hotel: Dolphin.

Swinford (Co Mayo). Spring salmon best from mid-March, grilse June onwards. Swinford AA issues permits, apply to Mrs Wills, Ballylahon Bridge (094 56221); Seamus Boland, Bridge St. **Lough Talt** is good brown trout lake, free.

Tributaries of the Moy

BUNREE. Joins just below Ballina. End of season salmon fishing, sea trout, brown trout. Free fishing.

GWEESTION. **Glore River** and **Trimoge River** join to become **Gweestion**, flowing from south easterly direction. Both have a large stock of small brown trout, with free fishing.

MULLAGHANOE and OWENGARVE. These two rivers flow from the **Charlestown** area westwards. They contain a good stock of browns to 1½lb. Fishing free, excellent on Owengarve d/s of Curry Village.

EINAGH. Joins main river from **Lough Talt** near **Aclare**. Brown trout to 3lb, but average at 10oz. Sea trout run; free fishing in river and lough (browns, av ½lb).

LOUGH CONN SYSTEM. Lough Conn, 12,000 acres, together with **L Cullin**, has free fishing for salmon, main run from end of March through April, grilse run from May through July. Salmon adhere to known localities, and are taken by trolling spoon or Devon minnow, a few on wet fly. Trout fishing starts around March 17. The vast majority of trout caught on Lough Conn are taken on wet flies during seasonal hatches. L Conn has one of the longest mayfly hatches in the country, from about 20 May until almost the end of June. Trout fishing slows in July, but improves in August. Specimen fish are sometimes taken. Several rivers run into **Loughs Conn** and **Cullin** which offer free fishing for game and coarse fish. From north west, **Deel River**: salmon in spring and summer, brown trout u/s of Deel Bridge. From the south, **Clydagh** and **Manulla Rivers,** and the outflow from **Castlebar Lakes** all join a few miles above lough. On Clydagh free salmon fishing; on Manulla free trout fishing between **Moyhenna** and **Ballyvary** bridges. Some free fishing for wild browns on location in **Islandeady Bilberry Lough**. **Upper** and **Lower Lough Lannagh** and **Lough Mallard**, nr **Castlebar**, have been developed as free trout fisheries. There is a wide range of accommodation approximate to the Lough Conn fisheries. Contact NWRFB, Ardnaree House, Abbey St, Ballina, tel: 096 22788, for further information on L Conn fishing.

SHANNON

(For close seasons, licences, etc, see The Shannon Regional Fisheries Board)

Largest river in these islands, 160m long with catchment area covering greater part of central Ireland. Enters Atlantic on west coast through long estuary. A typical limestone river, rich in weed and fish food, of slow current for most part, and though some its sources rise in peat, acidity counteracted by limestone reaches. Many of the adverse effects of hydro-electric scheme now overcome by re-stocking and other forms of fishery management. With exception of the famous Castleconnell stretch, Shannon mostly sluggish. Salmon run from March to May, grilse from end of May to September. Primary sea trout waters are **Rivers Feale** and **Doonbeg**. Permits from local tackle shops. Trout fishing is a feature of Shannon and tributaries, **Mulcair**, **Newport**, **Nenagh**, **Brosna**, **Little Brosna**, **Fergus**, and **Maigue**.

There is a mayfly rise, when excellent sport can be enjoyed, free of charge, in **Loughs Derg** and **Ree** at Athlone. Trolling is the usual method, otherwise; trout grow large. Salmon fishing rights on Shannon and tributaries are reserved by the ESB, and a permit is required, which is sold as st, wt, or dt, from ESB Fisheries Office, Ardnacrusha, tel: 061 345589, or ESB Shop, Limerick. Brown trout fishing is in part free, and in part leased to the Central Fisheries Board or fishing clubs. River has well-deserved reputation for its coarse fishing. Excellent fisheries for rudd, perch, shoals of bream and roach, at Plassey, O'Brien's Bridge, u/s of Portumna, Banagher, Shannonbridge. The three main pike fisheries of the system are R Shannon itself, Lough Derg, and R Fergus. There is a limit on the killing of pike: one per angler per day, max size, 3kgs. Coarse fishing may also be had in Derg and Ree. **Lough Allen**, northernmost lake of Shannon, specially good for pike. Eel fishing is growing more popular in Shannon region, which has sluggish stretches ideal for the species, large catches coming from Shannon, **R Fergus, L Derg** and **East Clare Lakes**; Mouth of Suck at Shannonbridge and mouth of Brosna are good spots to try. No state licence is required to fish for brown trout or coarse fish in the Shannon, but a licence costing £25 is required to fish for sea trout and salmon. For angling guide and information on angling services in Shannon region contact Shannon Development, Shannon Town Centre, Co Clare, tel: 061 361555 (903 Fax).

Kilrush (Co Clare). West Clare AA has fishing in this corner of Co Clare, on Lakes **Knockerra** (50 acres), **Knockalough**, **Doolough**, **Kilkee Reservoir**, all fly and worm only. Trout permits £5 from Jack Horgan, Cree PO and Doonbeg Tourist Office. Tackle shops: Clancy's, Henry St (065 51107), all local fishing information, and emergency tackle repairs; Michael O'Sullivan & Son, 49/50 Moore St, tel: 065 51071. Hotels: Strand, Kilrush Creek Lodge, both Kilkee. salmon and sea trout fishing locally on **Cree**, **Annageeragh** and **Doonbeg Rivers**.

Limerick (Co Limerick). On tidal Shannon. Clancy's Strand is the lowest bottom fishery on Shannon, mainly trout fishing, which can be very good, on fly, worm, dead minnow or spinner. ESB permit required. On outskirts of city is the Long Shore Fishery: wide, deep tidal water with spring salmon run; it can be fished from both banks. Good spring salmon fishing at **Plassey** (2m); 500 yds salmon fishing which peaks in May, and trout. ESB permit reqd. Limerick tackle shops: McMahon, Roches Street; Limerick Sports Stores, 10 William Street; J Donerty, 3 John St; Steve's Tackle, Michael St.

Castleconnell (Co Limerick). Principal centre for salmon angling on Shannon and within 3m of **Mulcair River**. Traditional big fish water; catches improved recently. Good run of spring salmon, grilse from May, and Sept fishing is usually good. Fishing on eight Castleconnell beats controlled by Regional Manager, Hydro Generation Region, Ardnacrusha, Nr Limerick, who will book beats and provide information. Permits £10 to £25, from Head Warden, M Murtagh, O'Briens Bridge, tel: 061 377289, or from Kingfisher Angling Centre. Advance booking advisable, from ESB, tel: 061 345588. Best beats to book are nos. 8, 4, 5, 1, 7, 6, 3, 2. Best spring beats are 8, 5, 7, 4, 1, 3, 2. Best months for spring salmon, April to mid-May, grilse mid-May to end June. Fly, spinning and worm. Trout fishing free. The best coarse fishing in Limerick area is located just below Castleconnell salmon fishery. This is free fishing. Tackle shop: Paddy Guerin, Kingfisher Angling Centre, tel: 061 377407, supplies boats, ghillies, hires tackle, also supplies permits and licences, and runs Kingfisher AC. Accommodation at Edelweiss, Stradbally, tel: 061 377397; J Moloney, Riverside, O'Brien's Bridge, tel: 061 377303.

Killaloe (Co Clare). At outlet from Lough Derg, good centre for trout and coarse fishing on lake. Trout angling can be very good in May and autumn; fish average 3-4lb. Boats for hire. **Doon Lough**, 8m west, is a fine coarse fishery, with a good stock of bream to 3lb, also boat fishing for large pike. Boats for hire. Good bream fishing at caravan park on west shore. Tackle shop: McKeogh's, Ballina. Hotel: Lakeside.

Scariff Bay (Co Clare). From Aughinish Point into bay there is good fishing for specimen pike, also stocks of bream, tench, perch and rudd. Boat essential. Further west shore centres for coarse fishing are **Mountshannon/Whitegate**: Church Bay contains large tench, pike, bream and rudd; **Williamstown Harbour**: big tench from boat, quay fishing for pike, perch and bream; **Rossmore** pier: good place for same species, and a nice spot for camping. Boats and ghillies are for hire.

Dromineer (Co Tipperary). Best centre for middle sections of **Lough Derg**. Large trout taken spinning or trolling; also good centre for dry fly and dapping; trout up to 10lb caught. Mayfly starts about first week in May. Coarse fishing very good at **Youghal Bay**, Dromineer, **Kilgarvan** and **Terryglass** from quays, harbour walls and shore; Carrigahorig Bay has shoals of big bream and large pike: boat essential; fishing free. Eight fishing clubs on lake are represented by Lough Derg AA. **River Nenagh** flows into R Shannon at Dromineer; a major trout fishery with small number of salmon; in wider stretches trout can reach 2lb, about ½lb in narrows. No coarse fish except between Ballyartella Weir and mouth of river (1m); 22m of fishable water. Fly fishing best Mar-May, wet and dry fly. Rivers Nenagh and tributary **Ollatrim** (trout fishery only, no maggot fishing) are controlled by Ormond AA; st from tackle shop: Whelan's, Summerhill, Nenagh, Co Tipperary.

Portumna (Co Galway). At northern inlet end of **Lough Derg**. Some good dapping bays within reach. Bream and rudd fishing in Shannon. Best pike months are March to May, and Oct. Good perch fishing in summer months. Local club membership £5 from tackle shop. Tackle shop: Garry Kenny, Palmerstown Stores, tel: 0509 41071. Hotels: Westpark; Portland House. Many guest houses.

Lough Rea (Co Galway). 19m NW of Portumna; fairly large limestone lake with trout, pike and perch. Fishing on lough and river open to members of Loughrea AA, which has improved and restocked water; trout average 2lb, pike run to over 30lb; for dt and boats contact Sweeney Travel, Loughrea, tel: 091 41552. Loughrea tackle shop: Beatty's, Church St. Hotel: O'Deas.

Banagher (Co Offaly). Brown trout, coarse fishing good: bream, rudd, hybrids, pike, perch, eels. River is wide at **Meelick**, with islands, pools and weirs. There is some east bank fishing for salmon, mainly from boat. Access to west bank is from **Kilnaborris**: bank fishing possible, in fast water. Occasional spring salmon, mainly grilse. **Brosna** and **Little Brosna River** and small tributary **Camcor River**, nr **Birr**, controlled by Central Fisheries Board; brown trout; a licence to fish required. Coarse fishing on **Grand Canal**. **Ferbane** is a good centre, with bream, rudd, pike. Shannon Regional Fisheries Board stock **Pallas Lake** (18m E) with rainbow and brown trout. Season 1 May-12 Oct. Bank fishing. Fly only. 6 fish limit. Permits from Jim Griffin, Tackle Shop, Rahan, Co Offaly; Al Conroy, Tackle Shop, Kilbride St (0506 21283), and Joe Finlay, 15 William St, both Tullamore, Co Offaly. Other tackle shops:, Donegans, Lyons, Kellerhers, all Banagher. Hotels: Brosna Lodge; Shannon.

Shannonbridge (Co Offaly). Junction of Shannon and **Suck** is a fine centre for coarse fishing; long stretches of bank ideal for bream, hybrids, tench and rudd. Hot water from the Power Station attracts tench. Eel and roach fishing also, is good here. Assn: Shannonbridge AA. Tackle and baits from Dermot Killeen, Bar & Grocery, Main St, tel: 0905 74112.

Athlone (Co Westmeath). Athlone AA has water within 20m radius; restocked with trout. Some salmon. Shannon and Lough Ree abound with trout (good rise to mayfly, late May to late June), pike, roach and bream; bank or boat. Tench plentiful on **Lough Ree. Lough Garnafailagh**, which has produced remarkable catches of tench and bream, may be fished from here. At Barrymore Point, Lough Ree, is good fishing for rudd and bream. Anglers accommodation: Mrs Duggan, Villa St John, Roscommon Rd, tel: 0902 92490; Mrs Denby, Shelmalier, tel: 0902 72245.

Lanesborough (Co Longford). Bream, rudd, rudd-bream hybrids, perch, pike, eels. Coarse fishing on **R Shannon, Suck, Lough Ree** and **Feorish River**. Good stock of big fish early in season on hot water stretch of Shannon below Power Station, from July these move out into lake. Baits from Holmes Tackle Shop; M Healey, Lakeside Stores. Tackle from Holmes Tackle Shop; Finns, Main St, Roscommon. Accommodation for anglers: Abbey Hotel, Roscommon, tel: 0903 26240; Mrs Mary Glennon, Rookwood, Athleague, tel: 0903 63810 (self-catering).

Strokestown (Co Roscommon). Free fishing in locality, some on £5 dt. Convenient centre for Shannon and **Lough Lea**, a chain of small lakes with rudd, perch, bream, pike and tench. **Cloonfree Lake**, one mile from town, is another good coarse fishery, especially for rudd. **Kilglass Lake**, a five-mile long chain, is 4 miles out on Dumsa Rd: plentiful bream and rudd. **Annamore Lake**, record rudd caught in 1995. **Lough na Blaith** has new fishing development with 70 fishing stands erected; rudd, bream, tench, roach. Local club, Strokestown AC. Approved accommodation: Mrs Cox, Church View House, Strokestown, tel: 078 33047, central for much local free fishing.

Rooskey (Co Leitrim). Centre for coarse fishing on Rivers Shannon, **Rinn** or **Rynn**, and many small lakes in the area. Bream, tench, rudd, perch, pike, roach. Some brown trout in Shannon. Good catches in **Drumdad Lake** near **Mohill**. Mohill is also a good centre for **Loughs MacHugh**, **Erril, Lakes Cloonboniagh** and **Creenagh**: fine waters for tench and bream, with pike. Tackle shops: Roosky Quay Enterprises; Lakeland Bait, Knocknacrory. Accommodation catering for anglers: Lakeland House; Mrs Davis, Avondale, tel: 078 38095; Mrs Duffy, Killianiker, tel: 078 38016.

Carrick-on-Shannon (Co Leitrim). Centre for **Shannon, Boyle, Loughs Key, Allen, Corry, Drumharlow** and many others. Trout and coarse fish. Boyle carries heavy head of roach. Good venues are: **Hartley Bridge, Drumsna, Carrick, Albert Lock**. Heavy catches are consistent. Tackle shops: The Creel, Main St; Tranquillity Tackle, Kilclare. Many guest houses and hotels offer special anglers accommodation, including Weir House, with 200m Shannon and 41 lakes within 6 miles; **Lough Bran**, with boats for hire; Aisleigh House; Ard-na-Greine House.

Drumshanbo (Co Leitrim). R Shannon rises in Cuilcagh Mountains a short distance N of here. Free coarse fishing on R Shannon, **Lough Allen** and twelve small lakes, incl. **Acres, Derrynahoo, Carrickport** and **Scur**. Trout fishing on Shannon, esp. below **Bellantra Bridge**, in fast water. Lough Allen Conservation Assn has stocked L Allen with over 100,000 trout in past five years. Lough also has a good stock of coarse fish, including specimen pike over 30lb and some big trout. However, as lough acts as a reservoir for the power station near Limerick and has sluice gates at lower end, the waters fluctuate considerably and at low water there are many hazardous rocks; and also there can be sudden strong winds. Local club is Lough Allen AC, visitors welcome, membership £10. Two trout streams run into L Allen, on which fishing is regarded as free. The **Yellow River** enters from east, a spate river, with brown trout in lower reaches. The **Owennayle** is a mountain stream entering from north. Trout average ½lb. Tackle shop: McGaurty's, The Square. Anglers accommodation: Paddy Mac's, High St, tel: 078 41128; Woodside Guesthouse, tel: 078 41106; Mrs Costello, Forest View, tel: 078 41243; McGuires Rent a Cottage, tel: 078 41033.

Principal Tributaries of the Shannon

DEEL. Enters estuary near Askeaton some miles below Limerick. Fishing stations; **Rathkeale** (Limerick), and **Askeaton** (Limerick), (best Feb-May), white trout (on summer floods), a few salmon and good brown trout (best mid-Mar to Sept). Parts of river preserved by Mrs R Hunt, Inchirourke, Askeaton, and Altaville Estate. Hotels at Rathkeale; Central, Madigan's. Deel AA issues st £5 for 15m at Rathkeale. nearest tackle shop at Limerick.

MAIGUE. Enters estuary between mouth of Deel and Limerick. Brown trout, and a few salmon.

Adare (Co Limerick). Adare Manor Hotel, tel: 061 396566, has 2m stretch for guests. Ghillie on site. Dunraven Arms Hotel has 1¼m fishing free to guests. Contact hotel for details of Bleech Lake, 5m, good trout and pike fishing. Rathkeale, 7m, trout, with ghillies and boats. Some free tidal water below town.

Croom (Co Limerick). Maigue AA has brown trout fishing. Season 1 March-30 Sept. Fly only. Bag limit 6 fish. Trout ¾lb-3lb. St £25, mt £17, wt £10, dt £5, from Hon Sec. Preserved water below town, free above to Bruree and beyond. Tributaries Camogue, Loobagh and Morningstar mostly free and very good for trout.

Kilmallock (Co Limerick). Kilmallock & Dist AC has brown trout fishing near town on **R Loobagh**, from Riversfield Bridge to Garrouse Bridge, fly only.

River is recovering from drainage scheme, and fish average small. Tickets from club members.

MULCAIR. Enters Shannon 4 miles east of Limerick, and is joined by **Slievenohera River**, which is a confluence of the Newport and Annagh Rivers. Mulcair River is spate system, mainly grilse, salmon from March, small brown trout d/s of Annacotty Bridge. The Slievenohera system gets spate runs of grilse from late June. St, wt and dt from Regional Manager, Hydro Generation Region, Ardnacrusha, Nr Limerick.

KILMASTULLA. Enters Shannon above O'Briens Bridge from east, near Montpelier. River holds some good trout at Shalee, and a moderate stock to 1lb immediately u/s of Kilmastulla Bridge. E.S.B. permit reqd.

FERGUS. Limestone stream with gin-clear water, trout fishing good; few salmon in spring. Fishing free. *See also Co Clare Streams and Loughs.*

Ennis (Co Clare). Good centre for fishing principal waters of Co Clare, including several coarse fish lakes and rivers (tench, pike, perch, rudd). Good brown trout fishing in Fergus and lakes it drains. **Knockerra Lake** has rainbow trout to 8lb. Tackle shop in Ennis: M F Tierney, Fishing & Cycle Centre, 17 Abbey St, tel: 065 29433. Accommodation: Auburn Lodge; Old Ground; Queen's; West Country Inn; G & J Finn, Druimin, tel: 065 24183.

Corofin (Co Clare). Numerous lakes very good for trout, others for perch, rudd and tench, and all for pike. Accommodation at number of family guest houses. Lakes Inchiquin, Atedaun and Ballycullinan and R Fergus close by; boats.

Tulla (Co Clare). Area is noted for its excellent bream fishing; also roach, tench and pike; fishing free in about 20 lakes within 10m radius (Ennis 10m).

BROSNA. Enters Shannon from the north east, at junction with Grand Canal, north of Banagher. A brown trout fishery, controlled by Inland Fisheries Trust, Dublin 9.

SUCK. Flows through 30 mile valley linking West Roscommon and East Galway, joins Shannon at Shannonbridge, between Banagheer and Athlone. Wild brown trout and excellent coarse fishing for tench, pike, bream and rudd. Tench to 6lb at Shannonbridge Power Station, where "hot water stretch" attracts fish. Specimen rudd in L Ree. Good fishing in Coreen Ford area, nr Ballinasloe.

Ballinasloe (Co Galway). River Suck deep and slow, providing excellent coarse fishing with large shoals of bream to 8lbs, bags of 100lbs common, also rudd to 2lbs. Other local waters include **Lough O'Flyn**, **Ballinlough**, 600 acres trout fishery, controlled by CFB. **Bunowen** and **Shiven** hold excellent stock of trout, especially good early in season. **Lough Acalla**, nr Kilconnell; rainbow trout, season 1 May to 30 Sept, st and dt purchased locally. Shannon Regional Fisheries Board permits from Keller Brothers. Hayden's Hotel offers anglers accommodation with salmon and coarse fishing in Rivers Shannon and Suck.

Ballygar (Co Galway). For middle R Suck and also tributaries, **Rivers Bunowen** and **Shiven**. Excellent coarse fishing. St £5 from Tom Kenny, Public House, The Square. Tackle from Hanley's Tackle Shop.

Roscommon (Co Roscommon). Coarse fishing on R Suck and **Lough Ree**. River is good for trout in mayfly season. Irish record rudd (3lb 1oz) caught in nearby **Kilglass Lake**. Roscommon Gun and Rod Club has Hind River; trout; dry-fly water. Hotels: Grelly's, Royal, O'Gara's, Abbey.

Castlerea (Co Roscommon). For upper R Suck reaches which hold trout in some areas. **Lough O'Flynn** now has excellent trout fishing, thanks to CFB improvement work. SRFB permit required, season £20, conc, day £5. Permits and boats from Padraig Campbell, O'Flynn Bar, Ballinlaugh. Trout and coarse fish in **Lough Glinn** and **Errit Lakes**. Hotels: Don Arms, Tully's.

INNY. A slow-flowing river densely populated with roach, pike, and large bream. Trout between Abbeyshrule and Shrule Bridge. Inny AA controls much fishing.

Mullingar (Co Westmeath). Many coarse loughs in area, including **Kinale** (roach, pike), **Slevins**, bream, trench, pike, perch, **Patrick** (tench), **Sheever**, (bream, tench, pike, perch), **Ballinafid** (specimen bream, carp), **Doolin** (carp, tench, bream), **Derravaragh** (pike, roach and trout); trout loughs are **Lene**, north of Collinstown, fly and trolling, good fly hatches on water; **Bane**, northeast of Mullingar, access through ghillies only, very large brown trout; **Glore**, 4km from Castlepollard, excellent stocks of wild browns, average over 2lbs, good fly hatches; famous limestone loughs, **Sheelin** ((4,654 acres, *see below*), **Ennell** (3,200 acres) and **Owel** (2,500 acres); and also **Mount Dalton Lake**, a small fishery stocked with brown trout. Season 1 March-12 Oct Ennell and Owel; on Ennell, wet fly fishing productive in March, fly hatches from May; on Owel, large hatches of fly from Mid Apr, and sedges from end of Jul to mid-Aug; on both lakes, dapping grasshopper and daddy longlegs in Aug. Mt Dalton season 1 May-12 Oct. Size limit 30cm. Bag limit 6 fish. Fly only on Mt Dalton Lake. St £20 and dt £5, from Shannon Regional Fisheries Board, Tudenham, Mullingar (044 48769); David O'Malley, *see below*. **Royal Canal** nr Mullingar contains tench, roach, rudd, tench, pike. West of Mullingar to Ballinea Bridge is one of Ireland's prime tench fisheries. Local assns: L Owel Trout PA, membership £7 p.a.; L Ennell Trout PA. Boats on L Ennell from Myles Hope, tel: 044 40807, or Jim Roache, tel: 044 40314; L Owel: Jack Doolan, Levington, Mullingar (044 42085), £22 per day with engine; Mount Dalton: Mrs C Gibson Brabazon, Mt Dalton, Rathconrath, Mullingar, (044 55102); L Sheelin: Stephen Reilly, Finea, tel: 043 81124. Tackle shops: David O'-Malley, 33 Dominick St (044 48300); Sams Tackle, Castle St, both Mullingar. Hotels: Bloomfield House, Greville Arms. Lakeside accommodation: Mrs A Ginnell, Lough Owel Lodge, tel: 044 48714; Mrs Kathleen Shaw, The Quarry Guest House, Mullingar, tel: 044 48261 (nr L Owel), boats and ghillies for hire; Mrs S T Kelly, Beechwood, tel: 044 71108; Mrs A Smyth, Whitehall Farm House, tel: 044 61140.

Castlepollard (Co Westmeath). Trout and coarse fish. **Lough Derravaragh** (2,700 acres), a limestone lake once famous for trout but in recent years trout stocks have decreased to be replaced by a large population of roach. **Lough Glore** (86 acres) holds excellent stock of wild brown trout; boat fishing only. **White Lake** (80 acres) is stocked annually with rainbow trout and some brown trout. Lakes controlled by Shannon Regional Fisheries Board. Season 1 March-12 Oct (Derravaragh and Glore); 1 May-12 Oct (White Lake). Bag limit 6 fish. St £9.50, dt £2; from Thomas Murphy, Fishing Tackle & Hardware, The Square (044 61137). Boats from Mrs Nancy McKenna, Fore (044 611781) for White Lake; Fergus Dunne, Oldcastle Rd, for L Glore.

Kilnaleck (Co Cavan). Brown trout fishing on **Lough Sheelin** (4,654 acres); rich limestone lough which produces and maintains a large stock of big brown trout. Fishing contolled by SRFB. Season 1 March-12 Oct. Mayfly from about mid-May to early June. hatches from Derry Point to curry Rocks, Merry Point, Sandbar, Plunkett's Point to Crane Island. Bag limit 6 fish. Coarse fishing is prohibited. No live bait fishing. Suitable flies and dt from Kilnahard Pier, Mountnugent, L Sheelin; dt also direct from Shannon Regional Fisheries Board, Mullaghboy, Ballyheelan, tel: 049 36144. Local assn: Lough Sheelin Trout PA. Tackle and Lough Sheelin information from Robert Chambers, Mullaghaboy, Ballyheelan, Kilnaleck (049 36682). Tackle and in-depth fishing information from Tom Murray, The Flying Sportsman, Carrick st, Kells, Co Meath (046 402050. Hotels: Sheelin Shamrock; Crover House, both Mountnugent. Boats from both hotels. B & B Accom at Sheelin House, Kilnahard: Josephine Leggette; boat and engine hire.

Two tributaries of the Inny are fishable, on a fisheries board permit: the **Tang River** joins Inny downstream of Ballymahon, and the **Rath River**, upstream. Both have a stock of small brown trout, and are best fished early in the season, before they run low. Permits from Sammy Smith, Tackle Shop, Castle St, or David O'Malley, Tackle Shop, 33 Dominick St, both Mullingar.

SLANEY

(For close seasons, licences, etc, see The Eastern Regional Fisheries Board)

Rises in corner between Barrow and Liffey watersheds and flows south 73m to Wexford Harbour. During most of course has rocky beds, rapids alternating with deep pools. Good spring salmon river, especially in Tullow-Bunclody reaches (Mar, April, May best; no autumn run) but of little account for brown trout save in upper reaches and in some tributaries. Good sea trout lower down and in tributaries Urrin and Boro. Best sea trout fishing in lower reaches, late June to August. Most salmon fishing private, but certain parts let from season to season and no permission needed to fish for salmon or sea trout from Enniscorthy Bridge to Ferrycarrig (Feb 26 to Sept 15). Fly fishing only, from 1 Apr to 31 Aug.

Wexford (Co Wexford). Garman AC has made efforts to restock. **Owenduff**; good white trout fishing in June, July and Aug. **Sow River** near Castlebridge good for brown trout and sea trout; permits from angling club. Fishing for brown trout on **Wexford Reservoir**. Sea fishing (inc. sea trout, bass and mullet) in estuary. Tackle shop: Bridges of Selskar, North Main Street. Hotels: Talbot, White's, County.

Enniscorthy (Co Wexford). Sea trout good; brown trout poor; free fishing downstream of bridge. Tackle shops: Paddy Lennon, 26 Main Street; Nolan, 3 Wafer Street, and C L Cullen, 14 Templeshannon. Hotels: Portsmouth Arms, Slaney Valley.

Bunclody (Co Wexford). Salmon and sea trout, browns and rainbows, coarse fishing for eels. Much fishing in area on Slaney, Clody and Derry, either free or for nominal fee. Bunclody Trout AC has fishing for visitors. Tackle shop (licences): John Nolan's Sports Shop, Ryland Rd. Accommodation: P Kinsella, Meadowside, tel: 054 77459.

Tullow (Co Carlow). Tullow Trout and Salmon AA have water on Slaney. Contact secretary. Trout and salmon fishing is free on Slaney from Rathvilly to Baltinglass, and also on **River Derreen** with permission from landowners. Hotel: Slaney.

The class fo fish to be encountered off Cahirciveen. 25lb. cod; 23lb. ling; 17lb. coalfish. Small wonder the place has been a by-word for a century!!

SEA FISHING STATIONS IN IRELAND

As elsewhere, the sea fishing in the Irish Republic has been growing in popularity. The inshore potential of these waters is now widely appreciated. Bass are much sought after along the south and west coasts, and pollack are abundant off the rocks. Deep-sea boats land specimen skate, conger, halibut, turbot and so on. Fishing facilities are improving all the time. There are however reports on the east coast of reduced sport for anglers, owing to over-fishing by trawlers. Space will not permit more than a few centres to be listed, but club secretaries and local tackle shops will be pleased to give further information and to help visitors.

Dundalk (Co Louth). Bay is shallow for the most part, but contains spurdog, ray and flatfish for boat anglers off north shore. Quay fishing from **Gyles Quay** at high water for flatfish and dogfish; the quay on **Castletown River** south bank, mullet in summer. 8m south at **Glyde** and **Dee** junction, spinning from southern breakwater for bass, mackerel, occasional sea trout. Good fishing rocks north of **Drogheda** at **Clogher Head**: pollack, coalfish, codling and mackerel. Club is North Louth Sea AC. Town also has two game angling clubs. Tackle shops: Macs Sports, Demesne Shopping Centre; Island Fishing Tackle, Park St (permits and licences); Military Connection, 8 Laurence St, Drogheda. Hotels: Ballymascanion, Imperial and others. Boats operate from **Carlingford**: Peadar Elmore, North Commons, Carlingford (042 73239, fax: 73733)

Dublin and **Dun Laoghaire** (Co Dublin). To north, **Howth Harbour** is popular venue: from piers, whiting, pollack, coalfish and codling; from rocks, mackerel, flatfish and others. Good boat fishing for large spurdog. Howth club holds annual festival. Estuary at **Sutton** is a good place to dig lugworm and clam. Ragworm can also be found. In Dublin Bay good points are: Dollymount Strand, (some large bass, flounder, eels, codling, good in autumn at evening); sea wall running south, (pollack, codling, whiting, bass and flounder); Liffey between Ringstead Basin and Pidgeon House Power Station (mullet and bass in large numbers); spinning below Poolbeg Lighthouse (bass, mackerel); Sandymount Strand, a large beach with gullies and pools, with bass, mullet, big flounder. This beach can be dangerous at flood tide. Ferryport at **Dun Laoghaire** provides pier fishing from West Pier: dabs and conger in summer, whiting, codling, pouting, coalfish in autumn/winter; also Coal Quay, for mullet fishing. Dublin has over thirty sea angling clubs affiliated to the Leinster Council of the IFSA. Dun Laoghaire Boat charter: Charles Robinson, Stella Maris, Church Hill, Wicklow (0404 68751); £20-£60 per angler, daily charter £200-£240. Several Dublin Tackle shops, and Dun Laoghaire Angling, George's St, Dun Laoghaire.

Arklow (Co Wexford). Local boats offer deep sea angling over inshore banks for dogfish, ray, codling, whiting, bull huss, plaice, flounder, and tope. Codling and dabs may be fished for from Roadstone Pier. Beach fishing on Clones Strand: codling, bass, flounder. There are more than two dozen good shore venues between Arklow and **Wexford**. Club: Arklow Sea Anglers. Tackle from Bolands, Pat Kelly, both Main St. Hotel: Arklow Bay.

Rosslare (Co Wexford). Good pier fishing for conger, occasional bass and flatfish. Access is difficult because of shipping. Fishing from shore at St Helens for bass, flatfish, mackerel and other species. Rock and surf fishing for bass and tope between Rosslare and **Kilmore Bay. Ballyteigue Lough** is a fine venue for flounders, and beach fishing is very good at **Cullenstown**, for bass and flounders. Ballytrent beach is good for flatfish by night. Boats can reach Splaugh Rock, a massive reef, and Tuskar Rock: mainly cod fishing.

Kilmore Quay (Co Wexford). Record Irish Pouting taken in 1983, and large coalfish taken recently. Fishing at high tide from pier produces flounder and occasional bass. Mullet may sometimes be taken by ground baiting. **St Patrick's Bridge**, reef of rocks to east of harbour, is boat mark for good bass fishing. Excellent pollack, bass and tope around **Saltee Islands**. Surf fishing for bass and tope at **Ballyteigne Bay**. Mullet and flatfish abound. Lugworm from harbour. **Burrow** shore is popular beach for competitions, best at night. Wexford Boat Charter: 143 The Faythe, Wexford (053 45888). Base, Kilmore Quay Marina. Club: Kilmore Quay SAC. Tackle shops in Rosslare, Wexford and Kilmore Quay.

Fethard Bay (Co Wexford). Bottom fishing for flounder, bass, plaice, best at night. Hook Head has spinning at high tide for pollack, coalfish, mackerel, bottom fishing for conger and other species. Along shore at Cummins Quay, **Ballyhack**, conger fishing.

Dunmore (Co Waterford. Shark, bottom and wreck fishing; base for charter boats. Contact J A O'Connor, Dunmore East Angling Charters, Pelorus, Fairy Bush, Dunmore East (051 383397). Daily charter £120-£200, 12 persons. Club: Dunmore East Sea Anglers.

Dungarvan Bay (Co Waterford). From **Ballinacourty** pier, bass, flatfish and dogfish, half flood to early ebb. Abbeyside and Barnawee; spinning for bass, bottom fishing for flounder. Fishing at Dungarvan for bass and flatfish. A number of large bass, 6lb to 9½lb are caught, but mackerel have been scarce. Pier at **Helvick** provides good sport with congers; distance casting catches ray. Mullet taken in Helvick Harbour. Fewer blue shark than there were. Conger, mackerel, pollack, wrasse (specimen taken) off Helvick Head. Crab and lugworm on foreshore. Local clubs are Abbeyside Sea Anglers and Dungarvan Sea Anglers, who concentrate on boat competitions. Boats from Dungarvan Sea Angling & Diving Service Ltd, 42 Lower Main St (plus information on all types of fishing), Dungarvan Charter Angling, or Gone Fishin', Lower Main St, (058 43514). £18 per angler daily, wreck, shark, or bottom fishing. Daily boat charter, Brian Barton (058 44962), £120 to £200.

Ardmore and **Youghal** (Co Cork). Several venues around Ardmore and Ram Head, incl surf fishing from Ballyquin Strand for bass and flatfish (flounder to 3½lb), Ardmore beach and pier, bass, flatfish; Goat Island and Whiting Bay, similar species. Fishing from Mangans Cove through Youghal, to Knockadoon Head and pier offers more than a dozen venues. Species caught include flounder, plaice (to 5lb), codling, ray, turbot, bass, dogfish, conger (to 41lb), ling (to 38lb), cod (to 28lb 12oz), pollack, coalfish, gurnard, whiting, wrasse, blue shark (135lb) and most deep sea species. Clubs: Ardmore Sea Anglers; Youghal Sea AC also has freshwater fishing on Blackwater and tributaries. Charter-boats: B O'Keeffe, tel: (024 92820), 6/8 anglers: £80, rods for hire; 'Shark Hunter', 31 ft, (024 92699). Hotels: Hilltop, Devonshire Arms, Avonmore Roseville and Green Lawn Guest Houses.

Ballycotton (Co Cork). One of the best-known of Irish sea fishing centres; large catches of prime fish and excellent facilities. Many specimen caught, including blue shark, conger, ling, pollack, coalfish, bass, hake, spur and spotted dog. Big cod in winter months. Fishing from pier at Ballycotton and **Knockadoon**, rocks from Knockadoon Head, Ballinwilling Reef and other marks, or boat; surf fishing at **Ballymona**; bass, flounder and codling. Good mullet in harbour. Lugworm may be dug at Ballycrennan and Ardnahinch. Boat hire: Ballycotton Angling Centre (£100 per boat min, 10.30 to 17.30) tel: 021 646773. Monthly competitions May to Oct. Local clubs: Ballycotton Deep Sea AC, c/o Sheila Egan, Main St; Aghada SAC, E Cull, Woodlands, Garryduff, Midleton. Tackle shops: T H Sports, Main St, Midleton. Hotels: Bayview (021 646746), Garryvoe (021 646718); Mrs B Murray (021 646713); Mrs M Tattan (021 646177). Many hotels around Midleton.

Cobh (Co Cork). Cobh Sea AC (c/o Geary's, *below*), runs an international sea angling festival each year in first week of September. Species caught include skate, bass, pollack, coalfish, tope, l s dogfish. Conger 44lb 12oz has been weighed in. For deep sea fishing there are charter boats from Geary's Angling Services, tel/fax: 021 812167, or Donnacha Geary, (021 813417). Club: Cobh Sea AC. Tackle shop: Cobh Tackle Shop, Town Centre. Hotel: Commodore. Guest house: Bellavista House (021 812450).

Cork (Co Cork). Fishing both inside and outside Harbour offers the following species: dogfish, codling, conger, pollack, turbot, plaice, ray, wrasse. 144lb blue shark caught in Harbour, and record angler fish. Various charter boats operate from Cork Harbour and **Crosshaven**, for shark, wreck and bottom fishing, incl: Cohb Angling Centre (0211 813417); Carrigaline Deep Sea Angling Charters, (021 372896); Barry Twomey, Crosshaven, (021 831843, fax 831679). Daily charges, £130. Tackle for hire. Club: Cork Sea Anglers. Tackle shops: Lee's, 40B Popes Quay; R Day & Son, 2 Bowling Green St, The Tackle Shop, Lavitts Quay.

Kinsale (Co Cork). Fine natural harbour. Old Head Sea AC holds closed competitions. Best-known centre on the south coast for deep-sea fishing, especially for shark, ling, conger, dogfish, ray, pollack, coalfish, red bream and wrasse. Well-equipped boats and experienced skippers; all operators offer rod and tackle hire. Kinsale Sea AC run many competitions during season. For full information contact Castlepark Marina Centre, Kinsale (021 774959, fax: 774958) Hotels: Trident, Actons, Perryville House; Atlantic, Garretstown.

Rosscarbery (Co Cork). Noted for surf fishing for flatfish, mackerel, occasional bass; three fine beaches. Bass and mullet also taken in small harbour, and from mouth of estuary. Mackerel spinning from pier. Lugworm and ragworm in estuary, sand eel from beach. Club: Rosscarbery SAC.

Baltimore (Co Cork). Shark (very good, July-Oct), skate, conger, tope, ling, cod, pollack and mackerel from boats; pollack, bass and mackerel from shore. Best June-Oct. Deep sea boat charter: T Brown, Baltimore Harbour Cottages, (028 20319); M Walsh, Marine Services, (028 20145/20352), £190, £30 per angler; Baltimore Angling Centre (028 20438), £180, £30 per angler; Nick Dent, (028 21709). Tackle shop: Kieran Cotter Ltd, Baltimore.

Mizen Peninsula (Co Cork). Fishing in harbours, rocks, coves, for pollack, mackerel, coalfish, flatfish, etc. Schull Pier offers bottom fishing for flounder, float fishing for mullet. Wreck fishing within easy reach. Schull boat operator: Cíarán O'Carroll, Mizen Charters, (tel/fax: 028 37370); good shark fishing and large skate; reef and drift fishing for large pollack, ling, coalfish, spurdog, bull huss. Tackle from Barnett's, Main St, Schull. Hotel: East End. B&B, Mary Murphy, Schull.

Bantry (Co Cork). Town is convenient centre for Bantry Bay deep sea fishing. Large conger are caught, ling, pouting, whiting, bull huss, l s d. Shore fishing best on south side of bay: thornback, dogfish, flatfish, wrasse, pollack. Boats operated by John Minehan, 4 Blackrock Rd, Bantry, (027 50318). Club: Bantry sea Anglers.

Castletownbere (Co Cork). Fine harbour for sheltered fishing in Berehaven and offshore at marks in Bantry Bay. Shark, pollack, ling, conger, tope, ray, skate, pouting, bass, bream, wrasse, spurdog, gurnard, flounder, plaice, grey mullet, whiting and mackerel. Boats are always available. Shore fishing at harbour pier, Muccaragh, Seal Harbour and Zetland Pier. Tackle shop and tourist agent: C Moriarty, The Square. Hotel: Cametrignane House. **Kenmare**: charter boats operated from Kenmare Pier by Seafari, 1 Reenkilla, Lauragh, Killarney (064 83171). £200 daily, £25 per angler.

Waterville (Co Kerry). Centre for Ballinskelligs Bay, which has various points for rock and surf fishing. Bass readily taken. Boats may be chartered for shark and other species; contact tackle shop: Tadhg O'Sullivan, Waterville; or Bealtra Boats, Bunavalla, Caherdaniel (066 75129).

Cahirciveen (Co Kerry) and **Valentia Island**. Rock fishing for pollack, wrasse, bull huss. Deep sea angling for bull huss, ling, cod, conger, pollack, and other species. Charter boats operate. Catches include conger (up to 72lb), turbot (to 26lb), red bream (to 9lb), bass (to 16lb). Also large gurnard, mackerel, garfish, tope, ling, pouting, whiting, cod and blue shark. Boat fishing most popular, but good sport also from shore. International Deep Sea Festival at Caherciveen in Aug. Club: Cahirciveen Sea & Shore AC. Boats from Hugh Maguire, Anchor Bar, (066 72049). At Valencia, Brendan and Kathleen Casey operate charter boat, (066 72437), shark and bottom fishing, £25 per angler, £140-£200 charter. Tackle from Anchor Bar & Tackle Shop.

Dingle Peninsula (Co Kerry). Rock fishing for pollack, wrasse, conger. Inshore fishing for ray; offshore for pollack, coalfish, bream, conger, ling, tope, cod, whiting, huss, spurdog, gurnard, pouting and shark. Club: Dingle SAC. Charter boats operate from Dingle: N O'Connor, Dingle Marina, (066 59947), £25 per angler, charter £200. Tackle shops: Walter Sheeny's, Dingle; Tim Landers, Tranlee.

Shannon Estuary. Locations for shore fishing on the south side are: **Beal Point** and **Littor Strand**, bottom fishing for dogfish, flatfish, and bull huss; several marks around **Carrig Island** and **Saleen Quay**, where good bottom fishing is to be had from rocks and quay: ballan wrasse, dogfish, bull huss, some tope. **Tarbert** and **Glin** piers are best at high tide for flatfish, conger at night; **Foynes** piers produce conger, thornback ray, codling, whiting and flounder. Best baits, crab, lugworm, mackerel. North side of estuary has pier fishing available at **Kildysart** (flounder, crab bait essential), and **Innishmurray** (bull huss, thornback, conger, freshwater eels), Kilrush, *(see below),* and **Carrigaholt** (bottom fishing for dab and flounder, spinning for pollack and wrasse). Beach fishing at **Shannakea** and **Killimer** for thornback, conger, dogfish and bull huss, and rock fishing at **Aylvaroo Point** for similar species, plus codling and whiting in winter, are among several other venues. Plenty of opportunities for bait digging. Charter boats for estuary from Kilrush. Car ferry runs from Killimer to Tarbert hourly, summer: 7 to 21.30, (Sundays: 9 to 21.30), winter: 7 to 19.30 (Sundays: 10 to 19.30).

Kilrush (Co Clare). Important sea fishing centre. Pier fishing from **Cappagh** pier, conger, whiting, flounder, dogfish on flood tide. Beach fishing at White Strand and Doughmore, Sandhills and Seafield Beachs. Mackerel and pollack fishing from Dunlickey cliffs and Bridges of Ross. Species commonly caught in Lower Shannon include large tope, pollock, conger, thornback ray, bullhuss, dogfish, bass. Several towns on the coast of Co Clare have charter boats available for shark, wreck and bottom fishing, 35 ft average, tackle for hire. At Kilrush, Atlantic Adventures, (065 52133, fax 51720), £30 per angler, £220 charter, 10 persons. Shannon Angling, Fort House, Cappa, Kilrush (065 52031), has boat charter and accom, as full holiday package. Kilrush Creek Marina (065 52072, fax 51692) has every facility for hiring and mooring boats, incl hoist and repair services, and accom, shops, bars, restaurants. Tackle and information from Michael O'Sullivan & Son, 49/50 Moore St, (065 51071) Martin Clancy, Henry St (065 51107), all sea and freshwater tackle, and all emergency repairs. **Liscannor** boats: W O'Callaghan, (065 21374, fax 21374). £300 daily charter, 12 persons. B&B: The Central (065 51332).

Galway Bay (Co Galway). **R Spiddal** enters on north side, with skate, tope, ray, huss, dogfish, monkfish, cod, ling, conger, flatfish. Boats and gillies for hire. Deep sea charter boats operate from **Spiddal**.

Clifden (Co Galway). First-class boat and shore angling in sheltered conditions. Blue shark, tope, coalfish, pollack, skate, ray, ling, cod, turbot, brill and plaice. Good marks include: Slyne Head; Barrister wreck off **Inishark**; Inishbofin; Inishturk and Fosteries Shoals. Other good bays are Mannin, Ballinakill, Killary, Roundstone, Cleggan and Bunowen. Tackle shops: E Sullivan, Main Street, and P Stanley, Market Street. Deep sea charter boats: J Brittain, (095 21073) £25 per angler daily; J Ryan, (095 21069), £35, £350 charter, tackle on board. Charter boats from **Letterfrack**: John Mongan, (095 43473), 31 ft, 12 persons, £15 per day. Club: Clifden Sea AC. Hotels: Clifden Bay, Alcock & Brown, Abbeyglen, Clifden House, Atlantic Coast and Celtic. Boats for hire at Bunowen and Roundstone.

Westport (Co Mayo). Good boat and shore fishing in shallow water. Local clubs run sea angling competitions in the area each year. Fish caught include: the record monkfish (69lb), skate (up to 167½lb), tope and conger (to 40lb and more), cod, codling, pollack, flounders, plaice, gurnard, coalfish, bass, wrasse, turbot, dog fish, white skate (146lb), blue shark, and porbeagle shark. Good marks include Tower in Inner Bay, off Lighthouse, Pigeon Point, Cloghormack Buoy. Sheltered sport in **Clew Bay**. 36 ft Boat available from Austin Gill, (098 64865), £150-£200 charter, 10 persons; F Clarke, (098 25481), £25 per angler, £125-£175 charter; R Roynon (098 26514), £17 per angler, £140 charter; Westport Sea Angling Boats, 33 ft, 10 persons, (098 25481), £150. Tackle shop: Hewetson's. Clubs: Westport Sea AC and Westport AC, which has trout fishing on Ballinlough, by Westport-Newport Rd: dt £10, incl boat. Hotels: Helm; Clew Bay; Grand Central.

Achill Island (Co Mayo). Excellent boat fishing; up to 40 species, incl pollack, conger, ling, ray, cod, etc; fish run large. Noted area for blue shark and porbeagle. Holds records for heaviest fish caught in Irish waters for both men and women: 365lb (man), 362lb (woman), plus blue shark record, 206lb. Pollack and wrasse fishing off rock produces specimens in 15lb class. Good marks are Carrick Mor,

Gubalennaun, Alennaun Beag, Dooega and Dugort. Flatfish from **Tullaghan Bay** on north side of island. Good shore fishing at Keel Strand and Keem Bay; Mackerel and pollack fishing from **Cloughmore Pier**. Sea trout late June to early Aug (plentiful and good size); mackerel; plaice etc. Charter boats from **Purteen Harbour**: Tony Burke, (098 47257), £120, one angler £25. Local club: Achill Sea AC. Tackle shops: Sweeney and Son, Achill Sound (098 45211); O'Malleys, Keel PO (98 43125, 43444 fax). Hotels: Island House, Dookinella, Keel (098 43180); Bervie Guest House, Keel (098 43114); Atlantic Breeze, Poolagh (098 43189), and many others. For Achill Deep Sea Angling Holidays, contact Mary Burke, Cashel, Achill (tel/fax: 098 47257).

Newport (Co Mayo). Central for Clew Bay, which has more than twenty popular shore fishing venues. At Newport Quay, bottom fishing for flounder; Rossmoney, casting over mud for dogfish, bullhuss and conger; Rossanrubble, bottom fishing for ray, dogfish and bullhuss; also Ross and Rossnakilly, dogfish, bullhuss, small pollack, flounder. Other species found in Clew Bay include mackerel, turbot, wrasse, coalfish, garfish, bass. Bait may be dug at Carrowmore Strand and Mallaranny (sand eel), Murrick, Rossbeg, Rossturk, Rossmurrevagh, Corraun (lugworm). Charter boat for shark and bottom fishing from Mary Gavin Hughes, Newport, (098 41562), £100 daily. Club: Newport Sea Anglers. Tackle from Hewetson's, Bridge St, Westport. Hotels: Black Oak Inn, Newport House.

Belmullet (Co Mayo). Rapidly rising in popularity as sea-fishing centre. Sheltered water. 38 species and many specimen caught to date, incl present Irish record red gurnard and halibut; turbot, bream and pollack especially good. Belmullet Sea AC (097 81076) has been active in improving sea fishing in the area. Local venues include Annagh Head: spinning for pollack, coalfish and mackerel from rocky outcrops, float fishing for wrasse, bottom fishing for dogfish and occasional conger; Cross: bottom fishing for flounder, dogfish and small turbot. Lugworm may be dug at various nearby localities, including the shore lying west of town. Deep-sea charter boats for shark, reef and bottom fishing from Belmullet: Padraic Sheeran (097 81105), £15 per angler, £80-£100 charter; **Blacksod Bay**: Vincent Sweeney, (097 85774), charter £100 per day min, £25 per angler; Martin Geraghty, (097 85741), charter £100; Michael Lavelle, (097 85669), charter £80.

Ballina (Co Mayo). Estuary of R Moy opens into Killala Bay. Lugworm may be found in sandy patches, sand eel, crab and clam are alternative baits. From Kilcummin Head at the west, to Lenadoon Point at the east, there are eight recognised shore fishing areas. These include Palmerstown Channel (Cloonoghmore Estuary), spinning for sea trout and bottom fishing for flounder; Ross Beacon, the same, Innishcrone Strand (beach fishing for flounder, dab, dogfish) and Pier (conger, dogfish, occasional ray, wrasse.

Donegal Bay (Co Donegal). There are more than twenty good shore fishing points around bay, from **Darbys Hole** in south through **Erne Estuary** (flounder), **Donegal Quays** (float fishing for mullet with ground bait), spinning from St John's Point, **Killybegs Harbour** (mackerel, etc from East Pier), beach fishing at Nun's Cove for flatfish, mackerel from **Muckross Pier** and Head, **Teelin Pier** (specimen conger, mackerel, flatfish) and White Strand (flatfish from beach plus mackerel). Shark fishing for blue shark Jul-Sept. Deep sea charter boats operating from **Killybegs**: E O'Callaghan, (073 31288); 36 ft charter boat for shark or bottom fishing, 6 rods shark, 10 rods bottom. £20, £160 charter; Brian McGilloway, (073 31144, mobile 087 2200982), 34 ft, 8-10 persons, £20-£25 per person, £100 charter; Antony Doherty, (073 31079), 39 ft fast fishing boat, up to 12 persons, 40m licence, £150-£200 charter. At **Teelin**, Smith Campbell, Teelin Bay Charters, Carrick, tel: (073 39117); 32 ft, 8 persons, £20, charter £100-£120. Species caught include pollock, ling, conger to 30lbs, cod to 15lbs, mackerel, coalfish, wrasse, flatfish and others. Local clubs are Donegal Bay SAC, Killybegs SAC and Kilcar SAC.

Rosapenna (Co Donegal). Boat fishing for tope. For deep-sea bookings apply Mrs C O'Donnell, The Fleets Inn, Downings. Boat charter: Pat Robinson, Dunfanaghy, (074 36290), 38 ft, shark, wreck, bottom fishing. £200. Other information from Donegal Deep Sea Angling Ltd, 1 Mount Southwell, Letterkenny. Tackle shop:

Co-operative Stores.

Lough Swilly (Co Donegal). Good fishing to be had locally, with haddock in June and July, and shark in Aug/Sept. There is an annual sea angling festival of Glengad-Malin at end of Aug. 1st Class wreck fishing in early morning, sea trout in estuaries. Shark and bottom fishing charter boat, The Cricket, 38 ft, operates at **Dunfanaghy**, 12 persons, £200. Pat Robinson, (074 36290). Species caught: cod, haddock, tope, charr, whiting, dogfish, ling, etc. At **Rathmullan** pier, 'Pegasus II', 33 ft, takes 8 rods shark fishing or 10 rods bottom fishing. £10, £70 to £100 charter. Tel: (074 58282), M Bowden. Tackle available from both.

Malin Head (Co Donegal). Charter boats operate from Bunagee and Culduff, species caught are whiting, haddock, cod, conger, ling, gurnard, pollock. Contact Inishowen Boating, J McLaughlin, Bunagee, Culduff, (077 70605). Hotels: Malin; McGrory Guest House; Mrs Ann Lynch, Culdaff and others.

Moville (Donegal). Haddock, pollack, cod, ling, whiting, wrasse, flatfish and others. Foyle Sea AC arranges Lough Foyle Festival of Sea Angling, an annual 8-day festival in August. Club owns boat and can arrange wreck fishing. Plenty of boats (20ft-30ft) and bait. Tackle from Pat Harkin, Malin Rd. Hotels: Foyle; Redcastle.

FISHING CLUBS ETC. IN IRELAND

The following is an alphabetical list of angling clubs and associations in the Ireland. Particulars of the waters held by many will be found, by reference to the Index, in the section headed 'Fishing Stations in Ireland', and the information about the others, which may not have their own water, could be had from the Secretaries, whose addresses are given. An addressed envelope should be enclosed with inquiries. Please advise the publishers (address at the front of the book) of any changed details for the next edition.

NATIONAL BODIES

Bord Fáilte (Irish Tourist Board)
Baggot Street Bridge
Dublin 2
Tel: Dublin 765871

Central Fisheries Board
Balnagowan House
Mobhi Boreen, Glasnevin,
Dublin 9
Tel: 379206/7/8
Fax: 01 360060

Department of Tourism, Fisheries and Forestry
Leeson Lane
Leeson Street
Dublin 2
Tel: 01 210111

Irish Federation of Sea Anglers
Hon. Sec.
67 Windsor Drive
Monkstown
Co Dublin
Tel: 01 806873/806901

Irish Specimen Fish Committee
Mohbi Boreen
Glasnevin, Dublin 9
Tel: Dublin 8379206

I.S.A.A.C.
Loughcarrig House
Midleton
Co Cork
Tel: 021 631952
Charter boats and accommodation for sea anglers

CLUBS

Abbeyfeale Anglers' Association
Pat O'Callaghan
Ballybehy
Abbeyfeale,
Co Limerick

Abbeyleix Anglers
M O'Brien
Ballyruan
Portlaoise
Co Laois

Abbeyside Sea Anglers
M Cowming
Clonea Road
Abbeyside
Dungarvan
Co Waterford

Achill Sea Anglers
Tony Burke
Cashel, Achill
Co Mayo

Ardfinnan Anglers
John Maher
Green View
Ardfinnan
Clonmel
Co Tipperary

Ardmore Sea Anglers
Mary Moloney
Fountain House
Ardmore
Youghal Co Cork

Arklow Sea Anglers
E Doyle
55 Fr Redmond Park
Arklow
Co Wicklow

Fishing Clubs

When you appoint a new Hon Secretary, do not forget to give us details of the change. Write to the publishers (address at front of the book). Thank you!

Athy Anglers
J Shaughnessy
c/o Athy Library
Athy
Co Kildare

Ballybofey and Stranorlar Angling Association
D McCollum
Edenmore
Ballybofey, Lifford
Co Donegal

Ballyduff Trout Fly Angling Association
Eamon Bolger
Post Office
Ballyduff, Co Waterford

Ballyhooly Trout Anglers
Jim Ahern
Ashgrove
Ballyhooly
Co Cork

Bannow Bay Anglers
J Whitty
Wellington Bridge
Co Wexford

Bantry Sea Anglers
Con O'Leary
Baurgorm
Bantry
Co Cork

Barrow Anglers
E Moore
Chaplestown
Carlow
Co Carlow

Belmullet Sea Anglers
Buddy Valkenburg
Belmullet
Co Mayo

Cappoquin Salmon and Trout Angling Club
Jeremy Nicholson
Littlebridge Inches
Cappoquin, Co Waterford

Carraroe Angling Club
Carraroe
Co Galway

Cahir and District Angling Club
W O'Donnell
Cahirabbey Upr
Co Tipperary
or
Tom Butler
Railway View
Cahir Abbey
Co Tipperary

Cahirciveen Sea and Shore Angling Club
Sean O'Shea
c/o Quirke's
Deelis
Cahirciveen
Co Kerry

Carrick-on-Suir Angling Club
N Power
Tinhalla
Carrick-on-Suir
Co Tipperary

Cashel, Tipperary and Golden Angling Club
James Doyle
2 Moor Lane, Cashel
Co Tipperary

Castlelyons Trout Anglers
P O'Dwyer
Glenarousk
Castlelyons
Co Cork

Chapelizod Anglers Club
Paul Deveroux
23 Liffey Terrace
Chapelizod
Dublin 20

Cavan Anglers
Brendan Coulter
Blaiwith, Ceighan
Co Cavan

Clane Angling Association
A McDonald
Downstown Lodge Stud
Maynooth, Co Kildare

Clodiagh Anglers Association
Timmy Delaney
Rathmoyle
Borrisoleigh
Co Tipperary

Clonbur Angling Club
Edward Lynch
Clonbur
Co Galway

Clonmel Salmon and Trout Anglers
John Kavanagh
West Gate Clonmel
Co Tipperary

Clonmel Anglers
John Carroll
3 Dr Croke Place
Clonmel
Co Tipperary

Cobh Sea Angling Club
Mrs Mary Geary
c/o Geary's Angling Services
Cobh, Co Cork

Corkeeran and Dromore Trout and Coarse Anglers' Association
Talbot Duffy
4 Lake View
Ballybay
Co Monaghan

Cork Salmon Anglers
J Buckley
Raheen House
Carrigrohane
Co Cork

Cork Sea Anglers
M Curran
22 Dundanion Road
Beaumont Park
Cork

Cork Trout Anglers' Association
J A O Connell
87 Patrick Street
Cork

Corofin Anglers' Association
Ned Cusack
Gortchalla
Moycullen
Co Galway

Culdaff Angling Association
c/o Faulkner's
Main Street
Culdaff
Co Donegal

Deele Angling Club
Billy Vance
Convoy, Lifford
Co Donegal

Donegal Bay Sea Angling Club
Joe Nash
Kilmacrennan
Letterkenny
Co Donegal

Drogheda and District Anglers' Club
c/o John Murphy
39 Anneville Crescent
Drogheda, Co Louth

Duff Angling Syndicate
John Fahey
Kinlough
Co Leitrim

Dundalk and District Brown Trout glers' Association
J Clarke
3 Mill Road
Forkhill
Co Armagh
BT35 9SJ

Dundalk and District Salmon Anglers' Association
Neil O'Neill, Mullaharlin Road
Heynestown
Dundalk, Co Louth

Dundrum and District Anglers
Sean Breen
Garryduff West
Dundrum
Co Tipperary

Dungarvan Sea Anglers
Mrs Anne Fuller
Friars Walk
Abbeyside
Dungarvan
Co Waterford

Dunmore East Sea Anglers
J Dunphy
68 Grange Heights
Waterford

Durrow Angling Club
Michael Walsh
18 Erkindale Drive
Durrow
Co Laois

Edenderry Coarse Angling Club
Pauric Kelly
48 Murphy Street
Edenberry
Offaly

Fermoy Salmon Anglers
E Glendon
21 Connaught Place
Wellington Road
Fermoy
Co Cork

Fermoy and District Trout Anglers' Association
M Fanning
41 Saint Mary's Terrace
Fermoy
Co Cork

Finn Angling Club
Francis Curran
1 Derry Road
Strabane
Co Tyrone

Foxford Salmon Anglers Association
Michael Tiernan
Riverside
Foxford, Co Mayo

Foyle Sea Angling Club
Droim A Mhaoir
Moville
Co Donegal

Fishing Clubs

When you appoint a new Hon Secretary, do not forget to give us details of the change. Write to the publishers (address at front of the book). Thank you!

Freshford Anglers
Mr Pearce
Doherty
Freshford
Co Kilkenny

Glebe Angling Club
William Cochrane
87 Mourne Park
Newtownstewart
Co Tyrone

Glengariff Anglers' Association
Patrick Power
Reenmeen
Glengariff, Co Cork

Greese Anglers
P Leigh
Woodhill, Narraghmore
Ballitore
Co Kildare

Headford Anglers Club
Michael Walshe
Ower Post Office
Galway

Inistioge Anglers Club
Bill Doherty
High Street
Inistioge, Co Kilkenny

Kells Anglers
John Flynn
Old School House
Kells
Co Kilkenny

Kenmare Trout Anglers
John O'Hara
21 Main Street
Kenmare
Co Kerry

Kilcar Sea Angling Club
Eileen McBrearty
Kilcar
Co Donegal

Killarney Sea Anglers
R O'Riordan
Inchycullane
Kilcummin
Killarney
Co Kerry

Killeshandra Angling Club
Jim Murphy
Coragh
Killeshandra
Co Cavan

Kilkenny Anglers' Association
Edward Stack
c/o Garda Station
Kilkenny
Permits from
Sports Shop
Kilkenny, Co Kilkenny

Killybegs Sea Angling Club
Mary Roullier
Evergreens
Killybegs
Co Donegal

Kilmore Sea Angling Club
B McLoughlin
Spencertown
Murrintown
Co Wexford

Kiltane Sea Angling Club
Seamus Geraghty
Shraigh West
Bunnahowan, Ballina
Co Mayo

Kinsale Sea Angling Club
Evelyn Morrissey
Butcher's Row
Kinsale
Co Cork

Letterkenny and District Anglers' Association
Gerry McNulty
Hawthorne Heights
Letterkenny, Co Donegal

Lismore Salmon Anglers
B Hogan
Main Street
Lismore
Co Waterford

Lismore Trout Anglers
B McCarthy
Main Street Lismore
Co Waterford

Lough Arrow and District Angling Club
Muriel Frazer
Ballindoon
Riverstown
Co Sligo

Lough Arrow Fish Preservation Association
J Hargadon
Annaghloy via Boyle
Co Sligo

Lough Owel Trout Preservation Association
S McKeown
Irishtown
Mullingar, Co Westmeath

Lough Sheelin Trout Protection Association
Paddy Lyons
Drumbee, Kilnaleck
Co Cavan

Monasterevin Anglers Club
P Moran
Rathangan Road
Monasterevin
Co Laois

Mountmellick Anglers
B Lynch
5 Wolfe Tone Road
Mountmellick
Co Laoise
Mountrath and District Anglers Club
Tom Watkins
6 Fintan Terrace
Mountrath
Co Laois
Newport Sea Anglers
Finola O'Malley
Comploom
Newport
Co Mayo
North Kerry Anglers' Association
Jim Horgan
6 The Square
Listowel, Co Kerry
Old Head Sea Anglers
Vincent McDwyer
Aghadoe
Carrigmore
Carrigaline
Co Cork
Ormond Angling Association
Joe O'Donoghue
Cameron
Gortlandroe
Nenagh, Co Tipperary
Portarlington Angling Club
Patsy Farrell
White Hart Lane
Kilmalogue
Portarlington
Co Laois
Rathdowney Anglers' Association
M White
Mooreville
Rathdowney
Co Laois
Rinnashark Sea Anglers
L Ryan
6 Lynwood
Ashley Court
Waterford
River Ilen Anglers' Club
A Taylor
Cois Abhann
Coolnagarrane
Skibbereen
Co Cork
Rossin and Slane Anglers
Ray Foster
181 Foxfield Grove
Raheny
Rosses Anglers' Association
John Ward
Dungloe, Co Donegal
353 73 31114
St Colmans Angling Club
Corofin
Co Galway
Schull Sea Angling Club
Kieren Higgins
47 Mountain View
Naas
Co Kildare
Shannonbridge Anglers' Association
c/o Dermot Killeen
Shannonbridge
Co Offaly
Slane, Rossin and District Anglers' Club
c/o "Mr Ace"
8 Laurence Road
Drogheda, Co Louth
or Secretary
Ray Foster
01 8315406
Sliabh Liág Anglers Association
Frank O'Donnell
Carrick Lower, Carrick
Co Donegal
Tallow and District Anglers' Club
Alan Sivyer
Bride View Bar
Tallow Bridge
Tallow, Co Waterford
Tar Trout Anglers' Association
Tony O'Brien
27 Fr. Sheedy Terrace
Clogheen
Co Tipperary
Thomastown Anglers
P Heafey
Castel Avenue
Thomastown
Co Kilkenny
Thurles/Hollycross/Ballycamas Anglers
Jimmy Purcell
Rathcannon
Holycross
Thurles
Co Tipperary
Tramore Anglers
J Cashin
33 Rockinham
Ferrybank
Waterford
Co Waterford
Tuam and District Anglers
Sonny Martyn
Esso Station
Galway Road
Tuam
Co Galway

Tullamore Coarse Fishing Club
Pat Gorman
Tullamore
Co Offaly
Tullow Trout and Salmon Anglers
Richard Burgess
The Lodge
Tullow
Co Carlow
Village Anglers
Arthur Campbell
Monvallet
Louth, Dundalk
Co Louth
Virginia Angling Club
Raymond Lloyd
Main Street
Bailieborough
Co Cavan
Virginia Coarse Angling Club
Pat McCabe
Rahardrum
Virginia
Co Cavan
Waterford Sea Anglers
J O'Brien
20 Beechwood Avenue
Lower Grange
Waterford
Co Waterford
West Clare Anglers' Association
Francis Meaney
Ennis Road
Kilrush, Co Clare
Westport Sea Angling Club
Julie Connolly
John's Row, Westport
Co Mayo
Youghal Sea Anglers
M Goggin
1 Ardrath
Youghal
Co Cork

FISHING ABROAD

The primary purpose of this section is to give the angler contemplating visiting, or even, in the case of Commonwealth countries, emigrating to, one of the countries listed a brief description of the fishing to be had. It is neither necessary nor practicable to enter into such detail as in the British sections, but the addresses of various authorities from whom further information can be obtained are given, together with that of the appropriate London tourist or Government information office, at the end of each description.

CENTRAL AFRICA

ZAMBIA. Most rivers and lakes carry good stocks of fish, giving very reasonable sport. But the angler must be prepared to travel long distances over rough roads, carrying his own camp equipment and finally making his camp beside the river he intends to fish. There are very few hotels off the main roads, and fewer still in fishing areas, though the Tourist Board is conducting a successful drive for more hotels and rest houses, particularly the lodges in the national wildlife parks, where good fishing is to be had on the rivers. For parties who appreciate camping holidays in the bush, some delightful trips can be planned, particularly in August and September, when there is little fear of rain and the nights are warm enough to make camping pleasant. Most of the rivers are either heavily wooded right down to the water or are swamp-edged, so the addition of a boat and outboard motor to the camp equipment is a sound policy. On the other hand, canoes and paddlers can be hired, and the latter are usually good guides to the best fishing grounds. Youths are also very helpful as camp attendants, and little trouble is normally experienced in hiring one or two to take care of the heavy work of the camp. The visiting fisherman must remember that the hippopotamus and crocodile are found in nearly all Zambian waters. Wading in rivers can be a dangerous pastime, and hippos, especially with calves, should be given a wide berth. An insecticide spray against tsetse fly and a malarial prophylactic are recommended.

Indigenous species. These include tiger-fish, which probably provide the best sport, and goliath tiger fish, a separate species running up to 80lb or more; fish of the Nile perch variety and their close relatives, giant perch (top weight around 200lb); giant vundu (sampa); large-mouthed, small-mouthed and humped bream; catfish; barbel; local pike; lake salmon; labeo; and nkupi. There are two species of fish which are referred to as nkupi, one is found in Lake Tanganika and is a cichlid, it is also called a giant yellow belly; and the other is a citharinid found in the middle Zambezi including Lake Kariba.

The great **Zambezi** and its large tributary, the **Kafue**, are outstanding among the rivers. A good centre for the Zambezi is **Livingstone**, though there is small, comfortable hotel Mongu, in Western Province. Another town which has become a tourist centre is Siavonga on Lake Kariba. There is an all weather road from Lusaka (capital of Zambia) to Siavonga, which can be reached within a two-hour drive. The centre has several modern lodges, some of which are air-conditioned. Sport fishing including angling and spearing are very important here. Good fishing centres on the Karfue are at Itezhi-tezhi, Lochinvar and the Lower Kafue, near Chirundu. At Itezhi-tezhi, the angler will come across the famous small yellow belly and the Kafue pike. At Lochinvar, bream are important sport fish and at Lower Kafue, vundu. All three centres are served by good lodges: Musungwa (at Itezhi-tezhi), Lochinvar (at Lochinvar near Monze), and Gwabi (at Lower Kafue near Chirundu).

Lake Tanganyika is another anglers' mecca and a good centre is **Kasaba Bay**, where there are three small lodges. A launch service is operated by the Zambia Travel and Touring Co Ltd. The lake holds giant perch, tiger-fish, yellow belly and vundu among a wide variety of sporting fish.

Apart from Nile perch and sampa, which call for heavy tackle, most of the fish mentioned can be landed with a spinning rod. Steel traces are necessary for tiger-fish, nkupi and pike. A light bait-casting rod will usually cover other species. Fishing is free as a rule and can take place all the year round, but most rivers are in spate during the rainy season from December to April.

Zambia is unlikely to prove to be a land in which trout will thrive, owing both to the high temperature range and the lack of suitable highlands, but an exception may be provided by the picturesque **Nyika Plateau**, north of **Chipata** on the Malawi border, where an experimental stocking with rainbow trout in the headwaters of the **Shire River** is being carried out.

Anglers are required to purchase an angling permit, obtainable from the offices of the Department of Fisheries in Chilanga. The department also has offices in all the major fishery areas, and permits may be bought from them.

Useful addresses are: **Department of Fisheries, Headquarters, Kafue Road, PO Box 350100, Chilanga** (tel: 260 1 278418); **Zambia Information Services, Block 26, Independence Avenue, PO Box RW 50020, Lusaka**. Tel: 217254; **Zambian National Tourist Board, 2 Palace Gate, Kensington, London W8 5NG**. Tel: 0171 589 6343; fax: 0171 581 1353.

ZIMBABWE. Zimbabwe offers some of the best fishing to be found in central Africa. The angler has scope to pit his skills against a diversity of species, ranging from the fighting tiger-fish of the **Zambezi** and **Save** river systems, to introduced species like the rainbow and brown trout in the mountain streams and dams of the Eastern Highlands.

Much of centre of the country acts as a watershed, with the streams forming rivers which flow north to the Zambezi river system, on which lies the huge expanse of Lake Kariba; south to the Limpopo; southeast to the Save and Runde; and east into the Pungwe system of Mozambique. Many dams exist on all of the rivers feeding the various systems. Not all of the 117 species of fish found here are of interest to the angler, but he will certainly find more than enough to suit his tastes. There is an excellent road, rail and air network ensuring that chosen fishing locations are readily accessible.

The main area of interest to fishermen is the Zambezi River, with **Lake Kariba** (250km in length with a surface area of some 5,250 square kilometres) and the **Victoria Falls** forming the chief focal points. Tourist facilities in both these locations are excellent, the visitor being able to choose from a varied list of accommodation ranging from basic camping and National Parks sites to luxury houseboats, lodges and hotels.

Tigerfish are most commonly taken using trolling or spinning methods, but they may sometimes be tempted with a fly. They are lightening-fast, fighting fiercely after the first vigorous take. The average size is between 2lb and 6lb, but double figure fish are common, especially in the legendary stretch above Victoria Falls. The current Zimbabwean and world record for this species stands at 34lbs 3oz.

Another freshwater fish which is proving popular with British anglers is the mighty vundu. The vundu is a giant catfish, in Africa, second only in size to the Nile perch. This species, although not often fished for by local anglers, is a formidable opponent, growing to well over 100lbs. Prospective fishermen would do best to try Lake Kariba first, using a sturdy boat rod and multiplier type outfit (capable of withstanding powerful runs often exceeding 100yds) plus the services of a guide.

The other most commonly sought after species are members of the tilapia and serranchromis families, known to local fishermen as bream. Besides being a popular table fish, the various species give an excellent account of themselves on light tackle and may be caught using a variety of methods ranging from conventional coarse fishing techniques to the use of spinners and flies.

Other indigenous species include the Cornish Jack, bottlenose, chessa, nkupe, hunyani salmon, purple labeo and the sharptooth catfish. Introduced species include the largemouth bass, a fine fighting fish introduced from USA several years ago and now widespread in Zimbabwean waters; rainbow, brown and brook trout, well stocked in the rivers and lakes of the Nyanga and Chimaniamni mountain ranges (a picturesque region often likened to Scotland); and carp, which are stocked in selected waters such as the **Mazowe Dam** near Harare and fish in excess of 50lbs have been caught.

The fishing season is any month with an 'R' in it and so ideally suits European anglers, who will, moreover, find that the high cost of the international airfare is pleasantly offset by the excellent value for money once there.

For more information, contact **Zimbabwe Tours and Travel, 3 Broadway, London N14.** (tel: 0181 519 6454).

MALAWI. Excellent sport with rainbow trout may be enjoyed in the bracing climate of the **Zomba, Mulanje** and **Nyika Plateaux** as a result of consistent restocking of rivers and streams by the Government. **Lake Malawi** holds over 400 species; including varieties of catfish, perch and carp. Most of these are found in the **Shire River** above **Livingstone Falls**, but below the falls the main species are related to those found in the **Zambezi**. They include the famous tiger-fish. Further information may be obtained from the **Angling Society of Malawi, PO Box 744, Blantyre, Malawi.**

EAST AFRICA

KENYA. Kenya is well-developed for the sporting tourist and offers a variety of fishing off the coast, in its rivers and in the lakes or the **Great Rift Valley**. Licence fees: are modest; accommodation of some variety is established at or near virtually all main centres.

The coast. Black, blue and striped marlin, broadbill swordfish, sailfish, yellow fin tuna, wahoo, barracuda, cobia, dorado, mako shark. Centres at **Mombassa, Shimoni**, for fishing in the famous **Pemba Channel**, a natural corridor between the mainland and Pemba Island, **Kilifi, Watamu, Lamu** and **Malindi**, the latter the largest. Accommodation at club premises or hotels. Charter boats. Good fishing almost all the year round, peaking Oct-April: at its least attractive May-June.

The mountain rivers. Stocked early in the century with brown trout, later with rainbows. Camps with rondavel accommodation at **Thiba, Thego, Kimakia, Koiwa.** Rest house at **Kaibabich**; lodges at **Ngobit** and **Kiandorogo**. A dozen or more specially recommended hotels and clubs. Camp accommodation may be primitive; nothing should be taken for granted. There are limits on size, method and bags, but wholesale poaching is an ever-present problem despite sincere governmental efforts to curb it.

The **lakes. Naivasha** is famous for black bass, but the angler in pursuit of them should forget any preconceptions he might have. Smallish coppery-tinted bar-spoons are the most successful lure and the bigger fish are found not so much in the shallows as in pockets of deeper water inshore, where they shelter in the papyrus. In **Lake Turkana** (formerly Rudof) the principal quarry are Nile perch and tiger-fish, the former growing to more than 250lb. Also in Turkana, the rare and beautiful golden perch, which may weigh 150lb. **Lake Baringo**, well off the beaten track, is noted for its tilapia fishing; also for its wildlife watching potential, but that is a bonus attaching to much of the Kenya fishing. Sport-fishing is now developing in **Lake Victoria** and the **Sasamua Dam**. Accommodation at all centres, but the extreme variety of types calls for detailed investigation in advance. The **Pemba Channel Fishing Club address is PO Box 86952, Mombasa**, tel: 313749; fax: 316875. The **Kenya Tourist Office** is at **25 Brook's Mews, London W1Y 1LF**. Tel: 0171-355 3144. Fax: 0171-495 8656.

TANZANIA. Tanzania can provide some of the finest big-game fishing in the world.

Big-game fishing: From October to March there is first-class sport with sailfish, shark, tunny, marlin, wahoo, horse mackerel and dolphin, particularly off **Dar es Salaam**, around **Bagamoyo, Latham Island** and **Mafia Island**, and also in the **Pemba Channel** off **Tanga**. Mafia offers some of the finest sport in the world in quantity, variety and excitement, and here particularly, and in addition to those already mentioned, can be found king fish, barracuda, red snapper and rock cod. There are two lodges on Mafia Island, with 30 and 12 air-conditioned rooms, respectively. Boats and equipment can be hired from the Seafaris Company. Flights to Mafia Island from the mainland (about 30 minutes run) are operated daily in each direction by air charter services from Dar es Salaam.

Lake fishing: the great **Lakes Victoria, Nyasa** and **Tanganyika** provide the best sport fishing where, from **Kigoma, Mwanza** and **Itungi**, it is possible to catch Nile perch, tiger fish and tilapia, which provide excellent sport. The **Great Ruaha River** and the **Rufiji River Basin** are further inland fishing grounds.

Trout fishing: At the moment, less organised than other branches of the sport, but can be arranged on request.

Further information (licences etc) may be obtained from the **Tanzania Tourist Board, PO Box 2485, IPS Building, Maktaba Street, Dar es Salaam**, and **PO Box 2343, Arusha**.

SOUTH AFRICA

EASTERN and WESTERN CAPE. Since the establishment of large-mouthed and small-mouthed black bass, the inland fisheries of the Cape area have been greatly extended; but this development has not been at the expense of the rainbow trout fisheries, which are as flourishing as ever. A few rivers hold brown trout, and brown trout were also introduced to upland waters some time ago. All the inland waters fall under the laws of the Cape Provincial Administration. In proclaimed trout rivers no fishing may be done at all except with the artificial fly and during the open season for trout, which extends from the beginning of September to the end of May. Trout licences are required but the charges are extremely moderate. In addition, however, the permission of riparian owners will be needed and sometimes a fee is payable.

Most of the rivers in the Western Cape are within a day's motoring of **Cape Town** on tarred roads, and some of the best waters are on State Forest Reserves, to which anglers have access on permit. This area has a winter rainfall and the best months are September, October and November, late April and early May. **Steenbras Reservoir** holds a rare hybrid known as 'tiger trout' which is a cross between brown trout and the American eastern brook trout.

The **Olifants River** in the **Citrusdal** and **Clanwilliam** districts provide excellent fishing for small-mouthed bass and the indigenous yellowfish, *Barbus capensis*. The latter takes artificial lures, is very game and runs as large as 20lb. Further afield, the mountainous area of **East Griqualand,** adjoining the **Transkei**, have rivers which provide boundless opportunities for the trout fisherman.

Sea fishing along the coastline is very good indeed, with hundreds of species to be caught. Cape Town has emerged as the world's leading Broadbill Swordfish fishing venue. The big-game potential is only beginning to be realised, and remarkable catches of yellowfin and longfin tuna have been taken. Tuna catches predominate throughout spring, summer and autumn; snoek in the winter months. Skiboat fishing is an interesting and highly successful technique for taking many varieties of off-shore fish. Every type of tackle is obtainable and accommodation is plentiful and comfortable.

KWAZULU-NATAL. The streams originating in the **Kwazulu-Natal Drakensberg** mountains, which rise to 11,000 ft, form several river systems before emptying into the Indian Ocean. Although the sources are in general too steeply graded to support fish life in any quantity, below the torrent source each river enters a series of pools and rapids suitable for trout and other fish. Moreover, the construction of numerous dams in the Kwazulu-Natal Midlands has been the means of providing many extra fishable waters.

Only waters at an altitude of about 4,000 ft and more have, in general, been stocked with trout. Below this level most rivers are too warm and silt-laden for the species to thrive. Black bass and carp have been established in a number of these midland dams with tilapia species inhabiting the warmer areas. However, other species to be caught are the indigenous 'scaly' (yellowfish), catfish, and eels. The State dams administered by the Kwazulu-Natal Parks, Game and Fish Preservation Board (Albert Falls, Midmar, Wagendrift, Spioenkop, Chelmsford, Hazelmere and Craigie Burn) not only provide abundant angling for many types of fish, including those mentioned above, but also provide a wide range of other recreational facilities and comfortable accommodation.

Rainbow and brown trout are the most important sporting fish of the Drakensberg area (midlands) and warm-water angling (carp, black bass, catfish, scaly, eels and tilapia) of the lower inland areas. The open season for trout streams is from September 1 to June 1, but dams are open throughout the year. The best fishing is usually obtained at the beginning and end of the season. From November to February the heavy summer rains and thunderstorms are apt to discolour the lower waters and render fly fishing difficult. It is almost always feasible, however, to obtain fishing on the headwaters or on artificial lakes and dams. The average size trout runs from about ½lb to 2lb, but on the larger waters, especially dams, much heavier fish can be expected and each season a few trout of more than 5lb are taken.

The province's record for a rainbow trout is 5.54kg (12lb 12oz) caught in the Swartberg district in May 1958.

Public waters and the Provincial nature reserves (where accommodation may be found close to fishing areas) are controlled by the Kwazulu-Natal Parks, Game and Fish Preservation Board; all queries regarding licences, accommodation etc should be directed to the **Kwazulu-Natal Parks Board Pietermaritzburg**, who will supply full information to visitors and handle reservations. Parks Board rangers are stationed at the more important public fishing areas to assist visitors and enforce regulations for the protection of trout, black bass, carp and indigenous fish.

Sea fishing. The majority of salt water anglers fish in the surf, casting their baits and lures from sandy beaches or from rocky promontories. Estuaries offer sport, while the open sea attracts those who have access to suitable craft. A wide variety of fish may be caught in the surf, ranging from sharks to small members of the bream family. Tackle varies accordingly, but a light fibre-glass rod of about 10-13ft together with a fixed-spool or multiplying reel gives a chance of catching many of the inshore species. Visitors should acquaint themselves with size restrictions and open seasons which apply to certain species of fish. Full details are obtainable from The Kwazulu-Natal Parks Board.

In June and July the annual migration of 'sardines' may attract game fish such as king mackerel into the surf and sport is likely to be fast and furious. The best estuarine fishing is **Lake St Lucia**, a nature reserve-controlled by the Kwazulu-Natal Parks Board; large numbers of grunter and kob enter the estuary leading to the main lake in spring and autumn. Deep sea angling takes place from ski-boats (small, speedy, flat-bottomed craft) as well as from the larger types of vessel. Advice on the organisation of deep sea trips will be provided by the Kwazulu-Natal Parks Board. Tackle for every branch of angling is obtainable. Innumerable hotels, holiday cottages, holiday flats and rest camps provide accommodation for visitors to the coastal resorts (with marlin, sailfish and tiger fishing).

NORTHERN PROVINCE and MPUMALANGA. Rainbow trout can be caught in a number of fine mountain streams at altitudes varying from 4,000 to 6,000ft in this north-eastern region of that was previously called the Transvaal. **Magoebaskloof, Sabie, Pilgrim's Rest, Lydenburg, Machadodorp, Belfast, Dullstroom** and **Waterval Boven** are the principal trout fishing centres. Some waters contain only fish over 3lb in weight. There is no closed season for trout fishing although fishing conditions are at their best in October and April. The rule is fly only, with dry and wet flies being used. Most waters are privately owned and, except where angling clubs have fishing rights, the permission of the riparian owner must be obtained. Good bass fishing is to be found in a large number of public, club and private waters. Large-mouth bass are widely distributed but some of the best waters are in the **White River** area of Mpumalanga: dams in that region, such as **Longmere, Klipkoppies, Witklip, Stanford** and **Dagama** have produced excellent fishing in recent times. Tiger-fish may be caught in the **Komati River** at **Komatipoort** and in the **Limpopo**. Minimum takeable size, 12in, daily bag limit, 6. Tiger-fish are best caught in September and October.

Yellowfish abound in the waters of the northern provinces There are four species, all belonging to the genus *Barbus*. In the **Vaal River** they grow to 30lb in weight and can be caught on mealiemeal dough, earthworms, grasshoppers or crabs. The two species of the east-flowing rivers grow to 15lb and take crab, earthworms, mealiemeal dough and spinners.

Tilapia, commonly known as 'kurper', is a very popular fish. There are two species, both being restricted to warmer waters. They can be caught on earthworms, mealiemeal dough (a paste bait) and spinners, with a light trout rod. They average about 1¼lb, but specimens of 4½lb are commonly caught. The best waters for this species are the **Hartebeestpoort, Rust der Winter, Roodeplaat, Loskop** and **Njelele dams**, also those in the White River area - although they may be caught in almost any lowveld water.

Not just the north, but the whole of the Republic of South Africa is a carp angler's paradise, with the fish attaining exceptional weights in very short periods, due to the nature of South Africa's waters. The record caught on rod and line is 48lb 10oz, although much larger specimens have been caught but not recorded, and the heaviest known fish was a monster of 83¼lb which was trapped in an irrigation furrow near **Bon Accord Dam** north of Pretoria.

Carp are found throughout South Africa in many public and private dams. No bag or size limits apply to these fish.

It is also possible to stay in and fish within some of South Africa's game reserves, including Loskop and Willem Pretorius.

General Information: Licences relative to the particular province can be obtained from Receivers of Revenue, magistrates' offices and reputable tackle stores throughout the Republic.

For further information contact the **South African Tourism Board, 5/6 Alt Grove, Wimbledon, London SW19 4DZ**, tel: 0181-944 8080; fax: 0181 944 6705.

Some time between May and July every year sardines in vast numbers migrate from east to west along the south coast of Natal, followed by large schools of shad, barracuda, shark and other predatory species of great interest to the angler. In certain conditions of wind and tide, sardines are washed ashore by the shoal to provide pickings for all present as in the picture.

FISHING IN AUSTRALASIA; INDIA; SRI LANKA AND MALAYSIA

AUSTRALIA

As a result of acclimatization and planned research in Australia, many of the lakes and rivers in the State of Tasmania, New South Wales, Western Australia and Victoria are well stocked with trout, which sometimes reach a large size. The island State of **Tasmania** is world-famous as a trout fishing centre, and continues to attract anglers from all parts of the Commonwealth each year.

Many rivers are still subject to flooding despite hydro schemes and this imposes a standstill on angling, so that the tendency is to reduce close seasons. The angler is strongly advised to check on river levels before going to fish. Before water temperatures have warmed up will be found to be the best times - midsummer is generally worst for trout fishing.

Freshwater Murray cod, perch and blackfish are found in good number in Australia. The **Murray River**, which forms the boundary of the eastern States of **Victoria** and **New South Wales**, and its many tributaries provide good sport for thousands of anglers, including trout in the upper reaches, Murray cod may weigh up to 150lb; another Murray River fish, the callop or golden perch, grows to over 50lb. Macquairie perch (to 11lb) and silver perch or grunter (to 6lb) are also taken. Another perch, or Australian bass, is taken in coastal streams and estuaries.

Australia was said by the late Zane Grey, noted big game authority, to possess the finest big game fishing grounds in the world. Centre of interest for sportsmen is **Montague Island**, off the coast of New South Wales, where there are marlin, tuna, shark and other big fish. The island is 14m from **Bermagui**, a safe harbour that can be used in all weathers. The tropical waters of the **Great Barrier Reef**, which extends for about a thousand miles along the east coast of Queensland, form Australia's most fascinating grounds; there are many unusual varieties of fish. There is good beach and rock fishing almost everywhere.

For further information contact **The Aussie Helpline, Beckett House, 60-68 St Thomas Street, London SE1 3QU**, tel: 0990 022000.

NEW SOUTH WALES. The streams near **Sydney** are mostly too small to support a large trout population, but good sport may be had in parts of the Blue Mountains area. Easily best from the fishing point of view, however, is the **Snowy Mountains** area. Very large reservoirs constructed as part of the hydro-electric scheme in the Southern Alps are now ranked equal to any in the world for brown and rainbow trout. The scenic beauty of the streams and these lakes is outstanding. **Lake Eucumbene** is the largest of the dams and in recent years has become the mecca of Australian trout anglers, but there are many other fine fisheries. Good accommodation and camping sites are to be found and many fine fishing waters are reached easily over good roads. Another good area for trout fishing is the **New England Tableland**, north of Sydney. Centred on the University Town of **Armidale**, the area's many streams and high altitude provide excellent fishing.

Apart from these new waters, one of the most renowned centres is **Cooma**, which has produced many of the heavier fish caught in the state. The **Murrumbidgee** and its tributaries near **Kiandra** are well worth fishing at the right time.

With the exception of a number of small spawning creeks, which have extended close seasons, and the larger impoundments, which are open all the year round, the trout streams are open to fishing from the mid-October to the end of June. Other inland waters are open the whole year. The most popular times for trout fishing are in the cooler months of the open season; that is October, November, March, April and May.

Anglers do not need a licence to fish in New South Wales. There are many attractive native species inhabiting the freshwater streams. Murray cod being perhaps the most popular, and the taking of fish up to 50lb is not uncommon; these fish do, in fact, run much larger. There are size and bag limits for trout and native fish and there is a closed season for Murray cod

Perth (WA) lawyer, John Byrne, caught this fine 25 lb spanish mackerel in Junction Bay, north of tropical Arnhem Land, Northern Territory. *Photo: Thomas Harmsworth.*

during September, October and November. Further information may be had by writing to **NSW Fisheries, Locked Bag 9, Pyrmont 2009**. Tel: 02 5667 800.

The State is noted for its attractive coastal lagoons and estuary fisheries. At many excellent resorts bream, flathead, whiting, black fish, etc, give good sport, while big game fish like tuna, marlin and shark abound in waters off the coast. Tourist information can be had from the **NSW Government Travel Centre, 19 Castlereagh Street, Sydney**.

NORTHERN TERRITORY. The **Northern Territory** has some of the most prolific fishing in Australia. With vast, unique wetlands, with their numerous freshwater rivers and billabongs (waterholes resulting from seasonal rivers drying up), it is the perfect environment for barramundi, and is commonly known as the centre for barramundi in Australia.

'The Top End,' as it is called, has two distinct seasons: the 'Tropical Summer' and the 'Dry.' On average 92% of the Top End's rainfall occurs during the tropical summer season, between November and April, and flooding can affect access to many inland areas by road. The Dry finds many rivers and creeks dried up, leaving isolated billabongs and lakes in difficult-to-access areas.

Fishing in the Territory is a year-round pursuit, and the different seasons offer different fishing opportunities, with the main attraction, barramundi, available all through the year. Known for its aggressive nature and fighting characteristics, the barramundi is found in both fresh and saltwater. It is the favourite quarry of the Australian angler, and can reach up to 50 kilos; 20 kilos being not uncommon. For fly fishermen, the saratoga offers good sport, and fights hard (average 2-3 kg; 5 kg being not uncommon).

The Northern Territory is also famous for its saltwater and estuary fishing in its many mangrove-lined creeks, tidal rivers, bays, offshore islands and reefs. Some of Australia's best light and medium tackle game fishing is found in the coastal waters of the Northern Territory, in **Arnhem Land,** which is territory set aside for Aborigines. Varieties include mangrove jack, queenfish, tuna, threadfin, bluenose salmon, trevally, spanish mackerel; even sailfish and marlin. Many species of fish have been caught on fly or lure in the **Goomadeer** river area, although lure is often more successful.

Reef fishing provides excellent sport for golden snapper, saddletail snapper, red-finned emperor, red emperor, estuary rock-cod, coral trout, moonfish, mangrove jack, bream, black jewfish, tuna, and spanish mackerel. The best times for barramundi are March to May, and October to December.

Mary river, east of **Darwin**, the **Daly river**, south of Darwin, and **Bathurst** and **Melville Islands** to the north of Darwin are very popular, but for exclusive and exceptional sport the estuaries and coast around **Goomadeer** river are perhaps unequalled. Specialist agents operate in this area and the only practicable way to fish there is through one of them. They have unique knowledge of some of the best fishing in the world; and their expertise is essential in terrain where the odd crocodile is active! Hat, sunglasses, 20+ factor sunscreen, long-sleeved cotton shirt, long cotton trousers in this tropical environment are a

This monster barramundi, the favourite catch of the Australian angler, weighed in at 65 lb and measured 130 cm. Sydney angler, Peter Kuzmiuk, captured this exceptional fish in the Goomadeer River, Arnhem Land, Northern Territory. So heavy was it that it was not long before he had to return it gently to the water, to watch it swim away. *Photo: Viv Thistlethwaite.*

must.

Weather and tides play an important role in fishing viability. The Northern Territory has large tidal changes and low tide can leave boats stranded for long periods with large tides often creating strong currents in the river systems. Obtaining tidal information before departing on fishing expeditions is a necessity. Such information can be obtained from local newspapers as well as from news and weather reports on radio and television. Regulations for recreational fishing deal mainly with bag limits and minimum size regulations. Details can be obtained from the **Department of Primary Industries and Fisheries, head office, Fisheries Division, Harbour View Plaza, corner of McMinn and Bennett streets, Darwin, NT 0800**. Tel: (089) 894 321 fax: (089) 811 475. The department will also supply names and addresses of fishing tour operators.

QUEENSLAND. There are no trout fishing centres, no licence fees and no close season except for Barramundi Angling (Nov 1 to Jan 31). Golden perch or 'yellow-belly' are found in the freshwater rivers of the south-west and as far north as the upper river of the **Dawson**. Murray cod are also caught in the south-western rivers, and freshwater perch or grunters (several species) are found in most inland streams. Barramundi are taken from all inland rivers of eastern Queensland north of and including the Dawson River. Nile perch have been introduced into a number of waters.

Off the coast are the **Greater Barrier** coral reefs (1,230 miles long), which abound in fish life. Big game fish are plentiful along the whole coastline, and the following species are commonly caught: Marlin, spearfish, tuna, bonito, Spanish mackerel, sharks (white pointer, mako, tiger, whalers, etc), amberjacks, emperor, trevally, etc.

Cairns and Tropical North Queensland are known world wide as a big game area for the big black marlin in the last quarter of the year. Large marlin are regularly landed.

The area off **Brisbane** provides one of the best light tackle game fish grounds in the world in the first half of the year particularly for tuna and sailfish.

The mainland coast provides excellent estuary beach and rock fishing for bream, whiting, flathead, tailor, trevally, giant perch, grunter, jew fish, and so on.

Further information can be had from the **Queensland Tourist and Travel Corporation, 392 Strand, London WC2R 0LZ**. Tel: 0171-240 0525. Fax: 0171-836 5881.

SOUTH AUSTRALIA. South Australia has very few freshwater streams if the **River Murray** is excluded. Relatively little trout fishing is to be found except in some streams near capital city of Adelaide and in farm dams. There is no closed season on trout fishing but there is a legal minimum length of 28cm.

The River Murray, which flows through the State to the sea, supports both commercial and recreational fisheries for native freshwater species, callop, silver perch and catfish and yabbies. Introduced species, including European carp and redfin may be caught, but must not be returned to the water alive. Fishing for Murray cod is now permitted between 1 Jan-31 Aug; Murray crayfish, silver perch and catfish are now fully protected in South Australia.

Very enjoyable and profitable sea fishing can be had along most of the coast of South Australia with rod and line or hand line. Amateur anglers do not require licences.

South Australia's premier saltwater table fish is the King George whiting and these are accessible to boat anglers in most waters of the State, including waters adjacent to Adelaide. Snapper up to 30lb or more and sweet tasting garfish are also taken by boat anglers in the relatively sheltered waters of **Gulf St Vincent** and **Spencer Gulf**. A large number of piers along the South Australian coast allow good fishing for a variety of species. Excellent sport fishing for Australian salmon (*Arripis trutta esper*, a sea perch, and not related to the family *Salmonidae*), sharks and large mulloway may be had by shore anglers along the surf beaches of the more exposed parts of the coast.

The coastal waters of the **Innes National Park** are home to a wide variety of fish life, and there are at least seven excellent beach and rock fishing locations where good catches of garfish, Tommy ruff, King George and silver whiting, squid, bream, mullet, flathead, and leather jacket may be had. Fishing boats take anglers on sea fishing trips from **Port Lincoln**, and commonly taken are snapper, various species of shark and tuna, and whiting.

Kangeroo Island, 4,500 square km, lying off the coast south-west of Adelaide, is an important national centre for wildlife and has a great potential for fishing. At Kingscote, Penneshaw and American River wharves garfish, tommy ruffs and snook may be caught on fast running tides; jetties at Emu Bay and Vivonne Bay produce good fishing at times; surf fishing at Emu Bay, Stokes Bay, D'Estrees Bay, Vivonne Bay and Middle River, where salmon, mullet, and large flathead may be caught; swallowtail are caught by rock fishing, and inland the Middle, Sou'West, Chapman and Cygnet Rivers, and the Western River mouth all provide excellent bream fishing; at the mouth of the Cygnet River, salmon trout, mullet and tommy ruffs are to be found. Charter boats operate on the island, found through information centres at Penneshaw and Kingscote, and snapper are caught along the north coast in large numbers, whiting to 1.5kg, and snook are also taken. Fishing in National Parks rivers or creeks is prohibited. Tourism is well organised on the island, and there is a wide range of good accommodation.

Anglers do not require a licence to fish with a rod or hand line, but must observe legal minimum lengths of fish, bag limits, boat limits, and closed areas, and must not take protected species. Fishing is not permitted in most Aquatic Reserves.

Tourist information can be had from the **South Australian Tourism Commission, Travel Centre, 1 King William Street, Adelaide**, tel: 1300 366770, or 8303 2033; and further information on fishery matters from the **Primary Industries SA Fisheries, GPO Box 1625, Adelaide SA, 5001,** and the **Honourary Secretary, South Australian Fly Fishers Association Inc, GPO Box 489, North Adelaide, SA 5006**. For houseboat hire in a wide range of river locations, often with fishing opportunity, contact **Houseboat Hirers Association Inc, 7 Gollop Cres, Redwood Park SA 5097**, tel: 08 8395 0999, fax 08 8263 5373.

TASMANIA. Tasmania, not without justification, describes itself as Australia's fly fishing capital. A multitude of lakes and rivers contain self-supporting populations of brown and rainbow trout, species which have achieved growth-rates on the island second to none. The size-bracket in which the angler expects his captures to fall spans 1-5 kg, with even larger trout an ever-present possibility. Most of the waters are within motoring distance of **Hobart** and **Launceston**. Mobile campers are widely employed. Guides operate in vicinity, and can arrange, where necessary, flies, lures, boats and accommodation.

Popular waters include **Great Lake**, 158 square km (situated in the central plateau of the island at an altitude of 1,000m, 83 miles from Hobart, the capital, and about the same distance from Launceston, second largest city in the island, situated in the north), **Lake King William, Lake St Clair, Lake Echo, Little Pine Lagoon**, (perhaps Tasmania's best known fly fishing water,) **Brady's Lake, Dee Lagoon, Arthurs Lake** (64.4 square km), **Lake Rowallan** and **Lake Pedder** (which reached a legendary peak in the late 1970s, with trout over 10kg. Now, trout average a more modest 1½ to 2kg). Other popular fishing waters are **Lake Leake** and **Tooms Lake** on the east coast, and **Lake Sorell** in the central midlands, 43 square km, at 823 m above sea level, with fine hatches of mayfly and caddis. Browns to 3kg are caught. Another popular group is the Bronte system, between Bronte Park and Tarraleah, as are the many small lakes in the Nineteen Lagoons district centred around **Lakes Ada** and **Augusta**. The **Western Lakes** are a scattering of countless lakes, lagoons and tarns across the Western Central Plateau (1150 to 1200m above sea level), between the Great Lake and the Cradle Mountain Lake, St Clair National Park. They are also know as the Wilderness Lakes. The more accessible amongst them include Howes Bay Lagoon, Carter Lakes, Lake Botsford, Lake Ada and Lake Kay. Mainly brown trout are to be found in the area. Other famous Tasmanian fisheries are **Brumbys Creek**, near Cressy and Longford, and the **Macquarie River**, flowing northwards through the midlands, with 'red spinner' mayfly hatches: stream fishing for small brown trout. **London Lakes** is a private trout fishery of 5,000 acres in the Central Highlands, with abundant stocks of wild browns, generally in the 1-1.5 kg size range. Contact London Lakes Lodge, P.O. Bronte Park, Tasmania 7140, tel: 03 628 91159 (fax 1122).

The northern part of the island is more richly endowed with trout streams than the south, having the **South Esk, North Esk, Macquarie** and **Brumby**. The north-west has the **Mersey, Forth, Leven, Blyth, Duck** and **Inglis**. In the south are the **Derwent**, and **Huon**.

Sea fishing abounds in Tasmania, mainly in the south east, but in the north Port Sorell and the **Tamar River** (65km, with jetty and estuary fishing) are popular venues, and in the west, Macquarie Harbour. The **Derwent River** at Hobart also provides many spots for jetty and estuary fishing, with catches of mackerel, flathead, cod, squid, barracouta, perch, bream, australian salmon. There are also many excellent beaches, particularly in the north from Cape Portland to Stanley, where flathead, Australian salmon, flounder and whiting are taken. Most of the rivers on the east coast from St Hellens to Bruny Island hold large populations of bream, best fishing in Nov. Bruny island also has excellent beach fishing. Bait is sold in many spots on the coast, and accommodation is first class.

Species caught either from shore or from boat are southern rock cod, leather jacket, blue eye, school whiting, barracouta, yellow-eyed mullet, black bream, flathead, warhou, leather-jacket, wrasse, mullet, silver trevally, southern garfish, greenback flounder, school, "gummy", marlin, various species of tuna, blue pointer, white pointer and bronze whaler sharks, elephant fish, Australian salmon, trumpeter, silver trevally, snapper, tailor, garfish, yellowtail kingfish. Boats may be chartered. There are various laws and restrictions practised, including bag limits; details should be obtained from **Dept of Primary Industry & Fisheries**, 03 6233 3515.

Angling licences are required. For inland waters these are: full season $40, 14 days $22, 3 days $13 and 1 day $8, with concessions for pensioners and juveniles, are sold at most sports stores, police stations and Tasmanian travel centres or the Inland Fisheries Commission. The *Tasmanian Angling Code*, which is free with each license should be consulted for details on fishing restrictions. The main season runs from the Saturday nearest 1 Aug to Sunday nearest 30 Apr. There are some exceptions. The principal angling associations are the Southern Tasmanian Licensed Anglers Association, the Northern Tasmanian Fisheries Association, and the North-Western Fisheries Association.

Further information can be obtained from **The Tasmanian Travel and Information Service, Level 13, Trafalgar Building, 110 Collins Street, Hobart**, tel: 03 6230 8250 (fax 8230), and **The Inland Fisheries Commission, 127 Davey Street, Hobart 7000**, tel: 03 6223 6622 (fax 4372).

VICTORIA. The smallest in area of the Australian mainland States, Victoria offers a considerable diversity of opportunities for freshwater river and lake, estuary, bay and inlet, beach and sea fishing. Many fishing locations are among or near National, State and other Parks which provide an attractive scenic environment and comprehensive touring/holiday experience. Anglers are able to use natural baits, artificial lures and flies in Victoria's public waters.

Freshwater Fishing. Victoria may be known for the **Yarra River** which passes through Melbourne, the capital of Victoria, but the State has many excellent opportunities for freshwater fishing. The Yarra R. has edible fish throughout its accessible length which is confined to bank fishing (headwaters are closed water catchment) with trout, blackfish, roach, redfin, carp, Macquarie perch, some Murray cod in the urban area and within 1 hour's drive from the city centre. The estuarine section from the city to Port Phillip Bay contains a wide variety of species fishable from the bank, including bream, mullet, luderick, some mulloway and tailor. Other major streams entering Port Phillip Bay are the **Maribyrnong** and **Werribee Rivers**, which have trout in the headwaters, coarse fish in the middle sections and estuary fish in the lower sections. Except in the far north-west of the State where it is very dry, there are numerous streams, lakes and reservoirs fishable from bank, shoreline or boat, throughout Victoria. Many waters have self-supporting fish populations, but Fisheries Victoria have active stocking programs of the native golden perch, Murray cod and Macquarie perch and the introduced brown trout, rainbow trout and chinook salmon into selected, suitable waters. Trout fishing is providing in hundreds of waters but is most popular in the north east (**Ovens River**. system, **Lake Dartmouth**), Wimmera region (**Toolondo Reservoir, Wartook Lake**), the south west (**Purrumbete Lake, Merri River**) and central (**Goulburn River, Lake Eildon**). Native fish angling for blackfish can be had throughout much of Victoria, and the waters of the northern half of the State provide Murray cod and golden perch in streams and lake systems draining into the Murray R. which forms the boundary between Victoria and New South Wales. Coarse fishing is practised State-wide with good populations of redfin, roach, tench and carp.

Saltwater Fishing. Melbourne and its suburbs are situated around **Port Phillip Bay**, which together with **Western Port Bay** about 1 hours drive to the south east, dominate Victoria's saltwater fishing scene, providing boat and shore anglers with a variety of fish including snapper to 11 kg (mainly October to March), flathead, whiting, mullet, garfish, trevally and gummy shark. Victoria's coastline has many estuaries, inlets, lakes, surf beaches and rocky shorelines that provide ample opportunities for shore, jetty, rock, beach and boat fishing. The most popular eastern area is the major **Gippsland Lakes** system where a series of large lakes provide excellent year-round fishing. Many of Victoria's coastal fishing areas are popular and well-serviced holiday locations complete with accommodation, facilities and boat hire. The **Glenelg River** in the west provides a 70 km estuary which is very popular for mulloway fishing. The commonly caught saltwater fish are bream, flathead, mullet, luderick, estuary perch, Australian bass, sharks, tailor, Australian salmon, sweep, leatherjackets and garfish.

There are too many angling locations around Victoria to mention individually. Tackle stores and newsagents provide numerous publications and video tapes about where and how to catch fish in the State. Two very useful books are *A Guide to Inland Angling Waters of Victoria*, 4th Edition 1991 - Tunbridge, Rogan and Barnham, Fisheries Victoria (FV), Department of Natural Resources and Environment (DNRE), 125 pp, 31 maps, (RRP $A14.95) ISBN 0 7241 0817 3, which provides excellent information about features and locations of more than 600 of Victoria's angling streams and freshwater lakes, the fish present, and advice about fish sizes and abundance; *Location Guide to Fishing Victoria's Coastline*, 1st Edition 1993 - Wilson, Australian Fishing Network, 96 pp, 30 maps, (RRP $A12.95), ISBN 062 621 427, which is designed to help the angler find and fish hundreds of locations along the coast.

Line anglers (unless exempted such as those under 16 years of age) require an Amateur Fishing Licence to fish inland waters, but do not require (at September 1997) a licence to fish in marine waters. Definitions of 'inland' and 'marine' waters together with full information on licensing and fishing regulations including bag limits, size limits and closed seasons are provided in the *Victoria Recreational Fishing Regulations Guide* which is provided with Amateur Fishing Licences and issued free from FV, DNRE and fishing tackle stores.

Licences can be purchased to cover periods of 28 days ($A10), 1 year ($A20) and three years ($A60) from DCNR offices and nearly 600 retail fishing and service businesses throughout Victoria.

Information on fishing regulations, locations and fish can be obtained from **Fisheries Victoria, Department of Natural Resources and Environment, 5/240 Victoria Parade** (P O Box 41), **East Melbourne, Victoria, Australia 3002** (Tel: 61 3 9412 4262, Fax. 61 3 9412 4260). Tourist information is issued by **Tourism Victoria, 7/55 Collins Street, Melbourne, Victoria, Australia 3000**. The address of the **Victoria Government Office** in London is **Victoria House, Melbourne Place, Strand, London WC2B 4LG** (Tel: 071 836 2656).

WESTERN AUSTRALIA. Stretching from the tropical north to the cool southern oceans, the vast coastal waters of Western Australia provide superb ocean sports fishing, and some of the best angling in the world can be found on the doorstep of Western Australia's major cities.

Around 300,000 West Australians go fishing at least once a year, and the state attracts many visiting anglers. Boat ownership is the highest in Australia.

Principal centres for ocean fishing are: **Kununurra, Broome, Port Hedland, Dampier, Exmouth, Carnarvon, Shark Bay, Kalbarri, Geraldton, Fremantle, Lancelin, Perth, Rottnest Island, Mandurah, Bunbury, Busselton, Augusta, Albany** and **Esperance**. Fishable rivers include **Margaret River, Kalbarri, Murry**. Species to be caught include: herring, silver bream, garfish, mulloway, whiting, tailor, tuna, Australian salmon, pink snapper, dhufish, barramundi, sailfish, flathead, whiting, black bream, and Spanish mackerel. Annual gamefishing classics are held in the tropical waters of **Exmouth** and **Broome** where marlin and other gamefish are target species. In the **Swan River**, on Perth's doorstep, locals hand-trawl for prawns and black bream. Flounder and flathead are also prolific. World famous western rock lobsters can be taken from the reefs around many mid-west coastal centres. Fishing boats operate from all principal centres.

A Recreational Fishing Licence must be held for the taking of lobster, maroon, freshwater fishing, abalone or to use a gill net, and is sold by Fisheries Department offices. Bag limits apply to all species of fish.

The **Fisheries Department** is located at **3rd Floor, SGIO Atrium, 168/170 St George's Terrace, Perth WA 6000**, and the address of the **Western Australian Government Office** in London is: **115 Strand, London WC2R 0AJ** (0171-240 2881).

NEW ZEALAND

Fishing in New Zealand divides into three parts - Trout, Salmon and Big Game angling.

Trout, both brown and rainbow, were introduced about 100 years ago and have long been fully distributed on both islands. Rainbow predominate in the North Island, and browns in the South, but many waters have a mixture of the two in varying proportions.

The main areas in the North are centred on **Lake Taupo** and the **Rotorua** district with its group of important lakes. The rivers flowing into and out of these lakes are also noted fisheries, particularly late in the season when the main runs commence. The **Tongariro, Waitahanui, Tauranga-Taupo** and others flow into Lake Taupo, while in the Rotorua area there are the **Kaituna, Ohau Channel**, and **Ngongotaha** to name a few. The summer trout fishing season runs from Oct to Apr in most districts. Winter trout fishing is found in the Taupo/Rotorua regions, with Apr/May. Sept/Oct the best months. May to Oct is the best time for the Tongariro. The top dry fly fishing in the more remote areas of the North Island is best Nov/Apr inclusive.

The South Island has thousands of miles of rivers and streams, and numerous lakes of all sizes. It was once calculated, at the turn of the century, that there are 17,000 miles of river fishing in New Zealand, and of course it is all open to the public, subject only to right of access and to reasonable accessibility. The best time for trout fishing in South Island is from Oct to May.

Good trout fishing is widely spread, and large trout can still be caught within an hour's drive of the main cities, but obviously many of the best waters are more remote and some are seldom fished, although helicopter or floatplane services operate out of the towns of **Queenstown, Wanaka** and **Te Anau** to reach places like **Lakes Alabaster** and **McKerrow**, or the **Pyke** and **Hollyford** rivers for example.

The main, and also the lesser, rivers of **Southland** and **Otago** provinces offer excellent dry fly and nymph fishing for brown trout, and fish of from 12 to 15 pounds are caught each season, but a good average would be from 3 to 4 pounds. Guide services are again easily found, although obviously concentrated somewhat in the more popular areas. An Angling Guides Association was formed some time ago, all professional guides are licensed, and are fully supported with 4-wheel drive vehicles and boats as necessary for their local areas.

In general, the open season is from Oct 1 until the end of April (North Island - 1 Oct to end of June) but some waters open early to take advantage of the runs of whitebait which provide feed for sea-run trout, while others, principally in the Taupo and Rotorua areas, stay open all the year, particularly the lower reaches of the larger streams feeding Lake Taupo, Rotorua and Wakatiou themselves.

Salmon, the Pacific Quinnat or King Salmon, introduced to the main **Canterbury** rivers, are fished for in about eight of them, the main ones being the **Waimakariri, Rakaia, Ashburton, Rangitata** and **Waitaki**. The fishing is mainly heavy spinning, with spoons most favoured as lures, in the lower rivers, estuaries and even in the surf at the mouths. A certain amount of fly fishing, using very large lures or flies, is done upriver, notably in the **Rakaia Gorge** area. In all the salmon rivers the fish are mostly in the 12 to 20 pound class, but larger are quite frequent. The rivers are often unfishable for many days at a time due to cloudy glacial melt water, and trips undertaken with salmon exclusively in mind are not to be recommended.

Big Game Fishing: the main bases for this are **Russell, Paihia** and **Whangerei** in the **Bay of Islands**, and also out from **Tauranga** to the **Mayor Island** area. There are ample charter boats, with professional skippers and hands, based in these places, catering for parties of up to four anglers. The tackle and bait are provided in the charter. Main species caught are striped, Pacific blue, and black marlin, broadbill, mako, thresher and hammerhead shark, yellowfin tuna, yellowtail, and are taken with natural bait or lure. The southern part of the West Coast of the South Island, known as 'Fiordland', is now assuming increased importance for big game fishing. Boats are now based there, at Milford Sound and elsewhere.

Big Game angling is mainly from January to the end of April, with the period from mid-February on offering fine sport.

Licences are needed for trout and salmon fishing. There is a special Tourist Licence which covers the whole country and is only sold at the Tourism Rotorua Information Office in Rotorua. Alternatively licences may be purchased from other districts which allow the visitor to fish in any district with the exception of Rotorua and Taupo, separate licences being needed for these two districts. Rods may be brought freely into the country, although airport agriculture officials may want to fumigate flies made with real feathers.

For further information and advice on angling in New Zealand, contact **New Zealand Professional Fishing Guides Association, Murphys Lodge, PO Box 16, Motu, Gisborne**, tel: 64 6 863 5822, fax: 64 6 863 5844; or **New Zealand Tourism Board, New Zealand House, Haymarket, London SW1Y 4TQ**. Telephone 0839 300 900. Calls charged at Premium Rate Services rates.

INDIA

One of the big attractions for the fisherman in India - in more senses than one - is the mighty mahseer. Mahseer country stretches between the Hindu Kush-Kabul-Kohistan watershed in the west all the way to the eastern tributaries of the Brahmapurta. It is found in some rivers in the Deccan plateau region and the River Kaveri in the south central plain region of Karnataka. Mahseer is essentially a migratory fish, running up and into side streams for spawning, at heights of up to 2000 metres during the monsoon. The fish avoids very cold water and therefore frequents the lower portion of the Himalayan streams during winter. Fish breeds three times a year, Jan-Feb, May-June, July-Sept, the peak season. The big ones are generally landed when returning from the breeding grounds when they chase shoals of minnows.

The mahseer can be taken on a spoon, but strong tackle is essential. It not only runs large - the biggest caught on rod and line weighed 119lb (Cauvery River, South India, 1919) - but is a splendid fighter. The sport has, in fact, been compared most favourably with salmon fishing.

Mahseer are generally found in the rivers of the Terai regions of the Himalayas, the Shivalik Hills in the north, and the river Kaveri in the south. The following river stretches have been specifically cited as mahseer fishing areas, and are accessible for accommodation or camping: **River Jhelum** (J & K), below the Wular lake on the Sopore-Rampur stretch 80 kms from Srinagar. **River Beas** (Himachal Pradesh and Punjab), from Dehra Gopipur up to the Pong Dam reservoir; Below Pong Dam at Talwara (Punjab); Harike barrage on the Ferozpur Road. Best seasons Feb-May, Sept-Nov. **River Ganga**, stretch above Tehri (10 km); Beashgat, and Gangalehri; **River Bhoroli** (Arunachal), 60 km from Tezpur, the river is fished between Tipee and Bhalukpong, as it flows through the Balipara reserved forest. Inflatable raft recommended; **River Manas** (Assam). Located in the famous Manas wildlife sanctuary; **River Kaveri** (Kamataka), 2½ hours by road from Bangalore. Mahseer of 43 kgs landed here on 20 Jan, 1985.

Kashmir is renowned for sport with brown and rainbow trout, which have thrived since they were introduced at the turn of the century. The snow trout is found in high altitude waters. The many streams in the area are regularly stocked from two large hatcheries and are divided into 'beats' of about two miles. Great variety is to be found, the rivers ranging from foaming torrents, when spinning is permitted, to gentle streams suitable for dry fly. There are 'fly only' beats. The most suitable flies are those usually included in every angler's selection, but in Kashmir they are usually dressed on hook sizes between No. 9 and No. 5 (old sizes). The season lasts from May to September. The major trout waters in Kashmir are as follows: **River Sindh**, flows along main Srinagar highway. Wide and shallow in places, upper beats are deep and narrow. Fishing early or late in the day is recommended; **River Lidder**, originates north of Pahalgam, and has two major tributaries, the **Aru** and the **Sheshnag**. excellent trout fishing, also for 'chush', a local species of bartel (inedible). Pahalgam is a convenient base for the system; **River Bringhi**, runs along the Anatnag-Dakshum road, beyond Acchabal. Narrow and boulder strewn, it has always been a great favourite with anglers. Three tributaries are the Dyus, Naubaug, and the Alhan. **Kokernag** and **Verinag** streams, springfed waters in the Kashmir valley, have easily accessible bank fishing, with good sized brown trout. There are a number of high altitude lakes in the north of the valley, well stocked with large brown trout. The average size of these waters is around 3000 sq meters, and they are only approachable by three-day treks, with camping necessary. Amongst these are lakes **Tarsar**, **Marsar**, approached from Pahalgam; **Kishensar**, **Vishensar**, **Gadsar** and **Gangabal**, approachable from Sonmarg, Gund or Nichnai.

India's rivers contain numerous other species. The **Jamuna** at **Okhla**, in **Delhi**, for instance, holds no fewer than eight species, including heavy catfish, the silund - a predator running up to 50lb, which can be taken on a spinner - and a humpbacked fish called the cheetul or moh, which will be seen constantly rising to the surface and turning over broadside. There is also plenty of huge carp in the slow-flowing rivers and the lakes and tanks. The sea fishing can be excellent, too, but is dependent upon seasonal migrations and the weather. A considerable body of angling literature has now been published by the **Bombay Natural History Society, 114 Apollo Street**.

While the tourist-angler should not expect to find luxurious cabins on his expeditions, numerous camping-sites and comfortable rest-houses have been provided, often in the most beautiful surroundings and at **Corbett**, the call of the tiger and the trumpeting of wild elephants may sometimes be heard.

So far as tackle is concerned, the trout or mahseer fisherman will be specially well catered for at **Srinagar**, capital of Kashmir, where he may obtain first-class gear, but rates are rising due to restricted imports, and it is preferable to take one's own equipment.

Further information from the **India Government Tourist Office, 7 Cork Street, London W1X 2LN** (Tel 0171-437 3677).

SRI LANKA (CEYLON)

Nuwara Eliya is the best centre for trout fishing. As it is above the 6,000ft level, the climate is temperate. There is good hotel accommodation. The fishing is, with few exceptions, restricted to fly only and most common patterns of wet fly are successful. Dry fly is rarely used, there being little natural fly. There is no statutory close season, though the club imposes one in parts following restocking. Size limits vary from 8in to 15in.

The main waters are: **Nuwara Eliya** stream (flows through the golf course and park); **Ambawela** stream (8m from Nuwara Eliya; jungle and grassland); **Bulu Ella** stream (2½m jungle); **Portswood Dam** (4m; tea estate); **Agra Oya** and **Gorge Valley** rivers (10-15m; tea estates), and the magnificently spectacular **Horton Plains** stream (30m; jungle and grassland, Nature reserve). Motor transport can be hired. On any of these waters it is possible to maintain an average of 1lb and several fish over 3lb are caught.

Trout fishing is now controlled by the Nuwara Eliya District Fishing Club. Stocking has so far been carried out in Portswood Dam, the Horton Plains, Agra Oya and Gorge Valley. For licences application should be made to the **Honourary Secretary, Nuwara Eliya District Fishing Club, Court Lodge Estate, Kandapola**. Visitors are advised to bring their tackle as fly tackle is scarce in Sri Lanka.

The two main species of indigenous sporting fish in Sri Lanka are the mahseer and the walaya (freshwater shark), found in the jungle rivers of the Low Country, particularly the **Mahawehi**, the upper reaches of the **Kelani** and the **Amban Ganga**. Ceylon mahseer, though small compared with those in some Indian rivers, provide good sport, but fishing for them can be somewhat difficult. Fishing for indigenous sporting fish in Sri Lanka is free. With a shoreline of 1,140 miles and a continental shelf of 10,000 square miles, the seas around Ceylon have an unlimited fishing potential hardly exploited.

The outfalls of 103 major river basins and hundreds of other estuaries, lagoons and coastal lakes all round the island are the most popular spots frequented by local surf casters as well as bait fishermen. Many varieties of game fish of the Carangid family, locally called paraw and know elsewhere as trevally, horse mackerel, etc, are taken. These swift and powerful carnivorous fish attain a length of 5ft and a weight of 150lb. The schooling habits of the caranx, their keen eyesight and some built-in sensory mechanism make them congregate in estuaries immediately after monsoons and rains.

Next in popularity among surf-casters come the barracuda and Spanish mackerel. Both these species of voracious predatory fish attain lengths of 6ft as do other species known locally as 'giant perch', 'threadfins' and 'tassel fish' which frequent the estuaries.

Trolling over the continental shelf yields catches of tuna ranging from the 2-3ft skipjack to the 6ft yellowfin and bluefin, the acrobatic dolphin, swordfish and marlin which attain a size to provide a challenge to the best big game fishermen of any country. The broadbill swordfish found in deeper waters reach a length of 15ft and a weight of well over 1,000lb. Though reaching only 10ft and 250lb, the sailfish compensate for their smaller size by their remarkable agility.

The monsoons regulate the fishing in Sri Lanka Seas. The western and southern coasts are favoured during the North-East monsoon (from October to April) and the east coast during the South-West monsoon (from May to September).

Further information can be obtained from **London Director, Sri Lanka Tourist Board, Sri Lanka Centre, 22 Regents Street, London SW1Y 4QD**, tel: 0171-930 2627 (9070 fax).

MALAYSIA

There is good sport in the jungle-covered highlands where fast-flowing, clean streams will delight the eye. These are well stocked with cyprinids or members of the carp family, which include the well-known mahseer of India, known locally as kelah. This group of which the most common species are kelah (up to 20lb), sebarau (up to 12lb), and kejor or tengas (up to 8lb), are sporting fish which fight well when hooked. Kelah and tengas are good to eat. They are best when curried and provide a good change or diet in the jungle when living on operational 24-hour pack rations.

All these fish will take an artificial bait; the most popular being a 1in or 1½in silver or silver/copper spoon. A normal salmon spinning outfit is ideal. For those who prefer it, a fixed-spool reel can be used provided it will hold sufficient line. Owing to the crushing power of the jaws of the kelah, extra strong treble or large single hooks should be used and some people recommend the use of a 2ft wire trace.

Taman Negara, on the borders of **Kelantan**, **Trengganu** and **Pahang**, provides the best fishing, and a visit to the HQ at **Kuala Tahan** is well worth the journey. It may be reached by rail to **Kuala Tembeling** and thence by water, in long, narrow, locally-built boats fitted with 40hp outboard motors which can do the journey up the **Sungaï Tembeling** in three to four hours depending on the condition of the river. At Kuala Tahan there are bungalows and a rest-house providing full board. A number of visitors' lodges and halting bungalows have been built throughout the park so the fishermen can stay near the river they are fishing.

From Kuala Tahan all onward movement is by smaller boats with lower-powered engines to negotiate the shallower rivers, such as the Tahan itself. There are many large pools well stocked with fish in the lower reaches, and above the **Lata Berkoh** barrier many pools and rapids, all excellent fishing water. Malay and Aborigine boatmen are happy to act as guides and are delightful companions.

It is easier and pleasanter to cast from the bank, but this will necessitate some wading where the bank is steep and overhung by the jungle. The water is pleasantly warm and waders would be far too hot to wear. Those with a good sense of balance can try fishing from a slowly paddled perahu, but as this is only a shell at the most 2ft wide, it is liable to be something of a circus act.

Most reliable times to fish are the months February/March and July/August, because in other months fishing will be spasmodic owing to the heavy rainfall. Spates and floodwater so colour the rivers that fishing is a waste of time.

In **Terengganu State** is the massive **Kenyir Lake,** a well known attraction to visiting anglers, where baung, toman, sebarau, kelah, kelisa and arowana can be caught, and house-boat holidays are organised: for information contact Jabatan Perhutanan, **Kuala Brang, Hulu Terengganu,** tel: 09 811259 for **Sekayu** area, or **Kenyir Lake Resort, Kenyir Dam, Hulu Terengganu,** tel: 09 950609, for **Kenyir Dam** area.

Apart from the fishing there is always the chance of seeing the wild animals of Malaysia at the many salt licks. There are usually monkeys, monitor lizard, snakes and flying foxes to be seen, as well as many varieties of birds such as hornbill eagle and kingfishers.

Intending visitors should write well before the date of their visit, giving as much information as possible on their special interests to the **Director-General, Dept of Wildlife and National Parks, Km10, Jalan Cheras, Kuala Lumpur, Malaysia,** so as to enable the Dept of Wildlife and National Parks to plan their itineraries.

FISHING IN NORTH AMERICA

CANADA

On the Atlantic side of the Dominion there are plenty of salmon rivers in **Quebec** and **New Brunswick**, and a good deal of fishing is open to the non-resident who takes out the appropriate provincial licence. There is a great deal of splendid trout fishing in many of the inland lakes and rivers, while in the **Great Lakes** region there are big muskellunge, and fine black bass fishing in various waters. The land-locked salmon is found in Quebec, both in the tributaries and discharge of **Lac St John**, and in some lakes in **Nova Scotia**, such as **Grand Lake** and **Beaver Bank Lake**. The 'trout' of this side of Canada are char *(Salvelinus fontinalis),* while some of them are migratory and become 'sea trout'. In the lakes are 'grey trout', some of which reach a great size. There are also char *(Salvelinus namaycush)* in the Arctic.

On the other side of Canada, British Columbia offers splendid opportunities of sport with Pacific salmon, steelhead and rainbow trout. Fishing for Pacific salmon has until recently been considered of necessity a matter for tidal waters. The **Campbell River, Vancouver Island**, has been the most favoured, and there quinnat (now known locally as tyee) up to 70lb have been caught on the troll. At **Prince Rupert** a 93lb quinnat was caught on a spoon in 1929 by Mr O P Smith, a professional fisherman. An 82lb tyee was caught in August, 1951, at **Rivers Inlet**. The coho has been caught on fly, also in tidal waters. Of late years it has become clear that quinnat will take in fresh water in certain conditions. To the far north there are evident possibilities of sport in **Yukon** and NW Territories.

So far as tackle is concerned, the trend is towards lighter outfits. Brook trout, for instance, are almost universally taken on a nine-foot, five-ounce fly rod, and many anglers use the same rod for steelhead or Kamloops trout, although this is probably foolhardy. Tackle should always be carefully geared to the area and quarry, and on-the-spot advice is desirable.

Much work is done by the Federal and Provincial hatcheries, and waters in various parts of Canada are supplied with fry of species suitable to their needs, chiefly salmonidae, but also bass and other kinds of the best big game fishing so far discovered anywhere.

Throughout Canada there are many regulations controlling all aspects of freshwater fishing, which vary from one province to another. Information on these laws is readily obtainable from a large number of public outlets.

Note: The Canadian Tourist Office has provincial brochures relevant to fishing in the country. For further information please contact The **Visit Canada Centre, 62-65 Trafalgar Square, London WC2N 5DY**, tel: 0891 715000 (Premium Rate Line, charged at 50p per minute).

ALBERTA. Alberta is fortunate in having more than 4,000 miles of good fishing streams and more than 1,000 lakes found in the mountains, foothills and prairies, and in the boreal forests of the northern region of the province.

There are 18 species of sportfish in Alberta of which there are 9 cold water and 9 warm water sportfish. The cold water sportfish include brook, brown, cutthroat, golden, rainbow, and lake trout, bull trout, Arctic grayling and mountain whitefish. These fish are generally found in the lakes and streams in the foothills and mountain areas in the west of the province.

The warm water sportfish include lake whitefish, walleye, perch, pike, goldeye, and lake sturgeon. These fish are generally found in rivers and lakes throughout the south east and northern areas of the province.

Since the 1960s, the total numbers of anglers fishing in Alberta has increased dramatically from 150,000 to nearly 350,000 in 1995. The number of fish caught each year has increased from 19 million in 1985 to 23 million in 1994. Perch, pike, walleye, trout, and lake whitefish are the most widely taken fish, accounting to 95% of total harvest but pike fishing is predominant. Fewer than half Alberta's lakes can produce game fish, owing to a short summer season when warm water temperatures produce sufficient aquatic insects, plants, and other food, and the supply of fish is supplemented by stocking. Hatchery production of

3.5 million trout are stocked annually throughout the province into lakes that do not contain native fish and which are readily accessible to the public.

As throughout Canada, there are many fishing regulations, which the angler must know before setting out. Licences are obligatory, and obtainable in most retail sports outfitters. Prices are as follows: Youths (under 16), none required. Non residents annual, $30; limited (5 day), $20.

Further information may be obtained by writing to **The Director, Fisheries Management Division, Alberta Natural Resources Service, Main Floor, North Tower, Petroleum Plaza, 9945-108 Street, Edmonton, Alberta, Canada T5K 2G6**.

BRITISH COLUMBIA. The province has a coastline (including islands) of 27,000 km and is drained by innumerable rivers and freshwater lakes. The game fish of British Columbia comprise five species of salmon: sockeye, chum, the chinook or spring (large specimens often referred to as 'Tyee'), the pink (tidal waters only), and the coho, which may be taken with the fly, but are more easily caught by trolling; all varieties of Pacific Coast trout, particularly the steelhead, the rainbow, and the cut-throat; Arctic grayling; two species of char, of which the commoner is the Dolly Varden; and the Eastern brook trout which has been introduced.

Some of the most important fishing areas are **Kootenay District**, **Okanagan District** (including **Beaver**, **Bear**, **Dee**, **Ideal**, **Mabel**, **Sugar**, **South** and **Woods Lakes), Kamloops District** (including **Adams, East Barriere, Murtle, Shuswap** and **Nicola Lakes**), **Cariboo District** (including **Quesnel**, **Horsefly** and **Canim Lakes,** and **Fraser** and **Thompson Rivers**), and **Merrit District**, which abounds with small productive, accessible lakes, such as **Chataway**, **Dot**, **Gypsum**, **Antler**, **Corbett**, **Peter Hope** and **Roche Lakes**. Most of the southern lakes and rivers are easily accessible, especially by car, and yield excellent fishing. Flying in to the less accessible waters is now a common practice. Lodges, cabins and boats are abundant.

The **Skeena Region** of northwest **British Columbia** has a wide variety of attractive fisheries. The **Burns Lake** area boasts a number of great trout fishing lakes, and **Terrace** is the centre of exceptional sport fishing for steelhead trout and chinook and coho salmon. Some restrictions apply on certain steelhead waters as conservation of this species poses particularly difficult problems. Information may be obtained from the Victoria address below.

Vancouver Island offers excellent cut-throat and steelhead trout fishing. The important waters are **Cowichan**, **Cameron**, **Sproat Lakes**, **Alberni** and **Qualicum Districts** and the **Campbell River** area. Steelhead trout are in **Sproat**, **Somass**, **Ash** and **Stamp Rivers**, to name but a few. Quinnat (or spring) salmon and coho are found in good quantities in many of the main rivers and streams draining into the Pacific Ocean. On Vancouver Island there is splendid salmon fishing in tidal water to be had near the following cities: **Campbell River**, **Comox**, **Nanaimo**, **Gold River**, **Port Alberni**, **Tofino**, **Ucluelet** and **Victoria**. On the mainland excellent fishing for salmon is to be found within 20 minutes drive from downtown Vancouver. Other famous salmon fishing locations include: **Pender Harbour**, **Powell River**, **Hakai Pass**, **Rivers Kitimat**, **Prince Rupert** and the **Queen Charlotte Islands**, including Langara Island.

Salmon conservation: there is a combined daily limit of 4 for all species of Pacific salmon in fresh and saltwater, and a limit of 2 chinook salmon. The annual limit of chinook is 15 or 30 fish, depending on area. There is also a size limit which varies according to species. A salmon conservation stamp must be purchased before fishing (*see below*). Stocks of coho have declined seriously in recent years, and additional conservation measures may be required. Before fishing contact nearest DFO office or phone, tel: 666 2828.

Licences are obligatory, and obtainable in most retail sports outfitters. Prices are as follows: Non residents annual, $55; 8 day, $30, one day, $15, and subject to change. Conservation surcharge stamps for fishing steelhead, salmon, rainbow trout, char, range from $10 to $40. For angling in tidal waters, the annual non-resident fee is $108.07; 5 dat $38.52; 3 day $20.33, 1 day $7.49. To fish for salmon, a stamp costing $6.42 is obligatory.

Further information (including details of licence charges and open seasons) can be had from the **Fisheries Branch, Ministry of Environment, Lands and Parks, 780 Blanshard Street, 2nd Floor, Victoria, BC V8V 1X4**, for freshwater fishing for species other than salmon, and **Department of Fisheries and Oceans, Suite 415, 555 W. Hastings St, Vancouver, B.C. V6B 5G3**, for saltwater fishing and salmon in freshwater. For travel information, write to **Tourism British Columbia, Parliament Buildings, Victoria B.C., V8V 1X4**. Tel: (250) 356-7285.

MANITOBA. Manitoba is at the centre of a country more than 4,500 miles wide, from **St John's, Newfoundland** on the east to **Victoria, British Columbia** on the west.

The province is enormous by British standards, covering 250,000 square miles and measuring 735 air miles from north to south. Lake Winnipeg, 40 miles north of the capital city of **Winnipeg**, is the seventh largest inland body of water in North America. The northern three-fifths of the province is laced with innumerable streams and rivers, and someone claims to have counted more than 90,000 lakes, although many are too small to even appear on a map.

The species most commonly fished are walleye, pike, channel catfish, lake trout, rainbow trout, brook (speckled) trout, arctic grayling, whitefish, smallmouth bass, lake sturgeon, Winnipeg goldeye (superior to eat, smoked), and carp. Trout fishing is some of the finest in North America, in particular, the **Knife** and **Gods Rivers** in north-eastern Manitoba is famous for trophy-sized brook and lake trout, northern pike and walleye. Lake trout *(Cristivomer namaycush)* are widely distributed from the south-eastern area of the province through to the northern boundaries in the deep, cold-water lakes of the Pre-Cambrian shield. Specimens over 35lbs are taken each year.

The Arctic grayling *(Thymallus arcticus)* is common along the north-western coast of Hudson Bay and its tributary streams, which include the **North Knife**, **Seal**, **Little Seal** and **Wolverine Rivers**. With its spectacular beauty, it is the delight of those fly-fishermen who are able to travel to the Churchill area or the fly-in area of **Nueltin** or **Nejanilini Lakes** in the far North.

Other fish. In the smaller lakes and streams in the southern part of the province, walleye, northern pike and yellow perch are plentiful. In **Lake Winnipeg** and the tributary **Red River**, carp and channel catfish to 30lbs are taken in large numbers at certain seasons. **Winnipeg River** is the locale for large walleye, and great northern pike, together with an abundance of smallmouth bass, which provide excellent sport.

Licences are required, and obtainable in most retail sports outfitters. Prices are as follows: Non residents annual, $40.50, regular; $22 conservation.

Further information (including details of licence charges and open seasons) can be had from **Travel Manitoba, Department RX8, 7th Floor, 155 Carlton Street, Winnipeg, Manitoba R3C 3H8**, tel: (204) 945-3777, ext RX8, fax: (204) 945-2302.

NEW BRUNSWICK. Atlantic salmon in the **Restigouche, Nepisiquit, Tabusintac, North-West Miramichi, South-West Miramichi, Little South-West Miramichi, Sevogle, Renous, Dungarvon, Cains, Rocky Brook, Clearwater Brook, St John River, Nashwaak,** (both closed to salmon angling for 1997, 1998 regulations unknown) and **Tobique** rivers. Salmon run large, fish from 30lb to 40lb are taken each year, and occasionally, 40lb to 50lb. New Brunswick rivers usually yield over 30,000 fish each season. Conservation methods such as hook and release are used, to ensure future stocks, and fishing is fly only. Non-residents are required to employ a guide while fishing for Atlantic salmon, but not for other species. Only grilse, fish 63cm or less in fork length, are allowed to be retained. The season varies from river to river. Licences are required, and obtainable in most retail sports outfitters. Seasonal prices range from $110 per season to $28.75 for 3 days, covering all species. Non-residents licences for all species except salmon cost £34 to £17.50.

In addition to salmon fishing, there is fishing for small-mouth bass in the south-west of the province. Several waters yield good-sized fish, and these are considered to be some of the best bass resources in North America. Other popular angling pursuits include spring Atlantic salmon, shad, brook trout, pickerel and land locked salmon. On the seashore, jigging for cod, casting for mackerel, and deepsea fishing are possible at some locations along the coast. A few striped bass are taken in the St John River and Bathhurst Harbour.

Non-resident licences must be obtained from a DNRE Service Office in the province. These must be carried by the holder at all times, but do not convey right of fishing on Crown-reserve waters or any private fishery without the consent of the lessee or owner. Further information, including details of licences and open seasons, can be had from the **Department of Natural Resources and Energy, Fish and Wildlife Branch, PO Box 6000, Fredericton E3B 5H1**, tel: 506 453 3981, fax: 506 444 4277, and outfitters may be contacted via the **New Brunswick Dept of Economic Development and Tourism, PO Box 12345, Fredericton E3B 5C3**.

NEWFOUNDLAND and LABRADOR. Newfoundland has probably some of the best game-fishing in North America. Almost a quarter of the island's area is water, and its many fine salmon rivers flow through unspoiled forest and hill country. During the 1994 season, anglers landed approximately 42,700 grilse, retaining 31,600 and releasing the rest. About 2,800 large salmon were caught, 474 were retained. Average catches vary, but may be as much as 1.49 salmon per rod day, on the **Sandhill River**, Labrador, or 0.65 per rod day on the **Grey River**, Newfoundland. Rivers with high productivity in 1993 included the **Eagle**, Labrador, 1,702 salmon in 2,067 rod days; the **Pinware River**, Labrador, 1,215 salmon in 3,158 rod days; the **Exploits River**, 4,694 salmon in 7,896 rod days; the **Humber River**, 2,932 salmon in 7,023 rod days, the **Gander River**, 3,313 salmon in 9,073 rod days, all Newfoundland. Ouananiche (land-locked salmon) are found in Newfoundland waters. Several kinds of trout - speckled, brown, rainbow and lake (char). Sea-run brown trout streams in the province are mainly concentrated along a 100-kilometre coastal area immediately south of St. John's; 15lb fish have been taken. Scheduled (licensed) rainbow trout waters comprise a small group of streams and ponds immediately north of St. John's; rainbows are also frequently caught in unscheduled water throughout the province. All the trout except the brown are at least as plentiful (and on average significantly larger) in Labrador as on the island; most Labrador angling waters are much more remote, however.

The salmon season varies among groups of rivers and from year to year, ranging from early June to mid-September, with most rivers open from mid-June to the first week in September, fishing is restricted to fly only. Scheduled rainbow trout waters are open from late May-early June to mid-September. The province has scheduled salmon rivers on the Island of Newfoundland and in Labrador, and scheduled rainbow trout streams.

Fishing in all inland waters in the province is restricted to rod, hook, and line, with a variety of baits and lures permissable in most unscheduled waters; angling in scheduled salmon rivers is further restricted to fly fishing only. There are bag limits in force, which are subject to change. These are at present: salmon, 2 retained per day, six per season. Lake trout, 2 per day; other trout species, 12 per day; northern pike, 2 per day; arctic char, 2 per day. Current regulations require that, except when angling within 800m of a provincial highway, a non-resident must either be accompanied by a resident relative, or engage the services of a licensed guide. This law is likely to be eased or dropped altogether in Newfoundland, but not in Labrador, which is more or less inaccessible wilderness.

Licence-fees for non-residents are as follows. Salmon: $50, $75 family; trout $5, $10 family. Special licenses are required to fish inland waters within the boundaries of National Parks. Anglers should consult with park officials regarding their fishing regulations. Licences are obtainable at most sports outfitters, tackle and hardware shops and department stores. Further information from **Department of Development and Tourism, Tourism Marketing Division, PO Box 8700, St John's, Newfoundland, Canada A1B 4J6**. Tel: (709) 729-3813, facsimile (709) 729-0057, or from **Department of Fisheries & Oceans, Communications Division, PO Box 5667, St Johns, Newfoundland**. Tel: 709 772 4421.

NOVA SCOTIA (including **Cape Breton Island**). Atlantic salmon in **St Mary's, La Have, Medway, Margaree, Stewiacke, Moser, Musquodoboit, Gold, North**, and **Liscomb** rivers; some 30 additional rivers have substantial runs of salmon but water levels and conditions are a major factor in the annual take. There are 16 rivers scheduled and posted for fly fishing only, but it should be noted Atlantic salmon may only be taken by fly; brook trout are common in streams and lakes, many of which are accessible from woods roads known as roads to resources; sea trout (brook and brown) in most tidal streams in the Northern and Eastern part of the province; salt water charter boats are hired for ground fishing in all areas except the upper reaches of the **Bay of Fundy**. Tuna charter boats operate in the **St George's Bay** and Halifax areas. Licence-fees for non-residents are as follows. Salmon: $120.75 season, $46 7 day; trout $46, $23.

The Department of Tourism publishes and distributes several brochures on outdoor sports activities. For further information please contact the **Department of Tourism, PO Box 456, Halifax, Nova Scotia B3J 2R5; Nova Scotia Salmon Association, Regional Council of the Atlantic Salmon Federation, P O Box 523, Halifax N.S. B3J 2R7**, fax: (902) 386-2334. NSalmon@ntcon.com; **Department of Fisheries and Oceans (Federal), 133 Church Street, Antigonish Mall, Antigonish, N.S. B2G 2E3**, tel: (902) 863-5670; **Department of Environment (Provincial), Suite 224, 1595 Bedford Highway, Halifax, N.S. B4A 3X4**, tel: (902) 424-7773.

ONTARIO. Brook trout are widely distributed in eastern Canada. In Ontario this excellent game-fish occurs from the **Great Lakes** northward to streams entering **Hudson Bay** and **James Bay**. Included in the eastern part of this area west of the **Québec** boundary are **Algonquin Park**, tributaries of the **Upper Ottawa River**, North Bay, Temagami Metachewan, the Porcupine, Matheson-Abitibi and Cochrane areas, the Moosonee and the Goose country.

The western and northern area includes waters draining into **Lake Superior** west of **Sault Ste Marie** to **Nipigon Bay, Nipigon River** (where the world record brook trout 14½lbs was caught, in 1916), **Lake Nipigon Forest Reserve**, the Lakehead District and the **Lake St Joseph** and the Albany wilderness. The numerous tributary waters of the **Albany River** offer some of the finest trout fishing to be found in Ontario.

In southern **Ontario**, west of the eastern area, the brook trout waters include the **Muskoka lakes**, the **Haliburton** and **Hastings** highlands and the **Magnetawan** area. Farther south and west, trout inhabit some streams tributary to **Lakes Huron, Erie, Ontario** and **Georgian Bay**. Lying between the eastern and western areas of northern Ontario there are numerous brook trout waters, among which are the **Sudbury, Manitoulin, Sault, Michipicoten, Mississauga, Gogama, Chapleau, Missinabi-White River-Franz, Elsas, Oba, Hornepayne, Hearst, Kapuskasing, Nakina** and **Albany** River areas.

The range of bass fishing, small-mouth and large-mouth, in Ontario extends from the **Ottawa** and **St Lawrence** rivers and Lake Ontario and Lake Erie to Temagami and the north channel of Georgian Bay. Included in this range are the following areas: **Long Point Bay** (Lake Erie), **Rideau lakes, Haliburton Lake District, Kawartha lakes, Muskoka lakes, Lake Nipissing**, the **French** and **Pickerel rivers**, and the Georgian Bay District areas. In the north-west section of Ontario bass are found in **Quetico Provincial Park**.

The muskellunge range in Ontario includes the Ottawa and St Lawrence rivers, Lake Erie, Lake St Clair and Georgian Bay, Kawartha Lake, Lake Nipissing, French and Pickerel rivers and tributary waters. The best fishing is in the mouth of the **Moon River** and the **Lake of the Woods** district in the north-western section of the province, an extensive area some 150m wide east to west, and 160m from the international boundary north. This district has hundreds of lakes, and large muskies are taken here every year. Lake trout, lake whitefish, yellow pickerel (walleye) and Gt Northern pike are fairly plentiful throughout the province. Rainbow and brown trout (neither is native to the province) have been stocked in limited areas. Rainbow trout fishing is booming in southern Georgian Bay, especially in the **Owen Sound-Collingwood** area. The rainbow fishing peaks in the spring and in the fall. In recent years rainbow trout fishing has also become popular in Lake Ontario in the **Port Hope** area.

Splake, a cross between lake trout and brook trout (speckled trout), have been introduced into some waters for a number of years now and are doing quite well. There exists now some good splake fishing at **Owen Sound, Parry Sound** and at **Providence Bay** on **Manitoulin Island**. Fishing for Pacific salmon, introduced into the Great Lakes, has escalated, especially in Lake Ontario where anglers flock to the **Port Credit-Niagara** area each year in late summer and early fall to catch large coho and chinook salmon. In the North Channel of Lake Huron and in Lake Superior pink salmon attract many anglers in early fall.

There are more than 500 fish and game associations in the province, many of which are federated with the **Ontario Federation of Anglers and Hunters (Rick Morgan, Executive**

Vice President, Box 2800, Peterborough, Ontario, K9J 8L5).

Apply to the **Natural Resources Information Centre, Room M1-73, Macdonald Block, 900 Bay Street, Toronto, Ontario M7A 2C1, Canada**, tel: 416 314 2000, fax: 416 314 1593, for Non-residents Fishing Licences and the Sport Fishing Regulations booklet published by the Ministry of Natural Resources.

PRINCE EDWARD ISLAND. This island, which lies in the Gulf of St Lawrence off the north coast of **Nova Scotia**, has an enviable reputation for its speckled trout fishing. The streams and rivers are spring fed, and the whole province may be considered a natural hatchery for trout and salmon. The salmon fishing, however, is not first class, and the best runs, with the exception of early runs on the **Morell** and **Trout Rivers**, do not begin until towards the end of the season. Both non-migratory and migratory trout are to be caught. Fishing for rainbow trout can be had in **Glenfinnan**, and **O'Keefe's Lakes**. Noted trout streams are the **West, Morell, Trout** and **Dunk** rivers, and large freshwater dams also afford good sport. Many estuaries contain white perch, and a few are home of the striped bass. During late summer and autumn, mackerel and smelt fishing is popular. There are bag limits of 10 trout per day, not more than 5 being rainbow, and one grilse per day, 7 per season. Salmon greater than 63 cm or less than 30 cm must be returned alive and unharmed. Trout and salmon season is from 15 April to 15 Sept, except Morell River, open June 1. Season is extended to Oct 31 on certain stretches of Rivers Morell, Midgell, Naufrage, Valleyfield, West, Dunk. Trout, Mill. Rainbow trout season on Glenfinnan and O'Keefe's lakes, April 15 to November 15. Non-residents trout day licences cost $6.51 + GST, Atlantic salmon licence $9.35 + GST, obtainable from sports outfitters or from Department of Fisheries and Environment.

Further information may be obtained from the **Prince Edward Island Visitor Services Division, PO Box 940, Charlottetown, PE1, C1A 7M5** and **Dept of Fisheries and Environment, Fish and Wildlife Division, PO Box 2000, Charlottetown, PE1, C1A 7N8**, tel: 368 4683.

QUÉBEC. Stretching over a vast expanse of territory, Québec boasts more than one million rivers and lakes. These waters teeming with fish offer the possibility of catching various species, including Northern pike, walleye, brook trout, Arctic char, landlocked salmon, lake trout, Atlantic salmon and bass. However, to fish in parks, wildlife reserves and ZECs (controlled zones), certain specific conditions apply over and above the general rules. In most parks and wildlife reserves, a reservation is required, and, just as for the ZECs, a right of access is emitted. Private firms offer outfitting services in Québec, including accommodation. Some hold exclusive fishing rights in specific areas. In Northern Québec, a right of access must be obtained from the Native authorities in question (Cree, Inuit, Naskapi) in order to fish in certain waters. On land under Inuit jurisdiction, fishermen must be accompanied by an Inuit guide. Any non-residents wishing to fish north of the 52nd parallel must use the services of an outfitter. Licence fees vary tremendously, depending on where and what is being fished for.

The Ministère de l'Environnement et de la Faune determines the rules governing recreational fishing. This information has been published in the brochures *Sportfishing in Québec, Main Regulations* and *Sportfishing for Salmon, Main Regulations*. For information on fishing in parks and wildlife reserves, users may consult the brochures *Activities and Services* and *Fishing by the Day*. These free brochures are obtainable from the **Ministère de l'Environnement et de la Faune, 150, boulevard René-Lévesque Est, Québec (Québec) G1R4Y1**. Tel: 1-800-561-1616. Télécopieur: 418-528-0834.

SASKATCHEWAN. Pike, perch and walleye are found throughout the province and represent the largest portion of the sport catch. Lake trout and arctic grayling are plentiful in the northern areas. Rainbow, brook, brown and lake trout are stocked in streams and lakes throughout the province. Current licence fee for those over 16 is $30.

For further information (including details of limits, accommodations, outfitters, and guides), write to **Tourism Saskatchewan, 500-1900 Albert Street, Regina, Saskatchewan S4P 4L9**, tel: 1 306 787 2300, fax: 1 306 787 5744; or visit at http://www.sasktourism.com.

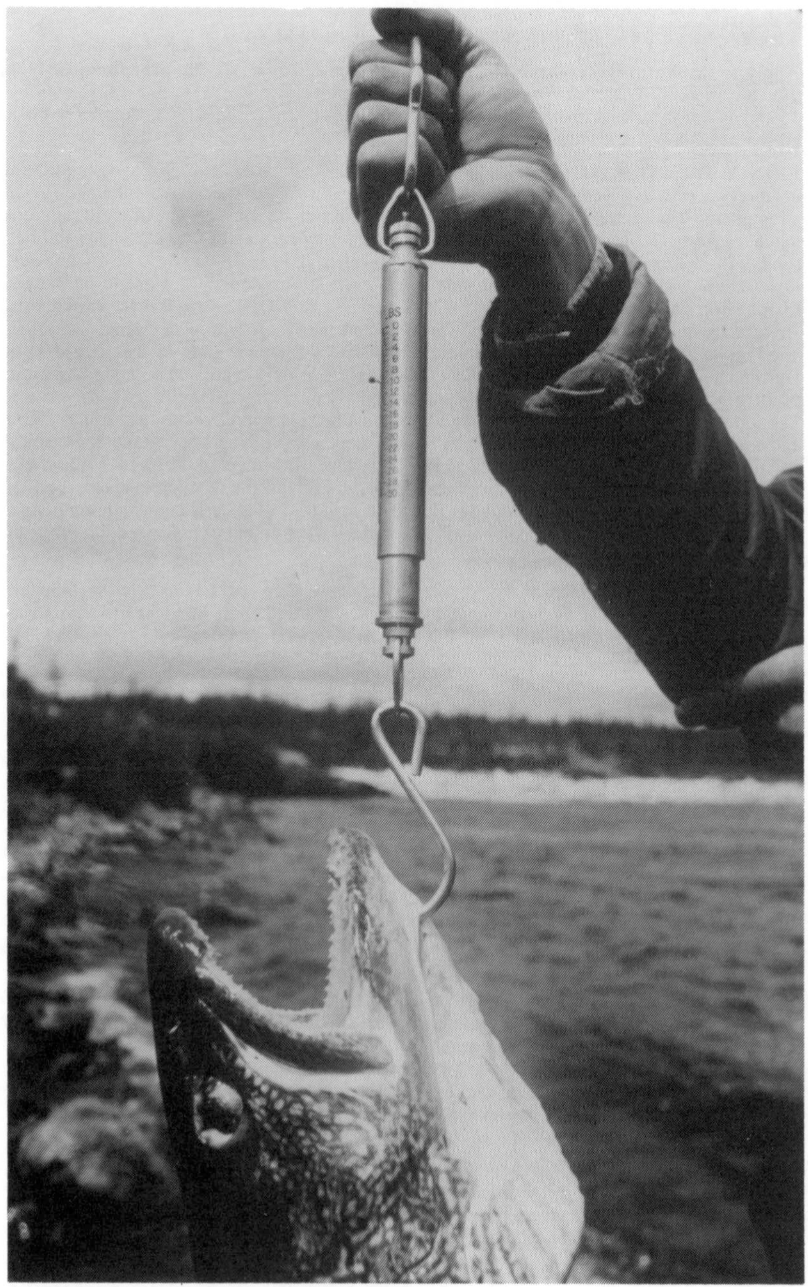

A Quebec lake trout that reached double figures before meeting an honourable and pain-free death. Respect for the quarry is at the heart of angling.

THE UNITED STATES OF AMERICA

The United States of America covers an enormous area of land and water space, offering everything between the near-Arctic conditions met in winter near the 49th parallel and the semi-tropical climate of Florida, Louisiana and Arizona, providing almost every conceivable environmental opportunity for freshwater or saltwater fish-species to exploit to their full advantage. This creates a great swathe of corresponding angling opportunities on such a scale that holidays spent fishing and camping in the backwoods have long been a commonplace of the American way of life as holidays on the coast - and, more recently, on the shores of the Mediterranean - have been of the British.

Such a demand compels a supply: and there is nowhere in the world where so sophisticated a blend of modern comfort and primitive atmosphere can be found at the waterside, made, as it were, to measure. And signs reading 'Keep out: fishing private' are not readily to be found in America. Apart from small lakes on private land immediately adjacent to private homes, the water and its inhabitants are the property of the community, managed expertly for the good of all by the community's public agencies. Fishing may not literally be 'free', but it is open to all with a few dollars to invest in recreation. The US population is four times Britain's; but the space open for it is ten times greater.

Because of the way in which, traditionally, exchange-rates and living costs have related, the USA has never in the past figured as a place where the adventurous British angler was likely to take a fishing holiday. All that, though, has now changed and it makes just as much sense, financially and otherwise, for an Englishman to holiday in **Tennessee**, fishing for large-mouth bass, or in **Minnesota** in search of *Esox masquinongy,* as for a Texan to come to Scotland to catch a Spey salmon. Going out from the **Florida Keys** in pursuit of marlin, sailfish or tarpon has for many years been a branch of the sport attracting a trickle of wealthy Britishers, but fishing American fresh waters has been a practice confined to angling writers and such, out to broaden their professional education.

Since it is the state geographically nearest to Britain, let us begin our review of the northern tier of states and their fishing with **Maine**, whose beaches offer the classical opportunity to contact the greatest of all saltwater sporting fish to be angled feasibly from the shore anywhere, the striped bass. Though scarcer now than in years gone by, unfortunately, there are still fine specimens to be taken by the persistent specialist surf-caster. Offshore, there are cod and pollack, the bluefin tuna, some of these registering on the beam-scale weights of more than 500lb.

Inland, there is a multitude of wilderness lakes and streams offering sport with smallmouth bass, brown and rainbow trout and the unique native of Eastern North America, the brook trout, actually a fine handsome member of the char family. Atlantic salmon which ran Maine's rivers by the ten thousand a hundred years ago suffered near-extermination, but are now being nursed back by conservation technology.

Moving west to the **Great Lakes,** thoughts turn back to another char, the 'lake trout', a fish which grows to great size in deep and cold water throughout this latitude and in Canada. One fishes for them in hopes of a 40-pounder. An attempt to pass over without comment the damage done to some waters, the Great Lakes included, by the consequences of unthinking industrialisation would be dishonest, but remedy is now the order of the day. None has been more spectacular in its success than the stocking of **Lake Michigan** with coho salmon from the Pacific shore. Here, a new and tremendously exciting sport-fishery has been created, as it were, out of nothing, based on a food-supply left uncropped by lake trout no longer present in sufficient numbers to preserve a natural balance. Most see that as a net gain. The coho gives better sport than the 'Mackinaw', as it is sometimes named farther north.

On to a state where water-area challenges land-space: **Minnesota**, as the North American Indian dialect-name implies, and the cream of the fishing for great northern pike (our pike), walleyes (resembling our zander) and the greatest lantern-jaw of them all, *Esox masquinongy,* the muskellunge or 'muskie'. While these predators are distributed throughout the region, Minnesota is the heartland. Muskies there may grow to 80lb weight and leap like trout when hooked.

Grace Oglesby fishing off Cape Hatteras, N Carolina, USA. *Photo: Arthur Oglesby*

Arthur Oglesby and 35lb. blackfin tuna, out from Corpus Christi, Texas, USA.

Passing through a varied landscape, some of it watered by trout streams, we arrive eventually among the foothills of the **Rockies**, where the brilliantly-coloured dolly varden and cut-throat trout (the former another char, to be pedantic) and representatives of the five sub-species of the so-called 'golden' trout join the ranks awaiting the angler's thinning, not to mention the sea-going rainbow trout, the steelhead. It was in the Rocky Mountain watershed that the rainbow, sedentary and sea-going, was first encountered and employed to provide the bloodstock for the eventual artificial populating of the entire temperate world with this enormously successful species.

Over the mountains: the ocean: and the feeding grounds of the Pacific salmon, five species, of which two, the king or 'Tyee' and the coho, are of sporting significance.

Going back East and starting again farther south, we traverse a band of warmer states, less favourable to the cold-water salmonids, but affording an ideal environment for pickerel (another pike-species) and for the small-mouth and large-mouth bass, the fish on which the romance of North American angling is largely founded. These big athletic cousins of the European perch (called there, incidentally, the 'yellow perch') hit surface flies and lures with astonishing ferocity, fight like tigers when hooked and lie habitually in the shade and cover of the water-plant zone where only the most expert of tackle-handlers can present the offering and cope with the ensuing seizure without disaster. As the cooler uplands are again reached, the typical population of the upland waters is met again, and the pattern replicates.

Repeat the journey starting in **Georgia**, and one covers territory with a yet warmer climate, swamplands, and then an area of low rainfall. Traditionally, what fishing there was did not enjoy sporting prestige. The image was one of a poor coloured man employing crude tackle to harvest cheap protein; a typical quarry, the Mississippi catfish. One is south of that section of the lowland region where water temperature falls low enough to permit salmonids to spawn successfully in natural waters.

But the water-demand for growing population growing also in affluence has necessitated the construction of chains of dams in the drier states; vast new sheets of deep water offering environments novel in their setting, with a variety of temperature regimes encouraging the successful introduction of some of the great sporting species found naturally to the north and west. Even **Arizona** - the 'dry county' itself - now provides fine fishing for sport, and offers it in hot sunshine, a combination of pleasures not frequently encountered by the proverbially frozen-fingered angler acquiring lumbago from his water-logged nether end.

It would not do to dismiss the terrific sport potential to be enjoyed generally in the U.S.A. without some mention of the fantastic angling offered in its largest state, **Alaska**. Known affectionately by Alaskans as the last frontier, it is comparatively untamed, but if you seek the five species of Pacific salmon, wild rainbow trout and Arctic grayling, it offers sport beyond your wildest dreams.

Providing you can gain access by boat or floatplane, and following payment of approx £25 in licence dues, all the fishing in Alaska is free. Most visiting anglers settle for residence in one of the many lodges which cater for those who do not wish to suffer any hardships when divorced from civilisation. Most of the best and more productive lodges are in the Bristol Bay area. This is easily accessible by hour-long scheduled flights from Anchorage to the little town of King Salmon. There, you are within short flying times by bush or floatplane to many of the best lodges.

Some lodges offer daily fly-outs to choice fishing venues, but this adds considerably to the expense and there are many advantages in seeking a lodge which offers fishing on the river at which it is sited, and where jet boats take you to good fishing within a matter of a half-hour boat ride. One lodge popular with British visitors (they even fly the Union Jack) is **Katmai Lodge** on Levelock Native land on the Alagnak river. This is but a mere 15 minute flight by twin-engined Otter from King Salmon to the lodge's own airstrip. Early July offers prime time for the king (chinook), sockeye and chum salmon. The pink salmon or "humpie" runs in late July (and only every other year), while the coho or silver salmon run in early August.

King salmon are not always easy to get on fly tackle, but those caught on baits may run to 60lb and more. Sockeye salmon may be taken on a single-handed fly rod but require a different technique to that used for Atlantic salmon here in Britain. The chum and coho have similar taking habits to Atlantic salmon, but it always pays to take great heed of your guide before assuming that you know it all.

Several sporting agencies in Britain have Alaskan fishing on offer, but if you wish to be accompanied by one of our well-known British salmon anglers, with long Alaskan experience, try contacting **Arthur Oglesby, 9 Oatlands Drive, Harrogate, North Yorkshire HG2 8JT**. Tel/Fax 01423 883565.

We have discussed none but the prime sporting species. They, however, are not the last word. US waters are inhabited also by others; carp, blue-gill sunfish, crappies and what-have-you, fish present in higher population densities and easier to catch, fish whose presence has traditionally ensured that the less expert members of the specialist angler's family on holiday may take their share of the pleasures and the triumphs. The travel business had now started international operations in this field and British anglers can expect a rapid growth in attractive opportunities.

MEXICO

Freshwater fishing: river trout fishing has been spoilt by local netting, but during the past few years black-bass fishing has become popular in Mexico, with exaggerated claims of 100 to 200 bass per day. For information about **Vicente Guerrero Dam**, near Ciudad Victoria, (fishing license 10 dollars per week), write to Sunbelt Hunting and Travel Inc., Box 3009, Brownsville, Texas 78520. For **Diaz Ordaz Dam**, contact Roberto Balderrama, Santa Anita Hotel, Los Mochis, Sinaloa. 8lb bass are common here, and at the San Lorenzo Dam, near Xicotencatl. Sea fishing: there are over 850 species to be caught, and in the Los Cabos region alone over 40,000 marlin and sailfish are hooked each year. Popular centres are Acapulco, Puerto Vallarta, Manzanillo, Mazatlán, Guaymas, Loreto, La Paz, Cancun, Cozumel, Tampico, Veracruz, Cabo San Lucas and San Jose del Cabo, with good facilities. Good charter boats are on hire, with expert crews. Amongst coastal species are pargo, yellowtail, rock bass, grouper, barracuda, totoava, snook, giant sea bass. Pelagic species include blue and striped marlin, yellowfin tuna, black marlin, bonito, sailfish, swordfish and mackerel. These are usually found a good distance from the shore. For more information contact Mexican

Fishing Federation, Londres 250, Mexico D.F. Bonefishing is a sport practised by U.S. anglers in Quintana Roo, near Cancun. Write to **Turismo Boca Paila S.A. de C.V., Apartado Postal 59, Cozumel, Quintana Roo, Mexico 77600**, tel: 00 52 987 211 76, fax: 00 52 987 20053.

The **Mexican Ministry of Tourism** has an office at **60/61 Trafalgar Square, London WC2N 5DS** (tel: 0171-734 1058, fax: 0171 930 9202) from which more detailed information can be obtained.

THE CARIBBEAN

Forty years ago, so little was the Caribbean exploited by the indigenous peoples dwelling on its islands and about its shores that the United Nations Food & Agriculture Organisation gave a priority to the encouragement of commercial fishing there. What little fish was eaten in Central America had come traditionally in the form of salted fillets imported from countries - Norway and North America particularly - which had well-established cold water fisheries for cod in the prolific waters of the North Atlantic and the Arctic.

Various geophysical features were thought at that time to inhibit the Caribbean from ever becoming a region rich in exploitable fish populations. That, in one sense, may have been correct, but there are more ways than one of exploiting a resource, a fact already known by that time to charter-boat proprietors operating out of Florida resorts to crop the wonderful harvest of American anglers in search of sport more dramatic than the salmon or the muskellunge could offer in freshwater.

Thus the possibilities of the **Gulf of Mexico** and the seas around the **Bahamas** became known - marlin, swordfish, sawfish, sailfish, barracuda, tarpon and tuna the quarry, individual fish which took angling statistics from measurement by the pound to measurement by the hundredweight. The same geophysical conditions which had led to doubts as to the possibility of upgrading national catches of readily marketable fish for human consumption in the region had concentrated the big predators at water-depths where they could be found and profitably angled for.

During these forty years, facilities for Big Game fishing as it soon became known, spread progressively throughout the area and one may now fish for these splendid creatures from bases in **Mexico**, **Honduras**, **Nicaragua**, **Costa Rica**, **Panama**, **Colombia**, **Venezuela** (which was the first country in the region seriously to exploit its fish stocks in the traditional fashion) and the oceanic islands all the way south to **Trinidad**.

Originally, the big fish were angled for with a trolled dead bait and tackle powerful enough to master a bolting horse. Nowadays they are sought for with the fly rod, too, reflecting the fact that official records are maintained not only for maximum species weights, globally speaking, but for tackle categories, too, expressed in terms of line-strength - i.e. IGFA rules.

Astonishingly, billfish - to use the up-to-date term for swordfish and sailfish species grouped together - five feet in length have been brought to the glove in ten minutes from hooking with a conventional fly rod and single-action fly reel.

Tourist offices in London maintained by Mexico and Islands in the West Indies give details on hotels, facilities for boat charter, (with professional help integral to the hire-package) and of what restrictions apply to limits, seasons, and species of fish and other marine quarry which are excluded locally from the angler's activities. These restrictions are not onerous.

ANTIGUA and BARBUDA

Antigua and **Barbuda** have developed their big game fishing. Marlin, sailfish, tuna, wahoo, snapper, grouper, angel, trigger, margate, amber jack, black jack, and barracuda are all present around the islands, according to the conformation of the sea-bed. There are many reefs and coral formations. Lobster fishing is particularly good around the wrecks off Barbuda, which number more than 50. Anglers should note that use of dynamite is strictly forbidden. Boats operate out of Marora Bay and from Catamaran Hotel, Falmouth, tel: 31036.

For further information contact the **Antigua and Barbuda Tourist Office, Antigua House, 15 Thayer Street, London W1M 5LD** (tel: 0171-486 7073/5).

THE BAHAMAS

The Bahamas comprise twelve major groups of islands spaced over 1,000 square miles or more of ocean. **Bimini** is probably the best known of the fishing centres and it was here that the largest Bahamian marlin recorded by an angler - a fish weighing more than 1,000 lbs - was brought into harbour.

Other notable islands are **San Salvador**, marlin, yellowfin, fine reef and flats fishing; **Exuma**, good bonefishing, reef fishing, and light tackle opportunities; **Long Island**, deep sea, bonefishing and reef fishing; **Cat Island**, for marlin and tuna; **Andros**, world class bonefishing, trophy sized bottom species, marlin and tuna; **Nassau**, bluewater fishing, for marlin and tuna, wahoo, kingfish, sailfish; **The Abacos**, deep and shallow water fishing, with a good variety, main attractions being yellowfin tuna, marlin, good flats and reef fishing; **Grand Bahama**, also good flats and reef fishing; **Chub Cay**, white marlin, dolphin and other species; and **Eleuthera**, with blackfin tuna, blue marlin, good bonefish flats and reef fishing, as well as big game. Seasons for best fishing:, bonefish Mar-Apr; snapper, spring summer, barracuda, Jun-Aug; blue marlin, May-Jun; white marlin, Mar-Jun; sailfish, Apr; broadbill and swordfish, Jun peak time; Allison tuna, Mar-May, blackfin, Jun; bluefin, May. Tournaments are held frequently throughout the islands, hotels catering specially for anglers abound, and there are many fishing lodges. Charter rates vary with duration of fishing trips and species sought.

One can buy four day's fishing for bonefish for $688, including three nights luxury accommodation, bait, packed lunches and a professional guide, or pay $200-$600 a day for the fishing alone. Contact **The Bahamas Tourist Office, 3 The Billings, Walnut Tree Close, Guildford, Surrey, GU1 4UL**, tel: 01483 448900, for more information.

BERMUDA

Licences are not required: charter boats in deep water produce catches of wahoo, greater

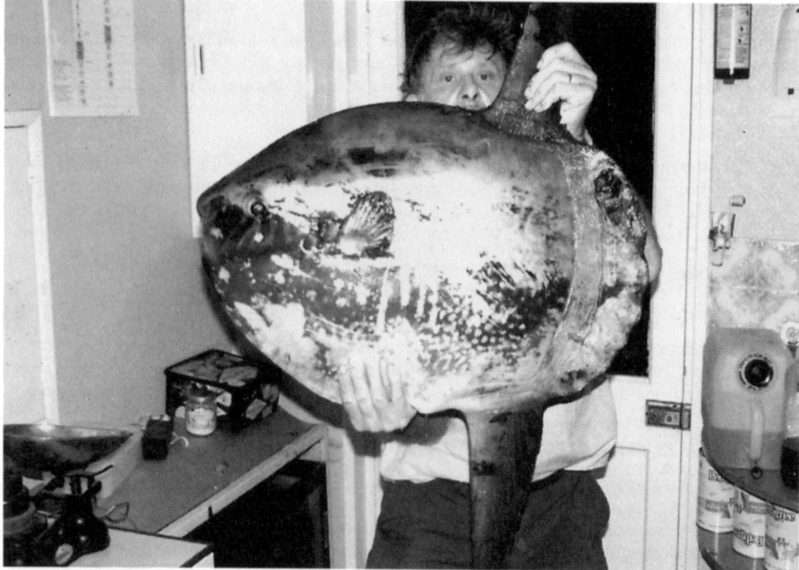

Sunfish weighing more than 3,000 lbs. and measureing 13 ft. in length (approx. 4 metres) have been recorded in the Caribbean. The specimen in the photograph, caught off Europe (a most unusual capture in that region) weighed 44 lbs. (approx. 23.25 Kg.).

amberjack, almaco jack, dolphin fish, grey and yellowtail snapper, great barracuda, rainbow runner, yellowfish, Atlantic blue and white marlin, little tunny, blackfin, yellowfin and skipjack tuna. Reefs produce greater amberjack, almaco jack, great barracuda, little tunny, Bermuda chub, grey and yellowtail snapper, and assorted bottom fish. Shore fishing from beaches, docks piers is fee, and may produce bonefish, palometa, grey snapper, great barracuda. Nineteen charter boats operate the year round, the majority independently, supply and demand peaking from May to November. Information given by the **Bermuda Tourist Office at 1 Battersea Church Road, London SW11 3LY** (tel: 0171-734 8813). **Bermuda Sport Fishing Association, Creek View House, 8 Tulo Lane, Pembroke HM O2**, tel: 295 2370, fax: 292 5535 (10 boats); **Charter Fishing Boat Association, PO Box SB 145, Sandys SB BX** ; and **St. George's Game Fishing and Cruising Association, PO Box GE 107, St. George's GE BX**, tel: 809 297 8093, (representing 7 boats). Hotel facilities are excellent. **The Bermuda Game Fishing association, PO Box HM 1306, Hamilton HM FX, Bermuda**, holds annual competitions.

LESSER ANTILLES

South of Puerto Rico is the chain of small islands known as the **Lesser Antilles** - the **Leeward** and **Windward** groups.

TRINIDAD AND TOBAGO

Finally, **Trinidad & Tobago**, the large islands which lie just off the coast of Venezuela and terminate the chain. Their waters, too, are abundantly supplied with billfish species, tuna, tarpon, barracuda and many other species of interest to the angler, if offering rather less dramatic sport than the 'stars' on the angler's stage. The tourist office, **8A Hammersmith Broadway, London, W6 7AL** (tel 0181-741 4466) supplies names and addresses of charter-boat operators in both islands.

SOUTH AMERICA

BRAZIL. This is a vast country in the same league as China, Canada, Australia and the United States of America. With the world's biggest river draining it, it lacks neither water nor fish.

Anglers from the USA have already explored its possibilities with exciting results, but little of the country has yet been opened to international angling and it is in the southern half of the sub-continent that the sport has been energetically developed.

ARGENTINA. Here, although the South Atlantic is probably now the world's most productive fishing zone, the emphasis in terms of sport shifts back to freshwater fishing. Salmonids were introduced from the northern hemisphere many years ago - land-locked salmon *(Salmo salar sebago)* the brown trout (in both its sedentary and migratory forms) and the brook trout *(Salvelinus fortinalis)*. The home of these species is in the Andean lake district. Specimen brook trout up to 10lbs, have been caught; in the case of the other species named, specimens topping 30lbs.

In the river-catchments of the lower-lying regions of the country, especially those of the **Parana** and **Plata**, there are two fine native species of fish, the dorado *(Salminus maxillosus)* and the perch *(Percicathys trucha)* which are rated as highly or higher than salmonids. The perch grows to weights approaching 20lbs, while the dorado reaches a weight of 50lbs.

In the same habitats are found other species which grow to be enormous - the mangururu (200lbs) the surubi (120lbs) and others which do not reach such spectacular weights but still offer splendid sport.

Spinning from a boat piloted by a guide is the usual method of fishing for dorado, but they will also take a fly (not exactly a blue winged olive!) and in an Argentinean torrent quite a challenge to the fly rod, also the fish it naturally feeds on, offered as either a live or a dead bait. This splendid sporting fish is found throughout the catchments of the rivers Plata and Parana. Centres specially recommended for the quality of the fishing guides, boats and accommodation are **Paso de la Patria** (Corrientes), **Isla del Carrito** (Chaco) and **Posadas** (Misiones).

The best fishing is in the summer - August to March. Annual competitions are held early in the season. Five vast National Parks offer the best of the fishing for salmonids, all of them on the west side of the country, in the uplands bordering Chile.

In **Patagonia**, the lakes and rivers in the mountainous region of **Cholila** contain abundant stocks of trout, usually fished with wet and dry fly, or Devon minnow. Average sizes are large: brook trout to 10lb, rainbow from 3-6lb with specimen fish running to 20lb, brown trout 3-8lb, with record from this area, 32lb. Other fishable species are landlocked salmon, perca, and Patagonian pejerrey. The principal lakes are **Lago Cholila**, the biggest in Cholila (15 km long), with beautiful surroundings. The water is very cold due to glacier melt; access via Estancia Lago Cholila; **Lago Lezama**, the highest and warmest in the area, deep, with permanent undercurrents of warm streams; **Lago Mosquito**, the smallest (8 km long, close to village, with small hostel alongside the lake. Largest rivers are **Rio Carrelefu**, **Rio Tigre**, **Rio Pedregoso**, and **Rio Blanco**. All these waters are excellent for fishing, and only a handful of anglers can be found in any one season for the place is virtually unknown internationally. Fishing holidays in this region are organised by **Arco Isis Tours** (*see below*).

From **Punta Piedras** in the north to **Tierra del Fuego** in the extreme south, Argentina has more than 2,200 miles of Atlantic coastline. The water so far south is too cold for tuna, billfish and tarpon, but their place is taken for the big game angler by all the Atlantic species of shark.

For the Argentineans themselves, though, the peak of the sea angling year is when the warm current from Brazil brings down the black corvina, whose shoals provide many specimens of 40lbs, and better. **San Clemente de Tuyu** is the most famous centre for fishing the corvina, where the fish arrive in December. They then work their way down the coast, arriving in **Bahia Blanca** in February. There is plenty of shore fishing, but boats are to be had, though not on quite the sophisticated scale to be met with in the Gulf of Mexico and the Caribbean.

Tourist information may had from the **Consulado General de la República Argentina, 27 Three Kings Yard, London W1Y 1FL**, tel: 0171 318 1340 (1349 fax); or the **Oficina Central de Información Turística, Av. Santa Fe 883, 1059 Buenos Aires,** tel: 312 2232/5550. For Cholila fishing, contact **Arco Isis Tours, 22 Palace Avenue, Llandaff, Cardiff CF5 2DW**, tel: 01222 554330.

CHILE. Chile's coastline matches that of the neighbouring Argentine, but the fishing promoted is that for introduced salmonids, especially in Chilean Patagonia. The trout run extremely large; the country in that region is thinly populated and attractively wild, the climate mild. The cities recommended as start-points for the angler are **Temuco, Puerto Montt** and **Coihaque**. All are accessible by air or rail from **Santiago**.

THE FALKLAND ISLANDS. One of the least known tourist attractions in the South Atlantic, but for the angler the best researched and the most promising. How else? - with its history of British colonisation, recently underlined by a military presence and a notable victory. From nowhere else south of the equator has *Where to Fish* received such comprehensive information. The whole development of sea trout fishing in the Falklands has taken place in less than a lifetime. Nature left the Islands with only the Falkland trout - *(aplochiton zebra)* which is not a trout or even a char, and a few minor species in its rivers. The first real trout *(Salmo trutta)* were introduced less than forty years ago, but a fast growing migratory strain quickly became established and spread around the islands, giving us today some of the finest sea trout fishing in the world.

Sea trout of five to ten pounds are common, and many fish in excess of ten pounds are taken every season. The best recorded sea trout taken on a fly to date was 22lb 12.5oz, caught on the San Carlos River by Alison Faulkner.

The main sea trout rivers - the **Warrah** and **Chartres** on West Falkland and the **San Carlos** on East Falkland - are ideal for fly fishing, with treeless banks being free of casting obstructions. However a strong wind often blows, so this is no place for a poor caster with mediocre tackle.

Most rivers have fair numbers of resident brown trout, but most are small, dark fish, typical of acid rivers.

Major sea trout rivers with visitor accommodation and guides.

West Falkland

Warrah River: Can be fished from **Port Howard Settlement**, where there is accommodation. The Warrah River is about 12 miles from the settlement, and the Chartres River about an hour drive. The main tributary, the **Green Hills Stream**, which is crossed on the way to the Warrah, is well worth fishing.

East Falkland

San Carlos River: Controlled by local farmers, the river is accessed from the Stanley Port - San Carlos track. Blue Beach Lodge offers comfortable accommodation.

Mullet fishing: as a bonus, you will probably come into contact with the Falkland mullet *(Eleginus falklandicus)* if fishing in tidal water. Like the British mullet, the Falkland species follows the tide right into shallow water, where it can be seen swimming just below the surface with a very obvious wake, but there the similarity ends. It is not even related to our mullet and is much larger, with fish recorded up to 20 pounds and mullet of 8 pounds are quite common. The dorsal fin runs virtually from head to tail along a tapering body, and the pectoral fins are huge in relation to the size of the fish.

The Falkland mullet is a powerful fish which makes long runs and would be much valued as a game fish if it existed in Britain. It often takes the sea-trout angler's fly or spinner, but the local method normally used is to suspend a piece of mutton (fresh sheep meat) on a size 4 or 2 hook a couple of feet below a small pike bung. This tackle is cast out wherever there are signs of mullet activity, and the response is rarely long delayed.

Small to medium mullet can be caught virtually on your doorstep at places like **Port Howard**.

The really large fish are often found in specific locations, at some distance from the settlements. It is worth considering setting aside a little time for a trip specifically for big mullet.

Flights leave Brize Norton on Mondays and Thursdays. Return flights leave Mount Pleasant in the Falklands on Wednesdays and Saturdays. The other routes of access are via South America.

There is Accommodation for fishermen at Stanley, Blue Beach, and Port Howard. There are also lodges in wildlife centres (fishermen may like to take some time off to see the large colonies of penguins, seals and other wildlife).

The **Falkland Islands Tourist Board** office is at **Falkland House, 14 Broadway, Westminster, London, SW1H 0BH**. (Tel 0171-222 2542).

NOTE. The tourist board strongly recommends that visitors travel with a recognised tour operator.

FISHING IN EUROPE

AUSTRIA

Austria is understandably popular with anglers from all over the world, with its abundance of streams and lakes, providing first-class sport with brown and rainbow trout, grayling, char, and coarse fish such as pike and pike-perch, huck, sheat-fish and carp. Some of the main centres tend to be overfished, so a car is immensely valuable; many mountain streams of indescribable beauty are easily reached by road. Much of the sport is on the lower reaches of these mountain rivers, but the more venturesome can often find better fishing on the high alpine streams and lakes. Grayling are highly regarded, often more so than trout, the **Traun** and the **Lammer** being two of the best grayling rivers in Europe. **Salza, Traisen, Erlauf, Steyt** and **Ybbs** are other recommended rivers.

To keep the sport at a high level, the authorities maintain strict conservation measures and a specially close watch is kept on pollution and abstraction. Generally speaking the rule is fly only for trout, grayling and char. Spinning is usually only permitted for larger fish such as lake trout, pike, huck, pike-perch (depending on the local authority) and so on, and natural bait and sheatfish only for coarse fisheries. Many waters are controlled by the two principal fishing associations, the Austrian Fishing Association (ÖFG) and the Association of Austrian Workers' Fishing Clubs (VÖAFV). The former issues temporary permits for several trout preserves as well as daily ones costing up to 600 Austrian schillings. Temporary permission and information can be obtained from the association's office. The same applies to the VÖAFV. There is a provincial fishing association in Upper Austria which issues licences *(see below for addresses)*.

Wherever he fishes, the visitor usually needs two permits, a general licence issued by the State and costing up to 350 Austrian schillings, according to the province - and a private permit from the local owner.

Accommodation is no problem, as many fine hotels offer anglers first class facilities on the more important lakes and rivers. More information and angling booklets can be obtained from the **Austrian National Tourist Office, PO Box 2363, London W1A 2QB**, tel: 0171-629 0461, fax: 0171 499 6038. Addresses of the main angling association are **Österreichische Fischereigesellschaft, 1010 Wien 1, Elisabethstrasse 22; Verband der Österreichischen Arbeiter-Fischerei-Vereine, A-1080, Wien, Lenaugasse, 14**; tel: 01 403 2176, telefax: 403 21 76/20; **Fischereiverband Oberosterreich Kärntnerstrasse 12, 4020, Linz**, telefax: 43(0) 732 603388; **Oo Fischerbund, Ziegeleistrasse 78, 4021 Linz**. For fishing in Upper Austria, contact **OÖ, Landesfischereiverband, A-4020 Linz, Karntnerstrasse 12**, tel: 07322/584-0.

BELGIUM

Although Belgium has never made a name for itself as a visiting fisherman's country, it has, in fact, in its many canals and rivers, most of the fish which British fishermen know, with sea fishing along its 40 miles of coast.

In general terms the freshwater fishing water can be divided thus: The **Scheldt** basin, with the rivers **Scheldt, Lys, Rupel, Dyle, Demer, Dendre** and **Nèthe** holding bream, roach, perch, pike, burbot, smelt, shad and eels; the **Meuse** basin, with the rivers **Meuse, Semois, Lesse, Sambre, Ourthe, Amblève, Warche** and **Vesdre** holding trout, grayling, chub, barbel, perch, roach, bream, pike, carp, tench and eels; and the streams between the Sambre and the Meuse, holding trout, grayling, chub, perch, pike, roach, bream, carp, tench and eels. Many waters of the lowlands and near industrial centres suffer from pollution and overfishing.

All Belgian waters fall into one of three categories; closed water, not subject to fishing laws; public, or navigable water, belonging to the State; preserved, or non-navigable water belonging to the landowners. Waters in the last two groups are subject to the fishing laws, and anyone fishing in them must possess a current licence. There are three different licences in Belgium: 1) sold by the Flemish authority, for fishing in the northern part of the country; 2) sold by the Brussels region, for Brussels; 3) sold by the Waloon government for fishing in Wallonia. The cost varies from 500 francs to 1500 francs, according to the type of fishing. Trout fishermen should note, for example, that they will need a 1500-franc licence to enter the water, in addition to any other permit necessary. Licences may be obtained at post offices. The close seasons are: Coarse fish, from the third Saturday of March until the third Saturday of June, with certain exceptions; trout, October 1 to third Saturday of March. Fly fishing falls off sharply on the Ardennes streams after June.

For visiting trout fishers the greatest attraction probably lies in the streams of the **Ardennes**, where there is a good deal of association water. These are mostly mixed fisheries on the lines of the Hampshire Avon in England, with trout and grayling predominating in the upper reaches and being increasingly joined by coarse fish on moving downstream. The best fishing will usually be found in the least accessible places. Standard British fly patterns will take fish on the Ardennes streams but the local flies should be tried where possible.

Sea fishing along the sandy, shelving coast is largely for dabs and plaice (Oct-June), flounders (all year) and sole (May-Oct), with piers and breakwaters providing sport with conger (all year), cod (Sept-Mar), and whiting (Oct-Jan). Turbot are occasionally taken (May-Sept) and rays, shad and garfish are also caught (Sept-Oct), **Zeebrugge**, **Ostend**, **Nieuwpoort**, **Blankenbergh**, and **Knokke-Heist** are good centres.

Belgian fishing legislation is extremely complex and anglers are strongly advised to consult the local tourist centres. For example, **Namur** province publishes a special angling brochure in French. Further detailed information (in English) from the **Belgian Tourist Office, 29 Princes Street, London W1R 7RG,** tel: 0891 887799, fax: 0171 629 0454 and, in Belgium itself, from the secretary of the **Fédération Sportive des Pêcheurs Francophones de Belgique. N H Balzat, rue de Wynants 33, 1000 Brussels,** tel: 25 11 68 48; and from the secretary of the **Fédération de Pêche en Mer, Parc Leopold 14, 8410 Wenduine**, tel: 50 41 33 92.

DENMARK

Fishing in Denmark is plentiful, varied and easy to come by. A few of the rivers hold salmon, and many of them sea trout, brown trout and grayling, as well as coarse fish, which are found also in many lakes.

In many places visitors can fish by purchasing tickets from the local fishing association. The association tickets are invariably cheap and sold at local tourist offices.

The principal rivers are all in **Jutland**. They are **Skjern Aa, Store Aa, Varde Aa, Ribe Aa** and **Karup Aa**. All are game-fish waters, but of them the best salmon fishing is probably to be had on the Skjern and the best sea trout fishing on the Karup. The water is generally good for fly fishing, and the flies used are much the same as those used in this country. Spinning is much practised. Added variety is given by the sea trout fishing which can be had from the rocks and from boats off both the mainland and the various Baltic islands.

For the coarse fisherman, the **River Guden** holds prolific stocks of bream and roach, and hundreds of lakes contain large bream, tench and other species, and are hardly ever fished. The lakeland area of East Jutland, for instance, produces very heavy net weights. Notable centres are Viborg, Sileborg, Ry, Århus, Skanderborg (beside **Lake Skanderborg**, teeming with fish), and Horsens.

The **Funen Islands** between Jutland and Zealand have been in recent years systematically developed into an important centre for breeding and increasing sea trout, as a response to dwindling native populations. More than two million fish have been introduced, barriers in the Funen river system have been removed by establishing fish passages and runs, and now, there exist ten different fishing locations on the coast round about **Odense**. Fishing is permitted all the year round, best times are Jan-May, and Aug-mid Nov. Normal methods are fly, and spinning with spoon or lure. A brochure may be obtained from **Fyn Tour, PO Box 265, DK-5700 Svendborg**. Fax: 45 62 20 13 33.

Denmark has a coastline of 7,500 kilometres, much of it unfished but nearly all stretches are accessible, with good possibilities for cod, coalfish, flatfish, tope, mackerel, garfish, whiting, ling and pollack, and for turbot, brill, plaice, sole, dab and flounder. One should not fish within 50 metres of a private dwelling place without the owners permission. Anglers are warned about the danger of breakwater fishing from **Jutland** west coast in rough weather, and on North Sea coast, jetty fishing is prohibited in several places for security reasons. Fishing boats will take anglers out to sea for a reasonable charge, and may also be chartered at Copenhagen, Elsinore, Korsør and Frederikshavn.

Salmon and sea trout fishing in fresh water is best from Apr/May to July, and September (salmon), June to Sept, and Oct/Nov, smaller rivers (sea trout).

A fishing licence is obligatory, and costs Dkr 100. It is obtainable from post offices or tourist offices. A tourist licence may be obtained for one day, cost Dkr 25, or one week, Dkr 75. Those under 18 or over 67 are exempt. Fishing rights in natural lakes and streams are nearly always private, but often let to local angling societies, who issue day or week cards. These are priced between Dkr 20-40 per day, Dkr 75-100 per week and may be bought at tourist offices. There are close seasons and size limits on game fish and large variety of other freshwater and sea fish.

Further information about both fishing and accommodation can be had from the **Danish Tourist Board, 55 Sloane Street, London, SW1X 9SY** (0171-259 5959); and **Danmarks Sportsfiskerforbund, Worsåesgade 1, DK-7100 Vejle** (75 82 06 99. Fax: 75 82 02 09).

FINLAND

Finland can offer the angler no fewer than 187,888 lakes and rivers, and some 3,000 miles of sea-shore and archipelago. In the north and centre of the country he can catch very big fish on very big, remote waters; conditions which, in Europe at any rate, are becoming increasingly harder to find. The long days of midsummer give plenty of fishing time - the best sport in fact is often enjoyed in the brief twilight which elsewhere is called 'night'. In the South and in the archipelago area the best fishing periods are spring and autumn. Ice fishing for perch is popular in the winter months, and spear fishing with a lamp is practised during autumn, in dark, calm, or cloudy weather.

Salmon, sea trout, brown trout and brook trout all run well above the European average, and the size of grayling, too, is often remarkable; four-pounders are not rare. There are also arctic char *(Salvelinus alpinus)* which in the right conditions will take a fly.

The cream of the sport is to be found in **Lapland**, though there are individual waters farther south which can match them in quality. Some of the best game fishing in Europe is to be found in the region north of **Lake Inari**, and especially the rivers emptying into the lake. A very good possibility is the lake itself, holding taimen, very big grayling and brown trout to 20lb and more. Best fished for during their migratory runs up the tributaries in late summer.

Although hydro-electric schemes have ruined the salmon runs in many famous waterways, rivers are recovering and several of them can be offered for salmon and sea trout fishing - the **Kiiminki**; the **Simo**; the **Lesti**; the **Tornio** which Finland shares with Sweden yielded in 1996 an estimated 20,000 kilos, the quieter stretches of Lappea producing more than 600 salmon, and the **Kymi River** produced 3,000 kilos, with salmon fishing well organised all the year round. The **Kuusinkijoki** at Kuusamo has been the venue of the world fly fishing championships.

There are problems, too, for the fly fisherman. Many rivers are so wide, deep and fast flowing that comfortable fishing from the bank is out of the question; it is often impossible to reach the salmon and sea trout lies, in fact. Hence on great rivers like the **Teno** (claimed to be the best river in the world for Atlantic salmon), and **Näätämö** which flow along the frontier with Norway, the fishing is mainly from a boat with an outboard motor from which large flies are cast by short but stout rods over enormous pools and streams - a technique known as 'harling'. Reels carrying 250 yards of line of up to 1mm thick and over 40lb breaking strain are employed.

These rivers, incidentally, are subject to special rules, involving the purchase of a permit from both countries in those parts through which the common national frontier passes. They are heavily poached. The spring fishing is usually best.

Another problem is transport - many of the best waters are 'off the beaten track' and although there are excellent air services between the main centres, after that the angler is on his own and must be prepared for a good deal of foot-slogging and camping. A car, with a fibreglass boat strapped to the roof, is a valid alternative where the roads are not too bad.

The Finnish coast with its large archipelago, not to mention the 6,500 **Åland Islands**, offers very good prospects for trout, salmon and perch-fishers, and the pike fishing is outstandingly good. Even the immediate surroundings of big cities should not be ignored. As to the catch - the sea area is best.

The coarse fisherman will find first-class pike fishing in high summer, trolling a popular method on Finnish lakes, and large perch, which are very edible, may be caught during this season by worming. Some very good coarse fishing is to be found in the south, notably for pike and perch and pike-perch - not, as many believe, a hybrid, but a separate species. Opportunities for the fly fisherman in the south have been extended in recent years by the stocking of ponds with rainbow, brown and brook trout.

The National Board of Forestry administers 85 fisheries, which it manages mainly by restocking. Most of these are in eastern and northern Finland.

Fishing regulations are strict and strictly enforced - there are game wardens even in remote districts. A licence is required. They can be bought at post offices or branches of Postipankki (closed Sat and Sun). Costs are as follows. Government fishing management fee is FIM 80 per year or FIM 20 per seven days. Lure fishing fee, entitling the purchaser to use lures in the waters of one province with one rod, reel and lure, FIM 150 per year or FIM 35 per seven days. Those under 18 or over 65 are exempt. Further, permission must be obtained from the owners of the local fishing waters. This does not necessarily cost anything.

Close seasons: salmon and trout, Sept 10-Nov 16; grayling fishing is allowed with rod and lures, April and May. In the Aland Islands shore fishing is banned between 15 Apr and 15 June, in order to protect nesting sea birds.

One important accessory for the angler is some form of repellant to ward off mosquito attacks, which can often be unbearable - some Finnish fishermen wear head-nets. There are many fishing holiday resorts in Finland, and many organised package fishing holidays.

Further information can be obtained from the **Finnish Tourist Board, UK Office, 30/35 Pall Mall, London SW1Y 5LP**. Tel: 0171-930 5871. Fax: 0171 321 0696.

FRANCE

Excellent sport with trout and some salmon fishing is open at reasonable cost in this country. French waterways are divided into the navigable public rivers, where fishing rights are owned by the State, and private rivers, where they belong to the riparian owner, fishing association or local authority. Even on the public rivers, however, anglers must belong to an angling and fish-breeding association and pay a tax based on the method of fishing adopted. Most rivers of this type provide coarse fishing only. Trout and salmon rights will nearly always be privately held, but the visitor should have little difficulty in obtaining a permit. Information should be sought from the local club or tackle dealer.

Close seasons vary a great deal according to the locality, especially for salmon, and it is best to make local inquiries. A rough guide, however, would be: salmon, Oct 1 to Jan 10; trout and char, from last Tuesday in Sept to third Friday in Feb; coarse fish, from Tuesday following April 15 to Friday following June 15.

Perhaps the best salmon fishing in France is to be found on a small number of fast flowing streams in the **Western Pyrenees**. The noted **Gave d'Oloron** is in this area. **Oloron**, **Sauveterre** and **Navarrenx** are good centres for this river. The **Gave d'Aspe**, which joins it at Oloron, and its tributary, the **Lourdios**, have provided good sport in recent years. They may be fished from **Lurbe**. At **Peyrehorade** the Gave d'Oloron is joined by the **Gave de Pau**, on which sport has also been improving, and Pau itself makes a fine place to stay. Salmon also run up the **Gaves d'Ossau** and **de Nive**.

Because of melting snow, the season begins later here than elsewhere in France, but it extends later, too. For the Oloron area the best months are from June to the end of August.

Brittany, too, provides some opportunities for the salmon fisherman, with 12,400 miles of water courses, though the fish are on the small side, especially on the **River Aulne**, which flows into the sea near **Brest**. Generally, March, April, then June to end of season is the best time for salmon. Try the **Châteaulinn** area until April and **Chateauneuf-du-Faou** later on. Châteaulinn is also a good centre for the **Ell'le** and from **Landerneau** and **Landivisiau** the **Ellorn** may be fished. This salmon and trout river has been improved, pruned, and made accessible by the local angling society. Other productive streams are the **Blavet**, which passes through many locks, and is a first-rate coarse fishing stream, **Laita** and **Odet**, which flow into the Atlantic; the **Trieux** and its tributary the **Leff**, with **Guingamp** a suitable venue. In Cotes d'Armor region, the **Guer** and **Guic** are excellent and easily accessible trout streams, also the **Jaundy**, and tributary the **Théoulas**, brown trout and occasional salmon.

Flowing northwards through picturesque countryside to feed the **Loire**, the **Allier** offers the best opportunities for salmon fishermen in **Auvergne**. This is a region comparatively unknown to British anglers. The place to make for is **Brioude**, on the upper reaches of the river. The **Bajace dam**, where salmon congregate before taking the leap, is half a mile away. **Vichy**, **Pont-du-Château**, **Veyre** and **Issoire** are other centres. The upper reaches of the Loire itself can provide good sport. **Cantal** in the heart of the Auvergne, has 2,500 miles of rivers and mountain streams, with abundant brown trout. Best time, March to June. **Roanne** is a suitable place to stay. In the **Languedoc-Roussillon** region of southern France, there are almost 1,800 miles of game fishing stretches, mostly on the three major river basins, the **Garonne**, the **Loire** and the **Rhône**, and a multitude of lakes, some 50 up in the mountains. 15 May to 15 June is the best time for fly fishing, April to Oct for coarse, and June, July, Sept for mountain lake fishing.

Some of the **Normandy** rivers have good runs of fish, but the best of the fishing is hard to come by, being largely in the hands of syndicates. The visitor may find opportunities, however, on the **Orne** and **Vire**, the **Sée**, the **Sienne** and the **Sélune**; **Pontfarcy**, **Quetteville**, **Avranches** and **Ducey** are suggested centres.

France is a splendid country for the trout fisherman, with an abundance of well-stocked streams flowing through glorious scenery. He may find solitude and beauty not very far from Paris - in fact, on the upper reaches of the **Seine** and its tributary, the **Ource**. A little farther south lies **Avallon**, from which the **Cure** and its tributaries may be fished.

But the visitor will find the **Pyrenees** very hard to beat for trout. The **Gave d'Ossau** is one of the best of the many first-class streams in this area, offering particularly fine sport at the **Fabrège dam**. From **Lurbe** the **Gave d'Aspe** and its tributary, the **Lourdios**, may be fished, and excellent sport may be had on the **Gave d'Oloron** above **Pont-de-Dognen**, the **Nive** above **Itxassou**, and the **Gave de Pau** upstream of **Pont-de-Lescar**. The best trout fishing is from the end of May, once the snow has melted, and from June for salmon; April/Nov for coarse fish.

In eastern France, the **Franche-Comté** region offers a wealth of fishing for trout and grayling in such fine rivers as the **Loue**, **Doubs**, **Ain**, the **Dessoubre**, **Bienne**, **Usancin**, **Breuchin** and **Saône**, as well as the **Saint-Point** and **Remoray** lakes, and the huge **Vouglans** reservoir. March is the best month for trout fishing with worm, dead minnow, and spinning, and very large fish are caught then. In May/July, dry fly and nymph. There is good coarse fishing to be found in the region, too, in June/July, and Sept/Oct

In the fascinating and comparatively unexplored regions of **Creuse**, **Haute-Vienne**, **Corrèze** and **Lot**, are innumerable streams with torrential upper reaches holding fine trout. Downstream they become less tumultuous and wider until, in the **Dordogne**, they harbour a variety of coarse fish. Figeac is a good centre for the trout. Farther east lies the wild, mountainous region of **Lozère**, where grand and beautiful rivers like the **Lot** and its tributary, the **Colagne**, may be fished. The **Bès** and **Truyère** should also be tried.

Wherever one turns in France, it seems, there are trout to be caught. In the **Savoy Alps** are innumerable streams of quality, like the **Isère** and **Doron**, near **Albertville**, and the **Sierroz**, **Tillet** and **Chéron** near **Chatelard-en-Bauges**, the **Arvan** and **Arc**, near **Saint-Jean-de-**

Anglers from Britian often visit France these days for the excellent carp fishing found in its kindlier climate. Dr. Bruno Broughton, Executive Director of the tackle trade's Angling Foundation, displays a fine specimen from a reservoir on the R. Lot. *Photo by the angler.*

Maurienne. Auvergne and the **Dauphiny Alps** are ideal for the explorer with a fly rod. **Grenoble** commands a number of valleys through which flow some noted trout streams.

Normandy has some trout fisheries of high repute, like Risle, Eure, Charenton and Andelles, but they are strictly preserved for the most part. Fishing on the streams of Brittany is more easily obtainable. **Quimper** is an excellent centre for the large fish of the **Odet** and its tributaries. Trout abound throughout **Finistère**, notably in the Aulne tributaries.

The lake fisherman is also well catered for in France, with some splendid opportunities in the Pyrenees, especially near **Luz-Saint-Sauveur**, and in the Alps. **Lakes Leman**, **Annecy** and, farther south, **Lauvitel** and **Beason** are good for trout.

One cautionary note for the fly fisherman - many French rivers are so torrential and boulder-strewn that they cannot be fished with fly. It is as well to check with a club or tackle dealer in the area to avoid disappointment. Best months of the fly are generally May, June and Sept in the north and before April and in Sept in the south. British patterns do well in the north, but are not so good in the south.

Further details from the **French Tourist Office, 178 Piccadilly, London W1V 0AL,** who will supply literature, including their *Angling in France* brochure, on receipt of £1 in stamps.

GERMANY

Bavaria and the **Black Forest** offer the best prospects for the trout fisherman. Although pollution and over-fishing are producing a decline in sport, Bavarian waters like the **Wiesent**, **Pegnitz**, **Loisach**, **Isar**, **Ammer**, **Saalach** and **Salzach**, to name only a few, still offer fishing of high quality amid beautiful surroundings. Brown and rainbow trout, as well as grayling, are widely distributed.

For anglers who like to fly-fish for trout and char from a boat, the **Hintersee** at **Berchtesgaden** is highly recommended - the char in particular are good, reaching weights of 6lb and more.

In the Black Forest, streams like the **Kinzig**, **Murg**, **Obere Wolf**, **Nagold** and **Bernbach** provide good sport with trout and grayling. The best waters are usually fly-only.

The **Harz** mountain area, south-east of **Hanover**, is also well worth exploring - the **Radau**,

A memorable 4lb. trout taken on a black wet fly from a tributary of the Danube. Stomach contents included a 6 ins. rainbow trout and a half-digested mole. *Photo: Cori Gebhart.*

fished from **Bad Harzburg**, is good. Trout are found, too, in some of the streams and lakes of the **Rhineland-Palatinate**, especially in the Eifel district, and in some parts of **North Rhine-Westphalia** and **Lower Saxony**.

Elsewhere there is good coarse fishing. In **Baden-Wuerttemberg** (apart from the Black Forest) carp, bream, tench, whitebait, roach, barbel, pike, eels and trout can be had in the **Neckar Valley,** the Hohenloe district, the **Swabian Forest** area and elsewhere, including trout, pike and barbel fishing in the **Danube**. Other coarse-fishing areas are the Rhineland Palatinate (Moselle, Ahr, Lahn), and most of Lower Saxony.

The angler will need a licence from the Landrats or Ordnungsamt (rural district council) or from the local police (Dm10 to Dm20) and a permit from the owner or lessee of the fishing. Many Hotels and clubs also have fishing rights. The principal seasons are as follows: river trout, Mar 2-Oct 9; sea trout, March 2-Oct 9; lake trout, Jan 1-Sept 30; river char, Jan 11-Oct 9; lake char, Jan 1-Oct 31; pike, May 1-Dec 31; pike-perch, July 1-Mar 31; huck, May 1 to last day of Feb. (The seasons vary slightly in the different Federal states).

General tourist information can be had from the **German National Tourist Office, 65 Curzon Street, London W1Y 8NE** (0171-493 0080).

HOLLAND

Fishing has become one of the most popular of outdoor sports in Holland. There are about 150,000 acres of fishing waters which hold eel, carp, pike, perch, pike-perch *(Stizostedion lucioperca),* roach, bream. To fish one must have a sportvisakte or national fishing document, which is inexpensive and can be obtained from any Dutch post office, angling club or tackle shop. It is valid for a year, from 1st January to 31st December. One also needs the right licence, and this is usually obtainable by joining one of the fishing clubs affiliated to the national angling organisation NVVS.

For information on Dutch angling clubs contact **Nederlandse Vereniging van Sportvissers-federaties, Afd. Voorlichting, Postbus 288, 3800 AG Amersfoort, Holland**. Tel: 033 463 4924; fax: 033 461 1928.

For general tourist information and details on accommodation, please contact the **Netherlands Board of Tourism, PO Box 523, London SW1E 6NT**. Tel: 0891 200 277, fax: 0171 828 7941.

ICELAND

There are five species of fish which are found naturally in fresh water: salmon, trout, char, common eel and stickleback. Rainbow trout were imported from Denmark about twenty years ago. Iceland has close on 100 salmon rivers, and at least twenty are regarded as first class. The Icelandic salmon is usually 4-12 pounds in weight and between 55-85 cm in length, but each year a few fish of up to 30lb are caught. Sea trout average between 1-4lb, occasionally caught to 20lb, and char, normally 1-2lb, although sometimes as much as 12lb. The salmon river fishing season is short, from May to Sept, numbers peak in July. Most salmon fishing is fly only, and the fishable rivers tend to be found in the west and north west regions. Sea trout fishing is best from Aug to Oct, brown trout and char from June to Sept. River owners are always pleased to arrange for catches to be smoked, frozen, or packed fresh, and will ship smoked salmon. Iceland has always been free of UDN and other freshwater diseases, and maintains a strict policy of disinfection. Visitors must have their tackle and other equipment disinfected (ten minute immersion in 2% formaldehyde) by local vets, and obtain a certificate to prove the fact.

Half an hour's drive away from **Reykjavík**, the **Laxa í Kjos** has a fishable length of about 15 miles. Further up the west coast is the **Langá**, fishable for 12 miles, on three beats. Nearby, the **Hítará** produces salmon over 20lb, most seasons. 75 miles north, the **Grímsá** is one of Iceland's most prolific salmon rivers, with a fishable section 19 miles long, and over 60 named pools. Fish are taken over 25lb. The **Laxá í Dölum**, 125 miles north of the capital, flows into Hvammsfjördur, and produces an average of 1,300 salmon each year. Also flowing into Hvammsfjördur is the **Flekkudalsá**, producing about 200 salmon per season. In the north east, 160 miles from Reykjavik, the **Vatnsdalsá** is especially known for its large fish, and the annual average catch, together with tributary, the **Álka**, is close on 1,000. The Vatnsdalsá also has a trout section of about 12 miles length. In the same region, the **Midjardará** system contains around 50 miles of fishable water, with more than 200 pools, and the **Vididalsá**, one of the best salmon rivers in Iceland. In the south west, the **Rangá** system has been improved over the past ten years, resulting in a catch of 1,500 salmon in 1994. The main river originates from cold underground springs, resulting in very clear water. Central north, is the beautiful **Fljótaá**, 250 miles from Reykjavík. Four rods permitted, fly, worm, spinner; annual average 234 salmon, fish over 20lbs each season, and 7,000 Arctic char. East of Akureyri is the **Laxá in Thingeyjarsysla**, the upper half of which is a fly only, brown trout fishery, with 5 and 7 pound fish taken regularly. Its lower half is the renowned salmon river, **Laxá i Adaldal**.

There are fewer than 100 lakes in the country of more than one sq km, and the largest of these is **Thingvallavatn**, 25 miles east of Reykjavík, surface area 82.6 sq km. The commonest fish caught there is the lake char, as well as brown trout of up to 26lb. Another big lake is **Thórisvatn**, 39 sq. miles, situated 120 miles east of the capital, with brown trout up to 4lb in weight. Twenty rods are permitted daily. There is fishing for char of 1-6lb on **Medalfellsvatn**, Kjosarsysla, half and hour away from Reykjavík. Open from May 1 to Sept 20. **Icelandair, 172 Tottenham Court Rd, London W1P 9LG**, tel: 0171 388 5599, issues a pamphlet on this and other lake fisheries in the vicinity, as well as information about salmon fishing holidays in Laxa/Kjos from £700 per day. The **Federation of Icelandic River Owners** publishes information about national fishing: **Bolholt 6-105, Reykjavík**. Tel: 354 1 31510, fax: 354 1 684363. An excellent 170 page fishing guide called *Veidiflakkarinn* is published by the **Icelandic Farm Holidays Association, Matnarstratil, 101 Reykjavík**, which gives full details of a large number of lake and river fishings.

Daily air services are operated by Icelandair. Travel within Iceland is mostly by air and bus services. Further tourist information may be obtained from the **Iceland Tourist Information Bureau, 172 Tottenham Court Road, London W1P 0LY**.

ITALY

In Italian rivers, mountain torrents and lakes above the 1,800 ft contour, trout, char, grayling may be fished for. The trout fishing close season is Oct 15 to Jan 15. Lowland waters contain mainly bleak, chub, carp, tench, pike, perch, roach, etc.

Sea fishing is first class. Deep-sea sport with tuna, albacore and swordfish has become increasingly popular, and so has underwater fishing. Underwater fishing with aqualung is prohibited in all Italian waters. Only those over sixteen are allowed to use underwater guns and such equipment. When submerged, an underwater fisherman is required to indicate the fact with a float bearing a red flag with a yellow diagonal stripe, and must operate with a radius of 50m of the support barge or the float bearing the flag. Fishing is prohibited: at under 500m from a beach used by bathers; 50m from fishing installations and ships at anchor. Sea sport fishing may be practised both from the shore and from a boat.

The most suitable coasts for underwater fishing are those of Sardinia, **Sicily**, **Aeolian Islands**, **Pontine Islands**, **Tremiti** Islands and the rocky shores of **Liguria**, **Tuscany**, **Latium**, **Campania**, **Calabria**, **Basilicata** and **Apulia**.

For fishing in rivers, streams, lakes and in all inland public and free freshwaters, a "Libretto di Pesca" and a "Licenza per la Pesca" issued by the Provincial Administration are required, and for foreigners cost about £20 in total. The Local Tourist Board will advise about further details for obtaining these. With exception of 10%, all waters liable to exclusive rights are managed by the Italian Angling Federation. Fishing in private waters requires the owners permission, while fishing in all other waters requires the Federation membership card, which may be obtained from Federazione address below, at cost of £10 per year.

Further information can be had from the **Italian State Tourist Board in London, 1 Princes Street, London W1** (0171-408 1254), from the **Federazione Italiana Pesca Sportiva e Attivita' Subaquee, Head Office, Viale Tiziano, 70-00196-Roma**, tel: 06 36858248, fax: 06 36858109, or from the provincial tourist boards (their addresses may be obtained from the Tourist Board in London).

LUXEMBOURG

Most of the rivers of Luxembourg are mixed fisheries holding trout, grayling and coarse fish, including pike, barbel, chub, roach, carp, eels, pike-perch and tench. There is a fine reservoir at the head of the Sûre, heavily stocked with lake trout, char and roach, and carrying a good head of pike, some of them very large. In inland waters, fishing is only allowed in public waters, that is, at present, the Mid-Sûre sector between the mouth of the Alzette at Ettelbruck, and the mouth of the Our at Wallendorf. Fishing is not allowed in the fish reserve between the Moestroff weir and the bridge at Reisdorf. In the ponds at Boulaide, Clemency, Clervaux-Reuler, Erpeldange/Ettelbruck, Fischbach/Mersch, Grevenmacher, Kockelscheuer, Lamadelaine, Olingen, Pétange, Pratz, Redange/Attert, Remerschen, and the lakes of Echternach and Weiswampach, fishing is allowed without any formality other than the payment of an indemnity.

A licence is required in order to fish in the Grand Duchy, costing 750 F per year, 150 F per month. The legislation regulating the practice of fishing is very complex and visitors are advised to contact the **Administration des Eaux et Forêts, PO Box 411, L-2014 Luxembourg,** tel: 40 22 01; or **Fédération Luxembourgeoise de Pêcheurs Sportifs, 14 rue du Fort Wallis, l-2714 Luxemburg,** tel: 48 88 74, for up-to-date information.

Tackle can be purchased, and local information gained, from **Maison Tony van der Molen, 16 rue de la Montagne, L-6470 Echternach, Grand Duchy of Luxembourg**. Further information, including details of hotels with fishing, from the **Luxembourg National Tourist Office, 122 Regent Street, London, W1R 5FE,** tel: 0171-434 2800; fax: 0171 734 1205.

NORWAY

Norway has acquired a world-wide reputation for its salmon and sea trout, which can be fished for in a superb setting of mountains and fjords, spectacular waterfalls and peaceful valleys. Beats on such renowned waters as the **Tana**, **Alta**, **Laerdal**, **Driva** and **Surna**, fetch very high prices and are in the hands of specialised agencies (inquire Hardy's of London and Sporting Services International). Excellent sport at more modest charges may be had from the many hotels with private stretches, especially in the north. The salmon season is from late May to Sept 5 (best in June and July) and the best sea trout fishing is to be had in August, although the season extends into Sept, the actual date varying in different districts.

Floating line fishing is becoming more widely practised, but it is more usual on the big rivers to employ heavy, fast-sinking lines and large flies, from size 3/0 upwards. Streamers and bucktails are popular for salmon, and sea-trout are often fished dry fly or nymph - in the clear waters the fish can often be seen and cast to.

Less well known, and much less expensive, is fishing for brown trout and char, which can be very good indeed. Countless streams and lakes well stocked with trout lie within easy reach of **Oslo**, while anglers prepared to travel further afield will be amply rewarded. Trout of 25lb and over have been caught in the lake **Steinsfjorden**, near **Vikersund**, and the **Randselven**, near **Kistefoss**, and **Lake Mjösa**, near **Gjövik**. Several fish of around this weight have fallen to fly.

Arctic char are mostly found in the deep and cold mountain lakes, where they can provide thrilling sport, though this is a difficult art. There are taxi flights to the lakes from the big towns. The brown trout season varies with altitude, the extremes being late May until mid-Sept. As several rivers have rather swift currents, strong tackle is recommended. Most fishing rights are owned privately, but there are vast areas of Crown land where good fishing may be enjoyed at no great cost. Any fisherman in Norway, in addition to the application fee, is required to take out a licence sold at post offices. It covers the entire country for a year, and prices vary. Many hotels in the country have their own rivers and lakes for brown trout fishing, making no charge to guests.

Dry-fly fishing is very popular, especially in smaller lakes and tarns or slow rivers. Most suitable gear is a fly-rod of 9½ft to 10½ft, with a No.7 line, which may be used anywhere at any time. Best flies are those in douce colours, such as March brown and Greenwell's Glory etc. For red char fishing, use stronger colours such as Red Cardinal, Butcher or

Leading salmon angler Arthur Oglesby with a 50 pdr. from Norway. Spinning slow and deep accounted for this exceptional fish - as it has accounted for many others in powerful Norwegian rivers.

Coachman, etc. The best all-round spinning lures are those with slow movements and in golden or red colours. For hooking, use Devon or Phantom lures, or artificial minnows. No gaff is required, but a large landing-net is desirable. Rubber boots or waders come in handy, practically everywhere.

Fishing regulations. Anyone over 16 fishing for salmon, sea trout, sea char or freshwater fish in waters on common land, has to pay an annual fee, 'fisketrygdavgift', of NOK 80. This can be done at any post office. The normal local fishing licence must then be purchased in addition. The cost of this varies from place to place. Licences are sold at sports suppliers, kiosks, tourist offices, hotels, and campsites etc. A licence generally covers the waters in a certain area, whilst some are valid for one lake or part of one only. A licence can be purchased for a day, a week, a month, or a whole season. Restrictions are normally stated on the licence. As a rule, a separate licence is needed for net or otter fishing.

Nets and crayfish tackle which have been used outside Norway, may not be utilised there: The same applies to gear used in waters found to be diseased, unless this gear has been disinfected. Crayfish tackle used in Norway has to be disinfected before it is employed again in the new season.

Live bait is forbidden in Norway. Also, to protect trout, char and salmon stocks, fish must not be transferred from one body of water to another. New restrictions have been introduced to protect stocks of anadromous salmonid fish.

For further details, contact the **Norwegian Tourist Board, Charles House, 5 Lower Regent Street, London SW1,** tel: 0171-839 6255. The Board publishes a comprehensive guide entitled *Angling in Norway,* which can be purchased from **MMW Production Ltd, 26 Woodford Square, London W14 8DP**.

PORTUGAL

Salmon and trout are found mostly in the **River Minho** and its tributaries in the far north, but the lack of controls has diminished sport. Very good sea trout fishing may be enjoyed in the Minho estuary near **Moledo** and on the **Lima** near **Viana do Castelo**. The fish are usually taken on bait or spinner, but fly fishing should prove productive. The coarse fisherman, too, can find sport. All Portuguese rivers hold barbel, while those in the centre and south of the country hold good carp and black bass.

The close season for salmon and trout fishing is from Aug 1 to end Feb and for other species from March 15 to end May. Licences for visitors are not as a rule required.

The sea fishing is excellent, partly owing to the structure of the continental shelf, and the narrow strip of 50 to 100 miles shallower water. More than 200 different species are taken. Among these are many of the fish known to British fishermen in home waters, but in the south it includes game species such as swordfish, blue and white marlin, tunny, bonito and amberjack, as well as blue porbeagle, thresher and mako sharks. School tunny and meagre (the so-called salmon-bass) are also taken.

Many of the fish known to British fishermen reach heavier weights in Portuguese waters. Bass of around 20lb are reported to be taken inshore from boats, for instance, and smaller fish of 10lb-14lb from the shore. Large shoals of mackerel up to 6lb were found by a British team fishing off Peniche in 1956. Good shore fishing for bass can be had more or less everywhere. Other fish regularly caught include: mullet (to 5lb), conger and dogfish, various types of bream, some running up to 25lb; pollack, cod, turbot, rock gurnard, wrasse, John Dory, tope and several others. Meagre attain weights up to 90lb, amberjack to 18lb, and school tunny to 80lb. The comparatively recent discovery of this vast potential has led to a rapid development of a number of small fishing ports. Boats and boatmen operate at most of them, and hotel accommodation is reported to be good. Most important of the new-found fishing centres is perhaps **Sesimbra**, south of **Lisbon**. Others are **Praia da Rocha** (near **Portimao)** and **Faro** in the south, **Cascais** (near **Estoril), Nazaré**, and **Ericeira** (all to the north-west of Lisbon) and **Sines** (south of Sesimbra). Apart from the fishing, most of these places have good beach and rock casting, and are good holiday and tourist centres. Boats are for hire at many places, including **Albufeira**, **Lagos** and **Monte Gordo**.

Visiting anglers will be made welcome at such clubs as the 'Clube dos Amadores de Pesca de Portugal', Rua do Salitre 175R/CD, Lisbon Tel: 684805 (for all kinds of angling, especially big game fishing), 'Clube Invicta de Pesca Desportiva' at Rua 31 de Janeiro 85-10, Tel: 321557, and the 'Amadores de Pesca Reunidos', at Largo dos Lojas 79 (second floor), Tel: 324501, both **Oporto**, where information on local fishing may be obtained and where all visitors will be treated as honourary members. In the **Algarve**, several hotels provide or can arrange sea fishing parties. They include the Hotels Praia, Algarve and Baleeira. The best centres in this region are in the **Sagres** and **Carvoeiro** areas where large mackerel are frequently taken. More information can be had from the ICEP/Trade and Tourism Office, 22/25A Sackville Street (2nd Floor), London W1X 1DE. Tel: 0171-494 144.

RUSSIA

The Kola Peninsula. Over the last few years the Kola Peninsula has built up a reputation for some of the most prolific Atlantic salmon and sea trout fishing to be found anywhere in the world. Situated in north-western Russia, jutting into the White Sea from its border with north-eastern Norway, the peninsula is approximately the same size as Scotland, with as many rivers supporting salmon and sea trout runs.

With few roads, a very small population, and lying mainly above the Arctic Circle, the peninsula is a truly remote wilderness, and it has taken some years to overcome the geographical problems this incurs. Although in recent times western fishermen have only fished the Kola since 1989, its rivers were a topic of great interest in the *Fishing Gazette* as long ago as 1925, a few Englishmen having fished there shortly after the turn of the century.

Hard work by a few western specialist organisations over the last few years has now made it possible to fish the Kola relatively easily. They have all combined their experience with Russian local knowledge, to build camps on the most productive and consistent rivers. The remoteness means that it is still not possible to fish there except through these organisations.

Salmon fishing. Varzuga. Kola. Russia. *Photo: Arthur Oglesby.*

To get to the rivers one must fly via Moscow, St Petersburg or Helsinki to the peninsula and then onward to the rivers by helicopter.

The season runs from the beginning of June, the winter snows having melted in May, until late September, when the onset of the severe Arctic winter prohibits access. The rivers may be grouped into those which flow north into the Barents Sea, and those which flow east and south into the White Sea.

The southern rivers were the first upon which fishing was organised. There, the main salmon run is in June and July, and a smaller run in September. Sea trout run throughout the season, not starting until July on some rivers. Large catches may be expected, with salmon of 5lb to 20lb being normal. The main salmon run in the northern rivers, which have only been fished seriously since 1991, is from mid-June to mid-July, although it does extend into August. To date, fish from these rivers have averaged 15lb to 20lb, with many in the 30lb to 40lb range. The 1993 season saw a fish caught exceeding 60lb.

The majority of fishing is on floating, intermediate or sink tip lines using traditional salmon flies. A sink line may be necessary on the northern rivers. A surprisingly large number of fish are taken on dry fly. The majority of the rivers require chest waders and wading staffs.

The rivers vary greatly in character. The **Panoi**, flowing east into the White Sea, is large, with prolific runs of salmon. Running South is the **Varzuga** system, including the **Pana** and **Kitsa**, which has, perhaps, the largest salmon runs in the world, and in parts is comparable with the Aberdeenshire Dee. The **Polanga**, **Babia**, **Likhodyevka** and **Pyalitsa**, fished together, are probably the prettiest rivers on the peninsula, requiring little wading and are similar to the Scottish Carron, Oykel and Cassley; their salmon run is not quite as prolific, but is boosted by large runs of sea trout. The **Kharlovka**, **Eastern Litsa**, **Varzina** and **Yokanga** in the north, all have runs of large salmon, but in places are very rocky and steep, with fast water and difficult wading.

Fishing is mostly fly only, and all rivers operate a policy of catch and release for salmon, allowing each rod no more than one or two fish a week for the table.

For further information contact **Nimrod Safaris Ltd, Water Eaton, Cricklade, Wiltshire SN6 6JU**. Tel: 01285 810132.

SPAIN

Spain is a well-endowed country, offering the most southerly fishing for Atlantic salmon in Europe; brown and rainbow trout, coarse fish including large carp and barbel, both in rivers, and shore fishing for sea bass, mackerel, mullet, conger and other species. Black bass, pike and Danube salmon are among comparatively recent introductions.

Twenty-six rivers draining the Cantabrian range and the Galician Coast are entered by salmon. The **Deva-Cares**, **Navia**, **Sella**, **Narcea**, and **Asón** provide the best sport. Arrangements for licences and permits for visitors are not uniform and the British angler contemplating salmon fishing in Spain is advised to contact the **Spanish Tourist Office, 57 St James Street, London SW1A 1LD** (tel: 0171-499 0901). Much the same is to be said of the trout fishing, applying equally to seasons and permitted methods. In some areas, trout grow impressively large. Spain has not yet become as notable for high-grade coarse fishing as it may at some future date, but few who have connected with large carp or barbel in a deep, fast-flowing Spanish river do not cherish ambitions to renew the experience.

The tourist office publishes an interesting full-colour map on fishing in the country.

SWEDEN

Sweden presents an inviting prospect for game and coarse angler alike, and with 9,000 km of coastline, a large variety of locations and species for sea fishing. Salmon fishing has a long tradition in the country, and western Sweden was explored for this purpose during the 19th century by British anglers. Several of these centrally located waters, the **Ätran**, **Säveån**, **Göta** and **Klarälven Rivers** still provide good sport, but there is more salmon fishing to be found than on the west coast alone. The whole coastline is dotted with attractive salmon rivers, and every year the most famous, **Mörrumsan**, **Emån** and **Dalälven** attract many anglers. Along the northern coastline there are a rich variety of rivers ideal for both spinning and fly-fishing. In recent years these have improved and produced more and larger salmon, weighing between 20 and 30 kg. During the 1990s a good quantity of very large salmon have come from the **Harnöbukten** area of southern Sweden. In addition, Sweden figures highly in the world's ratings for landlocked salmon. In summer, spinning and fly fishing are the most popular methods in the rivers, while trolling is favoured in the Baltic. In winter, trolling is popular in the two largest lakes **Vänern** and **Vättern**, where salmon of more than 17 kg have been caught.

For the game and coarse fisherman Sweden abounds in lakes. Amongst these, various in the **Hökensas** area near Lake Vättern have stocked rainbow and brown trout, and rainbow trout may be caught in the **Ångebytyärnet Lake** from jetty or shore. The **Svågadalen** wilderness has hundreds of lakes, tarns, rivers and brooks, and the main species are trout, char and grayling. The forest **River Svågan** runs through this area, with many exciting fishing spots. The brook trout, lake trout and sea trout run large in Sweden, lake trout to 17 kg, and may be caught in cold, fast-flowing water, on fly, spinner, jigger, or by trolling, depending on season and conditions. Pike fishing is wide spread in the country, and some lakes can produce pike around 20 kg, as well as large shoals of big perch. In the mountainous region of **Hemavan** are lakes with first rate trout and char fishing.

The Finnish **Åland** is an enormous archipelago, scattered out in the middle of the Baltic, easily accessible from Stockholm, with excellent pike, salmon and sea trout fishing. Fly fishing for pike is growing in popularity, as well as the more conventional methods of spinning and trolling.

Coastal fishing for sea trout may begin in January, and is popular on the coast of **Bleckinge**, where good spots include Björkenabben at Listerlandet, Lörby Skog in Pukaviksbukten, Sternö Island, and the coast east of Torhmans udde near Karlskrona. Bleckinge also has good pike fishing in its lakes, streams, and in the Baltic.

Lapland fishing for trout and grayling is well organised for small groups of anglers, and for this the following addresses may be contacted: **Länsturismen Västerbotten, Box 113, S-923 22 Storuman**, tel: 0951-141 10; fax: 0951-141 09; **Northern Hunt and Safari, Magnus Lindström, Blåsmarksvägen 140, S-944 92 Blåsmark**, tel/fax: 0911-393 11.

For salmon and trout fishing, licence charges vary considerably; charges for trout fishing in stocked lakes and ponds are somewhat higher than for natural waters. No charge is made to fish for grayling in the sea.

Ten of Sweden's foremost fisheries have entered into a partnership, with the purpose of encouraging angling in their respective areas. These include mountain, forest, rivers, lakes, and coastal fishing, for pike, rainbow trout, perch, carp, salmon, sea trout, brown trout, char, grayling and sea fish. The fishing is of a high quality, also the reception, accommodation and service, in the form of information, transport and guiding. Contact **Swedish Travel and Tourism, Box 8080 10361 Stockholm, Sweden**; or **Top 10 Fishing Sweden, 566 93 Brandstorp, Sweden,** tel: 46(0)502 502 00, fax: 46(0)502 502 02.

Close seasons vary widely. For salmon and sea trout it usually runs from Sept 1 to Jan 1, though fishing is prohibited in some waters after Aug 15.

Further and more detailed general information can be had from the year book published by **Sportfiskarna** (The Swedish Anglers Association), **Box 2, S-163 21 Spånga**, which lists about 1,800 fishing waters. The association cannot, however, answer detailed inquiries from abroad. These should be directed to the **Swedish Travel and Tourism Council, 11 Montagu Place, London W1H 2AL** (tel: 0171-724 5868, fax: 5872); or to **The National Board of Fisheries, Box 423, S-401 26 Göteborg, Sweden**. For a wide range of fishing holidays in Sweden, contact **EDA Travel and Tourist Centre, Stationsgatan, 1 SE-871 45 Härnösand, Sweden**, tel: 46(0)611-511010, fax: 46(0)611-51155.

SWITZERLAND

There is no shortage of water in Switzerland - 20,000 miles of rivers and streams, and 520 square miles of lakes within a small area - and as most of these waters hold trout, the country is a fly-fisherman's dream.

Unfortunately, the dream is often of brief duration, as the streams at appreciable altitudes are in snow spate often until July. But in the lower valleys there is sport to be had from May to the end of the summer. Lake fishing consists mainly in trolling at great depth. Swiss waters may be classed as follows:

The **Lakes**. Most of the lakes contain trout and char, pike, perch and other coarse fish. The trout and char (Ombre chevalier) run to a great size, but they lie at such depths that fly fishing or trolling with a rod is practically useless. Most of the lakes in the central plain are now suffering to some degree from pollution, but they still provide sport. Best results are obtained by spinning with light tackle.

The Great Rivers. Both the **Rhine** and **Rhône** hold very big trout. Spinning with a 2¼in silver Devon is the best method, though a small silver-bodied salmon fly will sometimes give good results. The Rhône, above the lake of **Geneva**, is fishable only till the middle of April. In summer months it is thick with snow water. Many Swiss rivers contain good stocks of coarse fish, including barbel, carp and pike.

Plain and Lower Valley Streams. Trout in these streams run from ¼lb to 2½lb or more. There is always a good hatch of fly, and the Mayfly is up on most of them from May to July. Wading is not as a rule necessary. Fine tackle is essential. Carry a couple of small silver Devons for thick water.

The Hill Torrents. Trout run four or five to the pound in the best of the hill torrents, rather smaller in the others. As the hatch of fly is usually poor, the upstream worm pays best. The coch-y-bondhu is sometimes useful, while in July and Aug the 'daddy-long-legs' is deadly. Wading is usually an advantage. Watch for the spate that often occurs towards midday owing to melting snow.

It should be said that Switzerland, in common with most European countries, is experiencing a growth of angling pressures, but the authorities, concerned to ensure that sport remains at a high level, release at least 100 million fish, mostly trout, from hatcheries every year.

The close season for trout runs most commonly from Oct 1 to Mar 15, and for grayling from Mar 1 to April 30.

Fishing regulations vary. Generally speaking the angler will require a canton licence and may also need a permit for private waters. Further information is obtainable from the local Tourist Offices in the area to be visited or from **Schweizer Sportfischer-Verband, Zentralsekretariat SSFV, Cuomo Beatrice, Corso San Gottardo 94, 6830 Chiasso, Switzerland**. General tourist information can be had from **Switzerland Tourism, Swiss Centre, Swiss Court, London W1V 8EE,** tel: 0171-734 1921; fax: 0171 437 4577.

Channel Islands sea angling draws visitors from far and wide. This 48lb conger (a monster, but only about a third of the weight of the current British record) was caught by an angler from Holland, fishing in the boat *Anna II* out from St Clement, Jersey. *Photo: Tony Heart.*

NOTABLE BRITISH AND IRISH FISH, INCLUDING THE OFFICIAL RECORDS

Until the British Record (Rod Caught) Fish Committee was set up in 1957, there was no recognised method of establishing a list of record fish. Such lists as did exist were based largely on data culled from books, the angling press and so on. Clearly, many of the claims were suspect, as the committee found when it examined the lists it had inherited and, as a result, discarded many so-called 'records'. Some have been discarded and replaced since the previous edition of **Where to Fish** was published.

Fisherman catching fish equal to or greater in weight than the established record should claim recognition of the fish through the Secretary of the appropriate governing body: National Federation of Anglers (coarse fish claims); National Federation of Sea Anglers (saltwater fish); The Salmon and Trout Association (game fish claims). The addresses appear in the preamble material to 'Fishing Clubs and Associations in England'. National claims for fish caught in Scotland, N Ireland or Wales will be processed by these officers. Some change in the arrangements is possible during the life of this edition of **Where to Fish** but if so the officers referred to will be in a position to advise. A claim should be made soon as possible after the capture of the fish, preferably by telegram or telephone and a confirmatory letter should give full details of the catch (date, time, tackle etc) and the names and addresses of two independent and reliable witnesses capable of identifying the fish, which should be retained for inspection, dead or alive, by the committee or its representative. Fish should not be weighed on spring balances, but on a steel-yard or scales which can be tested if necessary.

The committee is always pleased to receive similar details of any unusual catches. Only fish in the coastal waters of England (including the Channel Islands and the Isle of Man), Scotland, Wales and Northern Ireland are eligible. Fish caught in the Irish Republic should be reported to the Secretary, Irish Specimen Fish Committee, Balnagowan, Mobhi Boreen, Glasnevin, Dublin 9.

Fish marked as records in the following lists are those recognised by the BRFC after very careful examination of all the relevant factors, as the official record for the species.

Irish records, that is, those recognised by the Irish Specimen Fish Committee - are indicated thus † in the following lists. Note: The Irish keep separate records for rivers and lakes in respect of pike and brown trout.

For some years, there has been concern about British records awarded for game fish reared in conditions of semi-captivity. This dilemma has now been resolved by awarding separate records for: a) Fish from a naturally sustained population, as confirmed by the National Rivers Authority (marked with a single asterisk in the list); b) Fish stocked at under 2 years of age which have been accredited by scale reading, location and circumstances (marked with a double asterisk in the list); and c) Fish which have been farmed and reared for stocking at record weight (marked with a treble asterisk in the list). Records for category "c" (treble asterisk) have yet to be awarded for salmon, Arctic charr and grayling.

The other notable catches recorded here - ie those apart from the established records - are included for interest only and, because they have not been subjected to such rigorous scrutiny, should not be viewed as beyond question. Further data any of these fish would be welcome.

Official British Records are as updated at the meeting of the Committee 24/10/95.

GAME FISH

SALMON (*Salmo salar,* Linn)

69lb 12oz By the Earl of Home on Tweed about 1730. The "record" rod-caught salmon for the British Isles. This fish has been described as "somewhat legendary". In 1935, however, the Earl of Home sent a note giving evidence that the fish indeed existed.

67lb On the Nith at Barjarg by Jock Wallace in 1812. Wallace, a well-known poacher, is said to have played the fish from 8am to 6pm.

64lb On the Tay (Glendelvine water) by Miss G W Ballantine on Oct 7, 1922. Hooked in the Boat Pool at 6.15pm and landed half a mile below at 8.5pm. The fish took a spinning bait, a dace. The biggest salmon caught by a lady. Length 54in, girth 28½in. A cast of the fish was made and is at Glendelvine.
61lb 8oz On the Tay below Perth by T Stewart on the last day of the season, 1907, with a worm. It took an hour to land.
61lb J Haggart on the Tay in 1870.
61lb Mrs Morison on the Deverton on 1¼in fly (the weight probably was more as the fish was not weighed until 24 hours after capture), Oct 21, 1924.
60lb On the Eden by Lowther Bridge in 1888. Length 54in, girth 27in. Exhibited in the British Museum. It appears to be the biggest fish caught on fly in English rivers.
59lb 8oz On the Wye at Lower Winforton by Miss Doreen Dovey on Mar 12, 1923. This appears to be not only the record fish for the Wye, but also the biggest spring fish so far caught on a rod in Great Britain.
59lb On the South Esk by J K Somerville in Oct, 1922. Length 53in, girth 28in.
58lb Reported from the Shannon in 1872.
57lb 8oz On the Tweed (Floors water) in 1886 by Mr Pryor. This is usually accounted the biggest Tweed fish.
57lb† From the Suir by M Maher in 1874. The record fish for Ireland.
57lb On the Awe by Major A W Huntingdon on July 8, 1921. Length 52½in, girth 27½in.
56lb From the Deveron on Oct 31, 1920, by Col A E Scott. The fish took a 1in fly. Length 50in, girth 29in.
56lb On the Dee, Ardoe Pool, by J Gordon in 1886.
56lb From the Eden at Warwick Hall by G Mackenzie in 1892.
56lb On the Awe (Pol Verie) on June 12, 1923, By H G Thornton. Took a 5/0 fly and fought from 1pm till 3.30pm.

SEA TROUT (*Salmo trutta,* Linn)
25lb 5¼oz, J Farrant, River Test Estuary, Sept 1992.
22lb 8oz S Burgoyne, R Leven, Strathclyde, July 22, 1989.
22lb 8oz S R Dwight, Dorset Frome, at 11am, above the hatches at Bindon Mill, May 18, 1946.
21lb The Rev A H Upcher, Bothie Pool on the Awe on June 30, 1908. The "record" Scottish sea trout.
21lb Dorset Frome at Bindon in Mar, 1918, by R C Hardy, Corfe.
20lb 2oz V R Townsend, River Esk, Yorks, Sep, 1986.
20lb 2oz T Williams, the Dovey, in June, 1935. The "record" Welsh sea trout.
20lb G Leavy, River Tweed, Nov, 1983.
16lb 12oz T J McManus, Shimna River, Co. Down, N Ireland, Oct, 1983.

TROUT (BROWN) (*Salmo trutta,* Linn)
39lb 8oz On Loch Awe by W Muir in 1866. It was foul-hooked on a trout fly and took two and a half hours to land. It was set up, but the case was unfortunately lost in a fire.
30lb 8oz J W Pepper on spoon bait, Lough Derg, 1861. The Irish Times gave credence to this fish in 1903. The same angler claimed to have caught one of 24lb from Lough Corrib about the same period.
29lb On Loch Stenness in 1889 on a hand line. A "slob" or estuarine trout. A cast of this fish is in the Flyfishers' Club.
28lb 1oz D Taylor, Dever Springs, Hants, May 5, 1995.
27lb 8oz Colonel Dobiggin on the Tay at Murthly in 1842; length 39½in. Recorded by the late Duke of Rutland in his book on The Trout.
27lb 4oz Dr H H Almond, of Loretto, on the Inver about 1870. Said to have take a small salmon fly. Probably a fish from Loch Assynt.
26lb 2oz† From Lough Ennel by W Meares on July 28, 1894, on a spoon bait. (Irish lake record).
22lb From Loch Rannoch by F Twist in 1867.
21½lb Lough Derg by James Lucas, keeper at Derry Castle. The fish was preserved. Date of capture uncertain. (There was also a case containing a brace of trout, 16lb, 13lb, caught at the same time by trolling).
21lb 3½oz S Collyer, Dever Springs Trout Fishery, July, 1993.

21lb Loch Rannoch by Miss Kate Kirby in July, 1904. Probably the biggest trout ever caught by a lady.
20lb† From the Shannon in February, 1957, by Major H Place on a trolled silver Devon. (Irish river record.)
19lb 10¼oz A Thorne, from L Awe, April 1993.
19lb 9¼oz J A F Jackson, Loch Quoich, Invernesshire, 1978.
19lb 4½oz From Lower Lough Erne, Co Fermanagh, NI, by T Chartres, April 6, 1974.
19lb 2oz F Smith from Lough Corrib on spoon, Aug, 1971.
18lb 2oz K J Grant, Loch Garry, Tomdoun, on a Black Pennel fly, in July, 1965.
Note: Lt Col G F McDonald, proprietor of Strathgarve Lodge Hotel, Garve, Ross-shire, has a trout of 26lb in a glass case reported taken in Loch Garve on September 17, 1892, by Wm Ogilvy Dalgeish. Among notable Thames trout is a fish of 14lb taken by A Pearson (Shepperton) on fly in August, 1962.

TROUT (RAINBOW) (*Oncorhynchus mykiss*)
36lb 14½oz C White, Dever Springs Trout Fishery, Hants, 1995.
24lb 2¾oz J Moore, Pennine Fishery, Littleborough, Sept 15, 1989.
22lb 15oz† V Raymond, Dever Springs, Andover, July 4, 1989.
22lb 6oz B Hamilton, Pennine Fishery, Littleborough, Nov 19, 1988.
21lb 4oz D Graham, Loch Awe, Oct, 1986.
20lb 7oz P Cockwill, Avington, Sept, 1986.
19lb 8oz A Pearson, Avington Fisheries, Hants, 1977.
19lb 2oz R W Hopkins, Avington Fisheries, Hants, April, 1977.
18lb 9oz K Lynch, Hanningfield Reservoir, Essex, May 26, 1995.
18lb Richard Walker, Avington Fisheries, Hants, 1976.
18lb A Pearson, Avington Fisheries, Hants, June, 1976.
14lb 4oz J L Farmer, Avington Fisheries, Hants, July, 1975.
13lb 2oz Dr W J Drummond, Downton Tannery Stream (tributary of W Avon) Sept 28, 1974.
10lb ¼oz M Parker from a private lake in King's Lynn, July, 1970.
8lb 14oz Brian Jones, Packington Fisheries, May, 1970 (taken out of Trent RA season).
8lb 10oz C F Robinson, River Test at Stockbridge, Aug, 1970.
8lb 8oz From Blagdon in Sept, 1924, by Lieut-Colonel J Creagh Scott.
8lb 7oz† On Lough Eyes, Co Fermanagh, by Dr J P C Purdon on fly, in March, 1968. Irish record; Fish was just over 4 years of age.

TROUT (AMERICAN BROOK) (*Salvelinus fontinalis*)
5lb 13½oz A Pearson, Avington Fisheries, Hants, 1981.
5lb 6oz A Pearson, Avington Fisheries, Hants, 1979.

CHARR (*Salvelinus alpinus*)
8lb, F Nicholson, L Arkaig, 1992.
7lb 14½oz Roy Broadhead, June, 1991.
4lb 13oz P Savage, Loch Garry, May 1987.
3lb 5oz A Robertson, Loch Earn, 1985.
3lb 4oz S C Rex, Knoydart Dubhlochan, Oct, 1982.
1lb 12oz M C Imperiale, Loch Insh, Inverness, May, 1974.
1lb 11oz B A Richardson, Lake Windermere, April, 1973.
1lb 9oz A Stein, Lake Windermere, March, 1973.

GRAYLING (*Thymallus thymallus,* Linn)
7lb 2oz From River Melgum by J Stewart, July, 1949. The fish is believed to be somewhat legendary and was eliminated as a record by the British Record Fish Committee in 1968. 4lb 8oz Dr T Sanctuary on the Wylye at Bemerton in 1885. A fish of 4lb 12oz was netted from the Avon at Longford by G S Marryat and Dr Sanctuary in the same year and returned to the water.
4lb 4oz G Bryant on the Itchen.
4lb 3oz S R Lanigan (16 years old) Dorset Frome, Jan. 8, 1989.
4lb Three a fraction over this weight caught by H J Mordaunt and M Headlam on the Test (Oakley Stream) at Mottisfont on Boxing Day, 1905.
4lb E Chambers, Chess, near Chorley Wood, Jan, 1955. Mr Chambers had another of 3lb 13oz on the same outing, making a remarkable brace.

3lb 14oz E J Stanton, Driffield Canal, Sept, 1967.
3lb 12oz J Wigram on the Test near Stockbridge, in 1873.
3lb 12oz J W Gieve from the Test in 1917.
3lb 12oz M T Hooper, Loudsmill, Dorchester, 1988.
3lb 10oz I White, River Allen, Dorset, Aug, 1983.
2lb 13oz P B Goldsmith, R Test, 1981.
2lb 9¼oz D Hauxvell, R Teviot, Jan 12, 1980.

OTHER FRESHWATER FISH

BARBEL (*Barbus barbuss*, Linn)
16lb 2oz P Woodhouse, River Medway, 1994.
16lb 1oz C H Cassey, while spinning for salmon in the Hampshire Avon at Ibsley on March 6, 1960. Fish was foulhooked and therefore disallowed as a record.
15lb 7oz R Morris, River Medway, Jan 1993.
14lb 11oz D Taylor, River Medway, Nov 1992.
14lb 8oz D Taylor, River Medway, Nov 1992.
14lb 6oz D Williams, River Avon, Sept 1992.
14lb 6oz D Williams, River Medway, Sept 1992
14lb 6oz T Wheeler, Thames at Molesey in 1888.
14lb 6oz H D Tryon, Hampshire Avon (Royalty Fishery), Sept, 1934.
14lb 6oz F W Wallis, Royalty Fishery, Sept, 1937. The same angler had another of 14lb 4oz from the Royalty in Sept, 1933.
14lb 4oz R Jones, Thames at Radcot Bridge in 1909.
14lb 2oz P Reading, from a Wessex river, Aug, 1987.
14lb 1oz G Buxton, from a Wessex river, Sept, 1984.
14lb E A Edwards, River Kennet, 1954.
14lb Mr Simmons, Dorset Stour, Sept, 1930.
13lb 14oz C A Taylor, Hampshire Avon, Oct, 1934.
13lb 14oz P Mays, Troop Fishery, Dorset Stour, Oct, 1964.

BLEAK (*Alburnus alburnus*, Linn)
5¼oz Henry Stubbins, Nottingham, at Radcliffe-on-Trent, about 1890. Recorded by H Coxon in his Coarse Fish Angling, 1896.
4¼oz B Derrington, R, Monnow, Oct, 1982.
4oz 2dm F Brown on Trent at Long Higgin, 1959.
3oz 15dm D Pollard, Staythorpe Pond nr Newark, Aug, 1971.
3oz 8dm N D Sizmur, Thames at Walton, Surrey, 1963.

BREAM (COMMON) (*Abramis bramma*, Linn)
16lb 9oz M McKeown, from a private water in the South of England, June 1991.
16lb 6oz A Bromley, from a Staffordshire mere, Aug, 1986.
15lb 10oz J Knowles, Queensford lagoon, July, 1985.
(Part of a bag including other bream of 14lb 14oz, 13lb 11oz and 13lb 2oz, caught during two days.)
15lb 6oz A Nicholson, Queensford lagoon, Sept, 1984.
13lb 14oz C Dean, Oxford gravel pit, 1983.
13lb 12oz A Smith, Oxford gravel pit, Aug, 1983.
13lb 9oz M C Davison, Beeston Lake, Wroxham, Norfolk, July, 1982.
13lb 8oz A R Heslop, private water, Staffs, 1977.
13lb 8oz E G Costin, Chiddingstone Castle Lake, in Oct, 1945.
13lb R Willis, Duchess Lake, Bristol, Sept, 1949.
12lb 15oz F T Bench, Tring Reservoirs, Oct, 1945.
12lb 14oz G J Harper, Suffolk Stour, July, 1971.
12lb 14oz Caught by one of two brothers (Messrs Pugh), Tring Reservoirs, on July 28, 1933. They had two other bream, 12lb and 10½lb, on same day.
12lb 12½oz A J Fisher, July 30, 1931, Tring Reservoirs (thus beating an Irish fish of 11⅓lb, which had held the record for 49 years). Later that year Lord Rothschild reported a fish of

13lb 10oz found dying at Tring. Several other fish of 12lb and over have been taken from Tring.
11lb 12oz W Gollins, Ellesmere (Salop), 1970.
11lb 12oz† A Pike, River Blackwater (Co Monaghan), 1882.

BREAM (SILVER) (*Blicca bjoernka*, Linn)
4lb 8oz C R Rhind from Tortworth Lake, Gloucestershire, in 1923.
4lb 4oz K Armstrong, lake at Rugeley, Staffs, Jan, 1970.
4lb Two fish of this weight were caught by J Bowater from Yorkshire Derwent in July, 1933.
4lb G Burwash from Thames at Egham in Feb, 1922.
4lb J Bowater, Yorkshire Derwent, July, 1933.
3lb 7½oz A Engers from Plucks Gutter (Stour, Kent), July, 1949.
15oz D E Flack, Lakenheath, Aug 26, 1988.

CARP (*Cyprinus carpio,* Linn)
55lb 4oz A White, Mid-Northants Fishery, June 17, 1995.
51lb 8oz C Yates, Redmire Pool, Herefordshire, 16/6/80.
45lb 12oz R Macdonald, Yateley, summer 1984.
44lb Richard Walker on Sept 13, 1952, Redmire Pool, Herefordshire. The best of many huge carp from Redmire. "Dick" Walker himself had another of 31lb 4oz in June, 1954.
42lb R Clay, Billing Aquadrome, Sept, 1966.
40lb 8oz E G Price, Redmire Pool, Sept 27, 1959. King carp.
40lb 0½oz R Groombridge from a lake at Hemel Hempstead, July, 1956.
38lb 8½oz R Bowskill, Redmire Pool, Sept, 1966.
37lb 8oz J Sims, Wyver Pool at Belper, Derbys, July, 1968.
37lb 4oz D Stanley, W Sedgemoor Drain, Oct, 1986.
36lb 4oz W Quinlan, Redmire Pool, Oct, 1970.
35lb J Hilton, Redmire Pool, Oct, 1967.
34lb 8oz J Ward, pond near Wokingham, Berkshire, July 28, 1959.
34lb 4oz W Beta, Electricity Cut, River Nene at Peterborough, June, 1965. Thought to be the record river carp. The Electricity Cut has produced several big carp - one of 33lb 12oz was taken by P Harvey in Jan, 1965.
34lb P Chillingworth, Billing Aquadrome, June, 1970.
Fish of over 30lb (some of them more than 40lbs) have also come from the Ashlea Pool, Gloucester (two), Waveney Valley Lakes, the Layer Pits, near Colchester and from lakes and ponds in the home counties. Biggest catch of carp is thought to have been taken by Bob Reynolds from Billing Aquadrome. In August, 1957 he took carp of 26lb 1oz, 27lb 9oz, 27lb 13oz, and 28lb 4oz, making 109lb 11oz in all. The record Irish carp is a fish of 18lb 12oz taken by J Roberts from Abbey lake in 1958.

CARP (CRUCIAN) (*Carassius carassius,* Linn)
5lb 11½oz D Lewis, 6 acre Surrey pond, 1994.
5lb 10½oz G Halls, King's Lynn lake, June, 1976.
4lb 15½oz J Johnstone, Johnson's Lake, New Hythe, Kent, June, 1972.
4lb 11oz H C Hinson, Broadwater Lake, Godalming, 1938.
4lb 10oz M Benwell, Notts gravel pit, July, 1971.
4lb 9½oz B Cole, Kent lake, Sept, 1971.
4lb 8oz F J Axten, Bedfont Lake, July, 1964.
4lb 8oz B Burman, Shoebury Park Lake, Sept, 1971.
4lb 7½oz A Palfrey, South Ockendon pit, 1962.
4lb 7½oz F James, Leighton Buzzard pit, June, 1965.
4lb 7½oz A Donison, Guildford lake, Aug, 1968.
4lb 6½oz G Bott, Godalming lake, March, 1966.

CARP, GRASS (*Ctenopharyngodon idella*)
25lb 4oz D Buck, at Honeycroft Fisheries, Canterbury, Aug 1993.
16lb 1oz J P Buckley, Horton Fishery, Berks, July, 1990
16lb K Crow, from lake near Canterbury, July 1986.
9lb 12oz G A Gwilt, Trawsfynydd Lake, June, 1983.

CHUB (*Squalius cephalus,* Linn)

10lb 8oz Dr J A Cameron from the Annan in 1955.
8lb 14oz Caught out of season on the Wissey by J Roberts in May, 1960, while spinning for trout.
8lb 12oz J Lewis, River Mole, Oct, 1964.
8lb 10oz P Smith, River Tees, Durham, 1994.
8lb 8oz D Deeks from Sussex Rother, July, 1951.
8lb 4oz G F Smith from Avon at Christchurch, Dec, 1913.
8lb C Harmell, Royalty Fishery, Aug, 1964.
7lb 15oz P Minton, Yorkshire Ouse, Oct, 1964.
7lb 14½oz Mrs H M Jones, from Stour at Canford (Dorset) in Sept, 1937.
7lb 10oz P J Goddard, Bristol Avon, 1987.
7lb 6oz W Warren, Hampshire Avon, 1957.

DACE (*Leuciscus leuciscus,* Linn)
1lb 8¾oz S Horsfield, Derbyshire, Derwent, Jan, 1947.
1lb 8oz R W Humphrey, from tributary of Hampshire Avon, Sept, 1932.
1lb 7¾oz J S Upton, from the Penk, Dec, 1933.
1lb 7½oz F W Arnold, River Mole, Jan, 1934.
1lb 7½oz S Rolfe, Suffolk Stour, Feb, 1962.
1lb 7oz Abe Hibbard, near Sheffield, Feb, 1934.
1lb 5oz 2dm S Wilson, Llynfi, July, 1966.
1lb 5oz R Walker, Cam, July, 1938.
1lb 5oz J Cartwright, Cynon, 1965.
1lb 4¼oz J L Gasson, Little Ouse, Thetford, Feb, 1960.
1lb 2oz† J T Henry, River Blackwater, (Cappoquin), 1966.

EEL (*Anguilla anguilla,* Linn)
11lb 2oz S Terry, Kingfisher Lake, Hants, 1978.
8lb 10oz A Dart, Hunstrete Lake, July, 1969.
8lb 8oz C Mitchell, Bitterwell Lake in 1922. An eel of equal weight was taken from a trap on the Warwickshire Avon in Aug, 1960.
8lb 4oz J McFarlane, River Tees, 1964.
8lb 4oz J Taylor from pond at Arlesey, Bedfordshire, in July, 1958.
8lb R Jones, Monmouthshire lake, May, 1968. Mr Jones had another from the same lake of 7lb 8oz.
8lb M Bowles, Weirwood Reservoir, June 1986.
7lb 15oz P Climo, Monmouthshire lake, May, 1969.
7lb 13oz, M Hill, Arlesey Lake, Beds, Aug, 1970.
7lb 5¼oz B Young, Pluck Pond, Swansea, Aug, 1970.
7lb 1oz D Holwill, River Wallington, Fareham, Oct, 1968.
7lb W F Simmons from Dorset Stour at Christchurch in 1931.
An interesting catch was made by R Smith (13) and W Bush (14) from Hollows Pond, Whipps Cross, London, in Sept, 1958, when an eel weighing 6lb 8oz took both boys' baits.

GOLDEN ORFE (*Leusiscus idus*)
7lb 7¼oz D Smith, Church Lake, Horton, Beds, July 7, 1995.
6lb 11oz B Crawford, Lymm Vale, Cheshire, Oct 1990.
6lb 2oz, P Corley, at Lymm Vale, Cheshire, Sept 1993.
5lb 15oz G Sherwin, Lymm Vale, Cheshire, Oct 1990.
5lb 6oz M Foot, River Slea, Hants, 1978.
4lb 12oz J Moran, Burton Towers, N Wales, June 1986.
4lb 3½oz D R Charles, River Kennet, Aug, 1983.
4lb 3oz B T Mills, R Test, Jan, 1976.

GUDGEON (*Gobio gobio*, Linn)
5oz D H Hull, R Nadder, Jan 1990.
4¼oz M J Bowen, pond at Ebbw Vale, Gwent, 1977.
4¼oz Geo Cedric from the Thames at Datchet in Aug, 1933.
4¼oz W R Bostock from Hogg's Pond, Shipley, near Derby, in Oct, 1935.
4¼oz J D Lewin from the Soar in 1950.
4oz 1dm Caught at Sudbury by O S Hurkett, Mar, 1950.

PERCH (*Perca fluviatilis,* Linn)
5lb 15oz 6dm P Clark, Suffolk Stour, 1949.
5lb 14½oz D Florey from Farlows Lake, Dec, 1953.
5lb 12oz E V Hodd from Diana Pond, Hampton Court, in Aug, 1957.
5lb 9oz J Shayler from a private lake in Kent, 1985.
5lb 8oz† S Drum from Lough Erne, 1946.
5lb 4½oz H Green from Stradsett Lake, Norfolk, on Nov 9, 1936.
5lb 4oz Caught at Sandford Mill, Woodley, Berks, by Wm Leach in 1873.
5lb 4oz K Gardner from a lake in Norfolk, July, 1970. Other fish of over 5lb were reported from lakes in Worcester and Suffolk, and a pit in Colchester.
4lb 12oz S F Baker, Oulton Broad, 1962.

PIKE (*Esox lucius,* Linn)
53lb Lough Conn in July, 1920, by John Garvin. This fish is entitled to rank as the premier pike landed in Great Britain and Ireland. Mr Garvin caught a 30-pounder on the same day. Bigger pike than this have been reported, including a fish of 72lb from Loch Ken in 1774 and one of 60lb found dying at Dowdeswell. One approaching the weight Mr Garvin's fish 52lb is said to have been recovered when Whittlesey Mere, Cambs, was drained in 1851.
48lb Reported from Lough Corrib in 1905.
47lb 11oz T Morgan from Loch Lomond in July, 1945.
46lb 13oz R Lewis, Llandegfed Reservoir, S Wales, Oct, 1992.
45lb 6oz Gareth Edwards, Llandegfedd Reservoir, Gwent, 1990.
44lb 14oz M G Linton, Ardleigh Reservoir, Jan, 1987.
42lb D Amies, River Thurne, Aug, 1985.
42lb M Watkins, River Barrow (spoon), 1964, Irish river record.
41lb 8oz From Foxborough, Tulsk, Ireland, by P J Mannion in June, 1922.
41lb Mr Cawley from Lough Conn in Mar, 1918.
40lb 8oz From Lough Arrow. The fish was sent to The Fishing Gazette in 1900, together with another of 35lb. These fish were caught on "set lines".
40lb E Oulton from Lough Ramor in Nov, 1950.
40lb Lough Erne by John H Thompson in 1922. Hooked while the angler was playing another and smaller pike.
40lb P Hancock, Horsey Mere, Feb, 1967.
39lb C Loveland, Knipton Reservoir, 1967.
38lb 4oz P Emmings, Cheshunt pit, Dec, 1969.
38lb H Mumford Smith, Lough Conn, June 8, 1929.
38lb H A Robinson on Lough Mask in 1905. Various fish from this weight up to 40lb or more have been reported from Irish lakes, and there is little doubt that most of them have been authentic.
38lb† P Earl, Lough Ree (minnow), 1967 (Irish lake record).
37lb 8oz C Warwick, Avon at Fordingbridge, Oct, 1944.

PIKE PERCH (Walleye) (*Stizostedion vitrium*)
11lb 12oz F Adams, The Delph, 1934.

PIKEPERCH (Zander) (*Stizostedion lucioperca*)
18lb 10oz R Armstrong, River Severn, March 1993.
18lb 8oz R N Meadows, Cambridge stillwater, 1988.
17lb 4oz D Ditton, Gt Ouse Relief Channel, 1977.
16lb 6oz S Smith, Cut-off Channel, Oct, 1976.
15lb 5oz W G Chillingworth, Gt Ouse Relief Channel, February 1971. This angler had another of 12lb 13oz from the Relief Channel, Feb, 1971.
12lb 12oz Neville Fickling, Relief Channel, October, 1979. (This angler had another of 12lb 6½oz.) He had another of 12lb 7½oz from the same water the previous August.
12lb 5oz Dr R B Rickards, Relief Channel, Feb, 1970.

ROACH (*Rutilus rutilus,* Linn)
4lb 3oz R N Clarke, Dorset Stour, Oct, 1990.
4lb 1oz R G Jones, Gravel Pits, Notts, 1975.
3lb 14oz W Penny, Metropolitan Water Board's Lambeth Reservoir at Molesey, Sept 6, 1938 (118½in, g12⅝in).

3lb 14oz A Brown, Oakham gravel pit near Stamford, Lincs, 1964.
3lb 14oz Caught out of season on fly by F I Hodgson while fishing for trout in a spring-fed Lancashire pond in May, 1960.
3lb 10oz W Cutting, Hornsea Mere, Yorkshire, in 1917. On the same day he had another 3-pounder.
3lb 10oz A Whittock from the Hampshire Avon, Jan, 1953.
3lb 9¾oz T G Player from the Thames at Sonning in June, 1949.
3lb 9oz J Osborn, River Thurne, July, 1962.
Staines Reservoir produced three roach, each weighing 3lb 6oz in the autumn of 1962 and 1964.

RUDD (*Scardinius erythrophthalmus*, Linn)
4lb 8oz The Rev E C Alston on a mere near Thetford, July, 1933. He had another of 3lb 15oz during the month.
4lb 4oz Caught at Blackheath by J F Green, 1888.
3lb 15oz W Clews, Moor Lane Fisheries (Staines), 1957.
3lb 13oz A Oldfield from a mill pool in Cheshire, 1960.
3lb 13oz W Tucker, from the Thames at Chertsey, Jan, 1962.
3lb 12oz D A Fisher, pond at Stanmore, July, 1959.
3lb 12oz L Lindsay, Landbeach Lake, 1962.
3lb 12oz K Palfrey, Bridgwater and Taunton Canal, 1963.
3lb 10½oz E G Costin, Home Pond, Swanley, Oct, 1954.
3lb 10oz A Brogan, The Delph at Wisbech, July, 1935.
3lb 10oz Master D Denham, pit at Shepperton, July, 1954.
3lb 1oz† A E Biddlecombe, Kilglass Lake, on worm, 1963.

RUFFE (*Gymnocephalus cernus*)
5¼oz R J Jenkins, from farm pond in Cumbria, 1980.

TENCH (*Tinca tinca,* Linn)
14lb 7oz G Beavan, from a private gravel pit, Sept 1993.
14lb 3oz P A Gooriah, Wraysbury No One, June 1987.
12lb 8¾oz A Wilson from Wilstone Reservoir, Tring, 1985.
10lb 2oz E Edwards, undisclosed private water, 1983.
10lb 1¼oz A J Chester, Wilstone Reservoir, Herts, 1981.
10lb 1oz L W Brown, Peterborough Brick Pit, Aug, 1975.
9lb 1oz J Salisbury, gravel pit at Hemingford Grey, Hunts, 1963.
9lb G Young, Berkshire pond, Oct, 1964.
8lb 14oz K Baldock, Staplehurst pit, Aug, 1970.
8lb 12oz P Pilley, Middx lake, June, 1970.
8lb 9oz F Bailey, Lincolnshire drain, Aug, 1970.
8lb 8oz M Foode, Leicester Canal, Aug, 1950.
8lb 6oz K Morris, Cheshunt pit, Aug, 1964.
8lb 6oz J Brooksbank, Farningham pit, Dec, 1964.
8lb 4oz J Marshall, Grantham lake, 1961.
8lb 4oz R Hill, Bucks lake, Aug, 1970.
8lb 2oz A Lowe, Wraysbury pit (date unknown).
7lb 13¼oz† Raymond Webb, River Shannon, Lanesboro, 1971 (bread flake).
Tench of 11lb and 9lb 9oz 12dm were caught from a pit at Wraysbury, Middlesex, in July, 1959. The larger fish was returned to the water; the smaller one was sent to the London Zoo where it subsequently died. An autopsy showed it to be diseased and to contain 1lb 12oz of fluid. The larger fish was probably also diseased and neither could be allowed as a new record. Garnafailagh Lough, Westmeath, has produced a remarkable series of big tench in recent years, many over 7lb.

WELS (Catfish) *(Silurus glanis)*
62lb* R Garner, Withy Pool, Henlow, Beds, June 19, 1997.
57lb 4oz R Coote, Withy Pool, Henlow, Beds, Aug 23, 1995.
49lb 14oz S Poyntz, from Homersfield Lake, Norfolk, Sept 1993.
43lb 8oz R J Bray, Tring, 1970.

WHITEFISHES (*Coregonidae*)

These fishes are confined in the British Isles to a limited number of large, deep lakes where they are known under a variety of local names: Schelly (Haweswater, Ullswater) gwyniad (Bala) powan (Loch Lomond, Loch Eck) vendace (Derwentwater, Bassenthwaite Lake, Loch Maben) and pollan (Loughs Erne, Rea, Derg and Neagh). Although closely related to the salmonids, they do not grow large, nor have they attracted much attention by anglers. Although there is some confusion as to how many of the local names distinguish separate species rather than isolated populations of a single species, since March 18th 1988 no whitefish may be angled for lawfully in the United Kingdom of Gt. Britain and N. Ireland. At that date they were added under the nomenclatures *Coregonus albul* and *Coregonus lavaretus* to Schedule 5 of the Wildlife & Countryside Act 1981. The following records have been retained in these lists purely for their historical interest.

2lb 1½oz S M Barrie, Haweswater, 1986.
1lb 10oz W Wainwright, Ullswater, 1976.
1lb 7oz J M Ryder, Loch Lomond, 1972.
1lb 4oz J R Williams, Lake Bala, 1965.

Happiness in store. M.V. Bangor Crest heads for her mark at Killy Begs Sea Angling Festival.

SEA FISH:

ANGLER (*Lophius piscatorius*, Linn)

94lb 12¼oz	S M A Neill	Belfast Lough	Nov 1985
82lb 12oz	K Ponsford	Mevagissey	April, 1977
74lb 8oz	J J McVicar	Eddystone	Aug, 1972
71lb 8oz†	M Fitzgerald	Cork (Cobh)	July, 1964
68lb 2oz	H G Legerton	Canvey Island	1967

BASS (*Morone Labrax*, Linn)

19lb 9oz	P McEwan	off Reculvers, Herne Bay	1987
19lb	D L Bourne	Dover	Sept 3, 1988
18lb 6oz	R Slater	off the Eddystone	Aug, 1975
18lb 2oz	F C Borley	Felixstowe Beach	Nov, 1943
17lb 8oz	W G Byron (caught with a Gig-gan bait), l 12¼in, g 32½in	Castlerock, Derry	Oct 22, 1935
17lb 4oz	J Drysdale	Kinsale	Aug, 1943
16lb 6oz	T Browne	Bangor	July, 1935
16lb†	Major Windham. Reported taken with a fly on a trout rod	Waterville	1909

A fish of 18½lb was reported caught in the Teifi estuary by a salmon fisher in 1956.

BLACK-FISH (*Centrolophus niger*)

4lb 9oz	H G Lunt	Moggs Eye, Lincs	Nov 25, 1988
3lb 10½oz	J Semple	off Heads of Ayr	1972

BLUEMOUTH (*Helicolenus dactylopterus*)

3lb 2½oz	Anne Lyngholm	L Shell, S'way	1976

BOGUE (*Boops boops*)

1lb 15¼oz	S G Torode	Guernsey CI	1978

BREAM (BLACK) (*Spondyliosoma cantharus*, Gonelin)

6lb 14¼oz	J A Garlick	from wreck off Devon coast	1977
6lb 7¾oz	J L D Atkins	E Blackstone Rocks, Devon	Aug 1973
6lb 5oz	M Brown, jnr	Menai Straits	Oct, 1935
6lb 1oz	F W Richards	Skerries Bank	Sept, 1969
4lb 14oz	A Procter	Looe	Aug, 1953
4lb 12½oz	H Pavey	Littlehampton	1963

BREAM (COUCH'S SEA) (*Pagrus pagrus*)

1lb 10¼oz	D Fox-Reilly	off Guernsey	Sept 9, 1995
1lb 5¾oz	P Hutchins	Roselle Point, Alderney	Sept 25, 1995
1lb 4¼oz	T Mold	Roselle Point, Alderney	Sept 20, 1995

BREAM (GILTHEAD) (*Sparus aurata*)

10lb 5½oz	C Carr (aged 14 yrs)	Salcombe estuary	July 30, 1995
9lb 15¼oz	C Bradford	Salcombe	1991
9lb 8 oz†	R Simcox	off Salcombe	July 16, 1989
8lb 2oz	A Marquand	Guernsey	Sept, 1983
5lb 3oz	P King	Salcombe	July, 1983
5lb	A H Stratton-Knott	St. Mawes	1978

BREAM, RAY'S (*Brama brama*)

7lb 15¾oz	G Walker	Hartlepool	1967

BREAM (RED) (*Pagellus centrodontus,* De La Roche)

9lb $8\frac{3}{4}$oz	B H Reynolds	off Mevagissey	July, 1974
9lb 6oz†	P Maguire	Valentia	Aug, 1963
7lb 8oz	A F Bell	Fowey	July, 1925
6lb 3oz	Brig J A L Caunter	Nine miles of Looe	June, 1939
5lb $12\frac{1}{2}$oz	Brig J A L Caunter	Looe	1954

BRILL (*Scopthalmus rhombus,* Linn)

16lb	A H Fisher	Derby Haven, Isle of Man	1950
13lb 10oz	J L Williams	Brighton	1933

BULL HUSS (*Scyliorinus stellaris*)

22lb 4oz	M L Hall	Minehead	1986
21lb 3oz	J Holmes	Hat Rock, Looe	1955
21lb	F C Hales	Poole, Dorset	Aug, 1936
21lb	H Jupp	Brighton	Oct, 1953
20lb	F Matthews	Newhaven	Sept, 1954
19lb 14oz†	G Ebbs	Pwllheli	May, 1992
19lb 12oz†	M Courage	Bray	1969

CATFISH (*Anarhichas lupus*)

26lb 4oz	S P Ward	off Whitby	1989
24lb 3oz	N Trevelyan	Whitby	1980
15lb 12oz	E Fisher	off Filey, Yorkshire	1973
12lb $12\frac{1}{2}$oz	G M Taylor	Stonehaven, Scotland	1978

COALFISH, or **Saithe** (*Gadus virens,* Linn)

37lb 5oz	D Brown	S of Eddystone	1986
35lb 4oz	T Neatby	50m off Whitby	July, 1983
33lb 10oz	W H Saunders	off Dartmouth, Devon	Jan, 1983
33lb 7oz	L M Saunders	Start Point, Devon	1980
30lb 12oz	A F Harris	S of Eddystone	Feb, 1973
29lb $2\frac{1}{2}$oz	R Phillips	SE of Eddystone	Jan, 1973
27lb $12\frac{1}{2}$oz	J J McVicar	Eddystone	Jan, 1972
26lb 2oz	T J Trust	Start Point, Devon	1971
24lb 7oz†	J E Hornibrook	Kinsale	1967
23lb 8oz	Capt Hugo Millais	Land's End (Carnbase)	1921

COD (*Gadus callarias,* Linn)

58lb 6oz	N Cook	Off Whitby	Aug, 1992
53lb	G Martin	Start Point, Devon	June, 1972
46lb $0\frac{1}{2}$oz	R Baird	Firth of Clyde	Feb, 1970
45lb 14oz	D D Dinnie	Gourock	Jan, 1970
44lb 8oz	Brandon Jones	Barry (Glam)	Mar, 1966
42lb†	Ian L Stewart	Ballycotton	1921
34lb	The late R Blair	Ballycotton	1916
33lb 8oz	John E Timmins	Kinsale	Sept, 1962

A cod of 140lb landed at Hull Fish Dock in July, 1927, is worth adding to the record as a remarkable specimen, though it was not, of course, an angling trophy.

COMBER (*Serrana cabrilla*)

1lb 13oz	Master B Phillips	off Mounts Bay	1977

CONGER (*Conger conger,* Linn)

133lb 4oz	V Evans	from wreck off Berry Head	June 5, 1995
112lb 8oz		Over a wreck SE of Plymouth	July, 1992
110lb 11oz	H C Glausen	off Plymouth	1991
109lb 6oz	R W Potter	SE of Eddystone	Sept, 1976

102lb 8oz	R B Thomson	off Mevagissey	June, 1974
95lb 11oz	W K Oaten	Berry Head, S Devon	July, 1973
92lb 13oz	P H Ascott	Torquay	June, 1970
85lb	C E Chapman	Hythe (Hants)	June, 1970
84lb	H A Kelly	Dungeness	July, 1933

On the same day this angler had four more congers, 70lb, 33½lb, 21½lb, 15½lb.

80lb 8oz	H J West	Brixham	July, 1966
74lb	Mrs H Eathorne	Looe	1954
72lb†	James Green	Valentia	June, 1914
66lb	W H Pryce	Coverack	June, 1941
63lb 3oz	Miss B Klean	Hastings	1922

DAB (*Limanda limanda,* Linn)

2lb 12¼oz	R Islip	Gairloch	Aug, 1975
2lb 10¾oz	A B Hare	Skerries Bank	April, 1968
2lb 9½oz	M L Watts	Morfa Beach, Port Talbot	July, 1936
2lb 8½oz	L White	Netley Pier, Southampton	Nov, 1937
2lb 5½oz	C Stone	Ryde, IoW	Dec, 1934
2lb 4¼oz	N Coleman	Hastings	Jan, 1951
2lb 4oz	P A Heale	Southsea	Dec, 1933
1lb 12½oz†	I V Kerr	Kinsale	1963

DOGFISH, BLACK-MOUTHED (*Galeus melastomus*)

2lb 13½oz	J H Anderson	L Fyne	1977

DOGFISH (LESSER SPOTTED), or **Rough Head** (*Scyliorhinus caniculus,* Linn)

4lb 15oz†	S Ramsey	Abbey Burnfoot, Kirkudbrights	Aug 10, 1988
4lb 8oz	J Beattie	Ayr Pier	1969
4lb 2oz	B J Solomon	Newquay	Oct, 1976
3lb 15oz†	unknown	S Ireland	1980
3lb 12½oz	A Gibson	Firth of Clyde	July, 1967

FLOUNDER (*Platichthys flesus,* Linn)

5lb 11½oz	A G L Cobbledick	Fowey	1956
5lb 5½oz	D Clark	Littlesea	Mar, 1957
4lb 13oz	R Hitchman	Exmouth	1949
4lb 5oz	E F J Plumridge	Fowey Estuary	April, 1938
4lb 3oz†	J L McMonagle	Killala Bay	1963

FORKBEARD, GREATER (*Phycis blennoides*)

4lb 11¼oz	Miss M Woodgate	Falmouth	1969

GARFISH (*Belone belone,* Linn)

3lb 10¼oz†	E G Bazzard	Kinsale	Sept, 1967
3lb 8oz	Hanson Horsey	Kinsale	Oct, 1969
3lb 4¾oz	F Williams	Porthoustock, Cornwall	May 13, 1995
3lb	J Nardini	Penzance	1981
2lb 14oz	K C Ettle	Kinsale	Aug, 1968
2lb 14oz	D O'Donovan	Kinsale	Aug, 1968
2lb 13oz 14dm	Stephen Claeskens	Newton Ferrers	Aug, 1971
2lb 12oz	K C Ettle	Kinsale	Aug, 1968
2lb 12oz	M L Walsh	Ballycotton	June, 1967
2lb 11¾oz	Dennis Collins	Kinsale	1966
2lb 10½oz	J O'Sullivan	Courtmacsherry, Co Cork	Aug, 1971
2lb 10oz	Mrs Sandra Parker	Kinsale	Sept, 1969
2lb 9oz 2dm	A W Bodfield	Dartmouth	1963

2lb 9oz F T Goffin .... Coverack .... July, 1935

GREATER WEEVER (*Trachinus draco*)

2lb ¾oz T Griffiths .... Mounts Bay, Penzance 1994
2lb 4oz P Ainslie .... Brighton 1927
Record declared open at qualifying weight of 1lb 4oz.

GURNARD (GREY) (*Eutrigla gurnardus*)

3lb 1oz† B Walsh .... Rosslare Bay 1967
2lb 7oz D Swinbanks .... Caliach Point, Isle of Mull .... July, 1976
2lb 2oz D H Taylor .... Off Portrush, NI .... July, 1973
1lb 10oz D Cameron-McIntosh .... Isle of Arran 1971
1lb 6oz K R Manson .... Bressay, Shetland 1971

GURNARD (RED) (*Aspitrigla cuculus*)

5lb D B Critchley (captor aged 9) off Rhyl .... July, 1973
4lb 9½oz C Butler .... off Anglesey .... June, 1973
4lb 4¾oz W R Shaw .... Conway .... June, 1973
2lb 13¾oz B LeNoury (aged 14 yrs) .... Havre Cosselin, Sark .... Aug 31, 1995
2lb 8½oz D Relton .... 22m NW of Tobermory, I. O. Mull July, 1985

GURNARD, STREAKED (*Trigloporus lastoviza*)

1lb 6½oz H Livingstone Smith .... L Goil, Firth of Clyde 1971

GURNARD, YELLOW, or **Tub Fish,** (*Trigela lucerna,* Linn)

12lb 3oz G J Reynolds .... Langland Bay, Wales 1976
11lb 7¼oz C W King .... Wallasey 1952
10lb 8oz† C Gammon .... Belmullet 1970
10lb 2¼oz E Sederholm .... Belmullet .... May, 1969
9½lb W Adams .... Isle of Man 1907

HADDOCK (*Gadus aegifinus,* Linn)

13lb 11¼oz G Bones .... off Falmouth 1978
12lb 10oz Sub-Lieut K P White .... Manacles, Falmouth Bay .... Jan, 1975
10lb 13½oz† F A E Bull .... Kinsale, Co Cork .... July, 1964
10lb 12oz A H Hill .... Looe .... July, 1972
10lb 0½oz David Hare .... Valentia 1971
9lb 14½oz J O'Gilvie .... Valentia .... Aug, 1969
9lb 8¾oz L A Derby .... Kinsale .... June, 1965
9lb 4½oz Mrs M Morley .... Mevagissey 1969
9lb 2¼oz Eric Smith .... Kinsale .... July, 1963

HADDOCK, NORWAY (*Sebastes viviparus*)

1lb 13½oz T Barrett .... off Southend-on-Sea 1975

HAKE (*Merluccius merluccius,* Linn)

25lb 5½oz† H W Steele .... Belfast Lough 1962
20lb Frank Vinnicombe .... Falmouth .... Aug, 1960
17½lb Mrs J T Ashby .... Penzance 1911

HALIBUT (*Hippoglossus hippoglossus*)

234lb C Booth .... off Dunnet Head, Scotland 1979
212lb 4oz J A Hewitt .... off Dunnet Head .... Aug, 1975
196lb J T Newman .... off Dunnet Head, Caithness .... April, 1974
161lb 12oz W E Knight .... Orkney .... Aug, 1968
152¾lb† E C Henning .... Valentia 1926

He also had two, 128¾lb, 120½lb on another day in 1926.

135lb	J N Hearn	Ballycotton	1912

A Halibut weighing 500lb was landed by a commercial fishing boat at Grimsby in October 1957.

HERRING (*Clupea haringus*)

1lb 1oz	B Barden	off Bexhill-on-Sea	1973

JOHN DORY (*Zeus Faber,* Linn)

11lb 14oz	J Johnson	off Newhaven	1977
10lb 12oz	B L Perry	Porthallow, Cornwall	1963
8lb 8oz	J F Vallin	Mevagissey	1922
8lb 4oz	R Brown, Dreadnought SAS	Fowey	July, 1932

LING (*Molva molva,* Linn)

59lb 8oz	J Webster	off Bridlington	July 10, 1989
57lb 8oz	I Duncan	off Stonehaven	May, 1982
57lb 2½oz	H Solomons	off Mevagissey	1975
57lb 8oz	B M Coppen	off Eddystone	Mar, 1974
46lb 8oz†	A J C Bull	Kinsale	July, 1965
46lb	T D Walker	off Plymouth	Mar, 1974
45lb	H C Nicholl	Penzance	1912

LUMPSUCKER (*Cyclopterus lumpus*)

20lb 9¾oz	A J Perry	Weymouth pier	1987
14lb 3oz	W J Burgess	Felixstowe Beach	1970

MACKEREL (*Scomber scombrus,* Linn)

6lb 2½oz	W J Chapple	1½ miles off Penberth Cove, Cornwall	1984
5lb 6½oz	S Beasley	Eddystone Lighthouse	1969
4lb 11oz	L A Seward	Flamborough Head	1963
4lb 0½oz	F/Lt P Porter	Peel, Isle of Man	June 9, 1952
3lb 10oz	A Cave	Peel, Isle of Man	Aug, 1953
3lb 8oz	W Adams	-	1906
3lb 6oz†	J O'Connell	Valentia	1969

A fish of 4½lb was caught at Looe in June, 1935, by W C Butters on a handline.

MEGRIM (*Lepidohumbus wiffiagonis*)

3lb 12½oz	Master P Christie	Gairloch	Aug, 1973

MONKFISH (*Squatina Squatina,* Linn)

69lb†	Monsieur Fuchs	Westport	July, 1958
66lb	C G Chalk	Shoreham	1965
62lb	S Morris	Littlehampton	1919
62lb	A E Beckett	Porthcawl	1960

A fish of 68lb was reported from Beaulieu in August, 1953.

MULLET (GOLDEN GREY) (*Liza aurata*)

3lb ¼oz	J Reeves	E Coast, Alderney	1991
3lb ¼oz	D Heward	Christchurch Harbour	1994
2lb 13¼oz	C Fletcher	Rocquaine, Guernsey	1990
2lb 12¾oz	J Reeves	Alderney, CI	Sep 2, 1989
2lb 11½oz	D M Bohan	Fort Doyle, Alderney CI	1984
2lb 10¼oz	F Odoire	Alderney	Nov, 1983
2lb 10oz	R J Hopkins	Burry Port	1976

MULLET (GREY, THICKED-LIPPED) (*Chelon Labrosus*)

14lb $2\frac{3}{4}$oz	R S Gifford	Aberthaw, S Wales	1979
10lb 1oz	P/O P C Libby	Portland	1952
8lb 12oz	W E Wallis	Portland	1921
8lb 7oz	F V Daunou	Margate	About 1903

MULLET (GREY, THIN-LIPPED) (*Liza ramada*)

7lb	N Mableson	Oulton Broad	1991
6lb 4oz	H E Mephan	Kentish Rother	1981
3lb 7oz	D Davenport	Christchurch Estuary	Aug, 1983
3lb 2oz	J Corner	Christchurch Harbour	July, 1983

MULLET (RED) (*Mullus surmuletus*)

3lb 10oz	J E Martel	Guernsey	Oct, 1967
2lb 1oz 3dm	T F Cleal	Guernsey	Oct, 1967

OPAH (*Lampris guttatus*)

128lb	A R Blewitt	Mounts Bay, Penzance	1973

PELAMID (BONITO) (*Sarda sarda*)

8lb $13\frac{1}{4}$oz	J Parnell	Torbay	1969

PERCH, DUSKY (*Epinephelus guaza*)

28lb	D Cope	off Durlston Head, Dorset	1973

PLAICE (*Pleuronectes platessa,* Linn)

10lb $3\frac{1}{2}$oz	Master H Gardiner	Longa Sound	Oct, 1974
8lb 7oz	R Moore	Southbourne	June 18, 1989
7lb 15oz	Ian Brodie	Salcombe	Oct, 1964
7lb 13oz 1dm	W F Parker	Teignmouth	1961
7lb 6oz	D Brown	Dartmouth (Skerries)	June, 1963
7lb 6oz	J P Wright	Dartmouth	May, 1960
7lb 5oz 6dm	C Riggs	Teign Estuary	1949
7lb†	E Yemen	Portrush	1964

POLLACK, or **Lythe** (*Gadus pollachius,* Linn)

29lb 4oz	W S Mayes	Dungeness	1987
27lb 6oz	R S Milkins	Salcombe	1986
26lb 7oz	R C Perry	31 miles S of Salcombe	1984
25lb	R J Hosking	Eddystone	1972
23lb 8oz	G Bartholomew	Newquay	1957
22lb 8oz	W Digby	Looe	1955
21lb	Capt Hugo Millais	Land's End (Carnbase)	1921
Capt Millais had others of 17lb and 18lb at the same place			
20lb 8oz	Mrs Hugo Millais	Land's End (Carnbase)	1921
Mrs Millais also had a specimen of $19\frac{1}{2}$lb			
20lb 8oz	J H Layton	Lochinver	1920

POUTING (*Gadus luscus,* Linn)

5lb 8oz	R S Armstrong	Berry Head	1969
4lb 10oz	H B Dare	Coverack	Sept, 1935
4lb 10oz†	W G Pales	Ballycotton	1937
4lb 9oz	E Burton	Belfast Lough	April, 1968

PUFFER FISH (*Lagocephalus lagocephalus*)

6lb $9\frac{1}{4}$oz	S Atkinson	Chesil Beach	Oct, 1975

RAY (BLOND) (*Raia brachyura,* Lafont)

37lb 12oz	H T Pout	Salcombe	Oct, 1973
36lb 8oz†	D Minchin	Cork (Cobh)	Sept, 1964

35lb 9oz	A J Pearce	Portland	May, 1970
34lb 8oz	T Hutchinson	Cobh	Sept, 1967

RAY (BOTTLE-NOSED) (*Raja alba*)

76lb	R Bulpitt	off The Needles, IoW	1970

RAY (CUCKOO) (*Raio naevus*)

5lb 11oz	V Morrison	off Causeway Coast, NI	1975
5lb 6oz†	K Derbyshire	Causeway Coast, Co Antrim	Aug, 1971
5lb 3oz	P J Rankin	off Causeway Coast, NI	1974
5lb	N C McLean	Lamlash Bay, Isle of Arran	June, 1968

RAY (EAGLE) (*Myliobatis aquila*)

61lb 8oz	M Drew	off IoW	Aug 28, 1989
52lb 8oz	R J Smith	off Nab Tower, IoW	1972

RAY (ELECTRIC) (*Torpedo nobiliana*)

96lb 1oz	N J Cowley	off Dodman Point, Cornwall	July, 1975
47lb 8oz	R J F Pearce	Long Quarry, Torquay	Aug, 1971

RAY (MARBLED ELECTRIC) (*Torpedo marinurata*)

13lb 15¾oz	M E Porter	off Jersey	1990
5lb 8¼oz	M A Shales	Jersey CI	Aug 31, 1988
2lb 8½oz	B T Maguire	St Aubin, Jersey	July, 1983

RAY (SMALL-EYED) (*Raia microcellata*)

17lb 8oz	Mrs S Storey	off Watchet, N Somerset	1991
16lb 6½oz	J B Lush	off Minehead	April, 1982
16lb 4oz	H T Pout	Salcombe	Sept, 1973
14lb 8oz	T Pooley	nr Stoke Point, Devon	May 25, 1989
13lb 11½oz	H T Pout	Bolt Tail, Devon	1971
13lb 8oz	Mrs T Whippy	Pevensey Bay	Aug, 1969
12lb 1½oz	A T Scoones	Littlehampton	July, 1969

RAY (SPOTTED) (*Raia montagui*)

16lb 3oz	E Lockwood	Lerwick, Shetland	1970
14lb 3oz	W C Furnish	St Anne's Head, Pembroke	1970
8lb 5oz	D G Bowen	Mewslade Bay, S Wales	1980
8lb 4oz	G Brownlie	IoWhithorn, Galloway	June 15, 1989
7lb 12oz	J Cochrane	off Causeway Coast, NI	Aug, 1982
6lb 14oz	H A Jamieson	Causeway Coast, NI	1978

RAY (STING) (*Trigon pastinaca,* Linn)

68lb 4oz	K Rawlinson	off Aberdovey, Gwynedd	1993
65lb 8oz	J K Rawle	off Bradwell-on-Sea	1990
61lb 8oz	V W Roberts	off Pwllheli	1979
59lb	J M Buckley	Clacton-on-Sea	1952
52lb 8oz	T E Stone	Lymington River mouth	1938
52lb	J Manser	Brighton	June, 1954
51lb 8oz	P J Hill	Hastings	Oct, 1956

RAY (THORNBACK) (*Raia clavata,* Linn)

57lb	S G Lugger	Exmouth	July, 1951
38lb	J Patterson, Jnr	Rustington Beach	May, 1935
37lb†	M J Fitzgerald	Kinsale	May, 1961
31lb 7oz†	J Wright	Liverpool Bay	July, 1981

RAY (UNDULATE) (*Raja undulata*)

21lb 4½oz	S Titt	off Swanage	1987

21lb 4oz	K Skinner	St Catherine's Lghtho, Jersey, CI	Sept, 1983
20lb 12¼oz	F J Casado	off Corbierre, Jersey, CI	May, 1982
19lb 7oz	L R LePage	Herm, CI	1970

ROCKLING (THREE-BEARDED) (*Onos tricirratus*, Block)

3lb 4¼oz	G Hurst	off I.O.Wight	1992
3lb 2½oz	Mrs G Haves	off Dartmouth	1990
2lb 14¼oz	S F Bealing	Poole Bay	Oct, 1972
2lb 13oz 2dm	K Westaway	Portland Harbour	June, 1966

SCAD, or **Horse Mackerel** (*Trachurus trachurus*, Linn)

3lb 5¼oz	M A Atkins	Torbay	1978
3lb 4½oz	D O Cooke	Mewstone, Plymouth	1971
3lb 3oz	J B Thorton	Deal	July, 1934

SHAD (ALLIS) (*Alosa alosa*)

4lb 12½oz	P B Gerrard	Chesil Beach, Dorset	1977
3lb 4½oz	B H Sloane	Princess Pier, Torquay	1964

SHAD (TWAITE) (*Alosa finta*, Cuvier)

2lb 12oz	J W Martin	Garlieston, SW Scotland	1978
3lb 2oz	T Hayward	Deal	Nov, 1949
3lb 2oz	S Jenkins	Torbay	1954
2lb	S Gower	Poole Harbour	Oct, 1984

SHARK (BLUE) (*Carcharinus glaucus*, Linn)

218lb	N Sutcliffe	Looe	July, 1959
206lb†	J L McGonagle	Achill	Oct, 1959
184lb	T Robinson	Looe	1960
180lb	H Widdett	Looe	1955
180lb	F A Mitton	Looe	1960

SHARK (MAKO) (*Isurus oxyrhinchus*, Raf

500lb	Mrs J M Yallop	Eddystone Light	1971
498lb 8oz	K Burgess	Looe	July, 1966
476lb	W J Rogers	Falmouth	July, 1964
435lb	S G Miller	Looe	June, 1964
428lb 8oz	J E Sefton	Looe	1961

It was not until 1956 that the mako shark was positively identified as a British species, and it is probable that some of the fish listed earlier as porbeagles were, in fact, makos.

SHARK (PORBEAGLE) (*Lamna cornubica*, Gonetin)

507lb	C Bennett	off Dunnet Head, Caithness	March, 1993
465lb	J Potier	off Padstow, Cornwall	July, 1976
430lb	D Bougourd	South of Jersey	1969
367lb	B D Phillipps	Jersey, CI	June, 1960
365lb†	Dr O'Donnel Browne	Keem Bay, Co Mayo	1932
324lb	T Paince	Nab Tower	Aug, 1968
311lb	K C Wilson	Looe	1961
300lb††	J Eathorne	Looe	1951

The identification of the mako shark in British waters has thrown some doubt on the authenticity of this list. Dr O'Donnel Browne's fish was certainly a porbeagle, but the one marked †† is now thought probably to have been a mako. Fish caught since 1956 are definitely porbeagles.

SHARK, SIX-GILLED (*Hexanchus priseus*)

154lb†	A Bull	off Kinsale	Aug 28, 1968
9lb 8oz	F E Beeston	off Plymouth	1976

SHARK (THRESHER) (*Alopias vulpes,* Gonetin)

323lb	S Mills	Nab Tower, off Portsmouth	July, 1982
295lb	H J Aris	Dunose Head, IoW	1978
280lb	H A Kelly	Dungeness	1933
149lb	R Romilly Lunge	Christchurch	July, 1937

SHORT-SPINED SEA SCORPION (*Myoxocephalus scorpius*)

2lb 7½oz	B G Logan	Whitley Bay, Tyne & Wear	1982

SKATE (COMMON) (*Raia batis,* Linn)

336lb	Captor unknown	Beer	1934
227lb	P Banks	off Tobermory	1986
226lb 8oz	R S Macpherson	Shetland	Aug, 1970
221lb†	T Tucker	Ballycotton	1913
218lb 8oz	E C Henning	Valentia	1927
214lb	J A E Olsson	Scapa Flow	July, 1968
211lb	Dr C Ayton Marrett	Ballycotton	1912
208lb	Leonard F Hopkins	Clare Island, Co Mayo	Aug, 1971
205	A W Bowie	Kinsale	Aug, 1956

SMOOTHOUND (*Mustelus mustelus*)

28lb	A T Chilvers	Heacham	1969

SMOOTHOUND (STARRY) (*Mustelus asterias*)

28lb	R Grady	Maplin Sands, Essex	1980
23lb 2oz	D Carpenter	Bradwell on Sea	1972

SOLE (*Solea solea,* Linn)

6lb 8¾oz	N V Guilmoto	S Coast Boulders, Alderney	1991
6lb 8½oz	N V Guilmoto	S Coast Boulders, Alderney	1991
6lb 2oz	J Bartram	Nr Braye, Alderney, CI	1984
5lb 7oz	L Dixon	Alderney, CI	1980
4lb 8oz	H C L Pike	Alderney, CI	1978
4lb 3½oz	R Wells	Redcliffe Beach	Mar, 1974
4lb 1oz 14dm	R A Austin	Guernsey	Dec, 1967
4lb 1¾oz	M Eppelein	off Channel Islands	June, 1993
4lb	M Stinton	Clevedon Pier	Sept, 1943
3lb 4oz	S Hayman	Weymouth	Nov, 1956

SOLE (LEMON) (*Microstumus Kitt*)

2lb 7¾oz	W N Callister	Douglas, Isle of Man	1980
2lb 3oz	D R Duke	Douglas, Isle of Man	1971

SPANISH MACKEREL (*Scomber japonicus*)

1lb 5½oz	G Scammell	Lamorna Cove, Penzance	Aug 14, 1995
1lb 5½oz	M Prisk	Lamorna Cove, Penzance	Aug 14, 1995
1lb ½oz	P Jones	off Guernsey CI	1972

SPURDOG (*Squalus acanthias,* Linn)

21lb 3½oz	P R Barett	off Porthleven	1977
20lb 3oz	J Newman	Needles	May, 1972
17lb 1oz	S Bates	Deal	1971
16lb 12½oz	R Legg	Chesil Beach	1964
16lb 4oz†	C McIvor	Strangford Lough	June, 1969
15lb 12oz	John Rowe	Killala Bay, Sligo	Aug, 1967
15lb 5oz	J S W Fisher	Strangford Lough	Oct, 1971
15lb	W Hamilton	Strangford Lough	July, 1969
14lb 6oz	J C Nott	Clare Island	June, 1969

14lb 1oz	D R Angiolini	Valentia	Sept, 1968
14lb	R Wickens	Kinsale	Oct, 1962

SUNFISH (*Mola mola*)

108lb	T F Sisson	Saundersfoot	Aug, 1976
49lb 4oz	M G H Merry	Cornwall	Aug, 1976

TADPOLE FISH (*Raniceps raninus*)

1lb 13¾oz	D A Higgins	Whitley Bay	1977
1lb 5¾oz	N Conn	Seaham Beach, Co Durham	1990

TOPE (*Eugaleus galeus,* Linn)

82lb 8oz	R Chatfield	off Bradwell-on-Sea	1991
79lb 12oz	P J Richards	Bradwell-on-Sea	1986
74lb 11oz	A B Harries	Caldy Island	July, 1964
73lb 3oz (female)	L Andrews	Hayling Island	1949
65lb	Lt-Col R I P Earle	Studland	1956
64lb 8oz	J H Swan	Camel Estuary, Padstow	July, 1963
62lb 11oz	A J Drew	Herne Bay	1911
62lb 8oz (female)	R J Weston	Eastbourne	June, 1955
62lb 2oz (female)	A B Fitt	Herne Bay	June, 1951
62lb (male)	D S Southcombe	Weymouth	1946
61lb 8oz (female)	G T Northover	Herne Bay	June, 1936
60lb 12oz†	C McIver	Strangford Lough	1968

TORSK *(Brosme brosme)*

15lb 7oz	D J MacKay	Pentland Firth	July, 1982
12lb 1oz	D Pottinger	Shetland	1968

TRIGGER FISH (*Balistes carolinensis*)

5lb 14½oz	K Lydiard	Lynmouth rocks	Aug 20, 1995
5lb 5¼oz	D H Bush	Poole Quay	1990
4lb 9¼oz	E Montacute	Weymouth Bay	1975
4lb 6¾oz	E Bainbridge	Chesil Beach	Aug 31, 1989
4lb 6¾oz	A Kershaw	Chesil Beach	Sep 10, 1989

TUNA, BIG-EYE(*Thunnus obesus*)

66lb 12oz	S Atkinson	Newlyn Harbour	Oct 1985

TUNA BLUE-FIN (Tunny) (*Thunnus thynnus*)

The fish given in the following list were all caught in the North Sea tunny fishing grounds off Scarborough and Whitby:

851lb	L Mitchell-Henry,	1933
764lb	H W Holgate,	1934
812lb	Colonel E T Peel,	1934
763lb	G Baker,	1933
798lb	H G Smith,	1934
762lb	M W Holgate,	1935
798lb	Colonel E T Peel,	1932
749lb	S Cohen,	1949
785lb	Major R T Laughton,	1947
747lb	H E Weatherley,	1952
660lb	H E Weatherley,	1954

TUNA (LONG-FINNED) (*Thunnus alalunga*)

4lb 12oz	B Cater, Salcombe		1990

TURBOT (*Scopthalmus maximus,* Linn)

33lb 12oz	R Simcox	Salcombe, Devon	1980
32lb 8oz†	Unknown	S Ireland	1980
32lb 3oz	D Dyer	off Plymouth	May, 1976
31lb 4oz	Paul Hutchings (11)	Eddystone Light	July, 1972
29lb	G M W Garnsey	The Manacles	Aug, 1964
28lb 0½oz	T Tolchard	Dartmouth	1961
27lb 14oz	F S Stenning	Salcombe	1907
26lb 8oz	J F Eldridge	Valentia	1915
25lb 8oz	Mat Kearney	Cork Harbour	Aug, 1971
25lb 4oz	R Tolchard (age 12)	off Dartmouth	June, 1958

WHITING (*Gadus merlangus,* Linn)

6lb 12oz	N R Croft	Falmouth	1981
6lb 4oz	S Dearman Bridport	April, 1977	
6lb 3oz 3dm	Mrs R Barrett	Rame Head, Cornwall	1971
6lb	E H Tame	Shieldaig	Mar, 1940
5lb 2oz	H C Nicoll	Penzance	1912
5lb 1oz	H W Antenbring	Shieldaig	June, 1938

WHITING, BLUE (*Micromesistius poutassou*)

1lb 12oz	J H Anderson	Loch Fyne, Scotland	1977

WITCH (*Glyptocaphalus cynoglossus*)

1lb 2¾oz	T J Barathey	Colwyn Bay	1967
1lb 2¾oz	T J Barathey	Colwyn Bay	1967

WRASSE (BALLAN) (*Labrus bergylta,* Ascanius)

12lb 1oz	F A Mitchell-Hedges	Looe	1912
12lb	F A Mitchell-Hedges	Looe	1912
11lb 8oz	F A Mitchell-Hedges	Looe	1912
10lb 12oz	F A Mitchell-Hedges	Looe	1912
9lb 6oz	M Goodacre	Eddystone gully	1981
8lb 10¾oz	J le Noury	St Peter's Port Harbour, C.I.	March 1993
7lb 13½oz	D R Gabe	off Start Point, Devon	1978
7lb 10oz			
15dm	B K Lawrence	Trevose Head, Cornwall	1970
7lb 6oz†	A J King	Killybegs	1964

WRASSE (CUCKOO) (*Labrus mixtus*)

2lb 3/4oz	A B Welch	Lymm Bay	1990
2lb 2½oz	D Davies	off Plymouth	Dec 3, 1989
2lb 0½oz	A M Foley	Plymouth	Nov, 1973
1lb 14¾oz	R G Berry	Sennen, Cornwall	Sept, 1973
1lb 12½oz	L C Le Cras	Guernsey	Aug, 1972
1lb 10oz 8dm	B Perry	Torquay	Sept, 1971

WRECKFISH (*Polyprion americanus*)

10lb 10oz	B McNamara	off Eddystone	1980
7lb 10oz	Cdr E StJ Holt	Looe, Cornwall	1974

Index

INDEX OF ADVERTISERS